AF608496

Mondrian and Photography

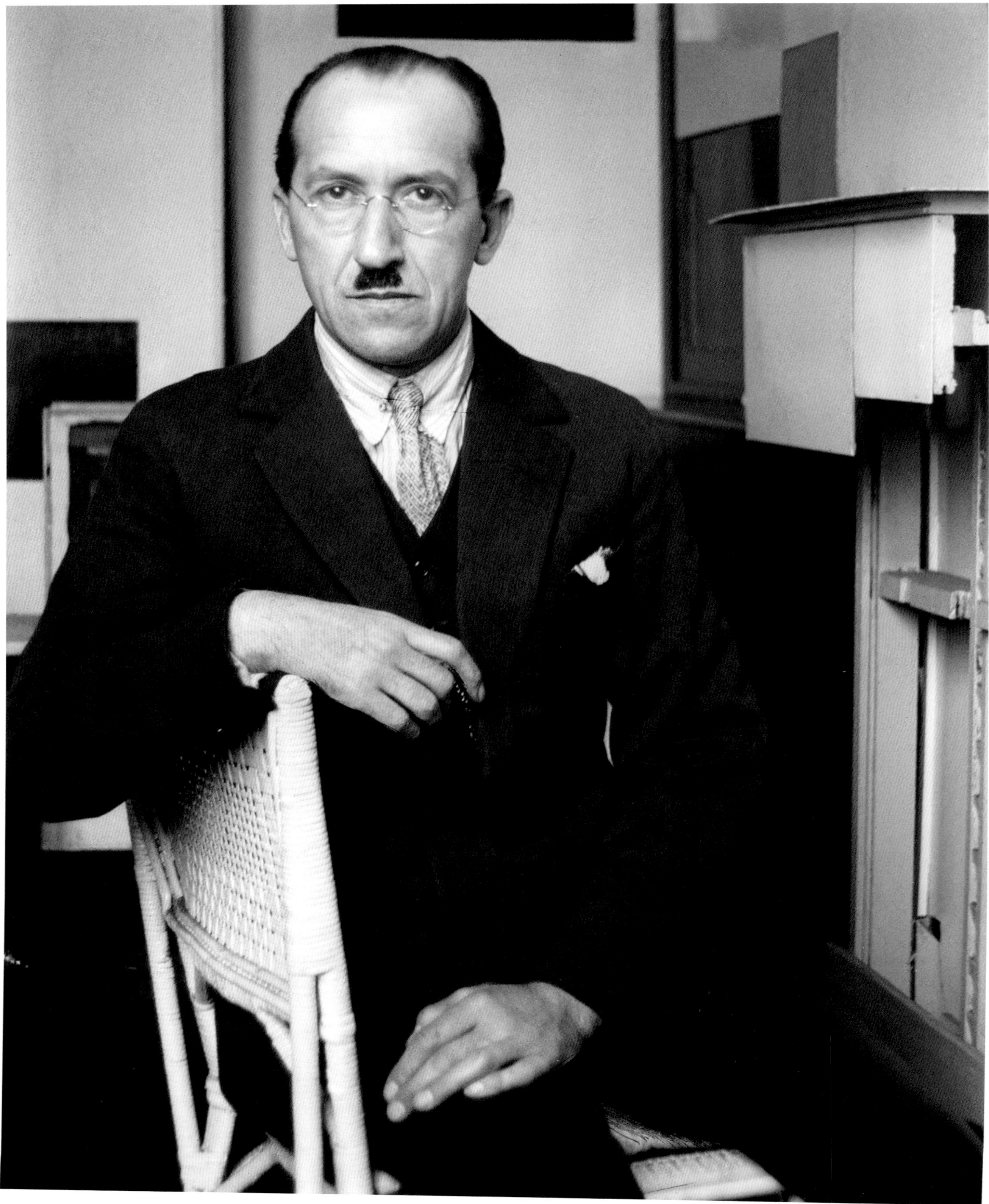

Mondrian and Photography

Wietse Coppes
Leo Jansen

Picturing the Artist and His Work

HATJE CANTZ

in collaboration with
RKD — Netherlands
Institute for Art History

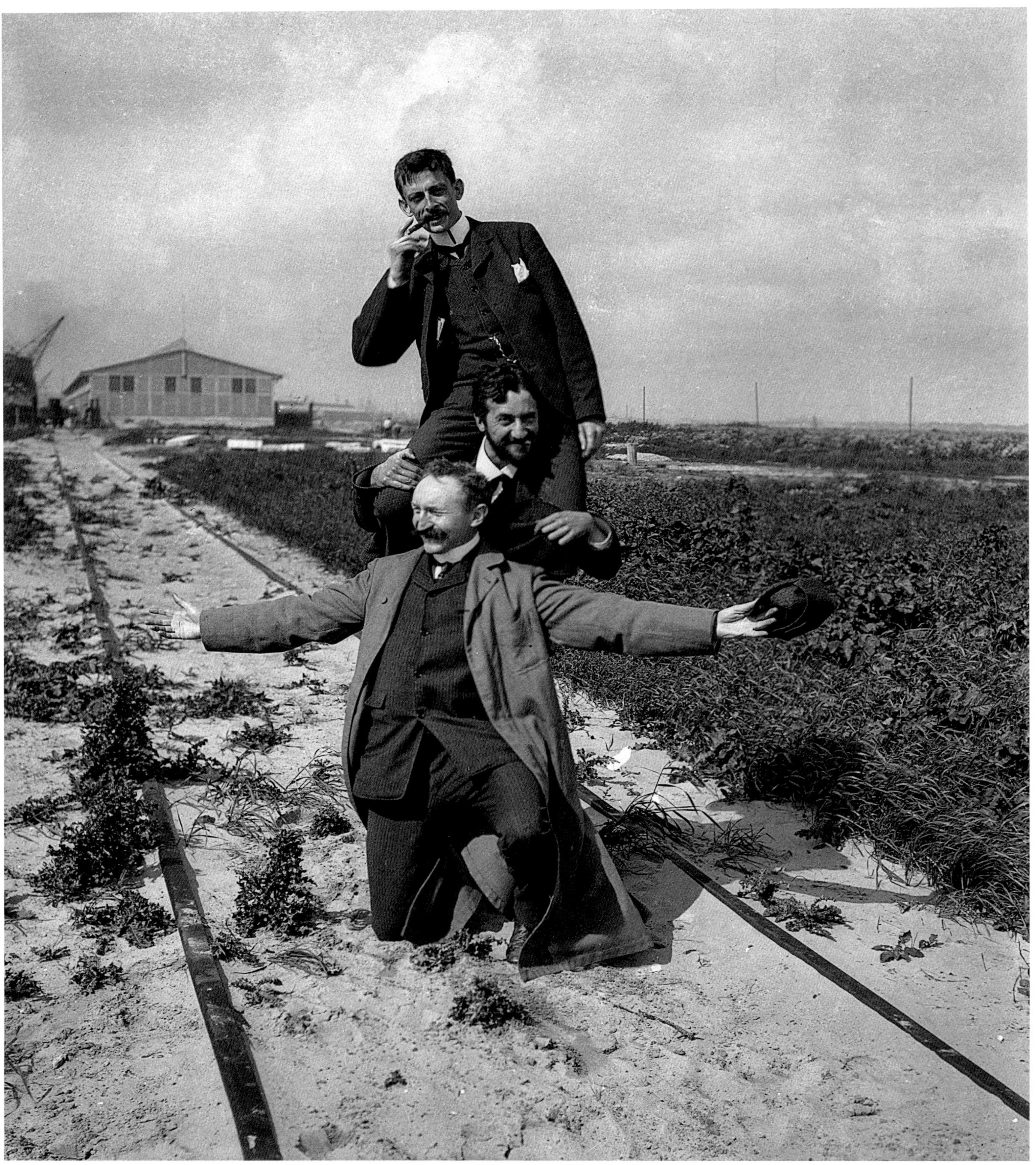

Page 2: Mondrian, between September 1926 and mid-February 1927. Photograph: André Kertész (cat. 99)

< Piet Mondrian with Frits Bodenheim on his shoulders and Simon Maris kneeling at the dock in IJmuiden, 28 August 1903 (detail). Photograph: Mies van de Water or Louise Bodenheim (cat. 20)

Foreword

The RKD — Netherlands Institute for Art History (The Hague) is one of the biggest art-historical archive organizations in the world. The Huygens Institute, part of the Royal Netherlands Academy of Arts and Sciences, is the leading research institution in the field of Dutch history and culture. Each of these bodies boasts a wealth of important archive collections, both digital and physical, which offer interested parties ranging from art lovers to professionals and researchers ample opportunity to study Dutch history, art and culture in an international context.

The archives relating to Piet Mondrian (1872—1944) and De Stijl occupy a prominent place among the many treasures held by the RKD. They constitute a national collection pertaining to this Dutch artist, who made an inestimable contribution to modern ('abstract') art. This collection runs to some seven hundred letters and dozens of personal documents, together with around a hundred photographs, which provide an unparalleled picture of the artist, his family, his friends and acquaintances, and his famous studios.

Besides taking care of these rich art-historical resources, the RKD and the Huygens Institute are naturally eager to make them available more widely through both digital and printed publications. Hence the joint initiative taken a few years ago to create a complete, scholarly online edition of Piet Mondrian's correspondence and theoretical writings. This online publication, the first volume of which is due to appear in late 2023 at https://mondrianpapers.org, is being prepared by Wietse Coppes, Mondrian and De Stijl Curator (RKD), and Leo Jansen, Senior Researcher at the Huygens Institute.

As part of their research for the publication, Coppes and Jansen compiled an inventory of the surviving photographs of Mondrian and his circle. It turned out that, besides the aforementioned hundred or so photographs in the RKD collection, there were not a further 150 to 200 out there waiting to be retrieved, as had been expected, but over 300, spread across some sixty institutions and public and private collections in the Netherlands and further afield. Within the pages that you are now reading, all these photographs have been brought together in the form of a book for the first time — a unique achievement in itself, but one that is also of immense importance to the study of the artist's life and work. The photographs offer a literal picture of the man, of the influential, international avant-garde network of which he was part, and of his famous studios, which he began to design from the 1920s onwards in keeping with his neo-plastic vision of art and architecture. The studios drew a great many curious visitors from all over the world, who found themselves immersed in an entirely different and new, stripped-down reality.

This book is also sufficiently comprehensive to alter the image that many will have formed of Mondrian, an image that has largely been shaped since the second half of the twentieth century by a few dozen photographs, which have been reproduced over and over again. These, almost without exception, convey a picture of Mondrian as an austere 'man-in-a-suit', who wished to be seen solely as the custodian and promoter of his uncompromising, neo-plastic art and artistic philosophy. Yet this supposed ascetic enjoyed life to the full. He regularly attended receptions, openings and dinners, and treated guests at his studio to wine, music and dancing. Following the publication of this book, no one will be able to maintain any longer, credibly, that Mondrian was some kind of monk or hermit.

Many of the photographs included here are not held by the RKD and, given their considerable number and how they are spread across institutions around the world, it hardly needs to be said that it was no easy matter to compile this publication. Elsewhere in their book, the authors offer personal thanks to all those who contributed to the research and the publication. But the publication would not have been possible without the generous assistance of many researchers, private individuals and archivists, and we would thus like to express our gratitude here on behalf of the RKD and the Huygens Institute for the kind cooperation of the owners and institutions that made their photographs available for this book. We also thank the International Music and Art Foundation (Vaduz) for the financial contribution that enabled its publication, as well as the publishers at Hatje Cantz and Fonds Mercator, Nicola von Velsen and Bernard Steyaert respectively. Their enthusiasm and unwavering belief in the project made it possible to publish two additional editions of the book, in English and French. We are especially indebted, lastly, to Tijdsbeeld publishers. Publisher Ronny Gobyn, consultant Jan Martens, project coordinator Ann Mestdag, designer Griet Van Haute, translator Ted Alkins and editor Ann Kay faced numerous challenges during the realization of this book; they were fully committed from the outset and the publication that *Mondrian and Photography* has become is due in no small part to them.

Chris Stolwijk, General Director RKD — Netherlands Institute for Art History

Dirk van Miert, Director Huygens Institute, Royal Netherlands Academy of Arts and Sciences (KNAW)

Piet Mondrian and Photography
Picturing the Artist and His Work

The prevailing image of Piet Mondrian is a cliché twice over. In terms of his art, almost everyone thinks straight away of his fascinating abstract works, made up of straight black lines arranged at right angles, along with a limited number of rectangular planes in primary colours, white, black and grey. This particular cliché stems from the largely posthumous success of Mondrian's pioneering work and from the influence his paintings exerted in the 20th century, not only on art but on architecture, design and fashion too. Like any cliché, though, it is overly narrow and fails to do justice to the reality. Namely that, before arriving at abstraction, Mondrian had travelled a long way as an artist, from the late 19th-century Dutch landscape tradition and on through symbolism, luminism and cubism before evolving towards the entirely new abstract style he called the 'nieuwe beelding', or neo-plasticism. During this cautious search for a style of his own, Mondrian produced many impressive works that are no less eloquent than his later, now iconic, non-representational paintings.

Mondrian the man — the way he looked — lives on in the collective memory in a similarly clichéd way. The picture is that of a stoic, intellectual hermit-artist: smart suit, clean-shaven, hair impeccably trimmed, living and working ascetically in a studio he fitted out according to his own aesthetic principles. A stock handful of portraits and a few dozen studio photographs have been reproduced time after time in newspapers, magazines, catalogues and other publications ever since the 1920s, resulting in an image that is remarkably aligned with the austere, sober visual language of his neo-plastic paintings. The work has come to be an extension, as it were, of the artist's character: an apparently perfect symbiosis of art and life. Most of the pictures in question were taken by professional photographers, some of them celebrities in their own right, and were carefully stage-managed. Their solid compositions directly embed themselves in our visual memory. Mondrian himself bears some of the responsibility for this one-sided image, given the control he exerted over how he was photographed and which pictures he allowed to be used in public. Only those that he felt correctly conveyed his persona as an artist were permitted. The resulting public image of Mondrian as an individual can thus be regarded as a successful marketing strategy on the part of the artist himself.

The image of the austere, smartly dressed artist reveals just one facet of Mondrian, both personally and professionally. He was also a relaxed, warm and humorous individual, who enjoyed the company of friends and acquaintances. Mondrian allowed himself to be photographed on all sorts of formal and informal occasions, including outings, visits, exhibition openings and parties, and he liked to mingle with artists and collectors, well known or otherwise, whether in the Netherlands, Paris or New York. His art sometimes required the sacrifice of seclusion, but the solitary life was definitely not enough for him. He repeatedly mentions the need for human contact in his letters, writing to his friend Lodewijk Schelfhout, for instance: 'I am not a hermit by profession either and I too, like you, must stand fully in life.'[1] Art needs, after all, to be nourished by life: 'art and humanity are one'.[2] A hundred or so photographs are known that offer a view of this other — and to many people surprising — Mondrian. They are brought together here along with famous, widely reproduced portraits and studio photos, as well as others that have rarely, if ever, been published before.

The story of Mondrian and photography occurred in parallel with the latter's rapid development in the decades between 1890 and 1940. Mondrian made strategic use of this new potential to promote himself, his ideas and his work, from the portraits shot by jobbing photographers around the turn of the century through to the pictures of himself and his famous studio taken by celebrity lensmen, whose job it was to satisfy the hunger of the burgeoning magazine industry. The first chapter discusses this parallel development. We then focus on the main categories into which the photographs can be subdivided, beginning with the portraits. These reflect how, for a long time, Mondrian regularly changed his appearance, before settling on the now familiar look. Next up are the studio photographs, which are some of the most important when it comes to disseminating his ideas on art, while also illustrating the development of his spatial application of those ideas. Mondrian's gregarious side is highlighted in a chapter on the group photos in which he can be seen. The boundaries between these three categories are not always clear-cut: the artist also appears in shots of his studio, for instance, while some group photographs were likewise taken in the studio. This is not the case with the final category, comprising the portfolio photographs that Mondrian commissioned to document and in some cases also to publicize his work and its development.

This book is not a photo-biography, nor does it claim to be an exercise in the history of photography. It hopes instead to offer a closer acquaintance with Piet Mondrian and to serve as a catalogue and reference for anyone who wishes to immerse themselves in the life and work of this exceptional artist.

>> Detail of cat. 369

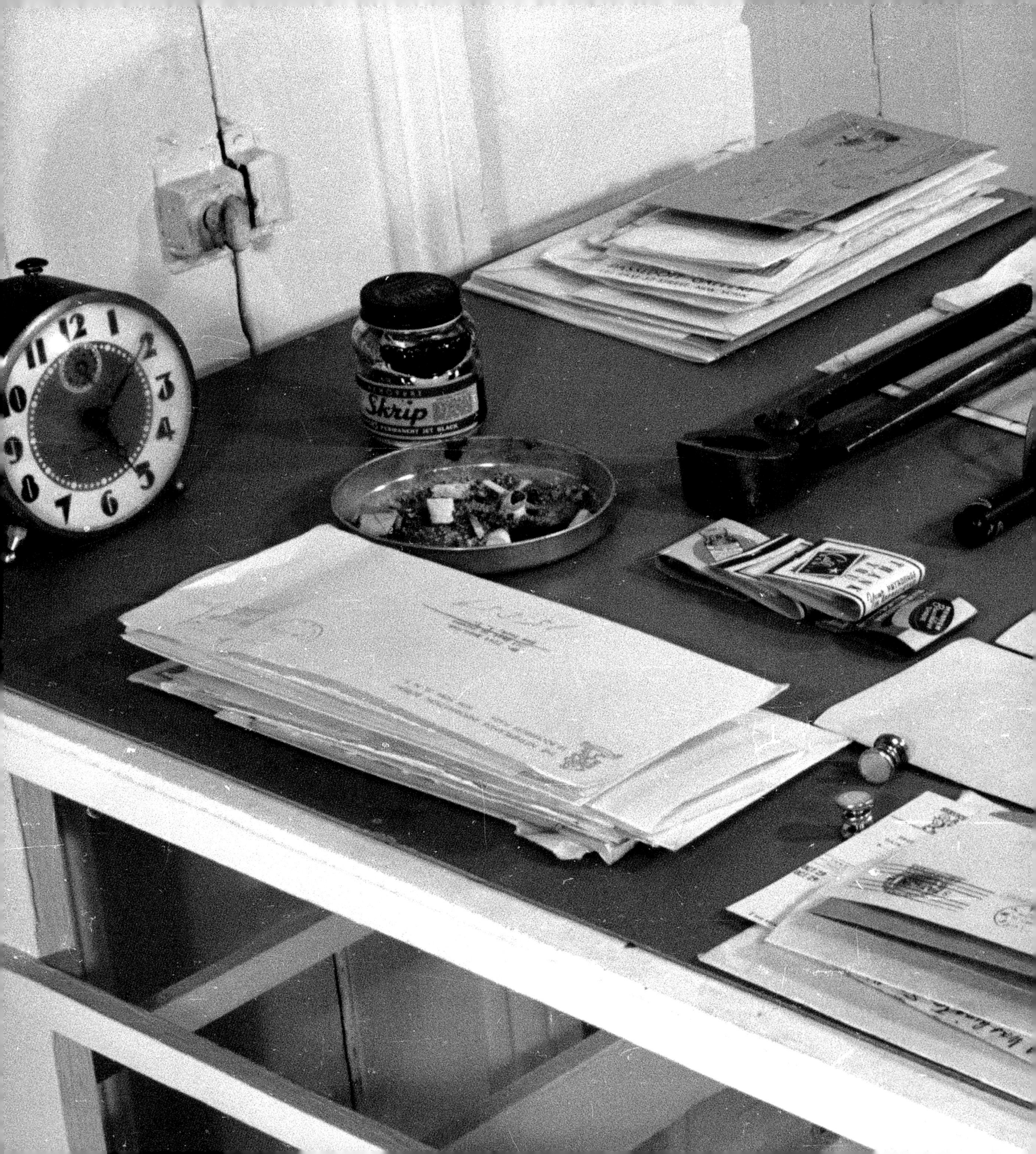
Skrip

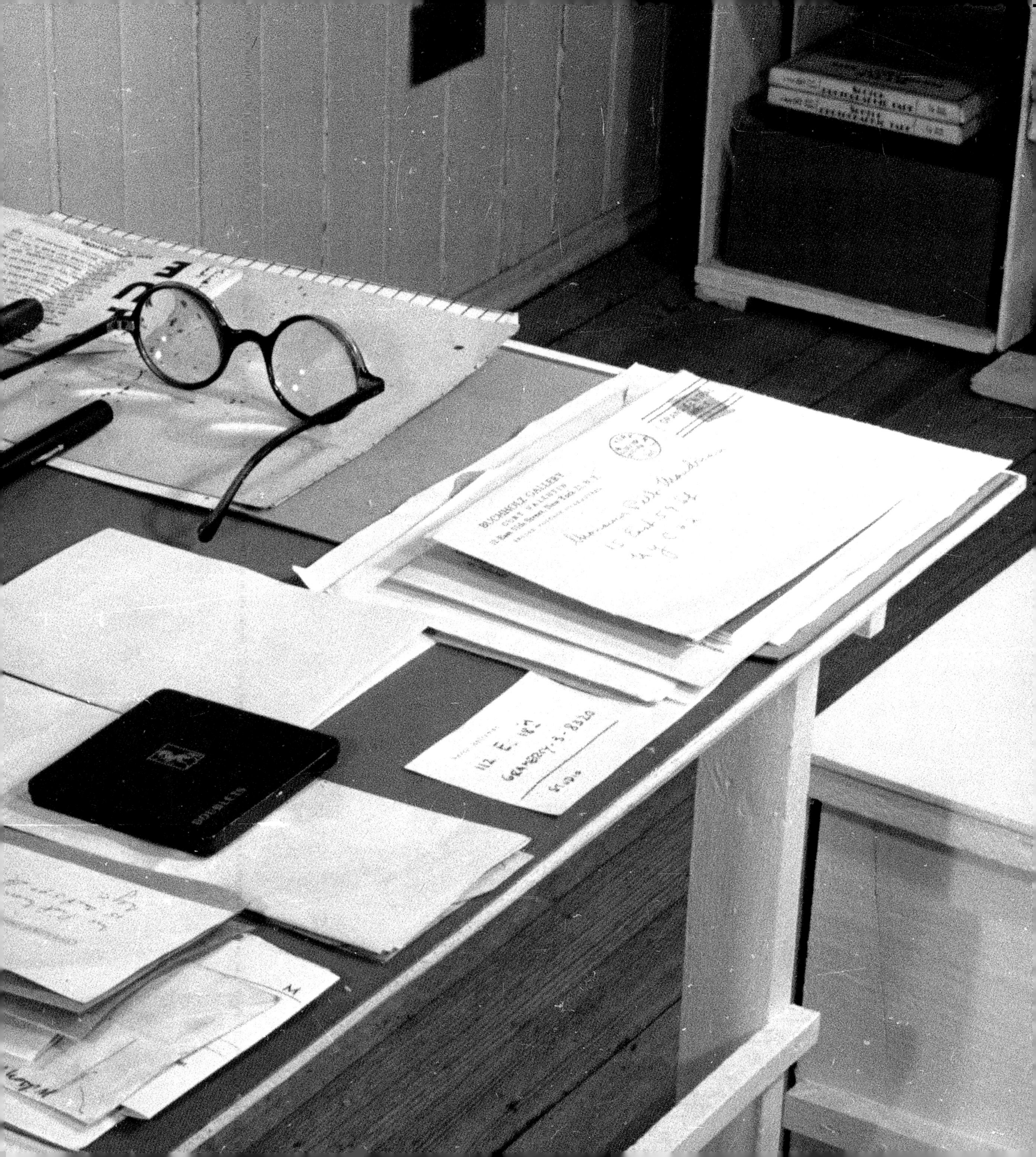
BUCHHOLZ GALLERY
CURT VALENTIN

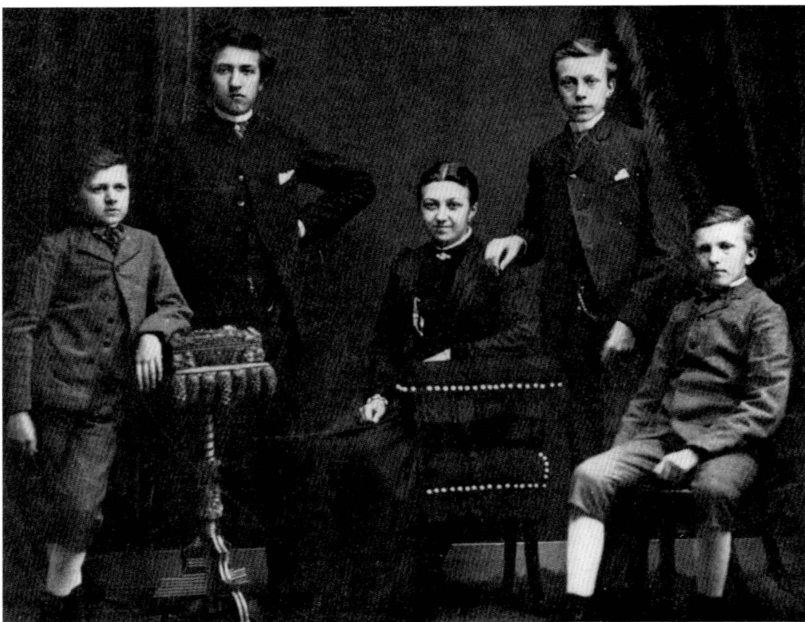

Fig. 1
The Mondriaan children, spring 1889 (?) (cat. 1)

> Fig. 2
Company at the opening of Gustave Buchet's exhibition at Galerie Zak, Paris, 22 November 1929 (detail) Photograph: Stanislaw Londynski (cat. 124)

Mondrian and the New Medium

Show how you want to be seen

The earliest photograph in which we get to see the future artist dates from around 1890 and shows Piet Mondrian (or Mondriaan, as he was still called at that point) posing for an unknown studio photographer with his sister and three brothers (fig. 1). As was customary in this type of picture, the Mondriaan children are dressed in their Sunday best, and they have been encouraged by the photographer to pose as naturally as possible. The set comprises a rear wall with imitation drapes, while the furniture that little Carel leans against on the left and Christina sits on in the middle are obvious studio props. Unlike their sister, the boys make no effort to put on a friendly expression. Perhaps they thought it more manly, although we should remember that the subjects had to keep perfectly still for several seconds, which obviously made it harder to relax. Whatever sense of spontaneity the poses might convey, the relative positions were carefully thought-out. As the eldest child, Christina is placed in the middle, with the two older brothers towering above her on either side. The youngest boys are situated lower down, flanking the trio. The symmetry of the arrangement is offset by the varying positions of their hands and arms, the way Christina turns as she sits on a chair placed sideways, and the standing and sitting poses of the boys on the left and right. This was a photographer who knew what they were doing.

The first photographic techniques date from around 1839, with the operation of large cameras and the process of developing and printing the plates initially limited to professionals. Technical and chemical knowledge was required and the equipment and other materials were expensive. Ordinary people had very little contact with the medium, unless they happened to come across a professional photographer working outdoors to capture an image of a building, city view or landscape.

This all began to change around 1870, by which time photographic technology had developed sufficiently to enable its commercial application. Professional photographers now sprang up everywhere to offer the group portraits that were gaining rapidly in popularity. They mostly worked from a studio equipped with sets and props, which meant that people tended to be immortalized in the same surroundings as many of their fellow villagers or townspeople. Group photographs like this had an aura of civic pride and harmony and were frequently taken to mark a noteworthy event such as a wedding or other anniversary, a jubilee, or a new addition to the family. Photographers could also

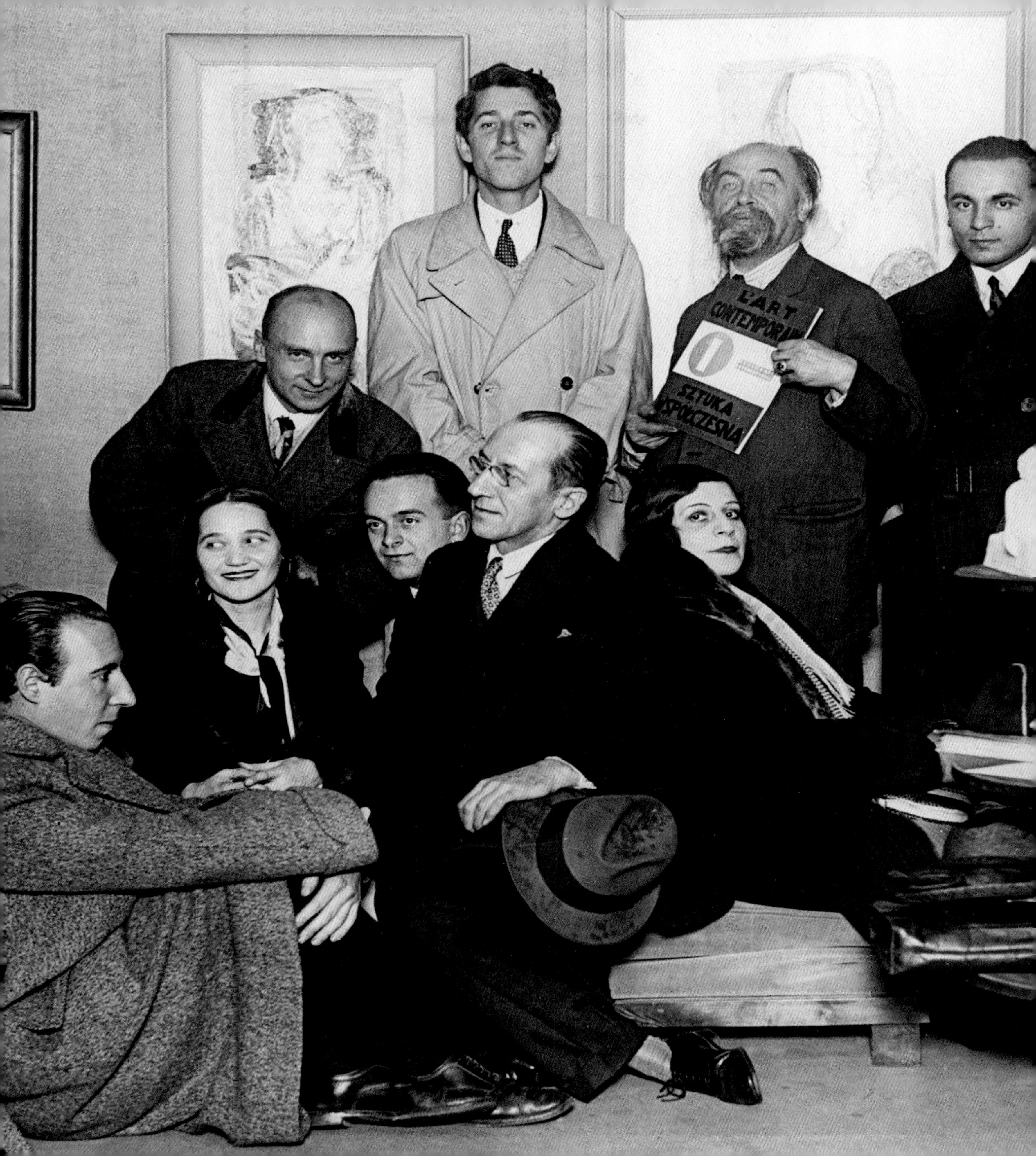
L'ART
CONTEMPORAIN
SZTUKA
WSPÓŁCZESNA

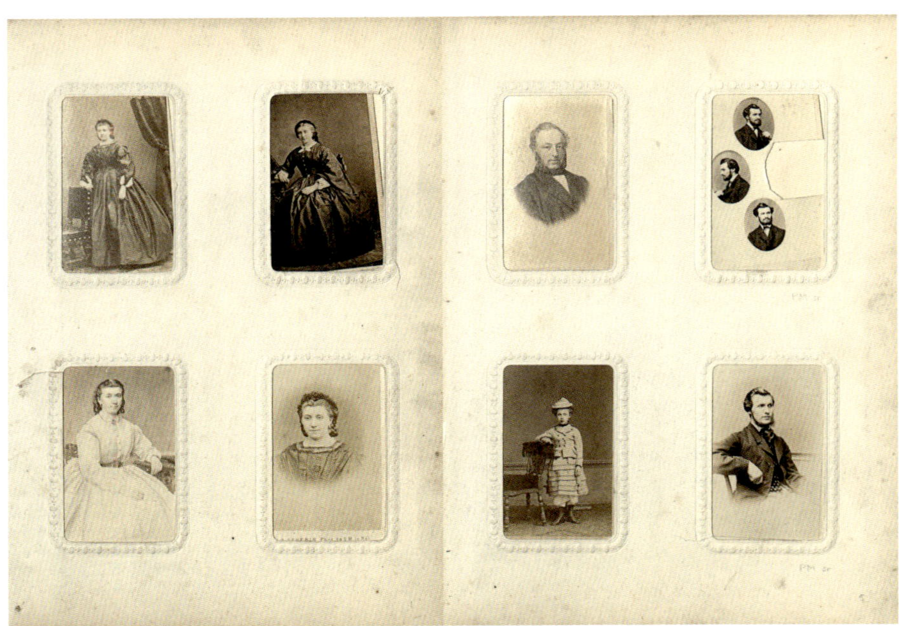

Fig. 3
Two pages from the Mondriaan family's *cartes de visite* album. Yale University, Beinecke Rare Book and Manuscript Library, New Haven

come and take pictures in situ, to provide a keepsake for the guests at a celebration, classmates at a school, a regiment of soldiers and so forth.

When the photograph of the Mondriaan children was taken, the family belonged to a middle class that was embracing the new medium to confirm its solid social position and make itself visible to others. This was especially important, because although Piet Mondriaan Senior was headteacher at a school in Winterswijk, he struggled to support his family and faced criticism of his teaching methods and social conduct.[3]

Another way to immortalize oneself was the *carte de visite*, which was patented in 1854 and was soon all the rage. It became the done thing in all strata of society to have professional portrait photos taken, small prints of which were then mounted on card. Photographers were also quick to start offering series of pictures devoted to themes such as different professions, local costume or famous individuals.[4] People kept the photos, swapped them with family and friends and collected them in special albums. Just such an album of portrait photographs was part of Piet Mondrian's estate. It contains numerous *cartes de visite* showing relatives from previous generations (fig. 3).

The idea behind the individual portrait was similar to that for the group portrait, but the pictures could be more personal, as the subject no longer had to fall in with the impression that the group as a whole wished to convey. All the same, people who had their photographs taken mostly wanted to show what likeable, successful or serious members of the family or society they were. *Cartes de visite* thus had something in common with the profiles we create nowadays on platforms like LinkedIn, which allow us to present ourselves to the world at large, both personally and professionally.

As photography continued to develop after 1900 and became increasingly ubiquitous, *cartes de visite* fell out of fashion as swiftly as they had arrived. Even so, the earliest portrait photographs of Mondrian — the oldest of which dates from 1899 — include pictures of this type from as late as 1908 or so (fig. 4). The portraits he himself arranged to have taken show that he was aware of what the camera had to offer from an early age. Mondrian broke with bourgeois conventions and wanted his portraits to convey a sense of self-confidence and individuality. It is there in his hairstyle, his clothes and his expression, as we will discuss in the following chapter.

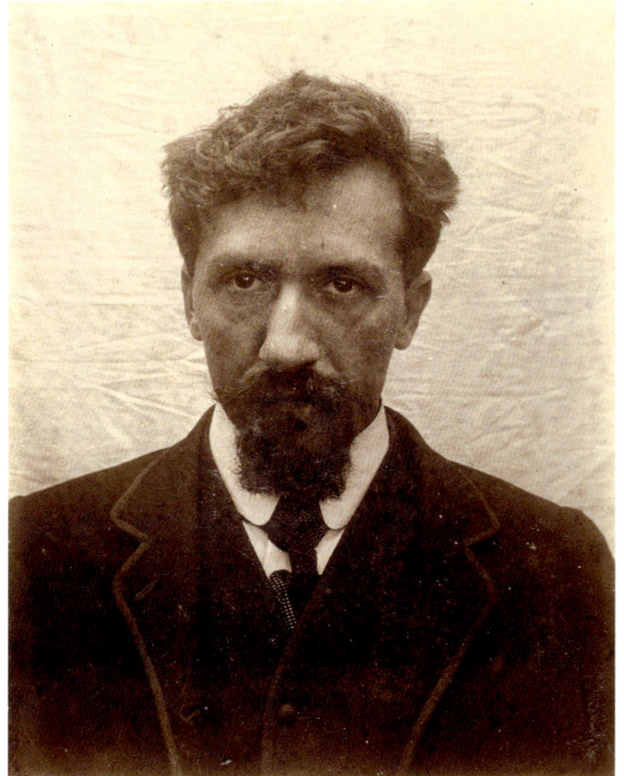

Fig. 4
Portrait of Piet Mondrian, c. 1908 (cat. 36)

The democratization of photography

Photography had been the preserve of a relatively limited group of professionals for about fifty years by the time amateur photographers began to appear around the turn of the century. It was in 1888 that George Eastman launched the first Kodak hand-held camera, paving the way for the widespread adoption, or 'democratization', of photography.[5] The device was easy to operate. You simply held the box in front of your stomach, pointed the lens and pressed the shutter. The compact size of the camera also allowed photography in all situations, even by non-professionals. Eastman's advertising slogan, 'You push the button, we do the rest', neatly summed up the process. Although photography still represented a fairly substantial investment for someone on an average wage, the Kodak camera brought it within reach of a much larger group of private users. The Eastman company continued to refine its product over the years, and sales grew exponentially, as did the number of photographs taken. This led in turn to the advent of the 'snapshot' — informal photos taken in a private context, such as family celebrations, daytrips, parties and tourist landmarks: the same moments, in other words, that we now capture daily by the hundreds of millions with our smartphones.

As the number of hand-held cameras for amateur photographers grew rapidly in the early part of the century, we gradually see Mondrian appearing in snapshots that offer a glimpse into his personal life. This is also where the story of the lesser-known Mondrian begins — the friend and artist who, alongside his dedicated and uncompromising artistic practice, liked company and felt the need for a social circle, in which he played an active part. Pictures of a trip to Spain (embarking at IJmuiden and travelling via France) with friends show that he did not attempt to hide this spontaneous side from the camera (fig. 5). There are later photos taken in the company of friends that likewise belong to the category of informal snaps shot by people who were present more or less by chance.[6]

The fact that the camera, even if it was still only affordable for the better off, was rapidly establishing itself in society and used increasingly frequently during social occasions, prompts the question of what we know about Mondrian as a photographer. It turns out there is little to go on. In the series of photos taken during the aforementioned trip to Spain with his friends Simon Maris (who owned a camera) and Frits Bodenheim, two were taken in which we see those two friends without Mondrian (figs 6—7), making it likely that he was the photographer. But those two are all there is: we have no further evidence of Mondrian as a photographer and no record that he ever owned a camera. We can only conclude that taking photographs in person did not especially appeal to him. On the other hand, he did have friends who were photographers — whether amateur or professional — from an early stage, and he appreciated the efforts that some of them made in pursuing their job or hobby.[7]

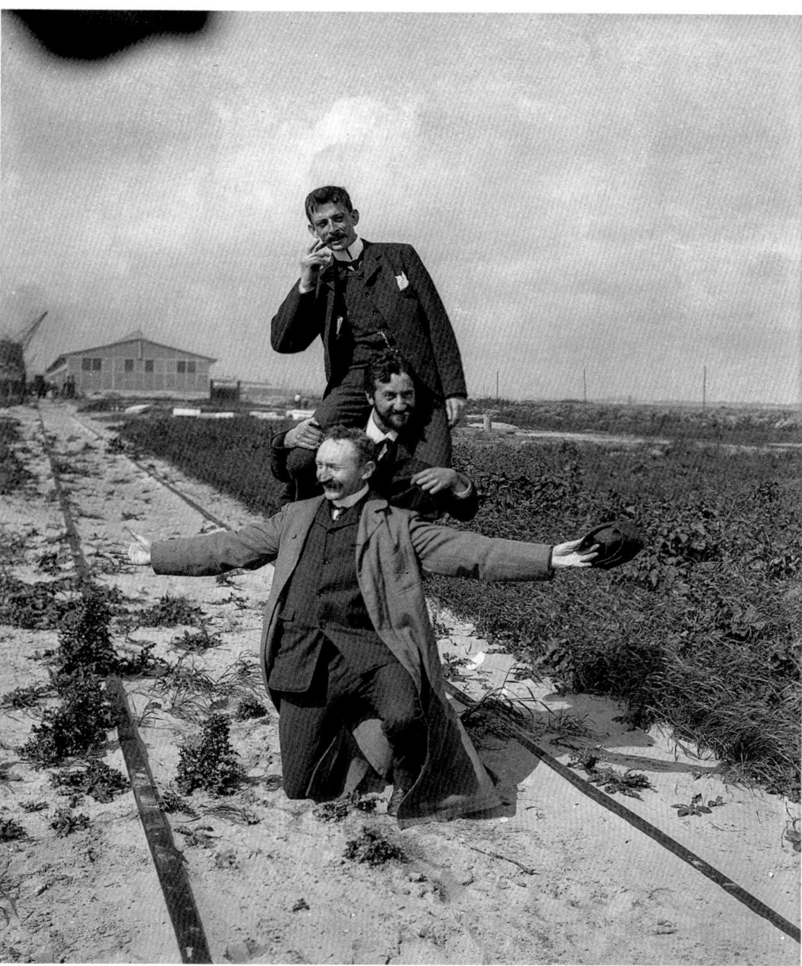

Fig. 5
Piet Mondrian with Frits Bodenheim on his shoulders and Simon Maris kneeling at the dock in IJmuiden, 18 August 1903
Photograph: Mies van de Water or Louise Bodenheim (cat. 20)

Photography and the artist

It did not take long for the invention of photography to start attracting the curiosity of artists. Although the idea that it might be an art form in its own right was still some way off, Edouard Manet, Camille Corot, Dante Gabriel Rossetti and later Paul Gauguin and Edvard Munch are famous examples of artists who made

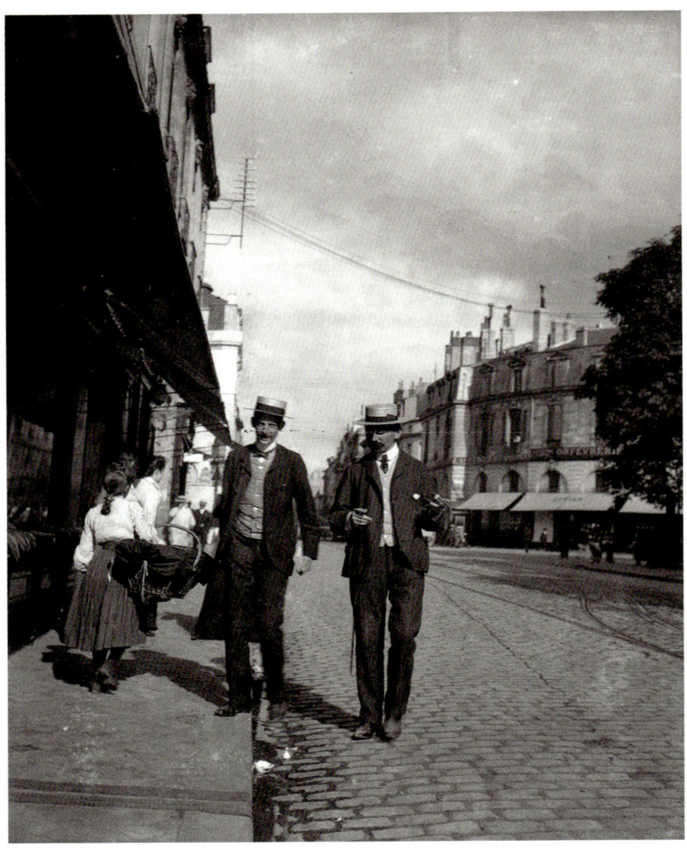

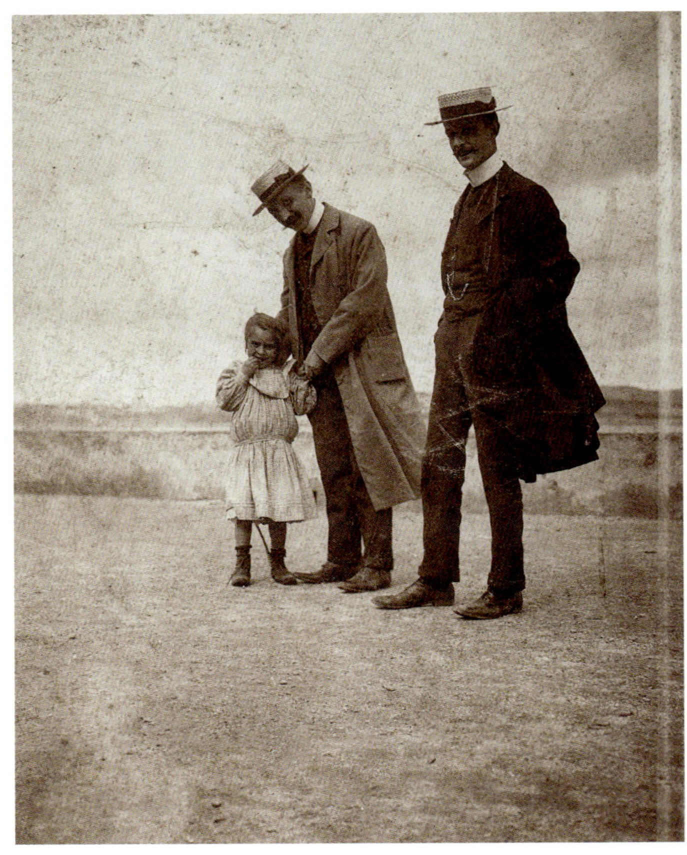

Figs 6–7
Simon Maris and Frits Bodenheim in Bordeaux (left) and at Las Arenas, Spain (right). Photographs by Piet Mondrian. The Hague, RKD, Simon Maris and Family Archive (0257), inv. 93

grateful use of photographs when preparing their work, even if it would be a long time before this was publicly admitted.[8] Edgar Degas was an early adopter, taking photographs even at the stage where this required a large, tripod-mounted camera and glass negatives. He took pictures of friends and family, but also of his models, the photographs of whom he could use as an example for his paintings. The lengthy exposure times that were still necessary meant that the subjects had to hold their pose for a prolonged period, and so most of Degas's photographs were carefully 'choreographed'.[9]

The invention of the hand-held camera had an enormous impact in this field too. Edouard Vuillard, Maurice Denis and Henri Rivière in France and Willem Witsen, George Breitner and Joseph Jessurun de Mesquita in the Netherlands were all artists who captured much more spontaneous scenes using the new, lighter cameras.[10] Photographs served different purposes for them. To some it was simply a means of documenting their private lives, whereas for others photography was incorporated in the creative (painting) process. Modern cameras offered short exposure times that could freeze movement, so that it could then be represented more accurately in a painting or print. Photographs could also be used to explore lighting effects or a motif, as had often been done in the past with sketches. All these types of picture were intended for use by the individual who took them or in their personal circle. They were not viewed as creative expressions or products of their maker, nor were they distributed, let alone published.

Photography did not play a significant role in Mondrian's studio practice: he did not feel that the medium was capable of penetrating more deeply into reality, which for him was the essence of his art. The fact that he used a photograph for a drawn self-portrait around 1908 is therefore very much the exception (see p. 24 for more). All the same, to earn his living, he did a lot of portrait commissions alongside his own, free work and it was not unusual for him to be asked to draw or paint a portrait based on a photograph: either because the subject was deceased or so that the sitter would not have to pose for long periods. The two earliest examples are a painted portrait of Dorothy

Gretchen Biersteker done in 1894 and a drawn portrait of her younger brother Noel from around 1897, both full-length. It is clear from the setting in which the toddlers are placed and their poses that both works were done after photographs taken by a commercial studio photographer.[11] In the case of another portrait, of 'Klein Jantje' ('Little Jan'), a boy whose name is unknown, both the painting itself and the original photograph (a *carte de visite*) have survived (figs 8—9). Comparison of the two clearly shows that Mondrian reproduced the studio decor, such as the painted backdrop and the wooden 'fence', fairly closely, but took the liberty of having the roots of the uprights grow more naturally into the soil, rather than depicting the base on which the photographer's scenery actually stood.

Mondrian viewed photography as a medium for reproduction, capable only of documenting a physical situation — whether of people, objects or locations. As far as this went, however, he was happy to embrace photography for use in his portraits, for recording works in his portfolio, and for depicting his studio.

New world, new media

Mondrian was in Paris from the spring of 1912 to July 1914 where, surrounded by the avant-garde of the day, he was able to give fresh impetus to his artistic quest, inspired by the recent cubism of Fernand Léger, Georges Braque and Pablo Picasso. His art underwent a fundamental change in the French capital. While he was visiting the neutral Netherlands in the summer of 1914, the First World War broke out, stranding him in his native country for the next five years. His work and ideas continued to develop during this interlude: from 1916 onwards, all reference to observable reality disappeared from his paintings, and he set out his views on art and society in several articles in the magazine *De Stijl*, which he co-founded in 1917.

Although *De Stijl* reproduced work by the likes of Picasso and Gino Severini during the war, Mondrian was unable for the most part to keep up with developments in the Paris art world from his base in the Netherlands. When he was eventually able to return to France, he was thus curious to find out how his fellow artists had been doing and what direction their work had taken in the meantime. To his immense disappointment, he discovered that the pre-war avant-garde mentality had been displaced by a 'retour à l'ordre', and so it took him a while to find a new circle of like-minded people in Paris. Although he had established his name among collectors and critics in the Netherlands, and even in Germany, and had sold work there too, he was obliged to start again from scratch in France.

Convinced that his entirely different development and ideas were the route to the future, he now made an even greater effort to promote them, publishing a number of articles in French, German and Dutch from the early 1920s onwards, in which he explored, among other things, the relationship between art and architecture in detail. Following his return to Paris, he put his neo-plastic aesthetic principles — in which the combination of art and everyday surroundings played an important part — into practice in his studio, which he henceforward decorated accordingly.

Mondrian's promotional strategy began to bear fruit in the second half of the 1920s. Several articles on his studio, in which he was presented on more than one occasion as a lone, spartan figure, living entirely for his art, were followed by the publication of the first photographs in newspapers and magazines, beginning in 1926. Having substantially refurbished his studio, he hired the photographer Pierre Delbo to document it between November 1925 and the spring of 1926.[12] Delbo's pictures (figs 10—11 and 38) are some of the most frequently reproduced records of the space. They swiftly began to crop up in periodicals in both France and abroad, including *Das Werk* (July 1926) and *i10* (January 1927).

Photographs of the studio were published elsewhere too (see pp. 32—43), a phase that would prove

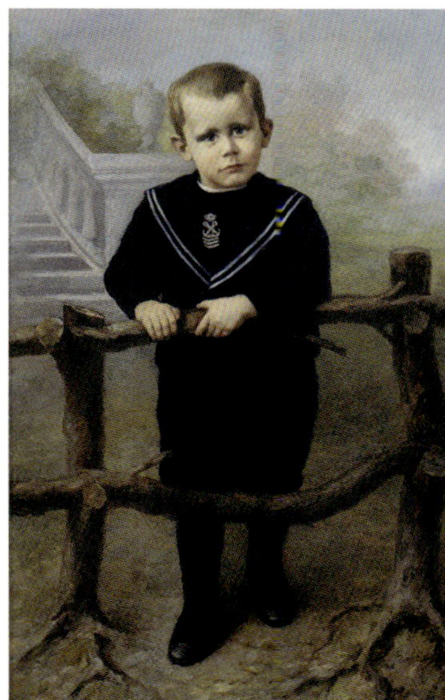

Fig. 8
Piet Mondrian
***Little Jan ('Klein Jantje')*, 1896**
Private collection

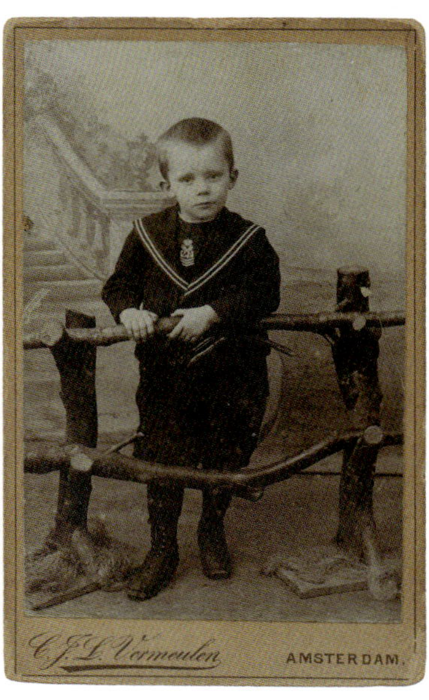

Fig. 9
***Carte de visite* with 'Little Jan', c. 1896**
Photograph: Atelier CA.J.L. Vermeulen
Private collection

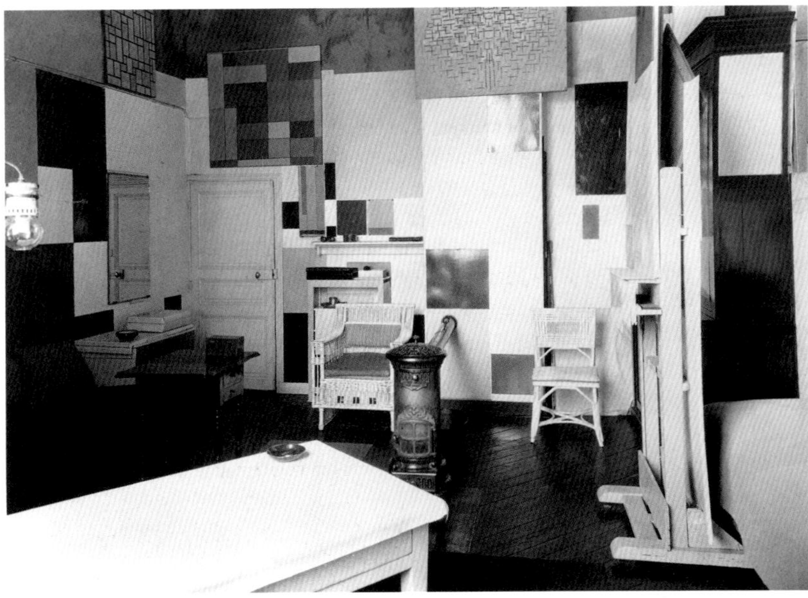

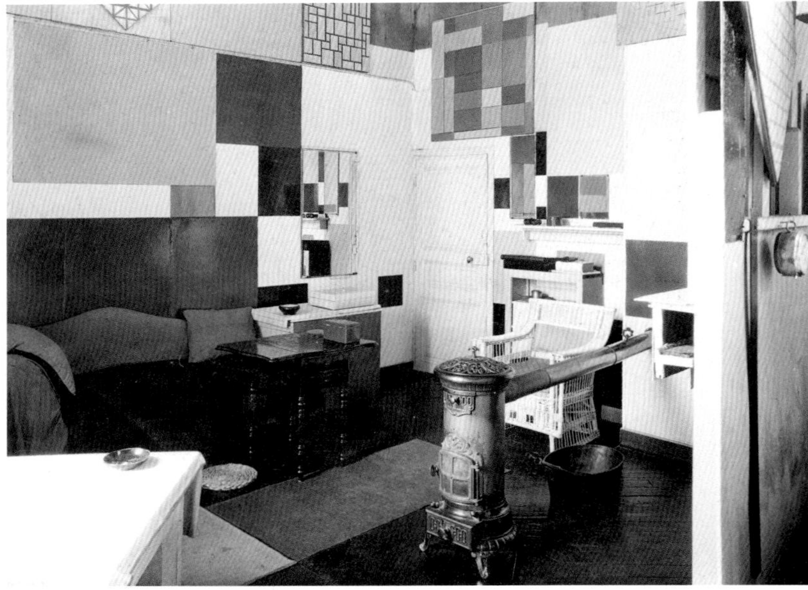

Figs 10–11
Pierre Delbo
Piet Mondrian's studio, c. late November 1925–March 1926 (cats. 75–6)

crucial to the artist's own construction of his image and myth, thanks to the convergence of several art-historical and wider developments. Firstly, there was an increasing recognition of Mondrian's ideas on painting and architecture, along with a growing appreciation of his work among art lovers, critics, curators and dealers: acknowledgment, in other words, of the quality of his art.[13] This customarily slow process had been accelerated in the meantime by the immense expansion of printed media and the associated thirst for visual material. Reproduction of photographs in newspapers and magazines had become steadily easier after the turn of the century. So rapid was this development that by the 1920s the mushrooming of illustrated papers and magazines had created an insatiable demand for photographs and photo reportage.[14] The parallel emergence of phenomena such as marketing and advertising was another source of demand. A visual culture now established itself and photographs became increasingly important to the transmission of news and other types of information.

This gave photography yet another boost, turning it into a source of income for a new professional group of documentary and press photographers. Many of the best-known practitioners of the 1920s and 1930s found their primary outlet in the magazines.[15] During that period (and also after the Second World War), Paris became a centre for pioneering photographers who went on to achieve fame, rubbing shoulders with one another in the same circles to which Mondrian now belonged. They included André Kertész, László Moholy-Nagy, Florence Henri, Rogi André and Rosie Ney, all of whom photographed Mondrian or his studio.

Mondrian's mission was buoyed up by this new tide. Having spent years cultivating his image as an artist with a view to highlighting the seriousness of the neo-plastic project, he became a sought-after subject from the late 1920s onwards for all sorts of photographers. He was now very much in vogue and would remain so for the rest of his life. After he moved to New York, for instance, the likes of Hermann Landshoff, Arnold Newman and Fritz Glarner were also quick to seek him out.

Photography as art form: The debate

One of the parallel historical developments mentioned above was the gradual emancipation of photography as an art form. It was long held in lower esteem than painting, in which the painter was not only expected to have mastered their medium, but also and above all to use those skills and tools to create *art*. Many had come to realize, however, that a photograph could be more than merely the clinical result of a mechanical process: the photographer's eye for staging, lighting and composition, how they applied their technique when shooting and the choices they made during the development process all contributed substantially to the eloquence of the result. Photographers sought initially to apply the principles of visual art, most notably painting, to the new medium. This was the underlying principle of 'pictorialism' — a strongly impressionistic strand in photography that arose towards the end of the 19th century but was superseded by modernism in the second decade of the 20th century, a development that accelerated in the 1920s.

The debate surrounding the potential or limitations of photography as an art form deserves to be considered separately, since Mondrian himself contributed to it — albeit somewhat ambiguously, as one might expect given his previously discussed views on the subject. Full use of photography was made at the Bauhaus from the moment the celebrated academy of art was founded in 1919. Even so, a true shift in attitude had to await the appointment in 1923 of László Moholy-Nagy, who developed his own vision of photography and began to use the camera as an artistic medium in its own right.[16] Moholy-Nagy's experiments had already prompted the article 'Produktion—Reproduktion' in *De Stijl* in 1922,[17] where he wrote, among other things: 'The camera captures light effects by means of a silver bromide plate positioned against its rear wall. We have so far only made secondary use of the device's function: to capture (reproduce) individual objects, how they reflected or absorbed the light. If we are to grant it a new function, we must use the light-sensitivity of the silver bromide plate in such a way that it captures and fixes the lighting effects (the momentary play of light) that *we ourselves have given shape* by means of mirrors and lenses. This too requires a good deal of experimentation.'[18]

The article turned out to be a prelude to the Bauhaus book *Malerei Fotografie Film* (Painting Photography Film), published in 1925, through which Moholy-Nagy would have a major influence on photography's reception as an art form. To his mind, the photographer shared the mission of the painter: 'Representation viewed from an artistic perspective becomes *creation*; without that perspective, it is merely *description*.'[19] He argued that recent developments in thinking about photography had led to a dichotomy between it and painting. Where the latter had initially been the domain in which reality was represented by means of colour and line, photography had now taken its place. The camera meant, after all, that its operator could come much closer to reality; even *reproduce* it. This in turn had triggered a change in painting: 'The mechanically exact process of photography and film provides us with an incomparably better functioning means of expression for *representing* than the manual methods of figurative painting we have known previously. From now on, painting can concern itself with the *pure expression of colour*. [...] The pure expression of colour shows that the "theme" of colour representation (painting) is *colour itself*; that through it, without reference to objects, a pure and primary, composed expression can be achieved.'[20]

For Mondrian — the forerunner since around 1915 of a non-figurative art in which visible reality had been abandoned — this was all grist to his mill. Rather than painting what he saw, he drew on his own convictions to search for an art capable of standing alone and that was based on the primordial principles underlying visible reality. Mondrian viewed the horizontal and vertical line, combined with the primary colours blue, red

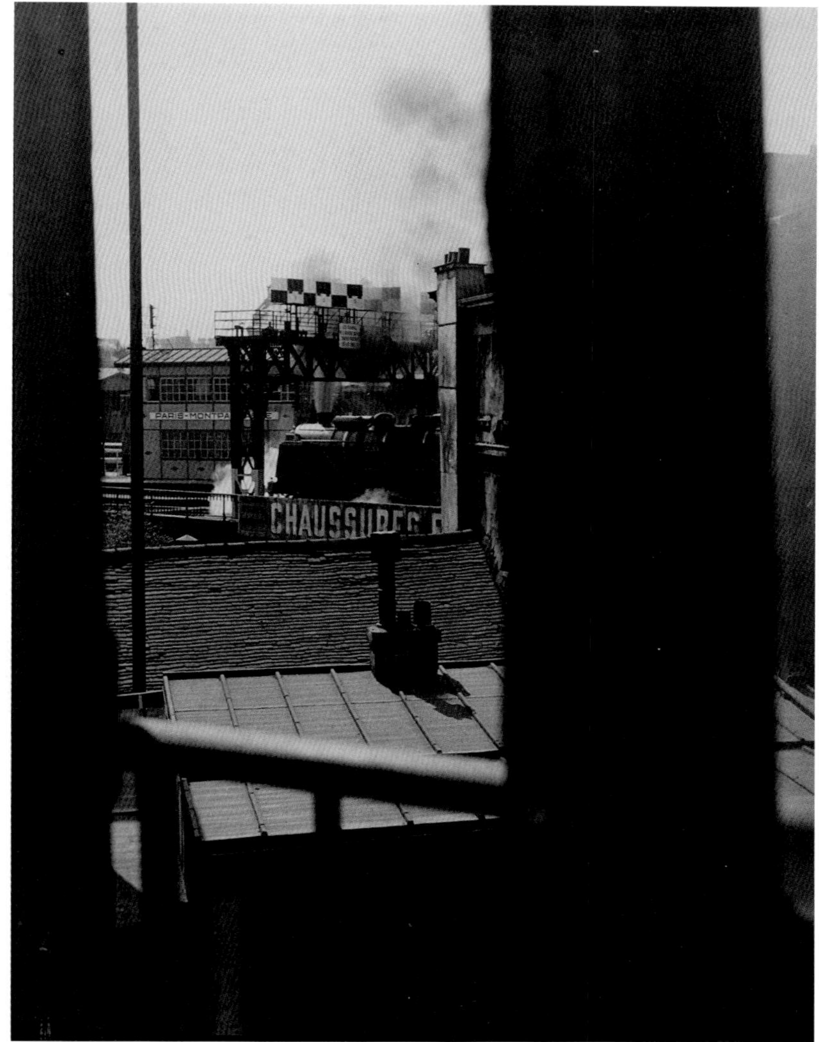

Fig. 12
László Moholy-Nagy
Gare Montparnasse viewed from Piet Mondrian's kitchen window, summer 1927 or summer 1930
(cat. 139)

and yellow, and the non-colours white, black and grey, as basic principles of reality. His work was entirely in keeping, in short, with Moholy-Nagy's vision of the painting of the future. This was not a coincidence, since Mondrian's aesthetics had been published in German in 1924 — once again in the Bauhausbücher (Bauhaus Books) series edited by Moholy-Nagy. The Hungarian was thus well informed about Mondrian's neo-plasticism at the time he wrote *Malerei Fotografie Film*. We do not know whether Mondrian was aware in turn of Moholy-Nagy's book, but it is by no means implausible.

We can infer Mondrian's attitude towards the ongoing debate regarding photography as art form from his response to another article on photography and painting. In 1927, at the editor Moholy-Nagy's request, Ernst Kállai published 'Malerei und Fotografie' in the Dutch journal *i10*.[21] While his point of departure differed from Moholy-Nagy's, Kállai likewise focused in his article on whether, and if so how, photography might be viewed as a form of art. Kállai took the opportunity to enumerate the differences between painting and photography, praising the painter's ability to use facture to generate different emotions.[22] Photography has no such possibility, since each photograph has the same, smooth surface due to the layer of gelatin containing grains of silver. Kállai clearly sided with painting, although he still concluded that it was threatened by film art, given the latter's ability to represent movement in a manner impossible for static painting.

Mondrian was one of several readers, including Moholy-Nagy, to respond to Kállai's article in a subsequent issue of *i10*. His short reaction makes it clear that he was still ambivalent towards photography as an art form:

> 'Although I substantially agree with Mr Kállai's interesting observations on "painting and photography", I feel we ought not to lose sight of the fact that it is the "artist" and not the "medium" that creates the work of art.
>
> The medium is certainly very important and is closely connected with the plastic expression of a work, but it is essentially the artist who determines that it is *purely plastic* and not imitative.
>
> All the same, it seems to me that the character of photography is more imitative than plastic. Photography in the customary sense is the appropriate medium for the *reproduction* of objectivity, and all art is *creation*.
>
> But it is difficult at present to predict the evolution of photography — indeed, so much effort has already been made in the field of pure plasticity that we might expect anything from photography. It is quite possible that the technique of photography will change, just as the technique of painting has changed, and Mr Kállai's comparisons and observations could help bring this about.'[23]

Contrary to what Moholy-Nagy had written in *De Stijl* in 1922, Mondrian continued to view photography as a medium of *registration* rather than one of *creation*. He considered his own neo-plasticism in painting to be a logical step after many decades, if not centuries, of painterly development. Photography, by contrast, was still in its infancy. As noted, Moholy-Nagy had already questioned this fundamentalist stance in *Malerei Fotografie Film*. He sidestepped the debate by making the tool subordinate to the artistic vision of the person wielding it; after all, in the hands of a mediocre painter, brush and paint are not sufficient to produce *art* either. The functional use that Mondrian made of photography throughout his life suggests that he did not share Moholy-Nagy's vision. Firstly, he had his work photographed in order to compile a portfolio for use in marketing his art. And secondly, he commissioned photographs of himself and his studio to communicate his style and image. So while Mondrian did use photography to serve his personal interests, he never viewed it as a creative, plastic tool in its own right.

Mondrian referred in his response to Kállai's article to the 'evolution of photography', indicating that, while promising, the medium's development to date was still insufficient in his view for photography to be considered an art form. It is hard to say, for instance, how familiar he was with the photograms that had recently been produced by Moholy-Nagy and Man Ray — two artists he knew personally and with whom he had varying degrees of contact. As a co-editor of *i10*, he is highly likely to have seen Moholy-Nagy's photograms in the magazine. And if he had a copy of *Malerei Fotografie Film*, he would also have come across photograms there by both Moholy-Nagy and Man Ray. It is quite plausible, besides, that Mondrian had already got to know Man Ray's work, since an exhibition had been held in 1925 featuring paintings by Mondrian and photographs by the American.[24] We can only speculate, however, as to whether the photographic efforts he mentions 'in the field of pure plasticity' refer to Man Ray and Moholy-Nagy's photograms.

There is nothing to suggest that Mondrian's views on photography changed after 1927. The most important exhibitions in the photographic field tended to be held in Germany, outside his patch. While he could keep up with new developments through magazines, newspapers, books and his many contacts with avant-garde photographers,[25] he did not offer any further opinion on photography as an art form in his letters or his other writings.

Two Mondrians

Given the role that photography played in Mondrian's life and his views on the medium, we can conclude that he used it mainly for practical purposes, primarily to promote himself and his work. This leaves the question of the relationship between the man and the image he created. How did Piet Mondrian's personal life relate to the cultivated artist as perceived by the outside world? He appeared in public as a serious and reserved man, immaculately dressed and coiffured. His expression is invariably grave and the space around him sober, austere and referring as a matter of course to his paintings. The inspirational link between it all is neo-plasticism and its significance to humanity and society. What was at stake was not Mondrian as an individual creator but his mission. Anything not directly related to the artist or his aspirations — his private life and human contacts, in other words — remained out of sight. The personal had to make way for the higher goal, just as it did in his art. Or did so in the eyes of the general public at least, which had to rely on what was published both during and after his life. Yet those who were close to him knew a quite different side to Mondrian. While there is no doubt that he opted uncompromisingly for a life devoted to art, many others played a part in that life too: relatives, friends, fellow artists, collectors, gallery owners, writers, patrons and curators. He also had a sense of humour that one might not expect going solely by the clichéd image of the artist. Anyone seeking to meet the 'true Mondrian' will thus find two of them. To do him justice, you need to overlay the one with the other.

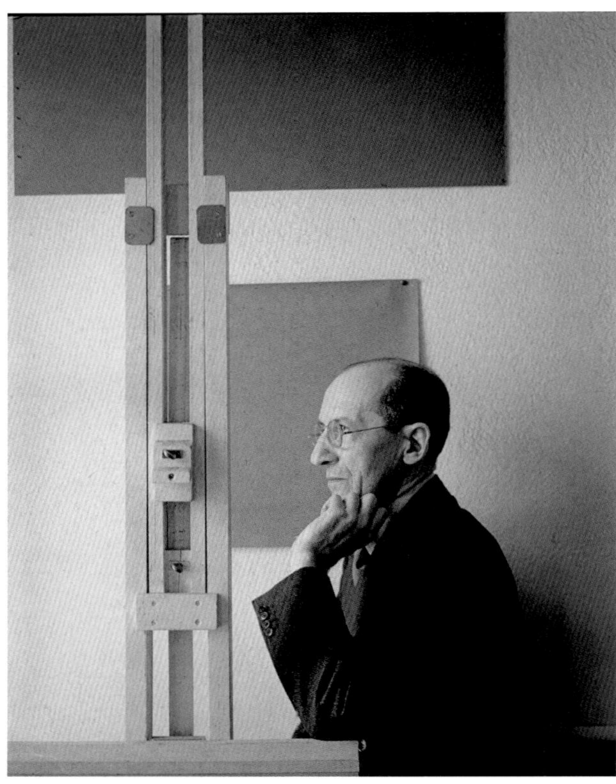

Fig. 13
Portrait of Piet Mondrian in his studio, between 29 April and 7 May 1942
Photograph: Arnold Newman
(cat. 239)

> Fig. 14
Detail from the Portrait of Piet Mondrian, autumn 1907, by Fotostudio Jac. Vetter, in which the retouching of Mondrian's pupils and hair are visible. The wrinkles also appear to have been retouched.
(cat. 35)

Portraits: Searching for the Right Look

Early portraits: Burgeoning self-confidence

Artists were defined around the turn of the century as individuals with special talents and aptitudes. This status of cultural flag-bearer did not translate into material wealth for every artist, yet something of a personality cult existed around poets, painters, sculptors, composers and other servants of 'Art' — an admiration for creators of beauty that could take flight the more famous the relevant artist became, with success begetting success. In so far as they made it to such Olympian heights, this often triggered a process of mythmaking (leaving to one side that something similar could also be achieved through provocative behaviour or a scandalous lifestyle).

Artists' portraits — whether done by themselves or others — are an ancient phenomenon. It goes without saying that outward appearance can influence public perception and is frequently taken as symbolic of the person's artistic temperament — Beethoven's wild hair, for instance, Tolstoy's simple smock, the glowering expression of Nietzsche, Proust's fastidious pocket handkerchief, or Picasso's self-assured virility.

The relatively limited effort and expense of a *photographic* portrait could raise awareness of the artist faster than ever before, especially when assisted by the press. *Onze moderne meesters* (Our Modern Masters), compiled by F. M. Lurasco, was published in 1907. The book's foreword contains a succinct description of what it contains: 'A collection of portraits of our [Dutch] contemporary painters, draughtsmen and sculptors, accompanied by a few brief biographical details'.[26] Mondrian was among those approached for the book, as was his uncle, the painter Frits Mondriaan. It was his first opportunity to present himself on a wider stage via a portrait photograph, which he had taken for this end at the Amsterdam portrait studio of Jacob Vetter. Mondrian appears to have prepared meticulously. He gazes confidently into the lens. The full, neat beard, the hair with the kiss curl and the wool waistcoat beneath the jacket give him the somewhat paradoxical appearance of a cultivated bohemian. No part of his appearance has been left to chance. The hair on the right, for instance, is cut straight as a ruler. His beard has been carefully trimmed in an angular style, with clipped sideburns flowing into his head-hair. A copy of the photograph, signed by Mondrian, has survived (fig. 14). In it, the irises, pupils and curl have all been retouched with black ink. It is not clear whether he did this himself, but we know from letters that he did not hesitate to adjust photographs.[27]

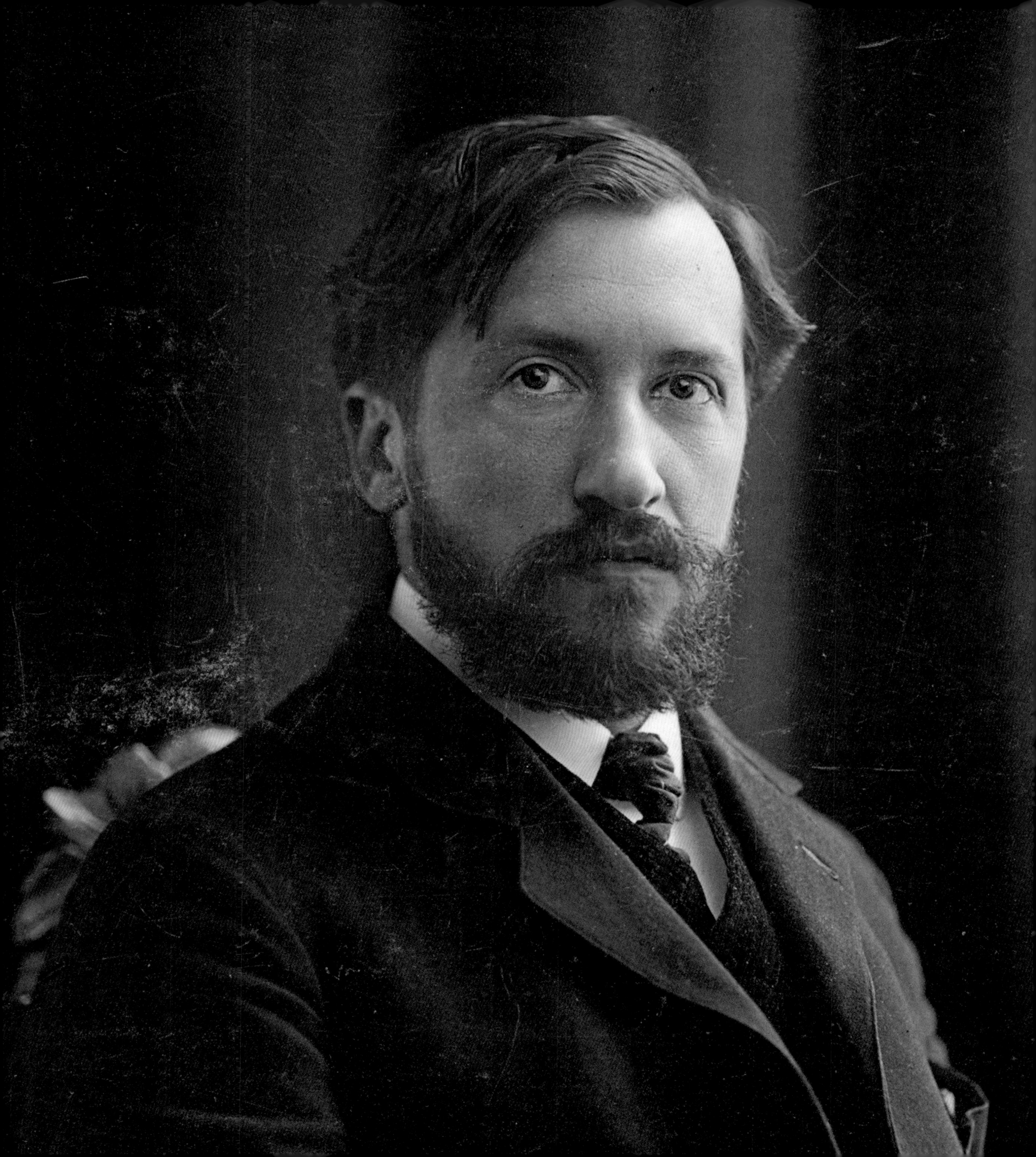

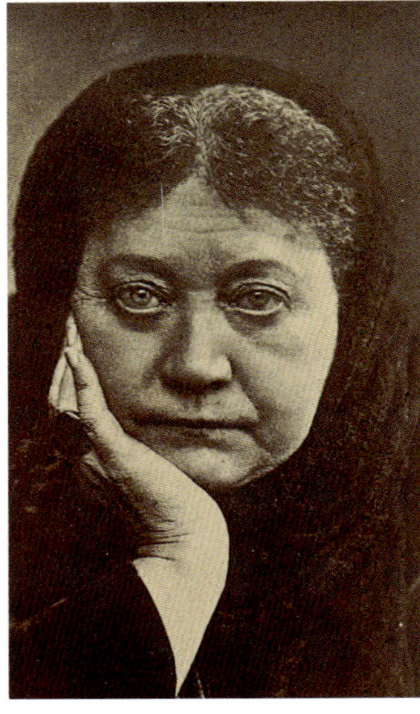

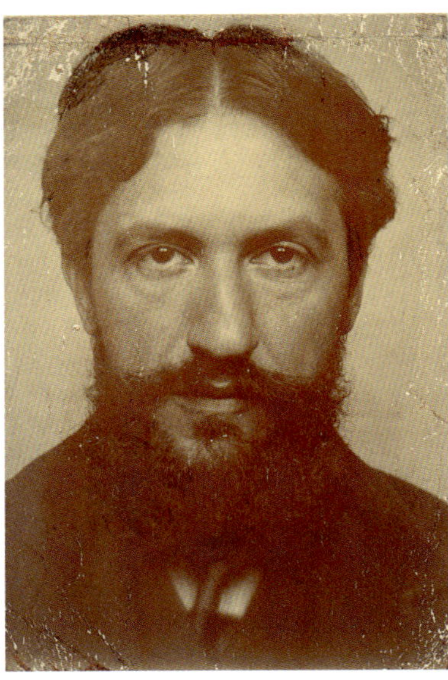

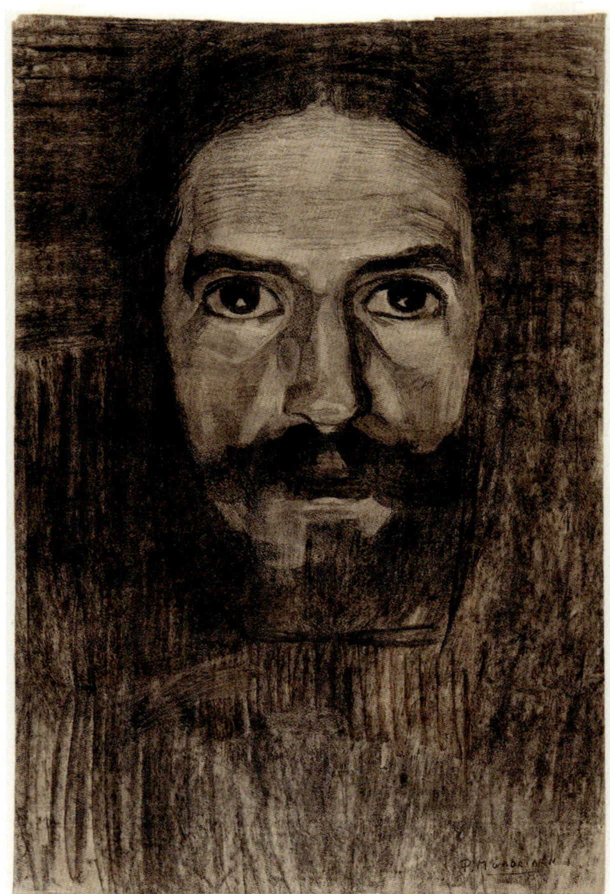

Mondrian further cultivated his artistic appearance in the years immediately following the Lurasco picture. The surviving portrait photographs and the studio shot from 1908–9 seem to allude to the artist's growing spiritual interests, most notably in Theosophy, which is also apparent in his work. He attended lectures by Rudolf Steiner (1908) and Annie Besant (1909) and immersed himself in Theosophical texts. In 1909 he wrote to the critic Israël Querido: 'I believe that you also acknowledge the strong connection between philosophy and art, but that is precisely what most painters deny; in the great masters it is subconscious, but I believe that conscious spiritual knowledge in a painter will have a much greater influence on his art — and that it is only a weakness within him, or a lack of genius, if that spiritual knowledge would harm his art. [...] I am trying to acquire occult knowledge for myself in order to understand things better.'[28]

Two portraits by an unknown photographer show the artist with slightly wavy hair and a curly beard (cats 37–8, fig. 16). Some have compared his appearance with that of the infamous Russian pilgrim, monk, faith-healer and schemer Rasputin. Superficial associations like this are not uncommon and have contributed to the myth surrounding him. Above all, however, they obscure Mondrian's true intentions.[29] If we insist on making a comparison at all, esoteric references would be more apt, given the striking emphasis on the wide-open eyes — a symbolic allusion to a state of spiritual vigilance that is also found in a portrait of Helena Petrovna Blavatsky, which Mondrian himself owned (fig. 15).[30] He used the two photographs to create a self-portrait in charcoal, in which the viewer is immediately drawn to the piercing gaze. It is clear that he even used the photos to determine the composition, as their folded edges correspond fairly accurately with the framing of the charcoal self-portrait (figs 16–17). This is one of the few surviving examples in which Mondrian demonstrably made use of photography in the creation of his non-commissioned art.

Fig. 15
Portrait of Helena Petrovna Blavatsky, c. 1895 RKD, Piet Mondrian Archive (0740), inv. 73.

Figs 16–17
Comparison between cat. 37 (pictured here reversed) and Piet Mondrian's *Self-Portrait*, c. 1908, Kunstmuseum, The Hague

One of the portrait photos can be seen in a photograph of the artist sitting at the table in the front room of his home and studio at Sarphatipark in Amsterdam (cat. 39). It stands on the cabinet to the right of Mondrian, in a mount in among the glass jugs.[31] Further to the right, we can see through into the back room, which Mondrian used as a studio. The artist is dressed in warm clothes and appears immersed in a heavy book, probably one of the occult sources to which he alludes in the letter to Querido. Three prints of this studio picture have survived, suggesting that the artist was pleased with the shot. He gave copies to two women friends and held onto a third print — a wonderful deep-blue cyanotype — for his whole life.

The fourth and final portrait of Mondrian with a full beard and loose hair dates from the spring of 1909 (fig. 18). There has been some speculation concerning the pose he adopted in it. Could it be a yoga position or a posture for meditation? It is tempting to interpret the picture in the light of Mondrian's growing interest in esotericism, but the key actually lies with the photographer — the Berlin-based doctor and phrenologist Alfred Waldenburg, who had probably been living in the Netherlands for some time when he met Mondrian in Amsterdam in late 1908.[32] Waldenburg and Mondrian shared an interest in the concept of 'evolution', which each approached from his own particular concerns. In Theosophy, for instance, it is a central concept applied to a person's spiritual development, whereas the scientist Waldenburg was drawn chiefly to the biological aspect of evolution. In addition to his practice as a phrenologist, the German engaged in a variant of anthropology grafted onto Darwin's theory of evolution. He believed that the shape of a person's skull revealed their predispositions and limitations. Waldenburg also took account of the development of other parts of the body, such as the hands, to determine which evolutionary step a person had attained. He photographed Mondrian in a pose that he also had other subjects of his adopt: hands raised, with the palm of one and the back of the other visible (fig. 19).[33]

The 'new Mondrian'

Mondrian's appearance underwent a metamorphosis in the middle of 1910. He shaved off his beard, combed his hair flat against his skull and swapped the loose-fitting shirt and wool waistcoat for impeccable three-piece suits. For the first time, we see the clear outlines of the Mondrian he would remain from then on: a man who presented himself with perfect grooming and sharp, conventional tailoring. The transformation did not go unnoticed within his circle, prompting him to write to one female friend: 'So, did you find me so very much changed? Well, that's just appearances: I'm still the same, just a little bit more balanced, if I'm not deceiving myself. The study of theosophy has helped a lot in that. This knowledge is of great benefit to me: it really is a guide to developing your consciousness. [...] I didn't think you had changed, in my case it's getting rid of the beard that's made me look strange.'[34] His hair was still parted in the middle at first, but at some point during the First World War, he started to comb it straight back. The only variations on this style that Mondrian later allowed himself were a toothbrush moustache he grew for a few years and spectacles from around 1922 onwards.

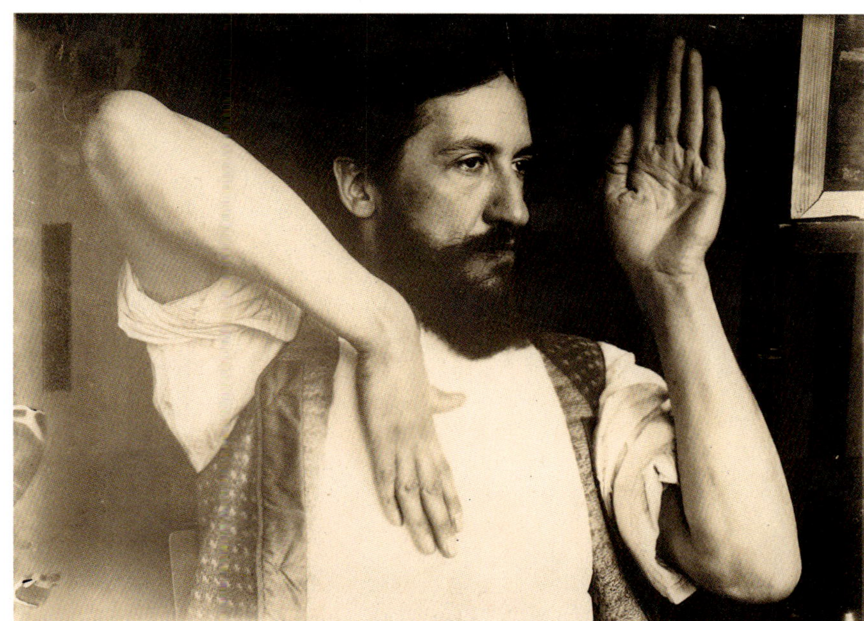

Fig. 18
Phrenological portrait of Piet Mondrian, c. April 1909
Photograph: Alfred Waldenburg, c. April 1909 (cat. 40)

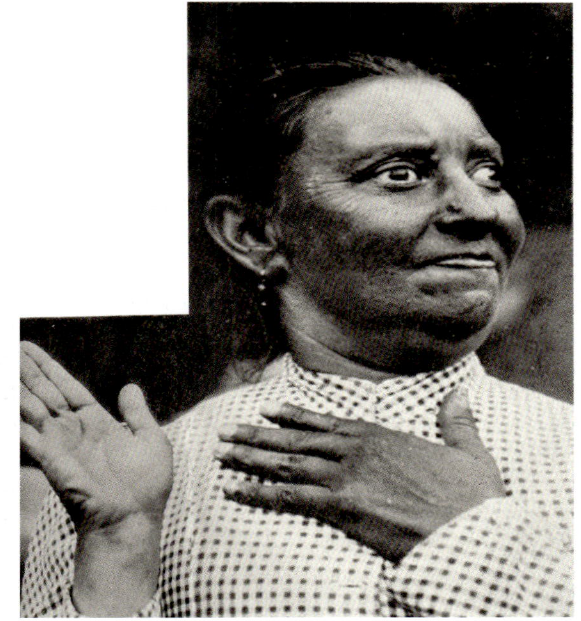

Fig. 19
Portrait of a forty-one-year-old epileptic from The Hague by Alfred Waldenburg, May–June 1907. The photograph was compiled from two separate images in the publication *Urschaedelform und Epilepsie*, based on a lecture that Waldenburg gave in Amsterdam in 1907.

To use the terms of the English essayist Joseph Addison, one might say at a stretch that Mondrian deliberately altered his aura in 1910 from 'natural genius' to that of 'learned genius'.[35] In other words, he used his appearance to show that he had exchanged the 19th-century poetics of the expressive artist for that of a more philosophically motivated, constructive approach. His change of appearance was decidedly not driven by superficial motives, but tied in with the previously described, fundamental artistic shift in Mondrian's work, which was definitively established during his first stay in Paris from 1912 to 1914.

Photographs of the 'new Mondrian' prior to his permanent move to Paris in 1919 are scarce. We do not know whether there were more of them at the time, but even if none existed, this would not mean that Mondrian attached less importance to the image he presented of himself. On the contrary: he was well aware that the public assumed a connection between the personality of the artist (as far as this can be made out in a portrait) and his art. His first comments on this connection also date from the same period. His work had begun to draw the attention of several prominent Dutch collectors, which made it important for him to get his image into circulation. Writing to his friend and collector Sal Slijper in May 1916, he commented: 'Now people are going to promote me so much, I'm starting to think there's a need for a portrait to be out there!!'[36] He drew and painted several self-portraits in the years 1916—18. A large, naturalistically executed example from 1918 is particularly noteworthy (fig. 20). The setting is Mondrian's small wooden studio in the countryside near Laren. There is a reference in the background to recent abstract canvases, with separately placed blocks of primary colours on a white ground.[37] Modern though he was, Mondrian followed the centuries-old tradition here in which artists use accoutrements to identify themselves. While these are often the tools of the painter's trade — there are any number of self-portraits featuring easel, brushes and palette — Mondrian preferred to present himself as a gentleman, with a reference in the background to his modernity and identity.

The photographer's eye

For the time being, the publication of Lurasco's portrait in 1907, taken especially for the occasion, remained a one-off. Although Mondrian's reputation was slowly but surely increasing and he was being discussed more frequently and at greater length by art critics, there was evidently no reason or opportunity for publicists to show the face of the artist himself. Mondrian was happy enough if one of his paintings was reproduced in a newspaper or magazine. This was to change at the beginning of 1922, when Theo van Doesburg asked him to send a portrait photograph for inclusion in a special issue to mark *De Stijl*'s fifth anniversary.[38] Mondrian had a new one taken at R. Rossetti photographer's studio on Rue d'Odessa, a stone's throw from his studio on Rue du Départ (fig. 21). The photograph appeared in the anniversary edition in December, accompanied by excerpts from his earlier texts on painting in the magazine and from the brochure *Le Néo-plasticisme*, which he had published in Paris in 1921. Little had changed in the past few years: Mondrian continued to devote great care to his appearance and he gazes directly into the lens, looking

Fig. 20
Piet Mondrian
***Self-Portrait*, 1918**
Oil on canvas,
88 × 71 cm
Kunstmuseum,
The Hague

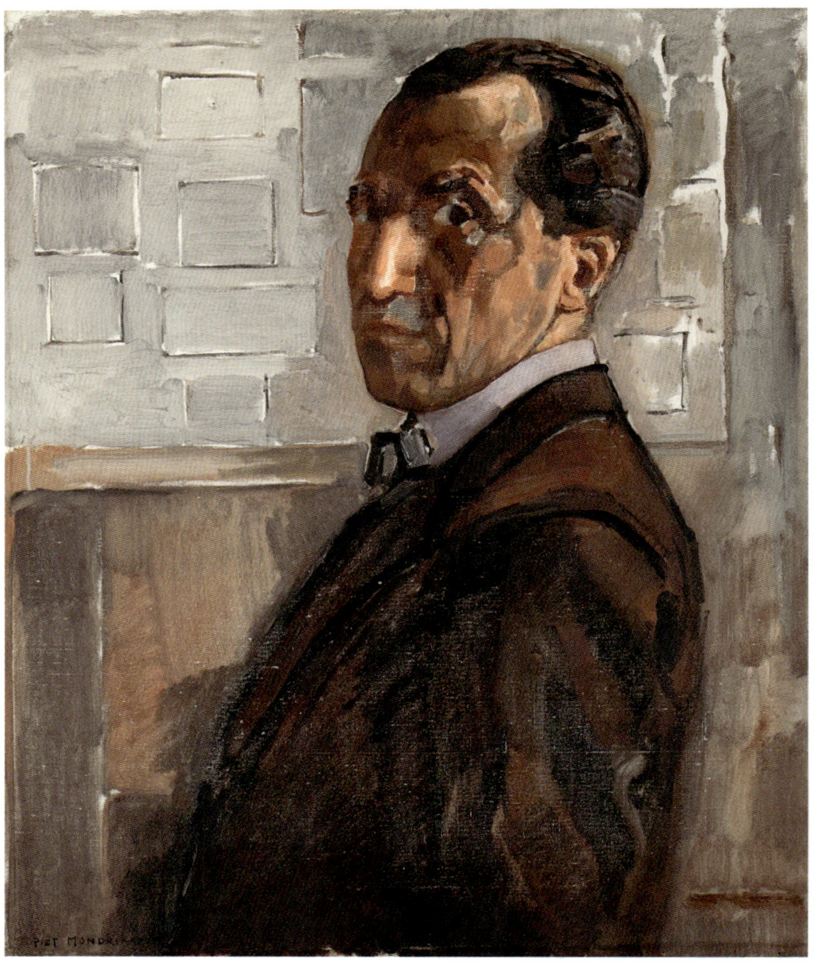

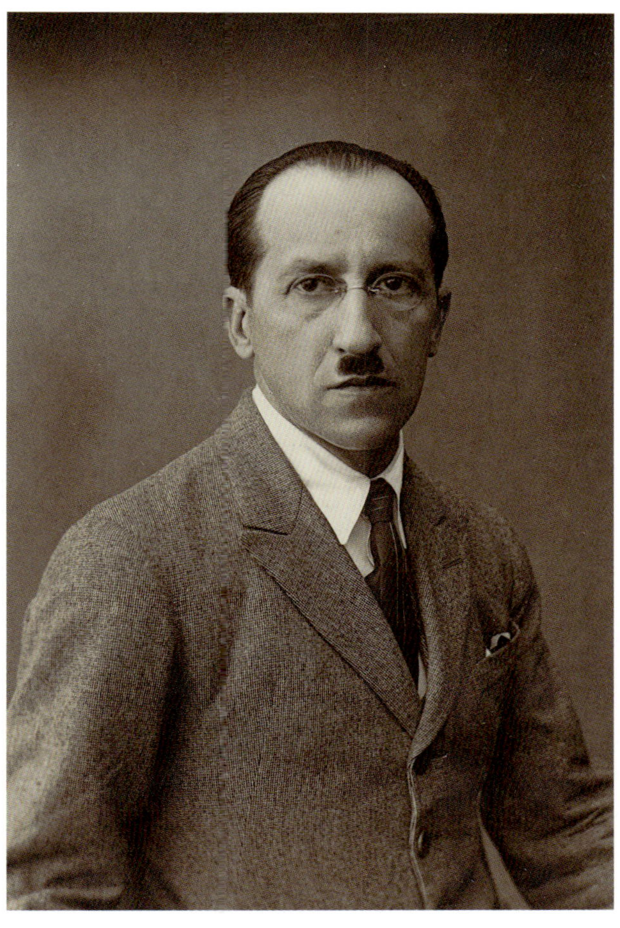

Fig. 21
Portrait of Piet Mondrian, spring (June) 1922
Photograph: R. Rossetti
(cat. 54)

Fig. 22
Piet Mondrian and Nelly van Doesburg in Mondrian's studio, early May 1923
Photograph: Theo Van Doesburg
(cat. 58)

The pictures of Mondrian taken in 1926 by André Kertész have a more staged or orchestrated character. The Hungarian photographer was introduced to the Dutchman in the summer of that year by the Belgian artist and writer Michel Seuphor.[40] In the months that followed, Kertész took several photographs of the artist and his studio, the first time that Mondrian was confronted by a professional, artistic photographer of the new generation. Kertész was one of the 'emancipated' photographers who wanted to use the camera to convey their own vision of reality and who saw photography as an autonomous medium of

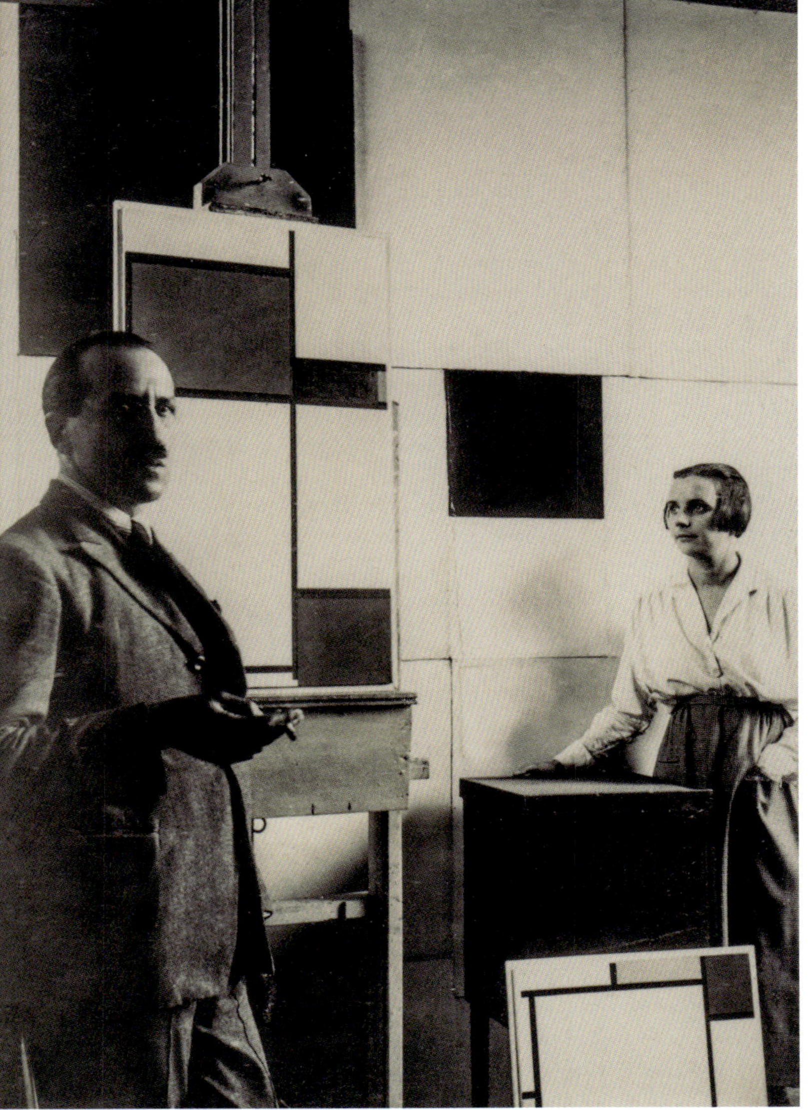

straight at the viewer. This is the first picture in which he wears spectacles — here a minimalist, frameless pince-nez. In the years that followed, Mondrian had himself photographed almost exclusively with glasses, from which we can see that he regularly changed models. Another new element is the toothbrush moustache, which Mondrian grew at some point after arriving in Paris and did not shave off until around 1928. Another photograph of Mondrian appeared in *De Stijl* in 1924, accompanying his article 'De huif naar den wind'.[39] On this occasion, Van Doesburg used a picture he himself had taken in Mondrian's studio, which also included his (Van Doesburg's) then girlfriend and future wife Nelly van Moorsel, as well as two recent paintings by Mondrian (fig. 22). Nelly was cropped out of the photograph as published in *De Stijl*, along with one of the paintings in the right foreground. Unlike the publication of photographs orchestrated by Mondrian himself, the reuse of a snapshot was enough for Van Doesburg on this occasion.

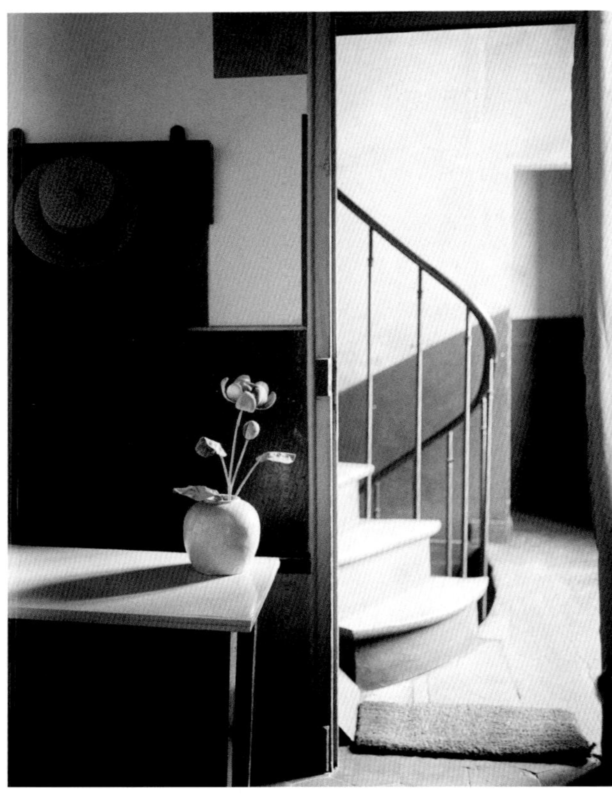

Fig. 23
***Chez Mondrian, Paris*, between September 1926 and mid-February 1927**
Photograph: André Kertész
(cat. 92)

expression. It is thanks to his artist's eye that images of Mondrian's pipe and glasses on the studio table and of the artificial flower, painted white, by the entrance have inscribed themselves in so many people's memories (fig. 23).

It is less well known that Kertész also took several portrait photographs of Mondrian, all of which are brought together for the first time in this book (cats 94–9). The meticulous orchestration of these pictures is evident from the contrast with a photograph Kertész took of Mondrian at an unguarded moment, in which we see the smiling artist pouring a glass of wine for one of his guests (fig. 24).

The Paris gallery Au Sacre du Printemps held an exhibition of André Kertész's work in 1927.[41] A damaged glass negative shows the proud photographer posing in front of a wall with a series of his pictures, including (directly behind his head) a photograph taken in Mondrian's studio (fig. 25). Another picture shows several people by a different wall containing photographs and abstract-geometric compositions by the Hungarian constructivist Ida Thal, which display some striking similarities with Mondrian's work (fig. 26). Two more photographs of Mondrian's studio hang on this wall, bringing the total to three: not bad out of a total of thirty-one exhibited pictures. Kertész's satisfaction with the technical and artistic quality of the photographs will undoubtedly have played a part in the selection, but this is also proof of the photogenic appearance of Mondrian and his studio.

Kertész preferred to work with natural light, but the use of artificial studio lighting offered new possibilities too, as beautifully reflected in a portrait taken around 1926 by Max Winisky (fig. 27). Little is known about this photographer, who advertised his 'artistic photography' and 'portraits d'art Max'. His relative anonymity is especially remarkable given the high quality of the portrait he made of Mondrian. It is certainly accurate to call it an 'artistic portrait': the light projected onto the wall behind the subject's head, for instance, evokes an intangible, artistic atmosphere. The face is lit strongly from the left, while the ear on the right is illuminated by another lamp, so that this half of the

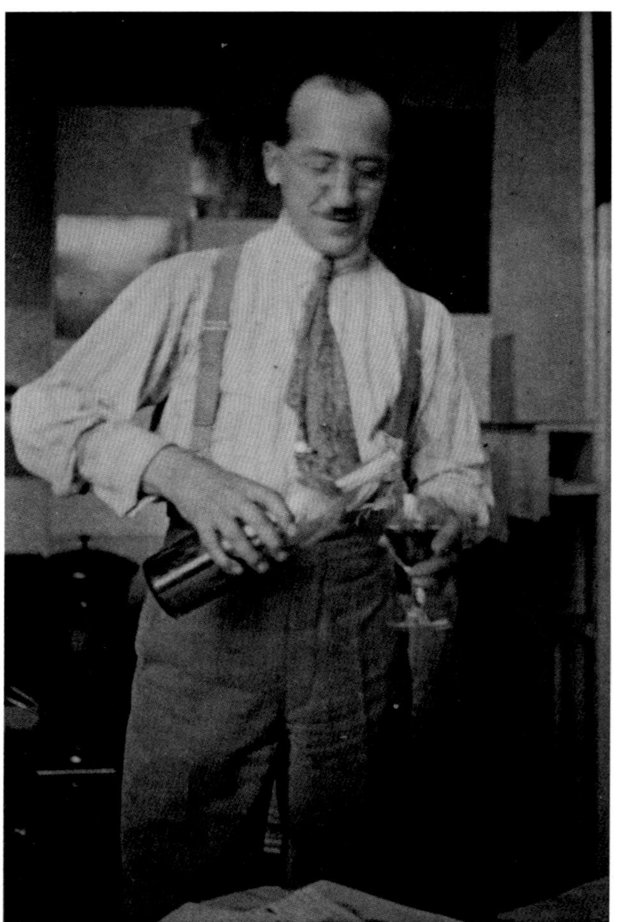

Fig. 24
Piet Mondrian pouring wine, 19 (?) August 1926
Photograph: André Kertész
(cat. 83)

Fig. 25
Self-portrait in the gallery Au Sacre du Printemps, Paris, March 1927
Photograph: André Kertész
Médiathèque du Patrimoine et de l'Architecture, Donation Kertész, Paris

Fig. 26
Jean Sliwinsky, Herwarth Walden and others in the gallery Au Sacre du Printemps, Paris, March 1927
Photograph: André Kertész
J. Paul Getty Museum, Malibu

Fig. 27
Portrait of Piet Mondrian, c. 1926
Photograph: Max Winisky
(cat. 73)

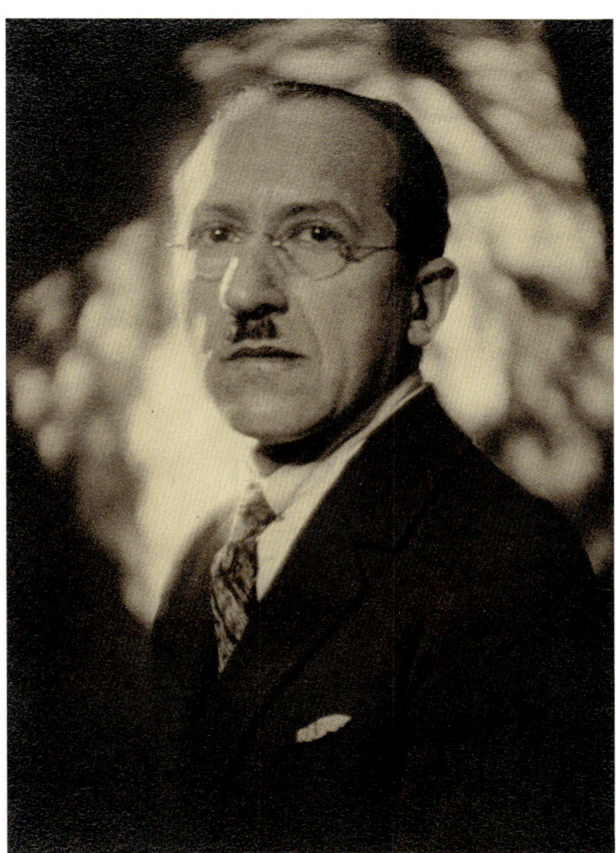

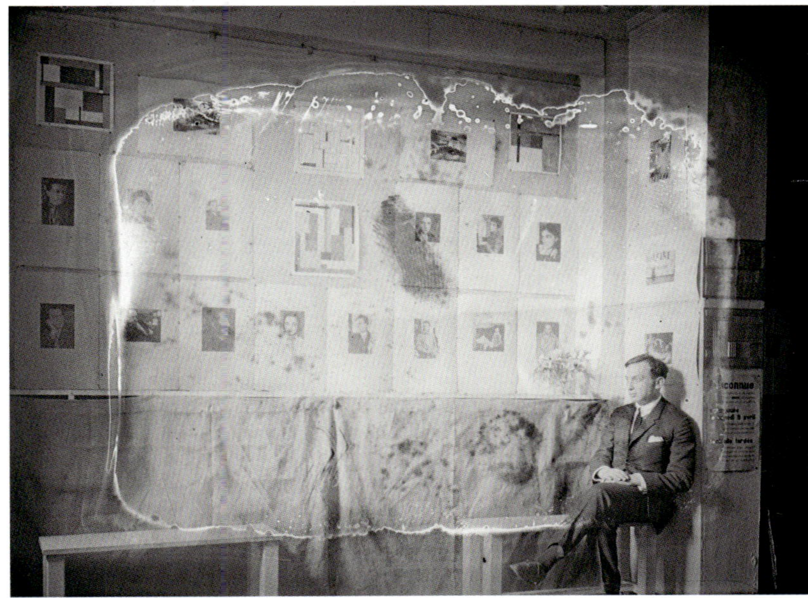

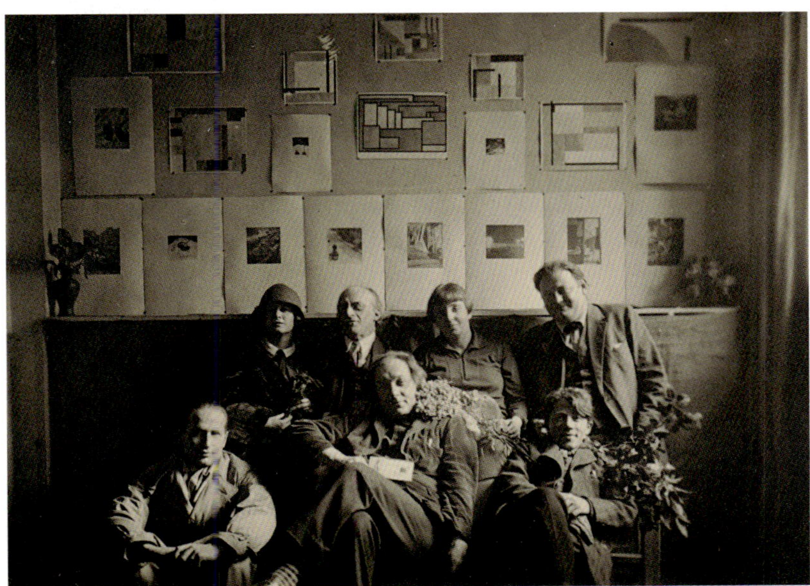

face does not disappear completely into darkness. The carefully thought-out composition and lighting gives the portrait an immense presence and it is one of the few photographs of himself that Mondrian would hold onto for the rest of his life. We can only speculate as to why the picture was never published during his lifetime, even though there were opportunities to use it. Perhaps he thought the shot too suggestive and insufficiently aloof. Whatever the case, when Paul Citroen was compiling a book on contemporary Dutch painting in 1929, he submitted a different portrait.[42]

Mondrian in private

There is a discernible shift towards the end of the 1920s in how Mondrian had himself photographed. From 1926 onwards, he focused attention on his distinctive studio and the message he wished it to convey. As far as we know, at least, it would be some considerable time before he had any posed photographs taken again — other than for official documents — which might be read as representing a person he wanted to be.

He was, by contrast, snapped in an informal context on multiple occasions. Examples include the pictures taken by Hannah Höch and Til Brugman during a visit to Mondrian in 1927, in which they take turns posing with the artist in his studio (fig. 29, cats 104—5). The quality of both photos is mediocre, with no trace of promotional or artistic aspirations. The same goes for the pictures that the Hungarian born American designer Eugene Lux took while paying Mondrian a visit in the spring of 1934. There are no allusions to his artistic practice in the portraits taken by Lux, unless one recognizes part of his easel in the wooden stand in the background (cats 155—61).[43]

Kurt Schwitters too shot a portrait of his friend and kindred spirit during a visit to Paris in 1936 (fig. 28). He photographed Mondrian in front of the stairs leading up to the mezzanine of his studio at 278 Boulevard Raspail, where the artist had recently moved. The staircase forms a striking oblique line in the composition — something that Mondrian loathed artistically to such a degree that when Theo van Doesburg introduced the diagonal into his work in 1924, it helped end the friendship between the two. The photograph must have been taken immediately before entering or exiting the studio, as Mondrian is dressed in a hat, scarf and overcoat — testifying once more to his efforts always to appear in public well dressed.

The only surviving photographs that document Mondrian's two-year stay in England (1938—40) are ones required for official travel documents (cats 187—88). He arrived in New York in early October 1940. Shortly afterwards, his American friend and future heir Harry Holtzman, who had met Mondrian on a visit to Paris in 1934, took him to his summer house in Great Barrington, Massachusetts, to recuperate after the stress of living in London during the Blitz and of a tiring transatlantic crossing. The picture Holtzman took of the artist in the garden of that house is probably the first to show him after his arrival in the United States (fig. 32).

A little later, Holtzman set up a photo session in his own Manhattan studio, not far from the location where he had put Mondrian up in New York. The Dutchman looks directly into the lens, with and without spectacles, alternately stern and remarkably amiable. There are also a few shots in which his eyes are closed. The series undoubtedly includes some of the most sympathetic surviving images of the artist (cats 193—207).

One of them continues to be used in a quite different context: the catalogue of Peggy Guggenheim's collection, *Art of This Century* (1942), includes pictures of the artists' eyes alongside the description of their works. For the text on Mondrian, a cut-out was used from one of Holtzman's portraits. Mondrian probably picked the photo himself: the contact print on which the eyes are marked has survived (figs 30—31). It is one of the few pictures taken by Holtzman in which

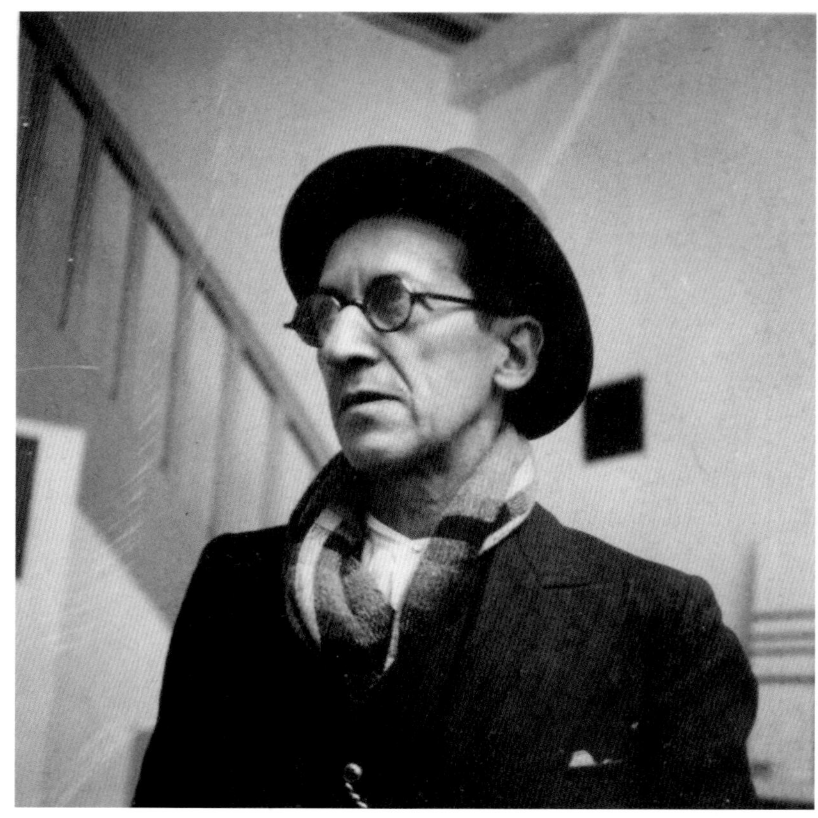

Fig. 28
Portrait of Piet Mondrian, between 20 and 24 March 1936. Photograph: Kurt Schwitters (cat. 174)

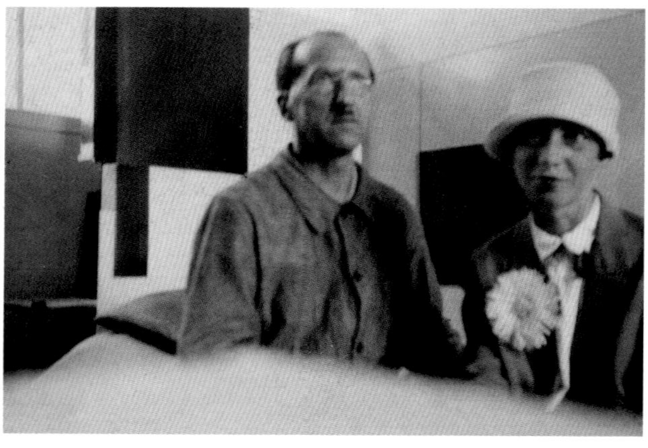

Fig. 29
Piet Mondriaan and Til Brugman in Mondrian's studio, September 1927 Photograph: Hannah Höch (cat. 104)

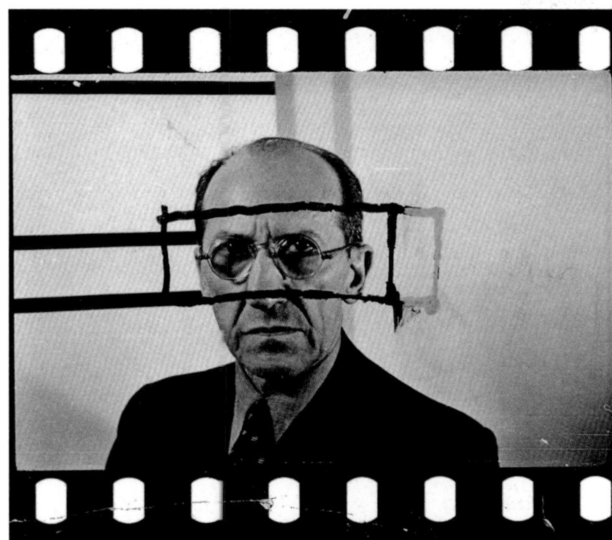

Fig. 30
Portrait of Piet Mondrian in Holtzman's studio, between 4 October 1940 and May 1942
Photograph: Harry Holtzman (negative) (cat. 195)

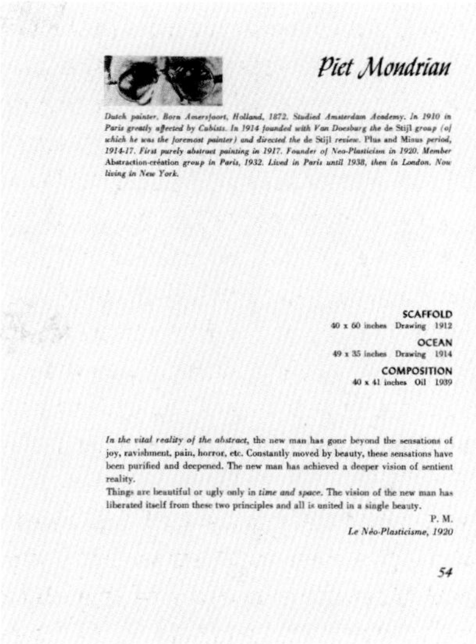

Piet Mondrian

Dutch painter. Born Amersfoort, Holland, 1872. Studied Amsterdam Academy. In 1910 in Paris greatly affected by Cubists. In 1914 founded with Van Doesburg the de Stijl *group (of which he was the foremost painter) and directed the* de Stijl *review.* Plus and Minus *period, 1914-17. First purely abstract painting in 1917. Founder of Neo-Plasticism in 1920. Member* Abstraction-création *group in Paris, 1932. Lived in Paris until 1938, then in London. Now living in New York.*

SCAFFOLD
40 x 60 inches Drawing 1912

OCEAN
49 x 35 inches Drawing 1914

COMPOSITION
40 x 41 inches Oil 1939

In the vital reality of the abstract, the new man has gone beyond the sensations of joy, ravishment, pain, horror, etc. Constantly moved by beauty, these sensations have been purified and deepened. The new man has achieved a deeper vision of sentient reality.
Things are beautiful or ugly only in *time and space*. The vision of the new man has liberated itself from these two principles and all is united in a single beauty.

P. M.
Le Néo-Plasticisme, 1920

54

Fig. 31
The cut-out of Mondrian's eyes marked on the negative was published in Peggy Guggenheim's collection catalogue *Art of This Century* in June 1942.

Mondrian faces the viewer seriously — severely, almost — and wearing glasses. As an artist, he preferred this image to the ones of the gentle, engaging man who also appears in many of the photographs from the same session. The choice of the stern photo shows that Mondrian was in control of the image of himself that appeared in the public domain until the end.

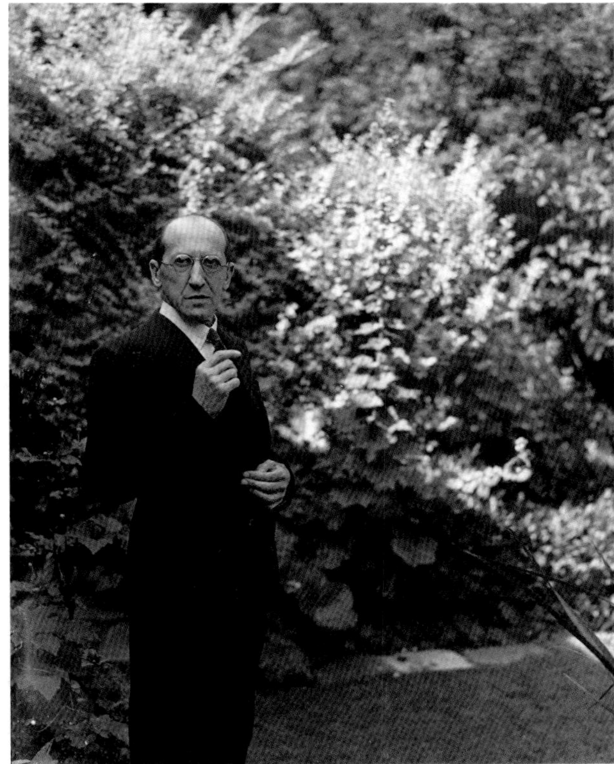

Fig. 32
Piet Mondrian in the garden of Harry and Eileen Holtzman's summer home in Great Barrington, autumn 1940 (?)
Photograph: Harry Holtzman (cat. 189)

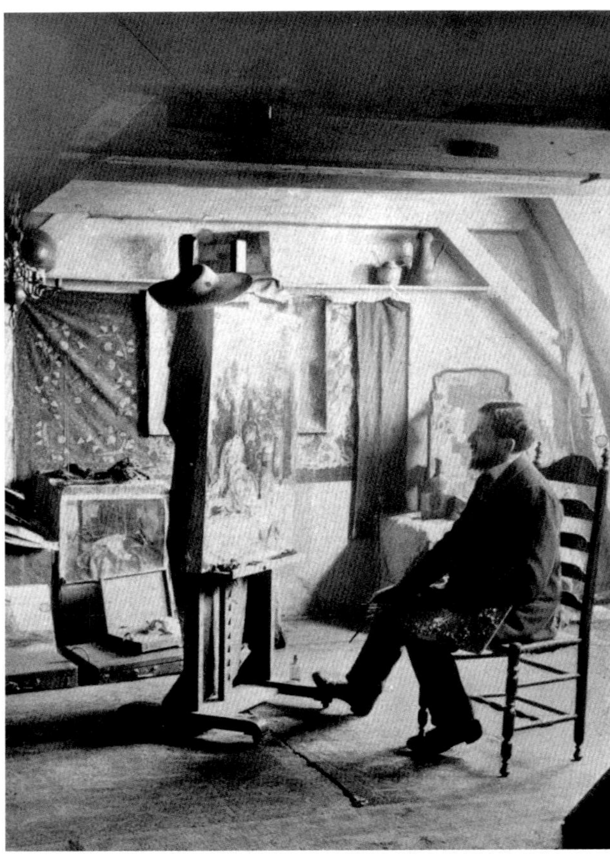

Fig. 33
Piet Mondrian in his studio at 10 Rembrandtplein Amsterdam, c. March 1906 (cat. 34)

> Fig. 34
Piet Mondrian's studio, c. March–April 1930 Photograph: Michel Seuphor or Rosie Ney (cat. 131)

Studio Photographs: A Means towards a Higher End

On the wall, as on the canvas

If Mondrian's distinctive appearance was widely photographed, so too was his studio. In this instance we are talking not only about the artist but also his art, his ambitions and his ideals, neatly summed up as 'the studio as self-portrait'.[44]

Mondrian appears in photographs taken relatively early in two of his Amsterdam studios, the interiors of which are firmly in the 19th-century tradition. He had himself photographed 'in action' in his workplace on the Rembrandtplein, palette and brush in hand, gazing thoughtfully at the canvas that stands before him on the easel (fig. 33). He is surrounded by references to his profession: painter's boxes, a stack of sketchbooks, a painter's hat hanging casually from the easel. A little later than this, at his Sarphatipark studio, he preferred to present himself as a contemplative *poeta doctus* in an introverted pose. Things around him, however, are hardly any different: we see ten or so of his works on the walls, several vases that he used to compose his still lifes, and paintings and frames stored in the studio space in the background (cat. 39). It is safe to assume that some tidying up had been done and props arranged for the shoot, but the photographs are otherwise likely to be a good reflection of reality. Fellow artists living more grandly often had themselves portrayed in sumptuously appointed studios. Mondrian's, by contrast, is unremarkable and makes a sober impression compared, say, to that of his less high-profile (but wealthier-born) friend Simon Maris (cat. 4).

We do not know a great deal about the interior of Mondrian's studios in the 1910s. He had a number of them in the Laren area during the war years, mostly small and poorly lit, but how they looked has not been documented either.[45] It was there, all the same, that he developed his 'nieuwe beelding', the personal aesthetics that, from 1917 onwards, would guide both his future artistic practice and the interior of his studios.

After settling permanently in Paris at the end of June 1919, Mondrian began to set up his studio in accordance with the principles of the nieuwe beelding, which he renamed *néo-plasticisme* for the benefit of the French. A single photograph has survived of his first attempts, made in this studio on Rue de Coulmiers, where he lived from 1 November 1919 to 21 October 1921. In it, hardly anything of the interior can be seen (cat. 52). The earliest images that genuinely capture the neo-plastic interior date from 1923–24, by which point the artist had moved to Rue du Départ, where he

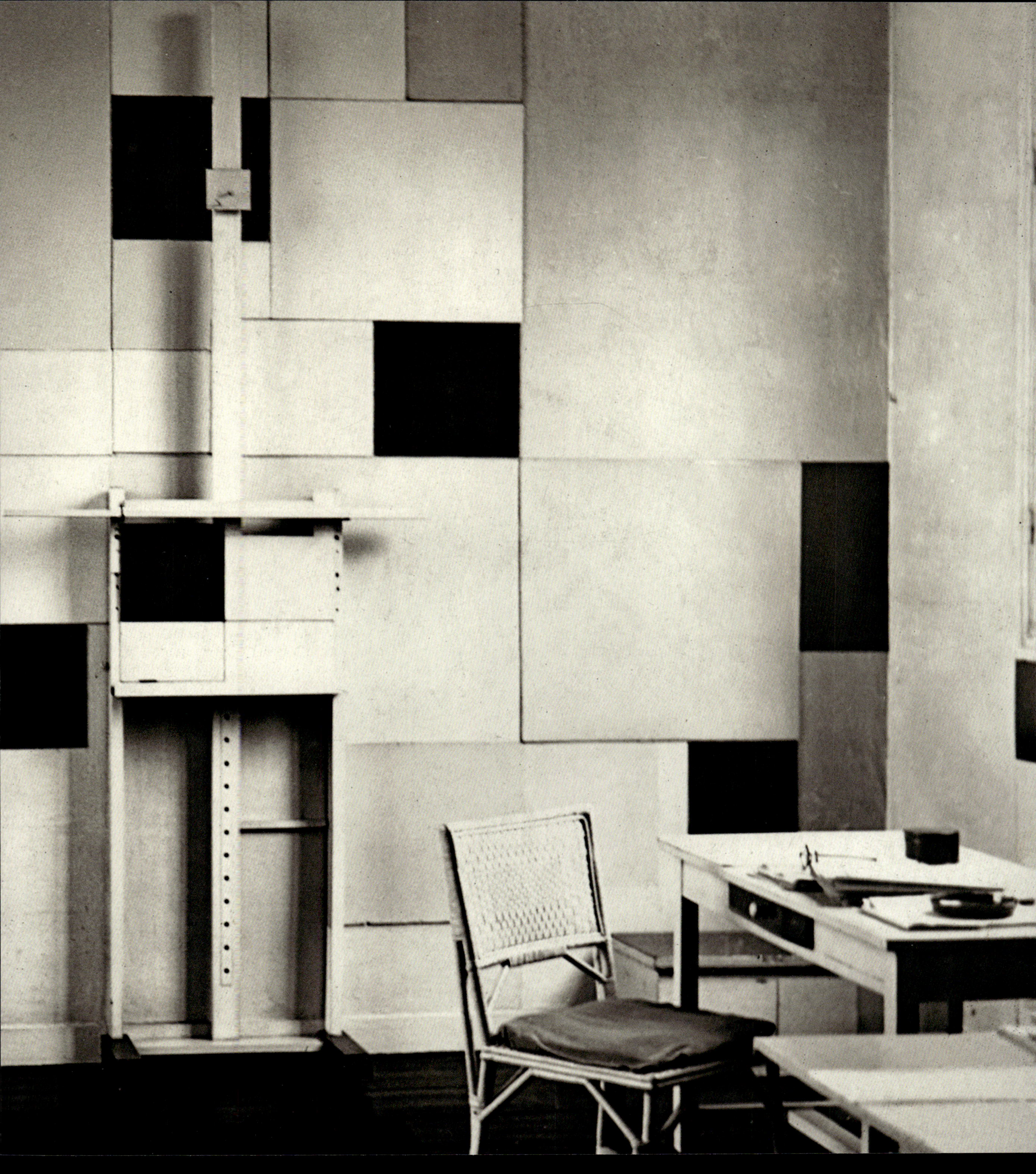

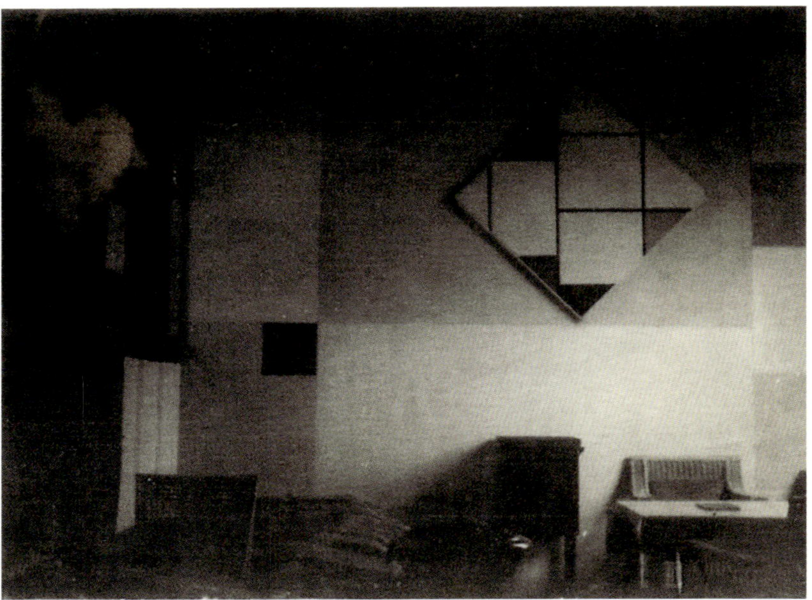

Fig. 35
Piet Mondrian's studio, July–August 1924
Photograph: Georges Vantongerloo (cat. 62)

had previously lived between May 1912 and June 1914. A picture taken by his colleague and friend Georges Vantongerloo in the summer of 1924 shows the rear wall of the studio (fig. 35). It is subdivided into large and smaller planes; a recent, diamond-shaped composition is displayed against one of the larger ones.

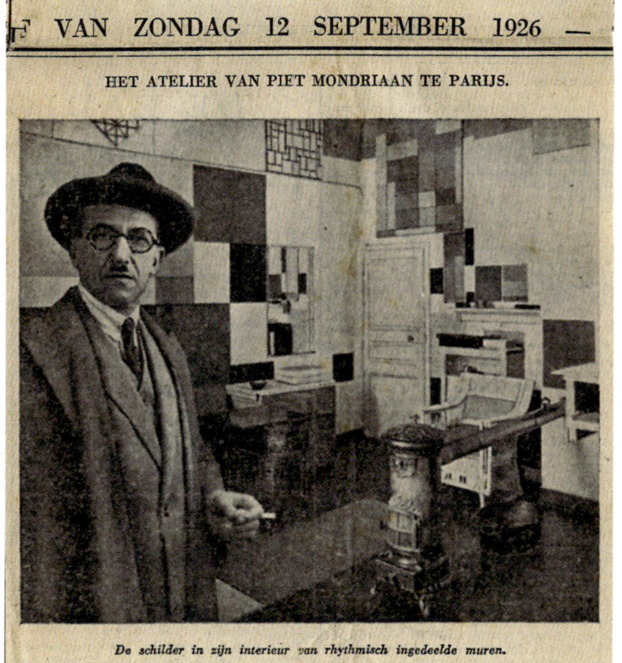

VAN ZONDAG 12 SEPTEMBER 1926 —

HET ATELIER VAN PIET MONDRIAAN TE PARIJS.

De schilder in zijn interieur van rhythmisch ingedeelde muren.

Fig. 36
Photomontage accompanying the article 'Bij Piet Mondriaan. Het kristalheldere atelier. Apologie van den Charleston', *De Telegraaf* (12 September 1926). Pierre Delbo took the studio photograph.

In the foreground we see the top of the pot-bellied stove, two chairs and a bed that Mondrian used for guests. The image is bounded on the left by a cabinet, to which a cardboard rectangle has been attached for decoration. If there is one thing that the photograph makes clear, it is that Mondrian's studio was not an everyday environment. The shabby exterior of the complex made the contrast with the spotless, sparkling interior space all the greater (fig. 37).

Mondrian's studio grew increasingly famous over the years. Several of the friends and acquaintances who visited sensed something sacred about it.[46] Journalists mentioned the special nature of the place in their interviews and articles, adding to its appeal. As his work and theoretical writings likewise became better known in France and abroad, Mondrian received more and more requests from interested parties wishing to visit his studio, among them the German critic, architect and future director of the Bauhaus, Hannes Meyer. As editor of the magazine *Das Werk. Schweizerische Zeitschrift für Baukunst/Gewerbe/Malerei und Plastik*, he was working on an article on the latest developments in art and architecture and was keen to include a photo of Mondrian's studio to illustrate modern developments in interior design. It gave Mondrian an excellent opportunity to introduce a new target group to the application of neo-plasticism in the interior, so he commissioned the photographer Pierre Delbo to take some shots of his studio, which he had recently refurbished.[47] The result was three photographs, of which the picture of (once again) the rear wall become the best known (fig. 38). This was the photograph that Meyer reproduced in *Das Werk* in July 1926, making it

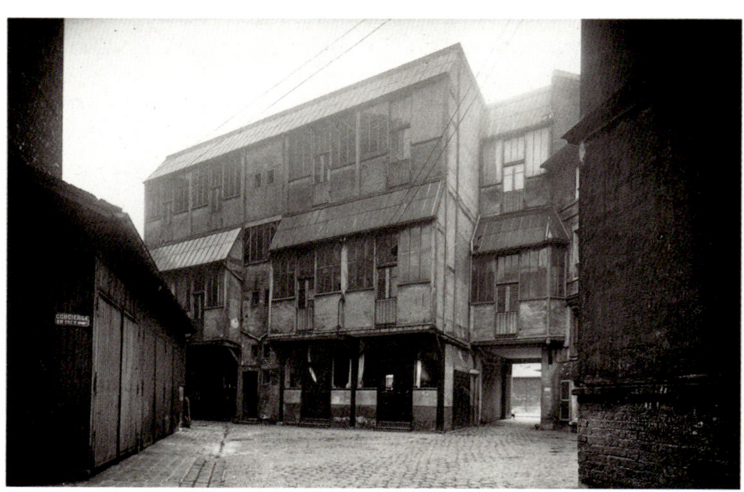

Fig. 37
26 Rue du Départ, Paris, 1927. Mondrian's studio windows, screened by white curtains, can be seen on the top floor in the recessed section to the right. Photograph: Photographe Seeberger Frères Bibliothèque historique de la Ville de Paris

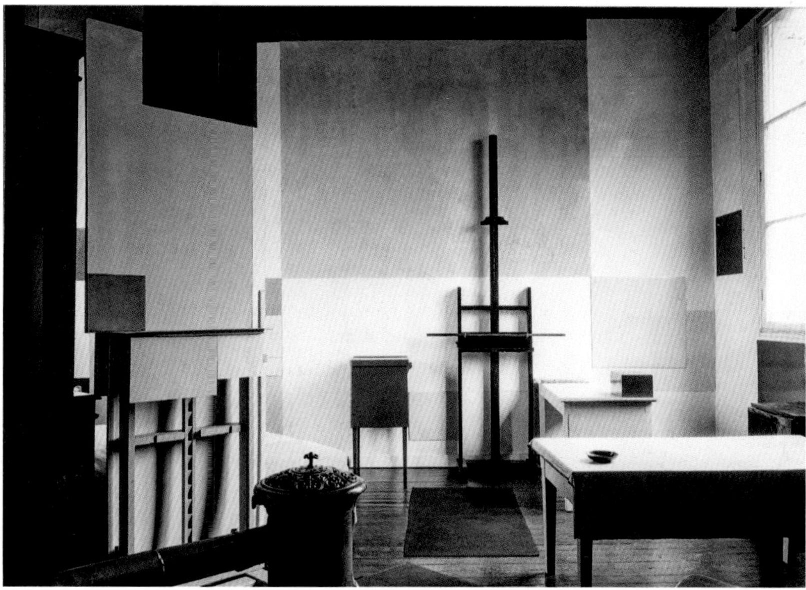

Fig. 38
Piet Mondrian's studio, c. end of November 1925–March 1926
Photograph: Pierre Delbo (cat. 74)

the first publication to include an illustration of Mondrian's studio.[48]

What is striking about the photograph is the absence of the artist himself. This might have been at Meyer's request, as it gave as general a view of the studio as possible. Had the painter posed in it, the result would have been a picture of a specific place at a specific moment in time, reducing some of its timelessness. This is certainly what Mondrian thought: when the American artist and collector Katherine Dreier visited him in April that same year and took a photograph of the studio (or had one taken), she noted on the back of the only surviving print (cat. 77): 'Mondrian's studio, Paris. He would not pose *in* it'.[49] It was a deliberate choice on the artist's own part: in other words, not to figure in the photograph himself. Photography functioned as a new medium for bringing neo-plasticism to the attention of the public. The important thing was his art, which strove for universal validity, and anything personal, accidental or random was to be banished.

As noted above, Delbo's photographs would be reproduced several more times in newspapers and magazines. One of them (cat. 76) was printed in September 1926 along with an article about Mondrian in *De Telegraaf*, one of the most widely read Dutch newspapers. To give an impression of both the studio and the artist who went with it, the newspaper shamelessly superimposed a photograph of Mondrian over one of Delbo's shots (fig. 36).[50]

Interior in motion

The decoration of the studio walls became increasingly dynamic after 1926. For a 1930 issue of the magazine *Cercle et Carré*, Mondrian combined the now celebrated photograph of the rear wall by Delbo with a new shot of it in order to illustrate his neo-plastic development.[51] By around 1928, studio experiments with smaller coloured units were already resulting in a dynamic complex of planes, in which Mondrian also sought to eliminate black as a dominant factor.[52] The result can be seen in a photograph of the rear wall taken in 1930 by Mondrian's good friend Michel Seuphor or by Rosie Ney (fig. 34). By printing Delbo and Seuphor/Ney's photographs together, the painter was able to make it clear at a glance that neo-plasticism had become considerably more dynamic in a period of just four years.[53] Thanks to the publication of studio photographs, Mondrian's workplace became one of the best-known avant-garde studios of the interwar period, and perhaps the only one in which artwork and working environment formed a perfect unity.

The artist benefited from this status, which brought him several new architect friends. He was on good terms, for instance, with Adolf Loos and Zlatko Neumann, and he also sold his work to the likes of J. J. P. Oud, Mart Stam, Pierre Chareau and Alfred Roth. In July 1928, Mondrian accompanied Stam and Roth — a Swiss employee of Le Corbusier, who went on to develop a successful career in his native country — on a visit to Garches, just outside Paris, to the Corbusier-designed home of Michael Stein, brother of the writer and collector Gertrude Stein.[54] Mondrian was also present when Stein hosted El Lissitzky and his wife in September that year. This led in turn to a photograph of Lissitzky in Mondrian's studio, presumably taken by Sophie Lissitzky-Küppers (cat. 116). The architecture critic Sigfried Giedion and his wife, the art historian Carola Giedion-Welcker, visited the studio later the same month, not only buying a painting there, but also taking a marvellous photograph of the now famous studio wall (fig. 40). Carola Giedion used it in March 1930 to illustrate her article 'Die Kunst des zwanzigsten Jahrhunderts: Experimentierzelle — Zeitseismograf' (Art of the Twentieth Century: Experimental Cell—Temporal Seismograph) in *Das Kunstblatt*. In it, she described Mondrian as the leader of the neoplastic movement, in which she also included Van Doesburg, Vantongerloo and Friedrich Vordemberge-Gildewart.[55] It says a lot about the status of Mondrian's studio that she preferred a photograph of it to a reproduction of a painting such as *Composition: No. I* (B193, 1927) from her own collection.

The picture taken by Sigfried Giedion documents an important transitional phase in the decoration of the studio. The easel, which was still black in the 1926 Delbo photographs, now has both white and black elements. In Seuphor/Ney's 1930 picture, the easel had been painted entirely white. This again emphasizes the fact that Mondrian's studio was not a static ensemble that assumed a particular form at a given moment: the artist constantly adapted a variety of elements, which formed part of the total artwork represented by the studio. Every element of the interior was subordinated to Mondrian's vision, as indicated not only by the painted easel, but also the position of the rugs, for instance, which were arranged differently each time.[56]

In November 1929, Mondrian allowed a picture of his studio to be reproduced in the catalogue of the A.S.B. exhibition at the Stedelijk Museum in Amsterdam (the letters stand for the disciplines of *architectuur*, *schilderkunst* (painting) and *beeldhouwkunst* (sculpture)). The photograph must have been taken by the Dutch architect Charles Karsten, one of the exhibition's organizers, who visited Mondrian several times from the late 1920s onwards, photographing the artist and his studio on several of those occasions.[57] The picture in the catalogue (fig. 39) shows three of the four Mondrian paintings featured in the exhibition. The easel stands in front of the rear wall, which is richly decorated with coloured planes. It is also decorated itself, with a composition comprising four cardboard rectangles, further integrating it into the decorative programme of the overall space. The boundaries between the traditional easel painting and the rest of the living environment are completely blurred in this photograph, which conveys the message that neo-plasticism offers an aesthetic application for the entire home and not just for a spot on the wall.

Another photograph taken by Karsten during one of his visits to Mondrian offers a wider view of the rear wall (fig. 41). What's more, the picture shows the fourth

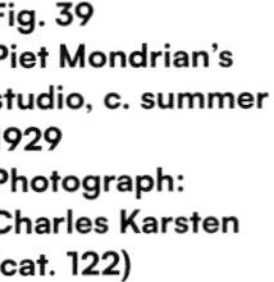

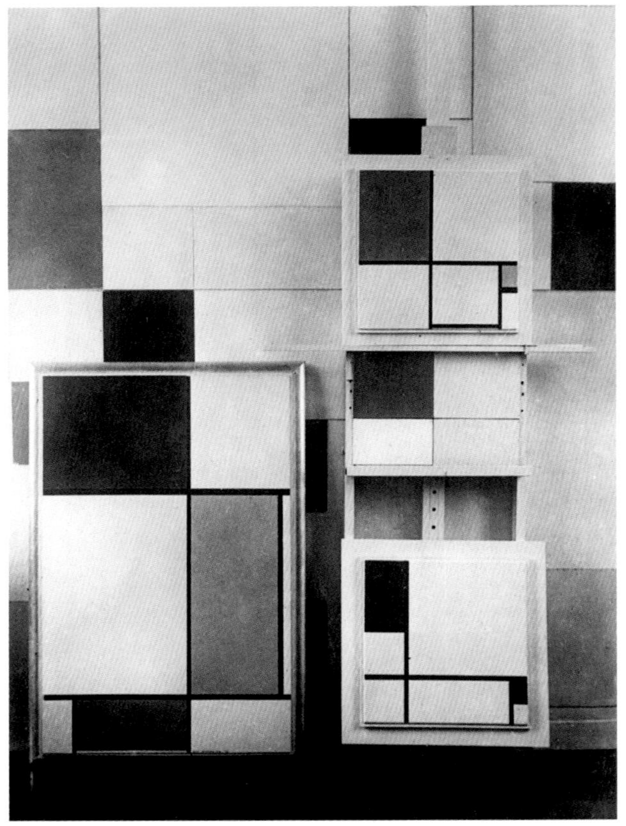

Fig. 39
Piet Mondrian's studio, c. summer 1929
Photograph: Charles Karsten (cat. 122)

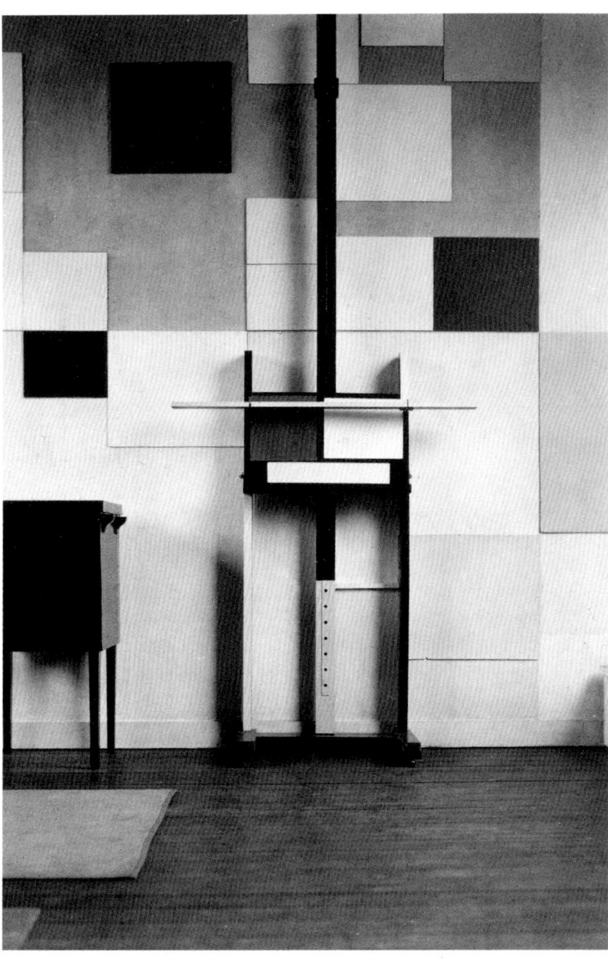

Fig. 40
Piet Mondrian's studio, September 1928
Photograph: Sigfried Giedion (cat. 117)

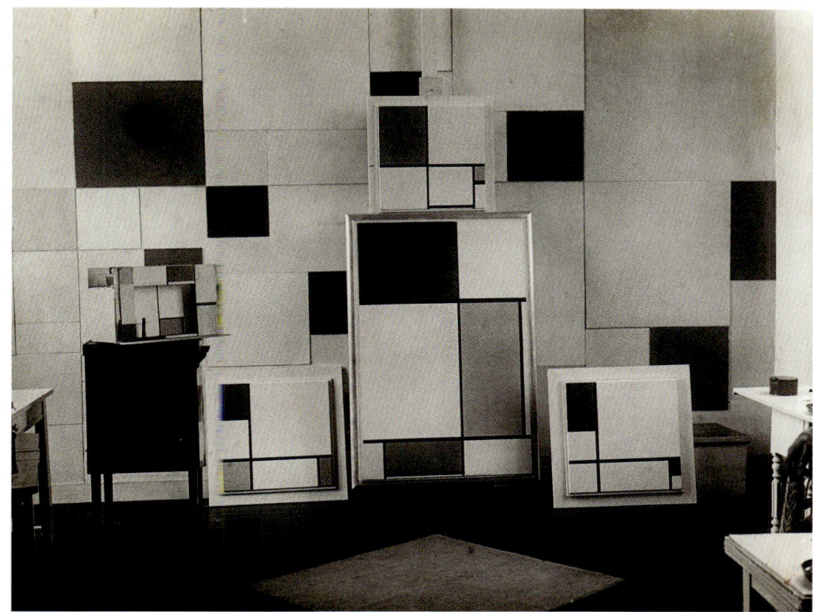

painting that the artist exhibited at the A.S.B. show, together with a model of the stage set for a play by Michel Seuphor, which Mondrian made in 1926 and of which André Kertész had taken several close-ups at the time.[58] A few pieces of furniture are still visible around the edges of the photograph, and on the right we see a hand (presumably Mondrian's) dangling casually over the edge of a chair. There is a rug in the foreground turned so that it forms a diamond, contrasting sharply with the mostly orthogonal lines that dominate the photograph and Mondrian's work alike. The paintings are arranged differently to one another than in the picture in the A.S.B. catalogue. Some deliberate staging has clearly occurred during the shoot: the works form a quadriptych, with the largest canvas placed at the centre to catch the eye. Towards the end of 1929, Mondrian sent a print of this photograph to the painter and photographer Paul Citroen, who was working at the time on a book containing 'a "Querschnitt" [cross-section] of the painting being done today in the Netherlands and by Dutch people abroad'.[59] He had written to Mondrian asking for information and received in reply the studio photograph along with album pages containing reproductions of paintings, a portrait photo, and a theoretical outline.[60] Citroen published Mondrian's essay, his portrait and the picture of the studio, but not the loose reproductions of his work.[61] The studio picture meant, however, that Mondrian stood out among the other painters in the book, who were represented solely by a portrait photograph and/or reproductions of their work.[62] The fact that the model of the stage set can also be seen in the studio photograph emphasizes the fact here, as in the A.S.B. catalogue, that Mondrian was not a traditional easel painter.

Fig. 41
Piet Mondrian's studio, c. summer 1929. Photograph: Charles Karsten (cat. 121)

Fig. 42
Piet Mondrian in his studio, mid-1929 Photograph: Rosie Ney (?) (cat. 120)

From self-fashioning to fashionable

The fame of Mondrian's studio now extended as far the United States. In 1929, the *Chicago Daily Tribune* published an article on the artist, in which he was described as 'one of the great figures in the art of today', residing in 'a Montparnasse atelier, which he decorated in the ultra-modern style'.[63] It was around this time that Mondrian adjusted his self-promotion strategy. Fewer photographs of the studio now appeared in publications, even as the number of photographers seeking him out was on the rise. A photograph dating from 1929 might have been taken by the Hungarian photographer Rosie Ney (fig. 42). Mondrian did pose in his studio in this instance, which could be interpreted as a newly acquired self-awareness. Meanwhile, the paintings that hung on the wall in Pierre Delbo's photographs had disappeared in the years between 1926 and 1929.[64] The five works from different stylistic phases had served a didactic purpose: Mondrian used them to explain the development of his work to visitors.[65] As his fame grew in the years after 1926, he apparently no longer saw the need to illustrate and elucidate the logic of that evolution and

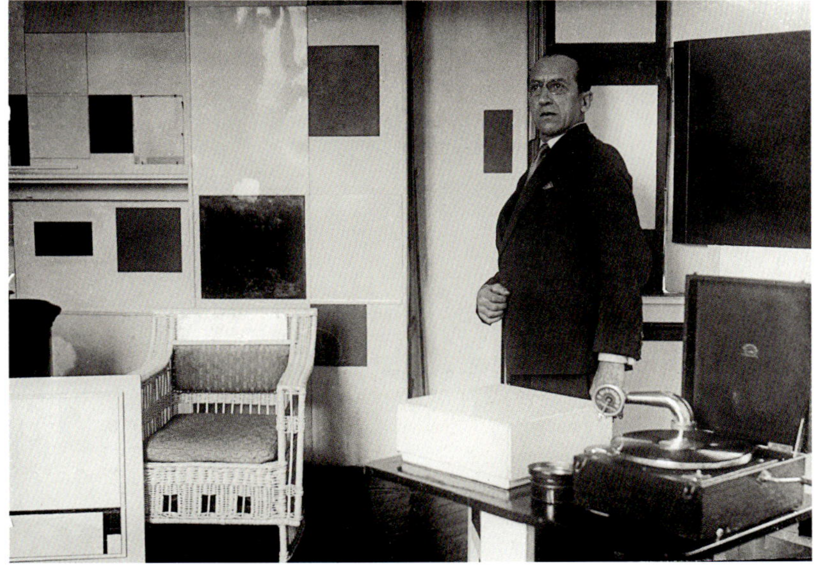

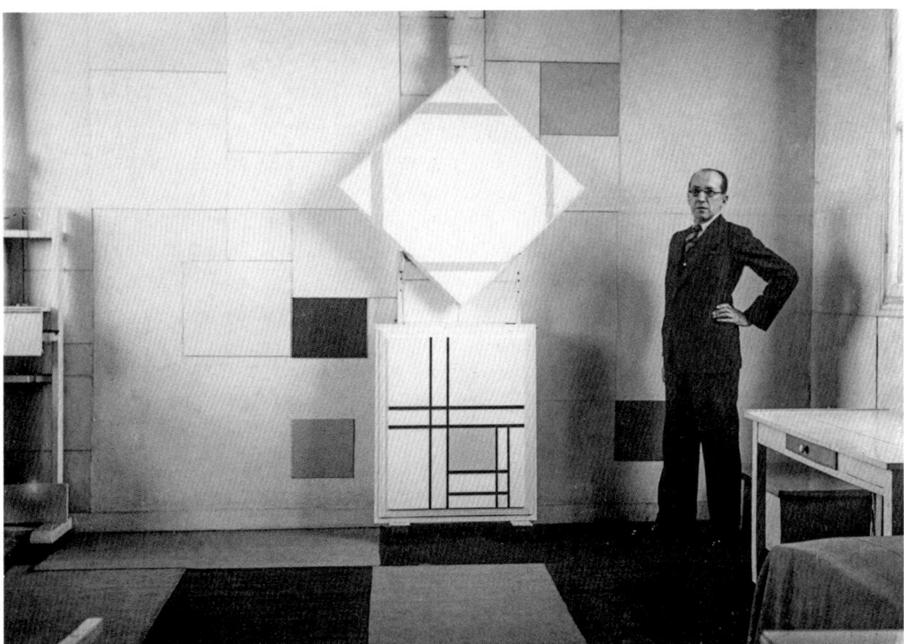

Fig. 43
Mondrian in his studio, September/October 1933
Photograph: Charles Karsten (cat. 148)

hence the 'self-explanatory' nature of neo-plasticism.[66] He surrounded himself in the 1929 photograph with a number of attributes that he (or the photographer) thought significant to his artistry. Positioned prominently in the foreground, we see the gramophone on which Mondrian played the jazz music he loved so much. His most recent painting is just about visible on the far left, leant casually against a chair.[67] With his dark suit and straight back, the artist himself is an element within the total composition of the studio: a vertical plane among the decoration on the walls. Although the photograph is likely to have been taken at Mondrian's request, it remained unpublished in his lifetime. All the same, it is clearly a picture in which Mondrian consciously had himself presented as master of his stylized environment.

Mondrian's connections with architects led to the publication of a photograph of his studio in the architecture journal *De 8 en Opbouw* in 1933. The magazine had been founded the previous year by two groups of architects, and was intended to promote the application of New Objectivity — a movement related to neo-plasticism — to building. Charles Karsten, one of those founders, had taken the photograph in *De 8 en Opbouw* during an earlier visit to Mondrian. It shows the artist next to his easel in front of the rear wall of the studio (fig. 43). Mondrian poses proudly with his most recent paintings, his back ramrod straight and his arm planted on his hip in a somewhat unnatural position, so that the angle of his arm echoes the diamond shape of the canvas on the easel.[68] The rugs have likewise been incorporated in the overall view once again, this time by positioning them orthogonally. Below the title 'Cavalcade', Karsten inserted a quotation from Le Corbusier: 'In the confusion of this disordered period, many have grown used to thinking against a black background. Yet the artwork of this age, so bold, so perilous, so bellicose, so domineering, seemingly expects us to think against a white background.'[69]

Mondrian painted the diamond-shaped canvas on the easel, *Lozenge Composition with Four Yellow Lines* (B241) in 1933 on the occasion of his sixtieth birthday. It was purchased by a group of admirers led by the artists Charley Toorop and Jacob Bendien — uncoincidentally also the driving force behind the aforementioned A.S.B. group — and ultimately donated to the Haags Gemeentemuseum in The Hague (now the Kunstmuseum Den Haag). Karsten must have provided Mondrian with multiple postcard-sized prints of the photograph. The artist was evidently pleased with it, as he sent copies to, among others, his brother Carel and his old friend Mies Elout-Drabbe in the Netherlands. He also pasted a print into a photo album of his work — his portfolio, to which we will return.[70] Following Mondrian's death, the photograph was widely used in catalogues and other studies on his life and work, making it one of the most reproduced and hence best-known images of the artist and his studio, along with Pierre Delbo's studio picture.

Mondrian had become so successful in cultivating his image and living environment by the early 1930s that photographers were increasingly likely to seek him out themselves rather than the other way around. This led in turn to a change in the photographs too: the mostly well-known photographers assumed control of the image, whether or not with the artist's input. There were quite a few Americans among the visitors to the studio, as they had been able to discover Mondrian's work at the Société Anonyme exhibition at the Brooklyn Museum and three other institutions between November 1926 and April 1927.[71] The show's organizer, the collector Katherine Dreier, included in the catalogue the photograph she had taken of Mondrian's studio, in which the artist had refused to pose (see

p. 35). She described him in the publication as the best Dutch painter since Rembrandt and Van Gogh,[72] which had the effect of opening up the US market to him.

This led in the years that followed to a steady flow of American dealers and collectors who wanted to get to know the painter and his work. They included Albert Eugene Gallatin, who paid his first visit to Mondrian in May 1933 and bought a work from him.[73] The American painter and collector would become an important business contact for the Dutchman, whom he visited again in the first half of 1934, taking two photographs of the painter in his studio.[74] He had Mondrian pose at his easel, wearing his painter's coat and holding a paintbrush (figs 44—5). After receiving prints of the photos, Mondrian wasted no time in writing to Gallatin to express his satisfaction with the results: 'I was truly touched by the superb photographs you sent me — magnificent in composition and execution and, I think, very good too as a reflection of my personality.'[75] This inadvertently shows that Mondrian had taken a new step in the way he wished to present himself via photographs: ten years earlier, he would never have tolerated access to, or the photographic expression of, his 'personality'.

If we compare these pictures with the ones taken by Eugene Lux, around the same time (March—May 1934), it is obvious how decisively the character of a visit or contact was for the way we see Mondrian. Lux's photographs show an exceptionally relaxed painter and gracious host to the photographer's wife (fig. 46). No question here of a highly stylized, posed artist gazing sternly into the lens: instead we find a gentle, charming man who, so the story goes, had Gwen Lux blushing with his 'constant flirting'.[76] This is a largely unknown Mondrian. The fact that he held onto prints of these photographs (they were found in his estate),

Figs 44—5
Portraits of Piet Mondrian, June 1934
Photograph: Albert Eugene Gallatin
(cats 172—73)

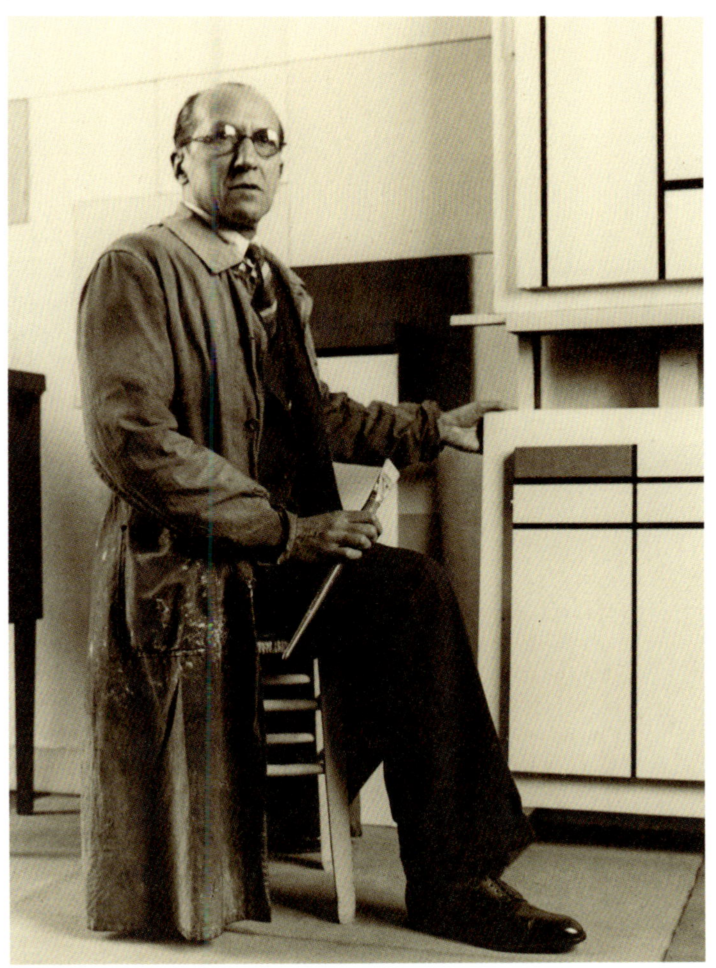

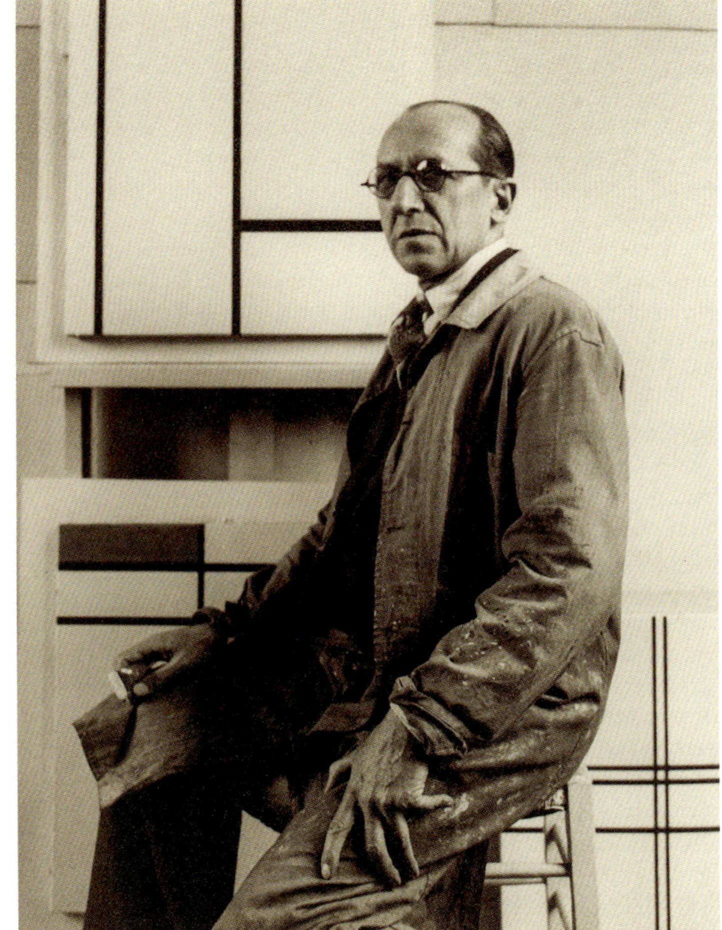

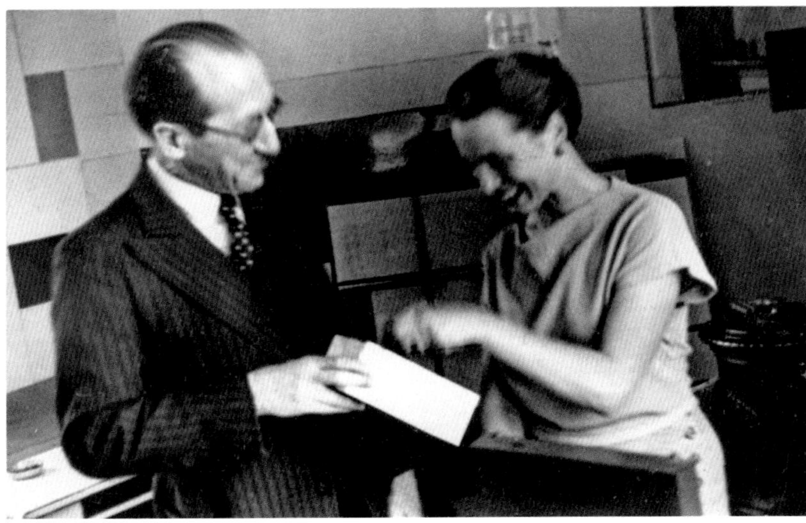

One of the photographers drawn to Mondrian's studio was the young Cas Oorthuys who, armed with a Rolleiflex, shot four portraits of the painter and two studio views in the summer of 1937 (cats 180–5).[80] The photographs display the low viewing angle characteristic of that type of camera, where the photographer looked down into the matt glass viewfinder rather than looking through one at eye level like most other models. A rare glimpse into Mondrian's working practice is provided by the picture showing several paintings in progress (fig. 48). It is clearly visible, for instance, that the lines in the painting on the left have been varnished but not the planes. Mondrian did this deliberately because the composition otherwise seemed 'lifeless' to him. Both of the works on the right of the photograph still show traces of the charcoal lines with which Mondrian set out his compositions.

suggests that he had no problem at all with having this side of his personality immortalized.[77]

A photograph by Rogi André in 1937, by contrast, *was* taken with a view to publicity (fig. 47). She learned her trade under André Kertész, to whom she had been married in the early thirties, and whose first name she adopted as her surname. Together with Man Ray and Florence Henri, she was commissioned in 1937 to photograph the artists taking part in the exhibition 'Origines et développement de l'art international indépendant' at the Musée du Jeu de Paume.[78] Although the pictures were not included in the exhibition catalogue, they were probably on display, since the publication explicitly mentions the photographers.[79] The portrait photograph is similar in many respects to one of Gallatin's 1934 shots, regarding which Mondrian had been so enthusiastic. The artist poses here with the same side turned towards the camera, standing to attention, as is so often the case. He does not wear his painter's coat in this 'official' portrait, however, while his upright position results in a more active and less traditional image. He gazes out of the picture to the right, his left arm resting on a small table. His rectangular palette and a ruler — positioned diagonally to the picture plane, possibly on purpose — lie on a stool next to him. The two paintings exhibited at the Jeu de Paume can be seen in the background. This is one of the few known pictures taken in the studio at 278 Boulevard Raspail, where Mondrian moved in March 1936 when the studio complex on the Rue du Départ was scheduled for demolition to make room for the expansion of Gare Montparnasse.

Fig. 46
Piet Mondrian and Gwendolyn Lux in Mondrian's studio, c. March–May 1934
Photograph: Eugene Lux (cat. 150)

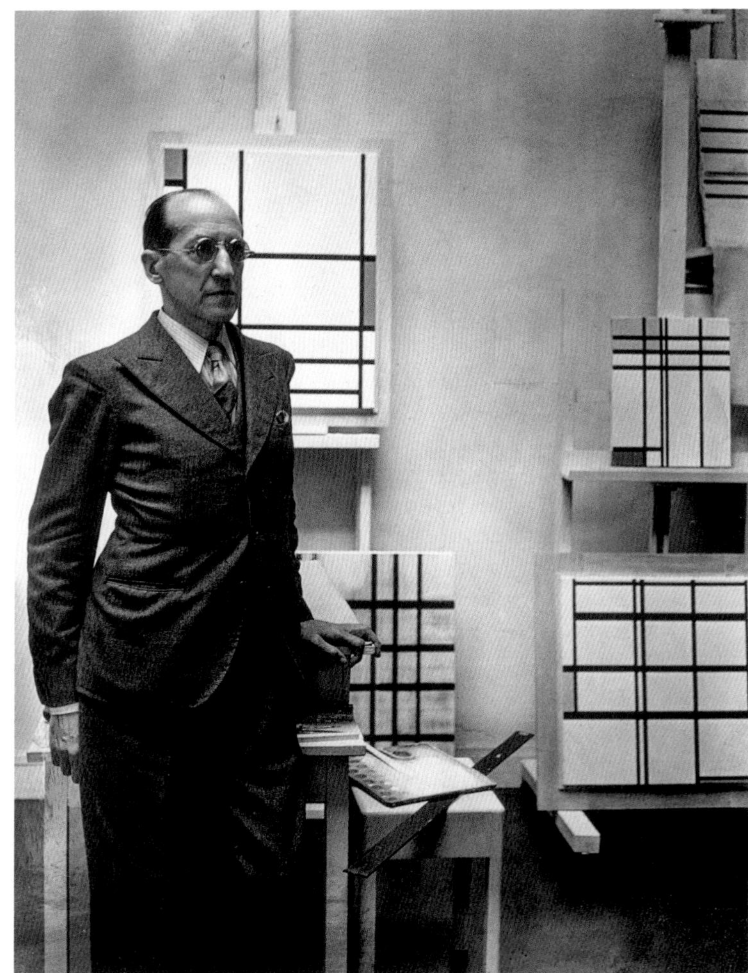

Fig. 47
Piet Mondrian in his studio, c. June–July 1937
Photograph: Rogi André (Rosza Klein) (cat. 179)

He would then move them around — by just a few millimetres in some cases — until he was satisfied with the composition, which he then executed in paint.

When Mondrian returned to Paris in 1919, he had been obliged to conclude that he was relatively alone with his art and ideas. Now, some fifteen years later, he had become a celebrated phenomenon in both the press and in progressive artistic circles in Western Europe and the United States. Within the image he had created over the years, his appearance, his work and his studio had become inextricably intertwined: reference to any one of them invariably evoked the others. Mondrian's fame had gathered momentum in what we would now call a successful example of 'branding'. In the meantime, the artist was approaching retirement age, but it was not in his character to rest on his laurels.

Crowning glory of the work (1)

Mondrian left Paris in September 1938 as the threat of war intensified. His work had featured the previous year in the 'Degenerate Art' exhibition organized in several German cities by the Nazis, meaning that the Hitler regime now posed a direct personal danger to him.[81] He travelled with the artist Winifred Nicholson and her children to London, where he would live for the next two years.[82] No photographs survive from that period, due partly to the fact that most of his friends had fled that city too before the start of the Battle of Britain in July 1940.[83] Mondrian decided to follow their example after a German bomb exploded near his house during the Blitz on 9 September.[84] With the financial assistance of his American friend Harry Holtzman, he boarded a ship for New York in Liverpool on 23 September 1940 and arrived in the United States in early October after a hazardous and exhausting crossing.[85]

Mondrian found a society in New York that was open to innovation, including abstract painting. What especially appealed to him about his new environment was the speed of urban life, the modernity, the functionalism of the latest buildings, the tangible, unflagging thirst for progress. The Museum of Modern Art had opened in the late 1920s and was led by the inspirational art historian Alfred Barr Jr, who had previously visited Mondrian in Paris and in the meantime had organized several trailblazing exhibitions.[86] Together with the likes of Peggy Guggenheim, Katherine Dreier and Albert Gallatin, Barr had opened a growing number of American minds to European innovators. As the latter began to arrive in the United States, they were thus

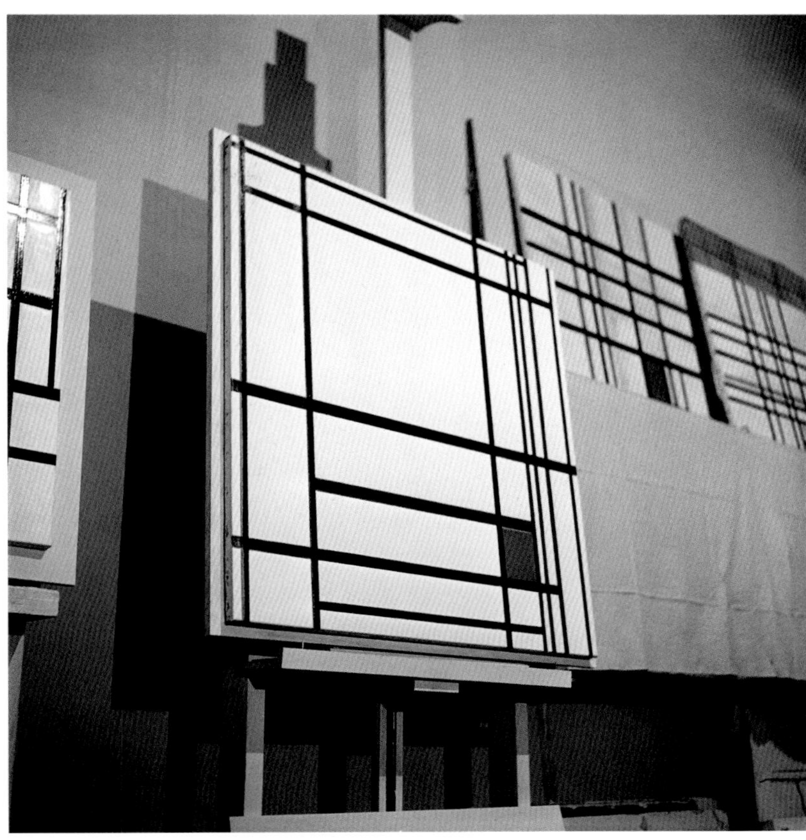

Fig. 48
Piet Mondrian's studio with *Composition de Lignes et Couleur: III* (B277) on the easel, August (?) 1937
Photograph: Cas Oorthuys (cat. 181)

received as respected and prominent members of the European avant-garde. This was the case not only for Mondrian, but also for artists like Max Ernst, André Breton, Marcel Duchamp, Jean Hélion, Fernand Léger and Marc Chagall — artists in exile who were warmly welcomed by their American kindred spirits, who took them up in their own ranks. These circumstances enabled New York to take over Paris's role as world capital of art after the Second World War.[87]

An article that testifies to this cultural earthquake was published in November 1941 under the title 'School of Paris Comes to U.S.' by the New York collector and future gallery owner Sidney Janis.[88] It appeared in *Decision: A Review of Free Culture*, founded by Klaus Mann. The short-lived magazine focused on contemporary developments in free, American society and called out the oppressive Nazi regime that had taken hold in Europe.[89] The tenor of the magazine matched Mondrian's own conviction, as set out in two articles from the late 1930s, in which he described Nazism and Communism as 'oppressive tendencies'.[90] Janis's article focused on four artists who had ex-

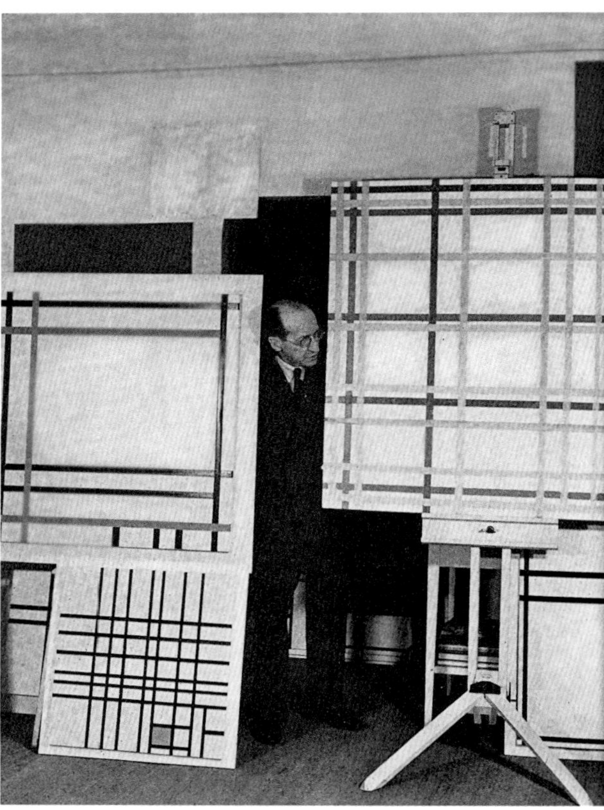

Fig. 49
Piet Mondrian in his studio with recent works, c. October 1941
Photograph: Emery Muscetra (cat. 190)

changed Europe for the United States to escape the war: besides Mondrian, they were Fernand Léger, Max Ernst and Roberto Matta Echaurren, a younger artist born in Chile but who had settled in Paris. To illustrate the piece, the photographer Emery Muscetra was commissioned to shoot portraits of the artists in their studios.[91] One picture of each of them was then printed (fig. 49). Two other unpublished shots of Mondrian have survived (cats 191—92). The interior of his studio is largely obscured in the photographs by the large canvases among which the artist poses. Janis nevertheless alluded to the importance of the studio in the article: 'The interior of his studio is a reflection of his personal discipline, of a piece with his paintings. It is brilliantly lighted, carefully planned, simply but ingeniously furnished, clinically clean. The white surfaces of the walls are broken by rectangular coloured areas of cardboard — red, blue, yellow, unequal in size — placed to form a typical Mondrian arrangement. To him the oblique is weak and the curve weaker still, so he has covered the curves on his studio doorway with rectangular shapes to eliminate the offending note. His paintings, arranged against the walls on the floor, fall in line as part of the composition of the room, and the effect of the whole upon the visitor is electrifying.'[92] So it was that the studio swiftly assumed the status of avant-garde topos in the United States too — a powerful example of Mondrian's self-promotion, the foundations for which had naturally been laid in Paris. Making his studio a neo-plastic experience enabled him both to amplify his personal reputation and to generate publicity for his still innovative ideas. The photographs encouraged interested parties to come and experience neo-plasticism for themselves in the studio, resulting in a large number of visitors.

Photographers too were now drawn to the studio again, among them the young American photographer Arnold Newman, who would make his name with dramatic portraits of artists and writers, many of them with European roots. Newman customarily shot about three dozen pictures during a session and is likely to have posed Mondrian for a similar number. The fact that only a small number of prints have survived from the shoot (cats 237—44) will have reflected Newman's critical selection of his material. He meticulously analysed the contact prints taken from the negatives and only printed those images he was entirely satisfied with after adjusting and correctly cropping them.[93] The resulting portraits have been described as 'unusually cool and distant'.[94] Newman seems to have been familiar with Mondrian's work and made clever use of the straight lines of the easel and the cardboard rectangles with which the studio was decorated. The result, in his own words, was 'stiff, linear and very formal, like the man', lending weight to the standard image that would persist.[95] Newman's photographs are simultaneously the result of his own skill and vision of the artist and of Mondrian's successful self-promotion. However, a variety of anecdotes from his personal life in the same period are known which once again reveal the opposite of his formal appearance. The way he frequented the newest jazz clubs with the artist Lee Krasner and her girlfriends, for instance, was enthusiastic and anything but aloof.[96]

Following Mondrian's death on 1 February 1944, Harry Holtzman carefully documented the studio with the assistance of Fritz Glarner — a Swiss painter who had likewise moved to New York and was an old acquaintance of Mondrian's from Paris. He had resumed painting in the American city, but made his living as a commercial photographer. Glarner had already done a documentary shoot with Mondrian in his studio in early 1943 and following the Dutchman's death took another

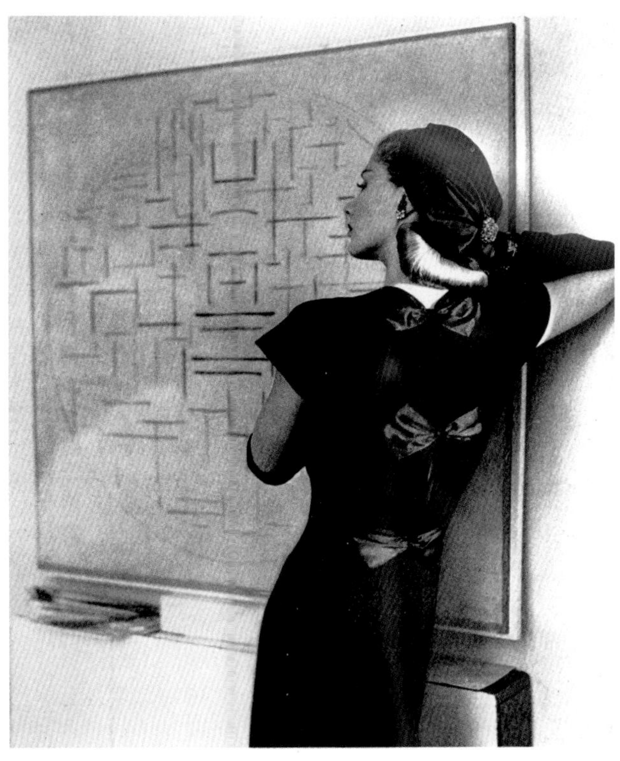

Fig. 50
Model in front of *Composition in Circle* (B75) in Mondrian's studio after his death, between 22 March and c. 3 May 1944
Photograph: Fernand Fonssagrives for *Town & Country* (cat. 410)

extensive series of pictures of his former workspace (cats 305—83). Holtzman did the same, but used colour film, producing what are the only surviving colour photographs of any of Mondrian's studios (cats 384—403). They offer a marvellous impression of the space, with radiant planes of colour against the whitewashed walls. Holtzman also shot some film footage, likewise in colour. What's more, he transferred the compositions on the walls to wooden boards and kept several cabinets and small tables that Mondrian had made himself and painted white.[97] For a few weeks after the artist's death, Holtzman opened the studio to interested visitors, reportedly including a large number of art school students.

The fashion photographer Fernand Fonssagrives was among those who took the opportunity to visit.[98] He shot a photo feature for *Town & Country* magazine, in which he had a number of models pose in the studio (cats 404—11, fig. 50). In doing so, he immediately built a bridge after the artist's death between Mondrian's abstract style and the world of design, advertising, fashion and pop culture: a development that would take off over the years, even while the image of Mondrian himself as an aloof, serious man persisted.

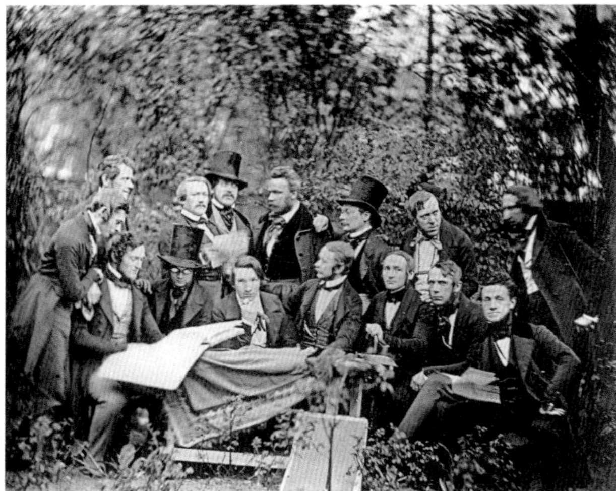

Fig. 51
***The Hamburg Artists' Association*, 1843**
Photograph: Carl Ferdinand Stelzner

> Fig. 52
***Die Surrealisten*, c. July 1942**
Photograph: Hermann Landshoff (cat. 245)

The Group Portrait: Individual versus Collective

Group identities

It will be more than clear by now that, contrary to the stock image of the artist as a rather stiff and serious loner, Mondrian was entirely human and a man with both social needs and skills. We have already mentioned the small groups in which he mixed privately, but he also regularly engaged with larger groups, mostly consisting of artists and people otherwise associated with the arts, with whom he was involved both professionally and socially. Group portraits shot during gatherings such as parties and opening nights provide a broader insight into the networks to which Mondrian belonged during successive stages of his life and within which he moved effortlessly, despite his repeated assertion that he had no desire to join groups. This ambiguous attitude is regularly if subtly apparent, therefore, in the group portraits.

Photographed group portraits are virtually as old as the medium itself. They were already being taken in the early 1840s, despite the very long exposures that were needed at first. The earliest examples include Carl Ferdinand Stelzner's *Hamburg Artists' Association* (1843), for which fifteen gentlemen in a garden did their best to remain motionless for some twenty to thirty seconds (fig. 51). It is evident from the result that not everyone succeeded. Nor could the lens avoid a degree of distortion around the edges.[99] The choice of example is not entirely random, as this too is a group of people linked by their involvement with the arts — in Hamburg in this instance. Consciously or otherwise, group portraits frequently testify to a shared identity — the subjects belong to a certain company of like-minded people, be they relatives of one another (the picture of the Mondriaan children, for instance, fig. 1), fellow churchgoers, members of a profession, a group of tourists, a sports team and so on. The phenomenon likewise pre-dates photography: paintings like Rembrandt's *Night Watch* or *The Syndics of the Drapers' Guild* are also regarded as expressions of group identity.[100]

There are plenty of group portraits of like-minded artists as well. A couple of noteworthy examples from Mondrian's time are the group photographs taken in May and September 1922 at the International Artists' Congress in Düsseldorf and the Congress of Constructivists and Dadaists in Weimar, respectively.[101] A ladder was used in the earliest photograph in order literally to connect the mainly Dadaist participants at the congress (fig. 53). The use of a firmly non-artistic prop places each of the artists on the same level,

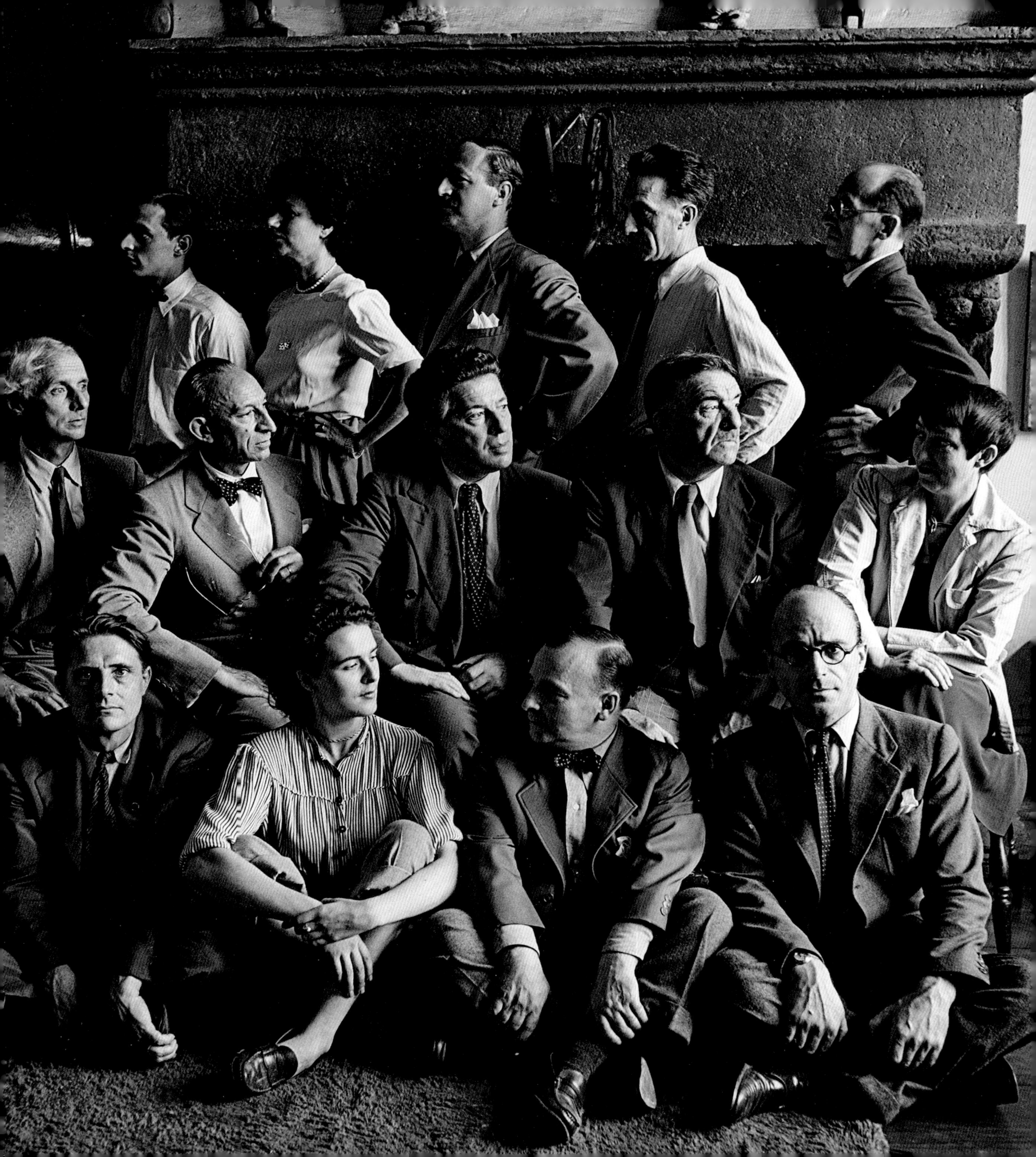

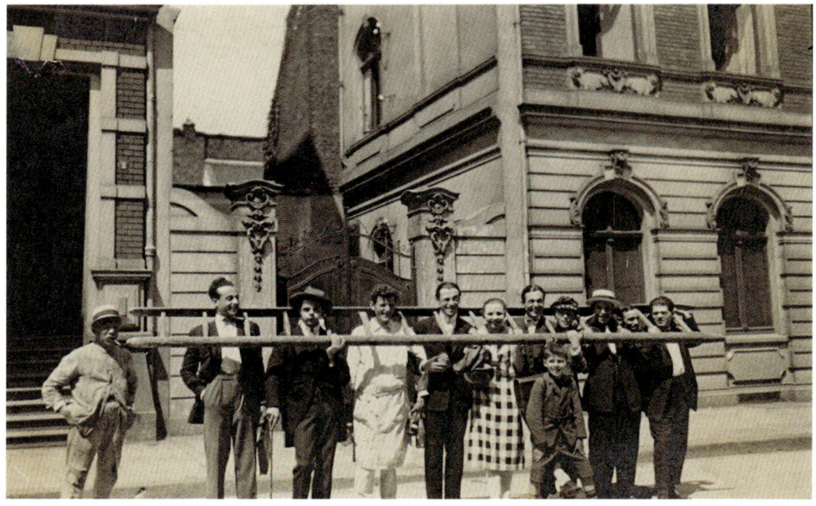

regardless of their different artistic and national backgrounds. The September photograph shows a motley group of conference-goers in Weimar (fig. 54). Most of the constructivists look into the lens, while most of the Dadaists look in different directions, resulting in a rather confusing image for the viewer, who seeks in vain for some kind of explanatory narrative. Both photographs can be read as successful expressions of the Dadaist group identity, as statements.

Mondrian certainly did not avoid club life and had immediately signed up to three associations when starting out as an artist: Kunstliefde in Utrecht, and Arti et Amicitiae and Sint Lucas in Amsterdam. He even held administrative posts in the latter group, as he later did at the Moderne Kunstkring, of which he was a cofounder in 1910. Clubs like this clearly offered the desired opportunities to show one's work and gain visibility in the associated network of fellow artists, critics/journalists and collectors. They thus served a professional purpose. Mondrian also belonged to the Dutch Reformed Church between 1893 and 1915, however, and in May 1909 he became a member of the Theosophical Society. Somewhat later, he joined forces with the indefatigable artist, networker, agitator and entrepreneur Theo van Doesburg to set up the magazine *De Stijl*, in which Mondrian frequently published, despite having assured Van Doesburg: 'I still don't feel anything for a new combination of artists. Do what you think is right, I will keep out of it all.'[102] This ambivalence — which, as noted, is also visible at times in the photographs — shows that Mondrian did not want to give up his individuality for the benefit of a collective: he invariably reserved the right to adopt his own, possibly divergent stance. The legendary movement De Stijl never consisted, moreover, of a strictly delineated group. Its participants were mostly in contact with one another via Van Doesburg and never met physically, and so there is no surviving picture of the full (or even partial) editorial team, let alone the entire movement.

Fig. 53
Participants at the International Künstlerkongress, Düsseldorf, May 1922
The Hague, RKD, Theo and Nelly van Doesburg Archive

Fig. 54
Participants at the Constructivists and Dadaists congress in Weimar, September 1922
The Hague, RKD, Theo and Nelly van Doesburg Archive

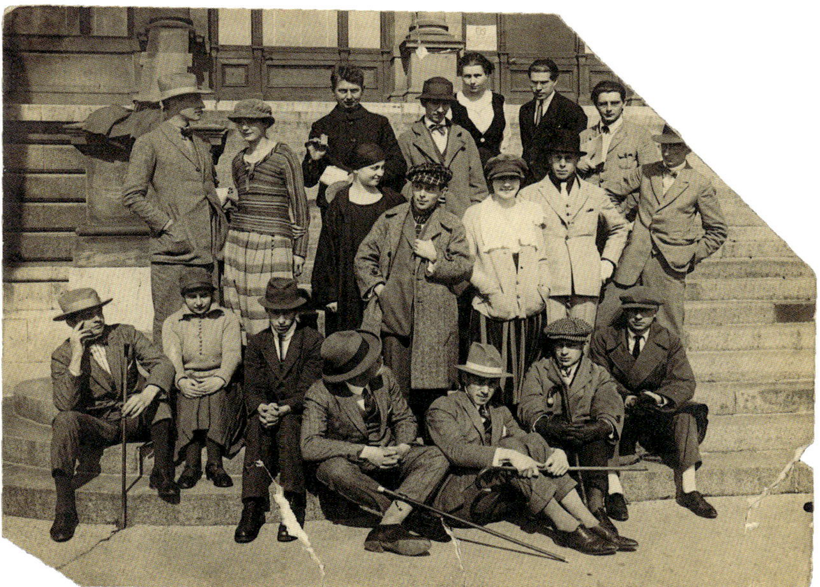

Some of the earliest surviving group photographs in which Mondrian can be seen were taken in Simon Maris's studio, before or after the opening of an exhibition at the progressive artists' association Sint Lucas (cats 10—13).[103] In them we see a group of painters and a lone critic. Mondrian, almost thirty at the time, makes a rather dreamy impression. He was still searching at that point for the right expressive possibilities in paint, and while he was considered a talented landscape painter, this was not yet the self-assured artist he would be in later years. The fact that the painters centred around Maris were friends too is apparent from two other group photographs taken a few years later by the river Gein (cats 29—30). With its picturesque nature, mills and farms, the meandering waterway to the south of Amsterdam was a popular spot for painters. Mondrian produced dozens of views of the buildings, groups of trees and meadows along the riverside. In one photograph, he poses with several people, including Simon Maris and the poet Hendrik Kroon, near De Vink — a popular inn, where boats could be hired and food and drink enjoyed.[104]

Several photographs have survived from the Sint Lucas period in which Mondrian appears as a member of the association. One was taken during a 1900 preview (cat. 6) and another in 1905 at the opening of the group's annual spring exhibition (fig. 56). What is striking about both pictures is that Mondrian is situated on the periphery of the group. The same goes for the group photographs taken in Maris's studio. Pictures of Sint Lucas fancy-dress parties nevertheless show that he did not shun the limelight. In 1909, for instance, Mondrian was asked to stage a bullfight for a Spanish-themed party, since he had attended such an event in Bilbao in 1903 (cat. 27). The events became quite legendary and were reported on in the press, to which end a photographer would also be sent along to snap the celebrating artists. The picture of the bullfight group shows Mondrian in the front row, to the right of what is presumably the 'toreador', who strikes a suitably martial pose towards the 'bull' (fig. 55). Another photo showing an informal moment at the party includes him, still wearing his costume, in a modest spot a little further back in the crowd (cat. 42). The more extrovert Simon Maris can be found a few places to the right of Mondrian, arms raised and doing his best to draw attention to himself.

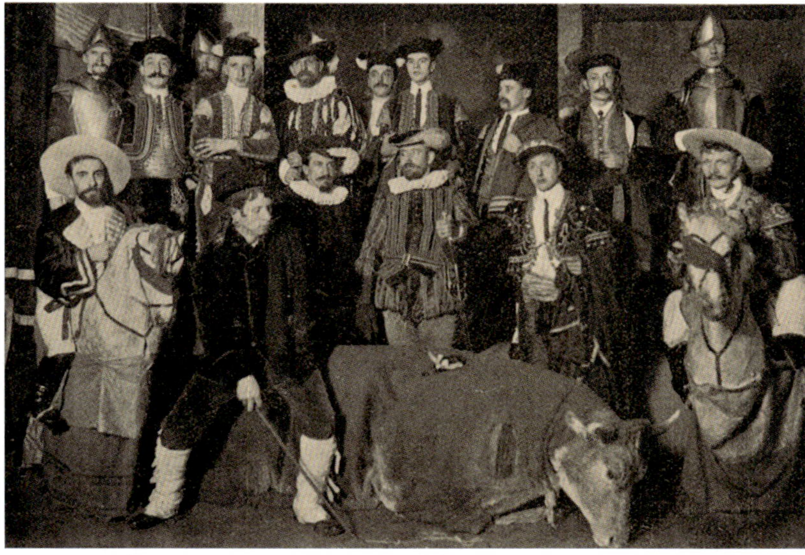

Fig. 55
***Tableau vivant* at the Spanish-themed party of the Sint Lucas artists' association, 13 November 1909 (cat. 41)**

Fig. 56
Visitors at the preview of the Sint Lucas association's spring exhibition at the Stedelijk Museum Amsterdam, May 1905 (cat. 32)

The convivial networker

Having made the acquaintance of cubism during a ten-day visit to Paris in the spring of 1911, Mondrian decided to settle in the French capital in early 1912. He stayed there two years, during which he worked hard to keep up with the latest developments in painting. We know from his Dutch colleague Jan van Deene, for instance, that he attended virtually every conceivable exhibition opening where modern painting was on view, earning him the teasing nickname 'Piet-can't-you-see-me' ('Piet Zie-je-me-niet').[105] A seasoned networker, he swiftly made contact with the innovators of the time, such as Diego Rivera, Fernand Léger, Gino Severini and Guillaume Apollinaire, thanks in part to introductions by Dutch artists who had been based in Paris for longer. Sadly, he was never captured on film with acquaintances like these.

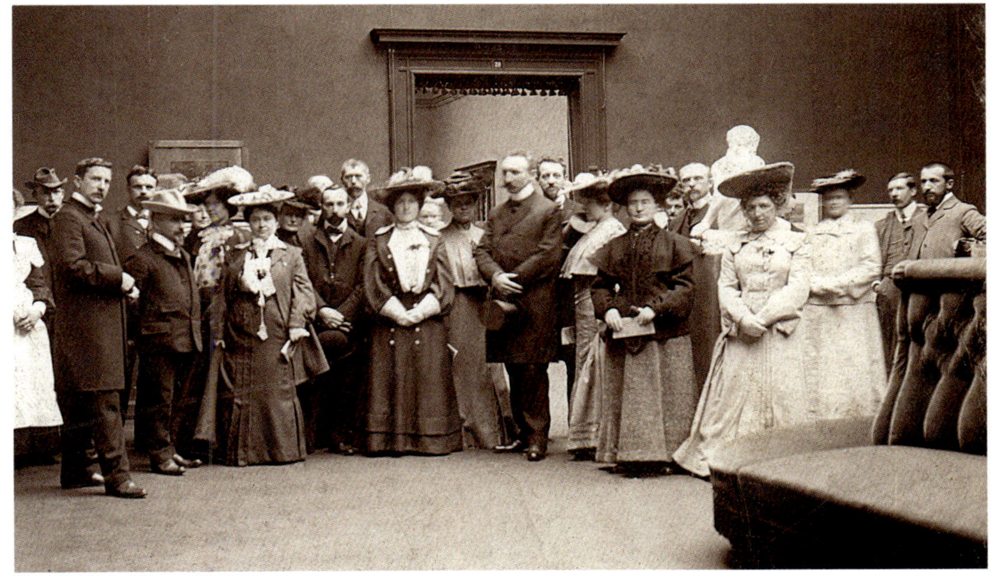

After returning to Paris in June 1919, Mondrian again abided only theoretically by his stated intention to 'keep out of it all'. In practice, he participated in all sorts of initiatives, including the magazines *L'Esprit nouveau* and *L'Art contemporain—Sztuka Współczesna*. Photographs were taken on more than one occasion during editorial meetings. Two of them — shot at the home of *L'Esprit nouveau*'s co-founder, the Belgian poet Paul Dermée, show Mondrian in a somewhat modest position (cats 102—3, fig. 57). The pictures offer a glimpse of the international and interdisciplinary character of the Paris avant-garde movement, including as they do the Italian painter and composer Luigi Russolo, the Polish painter and theorist Henryk Stażewski, the Belgian sculptor Georges Vantongerloo and the Romanian-

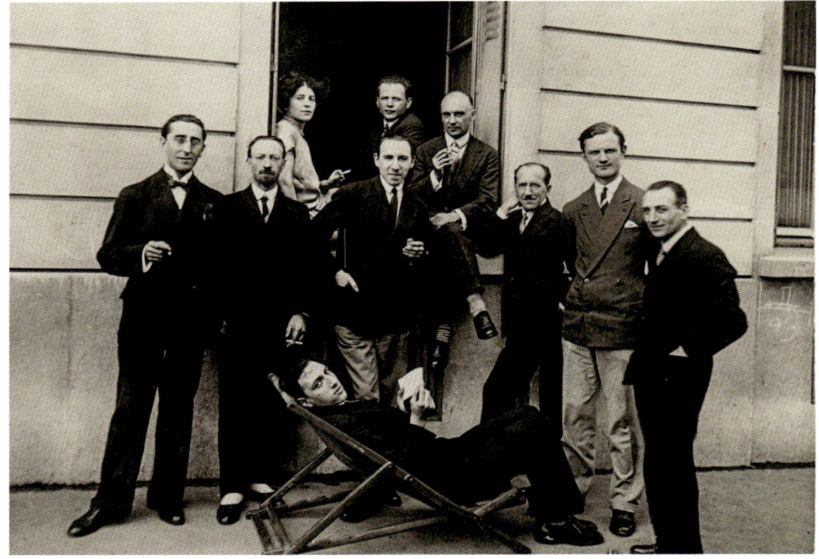

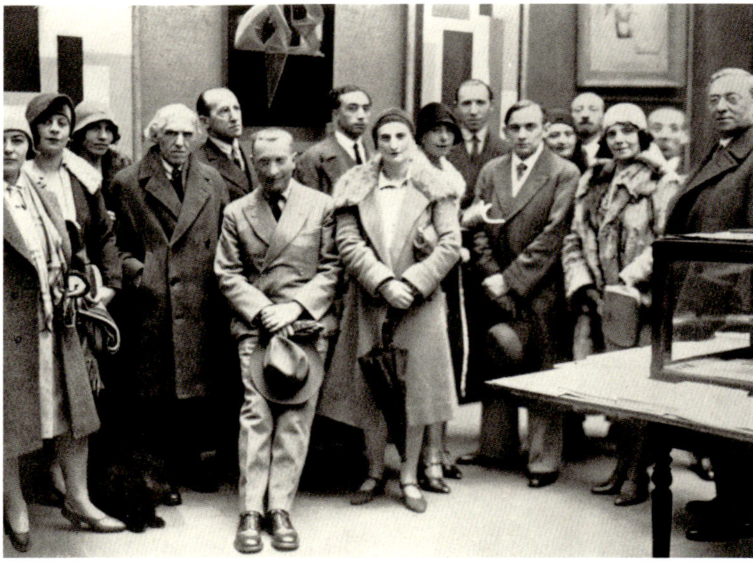

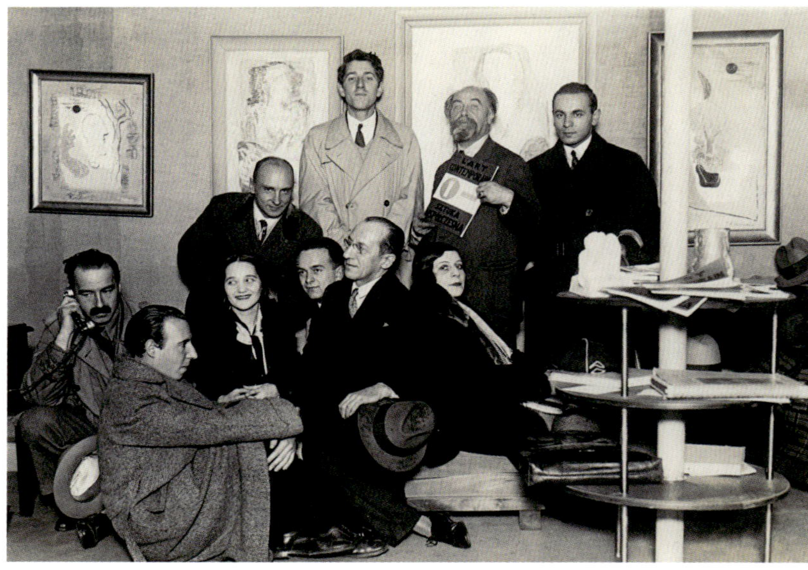

born poet Céline Arnauld. Mondrian takes a more prominent position, in the centre of the group, in the Franco-Polish magazine *L'Art contemporain—Sztuka Współczesna* (cats 124—25, fig. 58). Once again, we find a mixed company including the American photographer Florence Henri, the Belgian Michel Seuphor and the Russian-born photographer Pierre Choumoff, who proudly holds up the first issue of the magazine.

Fig. 57
Company in front of Paul Dermée's house, Paris, c. July 1927
Photograph: Stanislaw Londynski (cat. 103)

Fig. 58
Company at the opening of Gustave Buchet's exhibition at Galerie Zak, Paris, 22 November 1929
Photograph: Stanislaw Londynski (cat. 124)

Besides his magazine contributions in the shape of articles and reproductions of his work, Mondrian exhibited at several artists' associations in Paris, among them Cercle et Carré, which Michel Seuphor had founded in 1929.[106] The artists who showed at this society were almost exclusively foreigners who, like Mondrian, were staying in Paris for varying amounts of time. Although the Dutchman exhibited with the group, wrote for its magazine and attended its *jours* and *vernissages*, he wrote to Seuphor that he did not see himself as a member of any group and felt free to exhibit and publish elsewhere.[107] The pictures taken on 18 April 1930 at the opening of Cercle et Carré's first group exhibition (cats 134—36) show Mondrian to the rear of the group, which is otherwise made up of Joaquín Torres-García, Vera Idelson, Hans Arp, Ingeborg Bjarnason and Wassily Kandinsky, among others. In one of them (fig. 59), he gazes out of the picture with a rather surly expression rather than at the lens, as if to make the point that he was not an unconditional member of the association.

Fig. 59
Company at the opening of the Cercle et Carré exhibition at Galerie 23, Paris, 18 April 1930
Photograph: Ina Bandy (cat. 136)

On less formal occasions, by contrast, such as meals or get-togethers in his own studio or those of his friends, there was scope once more for Mondrian's other, more accessible, side. A photo dating from 1930 shows him at a Sunday evening gathering at Michel Seuphor's home in Vanves (fig. 60). The painter leans towards his neighbour, the photographer Florence Henri, who has placed a friendly elbow on Mondrian's shoulder. Another picture from the same period of visitors to Mondrian's studio likewise includes Florence Henri (fig. 61). Mondrian is similarly relaxed, sitting here in his white-painted wicker armchair. Judging by

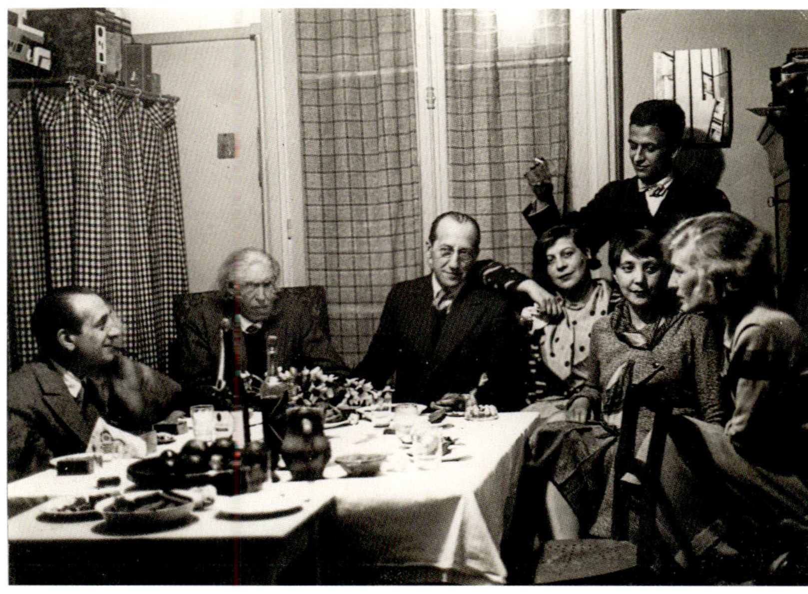

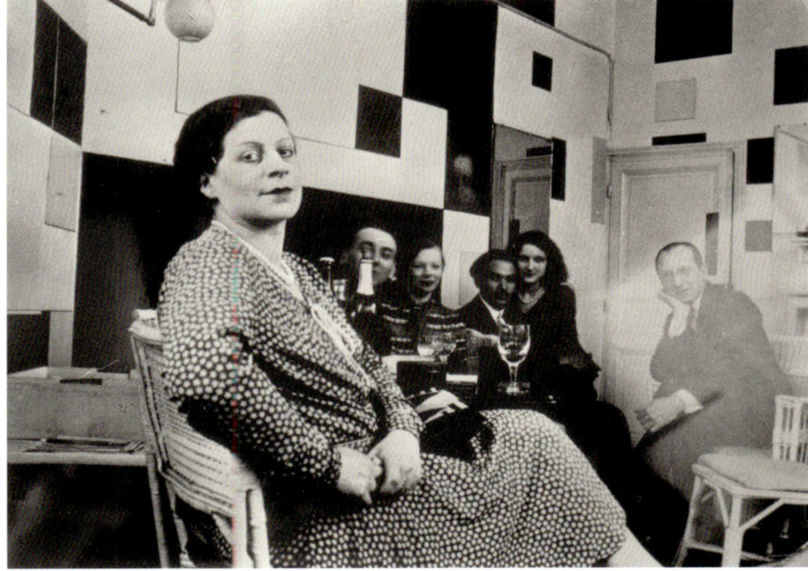

Fig. 60
Company in Michel Seuphor's home, Vanves, April 1930
Photograph: Michel Seuphor (cat. 137)

Fig. 61
Company in Piet Mondrian's studio, late 1929 (?)
Photograph: Michel Seuphor (?) (cat. 129)

the bottles and glasses on the table, this looks to have been an informal gathering of artist friends. Mondrian was also clearly at ease among the convivial company that Robert and Sonia Delaunay invited to Café Voltaire in May 1931 (cat. 144).

Crowning glory of the work (2)

Mondrian initially had to plot a strategic course to establish himself in the Paris art world, but when another war drove him to New York in 1940, he found the red carpet rolled out for him. The group portraits taken during those final years show that the artist enjoyed a different status in North America to the one he had in Europe. He joined the contingent of European artists in exile, who were welcome guests at artists' associations and gallery openings, including that for the 'Masters of Abstract Art' exhibition on 1 April 1942 at Helena Rubinstein's New Art Center. Mondrian, Hans Richter and Fernand Léger are invariably in the middle of the pictures, surrounded by the hostess and members of the emerging generation who had been united since 1936 in the American Abstract Artists association.[108] Almost all the photographs show the leading lights of that generation — artists like Harry Holtzman, Burgoyne Diller, Carl Holty and Gertrude Greene — clustered respectfully around Mondrian and the other émigrés (fig. 64, cats 233, 235).

The influence of established European painters and sculptors was thus substantial. An exhibition like 'Artists in Exile', organized by Henri Matisse's son Pierre, anticipated the inevitable shift in power towards New York as the pre-eminent centre of international art and culture. As the Second World War was laying waste to the Old Continent, European refugees created a new artistic and cultural spring in America. A series of photographs taken by George Platt Lynes in February 1942 for the 'Artists in Exile' catalogue typifies the aforementioned shift (cats 222—30). It is as if all the great figures had descended from their artistic Olympus into George Platt Lynes's photography studio. Looking at the series of pictures, we find a lively company of old friends.[109] They laugh, gesticulate and chat, while the photographer looks to create the perfect shot for the catalogue (fig. 63). Mondrian had one foot in this group, which consisted for the most part of surrealists. Despite the difference in style and artistic conception, they accepted him, albeit some of them more than others. His sense of humour certainly helped his relations with the group.[110]

Mondrian had his other foot in the group around the gallery owner and collector Peggy Guggenheim. Others too belonged to both circles, including Max Ernst (who was married to Guggenheim from 1942 to 1946), André Breton and Fernand Léger. The German-born photographer Hermann Landshoff recorded the Guggenheim group at their hostess's home. Landshoff, who was of Jewish origin, had only made the journey to New York from a now unsafe France in 1941.[111] He developed in the United States into a portrait and fashion photographer and must have understood

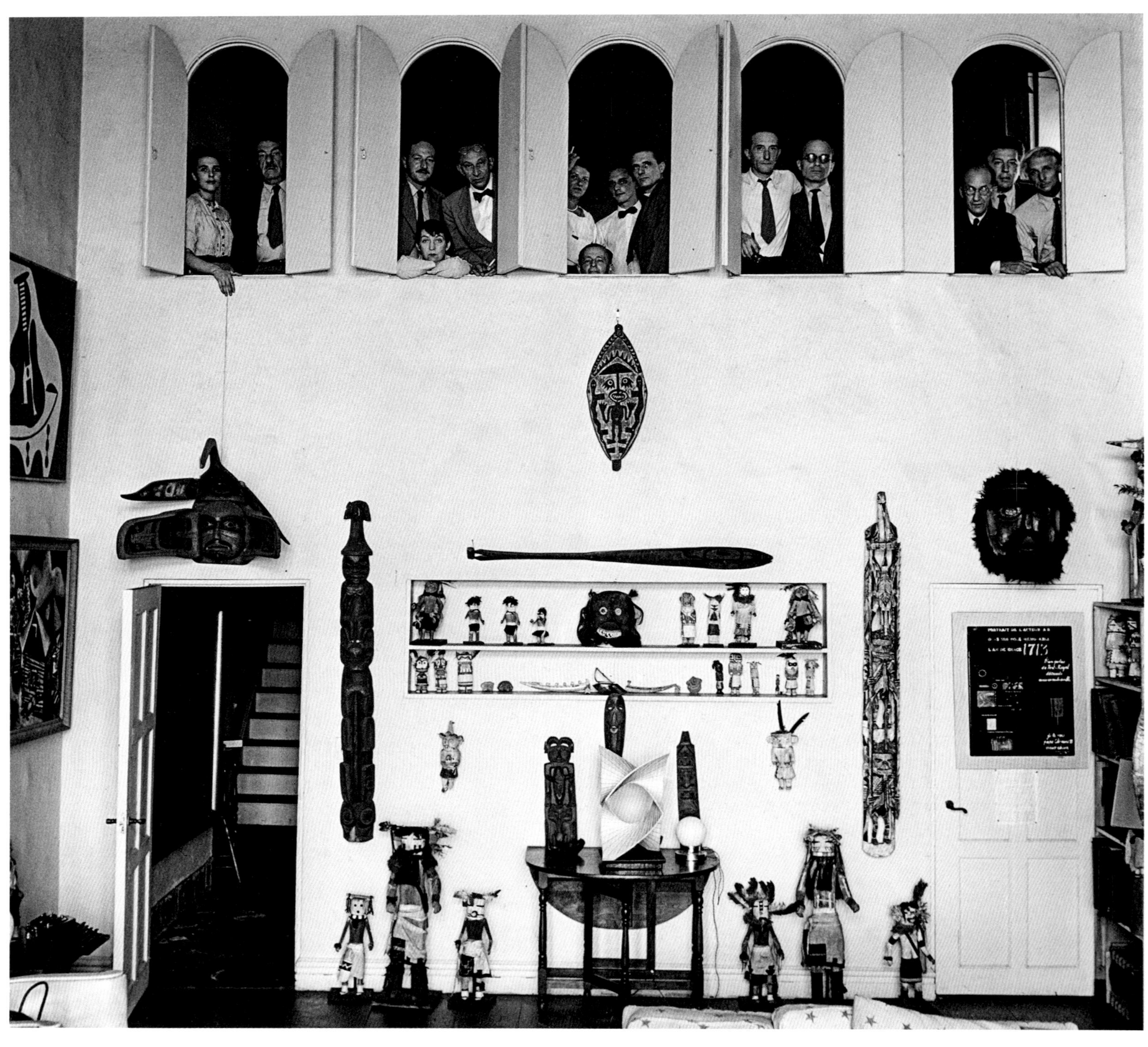

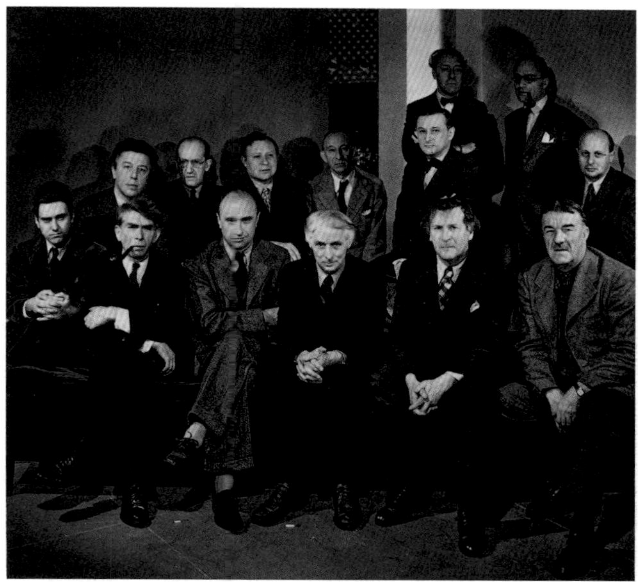

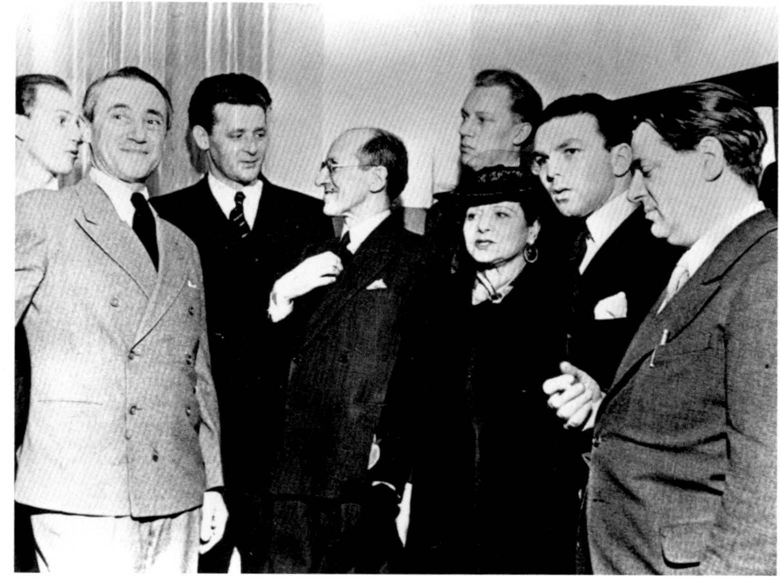

better than anyone what many of the artists he portrayed had been through. To stage one of the photographs (fig. 62), he made clever use of the architecture of Guggenheim's triplex apartment. Posed in different ways and at different levels, the artists form just as colourful an ensemble as the works of art lower down the same wall.

Mondrian shows no further inclination in the American group portraits to distance himself from the others through his pose or the direction of his gaze. According to many, his years in New York were the happiest of his life, a conclusion borne out if we look at the pictures. Mondrian no longer seems to have felt the need to be viewed as an outsider. His work was widely appreciated and well known by now, making him an accepted and even celebrated artist.

Fig. 63
Group portrait of participants in the 'Artists in Exile' exhibition, c. February 1942
Photograph: George Platt Lynes (cat. 223)

Fig. 64
Group photograph at the opening of the 'Masters of Abstract Art' exhibition, 1 April 1942.
Photograph: Lisette Model (cat. 235)

< Fig. 62
Group photograph at Peggy Guggenheim's house, c. July 1942
Photograph: Hermann Landshoff (cat. 247)

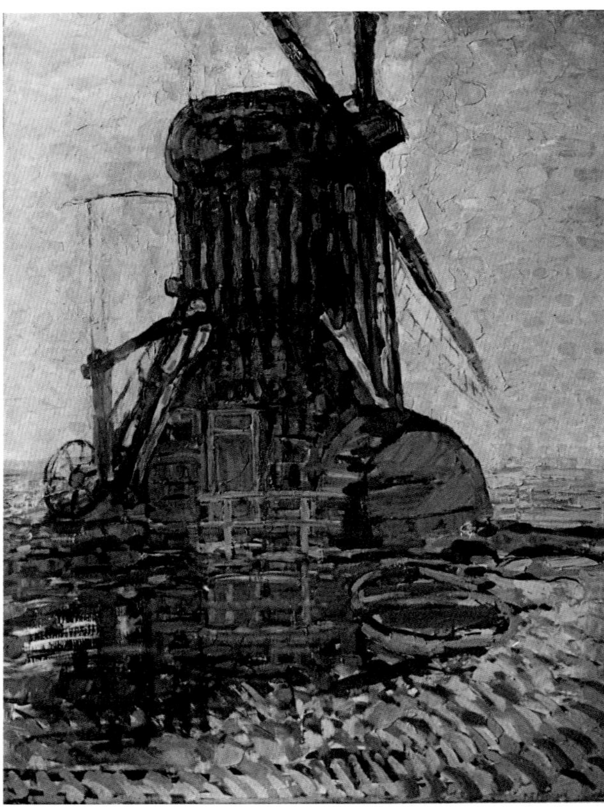

Fig. 65
Reproduction of *Mill in Sunlight: The Winkel Mill* (A654) by Piet Mondrian, c. 1908 (?)

> Fig. 66
***Composition A (No. I), with Red* (B260) unfinished in Mondrian's studio, c. March–May 1934 (detail) Photograph: Eugene Lux (cat. 166)**

Mondrian's Portfolio

Like many artists, Mondrian kept a portfolio — documentation of his work in the form of multi-purpose reproductions. Dozens of the photographs he had people take of his work have survived. Besides their immense art-historical importance, they represent a separate chapter in the story of Mondrian's relationship with photography.[112]

The survival of the portfolio photographs is twofold: some are spread across public and private collections, because Mondrian sent them to interested parties such as fellow artists, but also friends, critics, magazine editors and collectors. Inscriptions on the back in Mondrian's handwriting prove that they came from him personally. Where no such inscription is present, the paper type, printing technique and cropping make it likely that he was the source. Other photographs of his work have survived in two albums that came from the estate of Anna Bergman, a good friend of the artist (see p. 56).

Surviving photographs, especially those from the years before 1920, indicate the esteem in which Mondrian held his own work. It cost money, after all, to have pictures taken by professional photographers, so he did not have just any painting photographed. We can therefore conclude that he was satisfied with the works he did choose to record. The earliest surviving reproductions date from around 1907–8. They include a photograph of the painting *Mill in Sunlight: The Winkel Mill* (A654), which came in for a certain amount of criticism when Mondrian showed it in early 1909 at the Stedelijk Museum in Amsterdam (fig. 65). A reasonably representative number of reproductions still exist from the years after 1908, covering each successive phase in his oeuvre's development. There are photos, for instance, of work from the time he spent in the Dutch province of Zeeland (several pieces a year in the period 1909–11), the first Paris period (1912–14), the time he spent back in the Netherlands during the First World War (1914–19) and the second Paris period, during which the first classic neo-plastic work was produced (from 1920 onwards).

While he preferred professional photographers, if the opportunity presented itself, Mondrian did not hesitate to ask friends to take photographs of his work, thus saving costs. Examples include the pictures shot by Eugene Lux between May and June 1934 of a series of paintings (cats 163–70), which provide an exceptional insight into how this amateur reproduction process was approached. Mondrian orchestrated the photographs in this instance too by creating a neutral

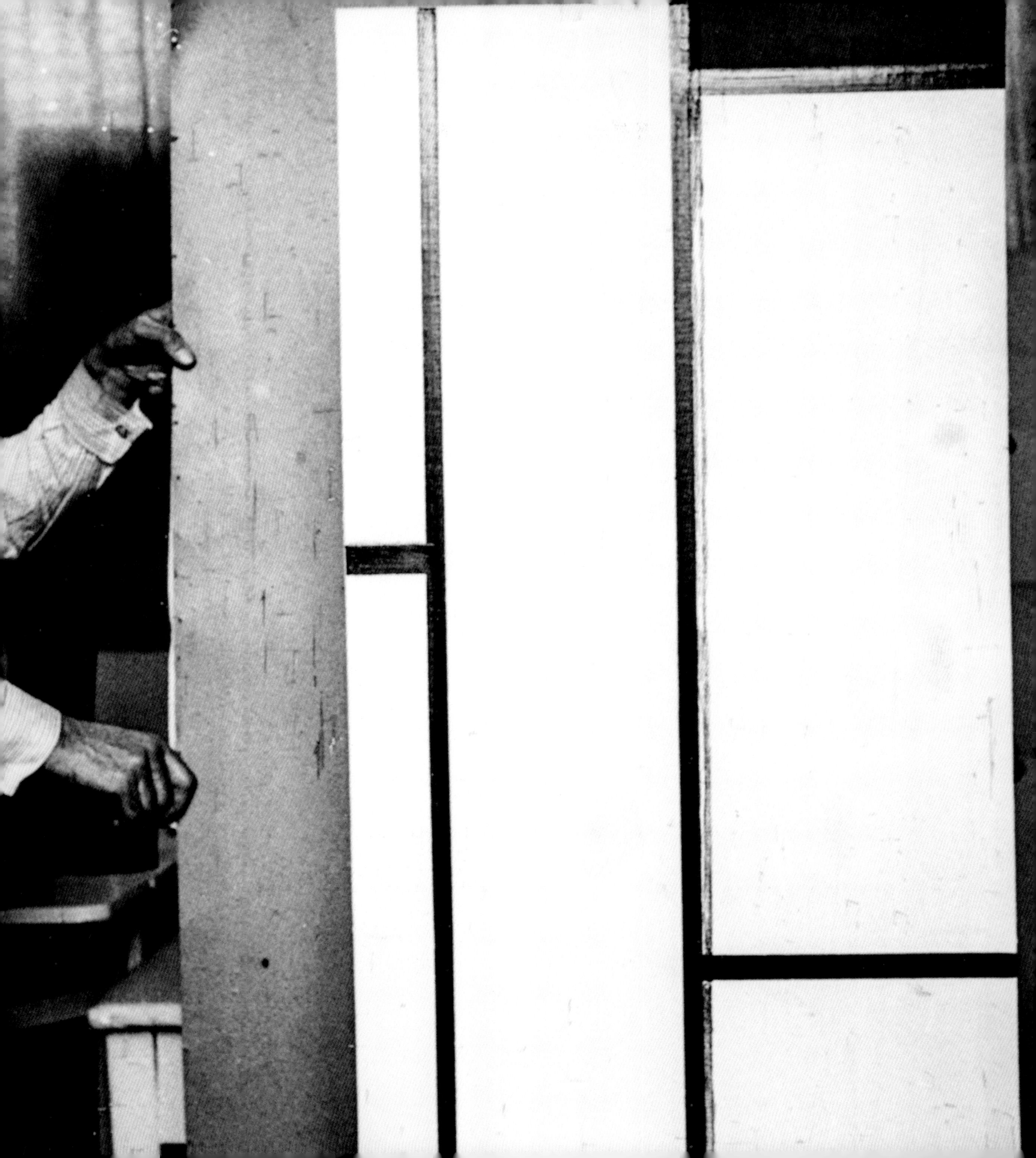

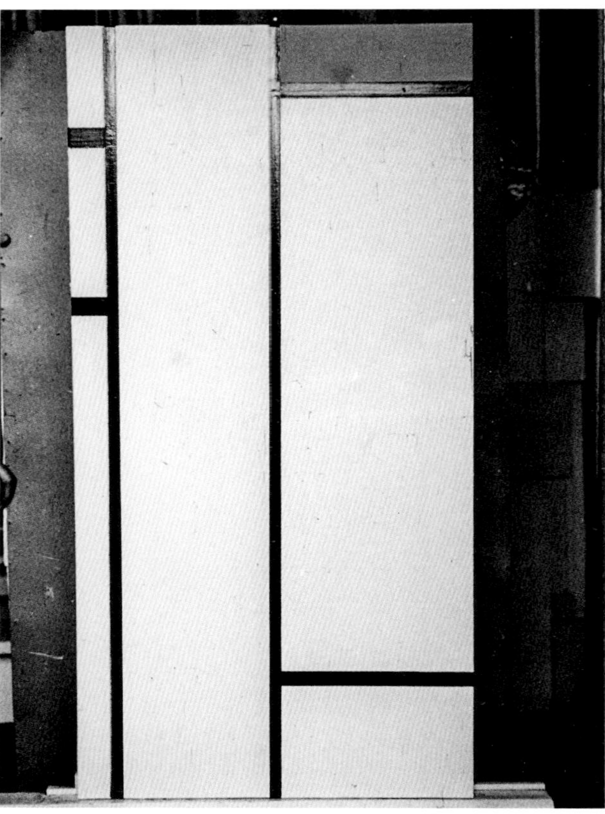

Fig. 67
Composition (No. III) blanc-jaune **(B257) unfinished in Mondrian's studio, c. March–May 1934 Photograph: Eugene Lux (cat. 165)**

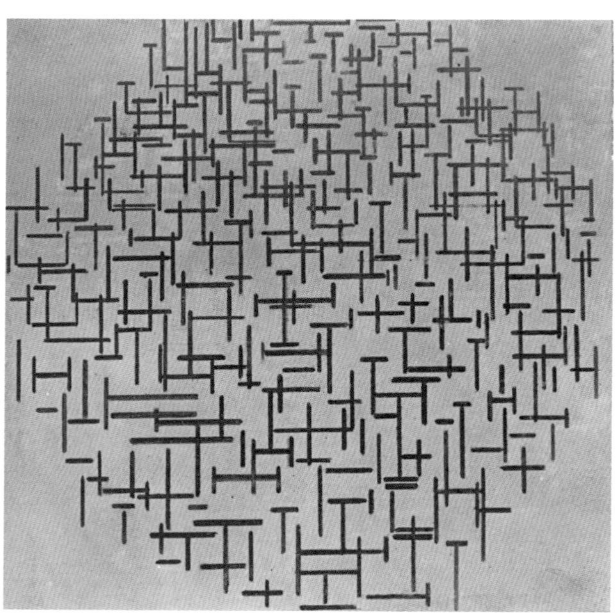

Fig. 68
Reproduction of *Composition in Line* (first state; B82, 1916) by Piet Mondrian, 1916

background using large sheets of paper or cardboard which he held behind his canvases. He undoubtedly trimmed the print afterwards so that his hands were no longer visible (fig. 66–7).[113]

The importance of reproductions

Photographic reproductions provide useful information about Mondrian's work. They generally date from shortly after the creation of the reproduced artwork and so capture it in its original state. A frame that was later lost might also be visible in the reproduction. In a few cases, Mondrian had a photograph taken of a painting that he later worked on further. Examples include his first entirely non-representational painting, *Composition in Line* (B82), from 1916–17. The fact that he had the work photographed suggests that he considered the first state of the painting in 1916 to be finished (fig. 68). He sent prints of the picture to various people, including Theo van Doesburg and the influential collector H. P. Bremmer, who purchased the painting for the high-profile collector Helene Kröller-Müller. The sale only took place, however, after Mondrian had completely reworked the painting in 1917. He had a photograph taken of the second state too. When this was reproduced in 1917 in the magazine *Beeldende Kunst*, of which Bremmer was the editor, it was one of the first times a painting of his had appeared in print. Without the picture of the first state, it would not have been known that Mondrian had overpainted the work or what it originally looked like.

Mondrian made a habit of adding colour notes to the back of black-and-white photographs of his neoplastic work, usually by writing in pencil the initial or the full name of the relevant hue in the place where the colour plane was located on the front of the picture. In some cases, these indications provide fresh information about a work. In 1926, Mondrian designed the stage scenery for a play by Michel Seuphor, photographs of which, taken by André Kertész, turned up in 2018. Mondrian sketched the different sets on the back of one of these — in black ink this time — and used a letter to identify the colour he had used in the various zones. Because of these notes, the colour scheme of the model recently became clear for the first time, revealing earlier interpretations to have been partially incorrect.[114]

Fresh understanding was also provided by another recently discovered colour-coded reproduction of a painting from 1926 — *Composition 1: Lozenge with Three Lines* (B169). Mondrian's notes on the back

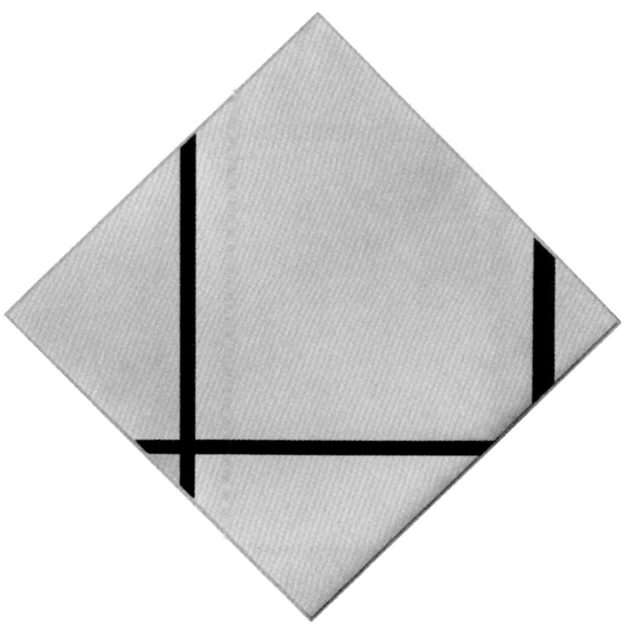

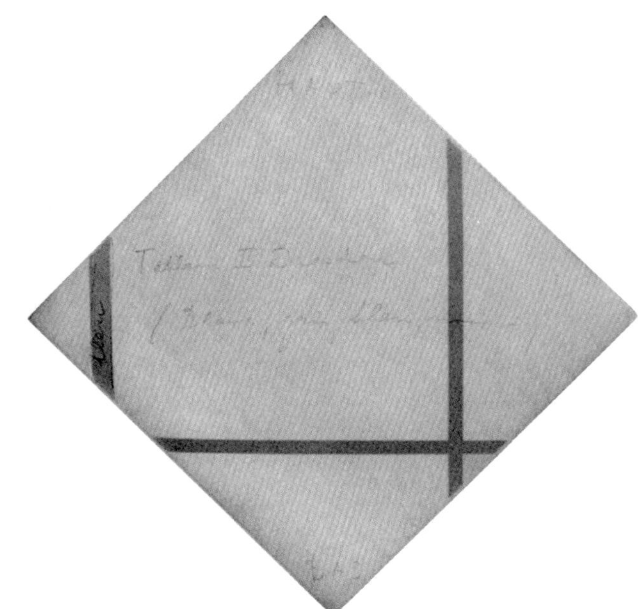

Figs 69—70 Reproduction (front and back) of *Composition 1: Lozenge with Three Lines* (B169) by Piet Mondrian, 1926

reveal that he painted the vertical line on the right-hand side of this composition blue rather than his customary black (fig. 69—70). It had previously been thought that he did not use coloured lines until 1933, and even then by way of great exception, in *Lozenge Composition with Four Yellow Lines* (cats 148—49, fig. 43). The discovery of the reproduction has thus shed new light on the development of Mondrian's neo-plastic work.[115] There are several cases too where a photographic reproduction is the only evidence of a painting's existence, a noteworthy example being the picture of a now lost diamond-shaped composition (fig. 71). Only two examples are currently known of this type of composition, based on a regular grid pattern with which Mondrian experimented in 1919. One is painted in the grey and ochre tones of early cubism, inspired by Picasso and Braque, which Mondrian applied around 1912—13. The other has the attenuated primary hues familiar from Mondrian's work in 1917. The surviving reproduction shows that there was a third diamond-shaped composition, signed like the others with the monogram 'P. M.' and dated 1919. Mondrian might have used saturated primary colours for this work, in which case it would have completed a triptych in which he took as his theme the development of colour use in neo-plasticism. This remains speculative, however, given the lack of colour indications. Another painting known only thanks to a photograph is *Composition No. XIV* (B180) from 1922, a reproduction of which originated in the Mondrian estate. When a hitherto unknown photograph turned up in 2017 showing a room in the 'Mondrian — Man Ray — Schwitters' exhibition in Dresden (1925), it was discovered that the painting had been exhibited there (fig. 72). Further investigation revealed that *Composition No. XIV* also featured in the catalogue raisonné under a different title where, given the lack of a visual reference, it was catalogued in the section 'Unidentified Works'. The gallery photograph thus allowed this

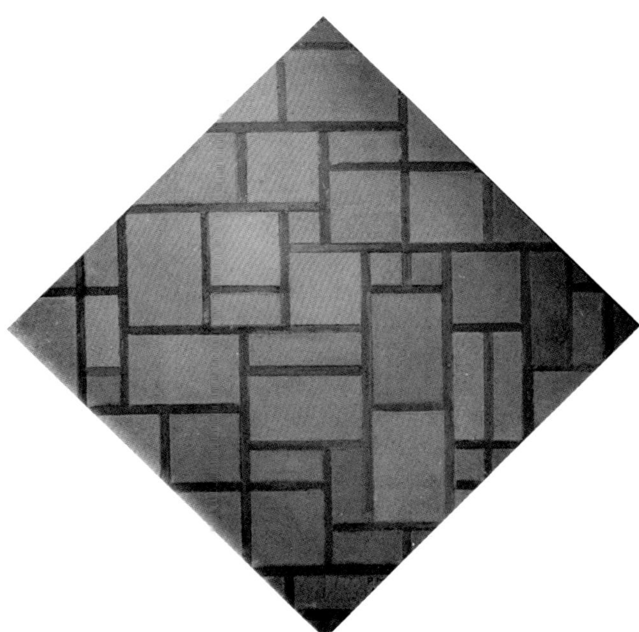

Fig. 71 Reproduction of *Composition with Grid 5a: Lozenge Composition with Colours* (B99a) by Piet Mondrian, 1919

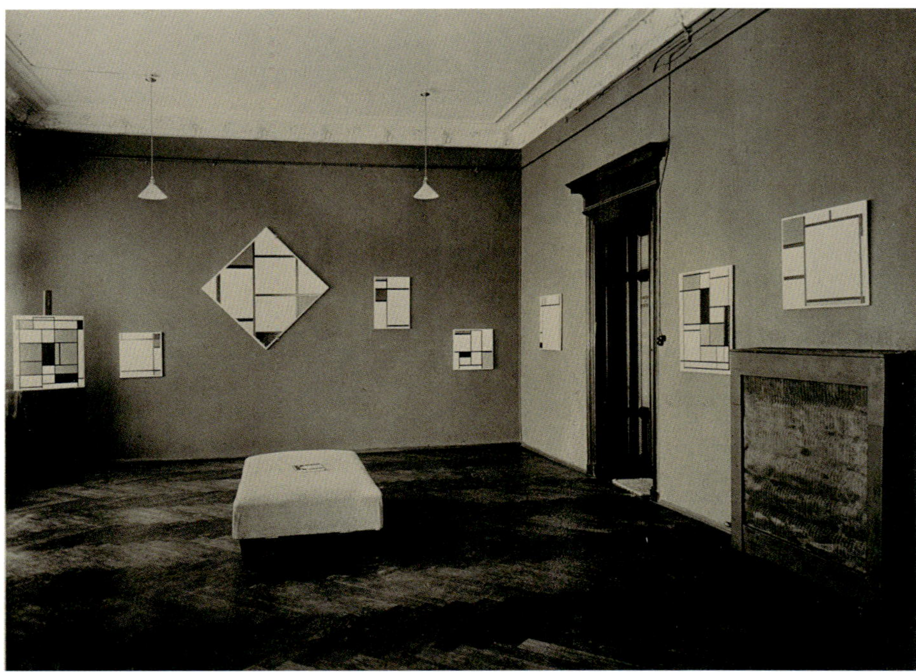

Fig. 72
View of the 'Mondrian — Man Ray — Schwitters' exhibition at Kunstausstellung Kuhl & Kuhn, Dresden, 1925. Photographic reproduction by Soichi Sunami, MoMA, undated. Mondrian's *Composition No. XIV* (B180, 1922) is the third painting from the right.

misunderstanding to be corrected. As far as we know, it is the only picture of a room at an exhibition of Mondrian's work held during his lifetime that is not included in *Piet Mondrian: Catalogue Raisonné*, published in 1998.[116]

Photo albums

In March 1922, Mondrian was interviewed on the occasion of his fiftieth birthday by a journalist from the Dutch newspaper *Het Vaderland*. Henri van Loon travelled to the studio in Paris, where Mondrian showed him a photo album: 'This is an album of photographs of my paintings from my earliest days until now. I started out as a naturalist but quickly felt the urge for a crisper summary and limiting of means. I have grown more abstract all the time. One period develops logically from another. What I myself see in that inner growth is above all the consistency. [...] I am sure that, if that growth is not yet finished, it will continue in the same direction, not go back.'[117] In other words, aside from documenting his own work and allowing it to be reproduced in publications, the albums served a didactic purpose, just like the aforementioned series of paintings from different stages of his development, which he had hung on the walls of his studio between 1922 and 1926.[118]

Sadly, the album reported by Van Loon, containing work from each stage of the artist's development to that point, has not survived. Two exceptional albums did emerge, however, in 2008, which had previously belonged to Mondrian's friend Anna Bergman. Mondrian had known her and her brother Cees since the turn of the century, when he was working in Amsterdam. He got on well with Cees Bergman, whose portrait he made. He also painted the wedding portrait of Bergman's fiancée Elisabeth Cavalini in 1901 and later produced portraits of the couple's children.[119] Mondrian kept in touch with both Cees and Anna Bergman until shortly before his death. Anna's estate later included letters, manuscripts and other personal documents from Mondrian, the two photograph albums among them.[120] The latter mostly contain reproductions of paintings from the mid-1930s and have thus been dated to around 1936. The smaller one also includes two studio photographs from 1933, taken by the architect Charles Karsten (cats 148–49). Mondrian himself is likely to have compiled the albums, although they were not purchased in Paris.[121] The fact that the photos passed through his hands is confirmed from the inscriptions on the back in his handwriting. He noted down not only the titles and colours of the paintings in the black-and-white photographs, but also which collection the work in question belonged to at the time. Another noteworthy feature is that some of the photos show an earlier state of a work, which Mondrian later adjusted. This is the case, for example, for *Rythme de lignes droites (et couleur?)* (B276) from 1937, to which Mondrian would add a further blue and red colour plane in New York (fig. 73).

Critical look

There are several letters showing that Mondrian could be extremely critical of reproductions of his work. In 1917, for instance, he wrote to Theo van Doesburg about fig. 74: 'I think that this photograph reflects the work (that I exhibited) very well: I want to convey something else in the next things, but the religious, etc. etc. is so good in this work; the placement of the three together is also expressive of things, wouldn't you agree? Van Hengelaar took an even bigger photo of the middle piece, but it needs some more work on it: the ground is too dark, etc.'[122] That same year, Mondrian apologized to Louis Saalborn, another

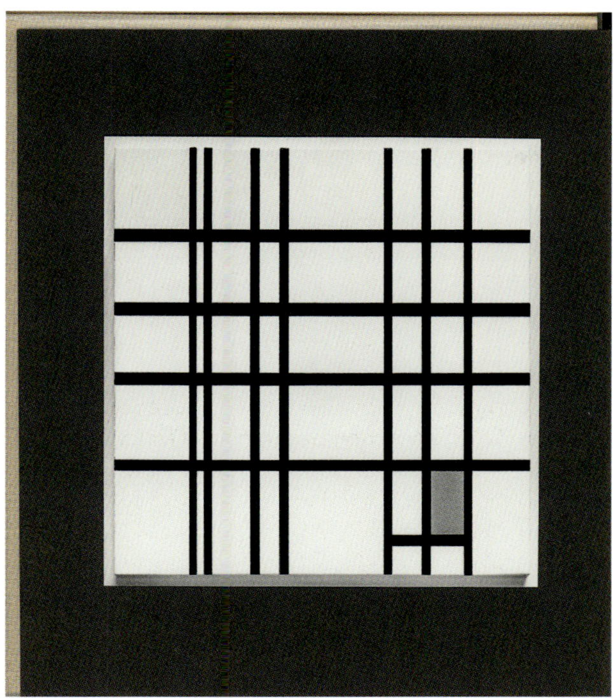

Fig. 73
Reproduction of *Rythme de lignes droites (et couleur?)* (B276) by Piet Mondrian, 1937. The photograph belongs to the 'large album' in the Anna Bergman Archive. The Hague, RKD, Anna Bergman Archive

friend, for the quality of a reproduction he had sent, noting on the back: 'The blue is too dark / the yellow too light'.[123] He reiterated his dissatisfaction with how a painting had been photographed in another letter to Van Doesburg in 1919: 'I don't like the picture anyway and so we shouldn't reproduce it. I think it would be better if you were to use the lozenge-shaped one if the occasion arises. The photographer tilted his camera again, turning them into trapeziums.'[124] All in all, Mondrian was not easily satisfied with the way his work was photographed and printed. Understandably so, given that the quality weighed even more in the case of works constructed from such sparse plastic means.

The limited ability of black-and-white photography to convey the vibrancy of his paintings was a problem for Mondrian. From his perspective, the grey tones did not give a good idea of the true colours, as was evident above. This prompted a discussion with Van Doesburg in 1919 about neo-plasticism, for which Mondrian was still using a uniform grid pattern as his basis at the time: 'It is true that there is the danger with a uniform arrangement of repeating oneself, but that can be countered in turn by opposition. Anything can become a system, be it irregular or regular. It simply depends on how it is solved. If I compare that work of mine, now reproduced in De Stijl, with the lozenge-shaped one that you (and I too) consider the best, I see that the latter is clearly put together better. It might be that the planes could differ more in size but I do not find it irksome in this one. I have also slowly found this way of working, as you can see clearly from the photos I sent you last year; the one you reproduced now is exactly the transition to the regular arrangement. I think we should each choose things like this ourselves and process them for ourselves: one will achieve more with this, the other with that.'[125] Mondrian returned to the matter a few months later, stating that it was the quality of the reproductions that had triggered the difference of opinion: 'I had just received De Stijl: it is another excellent issue, I read all the articles with pleasure. I think my reproduction is excellent. I also think now what you wrote at the time, that there is a touch of "repetition" in it; it was much less so in the original, due certainly to the colour values. All the same, I am now trying to avoid it in my new things.'[126] For all that they were indispensable to the exchange of ideas and concrete results, therefore, reproductions could also inadvertently lead to misunderstandings. Given that contacts between the various European avant-garde magazines and between artists

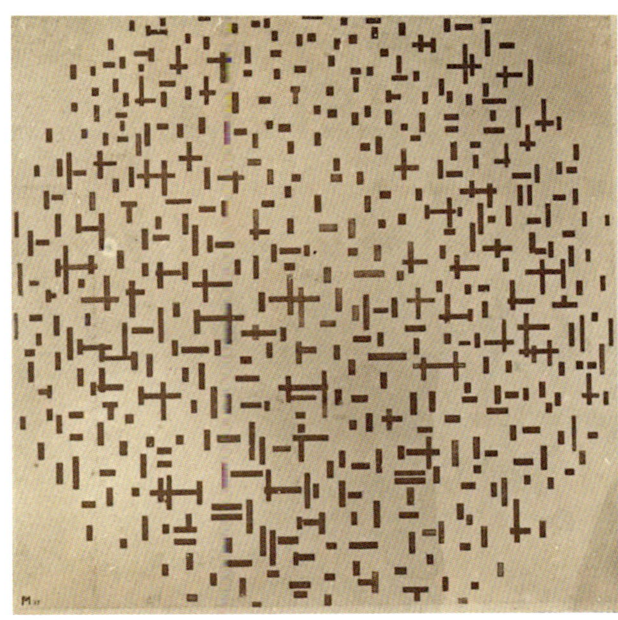

Fig. 74
Reproduction of Mondrian's *Composition in Line* (second state; B83), 1917 Photograph: Frits van Hengelaar

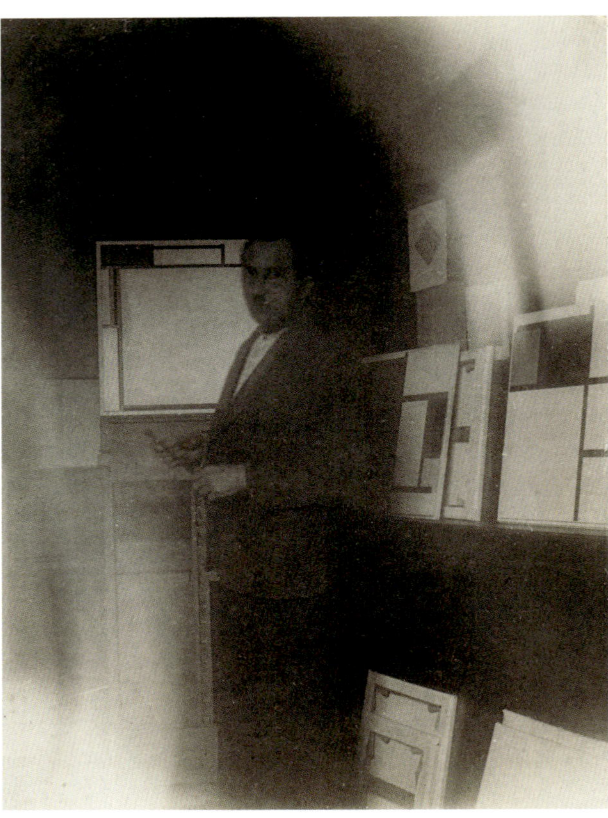

Fig. 75
Piet Mondrian in his studio, December 1923
Photograph: César Domela (cat. 59)

were kept up through the constant sending back and forth of black-and-white reproductions, it is important to realize that the absence of colour represented a loss of information. It thus makes sense that Mondrian began at some point to add colour notes to the back of reproductions.

Because of the exacting standards he imposed on the quality of reproductions, Mondrian preferred to work with professional photographers, as witnessed by comments in his letters and from the fact that many of the pictures are stamped with the photographer's name. Virtually all the reproductions in the two albums discussed above, for instance, were made by the same Swiss photographer, Hugo Paul Herdeg. He was active between 1932 and 1939 in Paris, where his clientele included several artists, among them Pablo Picasso, Hans Arp and Georges Braque. In 1934, moreover, he was appointed in-house photographer at the Musée de l'Homme.[127] Mondrian no doubt came into contact with Herdeg through word-of-mouth advertising by fellow artists. Like other professionals from whom Mondrian ordered photographs — among them Marc Vaux, J. Roseman and the previously discussed Pierre Delbo — Herdeg specialized in the photographic reproduction of artworks.

That this was a specific niche is apparent from the small number of reproduction photographers who worked for a large group of Paris avant-garde artists.[128] The fact that Mondrian was also a client of this select group of professionals is a further indication of his attitude toward photography, which he regarded as a medium ideally suited to *reproducing* reality. By opting for them wherever possible, he acknowledged the status of photography as a profession and of the professional photographer as a skilled practitioner. This is borne out by the reproductions of his own works that he hung on the walls of his studios in both Paris and New York (figs 75—6).

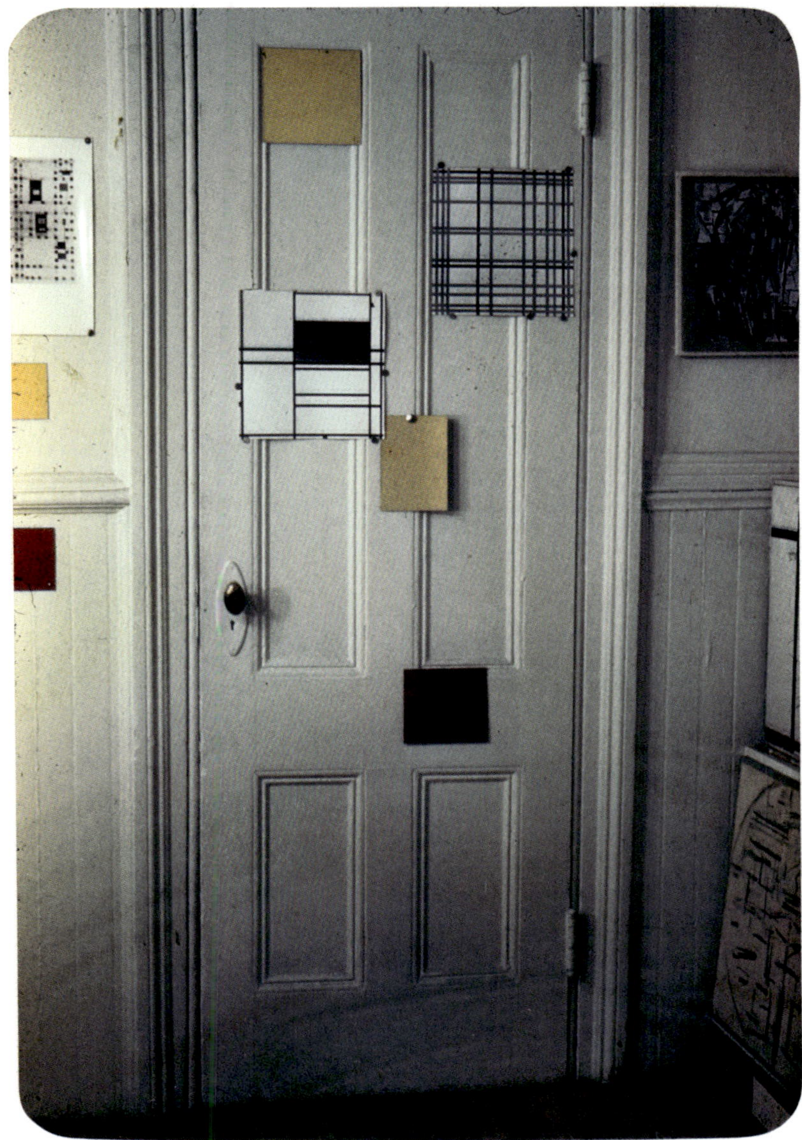

Fig. 76
The door of Mondrian's living area after his death, between 1 February and 22 March 1944
Photograph: Harry Holtzman
(cat. 402)

Closing Remarks

We have focused in the preceding chapters on how Mondrian successfully deployed photography to generate attention for his art and ideas. Part of this strategy was to construct his image as an artist — something he achieved so persuasively that it largely shaped the later, one-dimensional way he came to be perceived. Mondrian was effectively responsible for stereotyping himself. At the same time, the multitude of photographs that show him in the company of others confirm that he was not only a social creature, like most human beings, but also an accomplished and successful networker — albeit one who, given the choice, generally preferred the sidelines. The photographs likewise tell us a great deal about how Mondrian applied his neo-plasticism in the studio and, occasionally, his working methods.

What we have set out here is by no means the last word on the subject. What's more, this book offers the opportunity to compare Mondrian's studio and his strategic deployment of photography with that of other artists. An alternative example of how photography could be approached is provided by Pablo Picasso, who used the medium primarily to create an immense visual library,[129] on which he then drew gratefully for the creation of his own work. Surviving portrait photographs of him mostly present Picasso as a creative joker. The sculptor Constantin Brancusi, meanwhile, is known to have taken up photography himself to gain more effective control over the way his work was perceived by the public. Mondrian was not the only one, moreover, to use photography to create an image or to treat gallery openings as an opportunity to maintain and expand a network. What other network strategies did artists employ? Were there others who attracted the attention of photographers and, if so, why and where did it lead? The way all this relates to the emergence of a modern visual culture is one more field waiting to be explored. We very much hope that the encounter with Mondrian that this book offers will contribute towards answering these and other, new questions.

Notes

1 Letter from Piet Mondrian to Lodewijk Schelfhout, Paris, 12 June 1914. The Hague, RKD, Archive of Lodewijk Schelfhout and Albertine Schelfhout-Van der Meulen (0278), inv. 70.

2 Letter from Piet Mondrian to H. P. Bremmer, Laren, 2 April 1916. The Hague, Gemeente-archief, H. P. Bremmer archive (0836), inv. 01.

3 Cf. Mali et al. 1994, pp. 22–9.

4 The standard *carte de visite* was a card measuring approximately 10.5 x 6.5 cm on which a photograph of about 9 x 6 cm was pasted. 'Cabinet cards' were also common (photograph approx. 14 x 9.5 cm, card approx. 16.5 x 10.5 cm). Other formats existed too. See Mathews 1974, pp. 20–50; and Van den Dorpel et al. 1989, p. 7 and passim.

5 The characterization of this development, as well as many of the photo-historical backgrounds presented here in concise form, are derived from Rooseboom 2019 (p. 16) and Boom 1996, pp. 16–30.

6 This is not to say, of course, that a professional photographer like André Kertész did not take the occasional snapshot too.

7 One photographer with whom Mondrian was in contact in 1909–10 was Remelius Hora Adema, who belonged to and exhibited at the Nederlandse Club voor Foto-kunst, which was founded in 1907 (Leijerzapf 1984, vol. 1, p. 9). Mondrian mentions in a letter to Aletta de Iongh dated 30 January 1910 (Otterlo, Kröller-Muller Museum collection) that Hora Arema took his photography 'very seriously'.

8 Rooseboom 2019, p. 234.

9 Daniel 1998, p. 11.

10 Easton 2011.

11 *Dorothy Gretchen Biersteker*, 1894 (A25) and *Noel Biersteker*, c. 1897 (A26).

12 It has so far been assumed in the literature that Delbo's first name was Paul, but this does not appear to be correct. See the biography on Pierre Delbo on p. 122.

13 Cf. Bowness 1989, passim.

14 Rooseboom 2019, pp. 49–65.

15 Idem, p. 56.

16 Haus 1990, p. 15 et seq.

17 Moholy-Nagy 1922, pp. 98–101.

18 Idem, pp. 99–100.

19 Moholy-Nagy 1925, p. 6.

20 Idem, p. 7.

21 Kállai 1927, pp. 148–57. While Maholy-Nagy did not agree with most of the ideas expressed in the article, he published it in *i10* as 'I would like to open a debate in these pages'; see: Forgács 1994, p. 85.

22 See also Bool 1994, p. 69.

23 Mondrian et al. 1927; Mondrian's response, quoted here in its entirety, is on p. 235:

'Bien que je sois pour une grande partie d'accord avec les intéressantes observations sur la "peinture et la photographie" de mr. Ernst Kallai, il me semble nécessaire de ne pas perdre de vue que c'est "l'artiste" et non pas "le moyen" qui crée l'œuvre d'art.

Certainement le moyen est de grande importance et il est étroitement lié avec l'expression plastique d'une œuvre mais c'est l'artiste qui décide de son essence qu'elle est *purement plastique* et non imitative.

Néanmoins, il me paraît que le caractère de la photographie soit plutôt imitatif que plastique. La photographie dans le sens usuel est le moyen approprié pour *la reproduction* de l'objectivité, et tout art est *création*.

Mais à présent il est difficile de déterminer l'évolution de la photographie — en effet, de tels efforts ont déjà été réalisés sur le terrain de la plastique pure, que nous pouvons tout espérer de la photographie. Il est bien possible que la technique de la photographie se change, comme la technique de la peinture s'est changée et les comparaisons et observations de mr. Ernst Kallai peuvent aider à y arriver.'

24 The exhibition 'Mondrian — Man Ray — Schwitters' was held in September 1925 at Kunsthand-lung Kühl & Kühn in Dresden. Mondrian did not visit the show, but the combination will surely have piqued his curiosity about Man Ray's photographs. Both men belonged to the same artistic circles in Paris and must have crossed paths regularly.

25 One of the photographers with whom Mondrian had been in close contact since 1929 was Florence Henri. Writing in his autobiography, Michel Seuphor recalled that he had introduced Mondrian to Henri at her request. It led to a 'liaison' and to Henri moving in with Mondrian for almost two months. See Seuphor 1988, pp. 35–6.

26 Lurasco 1907, n.p.

27 Letter from Piet Mondrian to Theo van Doesburg, autumn 1915: 'I will drop into Laren on Sunday and send you a few photos I have heightened myself with chalk.' The Hague, RKD, Archive of Theo and Nelly van Doesburg (0408), inv. 134.

28 Letter from Piet Mondrian to Israël Querido, around September 1909. Quoted in Querido 1909.

29 See, more recently, Bramly 2012.

30 H. P. Blavatsky was the founder, along with Henry Steel Olcott and William Quan Judge, of the Theosophical Society in 1875. The portrait of her that Mondrian owned was part of Mondrian's estate. The Hague, RKD, Archive of Piet Mondrian (0740), inv. 073.

31 See also Coppes 2012, p. 264.

32 Regarding Waldenburg, see Coppes 2020.

33 Cf. Coppes 2020, p. 28.

34 Letter from Piet Mondrian to Aletta de Iongh, around October 1910, Otterlo, Kröller Müller Museum collection.

35 Cf. Kisters 2017, p. 47.

36 Letter from Piet Mondrian to Sal Slijper, 3 May 1916. The Hague, RKD, Sal Slijper archive (0150), inv. 147.

37 This is probably not an existing painting but an improvised composition, created by pinning rectangles of coloured card on the wall (Le Coultre 2015, p. 43).

38 An undated letter from Piet Mondrian to Theo van Doesburg (around March 1922) shows that Van Doesburg had asked him for a photo. The Hague, RKD, Archive of Theo and Nelly van Doesburg (0408), inv. 135.

39 Mondrian 1924, p. 86. The title refers to a Dutch proverb that literally means 'to hang one's *huik* [hooded cloak] towards the wind': i.e. to go with the flow/sail with the wind or to adapt to circumstances. It is not clear whether the use of *huif* rather than *huik* in the title was Mondrian's mistake or a type-setting error.

40 The first mention of a visit to Mondrian can be found on 19 August 1926 in one of Kertész's surviving diaries (Coppes/Jansen 2020, p. 84 and note 15 on p. 97).

41 'Photo-Kertész' ran from 12 to 24 March at the gallery Au Sacre du Printemps (Borhan 1994, pp. 20–21; and McCauley Lee/Canaan 2004, pp. 84–5).

42 See also p. 37.

43 See cats 150–71 for several other pictures taken by Lux during his visit to Mondrian.

44 Blotkamp 2006.

45 Cf. Le Coultre 2015.

46 Piet Zwart and Wim Schuhmacher's memories of the studio can be found in Coppes 2012, pp. 41 and 43.

47 Marek Wieczorek suggested in 2014 that it was Hannes Meyer who gave Delbo the commission. While not impossible, it seems more likely that Mondrian himself approached the photographer, albeit at Meyer's request, given that Lucien Lefebvre-Foinet, his regular supplier of art materials, was located just a few doors down the same street, Rue Vavin. See p. 22 and Wieczorek 2014, p. 63.

48 Meyer 1926; photograph on p. 209.

49 The photograph can be found in the Katherine S. Dreier papers/Société Anonyme archive, Beinecke Rare Book & Manuscript Library, Yale University, New Haven, CT, Box 109, Folder 2641.

50 See Röell 1926.

51 *Cercle et Carré* 3 (June 1930), p. [9]. The photographs must have served as illustrations for a short article by Jean Gorin on neo-plasticism and architecture on p. [3] (Gorin 1930), although this link is not made explicit in the magazine itself.

52 When a friend visited the studio in 1930, she noticed that the black had disappeared: 'Once I went to his studio and saw that something had changed; it was lighter, more radiant, as if the sun had broken through into the monk's cell. He was acting a little mysterious and did not immediately put on his latest gramophone record. His hair looked blacker and glossier than before, he was a little restless, until he suddenly announced that he was planning to marry. Now I realized what had changed in the studio: the black had gone. Black had to give way to his new vision of life.' Van Loon 1946, n.p.

53 It is also noteworthy that the decoration preceded the development of neo-plasticism as applied by Mondrian in his paintings, which continued to be dominated around 1930 by a small number of planes and lines. This would not change until about 1932, when Mondrian began to use double lines, resulting in more planes.

54 Also present on this visit was the Croatian architect Ernest Weissmann, who at the time worked for Le Corbusier; see cat. 113.

55 Giedion-Welcker 1930, p. 67; photograph on p. 66.

56 For the background to the changing studio, see Blotkamp 2010 and Coppes 2012.

57 In Karsten's estate, kept at Het Nieuwe Instituut in Rotterdam, is a portrait photo of Mondriaan from 1926. This photo may also have been taken by Karsten, although there is no further evidence of a visit by Karsten to Mondriaan in that year; see cat. 79.

58 For a detailed discussion of Kertész's photos of the stage model, see: Coppes/Jansen 2020.

59 Citroen 1931; quote on p. 6.

60 We know from an undated postcard sent in late 1929/early 1930 that Mondrian also sent several reproductions of paintings: 'Please find enclosed the photographs. Could you verify that they are placed correctly: printers often insert them upside-down, for instance. If you remove them from the card, you will see on the back which way is up.' The Hague, RKD, Archive of Paul Citroen (0398), inv. 7. Mondrian's essay was titled 'L'Art réaliste et l'art superréaliste (La Morpho-plastique et la néoplastique)'.

61 Citroen 1931, p. 76 (portrait); p. 77 (studio); pp. 76–82 (essay).

62 While a number of artists — Jacob Bendien and Theo van Doesburg among them — provided portrait photos showing them in their studio, Mondrian is the only one where the focus is on the studio as such.

63 Xceron 1929, p. 4.

64 We infer from an interview with Mondrian by the journalist Henri van Loon that the paintings had hung there since at least March 1922; see Van Loon 1922.

65 Ibid.

66 Mondrian presented his neo-plasticism as a logical, natural development in art. In 'De Nieuwe Beelding in de schilder-kunst', for instance, he wrote: 'If we see Painting gradually turning away from the natural appearance of things, this is, viewed superficially, a process of dissolution. It is, however, a *process of evolution*, which has slowly developed over the centuries and is now coming to the fore in a short space of time.' Mondriaan 1918, p. 132.

67 The painting can be identified as *Composition No. I* (B214) from 1929, which currently belongs to the Kunstmuseum Basel collection.

68 The paintings visible on the easel are *Lozenge Composition with Four Yellow Lines*, 1933 (B241) and (below) *Composition with Double Lines and Yellow*, 1934 (B242). It is not clear why the latter painting is dated 1934 in the catalogue raisonné of Mondrian's work, given that it appears finished in this photograph taken in 1933 (cf. Welsh/Joosten 1998-II, p. 370).

69 The photograph and the quote were reproduced in Opbouw 1933, p. 197.

70 The RKD has three prints of the photograph, and there is a fourth in the Koninklijke Bibliotheek in The Hague. They were all most likely given or sent by Mondrian to his friends, which is how they found their way into these respective collections.

71 The 'International Exhibition of Modern Art: Assembled by the Société Anonyme' ran from 19 November 1926 to 9 January 1927 at the Brooklyn Museum. It included two of Mondrian's paintings from 1926: *Tableau I: Lozenge with Four Lines and Grey* (B176) and *Tableau II* (B177). The exhibition then travelled to the Anderson Galleries, New York (25 January–5 February), the Albright Art Gallery, Buffalo (25 February–20 March) and the Toronto Art Gallery, Toronto (1–24 April) (Welsh/Joosten 1998-III, pp. 33–4).

72 Dreier 1926, pp. 48–9.

73 Gallatin acquired the 1932 painting *Composition with Yellow and Blue* (B236) on that occasion (Welsh/Joosten 1998-II, pp. 154 and 365–66).

74 Welsh/Joosten 1998-II, p. 156.

75 Letter from Piet Mondrian to A. E. Gallatin, 26 June 1934, New York, the New York Historical Society Collection.

76 Janssen 2016, p. 489.

77 The five prints by Lux in Mondrian's estate are kept in The Hague, RKD, Archive of Piet Mondrian (0740), inv. 065.

78 The exhibition ran from 30 July to 31 October 1937. Mondrian showed two works from 1937: *Composition en rouge, bleu et blanc* (B271) and *Composition en jaune, bleu en blanc* (B272) (Welsh/Joosten 1998-III, p. 41).

79 It is stated on the back page of the catalogue that 'Les artistes ont été / photographiés par: / Rogi André / Florence Henri / Man Ray' (Origines 1937, n.p.).

80 Welsh/Joosten 1998-II, p. 168.

81 The exhibition ran from 19 July to 30 November 1937 at the Gipsabguss-Sammlung of the Archäologisches Institut in Munich. It included two Mondrian paintings confiscated from public collections: *Komposition mit Gelb, Zinnober, Schwarz, Blau und verschiedenen grauen und weissen Tönen*, dating from 1923 (B149) (Provinzialmuseum Hannover), and *Farbige Aufteilung*, from 1928 (B202) (Museum Folkwang, Essen). The Nazi authorities probably destroyed both works some time between the end of 1937 and 1945 (Welsh/Joosten 1998-II, pp. 167, 308, 340–41 and III, pp. 40–41).

82 Darwent 2012, pp. 55–6.

83 It was long believed that a photograph of Piet Mondrian in the garden of Harry and Eileen Holtzman (cat. 189) had been taken by the British artist John Cecil Stephenson and that it showed Mondrian in a garden in Hampstead, the London district where he lived between September 1938 and September 1940. The picture seems actually to have been shot, however, by Harry Holtzman in the garden of his summer home in Great Barrington, Massachusetts.

84 Welsh/Joosten 1998-II, p. 173.

85 Janssen 2016, pp. 525–27.

86 Barr visited Mondrian in Paris in July 1935 while preparing the exhibition 'Cubism and Abstract Art', which ran from 2 March to 19 April 1936 at the Museum of Modern Art (Welsh/Joosten 1998-II, p. 168).

87 Harrison/Denne 2002, pp. 67–8.

88 Janis 1941.

89 Typescript by Klaus Mann on the principles underpinning *Decision: A Review of Free Culture*, Munich, Muenchner Stadtbibliothek, Nachl. Klaus Mann/Manuskripte (KM M 629).

90 For Mondrian's articles 'Liberation from oppression in art and life' and 'Art shows the evil of Nazi and Soviet oppressive tendencies', see: Holtzman/James 1986, pp. 320–30.

91 Welsh/Joosten 1998-II, p. 176.

92 Janis 1941, p. 90.

93 See Ewing et al. 2012, p. 92, for Newman's working methods. The RKD holds five contact prints of the session Newman did with Mondrian; in 2008, the Rijksmuseum in Amsterdam acquired an album with four contact prints (cf. Boom/Rooseboom 2012, pp. 182–83).

94 Boom/Rooseboom 2012, p. 182.

95 Arnold Newman, quoted in Ewing et al. 2012, p. 94.

96 Janssen 2016, pp. 538, 543–44.

97 See Troy 2013, pp. 71–126, for the background to and history of the *Wall Works* and studio furniture after Mondrian's death.

98 Fonssagrives was supposedly encouraged to shoot the piece in the study by *Town & Country*'s art director, Harry Bull (Henkels 1993, p. 40).

99 Cf. Sarl 1998, pp. 33–50, esp. p. 40.

100 Kettering 2006, p. 5.

101 Both photographs can be found in Den Haag, RKD, Archive of Theo and Nelly van Doesburg (0408), inv. 1568.

102 Letter from Piet Mondrian to Theo van Doesburg (1916). Den Haag, RKD, Archive of Theo and Nelly van Doesburg (0408), inv. 134.

103 See Gorter 2017 for more information on Mondrian's time with Sint Lucas.

104 There is another photograph showing Simon Maris sailing with a second person, who has been identified in the past as Mondrian by, among others, Leal 2010, p. 271, and Janssen 2013, p. 57. The individual in question is, however, Jan van der Hoeven Leonhard, a doctor and collector who had lots of artist friends (Gorter 2020, p. 40).

105 Van Deene 1977, p. 78.

106 Seuphor 1971, p. 7 et seq.

107 Letter from Piet Mondrian to Michel Seuphor, 15 March 1930; quoted in Leal 2010, p. 308.

108 Lansing/Colman 2013, p. 10.

109 According to an article in *Art News*, it had not been easy to get the artists together at the same time; see cat. 222.

110 Writing in his memoirs, Jimmy Ernst recalled an incident that took place in 1942 at the triplex his father Max shared with Peggy Guggenheim. Following a lunch with several surrealists, André Breton and Marcel Duchamp succeeded in loosening Mondrian's tongue. They were keen to find out what he thought of their work, which added elements to the art of painting, rather than omitting them. The Dutchman replied that he considered Yves Tanguy's latest work to be more abstract than his own recent paintings. Once he and Tanguy reached the end of their work, he continued, they would find they were still living together on the same planet. Ernst 1984, pp. 234–42.

111 Pohlmann/Landshoff 2013, p. 34.

112 The catalogue section of this book does not include the portfolio photos. See the explanation on p. 310.

113 Mondrian generally cropped the print so tightly that only the painting with the frame was visible, especially in the case of reproductions of his earliest neo-plastic work. He later began to leave a little of the background in too.

114 See Coppes/Jansen 2020.

115 See Wieczorek 2020, who published two reproductions demonstrating Mondrian's earlier use of coloured lines. In addition to *Composition 1: Lozenge with Three Lines*, there was *Painting No. II* (B177), also from 1926, in which Mondrian likewise incorporated a blue line.

116 The third part of *Piet Mondrian: Catalogue Raisonné*, compiled by Joop Joosten, lists exhibitions with Mondrian's work, and shows room overviews of exhibitions held during Mondrian's life in which his work can be seen. The photo of the exhibition in Dresden must not have been known to Joosten at that time. See Welsh/Joosten 1998-III, pp. 21–44.

117 Van Loon 1922.

118 Coppes 2012, p. 43.

119 For detailed information on these family portraits, see Draaijer 2022.

120 Both photo albums are located in The Hague, RKD, Archive of Anna Bergman (0662), inv. 31 and 32.

121 The front cover of the smaller of the two albums has gold letters spelling out *Foto's* in Dutch, while a sticker in the larger one shows that it was purchased at the Dutch department store De Bijenkorf. Mondrian might have been given them as a gift by Bergman or another Dutch visitor, given that he did not return to his native country after 1919. The albums also contain notes in another hand. Assuming that Mondrian compiled them, it is plausible that he handed the albums to Cees or Anna Bergman when he moved to London in 1938, at which point he had to leave many of his possessions behind.

122 Letter from Piet Mondrian to Theo van Doesburg, 7 July 1917. The Hague, RKD, Archive of Theo and Nelly van Doesburg, (0408), inv. 134.

123 The words are found on a photographic reproduction of the painting *Composition with Colour Planes 1* (B87), 1917, that

Mondrian sent to Louis Saalborn. Reproduced in Hoek 1982, p. 63.

124 Letter from Piet Mondrian to Theo van Doesburg, augustus 1919. The Hague, RKD, Archive of Theo and Nelly van Doesburg (0408), inv. 102–3.

125 Letter from Piet Mondrian to Theo van Doesburg, 18 April 1919. The Hague, RKD, Archive of Theo and Nelly van Doesburg (0408), inv. 136.

126 Letter from Piet Mondrian to Theo van Doesburg 6 September 1919. The Hague, RKD, Archive of Theo and Nelly van Doesburg (0408), inv. 136.

127 Gasser 2007.

128 Coppes 2010, p. 153.

129 Baldassari 1997, passim.

THE DUTCH PERIOD 1872–1919

The artist Piet Mondrian, who would play a key role in 20th-century modern art, was born Pieter Cornelis Mondriaan in Amersfoort, near Utrecht, on 7 March 1872. When he was eight years old, his family moved to Winterswijk in the province of Guelders. His formal schooling was limited to just eight years of primary education at schools headed by his father in those same two Dutch towns. This was followed by years of self-study in preparation for the lower and intermediate drawing certificate (*tekenakte*), which he attained in 1889 and 1892 respectively. The idea was to earn his living as a drawing teacher. He inherited his talent in this regard from his father. During the same period, he was given painting lessons by his uncle, Frits Mondriaan, who lived in The Hague and is best known as a landscape painter. From time to time, Frits visited his brother's family to paint *en plein air*. The young Mondrian also received guidance in drawing and painting from Jan Braet von Überfeldt — an artist who had trained at the Rijksacademie in Amsterdam and was living at the time in Deventer. Work by Mondrian was shown as early as 1890 in an exhibition of 'living masters' in The Hague.

He moved to Amsterdam in the autumn of 1892 and embarked on a two-year course at the Rijksacademie van Beeldende Kunsten (National Academy of Fine Arts), supported financially by an annual allowance of 100 guilders from Queen-Regent Emma. Mondrian also took an evening course in life-drawing in 1894—95 and another to learn etching techniques in 1896—97.

Amsterdam was rapidly developing into a major national centre of the arts at that time, which saw the opening of the Rijksmuseum (1885), the Concertgebouw (1888) and the Stedelijk Museum (1895). Mondrian quickly found his way into artistic circles, via his membership of artists' associations at which he regularly showed his work and friendships with fellow students and colleagues, including Simon Maris, who came from a famous family of painters. He paid his way chiefly through portrait commissions, while also making copies of paintings in museums and painting still lifes for the art trade. There were occasional book illustrations and designs for decorations too, and he had a small number of pupils. The main motifs in his independent work, rooted in the Dutch tradition of the previous century, were landscapes, country villages and cottages, cityscapes (mostly industrial) and still lifes. The rural subject matter that began to dominate after the turn of the century was mostly drawn from Amsterdam and the surrounding area.

Mondrian fled Amsterdam in early 1904, due to unspecified problems. He spent almost the entire year in the Brabant village of Uden, close to his lifelong friend Albert van den Briel, who was employed there as an agricultural engineer. Van den Briel later recalled that Mondrian was experiencing an existential crisis and that they had had numerous conversations about philosophical and religious subjects.

The character of his work altered after Mondrian returned to Amsterdam. The colours grew brighter and his landscapes became charged with a tranquil, timeless atmosphere. He was looking for a spiritual art, which would allow the inner essence of things to be perceived beneath their outer manifestation. Mondrian had probably been drawn to Theosophy for a while, but his interest intensified during this period. In May 1909 he joined the Theosophical Society, of which he would remain a member for the rest of his life.

Mondrian's use of colour in his work changed around 1908–9. The colours of nature gave way to highly saturated shades of blue, purple and orange, applied with a divisionist touch. Together with Jan Sluijters, Jan Toorop and Leo Gestel, Mondrian formed part of a 'luminist' avant-garde that attracted considerable attention from both the public and art critics. He found the conservative artistic climate in the Netherlands less and less conducive. From 1908 to 1915, he spent several weeks each summer at an artists' colony in Domburg, where Jan Toorop was at the centre of a circle of painters searching for renewal. Mondrian was among the founders in 1910 of the Moderne Kunstkring (Modern Art Circle) — an initiative to create more opportunities in the Netherlands for the most progressive artists to show their work. He followed up in 1911 by cancelling his membership of the Arti et Amicitiae and Sint Lucas artists' associations in Amsterdam, which he now considered overly conventional. When it came to showing his own work, Mondrian also looked abroad. He exhibited in Brussels (1909 and 1910), in Nantes (1911) and, in what was a personal milestone for him, at the Société des Artistes Indépendants in Paris (1911).

Mondrian spent ten days in Paris in May 1911 to see his work at the latter exhibition and to prepare for his first show at the Moderne Kunstkring. He recognized the importance of the new cubist movement and for the remainder of his life would acknowledge his debt to Pablo Picasso. The impact of this experience can already be detected in several of his works as early as the summer of 1911. So inspiring were these contacts that he decided in early 1912 to move to Paris, after first breaking off a betrothal he later described as 'merely an illusion'. His entry into the art scene in the world capital of modernism was smoothed by other Dutch avant-garde artists working there.

>> Detail of cat. 39

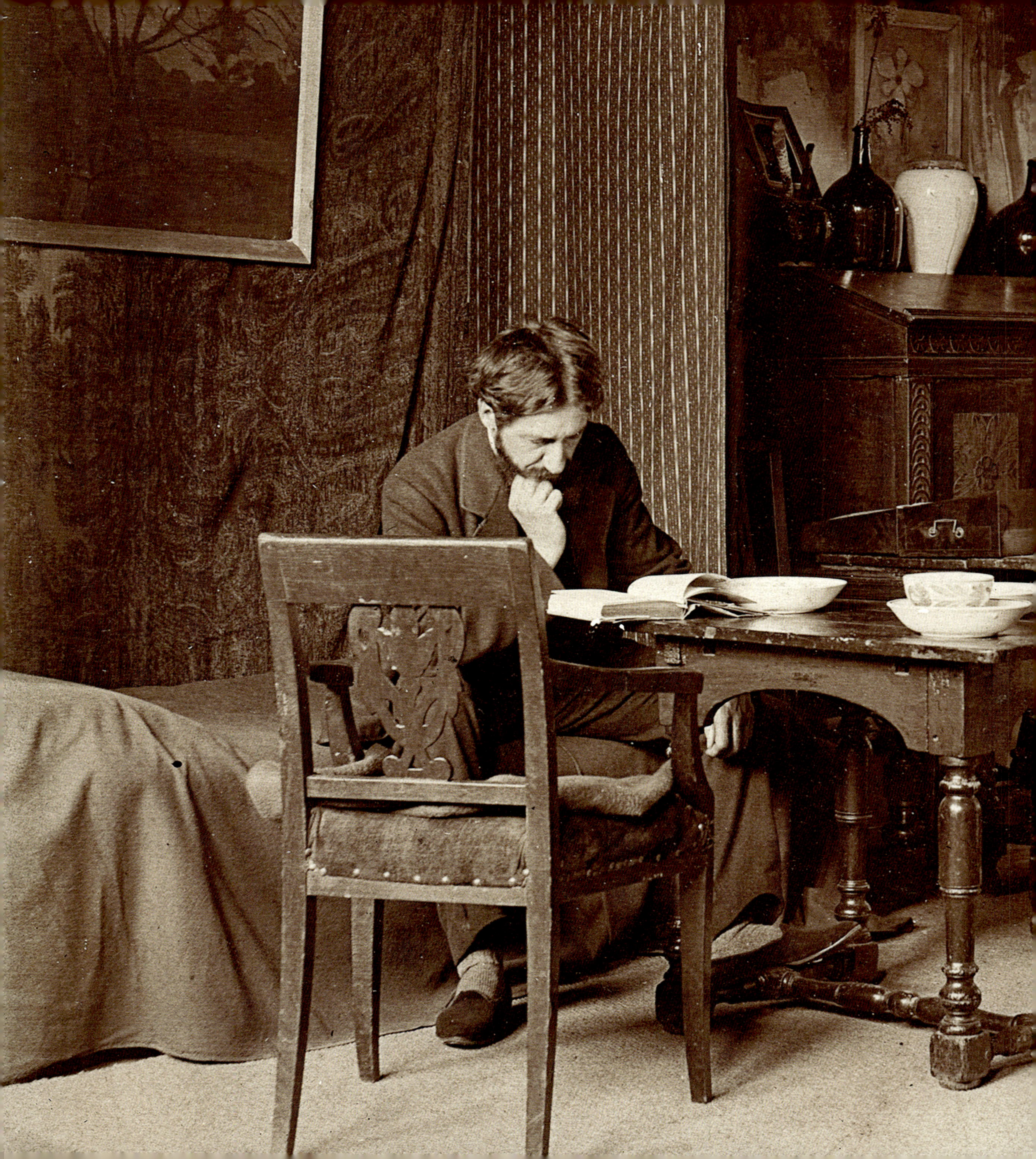

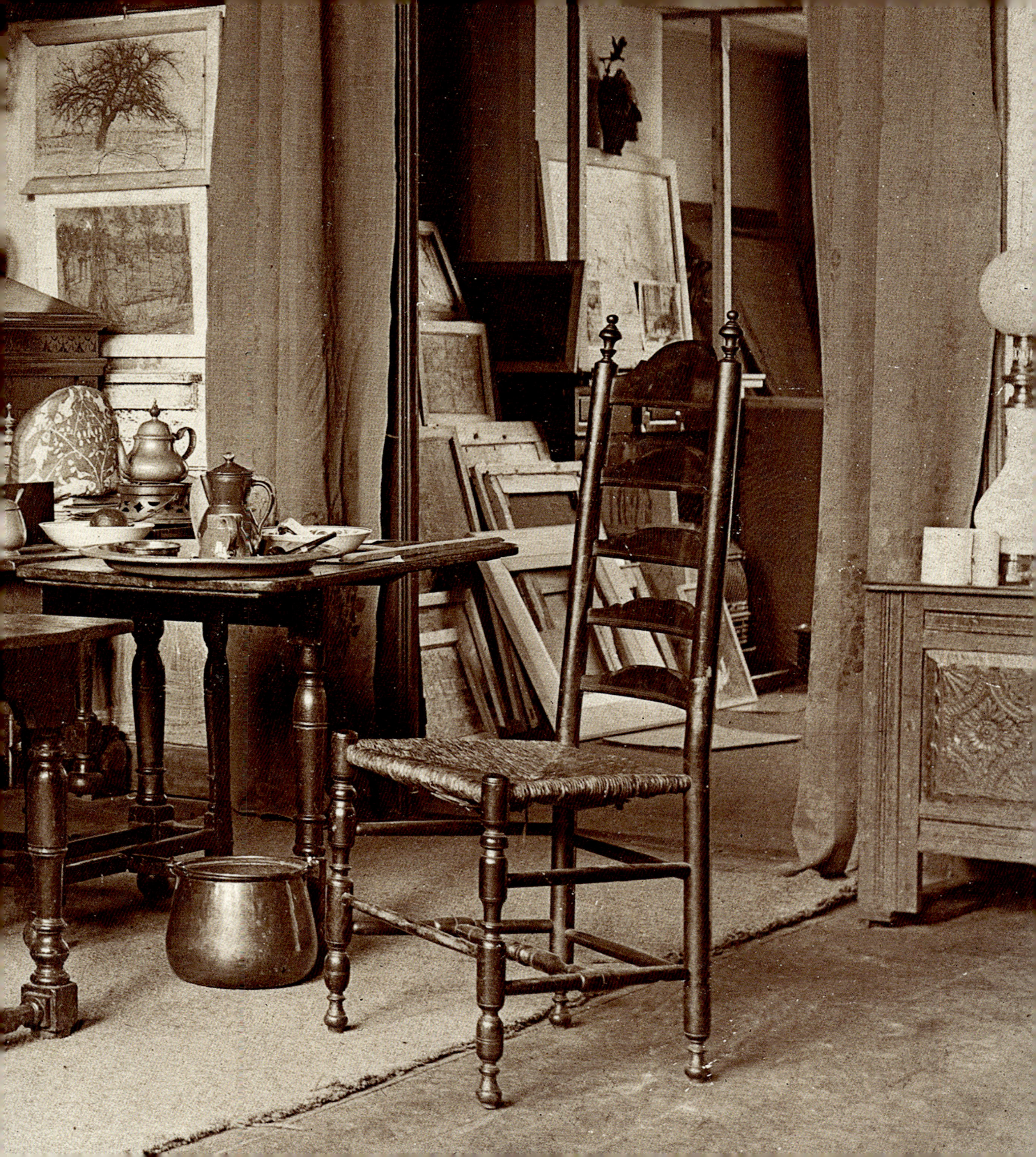

Mondrian's Paris years — 1912–14, interspersed by summers in the Netherlands, including visits to Domburg — marked a turning point in his work. By studying a restricted number of motifs (most notably trees, facades and the sea), he set out to unite cubist principles with his own vision. Motifs became less and less of a subject as such: they were reduced instead to the prompt for a painterly quest for their essence. These were Mondrian's first steps towards abstraction.

He planned his summer visit in 1914 so that he was just able to see the solo exhibition of his recent work at the Willem Walrecht art gallery in The Hague. Remarkably, he sold no fewer than six of the sixteen works, which were entirely out of the ordinary for the Netherlands. Three of them went to the collector Hendrik van Assendelft from Gouda, who would become a close friend of Mondrian.

The outbreak of the First World War in August 1914 meant that Mondrian was unable to return to his Paris studio to continue his work. After one or two detours, he found his way in the summer of 1915 to the artists' village of Laren in the Dutch countryside. The writers, poets, artists and thinkers he met there turned out — for a while at least — to be kindred spirits: the philosopher Mathieu Schoenmaekers, for instance, and the artist Bart van der Leck. He also befriended broker Sal Slijper, who would go on to buy a large number of Mondrian's works in the years that followed. Although he missed Paris, the war years spent in the Netherlands proved to be a crucial phase in the development of his work and in his thinking about the nature and function of his art.

In the autumn of 1915, Mondrian's work was spotted at an exhibition by Theo van Doesburg, an artist, critic, poet, magazine editor, agitator and networker. He devoted an article to Mondrian, bringing the two into direct contact. This marked the beginning of a ten-year friendship that would prove highly significant for both men. They were joint founders of *De Stijl* magazine — edited by Van Doesburg — and became the figureheads of modern art in the Netherlands, with a broad network in the European avant-garde. It was in a long series of articles in the early volumes of *De Stijl* (1917–18) that Mondrian first published the principles underpinning his artistic thinking and practice, which he gave the name 'nieuwe beelding' or neo-plasticism. It served as the foundation for numerous other art-theoretical articles subsequently published both there and in a whole series of international journals.

By 1917, Mondrian's art had reached the stage of full abstraction. His painterly experiments led to what he considered the essential pictorial elements of the new art of painting that would bring him international fame: the horizontal and vertical black lines, between which lie coloured rectangles in variations of primary colours and black, white and grey. Mondrian viewed these elements as the logical consequence of cubism: the spatial effect was destroyed and every reference to visible reality abandoned. What's more, colour had been reduced in his eyes to its purest manifestation.

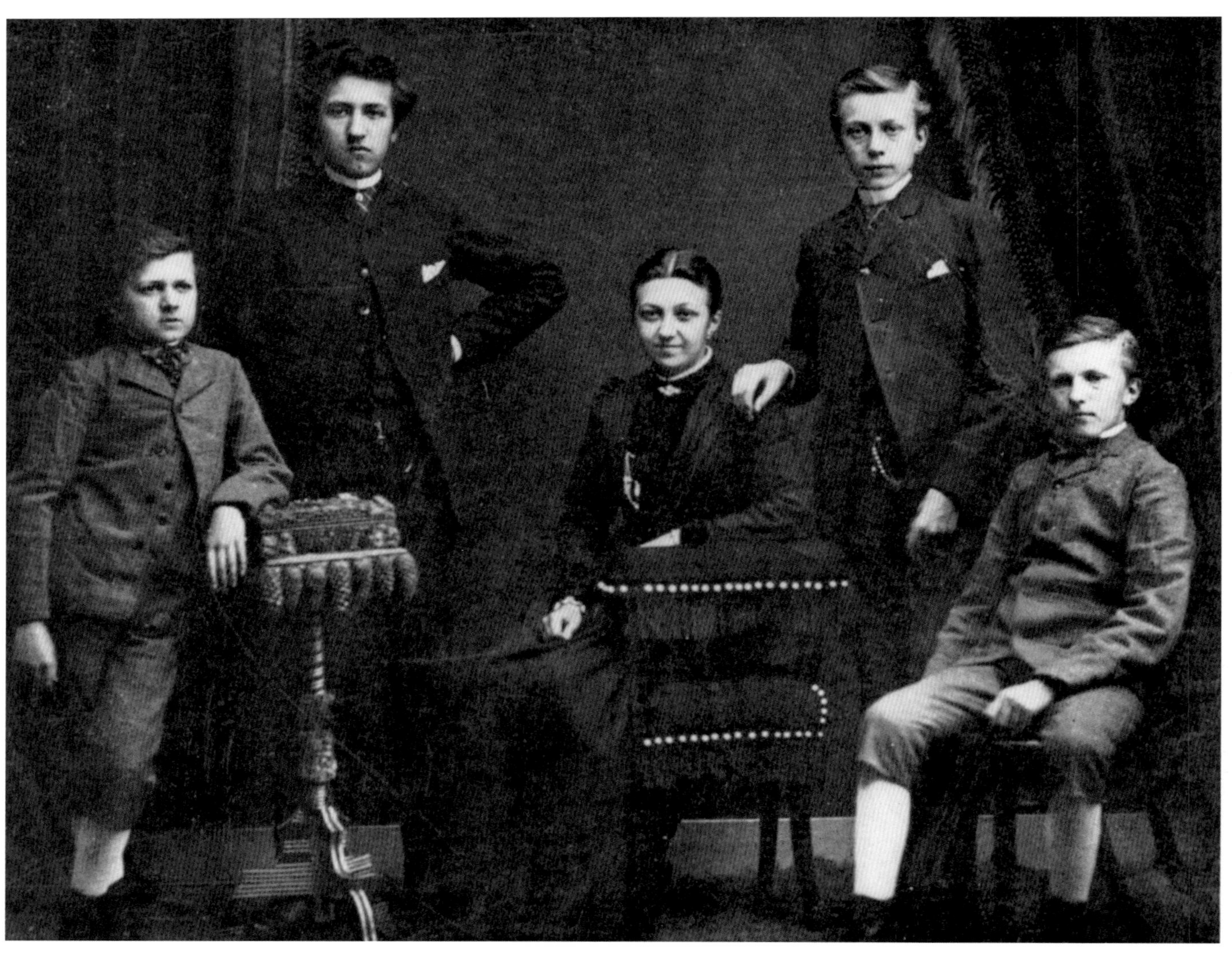

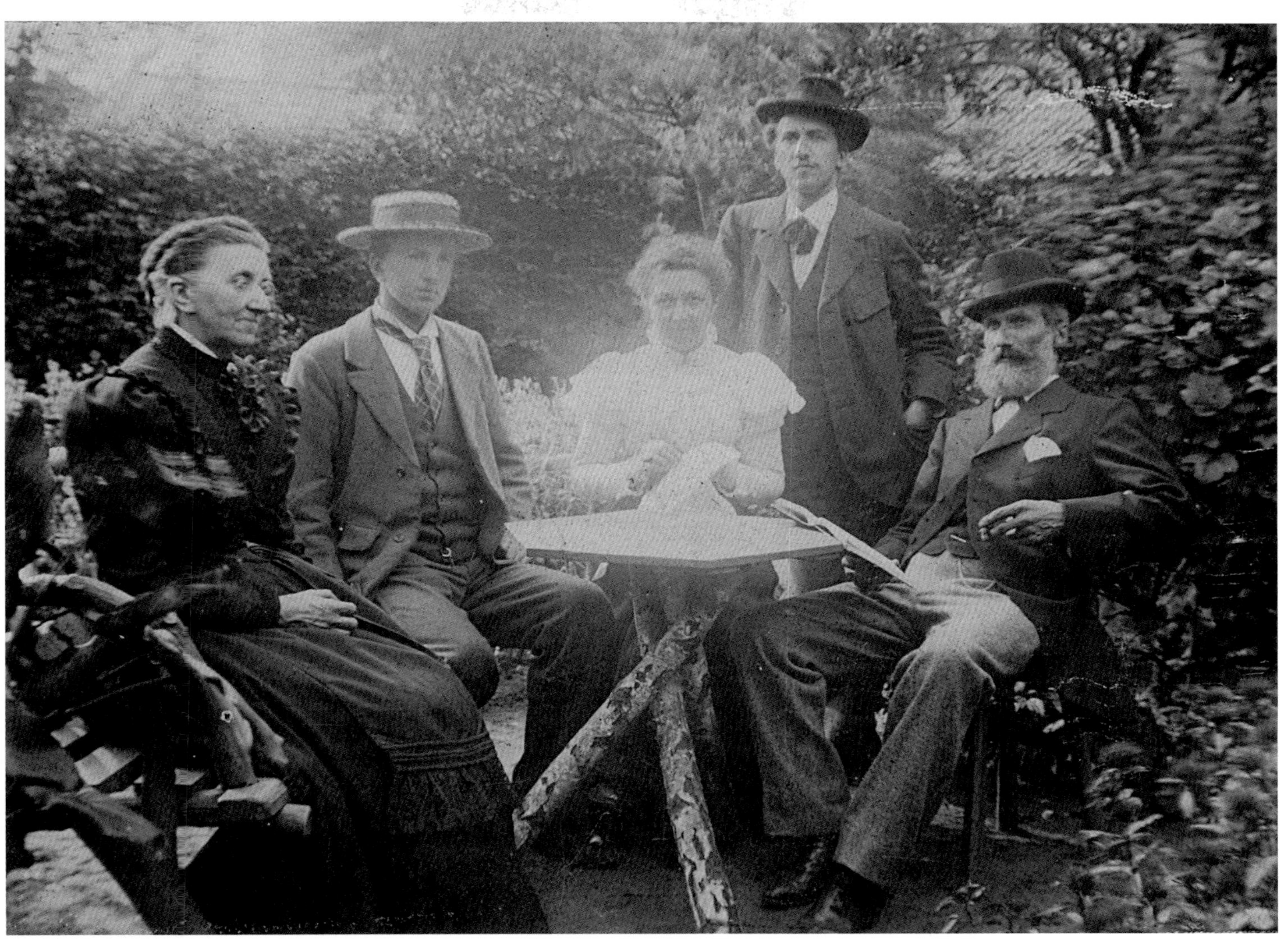

CAT. 1 **Unidentified photographer**
The Mondriaan children, spring 1889 (?)
Left to right: Carel, Piet, Christien, Willem, Louis. Assuming that Piet Mondriaan/-ian is between fifteen and twenty years old, the photograph might have been a gift to mark their parents' twentieth wedding anniversary on 12 May 1889.

CAT. 2 **Louis Mondriaan (?)**
Members of the Mondriaan family, c. 1894
Left to right: Johanna Mondriaan-de Kok, Carel, Christien, Piet, Pieter Mondriaan Sr. Two of the sons are absent: Louis, who probably took the picture, and Willem Frederik, who was in Suriname in 1894 as personal secretary to the aristocrat *Jonkheer* Van Asch van Wijk.

CAT. 3 See catalogue

In Simon Maris's Studio

CATS 4—5, 8—14

Simon Maris (1873—1935) was the son of the celebrated Hague School painter Willem Maris, whose brothers Jacob and Matthijs were artists too, and so Simon was brought up on art from the earliest age. He trained at the academies in The Hague and Antwerp, before setting up in 1900 in a former photographer's studio in the centre of Amsterdam, which is where he met Piet Mondrian.[1] Both men belonged to the Sint Lucas artists' association and had lots of friends and acquaintances in the city's artistic circles. Maris was active in several genres, but he became best known for his portrait paintings, while also trading in art and antiques. It was in this latter capacity that he made several efforts to sell Mondrian's work. They remained friends until Maris's death.

Thanks to his father's success, Maris was relatively well off for an artist at the beginning of his career. In the studio where the following photographs were taken between 1900 and 1902, he held what he called *jours*, for which a circle of friends consisting of artists, writers and critics of both sexes were invited to socialize, discuss, eat and drink. The painter Lizzy Ansingh recalled the events some thirty years later, praising Maris's hospitality and courtesy: 'Saturday afternoons at your studio, that long narrow room on the Spui, so high up! [...] where the women painters served tea and a softly mumbling Piet Mondrian tried to explain his ideals.'[2]

The group photographs in Maris's studio show almost all of them several times, suggesting that this was a close-knit group of friends. They also confirm Mondrian's need for social contact with like-minded people. Although the friends practised different disciplines and art forms, they belonged to the same artistic generation and conformed to the tone set by their predecessors in the late 19th century. In the case of the painters, this meant the Hague School in terms of landscape and rural life, and Amsterdam impressionism, which focused on more modern, urban motifs. Mondrian was the only one to break free over the next few years and he would ultimately make a name for himself — more so than any other member of the group. Ansingh's take on this was that 'He has been Mondrian [that is, with a single 'a'] for years now, he mumbles in French and it is all check shapes that he does down there in Paris [...] but he has remained an idealist and has grown famous.'[3]

The setting for the photos is a traditional 19th-century studio, with drapes and carpets, sketches and studies on the floor and on the wall, and props for still lifes on the mantelpiece. There is no sign of painting materials, though, aside from a few glimpses of a large, hard-to-conceal easel, used as a coat rack (cats 4—5). We do not know what type of camera was used, but the varying feel of the pictures suggests that different photographers took them. The people being photographed were aware of the camera in each case. In some cases the poses are a little more casual and the subjects are looking in different directions, while in others they are clearly holding still, ready for the picture to be taken. In other words, while the photos do capture a real moment in time, they are not entirely natural or unposed. They were mostly taken as mementos.

1 Welsh/Joosten 1998-I, p. 121. P. Gorter has suggested that they could have met as early as 1888 through Mondrian's uncle Frits, who took painting lessons from Simon's father in The Hague (Gorter 2020, p. 1). This is only speculation, however.

2 'de middagen, des Zaterdags, in uw atelier, die lange pijpela op het Spui, heel hoog! [...] waar de schilderessen thee schonken en Piet Mondriaan zachtjes mompelend zijn idealen poogde duidelijk te maken.' Anonymous 1933.

3 'Hij heet sedert jaren Mondrian, mompelt in het Fransch en het is ál geblok, wat hij maakt, daar in Parijs [...] maar een idealist is hij gebleven en beroemd is hij geworden.' Ibid.

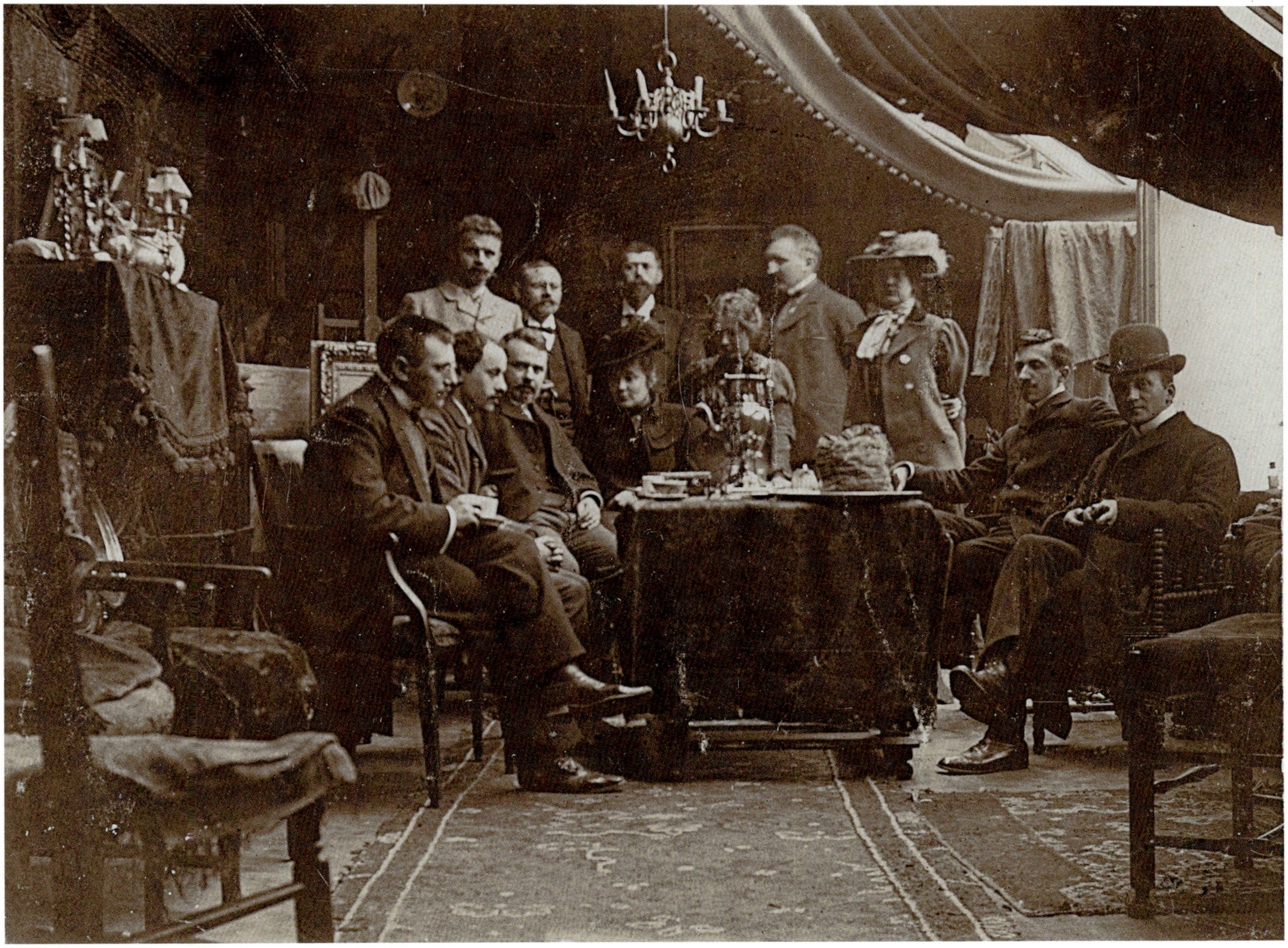

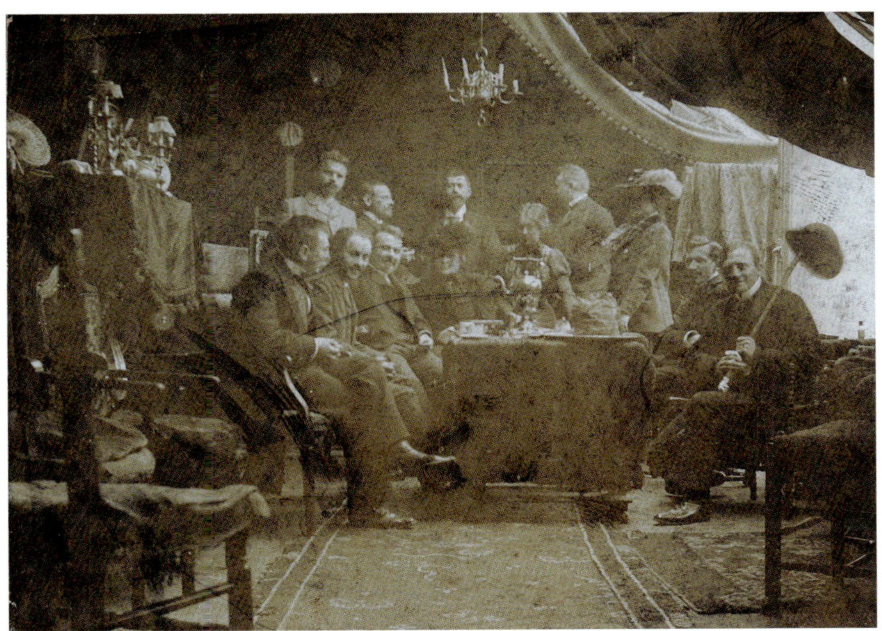

CATS 4–5 **Unidentified photographer**

Group photo in Simon Maris's studio, 1900

Left to right, standing: Arnold Gorter, unidentified man, Jan Hanau, Lizzy Ansingh, Simon Maris, Thérèse Ansingh; sitting: Frans Deutmann (?), Marinus van Raalte, Hendrik Kroon, Nelly Bodenheim, Piet Mondrian and Jan Kleintjes (?).

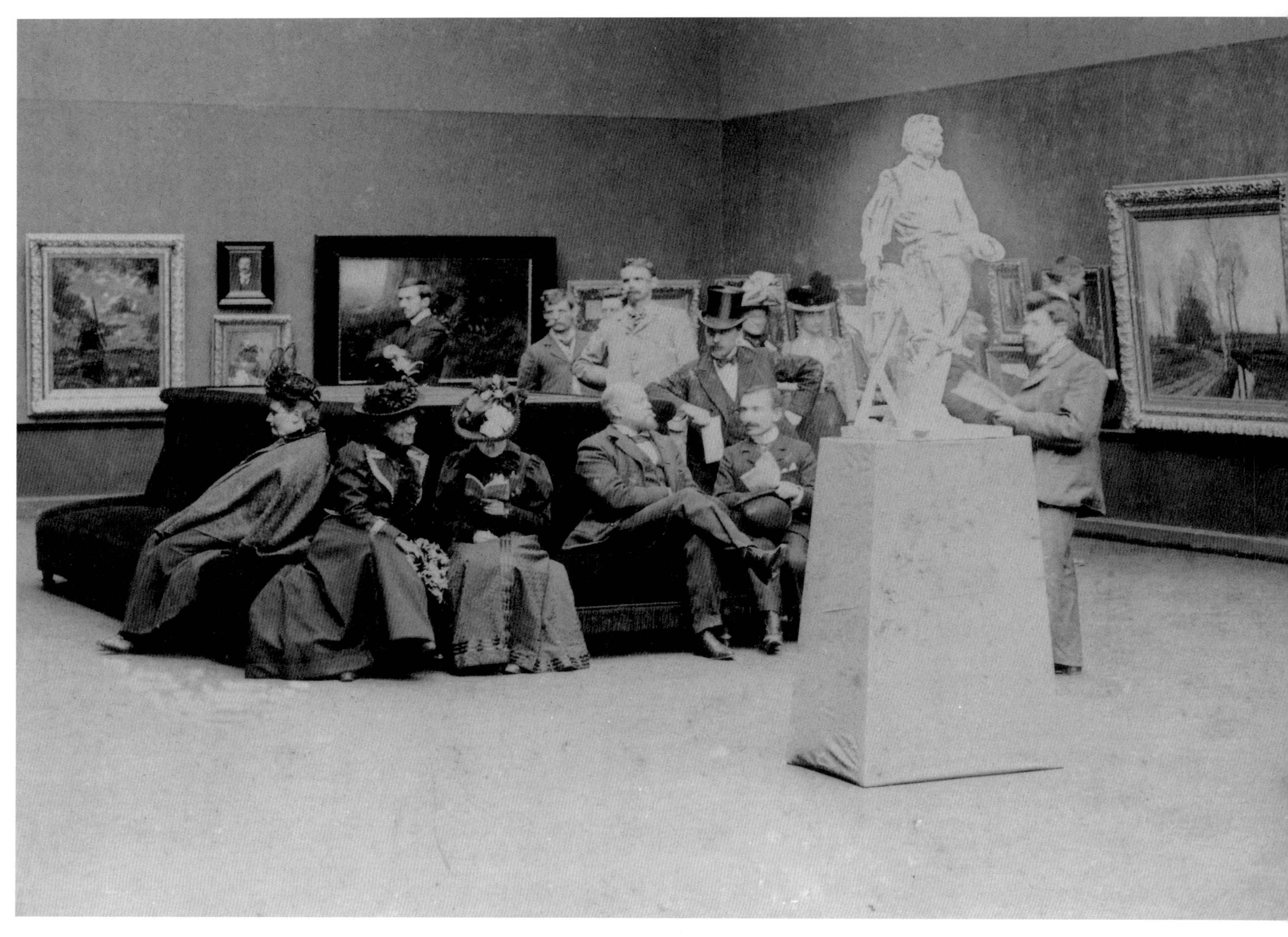

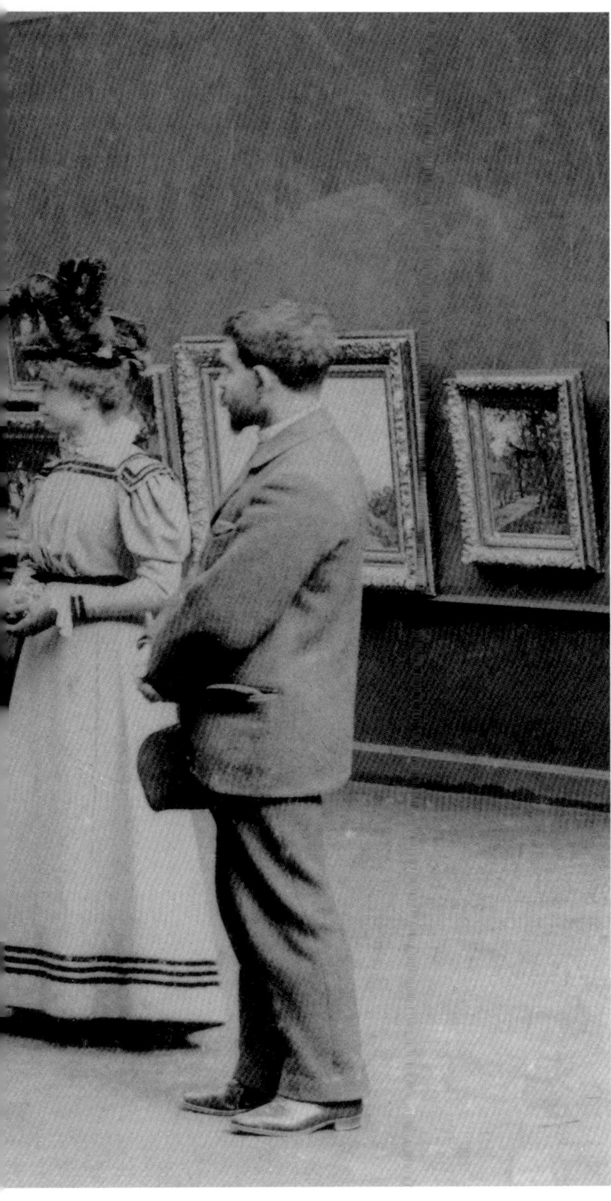

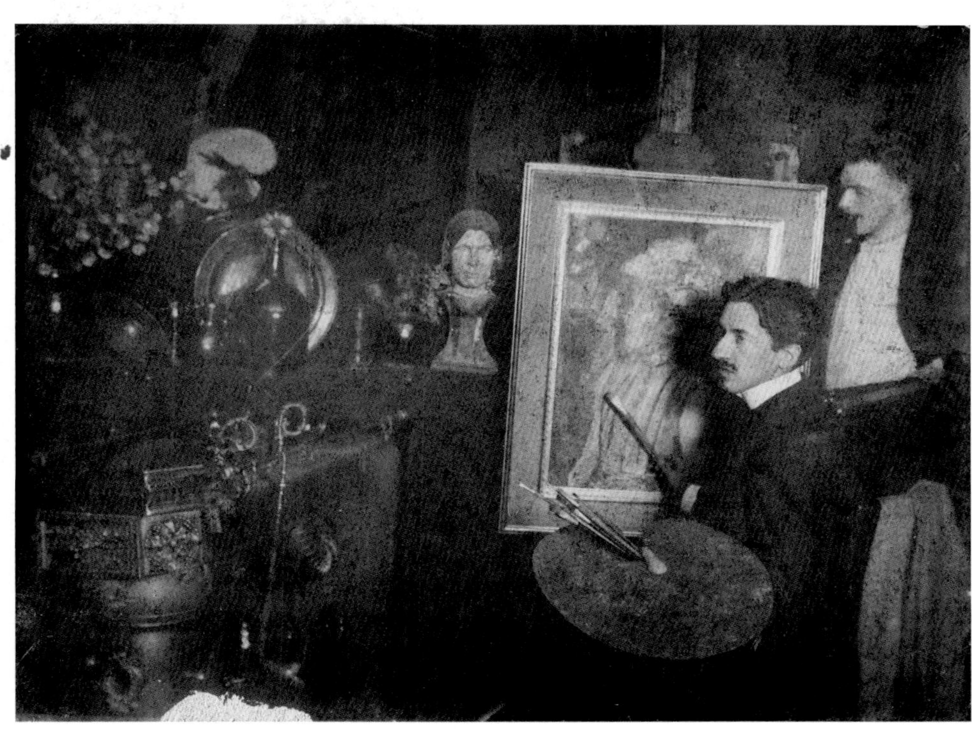

CAT. 6 **Unidentified photographer**
Preview of the Sint Lucas association's spring exhibition at the Stedelijk Museum, Amsterdam, 18 or 19 May 1900
Piet Mondrian stands at the back to the left with his arms folded.

CAT. 7 **Unidentified photographer**
Piet Mondrian and Cees Bergman (?) in Mondrian's studio, c. 1901
The man on the right behind Mondrian could be the commissioner of the painting, the coffee merchant Cees Bergman. He married Elisabeth Cavalini, the woman in the portrait, a short time later. Several of the props seen on the left feature in Mondrian still lifes from this period.

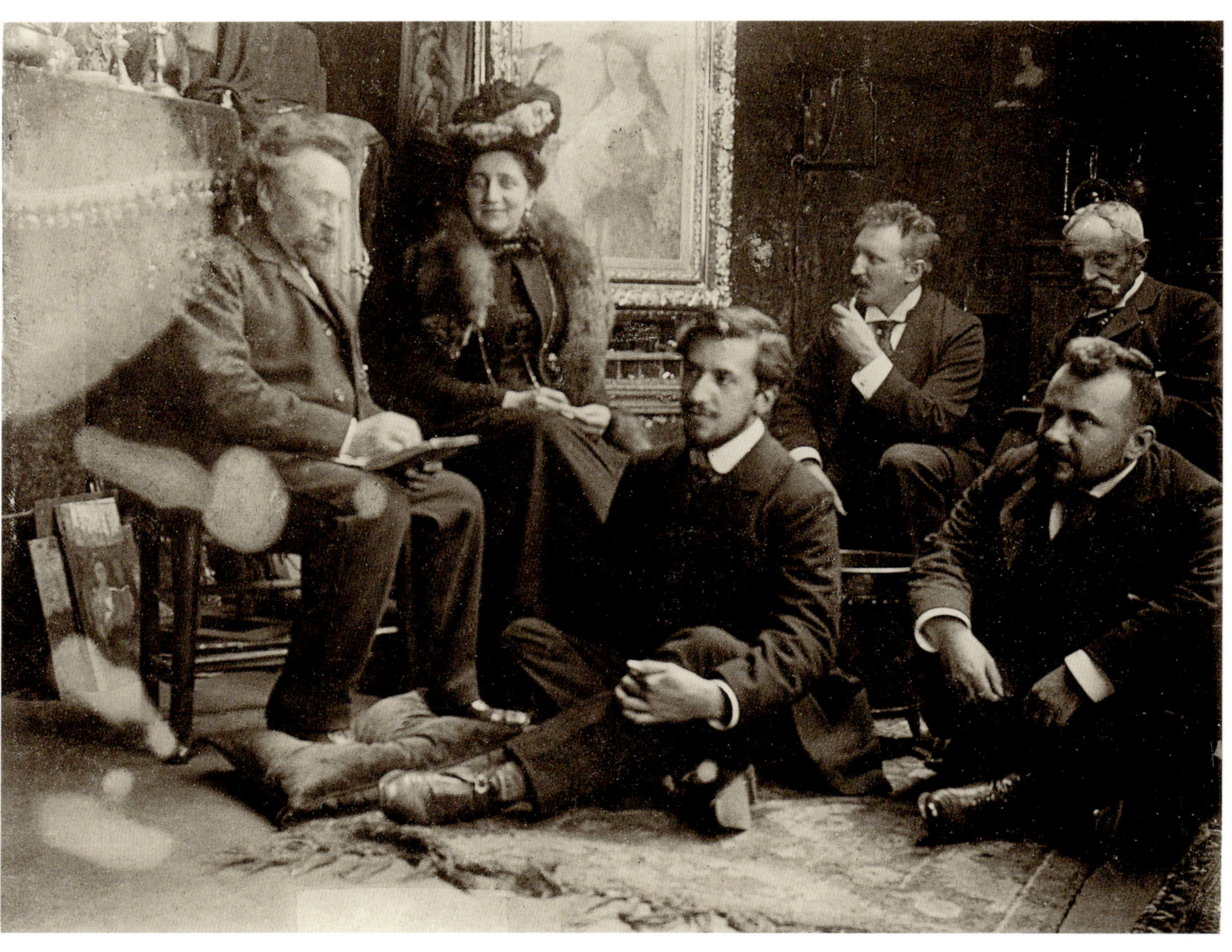

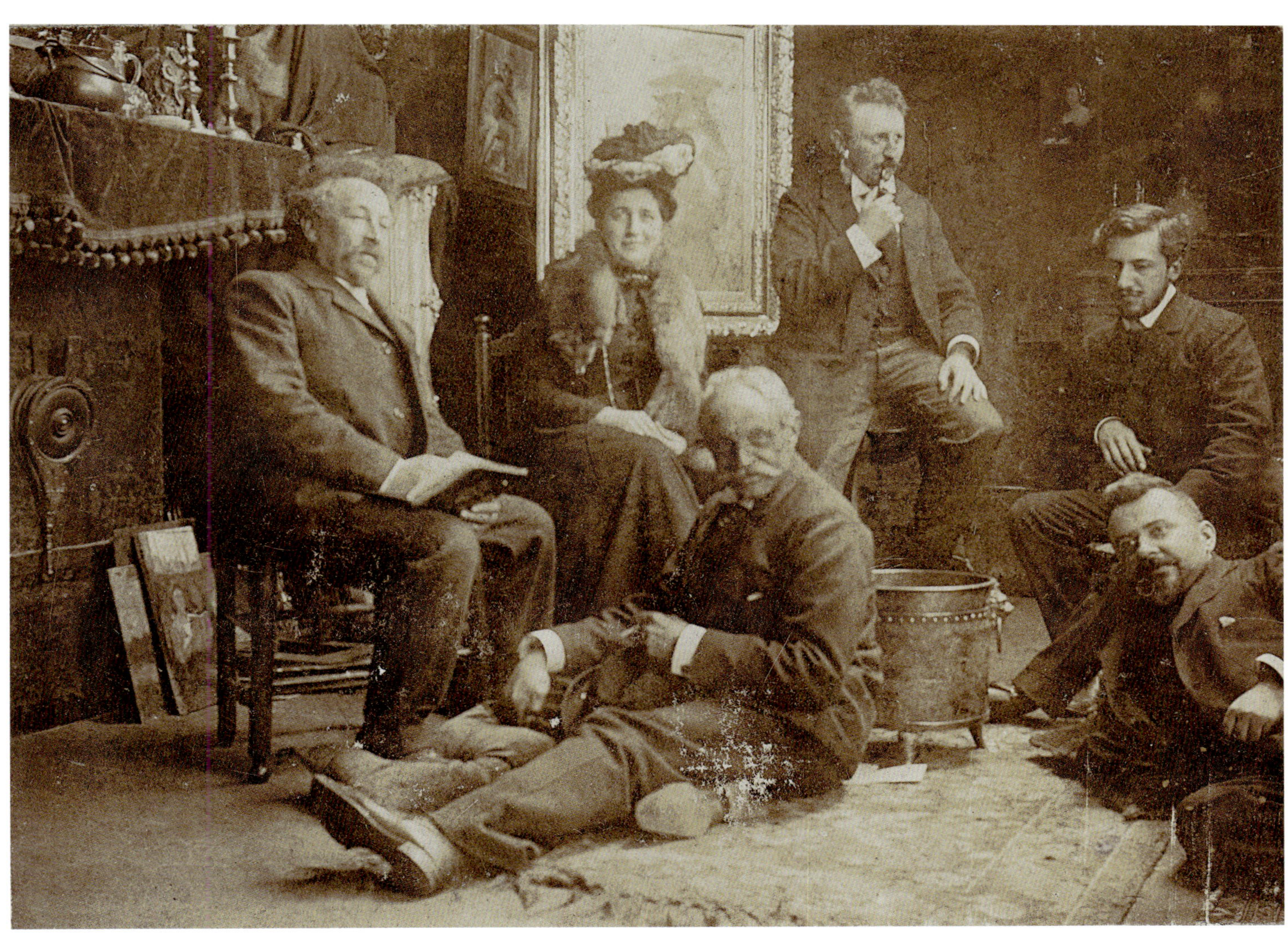

CAT. 8 **Unidentified photographer**
Group photo in Simon Maris's studio, c. 1901
Left to right, back row: Willem Maris, Johanna van Bijlevelt, Simon Maris and Marinus van der Maarel; front row: Piet Mondrian and Hendrik Kroon.

CAT. 9 **Unidentified photographer**
Group photo in Simon Maris's studio, c. 1901
Left to right, back row: Willem Maris, Johanna van Bijlevelt, Simon Maris, Piet Mondrian; front row: Marinus van der Maarel and Hendrik Kroon.

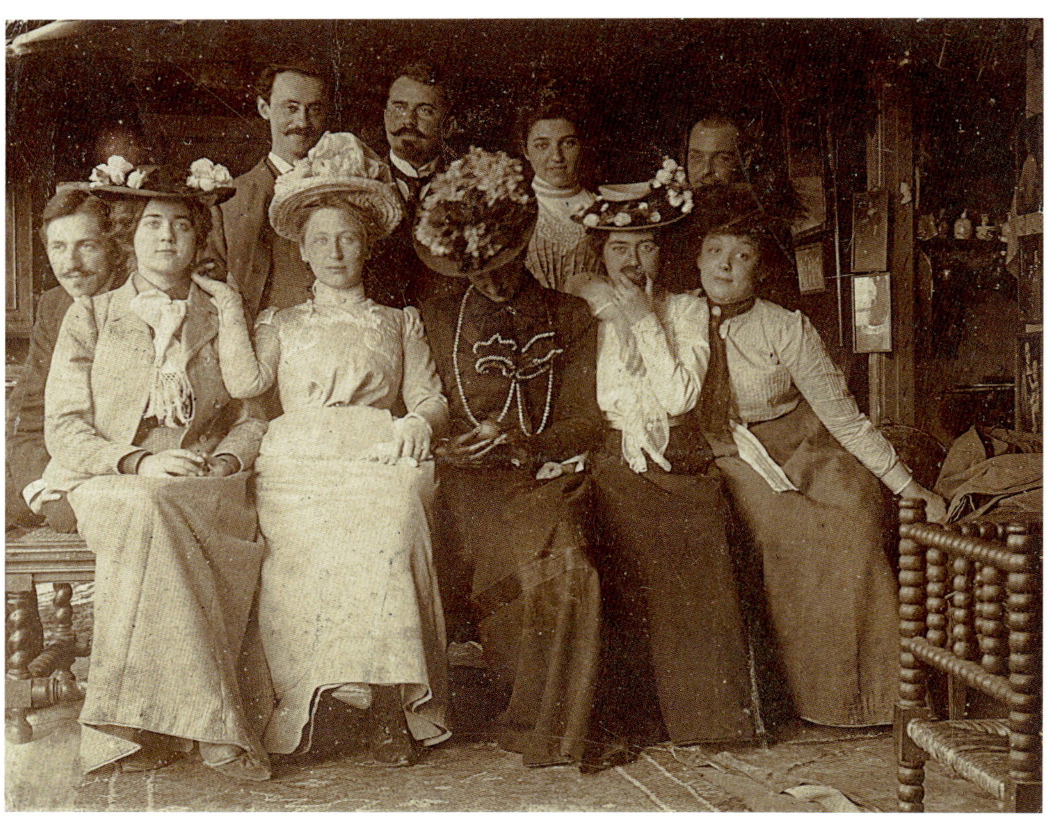

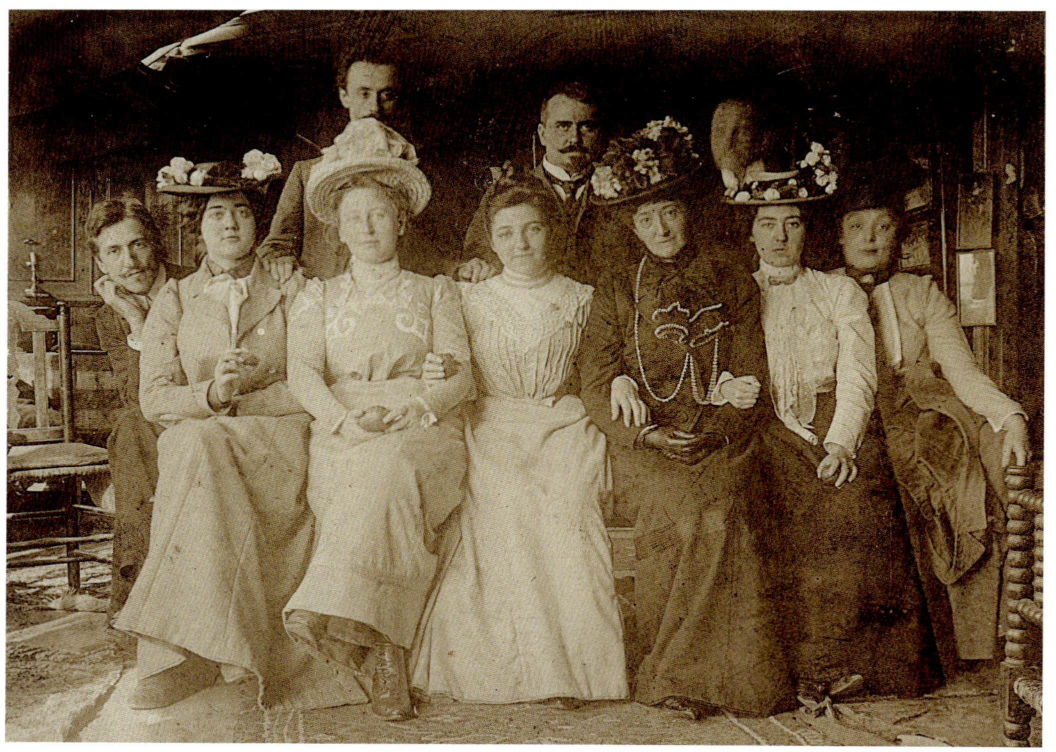

CAT. 10 **Unidentified photographer**

Group portrait in Simon Maris's studio following the opening of the exhibition at Sint Lucas, 8 June 1901

Left to right, standing: Marinus van Raalte, Hendrik Kroon, Jet Hendrix, Chris Huidekoper; sitting: Piet Mondrian, Thérèse Ansingh, Jo Stumpff (?), Georgine Schwartze, Lizzy Ansingh, Nelly Bodenheim.

CAT. 11 **Unidentified photographer**

Group portrait in Simon Maris's studio following the opening of the exhibition at Sint Lucas, 8 June 1901

Left to right, standing: Marinus van Raalte, Hendrik Kroon, Chris Huidekoper; sitting: Piet Mondrian, Thérèse Ansingh, Jo Stumpff (?), Jet Hendrix, Georgine Schwartze, Lizzy Ansingh, Nelly Bodenheim.

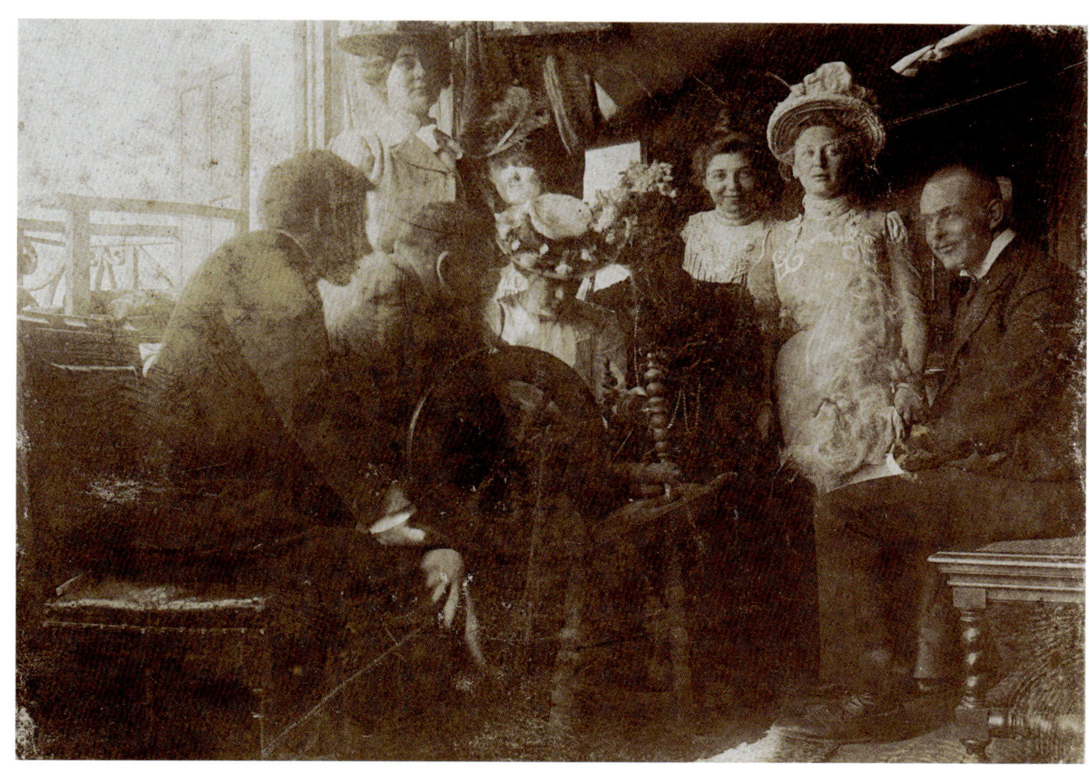

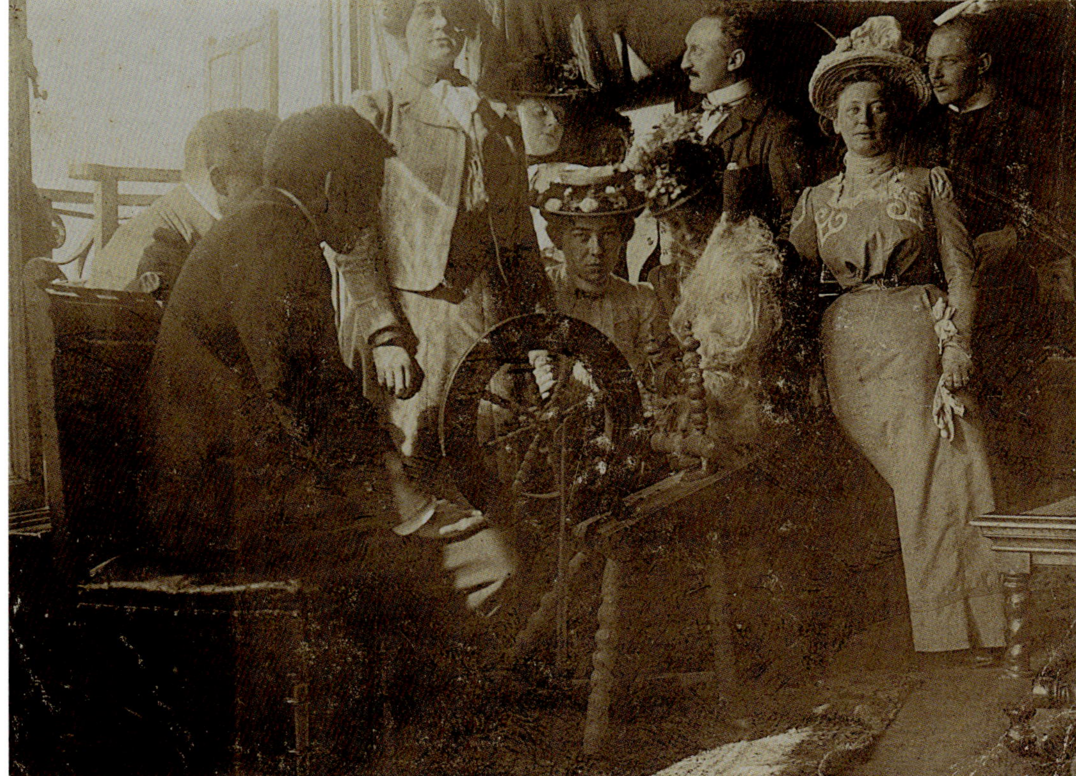

CAT. 12 **Unidentified photographer**
Group portrait in Simon Maris's studio following the opening of the exhibition at Sint Lucas, 8 June 1901
Left to right, standing: Thérèse Ansingh, Nelly Bodenheim, Jet Hendrix, Jo Stumpff (?); sitting: Piet Mondrian, Hendrik Kroon, Lizzy Ansingh, Georgine Schwartze, Chris Huidekoper.

CAT. 13 **Unidentified photographer**
Group portrait in Simon Maris's studio following the opening of the exhibition at Sint Lucas, 8 June 1901
Left to right, standing: Thérèse Ansingh, Nelly Bodenheim, Simon Maris, Jo Stumpff (?), Chris Huidekoper; sitting: Hendrik Kroon, Piet Mondrian, Lizzy Ansingh, Georgine Schwartze.

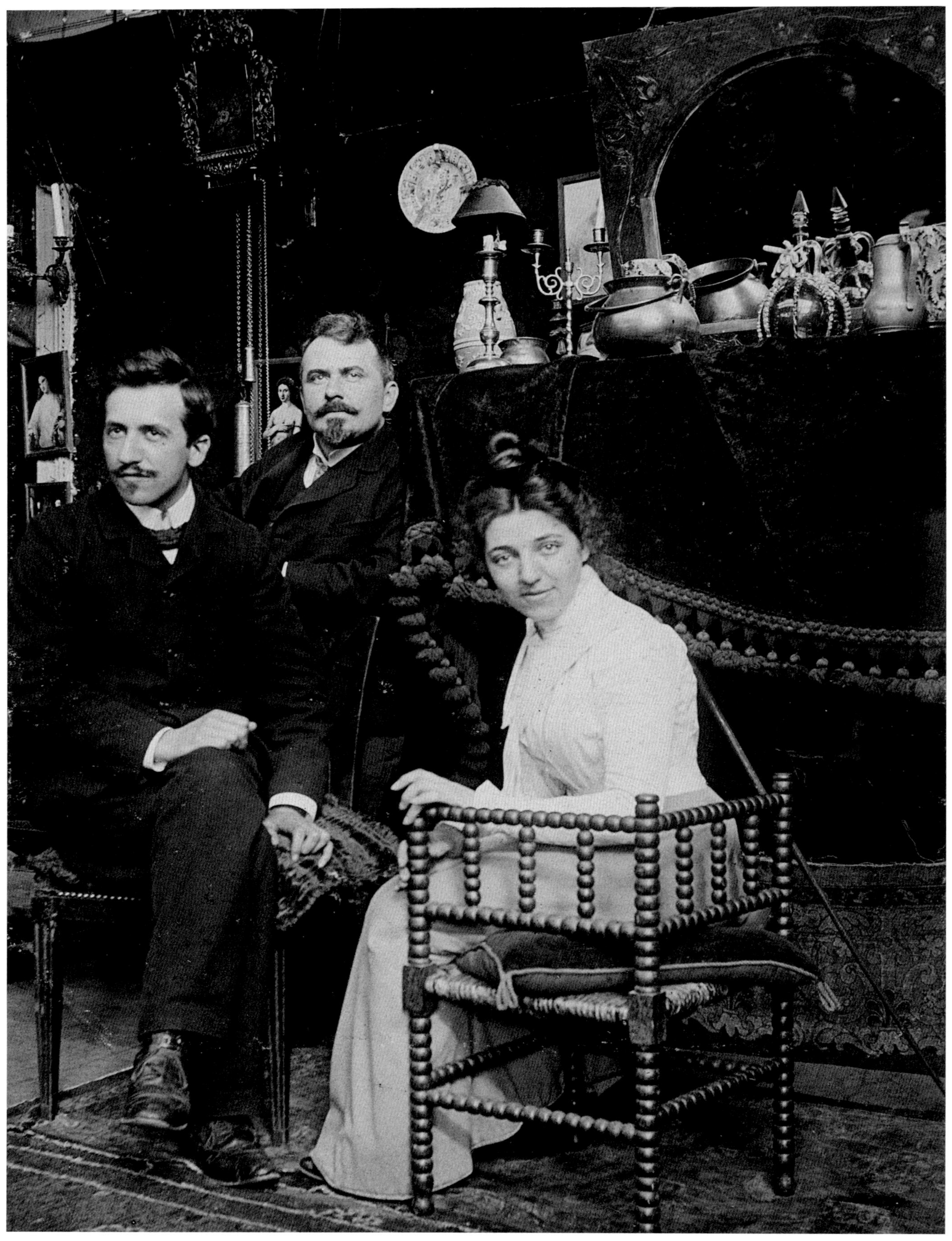

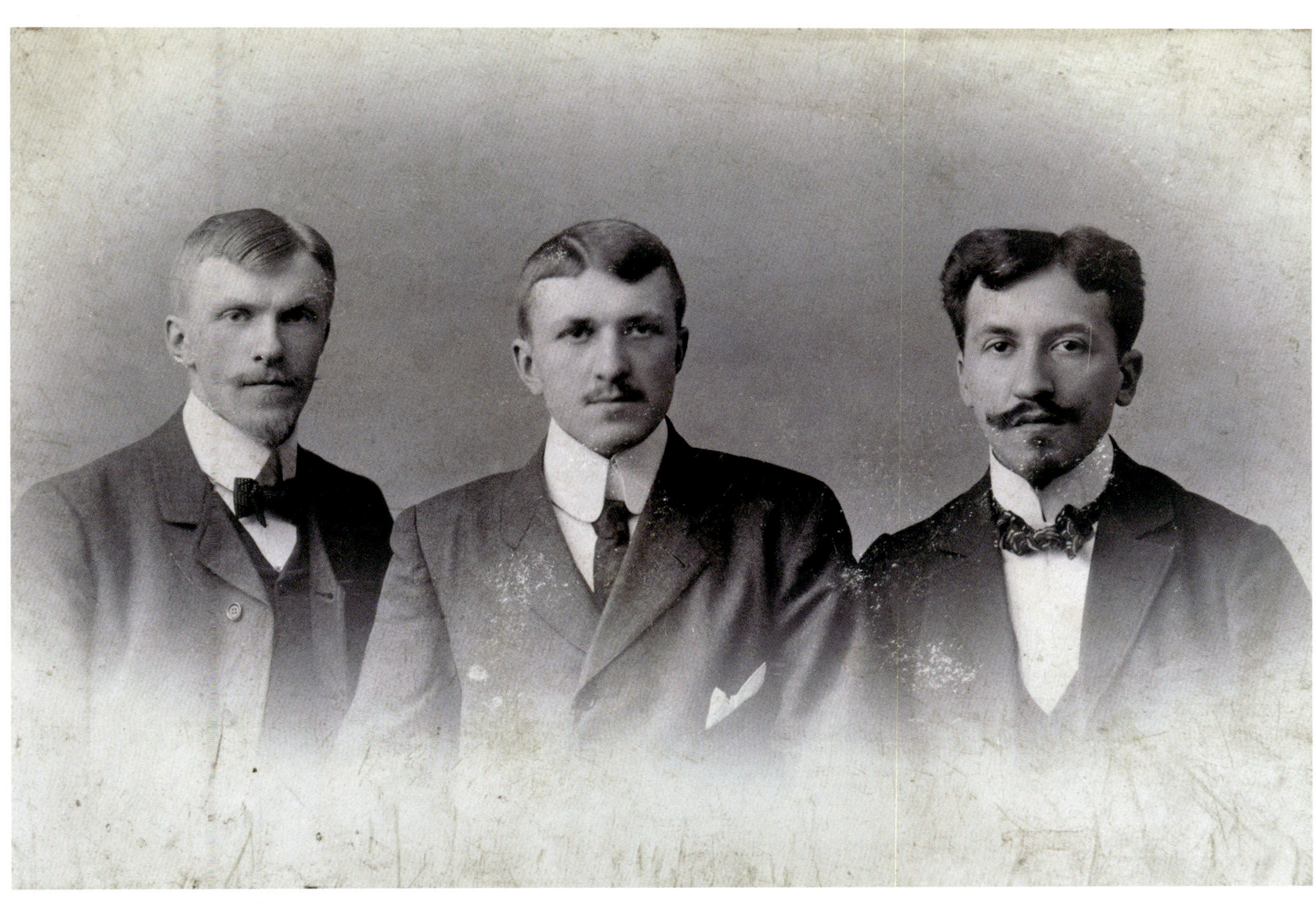

CAT. 14 **Unidentified photographer**
Piet Mondrian, Hendrik Kroon and Jet Hendrix in Simon Maris's studio, second half 1901

CAT. 15 **Unidentified photographer**
Louis, Carel and Piet Mondrian, c. 1902

>> CAT. 16 **Paul Götte**
Group photo of guests at an Oriental-themed party at the Sint Lucas artists' association, 21 February 1903
Front row, left of centre, Piet Mondrian. The annual fancy-dress parties at Sint Lucas were renowned. The highlight of the 1903 event was a performance of the play *The Judgment of Solomon*, written specially for the occasion by Hendrik Kroon.

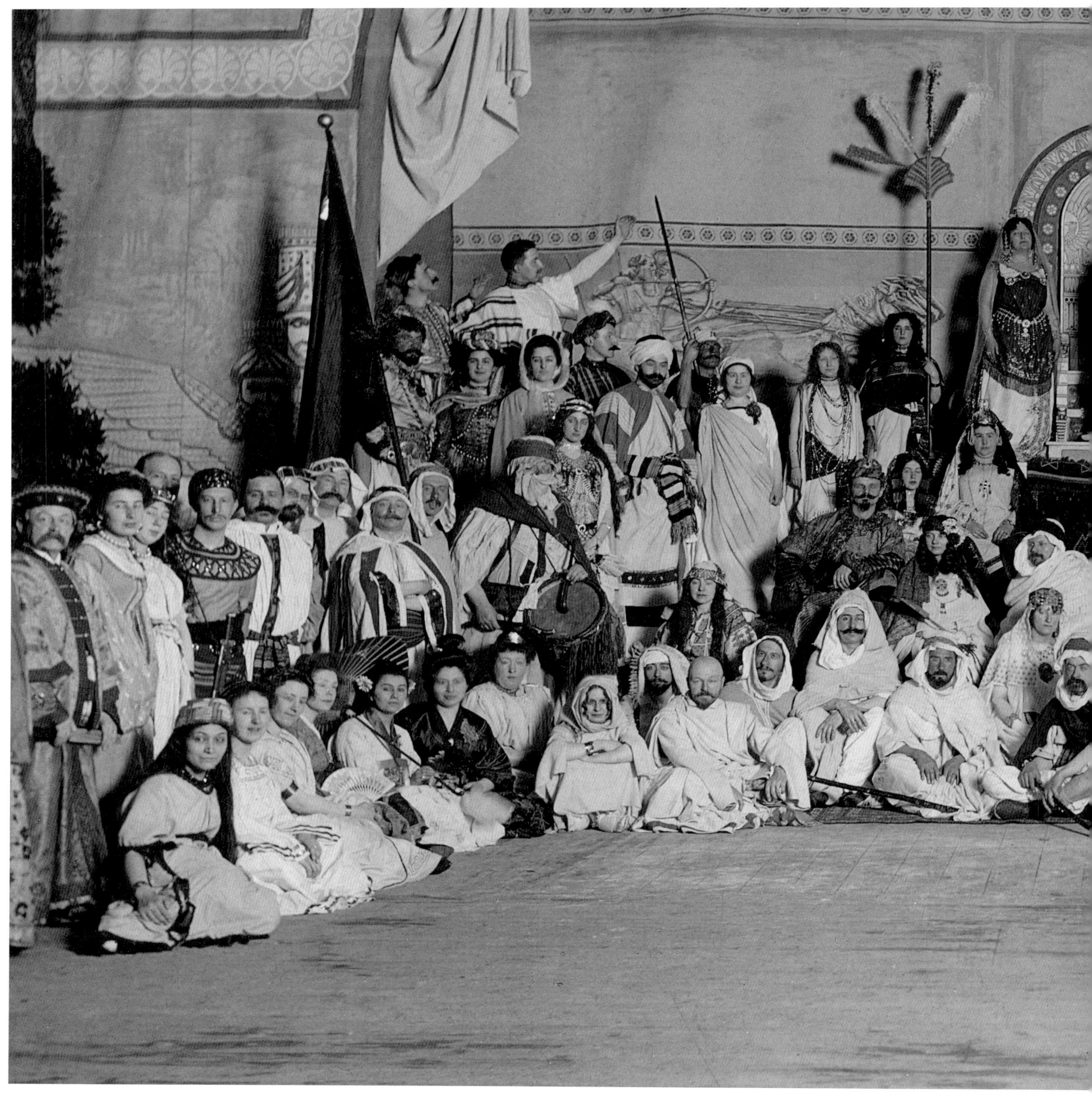

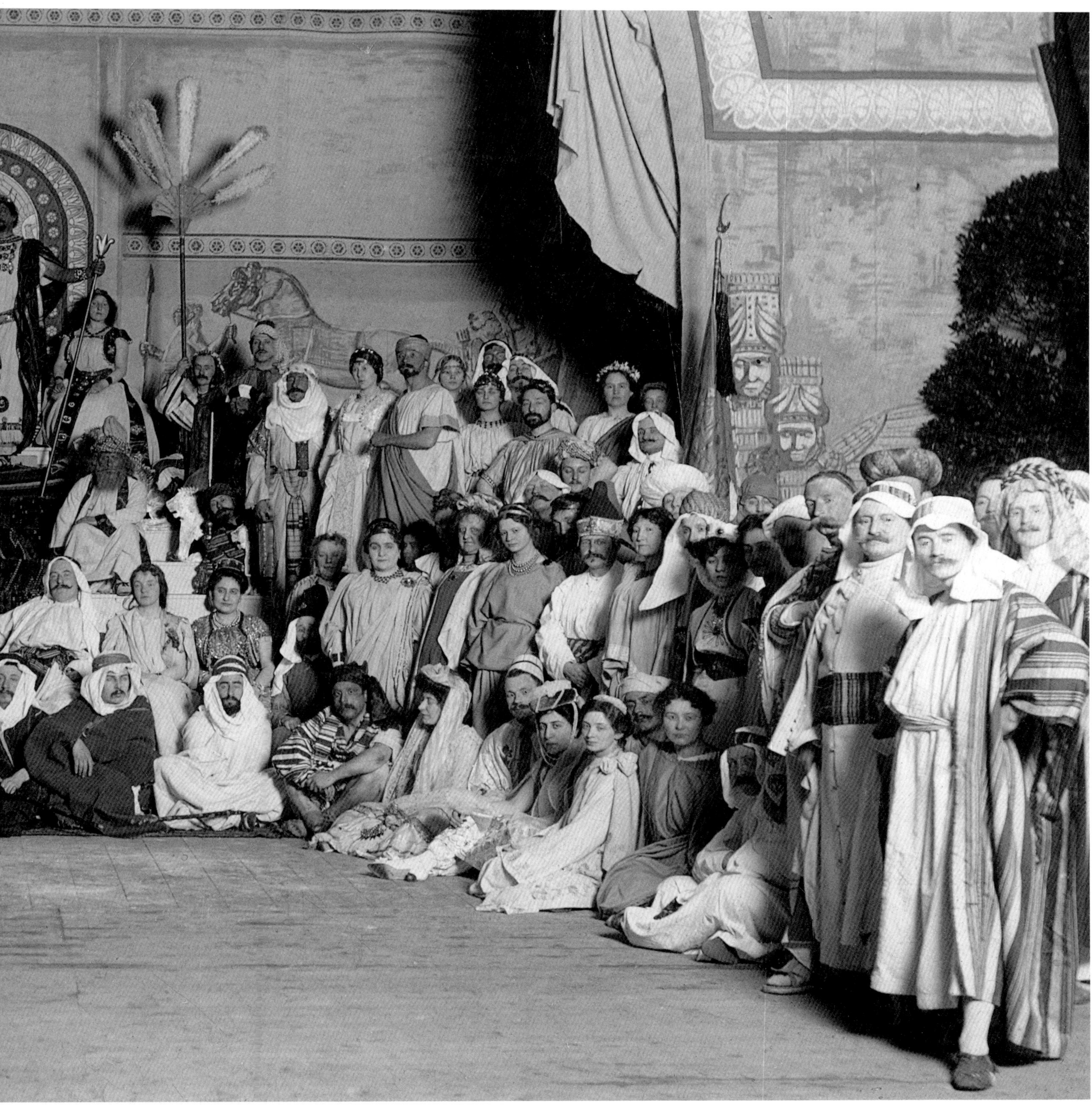

Trip to Spain in 1903

CATS 17—28

Mondrian was not a big traveller. We know of only three trips that he made abroad before he was forty: Cornwall in 1900, Bilbao in 1903 and Paris in 1911. Of these, the visit to Spain is the best documented, as several photographs have survived. His precise reason for going there is not known, but the adventure of the journey might have been a goal in itself. At any rate, no sketches or paintings by Mondrian have been preserved that can be linked to his stay in Spain or southwest France. The journey began on 28 August 1903, when Mondrian boarded the coaster SS *Orion* in IJmuiden accompanied by Simon Maris and Frits Bodenheim. Before embarking, the intrepid trio posed full of bravado on the quayside before their ladies escorted them onto the ship. Several photos were also and his friends enjoying a meal at a pavement café and toasting their safe arrival (figs 23–4). The most dynamic (and least posed) photo of the trip was likewise shot in Bordeaux by Mondrian himself — one of only two photographs he is known to have taken (see fig. 6 on p. 16). In it, we see Maris and Bodenheim walking across Place Gambetta — an action photo of which there are very few from the trip. Mondrian's picture recalls the street photographs that the Amsterdam painter and photographer George Breitner took ten to fifteen years earlier, albeit with less radical cropping.

After Bordeaux, the group continued their journey to Bayonne and nearby Biarritz. The *Orion* was already on its way back to Amsterdam, having picked up a load of wine, cognac attributed to him with any certainty (see fig. 7 on p. 16). On the nearby beach of La Arena, he photographed Maris and Bodenheim in the company of a young girl. The picture was taken from a low angle, giving it a strikingly high horizon. The imposing mountains that surround La Arena are not included.

Fourteen days after setting foot in Bordeaux, they re-embarked on the *Orion*, which had docked once more from Amsterdam, to make the five-day return voyage to the Netherlands. They arrived back in IJmuiden on 23 September, just under a month after they first departed. The series of pictures clearly shows that photography was already a widespread phenomenon by the early years of the 20th century. Cameras had become so con-

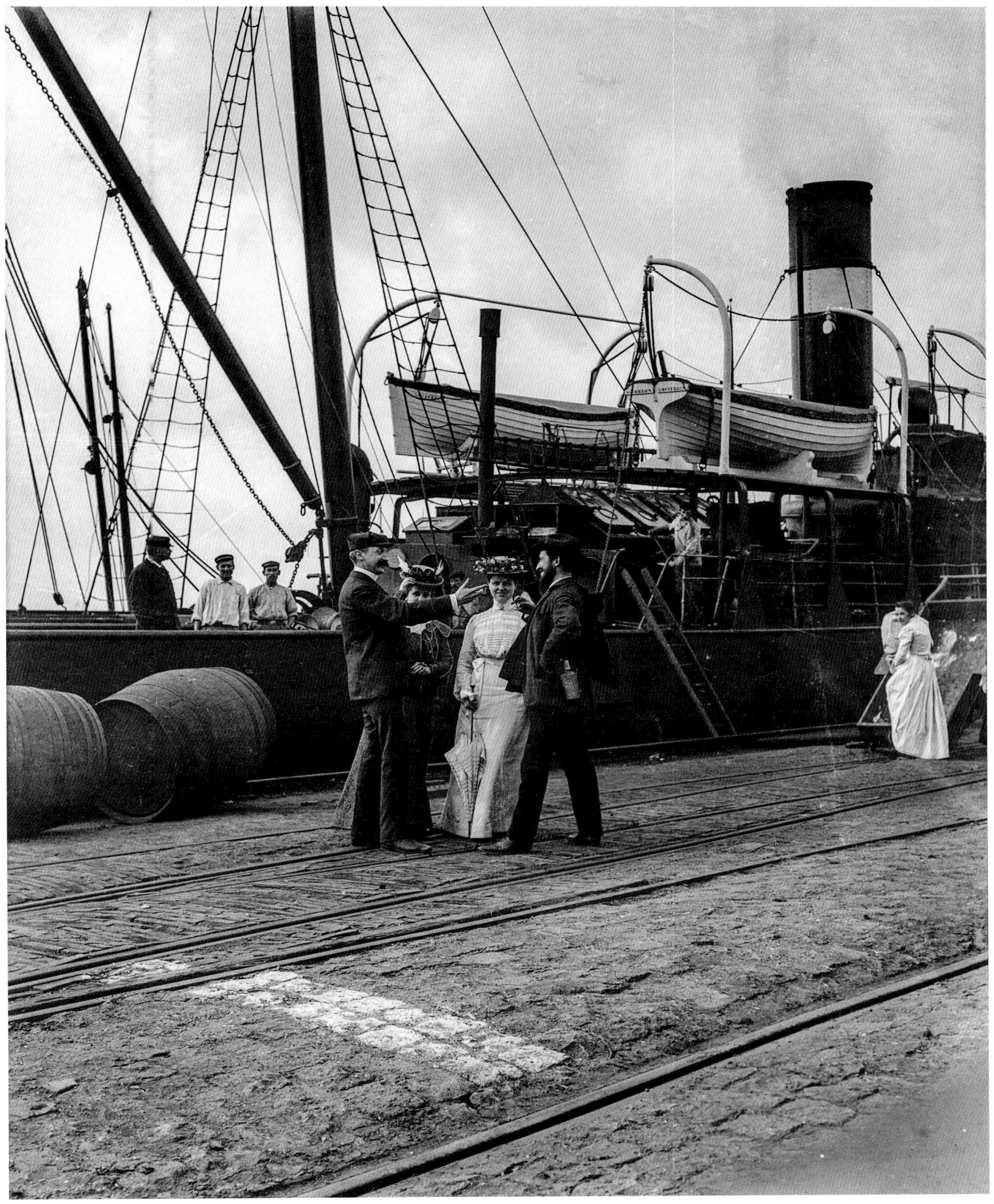

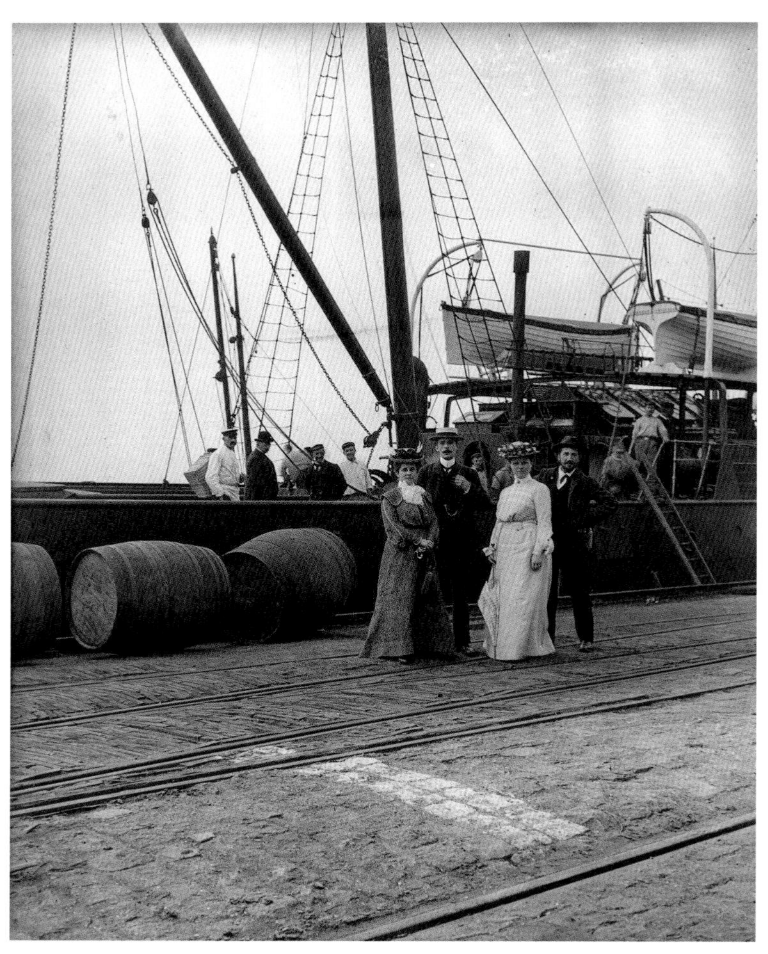

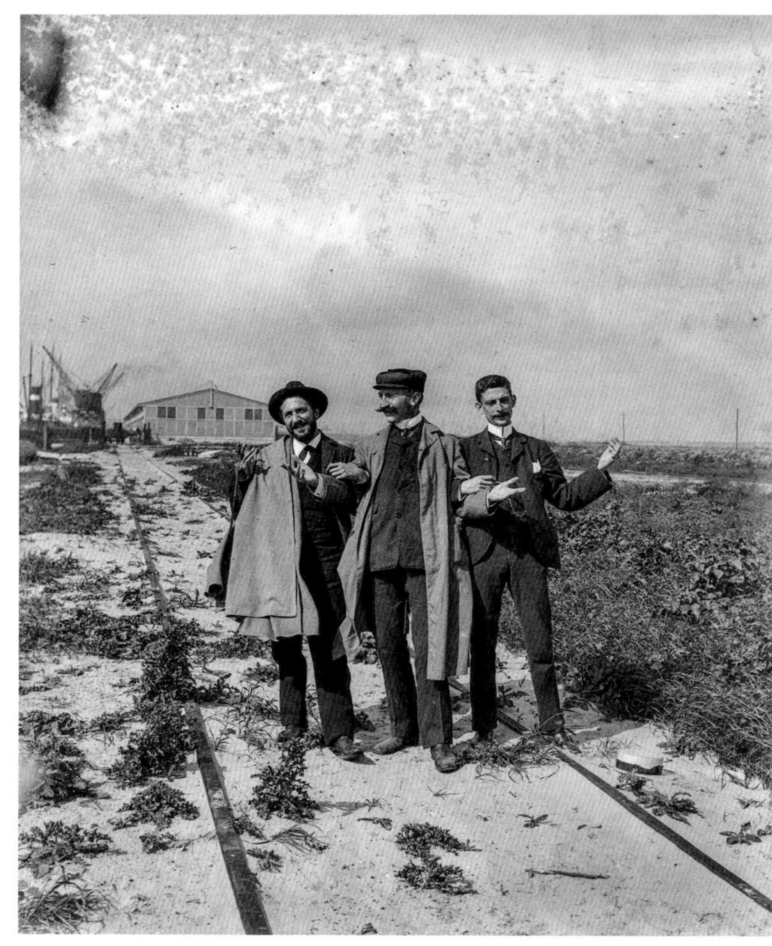

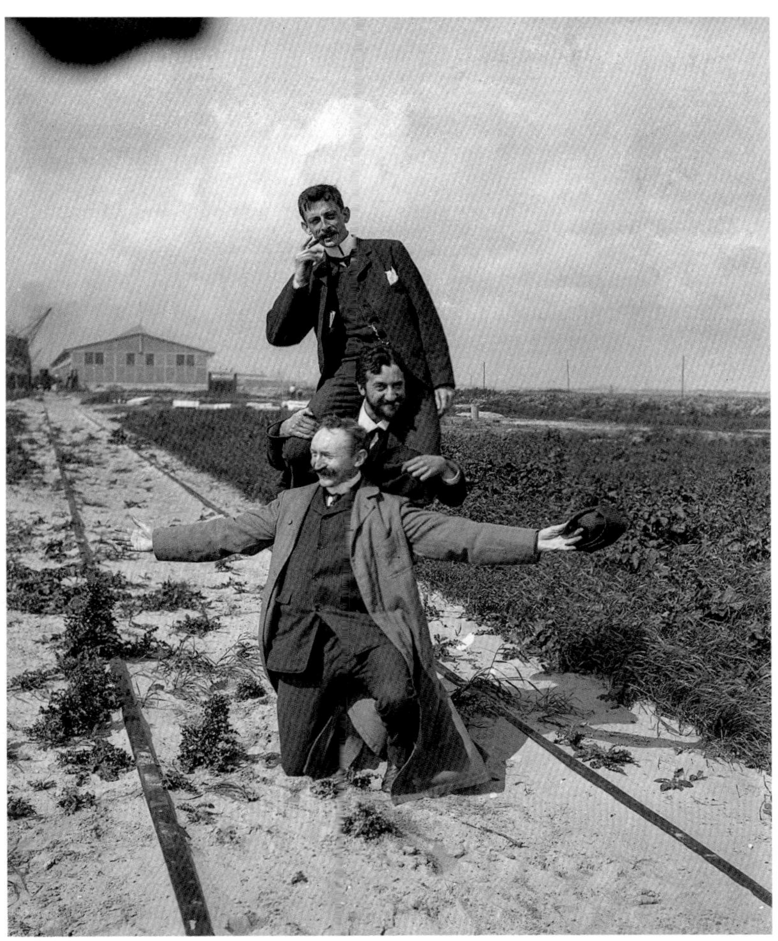

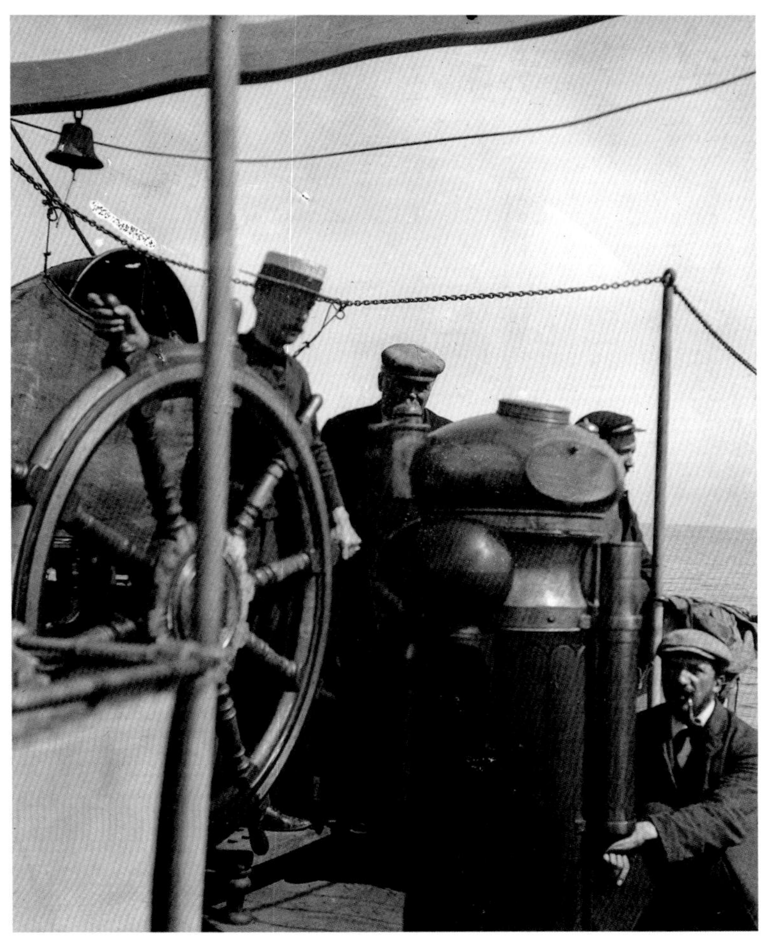

CAT. 18 **Simon Maris**
Louise and Frits Bodenheim, Mies van de Water and Piet Mondrian at the dock in IJmuiden, 28 August 1903

CAT. 19 **Mies van de Water or Louise Bodenheim**
Piet Mondrian, Simon Maris and Frits Bodenheim at the dock in IJmuiden, 28 August 1903

CAT. 20 **Mies van de Water or Louise Bodenheim**
Piet Mondrian with Frits Bodenheim on his shoulders and Simon Maris kneeling at the dock in IJmuiden, 28 August 1903

CAT. 21 **Simon Maris**
Frits Bodenheim, Piet Mondrian and two crew members on board the SS *Orion*, August–September 1903
Far left: Frits Bodenheim; far right: Piet Mondrian.

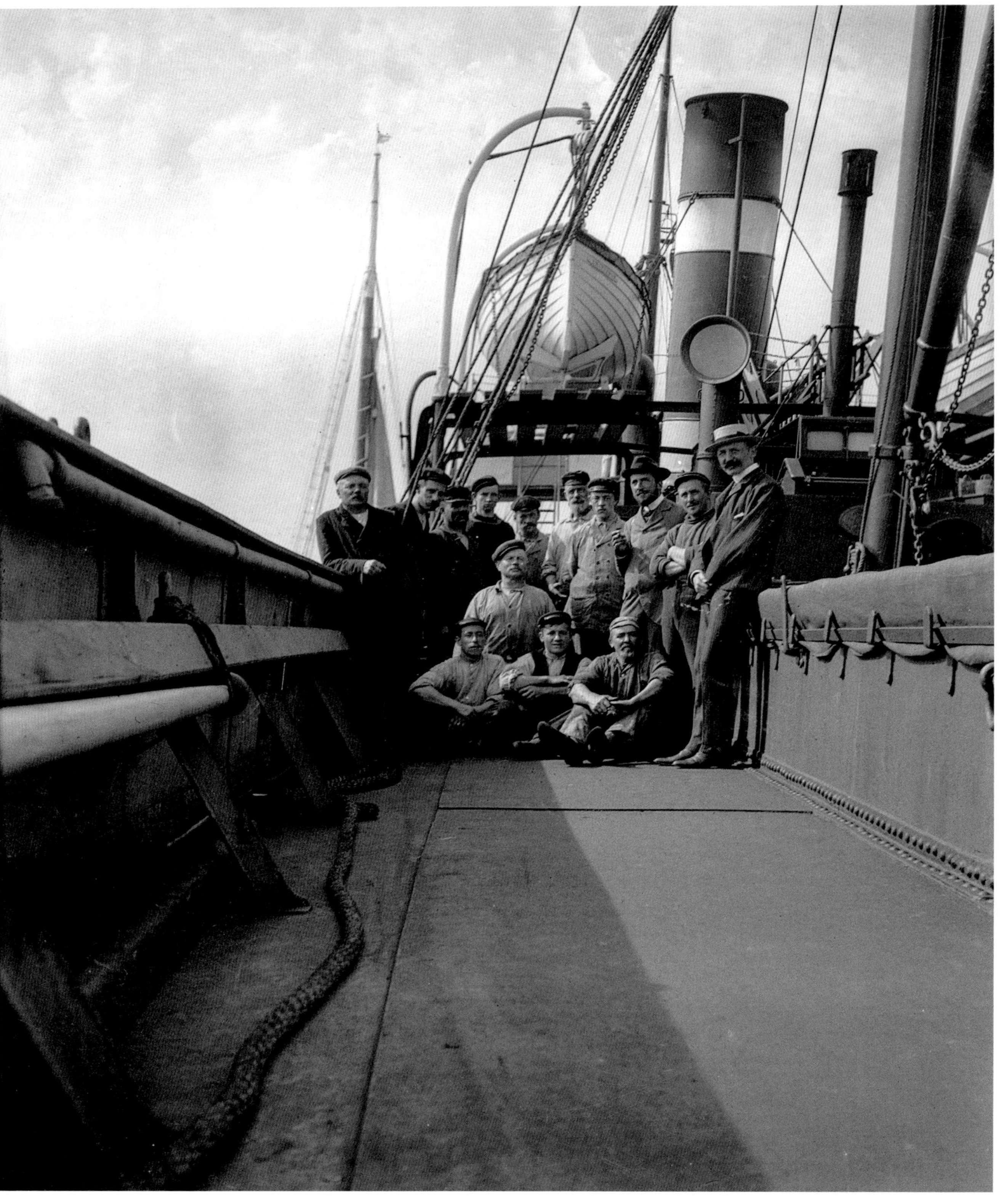

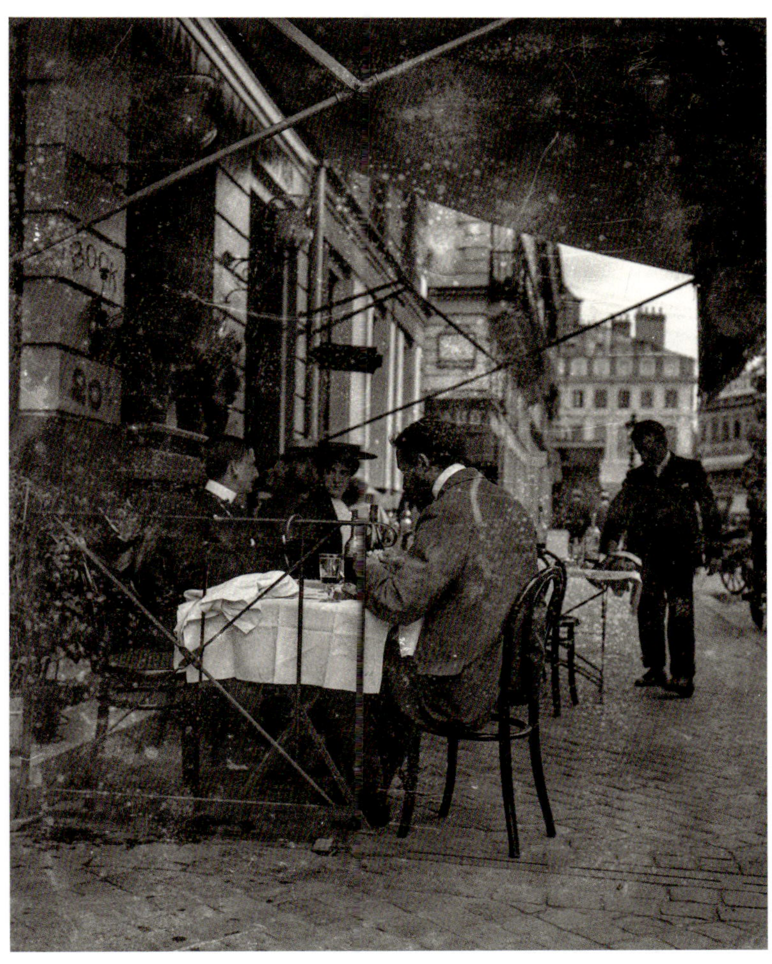

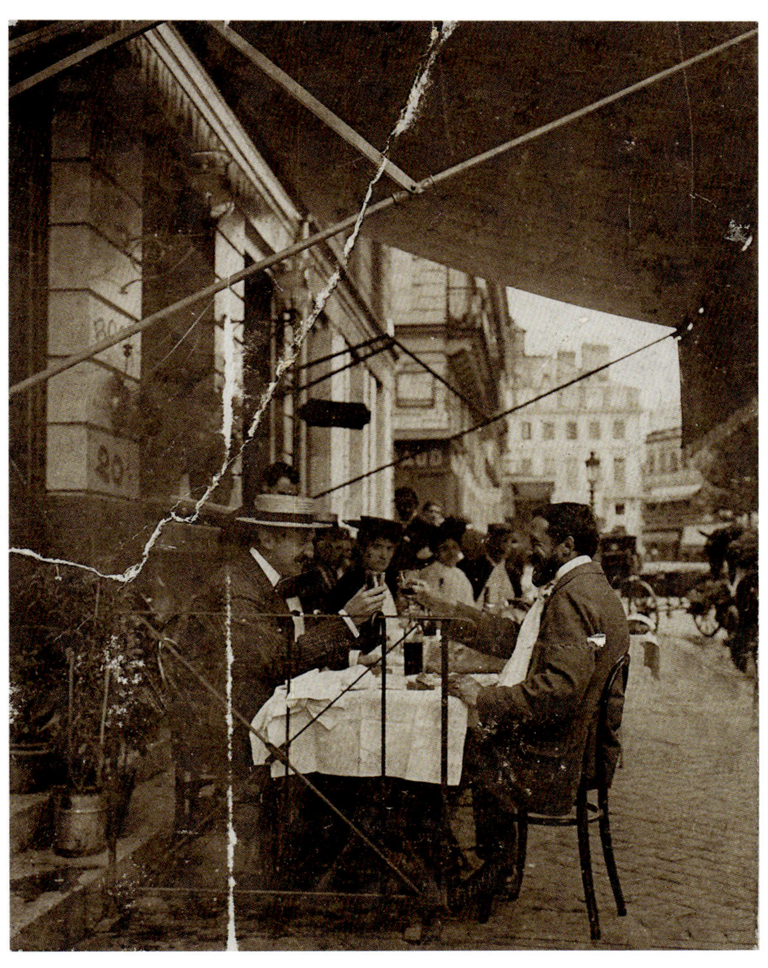

CAT. 22 **Frits Bodenheim**
Piet Mondrian, Simon Maris and crew members on board the SS *Orion*, August—September 1903
Third from right: Piet Mondrian; far right: Simon Maris.

CAT. 23 **Simon Maris**
Piet Mondrian and Frits Bodenheim dining in Bordeaux, 2 September 1903
Mondrian in the foreground, seen from the back.

CAT. 24 **Frits Bodenheim**
Simon Maris and Piet Mondrian dining in Bordeaux, 2 September 1903

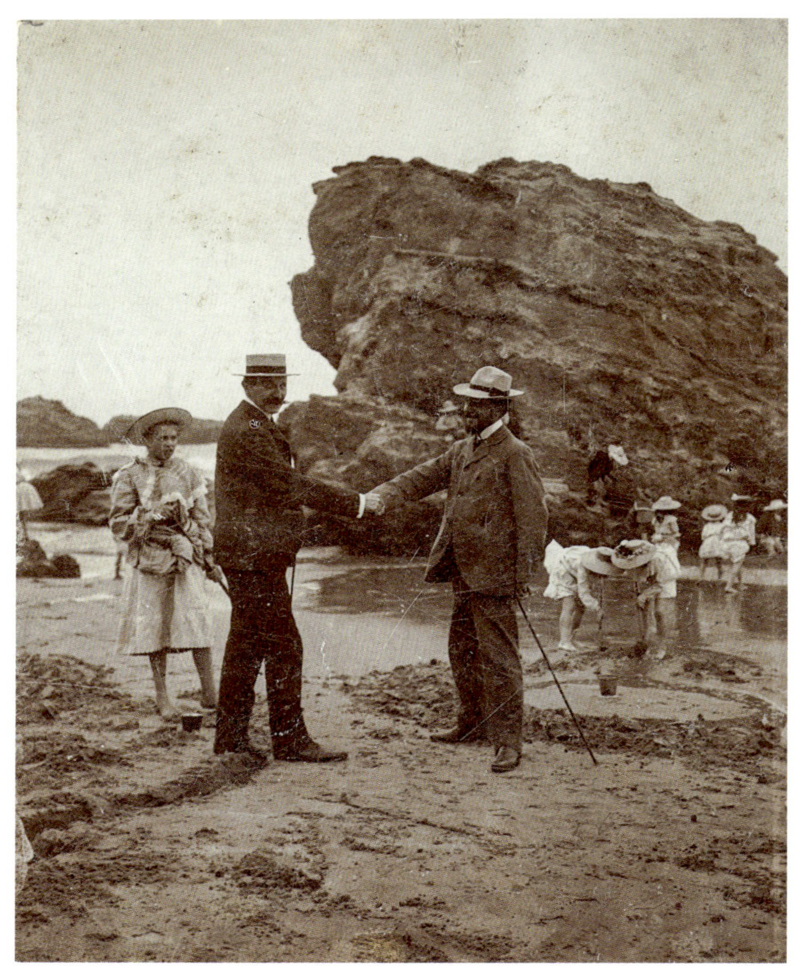

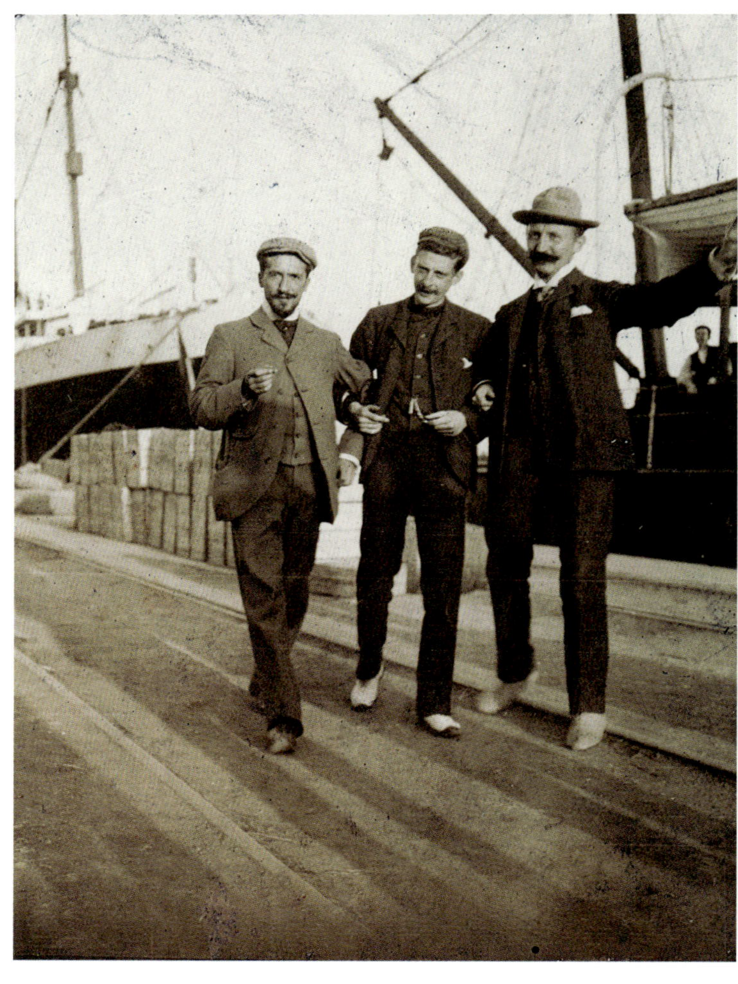

CAT. 25 **Frits Bodenheim**
Simon Maris and Piet Mondrian on the beach in Biarritz, 4 September 1903

CAT. 28 **Unidentified photographer**
Piet Mondrian, Frits Bodenheim and Simon Maris on the dock in Amsterdam, 23 September 1903

> CAT. 27 **Frits Bodenheim**
Simon Maris and Piet Mondrian at the arena in Bilbao, September 1903

CAT. 26 See catalogue

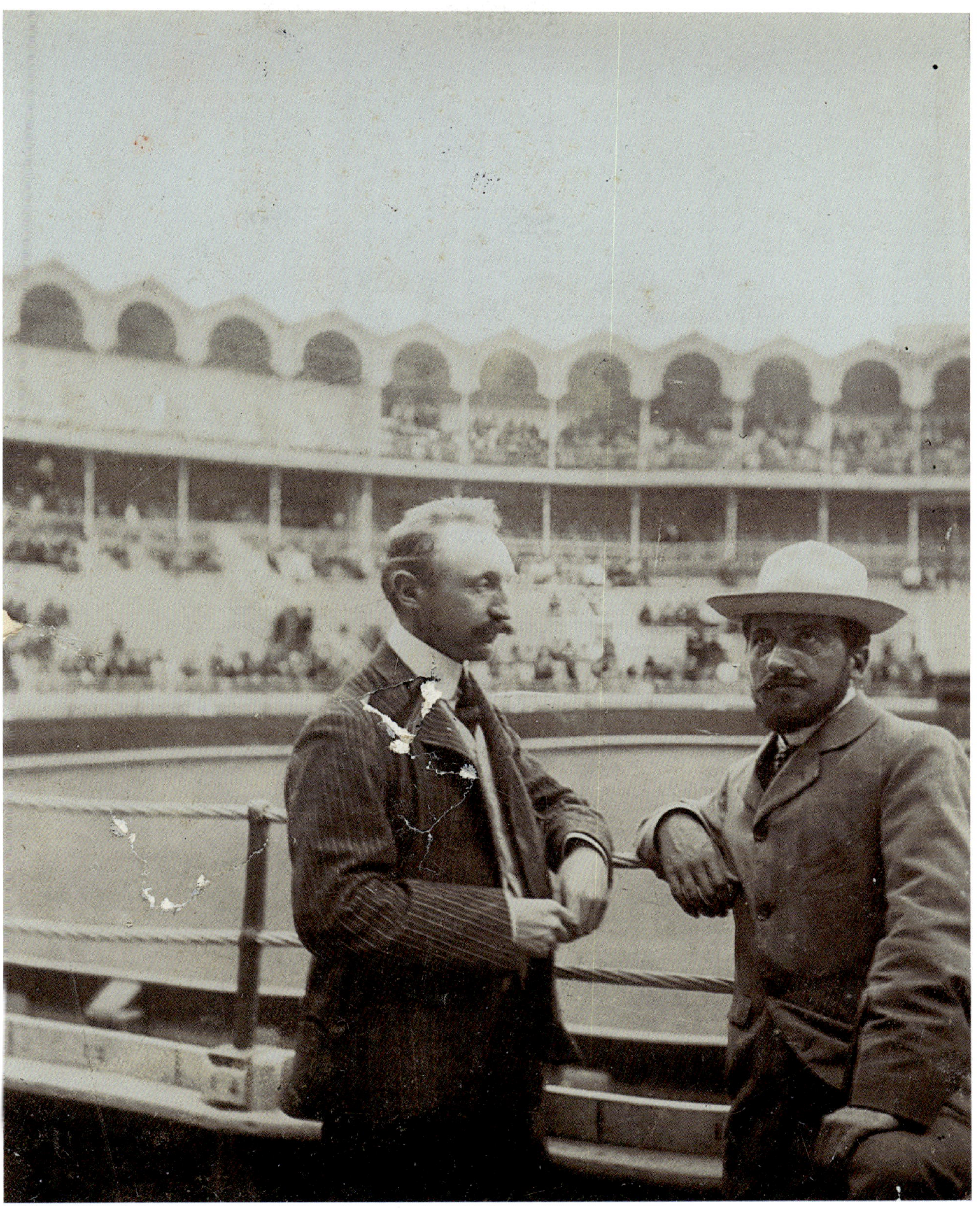

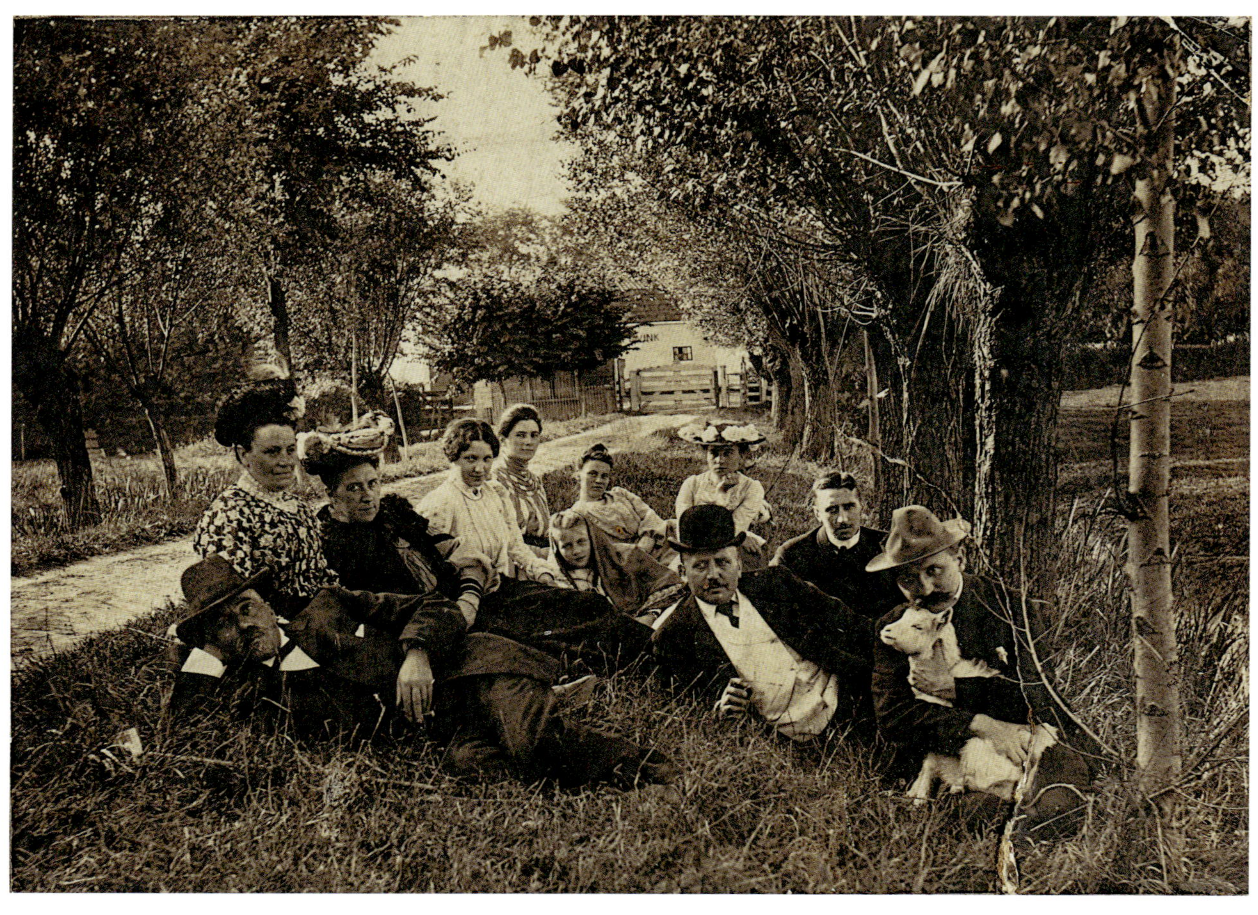

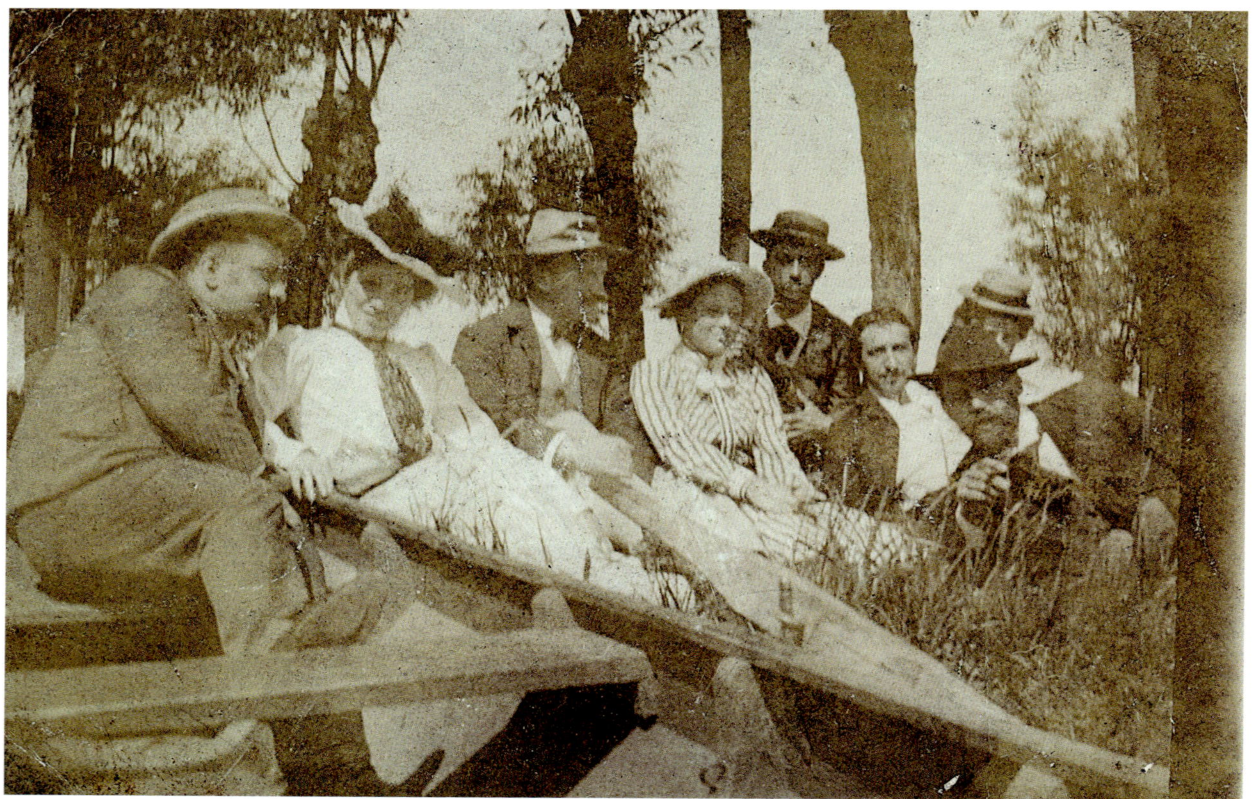

CAT. 29 **Unidentified photographer (possibly Adriaan Boer)**
Piet Mondrian and friends by the Gein, June 1904
Left to right: unidentified man and woman, Betsy Repelius (?), Cornelia den Breejen, unidentified persons, Piet Mondrian and Simon Maris with a goat. The river Gein and its surroundings were a popular daytrip destination for people from Amsterdam.

CAT. 30 **Unidentified photographer**
Piet Mondrian and friends at the Gein, c. summer 1904
Left to right: Hendrik Kroon, unidentified woman, Simon Maris, unidentified woman, Albert Hulshoff Pol, Piet Mondrian, Joop Siedenburg, Cornelia den Breejen.

CAT. 31 **Unidentified photographer**
Portrait of Piet Mondrian, c. 1905

CAT. 32 **Atelier Herz, Amsterdam**
Visitors at the preview of the Sint Lucas association's spring exhibition at the Stedelijk Museum, Amsterdam, May 1905
Mondrian, with strikingly short hair, can be seen on the far right. Several of his acquaintances and friends appear in the photo: Arnold Marc Gorter (bow tie, third from the left), Hendrik Kroon (with hat) in front of him, Simon Maris (hat in hand) in the middle, and the doctor and collector Jan van der Hoeven Leonard next to him.

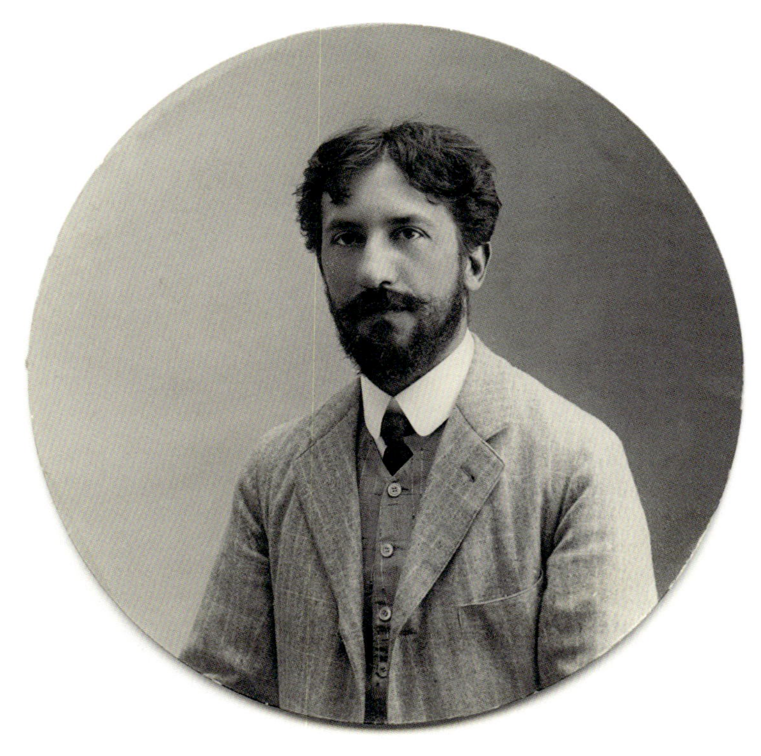

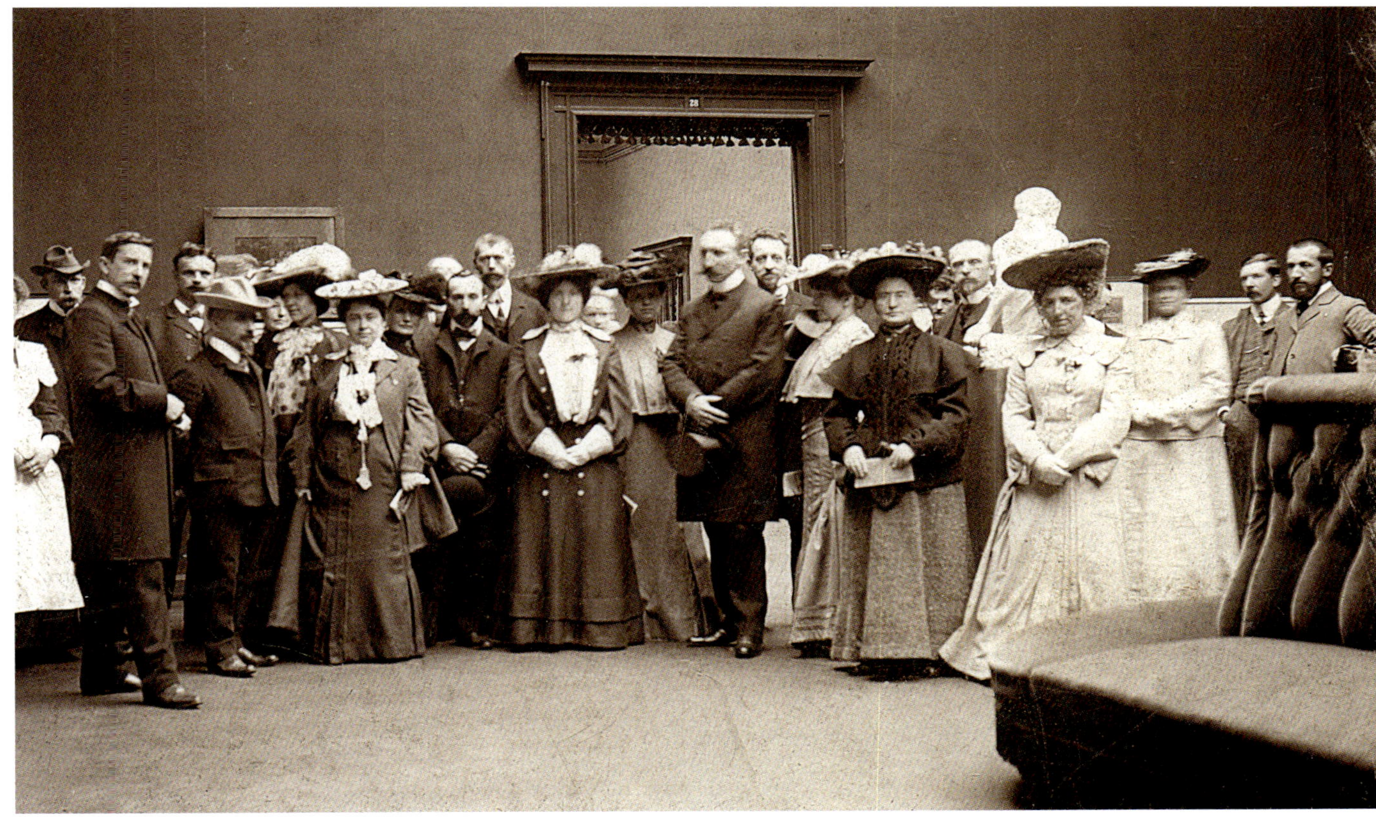

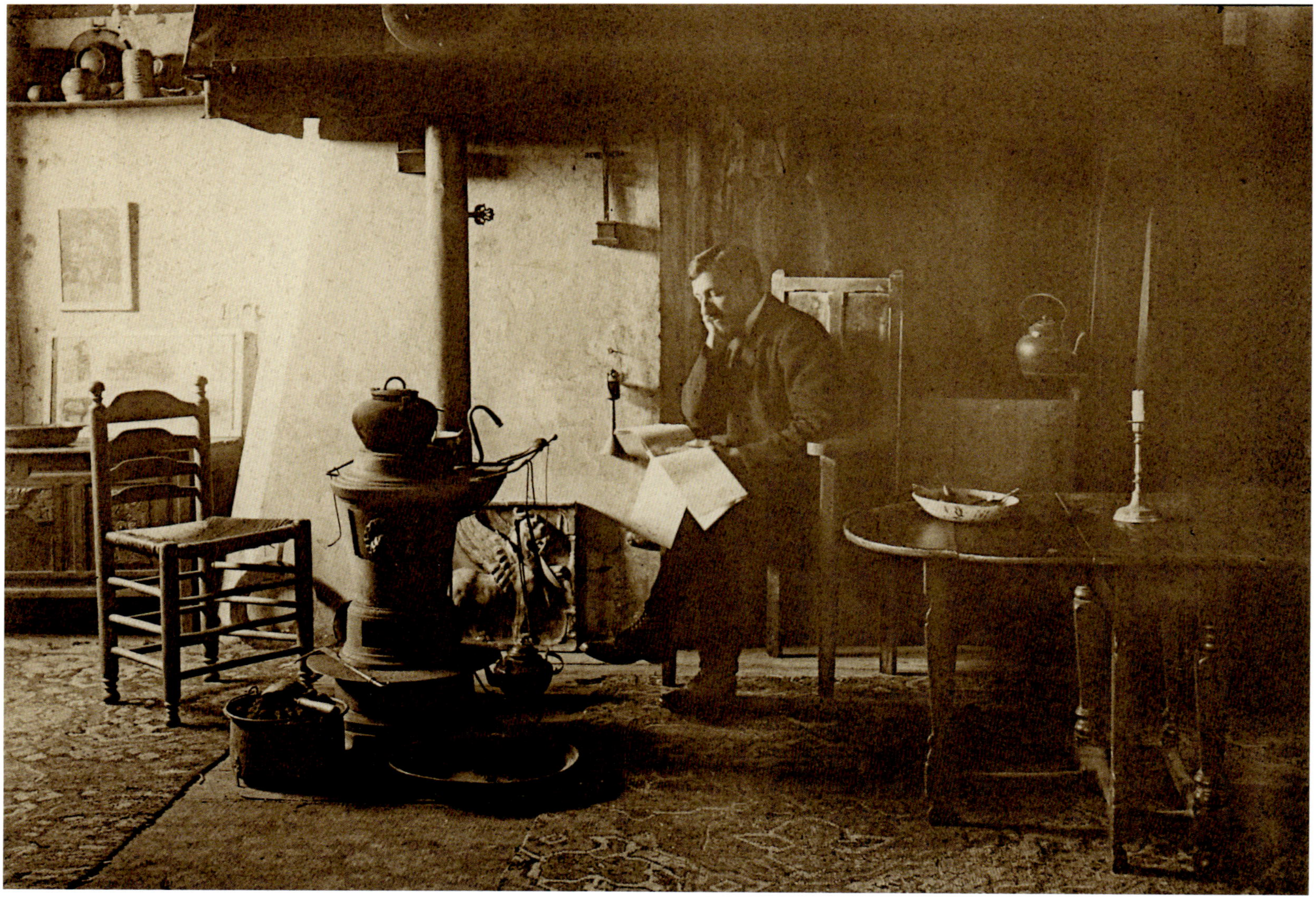

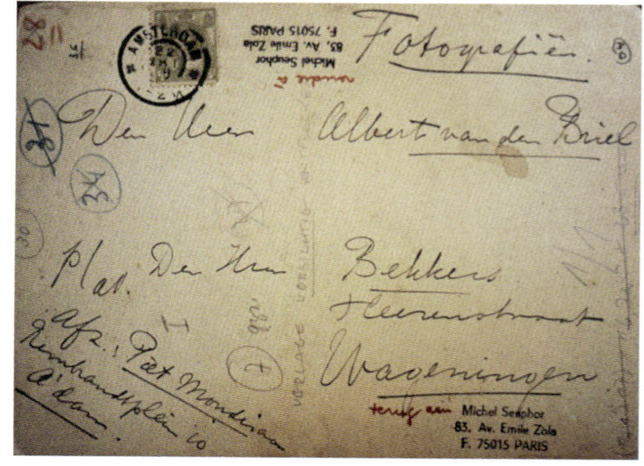

CAT. 33 **Unidentified photographer**
Piet Mondrian in the living area of his studio at 10 Rembrandtplein, Amsterdam, c. 1905 (?)
Mondrian kept this studio from February 1905 to June 1906.

CAT. 34 recto/verso **Unidentified photographer**
Piet Mondrian in his studio at 10 Rembrandtplein, Amsterdam, c. March 1906
The painting on the easel is the *Still Life* for which Mondrian was awarded the Willink van Collen Prize for the encouragement of young artists in April 1906.

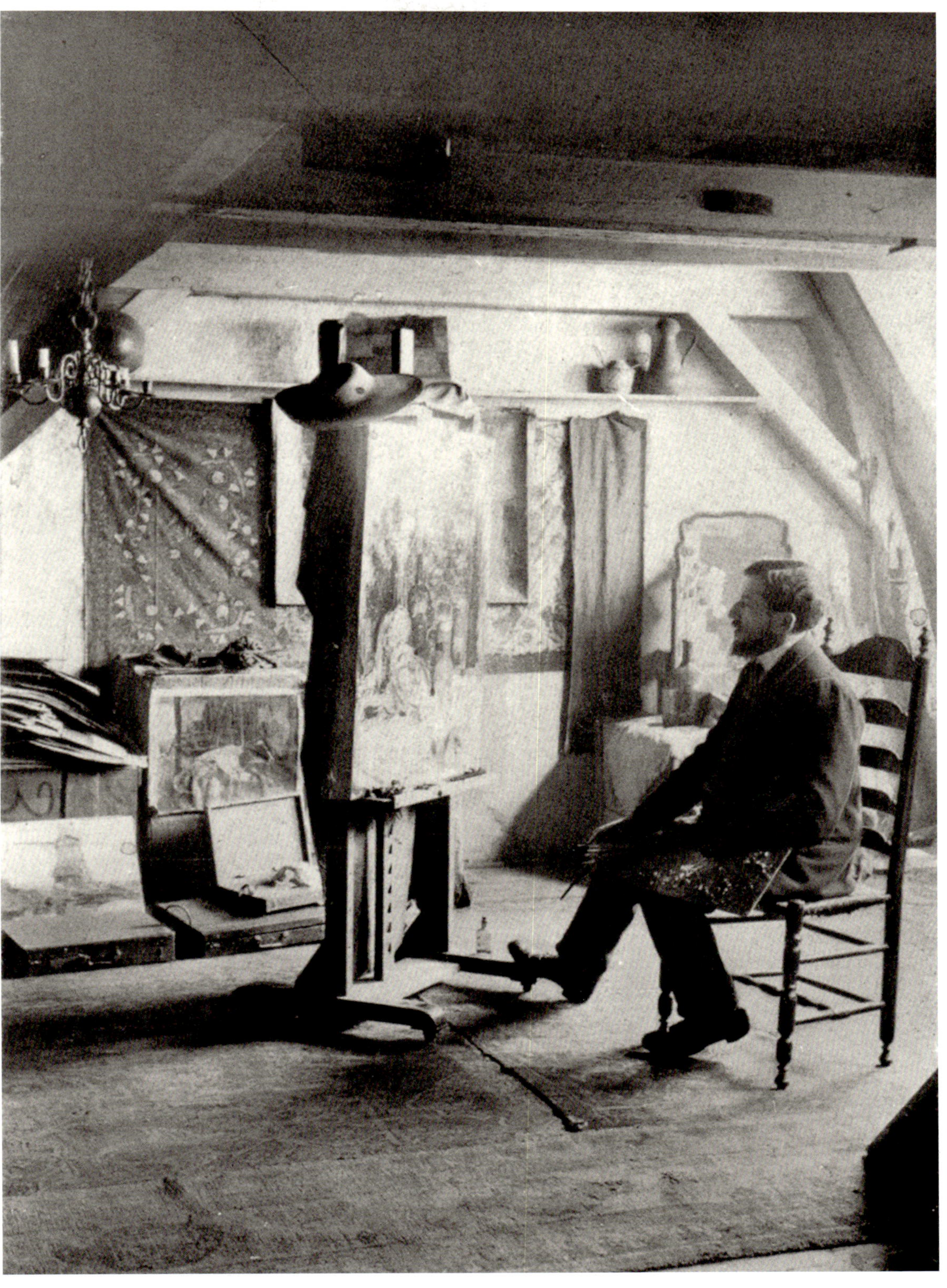

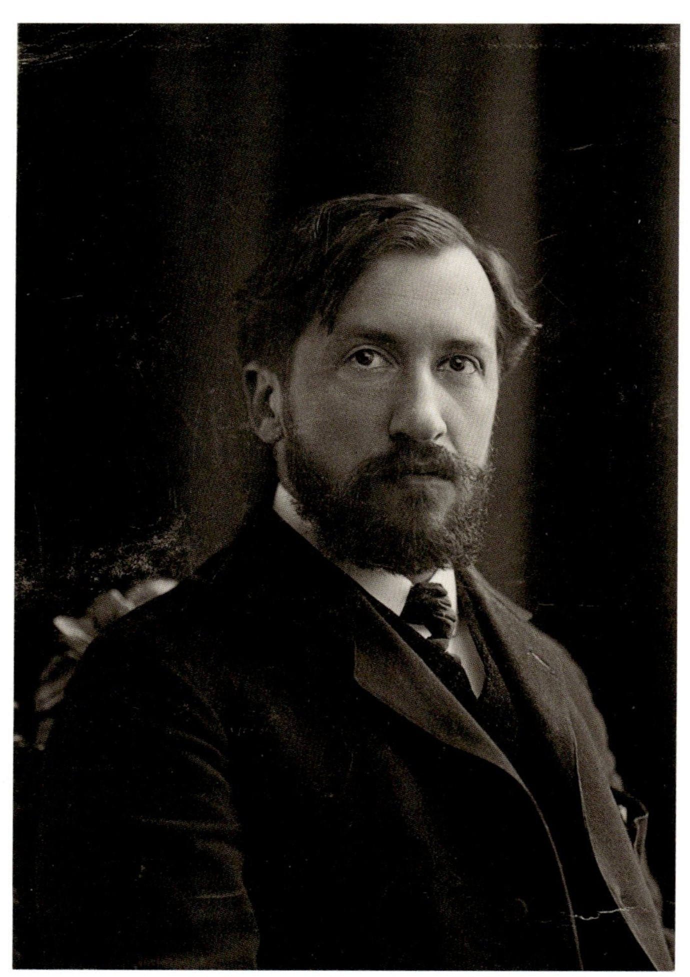

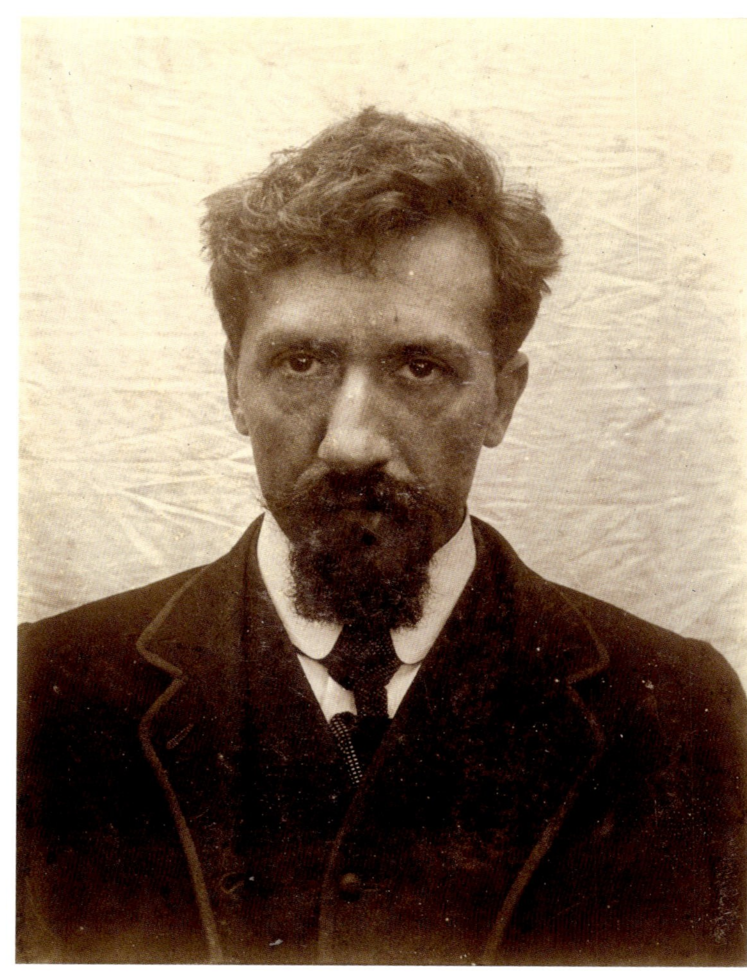

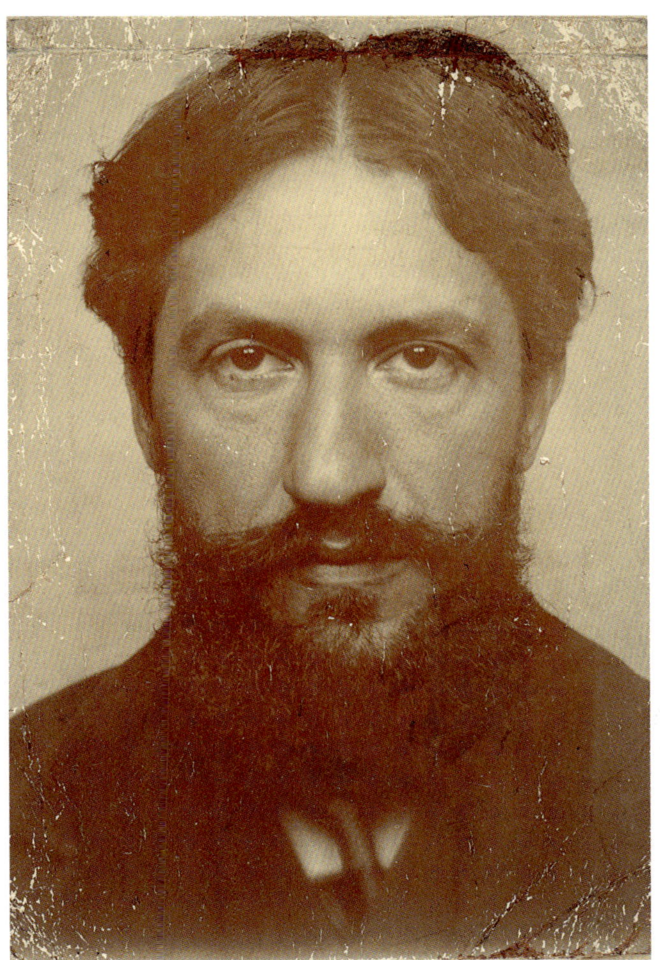

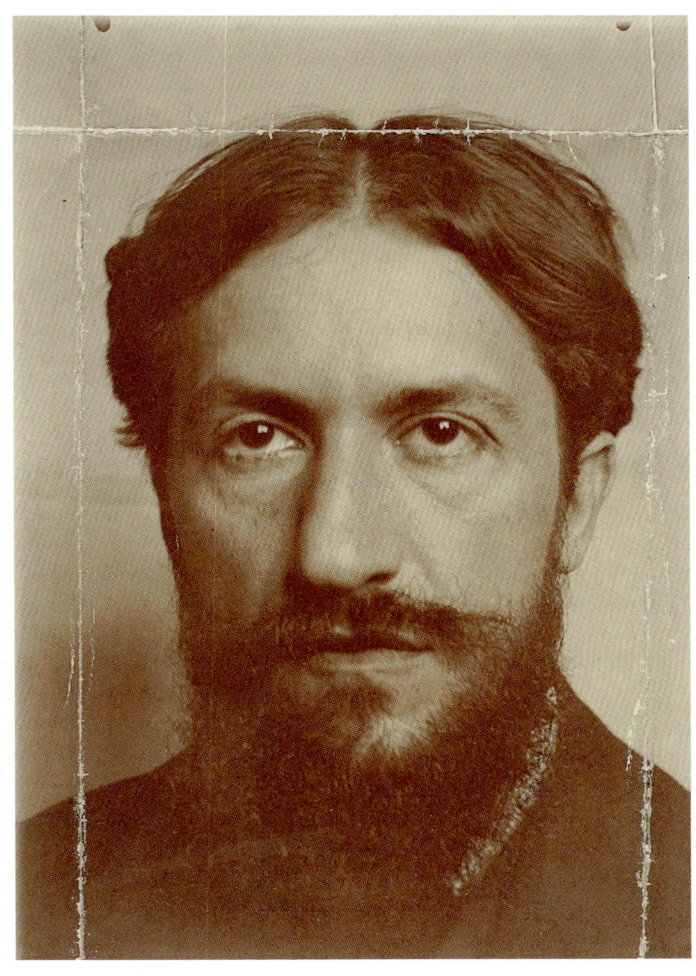

CAT. 35 **Fotografisch atelier Jac. Vetter**
Portrait of Piet Mondrian, autumn 1907
Mondrian gave the print reproduced here to the painters' model Cornelia den Breejen (usually called 'Noot' or 'Noor'), who had married his friend Simon Maris in 1905. He sent another copy to his brother Willem Frederik in South Africa.

CAT. 36 **Unidentified photographer**
Portrait of Piet Mondrian, c. 1908

CATS 37–8 **Unidentified photographer**
Portrait of Piet Mondrian with beard and centre parting, c. 1908
This photograph, or its companion, cat. 38, can be seen in the picture that Reinier Drektraan took of Mondrian's studio in the Sarphatipark (cat. 39). Both pictures were used as a basis for Mondrian's large *Self-Portrait* in charcoal and chalk of 1908–9. Mondrian determined the composition of the drawing by folding over the edges of the photos.

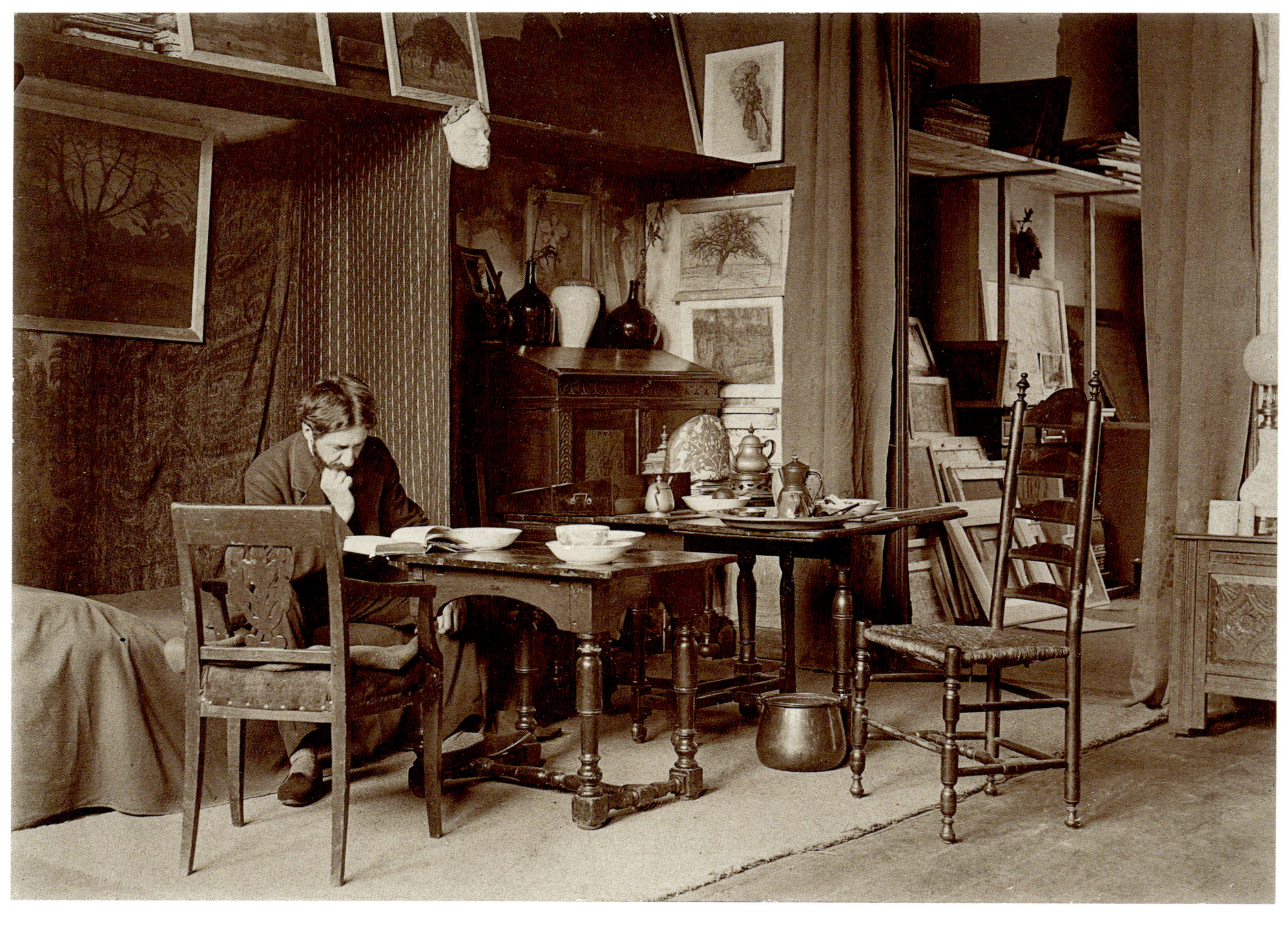

CAT. 39 **Reinier Drektraan**

Piet Mondrian in the living area of his studio at 42–1 Sarphatipark, Amsterdam, autumn 1908

Cat. 37 or 38 can be seen in a mount behind the vases. The differences between the prints are due to the techniques used (see catalogue).

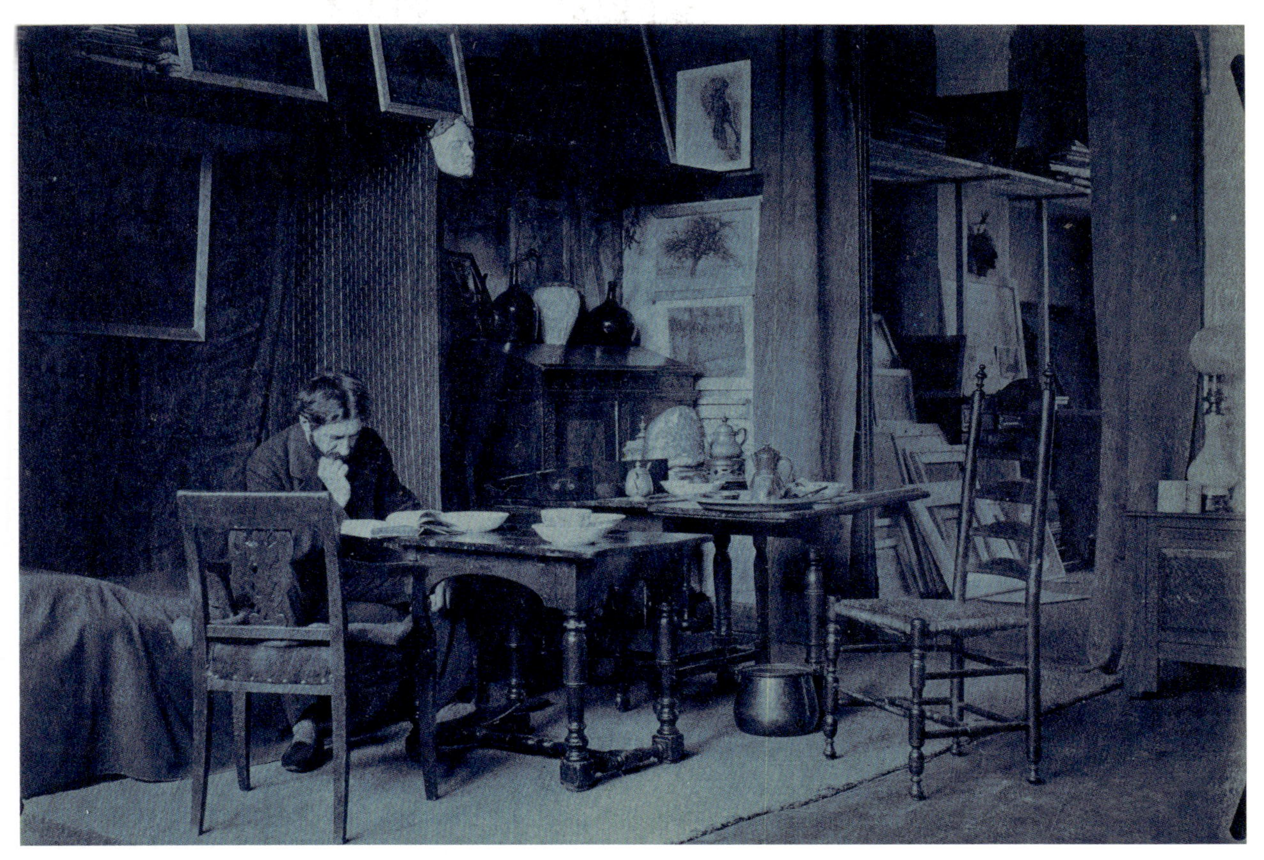

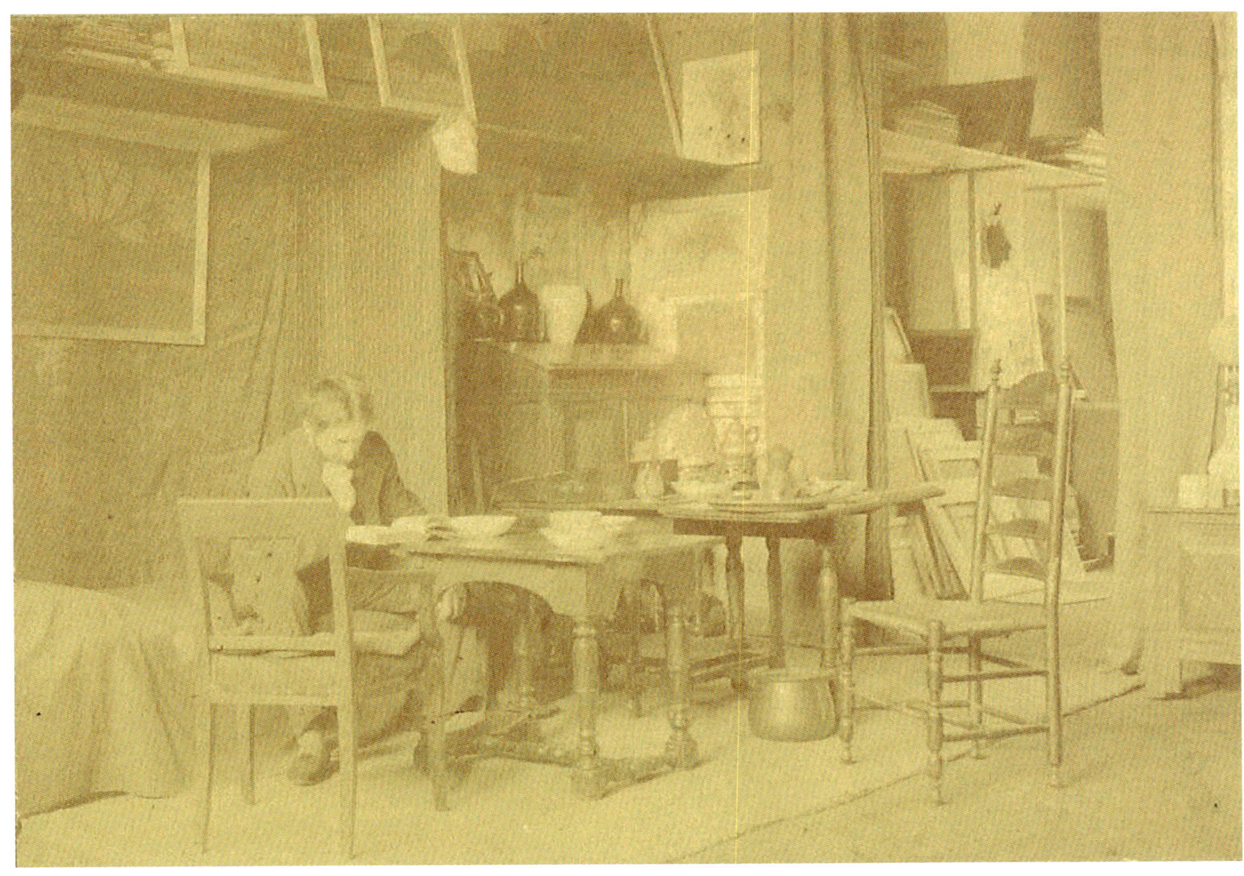

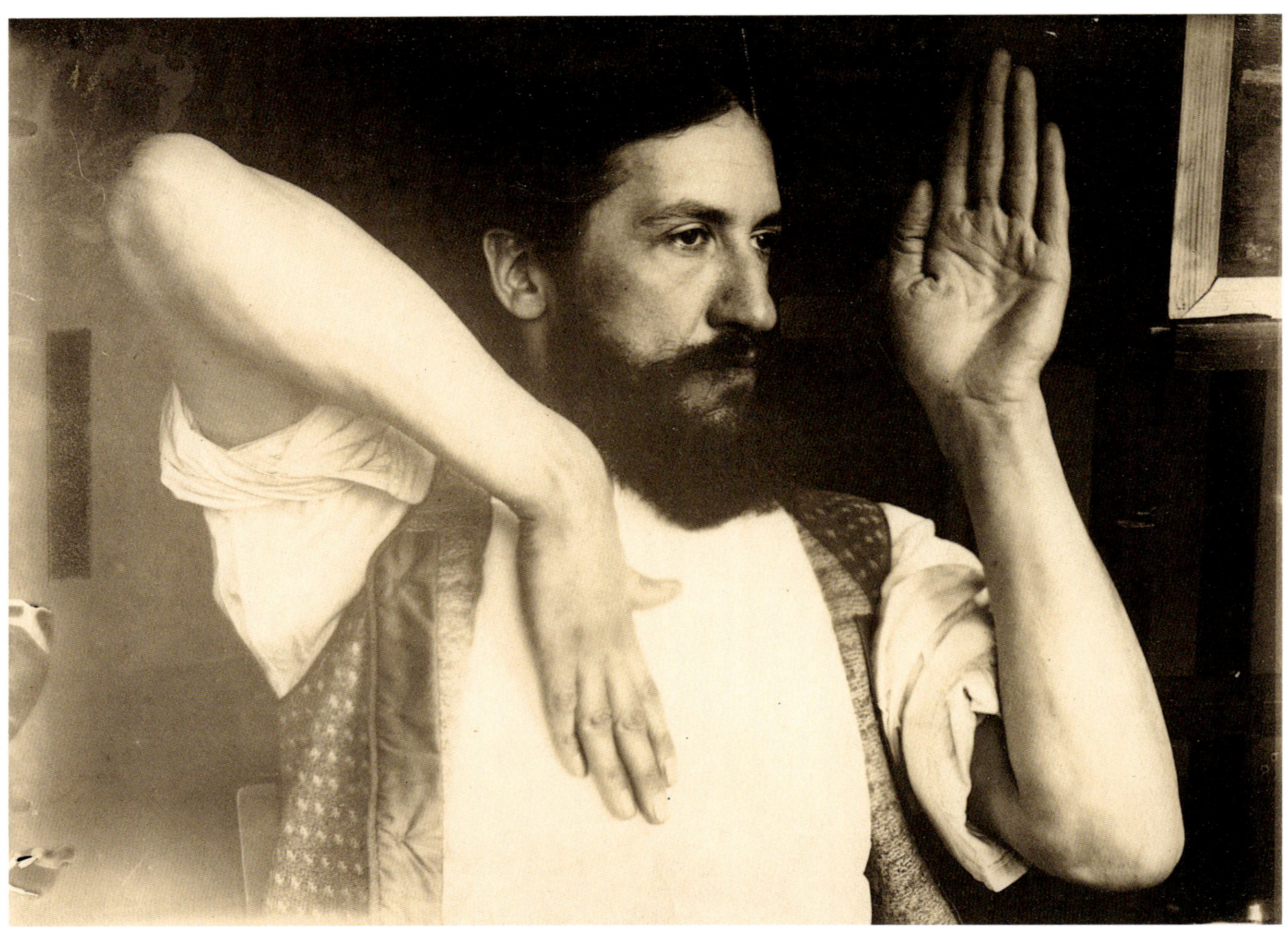

CAT. 40 **Alfred Waldenburg**
Phrenological portrait of Piet Mondrian, c. April 1909
Alfred Waldenburg was an evolutionary anthropologist and phrenologist from Berlin. He lived in the Netherlands from about 1905 until his death in 1942. Mondrian met the 'skull measurer' in around 1909 and was invited to strike a 'phrenological pose' for a photograph. It was important for the back of one hand and the palm of the other to be visible.

CAT. 43 **Unidentified photographer**
Portrait of Greta Heijbroek and Piet Mondrian, c. September 1911
Mondrian proposed to Greta Heijbroek, a merchant's daughter from Amsterdam, around September 1911. The engagement was broken off for unknown reasons before the year was out.

CATS 41–2, 44–5 See catalogue

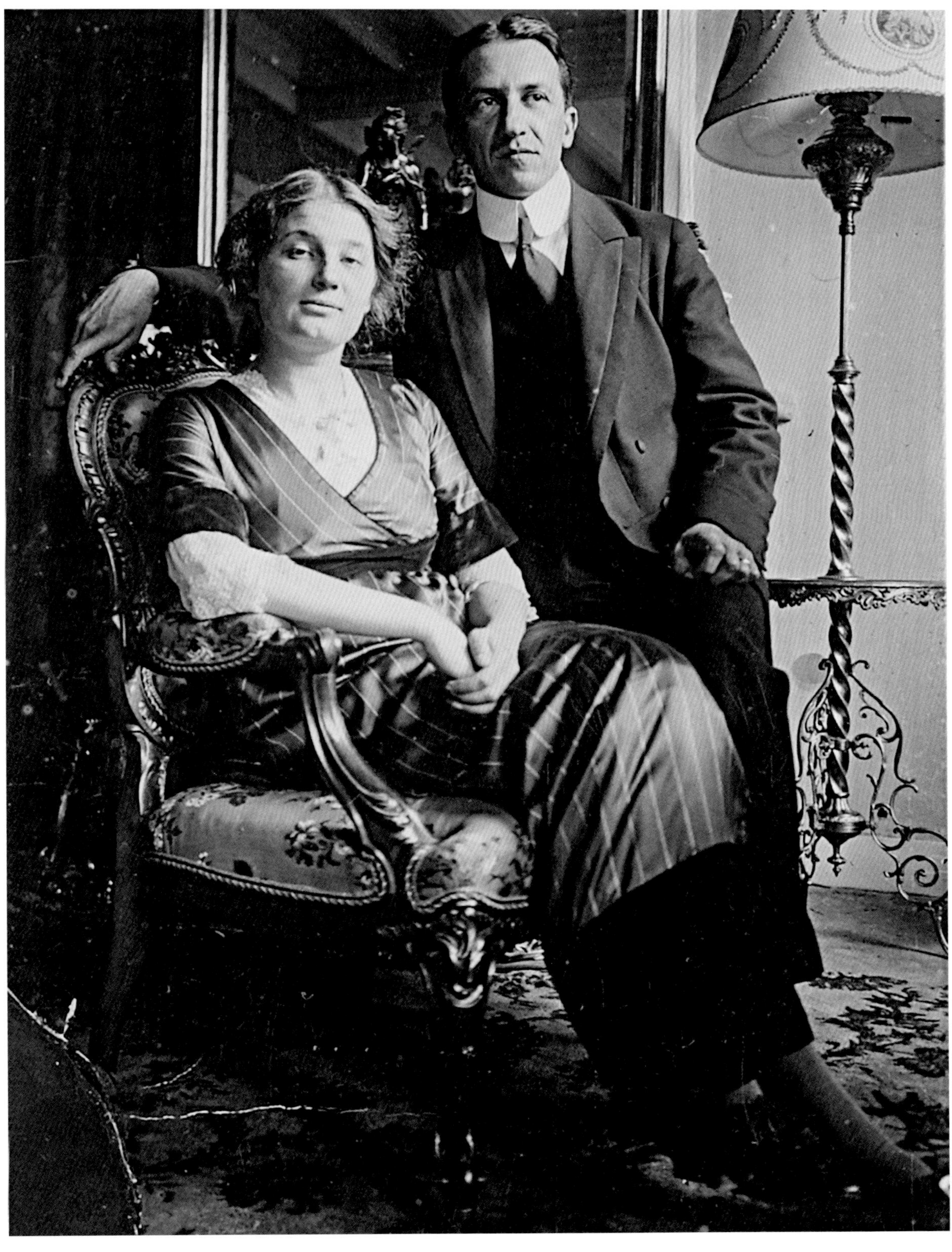

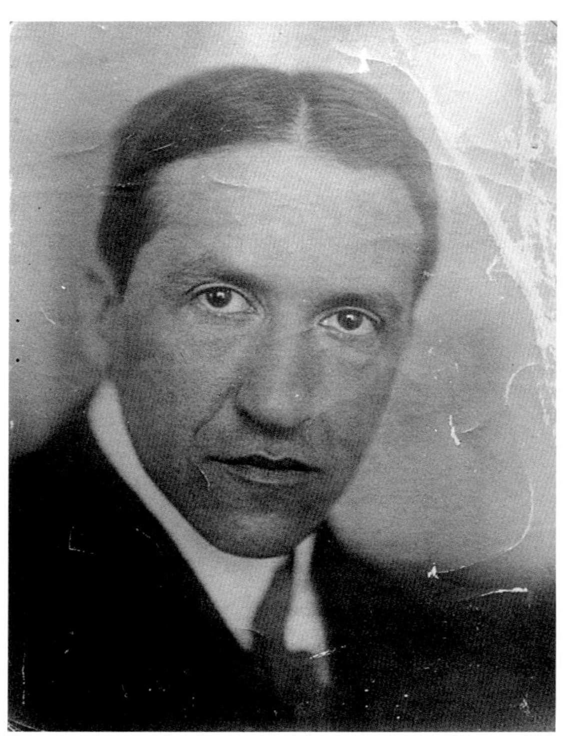

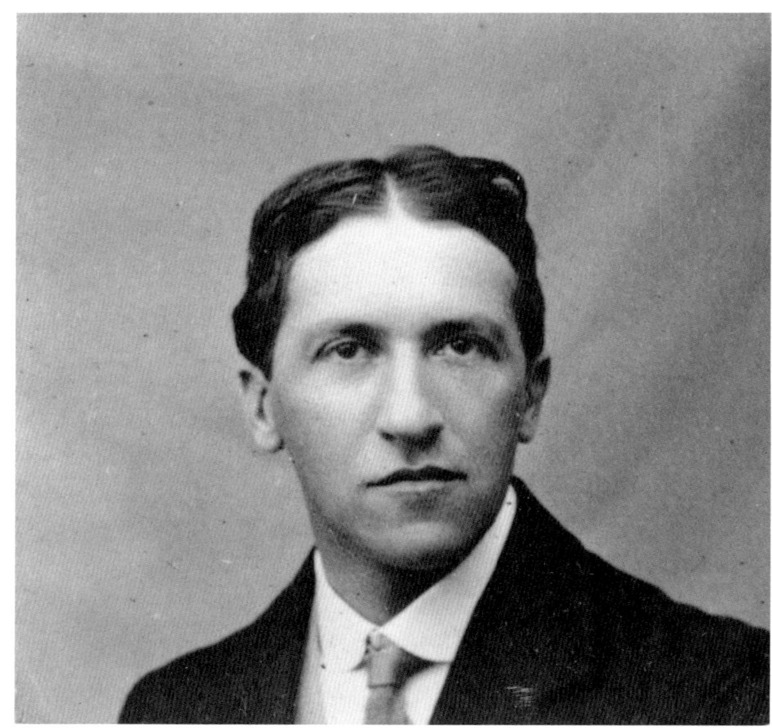

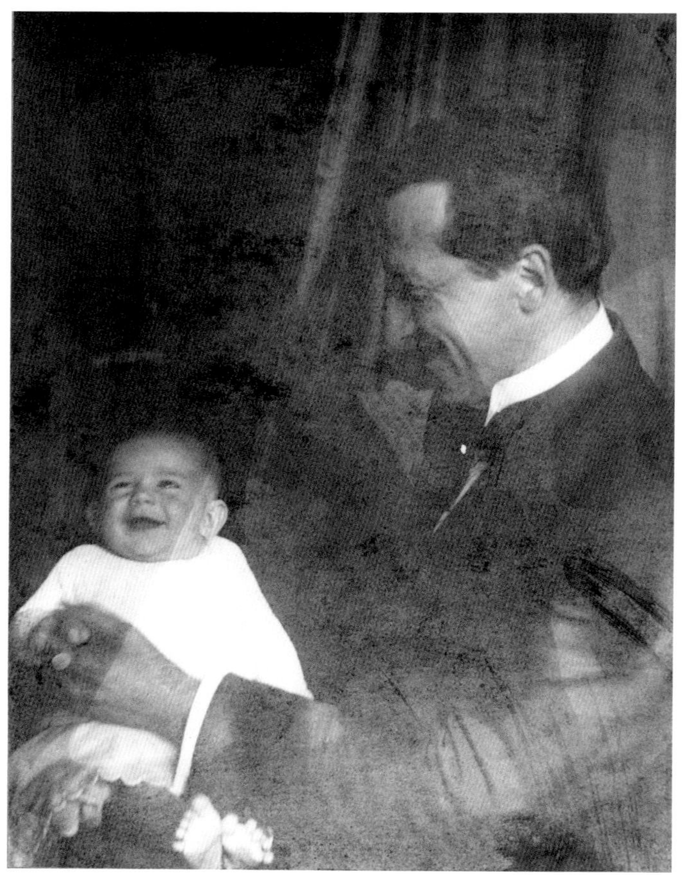

CAT. 46 **Unidentified photographer**
Portrait of Piet Mondrian, 1911
Mondrian's appearance changed drastically in the late summer of 1910. He abandoned his bohemian hairstyle and beard (see cats 37–8) for a clean-shaven look, with his hair slicked back against his skull.

CAT. 47 **Unidentified photographer**
Portrait of Piet Mondrian, 1912 (?)
The photograph is known from the copyist card issued to Mondrian for the Louvre.

CAT. 49 **Unidentified photographer**
Piet Mondrian with Hugues Raymond Colin on his knee, September–October 1914
Mondrian met the Franco-Dutch couple Raymond Colin and Marie Colin-Penning in Paris around 1912. Mondrian and the Colin family were all in the Netherlands when the First World War broke out.

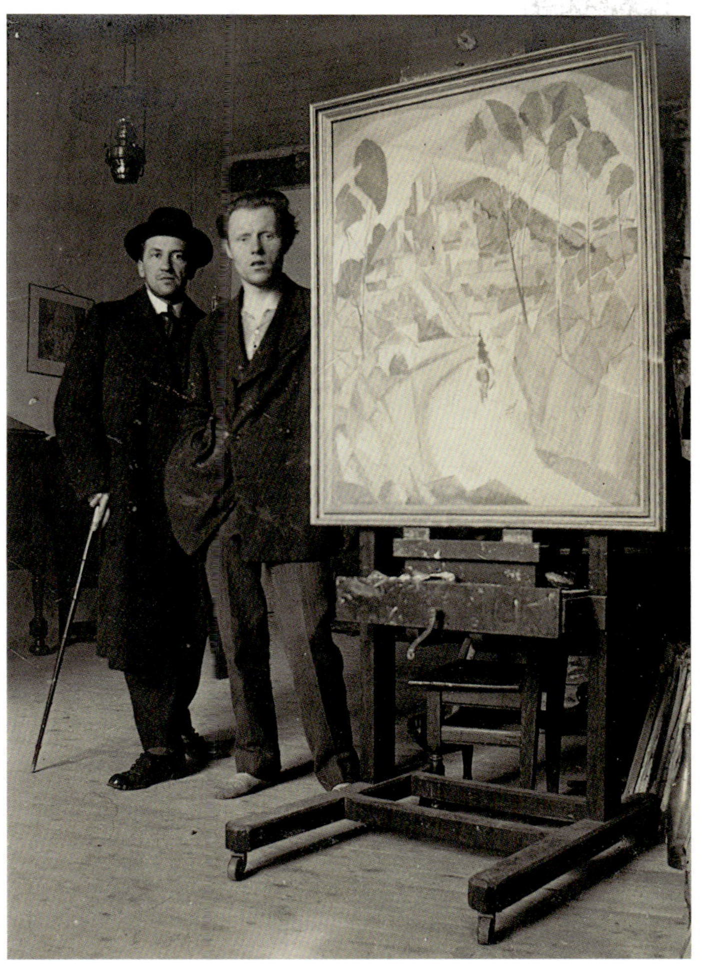

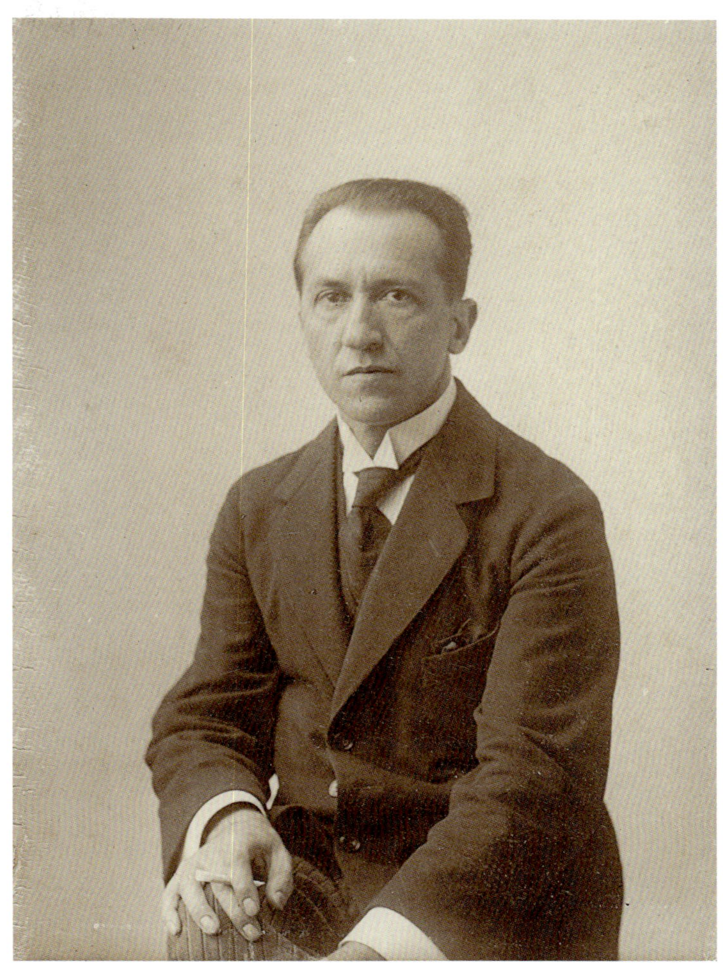

CAT. 48 **Conrad Kickert**

Piet Mondrian and Lodewijk Schelfhout in the latter's studio, 1912

Mondrian and Schelfhout pose here by the latter's cubist *View of Villeneuve-lès-Avignon* (1912). In early 1912, Mondrian, Schelfhout and Conrad Kickert rented studio spaces at 33 Avenue du Maine. The trio moved on in May 1912 to the studio complex at 26 Rue du Départ.

CAT. 51 **Unidentified photographer (Peter Alma?)**

Portrait of Piet Mondrian, c. 1918 (?)

This is the last photograph taken of Mondrian in the Netherlands. A copy of it was also used for his residence permit in Paris.

CAT. 50 See catalogue

THE PARIS YEARS 1919–38

Following his unplanned five-year sojourn in the Netherlands, Mondrian returned to Paris in late June 1919. The studio he had left behind in the summer of 1914 in the belief that he would only be away for a few weeks had been occupied in the meantime by someone else, obliging him to make do with another, darker one in the same complex on the Rue du Départ, adjacent to the Gare Montparnasse. Fortunately, the works he had left behind had been safely stored. What's more, Sal Slijper, his friend from Laren, had bought them all sight unseen, providing Mondrian with some reassuring basic capital. In early August, he wrote to Theo van Doesburg, leader of De Stijl, with whom he kept in close contact: 'I am happy to be here again because I feel the seriousness of the big city strongly. It is all so childish in Holland.'[1]

He moved in November 1919 to a studio at 5 Rue de Coulmiers, where he applied his neo-plastic ideas spatially for the first time, decorating his ascetically furnished studio with primary-coloured rectangles on the walls. A Dutch journalist who interviewed him was impressed by this absolute novelty: 'the studio speaks on his behalf. The walls of this space, which already has a pleasant stereometric form, are arranged with unpainted canvases or ones executed in a basic colour, so that each wall forms a kind of block painting in itself, enlarged several times.'[2] Mondrian took the view that neo-plasticism could also be achieved architecturally. Sadly, of this studio, which Mondrian continued to use until 21 October 1921, only one photograph survives, which does not offer a clear enough view. He subsequently moved back to the familiar complex on the Rue du Départ, but now in a different, better-lit studio.

A disappointed Mondrian was forced to conclude that Paris had lost some of its pre-war innovative drive. Artists like Picasso and Diego Rivera were working naturalistically again, a development that would later be described as a 'retour à l'ordre'. Ever the networker, though, he renewed his old contacts and made new ones too. He took part in exhibitions in both the Netherlands and Paris in 1921 and 1922. Léonce Rosenberg's L'Effort Moderne was one of the few French art galleries to show an interest in his geometric-abstract paintings. Rosenberg showed recent work by Mondrian several times and in February 1921 he published an abridged version of his artistic philosophy that had previously appeared in *De Stijl*, with the title *Le Néo-plasticisme*. Although Mondrian continued to publish articles in the movement's magazine, his texts now also appeared regularly in foreign periodicals, whether or not directly solicited.

1 'Ik ben blij weer hier te zijn omdat ik den ernst van de groote stad sterk voel. Alles is toch kinderwerk in Holland.' Letter from Piet Mondrian to Theo van Doesburg, 1 August 1919. Theo and Nelly van Doesburg archive, The Hague, RKD — Netherlands Institute for Art History, 0408.136.

2 'het atelier spreekt namens hem. De wanden van dit vertrek, dat uit zichzelf al een aangenamen stereometrischen vorm heeft, zijn nl. ingedeeld door onbeschilderde of in de grondkleur geschilderde doeken, zoodat elke wand op zichzelf een soort blokjesschilderij vormt, ettelijke malen vergroot.' Röell 1920. The term 'ground colour' is misleading; Röell means 'primary colour'.

Several close acquaintances — with Sal Slijper taking the lead — marked his fiftieth birthday in 1922 with a retrospective of almost sixty paintings at the Stedelijk Museum in Amsterdam. Despite the growing interest in his work and ideas as the 1920s progressed, Mondrian was going through a difficult period financially. Living in Paris was expensive and sales of his work were not bringing in substantial sums. He made ends meet by producing dozens of drawings, watercolours and oil paintings of flowers, which contacts in the Netherlands sold on his behalf.

His money woes did not prevent him from producing a large number of neo-plastic works, in which he moved steadily towards ever more sober compositions. Recognition for his art came in from various quarters. Friends, both Dutch and foreign, supported him by buying or commissioning his work, by taking it on consignment or otherwise helping out. German admirers of modern art began to develop a taste for his art too, partly because several prominent Bauhaus artists, including László Moholy-Nagy, admired and had written about it. Mondrian was shown in German galleries and museums and he hosted interested parties from numerous European countries and from America at the Rue du Départ.

In addition to his work, the studio itself attracted visitors because of its neo-plastic interior design. It assumed almost mythical status and became a must-see for those in the know who visited Paris, whether or not for that specific purpose. Mondrian decided to have the space documented by the photographer Pierre Delbo towards the end of 1925 or early in 1926. The pictures appeared in magazines here and there, which only added to the studio's fame. In the years that followed, it would be photographed countless more times by photographers both famous and less so.

The Montparnasse district of Paris where Mondrian lived was a melting pot at the time of avant-garde groups and their activities. He made friends with Dadaists, surrealists and geometric-abstract artists and was involved in exhibition and magazine initiatives, such as the artists' association Cercle et Carré, founded in 1929. His circle of acquaintances included all sorts of prominent artists and architects — Marcel Duchamp, Man Ray, André Kertész, László Moholy-Nagy, El Lissitzky, Le Corbusier, Hans Arp and his wife Sophie Taeuber, Adolf Loos, Joaquín Torres-García, Sonia and Robert Delaunay, and Naum Gabo, to name just a few. One important friendship was with the Belgian artist and publicist Michel Seuphor, who was one of

>> Detail of cat. 75

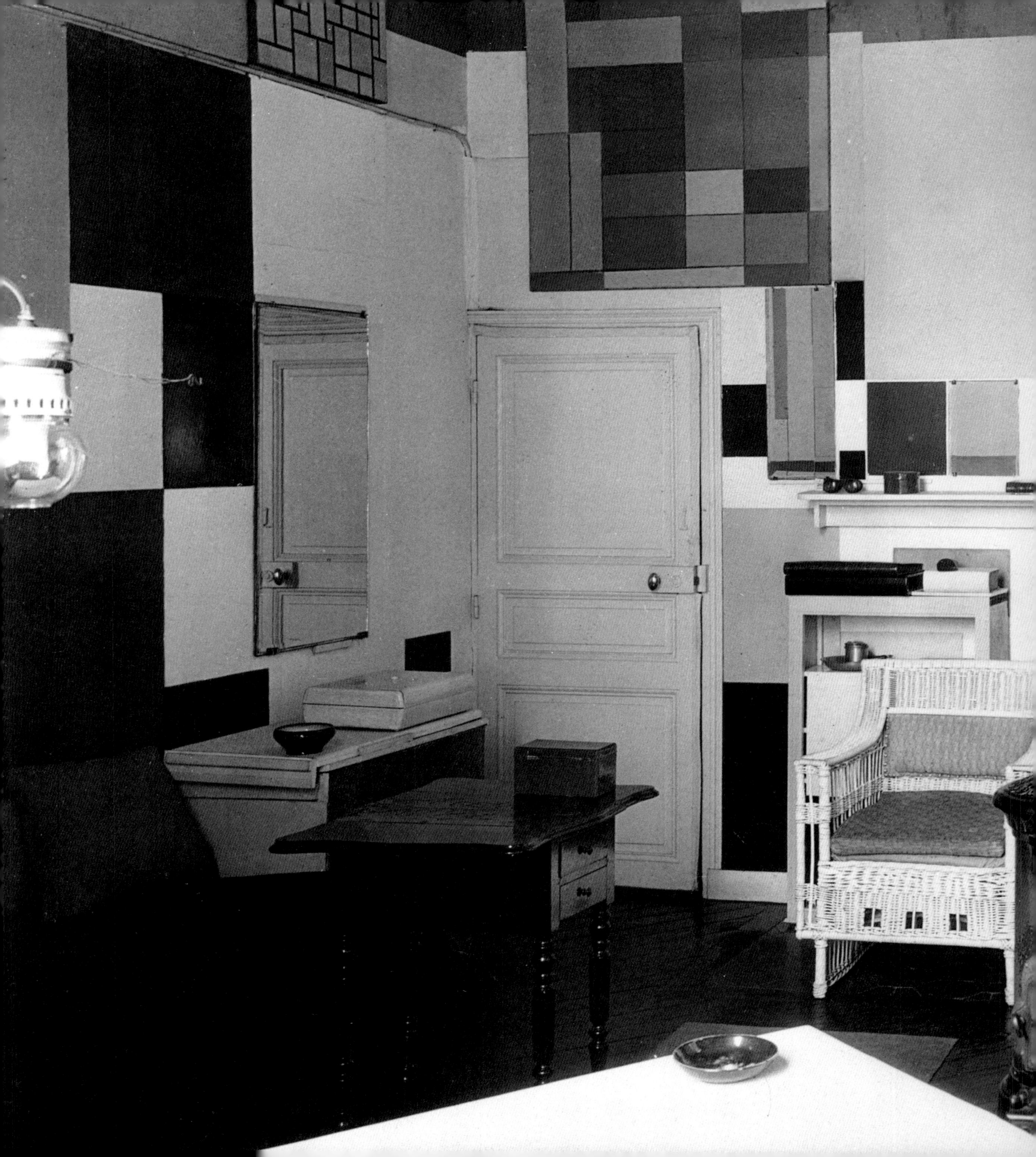

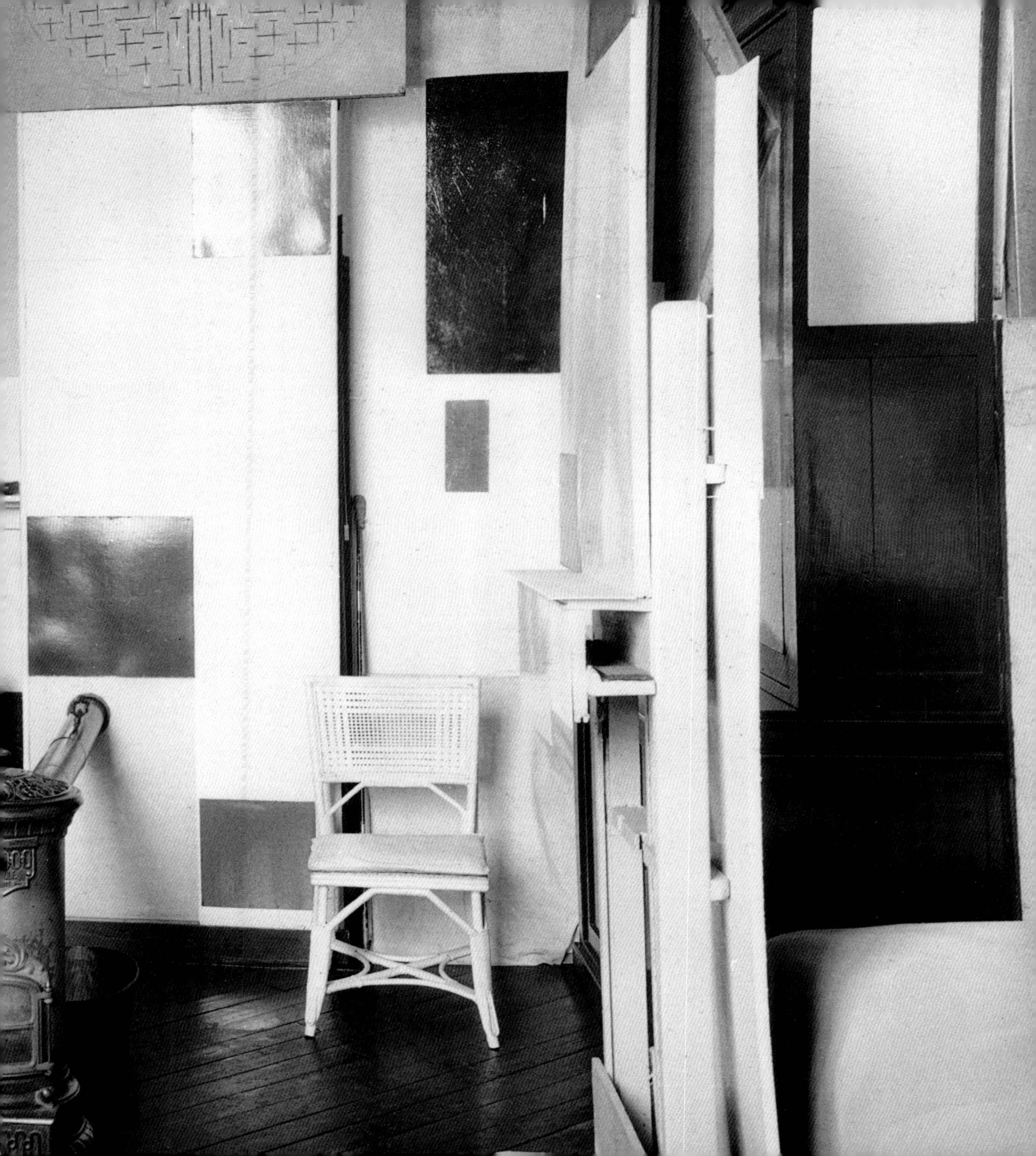

the few people with whom Mondrian created a collaborative work of art (*Tableau-Poème*, 1928 (B205)). Seuphor also went on to write the first comprehensive image-defining biography of Mondrian in 1956.

Mondrian was no stranger to Montparnasse nightlife either: he enjoyed visiting restaurants, bars and clubs to meet up with friends, listen to jazz and to dance — a serious pastime of his, which he had previously indulged in Amsterdam and Laren. There was a gramophone and a collection of jazz records in his studio, where he regularly treated visitors to music and dancing.

Mondrian established his name as an artist in the course of the 1930s. Collectors, dealers and museum directors from all over the world sought him out to acquire, sell or exhibit his works. Sales grew in Switzerland and the United States in particular, and from 1936, Mondrian even had a permanent art dealer in the United States in the shape of Frank Valentine Dudensing.

It was in March of that year that he had to quit his by now legendary studio in the Rue du Départ, as the building was scheduled for demolition. He found a new base on Boulevard Raspail, also in Montparnasse. The few known photographs show another neo-plastic interior design. It was around this time, however, that the Nazi threat grew steadily more acute in Europe, and artists in Paris began to feel increasingly unsafe. An exhibition of 'Degenerate Art' organized by the Nazis was a sign of things to come. Held in several German cities in 1937, it included work by Mondrian. His friends Ben and Winifred Nicholson — British artists who were married but living separately in Paris — urged Mondrian to come with them to a relatively safe London, while his American friend, colleague and admirer Harry Holtzman even offered to set him up in New York. As much as Mondrian loved the French capital, he had to get away before the Nazis turned up at the gates of Paris. So it was at the end of September 1938 that he travelled to London with Winifred Nicholson and her children.

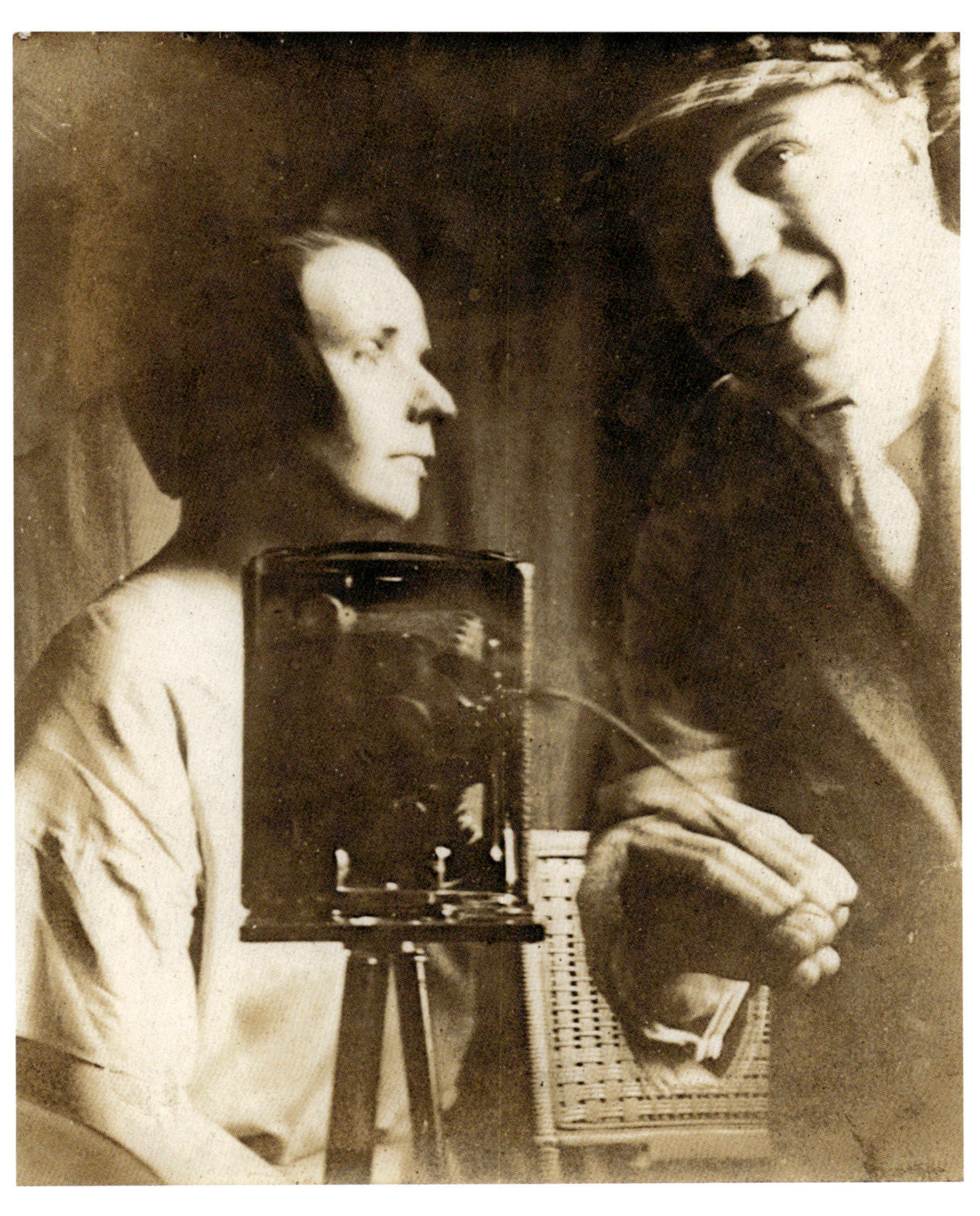

CAT. 52 **Theo van Doesburg**

Self-portrait of Theo and Nelly van Doesburg in Piet Mondrian's studio, between 28 March and 9 April 1921

This is the only photograph known to have been taken in Mondrian's studio at 5 Rue de Coulmiers, where the artist lived from 1 November 1919 to 21 October 1921.

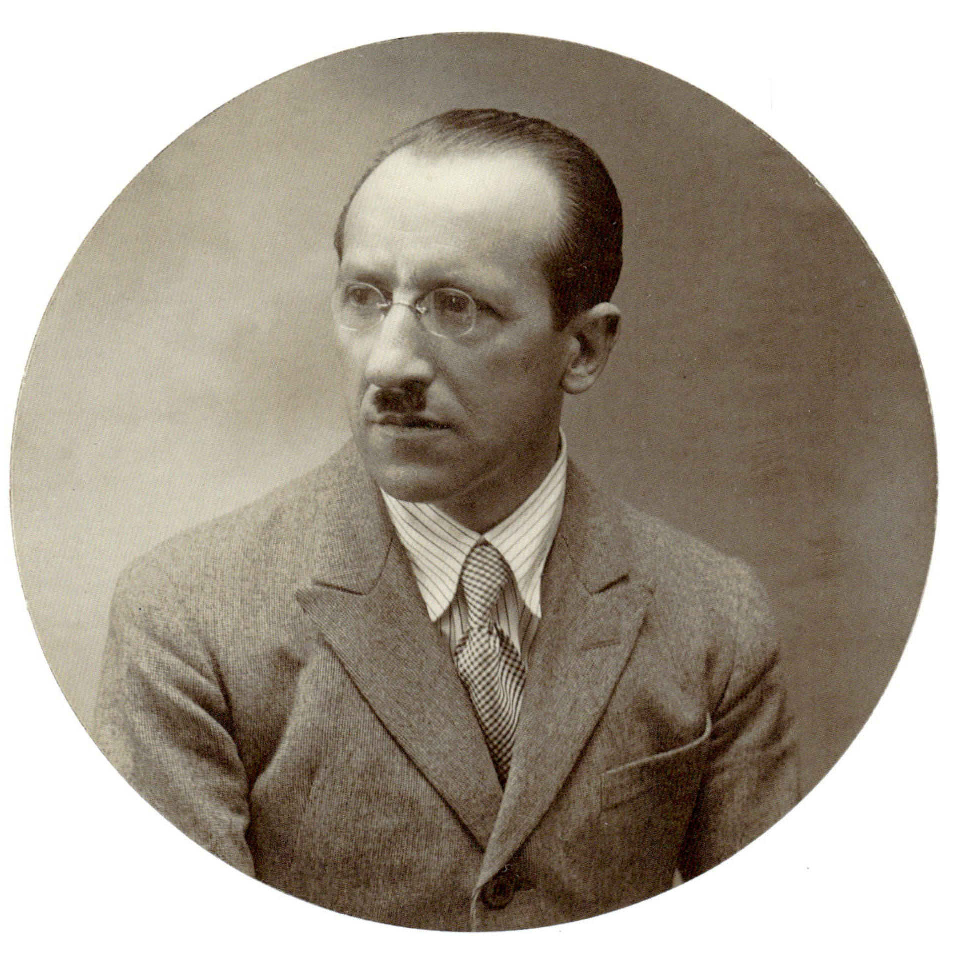

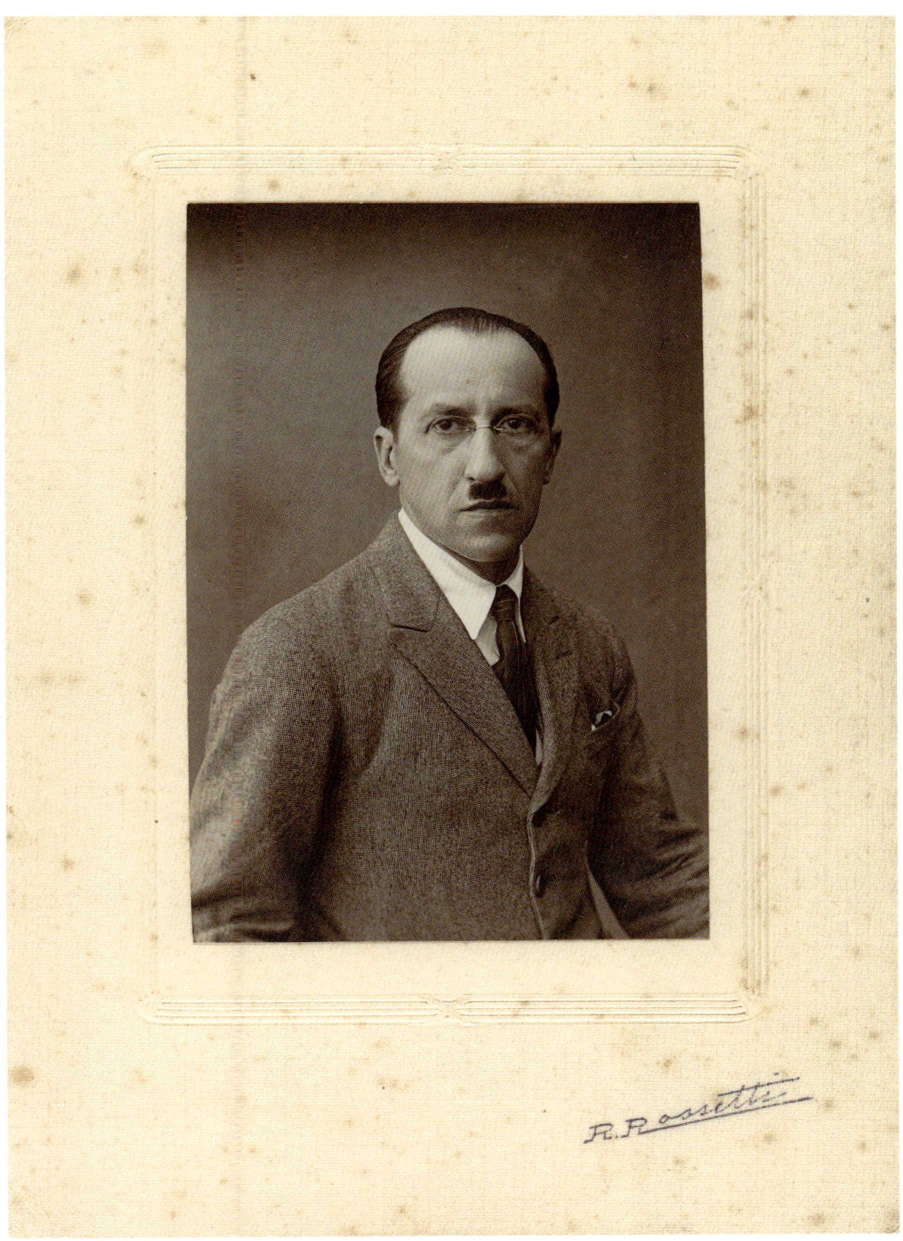

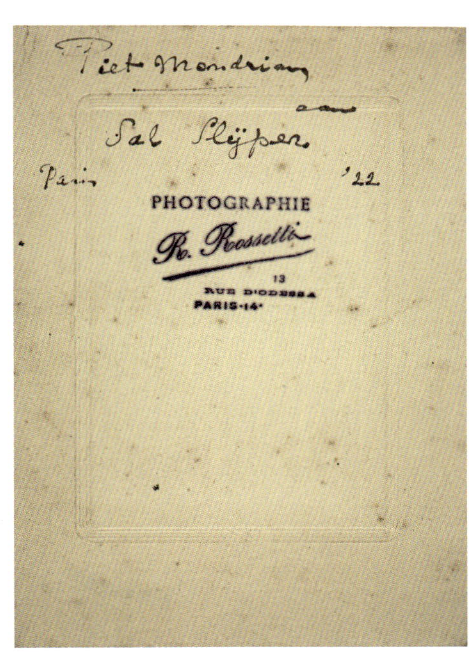

CAT. 53 **Unidentified photographer**
Portrait of Piet Mondrian, c. 1922

CAT. 54 recto/verso **Photographie R. Rossetti**
Portrait of Piet Mondrian, summer (June?) 1922
Around March 1922, Theo van Doesburg asked in a letter for a portrait photograph of Mondrian for use later that year in the anniversary issue of *De Stijl*. Mondrian might have had this portrait taken in response.

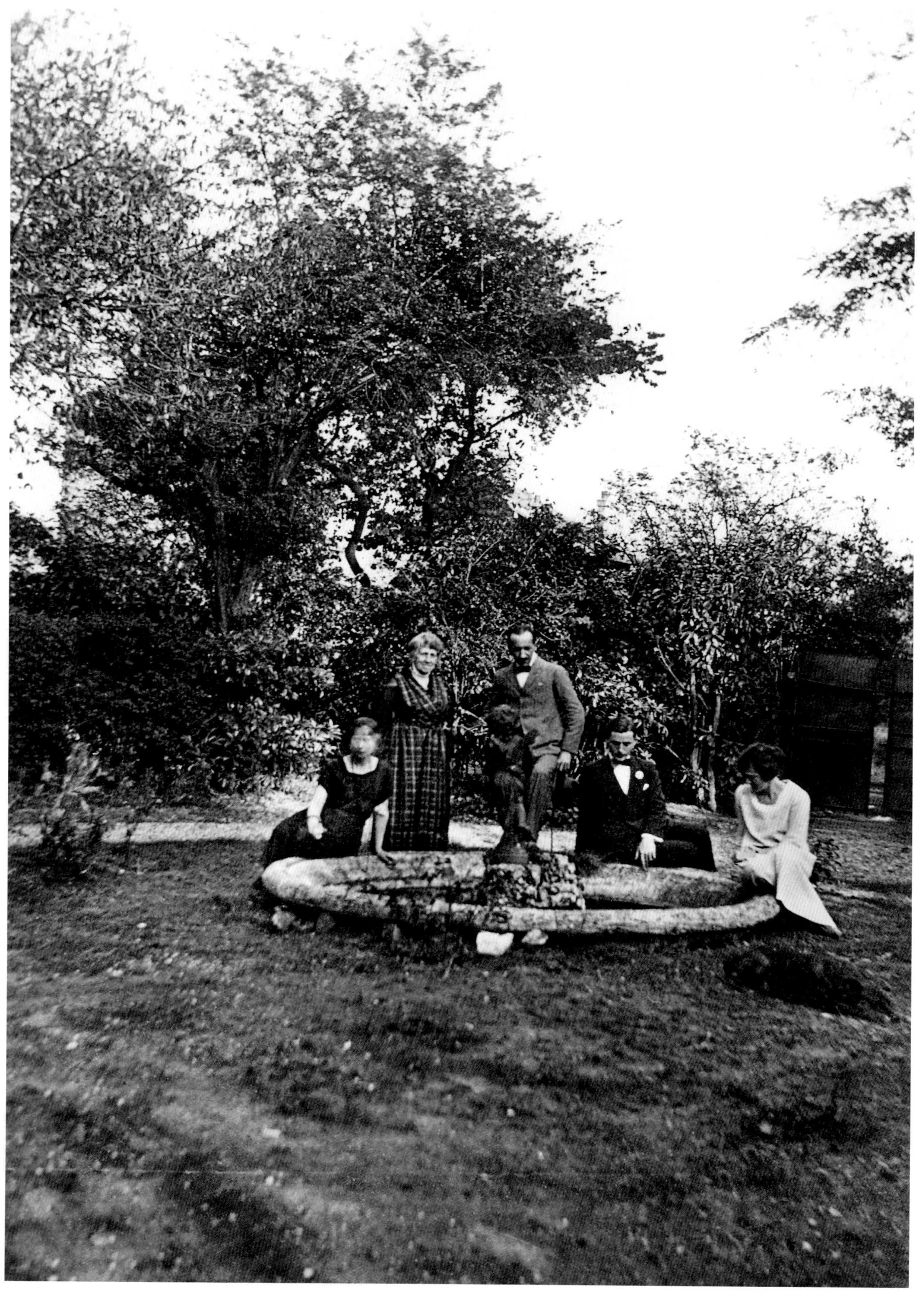

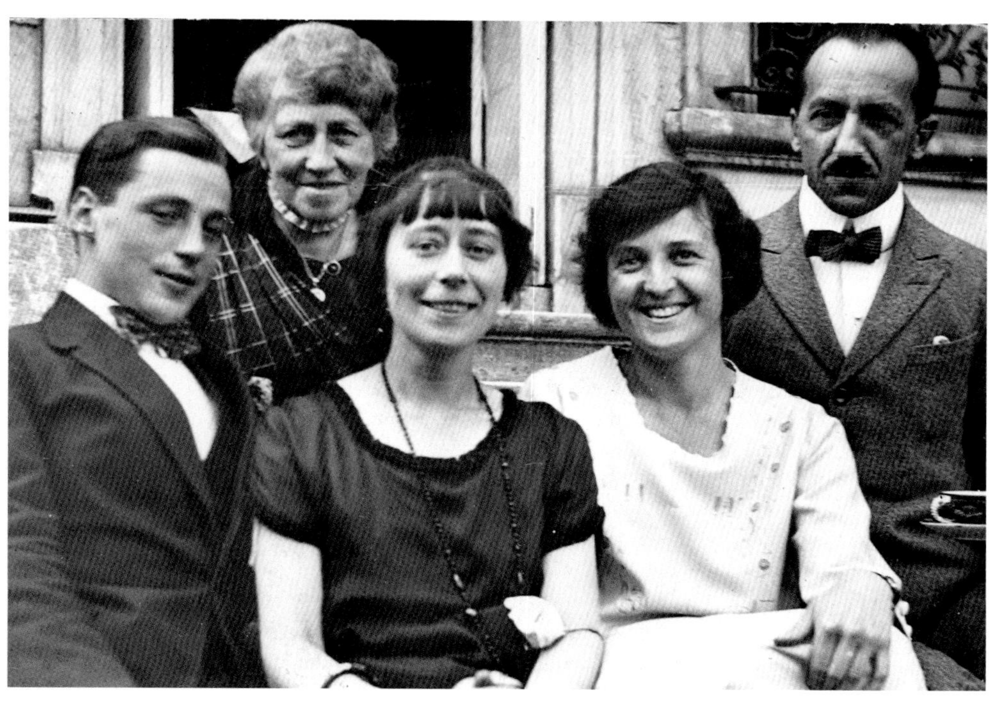

CAT. 55 **Unidentified photographer**
Company in the Colin-Penning family's garden, summer 1922
Left to right: Marinus Ritsema van Eck, Dina Penning-Elemans, two unidentified women, Piet Mondrian.
Mondrian was in contact with Raymond Colin and Marie Colin-Penning from the beginning of his time in Paris. Around 1922, the couple rented a villa in the Parisian suburb of Clamart, where they held Sunday afternoon dance parties.

< CAT. 56 **Unidentified photographer**
Company in the Colin-Penning family's garden, summer 1922
Left to right: unidentified woman, Dina Penning-Elemans, Piet Mondrian, Marinus Ritsema van Eck and unidentified woman.

CAT. 57 See catalogue

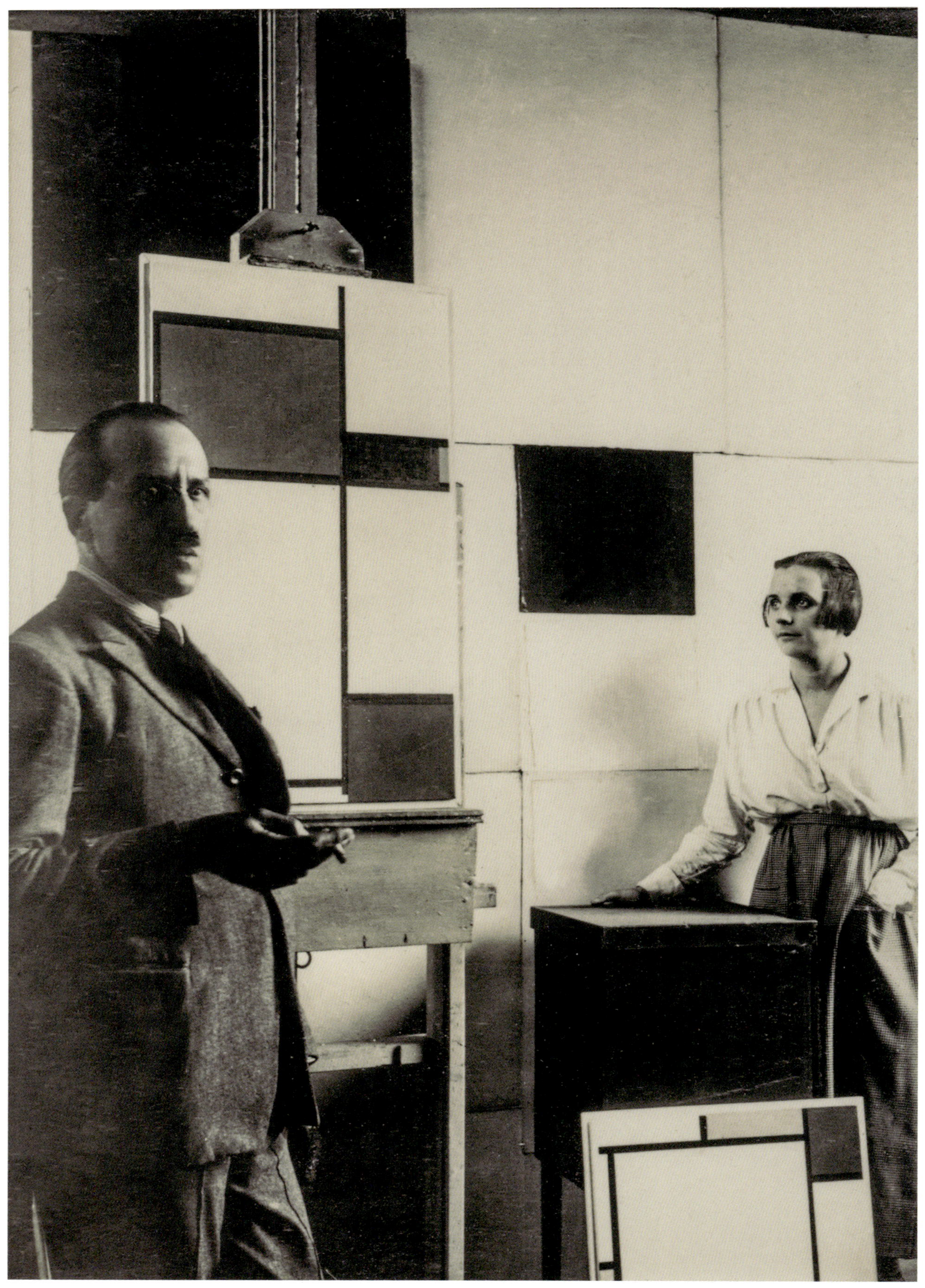

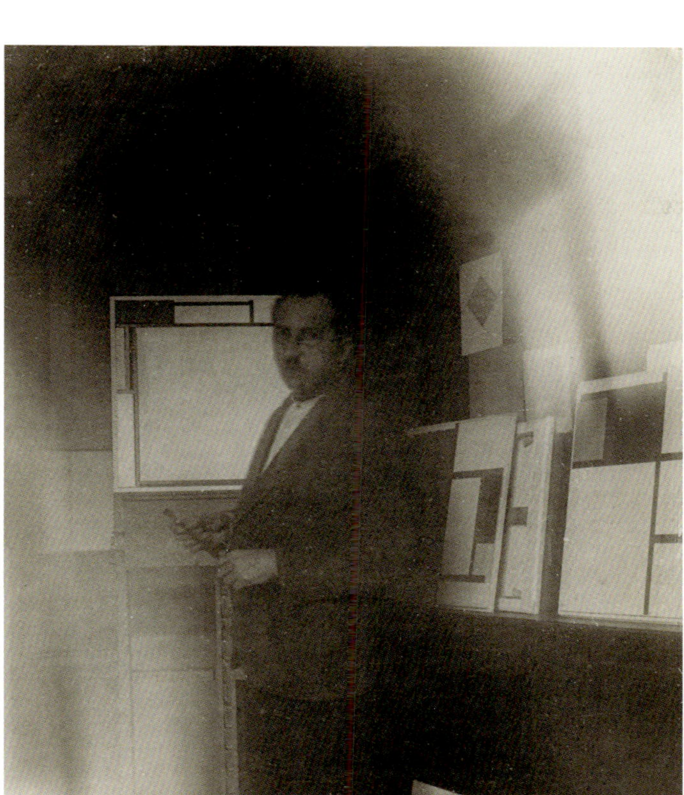

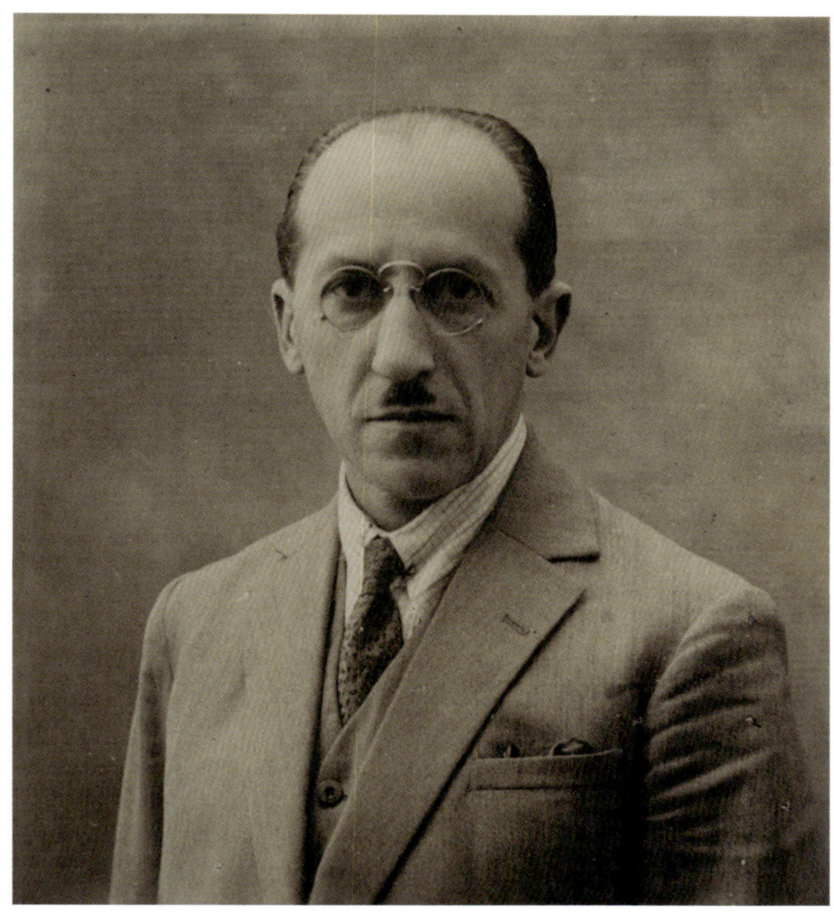

CAT. 58 **Theo van Doesburg**
Piet Mondrian and Nelly van Doesburg in Mondrian's studio, early May 1923

CAT. 59 **César Domela**
Piet Mondrian in his studio, December 1923
To the right of Mondrian's head hangs Supplement XIX of *De Stijl*, vol. 2, no. 10 (August 1919): a reproduction of the artist's *Composition with Grid 5: Lozenge Composition with Colours* (B99, 1919).

CAT. 60 **Unidentified photographer**
Portrait of Piet Mondrian, c. 1924 (?)

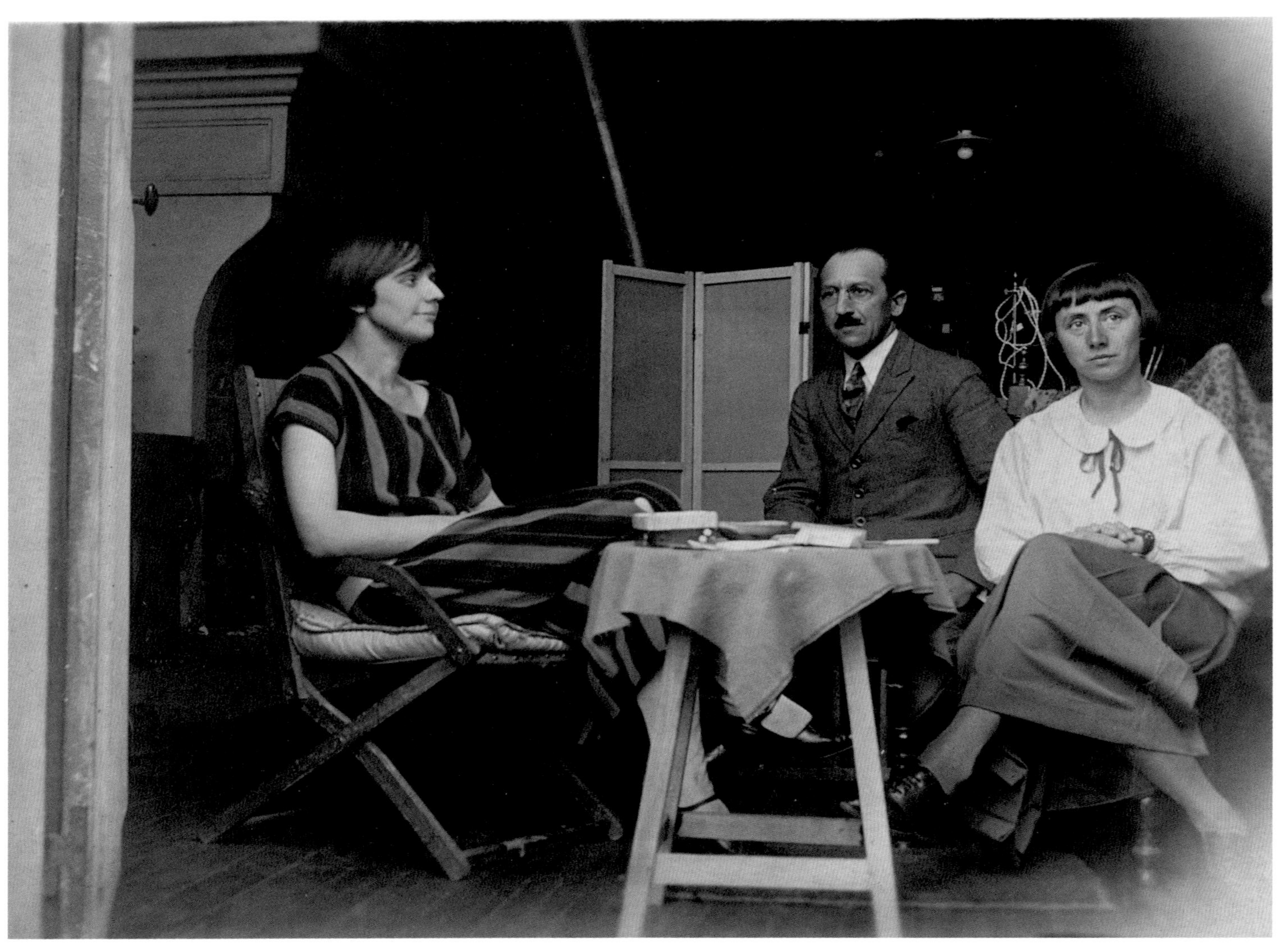

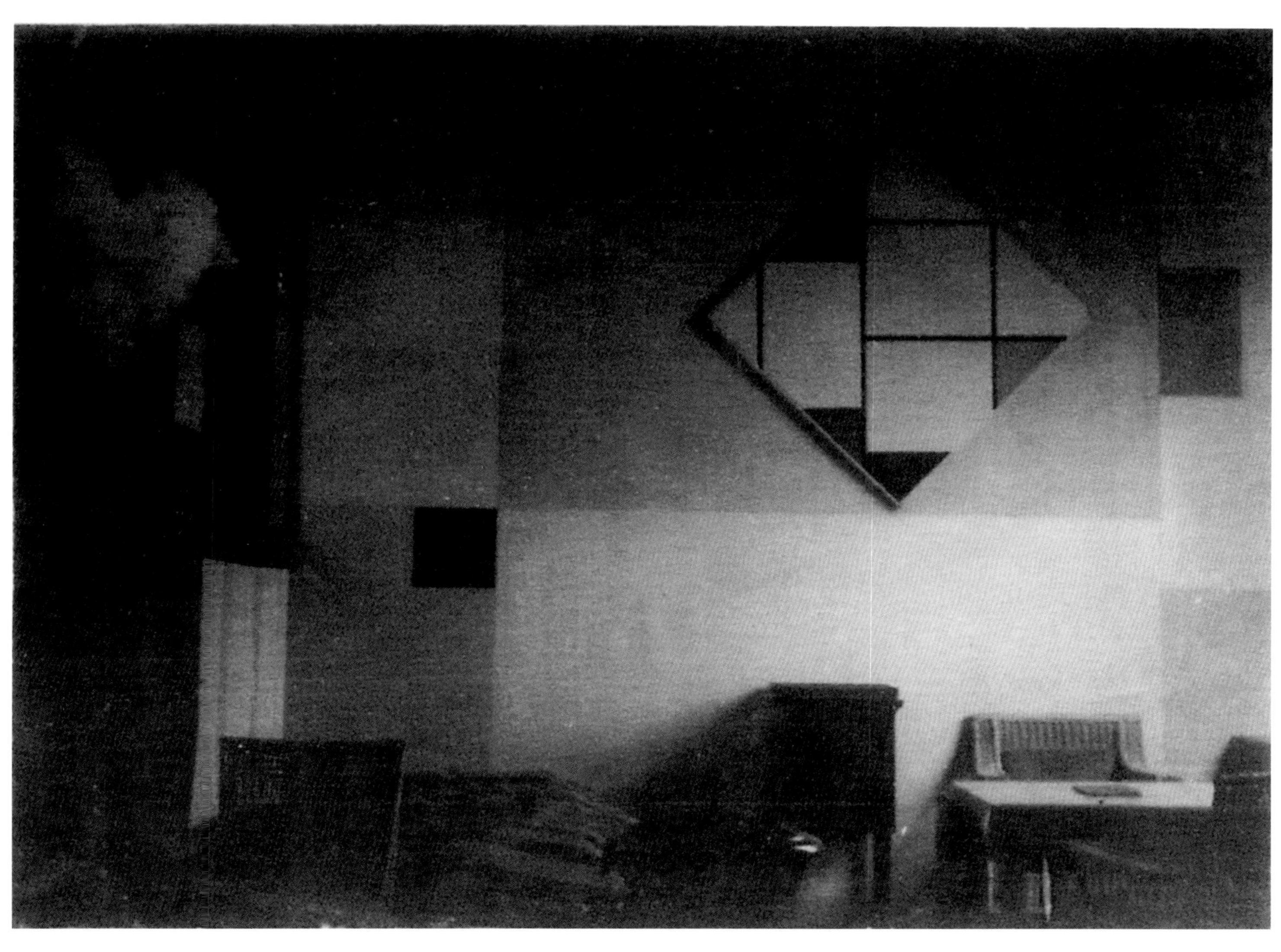

CAT. 61 **Theo van Doesburg**
Nelly van Doesburg, Piet Mondrian and the German artist Hannah Höch in the Van Doesburgs' studio, 27 April 1924
Theo and Nelly van Doesburg had a studio at 64 Avenue Adolphe Schneider in Clamart.

CAT. 62 **Georges Vantongerloo**
Piet Mondrian's studio, July—August 1924

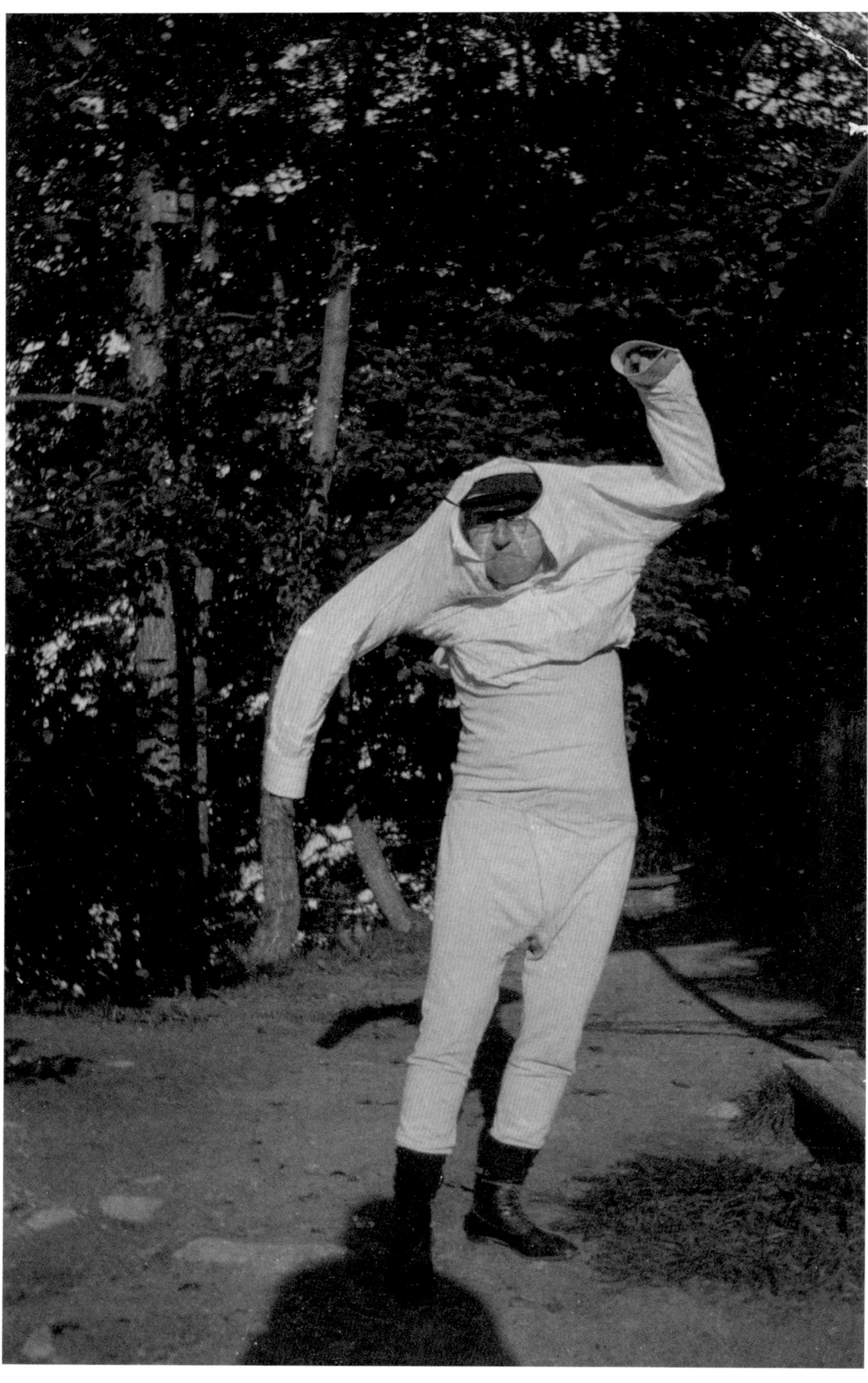

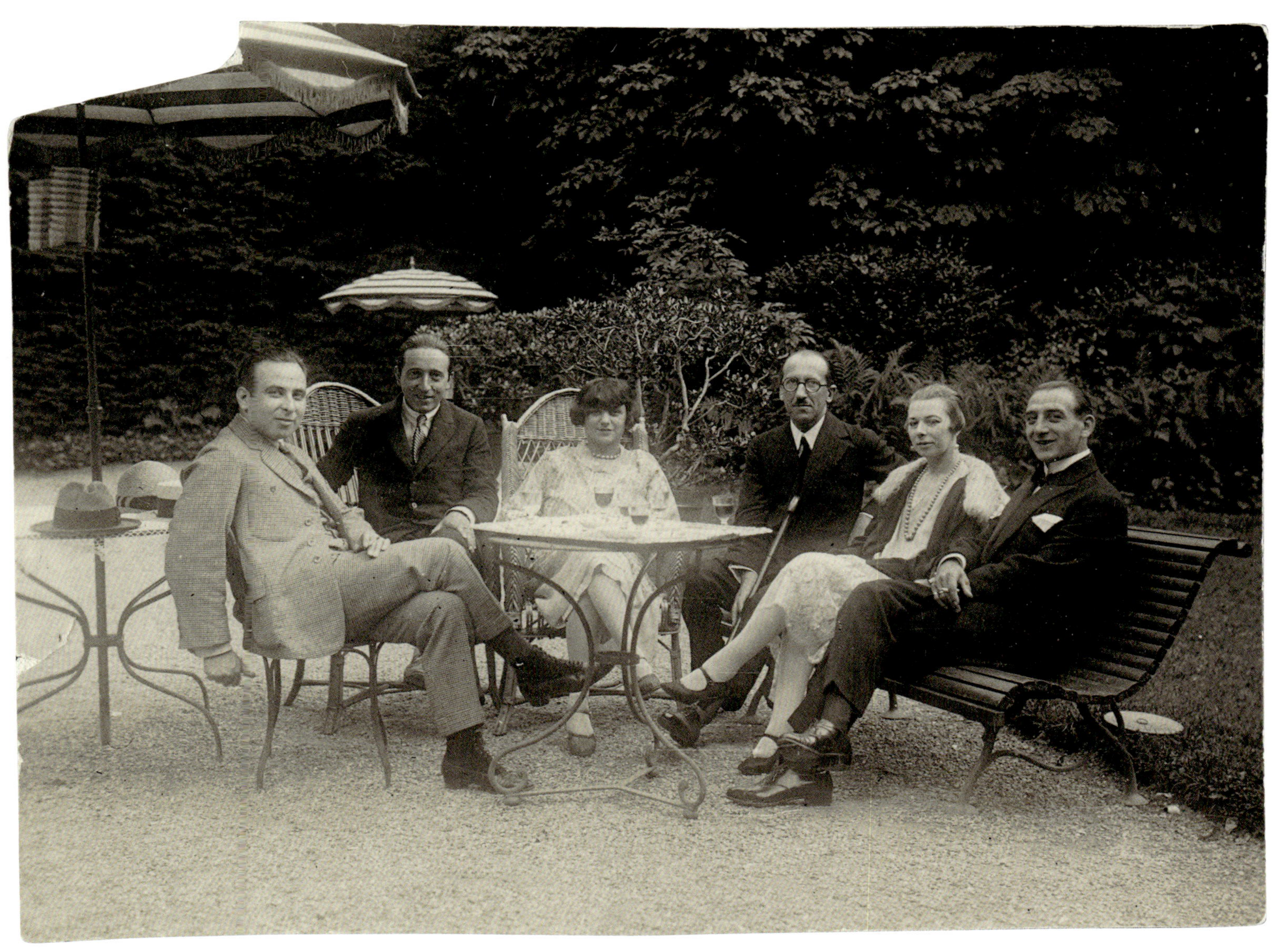

CAT. 63 **Agatha Zethraeus**
Piet Mondrian in Agatha Zethraeus's garden, Clamart, c. 1925

CAT. 64 **Liesbeth Sanders-Herzberg**
Mondrian and friends in a garden in Saint-Germain-en-Laye, 15 July 1925
Left to right: Paul Sanders, Jacques Tas and Frieda Tas-Herzberg, Piet Mondrian, Tine and Georges Vantongerloo. The photograph was taken during a visit to Paris by the sisters Frieda and Liesbeth Herzberg and their husbands Jacques Tas and Paul Florus Sanders. Mondrian also visited the Exposition des Arts Décoratifs with the Sanders and Vantongerloos, as seen in cats 65–6.

CATS 65–6 See catalogue

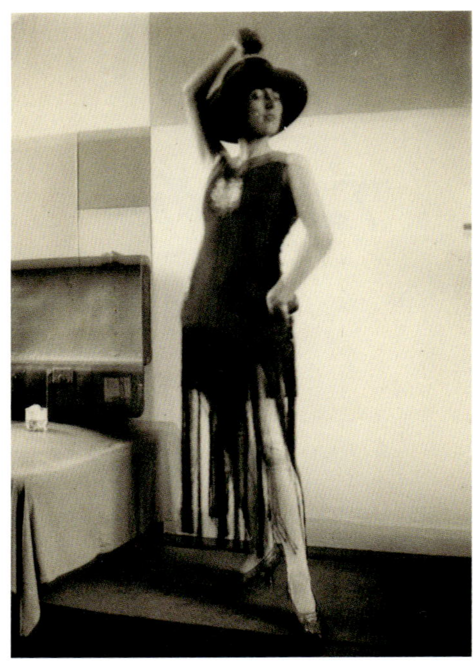
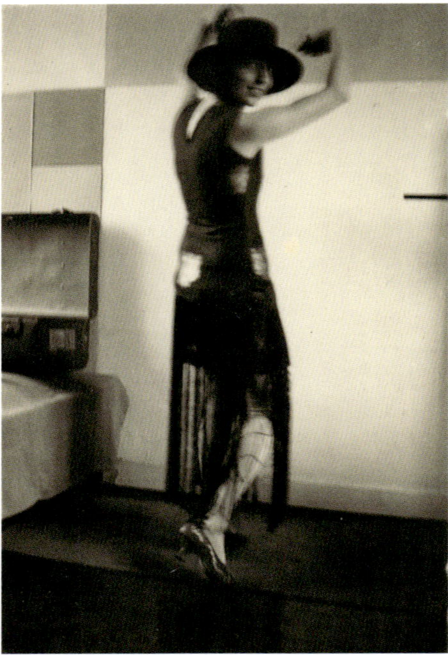
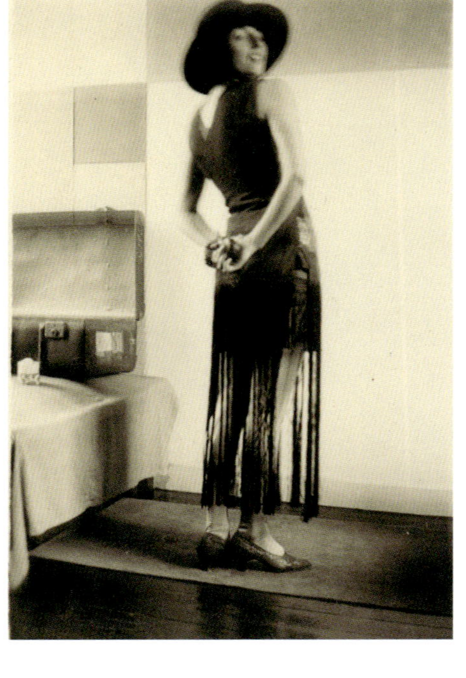
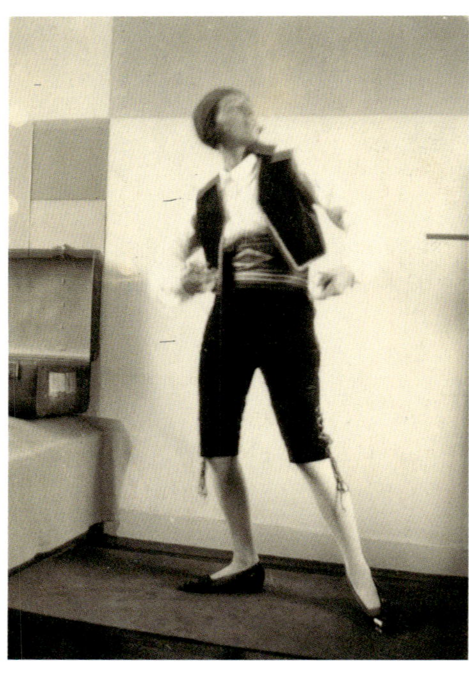
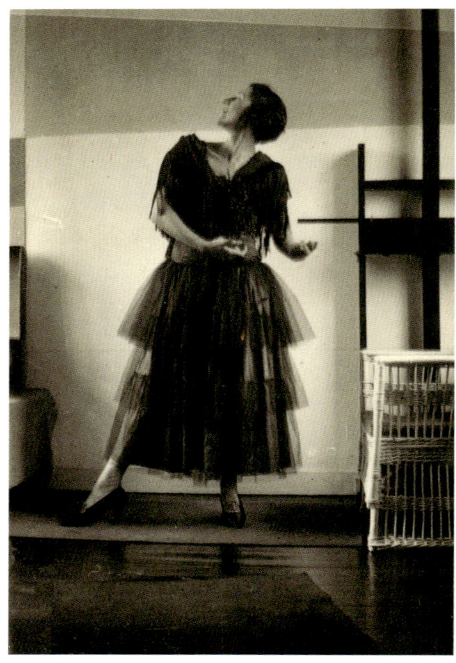
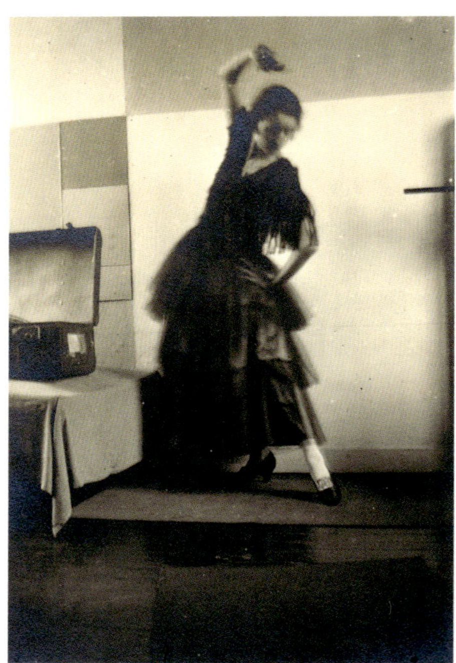

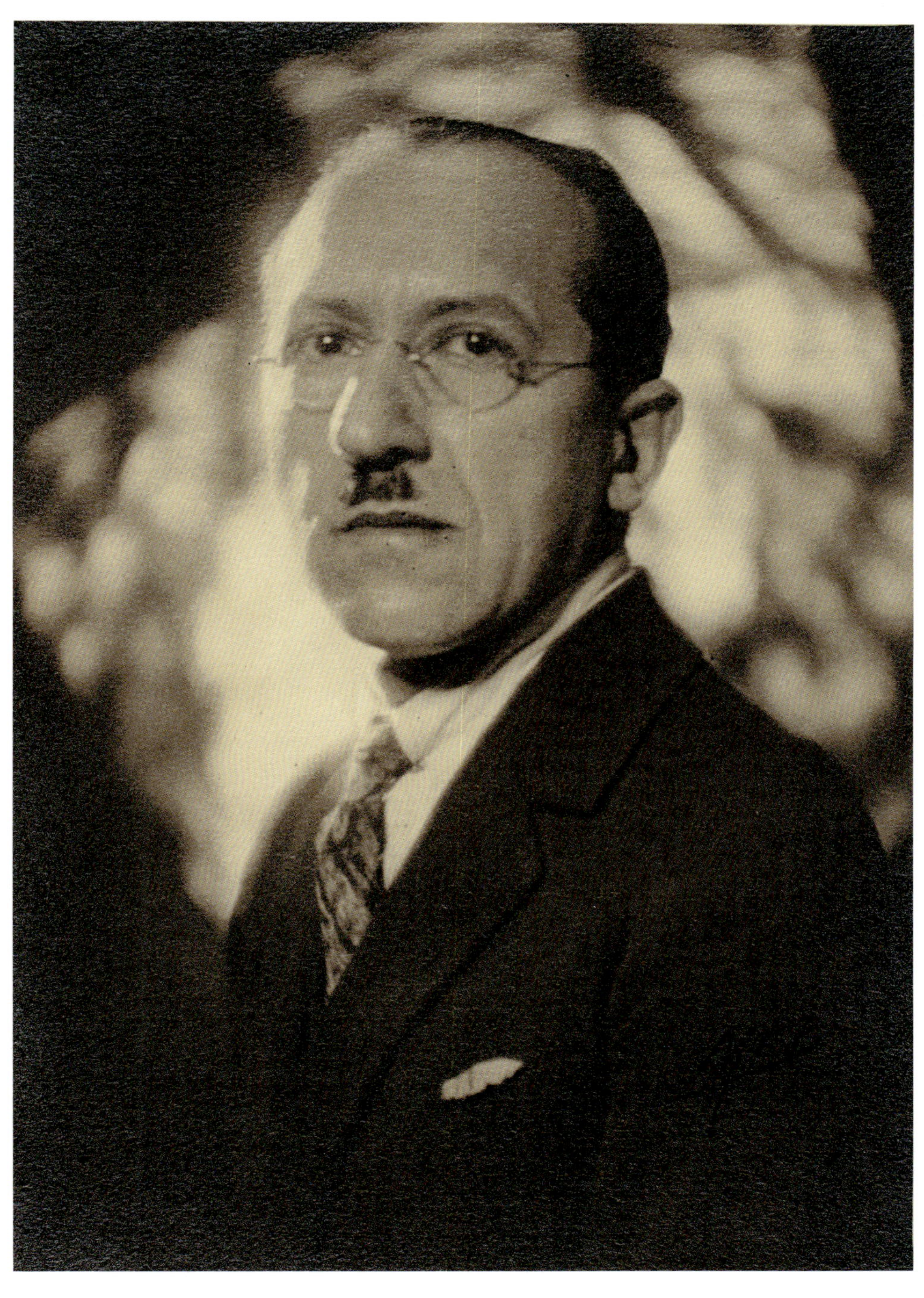

CATS 67–72 **Unidentified photographer (César Domela?)**

The dancer Kamares (Willy van Aggelen) in Piet Mondrian's studio, late December 1925

The Dutch dancer Wilhelmina van Aggelen, whose stage names included 'Kamares' and 'Taï Aagen (Taïta) Moro', was invited by Mondrian's friend and colleague César Domela to pose, costumed, in Mondrian's studio.

CAT. 73 **Max Winisky**

Portrait of Piet Mondrian, c. 1926

Pierre Delbo

CATS 74—6

The Parisian photographer Pierre Delbo took a series of iconic pictures of Mondrian's studio on the Rue du Départ sometime between November 1925 and the spring of 1926. The fame of his photographs contrasts sharply with what little is known about Delbo's life. Not even his name is certain: he is customarily referred to in the Mondrian literature as Paul, whereas contemporary sources — including the lists of names in *Photo-Annuaire* — exclusively call him Pierre. Where 'Paul' came from is unclear: it appears to be a mistake that was then repeated in subsequent publications. We have therefore assumed that the photographer who shot Mondrian's studio was actually named Pierre Delbo.

What we do know is that Delbo had a photography studio at 9 Rue Vavin in Paris.[1] Mondrian visited the street regularly, as the company run by Lucien Lefebvre-Foinet, Mondrian's regular delivery service and supplier of painting materials, was located at number 19.[2] Surviving advertisements suggest that Delbo targeted clients from artistic circles, no doubt reflecting the fact that numerous artists kept studios in the Montparnasse district. In the spring of 1926, several Paris exhibition catalogues contained ads for the firm 'Pierre Delbo', which promised a 'Fast service for photographing paintings, sculptures, drawings and all documents'.[3]

'P. Delbo' was listed as an exhibitor in February 1926 at a major photographic exhibition in Paris.[4] Details of Delbo's work are, sadly, also scarce. He provided the reproductions in 1925 for a catalogue of watercolours by Paul Klee, and in the same period he photographed a series of dolls by the Russian artist Marie Vassilieff, who worked in Paris.[5] Delbo appears to have developed or reproduced photographs for Man Ray around 1930.[6]

In late October 1925, Mondrian was visited by the Swiss architect and critic Hannes Meyer, on the recommendation of J. J. P. Oud.[7] It has generally been assumed that it was Meyer who asked Mondrian for a picture of his studio, prompting the artist to hire Delbo.[8] No evidence has been found to support this claim, however, aside from the fact that Meyer was the first to publish one of Delbo's studio photographs. If it was indeed Meyer who requested a photo from Mondrian, the pictures might have been intended for publication in the architecture magazine *ABC: Beiträge zum Bauen*, the May issue of which he was preparing. Mondrian wrote to Oud on 26 December: 'H. Meyer is going to write about the new painting in his A.B.C., or at least to include some photographs.'[9] In the same issue, Mondrian himself published an article titled 'Die Malerei und ihre praktische "Realisierung"' (Painting and Its Practical 'Realization'), in which he discussed the relationship between art and architecture.[10] Rather than Delbo's studio photos, however, the piece was accompanied by reproductions of two paintings (B161, B165). Meyer then published the picture of the studio (cat. 74) two months later in the magazine *Das Werk*.[11]

We can tell that Mondrian was pleased with Delbo's photo of the rear wall from the fact that he sent copies to friends, including Sal Slijper, César Domela and Albert van den Briel. The photograph was used in 1927 to illustrate Mondrian's article 'Neo-Plasticisme. De Woning — De Straat — De Stad' (Neo-plasticism. Home — Street — City) in the Dutch magazine *i10*.[12] The other two studio photographs taken by Delbo must also have circulated within Mondrian's circle. Cat. 76, for instance, was reproduced in the Dutch newspaper *De Telegraaf* in September 1926 and in *Der Querschnitt* in February 1928.[13] The latter magazine was supported (and initially published) by Wilhelm Graf Kielmansegg, an admirer and collector of Mondrian's work. The studio photographs taken by Delbo have since been reproduced dozens of times in studies on Mondrian and De Stijl. But while his pictures became iconic, the photographer himself has been largely forgotten.

1 The back of the surviving original prints of the studio photograph taken by Delbo (cat. 74) is stamped with a name (P. Delbo) and address.
2 Coppes 2010, p. 154. The Lefebvre-Foinet building was located on a corner, with entrances at both 19 Rue Vavin and 2 Rue Bréa.
3 Société 1926-1 and Société 1926-2.
4 Anonymous 1926, p. 31. It is not known which of Delbo's photographs featured in the exhibition.
5 Klee 1925; for Vassilieff, see https://www.das-verborgenemuseum.de/exhibits/exhibit/women-artists-in-dialogue-en, accessed 12 April 2022.
6 University of Buffalo, James Joyce Collection, XVII.9.6: Man Ray, *Portrait of Giorgio and Helen Fleischman Joyce*, Paris, c. 1930. Inscriptions: recto, in typescript: 'Copyright by Man Ray, Paris'; embossed printing: 'P. Delbo, 9 Rue Vavin, Paris'; verso, stamp: 'P. Delbo, 9 Rue Vavin, Paris'.
7 Droste/Opel 2019, pp. 120–21.
8 Welsh/Joosten 1998-II, p. 132; Wieczorek 2014, p. 63; Hanssen 2015, pp. 315–16.
9 Postcard from Piet Mondrian to J. J. P. Oud, Paris, 26 December 1925. Paris, Fondation Custodia, J. J. P. Oud archive.
10 Mondriaan 1926.
11 Meyer 1926, p. 209.
12 Mondriaan 1927.
13 See the relevant catalogue entry.

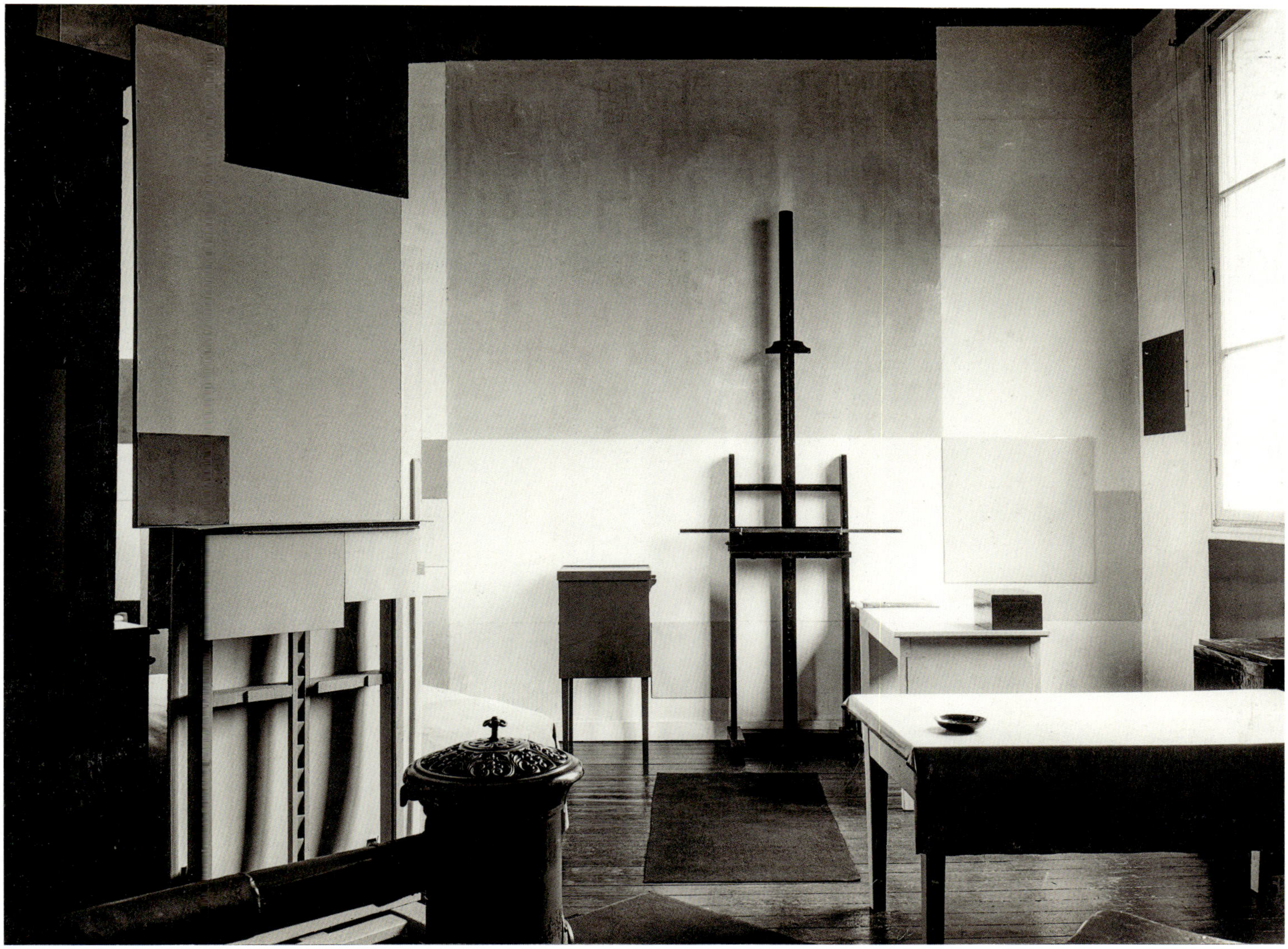

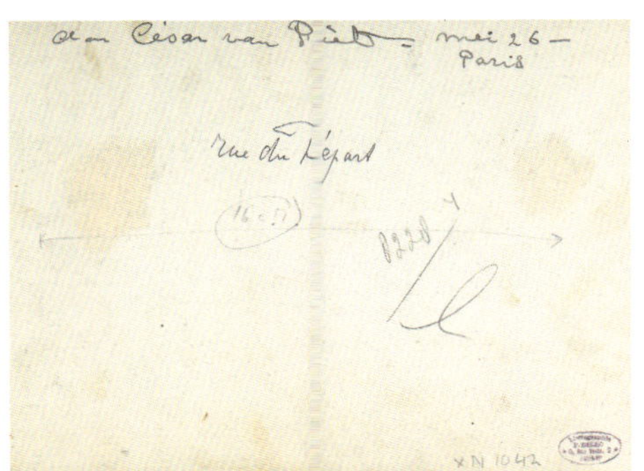

CAT. 74 recto/verso **Pierre Delbo**

Piet Mondrian's studio, c. late November 1925–March 1926

This photograph of Mondrian's studio was the first to be published. Together with Delbo's two other shots, it is among the best-known and most frequently reproduced pictures of Mondrian's neo-plastic interior.

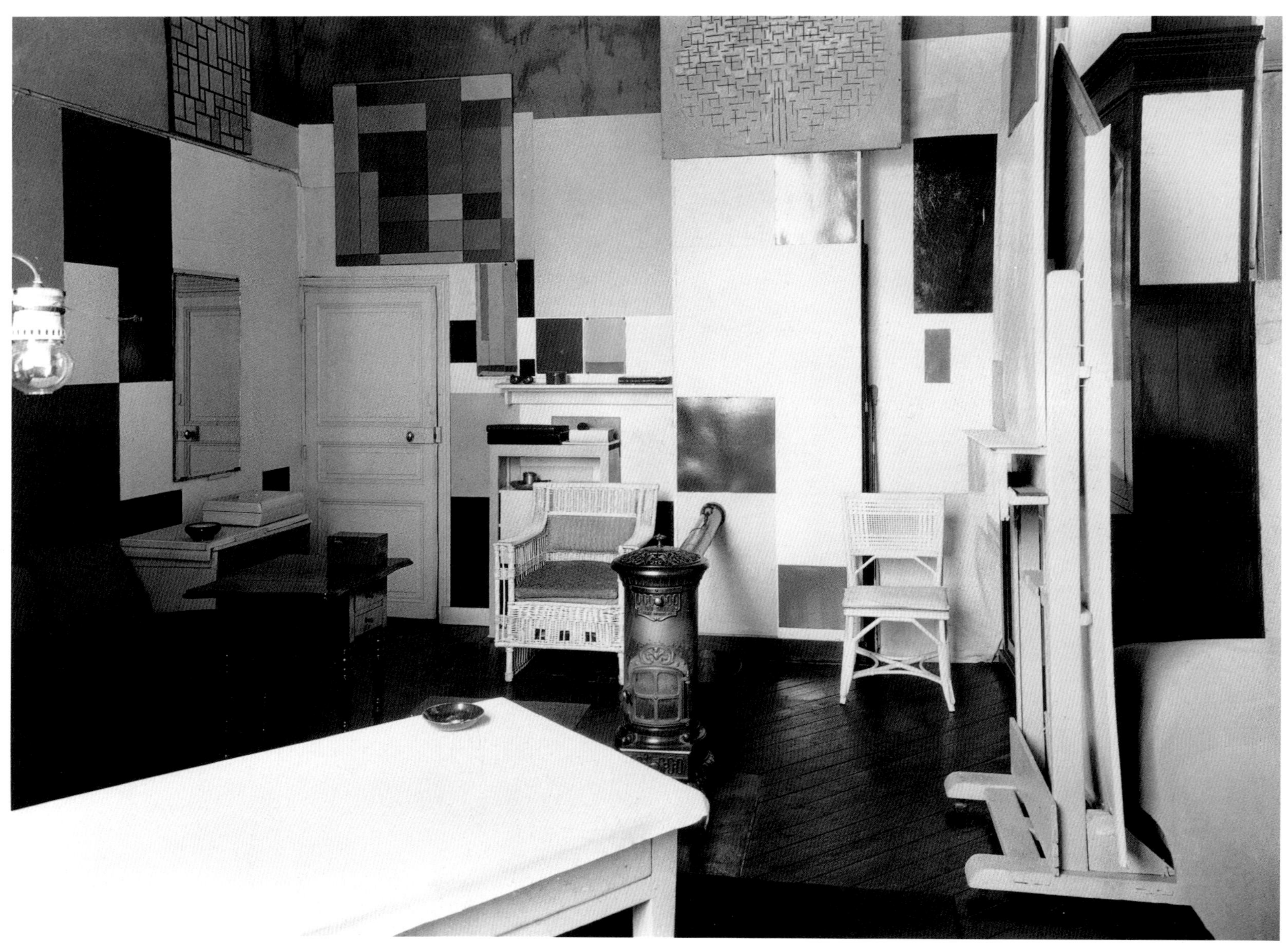

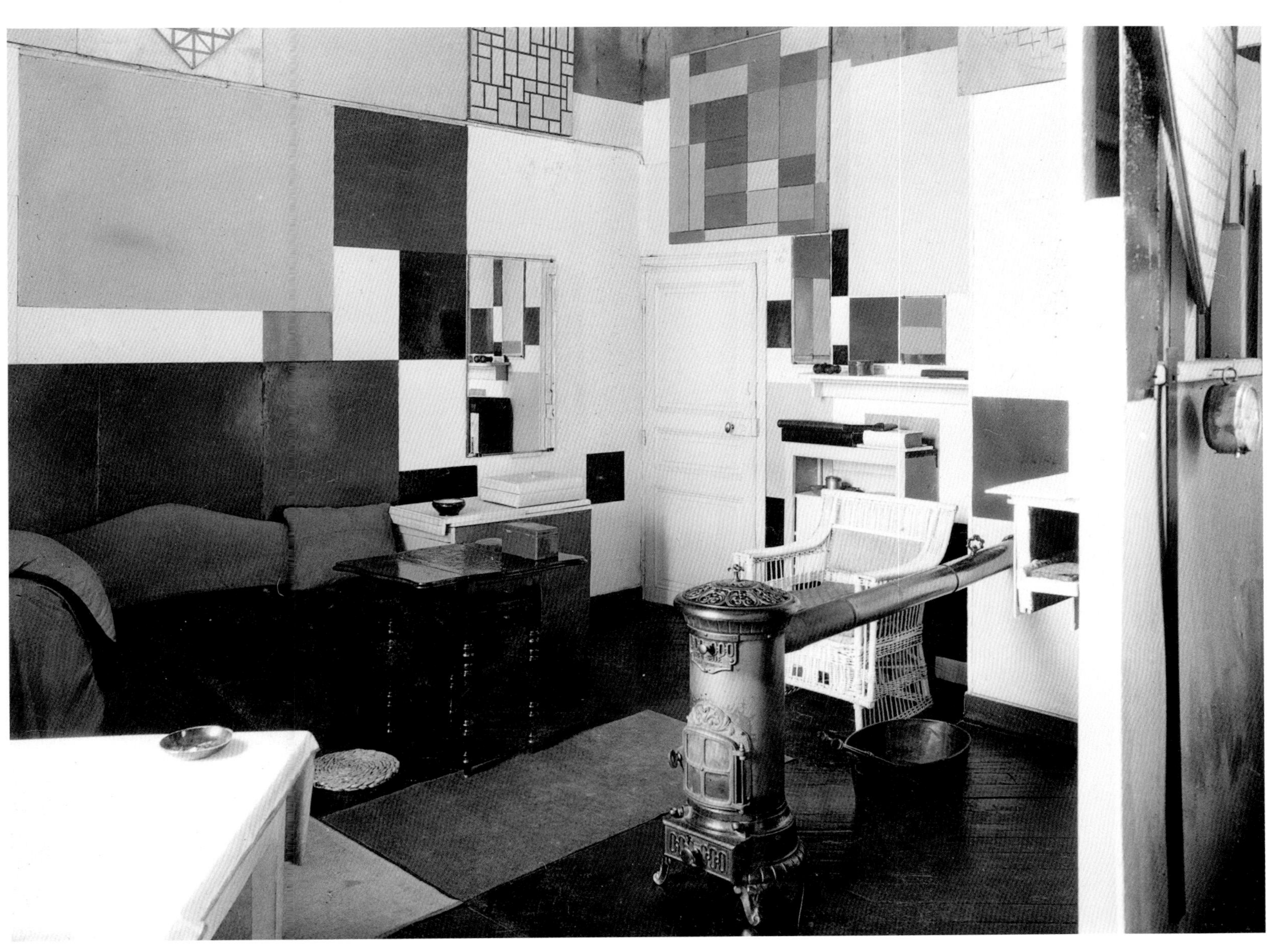

CATS 75–6 **Pierre Delbo**
Piet Mondrian's studio, c. late November 1925–March 1926

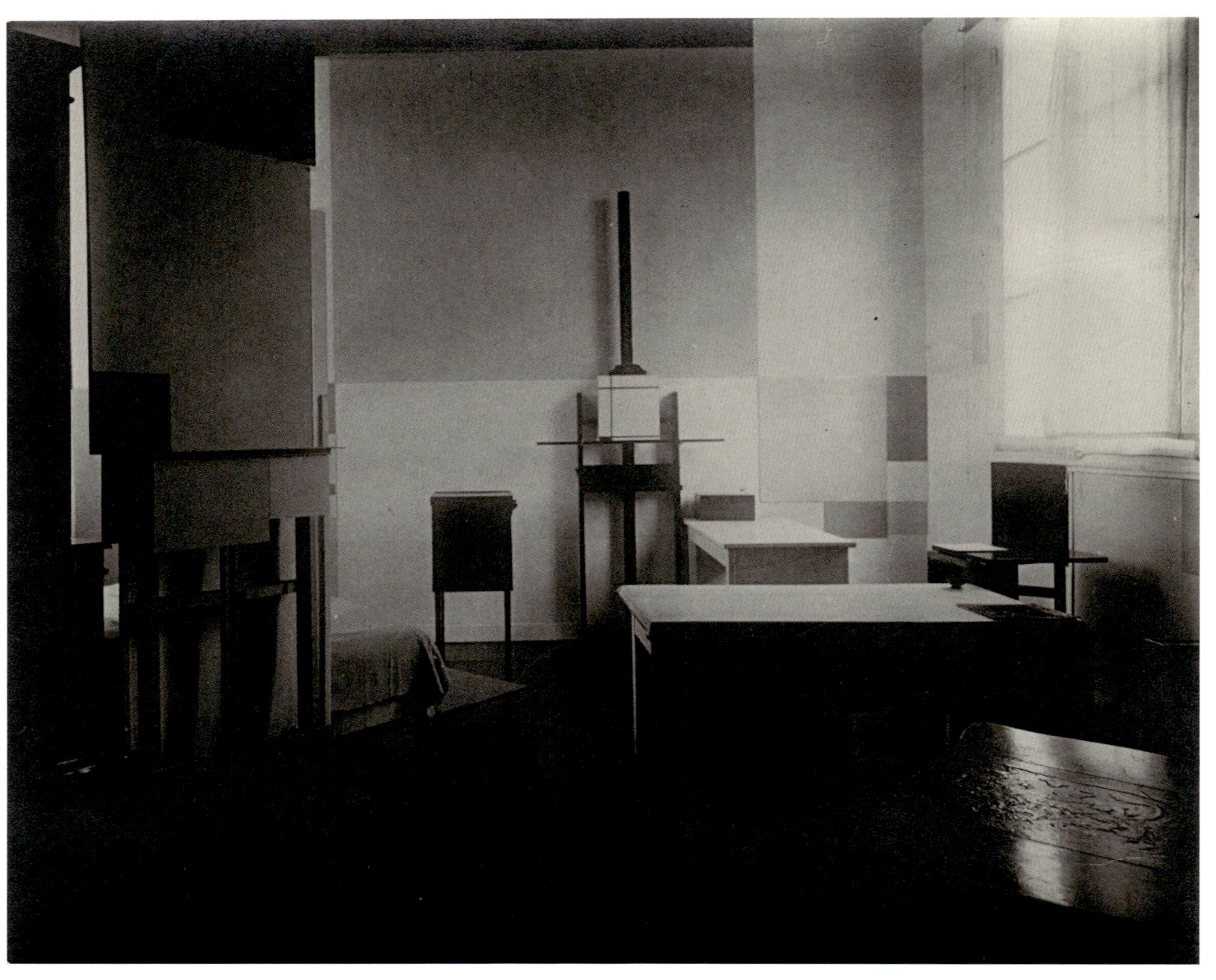

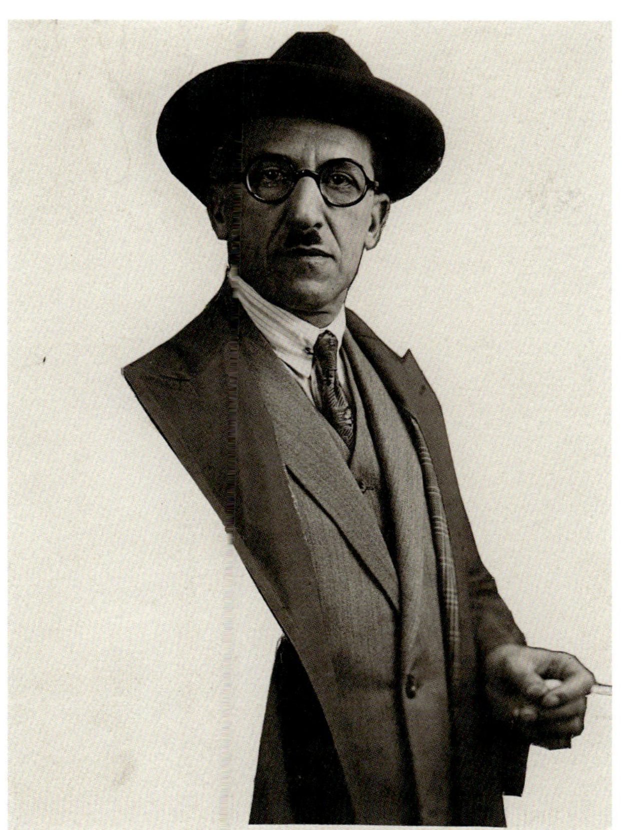

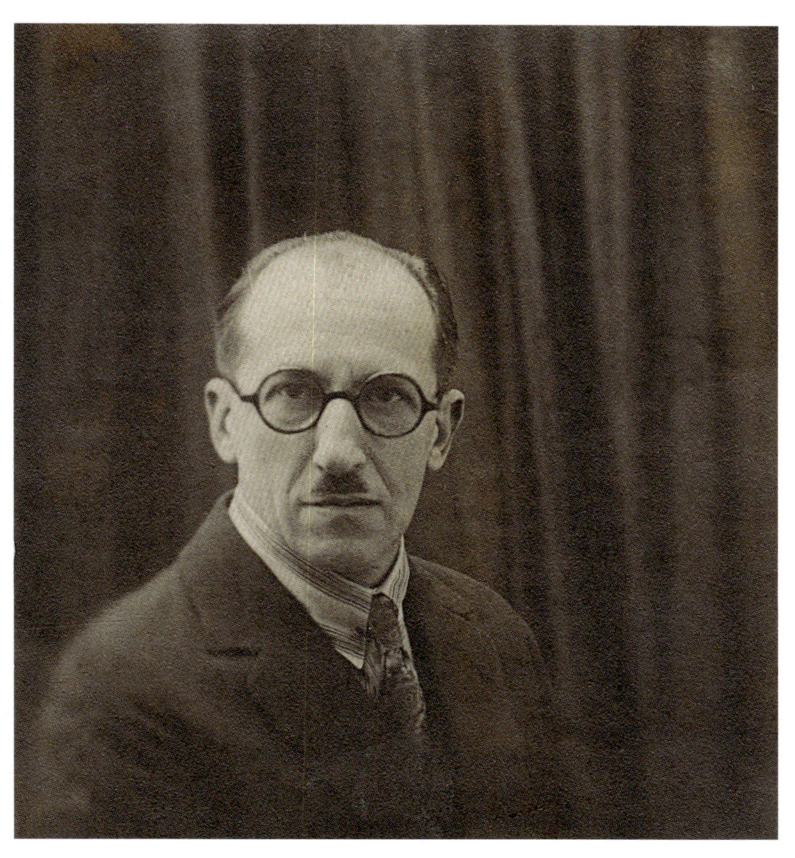

CAT. 77 **Unidentified photographer**
Piet Mondrian's studio, 7 April 1926
The photograph was taken during the visit to Mondrian's studio by Katherine S. Dreier. The American artist and collector wanted to borrow work for the 'International Exhibition of Modern Art', which she was organizing at the Brooklyn Museum, New York, from 19 November 1926.

CAT. 78 **Unidentified photographer**
Portrait of Piet Mondrian, c. September 1926

CAT. 79 **Unidentified photographer (Charles Karsten?)**
Portrait of Piet Mondrian, c. summer/autumn 1926

André Kertész

CATS 80—101

The work of the Hungarian photographer André Kertész (1894—1985) is world-famous. He began taking photographs in his native country after buying his first camera in 1912 from his earnings as an accountant at the stock exchange. Although he was self-taught, his special talent and keen eye for composition quickly became apparent. Kertész's early photographs include several that have become part of the collective photographic memory: *The Lovers (Budapest*, 1915), for instance, and *Underwater Swimmer* (Esztergom, 1917). He left Hungary in 1925 and settled in Paris, where he soon became part of the international artistic amalgam of the French capital. Kertész quickly made the acquaintance of several Central and Eastern European artists, whom he met at one of the many artists' cafés in Montparnasse. He came into contact through a mutual acquaintance with the Belgian Michel Seuphor, who took him to Mondrian's studio in August 1926.[1]

Several of the photographs that Kertész took of Mondrian and his studio in 1926—27 are among his best-known work and already featured in the first exhibition of his pictures held in Paris in March 1927.[2] Although Seuphor later claimed to have shown Kertész which corners of Mondrian's studio to shoot, it was ultimately the photographer himself who was responsible for famous pictures like *Chez Mondrian* (cat. 92) and *Nature morte (Les Lunettes et la pipe de Mondrian)* (cat. 93).[3]

Almost all the glass negatives of Kertész's photographs have been preserved and prints of a large number of them have likewise survived.[4] They reveal that he continued to make choices while printing — cropping an image more tightly, for instance. In some cases, he also finished off prints by retouching them.

The photographs in which Mondrian himself can be seen can be divided into two groups. First of all, there are photographs of Mondrian by himself, most of which may be viewed as portraits or portrait studies (cats 94—9). An example of a retouched portrait photograph is the print in the MoMA collection (cat. 94.2), in which Kertész accentuated the hairline and reduced the lines running from the nose to the mouth.[5] There are also photos of Mondrian with other people in his studio, indicating that it was a meeting place for avant-garde artists and literati. We see Mondrian in the company, for instance, of the German painters Julius Herburger and Willi Baumeister, the Belgian publicists Paul Dermée and Michel Seuphor, the Italian futurist artist Enrico Prampolini and the Hungarian painter Gyula Zilzer — a diverse international company that illustrates the variety of the Parisian art world. Mondrian did not just happen to be one of their number, he also acted as host by opening his studio to gatherings of various kinds. The fact that he received so many visitors meant that the status of his studio as an avant-garde topos rose sharply from the second half of the 1920s onwards. Word-of-mouth drew other artists and collectors who also wanted to take a look at the studio.

Kertész's photographs further contributed to the studio's status, featuring as they did in exhibitions and all kinds of publications. The previously mentioned *Chez Mondrian* and *Nature morte (Les Lunettes et la pipe de Mondrian)* in particular came to symbolize the artist's distinctive living space. The artificial white tulip by the studio entrance was at odds with the geometric-abstract paintings and seems at first glance to clash with the visitor's expectations. Yet Mondrian incorporated this element too in the overall composition of the studio. Kertész later recalled his first visit to Mondrian in the following terms: 'I went to his studio and instinctively tried to capture in my photographs the spirit of his paintings. He simplified, simplified, simplified. The studio with its symmetry dictated the composition. He had a vase with a flower, but the flower was artificial. It was coloured by him with the right colour to match the studio.'[6] *Nature morte* has exactly the simplified composition that Mondrian was aiming for in his paintings. An ashtray containing a pipe and two pairs of his spectacles are arranged in the corner of a table. The sharp lines and sober elements evoke a similar atmosphere to Mondrian's own abstractions, making this a portrait of the artist without his being physically present.

1 Phillips et al. 1985, p. 28.
2 The exhibition 'Photo-Kertész' ran from 12 to 24 March 1927 at the gallery Au Sacre du Printemps. Kertész's photographs were alternated with abstract-geometric compositions on paper by the artist Ida Thal (Borhan 1994, pp. 20—21).
3 De Mondenard 2010, p. 112.
4 Where a glass negative still exists, we have used them for our prints of Kertész's photographs, since the negatives almost invariably contain a larger image (and hence more information) than the prints taken from them.
5 Reinhold 2014, p. 6.
6 Kertész/Adam 1985, pp. 52—3.

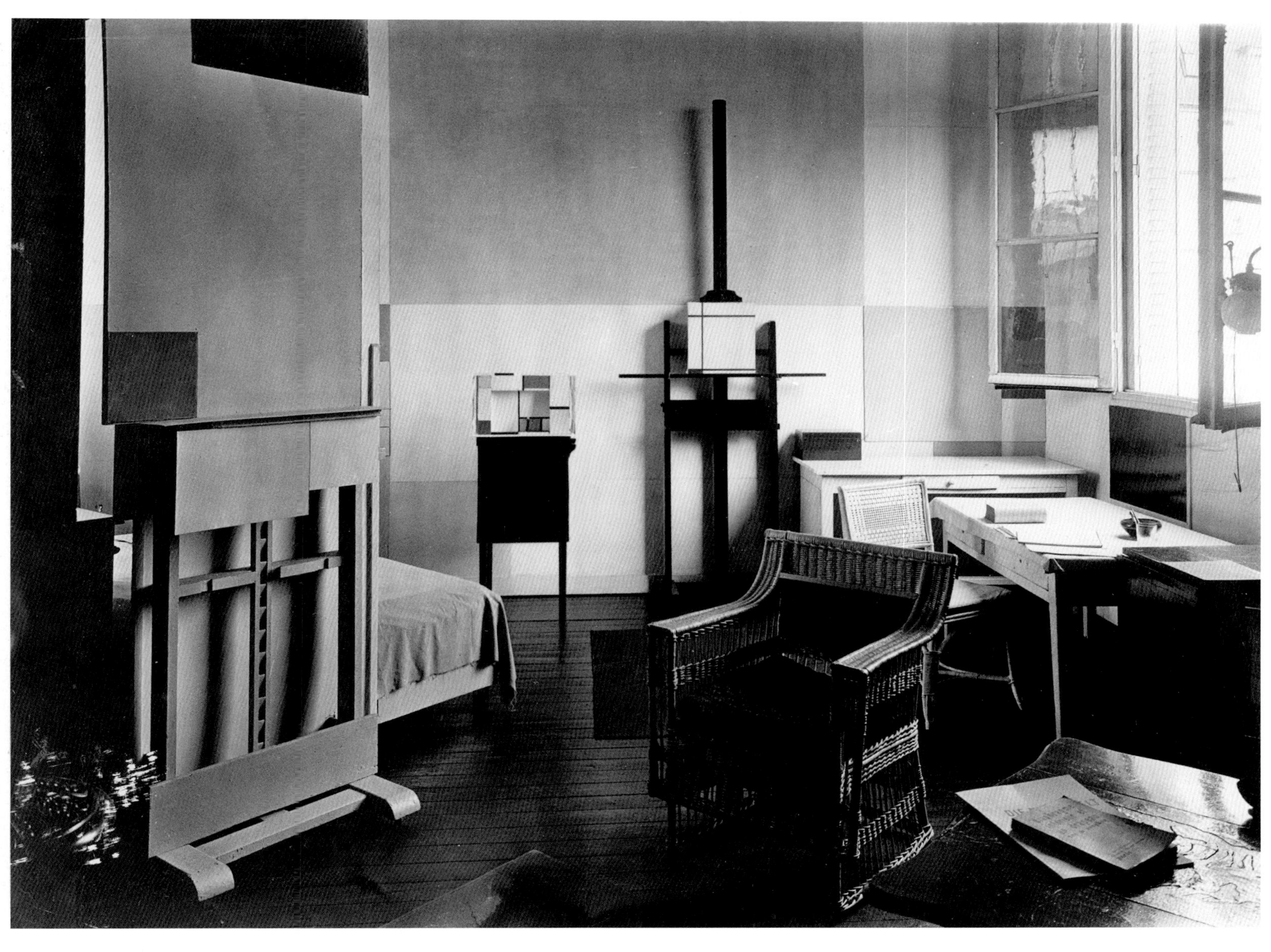

CAT. 80 **André Kertész**

Piet Mondrian's studio, 19 (?) August 1926

Michel Seuphor's poetry collection *Diaphragme intérieur et un drapeau* can be seen on the table in the right foreground. Below it is the July 1926 issue (presumably an offprint) of *Das Werk*, in which Hannes Meyer published his article 'Die neue Welt', as we read on the white cover, and in which Delbo's famous studio photo (cat. 74) was printed. This shot, too, by Kertész is one of the most famous studio photographs.

Mondrian's stage-set design, reproduced in cats 84–6 and 121, can be seen against the back wall on the left.

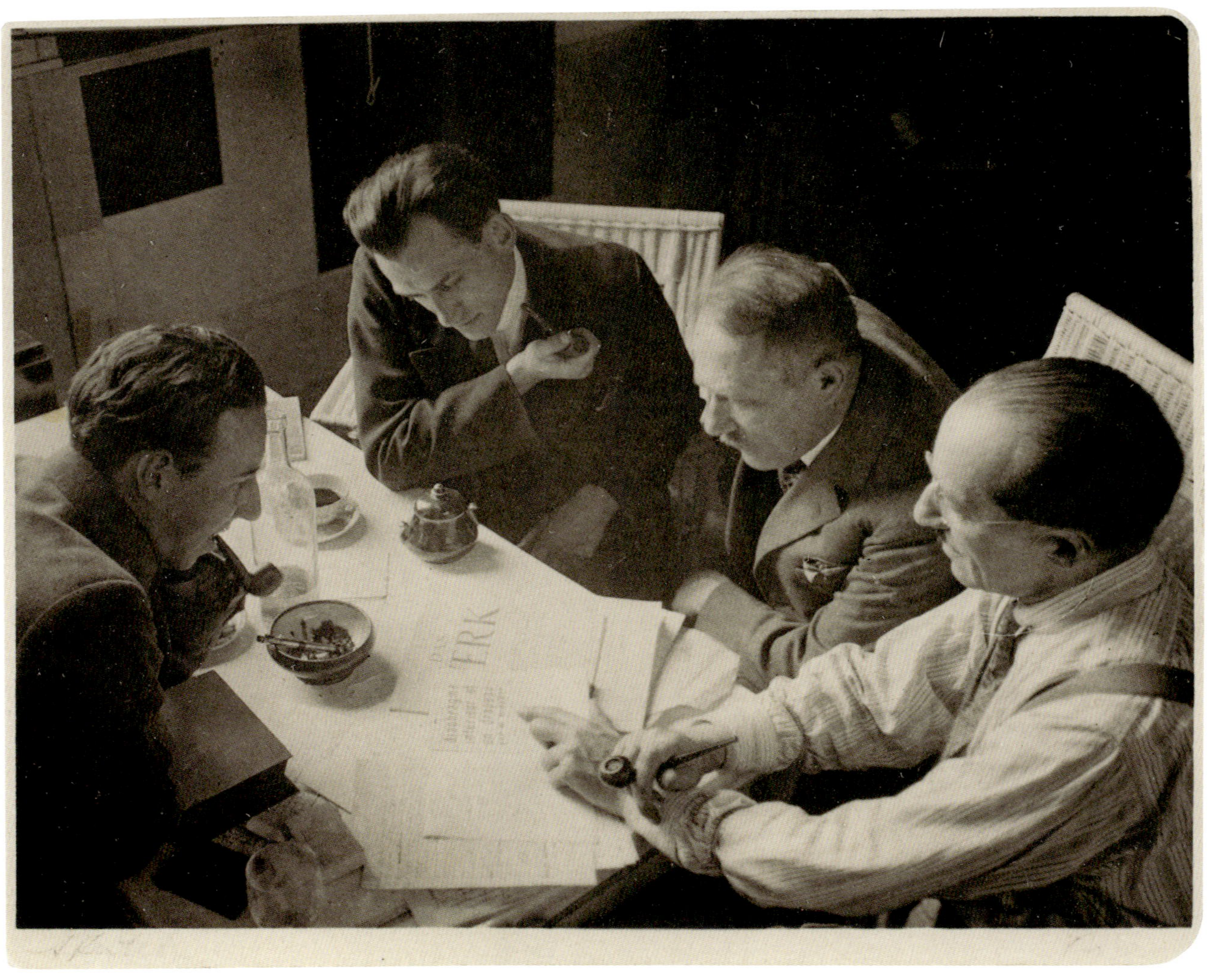

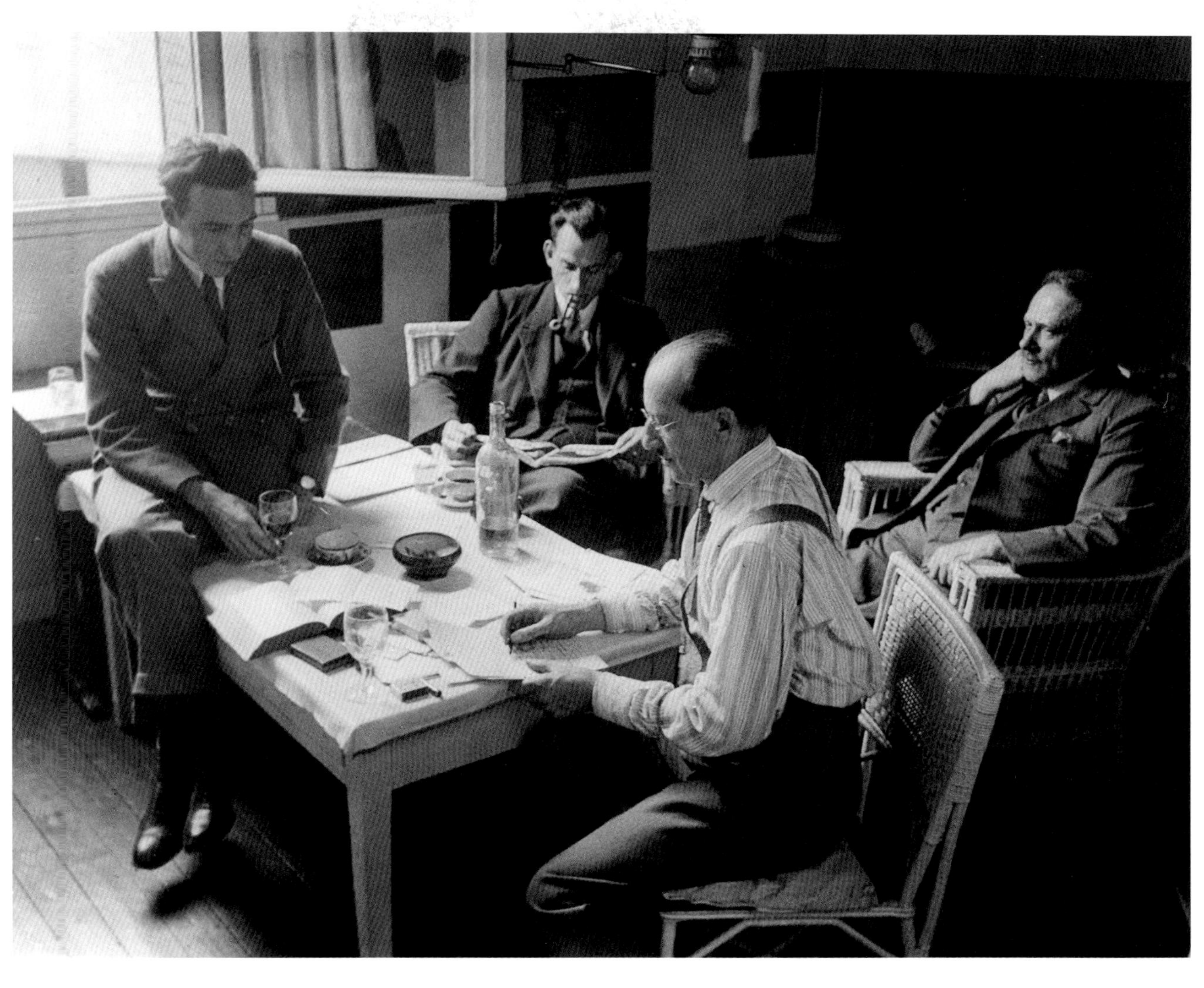

CATS 81–2 **André Kertész**
Michel Seuphor, Gyula Zilzer, unidentified man and Piet Mondrian in Mondrian's studio, 19 (?) August 1926

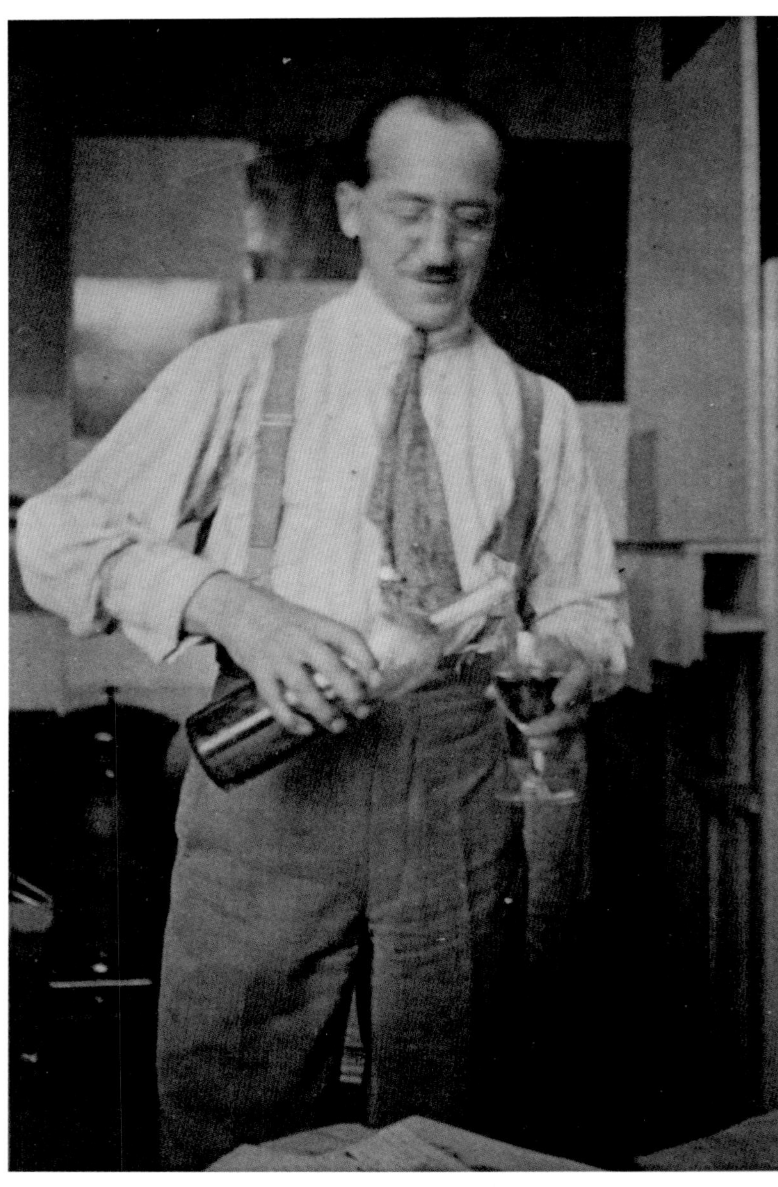

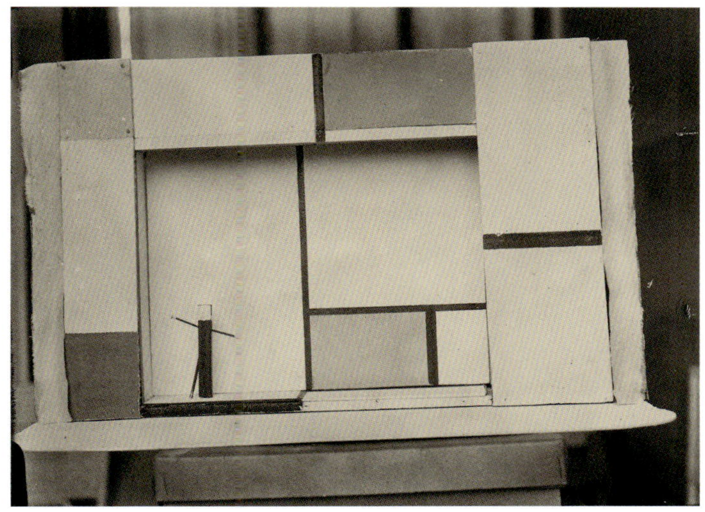

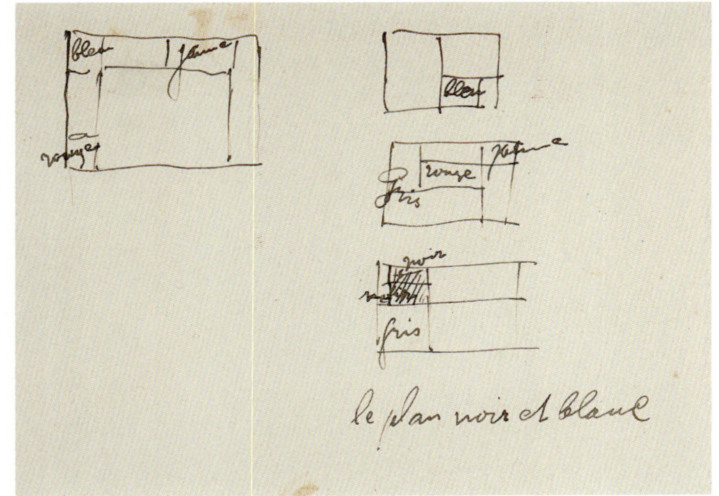

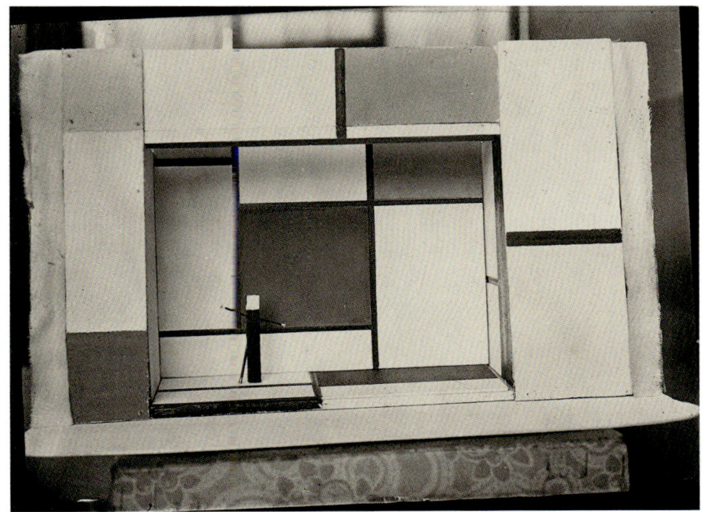

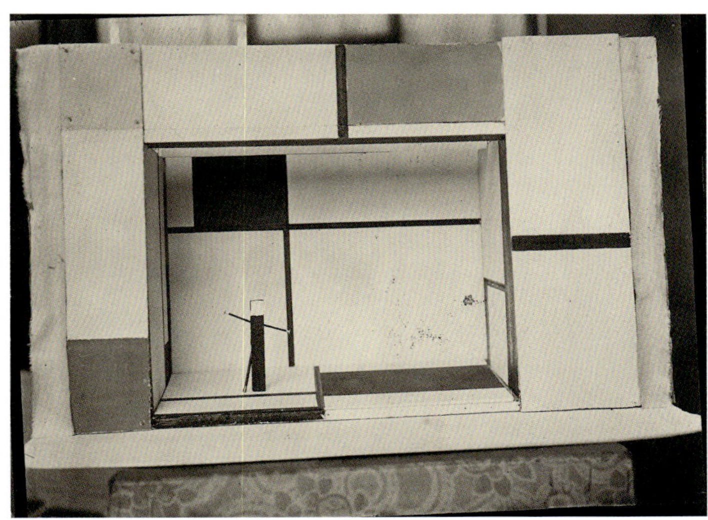

CAT. 83 **André Kertész**
Piet Mondrian, pouring wine, 19 (?) August 1926

CATS 84 recto/verso, 85–6 **André Kertész**
Model of Mondrian's stage design for Seuphor's play *L'Ephémère est éternel*, first act, between 19 August and 20 December 1926
Mondrian designed the set in a few days, after Seuphor let him read the text of the 'anti-theatre', three-act play *L'Ephémère est éternel*. Neither the set nor the play were staged in Mondrian's lifetime.

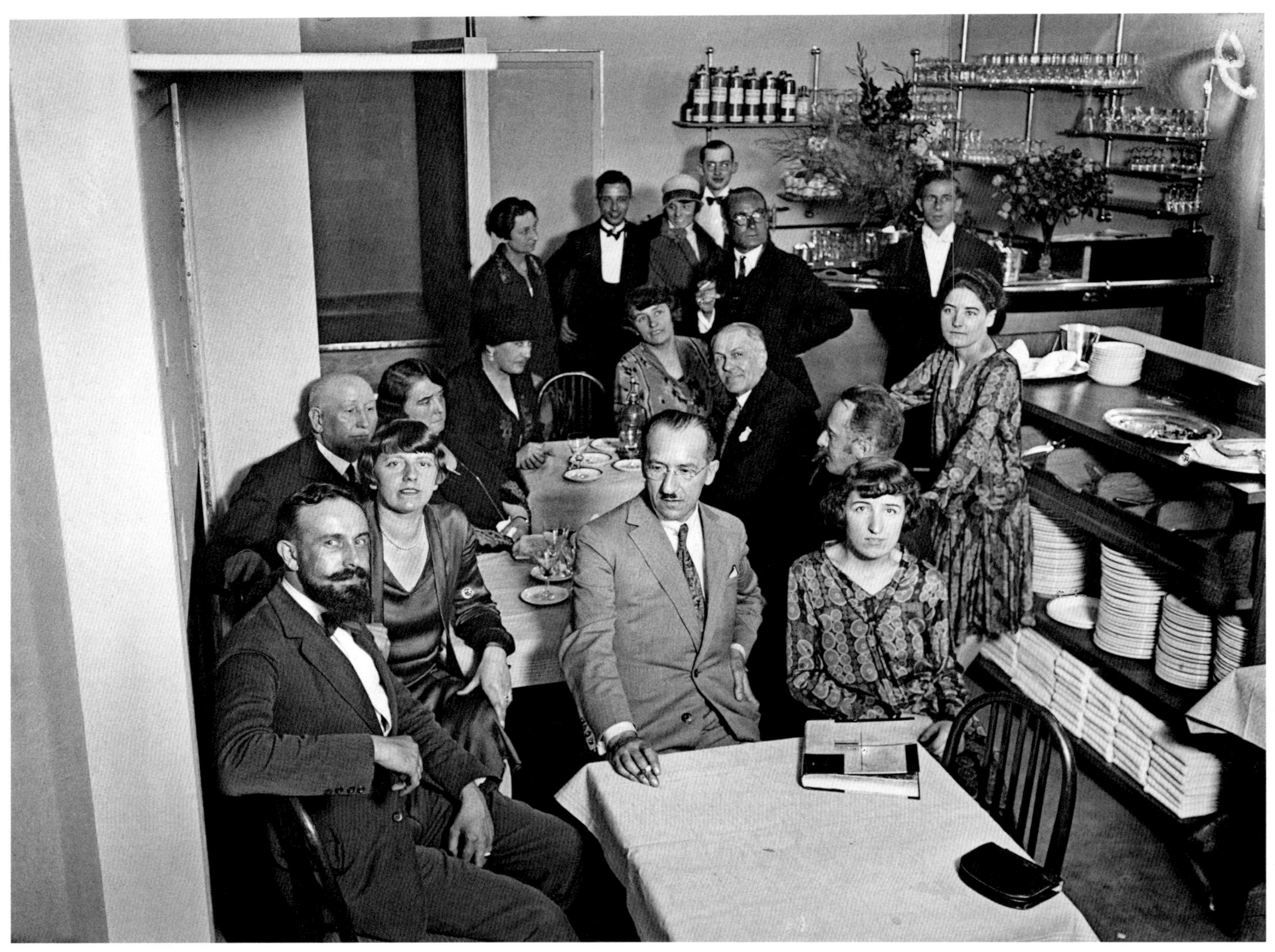

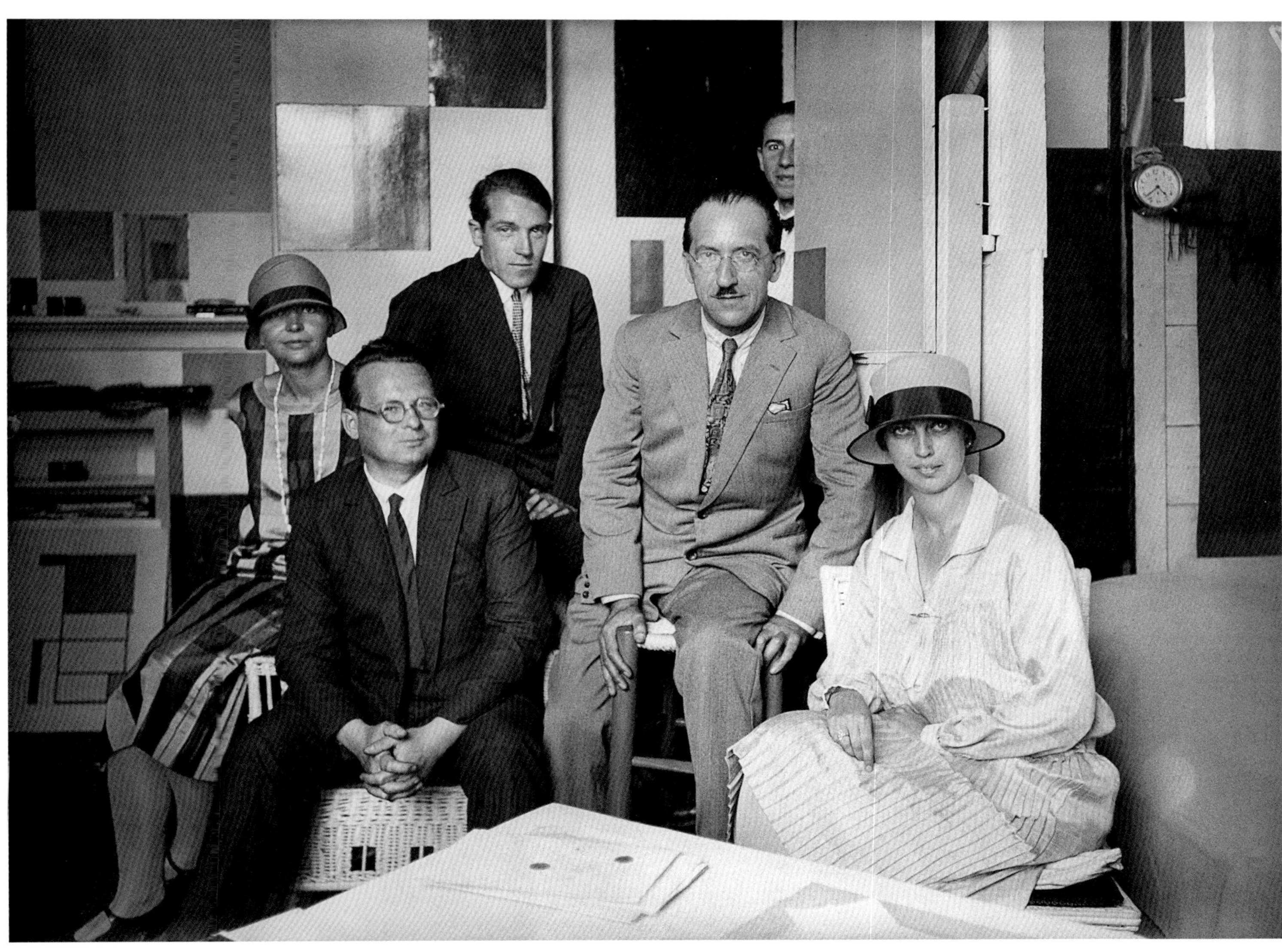

CAT. 87 **André Kertész**

Company at the opening of the restaurant Bij Leo Faust, 2 September 1926

Front, far left: Vilmos Huszár; centre: Piet Mondrian; rear (with cigarette): Piet Zwart.

The Dutch journalist and writer Leo Faust had moved to Paris as a foreign correspondent shortly before the First World War, but refocused on the catering business. His restaurant Bij Leo Faust, at 36 Rue Pigalle, targeted his compatriots in the French capital by serving typically Dutch food and drink. The restaurant was designed by Piet Zwart, another Dutchman.

CAT. 88 **André Kertész**

Company in Piet Mondrian's studio, 2 September 1926 (?)

Left to right: Gertrud Stemmler, Willi Baumeister, Julius Herburger, Piet Mondrian, Michel Seuphor and Margarete Baumeister.

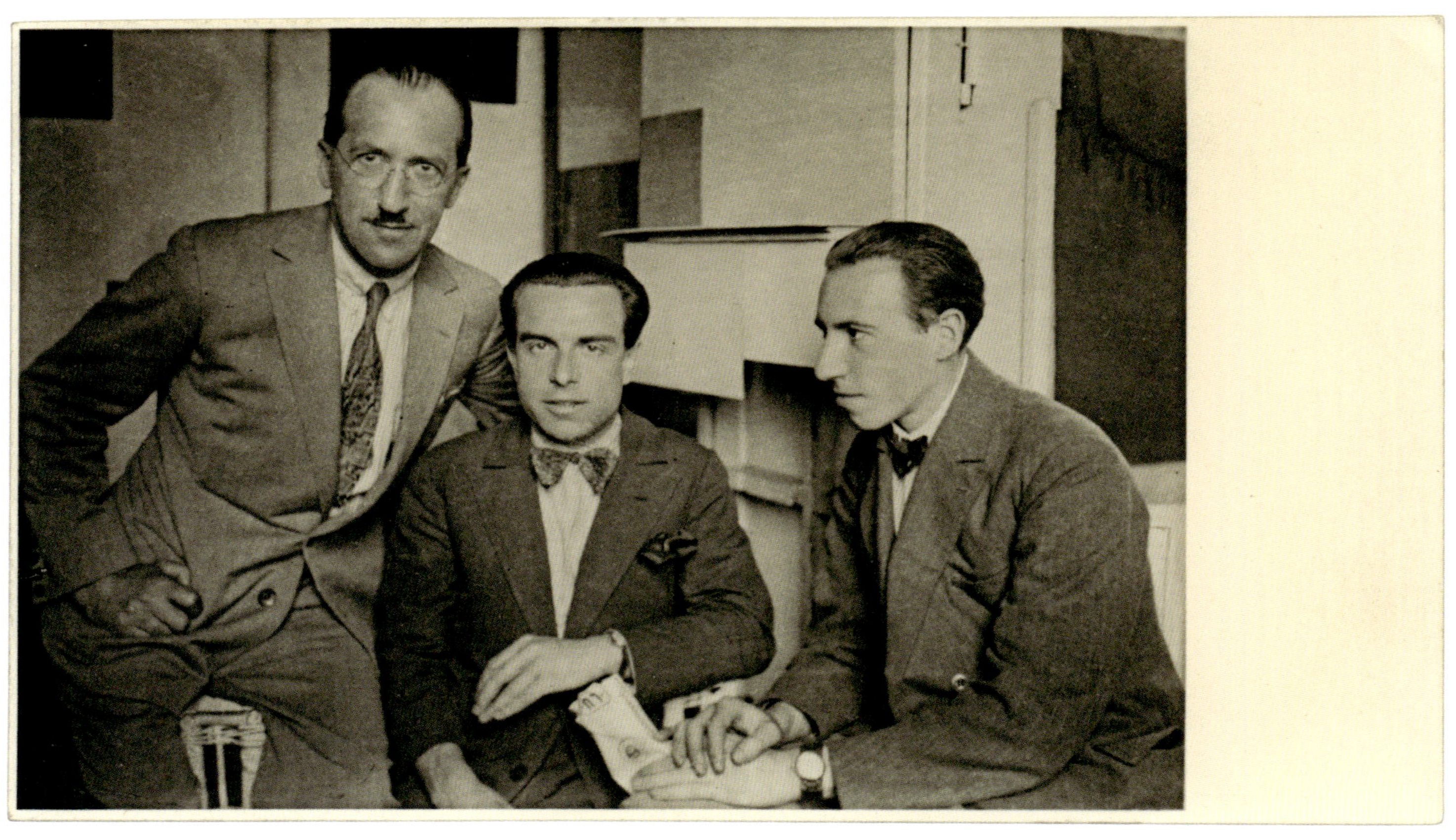

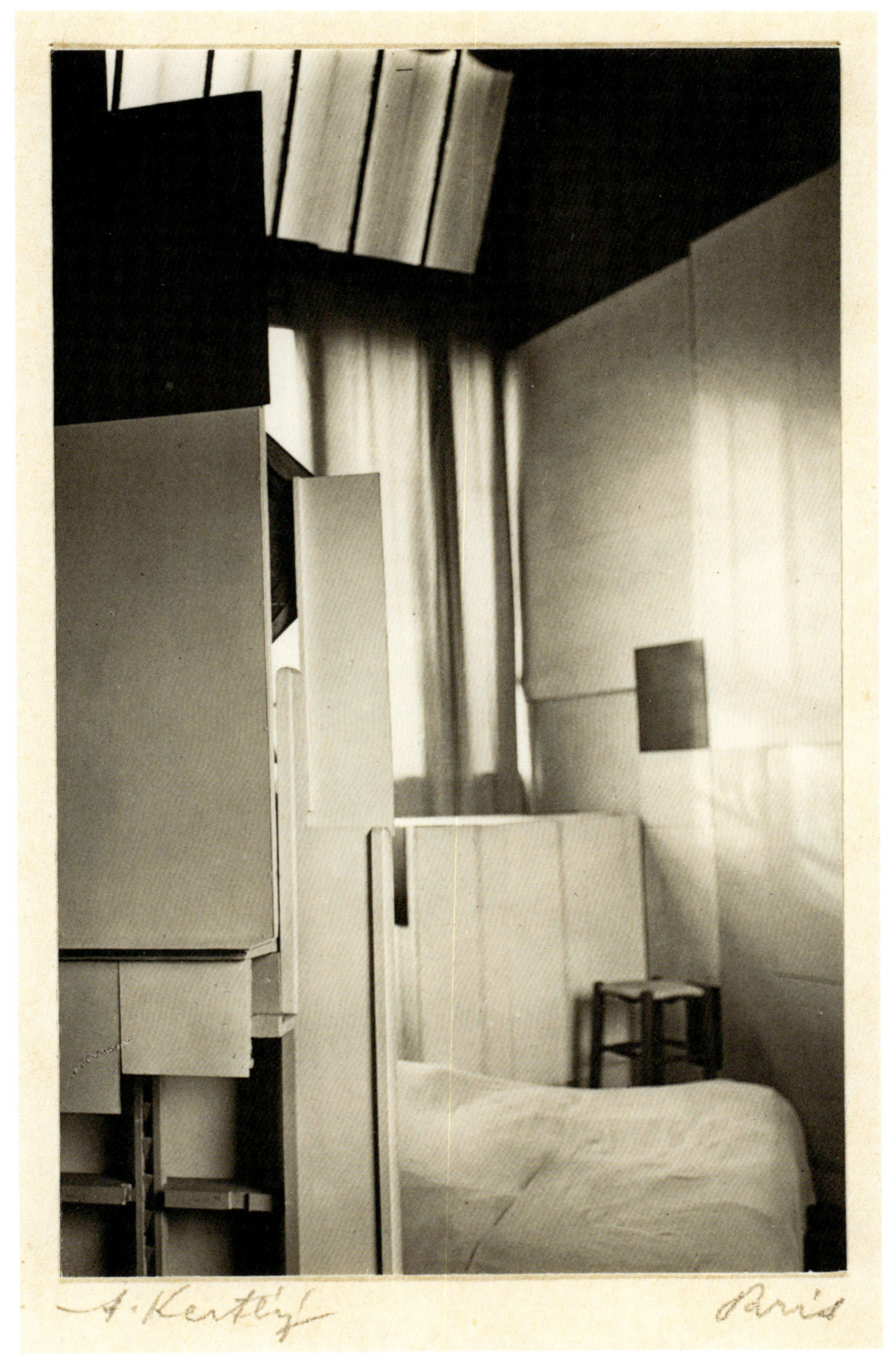

CAT. 89 **André Kertész**
Piet Mondrian, Enrico Prampolini and Michel Seuphor in Mondrian's studio, 2 September 1926 (?)

CAT. 90 **André Kertész**
Piet Mondrian's studio, between September 1926 and mid-February 1927

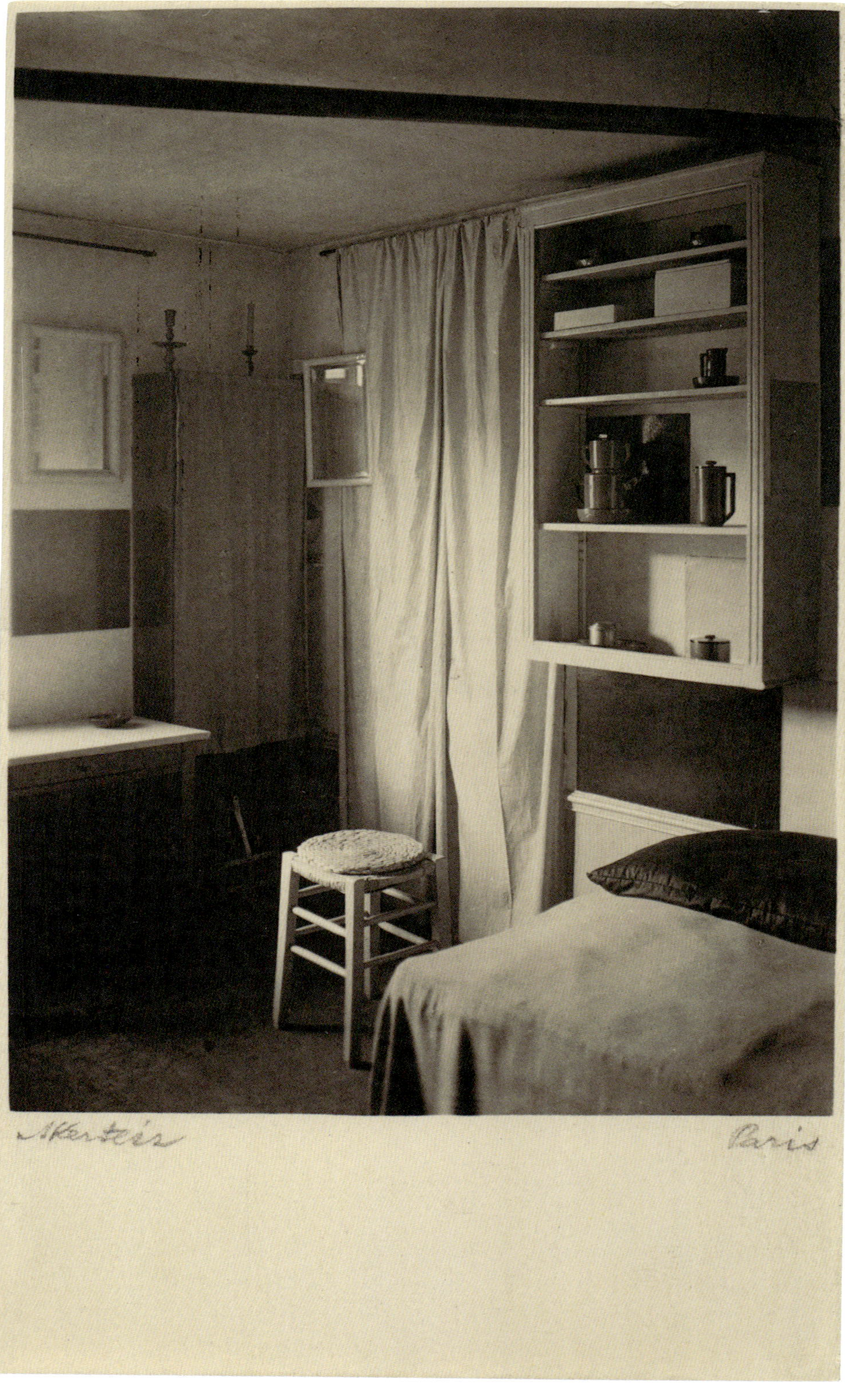
A.Kertész
Paris

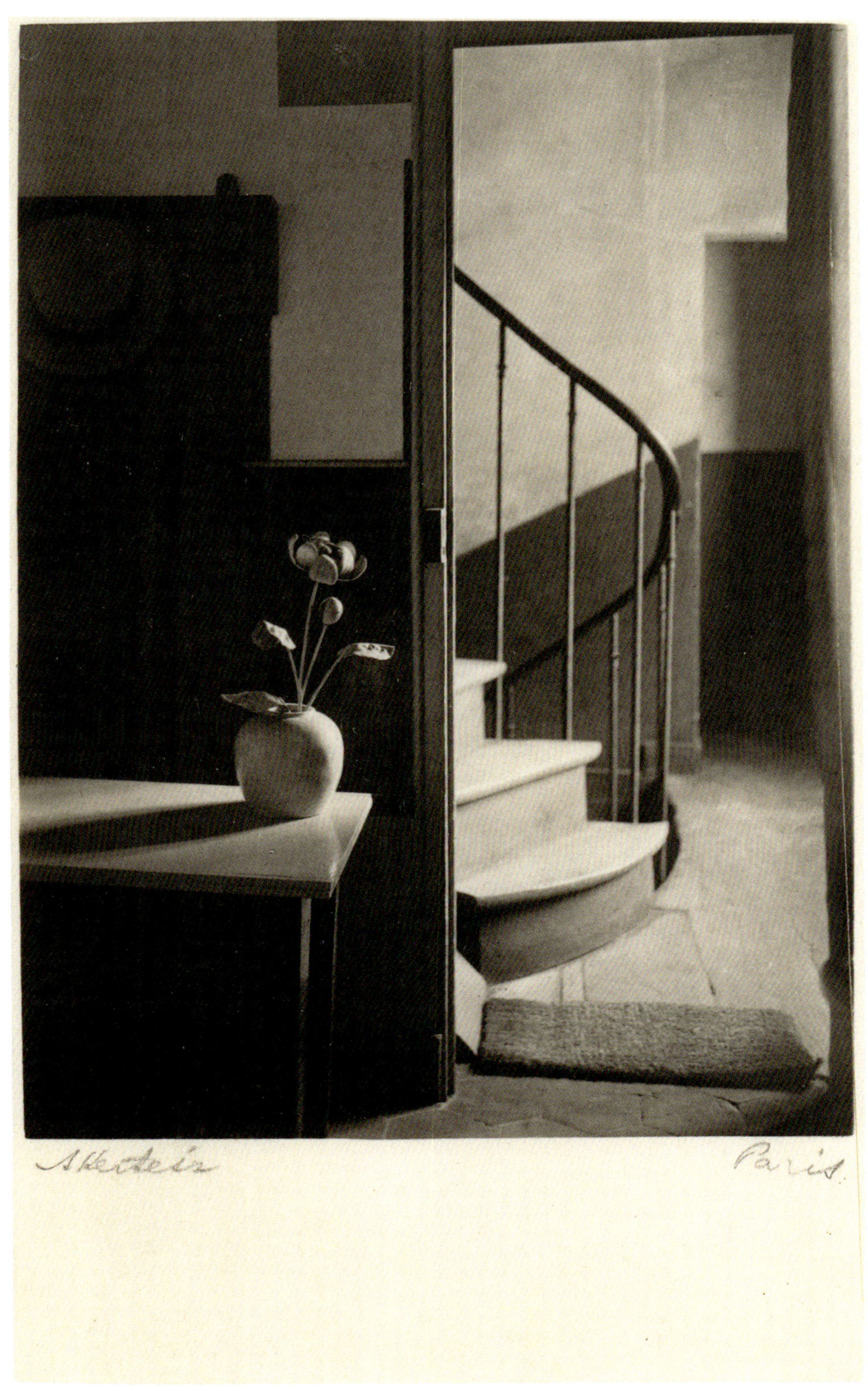

CAT. 91 **André Kertész**
Piet Mondrian's living quarters, between September 1926 and mid-February 1927

CAT. 92 **André Kertész**
***Chez Mondrian*, Paris, between September 1926 and mid-February 1927**
This is one of the best-known photographs of Mondrian's interior. The title comes from Kertész himself.

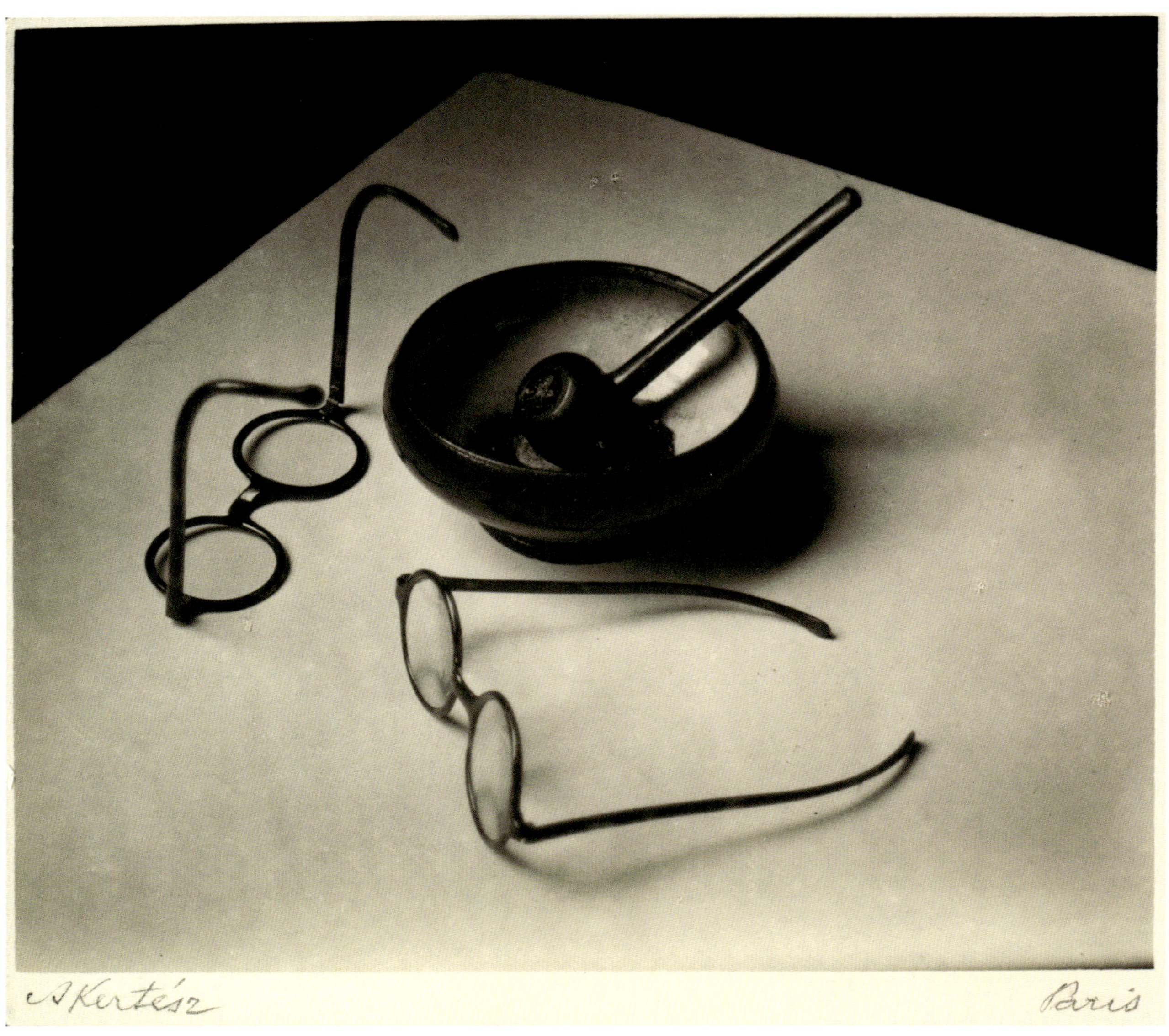
A Kertész
Paris

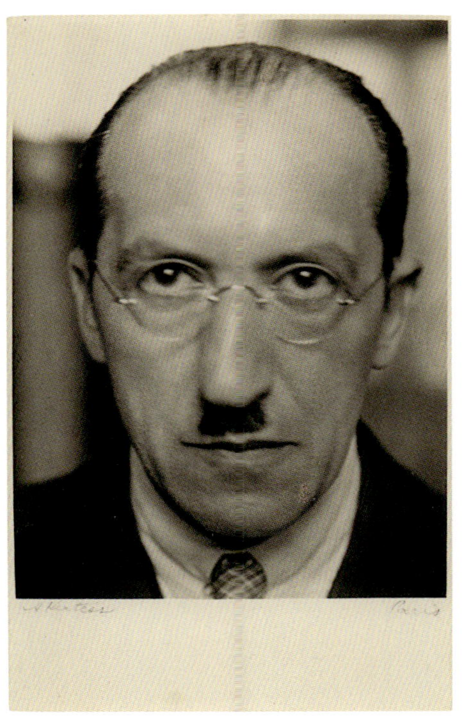

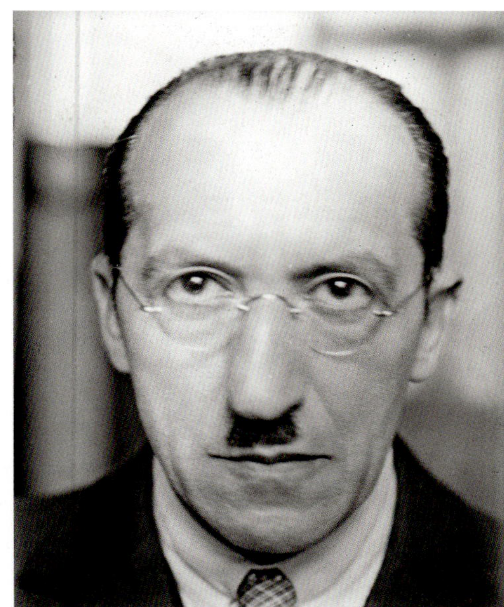

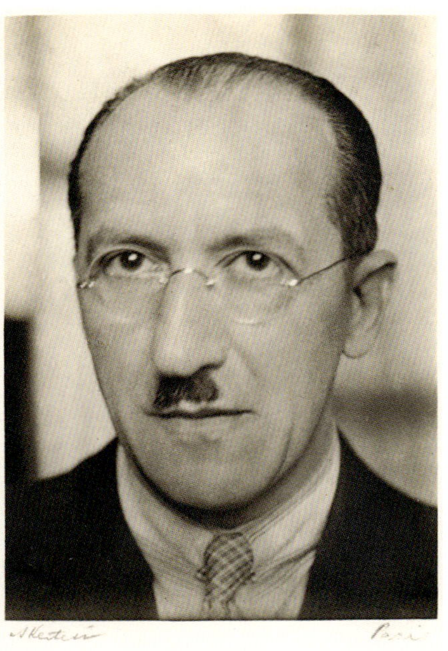

CAT. 93 **André Kertész**
***Les Lunettes et la pipe de Mondrian/Nature morte*, between September 1926 and mid-February 1927**
Kertész used both titles ('Mondrian's glasses and pipe' and 'Still life') for this picture, which he exhibited several times.

CAT. 94 **André Kertész**
Portrait of Piet Mondrian, between September 1926 and mid-February 1927
Kertész edited the portrait on the print to give Mondrian a more flattering look.

CAT. 95 **André Kertész**
Portrait of Piet Mondrian, between September 1926 and mid-February 1927

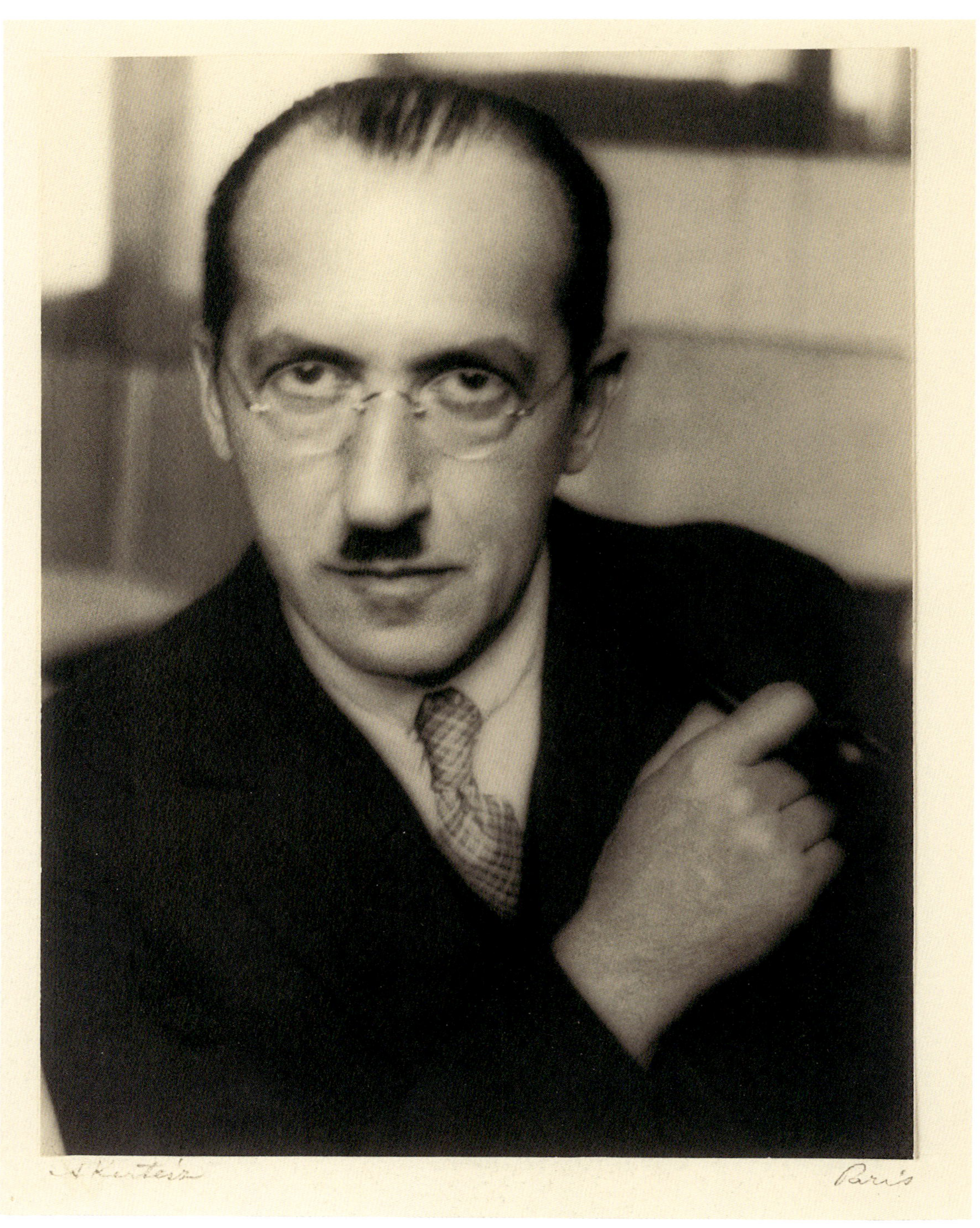
A Kertész
Paris

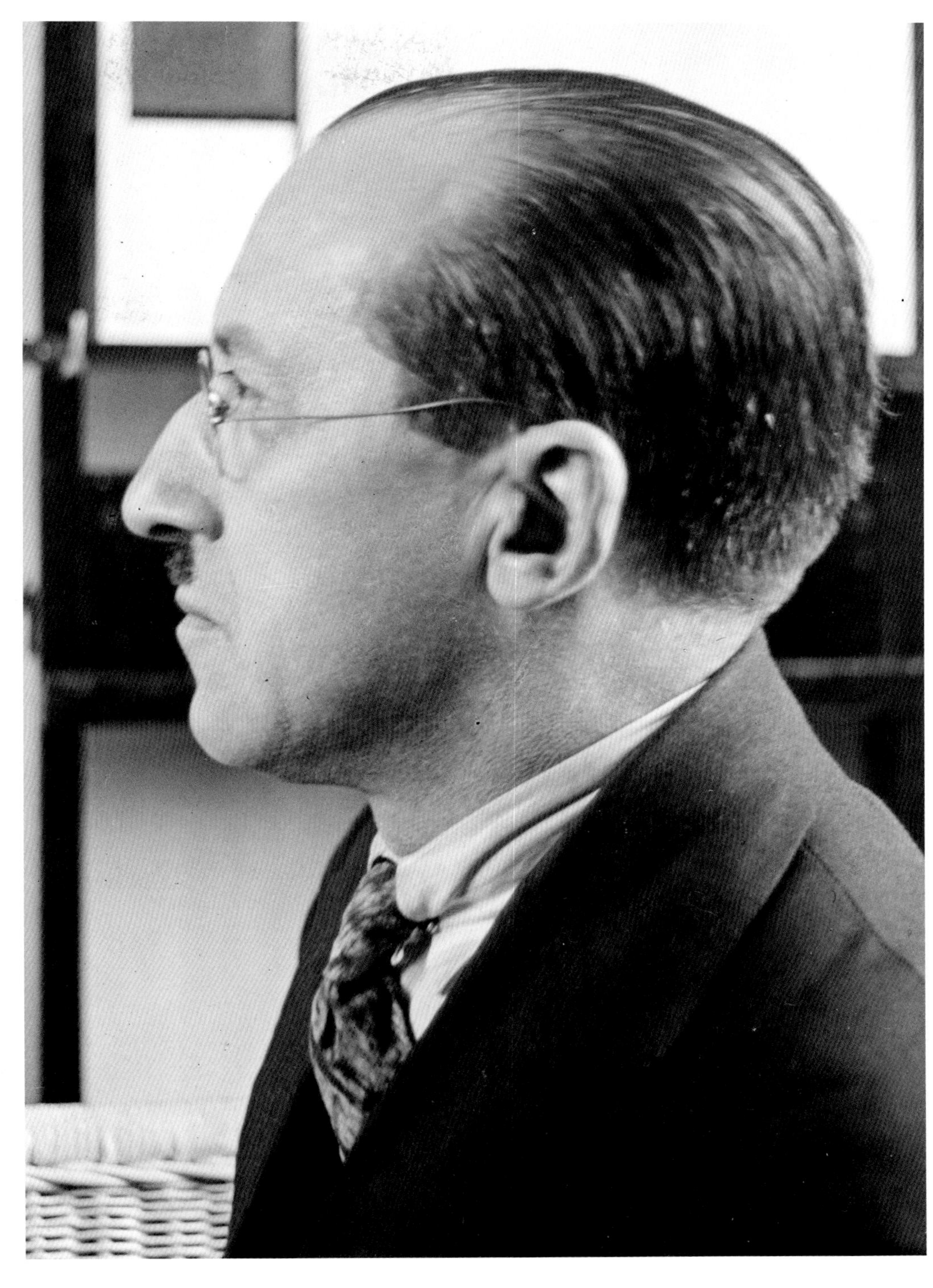

CATS 96–7 **André Kertész**
Portrait of Piet Mondrian, between September 1926 and mid-February 1927

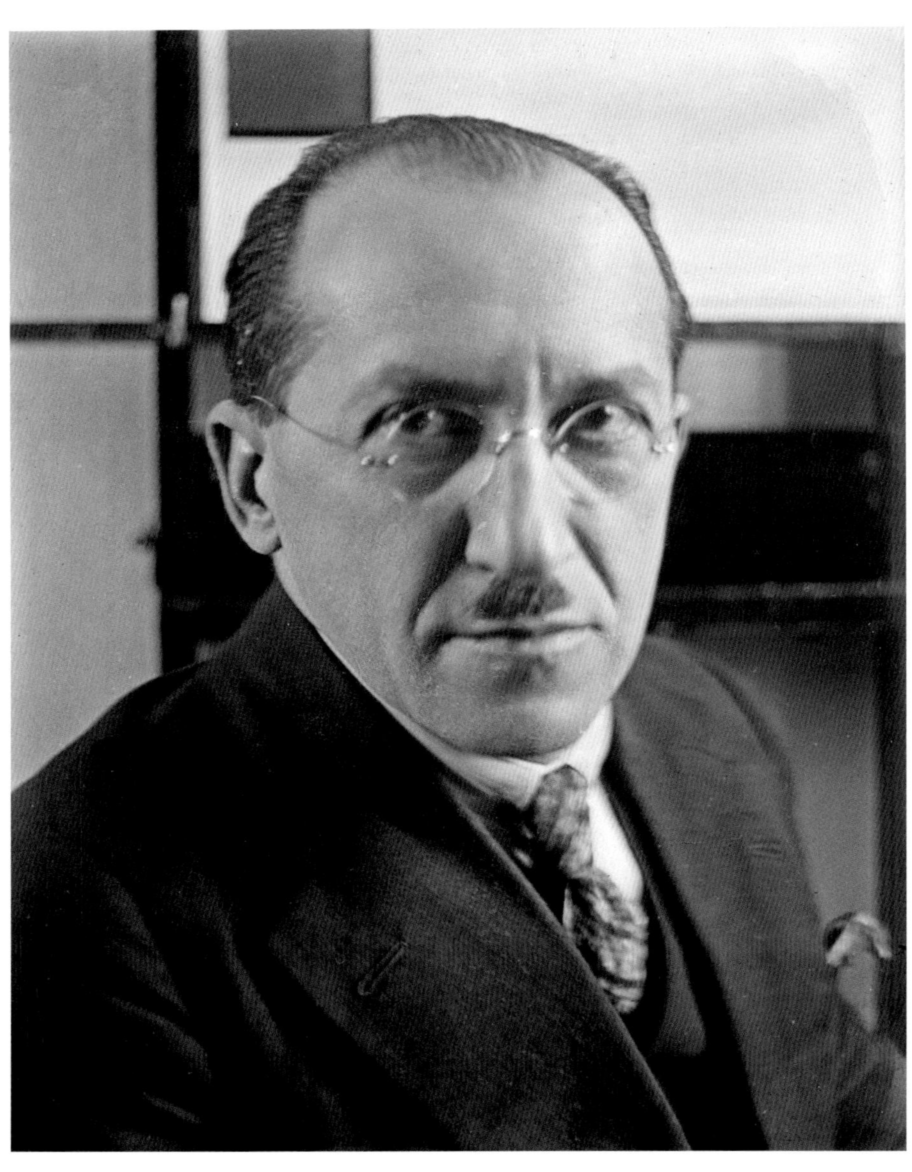

CAT. 98 **André Kertész**
Portrait of Piet Mondrian, between September 1926 and mid-February 1927

CAT. 99 **André Kertész**
***Mondrian*, between September 1926 and mid-February 1927**
The title comes from Kertész himself.

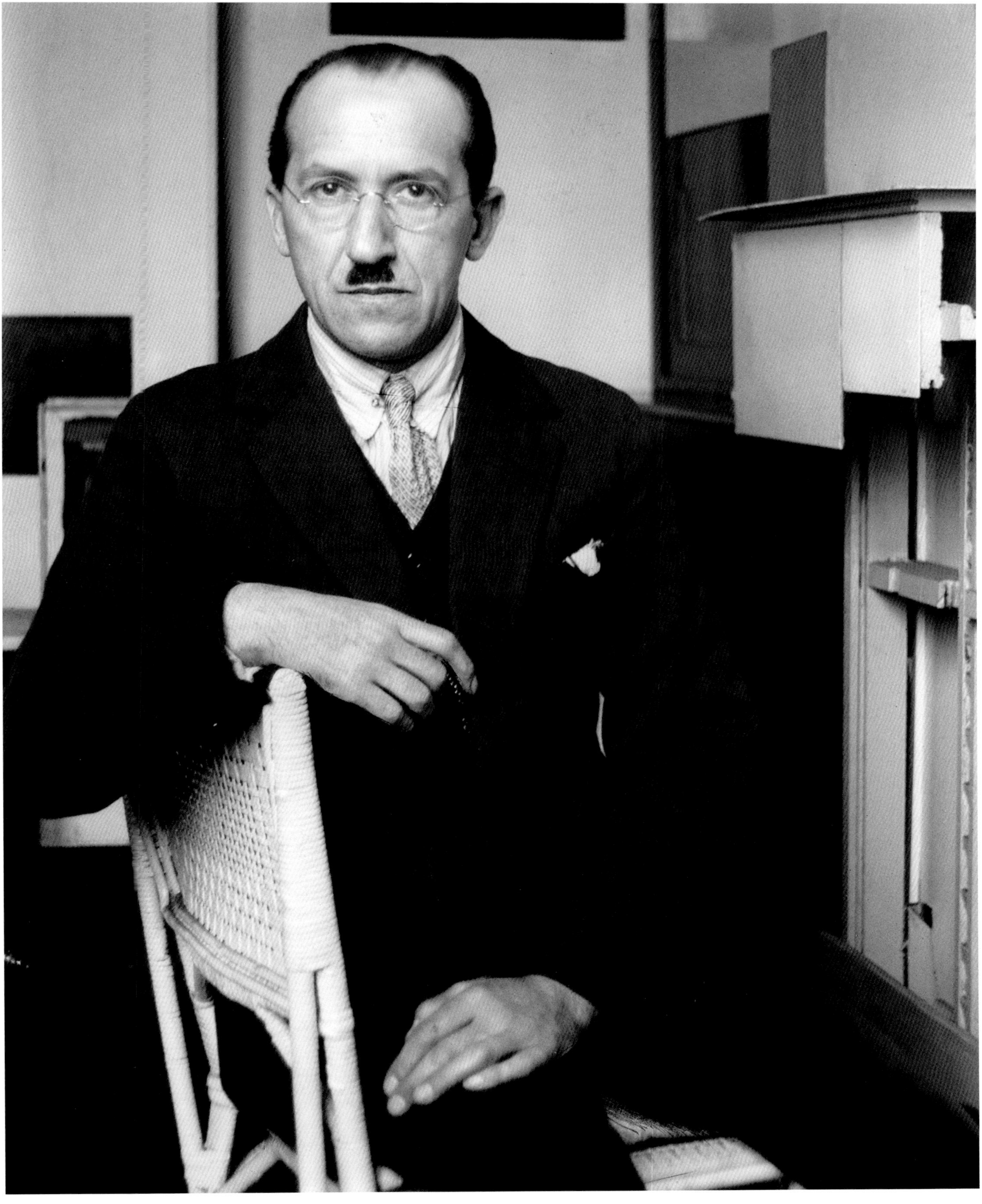

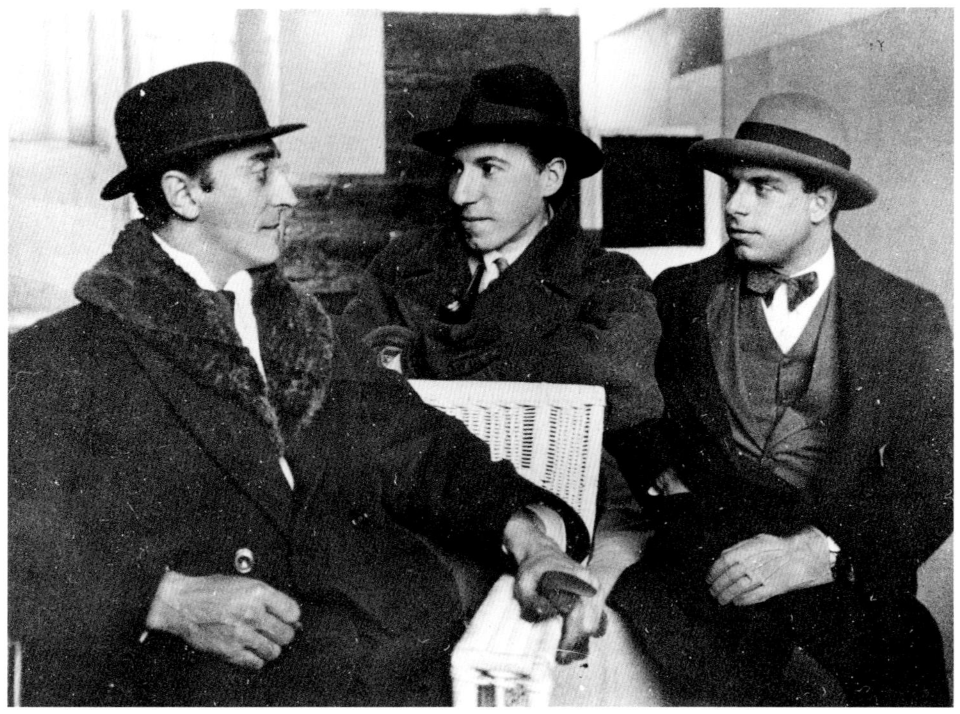

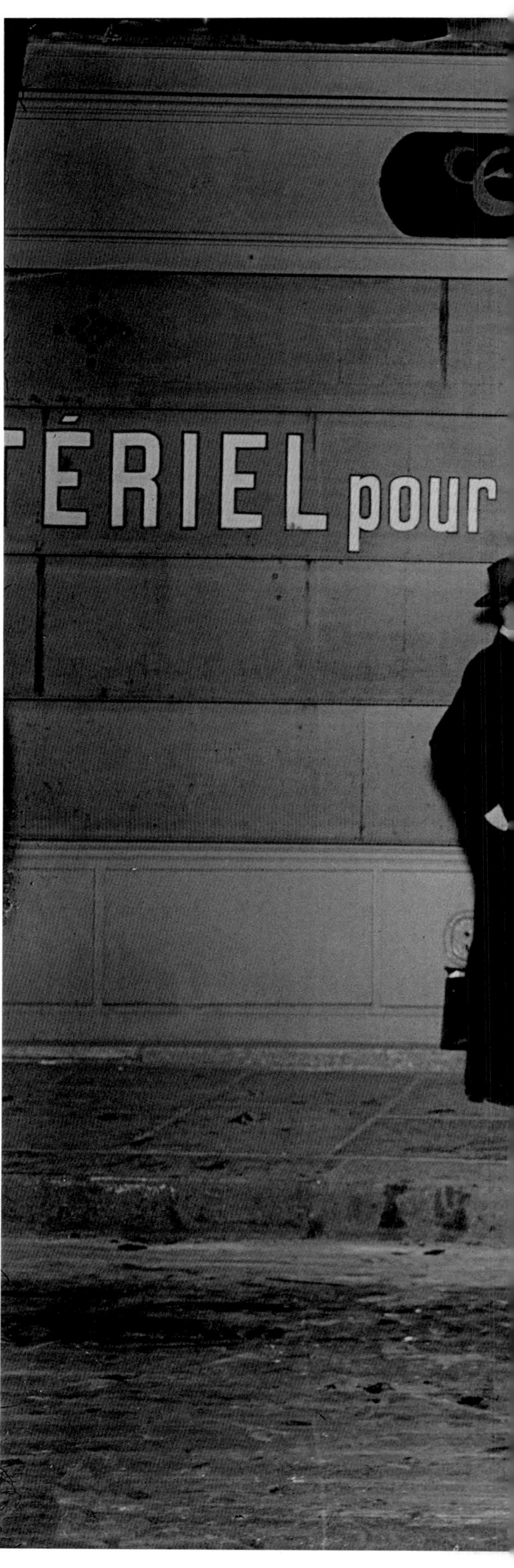

CAT. 100 **André Kertész**

Paul Dermée, Michel Seuphor and Enrico Prampolini in Piet Mondrian's studio, winter 1926–27

The three artists formed the editorial team at *Documents internationaux de l'esprit nouveau*, the first (and only) issue of which appeared in January 1927. It included the photographs of Mondrian's design for Michel Seuphor's play *L'Ephémère est éternel* (cats 84–6).

CAT. 101 **André Kertész**

Company after the opening of the 'Photo-Kertész' exhibition in the gallery Au Sacre du Printemps, 12 March 1927

Left to right: Franz Waldraff, Max Ackermann, Bertel Schleicher, Julius Herburger, Piet Zwart, Enrico Prampolini (with the wrapped-up painting), Willi Baumeister, Ida Thal-Hackmüller (whose abstract-geometric work was on display at Au Sacre du Printemps at the same time as Kertész's photos), Mario Sotgia-Rovelli, Zlatko Neumann, Adolf Loos, Piet Mondrian and Michel Seuphor.

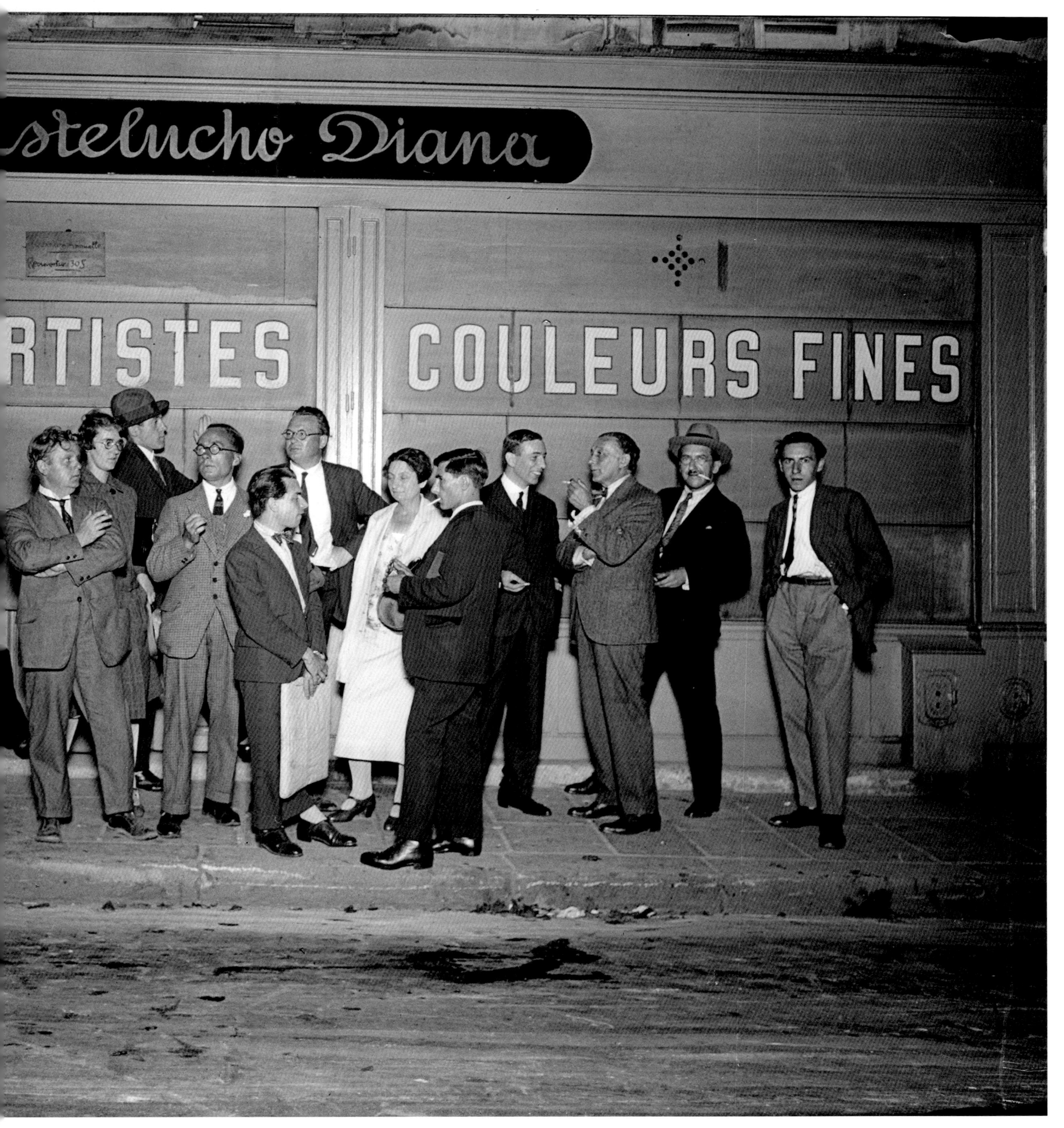

stelucho Diana
RTISTES
COULEURS FINES

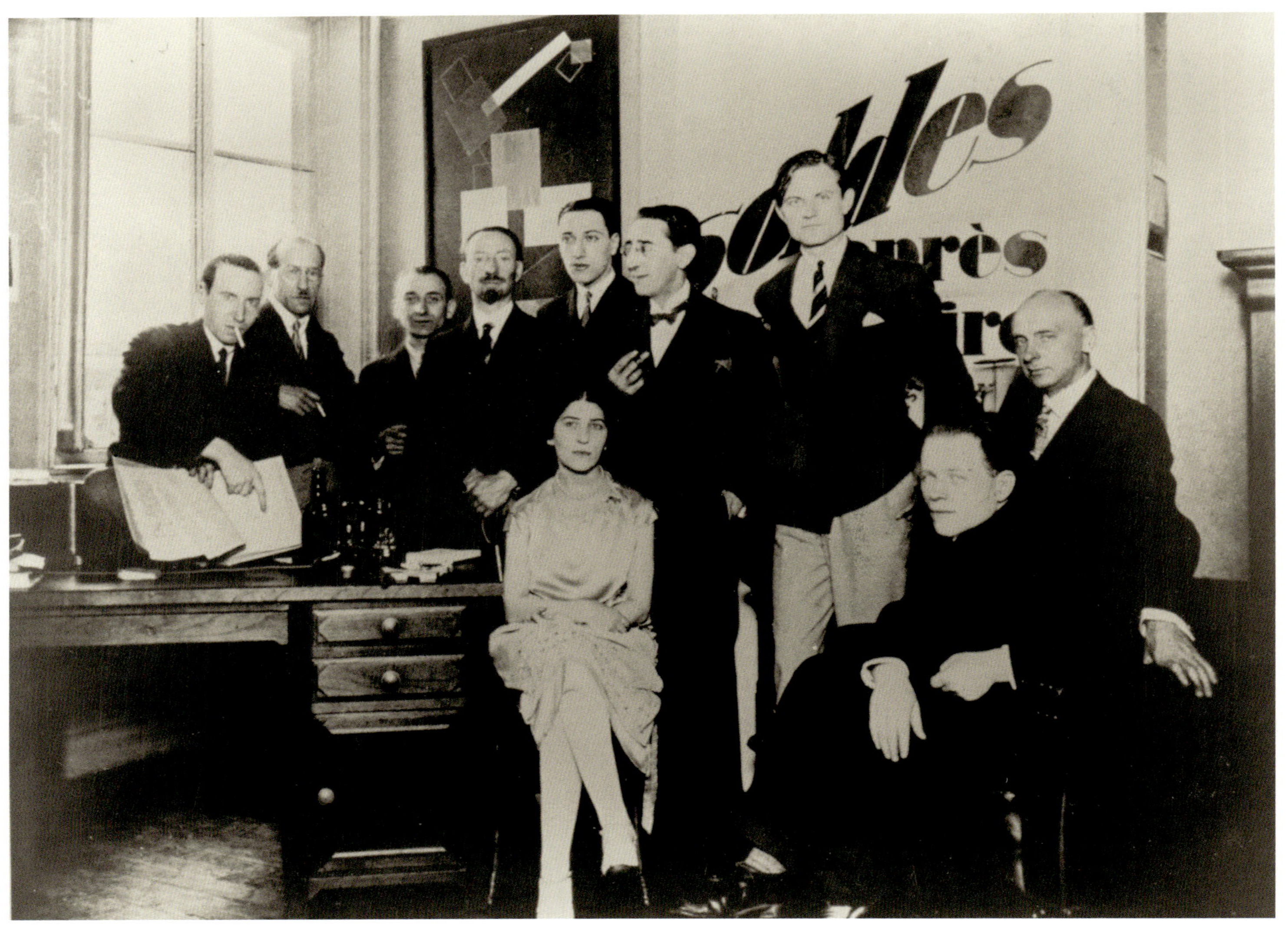

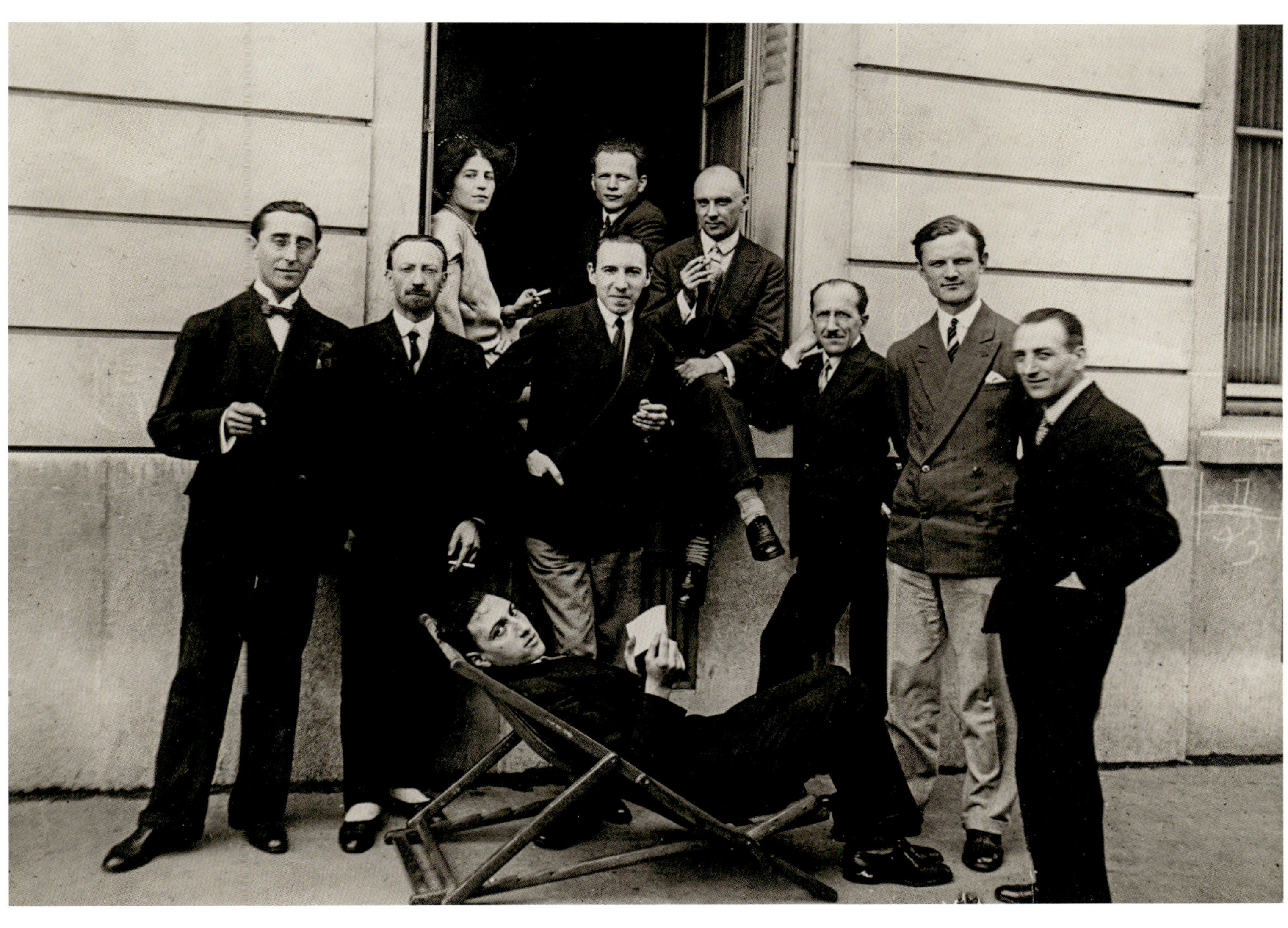

CAT. 102 **Stanislaw Londynski**
Company at Paul Dermée's house, Paris, c. July 1927
Left to right, front row: Céline Arnauld, Aleksander Rafalowski, Henryk Stazewski; second row: Michel Seuphor, Piet Mondrian, Georges Vantongerloo, Luigi Russolo, Ilarie Voronca, Paul Dermée, Juozas Tysliava. Paul Dermée was a Belgian-born writer, poet and critic; his wife Céline Arnauld was a Dadaist poet.

CAT. 103 **Stanislaw Londynski**
Company in front of Paul Dermée's house, Paris, c. July 1927
Left to right, standing: Paul Dermée, Luigi Russolo, Michel Seuphor, Piet Mondrian, Juozas Tysliava, Georges Vantongerloo; sitting on the windowsill: Céline Arnauld, Aleksander Rafalowski, Henryk Stazewski; reclining in the chair at the front: Ilarie Voronca.

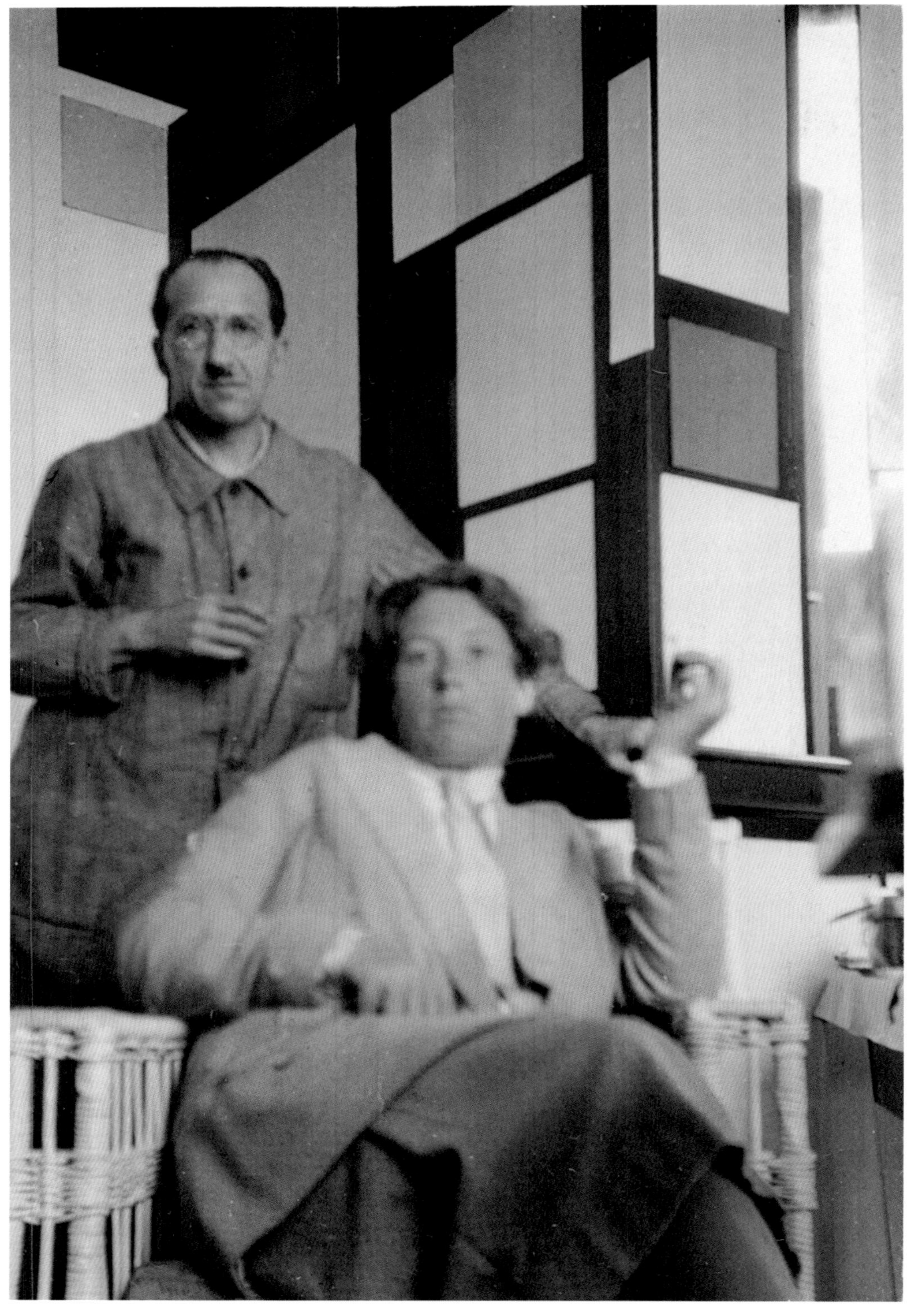

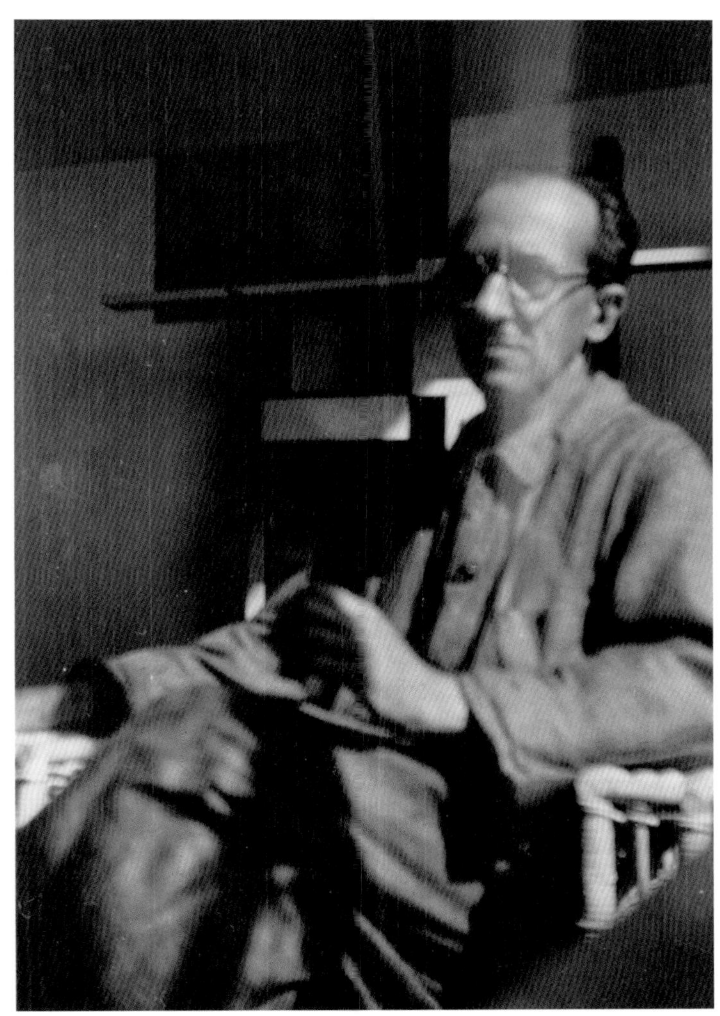

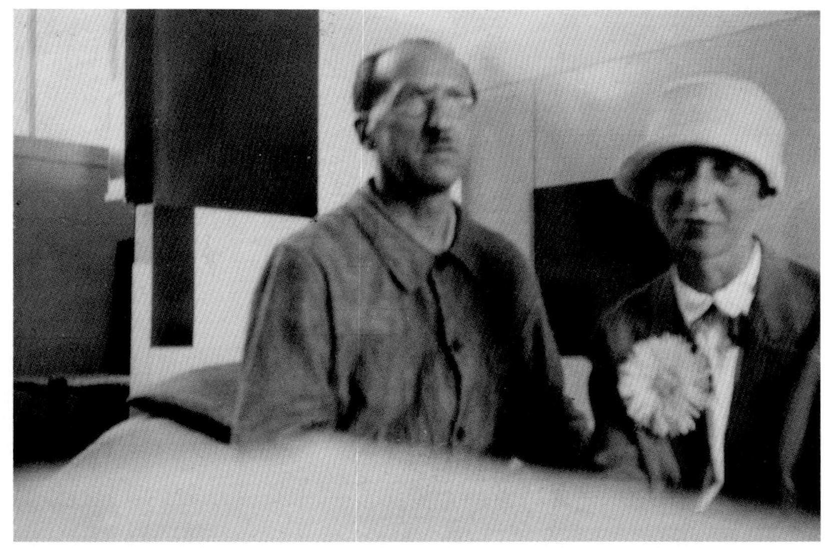

CAT. 104 **Hannah Höch**
Piet Mondrian and Til Brugman in Mondrian's studio, September 1927

CAT. 107 **Hannah Höch**
Portrait of Piet Mondrian, September 1927

CAT. 105 **Til Brugman (?)**
Piet Mondrian and Hannah Höch in Mondrian's studio, September 1927

CAT. 106 See catalogue

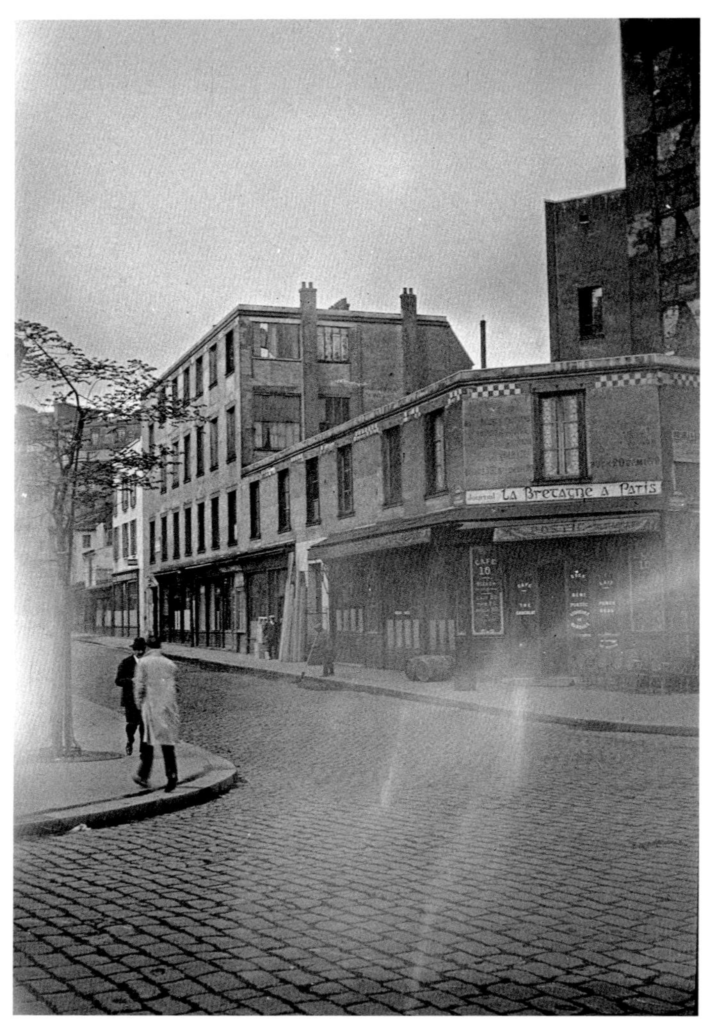
La Bretagne à Paris

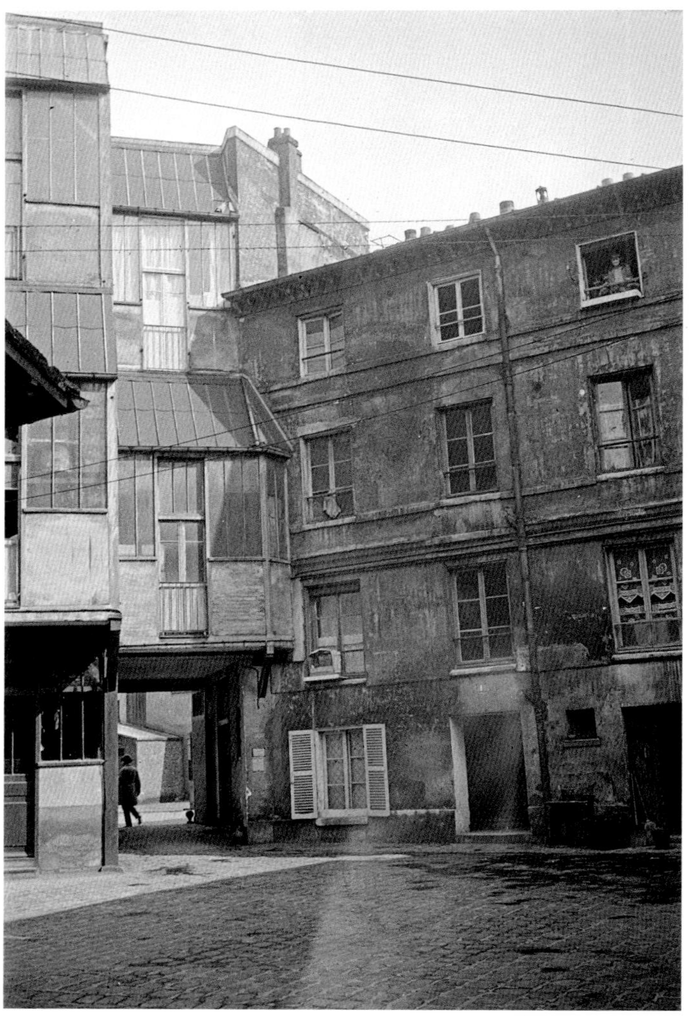

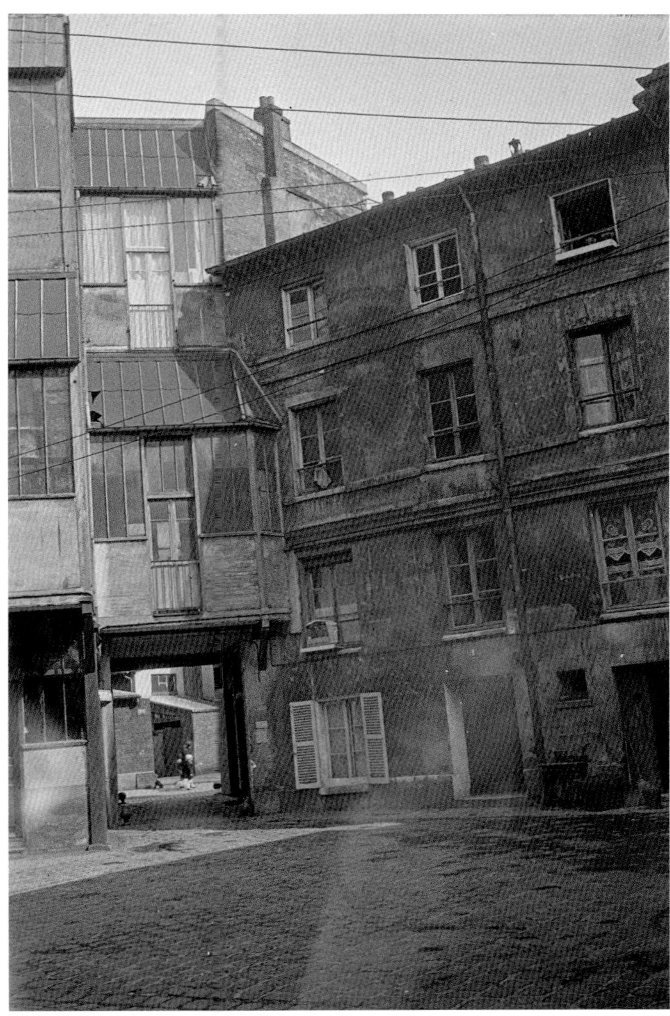

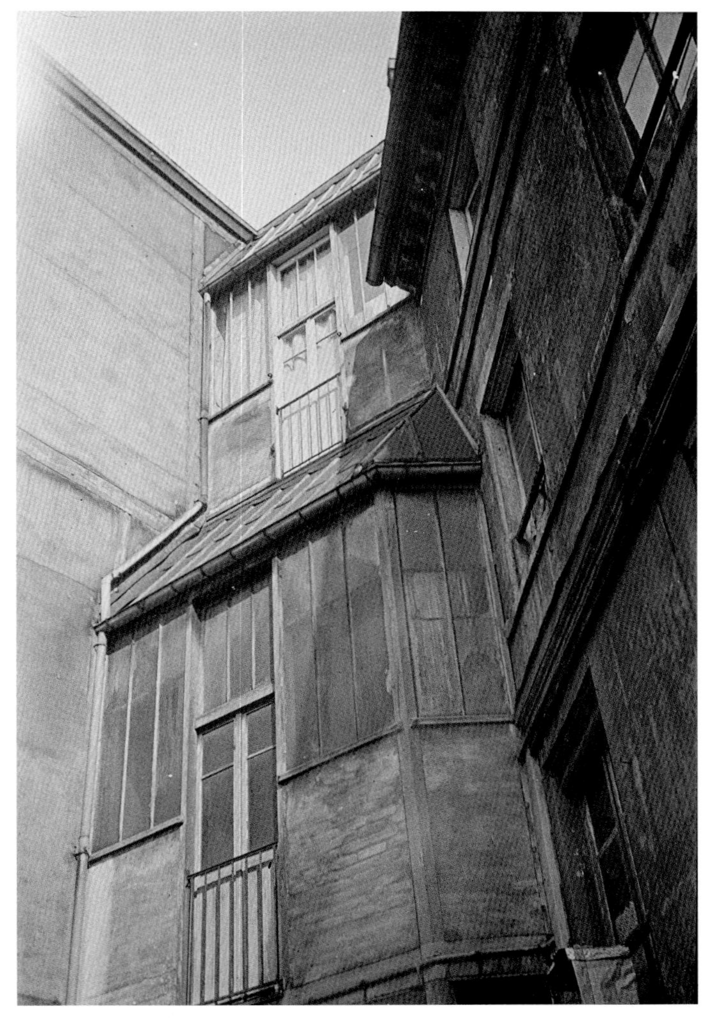

CAT. 108 **Alfred Roth**
Studio complex at 26 Rue du Départ, spring 1928
Mondrian's studio was on the left in the tall building.

CATS 109–10 **Alfred Roth**
Courtyard of the studio complex at 26 Rue du Départ, spring 1928
The window of Mondrian's studio is on the second floor above the passageway.

CAT. 111 **Alfred Roth**
Window of Piet Mondrian's studio (top floor), viewed from the courtyard at 26 Rue du Départ, spring 1928

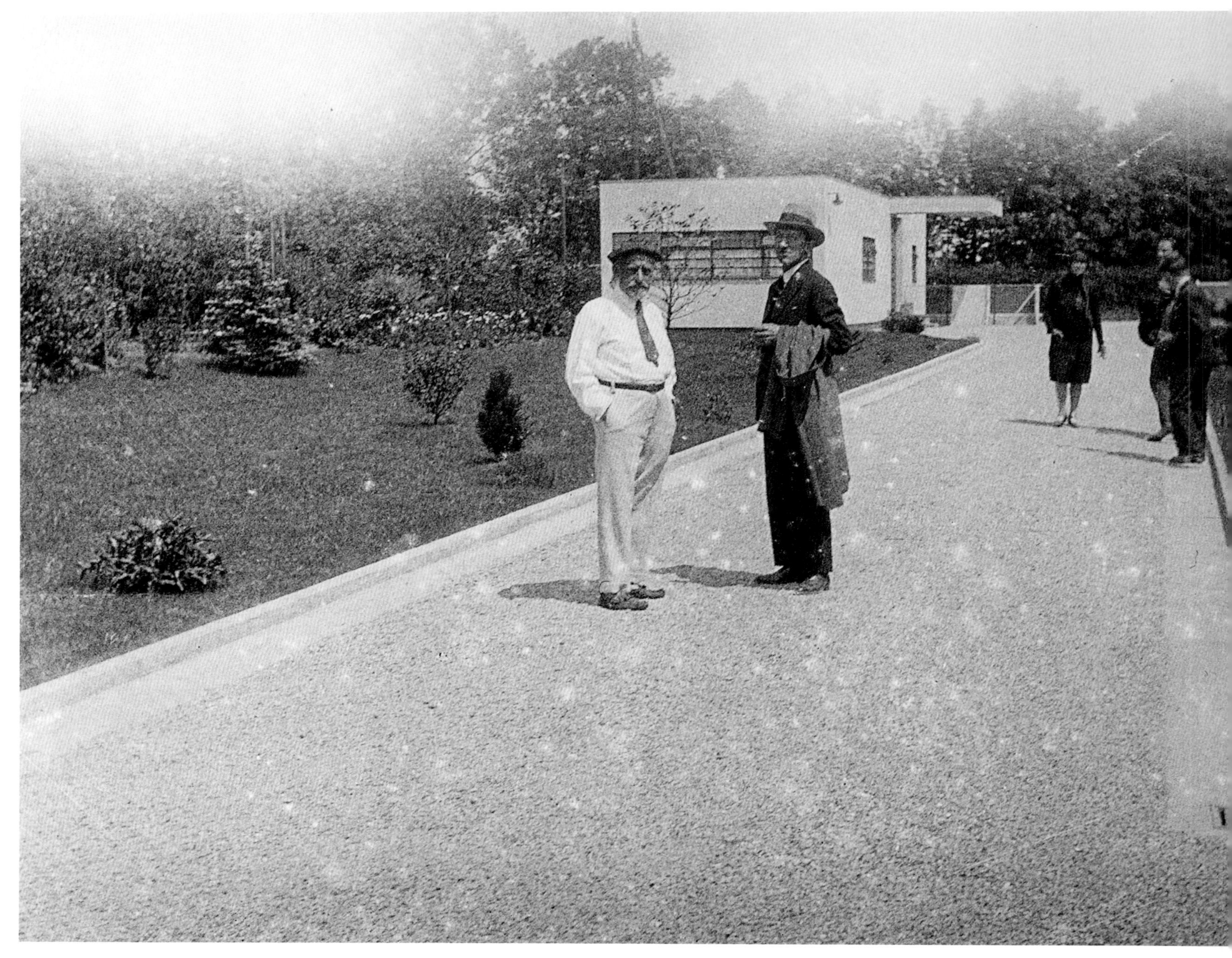

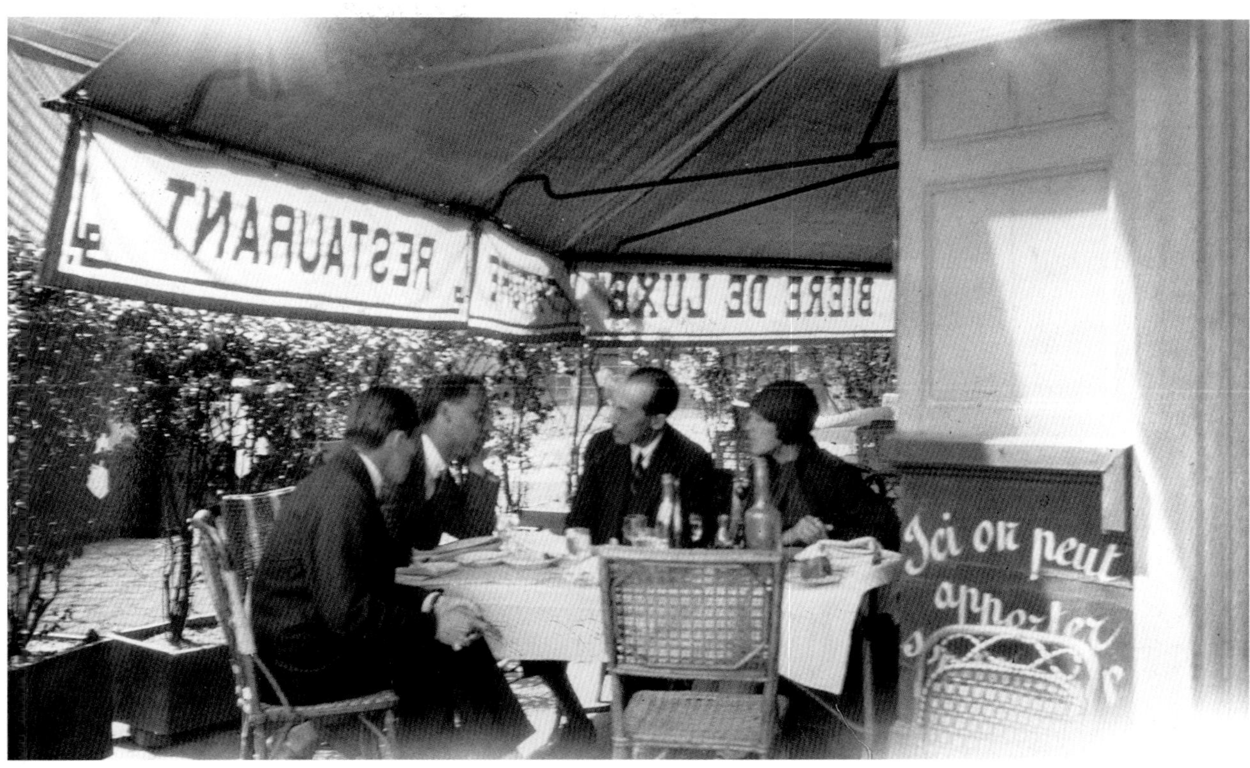

CAT. 112 **Alfred Roth**

Michael Stein and Piet Mondrian at the entrance of Villa Stein-de Monzie, Garches, 1 July 1928

Piet Mondrian visited the Villa Stein-de Monzie, designed by Le Corbusier, with his friends, the architects Alfred Roth and Mart Stam. Visible in the background are Mart Stam, Ernest Weissmann — a Croatian architect who had worked for Le Corbusier's firm since early 1928 — and a woman who might be Stam's wife Lena Lebeau.

CAT. 113 **Ernest Weissmann (?)**

Alfred Roth, Mart Stam, Piet Mondrian and an unidentified woman (Stam's wife Lena Lebeau?) on a terrace, 1 July 1928

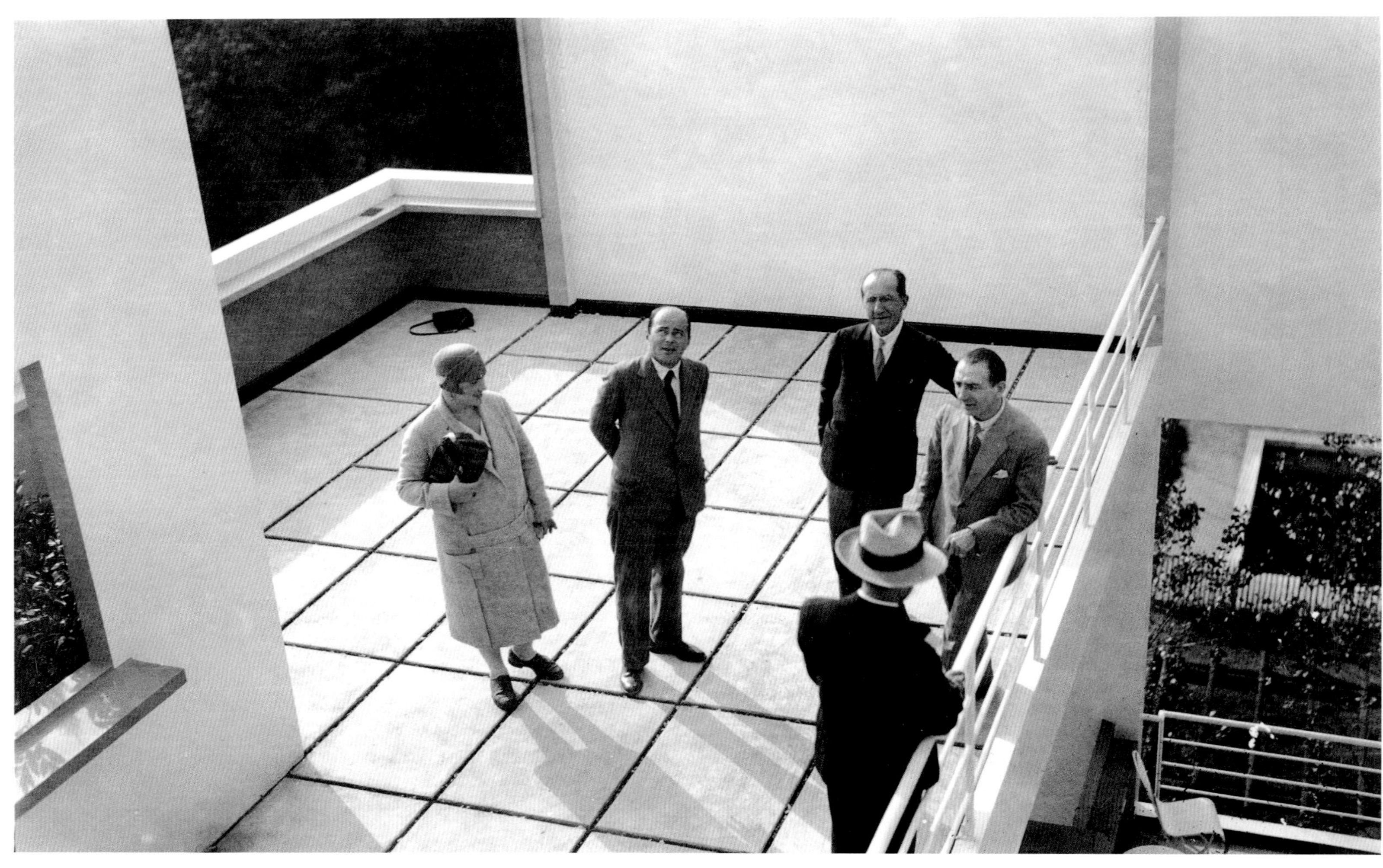

CAT. 115 **Unidentified photographer**
Company on the roof terrace of Villa Stein-de Monzie, Garches, early September 1928
Left to right: Sophie Lissitzky-Küppers, El Lissitzky, Piet Mondrian, Georges Vantongerloo and Mart Stam (viewed from the back).

CAT. 114 **Unidentified photographer**
Company on the roof terrace of Villa Stein-de Monzie, Garches, early September 1928
Following an earlier visit on 1 July 1928 (see cat. 112), Mondrian returned to the house designed by Le Corbusier in early September 1928. Above, left to right: Mart Stam, Georges Vantongerloo, Sophie Lissitzky-Küppers and her husband El Lissitzky. To the left of Mondrian, Sarah Stein-Samuels, who was married to Michael Stein.

CAT. 116 See catalogue

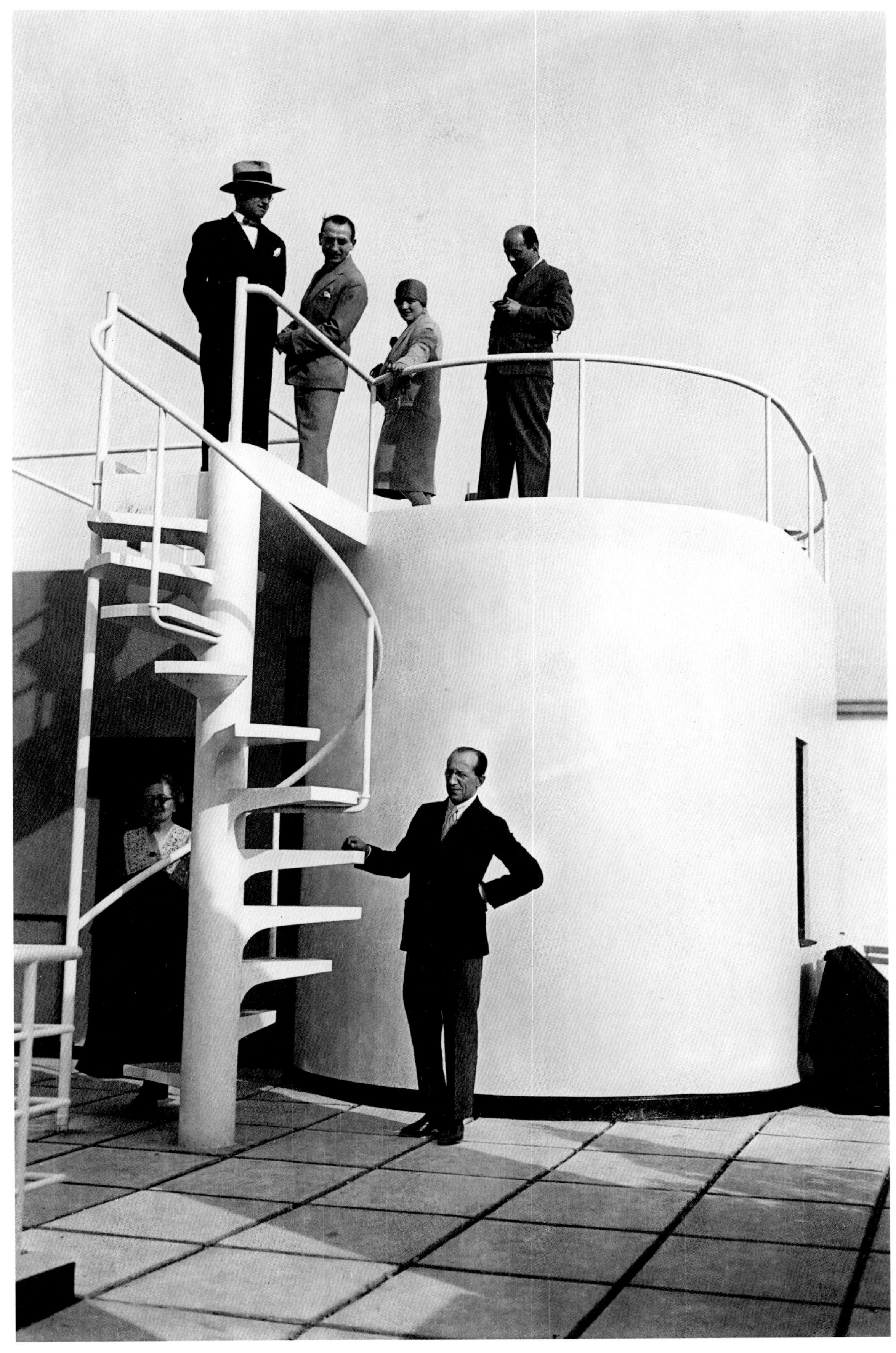

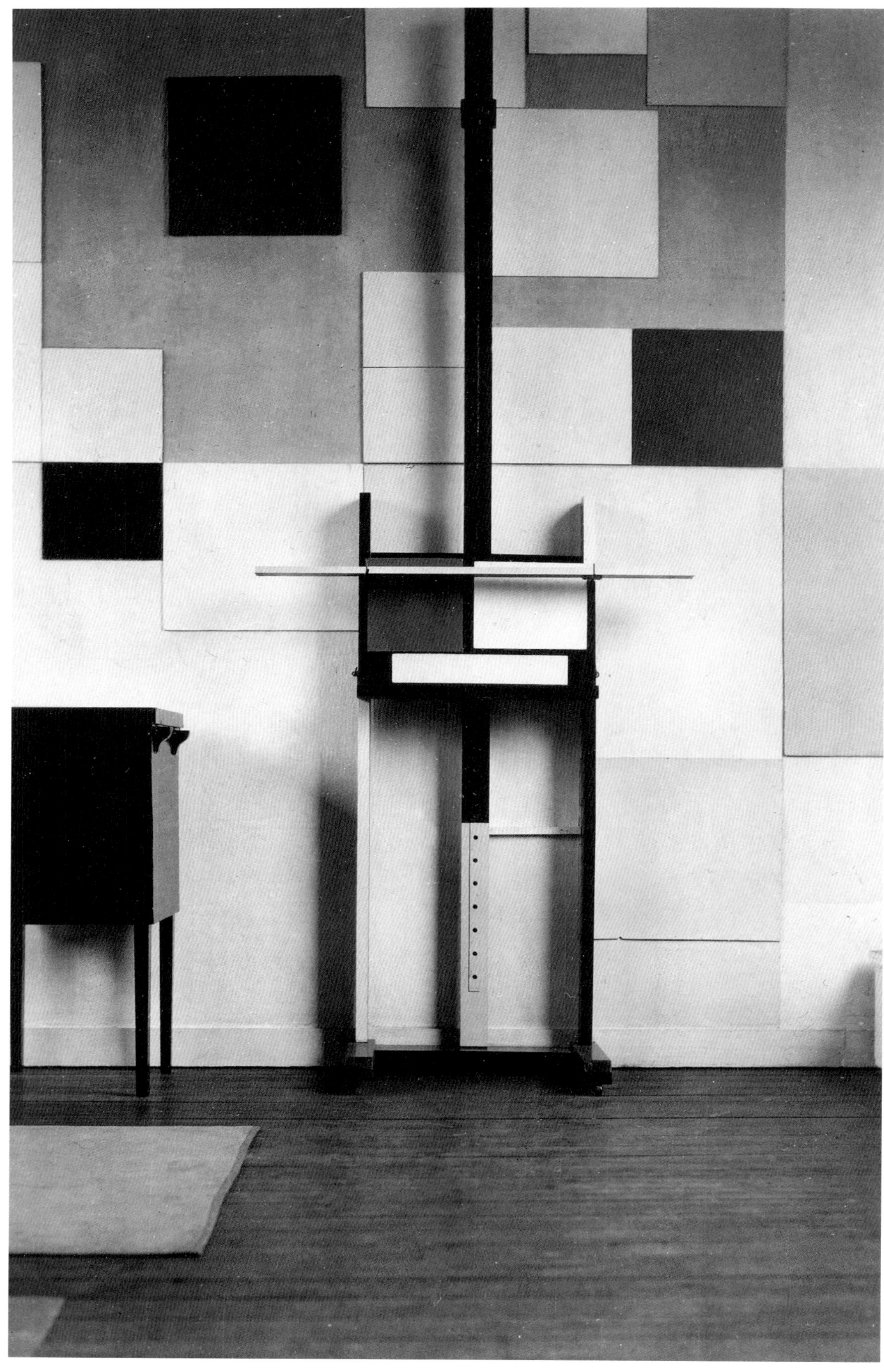

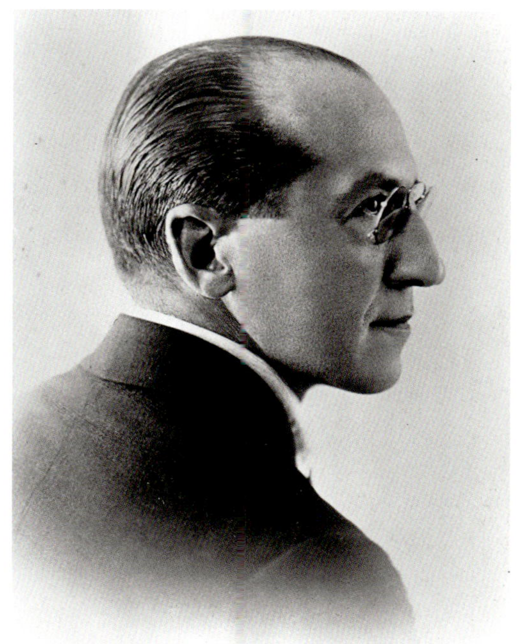

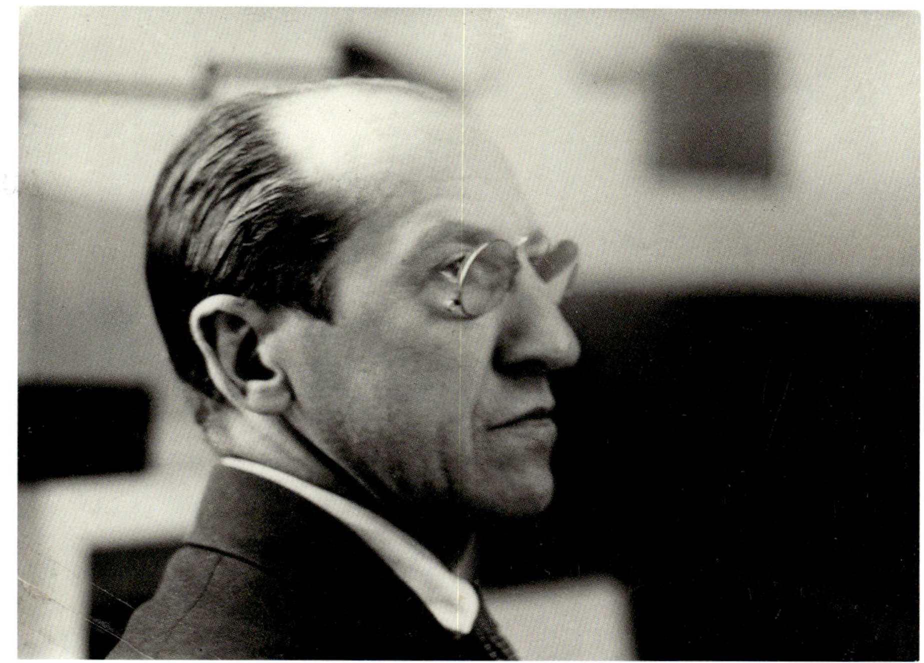

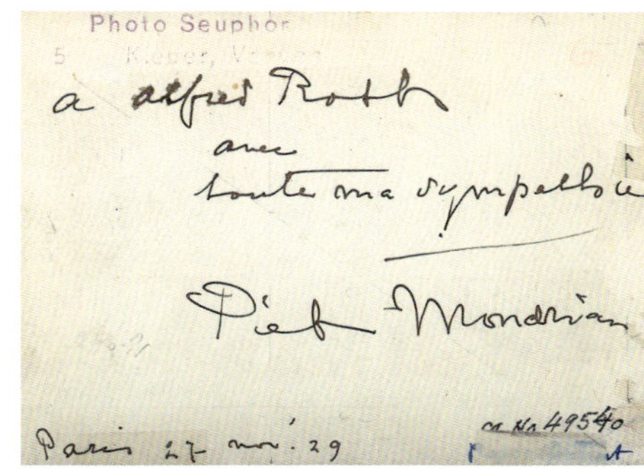

CAT. 117 **Sigfried Giedion**
Piet Mondrian's studio, September 1928
The easel, painted half-black and half-white, can also be seen in the photo of El Lissitzky in the studio, which was taken in the same month (cat. 116).
Carola Giedion-Welcker printed the photograph in March 1930 to illustrate her article in *Das Kunstblatt*.

CAT. 118 **Unidentified photographer**
Portrait of Piet Mondrian, c. 1929
Apart from the vignette effect, Mondrian's face also seems to have been retouched. The creases in the skin, for instance, which can be seen in the picture taken around the same time by Michel Seuphor (cat. 119), are entirely absent here, making Mondrian look much younger.

CAT. 119 recto/verso **Michel Seuphor**
Portrait of Piet Mondrian, mid-1929 (?)
Mondrian's appearance — without moustache and with pince-nez — is similar to the anonymous portrait cat. 118.

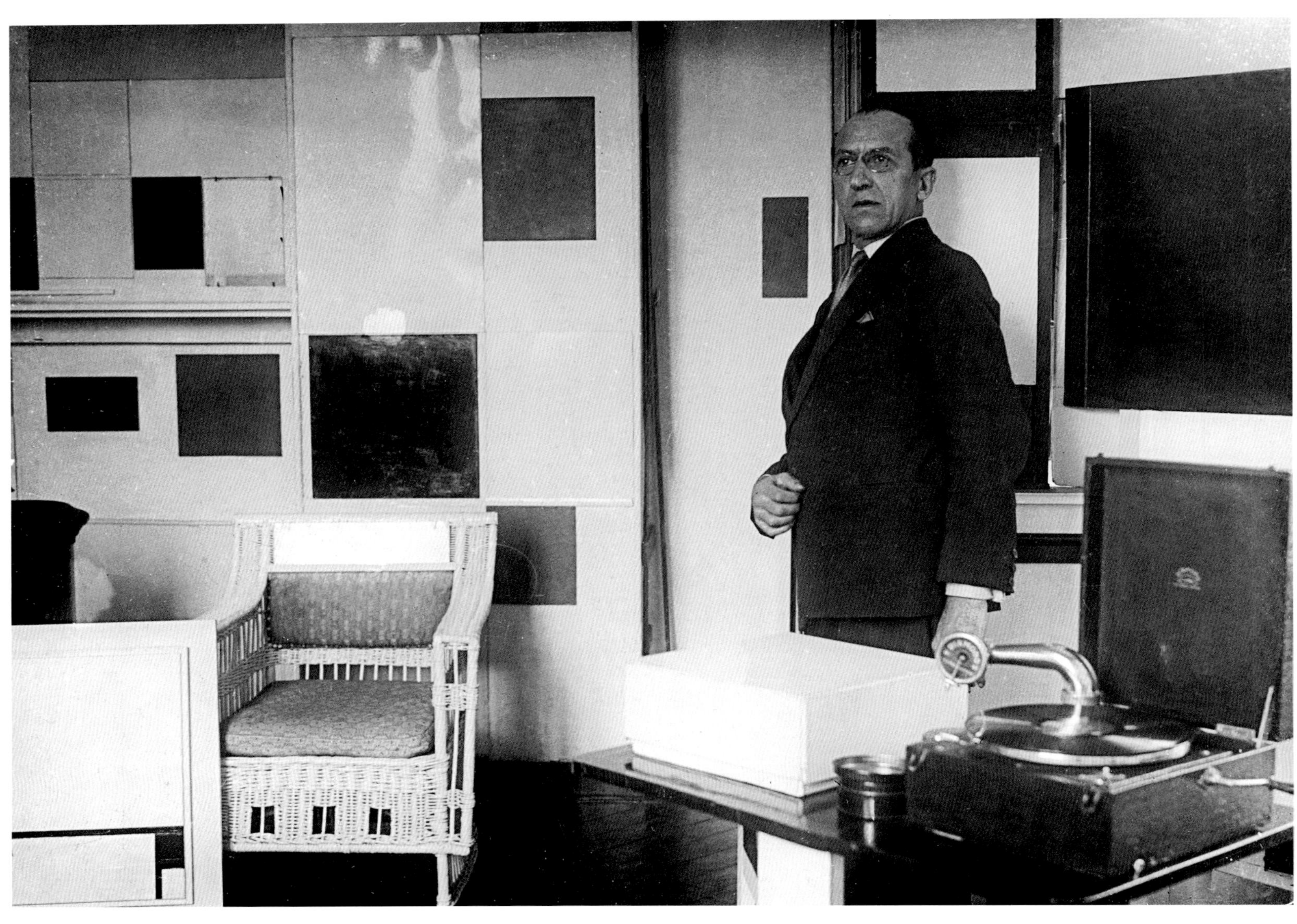

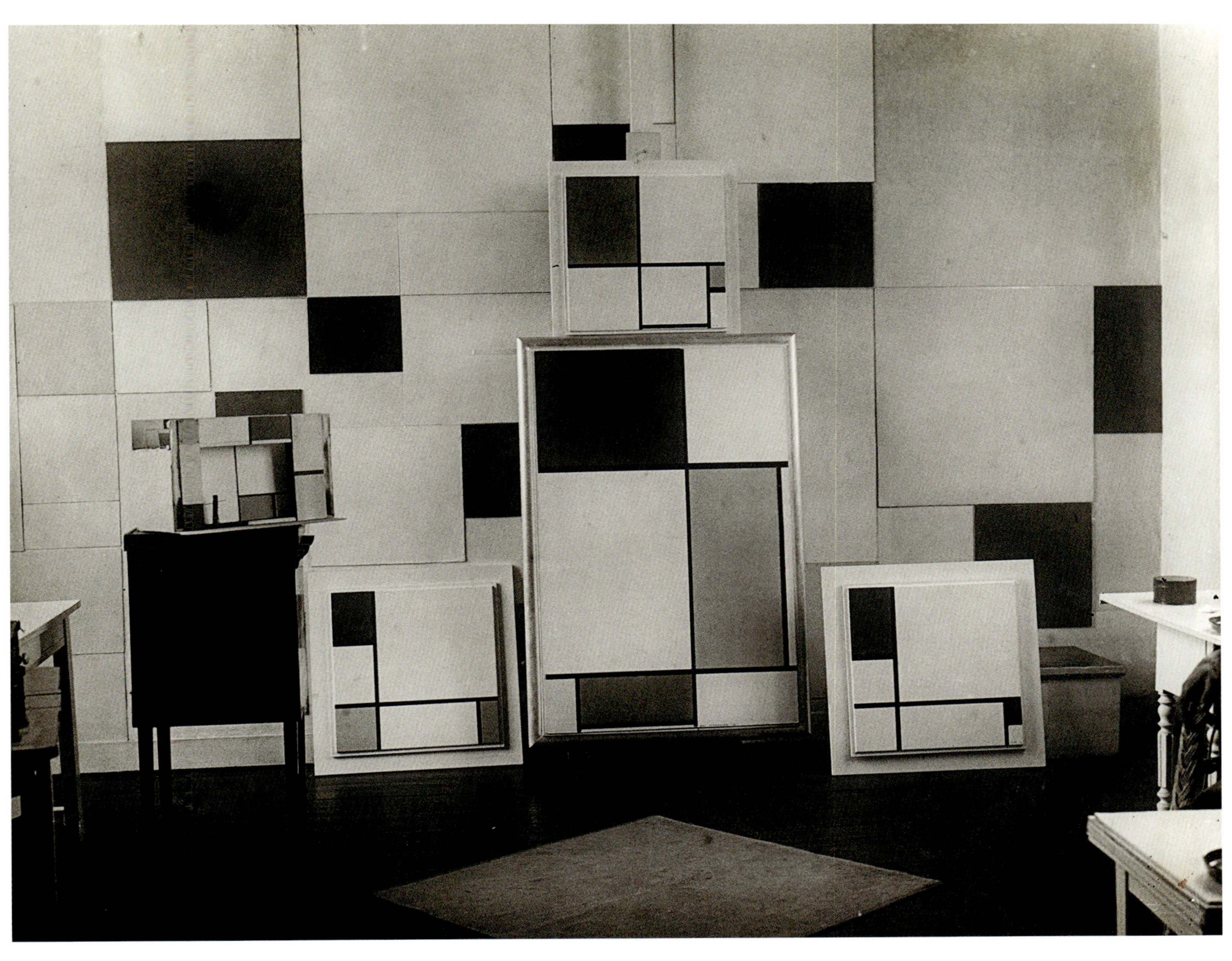

CAT. 120 **Rosie Ney (?)**
Piet Mondrian in his studio, mid-1929 (?)

CAT. 121 **Charles Karsten**
Piet Mondrian's studio, c. summer 1929
Mondrian's stage-set design, reproduced in cats 80 and 84–6, can be seen against the back wall on the left.

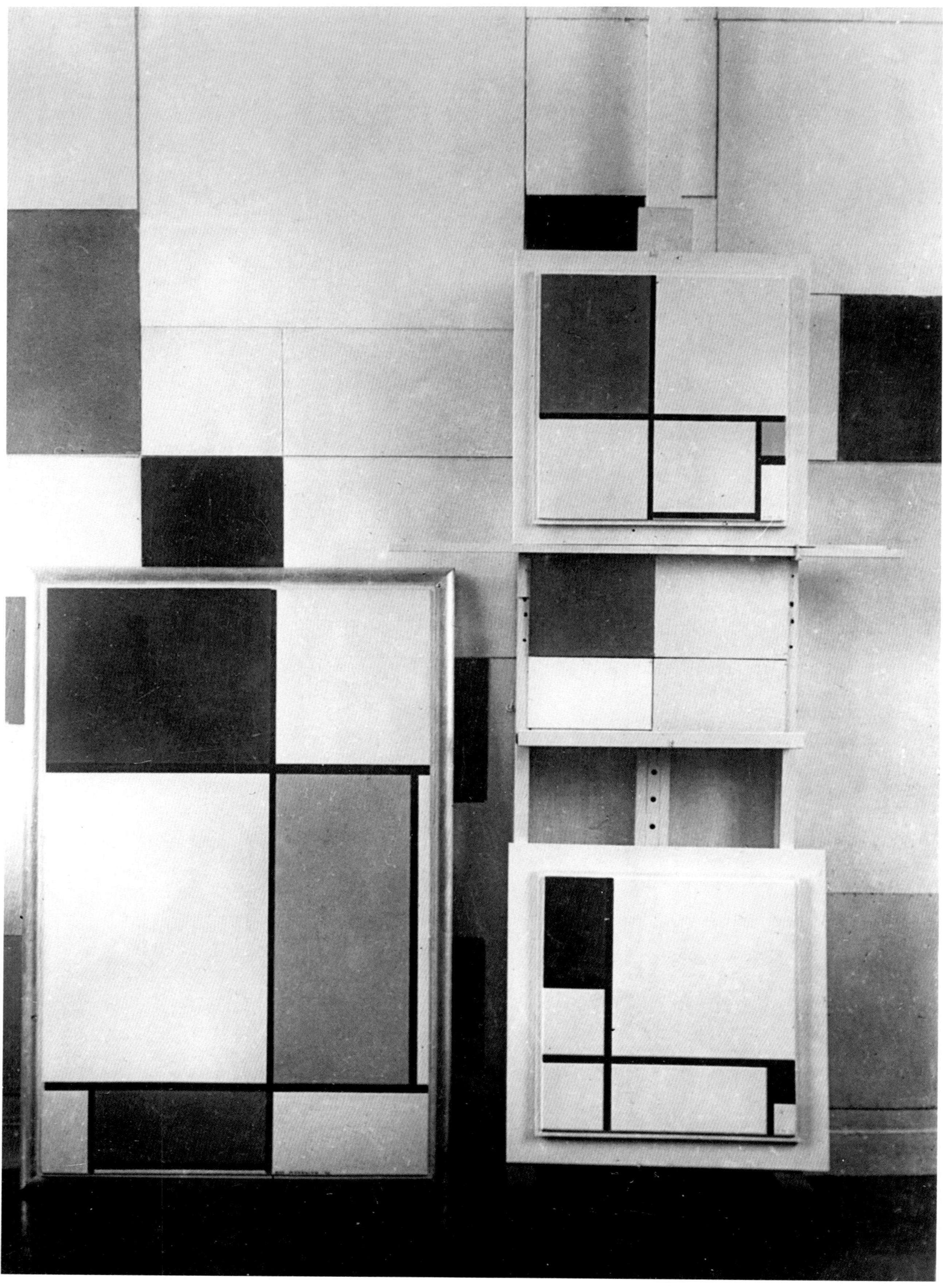

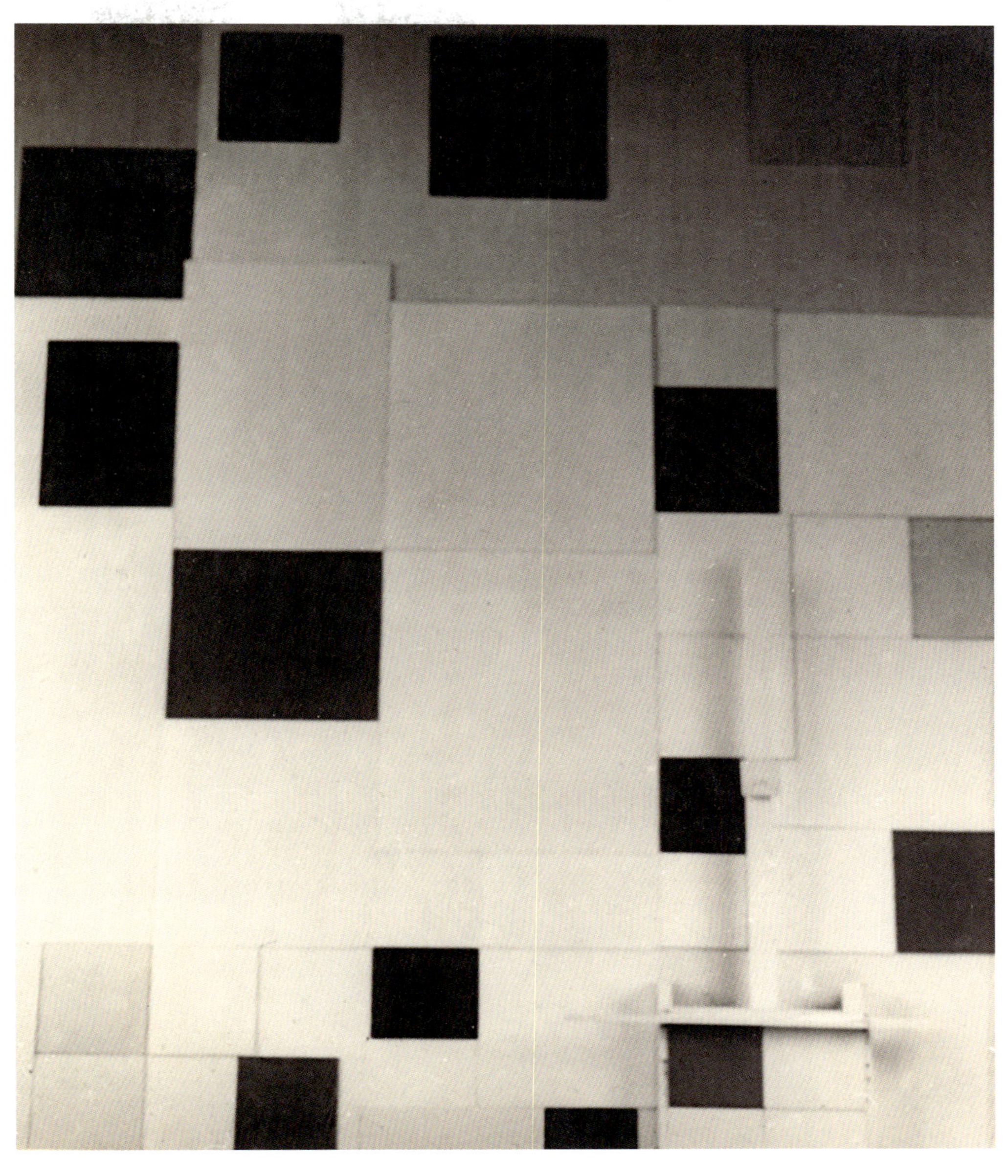

CAT. 122 **Charles Karsten**
Piet Mondrian's studio, c. summer 1929

CAT. 123 **Unidentified photographer**
Piet Mondrian's studio, c. summer 1929
This picture provides a view of the rear wall, specifically the upper part above the easel. It shows that Mondrian continued his neo-plastic interior design to a height of at least three metres above floor level.

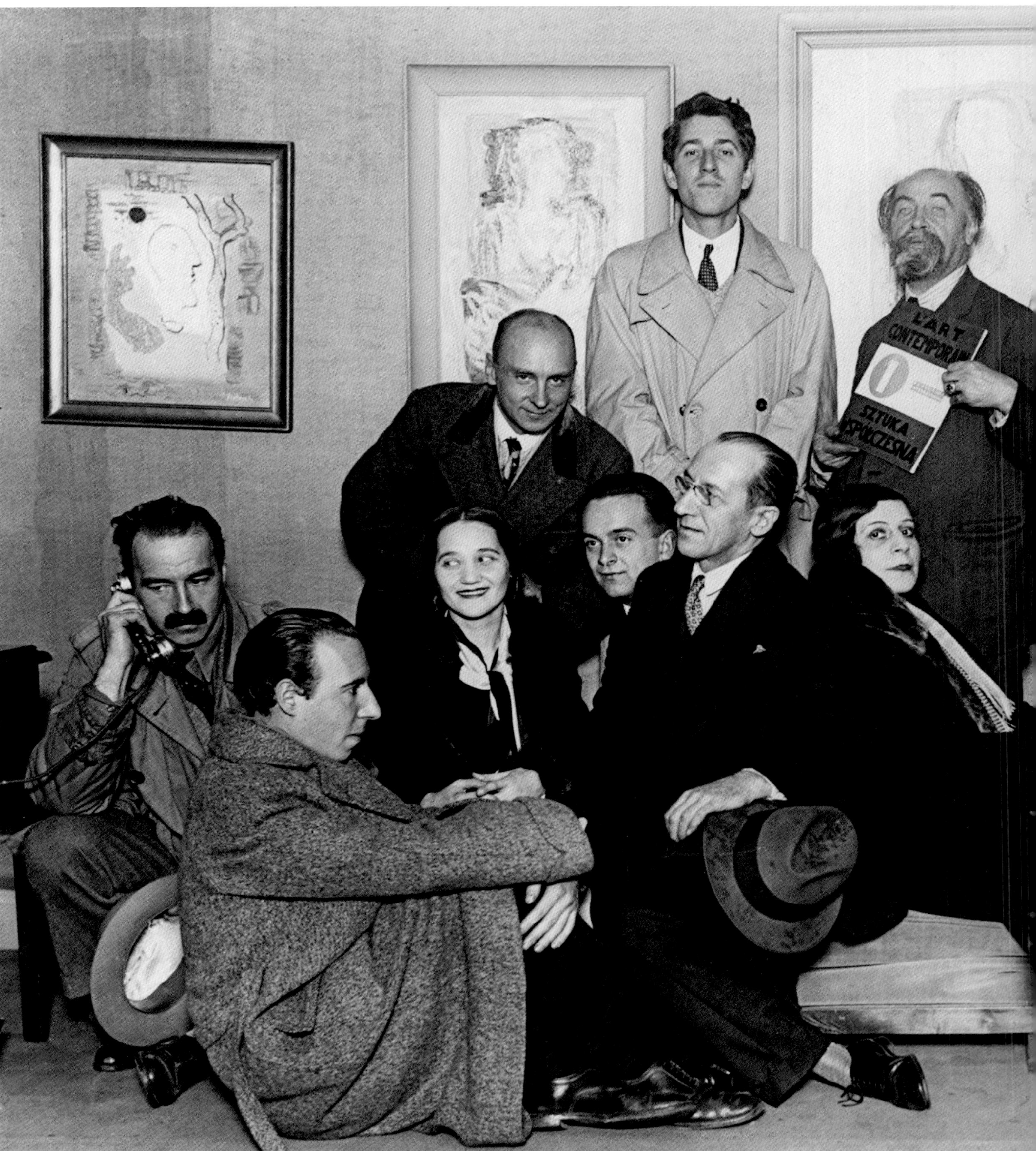
L'ART
CONTEMPORAIN
SZTUKA
SPÓŁCZESNA

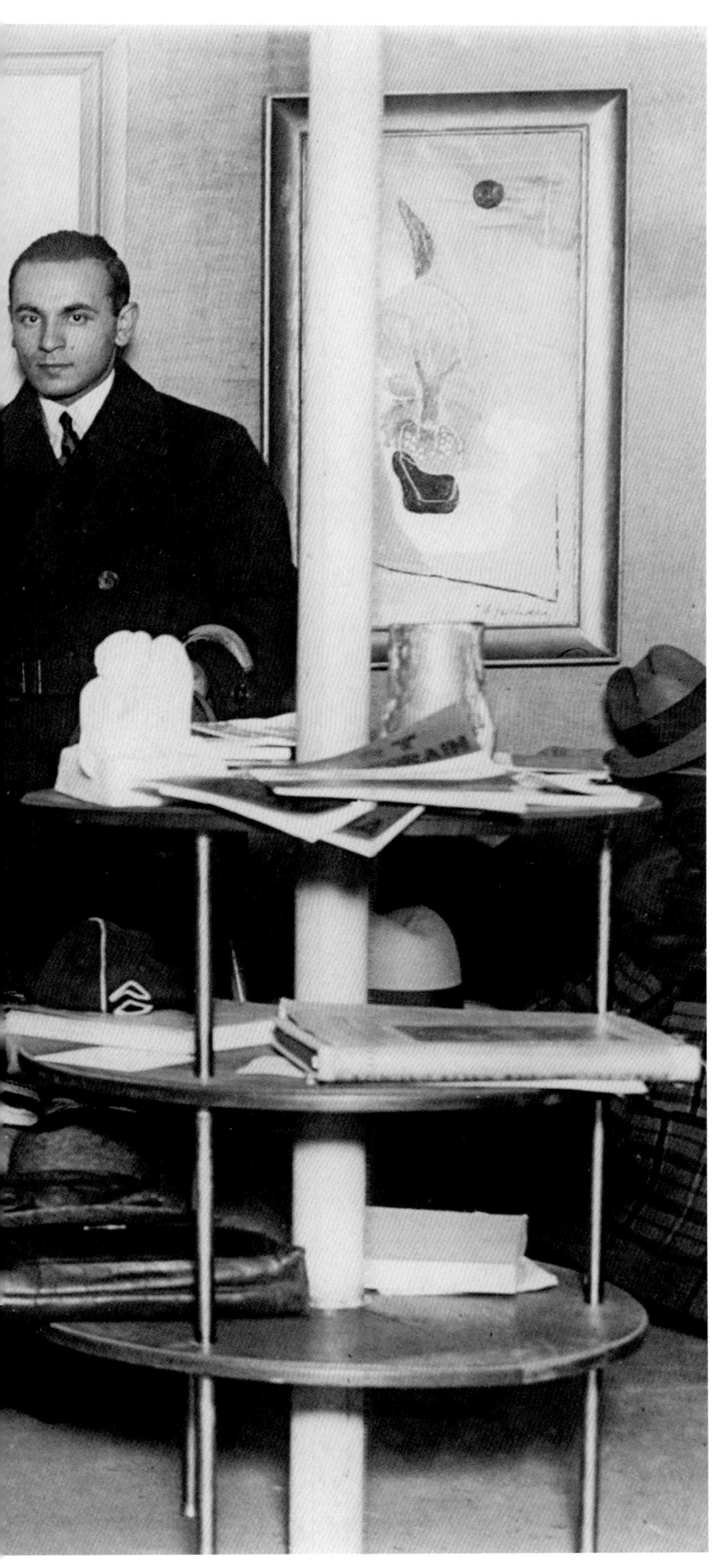

CAT. 124 **Stanislaw Londynski**

Company at the opening of Gustave Buchet's exhibition at Galerie Zak, Paris, 22 November 1929

Left to right, sitting: Auguste Zawoyski, Michel Seuphor, Nadia Grabowska, Jan Brzekowski, Piet Mondrian, Florence Henri; standing: Henryk Stazewski, Stanislaw Grabowski, Pierre Choumoff and an unidentified man. Choumoff is holding up the first issue of *L'Art contemporain—Sztuka Współczesna*, which appeared in April 1929.

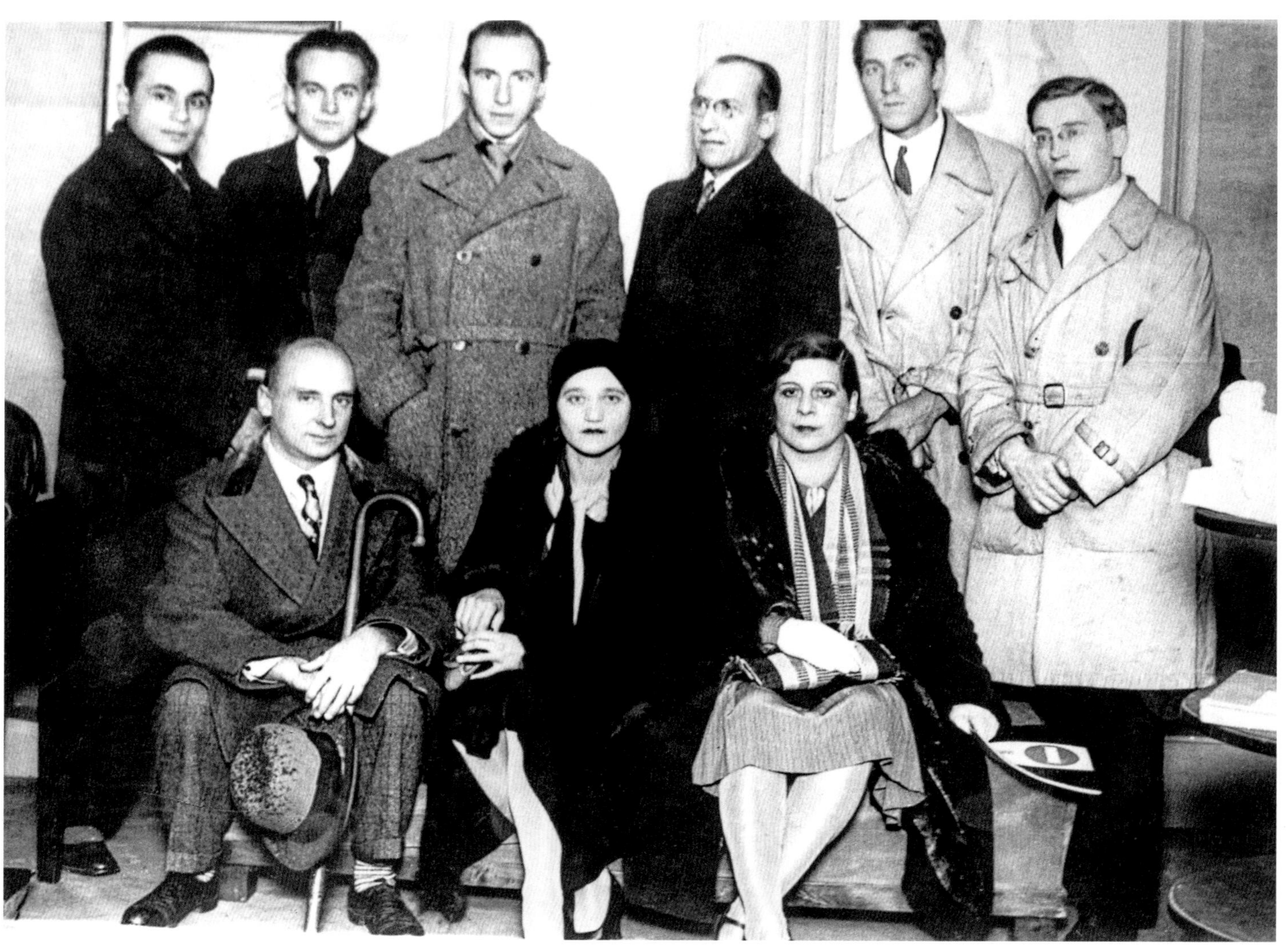

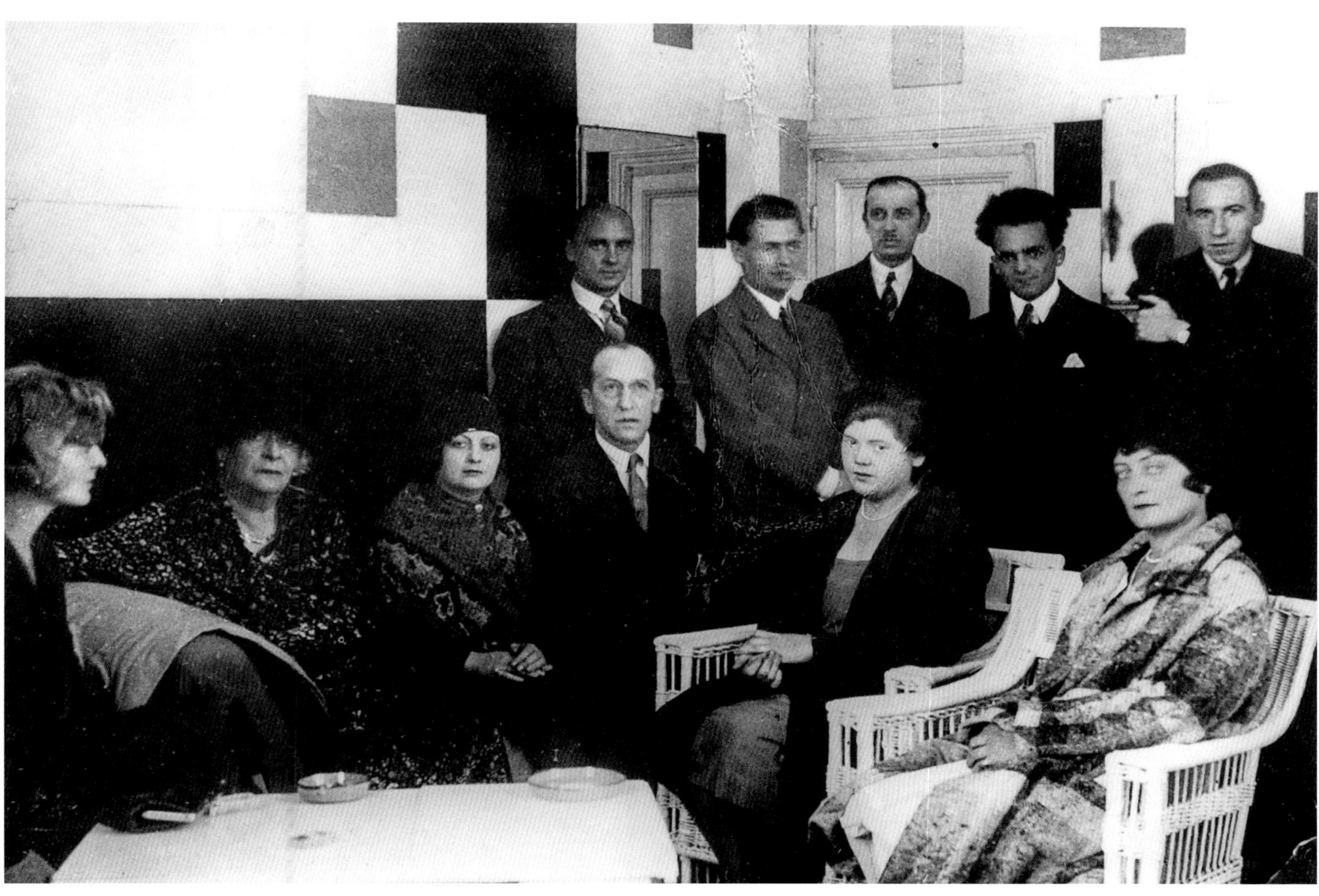

CAT. 125 **Stanislaw Londynski**

Company at the opening of Gustave Buchet's exhibition at Galerie Zak, Paris, 22 November 1929

Left to right, sitting: Henryk Stazewski, Nadia Grabowska, Florence Henri; standing: unidentified man, Jan Brzekowski, Michel Seuphor, Piet Mondrian, Stanislaw Grabowski, unidentified man.

CAT. 127 **Henri Glarner**

Company in Piet Mondrian's studio, c. autumn 1929

Left to right, sitting: Ingeborg Bjarnason, Alexandra Exter, Vera Idelson, Piet Mondrian, Lucy Glarner, Brigida Pessano; standing: Henryk Stazewski, Fritz Glarner, Arturo Martini, Lancelot Ney, Michel Seuphor.

CAT. 126 See catalogue

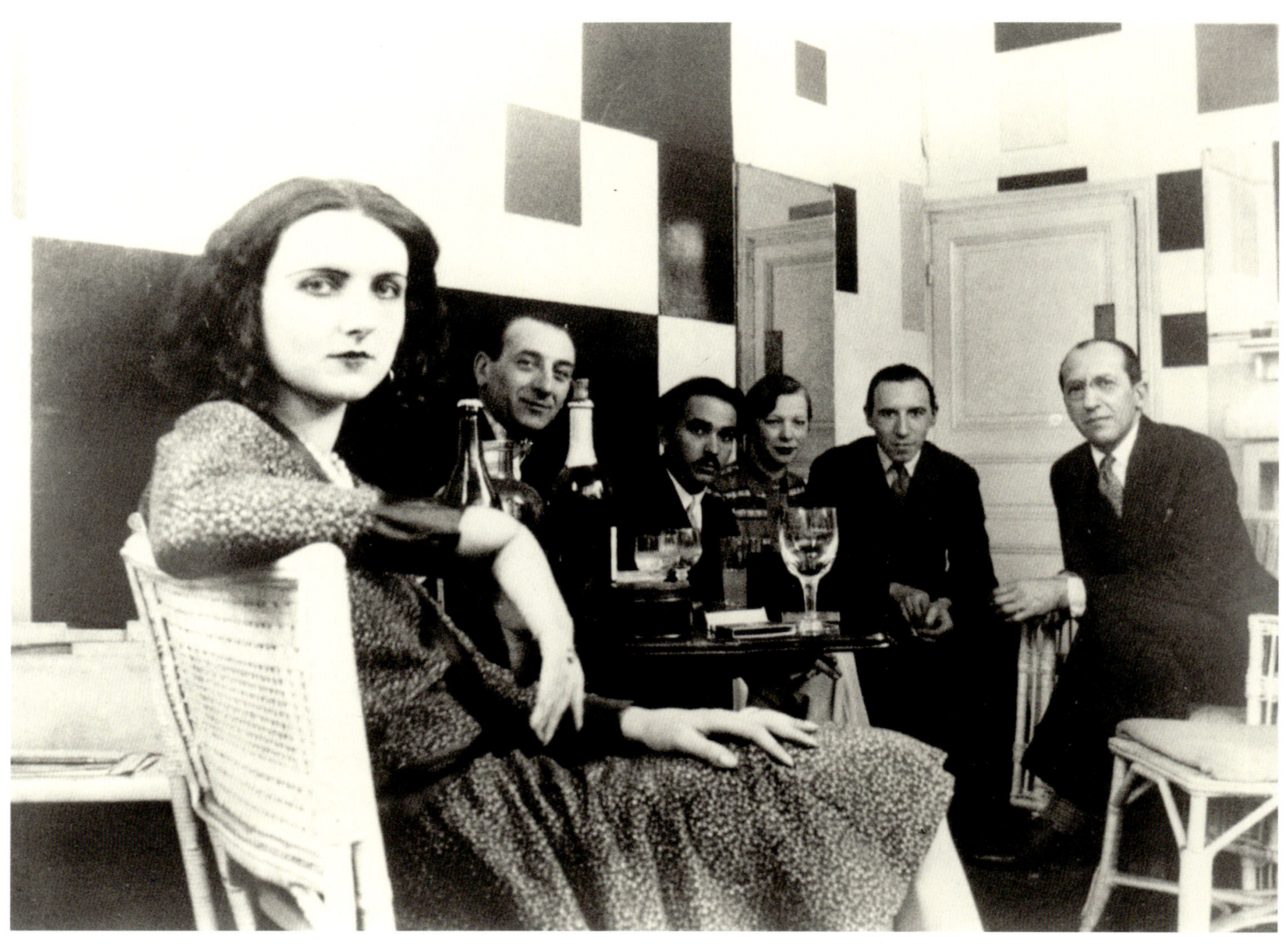

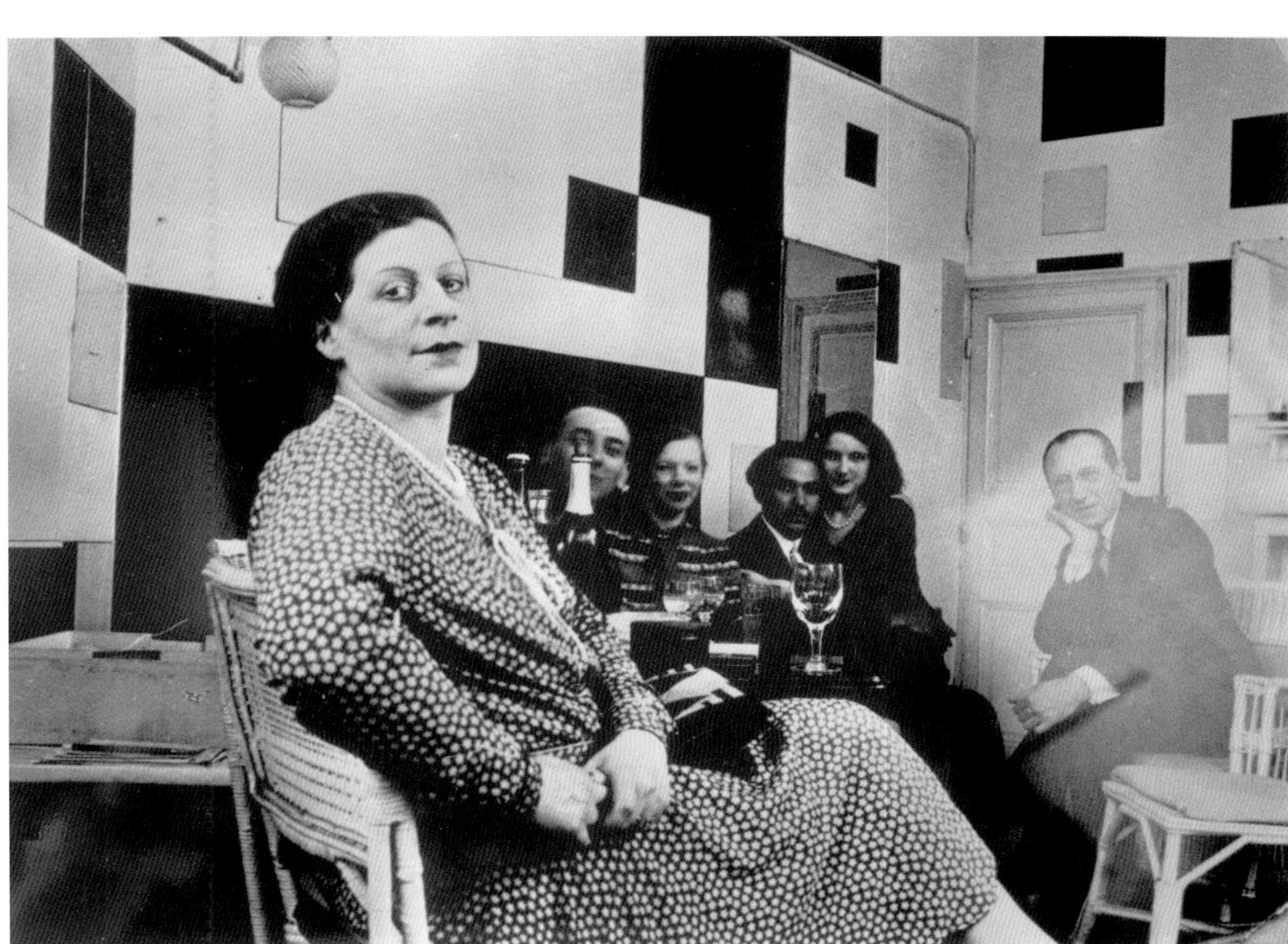

CAT. 128 **Florence Henri (?)**
Company in Piet Mondrian's studio, c. autumn 1929
Left to right: unidentified woman, Georges Vantongerloo, unidentified man, Tine Vantongerloo, Michel Seuphor, Piet Mondrian.

CAT. 129 **Michel Seuphor (?)**
Company in Piet Mondrian's studio, c. autumn 1929
Left to right: Florence Henri, Georges and Tine Vantongerloo, unidentified couple, Piet Mondrian.

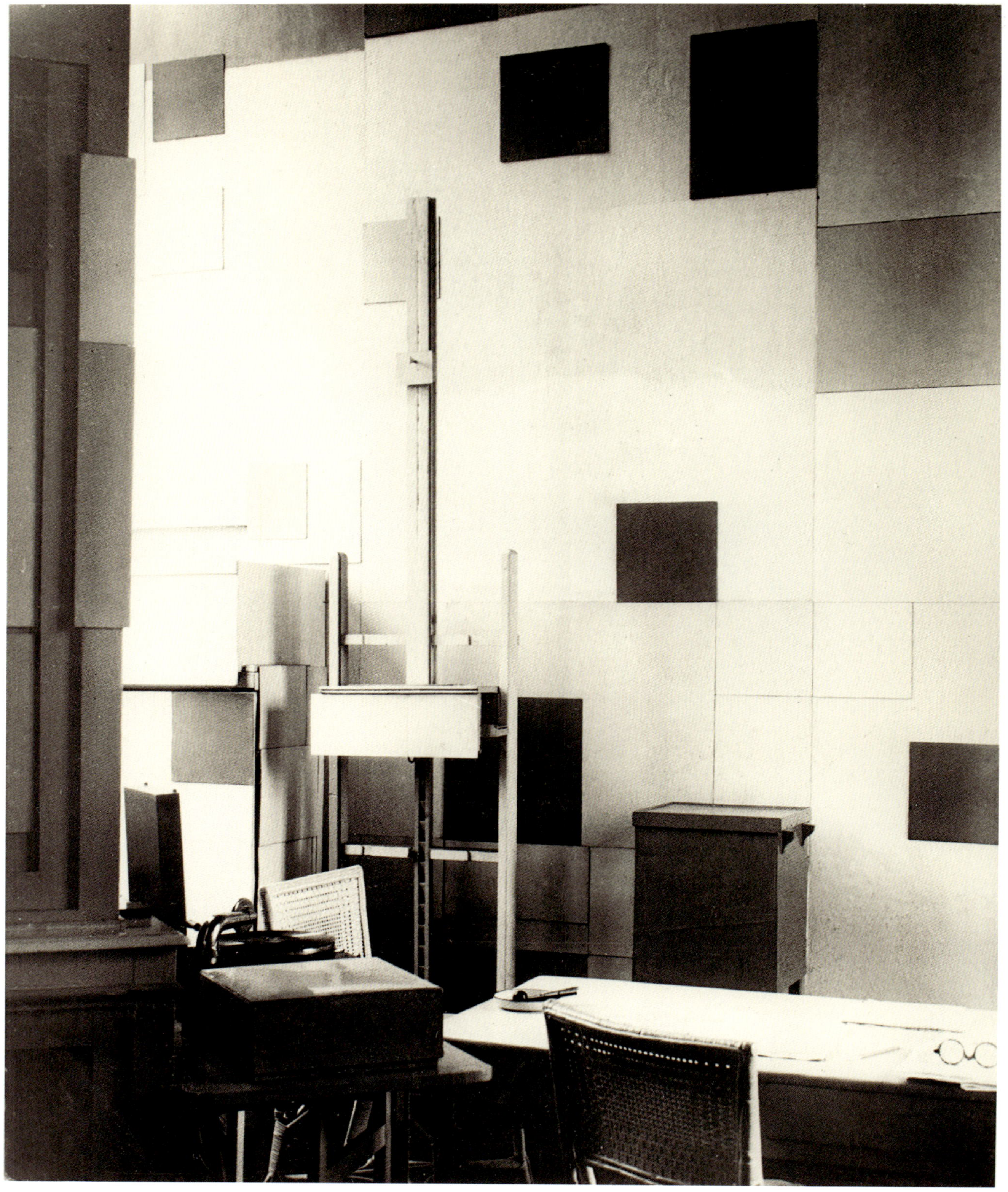

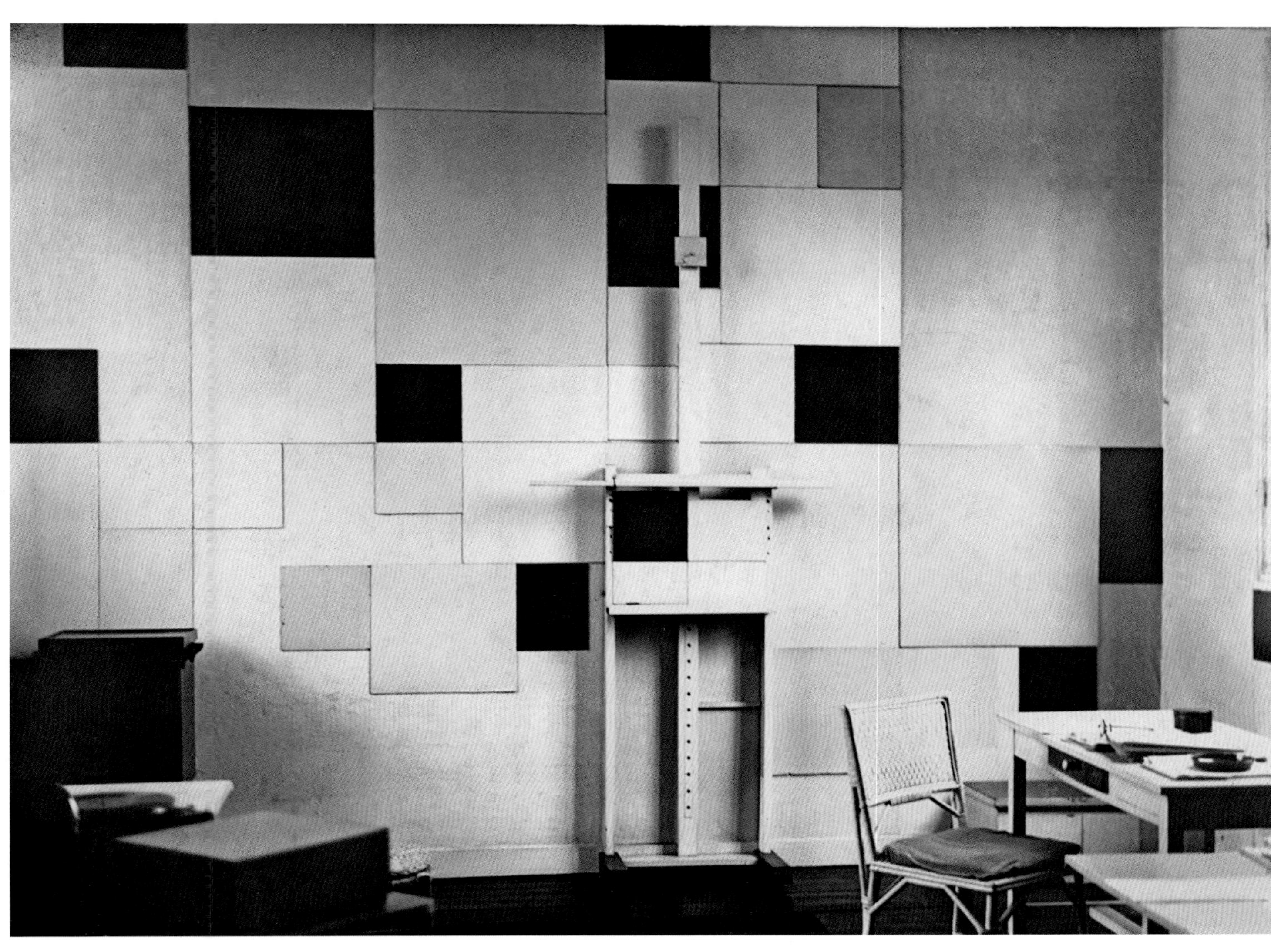

CAT. 132 **Michel Seuphor or Rosie Ney**
Piet Mondrian's studio, c. March–April 1930

CAT. 130 **Michel Seuphor or Rosie Ney**
Piet Mondrian's studio, c. March–April 1930
This photograph was published in *Cercle et Carré* in June 1930, where it appeared in combination with Pierre Delbo's 1925/26 studio photograph (cat. 74). The juxtaposition of the two pictures was intended to illustrate how neo-plasticism had developed in the intervening years.

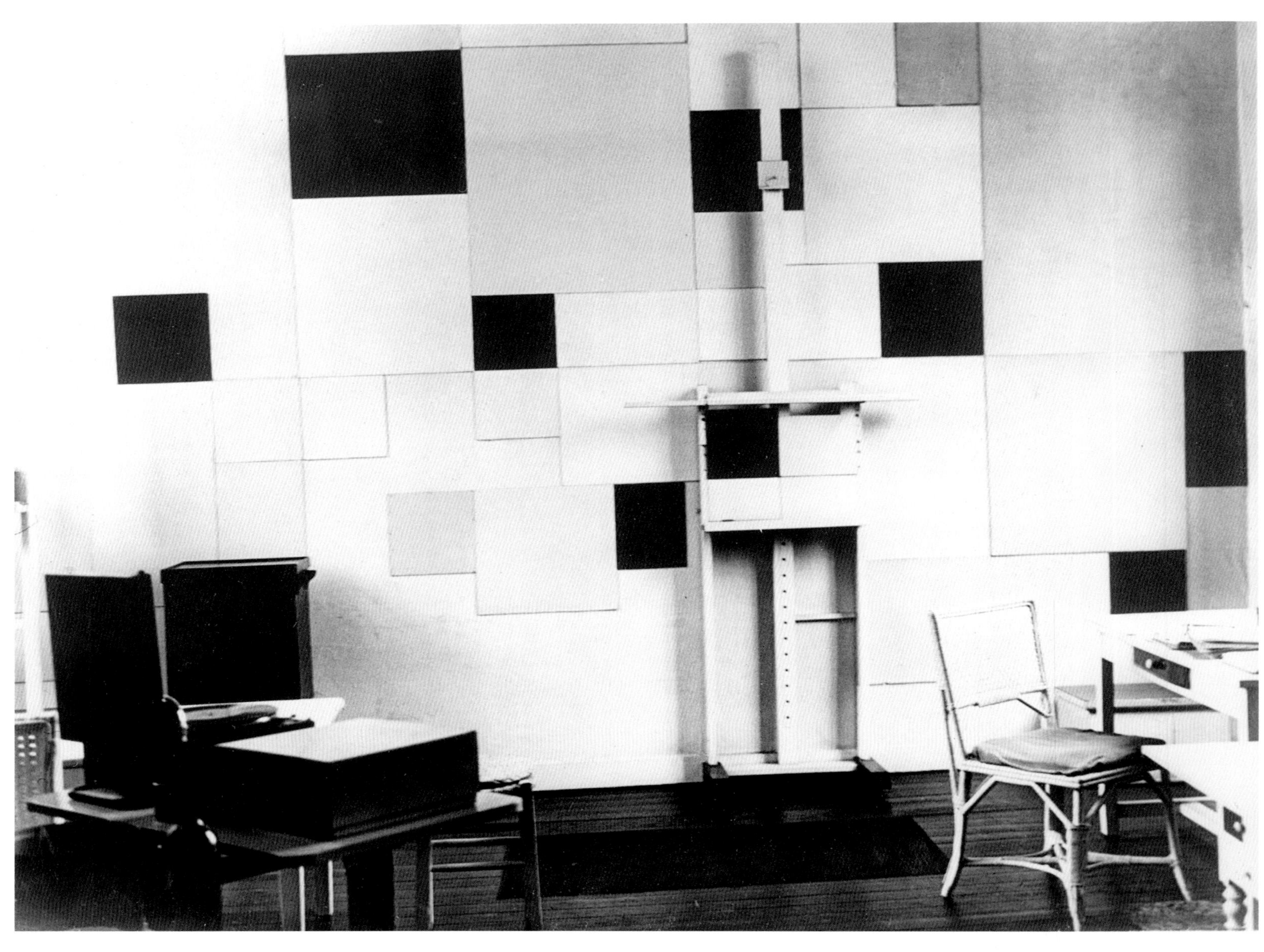

CATS 131, 133 **Michel Seuphor or Rosie Ney**
Piet Mondrian's studio, c. March–April 1930

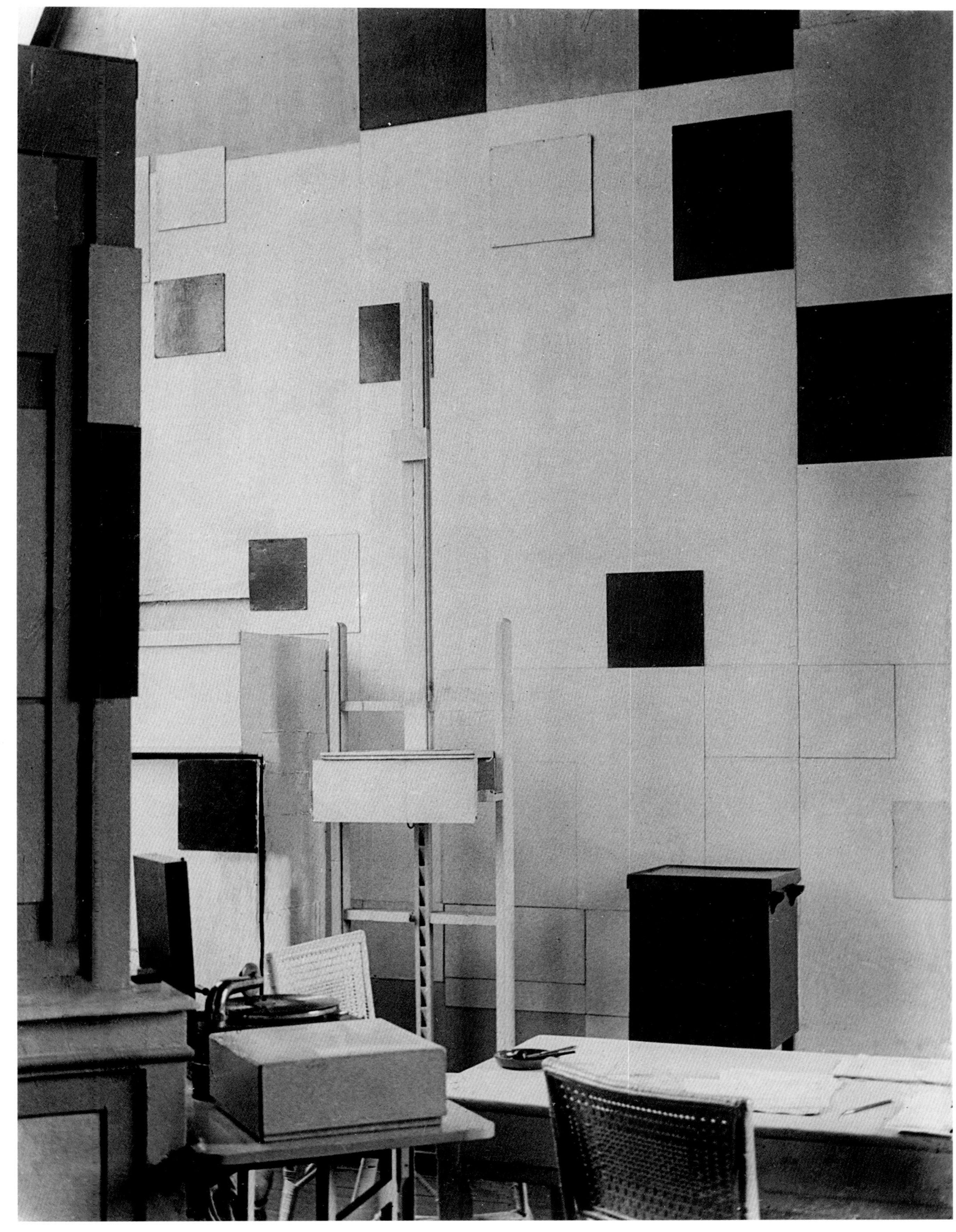

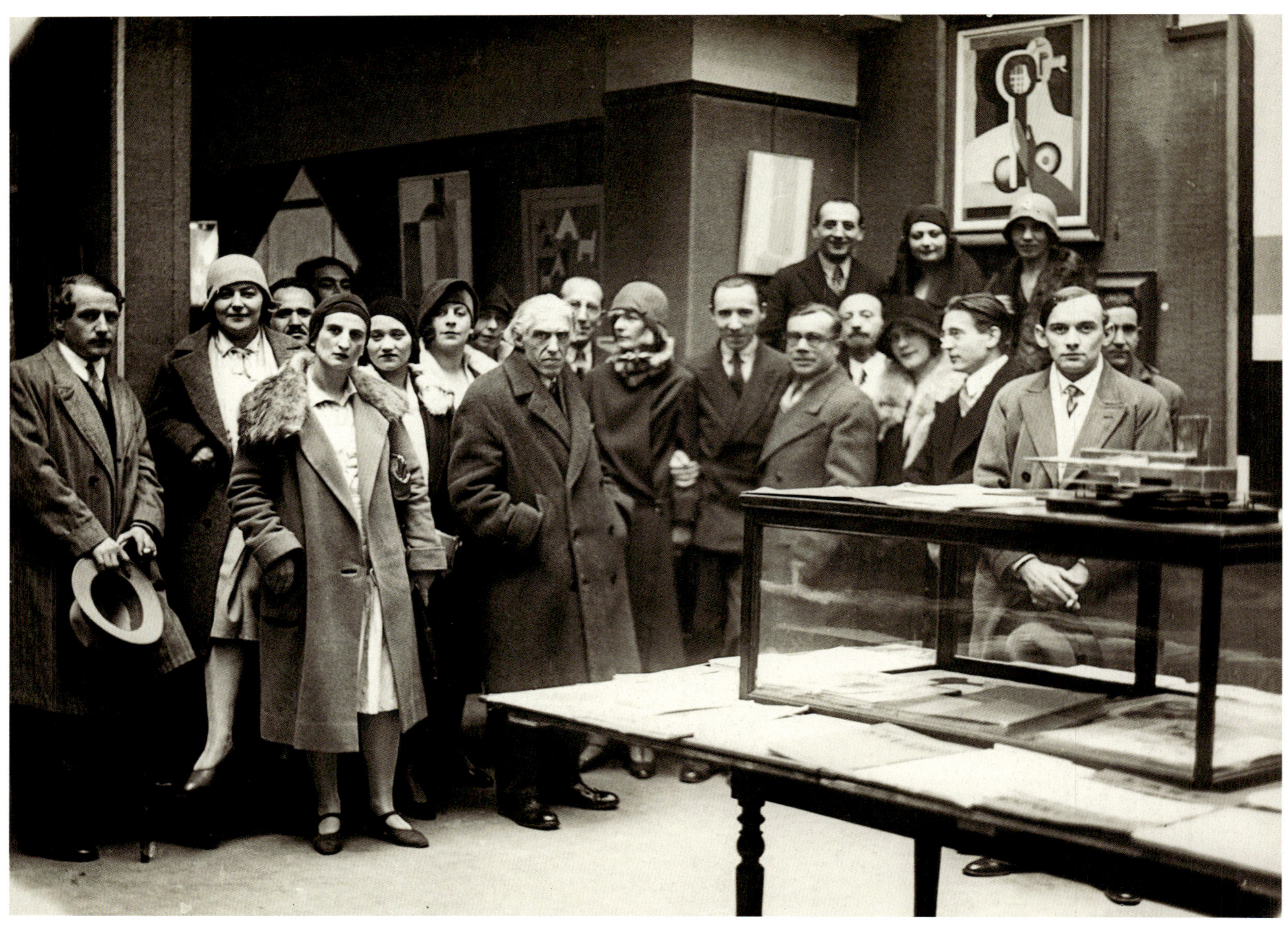

CAT. 135 **Ina Bandy**

Company at the opening of the Cercle et Carré exhibition at Galerie 23, Paris, 18 April 1930

Left to right: unidentified man, Franciska Clausen, unidentified man, Pierre Daura, Marcelle Cahn, Nadia Grabowska, Florence Henri, Sophie Taeuber-Arp, Joaquín Torres-García, Piet Mondrian, Ingeborg Bjarnason, Michel Seuphor, Jean Gorin, Luigi Russolo, Wanda Wolska, Stefan Moszczynski, Friedrich Vordemberge-Gildewart, Germán Cueto; higher up: Georges Vantongerloo, Vera Idelson, Manolita Piña Torres-García.

Cercle et Carré was a group of constructivist artists founded by Joaquín Torres-García and Michel Seuphor. The group exhibition was a one-off: Cercle et Carré disintegrated a few months later.

CAT. 134 See catalogue

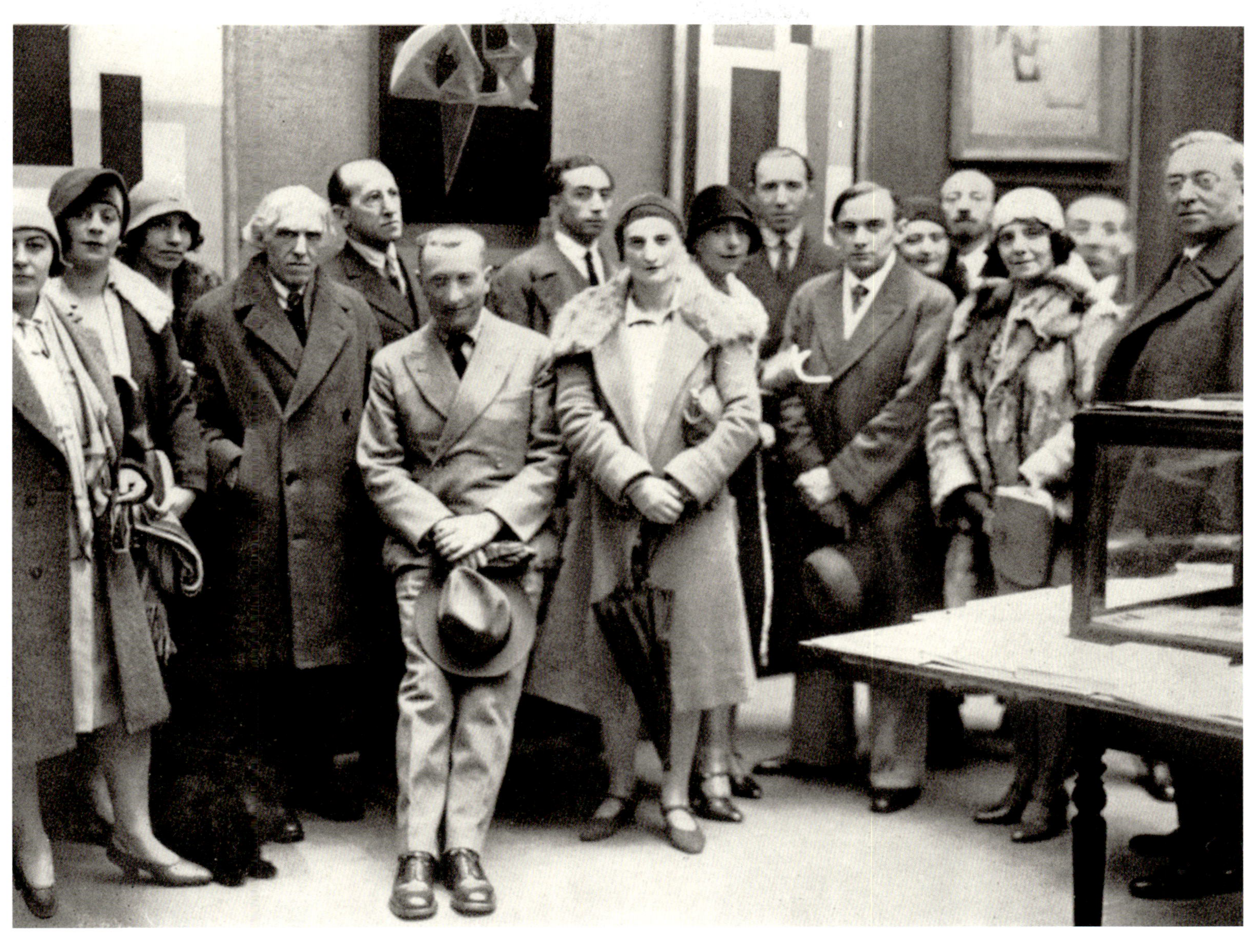

CAT. 136 **Ina Bandy**

Company at the opening of the Cercle et Carré exhibition at Galerie 23, Paris, 18 April 1930

Left to right: Franciska Clausen, Florence Henri, Manolita Piña Torres-García, Joaquín Torres-García, Piet Mondrian, Hans Arp, Pierre Daura, Marcelle Cahn, Sophie Taeuber-Arp, Michel Seuphor, Friedrich Vordemberge-Gildewart, Vera Idelson, Luigi Russolo, Nina Kandinsky, George Vantongerloo, Wassily Kandinsky, Jean Gorin.

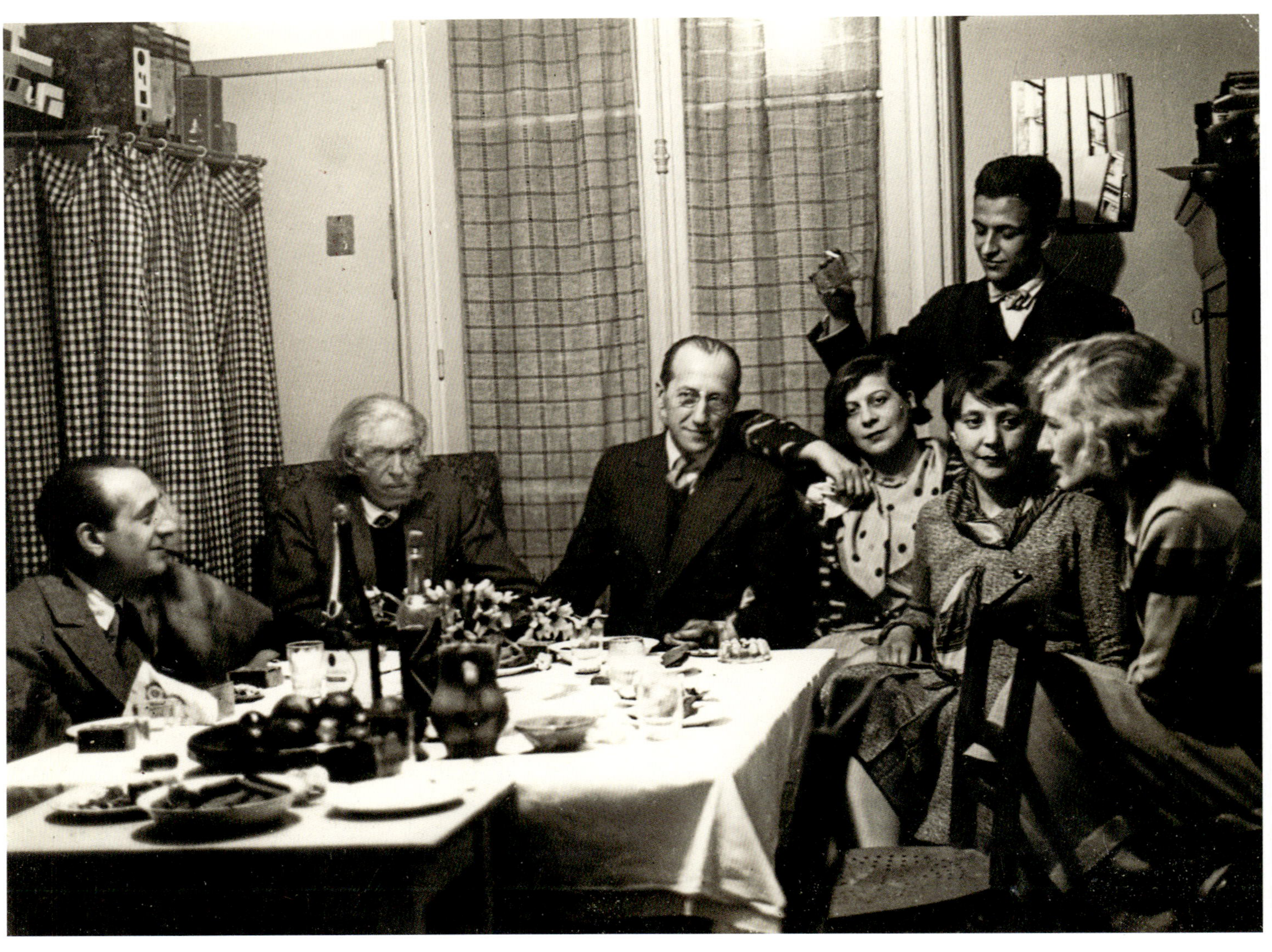

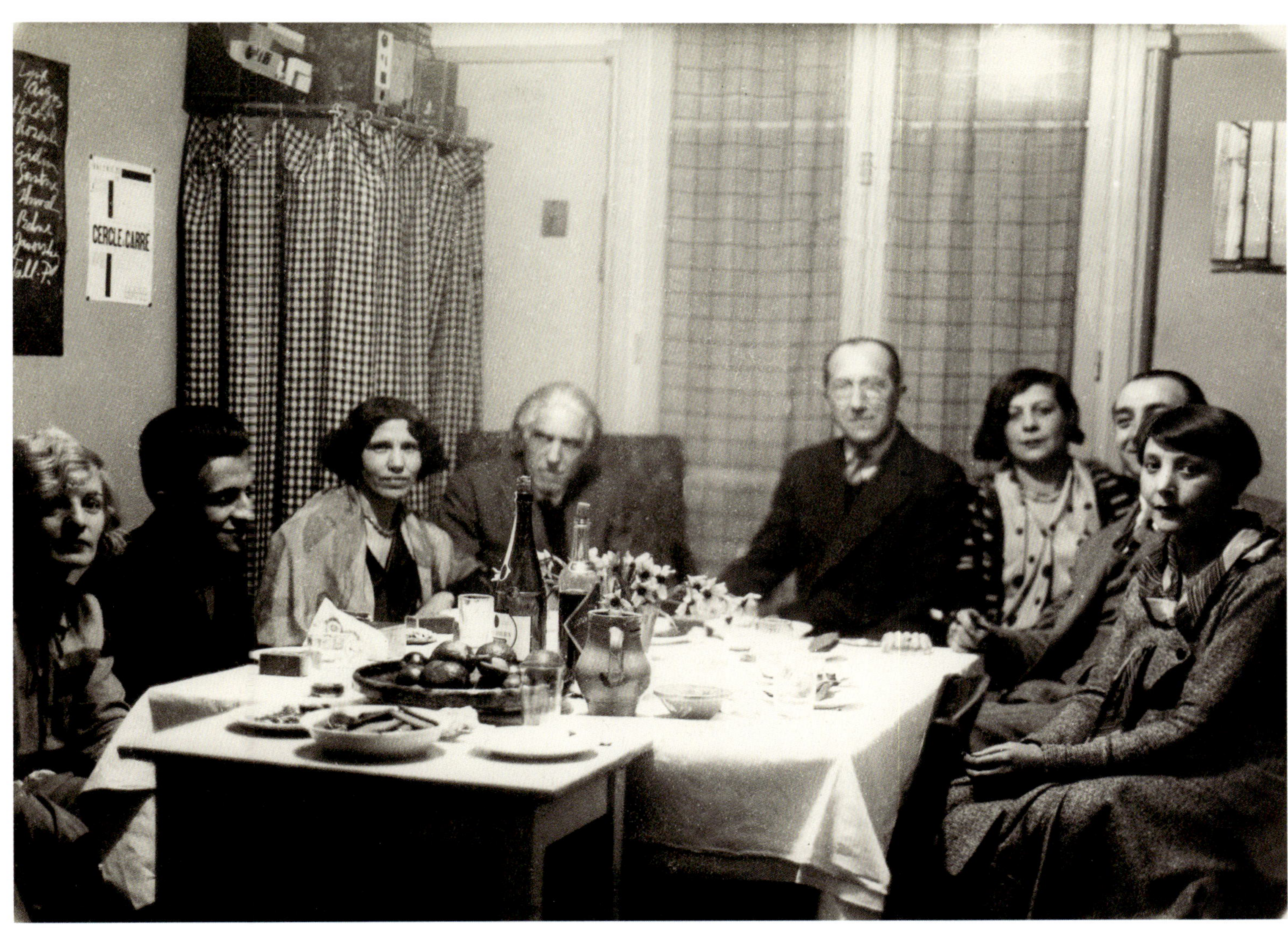

CAT. 137 **Michel Seuphor**

Company in Michel Seuphor's home, Vanves, April 1930

Left to right: Georges Vantongerloo, Joaquín Torres-García, Piet Mondrian, Florence Henri, Denis Honegger, Margaret Schall, Ingeborg Bjarnason.

Like cat. 138, this photograph was taken during one of the meetings of the group associated with the magazine *Cercle et Carré*, which were held on Sunday evenings at Seuphor's studio in the Paris suburb of Vanves.

CAT. 138 **Michel Seuphor**

Company in Michel Seuphor's home, Vanves, April 1930

Left to right: Ingeborg Bjarnason, Denis Honegger, Manolita Piña Torres-García, Joaquín Torres-García, Piet Mondrian, Florence Henri, Georges Vantongerloo, Margaret Schall.

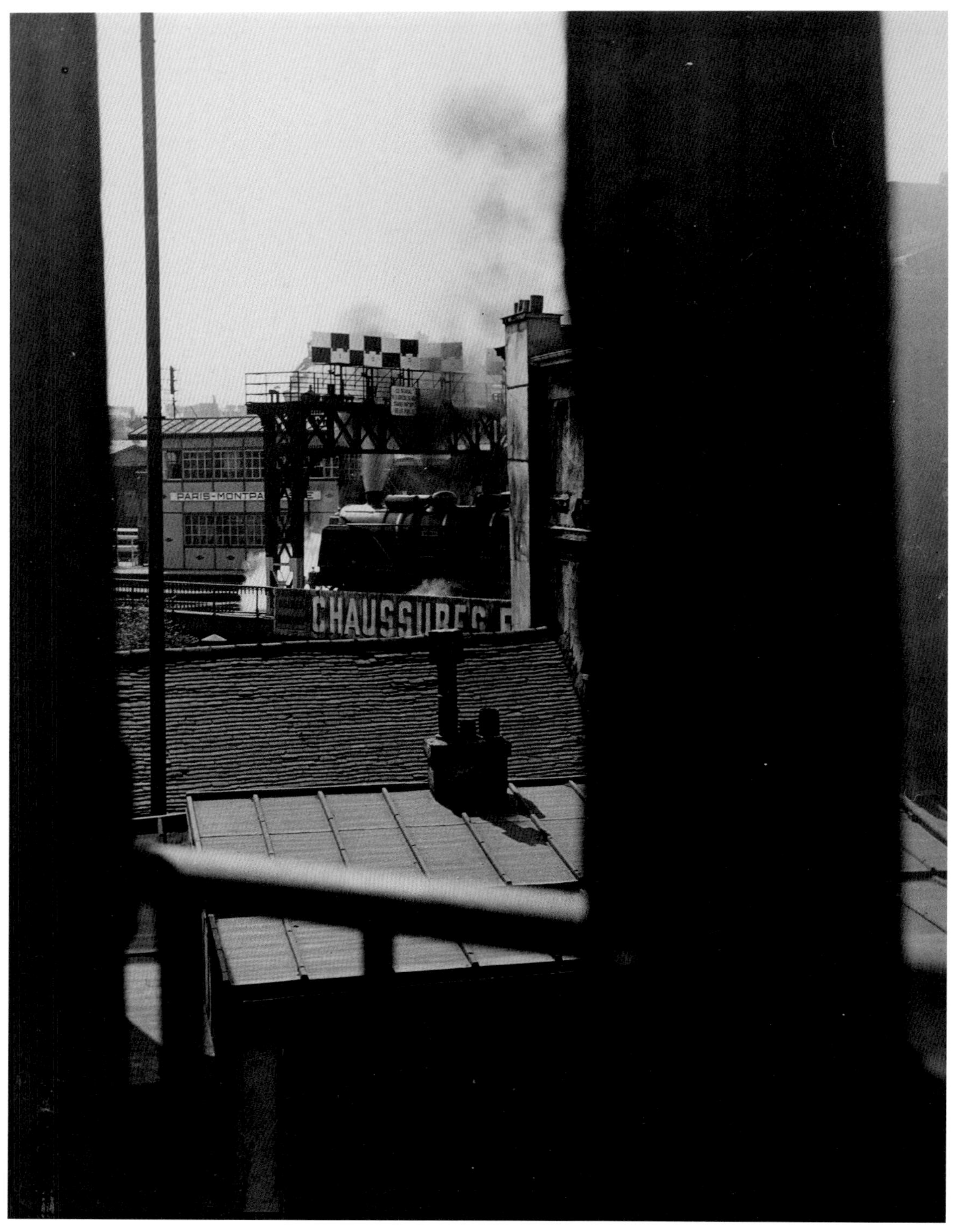
PARIS-MONTPA
CHAUSSURES

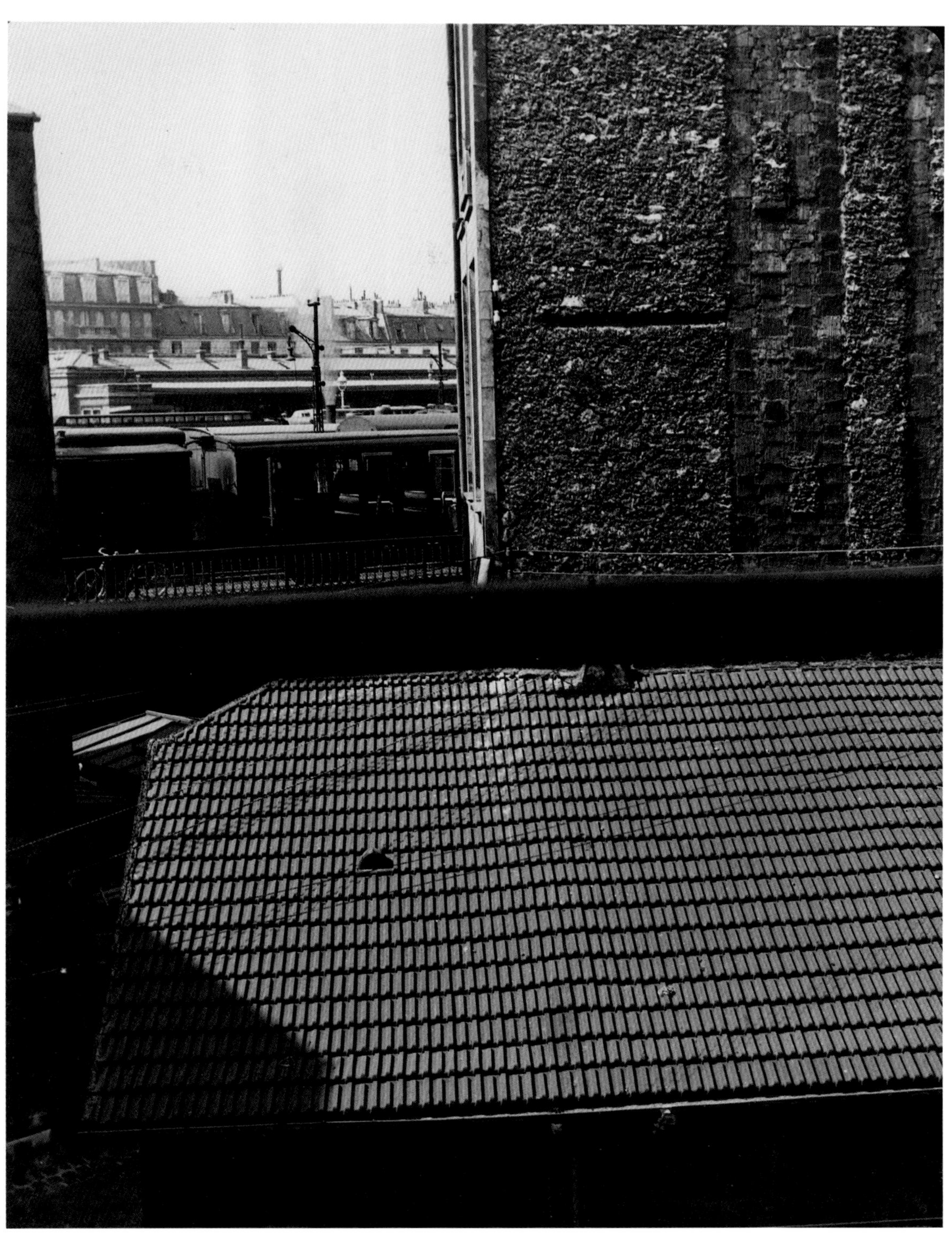

CAT. 139 **László Moholy-Nagy**
Gare Montparnasse viewed from Piet Mondrian's studio, summer 1927 or summer 1930
This photograph was taken from Mondrian's studio at 26 Rue du Départ. The railway tracks of the Montparnasse station could be seen from the window.

CAT. 140 **László Moholy-Nagy**
Gare Montparnasse viewed from Piet Mondrian's kitchen window, summer 1927 or summer 1930

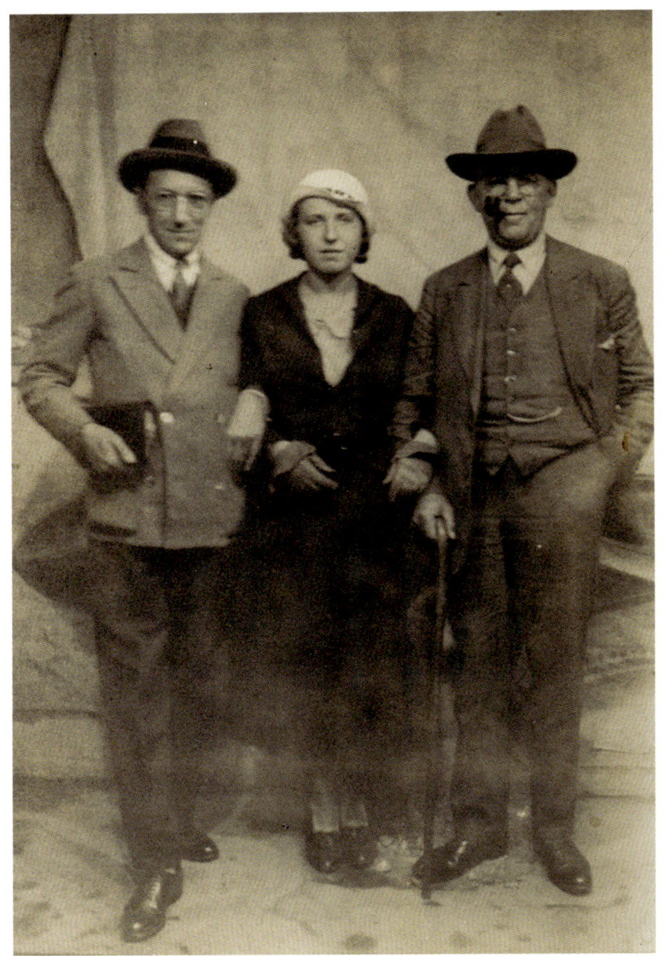

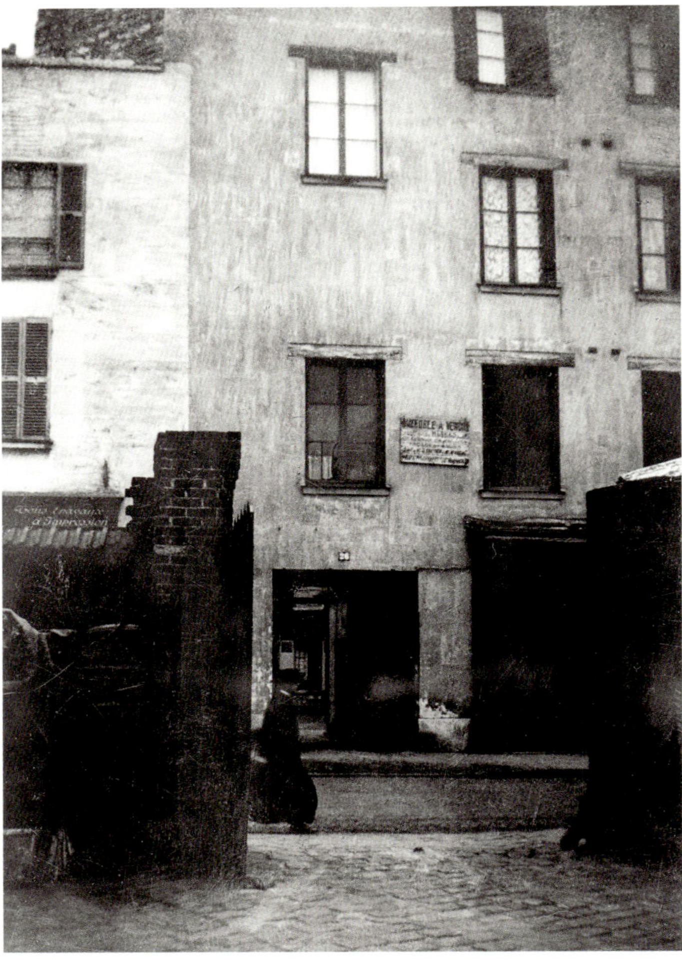

CAT. 141 **Unidentified photographer**

Piet Mondrian, an unidentified woman and Berend Groeneveld, c. 1930

The Dutch amateur painter Berend F. Groeneveld was on good terms with both Mondrian and the latter's friend and fellow artist Simon Maris. He made regular, extended visits to Paris, where he socialized a great deal with Mondrian.

CAT. 143 **Jan van den Briel**

Studio building on Rue du Départ, 1931

The second window above the passageway belonged to Mondrian's studio. This one faced south; the north-facing studio window is shown in cats 109–11.

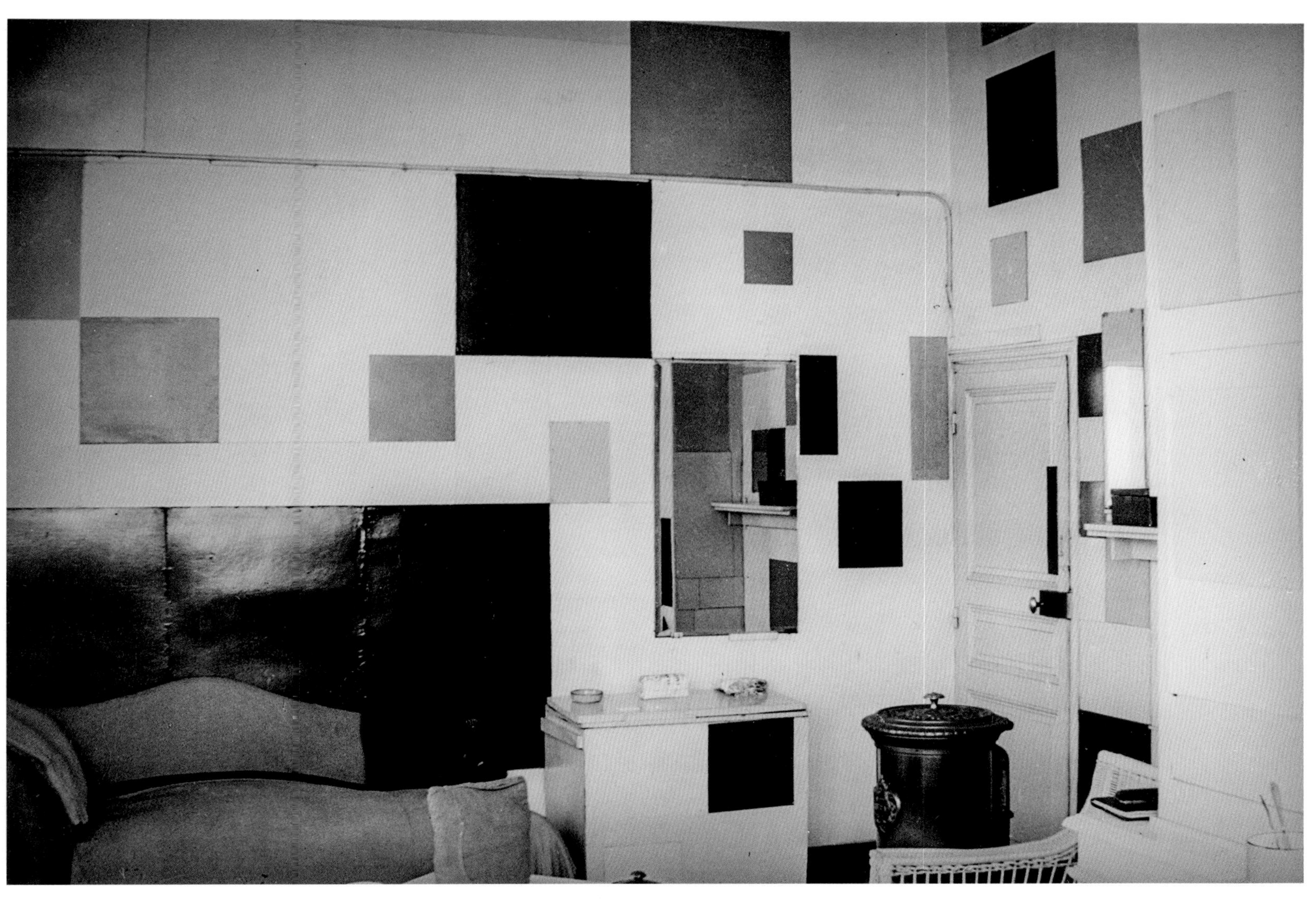

CAT. 142 **Jan van den Briel**

Piet Mondrian's studio, 1931

Johan (Jan) Kees van den Briel was the son of Mondrian's close friend Albert Pieter van den Briel. Mondrian and Van den Briel Senior met in Amsterdam around the turn of the century. After Mondrian had left the Netherlands for good in 1919, Van den Briel visited him almost twice a year in Paris, until Mondrian moved on again to London in September 1938. Van den Briel evidently brought his son along on some of his trips to Paris.

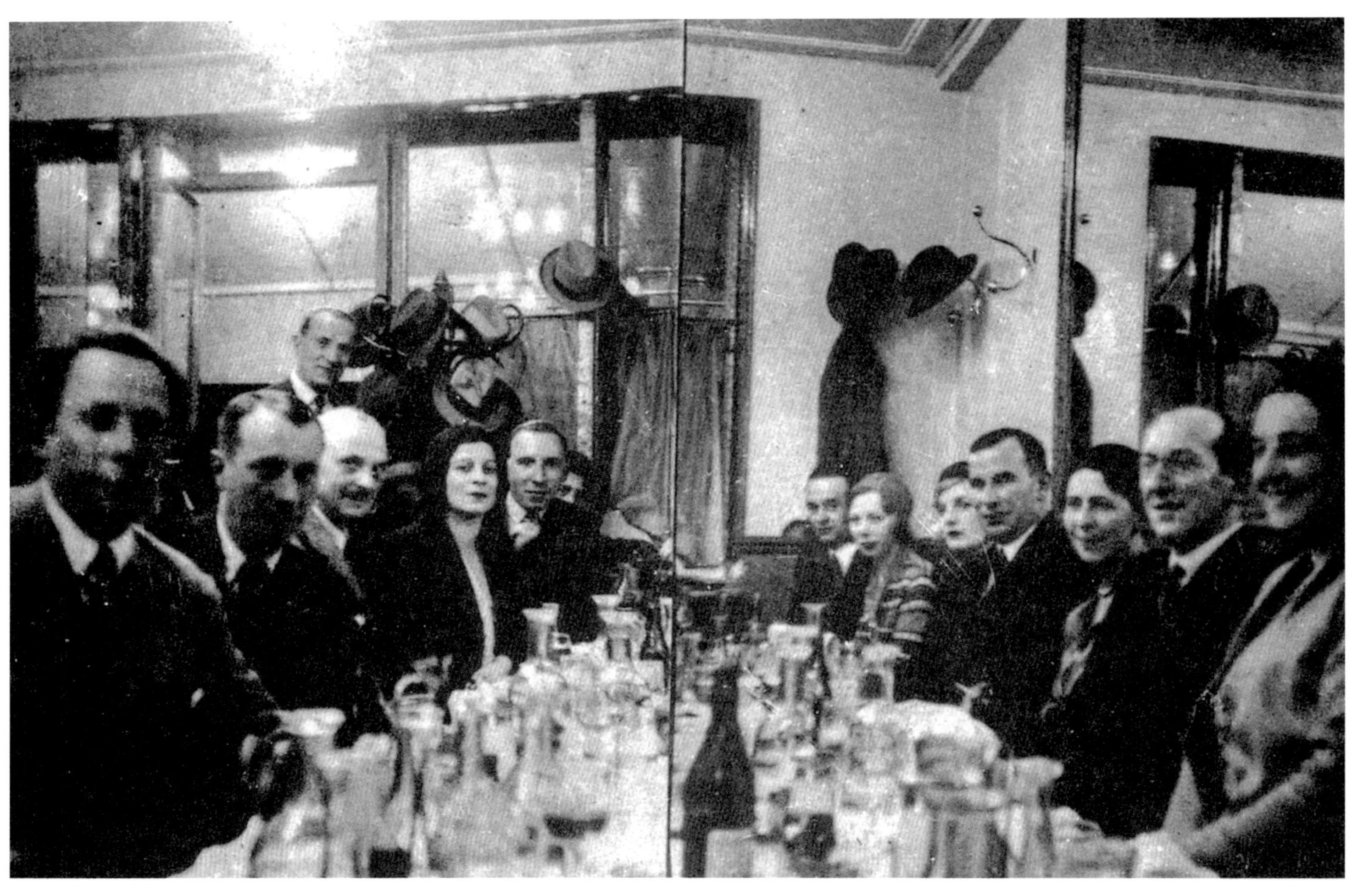

CAT. 144 **Unidentified photographer**

Company at Café Voltaire, Paris, May 1931

Left to right: Robert Delaunay, Hans Arp, Henryk Stazewski, Arturo Ciacelli, Florence Henri, Michel Seuphor, Pouma, Jan Brzekowski, Tine Vantongerloo, Woti and Theodor Werner, Sophie Taeuber-Arp, Piet Mondrian, Sonia Delaunay.

The picture was taken during one of the *jours* that Robert Delaunay organized on Saturdays at Café Voltaire on the Place de l'Odéon.

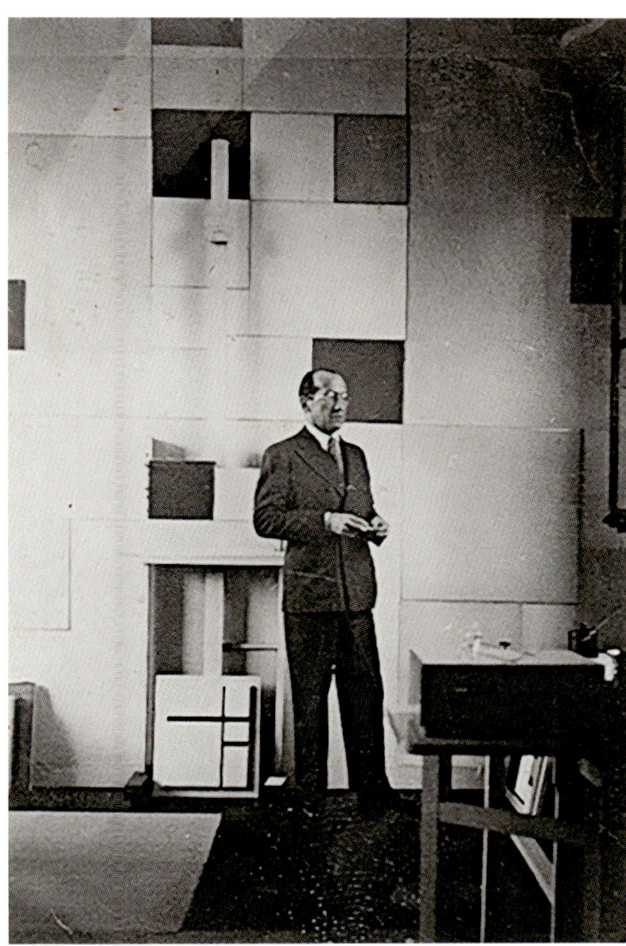

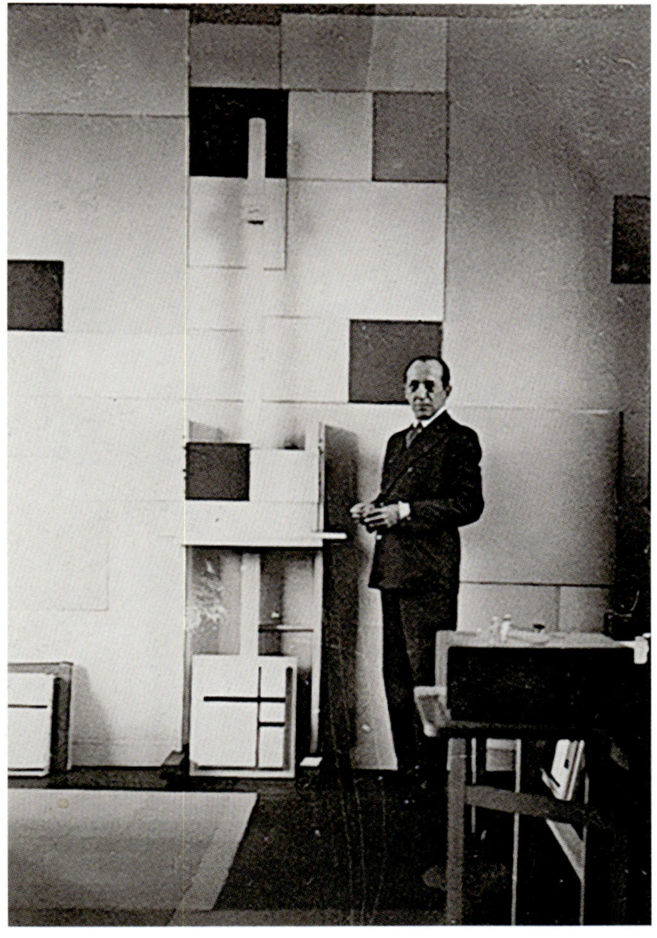

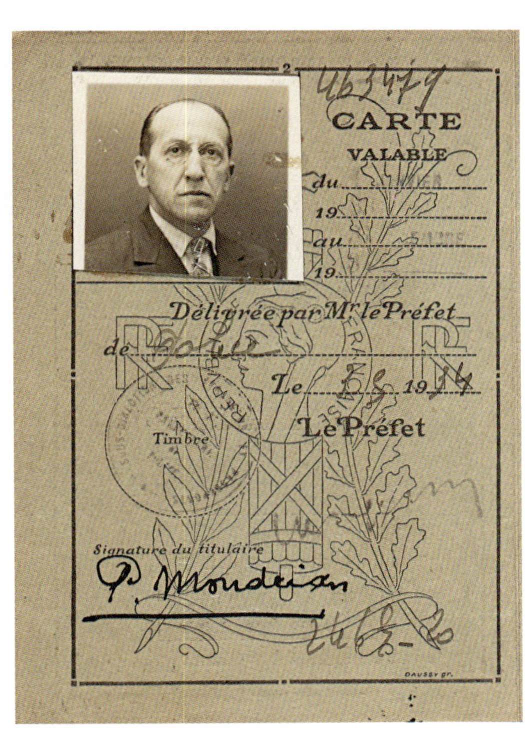

CARTE
VALABLE
du
19
au
19
Délivrée par Mr le Préfet
de
Le 19
Le Préfet
Timbre
Signature du titulaire
P. Mondrian

CATS 145–46 **Charles Karsten**

Piet Mondrian in his studio, August 1931

The architect Charles Karsten visited Mondrian in August 1931, when he took both this photograph and cat. 146. The painting on the easel, *Composition II* (B223) of 1930, had been included in the '1940' exhibition held in Paris in June 1931. After visiting Mondrian, Karsten must have taken the painting back to the Netherlands to sell on commission. It remained in his possession until 1950.

CAT. 147 **Unidentified photographer**

Portrait of Piet Mondrian, c. June 1933

This photograph was used for both Mondrian's French identity card and the receipt for its issue.

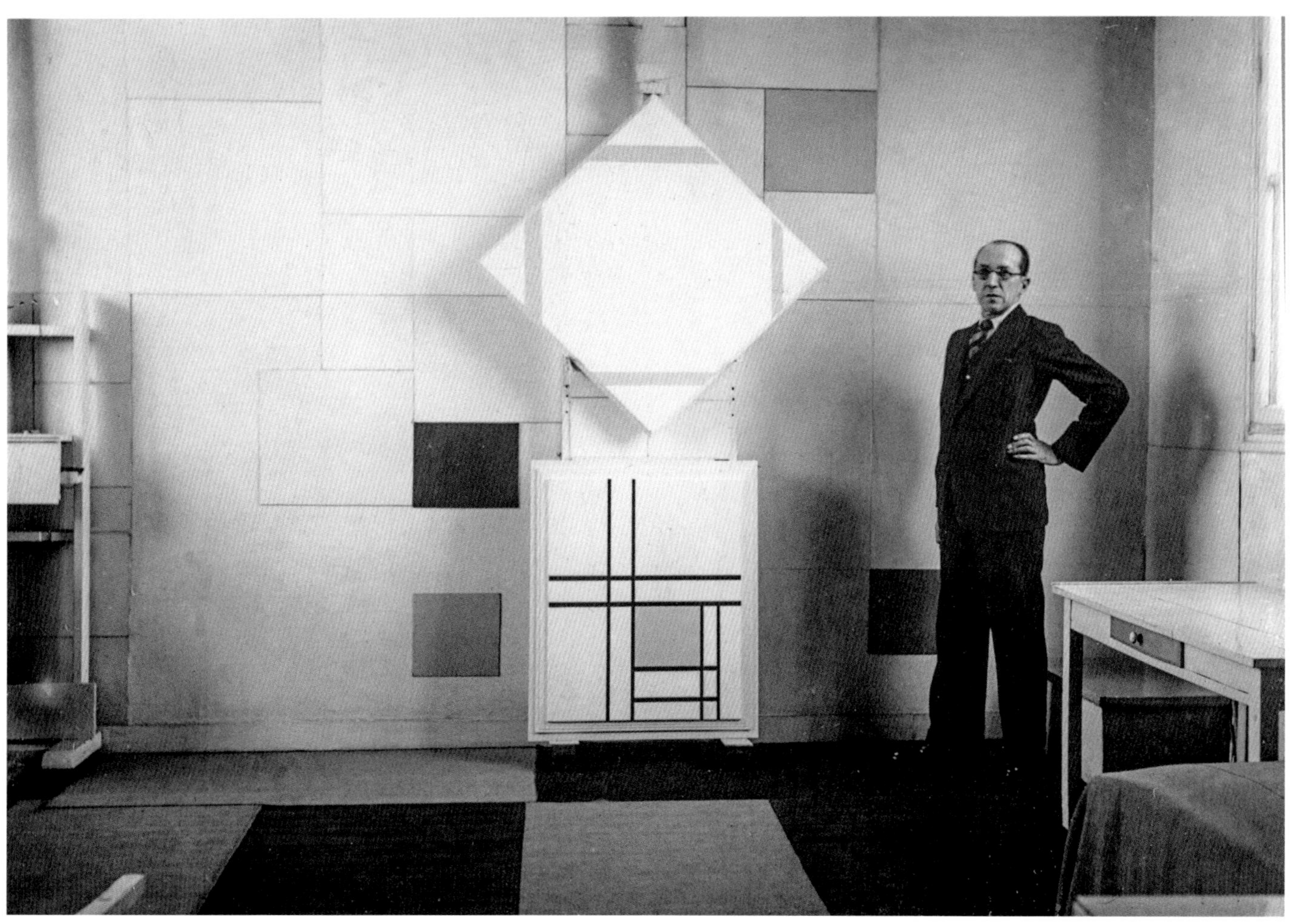

CAT. 148 **Charles Karsten**
Mondrian in his studio, September/October 1933
A group of artist and architect friends, Karsten among them, donated the uppermost painting on the easel, *Lozenge Composition with Four Yellow Lines* (B241, 1933), to the Gemeentemuseum in The Hague in November 1933. The work at the bottom, *Composition with Double Lines and Yellow* (B242), was bought in 1934 by the Swiss couple Emil and Clara Friedrich-Jezler. It is assumed lost during the Second World War.

CAT. 149 **Charles Karsten**
Piet Mondrian's studio, with *Lozenge Composition with Four Yellow Lines* (B241) and *Composition with Double Lines and Yellow* (B242) on the easel, September/ October 1933

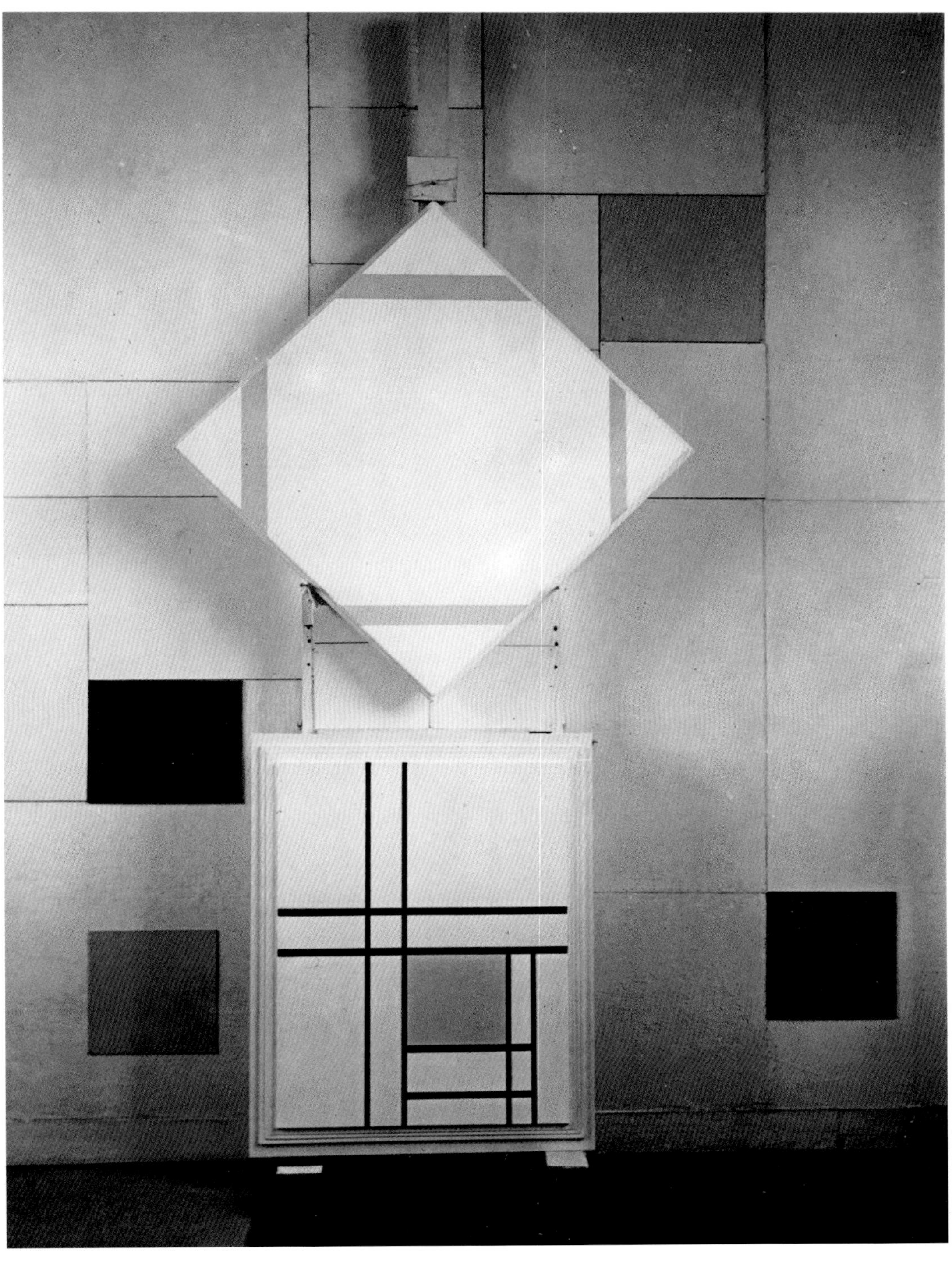

Eugene Lux

CATS 150—71

Hungarian-born Eugene Lux (1900—1985) was, among other things, a sculptor and a graphic and industrial designer. He studied art history, in particular focusing on wood-carving and sculpture, and in 1926 emigrated to the United States, where he established himself as an industrial designer. There, he created a number of clock designs that, although functional, he treated as aesthetic objects. He believed that every object should have formally beautiful properties.[1] In 1928 he married the American sculptor Gwendolyn Wickerts,[2] and in 1930 the couple went to Europe for the first time, returning to the USA in 1932. The reason for this trip, especially to Paris, was Gwen's interest in abstract art. In 1933 they left America once more to visit the main European capitals.

It was during these years that Lux became acquainted with Piet Mondrian, and he would later define their relationship as 'good friends'.[3] This is borne out by a letter of 1934 from Mondrian to Lux, in which he writes: 'By your homogeneous spirit and equivalent sensitivity, you two always inspire me. You understand that I miss you a lot here.'[4] In Paris, Lux and Mondrian saw a great deal of each other. They shared the same artistic interests, and supposedly often had discussions about Mondrian's work. From Mondrian's letters it can be deduced that Eugene and Gwen stayed in Paris around March—May 1934.

During one or more of his visits to Mondrian's studio, Lux took a series of photographs of the artist, including portraits of him in the studio, as well as photos for Mondrian's portfolio.[5] Shortly after their stay in Paris had ended, Mondrian wrote that he missed them 'because we are so much alike in spirit and mentality'.[6] Mondrian's empathy with Gwen is evidenced by the photographs of them together, and on the back of one such photograph — which was probably sent or given to Mondrian later — she wrote: 'To my dear friend Mondrian' (cat. 152). Soon after the couple left Europe in 1934, they were divorced, and Eugene then travelled through Mexico for a long time and lost contact with Mondrian — much to his regret.

1 Joop M. Joosten, 'Biography of Lux' [not published], The Hague, RKD, Joop Joosten Archives.

2 'Eugene Lux', https://rkd.nl/en/explore/artists, accessed 16 December 2021.

3 Letter from Eugene Lux to Joop Joosten, The Hague, RKD, Joop Joosten Archives.

4 'Par votre esprit homogène et sensibilité equivalente, vous deux m'inspirent toujours. Vous comprenez que je vous manque beaucoup ici.' Letter from Piet Mondrian to Eugene Lux, 17 November 1934, The Hague, RKD, Eugene and Gwen Lux Archives (0954), inv. 006.

5 Welsh/Joosten 1998-II, p. 156. In a letter from 27 July 1934 Mondrian wrote to them: 'Les photos de Mr. Gallatin [MM105—6] sont bien mais ne pas si vivantes que les votres et trop académiques'. The Hague, RKD, Eugene and Gwen Lux Archives (0954), inv. 003.

6 'parce que nous sommes si pareils d'esprit et de mentalité'. Letter from Piet Mondrian to Eugene and Gwen Lux, 27 July 1934, The Hague, RKD, Eugene and Gwen Lux Archives (0954), inv. 003.

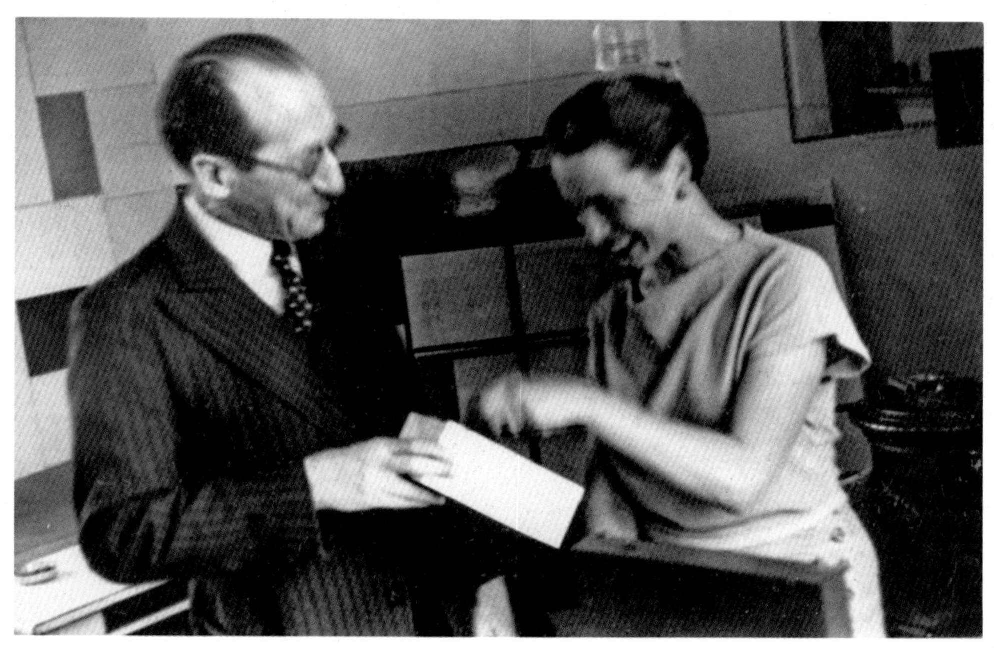

CAT. 150 **Eugene Lux**

Piet Mondrian and Gwendolyn Lux in Mondrian's studio, c. March–May 1934

Eugene Lux and his wife Gwen Lux-Wickerts stayed in Paris from 1932 to 1934. Around March–May 1934, Eugene took several photographs during one or more of their visits to Mondrian — both portraits and studio and portfolio pictures.

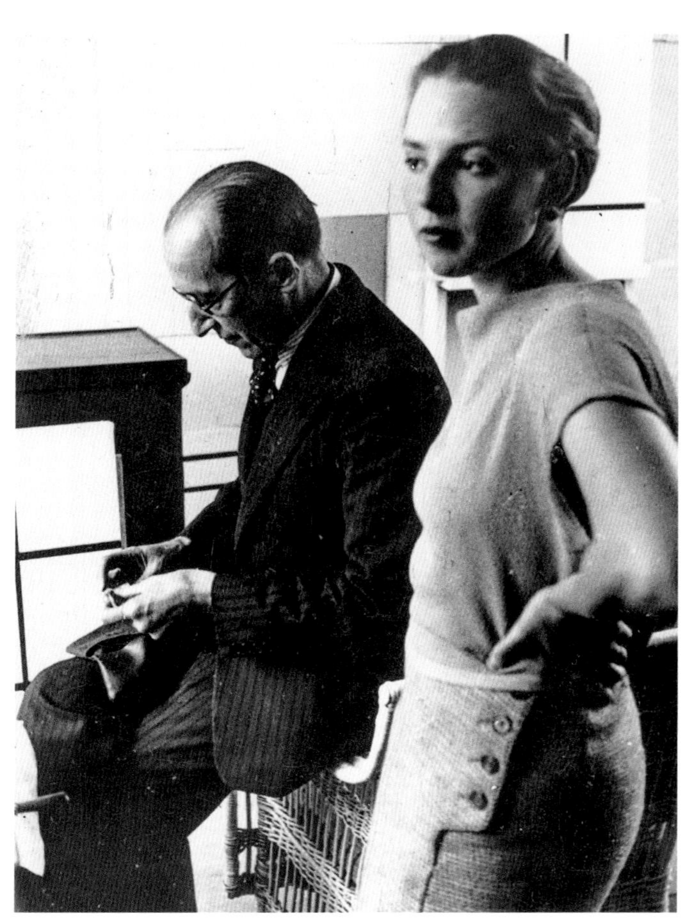

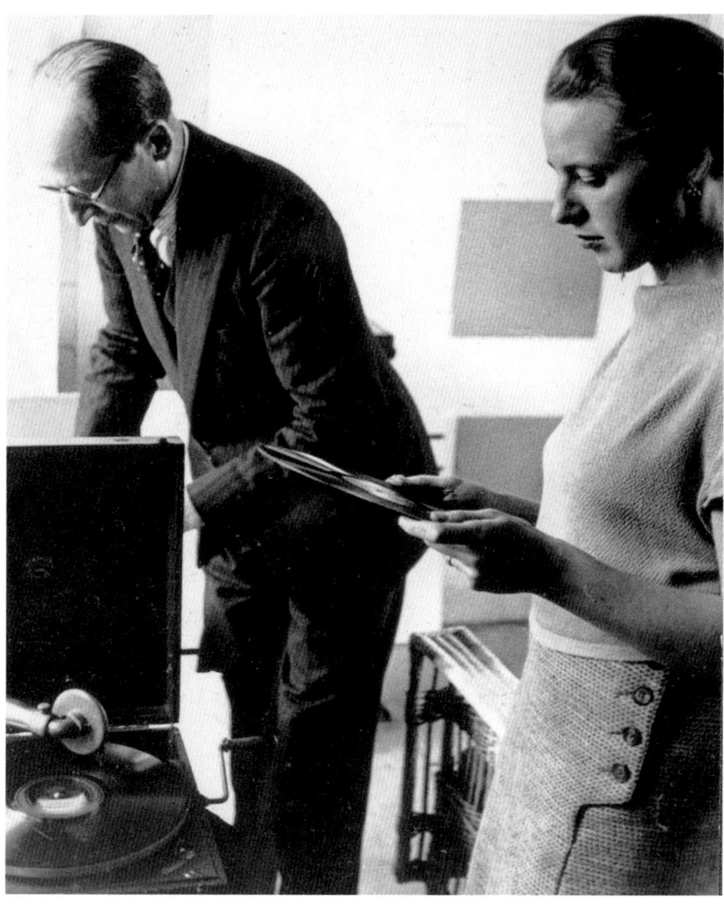

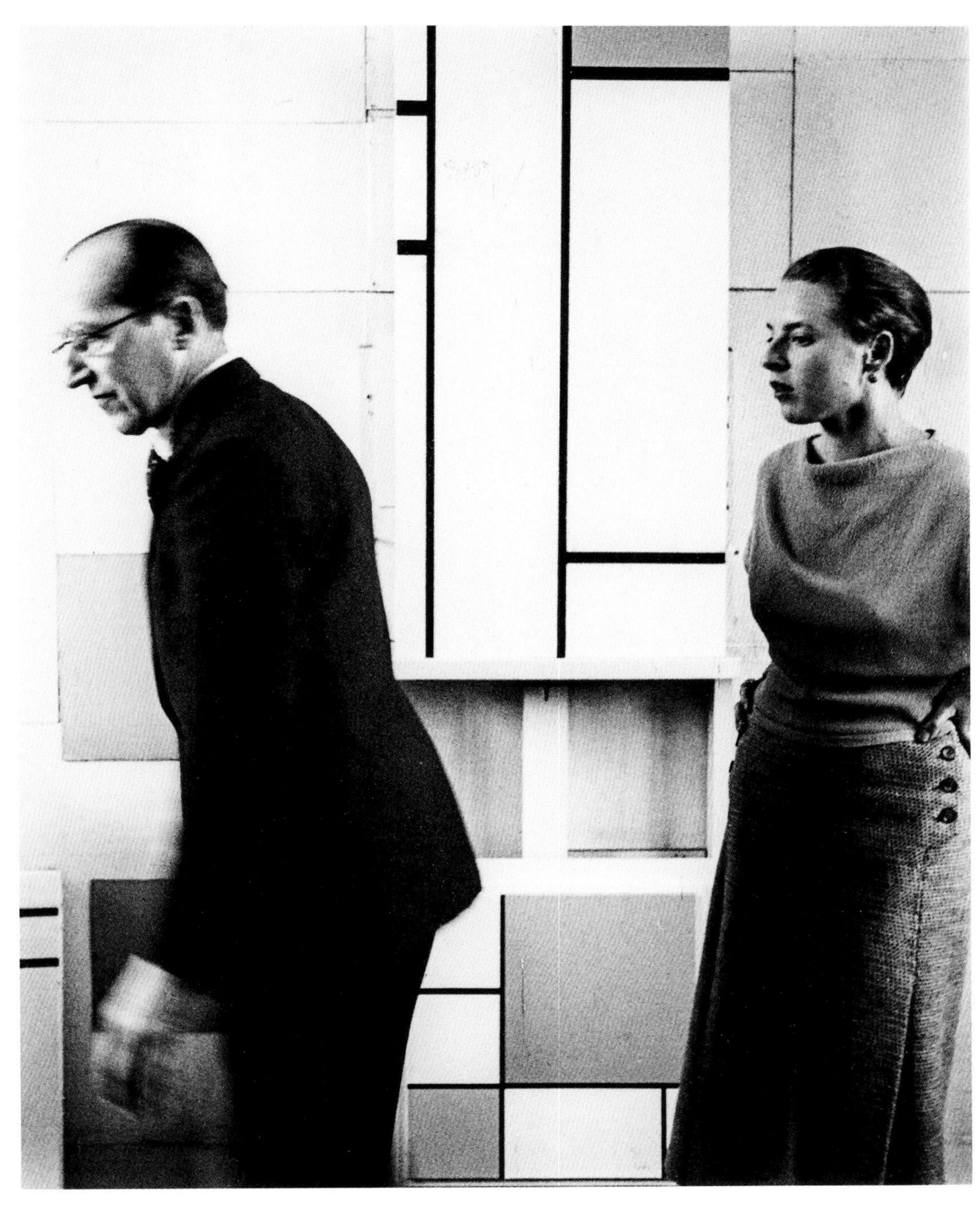

CATS 151–53 **Eugene Lux**
Piet Mondrian and Gwendolyn Lux in Mondrian's studio, c. March–May 1934

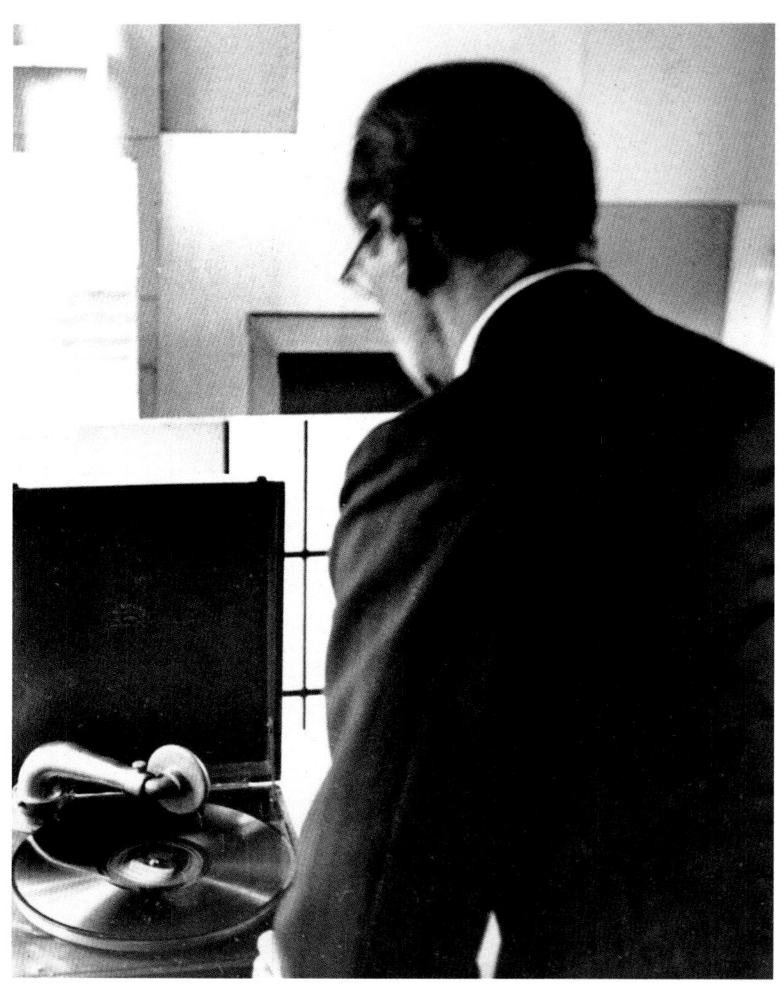

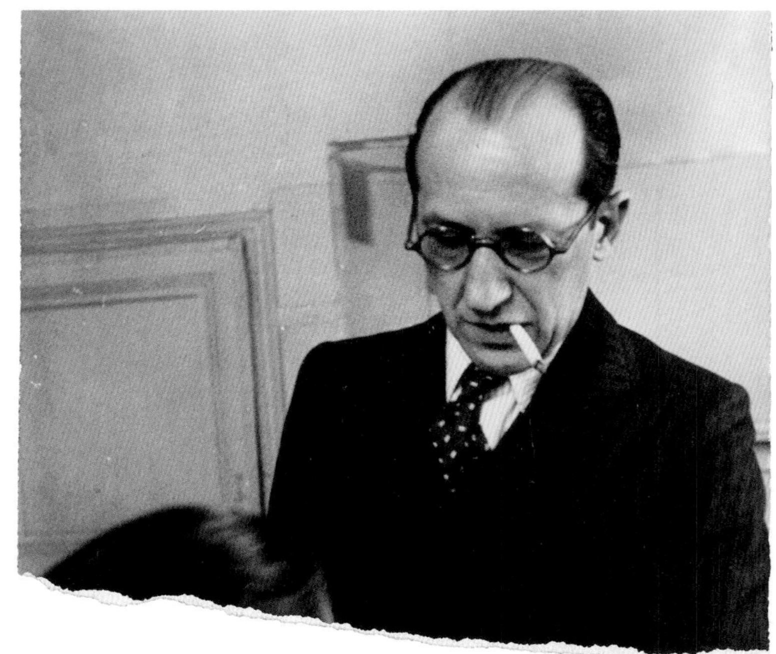

CAT. 154 **Eugene Lux**
Piet Mondrian with gramophone, c. March–May 1934

CAT. 157 **Eugene Lux**
Piet Mondrian and Gwendolyn Lux in Mondrian's studio, c. March–May 1934
For unknown reasons, the lower half of the photograph has been torn off.

CATS 160–61 **Eugene Lux**
Portrait of Piet Mondrian, c. March–May 1934
Cat. 160 was published in January-February 1939 in *Living Art in England*, a special double issue of the surrealist magazine *London Bulletin*.

CATS 155–56, 158–59 See catalogue

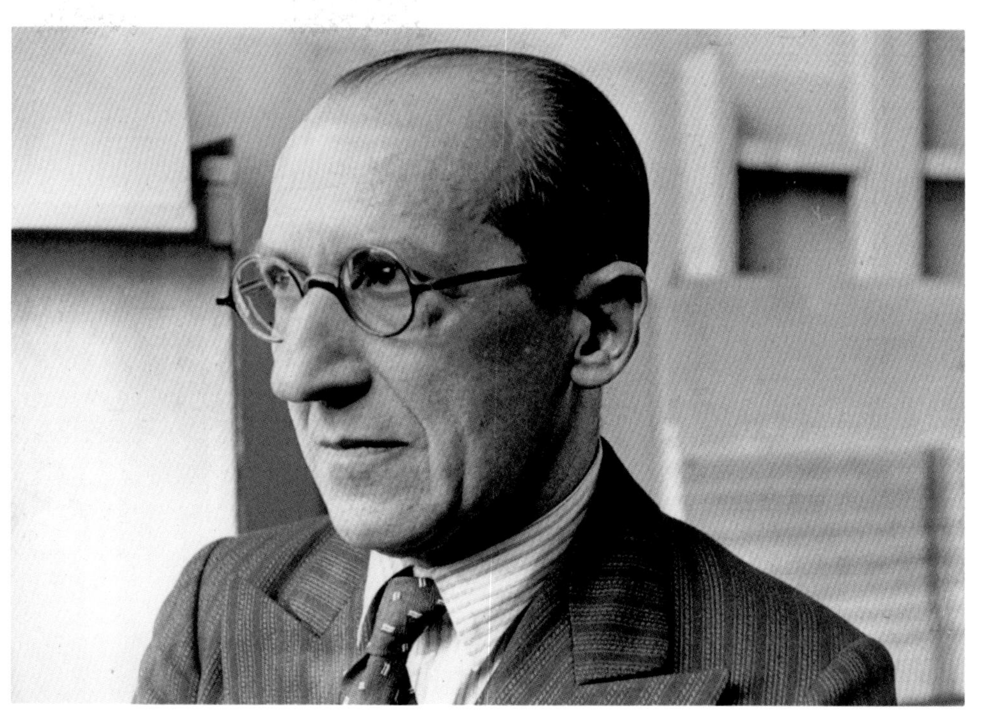

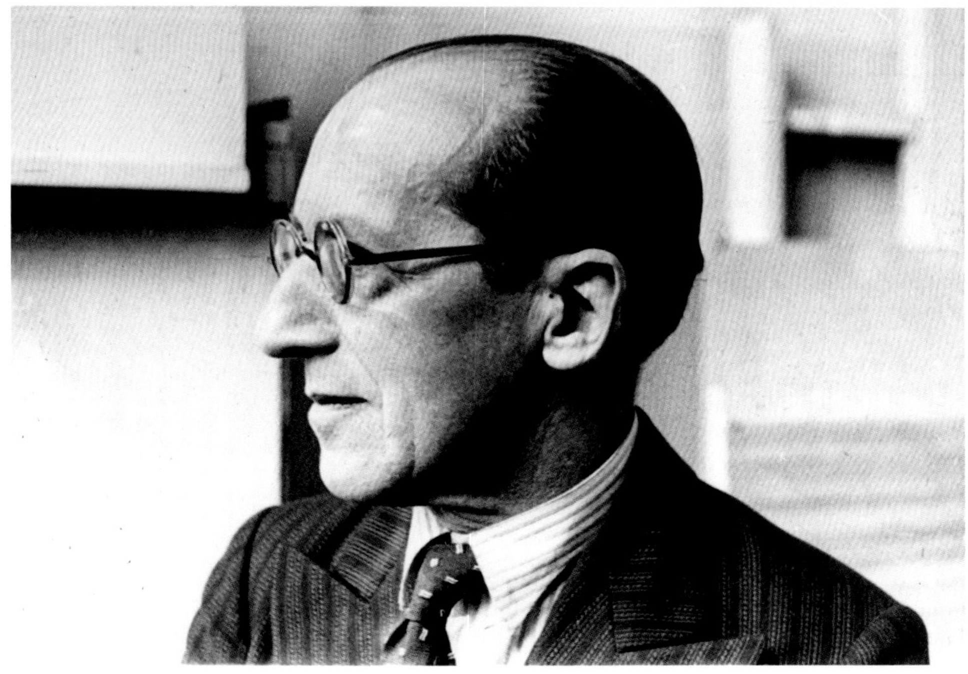

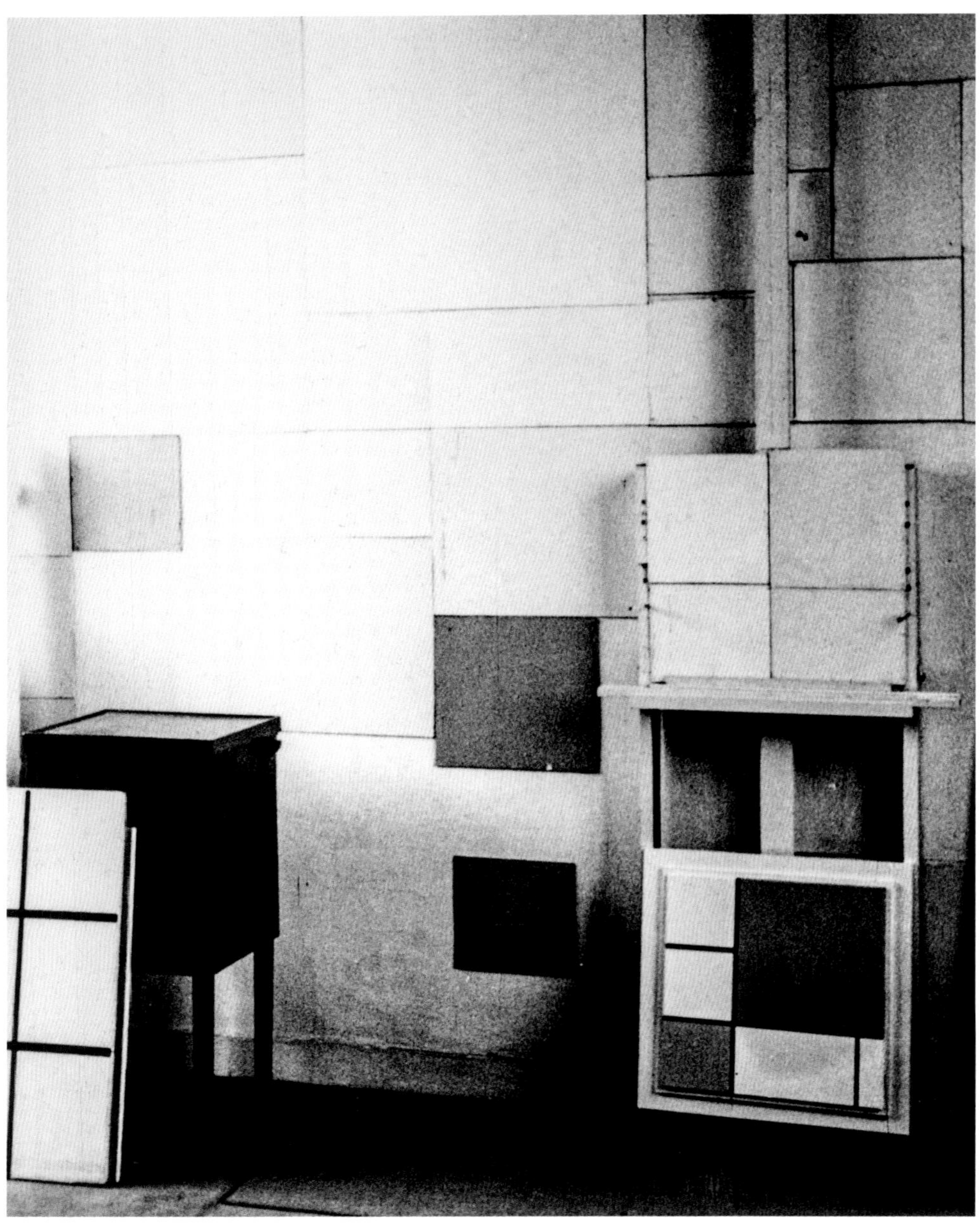

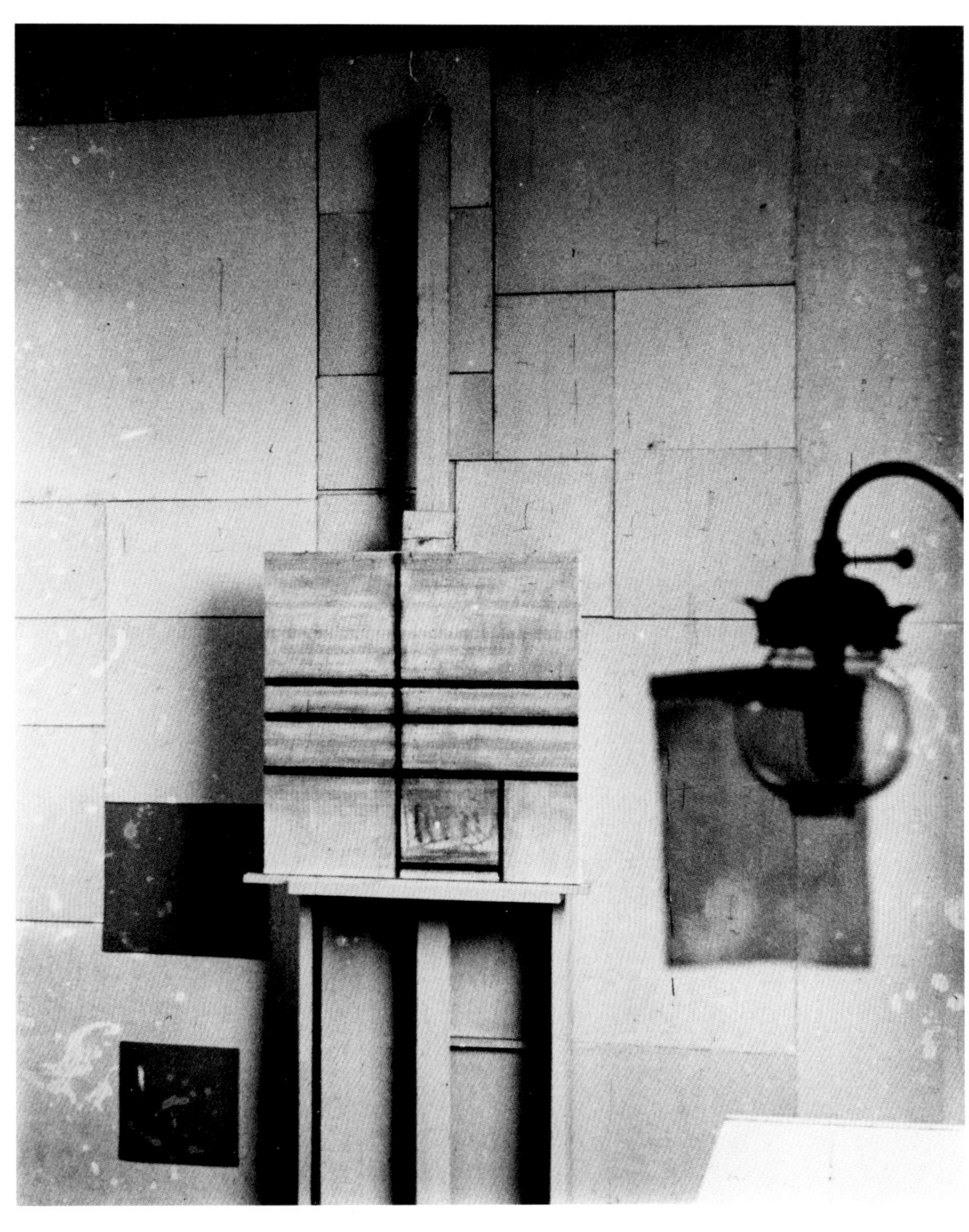

CAT. 162 **Eugene Lux**
Piet Mondrian's studio, c. March–May 1934
Composition with Blue and Yellow (B235, 1932) is shown leaning against the easel, while on the left we see an unfinished *Composition B/(No. II), with Red* (B254, 1935). The latter is also visible in cat. 168.

CAT. 163 **Eugene Lux**
Piet Mondrian's studio, c. March–May 1934
The work on the easel is *Composition with Double Line (Unfinished)* (B247, 1934). Lux's photographs are the only evidence of the painting in this state.

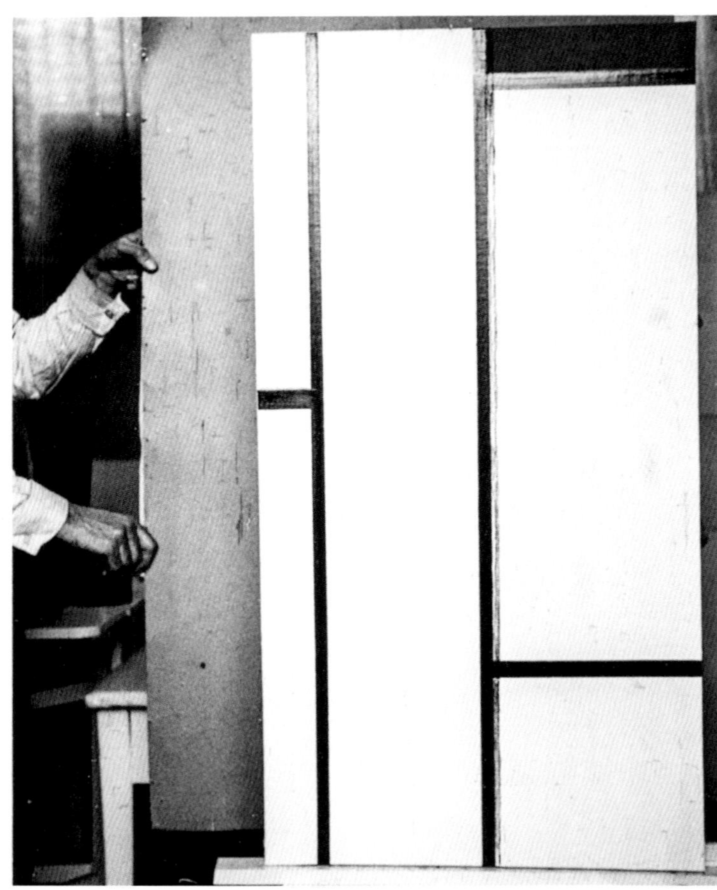

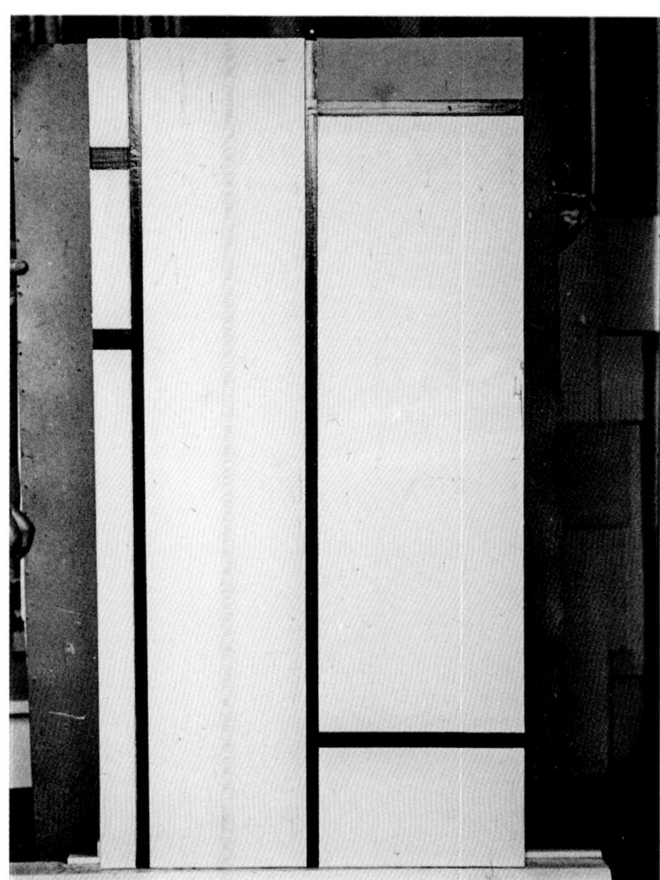

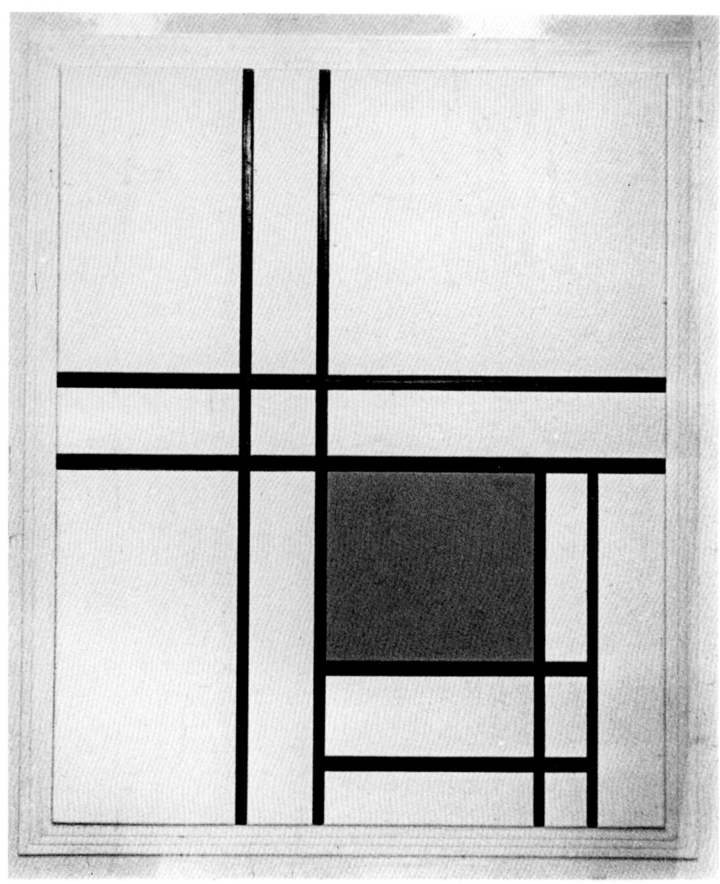

CAT. 164 **Eugene Lux**
Composition A (No. I), with Red **(B260)**
unfinished in Mondrian's studio, c. March–May 1934

CAT. 165 **Eugene Lux**
Composition (No. III) blanc-jaune **(B257) unfinished in Mondrian's studio, c. March–May 1934**

CAT. 166 **Eugene Lux**
Composition with Double Lines and Yellow **(B242)**
in Mondrian's studio, c. March–May 1934

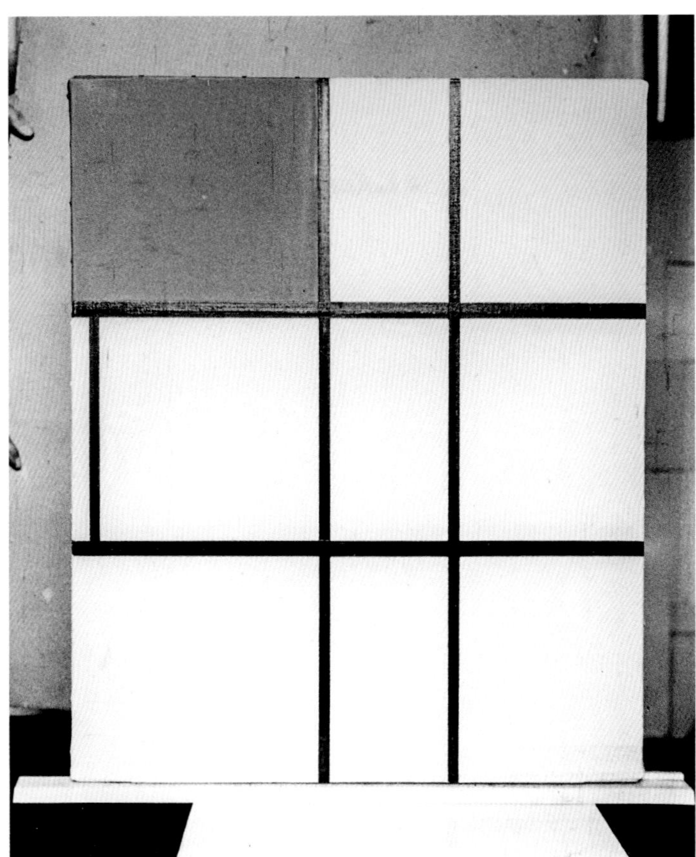

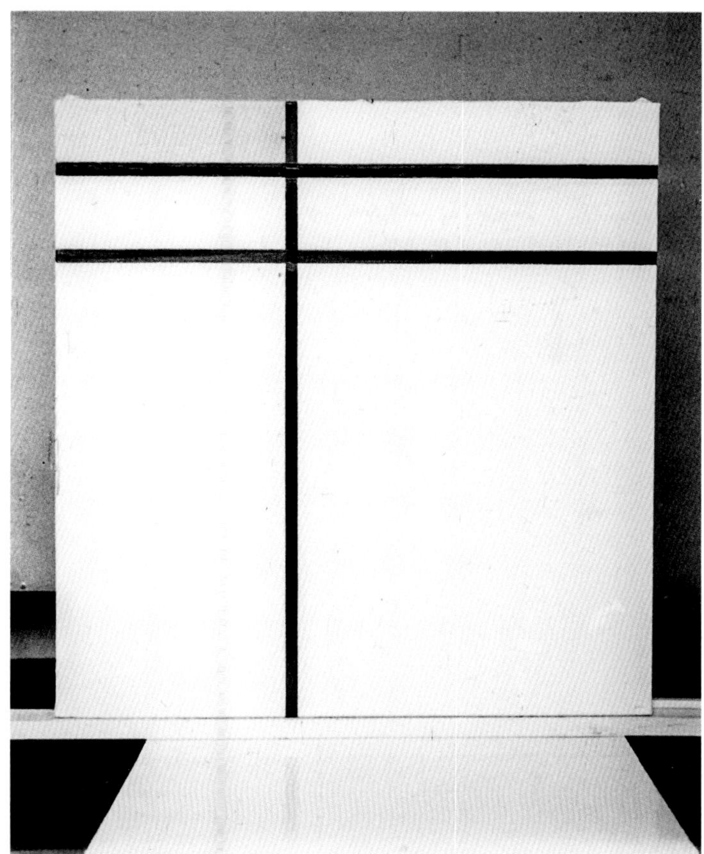

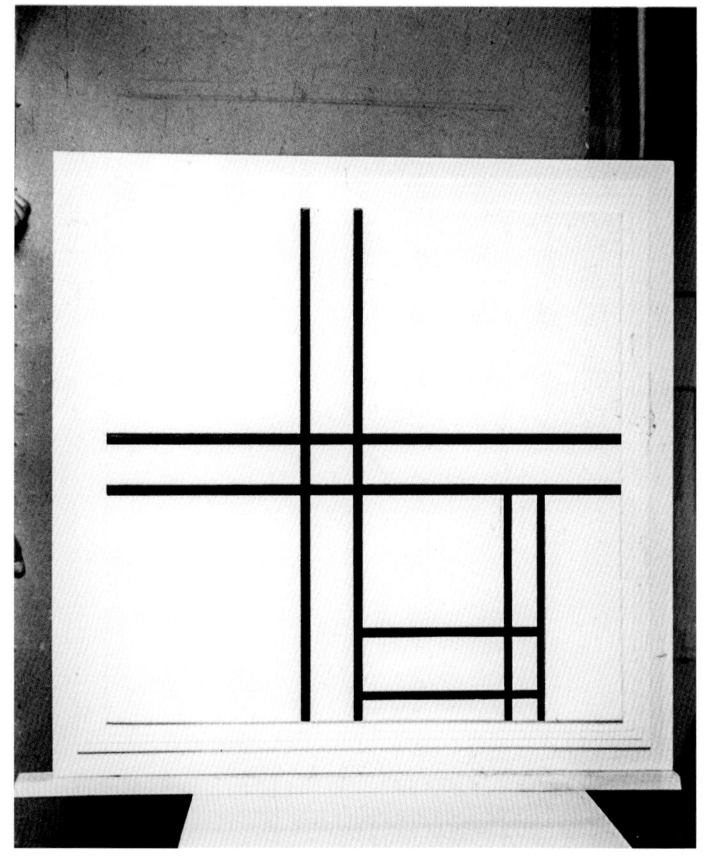

CAT. 167 **Eugene Lux**
Composition **(B252) unfinished in Mondrian's studio, c. March–May 1934**

CAT. 168 **Eugene Lux**
Composition B/(No. II), with Red **(B254) unfinished in Mondrian's studio, c. March–May 1934**

CAT. 169 **Eugene Lux**
Composition A, with Double Line and Yellow **(B253) unfinished in Mondrian's studio, c. March–May 1934**

CAT. 170 **Eugene Lux**
Composition in Black and White, with Double Lines **(B243) in Mondrian's studio, c. March–May 1934**

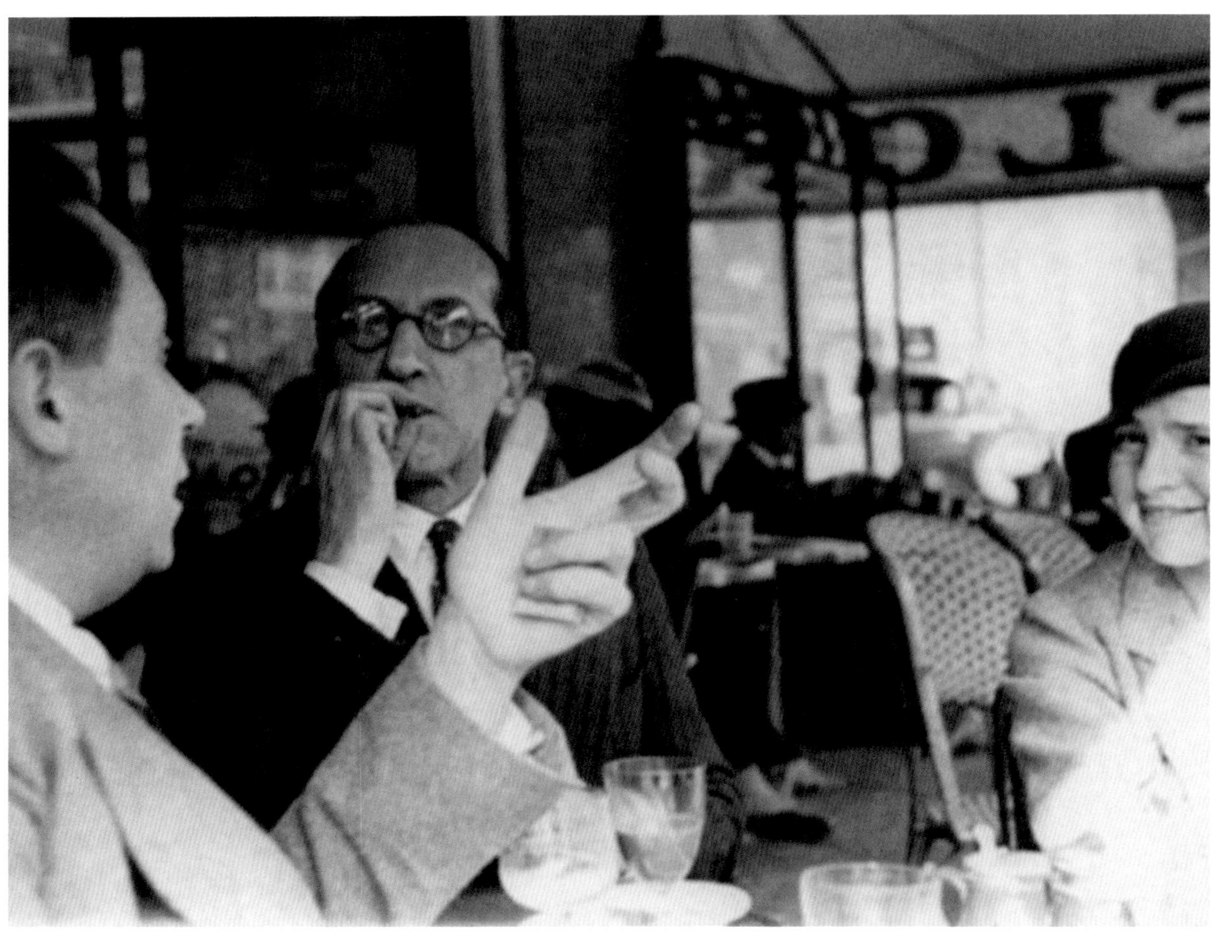

CAT. 171 **Eugene Lux**

Robert Delaunay, Piet Mondrian and an unidentified woman on the terrace of Café de Flore, Paris, c. March—May 1934

Café de Flore was one of the famous establishments in the Saint-Germain-des-Prés district, where artists, writers, philosophers and other intellectuals met.

CAT. 172 **Albert Eugene Gallatin**

Portrait of Piet Mondrian, June 1934

Mondrian expressed his satisfaction with the results of cats 172–73 in a letter to Albert Gallatin: 'I was truly touched by the superb photographs you sent me — magnificent in composition and execution and, I think, very good too as a reflection of my personality.' By contrast, in another letter, to the Luxes (see cat 150), he described Gallatin's photographs as 'too academic'.

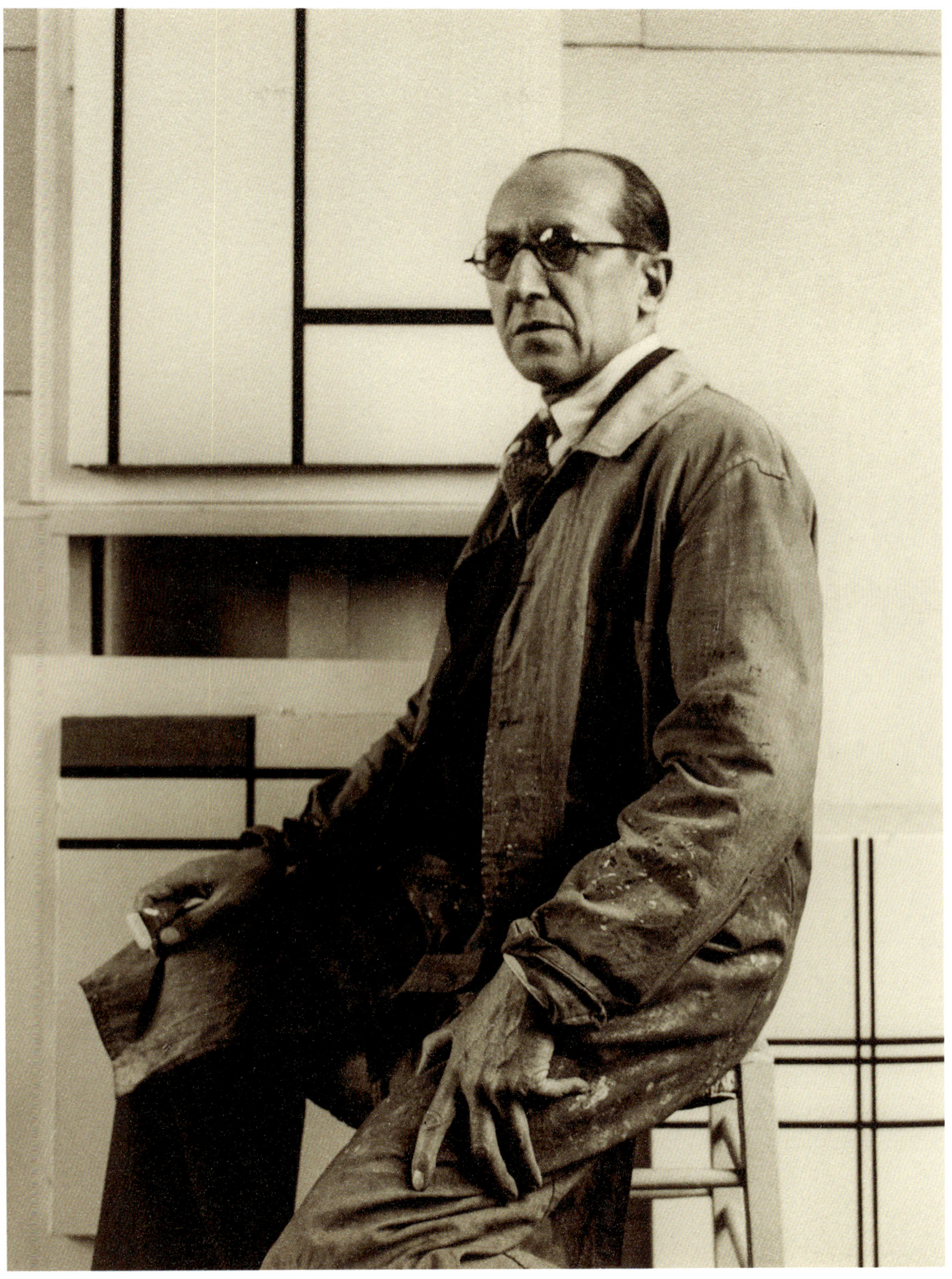

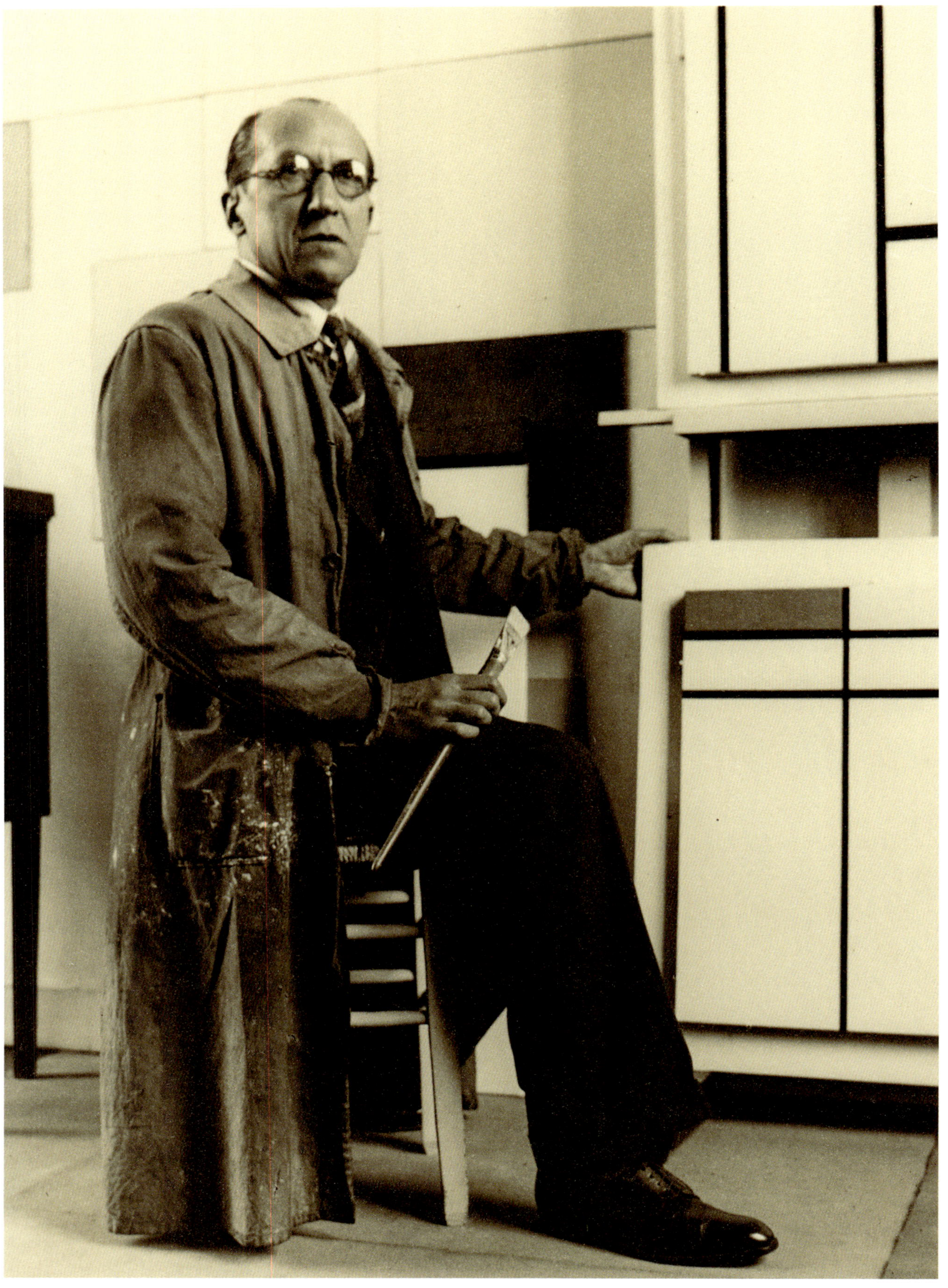

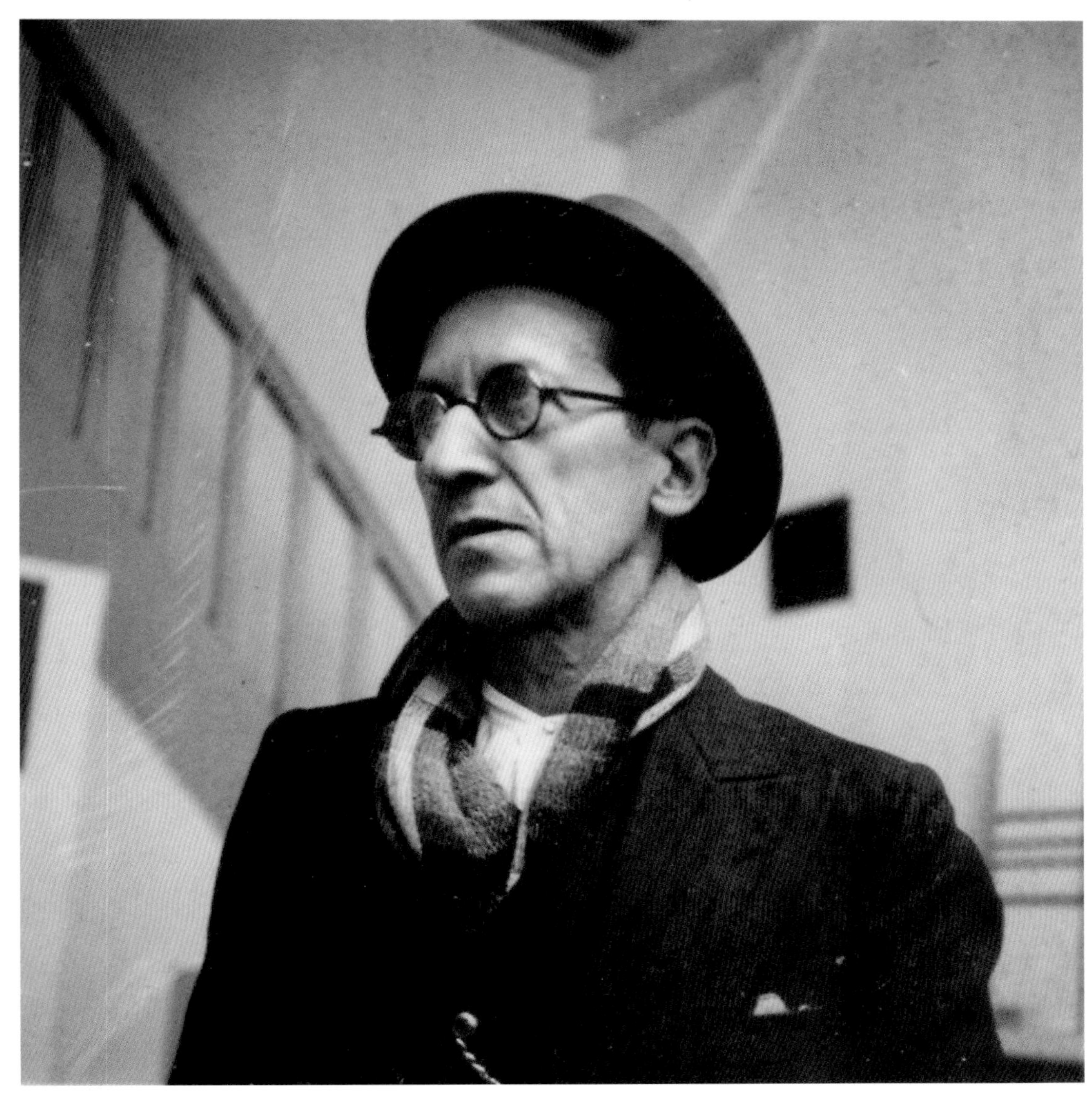

CAT. 173 **Albert Eugene Gallatin**
Portrait of Piet Mondrian, June 1934

CAT. 174 **Kurt Schwitters**
Portrait of Piet Mondrian, between 20 and 24 March 1936
This is the earliest known photograph of Mondrian in his studio at 278 Boulevard Raspail, which he moved into on 20 March 1936. The German Dadaist Kurt Schwitters was one of the first to visit him after his relocation.

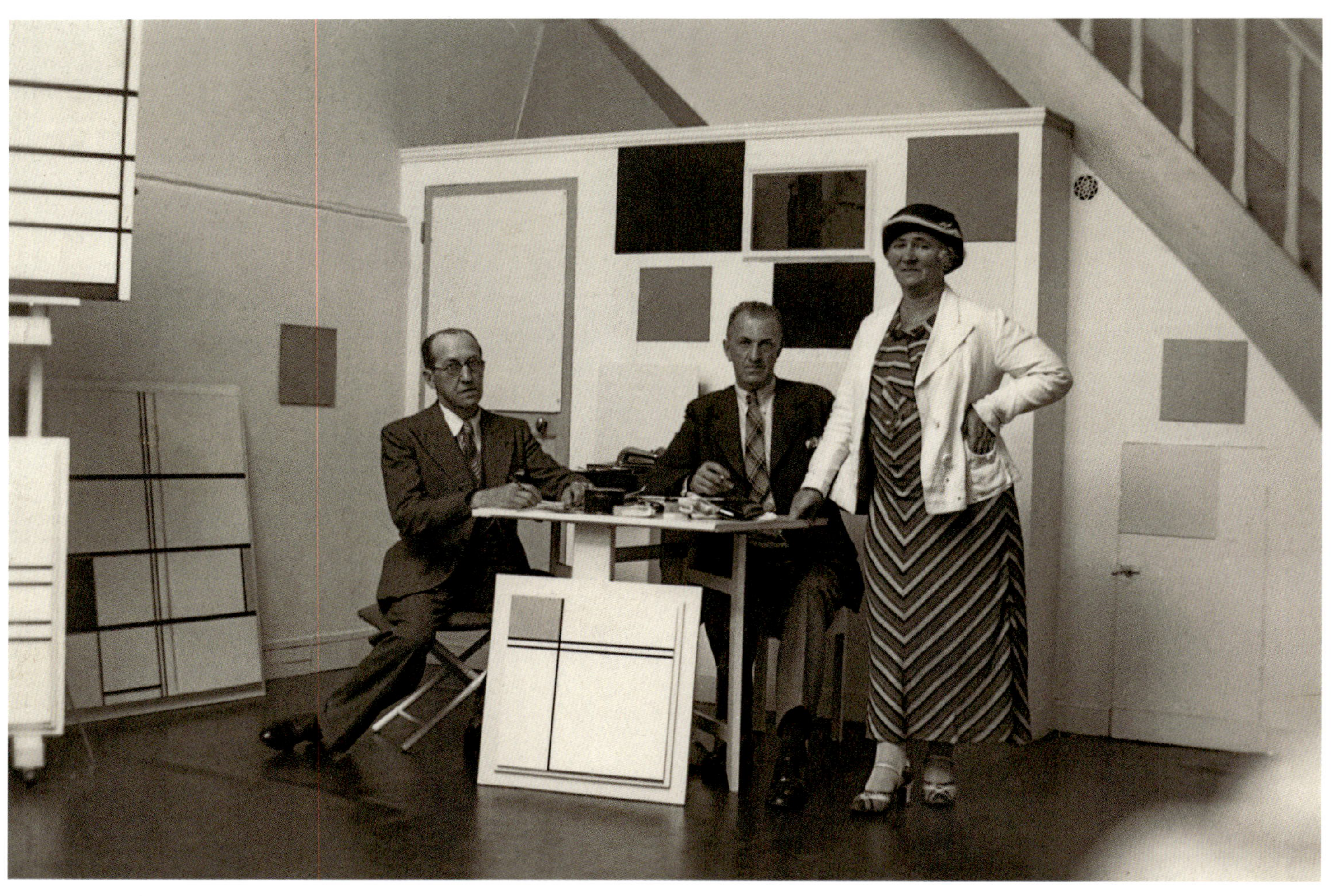

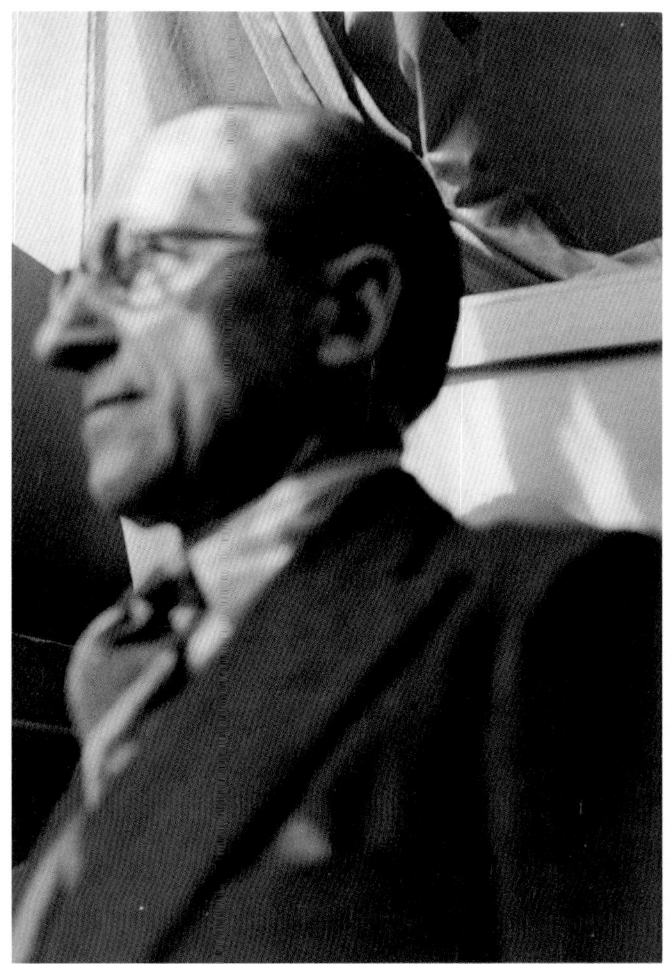

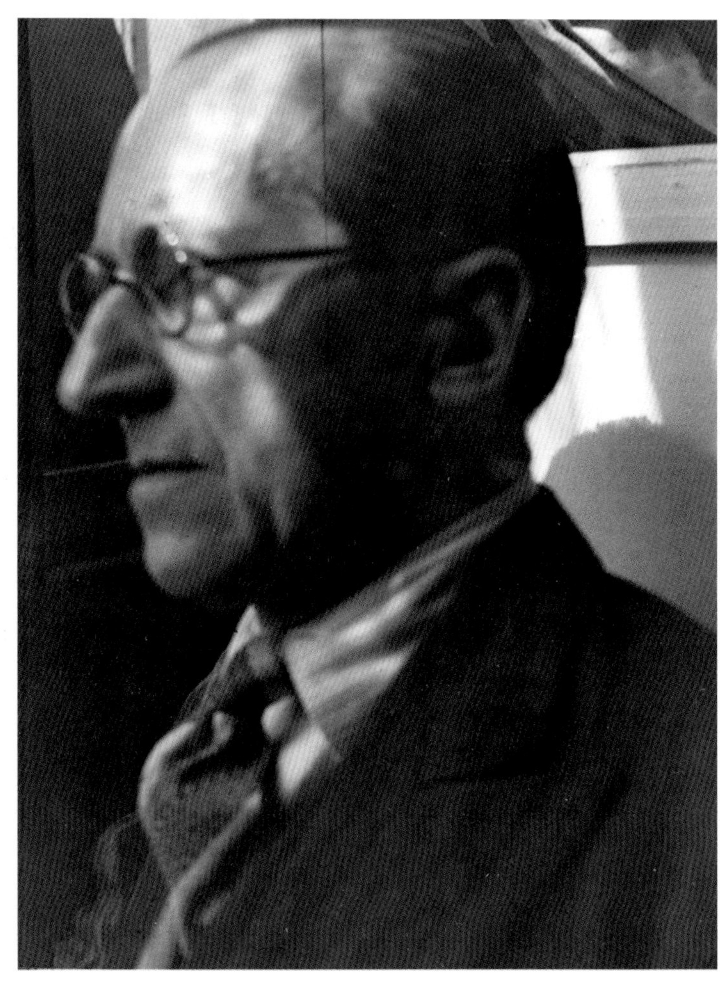

CATS 176 **Unidentified photographer**
Piet Mondrian, Carel Mondriaan and his fiancée Maria van den Berg in Mondrian's studio, August 1936

CATS 177–8 **Unidentified photographer**
Portrait of Piet Mondrian, c. 1937

CAT. 175 See catalogue

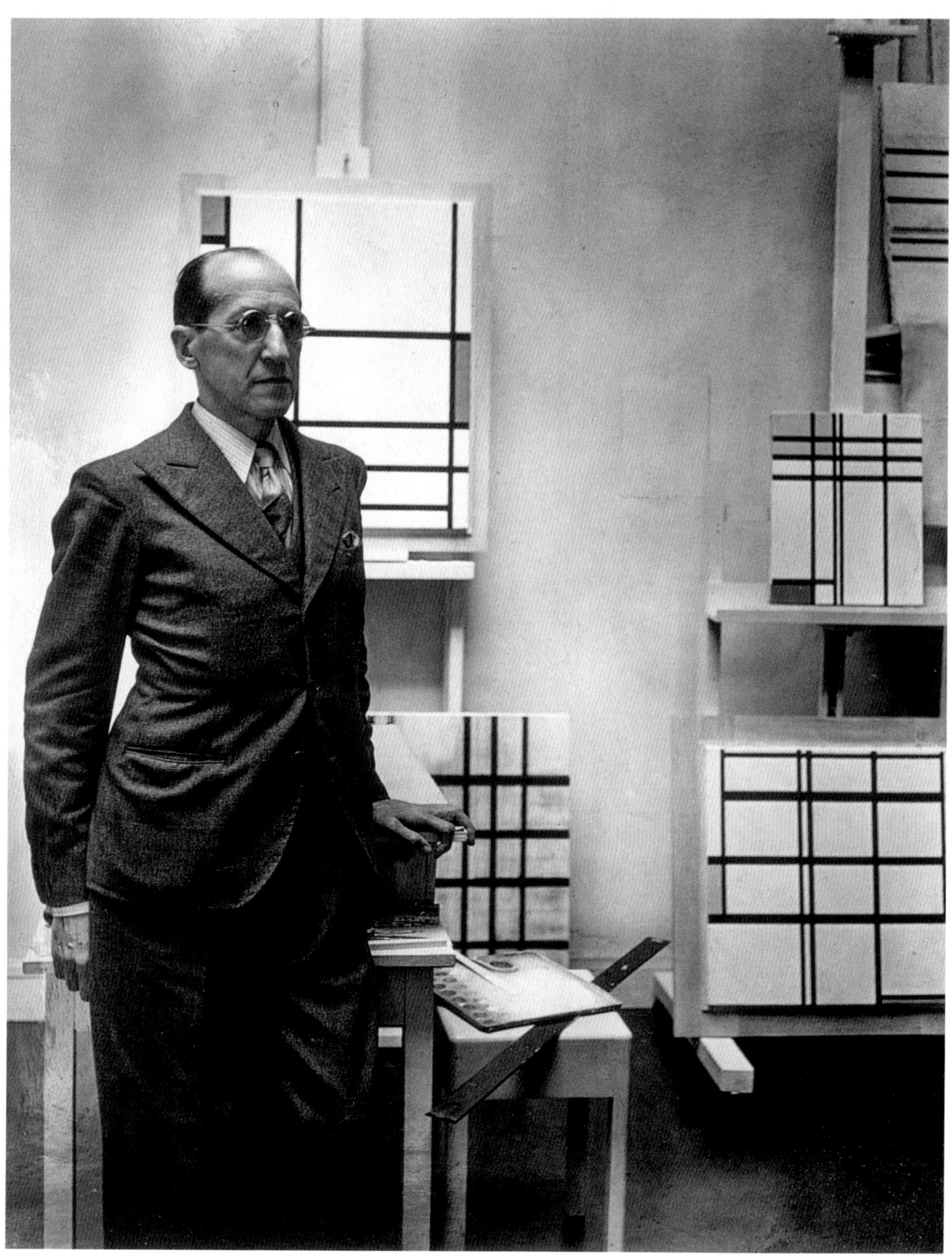

CAT. 179 **Rogi André (Rosza Klein)**
Piet Mondrian in his studio, c. June—July 1937
The Hungarian-born photographer Rogi André (pseudonym of Rosza Klein) took this picture in 1937 when she was commissioned along with Man Ray and Florence Henri to photograph the artists due to take part in the exhibition 'Origines et développement de l'art international indépendant' at the Jeu de Paume in Paris.

Cas Oorthuys

CATS 180—85

The Dutch photographer Cas Oorthuys (1908—1975) trained as an architect, but took up photography at an early age.[1] He spent two years as an architect working for Haarlem city council until he was fired in 1932, following which he devoted himself to photography and graphic design — disciplines he would frequently combine. Oorthuys had been interested since an early age in all things new and modern in the fields of politics, technology and society. This was expressed in the powerful political engagement communicated by the entirety of his photographic practice. He associated himself with socialist and communist magazines, groups and campaigns and joined the Vereeniging van Arbeiders-Fotografen (Worker-Photographers' Association), founded in 1931. Social relations and injustice and the rise of fascism were important themes in his work in the 1930s.

Oorthuys was largely self-taught, but he quickly came into contact with young photographers in Amsterdam who frequently applied their work to political ends. For a short while in 1931, he took lessons from the communist film-maker Joris Ivens. His generation was influenced by avant-garde photography in Germany and Russia — New Photography, which was linked to constructivist art and the Bauhaus, where László Moholy-Nagy placed modern photography on the curriculum. New Photography viewed the medium's mechanical aspect as a strength: it enabled what was literally a new way of looking at reality, rather than aestheticizing or reproducing it.[2] Photography had a political function (raising awareness and liberating the working class) and was used for propaganda, often in the form of photomontages and collages. The diagonal visual composition, the direct approach to the subject, and the framing of Oorthuys's work, can all be traced back directly to the principles of New Photography.

Oorthuys visited Paris in the summer of 1937 to attend a number of exhibitions in the company of a fellow left-winger, the artist and printmaker Peter Alma.[3] Alma was an old friend of Mondrian's, whose paintings he admired, although contact between them had faded somewhat. He had made repeated efforts in the 1920s to persuade Dutch museums to recognize and acquire his friend's work.[4]

By the time Oorthuys visited Mondrian with Alma, he had earned a reputation as a documentary photographer, which is apparent to some extent in the photographs he took during the visit. They fall into two small groups: four portraits and two photos of the studio, with paintings in progress forming the main motif. We can recognize Oorthuys's hand, or rather his eye, in both groups. The portraits were shot close-up, so that Mondrian's head almost touches the top edge of the frame, leaving space below for his characteristically dapper clothes. On the other hand, the shots were taken from a somewhat low and oblique angle, which was unusual for a standard portrait. The low viewpoint adds dynamism to the image, offsetting the solidity of the square format.

The same also applies to the two shots of the paintings in the studio. In one of the two, Alma's hand and head can be seen in the lower right corner (cat. 180), while in the other, the painting on the easel rises — both literally and figuratively — above the viewer, and the double lines of the composition radiate out from the picture plane in all directions (cat. 181). The subject is cropped at such an angle in both studio pictures that the diagonal effect is very strong, despite the many rectangles in the image.

Mondrian will not have liked this aspect very much in terms of representing his paintings. Depth effects and diagonals in his work were anathema to him, with the result that pictures he commissioned of them himself, as well as the staged studio photographs, were entirely frontal for the most part. Oorthuys might not have been very enthused by the photographs either: he never reproduced any of the six in the many books of his work that he compiled through the course of his life.

1 Information on Oorthuys is drawn from Hekking 1982, pp. 12—24.
2 Cf. Rooseboom 2019, pp. 118—21.
3 Welsh/Joosten 1998-II, p. 168.
4 Jooren 2016, pp. 20—22.

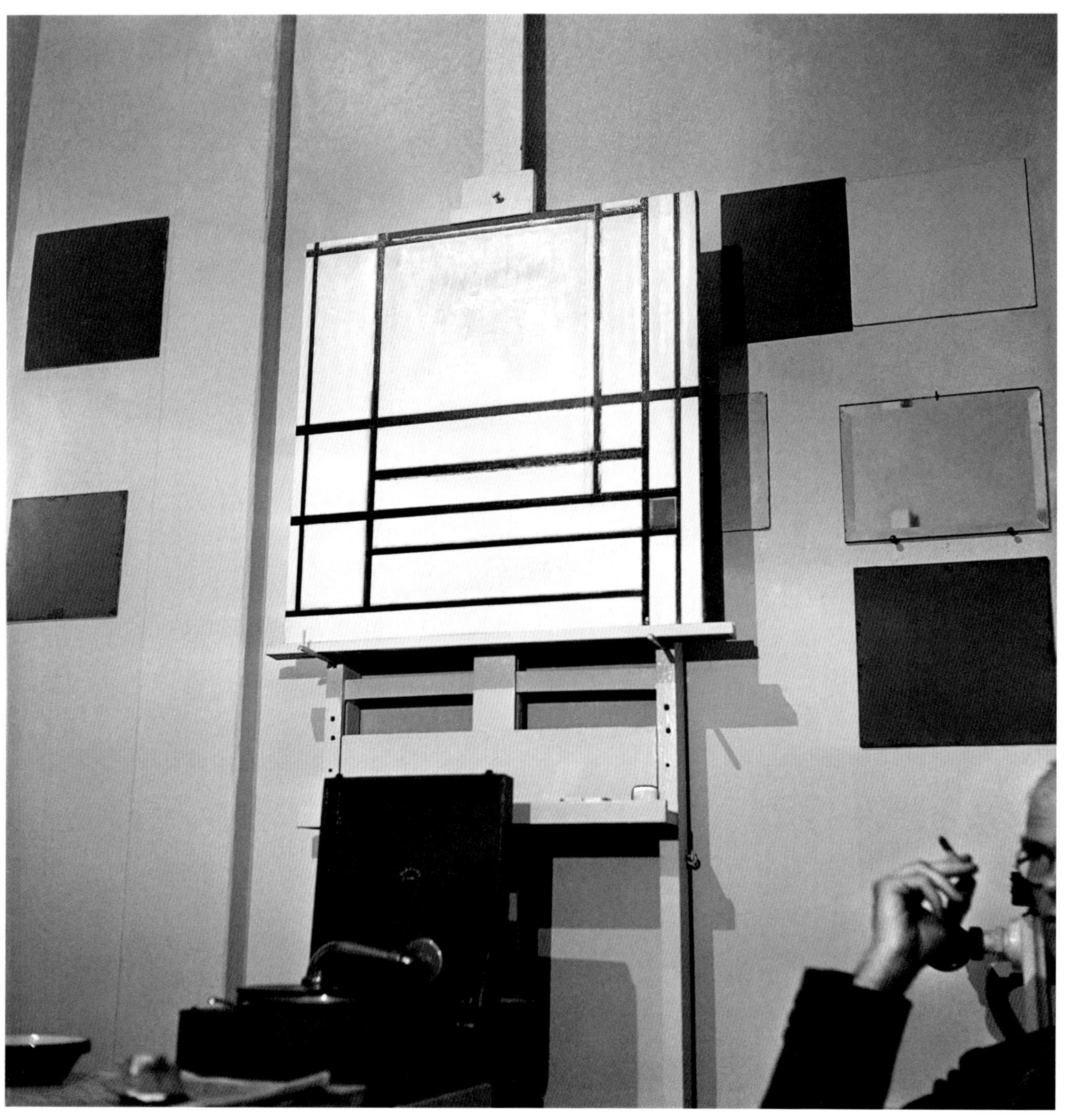

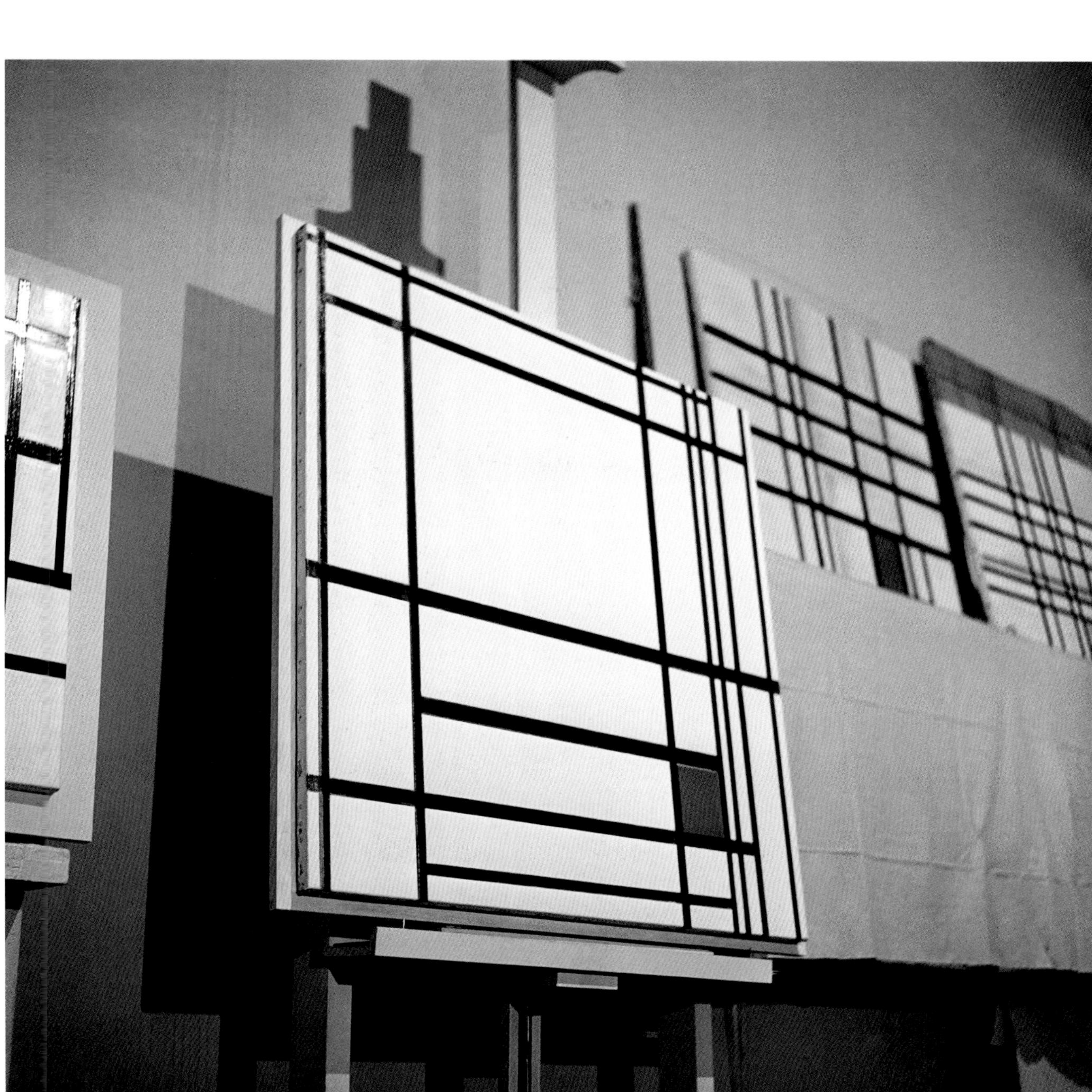

CAT. 180 **Cas Oorthuys**

Piet Mondrian's studio with *Composition of Lines with Red* (Unfinished) (B278) on the easel, August (?) 1937

The person just visible on the right is the artist Peter Alma, a friend of Mondrian's since around 1912.

CAT. 181 **Cas Oorthuys**

Piet Mondrian's studio with *Composition de lignes et couleur: III* (B277) on the easel, August (?) 1937

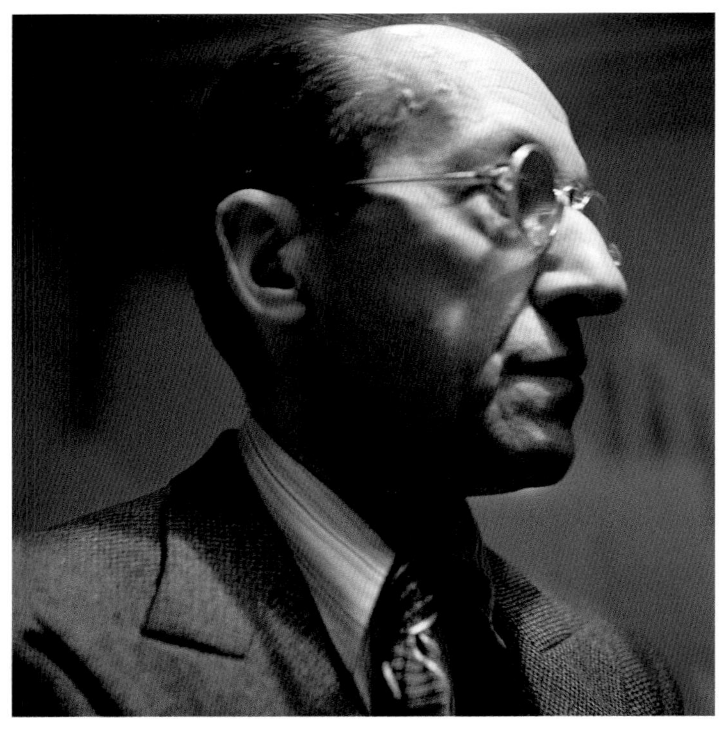
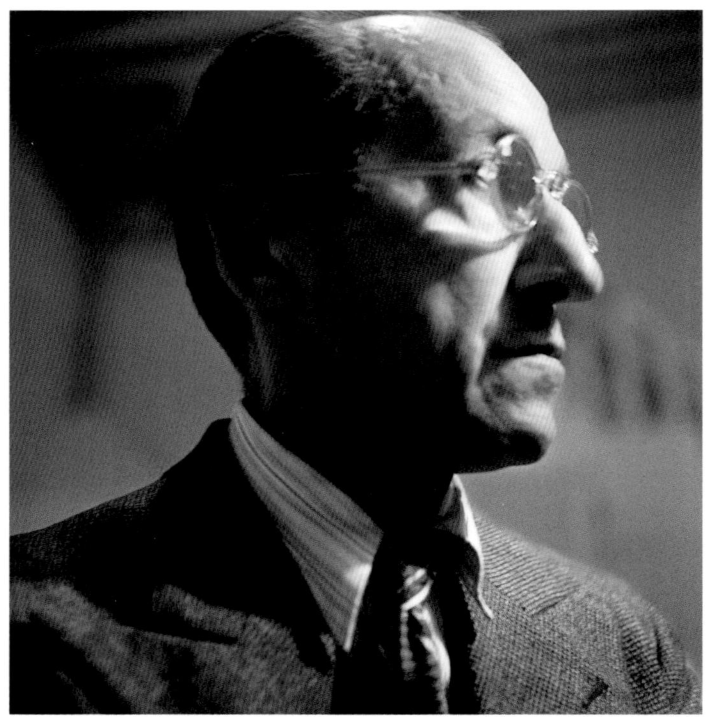
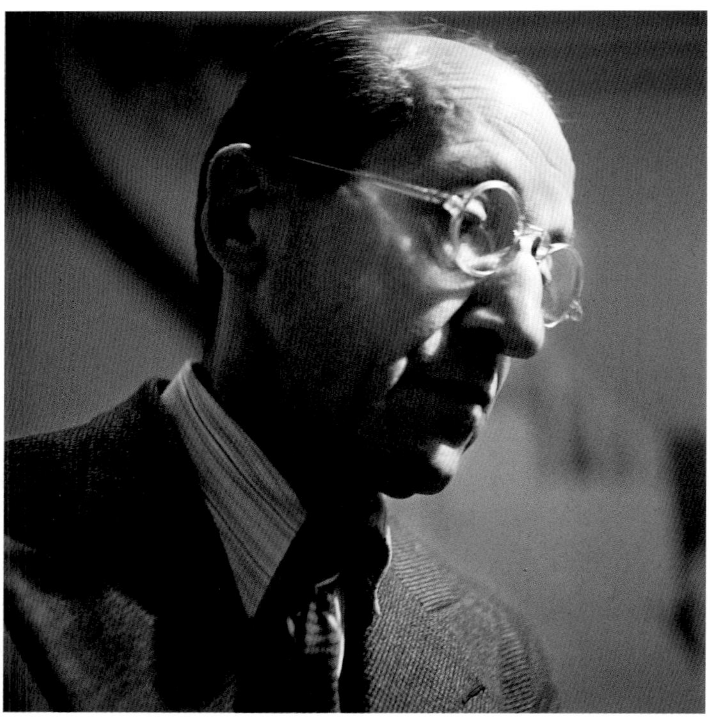
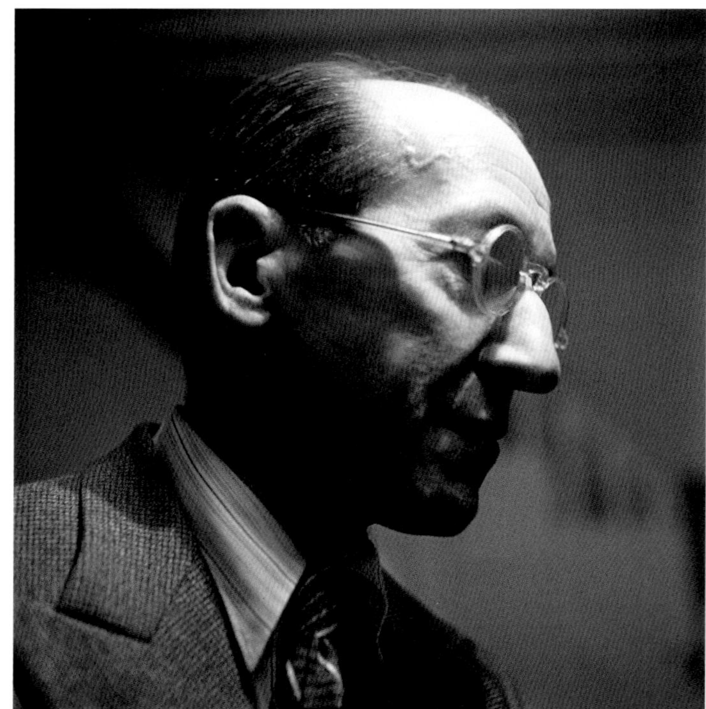

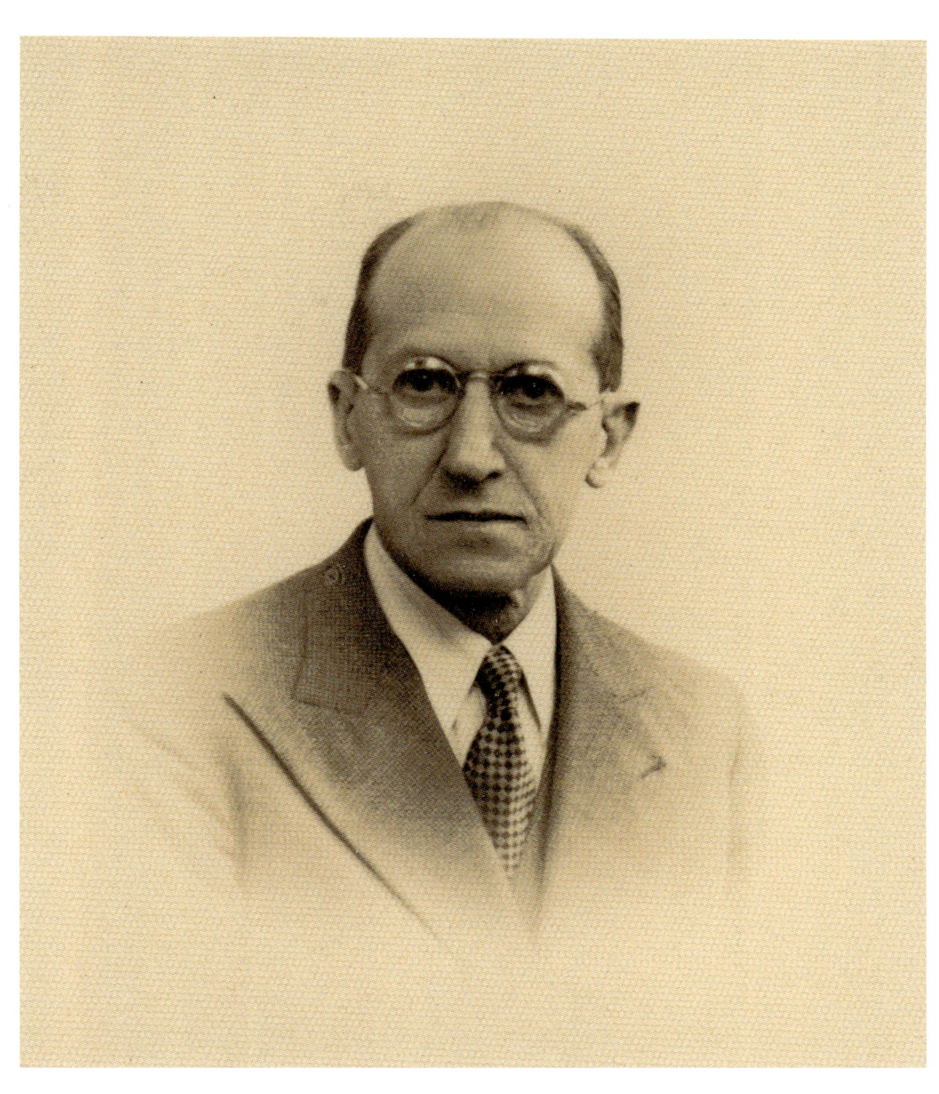

CATS 182–85 **Cas Oorthuys**
Portrait of Piet Mondrian, August (?) 1937

CAT. 186 **Unidentified photographer**
Piet Mondrian's passport photo, 12 September 1938
Mondrian had this photo taken for his new passport, which was issued by the Dutch embassy in Paris on 13 September 1938. It is the final picture from France: on 20 September 1938 Mondrian sailed from Calais to Dover.

THE LONDON AND NEW YORK YEARS 1938–44

Within a few days of his arrival in London, Mondrian was able to move into a spacious studio at 60 Parkhill Road in the quiet suburb of Hampstead. He was presumably helped by his friend Ben Nicholson, whose studio Mondrian could see from his own workplace on the first floor. Sadly, no photographs have survived from this period, apart from a passport photo taken shortly before Mondrian left for the United States. We do know from his correspondence, however, and from other testimony that the studio walls were whitewashed and that the artist immediately painted primary-coloured rectangles on them again, just as he had done in Paris. He got hold of some simple pieces of furniture, which he painted white. Mondrian then continued to work on canvases he had begun in Paris and quickly started several new, large ones.

He swiftly felt at home in London, which he found cleaner and more pleasant than the French capital. Thanks to his many friends there, he immediately had a social life. Also active in the city was a small group of geometric-abstract artists who viewed Mondrian as an important pioneer. It was in London that he liberated the block of colour from enclosure by black lines or the painting's edge, and where small, disconnected rectangles in red, yellow and blue made their appearance, marking a new phase in his work. Mondrian's paintings could also be seen by the London public in 1939: at the Guggenheim Jeune gallery, for instance, run by Peggy Guggenheim, who met Mondrian in London and would play a further part in his career in New York.

In September 1939, Britain became involved in the Second World War and London came under threat of being bombed. Although Mondrian's friends tried to persuade him to follow them to the safer countryside, he remained in the city and continued to work. He also wrote several unpublished texts in which he argued that freedom could be achieved if we organized our lives according to the same principles that hold sway in art (that is, Mondrian's), based on the balance of opposite but equal elements. In 1940, however, having decided to cross the Atlantic to New York after all, Mondrian started the application for the necessary visa. The Blitz began on 7 September of that year: the Germans regularly bombarded London from that moment on. A German bomb dropped close to his studio, shattering his windows. The panes had been blacked out using paper blinds, so that he escaped with a fright and a few splinters of glass. Mondrian had an involuntary introduction to the phenomenon of the air-raid shelter. With the help of friends on both sides of the ocean, he was able to leave a threatened and badly mauled England on 23 September 1940, when he embarked in Liverpool on SS *Samaria*, bound for New York.

The first leg of the voyage was still subject to the dangers of war, such as roving U-boat packs, but on 3 October the *Samaria* docked in New York unscathed. Mondrian's friend Harry Holtzman was waiting for him when he disembarked. He booked a room in a comfortable hotel so the artist could gather his strength and then rented an apartment for him at 353 East 56th Street, near his own home. Several carefree years now began for Mondrian. The wealthy Holtzman covered many of his costs and the artist's work sold reasonably well, albeit not for especially high prices. He liked the modernity of New York and took great pleasure from Hollywood movies and listening to jazz in bars and clubs. His response to discovering the staccato rhythms of boogie-woogie was 'enormous, enormous'.

More importantly for Mondrian, for whom art always took priority in his life, New York offered an artistic climate in which he could flourish. European intellectuals and artists like himself fled the Old World en masse, many of them settling in the same US city, turning New York overnight into the world centre of modern art, which it would remain for decades after. Mondrian was reunited there with the artistic vanguard he had left behind in Paris when he fled to London, among them Marcel Duchamp, Fritz Glarner, Max Ernst, André Breton and Fernand Léger.

His geometric-abstract work meant that Mondrian was something of an outsider compared to these artists. All the same, America had been prepared for his highly abstract art in the preceding years by young artists — some of them united in the American Abstract Artists group — who now welcomed him with open arms. Mondrian's paintings had also been brought to the attention of a wider public at the Museum of Living Art, run by the collector Albert Gallatin, and by the gallery owner Valentine Dudensing. His work was well received at the recently opened Museum of Modern Art by the influential director Alfred Barr Jr and the curator James Johnson Sweeney.

Once again, he turned his apartment cum studio into a neo-plastically decorated space that attracted a great deal of attention in New York too. Collectors came to visit, journalists to interview him, and his work and ideas were discussed in catalogues and other publications on modern art and architecture. In October 1943, Mondrian was able to move into a lighter studio and dwelling belonging to an artist couple of his acquaintance, Boris and Jan Margo. Located at 15 East 59th Street, it was here that he continued to work on a painting he had begun in 1942 — the diamond-shaped *Victory Boogie Woogie*. Its black lines were initially replaced by coloured ones, which were later broken up into primary-coloured blocks. Even though Mondrian was in his seventies by now, his neo-plastic quest continued unabated.

>> Detail of cat. 243

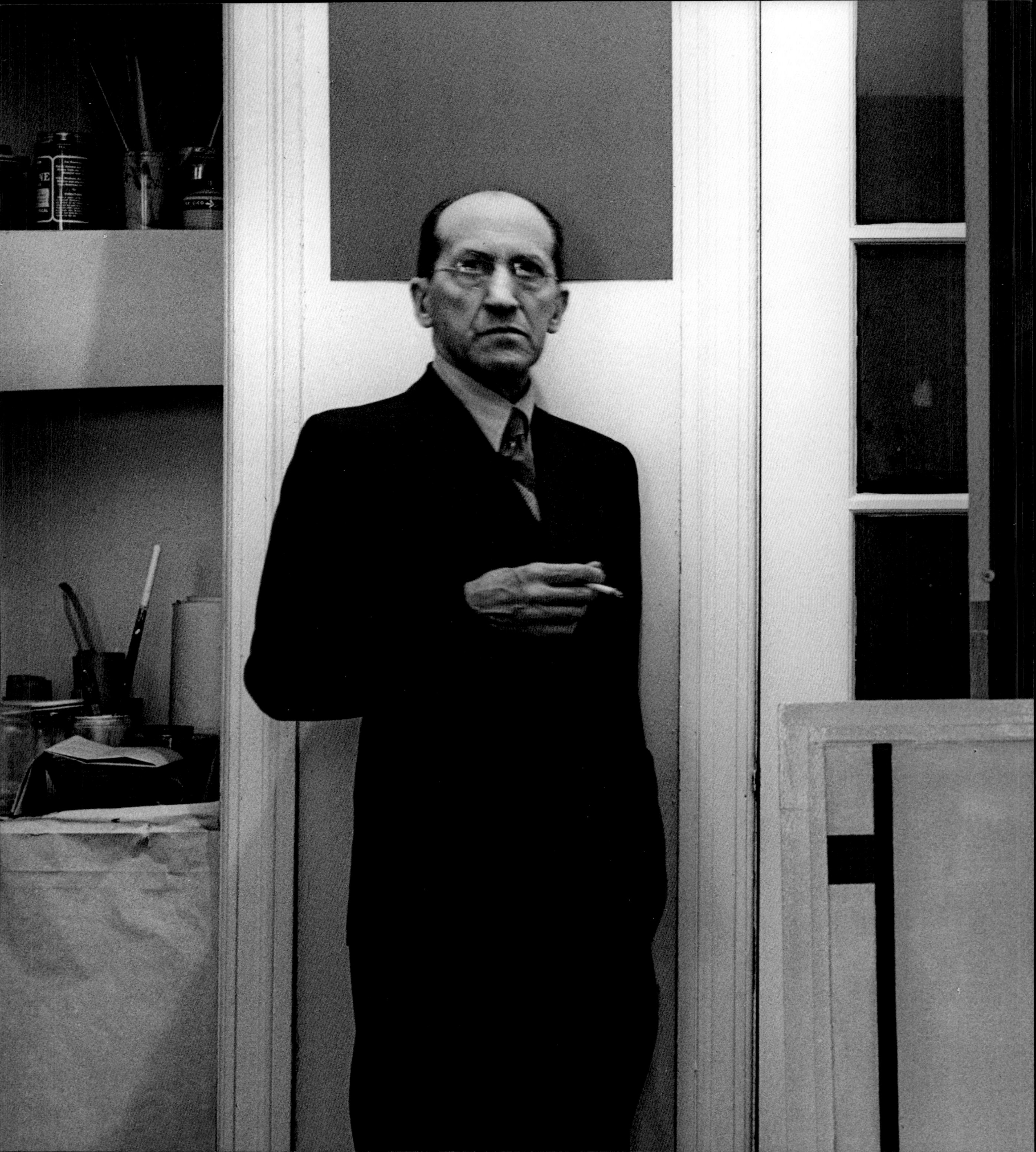

Victory Boogie Woogie was destined to remain unfinished, however. The artist's health had never been robust and he fell ill in January 1944, with what he described as bronchitis. Friends visiting on the 26th of that month were concerned by his condition and summoned a doctor, who diagnosed severe pneumonia. Mondrian was admitted to Murray Hill Hospital, where he died on 1 February 1944, shortly before turning seventy-two. A memorial service was held for him at a chapel on Lexington Avenue on 3 February, attended by around two hundred artists, writers, collectors and other art lovers. He was buried in a simple grave in the Cypress Hills Cemetery in Brooklyn.

Harry Holtzman arranged for Mondrian's famous studio to be opened to interested parties in the weeks that followed and he and Fritz Glarner took a series of unique photographs of the neo-plastic silence that Mondrian left behind.

TRIPLICATE
(To be given to declarant when originally issued; to be made a part of the petition for naturalization when petition is filed; and to be retained as a part of the petition in the records of the court)

UNITED STATES OF AMERICA

No. 501621

DECLARATION OF INTENTION
(Invalid for all purposes seven years after the date hereof)

bec ss: In the ... Court of ... at ...

(1) My full, true, and correct name is PIETER (PIET) MONDRIAN (Full, true name, without abbreviation, and any other name which has been used, must appear here)

(2) My present place of residence is 353 E. 56 St., NY NY NY (Number and street) (City or town) (County) (State) (3) My occupation is artist

(4) I am 69 years old. (5) I was born on March 7, 1872 (Month) (Day) (Year) in Amersfoort, Netherlands (City or town) (County, district, province, or state) (Country)

(6) My personal description is as follows: Sex male, color white, complexion medium, color of eyes brown, color of hair dk. brown, height 5 feet 8 inches, weight 138 pounds, visible distinctive marks slightly bald, race white, present nationality Dutch

(7) I am not married; the name of my wife or husband is ...; we were married on ... (Month) (Day) (Year) at ... (City or town) ... (State or country); he or she was born at ... (City or town) ... (County, district, province, or state) ... (Country) on ... (Month) (Day) (Year); and entered the United States at ... (City or town) ... (State) on ... (Month) (Day) (Year) for permanent residence in the United States, and now resides at ... (City or town) ... (County and State)

(8) I have no children; and the name, sex, date and place of birth, and present place of residence of each of said children who is living, are as follows:

(9) My last place of foreign residence was London England (City or town) (County, district, province, or state) (Country) (10) I emigrated to the United States from Liverpool England (City or town) (Country) (11) My lawful entry for permanent residence in the United States was at New York, NY (City or town) (State) under the name of Pieter Cornelis Mondriaan on October 3, 1940 (Month) (Day) (Year), on the SS Samaria (Name of vessel or other means of conveyance)

(12) Since my lawful entry for permanent residence I have not been absent from the United States, for a period or periods of 6 months or longer, as follows:

Departed from the United States			Returned to the United States		
Port	Date (Month, day, year)	Vessel or Other Means of Conveyance	Port	Date (Month, day, year)	Vessel or Other Means of Conveyance

(13) I have not heretofore made declaration of intention: No. ..., on ... (Month) (Day) (Year) at ... (City or town) ... (County) ... (State) in the ... (Name of court)

(14) It is my intention in good faith to become a citizen of the United States and to reside permanently therein. (15) I will, before being admitted to citizenship, renounce absolutely and forever all allegiance and fidelity to any foreign prince, potentate, state, or sovereignty of whom or which at the time of admission to citizenship I may be a subject or citizen. (16) I am not an anarchist; nor a believer in the unlawful damage, injury, or destruction of property, or sabotage; nor a disbeliever in or opposed to organized government; nor a member of or affiliated with any organization or body of persons teaching disbelief in or opposition to organized government. (17) I certify that the photograph affixed to the duplicate and triplicate hereof is a likeness of me and was signed by me.

I do swear (affirm) that the statements I have made and the intentions I have expressed in this declaration of intention subscribed by me are true to the best of my knowledge and belief: SO HELP ME GOD.

Pieter (Piet) Mondrian
(Original and true signature of declarant without abbreviation, also other name if used)

Pieter Cornelis Mondriaan.

Subscribed and sworn to (affirmed) before me in the form of oath shown above in the office of the Clerk of said Court, at New York, NY this 22nd day of September, anno Domini 1941. I hereby certify that Certification No. 2-905151 from the Commissioner of Immigration and Naturalization, showing the lawful entry for permanent residence of the declarant above named on the date stated in this declaration of intention, has been received by me, and that the photograph affixed to the duplicate and triplicate hereof is a likeness of the declarant.

[SEAL]

GEORGE J H FOLLMER
Clerk of the U S DISTRICT Court.
By ... Deputy Clerk.

Form N-315
U. S. DEPARTMENT OF JUSTICE
IMMIGRATION AND NATURALIZATION SERVICE
(Edition of 1-13-41)

16—19119 U. S. GOVERNMENT PRINTING OFFICE

CAT. 188 **Unidentified photographer**

Portrait of Piet Mondrian, between 24 August and 22 September 1941

This passport photo was used for Mondrian's application for US citizenship.

CAT. 187 See catalogue

Harry Holtzman

CATS 189, 193–221, 384–403

Towards the end of 1934, the twenty-two-year-old American artist Harry Holtzman (1912–1987) sailed from New York to Europe, curious about life in Paris, the world capital of art. He was eager to meet the maker of the abstract work that had so fascinated him when he came across it in Gallatin's Gallery of Living Art at the University of New York. According to his own account, he knocked on the door of Mondrian's studio one afternoon in December 1934, having tracked down the address via an artists' café in the city. Mondrian tended not to welcome unannounced visitors, but he made an exception for the young American who had travelled such a long way. It was the beginning of a friendship that would last until Mondrian's death, just over nine years later.

Holtzman returned to America in April 1935, but despite their physical distance, the two men kept up a friendly correspondence. Holtzman, whose wife was heiress to a Kansas oil magnate, supported Mondrian both morally and financially when the artist started planning his emigration to New York in 1940, having already fled Paris for London in September 1938 in the face of the Nazi advance. Holtzman's ongoing support earned him Mondrian's deep sympathy. Shortly after the Dutchman arrived in New York, Holtzman took him to his summer house in Great Barrington, Massachusetts, to gather his strength after a physically and emotionally draining crossing. It was there that Holtzman took the first photograph of Mondrian on American soil (cat. 189). Two further series of photographs would follow, the first consisting of portraits of Mondrian by Holtzman in the latter's studio (cats 193–221). Some feature the two men together, others Mondrian on his own. Holtzman will have used a self-timer to take the pictures in which both artists appear. The ungainly shadows suggest the pictures were lit either by flash or powerful lamps. The friends pose together in various settings, surrounded in each case by Holtzman's neo-plastic work. In some cases they smile at each other (cat. 211), while in others they gaze out of the picture with serious expressions.

The portraits Holtzman took of Mondrian on his own during the same session are undoubtedly some of the most sympathetic images of the artist, who looks genially into the lens. The photographs in which he has removed his glasses in particular show a less familiar Mondrian — the soft, accessible personality rather than the rigid and aloof painter of horizontals and verticals.

The second series of photos was taken a few years later, shortly after Mondrian's death on 1 February 1944 (cats 384–403). As the sole heir, Holtzman took ownership of and responsibility for Mondrian's artistic and physical legacy. He viewed the studio as an integral part of Mondrian's practice and opened it up to interested parties for several weeks after his friend's death. It seems to have been of particular interest to art-school students. The series of photographs Holtzman took of the space was intended to document the artist's final studio, prompting him to take colour photographs. Holtzman used Kodachrome still film, relatively new at the time, to capture the special location as effectively as possible. The results were sharp and chromatically correct, offering a vibrant image of the studio. It makes for a substantial contrast with the earlier black-and-white photos of Mondrian's Paris studios. The pictures taken by Holtzman are indeed the best in terms of conveying the dynamism the artist was able to create by placing primary-coloured cardboard rectangles on the wall. The series provides a marvellous impression of Mondrian's everyday surroundings, in which art and life merged in a perfect symbiosis.

Holtzman eventually dismantled the studio, carefully tracing the compositions on the walls and then transferring them to large wooden panels, painted white like the interior of the studio. He exhibited these *Wall Works*, as he called them, several times during his lifetime, together with the studio furniture. At some point, both the *Wall Works* and the furniture were lost, leaving the colour photographs as the only surviving testimony to Mondrian's final living and working space.

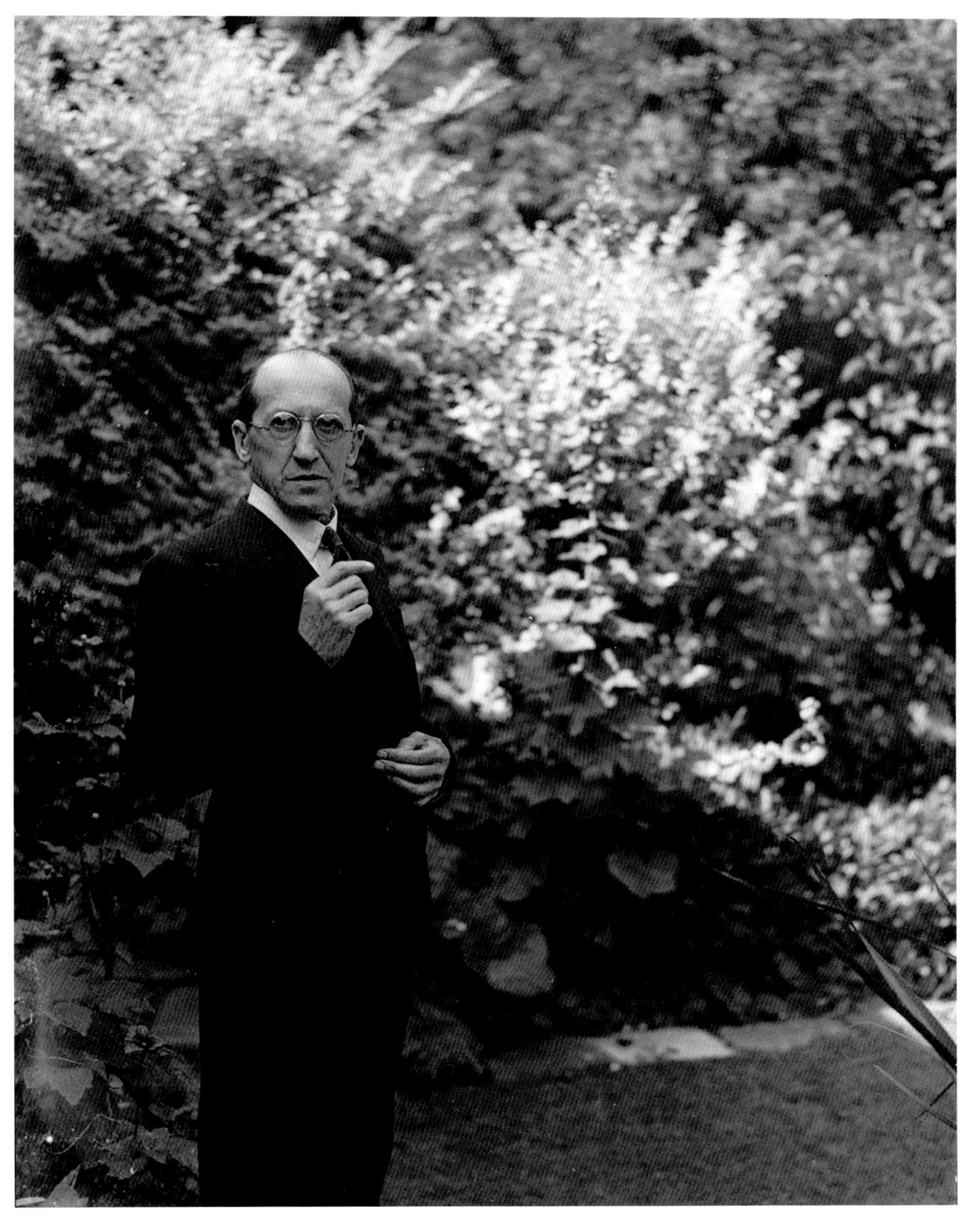

CAT. 189 **Harry Holtzman**
Piet Mondrian in the garden of Harry and Eileen Holtzman's summer home in Great Barrington, autumn 1940 (?)

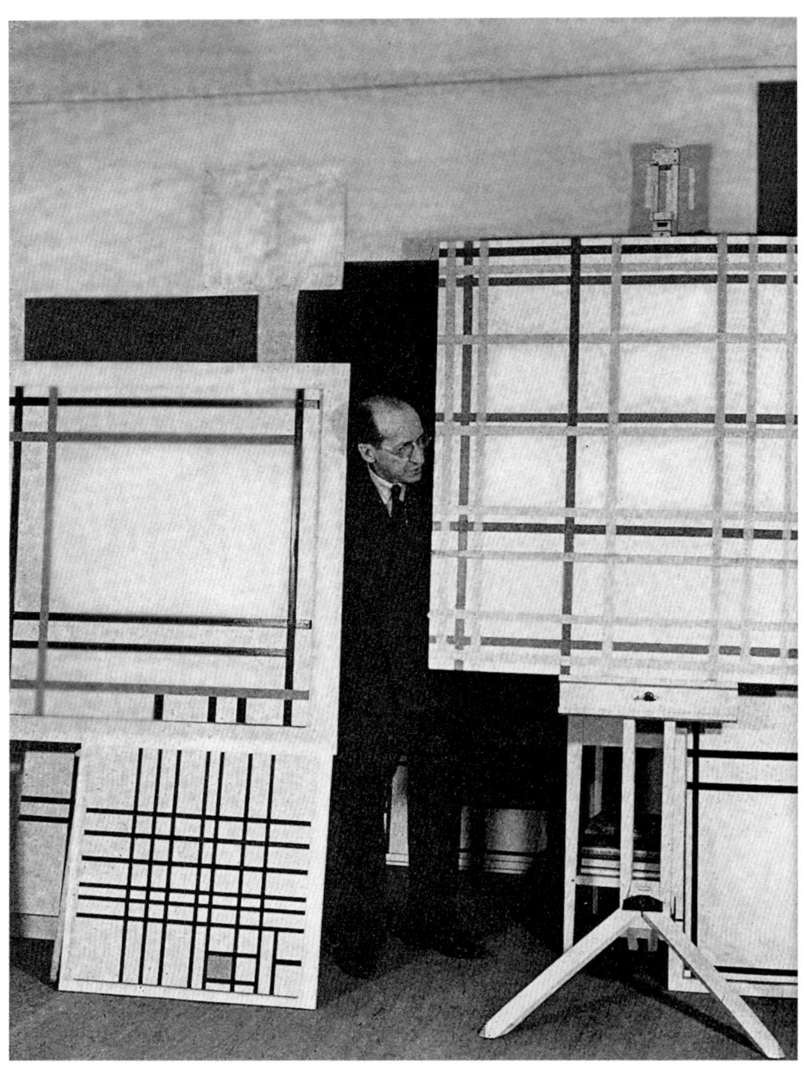

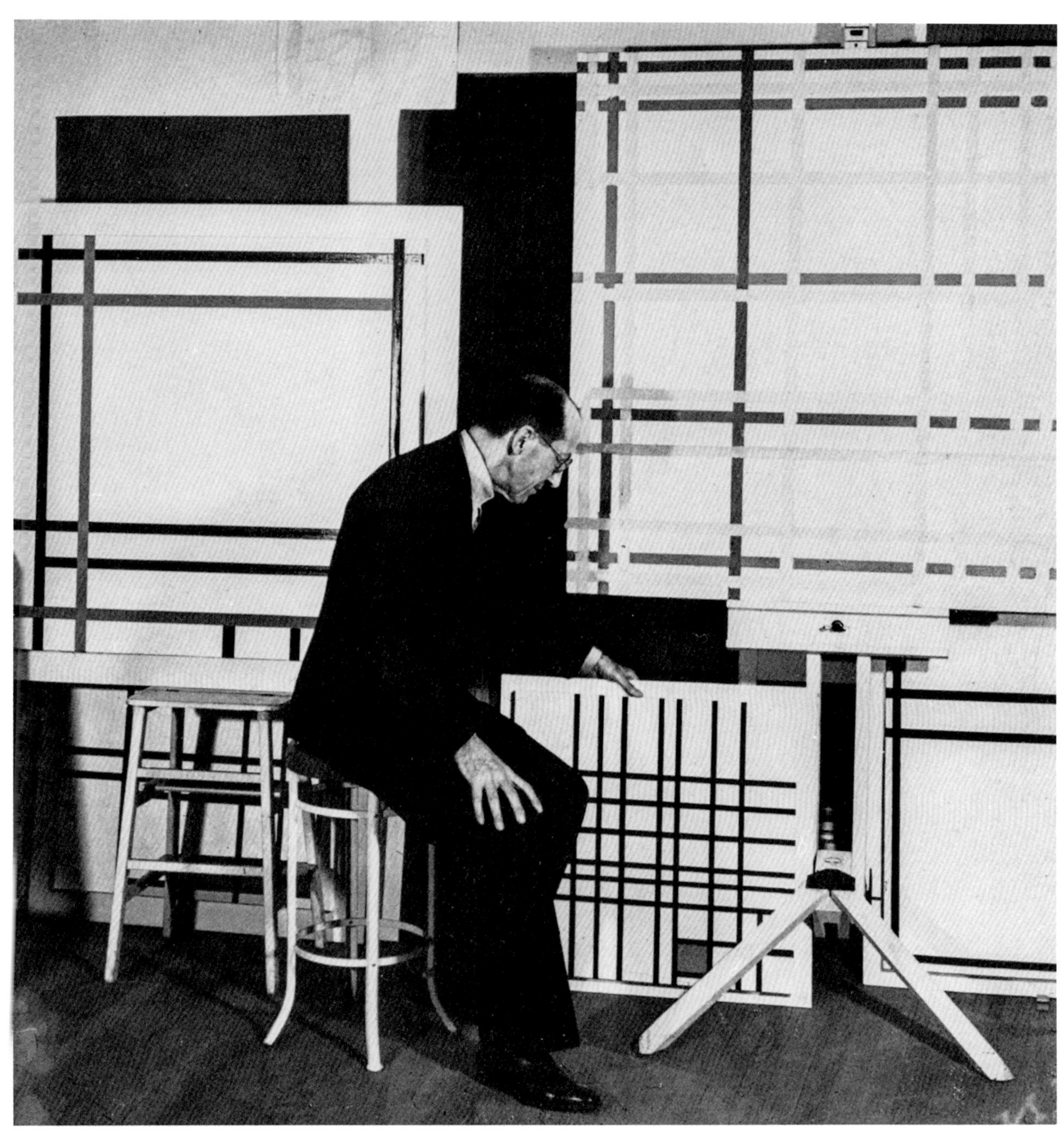

CATS 190—91 **Emery Muscetra**
Piet Mondrian in his studio with recent works, c. October 1941

CAT. 192 See catalogue

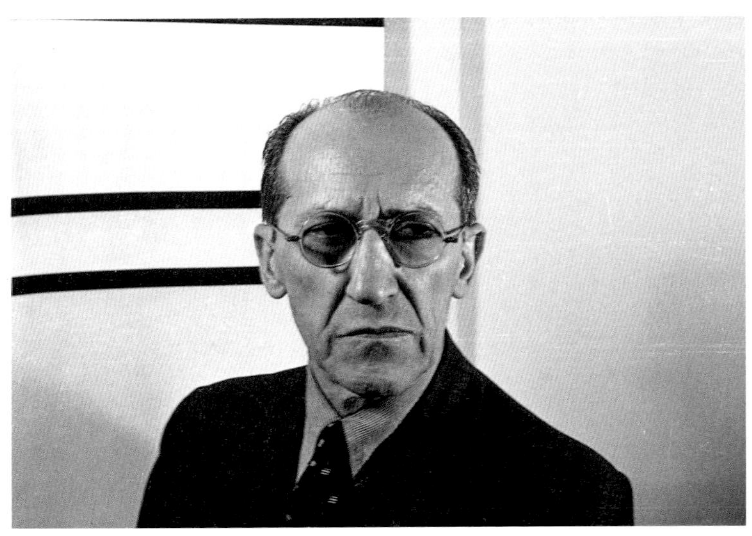
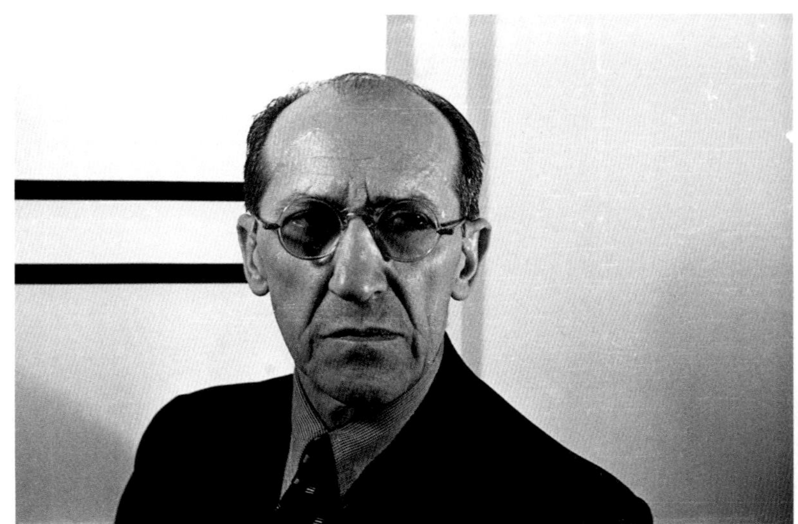
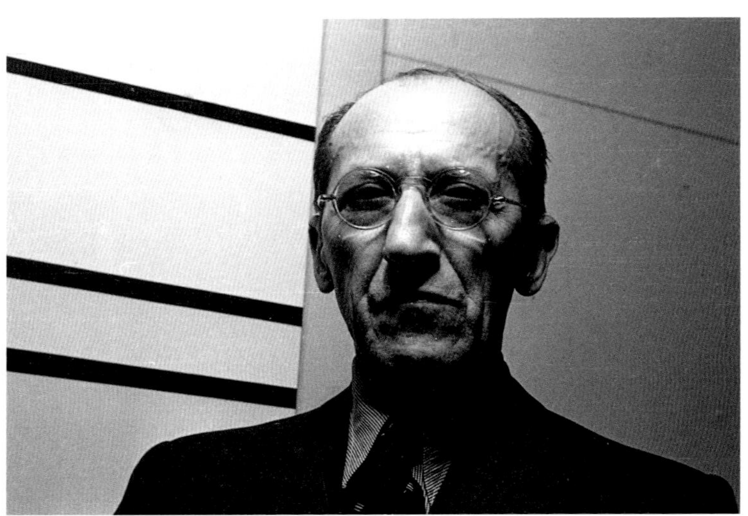
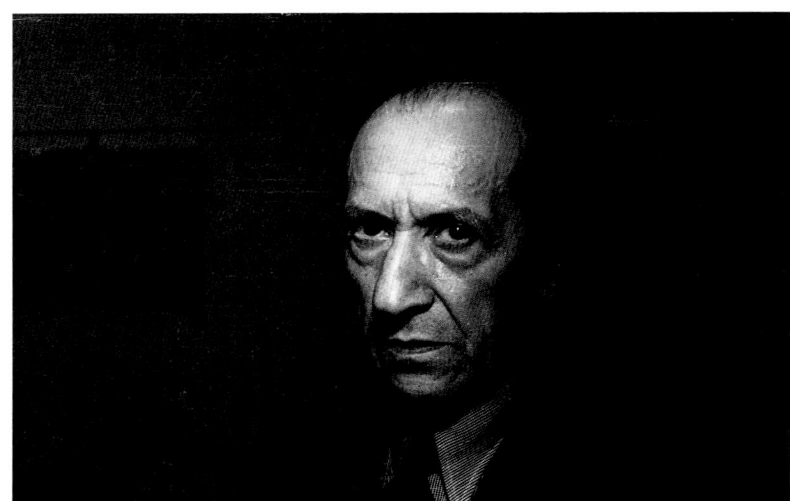

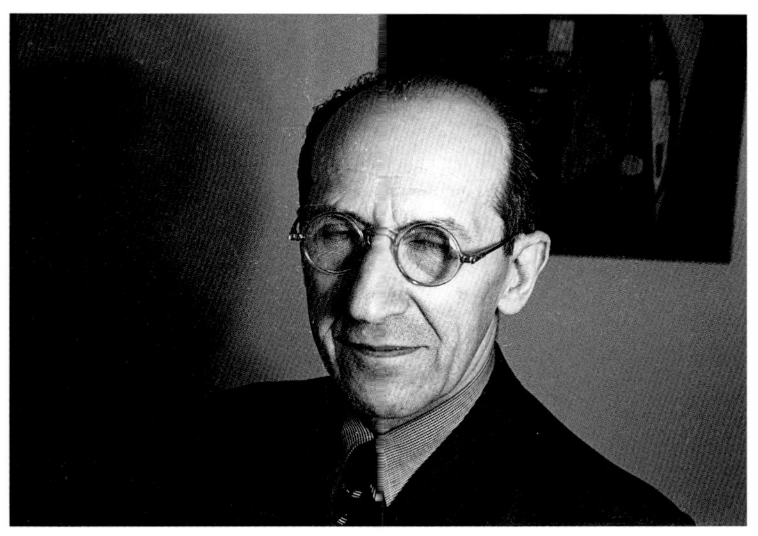

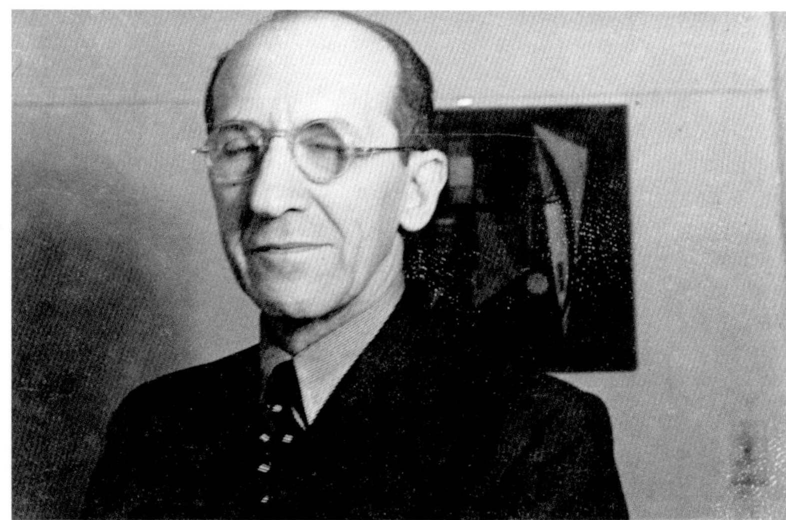

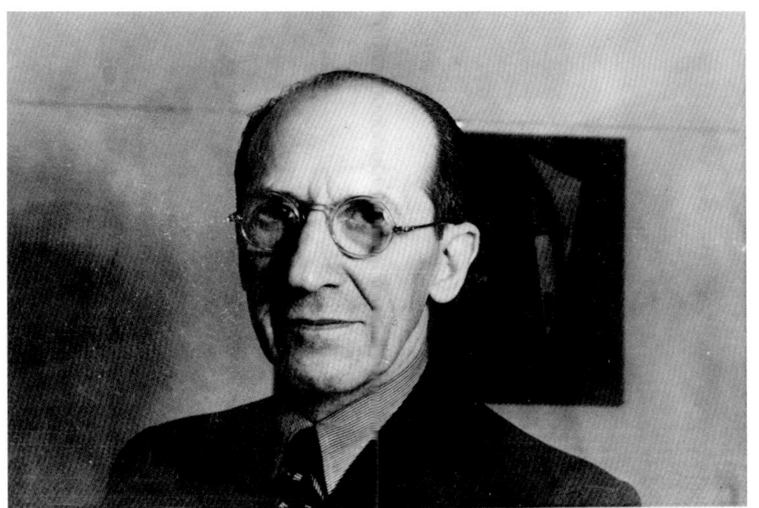

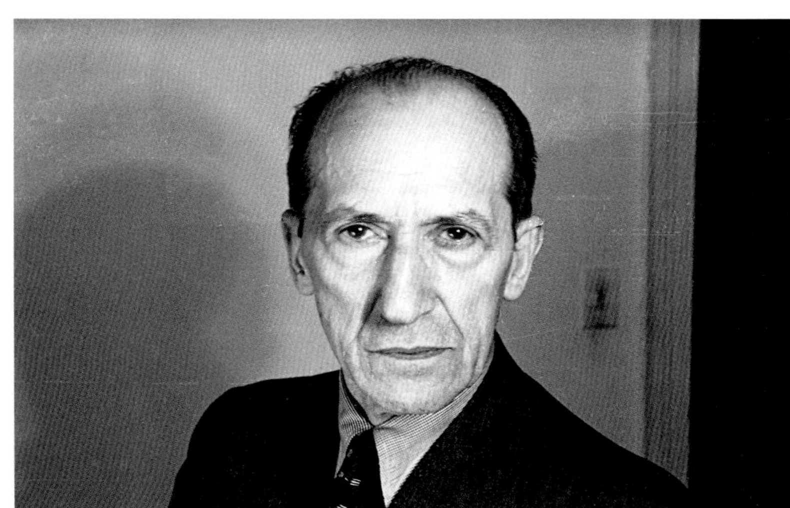

CATS 193–94, 196–201 **Harry Holtzman**
Portrait of Piet Mondrian in Holtzman's studio, between 4 October 1940 and May 1942

CATS 195, 202–10 See catalogue

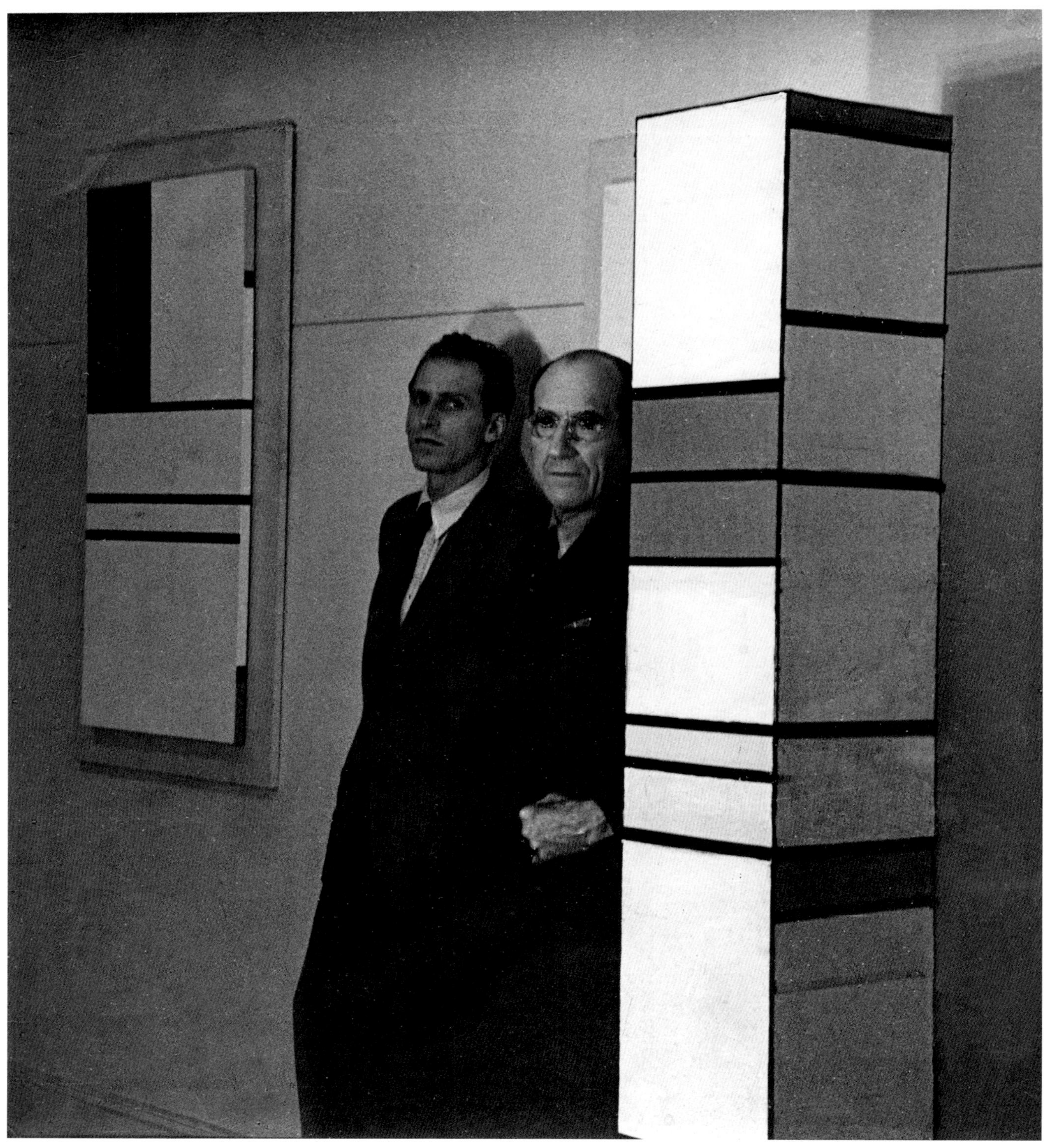

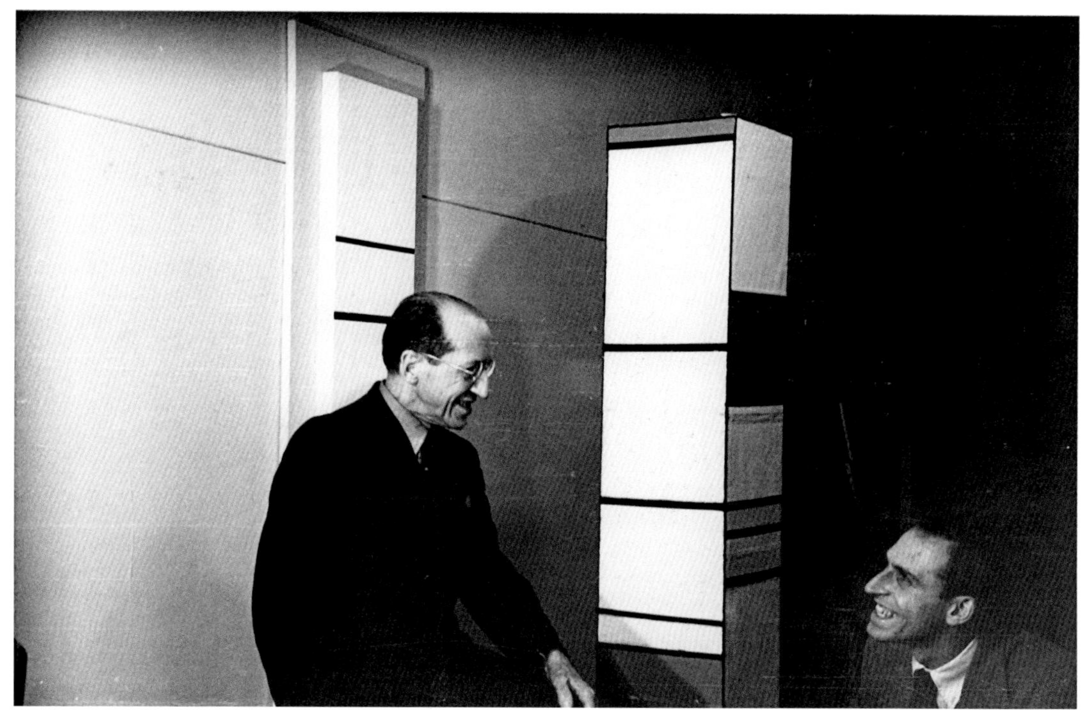

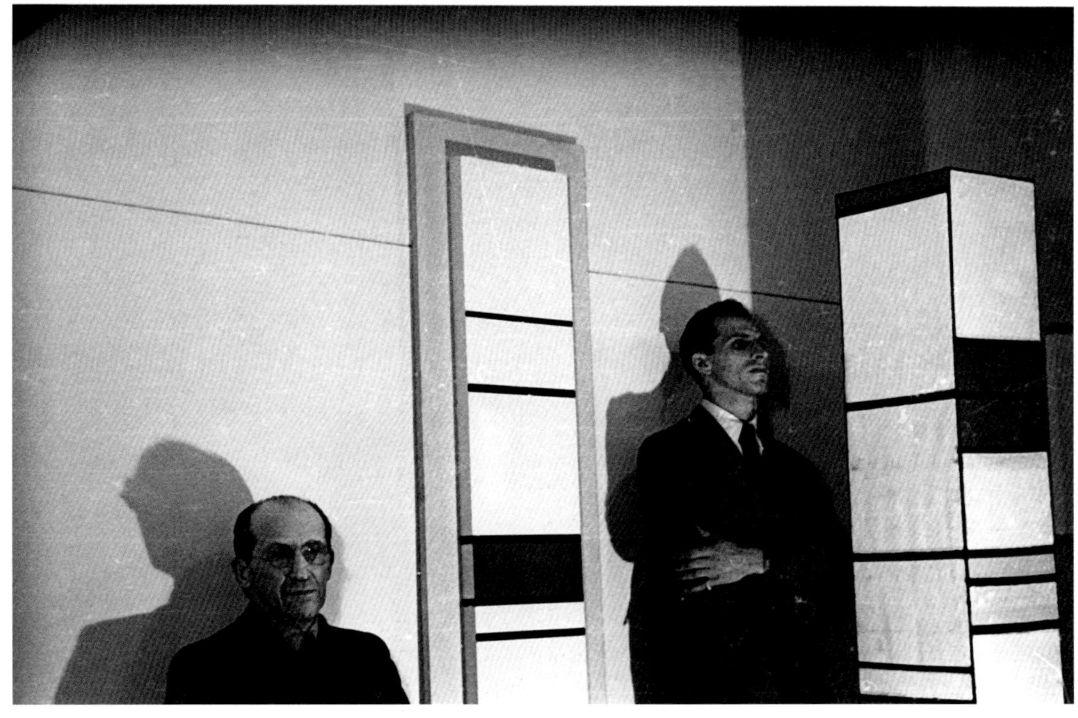

CATS 214, 211, 215 **Harry Holtzman**
Piet Mondrian and Harry Holtzman in Holtzman's studio, between 4 October 1940 and May 1942

CATS 212–13 See catalogue

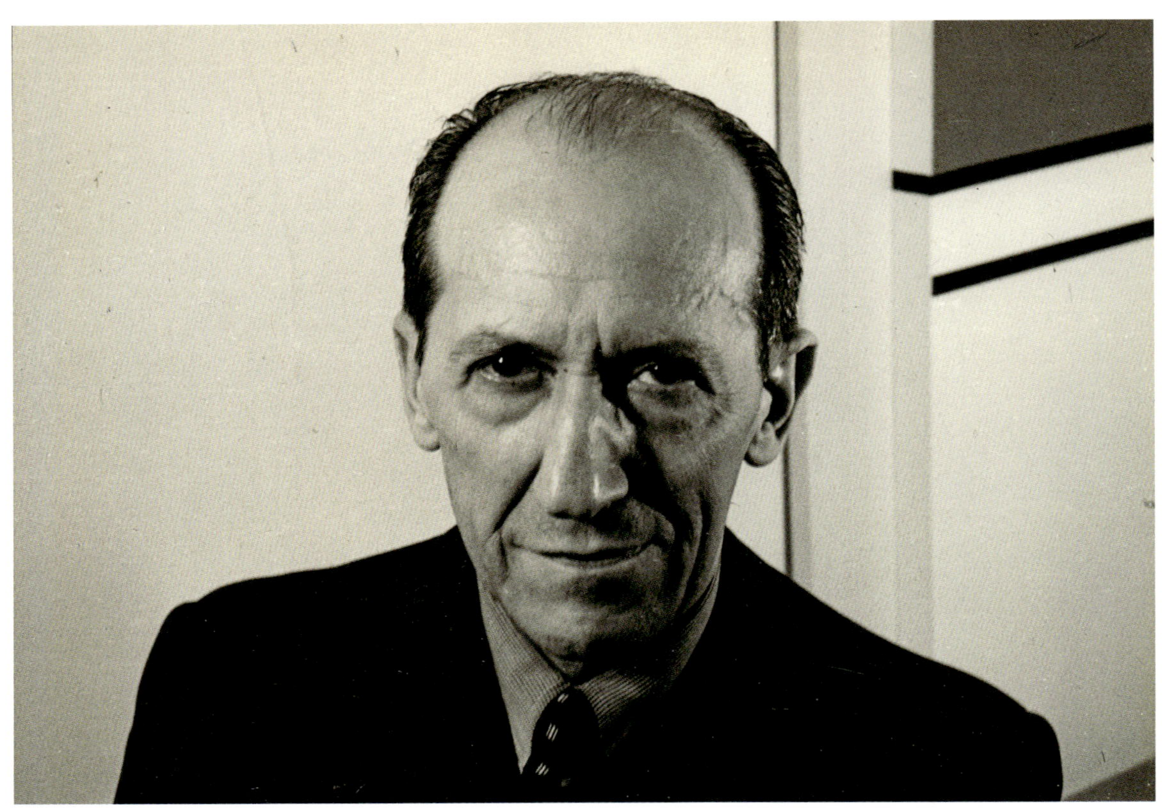

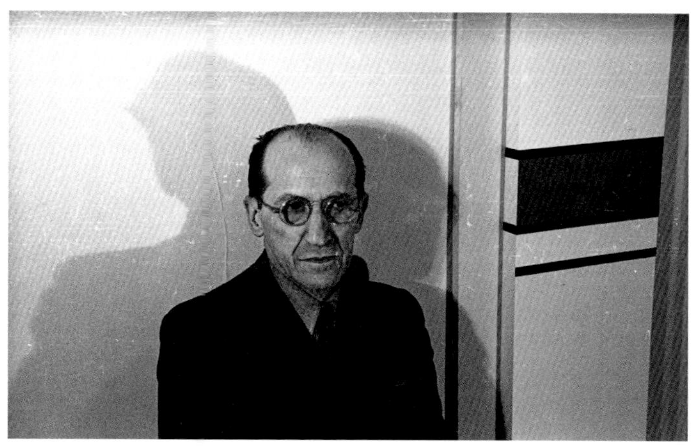
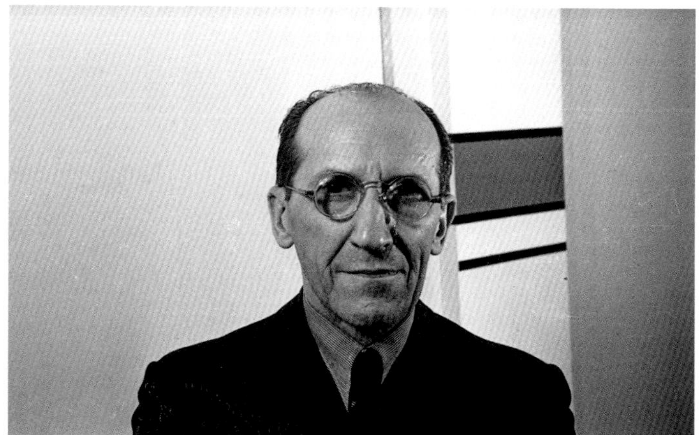
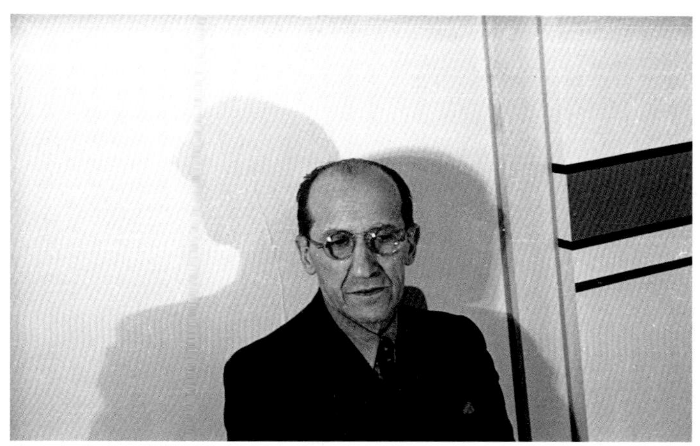
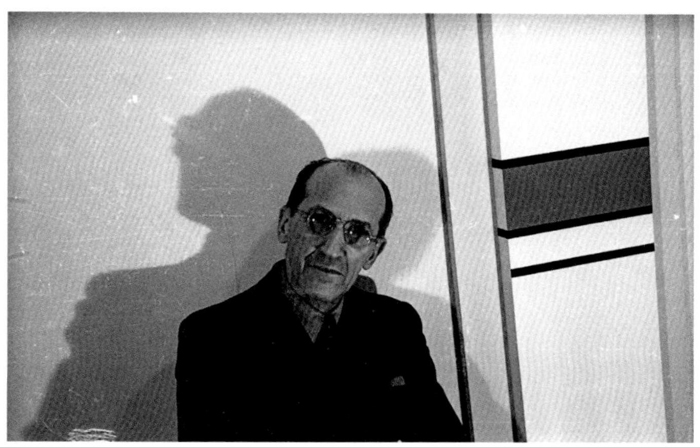
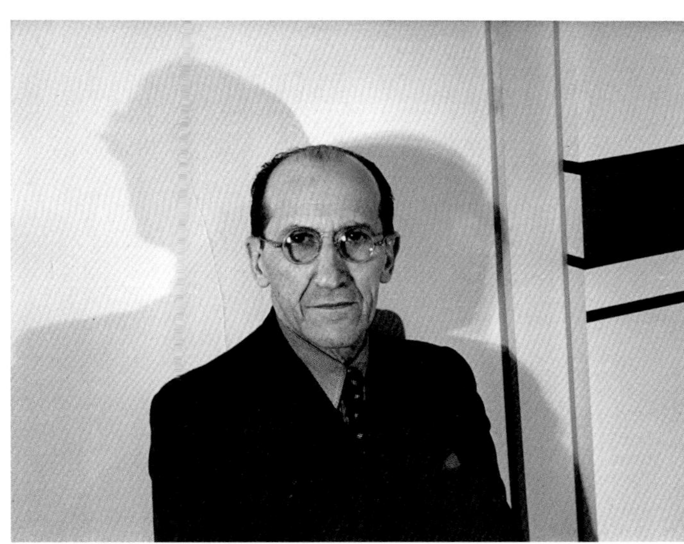

CATS 221, 216–220 **Harry Holtzman**
Portrait of Piet Mondrian in Holtzman's studio, between 4 October 1940 and May 1942

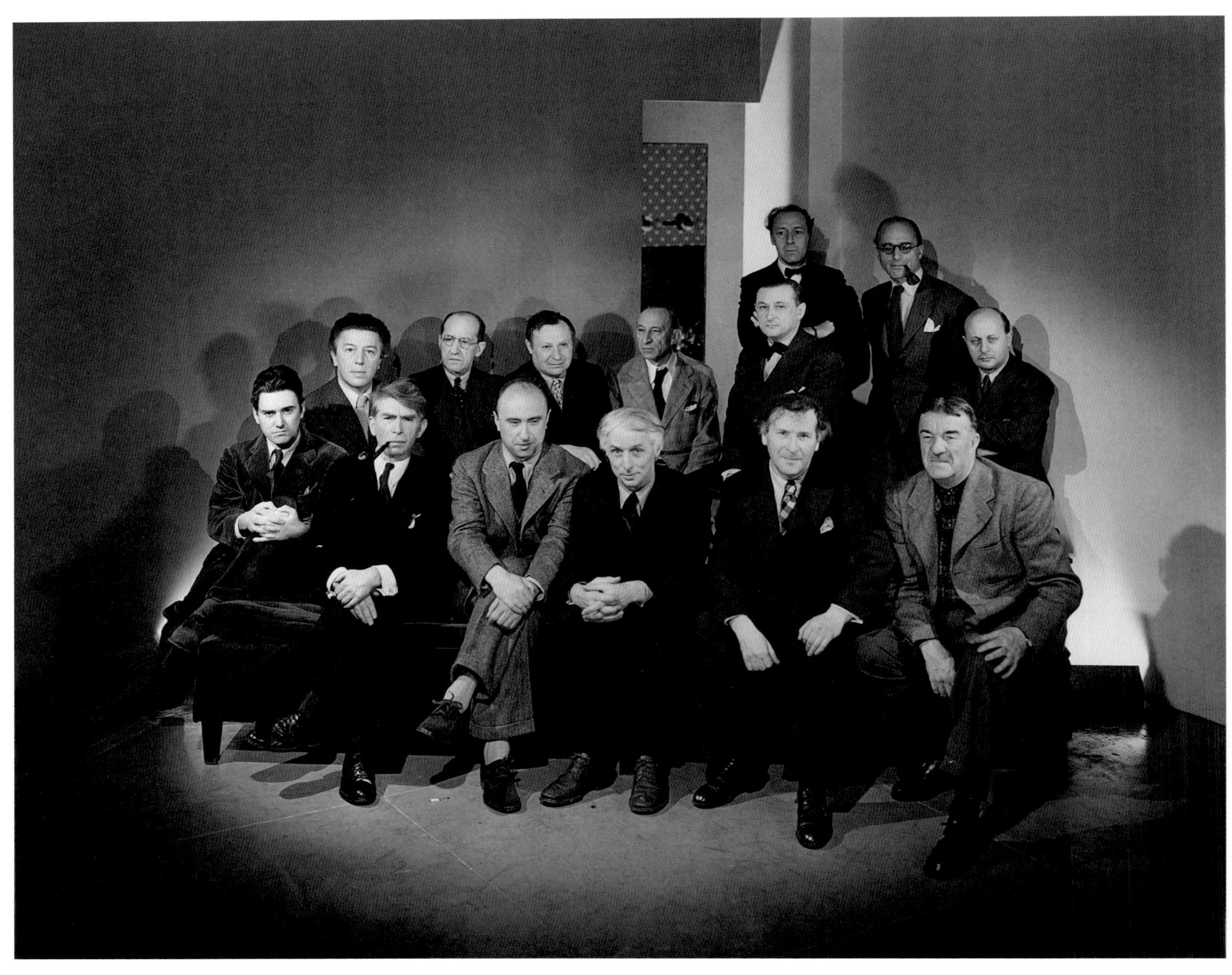

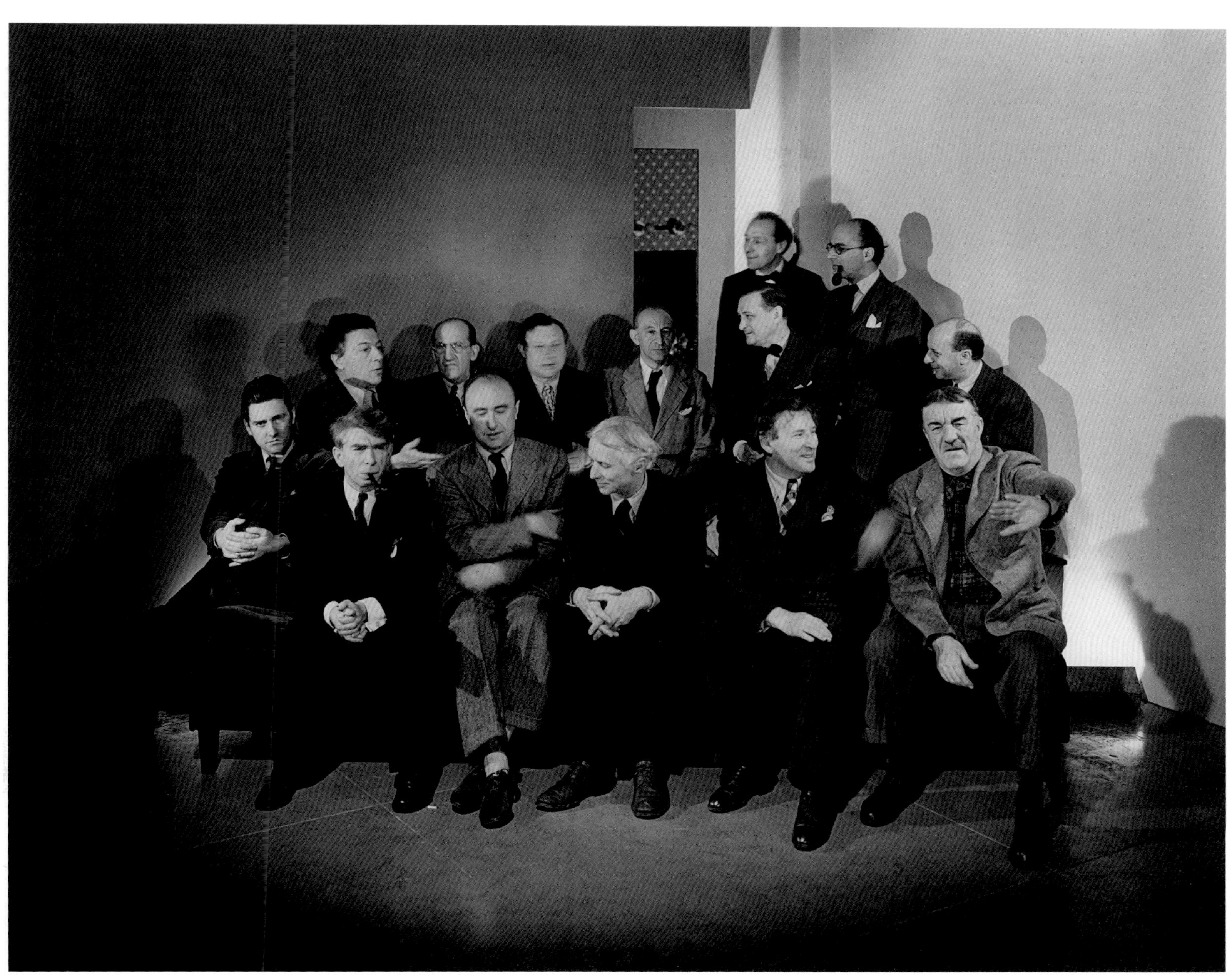

CATS 222, 224 **George Platt Lynes**

Group portrait of participants in the 'Artists in Exile' exhibition, c. February 1942

Left to right, front row: Matta Echaurren, Ossip Zadkine, Yves Tanguy, Max Ernst, Marc Chagall, Fernand Léger; middle row: André Breton, Piet Mondrian, André Masson, Amédée Ozenfant, Jacques Lipchitz, Pavel Tchelitchew; back row: Kurt Seligmann, Eugène Berman.

CATS 223, 225–227 See catalogue

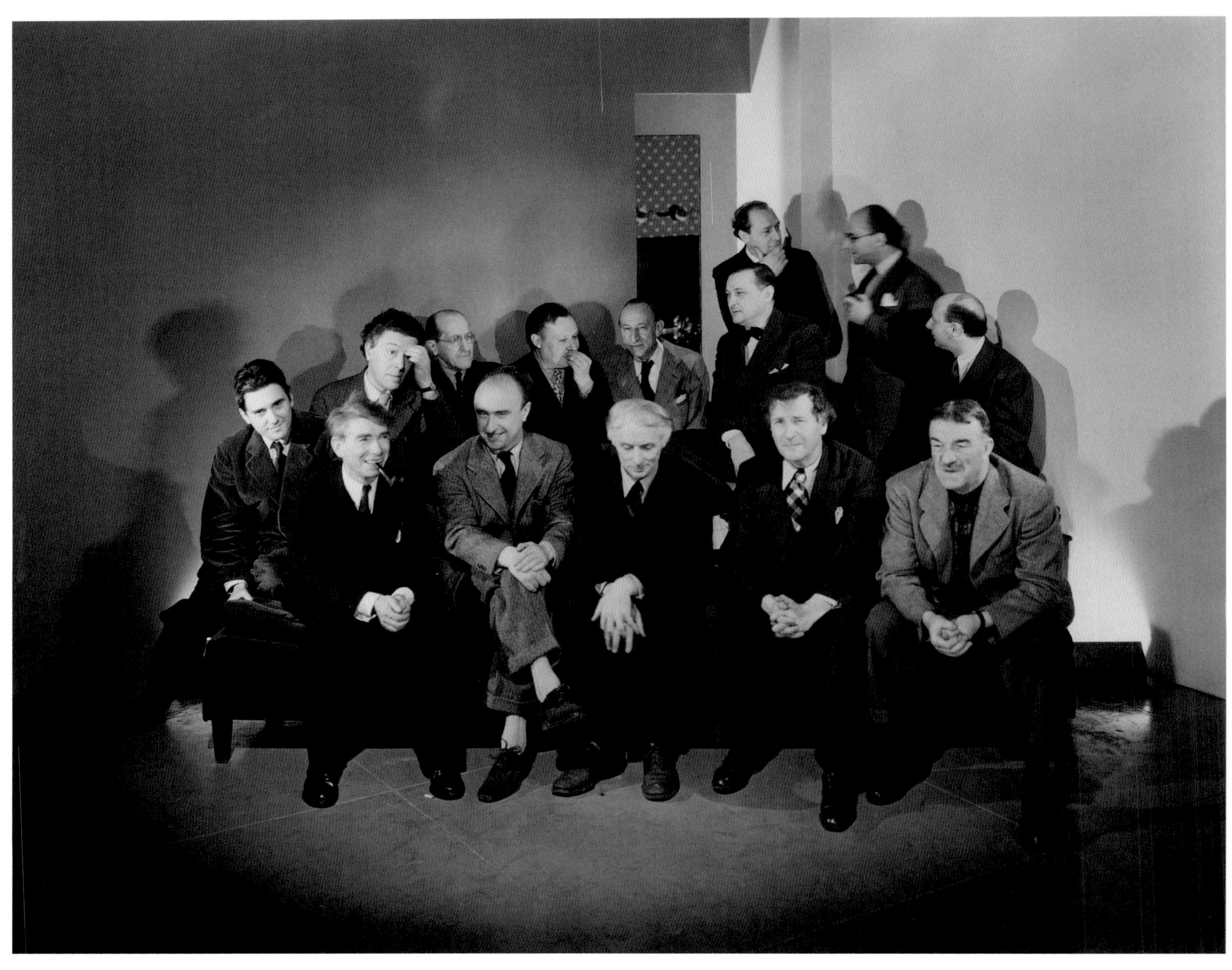

CAT. 228 **George Platt Lynes**

Group portrait of participants in the 'Artists in Exile' exhibition, c. February 1942

Left to right, front row: Matta Echaurren, Ossip Zadkine, Yves Tanguy, Max Ernst, Marc Chagall, Fernand Léger; middle row: André Breton, Piet Mondrian, André Masson, Amédée Ozenfant, Jacques Lipchitz, Pavel Tchelitchew; back row: Kurt Seligmann, Eugène Berman.

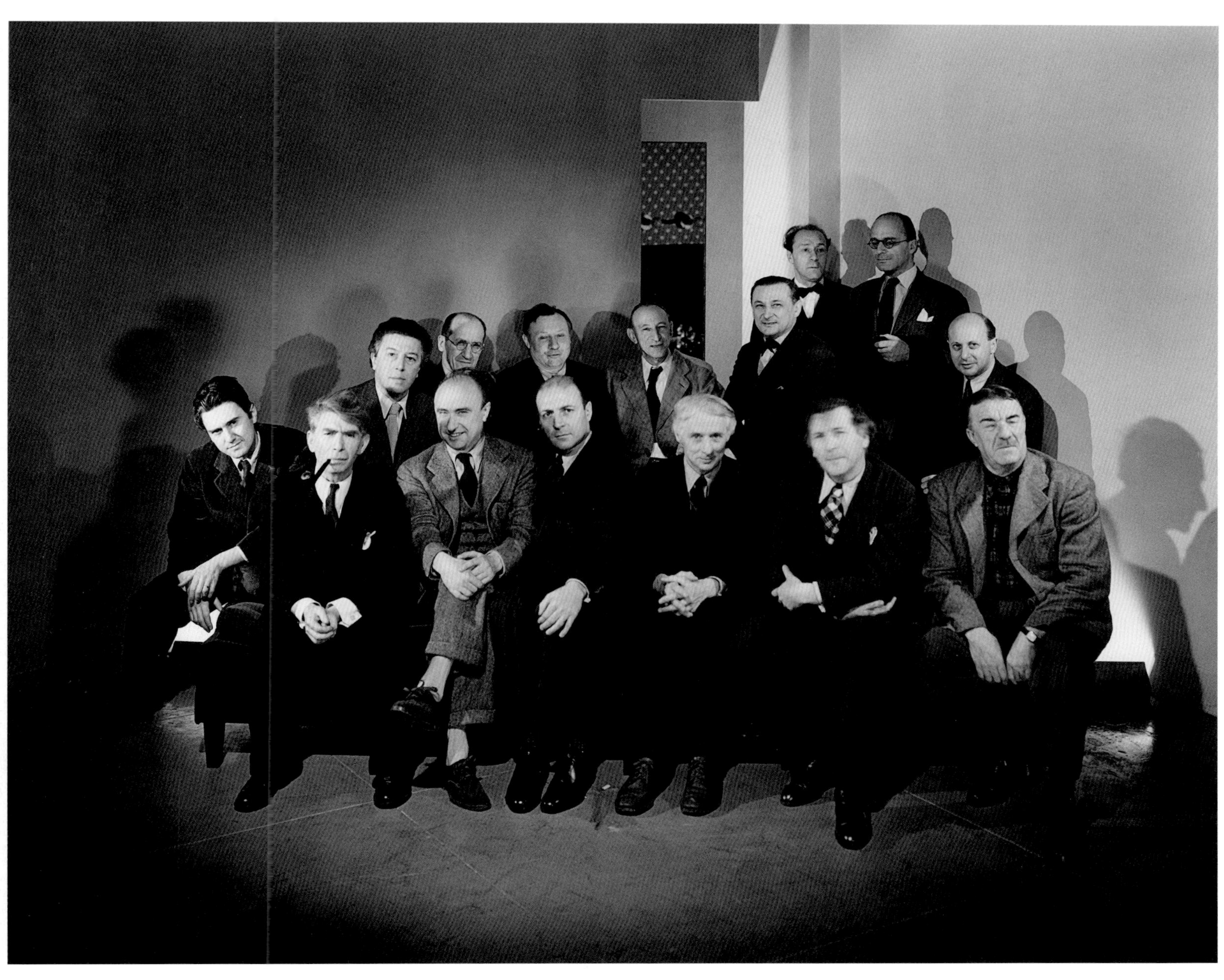

CAT. 229 **George Platt Lynes**

Group portrait of participants in the 'Artists in Exile' exhibition, c. February 1942

Left to right, front row: Matta Echaurren, Ossip Zadkine, Yves Tanguy, Pierre Matisse, Max Ernst, Marc Chagall, Fernand Léger; middle row: André Breton, Piet Mondrian, André Masson, Amédée Ozenfant, Jacques Lipchitz, Pavel Tchelitchew; back row: Kurt Seligmann, Eugène Berman.

CAT. 230 See catalogue

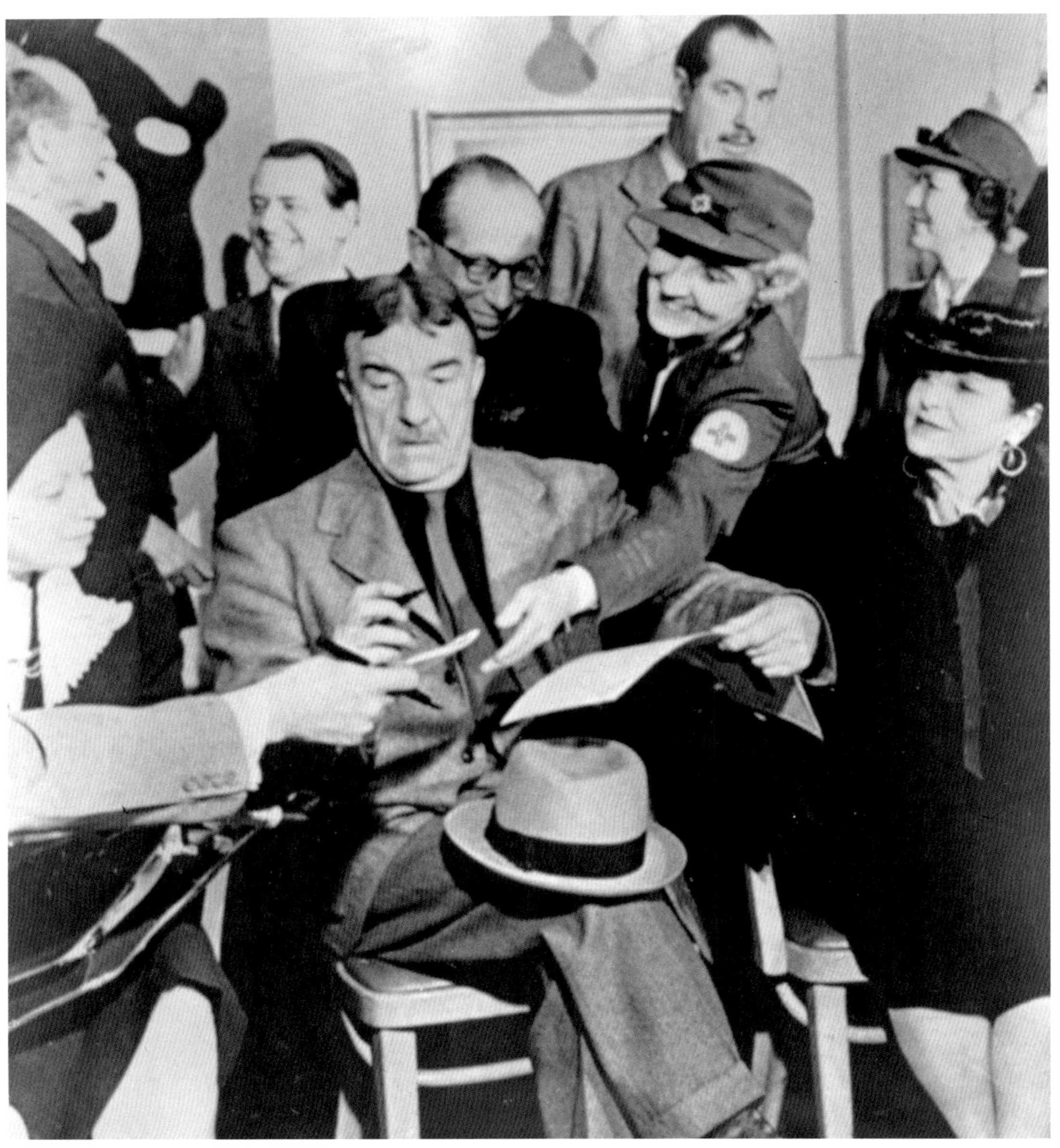

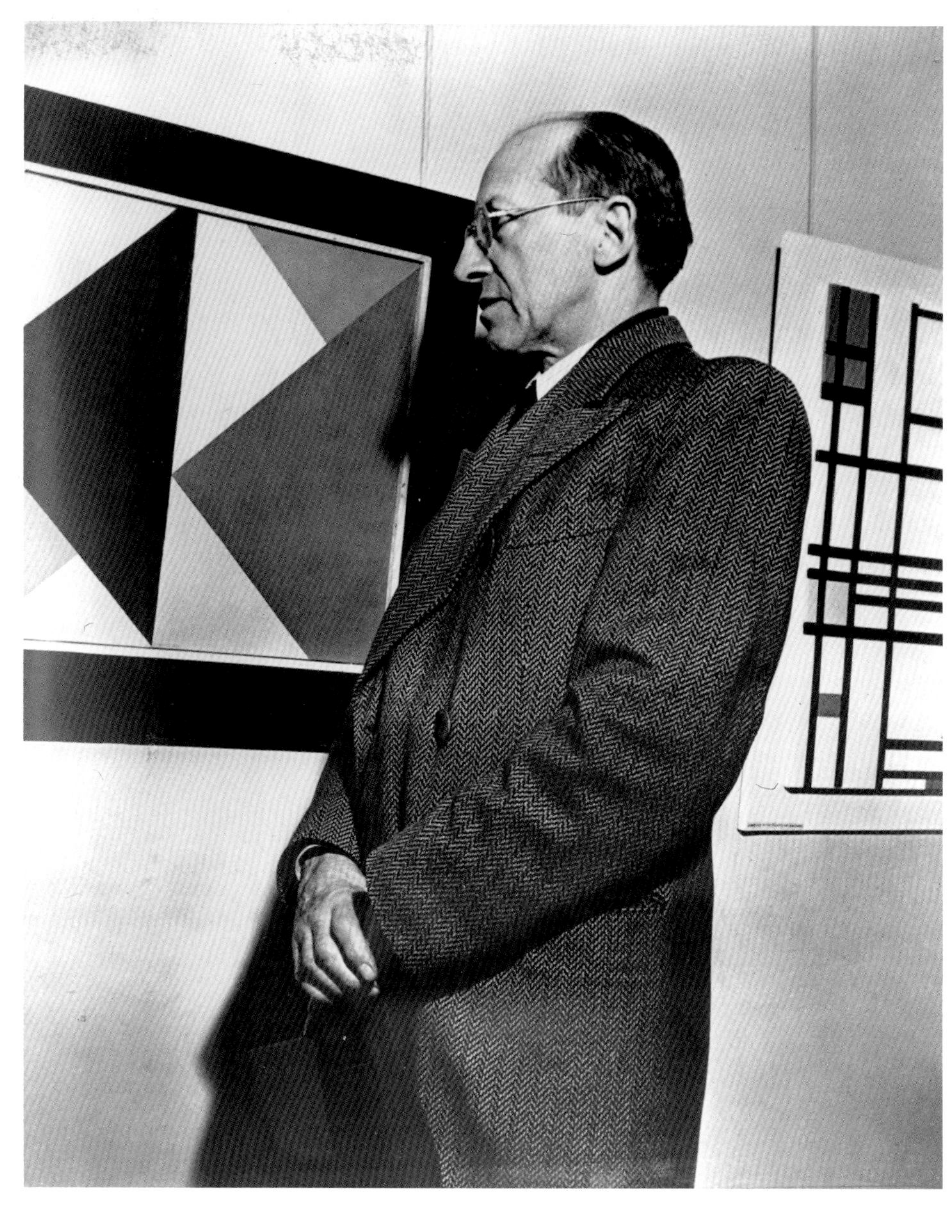

CAT. 232 **Lisette Model**

Fernand Léger signing autographs at the opening of the 'Masters of Abstract Art' exhibition, 1 April 1942

Left to right: unidentified woman, Piet Mondrian, Fritz Glarner, Fernand Léger (sitting), Kurt Seligmann, Charles Shaw, two unidentified women from the American Red Cross, Helena Rubinstein.

CAT. 231 **Lisette Model**

Piet Mondrian at the opening of the 'Masters of Abstract Art' exhibition, 1 April 1942

Mondrian poses here with Theo van Doesburg's *Contra Composition XIII*, from the Peggy Guggenheim collection. His own *Composition No. 5 with Blue, Yellow and Red* (B[286].314, 1938/1942) can be seen hanging on the right.

CAT. 233 See catalogue

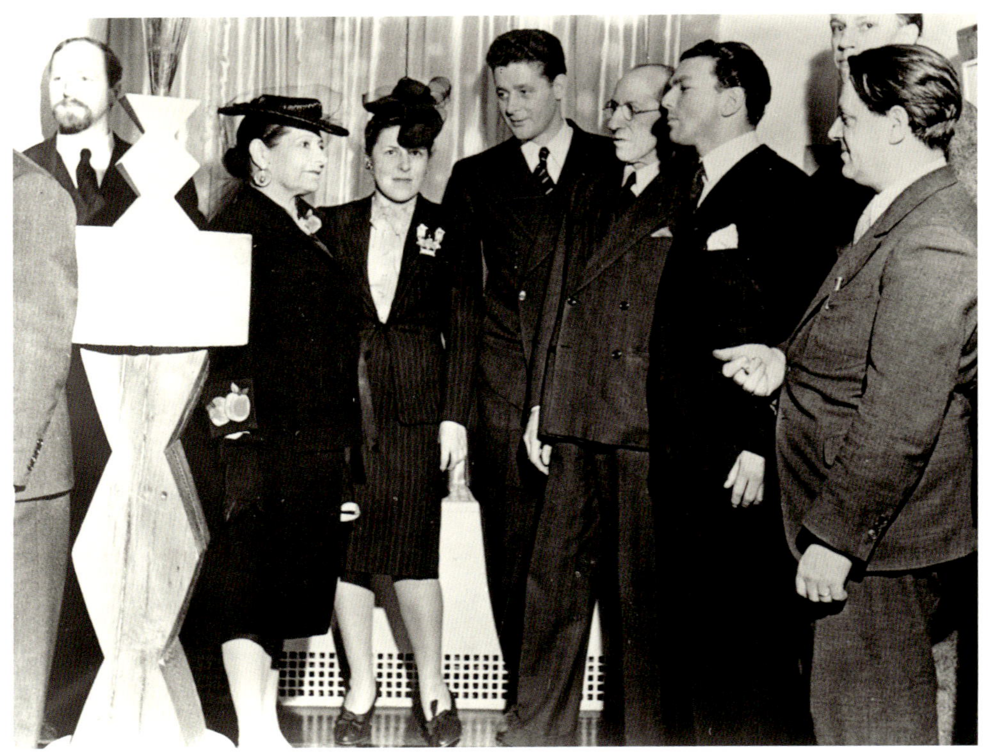

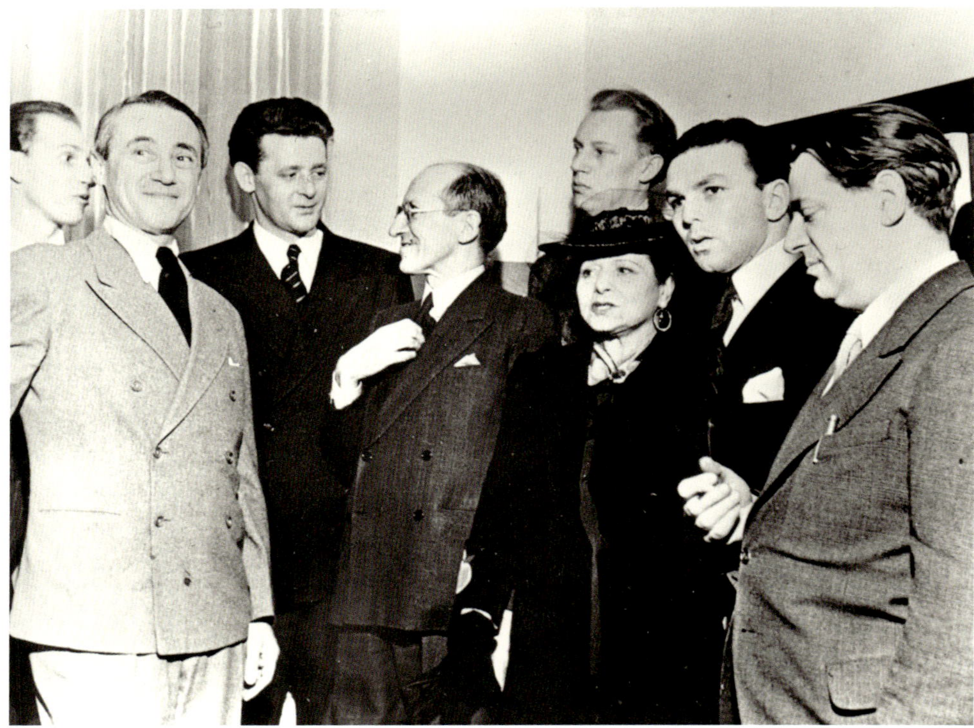

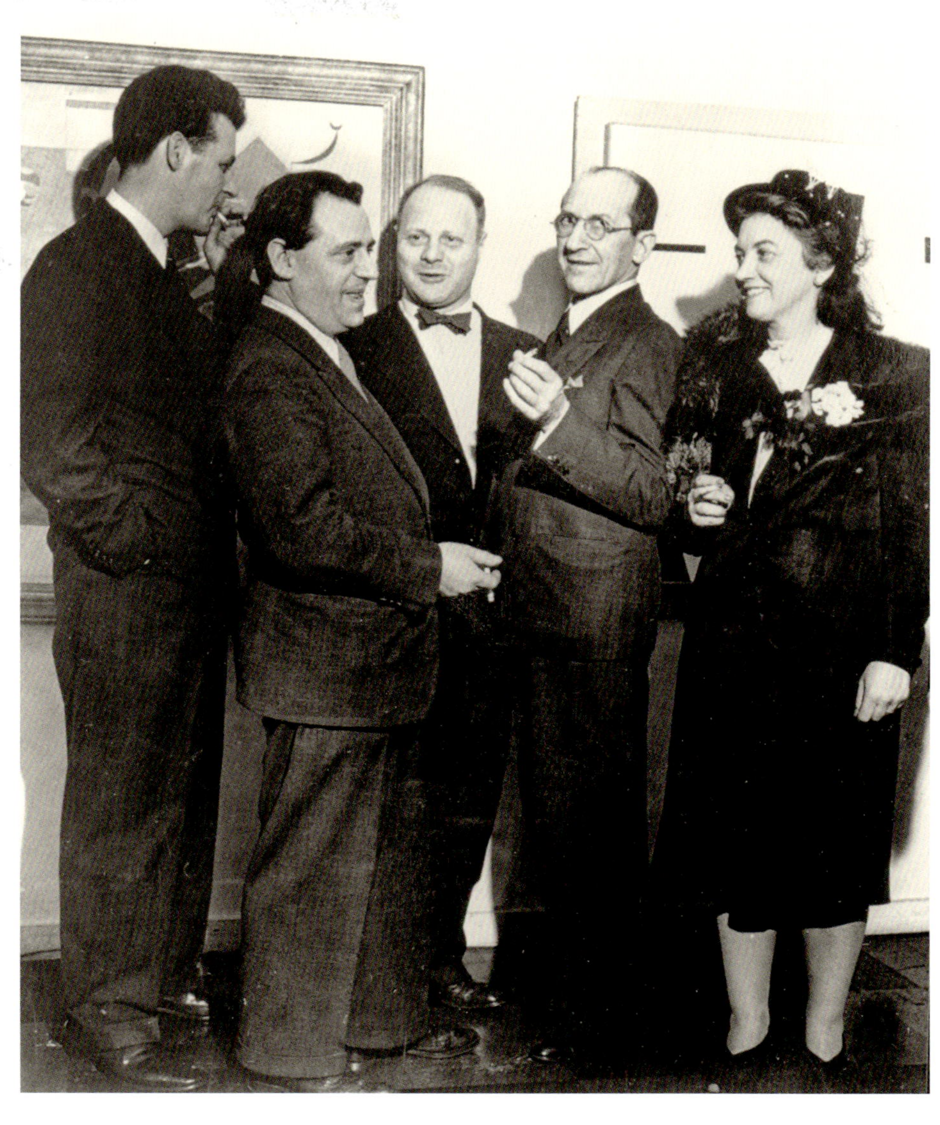

CAT. 234 **Lisette Model**
Group photograph at the opening of the 'Masters of Abstract Art' exhibition, 1 April 1942
Left to right: John Ferren, Helena Rubinstein, Gertrude Greene, Burgoyne Diller, Piet Mondrian, Stephan Lion, unidentified man, Fritz Glarner.

CAT. 235 **Lisette Model**
Group photograph at the opening of the 'Masters of Abstract Art' exhibition, 1 April 1942
Left to right: unidentified man, Hans Richter, Burgoyne Diller, Piet Mondrian, unidentified man, Helena Rubinstein, Stephan Lion, Fritz Glarner.

CAT. 236 **Lisette Model**
Group photograph at the opening of the 'Masters of Abstract Art' exhibition, 1 April 1942
Left to right: Burgoyne Diller, Fritz Glarner, Carl Holty, Piet Mondrian, Charmion von Wiegand.

Arnold Newman

CATS 237—44

Arnold Newman (1918—2006) began his career in photography at the age of twenty in Philadelphia, PA, and quickly began working in abstract and documentary photography. In 1941, Beaumont Newhall (Curator of Photography at the Museum of Modern Art) and American photographer Alfred Stieglitz (1864—1946) invited Newman to exhibit at the A.D. Gallery, New York, which would jumpstart his career.[1] Over the years, Newman has acquired fame both as the pioneer of the environmental portrait and as a prominent figure in still-life and abstract photography. Today, he is considered one of the most influential photographers of the 20th century.

In 1942 Newman met Piet Mondrian and the two struck up a friendship that would have significant consequences for both of them. Many of Newman's famous photographs were made in the years between 1941 and 1946, and some of these were influenced by his friendship with Piet Mondrian — more specifically the formal qualities of his work.[2] Newman recalled that he 'visited Mondrian a number of times during the spring and fall of 1942 and watched him work'.[3] In one of these sessions, Newman remembered that the painter turned from his canvas to ask him 'what would you do?' and Newman replied, 'I'd move that line one-eighth of an inch.' Mondrian, agreeing, complied, according to the story told by Newman.[4] This recollection shows the depth of personal and artistic respect that the two men had for each other.

Newman created the iconic series of portrait photographs of Piet Mondrian in the painter's studio at 353 East 56th Street, New York, shortly after 27 April 1942 (cats 237—44). The meeting was arranged through a letter that Mondrian sent Newman that same day, offering him two dates the following week to choose from.[5] Newman described Mondrian, in his posing, as 'stiff, formal and very polite'. 'We had a very successful sitting, although several of the exposures were ruined because he was hard of hearing and he was playing jazz music quite loud and every time I'd say "hold it" he'd say "what?"' For this reason Newman started to communicate with Mondrian by raising a finger to signify that he should stay still.[6]

As the photographs show, Mondrian is carefully staged and so we can probably assume that the painter must have complied with Newman's requests to take up specific attitudes in order to create a dramatic effect. Mondrian is standing stiffly near, or leaning on, his easel. Yet the use of natural lighting makes the photographs appear personal and intimate — a common feature of Newman's work, as he typically attempted to portray a person in relation to their personal space. For this reason, a lot of space is given over to the studio and the environment surrounding Mondrian, another characteristic aspect of Newman's photography. The photographs that came out of this session are without question the most well-known photo portraits of Mondrian during his time in New York.

1 Flukinger 2013, pp. 12—17.
2 Ewing et al. a.o. 2012 2012, pp. 90—97.
3 Newman/Geldzahler 1980, p. 13.
4 Newman 1996, p. 28.
5 Letter from Piet Mondrian to Arnold Newman, 27 April 1942, Arnold Newman Papers and Photography Collection, Harry Ransom Humanities Research Center, Austin, TX. Newman may have shown Mondrian the finished result on 25 May, as he recalled visiting Mondrian that day when the Memorial Day parade passed by the studio; see Piet Hoenderdos, *Mondriaan in New York*, film, Netherlands Institute for Sound and Vision [Nederlands Instituut voor Beeld & Geluid], 1980, timestamp: 31.45, at https://www.youtube.com.
6 Hoenderdos, timestamp: 31.46.

CAT. 237 **Arnold Newman**
Portrait of Piet Mondrian in his studio, between 29 April and 7 May 1942

CAT. 238 See catalogue

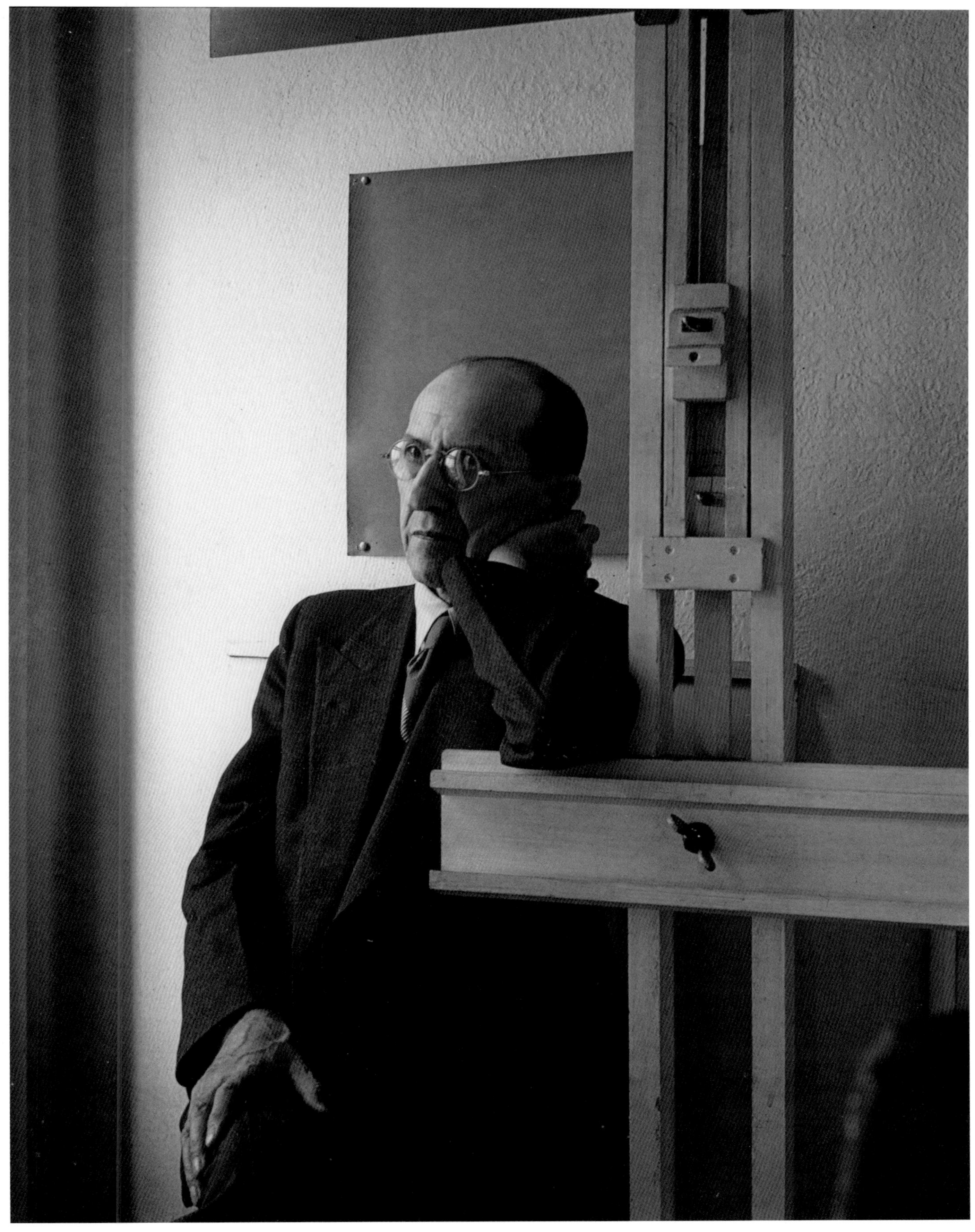

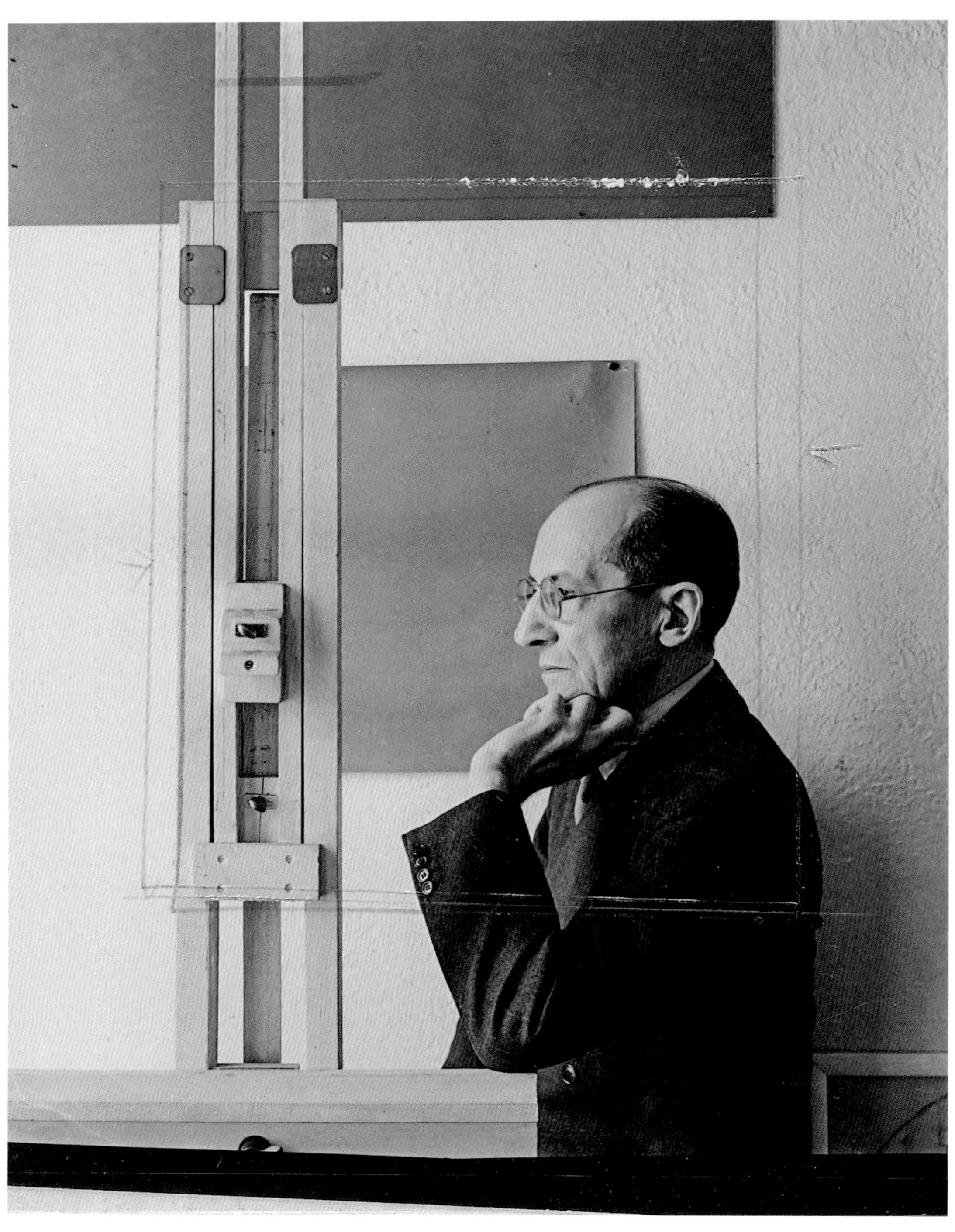

CATS 240, 239 **Arnold Newman**

Portrait of Piet Mondrian in his studio, between 29 April and 7 May 1942

The rectangle on photograph cat. 240 shows how Newman wanted the image to be cut out. The end result (cat. 230), however, is different.

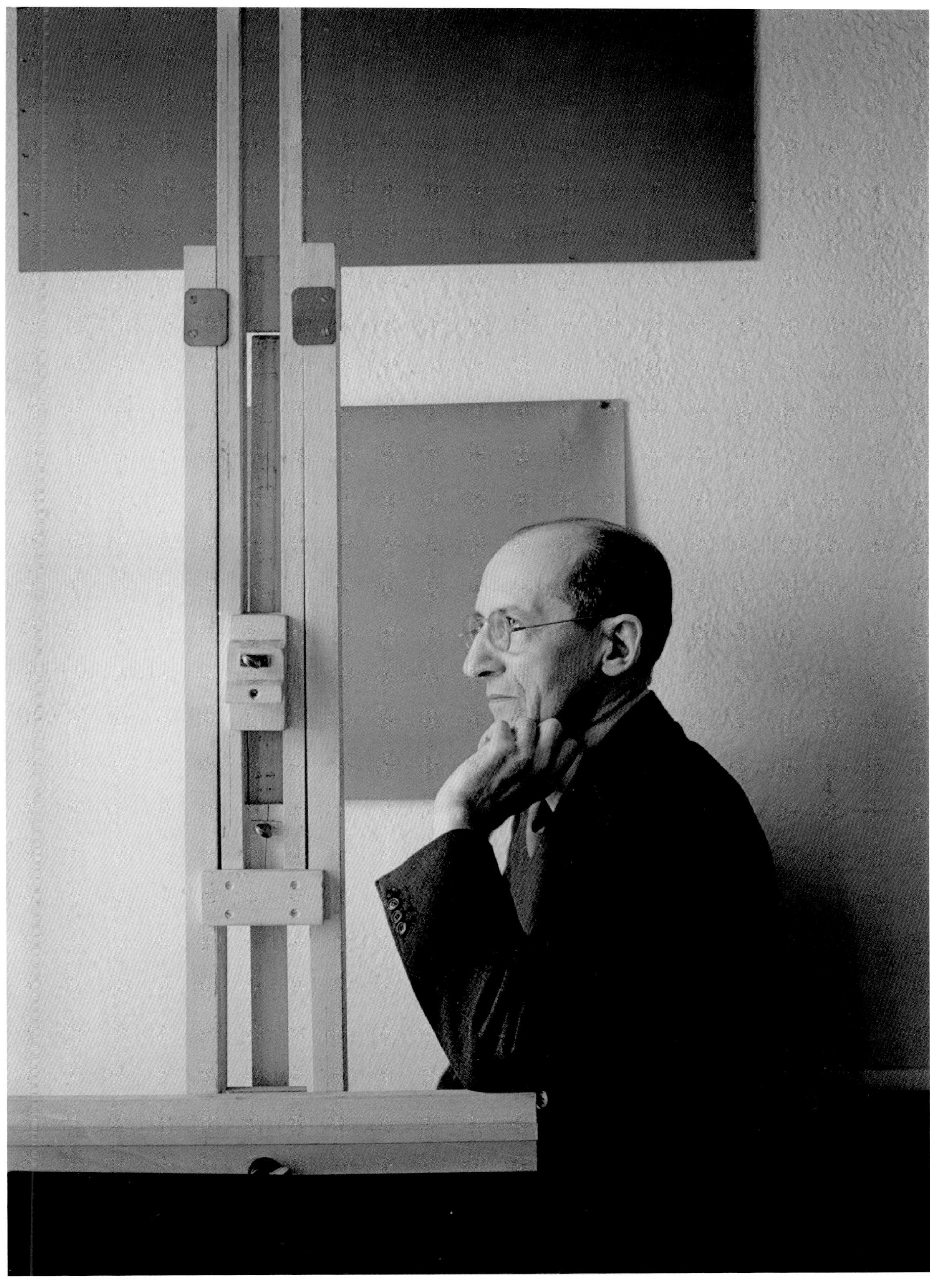

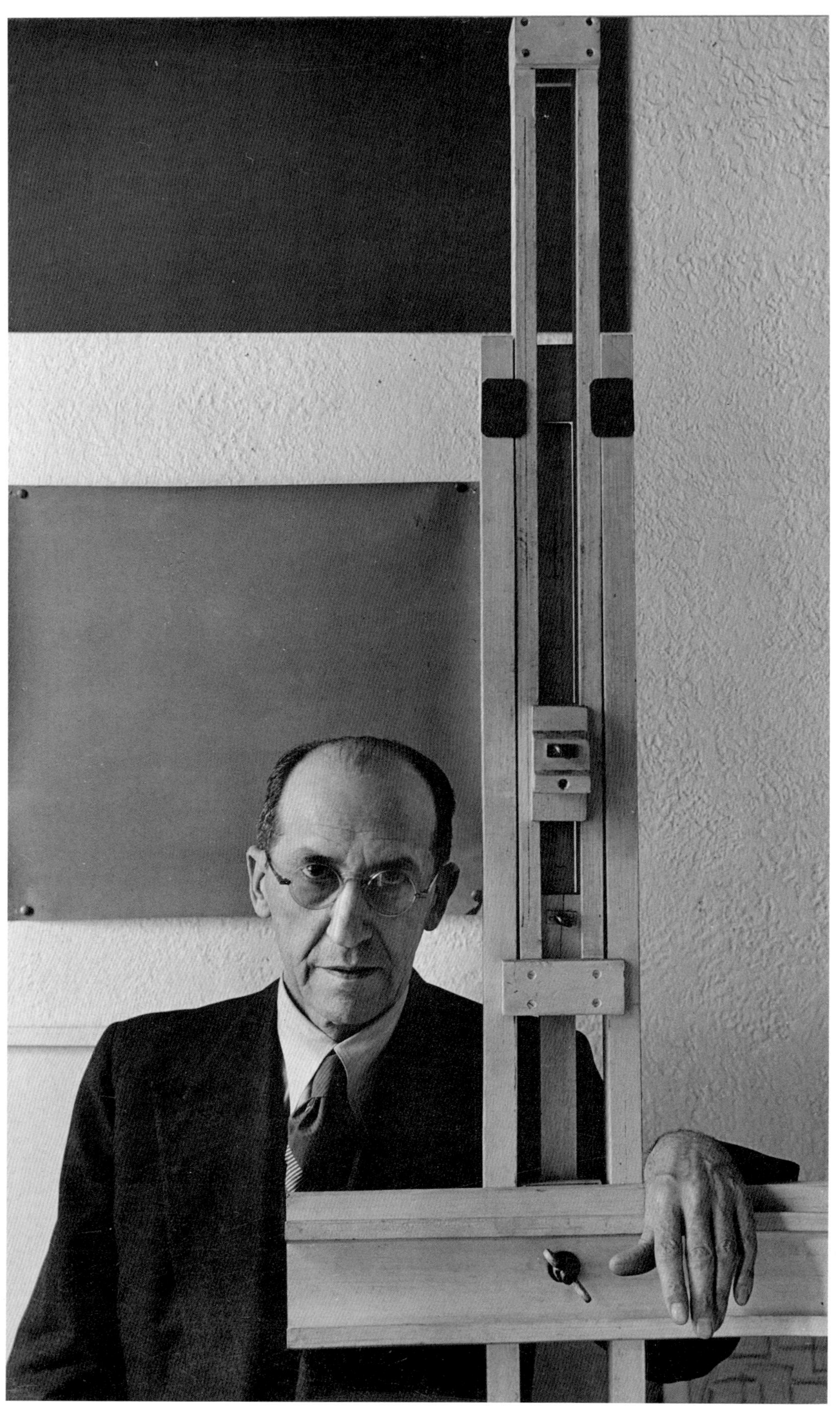

CATS 241, 243 **Arnold Newman**
Portrait of Piet Mondrian in his studio, between 29 April and 7 May 1942

CATS 242, 244 See catalogue

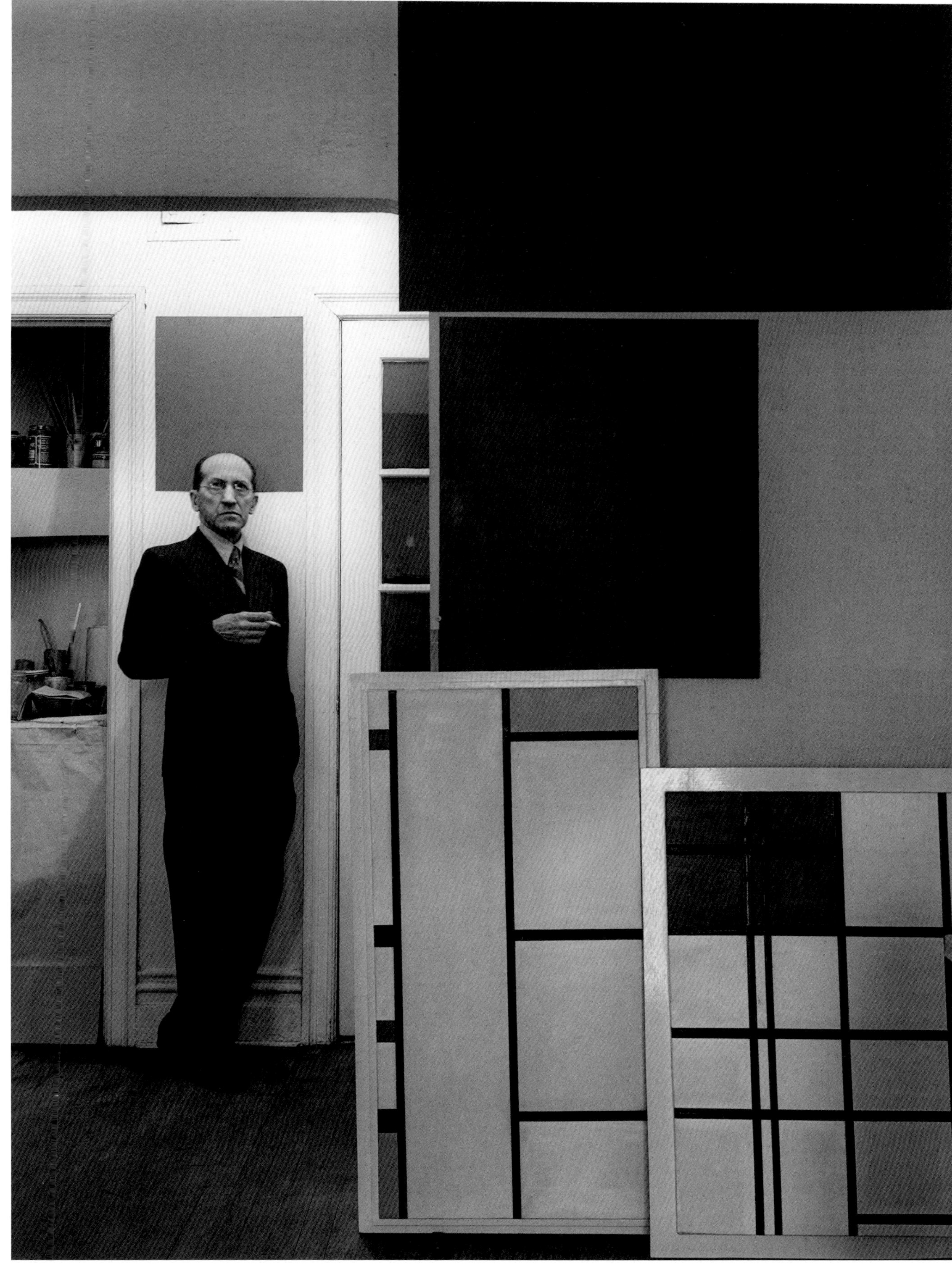

Hermann Landshoff

CATS 245—49

Hermann Landshoff (1905—1986) was born in Munich and trained as a graphic designer and typographer, before working in the latter capacity for several years.[1] He was also a talented caricaturist and began to publish cartoons in 1927, often featuring prominent Munich figures. His work appeared in, among other publications, the famous satirical magazine *Simplicissimus*. Sales opportunities for his work contracted in 1930, due primarily to the previous year's stock market crash, but his discovery of photography offered him a fresh perspective. He later said of this time: 'I took my first photograph when I was twenty-four. I have been living and sleeping in my darkroom ever since. As a photographer, I was self-taught from the outset.'[2] Photography had boomed since the previous decade and the insatiable demand for material from the numerous illustrated magazines provided opportunities for a burgeoning group of commercial photographers.

As a Jew, Landshoff was banned from practising his profession in the wake of the Nazi takeover in 1933. He moved to Paris, where he focused on fashion photography and reportage for magazines like *Vogue* and *femina*, which published the work of numerous celebrated photographers. He was guided in his shoots more by intuition than technique. 'Meanwhile your hands have to operate the camera blindly, working entirely by themselves. Like perfect machines, running without control or supervision. If you are a slave to the camera when taking photographs, you would be better off leaving it alone.'[3] Landshoff preferred to work in this period with a medium-format Rolleiflex 6x6 or 6x9. His mastery of the camera and darkroom reached immense heights in Paris. He was a champion and practitioner of the 'straight print' — printing the entire negative without further cropping. The composition was thus determined while shooting, with subsequent editing and manipulation of the picture kept to a minimum. Landshoff viewed his work as art and art as a matter for the elite.

When Paris too was threatened by the Nazis, Landshoff emigrated to New York in May 1941. After a difficult initial period, his work began to be published in the leading fashion magazine *Harper's Bazaar*. Together with photographers like Lillian Bassman and above all Richard Avedon, he took fashion photography out of the aestheticizing and idealizing studio environment by turning to street photography and placing the models in more realistic settings. He also became a noteworthy portrait photographer of famous figures from a variety of artistic circles, including movie actors, writers, artists and fellow photographers. While Landshoff owed his fame to these two genres, he remained a generalist throughout: his work likewise includes a great many photographs of landscapes, still lifes and architecture.

New York enjoyed a rich émigré culture in the 1940s (and long after), thanks to the many actors, artists, art dealers, publishers, writers and so on who had fled Europe because of the war. Landshoff met old acquaintances there and made new contacts among the elite. He was associated especially closely with the group of artists — mostly surrealists — who gathered around the wealthy collector and patron Peggy Guggenheim. There is nothing to suggest that Landshoff was in personal contact with Mondrian, but he certainly met him in that circle, even if the Dutchman was far from being a surrealist. Mondrian knew many of them from his Paris years, though, and had also met Guggenheim in London a few years earlier, following which she bought several of his works.

The group of five photographs in which Mondrian can be seen reveal different aspects of Landshoff's skills. Best known are the two group photos in which Peggy Guggenheim and thirteen of her guests (including her husband Max Ernst) pose in three rows in front of the large fireplace in the living room of her triplex home in Manhattan (cats 245—46). While they are still managed group portraits, they lack the static feel that often accompanies such photographs. The positioning injects a touch of dynamism into the pictures, along with a suitably surrealistic and humorous undertone.

The photograph of the artists looking down from the gallery on the upper floor (cat. 247) is of a different order: it might be interpreted as a subtle portrait of Peggy Guggenheim as a collector of artists as well as their art.

There is also a snapshot of Leonora Carrington and Mondrian, taken from a low angle and with strong lighting effects (cat. 249). Although the two subjects appear to be conversing, Landshoff does not show them actually talking, but captures instead a moment when the conversation has paused: Mondrian blows cigarette smoke upwards out of respect for his companion, so that there is a momentary break in contact between the interlocutors.

The portrait of Mondrian, Léger and Ozenfant (cat. 248) is clearly posed once again, yet there is no trace of immobility. The differences in position, pose and gaze lend something special and distinctive to each of the people in the portrait. Ozenfant looks friendly, Léger expressionless and Mondrian literally and figuratively somewhat out of place. Three artists, three personalities. Three portraits in one, thanks to the fourth personality behind the camera.

1 Details of Landshoff's life and career are drawn from Pohlmann/Landshoff 2013.

2 'Mit 24 Jahren habe ich mein erstes Photo gemacht. Bis heute wohne und schlafe ich seitdem in meiner Dunkelkammer. Als Photograph war ich von Anfang an Autodidakt.' Quoted in Pohlmann/Landshoff 2013, p. 26.

3 'Deine Hände müssen währenddessen an der Kamera blind, für sich allein arbeiten. Wie perfekte Maschinen, die unbeaufsichtigt ohne Kontrolle laufen. Wer beim Photographieren der Sklave seiner Kamera ist, sollte besser die Finger davon lassen.' Idem, p. 31.

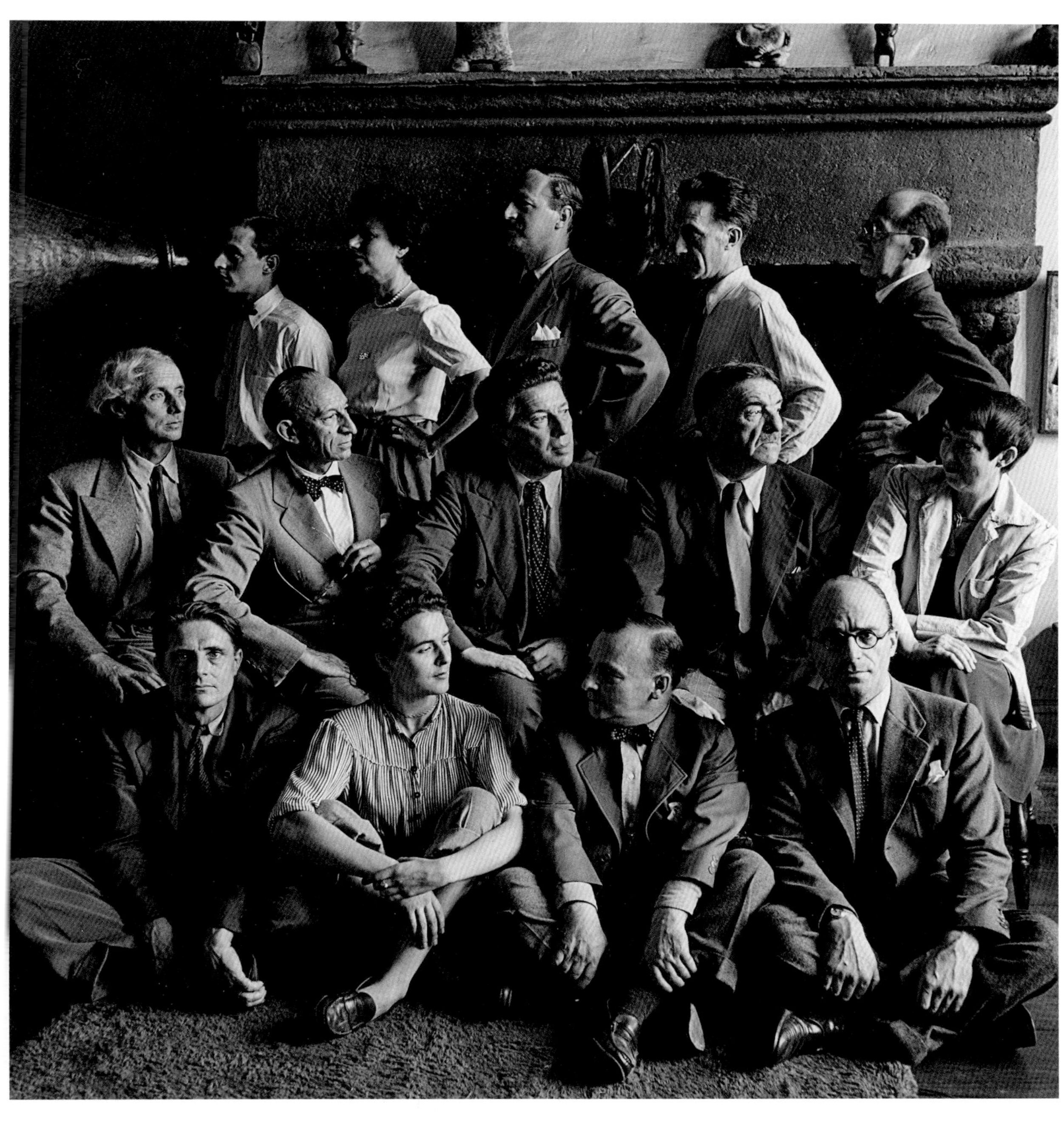

CAT. 245 **Hermann Landshoff**

***Die Surrealisten*, c. July 1942**

Left to right, front row: Stanley William Hayter, Leonora Carrington, Frederick Kiesler, Kurt Seligmann; middle row: Max Ernst, Amédée Ozenfant, André Breton, Fernand Léger, Berenice Abbott; back row: Jimmy Ernst, Peggy Guggenheim, John Ferren, Marcel Duchamp, Piet Mondrian. The title *Die Surrealisten* comes from Landshoff himself.

The series of photographs (cats 245–49) was taken during a meeting of artists and architects at Peggy Guggenheim's house in New York.

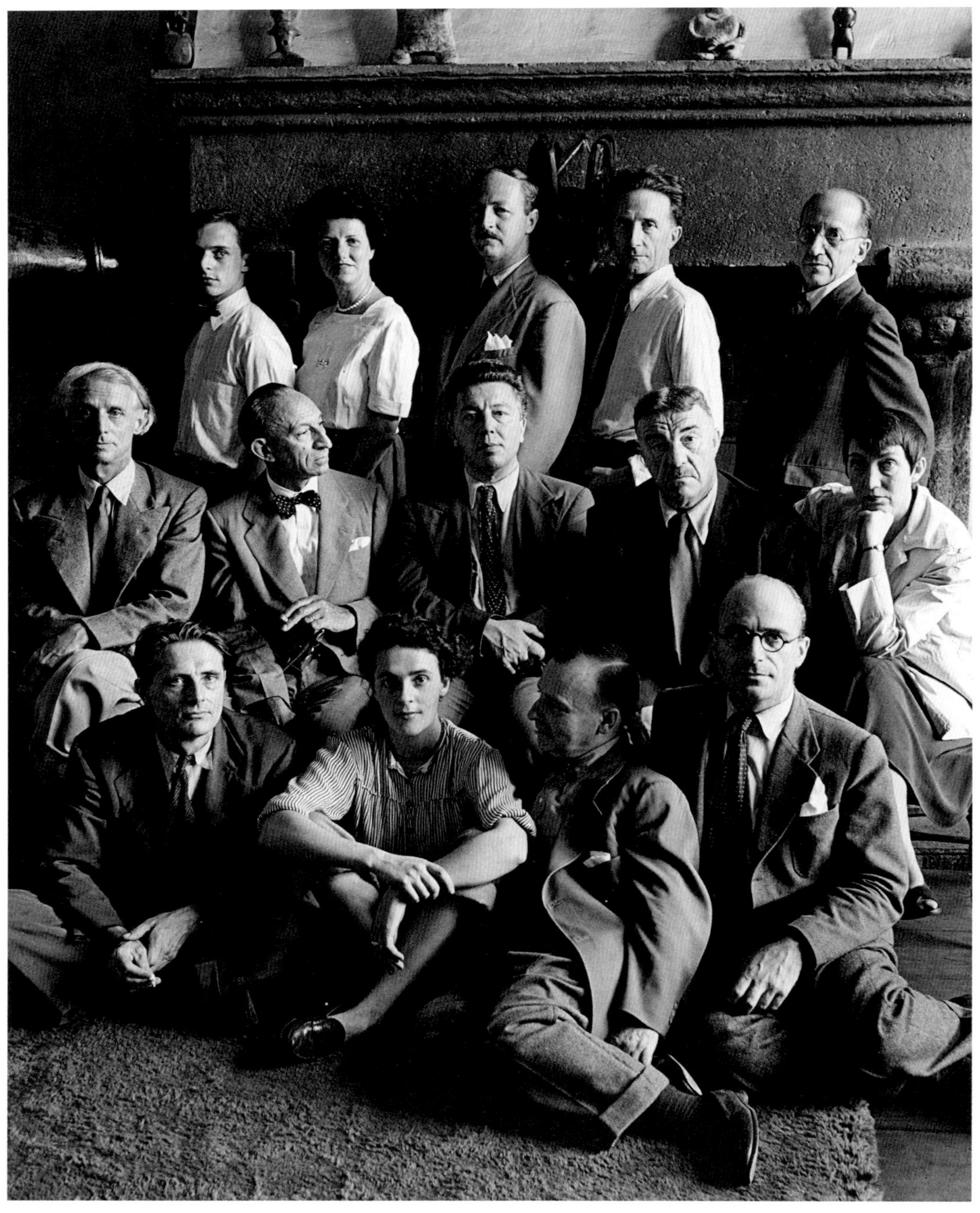

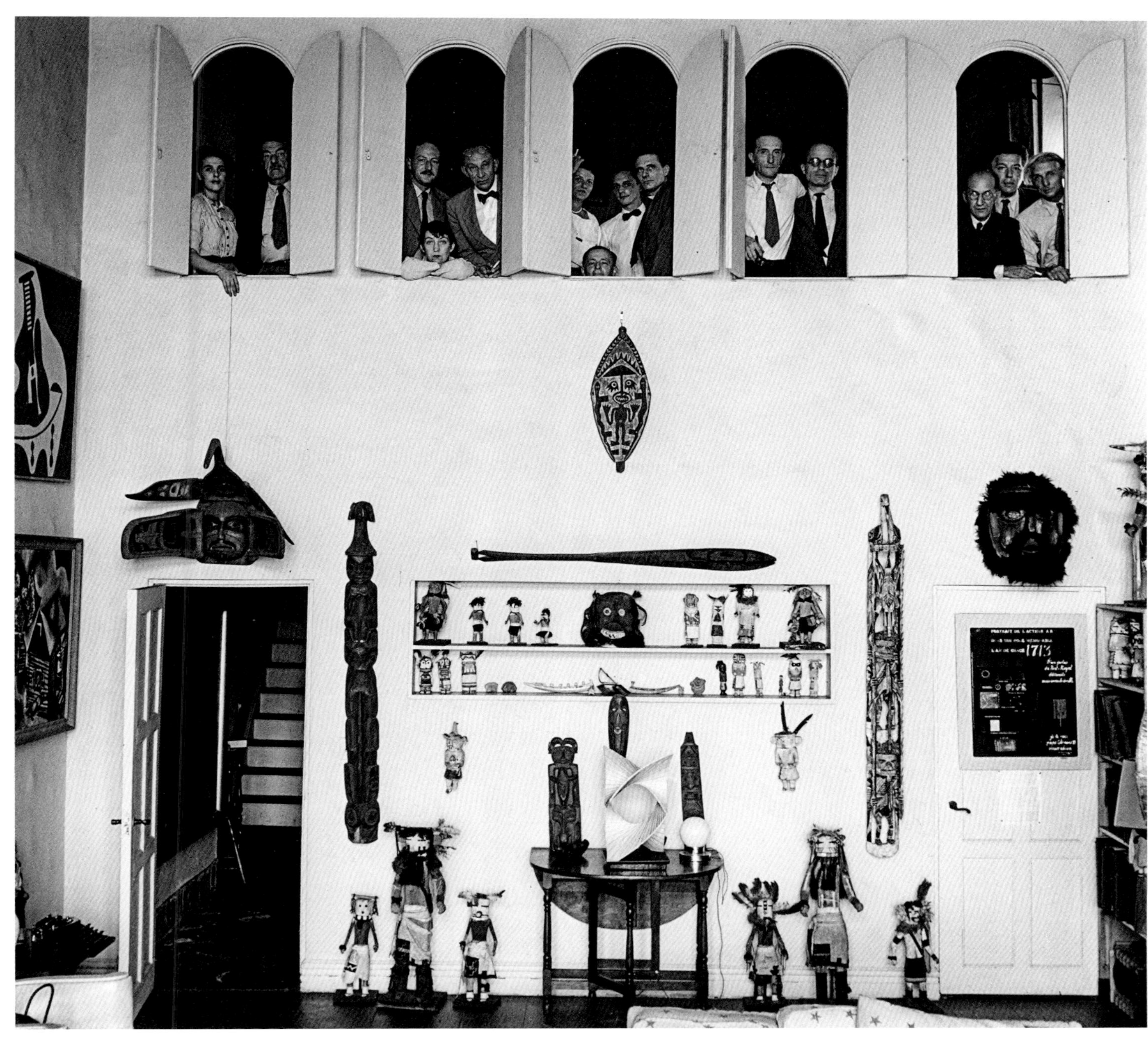

CAT. 246 **Hermann Landshoff**
***Die Surrealisten*, c. July 1942**
See cat. 245

CAT. 247 **Hermann Landshoff**
Group photograph at Peggy Guggenheim's house, c. July 1942
Left to right: Leonora Carrington, Fernand Léger, John Ferren, Berenice Abbott, Amédée Ozenfant, Peggy Guggenheim, Frederick Kiesler, Jimmy Ernst, Stanley William Hayter, Marcel Duchamp, Kurt Seligmann, Piet Mondrian, André Breton, Max Ernst.

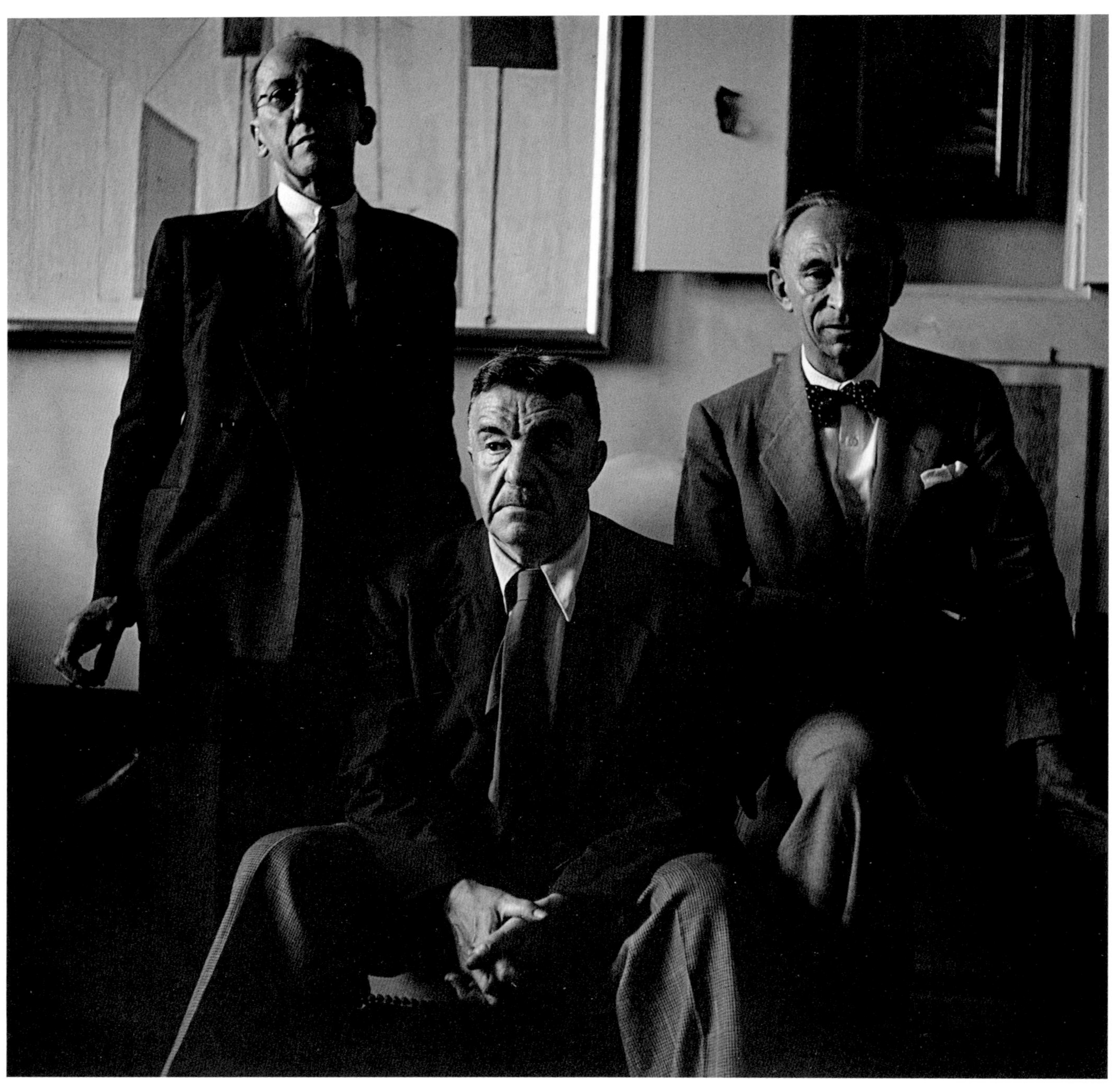

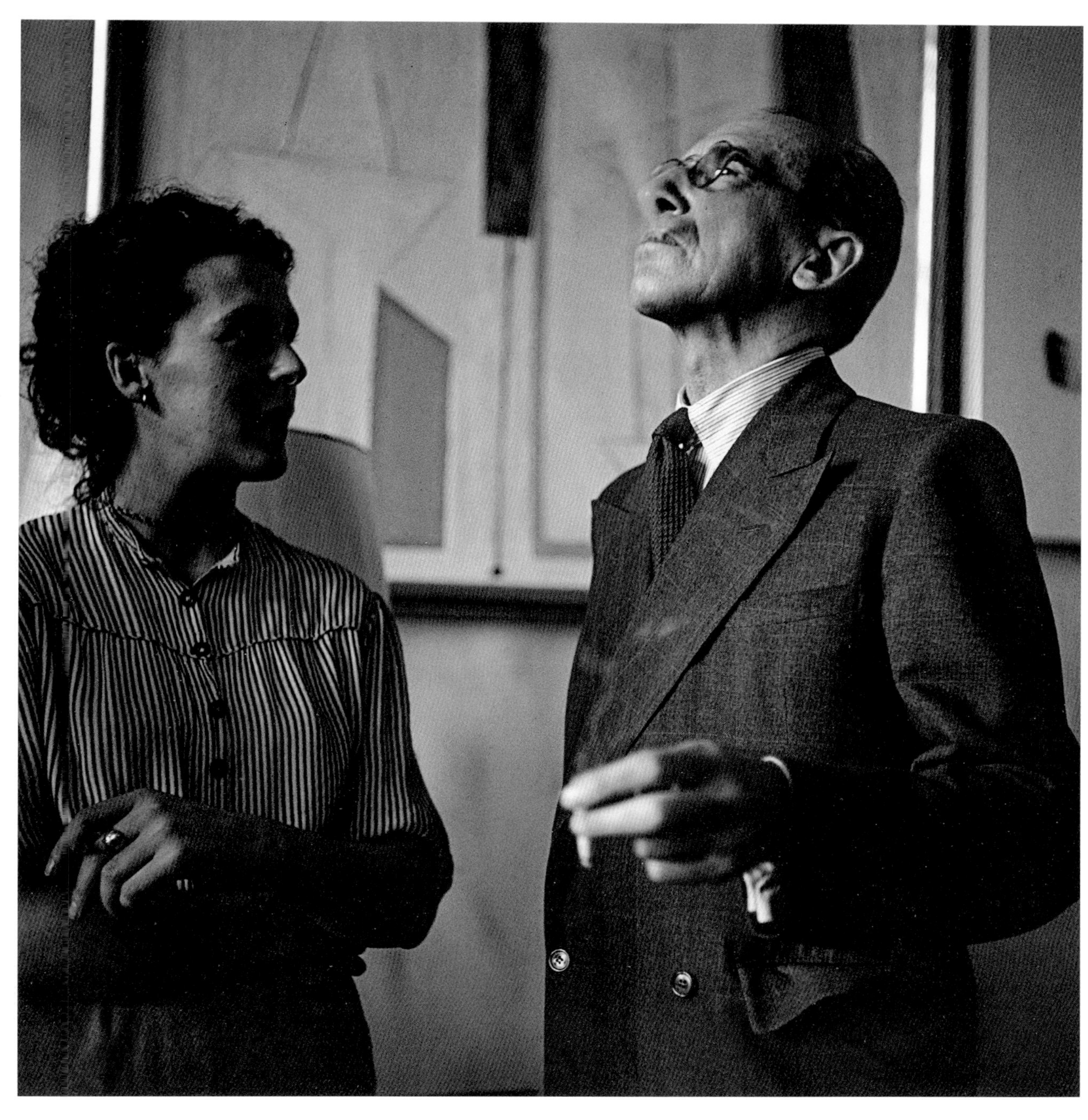

CAT. 248 **Hermann Landshoff**
Piet Mondrian, Fernand Léger and Amédée Ozenfant at Peggy Guggenheim's house, c. July 1942

CAT. 249 **Hermann Landshoff**
Leonora Carrington and Piet Mondrian at Peggy Guggenheim's house, c. July 1942

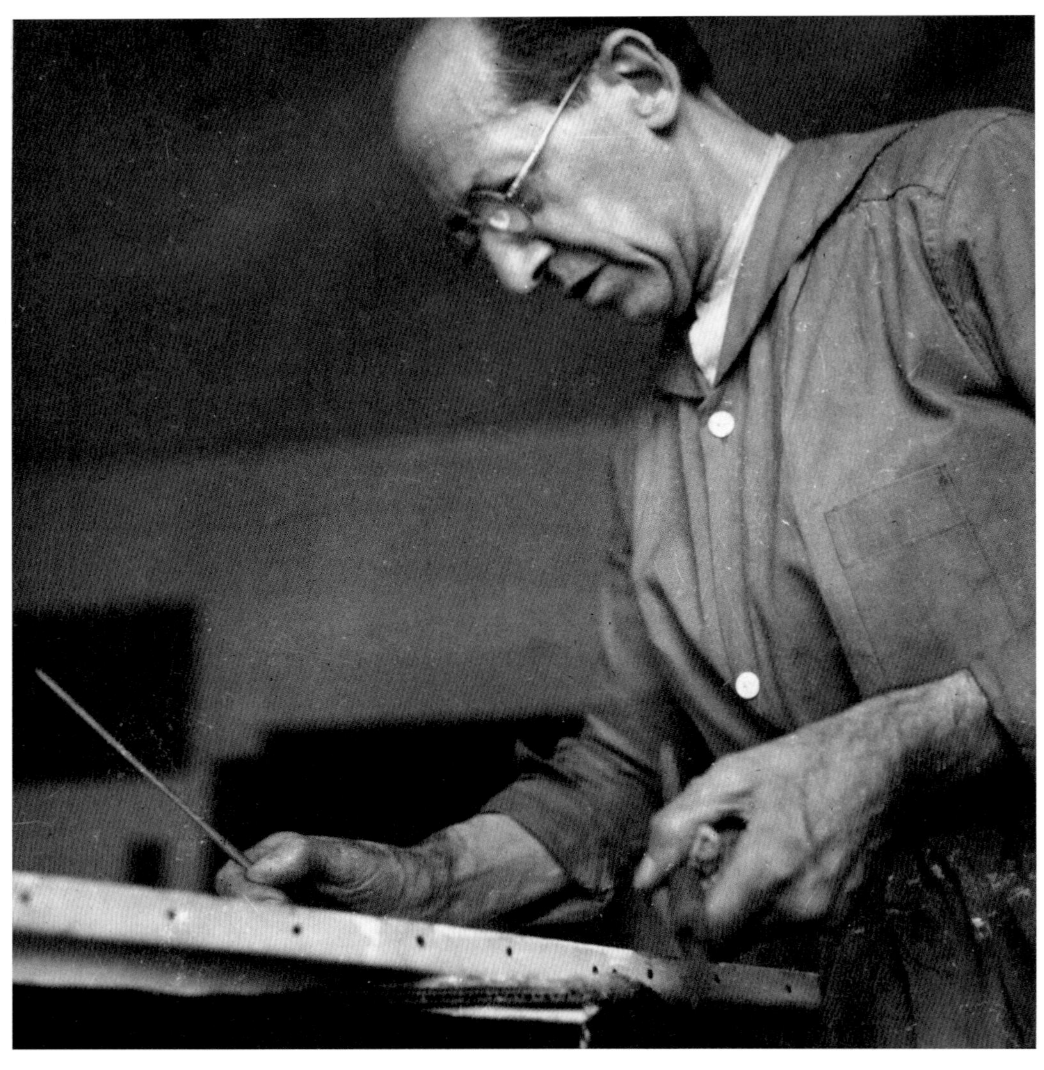

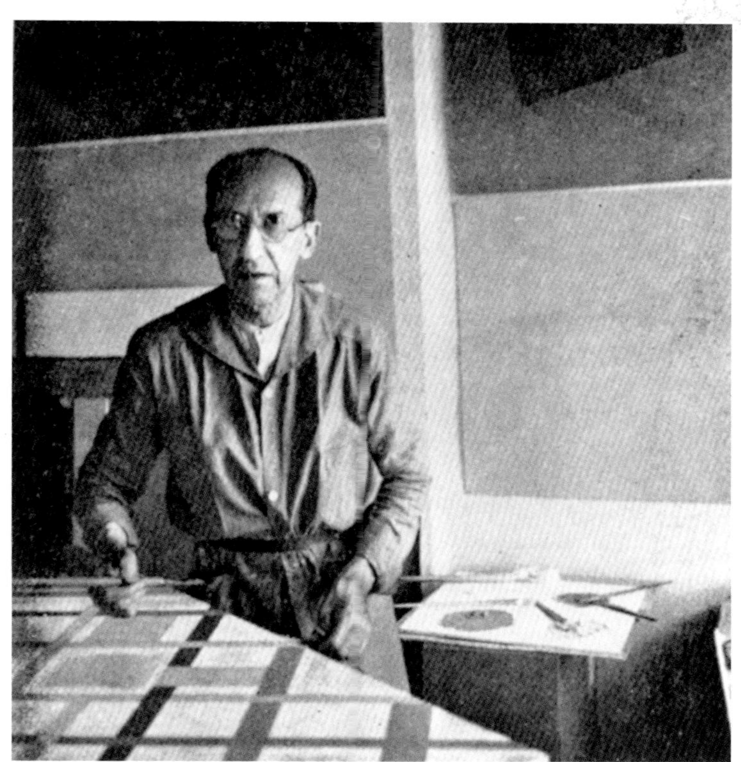

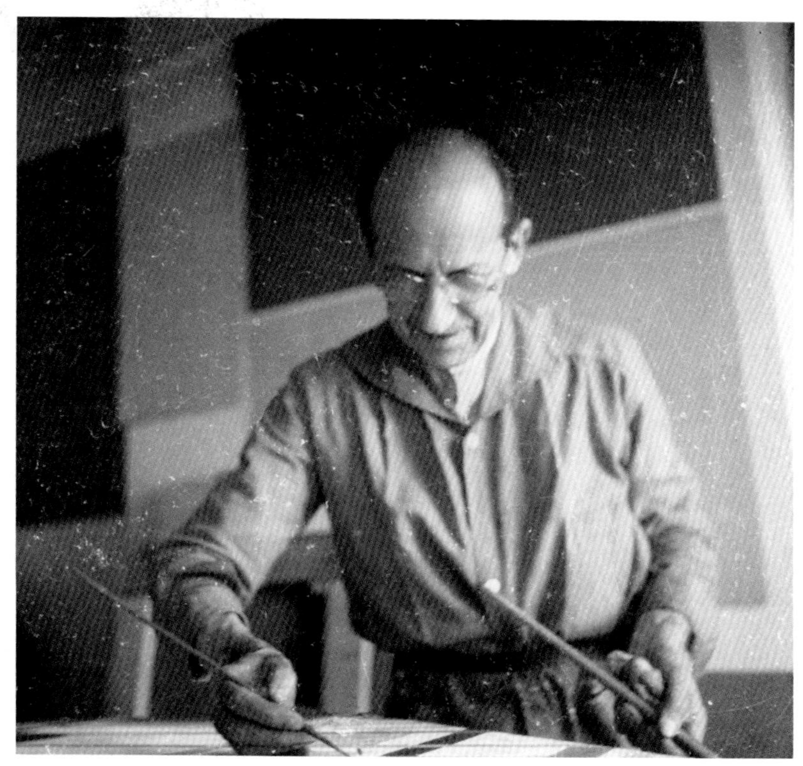

CATS 251, 250, 252 **Kate Steinitz**
Piet Mondrian working on *Victory Boogie Woogie* (B324), between June and the end of August 1942

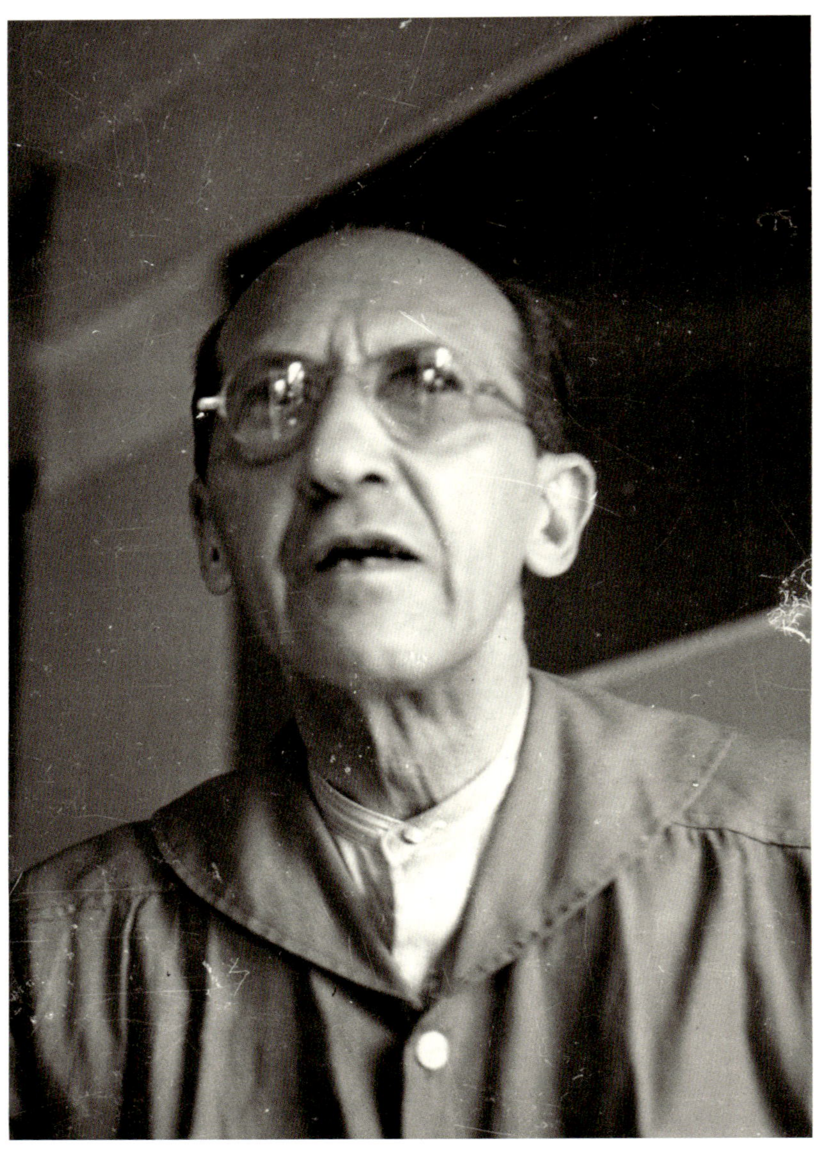

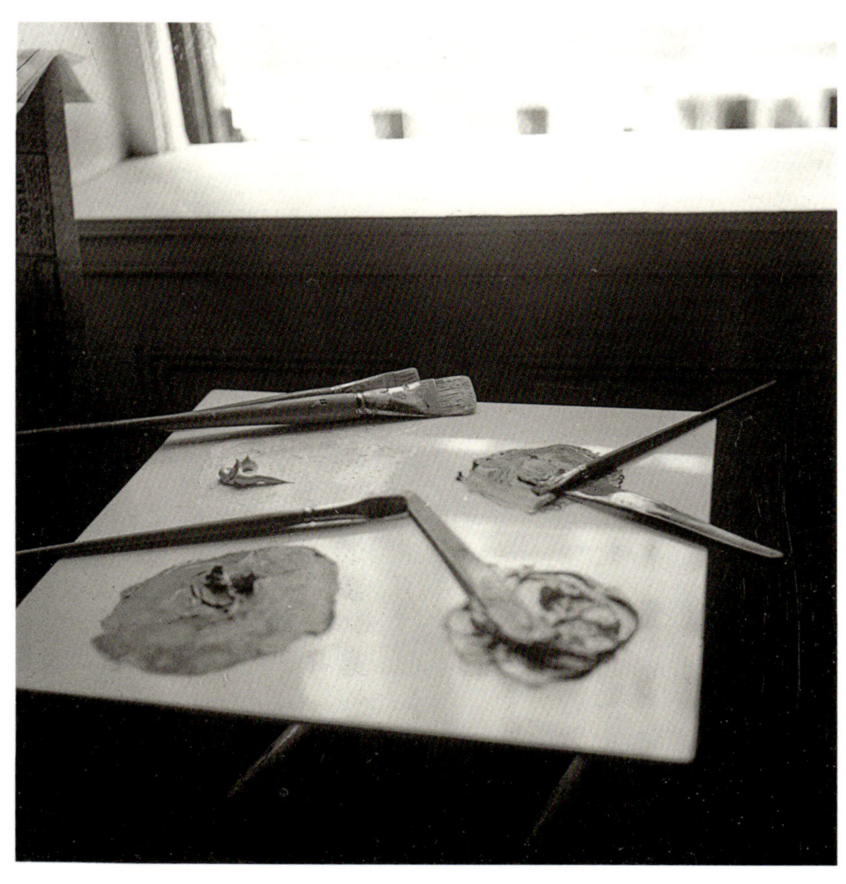

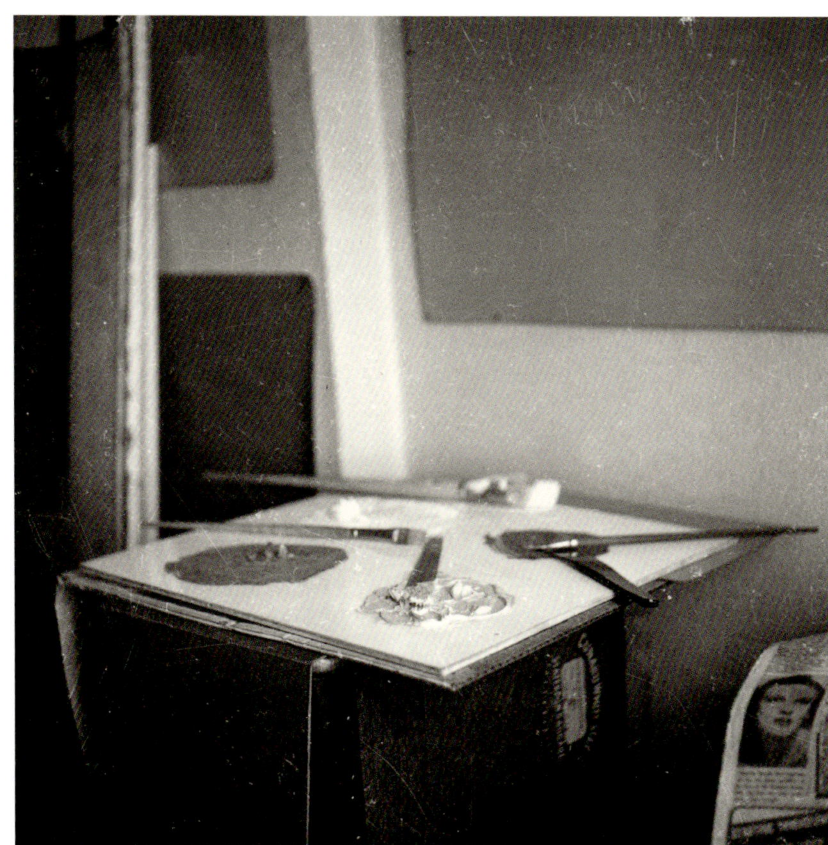

CAT. 253 **Kate Steinitz**
Portrait of Piet Mondrian, between June and the end of August 1942

CATS 254–55 **Kate Steinitz**
Piet Mondrian's palette, between June and the end of August 1942
The palette is a flat square stone on which brushes, palette knives and four colours of paint are arranged.

Fritz Glarner

CATS 256–95, 305–83

Born in Zurich, Fritz Glarner (1899–1972) had started painting by the age of thirteen. He later attended the Royal Academy of Fine Arts in Naples, yet he never got a diploma and his art techniques were mainly self-taught. In 1923 he moved to Paris, where he stayed until 1935, and in 1928 married Lucie (or Lucy) Powell (?–1979), an American artist of Russian descent.[1] The couple came into close contact with the most important avant-garde artists of the time in Paris; Glarner himself, however, still painted too traditionally at that point to join such circles. The Glarners are said to have first met Piet Mondrian in 1929, possibly in one of the cafés frequented by artists.[2] During this Parisian period, Mondrian and Glarner remained no more than acquaintances, although a photograph from the time, supposedly taken by Henri Glarner, one of Fritz's brothers, makes it clear that Glarner did visit Mondrian's studio on at least one occasion (cat. 127).

After Glarner emigrated to the United States in 1935, his artistic style and career underwent major changes. During his first years in New York, he became part of the artists' asssociation called the American Abstract Artists and developed a greater interest in the artistic experiments of the 20th century, especially in working with De Stijl-based compositional approaches.[3] Glarner defined his new works as 'Relational Painting', and for this reason he has often been described as a follower of Mondrian — according to Glarner's own account, he described Mondrian as his 'master'.[4] It was in New York that Glarner became reacquainted with Piet Mondrian but at a more personal level, forging a much closer friendship than before until Mondrian's death in early 1944. Several of Mondrian's letters from these years attest to this: on numerous occasions Mondrian wrote to other friends, recalling meetings and exchanges of artistic ideas and other information with the Glarner couple.

During his New York period, Glarner supported himself financially by working as a photographer, assisted by his wife. Mondrian was a frequent visitor to the Glarner residence and, likewise, they would often meet in Mondrian's studio. Between 1941 and 1944 the couple took many photographs of Mondrian, almost all of which were shot in the artist's studio on 353 East 56th Street. The pictures show Mondrian at work, looking at paintings or putting on a gramophone record. In these photographs he can be seen wearing his painting coat and smoking cigarettes. Although Mondrian seems to be posing in some of the shots, the character of the actions, and the style of the pictures, give them a personal atmosphere. On some occasions, Glarner was asked to take pictures of Mondrian's paintings; as Mondrian writes in a letter from March 1943 to fellow artist Harry Holtzman: 'Glarner made a photo of it but it does not represent quite well the picture so it is no good to send it to you. Dudensing did take photos also, but less good.'[5] Glarner's photography, while not always technically perfect, is effective at showing movement and action, giving us a glance into Mondrian's studio space and practices.

Over the following years, Glarner continued his exploration of abstract painting, based on Mondrian's theory of neo-plasticism. He was part of a circle of artists that included many of the people in close proximity to Mondrian during his final years, such as Harry Holtzman, Ilya Bolotowsky, Burgoyne Diller and Charmion von Wiegand. While Glarner developed variations of colour and form compared to Mondrian, for instance using grey lines instead of black and adding oblique angles and lines, Mondrian's influence on Glarner was undeniable and long-lasting. In 1971 Glarner moved back to Switzerland, where he passed away the following year.

1 Knight 1989.
2 Welsh/Joosten 1998-II, p. 142.
3 Knight 1989.
4 Forman 1971.
5 Letter from Piet Mondrian to Harry Holtzman, 25 March 1943 (The Hague, RKD, Archive of Mondrian (0740), inv. 126.

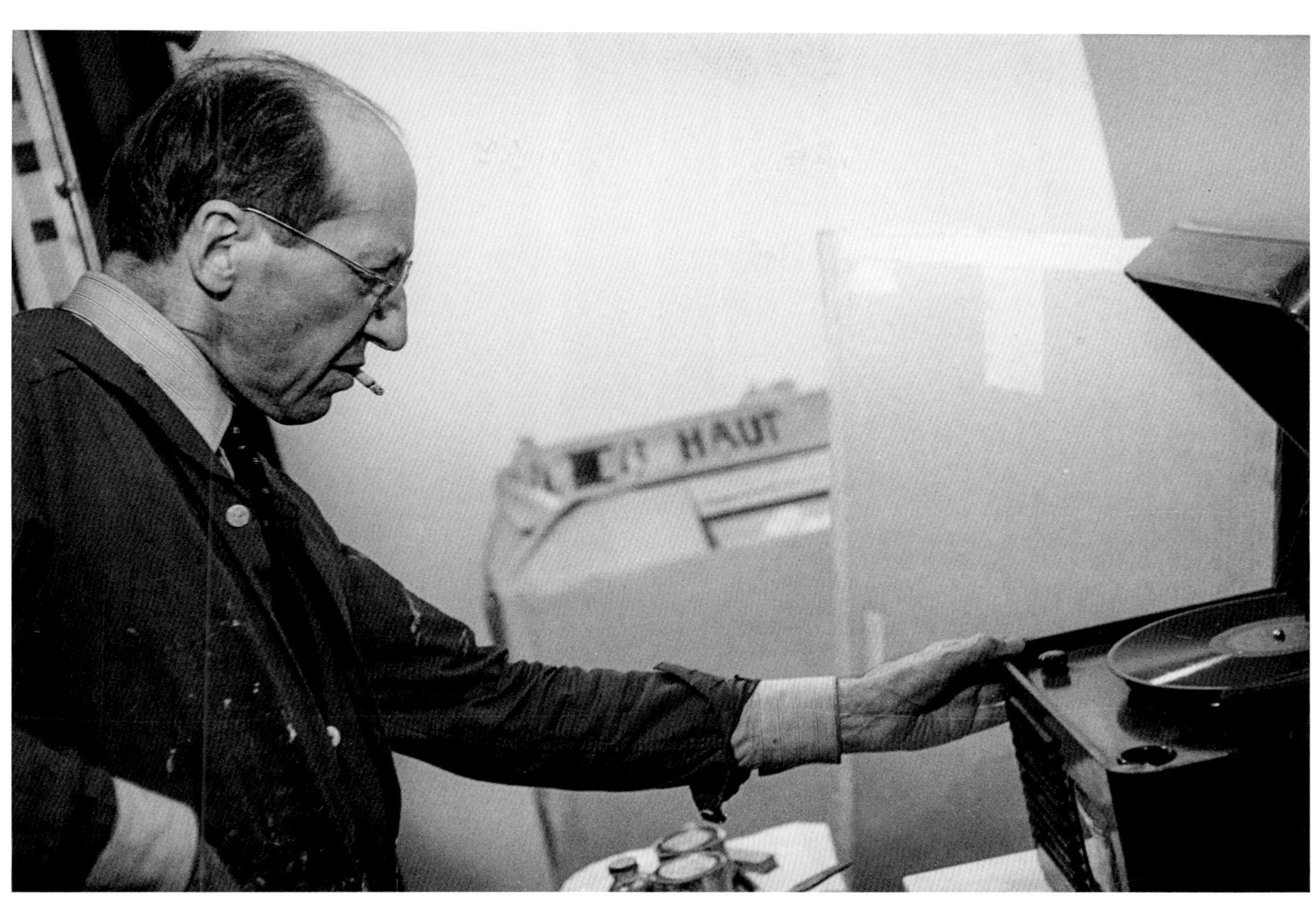

CAT. 256 **Fritz Glarner**
Piet Mondrian in his studio with his gramophone, between c. late 1942 and mid-March 1943

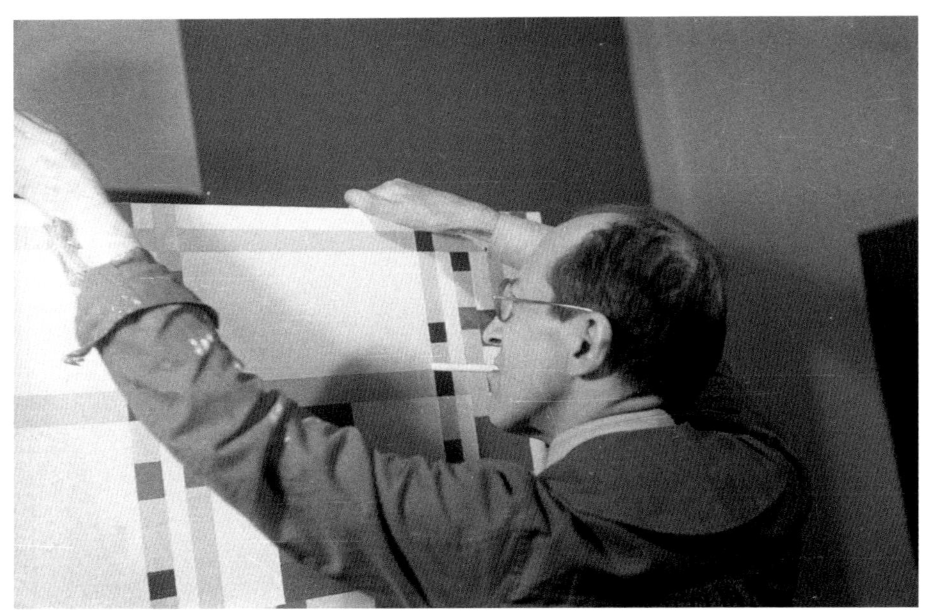

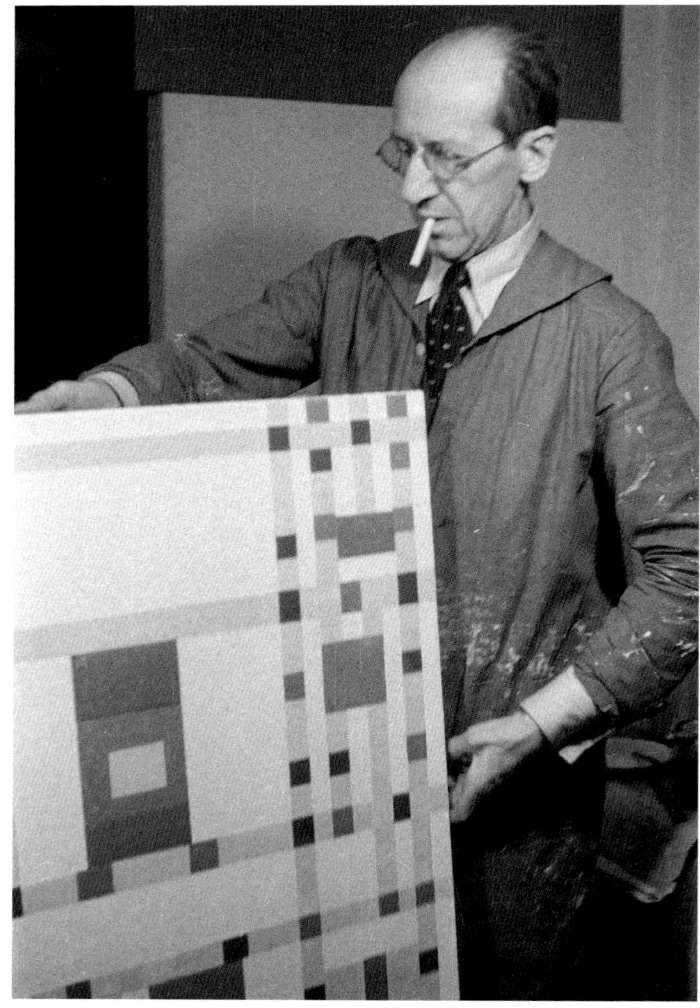

CATS 261, 263, 265, 267 **Fritz Glarner**
Piet Mondrian in his studio, with *Broadway Boogie Woogie* (B323), between c. late 1942 and mid-March 1943

CATS 257–60, 262, 264, 266 See catalogue

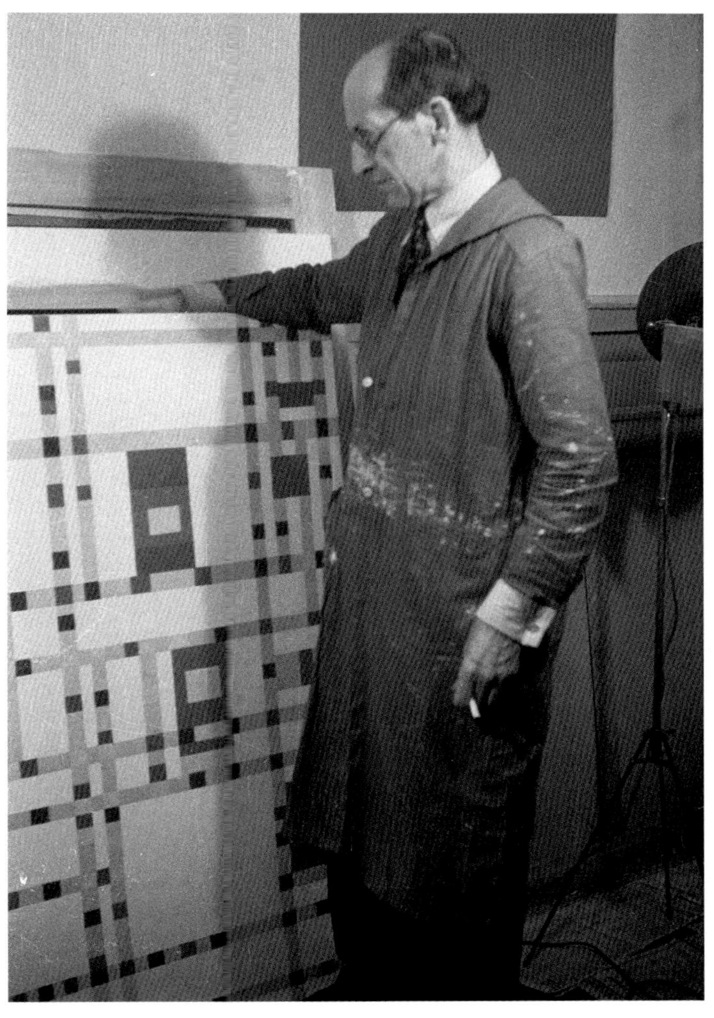

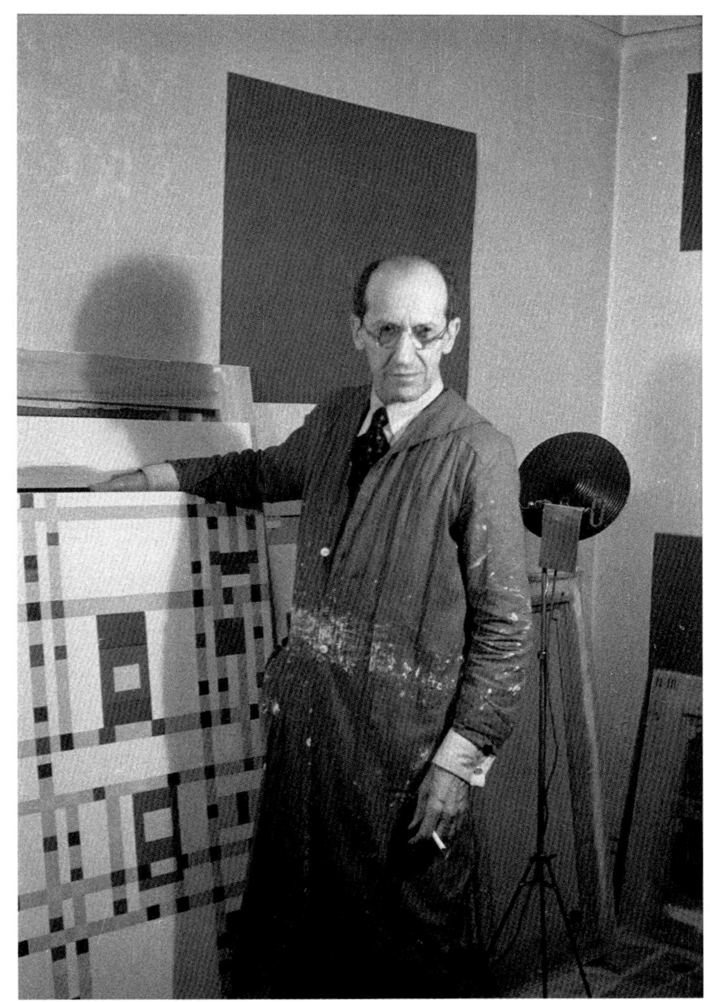

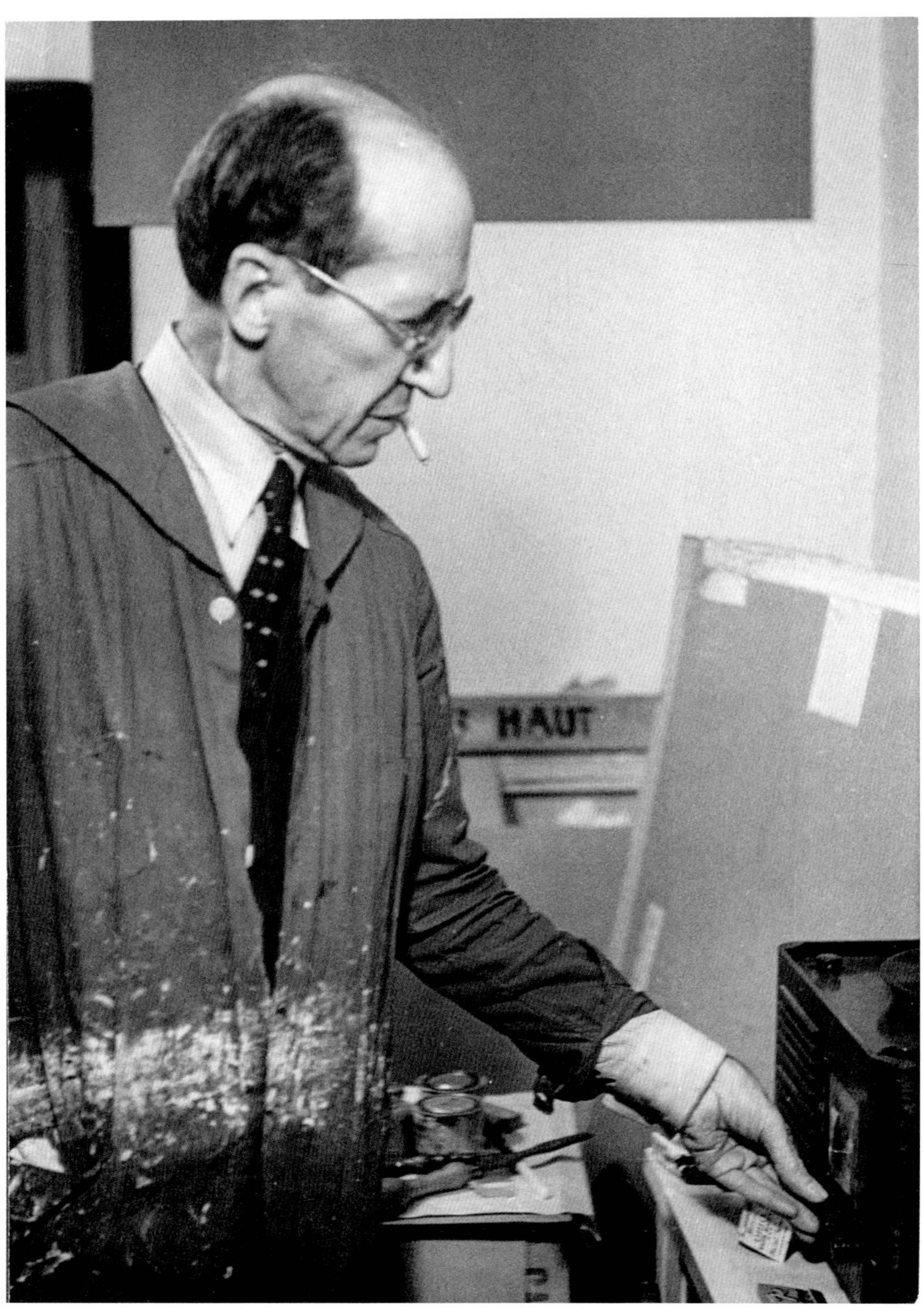

CAT. 272 **Fritz Glarner**
Piet Mondrian in his studio with his gramophone, between c. late 1942 and mid-March 1943

CAT. 270 **Fritz Glarner**
Piet Mondrian in his studio, between c. late 1942 and mid-March 1943

CATS 268–69, 271 See catalogue

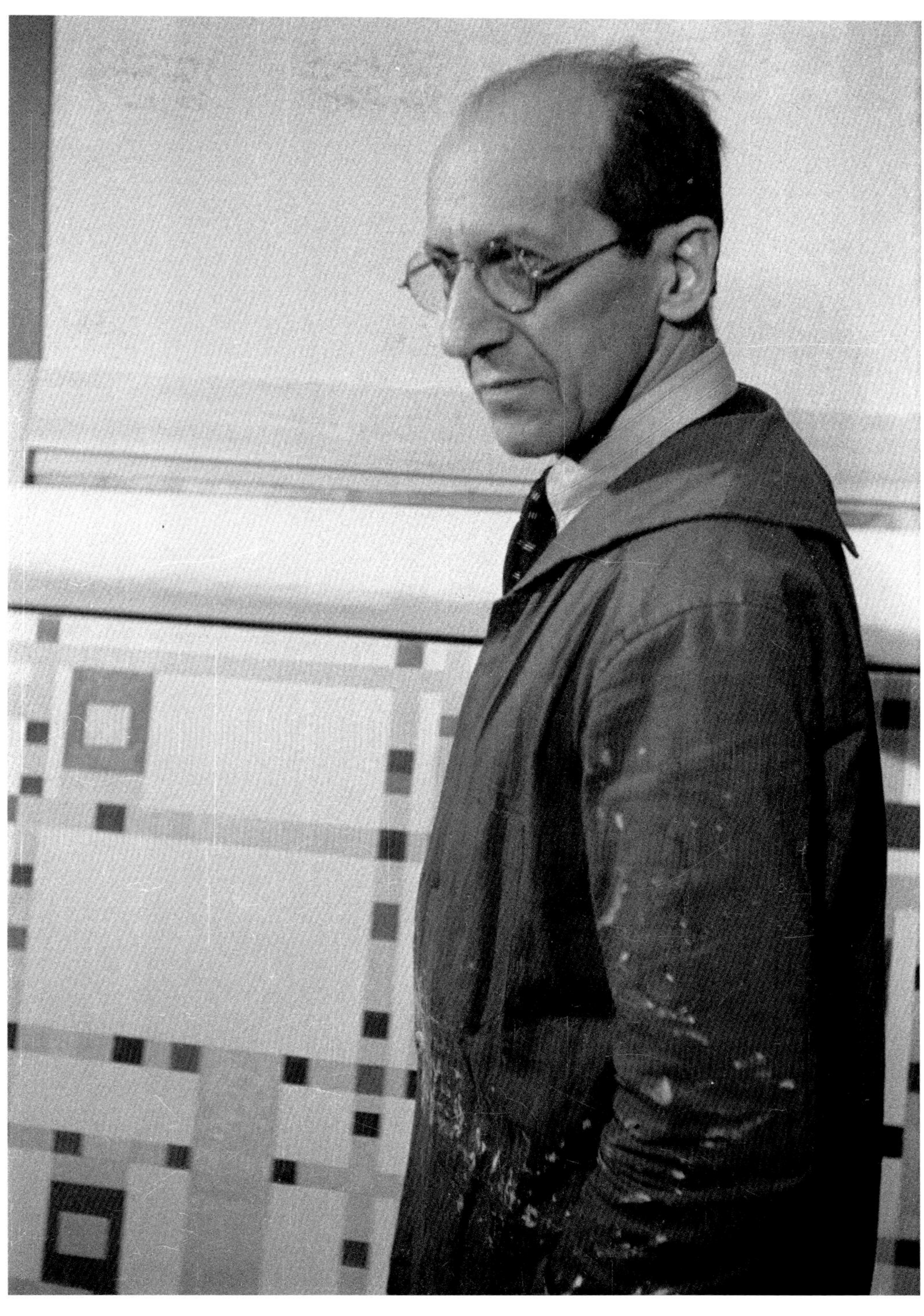

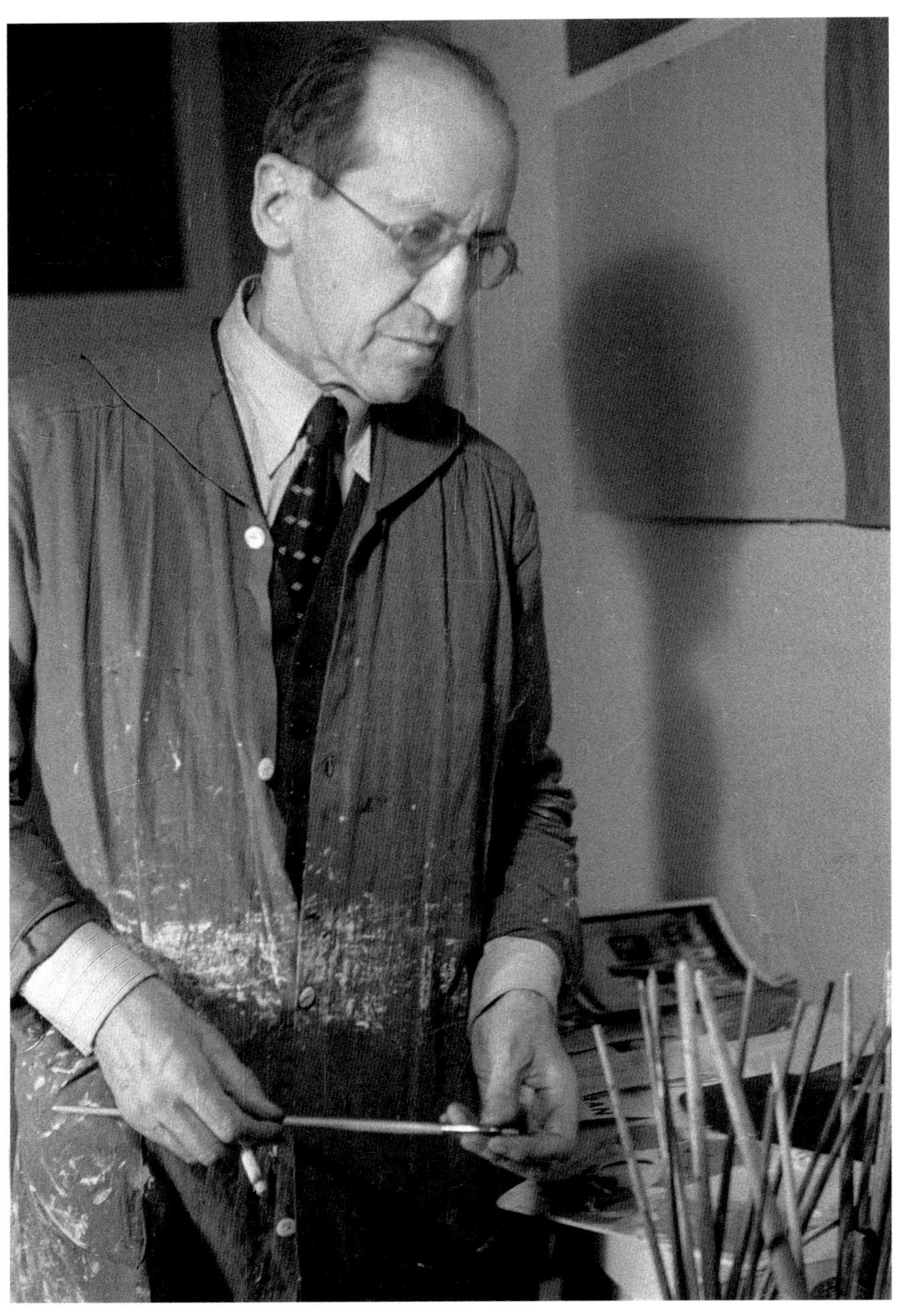

CAT. 275 **Fritz Glarner**
Piet Mondrian working in his studio, between c. late 1942 and mid-March 1943

CAT. 276 **Fritz Glarner**
Piet Mondrian in his studio, with *Place de la Concorde*, between c. late 1942 and mid-March 1943

CATS 273–74, 277 See catalogue

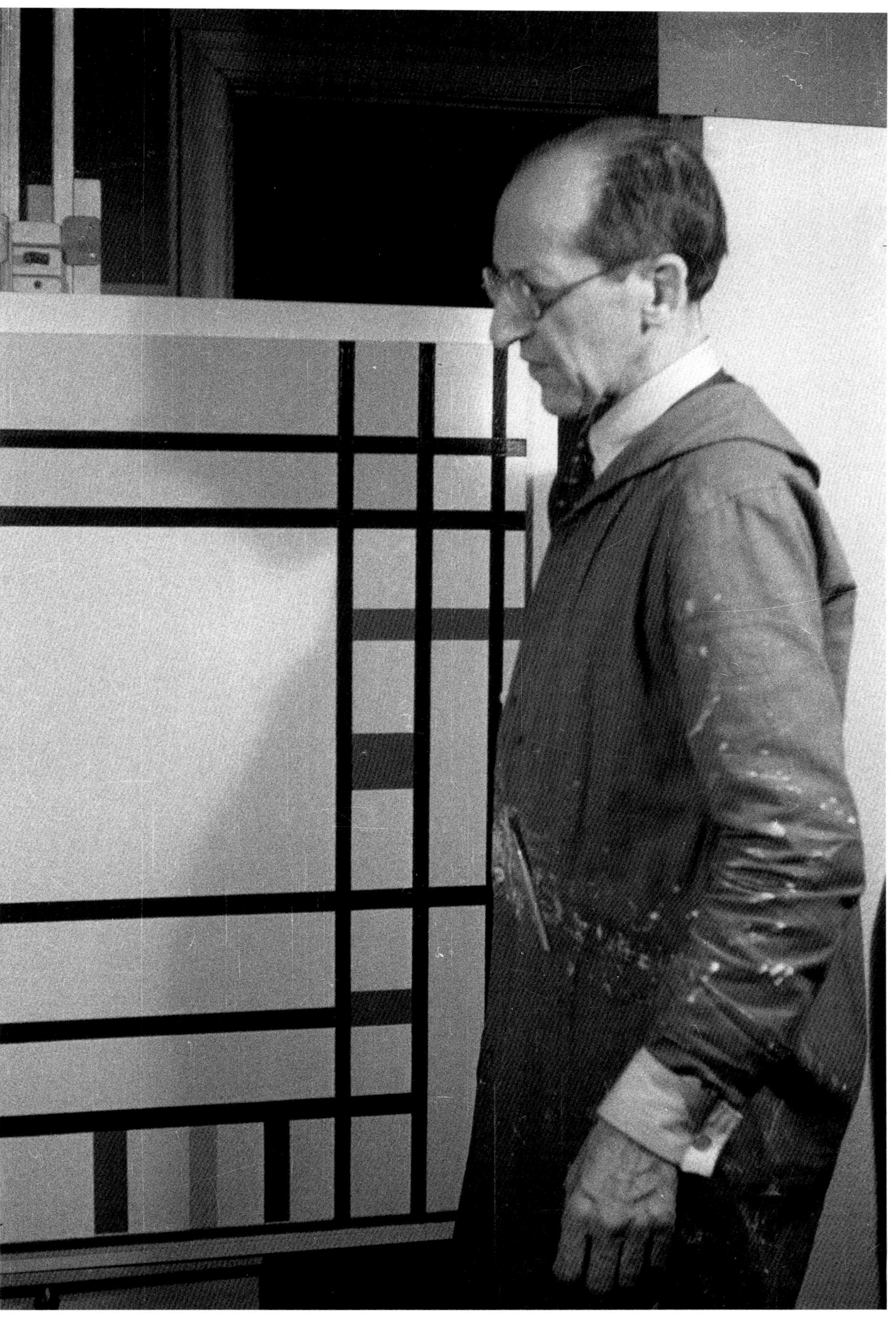

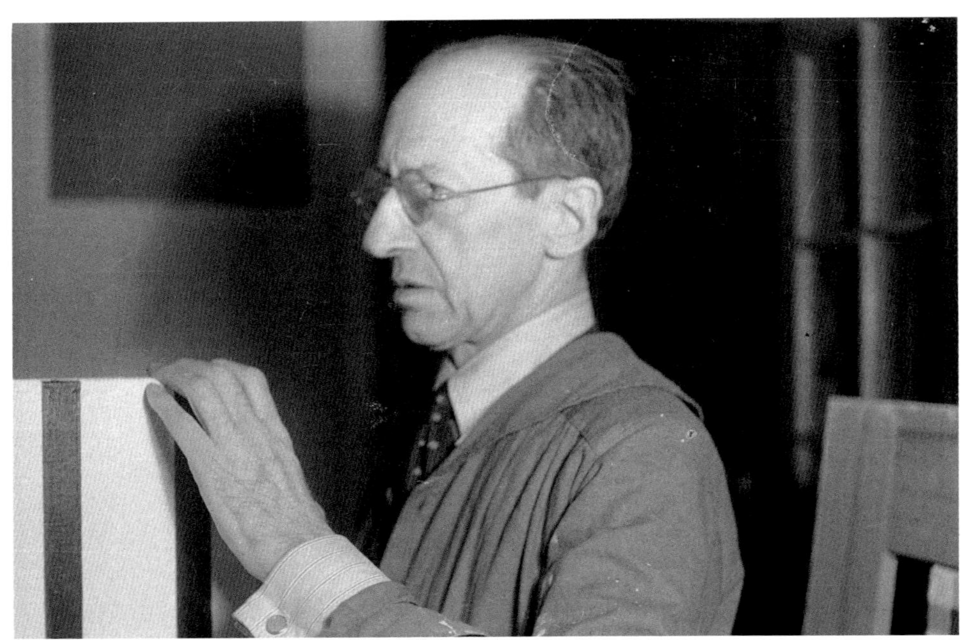

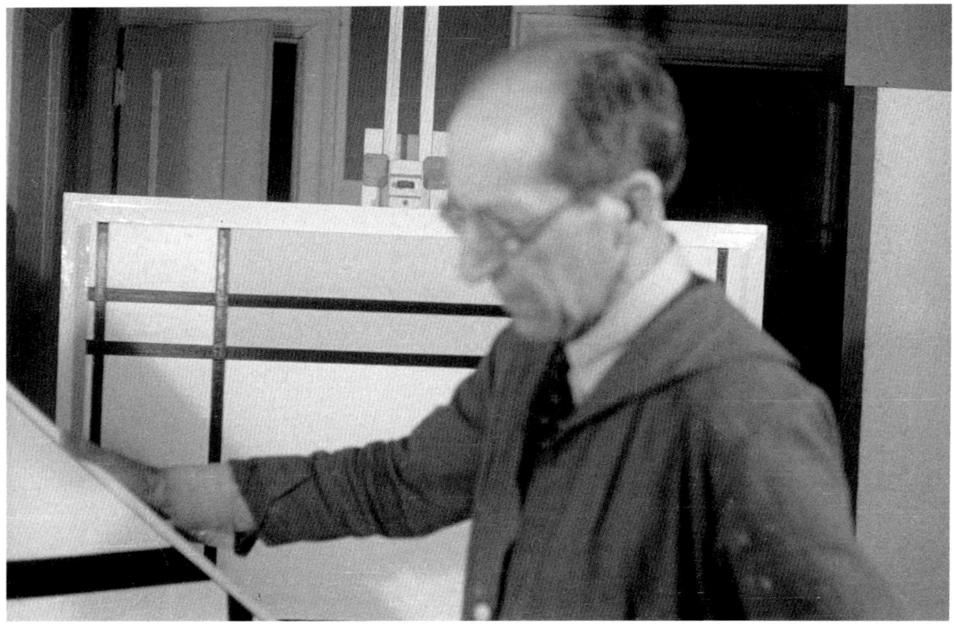

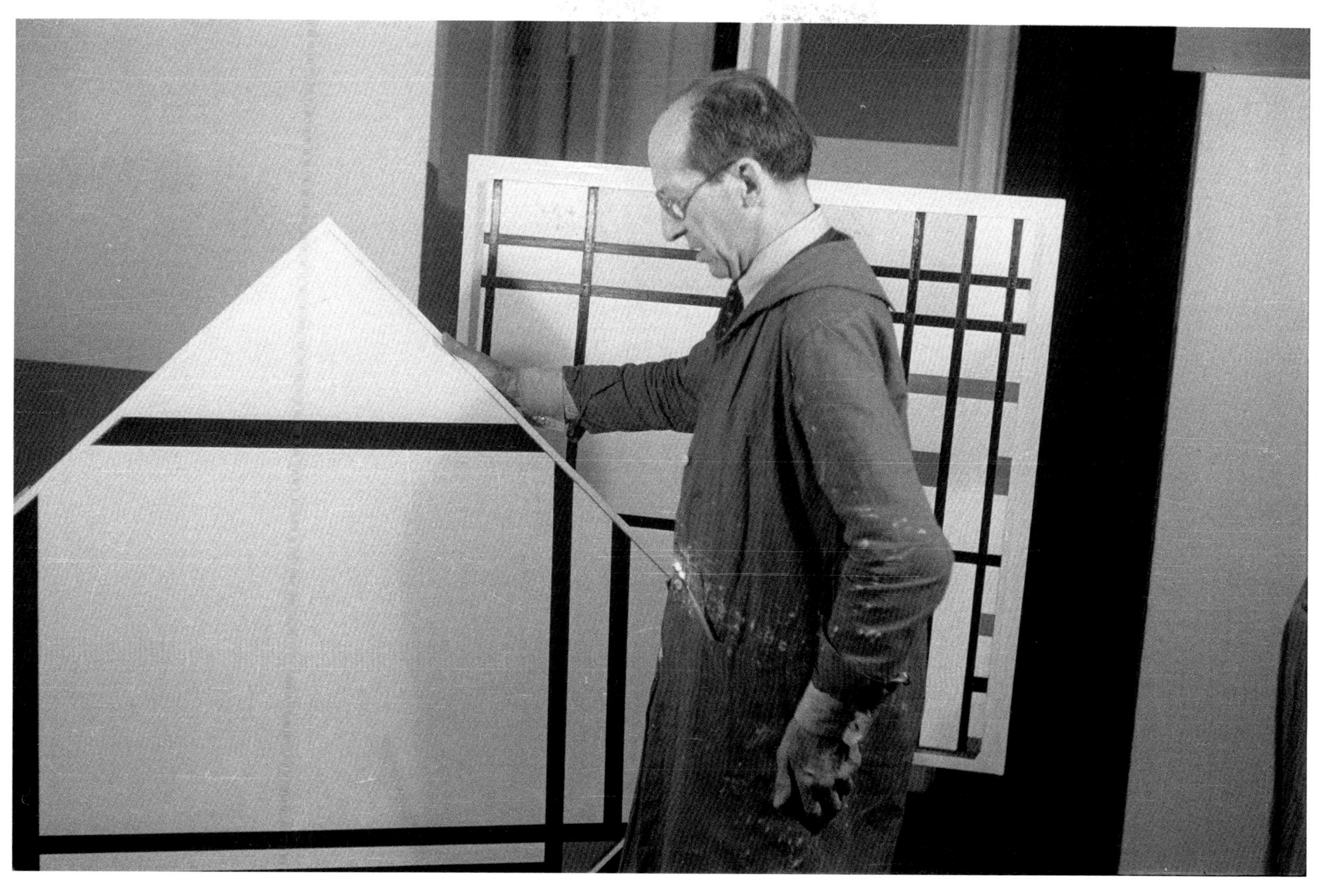

CAT. 278 **Fritz Glarner**
Piet Mondrian in his studio, between c. late 1942 and mid-March 1943

CATS 280, 282 **Fritz Glarner**
Piet Mondrian in his studio, with *Picture No. III* (B282), between c. late 1942 and mid-March 1943

CATS 279, 281 See catalogue

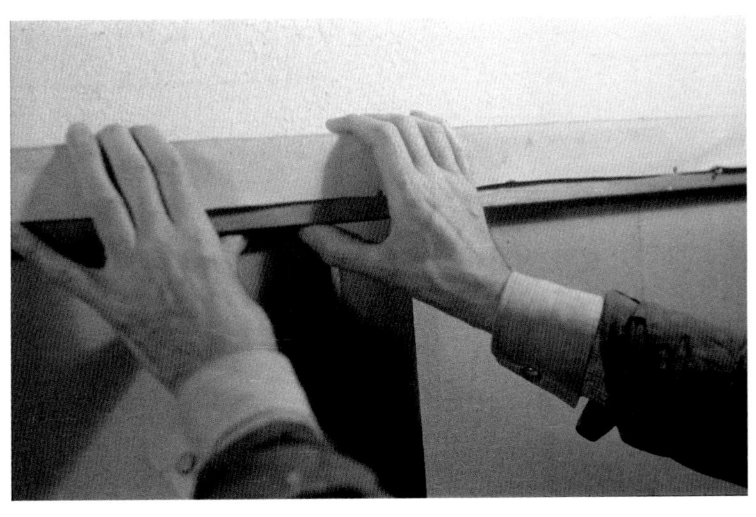

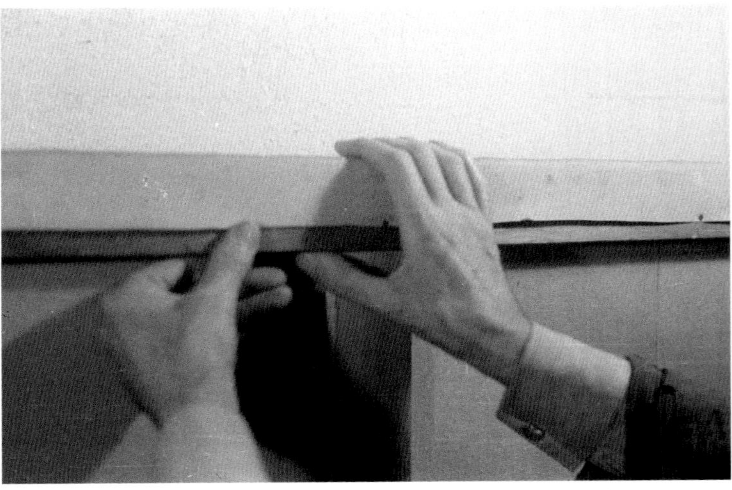

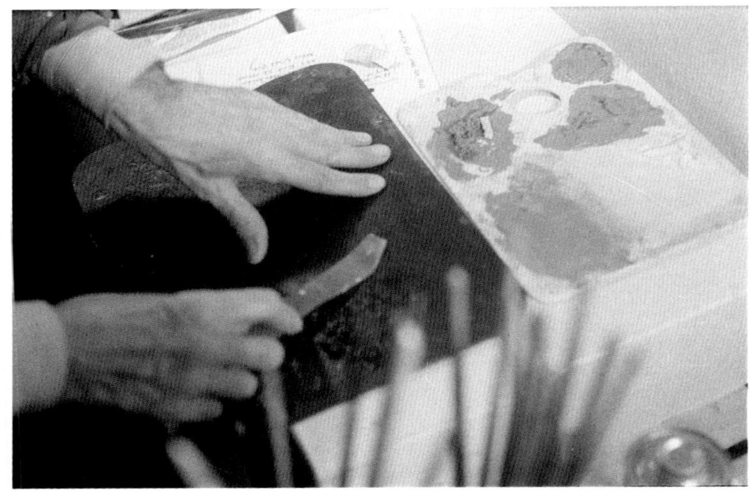

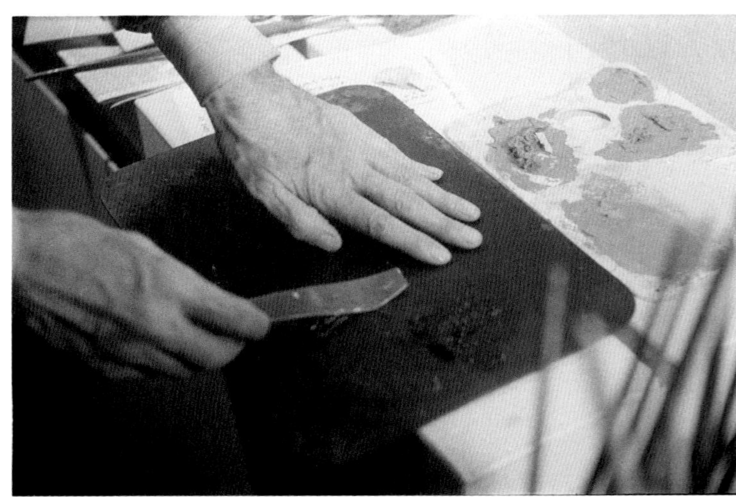

CATS 283–90 **Fritz Glarner**
The hands of Piet Mondrian,
between c. late 1942 and mid-March 1943

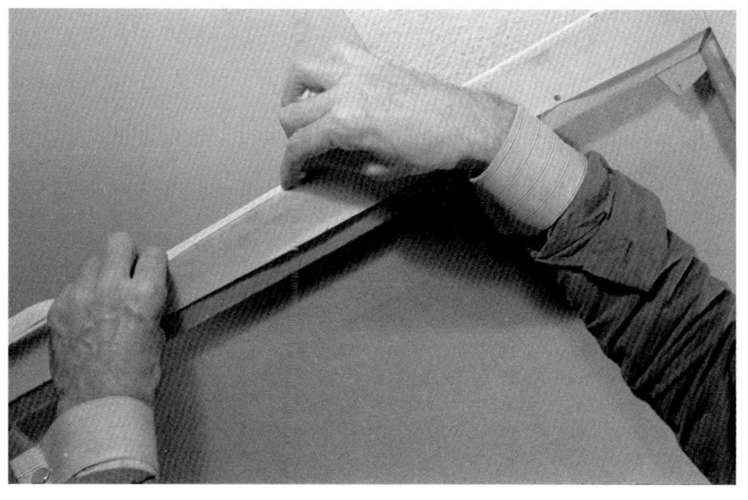
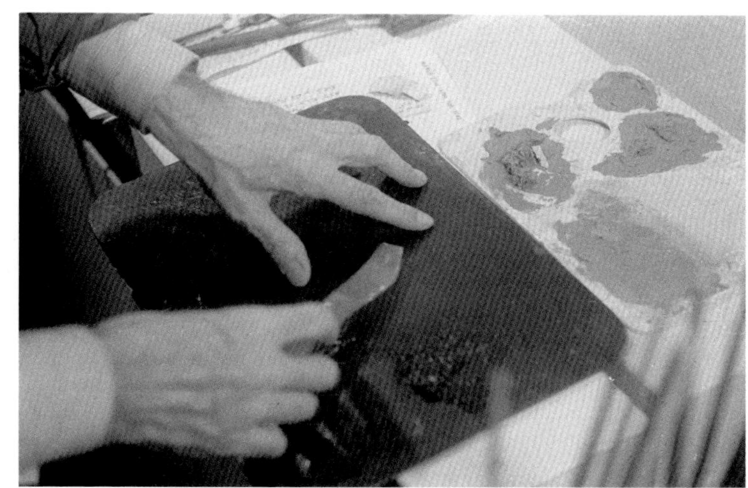
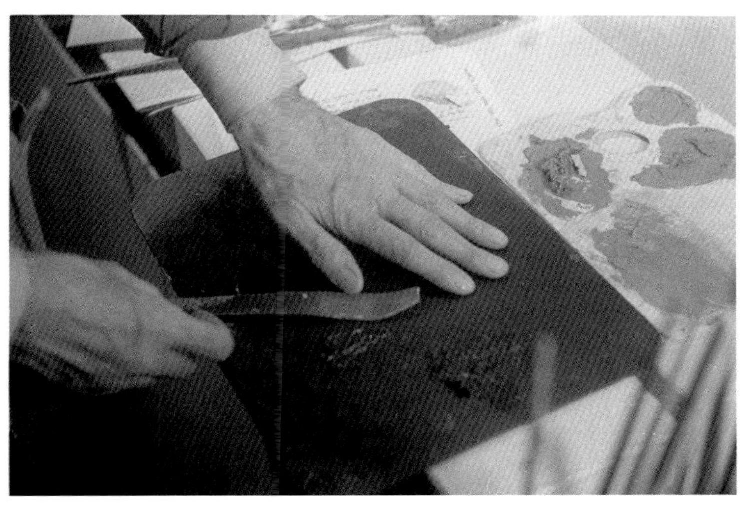
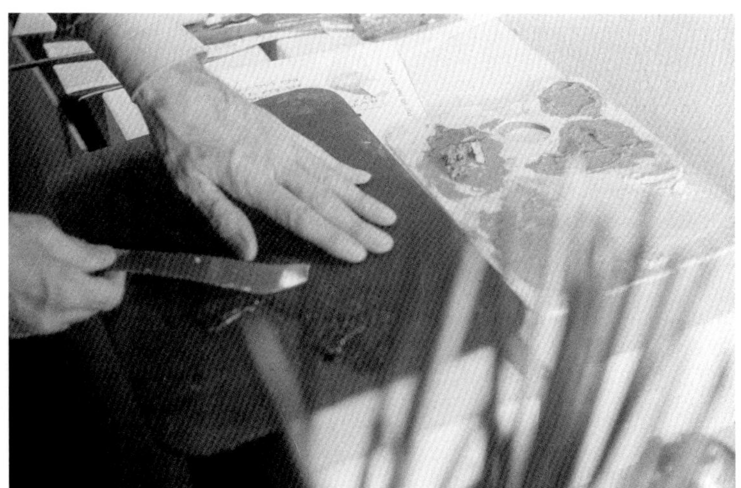

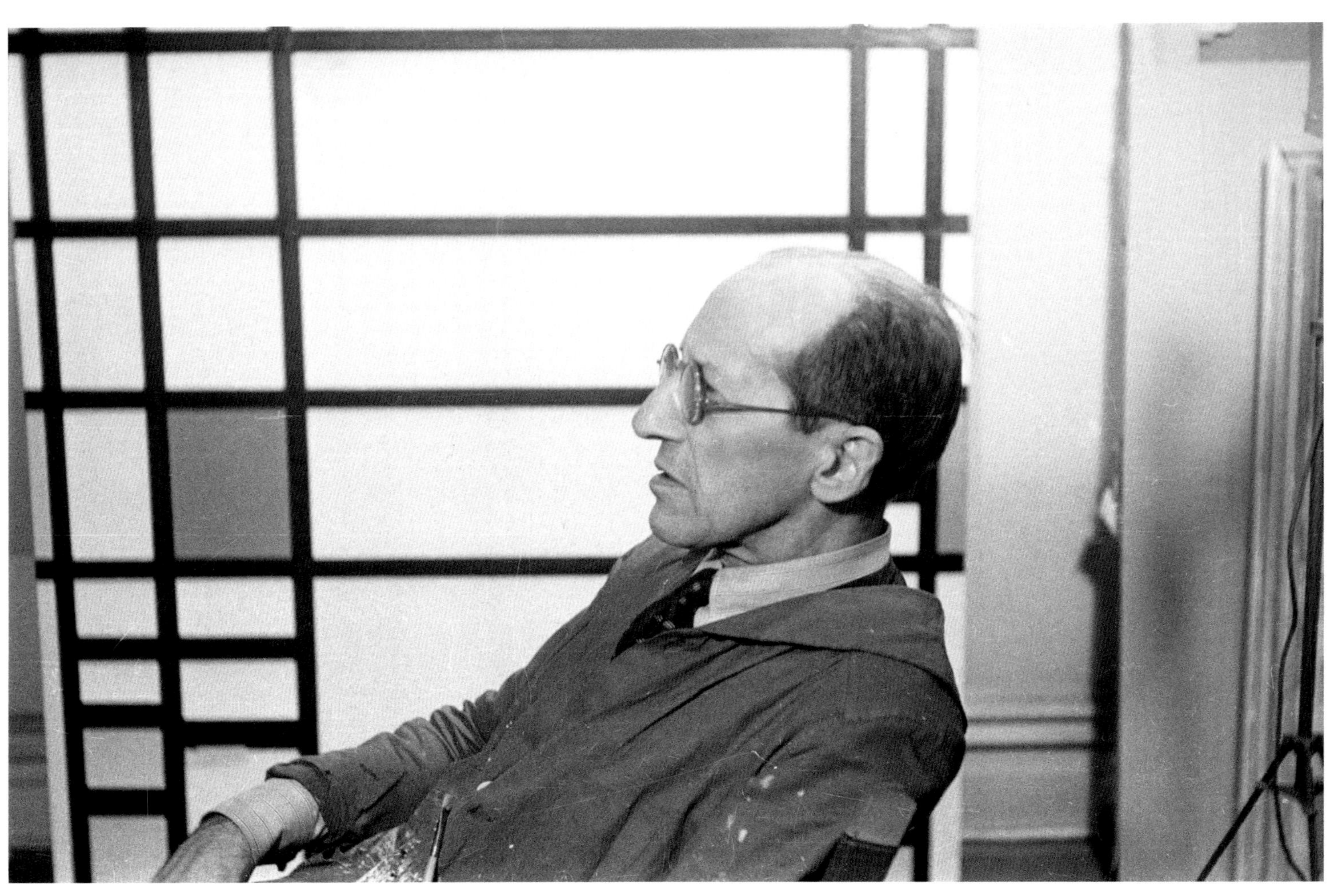

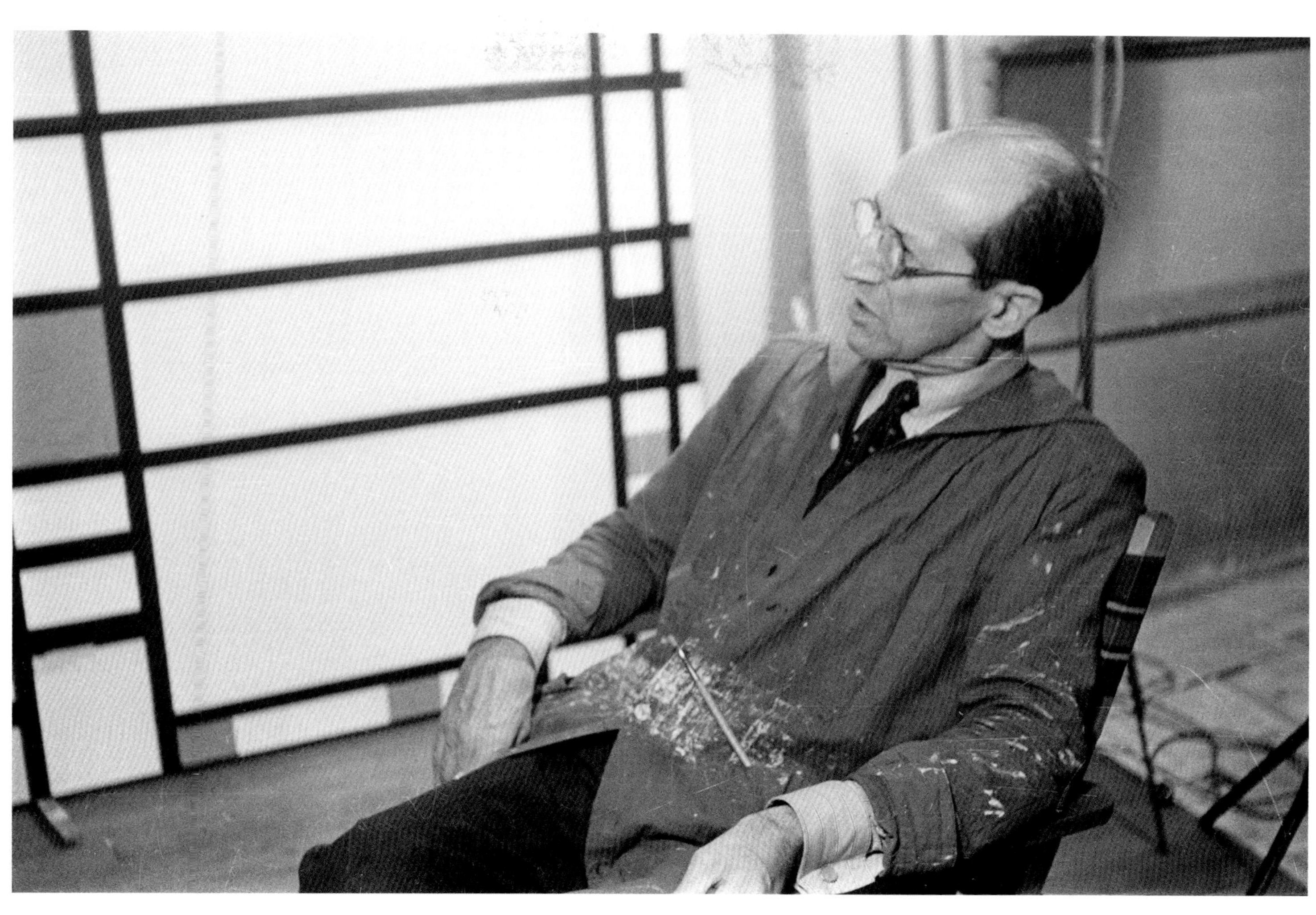

CATS 292, 294 **Fritz Glarner**
Piet Mondrian in his studio, between c. late 1942 and mid-March 1943

CATS 291, 293, 295 See catalogue

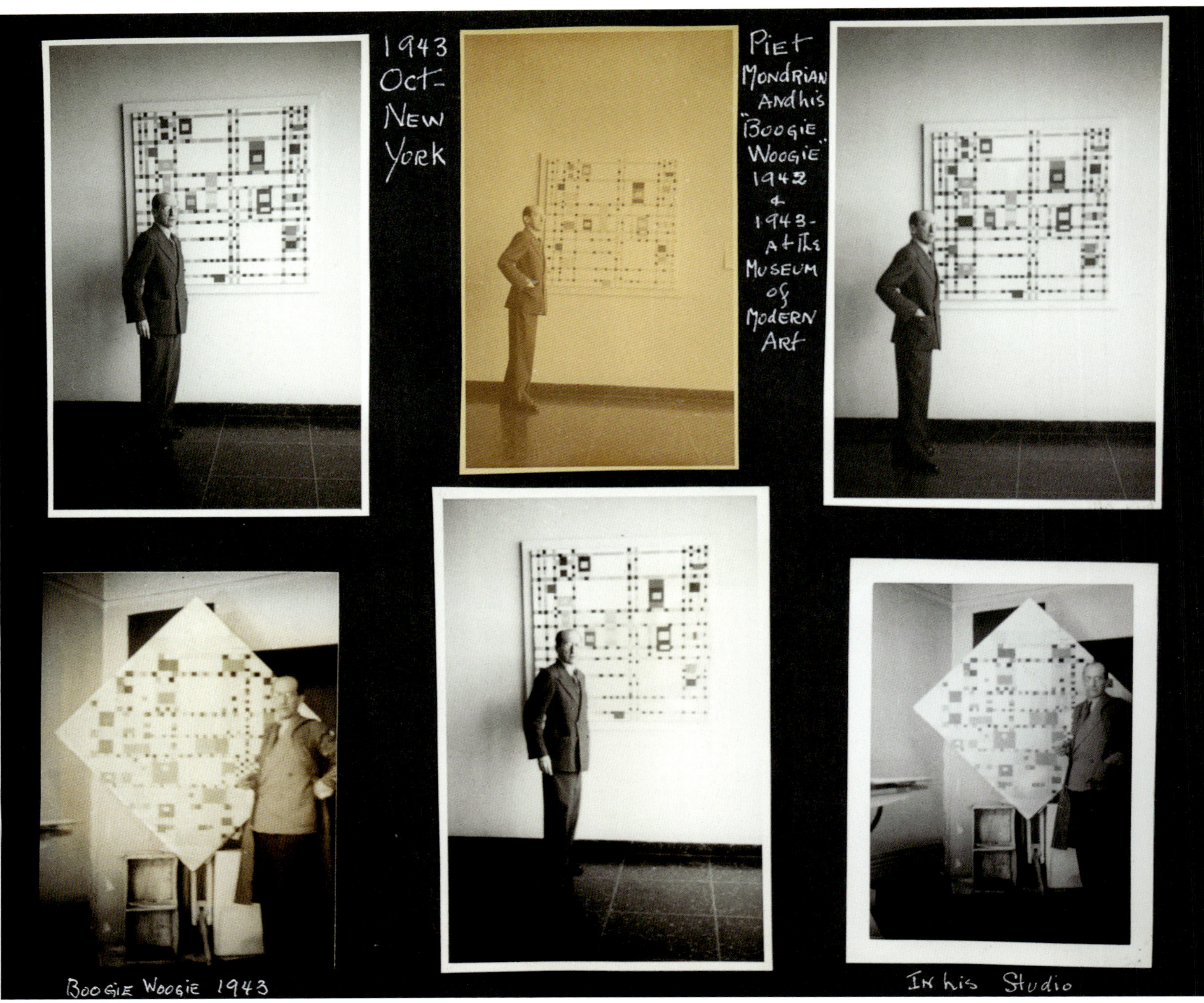
1943
Oct.
New
York
Piet
Mondrian
And his
"Boogie
Woogie"
1942
&
1943-
at the
Museum
of
Modern
Art
Boogie Woogie 1943
In his Studio

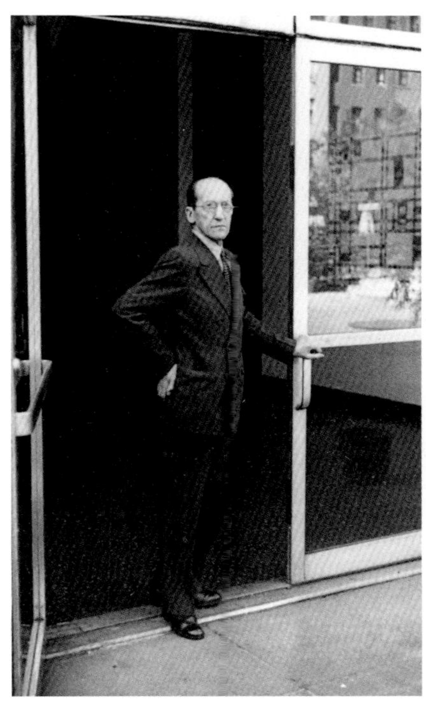

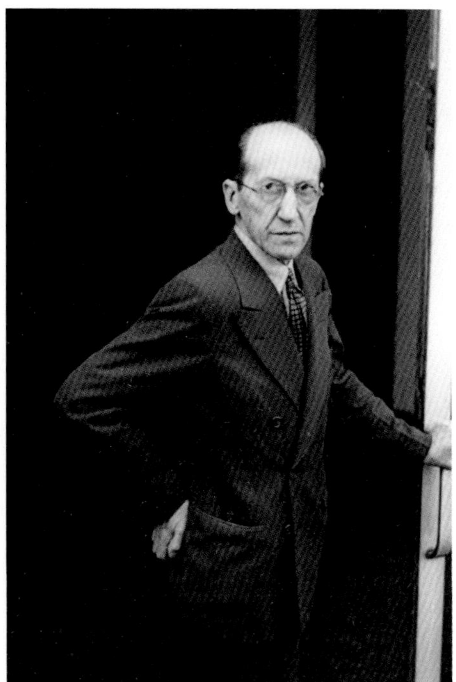

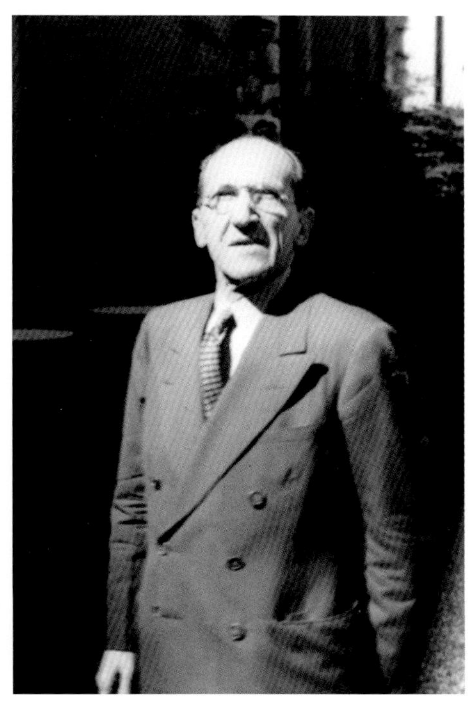

CATS 296–99 and 303–4 Page with photographs from an album belonging to Elizabeth 'Bobsy' Goodspeed Chapman, a wealthy collector and amateur photographer and film-maker from Chicago. In October 1943 she visited the Museum of Modern Art in New York in the company of Mondrian. Earlier that year the museum had obtained Mondrian's painting *Broadway Boogie Woogie* (B323) through an anonymous donation.

CATS 300–301 **Elizabeth 'Bobsy' Goodspeed Chapman**
Piet Mondrian at the entrance to the Museum of Modern Art's sculpture garden, October 1943

CAT. 302 **Elizabeth 'Bobsy' Goodspeed Chapman**
Piet Mondrian in the Museum of Modern Art's sculpture garden, October 1943

POSTHUMOUS PHOTOGRAPHS

Mondrian died on 1 February 1944 from a neglected bout of pneumonia. His possessions, including his studio and all its contents, passed to his heir, Harry Holtzman. The American continued to rent the studio until the middle of June, keeping the space more or less as the artist had left it.[1] From his very first visit to Mondrian in 1934, Holtzman understood the special status that the studio occupied in the Dutchman's overall body of work and so, some time between 2 February and 21 March 1944, he meticulously documented the interior at 15 East 59th Street, where Mondrian spent the final four months of his life.[2] He carried out the task with Fritz Glarner, a Swiss-born painter and photographer, who had met Mondrian in Paris around 1929. Together they photographed the most important rooms, with Holtzman taking a total of twenty colour photographs of the studio and filming the space in colour, while Glarner systematically recorded the various spaces in dozens of black-and-white shots. Some time later, Holtzman used large sheets of paper to trace the composition of coloured paper rectangles with which Mondrian had decorated the walls, before they were finally taken down.

Whether Holtzman and Glarner took their pictures on the same day is not clear, but it would seem likely. In some cases, for instance, the camera position is almost identical and the photographic lamps that were used are visible in both black-and-white and colour photographs (see, for example, cats 359 and 385). The lamps will have been set up in the studio for the photo session.[3] Their use resulted in sharp shadows in several photos. Not all of the pictures were taken in artificial light: comparison of cats 305 and 384 show abundant daylight in the black-and-white shot, while it is pitch black outside in the colour photograph. This suggests that the work took a good part of at least one day, which makes sense considering the large amount of shooting and the constant repositioning of lights and camera.

1 The posthumous photographs show that certain items of furniture, such as the table with Mondrian's palette, changed location during the session(s): compare, for example, cats 305 and 382.

2 It cannot be determined on which precise day after 2 February 1944 the photographs were taken, but it must have been before 22 March, the date on which Holtzman opened the studio for a few weeks to friends and other interested parties (Welsh/Joosten 1998-II, p. 182).

3 Glarner chiefly earned his living in New York from photo-reportage and must have had access to the necessary tools, including photographic lamps.

4 The opening is thought to have lasted until around 3 May 1944. The rental contract was not terminated until 14 June (Troy 2013, p. 83).

5 Anonymous 1944, p. 20.

Holtzman opened the studio to interested parties for about six weeks, beginning on 22 March,[4] 'so that artists and students can visit the place and glean what information they can about the master's methods'.[5] Several hundred people appear to have taken the opportunity, including members of Mondrian's circle and a not insignificant number of art school students.[6] The celebrated fashion photographer Fernand Fonssagrives also visited the studio at the request of Henry Bull, editor-in-chief of *Town & Country* magazine.[7] As far as we know, he took eight pictures of the studio, four of which show a model posing among Mondrian's paintings. The other four were shot without a model, three of them in the studio and one in Mondrian's living quarters.[8] Fonssagrives's photographs are probably the last to be taken in Mondrian's studio and can be seen as one of the earliest signs of the popularization of Mondrian's visual language. The magazine shoot is symbolic, therefore, of a phenomenon that would only grow after the artist's death.

Fritz Glarner is thought to have moved into the studio after Holtzman ended the tenancy on 14 June 1944. By that point, Holtzman had already cleared the studio, including all the furniture, remaining paintings, personal effects and the compositions on the walls. He transferred the last to white-painted wooden panels in the early 1980s.[9] Mondrian's furniture and part of these *Wall Work* compositions were later lost.[10] The following photographs are thus the most important documents for anyone looking for a clear impression of Mondrian's final studio and living quarters, and of his spatial application of neo-plasticism to his interior. Because of the systematic way in which the space was photographed, it is also the best documented of Mondrian's studios.

6 Holtzman opened the studio for an average of two afternoons a week. He sent out invitations to visit but also placed an advertisement in the newspaper (Anonymous 1944, p. 21).

7 Henkels 1993, pp. 39–40.

8 Henkels suggests in his 1993 book that Fonssagrives took the three pictures of the studio on a different day to those with the model. The latter, he argues, were shot during 'a fashion show that had taken place in Mondrian's studio' (Henkels 1993, p. 40). It seems more likely, however, that Fonssagrives took the pictures both with and without the model in the course of a single session.

9 Troy 2013, p. 105.

10 For a detailed account of what happened to the furniture and the Wall Works after Mondrian's death, see the chapter '(Un)Becoming art: Mondrian's furniture and the walls of his New York studio', in Troy 2013, pp. 71–126.

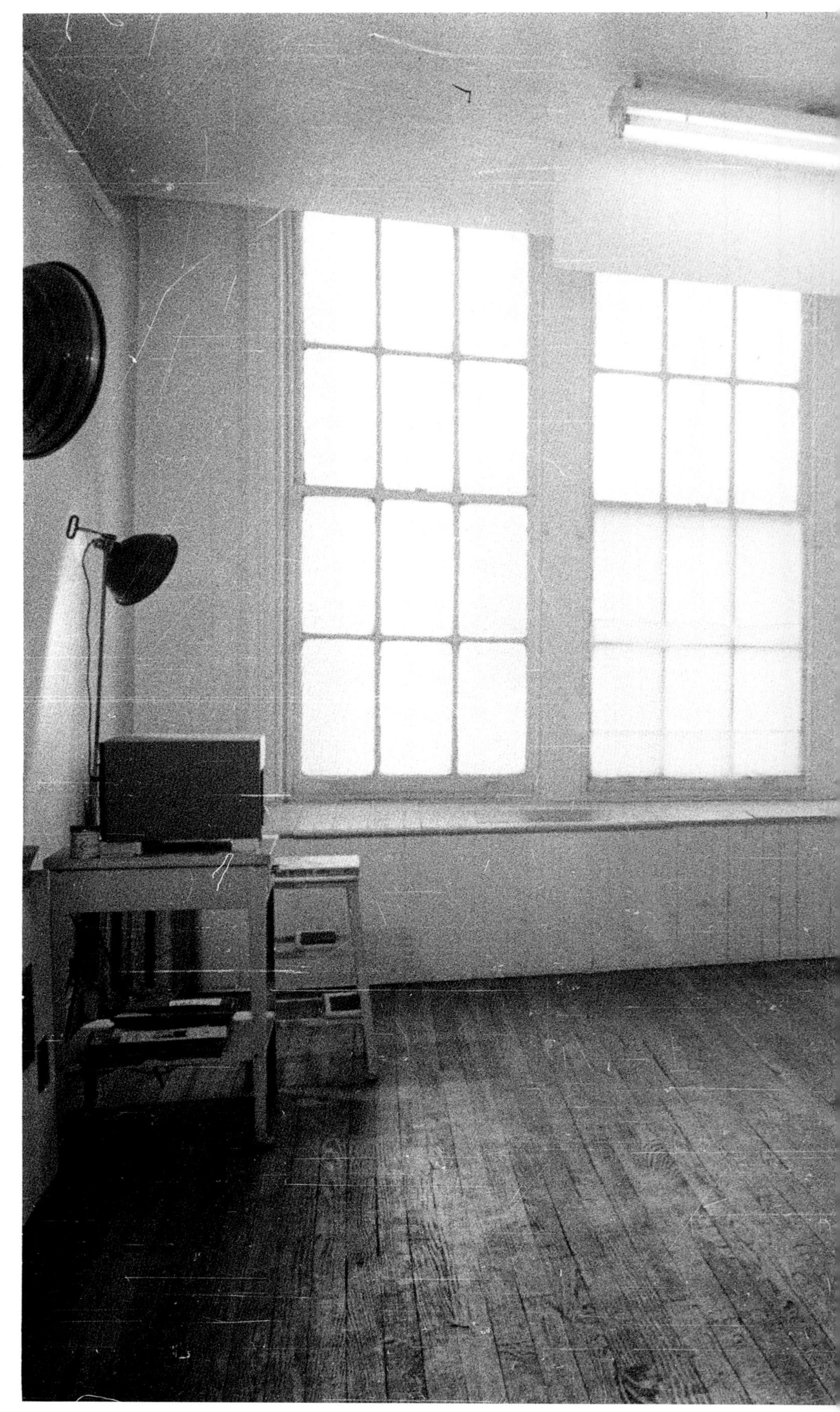

CAT. 306 **Fritz Glarner**
Mondrian's studio after his death, between 2 February and 21 March 1944

CATS 305, 307 See catalogue

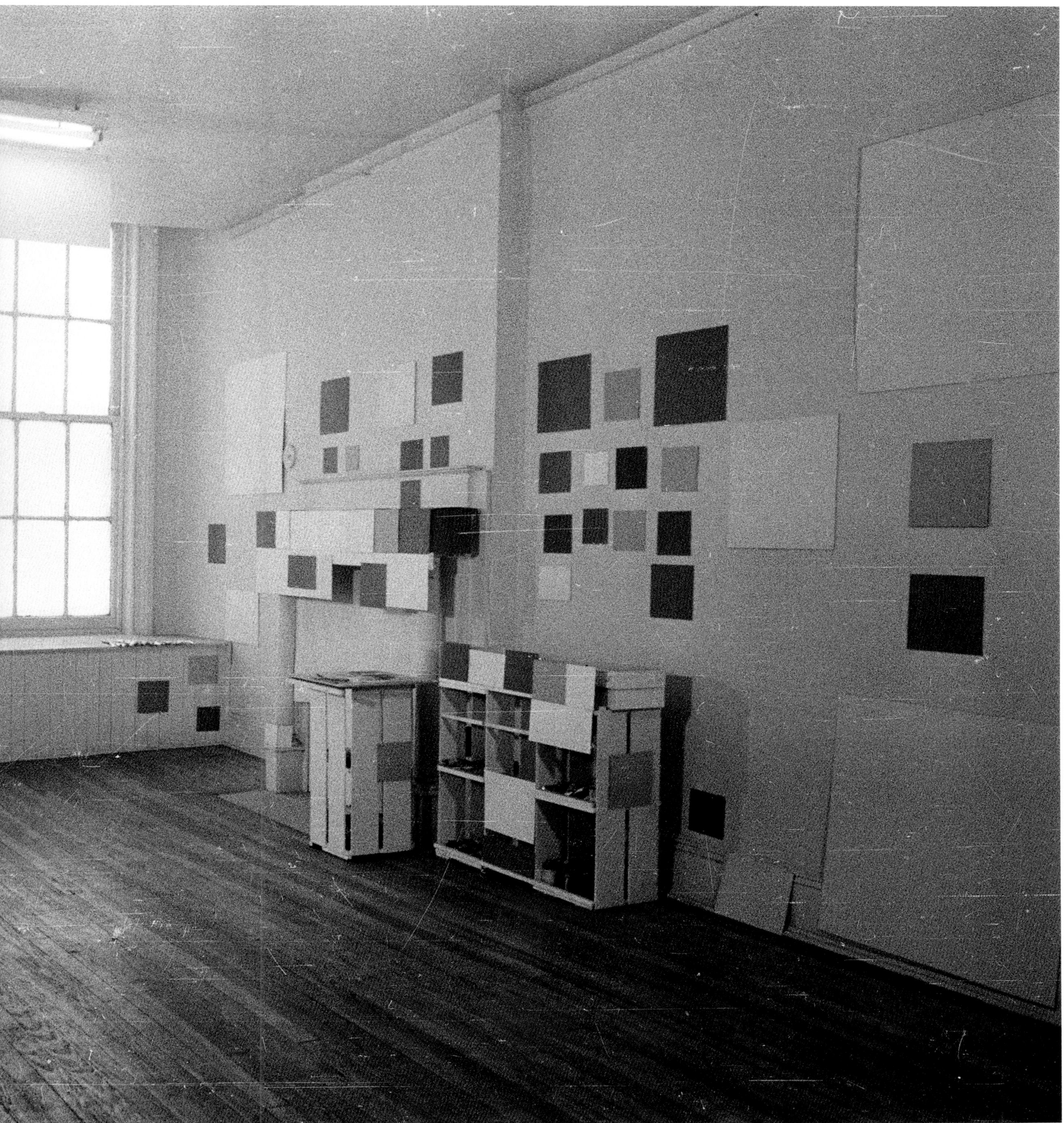

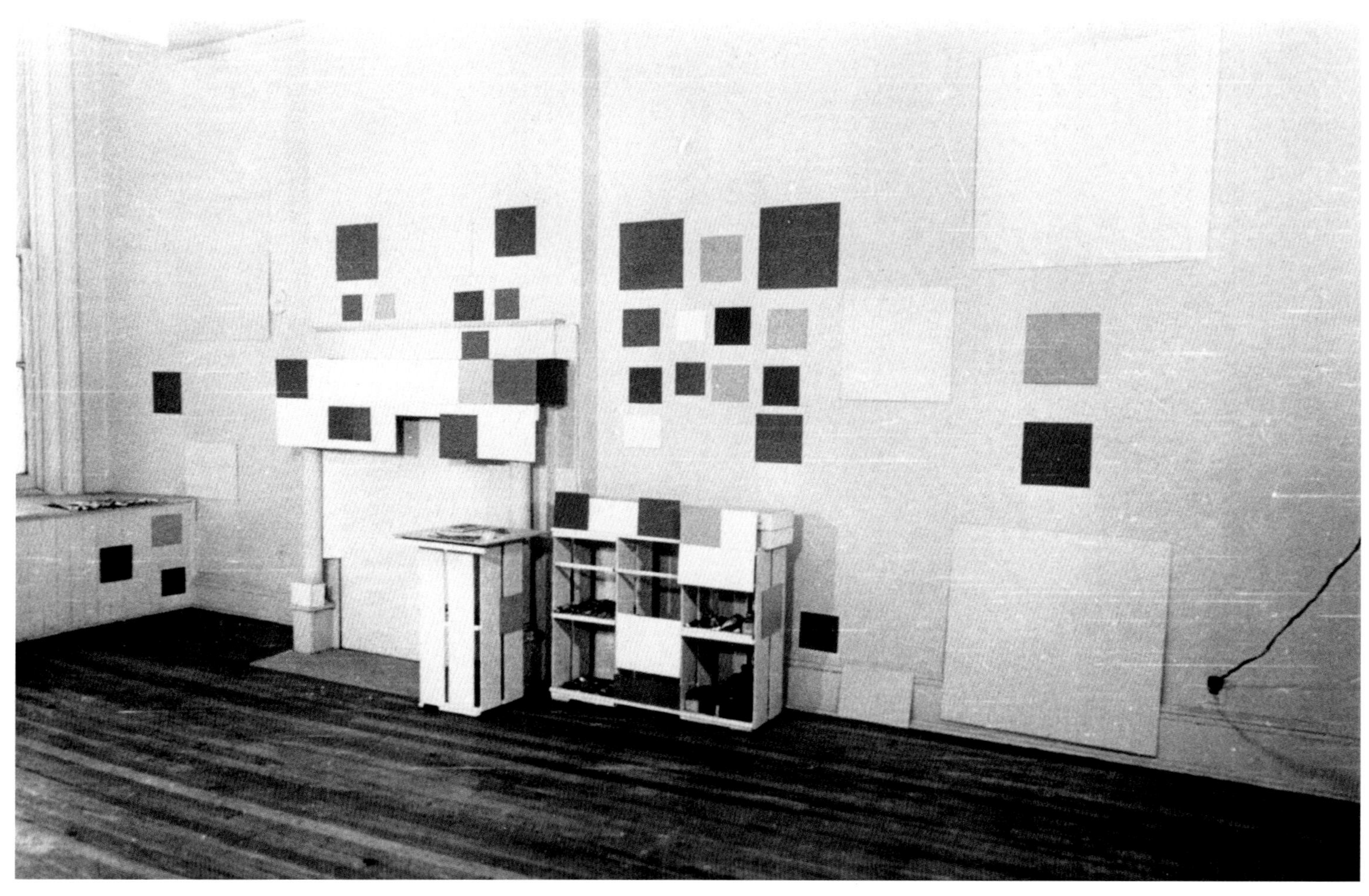

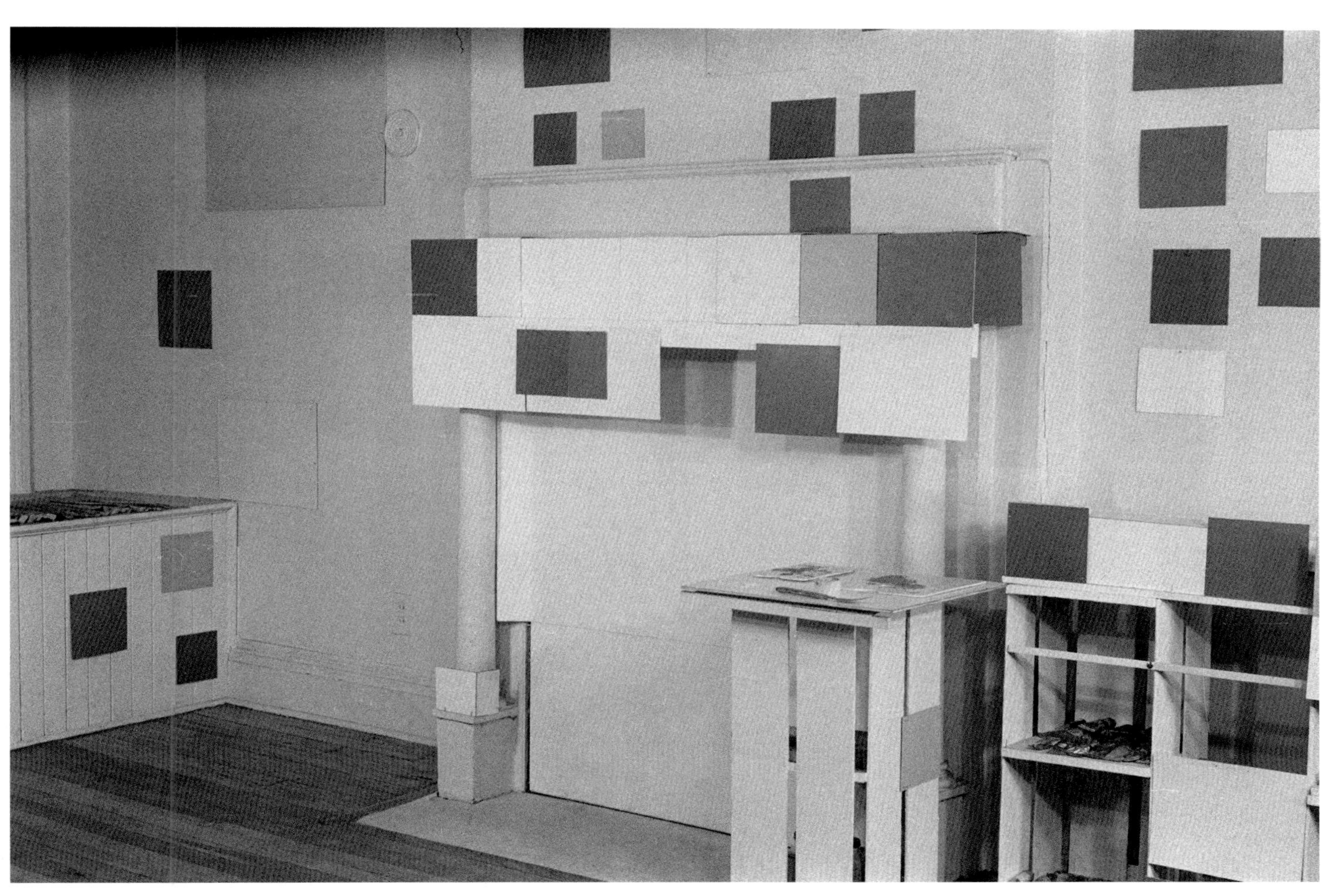

CAT. 308 **Fritz Glarner**
Mondrian's studio after his death, between 2 February and 21 March 1944

CAT. 309 **Fritz Glarner**
Mondrian's studio after his death, with his palette table in the middle, and a shelf-unit with painting materials on the right, between 2 February and 21 March 1944

CATS 310–11 See catalogue

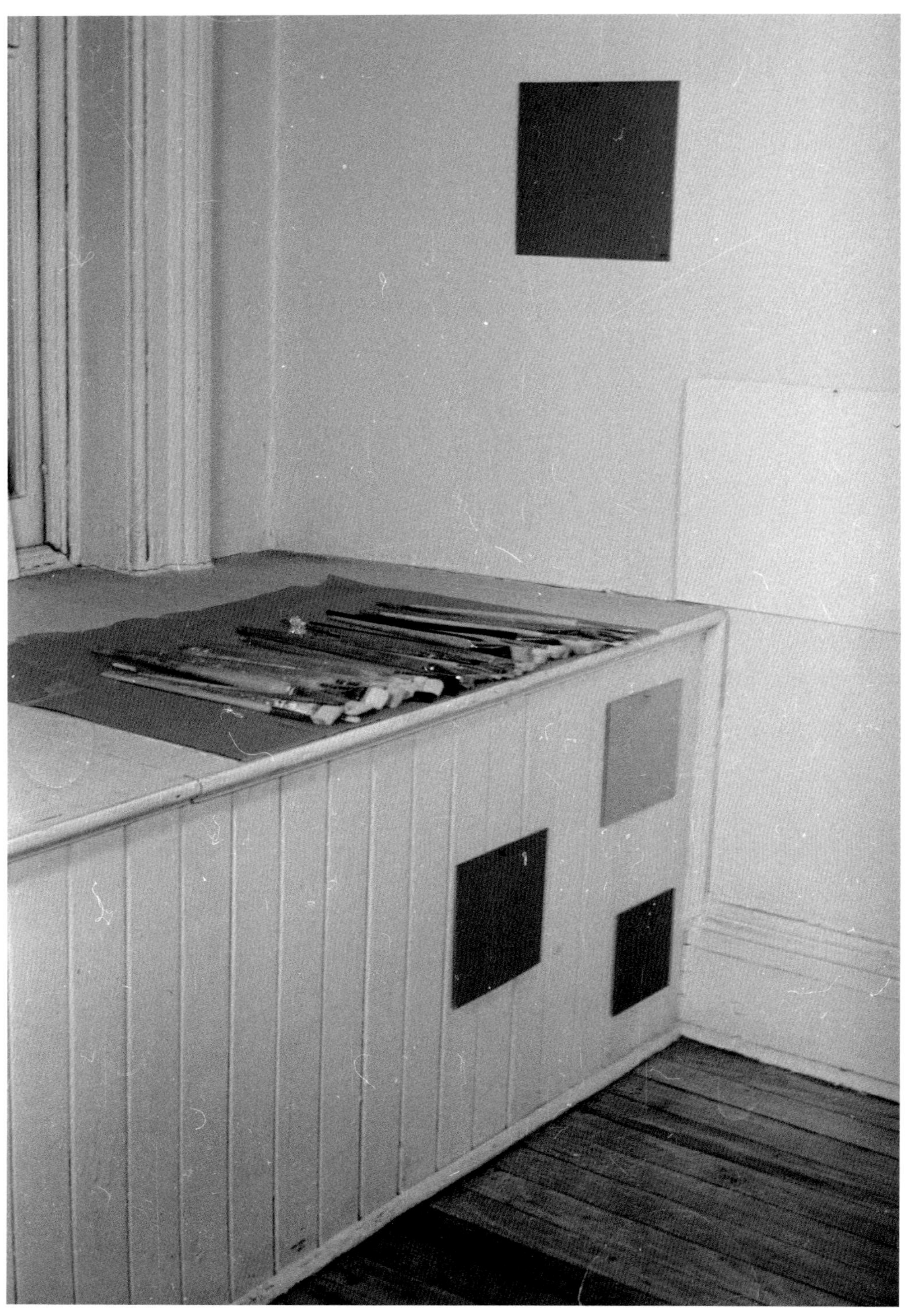

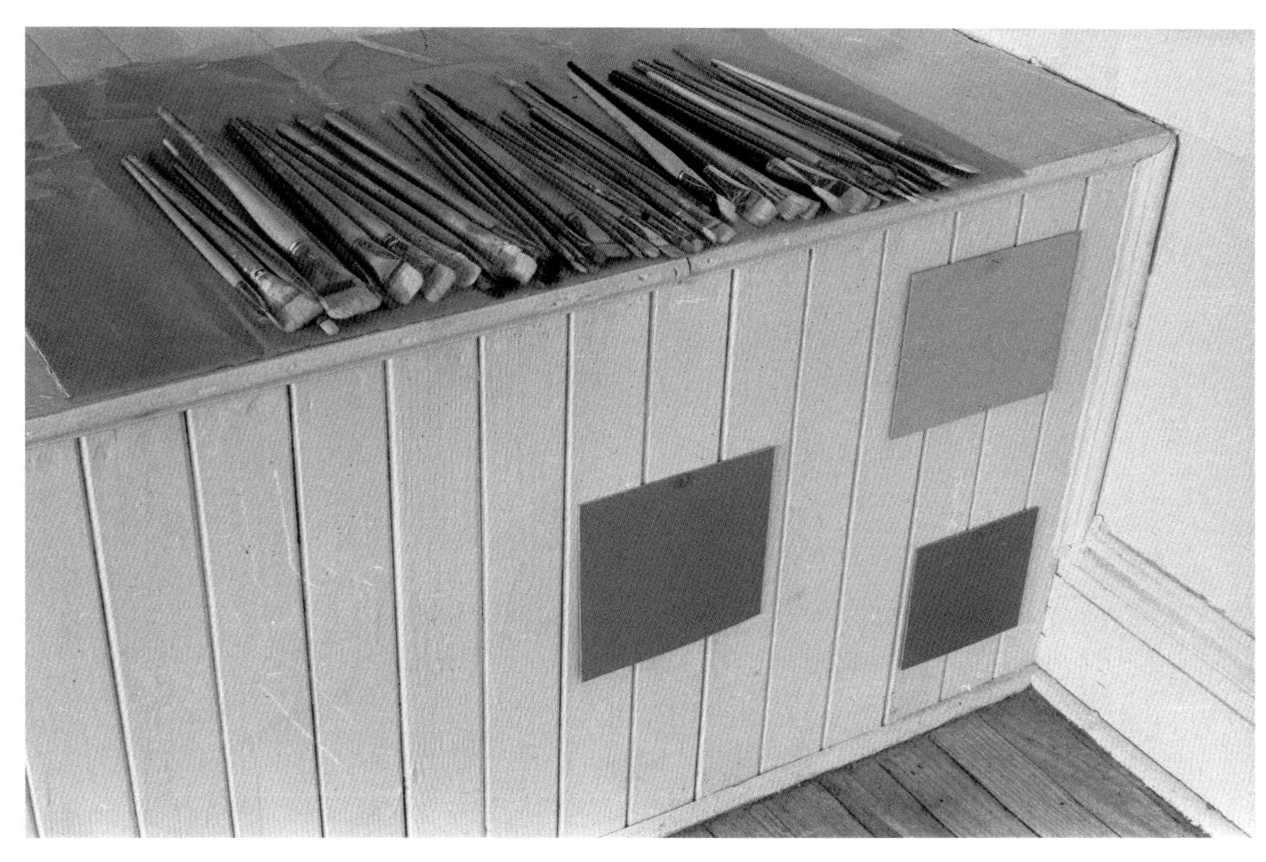

CATS 312, 315 **Fritz Glarner**
Paintbrushes in Mondrian's studio after his death, between 2 February and 21 March 1944

CATS 313–14 See catalogue

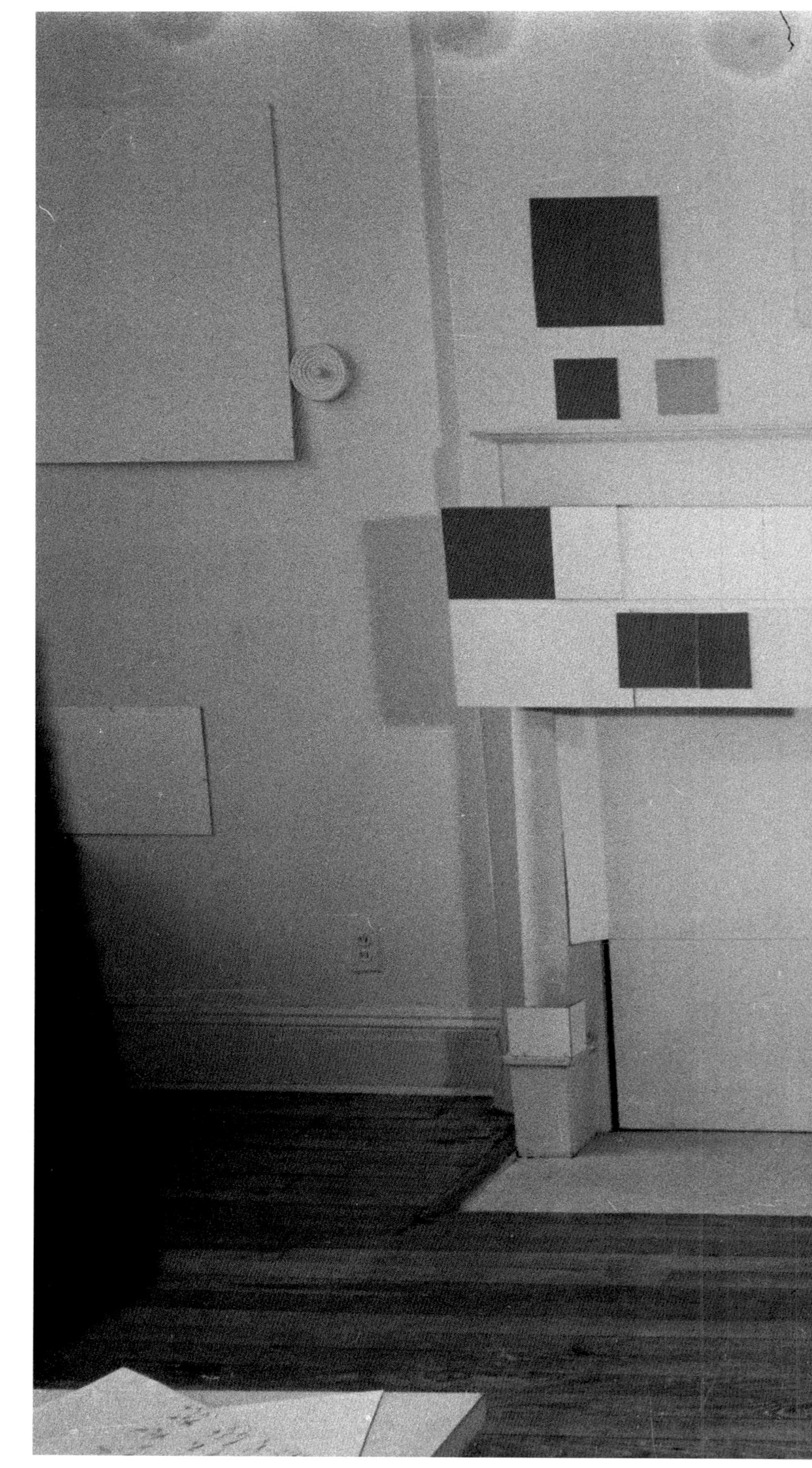

CAT. 317 **Fritz Glarner**

Mondrian's studio after his death; view of the east wall, with his palette table in front of the fireplace, alongside a shelf-unit with painting materials, between 2 February and 21 March 1944

CATS 316, 318—35 See catalogue

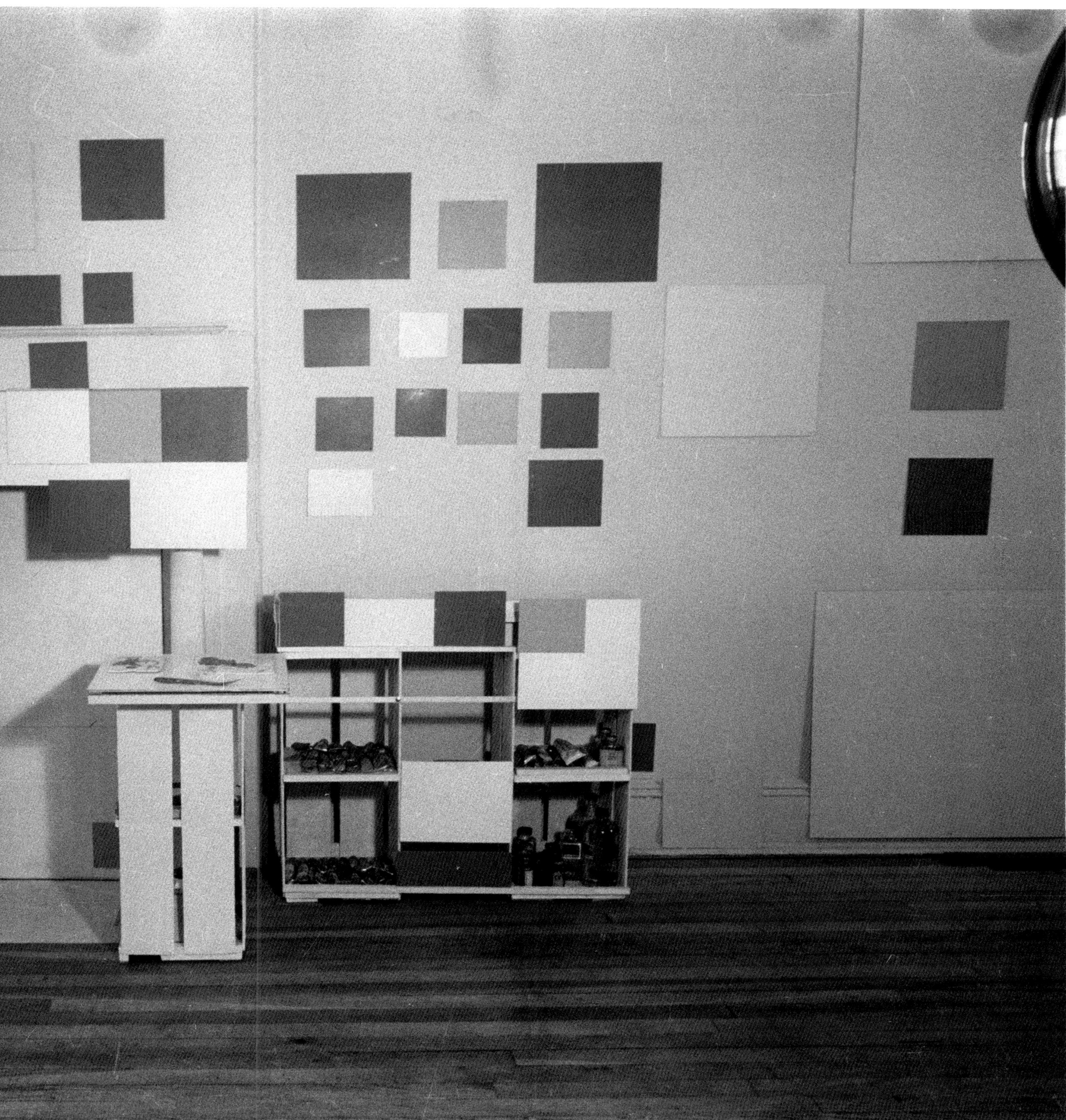

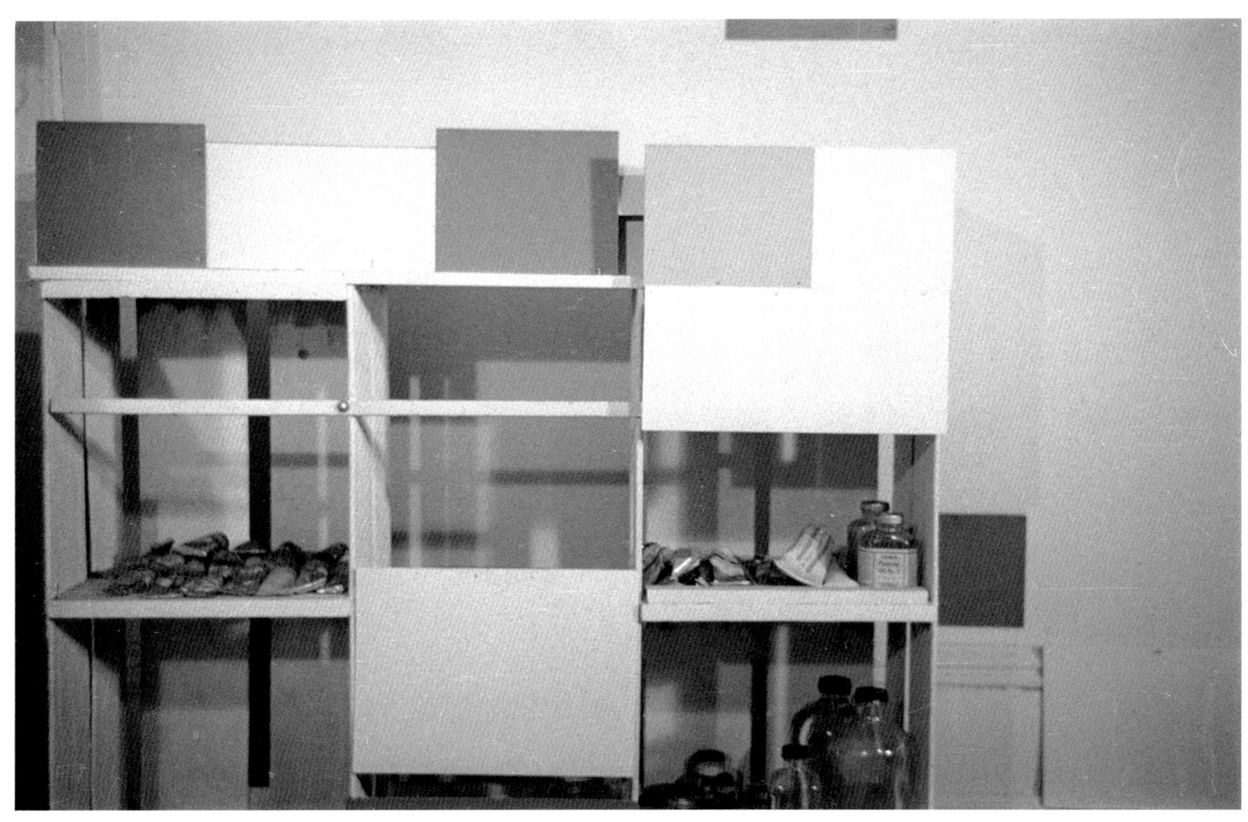

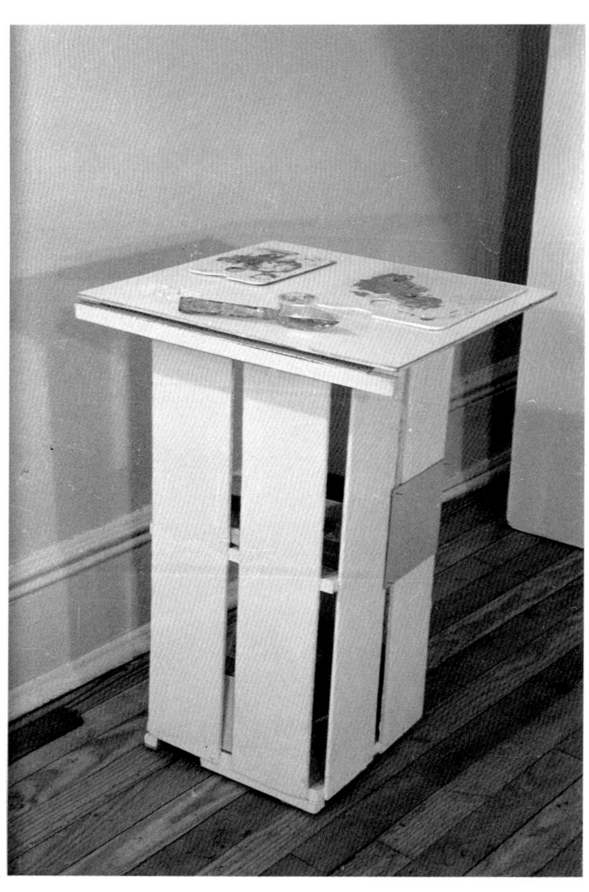

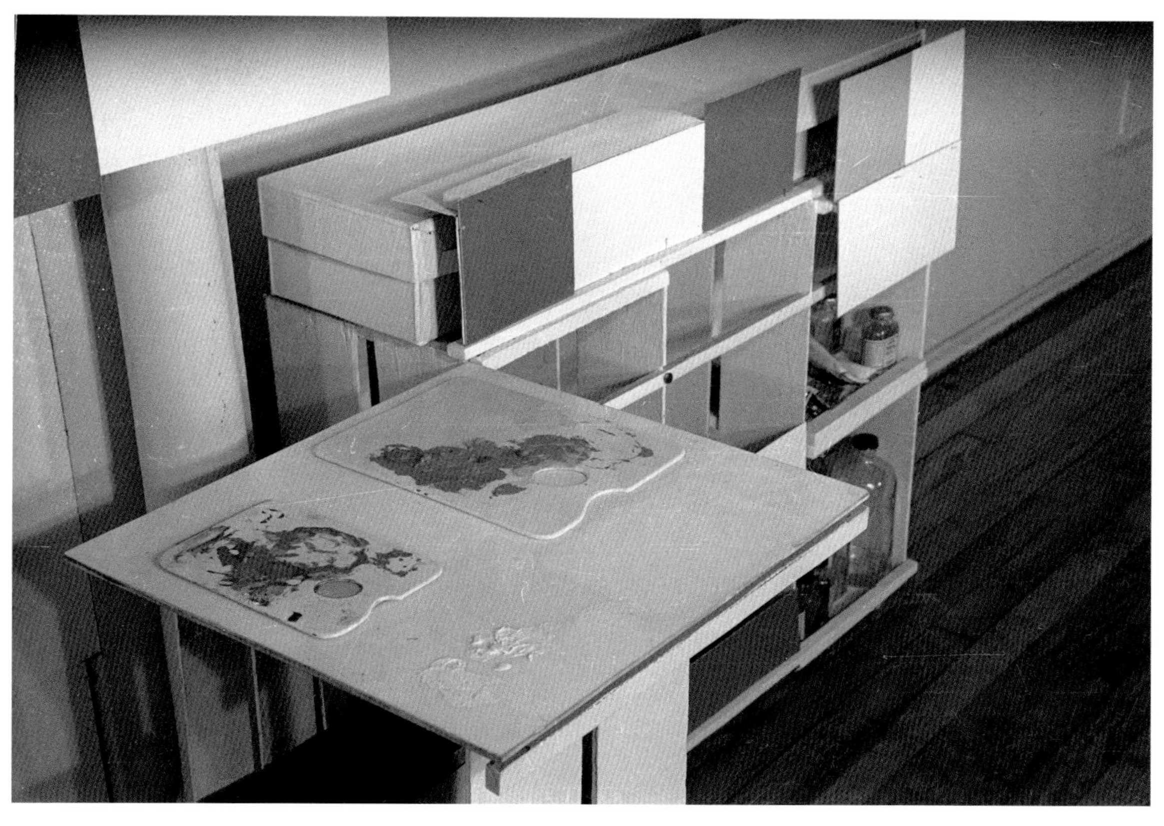

CAT. 336 **Fritz Glarner**
Shelf-unit with Mondrian's painting materials in his studio after his death, between 2 February and 21 March 1944

CAT. 343 **Fritz Glarner**
Palette table with palettes and a shelf-unit with painting materials in Mondrian's studio after his death, between 2 February and 21 March 1944

CAT. 344 **Fritz Glarner**
Palette table with palettes and a palette knife in Mondrian's studio after his death, between 2 February and 21 March 1944

CATS 337–42 See catalogue

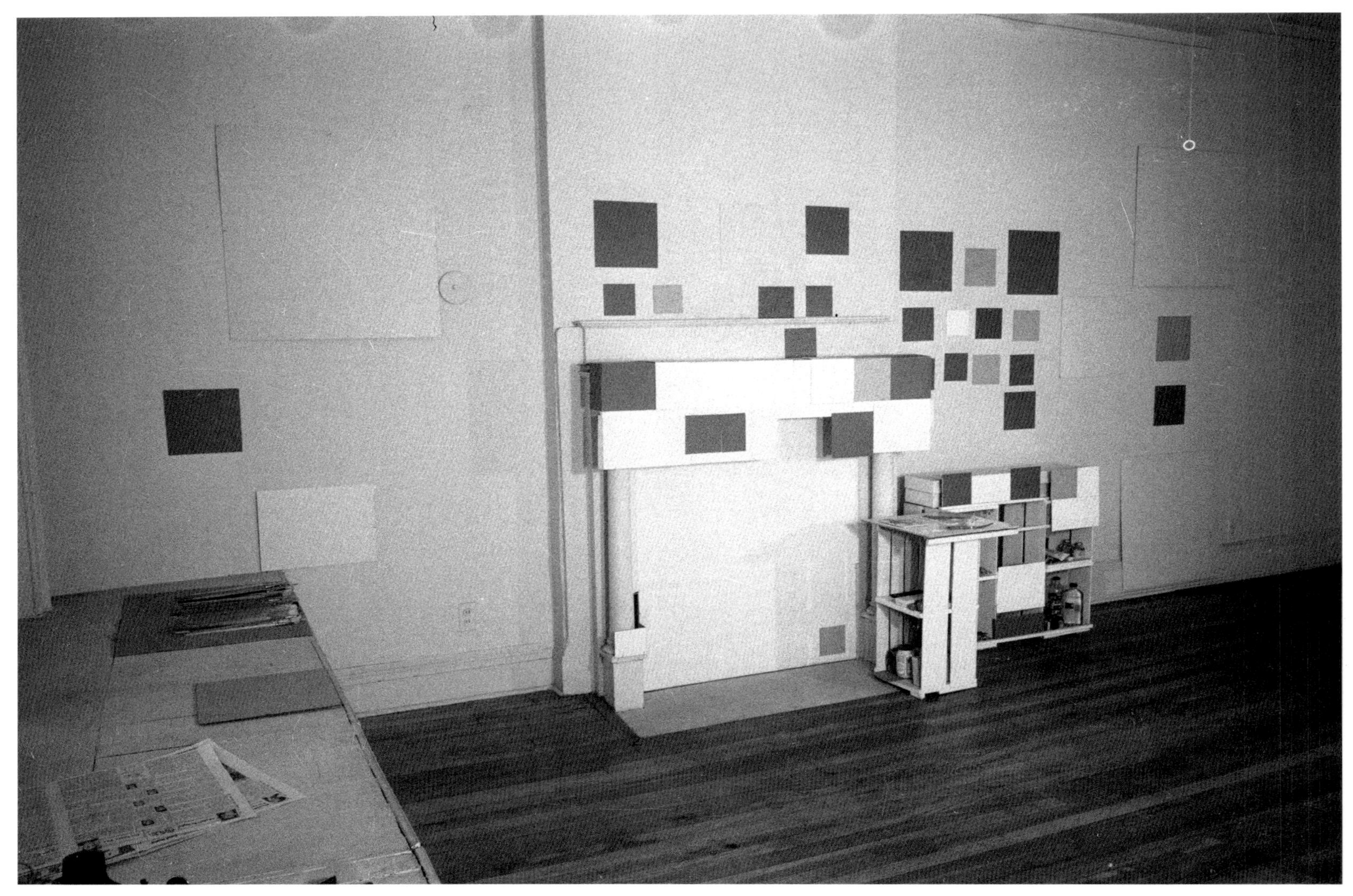

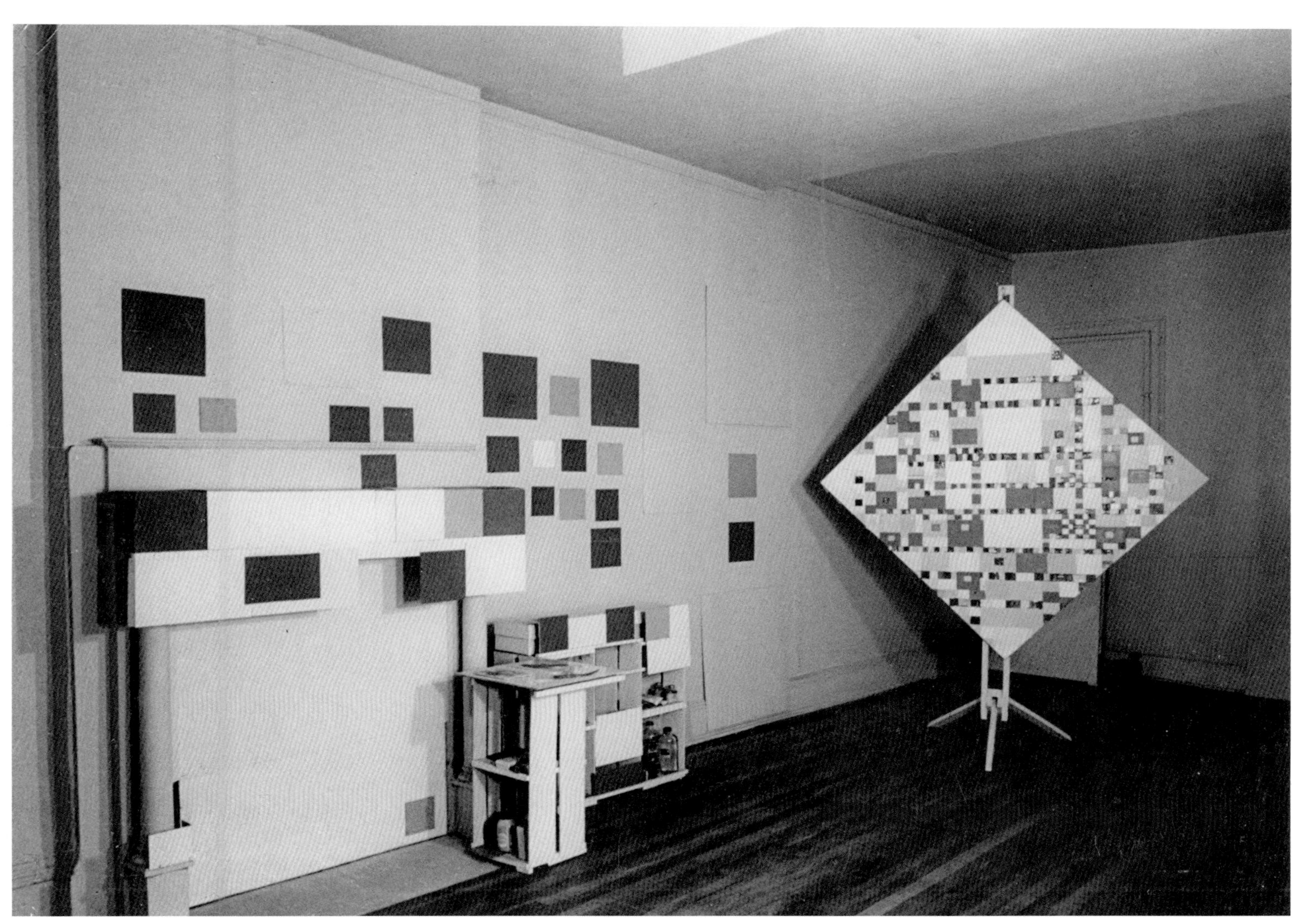

CAT. 347 **Fritz Glarner**
Mondrian's studio after his death, east wall, between 2 February and 21 March 1944

CAT. 348 **Fritz Glarner**
Mondrian's studio after his death, east wall, with *Victory Boogie Woogie* (B324) on the easel, between 2 February and 21 March 1944

CATS 345–46 See catalogue

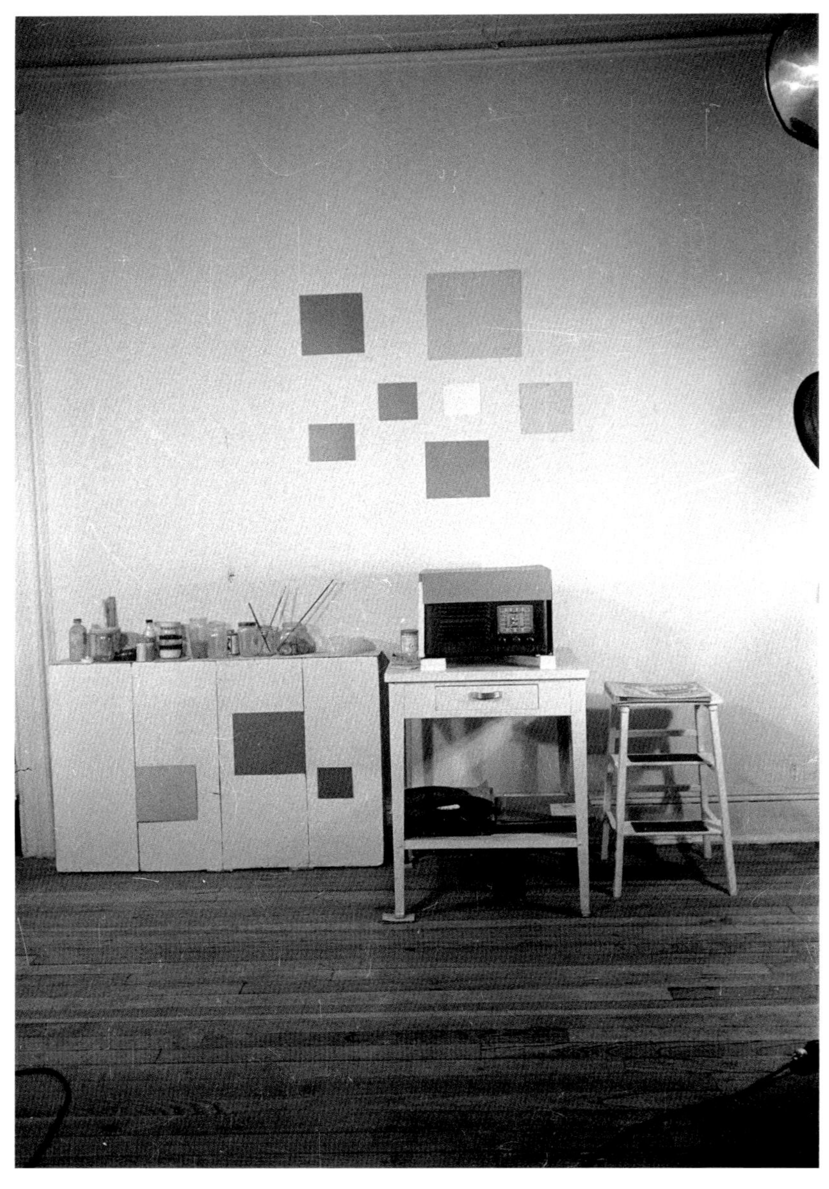

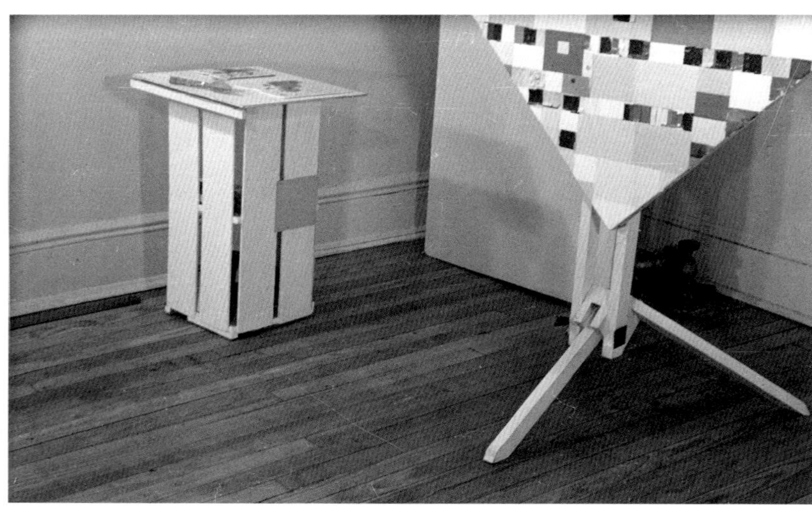

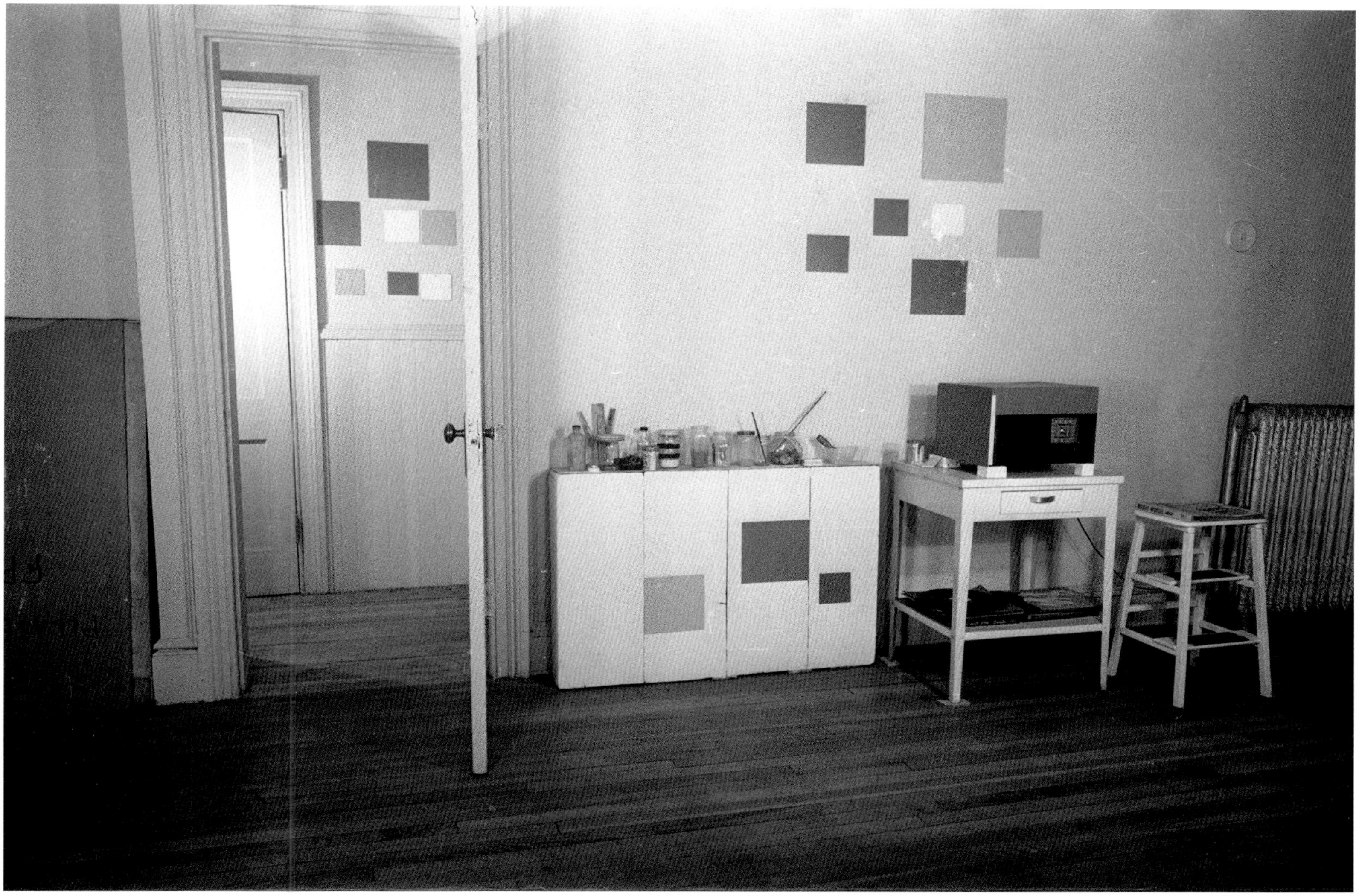

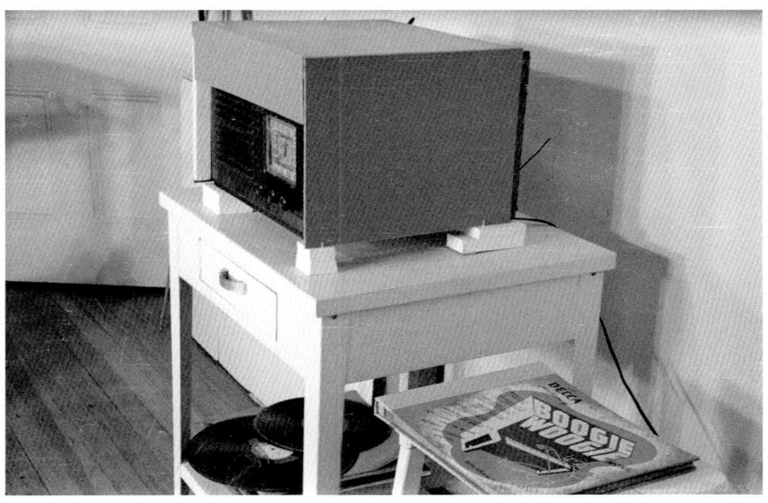

CAT. 359 **Fritz Glarner**
West wall of Mondrian's studio after his death, with furniture and gramophone, between 2 February and 21 March 1944

CAT. 352 **Fritz Glarner**
Palette table with palettes and palette knife next to *Victory Boogie Woogie* (B324) in Mondrian's studio after his death, between 2 February and 21 March 1944

CAT. 354 **Fritz Glarner**
Part of the west wall and furniture in Mondrian's studio after his death, with a view through to the landing, between 2 February and 21 March 1944

CAT. 364 **Fritz Glarner**
Mondrian's gramophone after his death, between 2 February and 21 March 1944

CATS 349–51, 353, 355–63 See catalogue

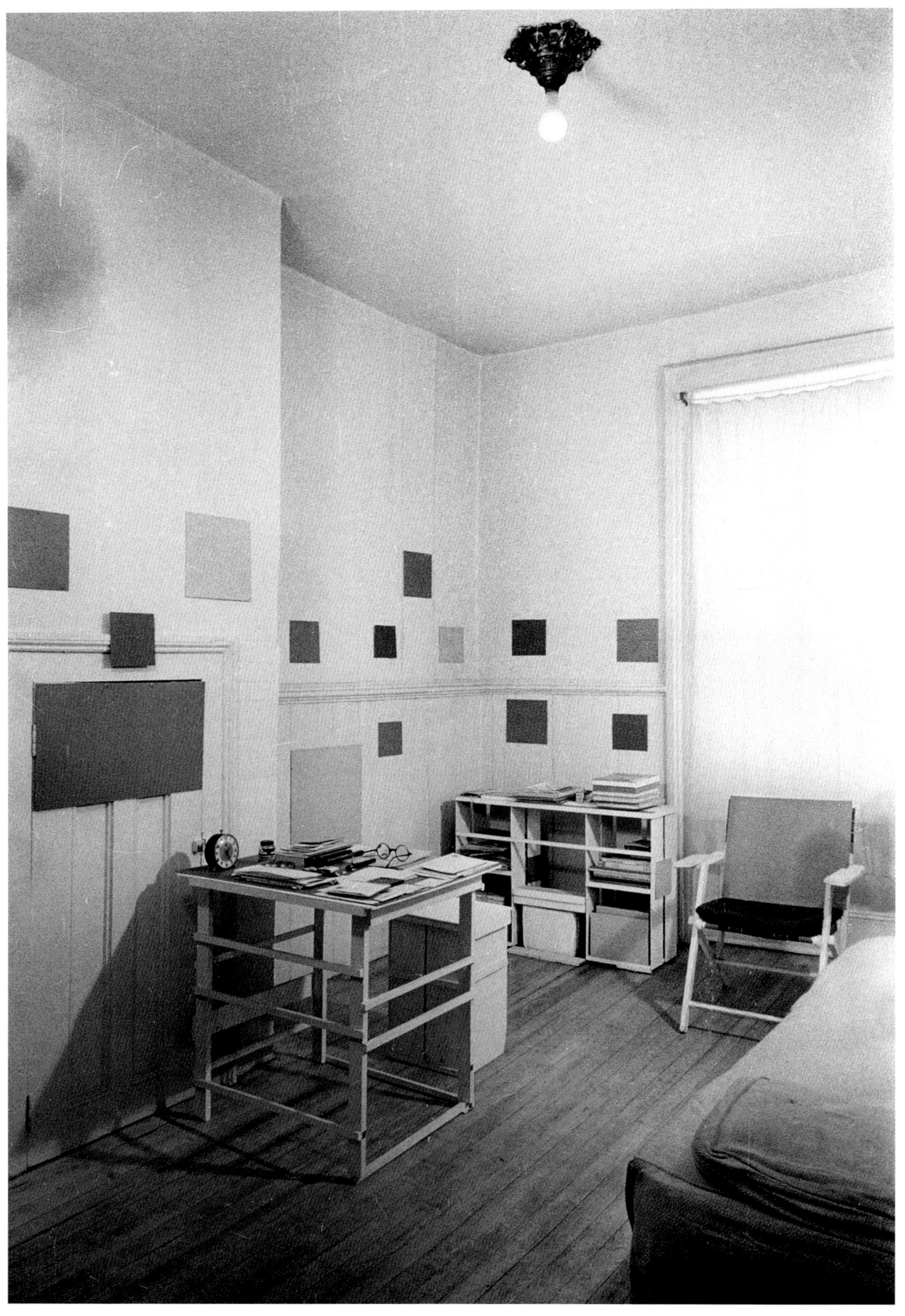

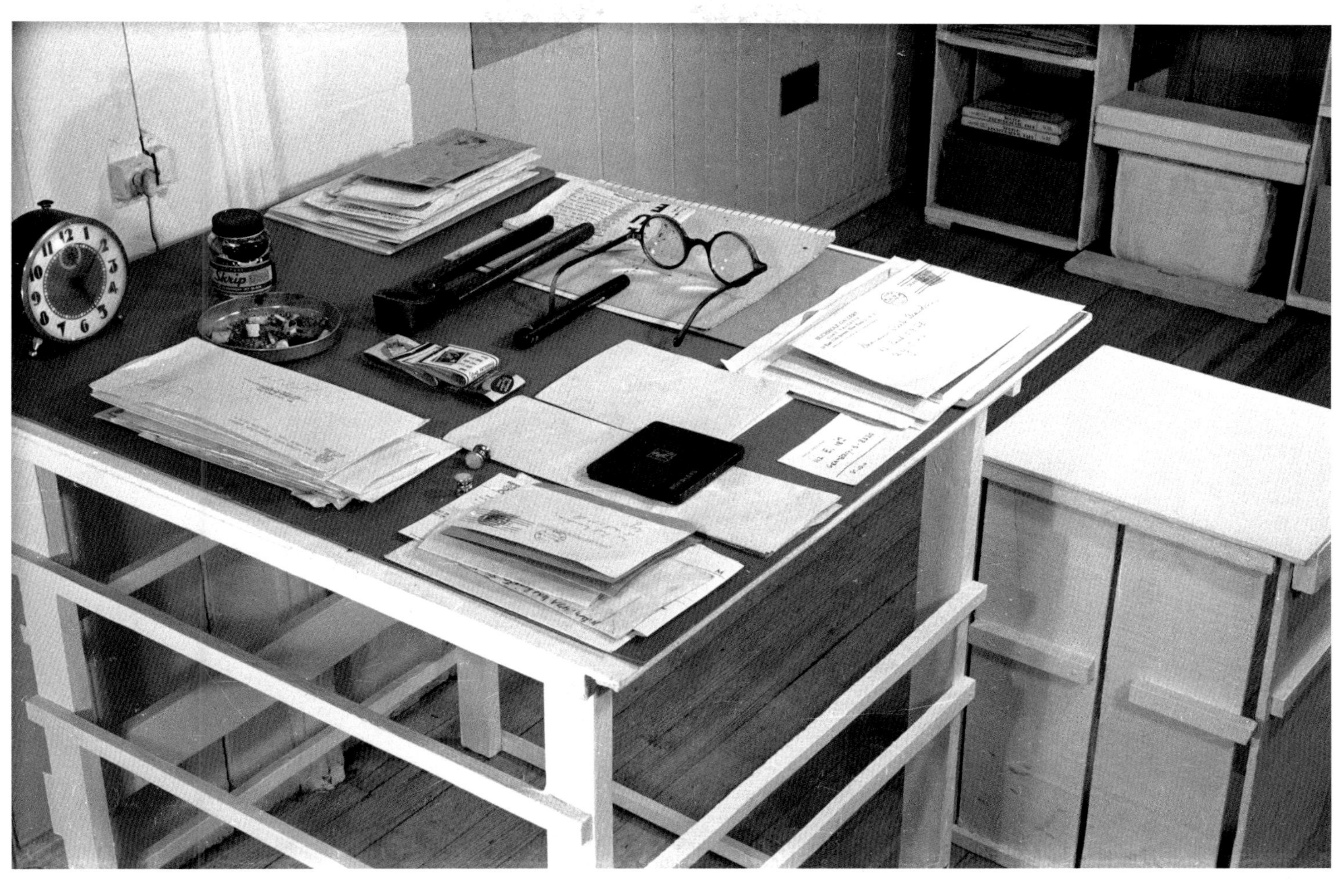

CAT. 366 **Fritz Glarner**
Mondrian's living quarters after his death, between 2 February and 21 March 1944

CAT. 369 **Fritz Glarner**
Writing table in Mondrian's living quarters after his death, between 2 February and 21 March 1944

CATS 365, 367–68 See catalogue

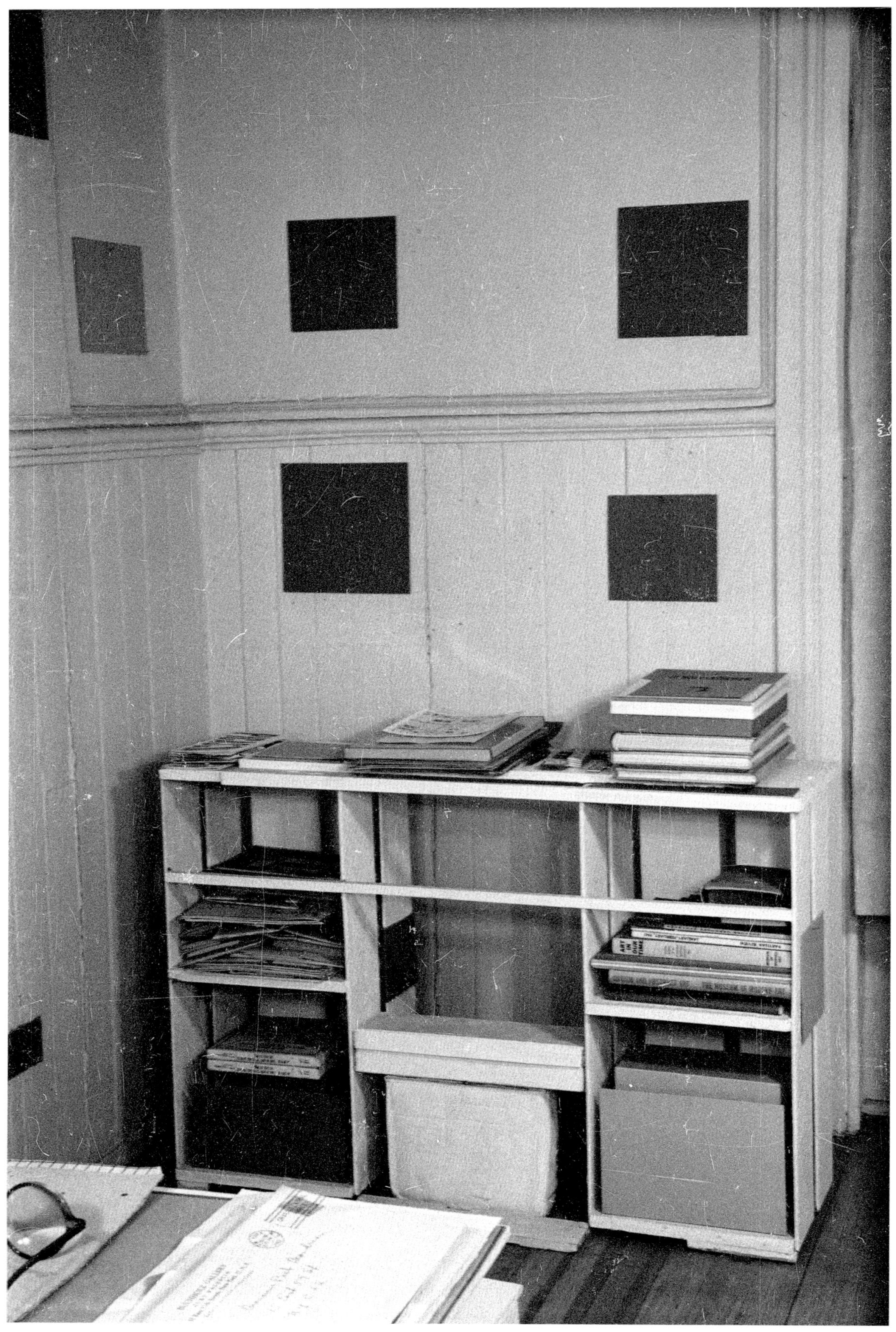

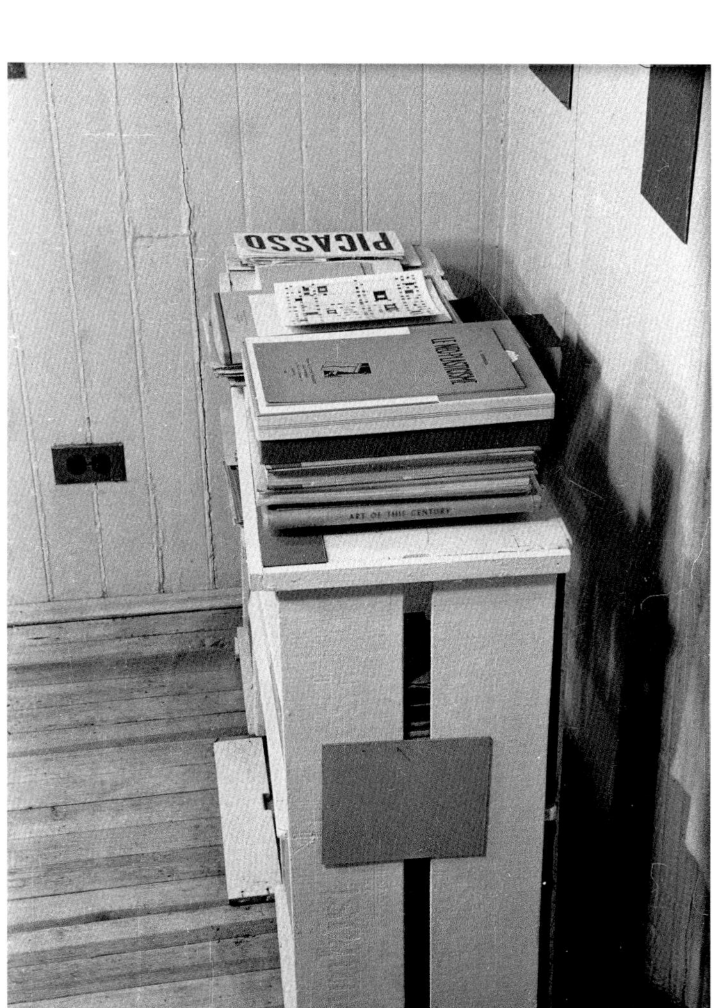

CATS 371, 373 **Fritz Glarner**
Bookcase in Mondrian's living quarters after his death, between 2 February and 21 March 1944

CATS 370, 372 See catalogue

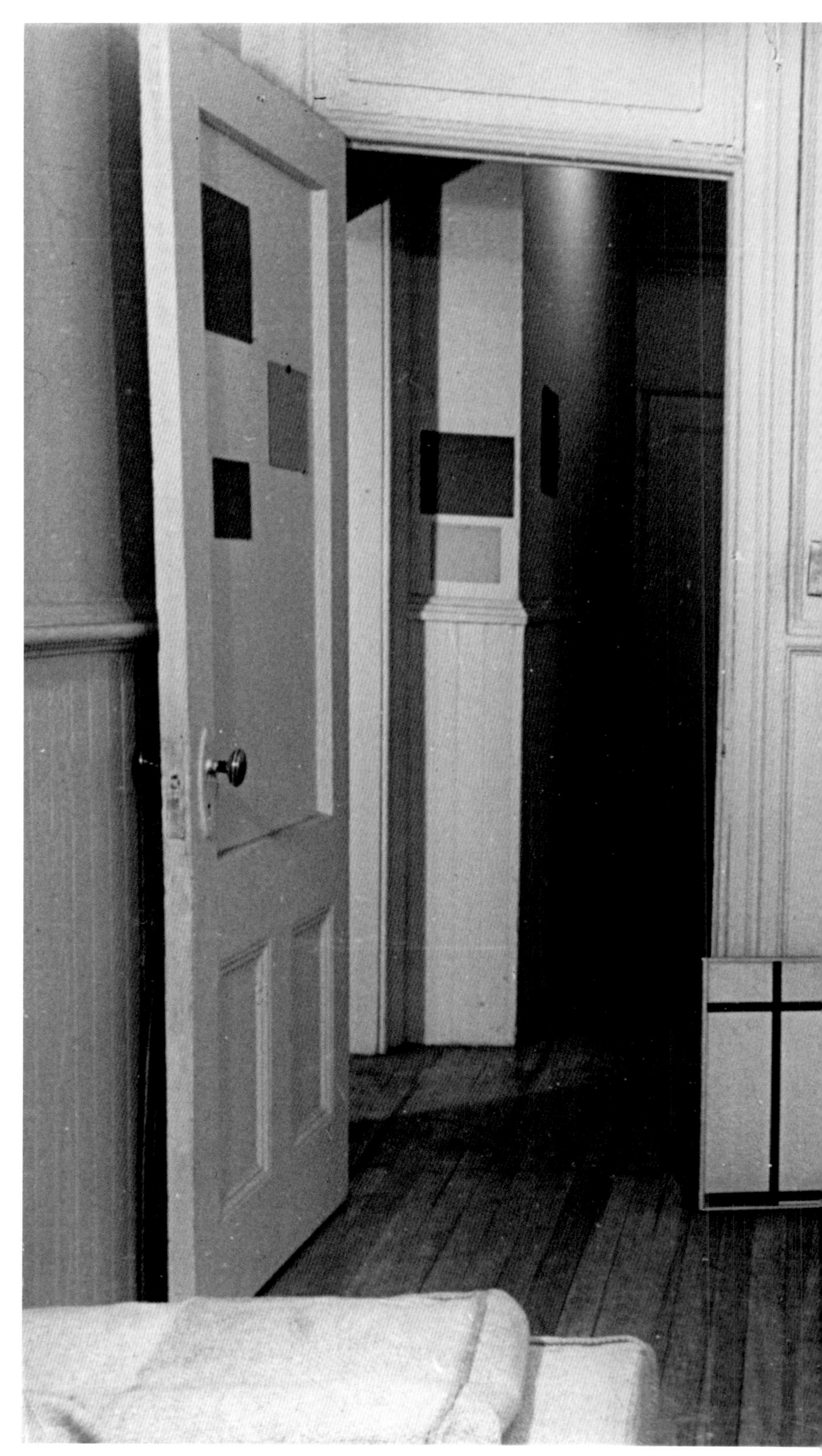

CAT. 374 **Fritz Glarner**
Mondrian's living quarters after his death, between 2 February and 21 March 1944

CAT. 375 See catalogue

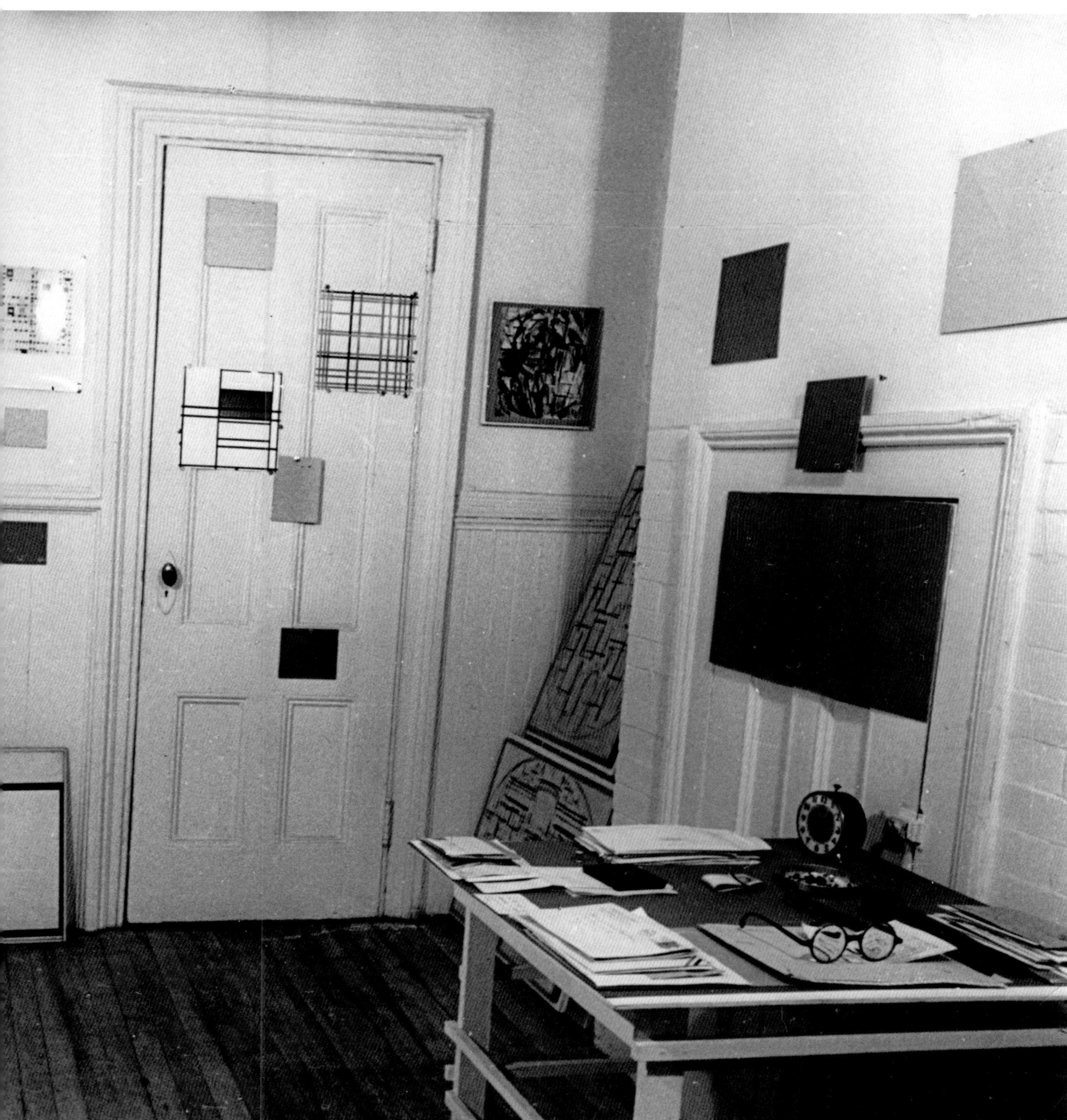

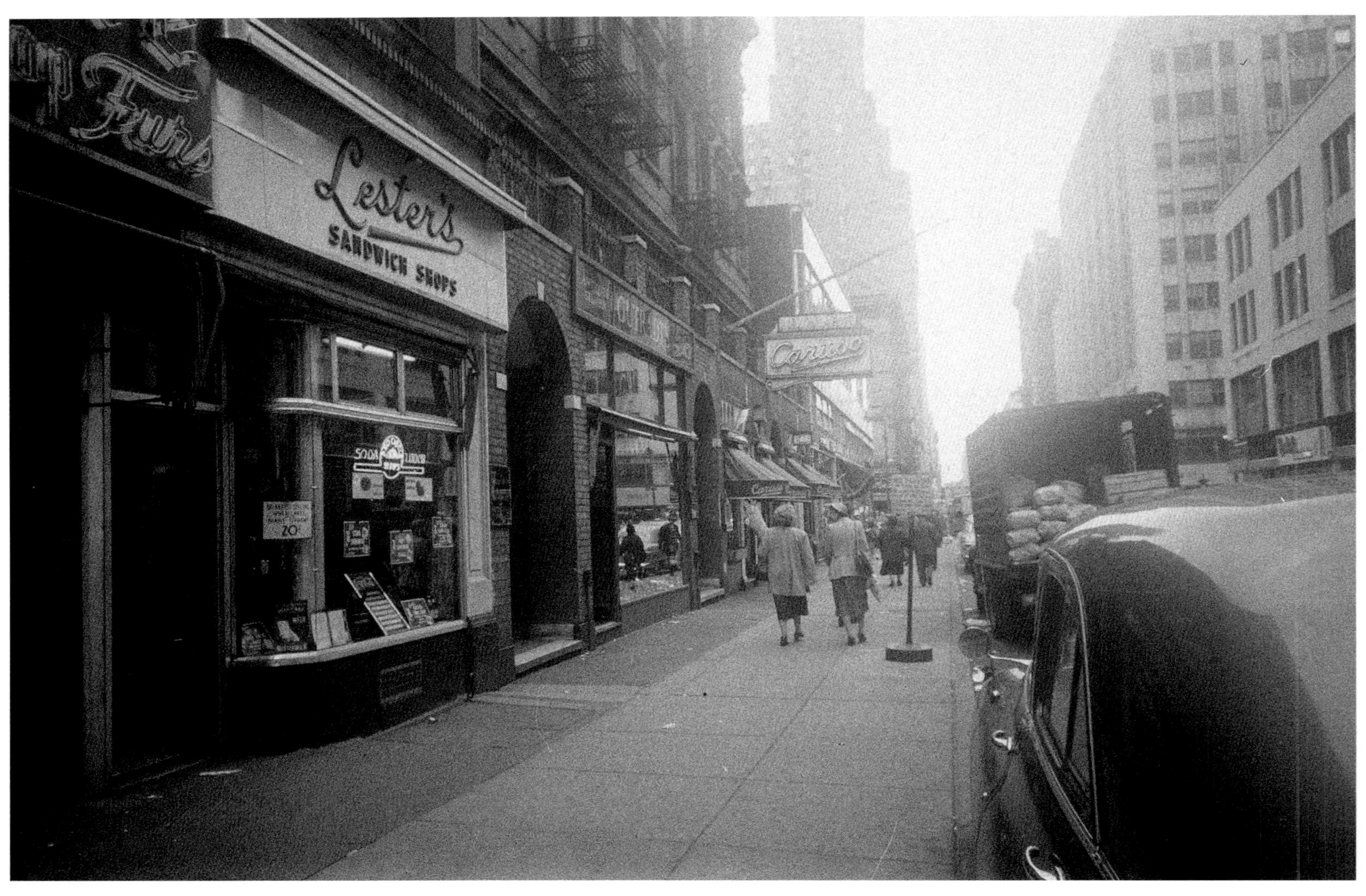
Furs
Lester's
SANDWICH SHOPS
SODA
20¢

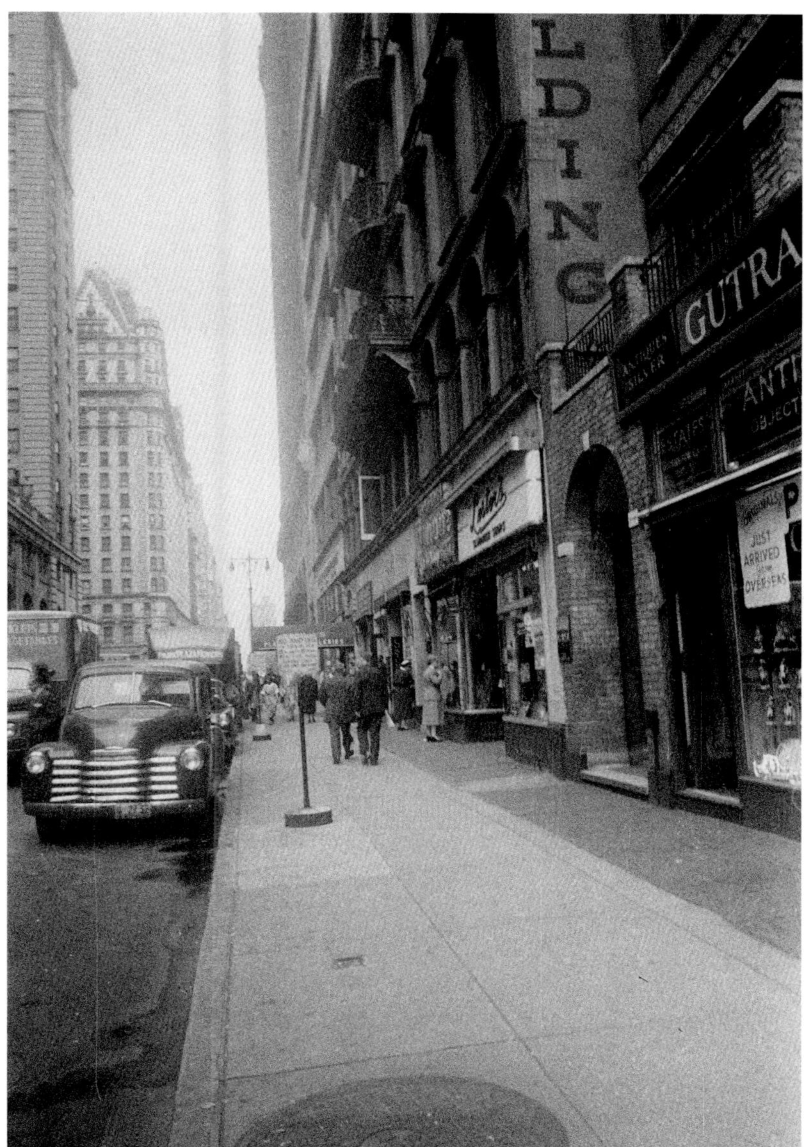

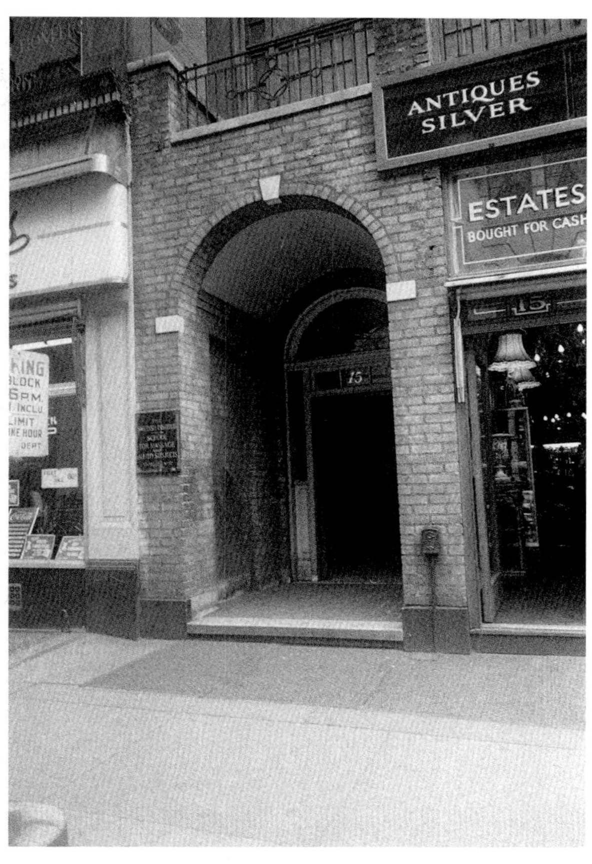

CATS 376, 381, 383 **Fritz Glarner**
View of East 59th Street; on the left, the archway leading to Mondrian's studio and apartment at no. 15, between 2 February and 21 March 1944

CATS 377–80, 382 See catalogue

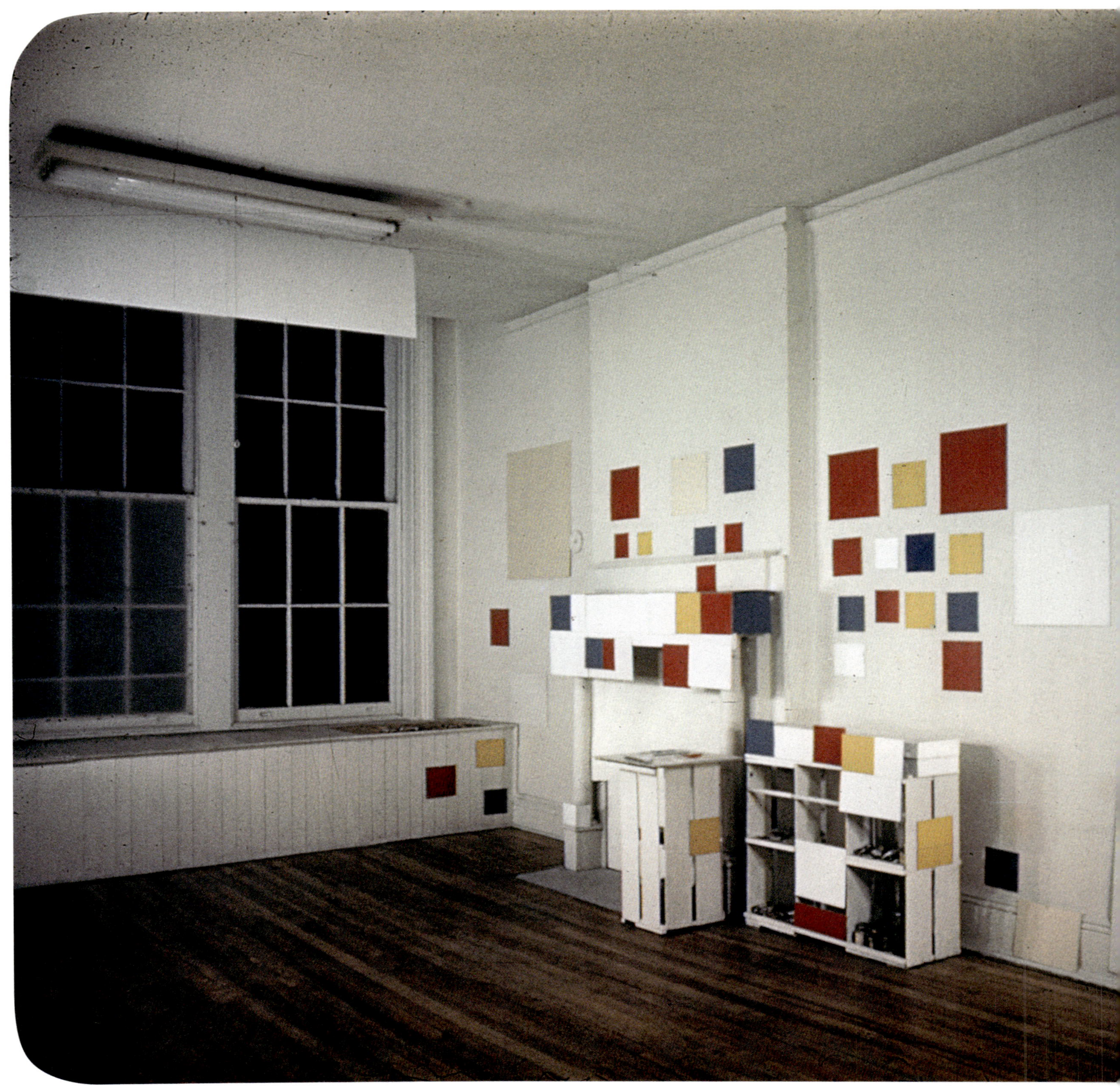

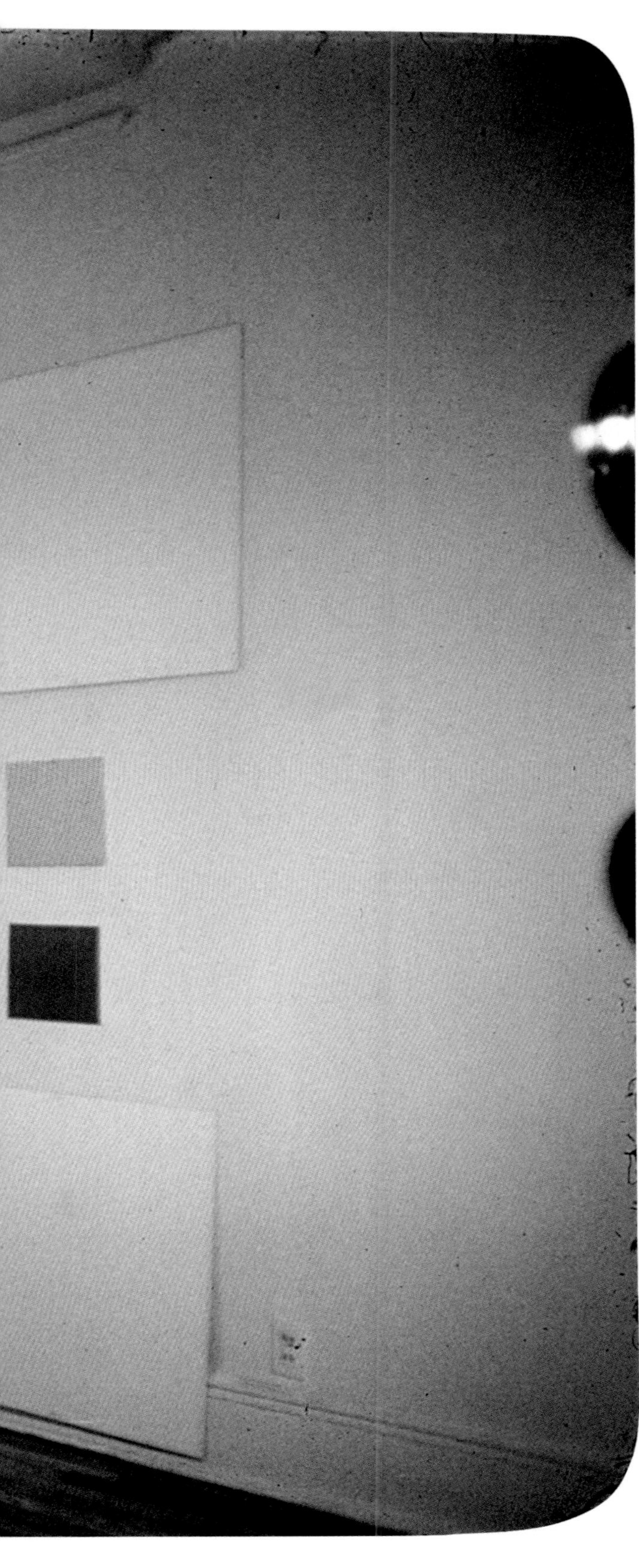

CAT. 384 **Harry Holtzman**
Mondrian's studio after his death, between 2 February and 21 March 1944

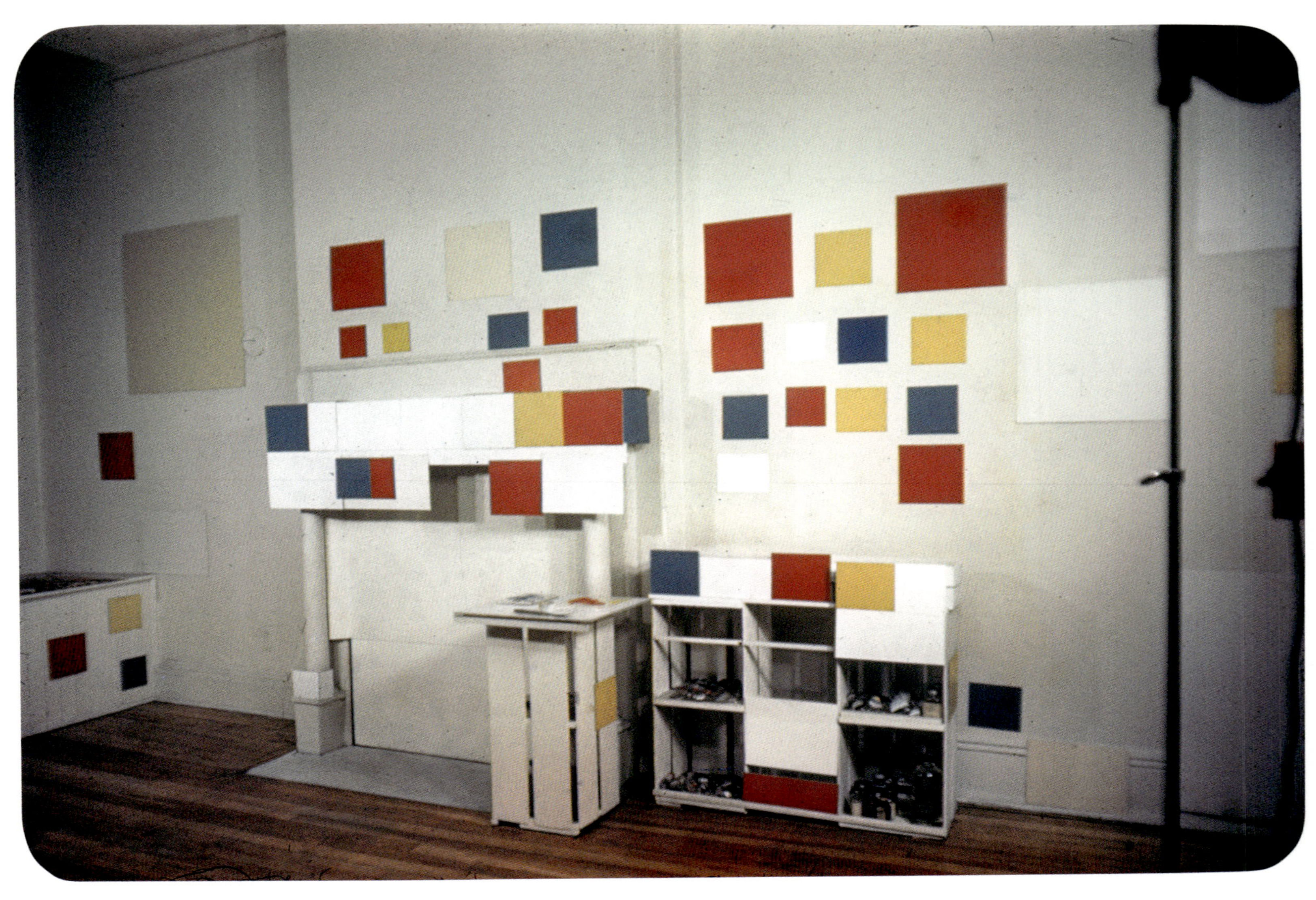

CAT. 385 **Harry Holtzman**

Mondrian's studio after his death, with his palette table and a shelf-unit with painting materials, between 2 February and 21 March 1944

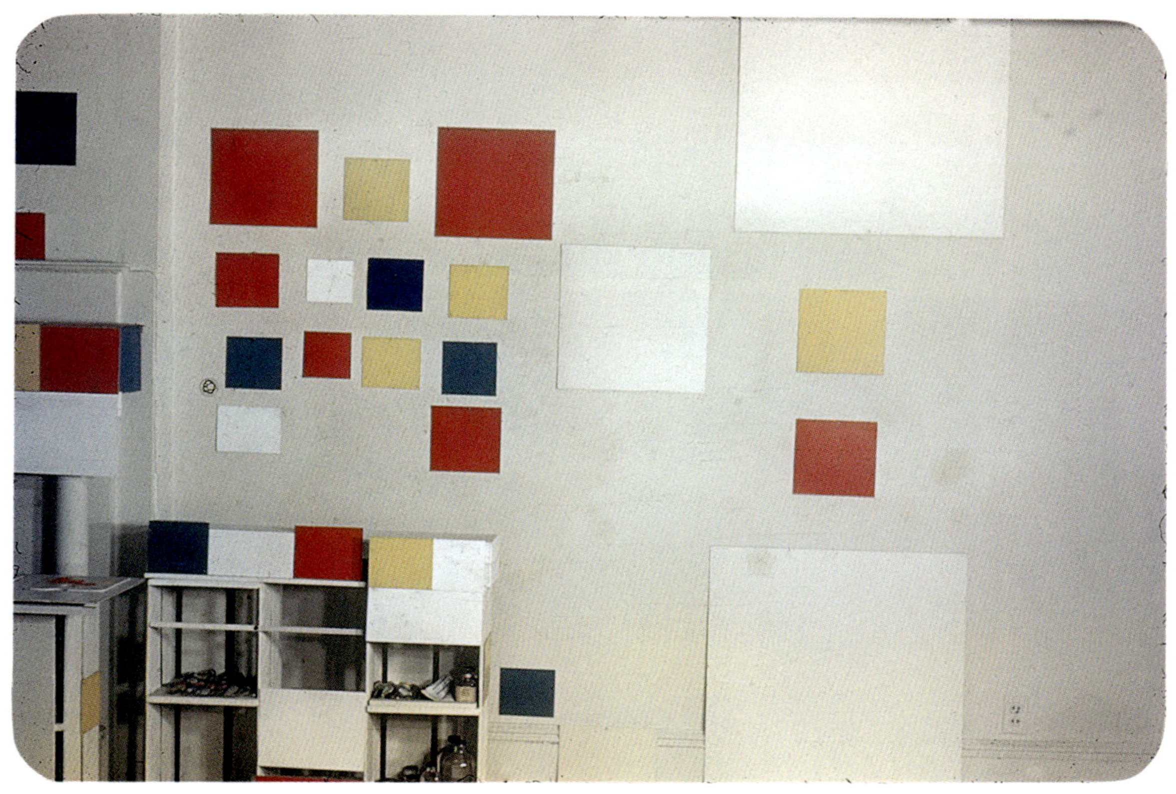

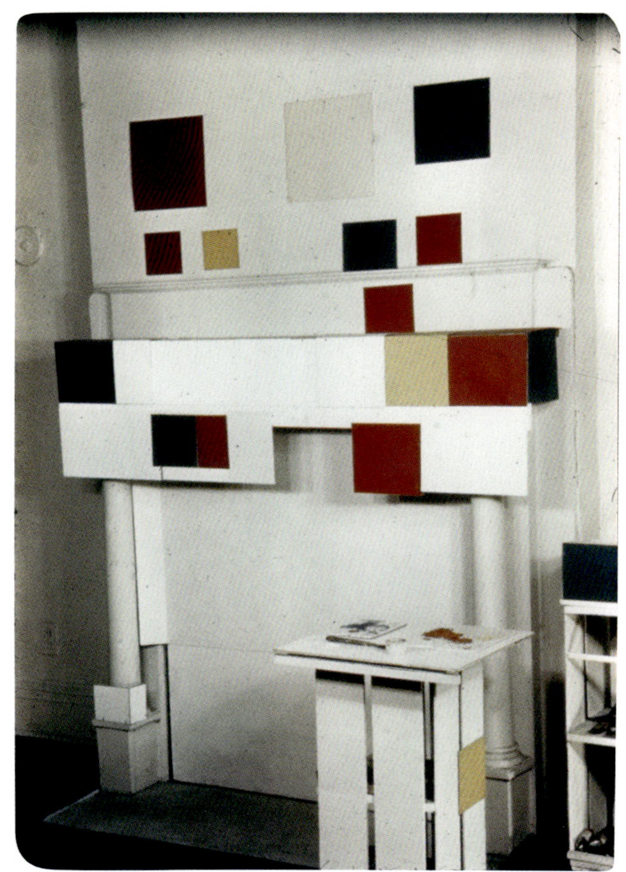

CAT. 386 **Harry Holtzman**
Mondrian's studio after his death, with his palette table in the foreground, between 2 February and 21 March 1944

CAT. 387 **Harry Holtzman**
Wall decoration and furniture in Mondrian's studio after his death, between 2 February and 21 March 1944

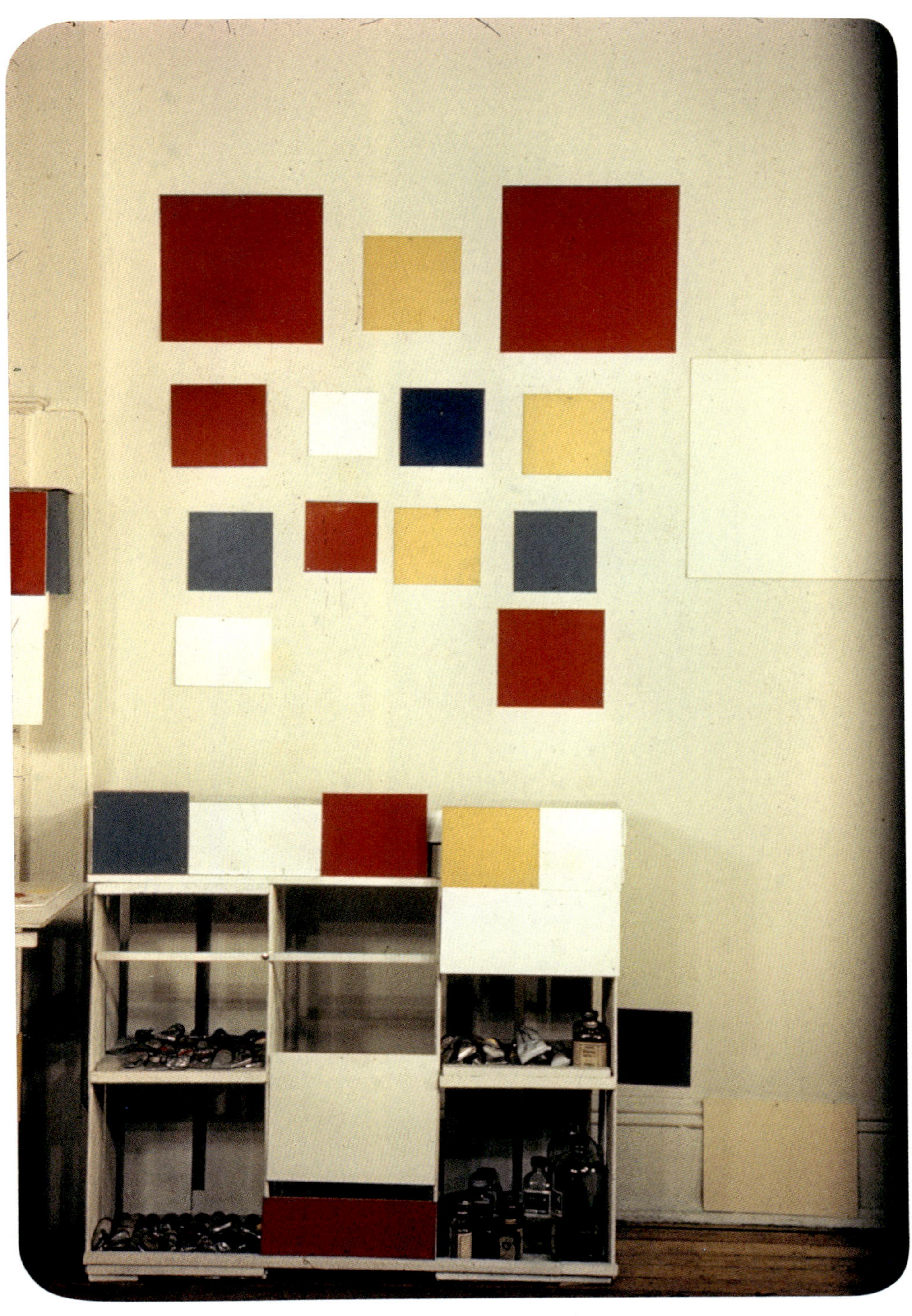

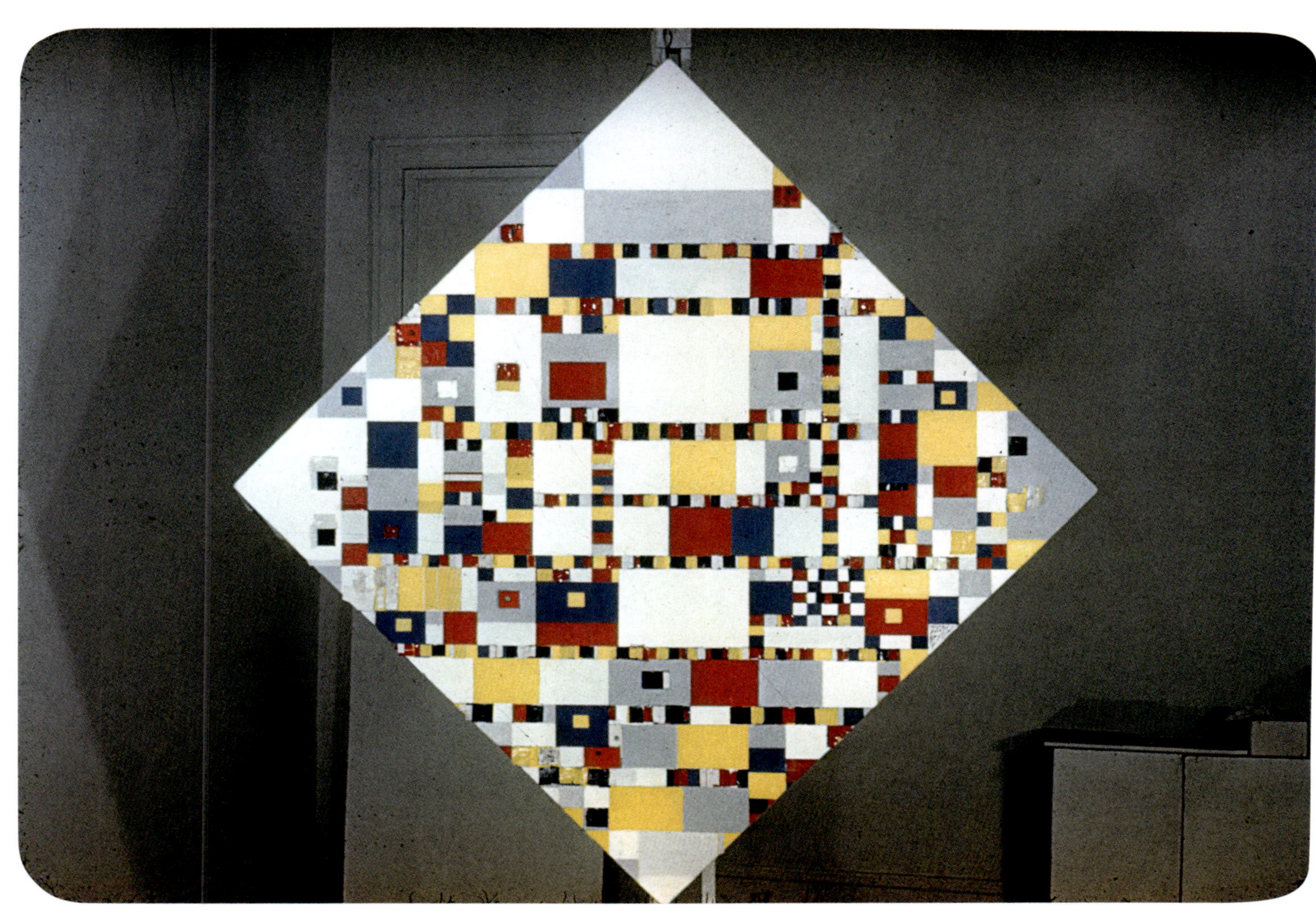

CAT. 388 **Harry Holtzman**
Wall decoration and shelf-unit with painting materials in Mondrian's studio after his death, between 2 February and 21 March 1944

CAT. 391 **Harry Holtzman**
***Victory Boogie Woogie* (B324) in Mondrian's studio after his death, between 2 February and 21 March 1944**

CAT. 389 See catalogue

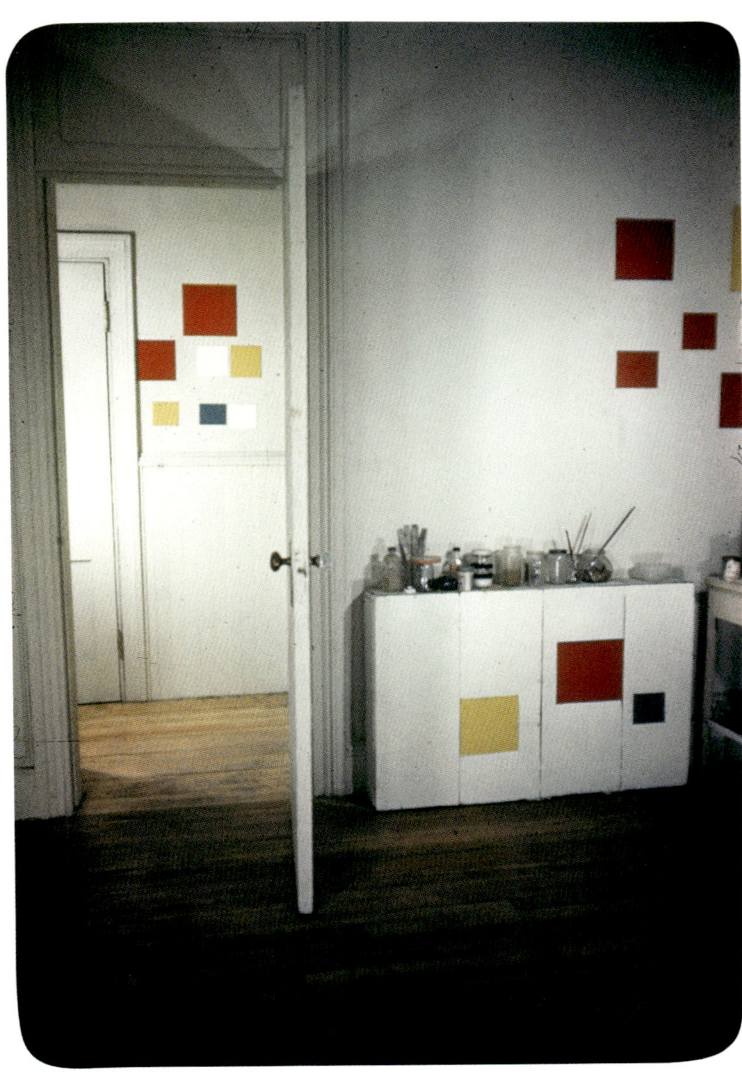

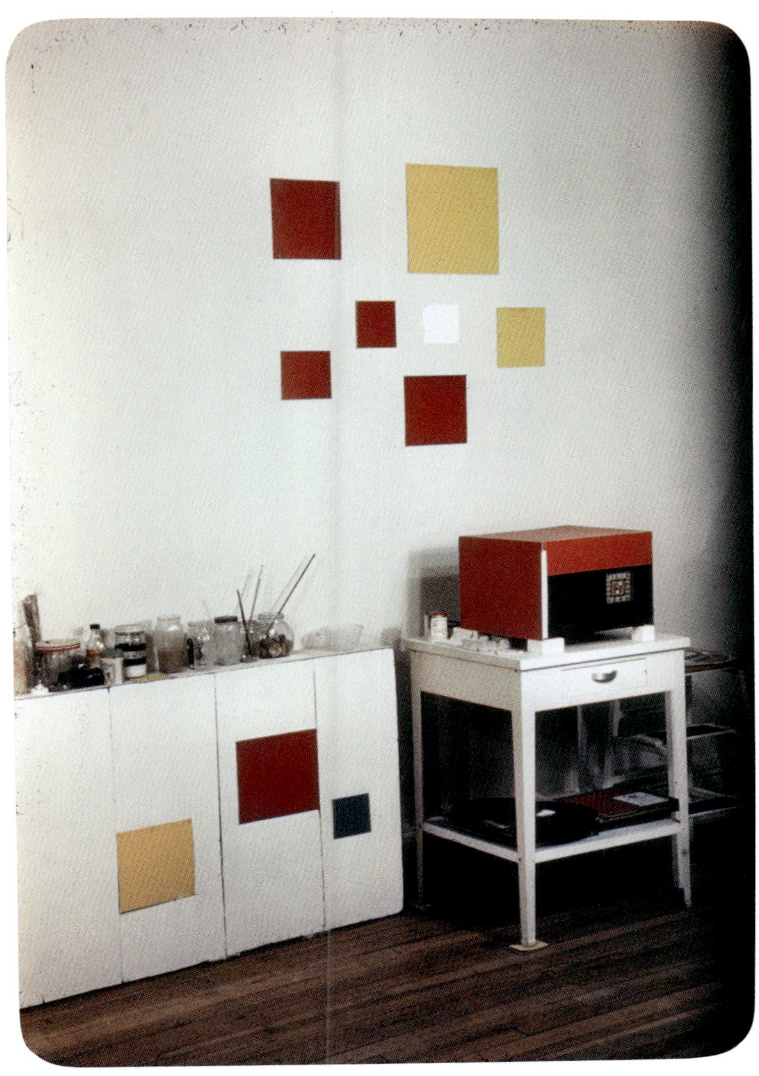

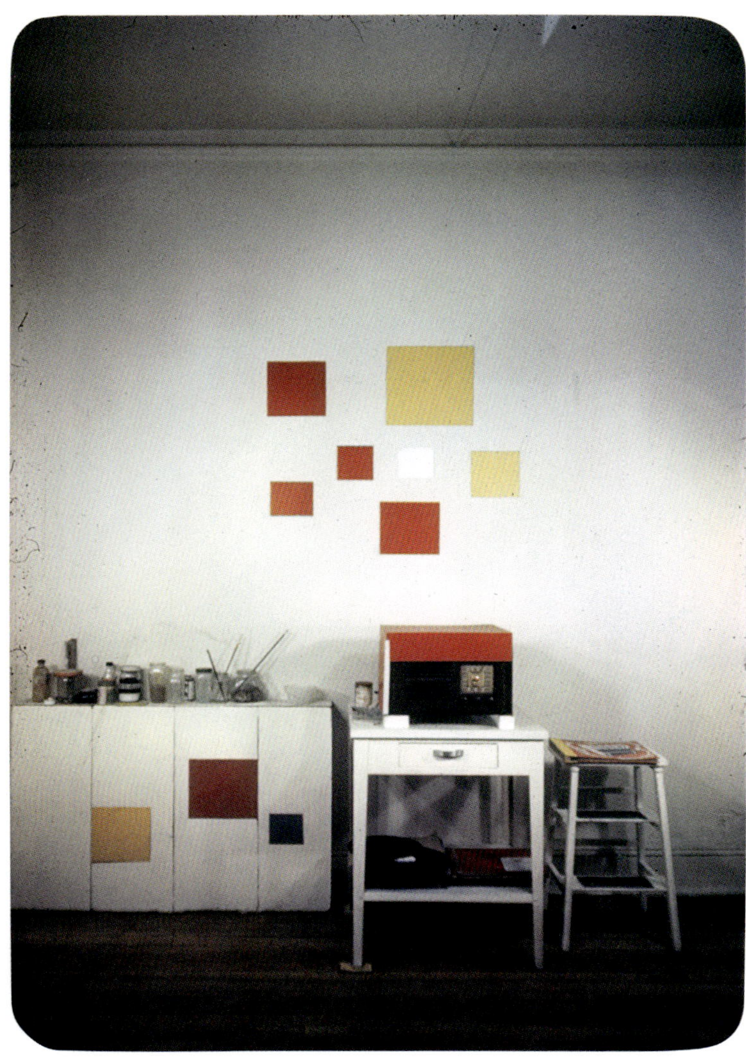

CATS 392–94 **Harry Holtzman**

Decoration of walls and furniture in Mondrian's studio after his death, between 2 February and 21 March 1944

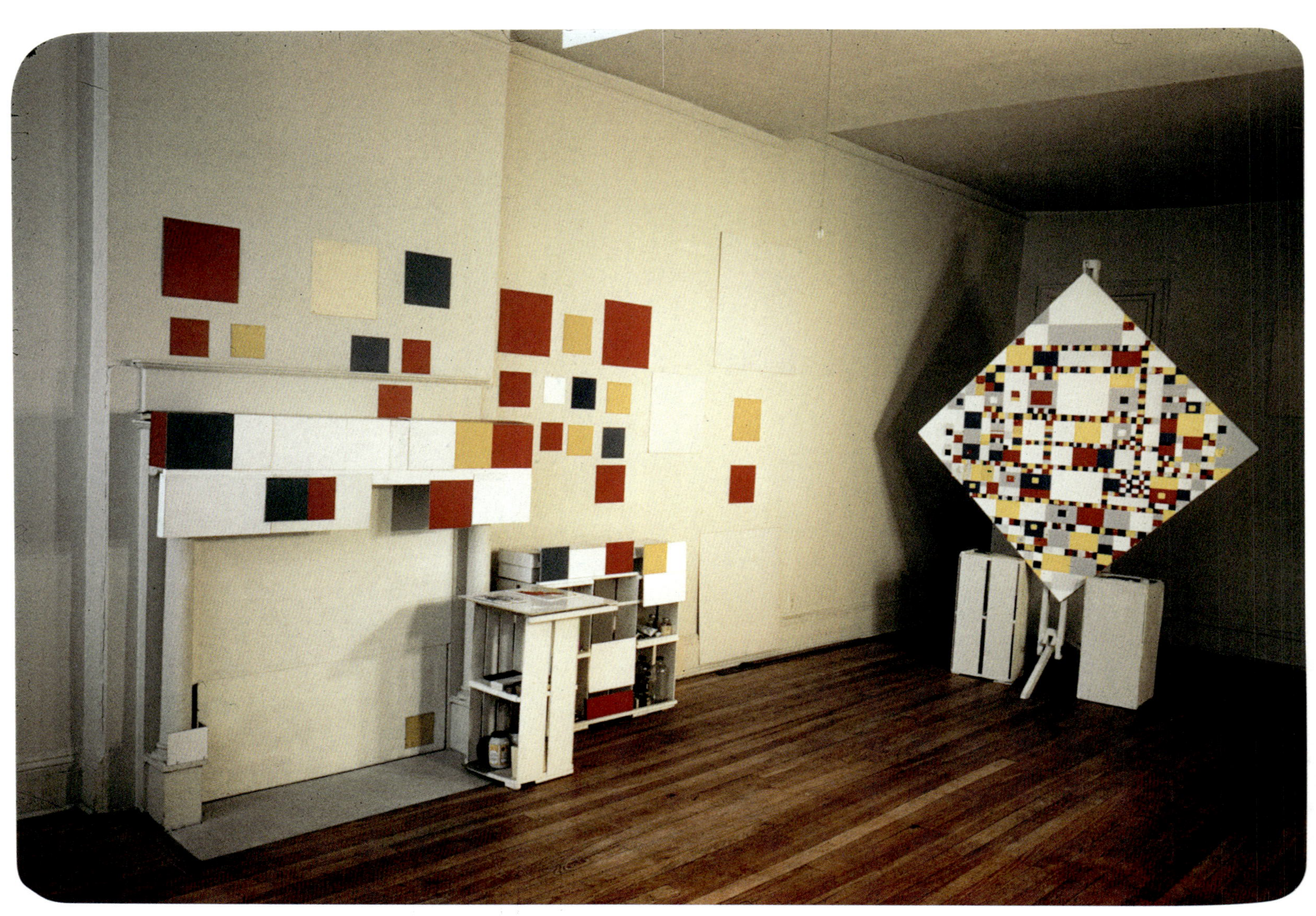

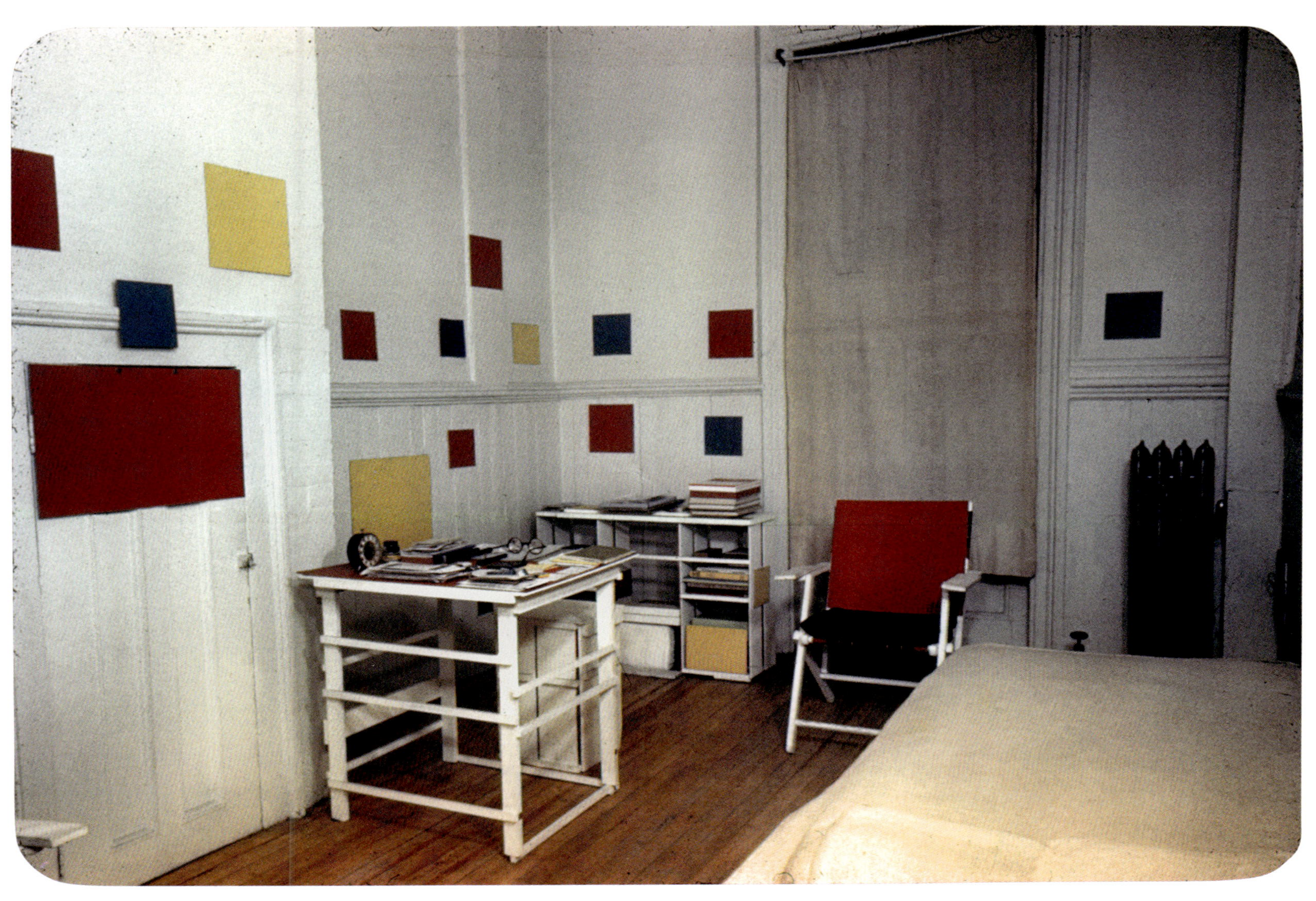

CAT. 390 **Harry Holtzman**
Mondrian's studio after his death, with *Victory Boogie Woogie* on the easel (B324), between 2 February and 21 March 1944

CAT. 395 **Harry Holtzman**
Mondrian's living quarters after his death, between 2 February and 21 March 1944

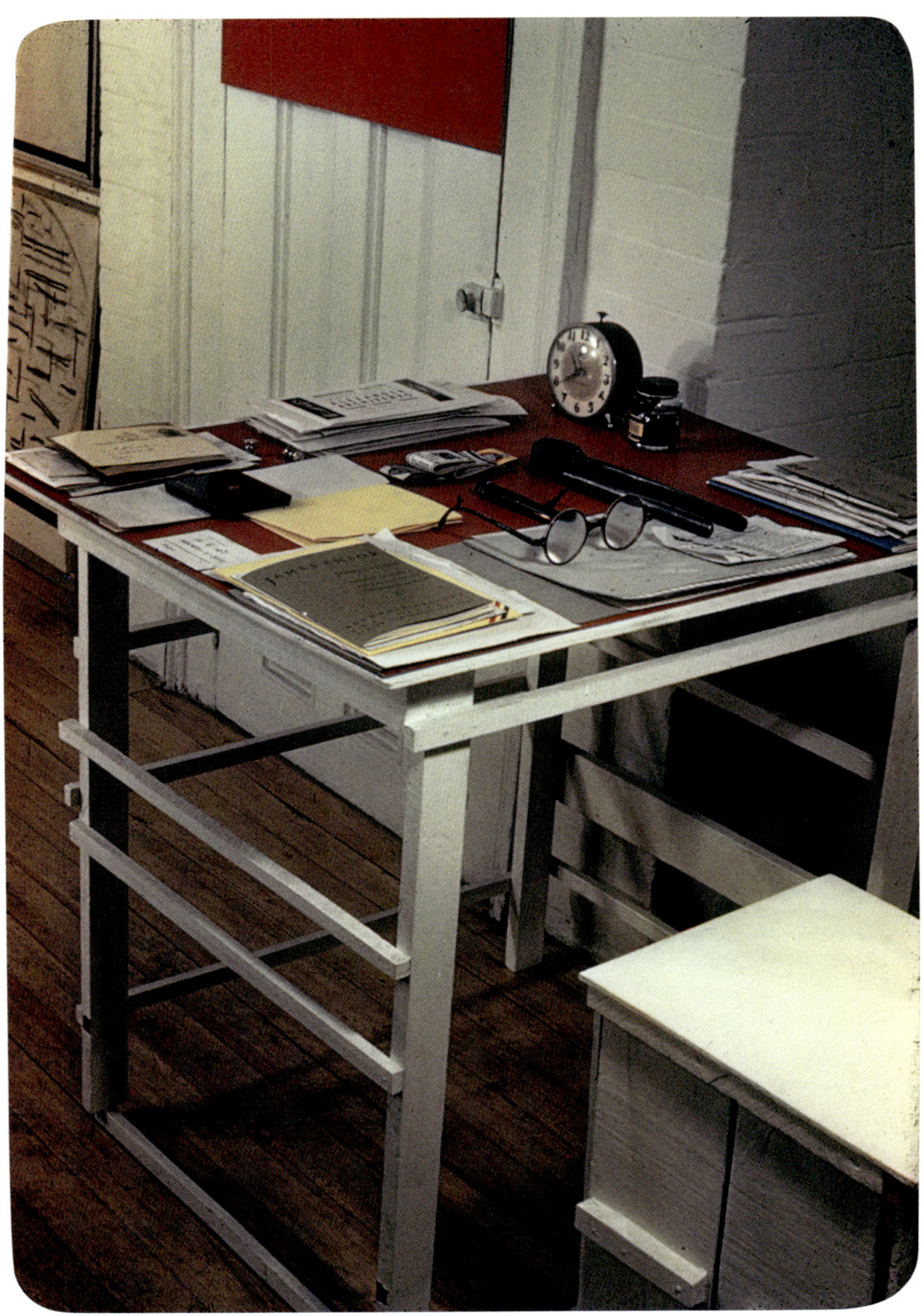

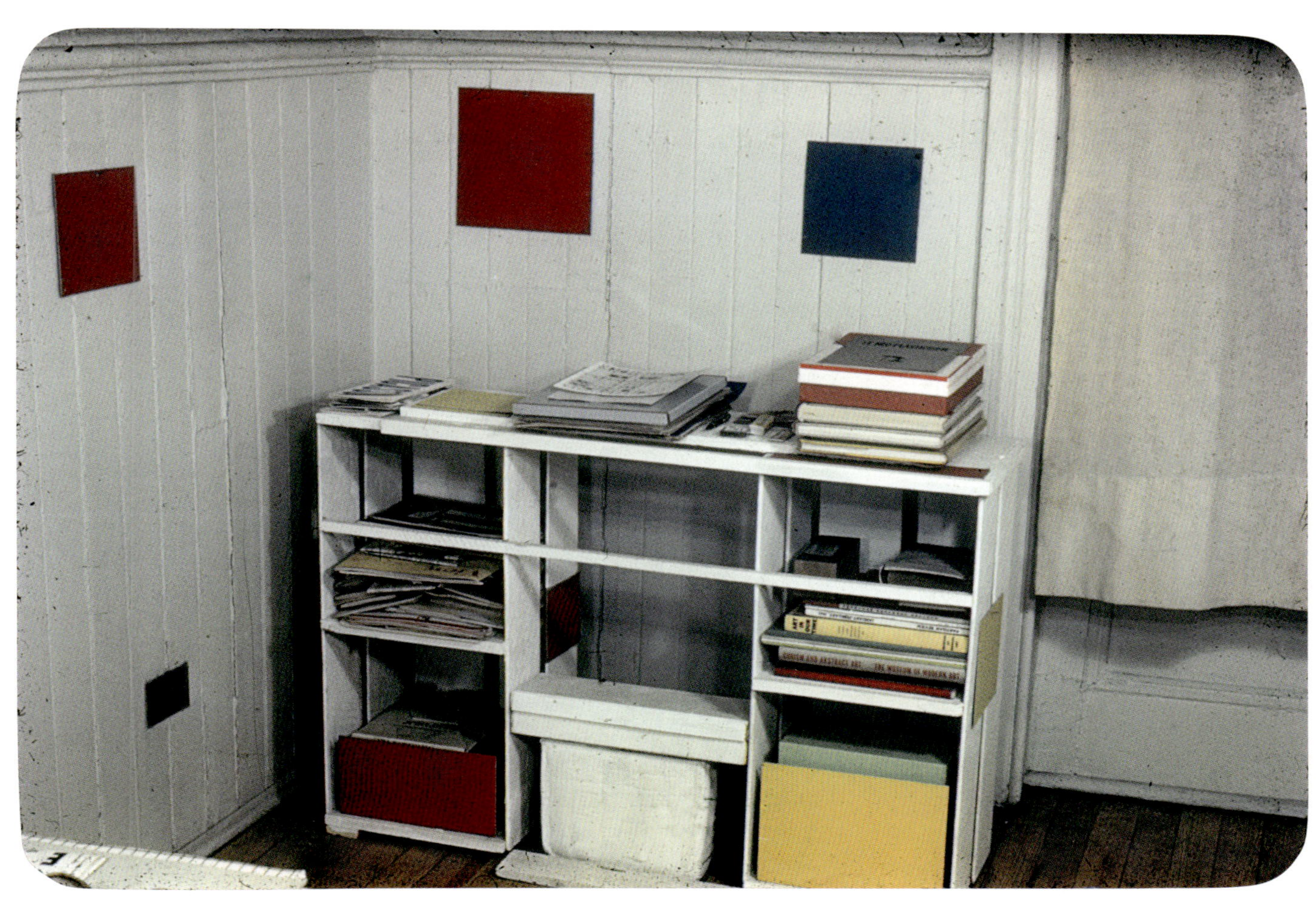

CAT. 398 **Harry Holtzman**
Writing table in Mondrian's living quarters after his death, between 2 February and 21 March 1944

CAT. 399 **Harry Holtzman**
Bookcase in Mondrian's living quarters after his death, between 2 February and 21 March 1944

CATS 396–97 See catalogue

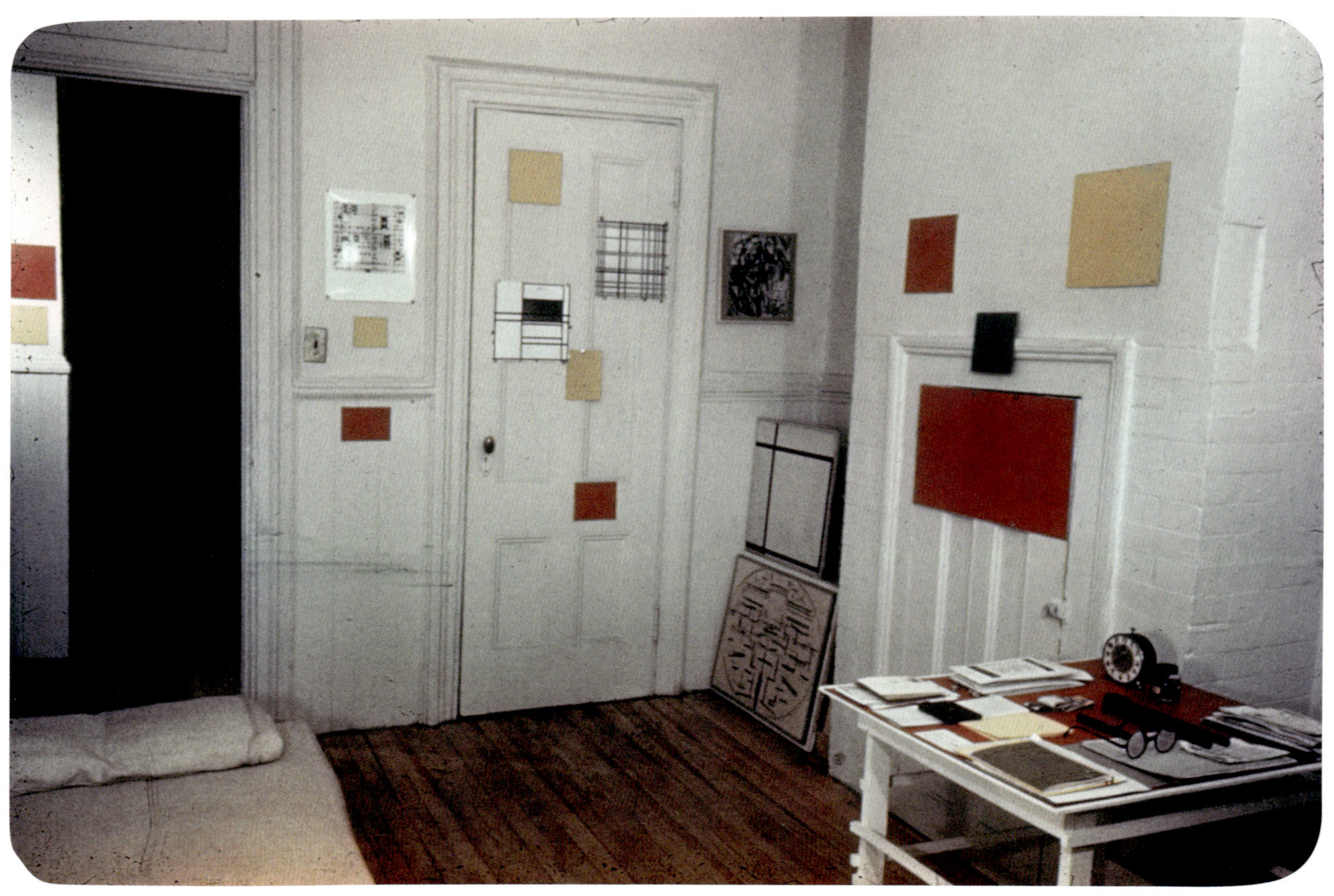

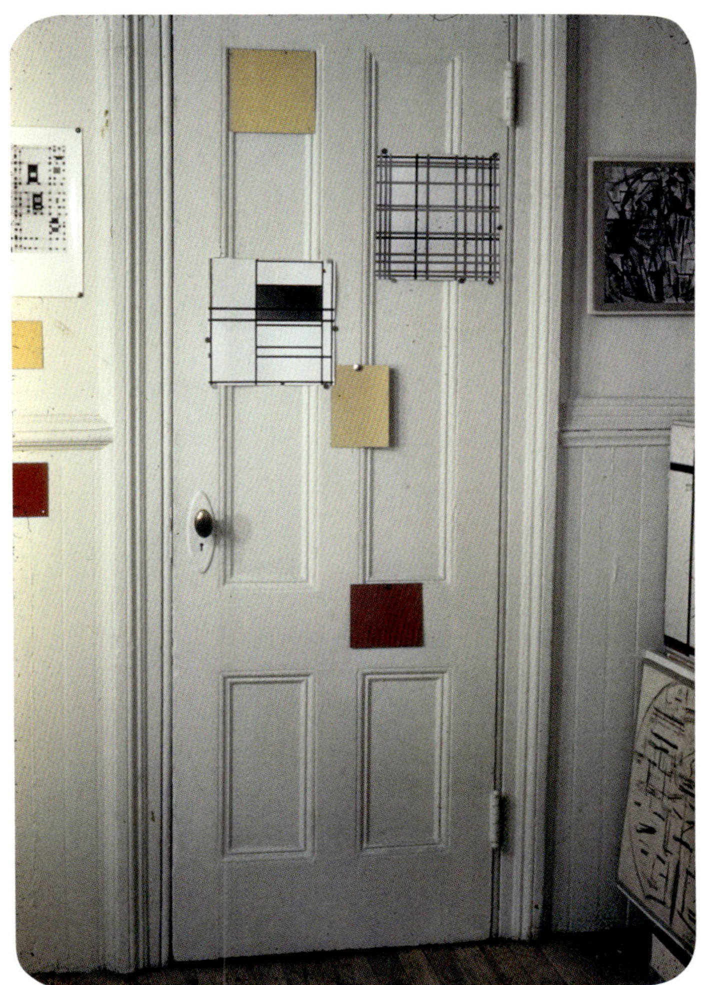

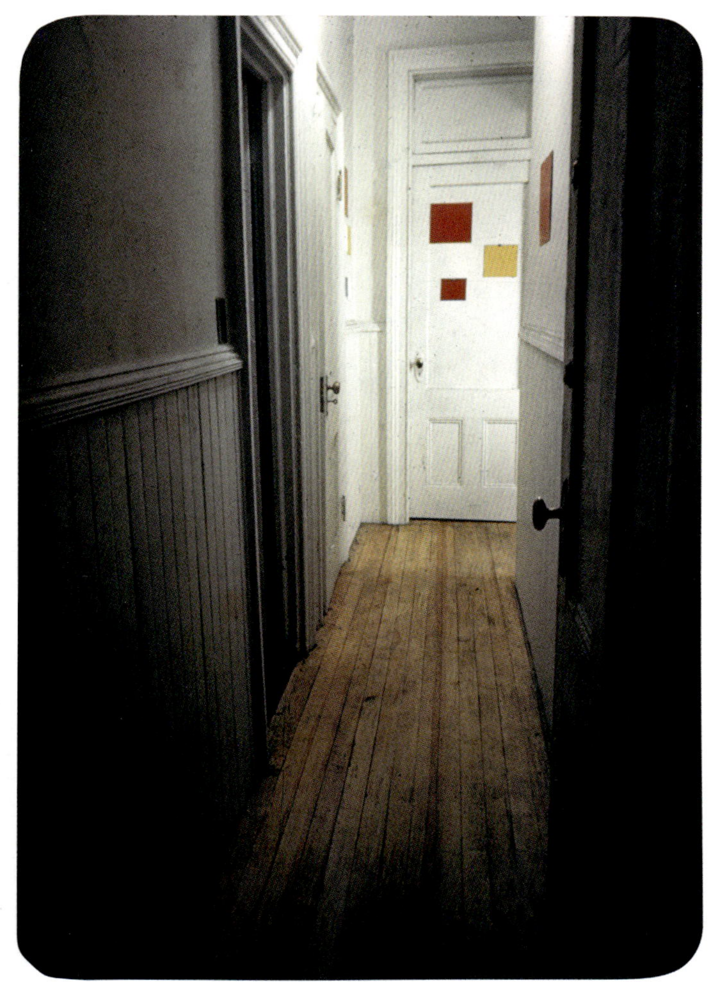

CAT. 400 **Harry Holtzman**
Mondrian's living quarters after his death, between 2 February and 21 March 1944

CAT. 402 **Harry Holtzman**
The door of Mondrian's living quarters after his death, between 2 February and 21 March 1944

CAT. 403 **Harry Holtzman**
The corridor of Mondrian's apartment after his death, between 2 February and 21 March 1944

CAT. 401 See catalogue

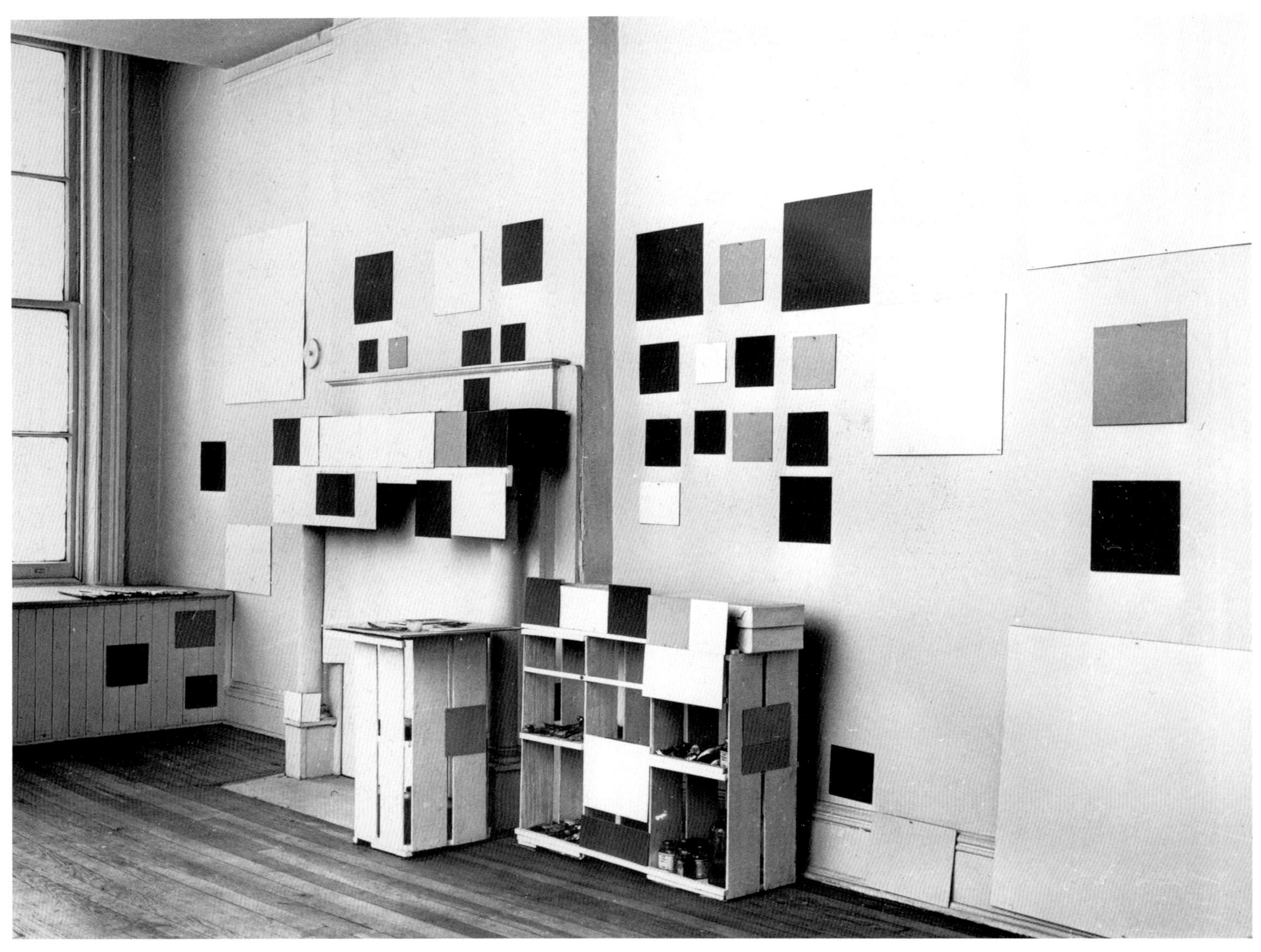

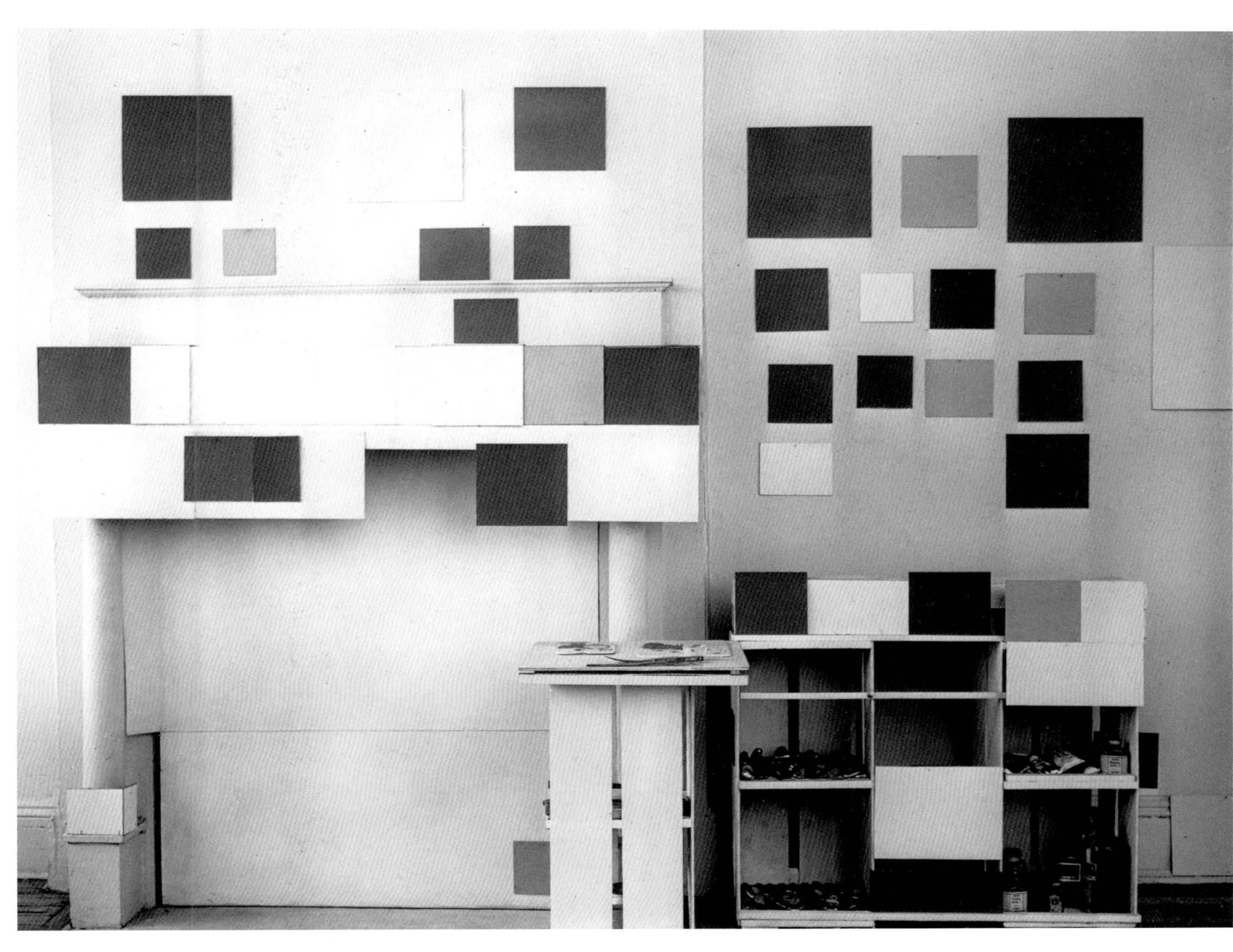

CATS 404–5 **Fernand Fonssagrives**
Mondrian's studio after his death, between 22 March and c. 3 May 1944

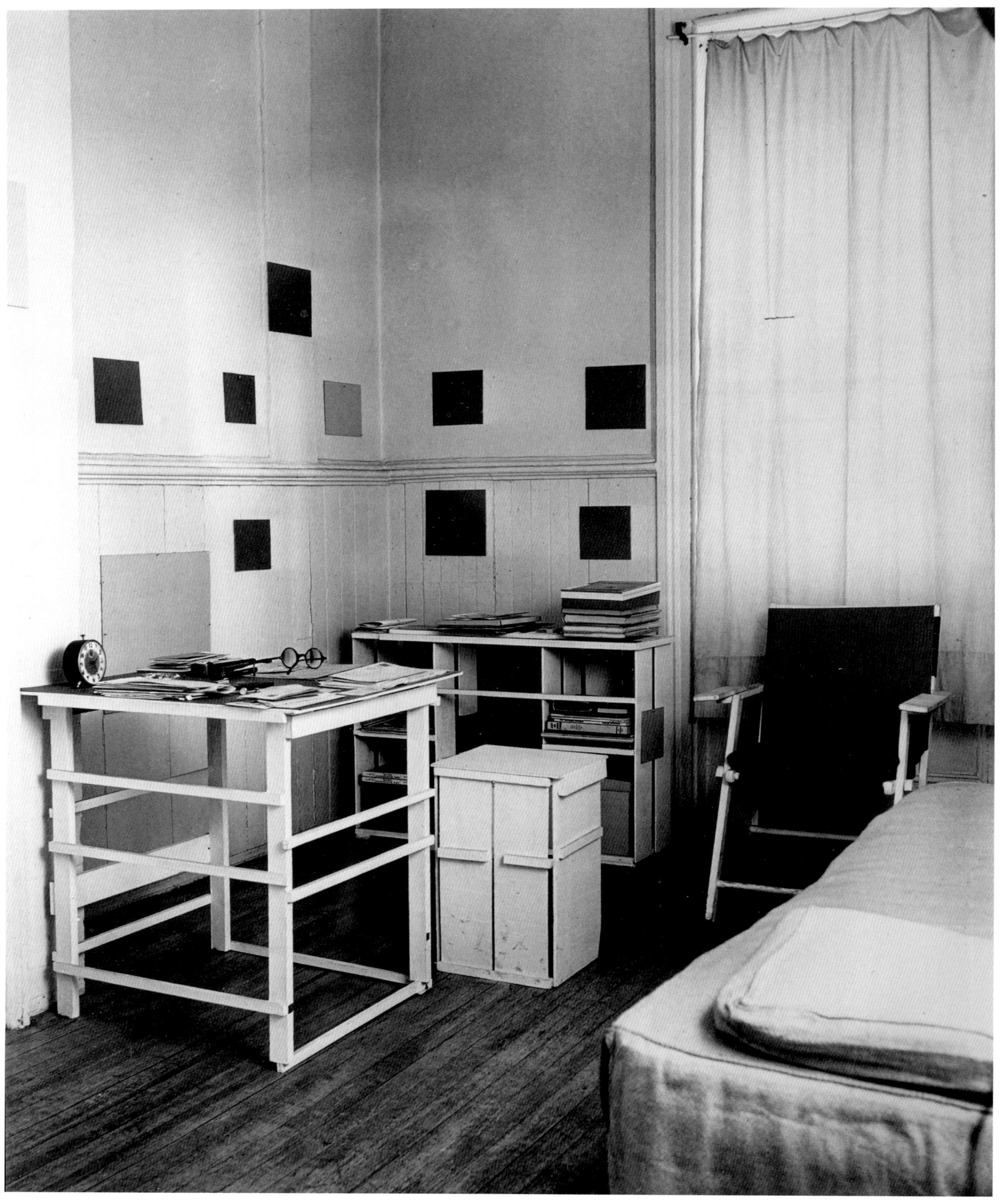

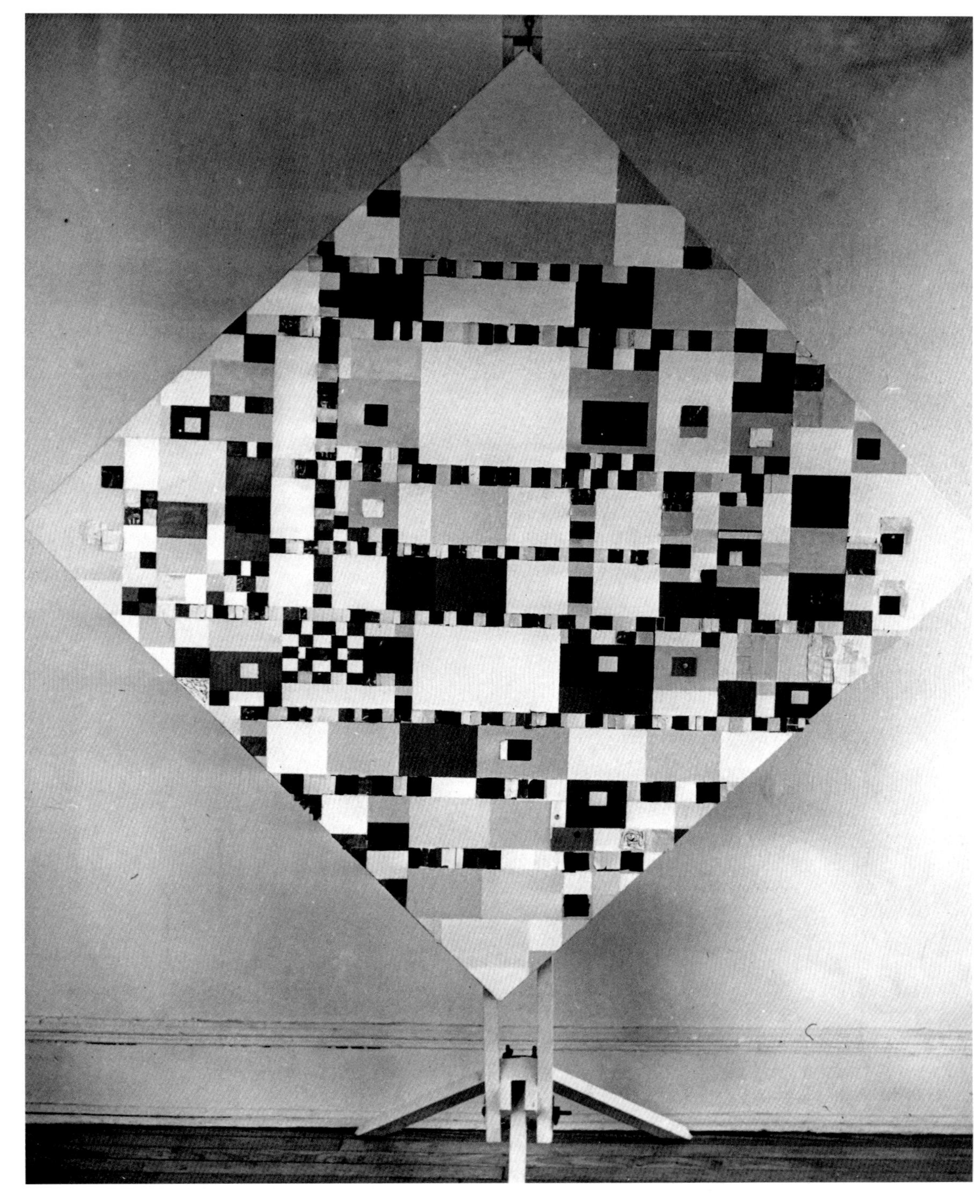

CAT. 406 **Fernand Fonssagrives**
Mondrian's living quarters after his death, between 22 March and c. 3 May 1944

CAT. 407 **Fernand Fonssagrives**
***Victory Boogie Woogie* (B324) in Mondrian's studio after his death, between 22 March and c. 3 May 1944**

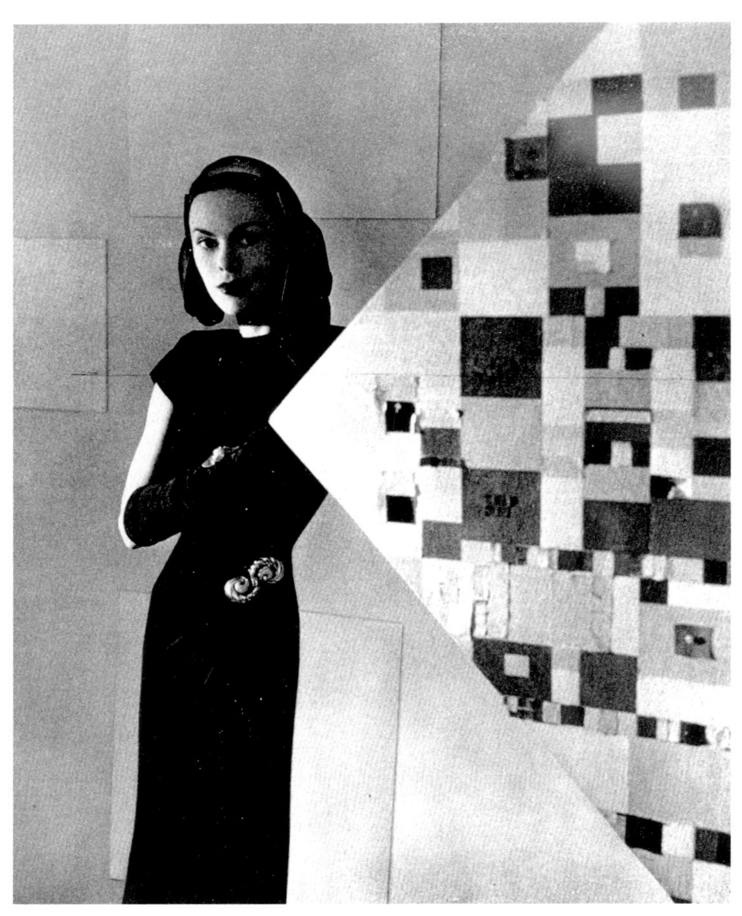

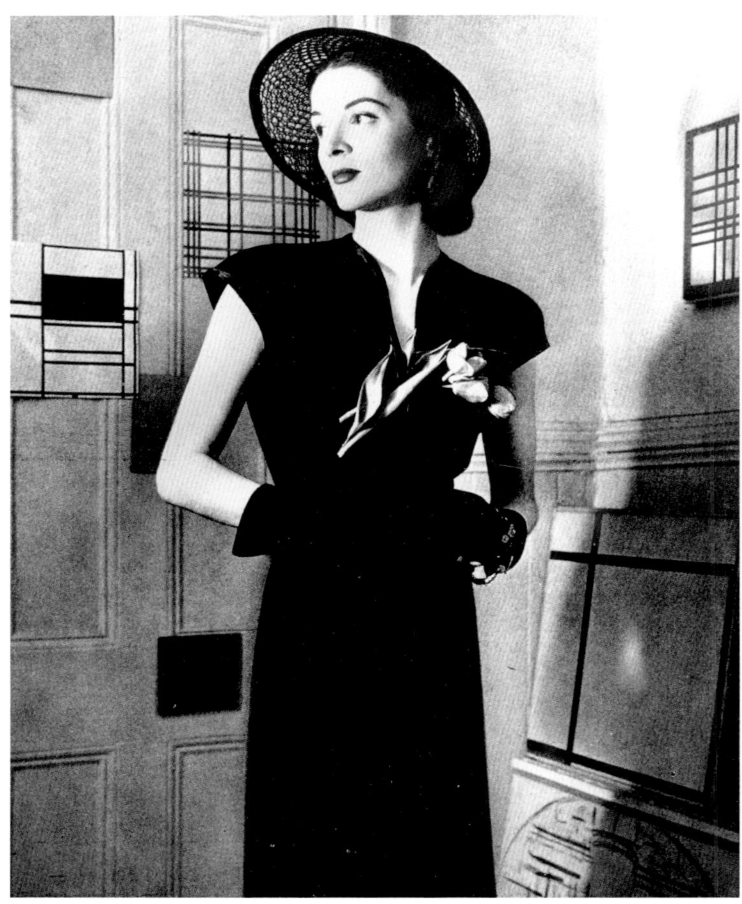

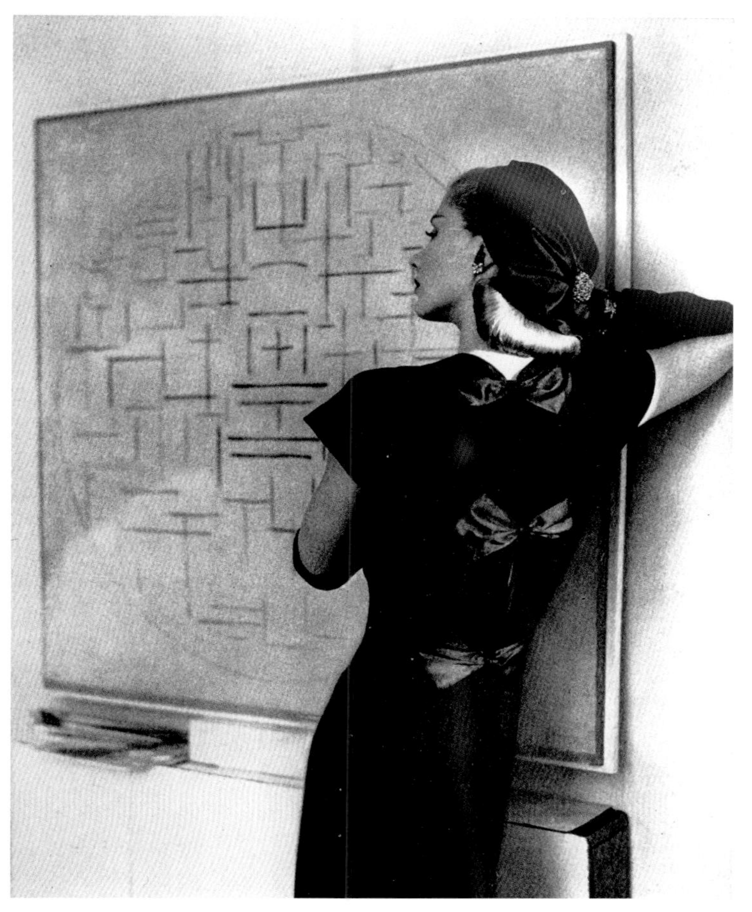

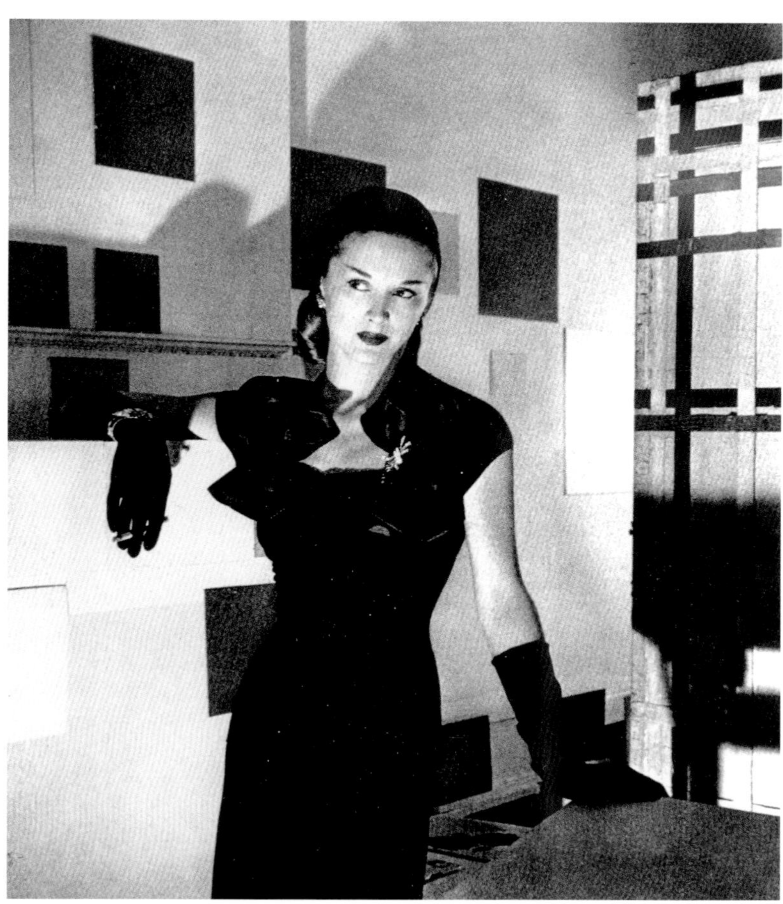

CAT. 408 **Fernand Fonssagrives**
Model next to *Victory Boogie Woogie* (B324) in Mondrian's studio after his death, between 22 March and c. 3 May 1944

CAT. 409 **Fernand Fonssagrives**
Model in Mondrian's living quarters after his death, between 22 March and c. 3 May 1944

CAT. 410 **Fernand Fonssagrives**
Model in front of *Composition in Circle* (B75) in Mondrian's studio after his death, between 22 March and c. 3 May 1944

CAT. 411 **Fernand Fonssagrives**
Model next to *New York City 1* (B300) in Mondrian's studio after his death, between 22 March and c. 3 May 1944
The painting appears to have been placed on an easel especially for the photograph, as this work cannot be seen in other posthumous pictures of the studio.

Notes for the Reader

The starting point for this book was to compile as complete an overview as possible of two categories of photographs that are relevant to the contemporary reception of the life and work of Piet Mondrian (1872–1944): photographs showing the artist on his own (portraits or studio shots) or in company; and photographs taken during his lifetime that capture his living and working environments. The criterion for this second category was that the pictures should have been taken *because* there was a connection at the time of shooting between the subject matter and the artist.[1] We also include in this latter category the series of photographs of the artist's final studio and apartment in New York, which Fritz Glarner, Harry Holtzman and Fernand Fonssagrives shot immediately after Mondrian's death on 1 February 1944. These respective sets offer such a comprehensive survey of the neo-plastic decoration and furnishing of Mondrian's living and working quarters (Holtzman's photographs are in colour too) and are of such art-historical importance that we felt they had to be reproduced here. We have placed them at the end of the catalogue.[2]

There are several photographs in the Mondrian literature, meanwhile, in which one of the people depicted has, in our view, been wrongly identified as Piet Mondrian. These have not been included in the catalogue.[3]

Mondrian and Photography came about against the background of the Mondrian Edition Project (MEP), a collaborative venture between the RKD — Netherlands Institute for Art History in The Hague, and the Huygens Institute of the Royal Netherlands Academy of Arts and Sciences in Amsterdam. The MEP has set out to publish all of Piet Mondrian's letters and theoretical writings online, accompanied by notes and English translations of all the texts (https://mondrianpapers.org).

The RKD's archives hold around a hundred of the original prints published here.[4] The remaining images, some of them original, some later prints, are located at dozens of separate locations around the globe. It is, of course, possible and even likely that new photographs will emerge after this book is published: pictures that would have been worthy of inclusion here, and which might also have shed fresh light on the ones we have reproduced. While we have attempted to be complete, therefore, this can obviously only extend as far as our current knowledge allows.

Structure

This book comprises three main sections: an introductory essay, a plate section and a catalogue section.

The introduction seeks to frame the role that photography played in Mondrian's life and the use that he made of the medium in the context of his time.

The plate section offers a selection of photographs that deserve extra space for a variety of reasons, such as their informative nature or their quality. Captions are provided for a number of photos containing background information, such as the identity of the people and the reason the picture was taken.[5] The photographs are arranged chronologically in four sections: the Dutch years until Mondrian left the Netherlands for good (c. 1889—1919, which also includes his first two-year stay in Paris, 1912—14, of which just one photograph is known); the years Mondrian lived in Paris (1919—38); the years he spent in London and in New York (1938—40 and 1940—44 respectively); and, lastly, the previously mentioned posthumous section. The first three of these sections are each preceded by a brief biography of Mondrian during the years in question, while the introduction to the fourth describes the circumstances of the shoots conducted at Mondrian's final studio shortly after his death by Glarner, Holtzman and Fonssagrives.

Several sequences of related photographs have been provided with a brief introduction, including the pictures of Mondrian's trip to Spain with friends in 1903, as well as series by photographers who we feel deserve further explanation for a number of reasons. Where these notes relate to the photographers, they are largely limited to the context of this publication.

The third section, the catalogue, contains a complete overview of the photographs we collected, together with documentary and technical data, in so far as these could be ascertained. See also below.

The photographs

We sought to reproduce as many vintage prints of the photographs as possible by requesting high-quality scans from the owners or the institutions at which they are located. For various reasons, original prints could not be traced in many instances. Where that was the case, we had to resort to earlier reproductions of them, possibly black-and-white photographs of the originals or images from newspapers, magazines or other publications. Consequently, the quality of these images is not always of the highest standard but we decided to include them in the catalogue anyway, as we felt it was not desirable to omit them from an overview that sets out to be comprehensive.

Another form in which photographs may have survived is the negative, whether film or glass. Where a negative exists as well as a vintage print, we have reproduced them both with the same catalogue number (plus an added sequential number) if we felt it was useful to be able to compare the cropping of the print with the full negative; see cats 96.1 and 96.2, for instance. It can also be the case that a negative has survived without a vintage print. All the negatives we printed ourselves were processed digitally and reproduced in positive form. Original prints from the same negative but which differ significantly, as in the case of the studio shot by Reinier Drektraan (cat. 39.1—3), have also been included under the same catalogue number.

The almost three hundred contact prints of shots by Fritz Glarner, kept at the Kunsthaus Zurich, are a special case: they show that the prints that were known prior to the publication of this book only represent part of the series of photographs that Glarner took in Mondrian's studio in 1942/3 and shortly after the artist's death in 1944. What's more, during the final session Glarner took several shots from the same vantage point, but with varying lighting and/or shutter speed. For the purposes of the catalogue entry, we chose the contact print that provided the best or most complete picture. In addition to the variations in exposure, there were some slight differences in viewpoint, which do not, however, offer any additional information. All the same, we consider these to be separate shots and so they have been given a catalogue number of their own.

Photographs are delicate objects: the condition in which they have survived depends on numerous factors, including exposure to daylight, being sent to a print shop for reproduction, the care with which they have been handled, being mailed out in envelopes, neglect and more besides. Factors like this leave their mark on the print. The photographs presented in this book have been meticulously post-processed by Tijdsbeeld publishers to extract as much information from the shots as possible. Scratches and other instances of mechanical damage have been retouched, obtrusive reflections corrected, contrasts balanced and, as noted already, negatives converted into positive images.

Titles and dating

Very few photographs were given an 'official' title by their creators — a few by André Kertész (cats 92 and 93) and group photographs by Hermann Landshoff (cats 245 and 246). We have assigned factual, descriptive titles to the remaining pictures, which means that similar photos can have identical titles. We felt that it was better to accept this and to keep our descriptions as neutral as possible rather than coming up with contrived alternatives.

The dates we have assigned to the photographs are based on what we know from the correspondence — Mondrian's in particular — and existing literature on the artist, the photographer and other contemporaries. It was often impossible to identify a precise date and so we have made do with a rough dating, such as 'between date x and date y' or '1889 (?)'. Photographs like this are included in the chronology based on the earliest date in the stated range. In the case of our two examples, this would mean 'date x' and the beginning of 1889 respectively.
The reasoning behind our dating is set out in the supplementary data (see below).

Supplementary data

Data of a more technical and documentary nature has been placed in the catalogue section. Where available, the following information is provided there: technique, dimensions, any relevant inscriptions, and the whereabouts of the reproduced print and/or negative. The dimensions stated for extant original prints refer to the photographic paper, including any borders (see some of André Kertész's prints, for instance).

Several types of additional information are also provided, including the reasons for our dating, references in the literature, references to other catalogue numbers and so forth. For photographs published during Mondrian's lifetime, a reference to the relevant publication(s) is provided.

Realization

We have been supported in our work in a variety of ways. Assistant researcher Laurens Kleine Deters spent around six months helping to prepare the catalogue, based in part on inventories drawn up by Evelien de Visser (former documentalist of the Mondrian Edition Project) and by intern Aurora Wilson Dyer Gough. Akiko Hakuno managed some of the image requests, a complex task which was completed by Ann Mestdag.

Draft versions of several texts were written by Laurens Kleine Deters (introduction to Pierre Delbo) and Clarissa Frascadore (introductions to Fritz Glarner, Eugene Lux and Arnold Newman). It goes without saying that we, the authors, are wholly responsible for the content of this book.

1 This means, for instance, that the photographs of the studio building on Rue du Départ, which Mondrian's friend Alfred Roth took during a visit, are included in the catalogue (cats 108–11), but not so Seeberger Frères' photograph of the same building (see illustration on p. 34). Non-contemporary photographs of Mondrian's homes/studios have not been included in the catalogue either.

2 The catalogue does not, therefore, include the portfolio photos (see pp. 52–9). An overview of these photographs with any degree of accuracy is currently lacking, making it difficult to determine to what extent the known portfolio pictures are representative of all such pictures that Mondrian asked to be taken.

3 A photograph of three people in a rowing boat, for instance, shows Simon Maris and Mies van de Water, but rather than Mondrian (Leal 2010, p. 271) the third man is Jan van der Hoeven Leonard (Gorter 2020, p. 40). A picture of several people in the garden of the De Vink tavern near the river Gein in Amsterdam includes someone who was incorrectly identified as Mondrian in 2008 (Janssen 2008, p. 68), but is actually a friend of the artist, namely the art dealer Joop Siedenburg. A photograph of a musical evening attended by members of the Sint Lucas association in Amsterdam, taken around 1910, includes a strongly backlit figure at the back of the large company. We consider the image to be too indistinct to endorse the earlier identification of this person as Mondrian (Bax 1994, p. 35). Another picture, lastly, shows the painter Moïse Kisling next to a person we believe has been wrongly identified as Mondrian (Portevin 2010, p. 16).

4 In several cases, a more appropriate vintage print was found in a collection outside the RKD. We selected the best image in each case, and so not all of the one hundred or so vintage prints held by the RKD feature in this book.

5 Paintings that appear in photographs have only been identified where they feature prominently in the scene or the action being performed (by Mondrian); not so, therefore, when they were simply part of the decoration. The titles of Mondrian's works are drawn from *Piet Mondrian: Catalogue Raisonné* (1998) by Robert Welsh and Joop Joosten. The principle adopted by Welsh/Joosten 1998 when assigning titles to Mondrian's works means that they can be multiple and in different languages (see Welsh/Joosten 1998-I, pp. 138–39 and 1998-II, pp. 186–89). For the most part, we use the first title they give, and provided with the number from the catalogue raisonné.

Catalogue

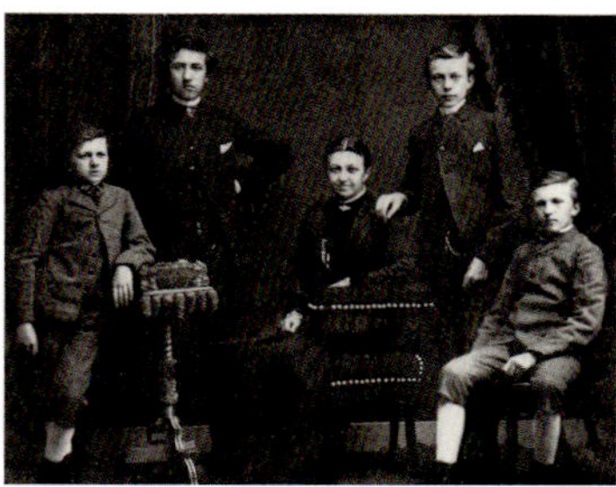

CAT. 1 Unidentified photographer

The Mondriaan children, spring 1889 (?) (see p. 70)

A vintage print has not been traced: the photograph reproduced here is a later print (The Hague, RKD, Artist Portraits Collection).

The suggestion that the photograph was a twentieth-anniversary gift to their parents in 1889 is based partly on the fact that Mondrian also gave them a photograph to commemorate their anniversary ten years later (see cat. 3).

The picture might have been taken by H. Bulens, a photographer in Winterswijk, who also supplied Mondrian's parents with *cartes de visite* around this time.

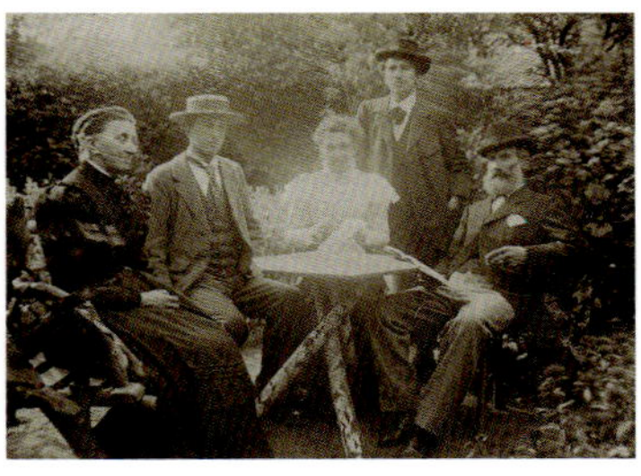

CAT. 2 Louis Mondriaan (?)

Members of the Mondriaan family, c. 1894 (see p. 71)

Gelatin printing-out paper, 9.8 x 12.8 cm (mount)

The Hague, RKD, Carel Mondriaan Archive (0929), inv. 14

The date is based on Mondrian's appearance without the beard or goatee he grew a few years later (see cat. 3) and the absence of Willem Frederik from the picture.

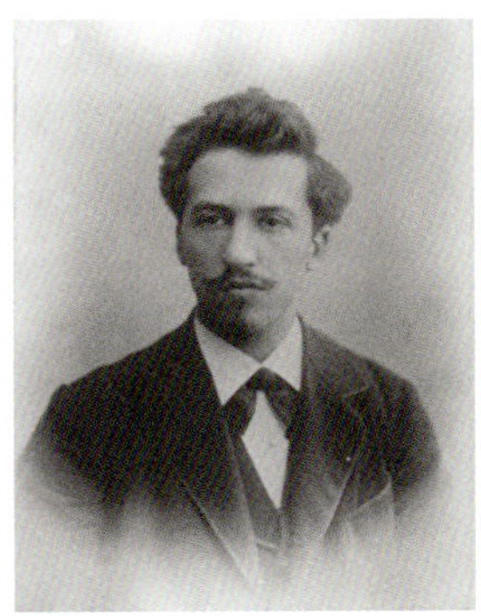

CAT. 3 Fotostudio Cosman, Amsterdam

Portrait of Piet Mondrian, 1899

Unidentified technique, 16.5 x 11 cm (card)

Verso, in Piet Mondrian's handwriting: '12 mei '99 / Aan Vader en Moeder / *Piet*' ('12 May [18]99 / to Father and Mother / *Piet*'); stamp: 'Michel SEUPHOR / 83 Avenue Emile Zola / PARIS (15e)'

The inscription on the back shows that Mondrian gave the photograph to his parents, who celebrated their thirtieth wedding anniversary on 12 May 1899.

A vintage print has not been traced: the photograph reproduced here is a later print (The Hague, RKD, Joop Joosten Archive (0838), inv. 808).

The stated dimensions are based on other known *cartes de visite* by Fotostudio Cosman from the same period in the RKD collection.

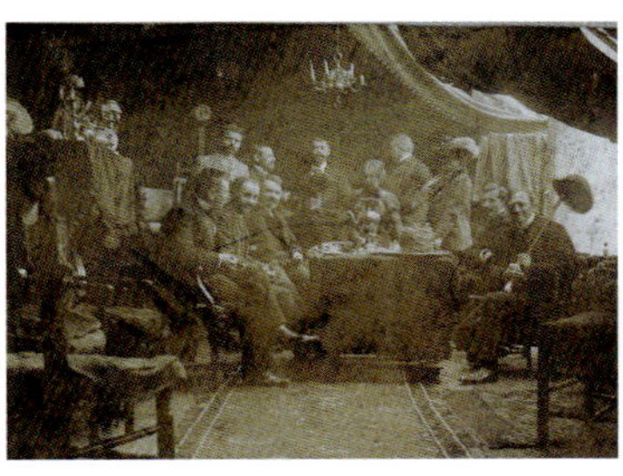

CAT. 4 Unidentified photographer

Group photo in Simon Maris's studio, 1900 (see p. 73)

Collodion printing-out paper, 8 x 11 cm

The Hague, RKD, Simon Maris and Family Archive (0257), inv. 93

For the dating and identification, see Gorter 2020, pp. 5–6.

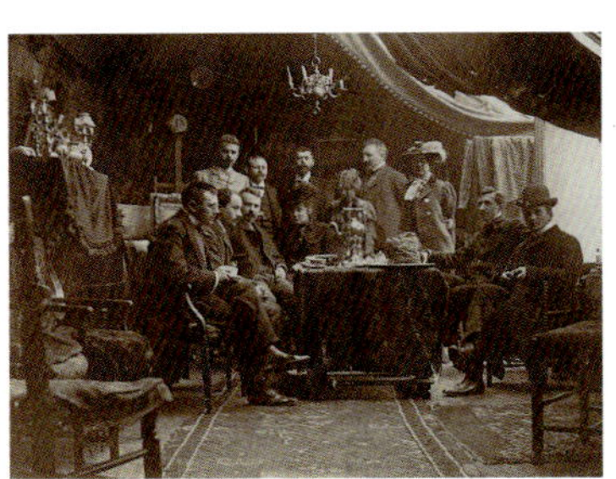

CAT. 5 Unidentified photographer

Group photo in Simon Maris's studio, 1900 (see p. 73)

Gelatin printing-out paper, 8 x 10.2 cm

The Hague, RKD, Simon Maris and Family Archive (0257), inv. 93

For the dating and identification, see Gorter 2020, pp. 5–6.

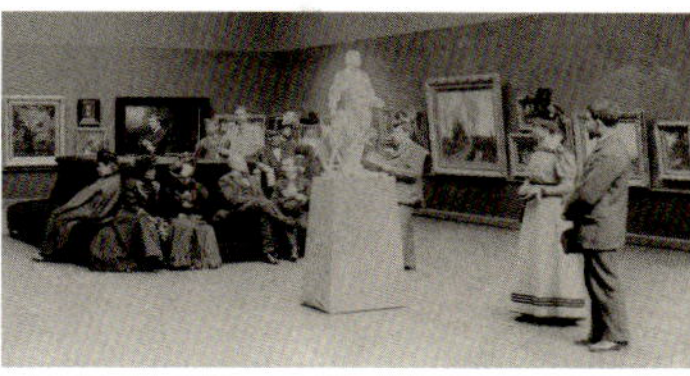

CAT. 6 Unidentified photographer

Preview of the Sint Lucas association's spring exhibition at the Stedelijk Museum, Amsterdam, 18 or 19 May 1900 (see pp. 74–5)

Technique unknown, 22 x 30 cm

Collection Paul Gorter

The exhibition opened on 19 May 1900. Since this was a preview, the possible date extends beyond the opening date itself (Gorter 2020, p. 16).

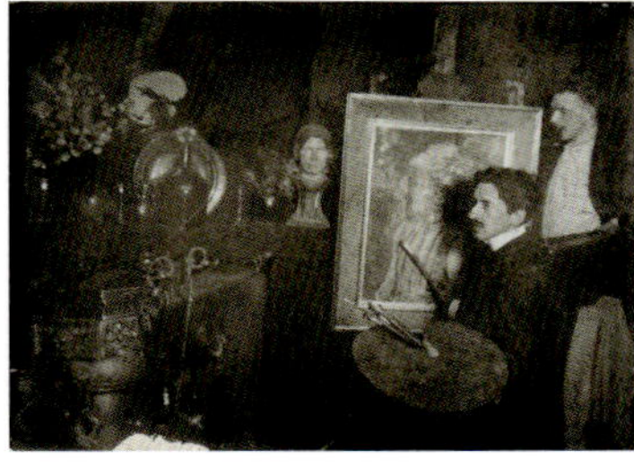

CAT. 7 Unidentified photographer

Piet Mondrian and Cees Bergman (?) in Mondrian's studio, c. 1901 (see p. 75)

Gelatin printing-out paper, 8.9 x 12.1 cm

The Hague, RKD, Simon Maris and Family Archive (0257), inv. 93

Mondrian is sitting in front of his *Portrait of Elisabeth Sophia Maria (Betsy) Cavalini* (A385a), which is dated 1901. The dating of the photograph takes account of the fact that the depicted portrait is framed and must therefore have been finished (or virtually so).

For the suggestion that the man on the right is Cees Bergman, see Draaijer 2022, photo section (n.p.).

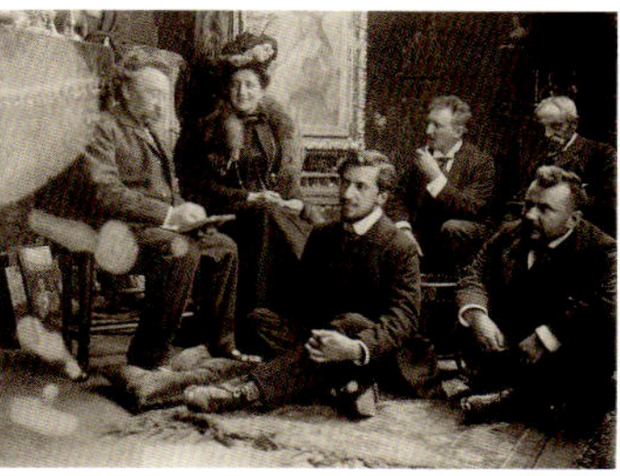

CAT. 8 Unidentified photographer

Group photo in Simon Maris's studio, c. 1901 (see p. 76)

Gelatin developing-out paper, 8.2 x 11.3 cm

The Hague, RKD, Simon Maris and Family Archive (0257), inv. 93

For the dating and identification, see Gorter 2020, pp. 7–8.

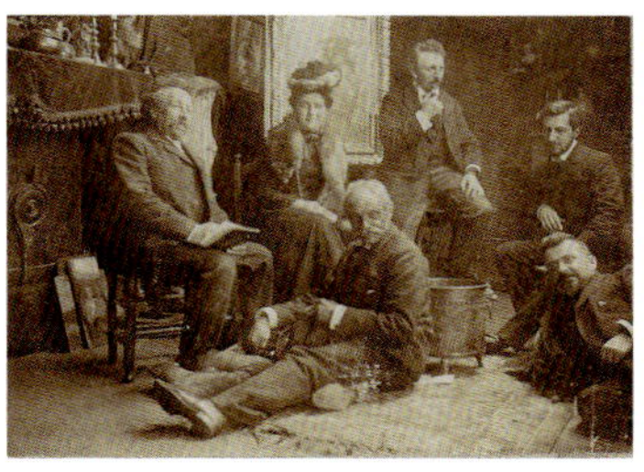

CAT. 9 Unidentified photographer

Group photo in Simon Maris's studio, c. 1901 (see p. 77)

Gelatin developing-out paper, 8.2 x 11.3 cm

The Hague, RKD, Simon Maris and Family Archive (0257), inv. 93

For the dating and identification, see Gorter 2020, pp. 7–8.

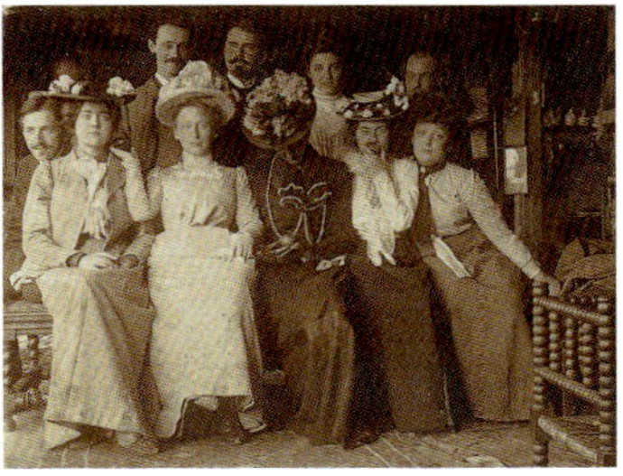

CAT. 10 Unidentified photographer

Group portrait in Simon Maris's studio following the opening of the exhibition at Sint Lucas, 8 June 1901 (see p. 78)

Gelatin printing-out paper, 8 x 11.3 cm

Recto, in Cornelia den Breejen's handwriting: 'Piet Mondriaan, Th. Ansingh, M v Raalte, ?, G. H. Kroon, G. Schwartze, H. Hendriks, Lizzy Ansingh, Huidekoper, Nelly Bodenheim'; in right margin: 'Foto op atelier Simon Maris 8/6. 1901 op 't Spui na de St. Lucastentoonstelling' ('Photo at Simon Maris's studio 8 June 1901 at the Spui after the Sint Lucas exhibition')

The Hague, RKD, Simon Maris and Family Archive (0257), inv. 93

The dating is based on the inscription.

For the identification, see also Gorter 2020, pp. 11–12.

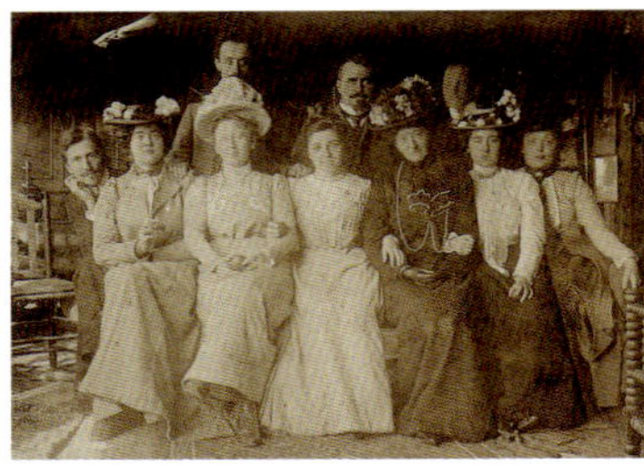

CAT. 11 Unidentified photographer

Group portrait in Simon Maris's studio, following the opening of the exhibition at Sint Lucas, 8 June 1901 (see p. 78)

Collodion printing-out paper, 8.2 x 11.3 cm

Recto, in Cornelia den Breejen's handwriting: 'Mondriaan, Th. Peizel Ansingh, M v Raalte, ?, Jet (Holst) Hendriks, G. H. Kroon, Georg. Schwartze, ?, Lizzy Ansingh, Nelly Bodenheim'

The Hague, RKD, Simon Maris and Family Archive (0257), inv. 93

The dating is clear from the inscription on another photograph from the same group (see cat. 10).

For the identification, see also Gorter 2020, pp. 11–12.

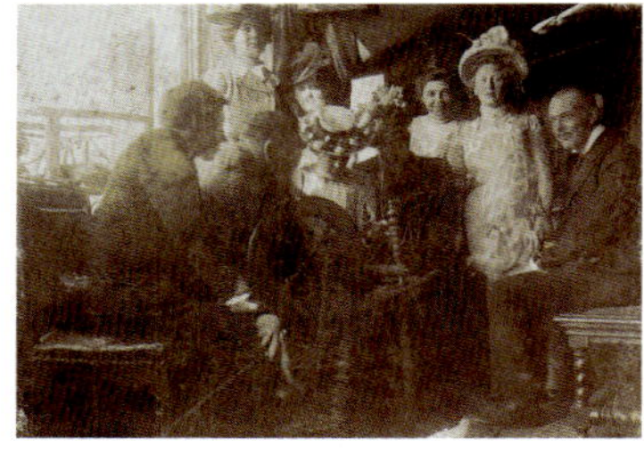

CAT. 12 Unidentified photographer

Group portrait in Simon Maris's studio, following the opening of the exhibition at Sint Lucas, 8 June 1901 (see p. 79)

Gelatin printing-out paper, 8.2 x 11.2 cm

Recto, in Cornelia den Breejen's handwriting: 'P. Mondriaan, Th. Peizel, G. Kroon, Nelly Bodenheim, Lizzy Ansingh, G. Schwartze, J. Hendriks, ?, Huidekoper'

The Hague, RKD, Simon Maris and Family Archive (0257), inv. 93

Everyone here is dressed the same way as in cats 10–11, so the picture must have been taken on the same afternoon.

For the identification, see also Gorter 2020, pp. 13–14.

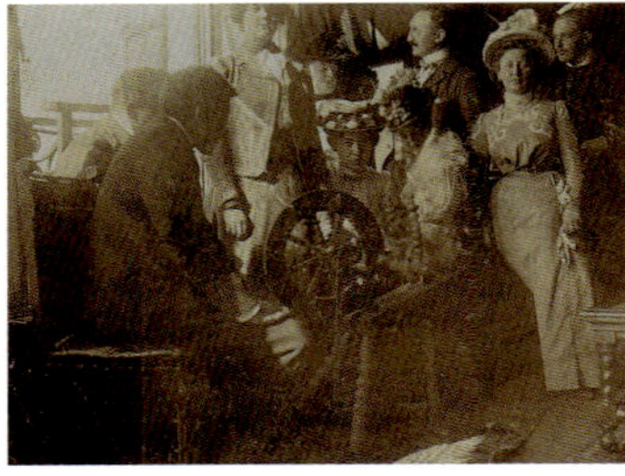

CAT. 13 Unidentified photographer (Jet Hendrix?)

Group portrait in Simon Maris's studio, following the opening of the exhibition at Sint Lucas, 8 June 1901 (see p. 79)

Gelatin printing-out paper, 8.2 x 11.1 cm

The Hague, RKD, Simon Maris and Family Archive (0257), inv. 93

Simon Maris has taken the place of Jet Hendrix compared to cat. 12, suggesting that it might now have been the latter operating the camera.

The dating is clear from the inscription on another photograph from the same group (see cat. 10).

For the identification, see also Gorter 2020, pp. 13–14.

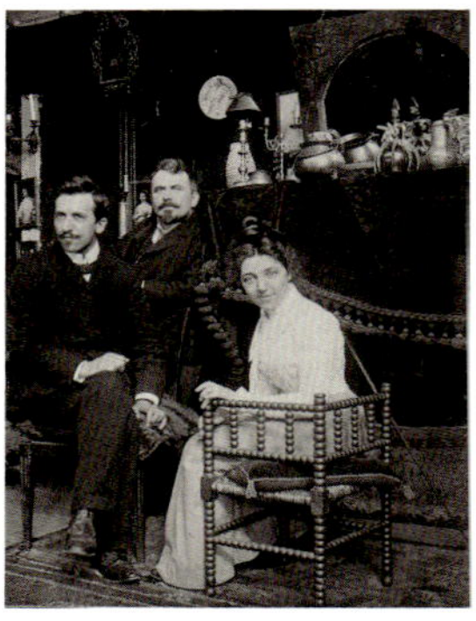

CAT. 14 Unidentified photographer

Piet Mondrian, Hendrik Kroon and Jet Hendrix in Simon Maris's studio, second half 1901 (see p. 80)

Gelatin printing-out paper, 11.1 x 8.3 cm

The Hague, RKD, Simon Maris and Family Archive (0257), inv. 93

For the dating and identification, see Gorter 2020, p. 9.

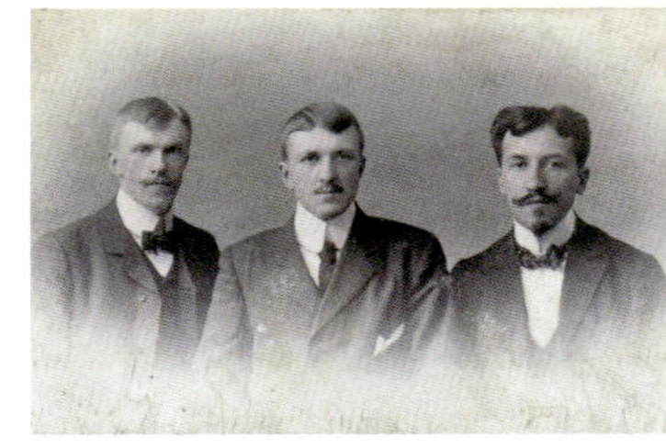

CAT. 15 Unidentified photographer

Louis, Carel and Piet Mondrian, c. 1902 (see p. 81)

Collodion printing-out paper, 10.3 x 12.9 cm

Recto, in Willem Frederik Mondriaan's handwriting: 'Louis Carel Piet'

Private collection

The bright vignetting effect (most visible at the bottom), the composition and the clothes worn by the sitters all suggest that a professional photographer took this picture.

It can be dated from Piet Mondrian's hairstyle to around 1902.

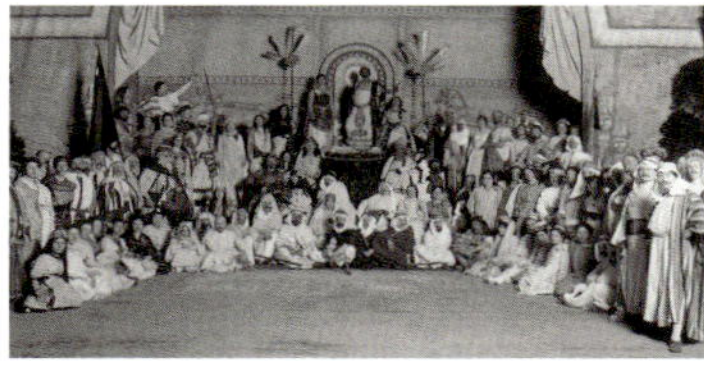

CAT. 16 Paul Götte

Group photo of guests at an Oriental-themed party at the Sint Lucas artists' association, 21 February 1903 (see pp. 82–3)

Technique unknown, 22 x 28 cm

Collection Paul Gorter

The photograph was published in the newspaper *Dagblad van Zuid-Holland en 's Gravenhage*, where it was captioned: 'Fancy-dress ball of the "Sint Lucas" artists' society in Amsterdam. / Shot under artificial light by P. F. Götte, Amsterdam.' See Gorter 2017, pp. 19 and 34 n. 29.

Publication: *Dagblad van Zuid-Holland en 's Gravenhage*, 8 March 1903

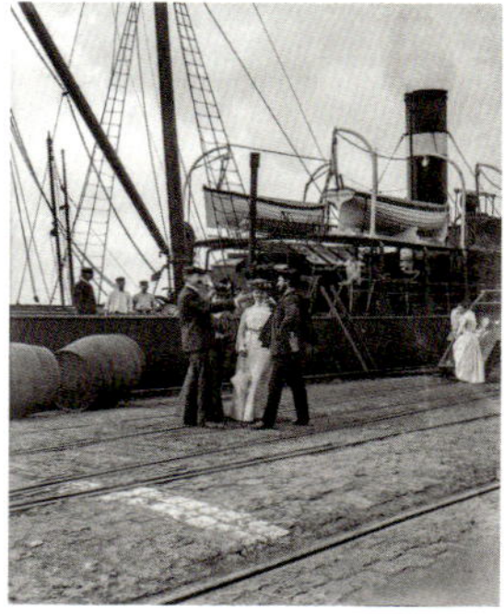

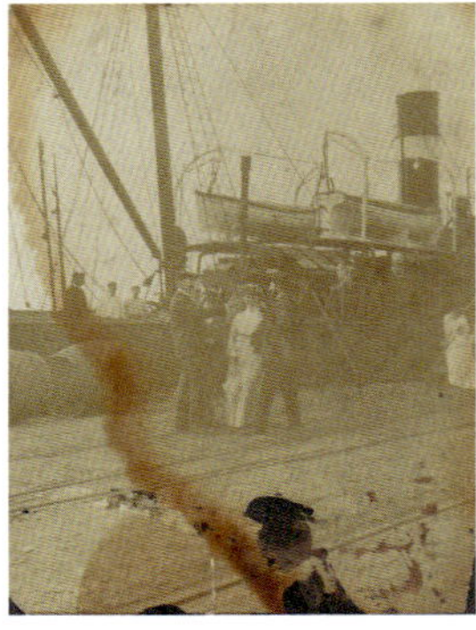

CAT. 17.1; 17.2 Frits Bodenheim

Simon Maris, Louise Bodenheim, Mies van de Water and Piet Mondrian at the dock in IJmuiden, 28 August 1903 (see p. 85)

(1) Negative, digitally processed, 12.3 x approx. 10.5 cm; (2) Gelatin developing-out paper, 11.8 x 9 cm

(1) (2) The Hague, RKD, Simon Maris and Family Archive (0257), inv. 93

Regarding the journey and the date, see Gorter 2020, pp. 16–17.

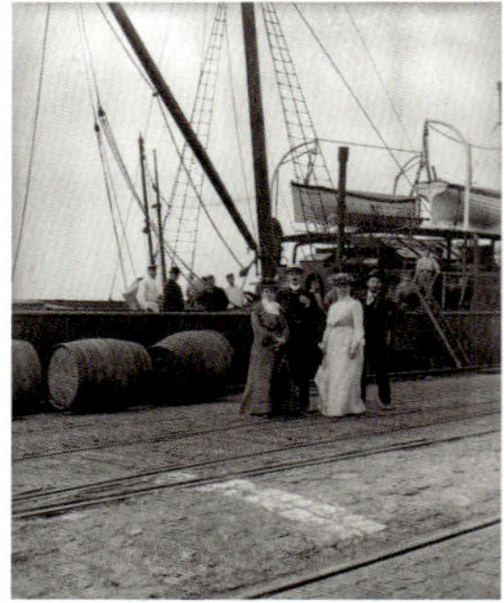

CAT. 18 Simon Maris

Louise and Frits Bodenheim, Mies van de Water and Piet Mondrian at the dock in IJmuiden, 28 August 1903 (see p. 86)

Negative, digitally processed, 12.3 x approx. 10.5 cm

The Hague, RKD, Simon Maris and Family Archive (0257), inv. 93

Regarding the journey and the date, see Gorter 2020, pp. 16–17.

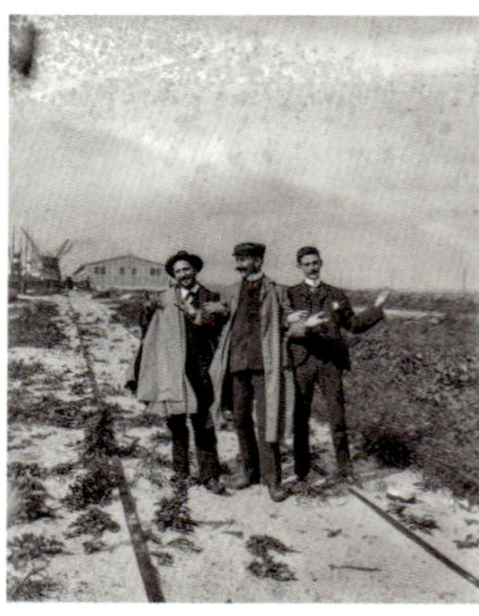

CAT. 19 Mies van de Water or Louise Bodenheim

Piet Mondrian, Simon Maris and Frits Bodenheim at the dock in IJmuiden, 28 August 1903
(see p. 86)

Negative, digitally processed, 12.3 x approx. 10.3 cm

The Hague, RKD, Simon Maris and Family Archive (0257), inv. 93

The picture is likely to have been taken by one of the two women who came to wave them off; see cats 17–18.

Regarding the journey and the date, see Gorter 2020, pp. 16–17.

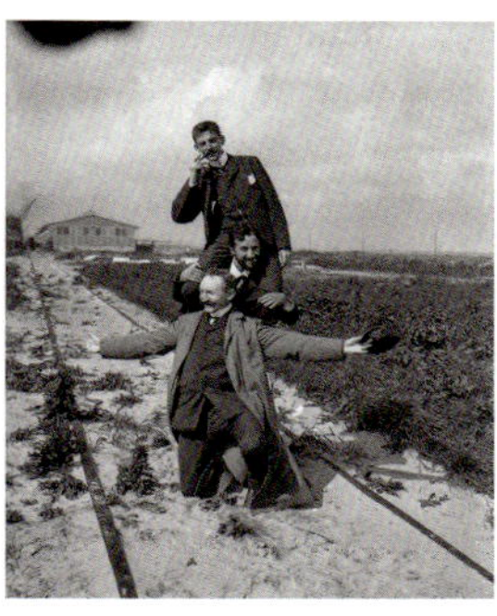

CAT. 20 Mies van de Water or Louise Bodenheim

Piet Mondrian with Frits Bodenheim on his shoulders and Simon Maris kneeling at the dock in IJmuiden, 28 August 1903
(see p. 87)

Negative, digitally processed, 12.3 x 10.2 cm

The Hague, RKD, Simon Maris and Family Archive (0257), inv. 93

The picture is likely to have been taken by one of the two women who came to wave them off; see cats 17–18.

Regarding the journey and the date, see Gorter 2020, pp. 16–17.

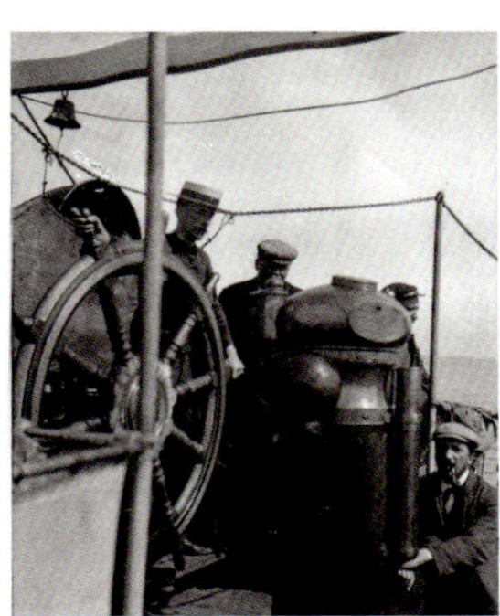

CAT. 21 Simon Maris

Frits Bodenheim, Piet Mondrian and two crew members on board the SS *Orion*, August–September 1903
(see p. 87)

Negative, digitally processed, 12.3 x 10 cm

The Hague, RKD, Simon Maris and Family Archive (0257), inv. 93

Regarding the journey and the date, see Gorter 2020, pp. 16–17.

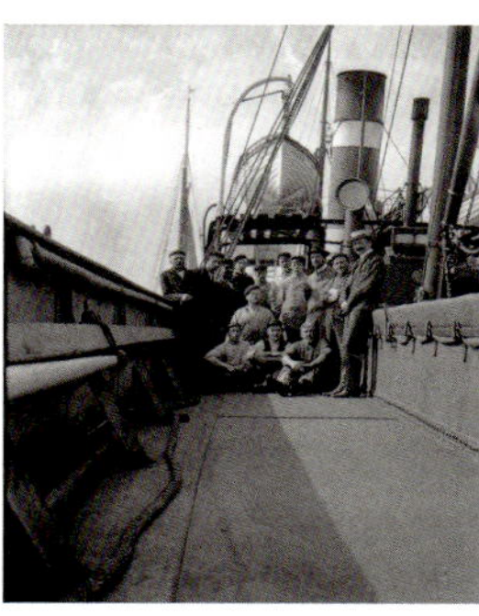

CAT. 22 Frits Bodenheim

Piet Mondrian, Simon Maris and crew members on board the SS *Orion*, August–September 1903
(see p. 88)

Negative, digitally processed, 12.3 x 10.4 cm

The Hague, RKD, Simon Maris and Family Archive (0257), inv. 93

Regarding the journey and the date, see Gorter 2020, pp. 16–17.

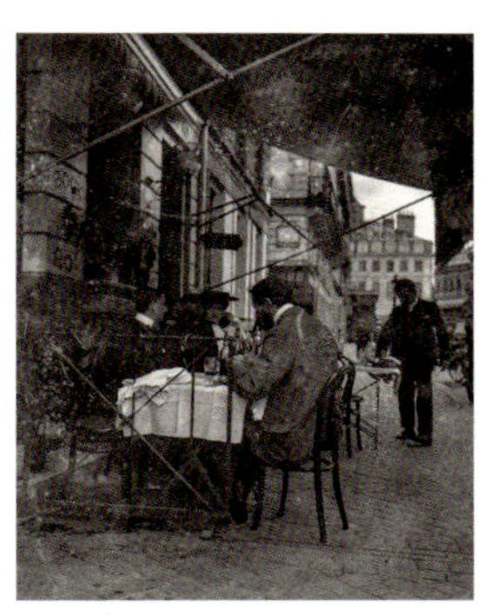

CAT. 23 Simon Maris

Piet Mondrian and Frits Bodenheim dining in Bordeaux, 2 September 1903 (see p. 89)

Negative, digitally processed, 11.6 x 9.2 cm

The Hague, RKD, Simon Maris and Family Archive (0257), inv. 93

Regarding the journey and the date, see Gorter 2020, pp. 16–17.

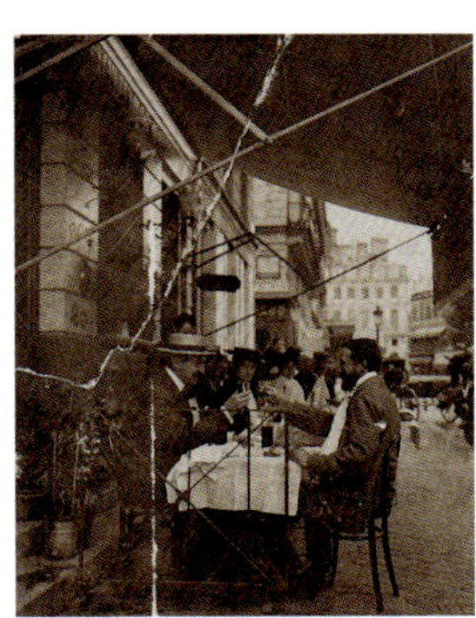

CAT. 24 Frits Bodenheim

Simon Maris and Piet Mondrian dining in Bordeaux, 2 September 1903 (see p. 89)

Gelatin printing-out paper, 11.6 x 9 cm

Recto, in Simon Maris's handwriting: 'Simon Maris & Piet Mondriaan te Bordeaux' ('Simon Maris and Piet Mondrian in Bordeaux')

The Hague, RKD, Simon Maris and Family Archive (0257), inv. 93

Regarding the journey and the date, see Gorter 2020, pp. 16–17.

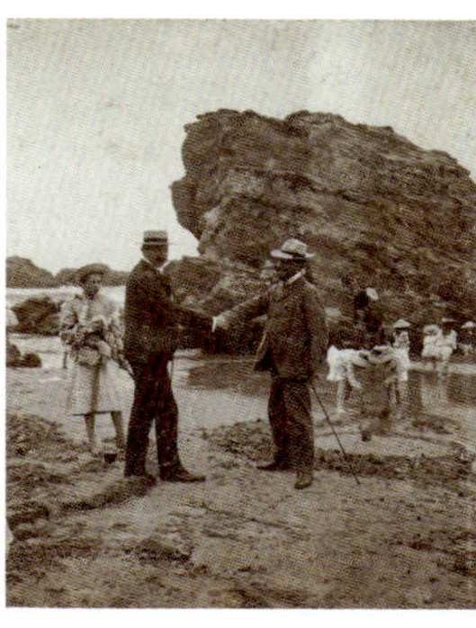

CAT. 25 Frits Bodenheim

Simon Maris and Piet Mondrian on the beach in Biarritz, 4 September 1903 (see p. 90)

Gelatin printing-out paper, 11.7 x 9.3 cm

Verso, in Simon Maris's handwriting: 'Biarritz, 4 sept. 1903'

The Hague, RKD, Simon Maris and Family Archive (0257), inv. 93

Regarding the journey and the date, see Gorter 2020, pp. 16–17.

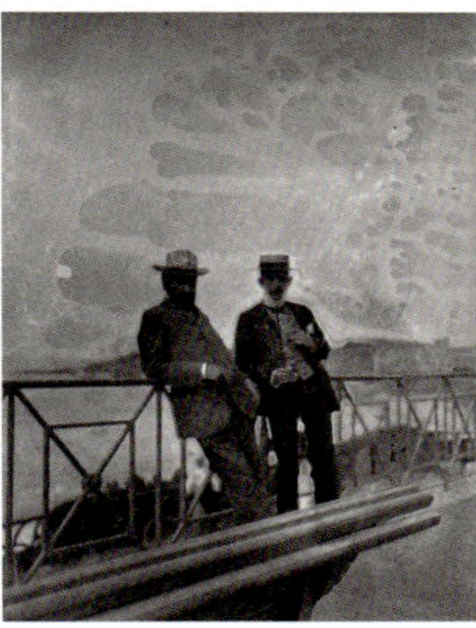

CAT. 26 Simon Maris

Piet Mondrian and Frits Bodenheim in Biarritz, 4 September 1903

Negative, digitally processed, 11.7 x 9.5 cm

The Hague, RKD, Simon Maris and Family Archive (0257), inv. 93

Gorter suggests that the photograph was taken on the coast near Bilbao (Gorter 2020, p. 30). The distinctive imitation wood fence behind the railing on which Mondrian and Bodenheim are leaning confirms, however, that this must have been Biarritz.

According to Gorter's chronology, the pictures were shot in Biarritz on 4 September 1903 (Gorter 2020, pp. 16–17).

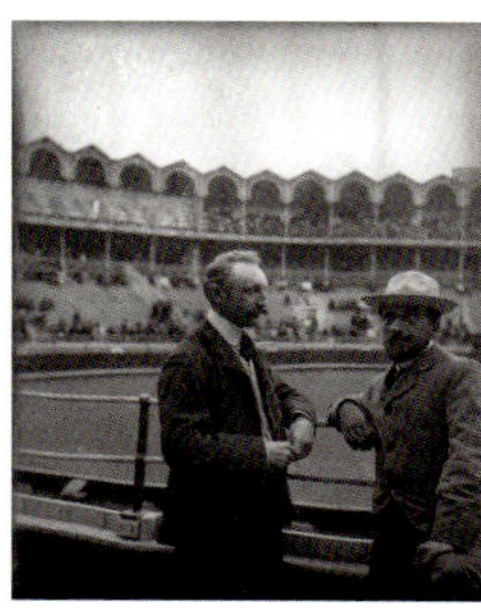

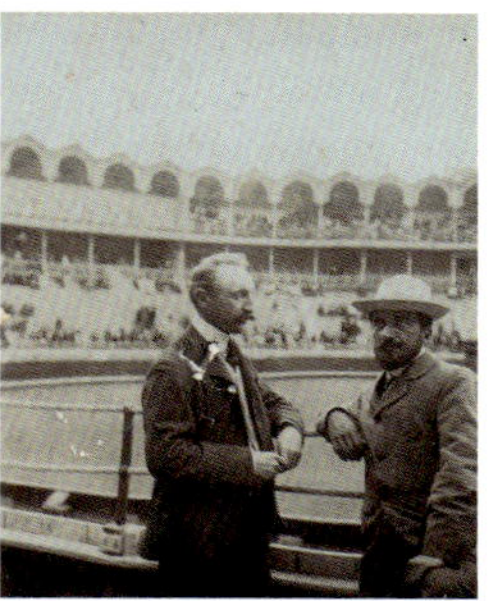

CAT. 27.1; CAT. 27.2 Frits Bodenheim

Simon Maris and Piet Mondrian at the arena in Bilbao, September 1903
(see p. 91)

(1) Negative, digitally processed, 11.7 x 9.5 cm; (2) gelatin printing-out paper, 11.7 x 9.2 cm

Recto (2): 'Bilbao Spanje. Maris – S'

The Hague, RKD, Simon Maris and Family Archive (0257), inv. 93

Regarding the journey and the date, see Gorter 2020, pp. 16–17.

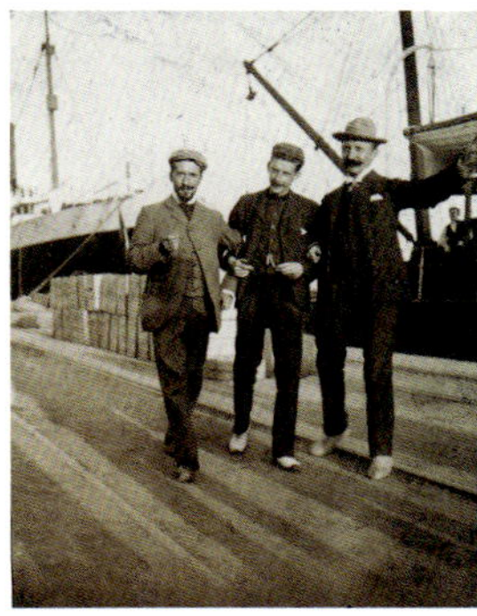

CAT. 28 Unidentified photographer

Piet Mondrian, Frits Bodenheim and Simon Maris on the dock in Amsterdam, 23 September 1903
(see p. 90)

Gelatin printing-out paper, 11.8 x 9 cm

The Hague, RKD, Simon Maris and Family Archive (0257), inv. 93

Regarding the journey and the date, see Gorter 2020, pp. 16–17.

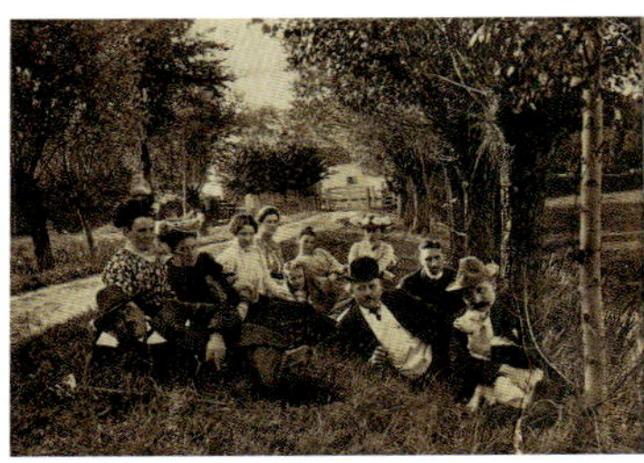

CAT. 29 Unidentified photographer (possibly Adriaan Boer)

Piet Mondrian and friends by the Gein, June 1904
(see p. 92)

Collodion printing-out paper, 10 x 13.4 cm

Verso, in Simon Maris's handwriting: 'juni 1904', 'Tusschen stadsbewoners...' ('June 1904', 'Among city-folk...')

The Hague, RKD, Simon Maris and Family Archive (0257), inv. 93

For the photographer, dating and identification, see Gorter 2020, pp. 34 and 39. Gorter has suggested that this picture might have been taken by Adriaan Boer, based on another photograph in the Maris archive that shares the same quality and tone. The latter is monogrammed 'A. B.', which Gorter thinks are most likely the initials of Adriaan Boer.

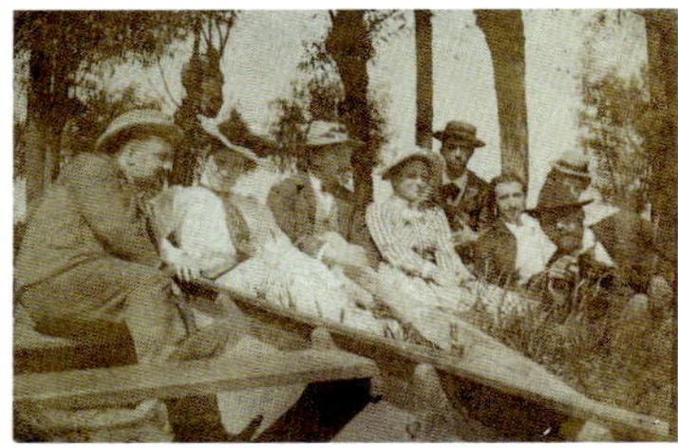

CAT. 30 Unidentified photographer

Piet Mondrian and friends at the Gein, c. summer 1904 (see p. 92)

Collodion printing-out paper, 5.8 x 8.9 cm

The Hague, RKD, Simon Maris and Family Archive (0257), inv. 93

For the identification, see Gorter 2020, p. 36.

Janssen dates the photograph to the summer of 1904 (Janssen 2013, p. 57). Gorter places it around 1907–8 based on Mondrian's hairstyle (Gorter 2020, p. 36). Given the similar atmosphere and setting to cat. 29, we also date the photograph to around the summer of 1904.

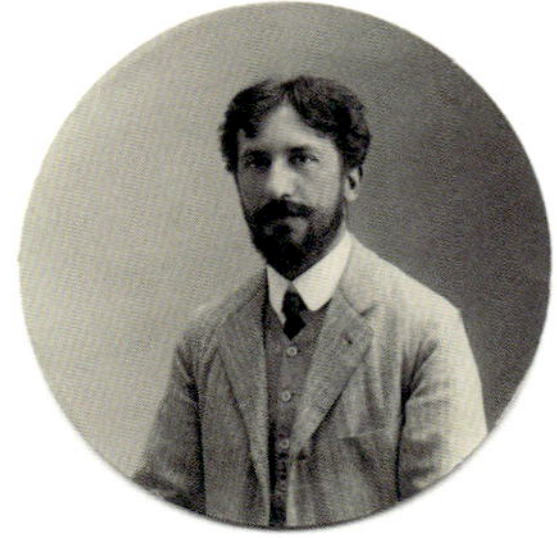

CAT. 31 Unidentified photographer

Portrait of Piet Mondrian, c. 1905
(see p. 93)

Gelatin developing-out paper, 8.3 x 8.3 cm

Verso, in unidentified handwriting: 'Piet Mondriaan' (2x), '1906' (corrected to '1908'), 'Blankenbergen'

The Hague, National Archives, Spaarnestad Collection

For the dating, we follow Janssen, who dated the photograph to around 1905, based on Mondrian's hairstyle and youthful appearance (Janssen 2013, p. 85).

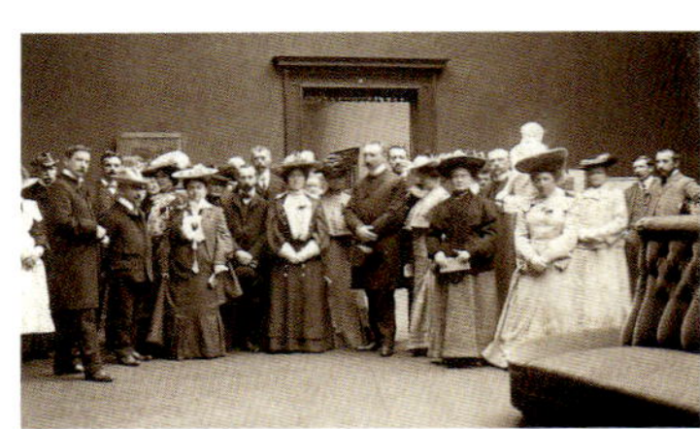

CAT. 32 Atelier Herz, Amsterdam

Visitors at the preview of the Sint Lucas association's spring exhibition at the Stedelijk Museum, Amsterdam, May 1905 (see p. 93)

Technique unknown, 10 x 14 cm

Collection Paul Gorter

For the identification, see Gorter 2017, p. 22.

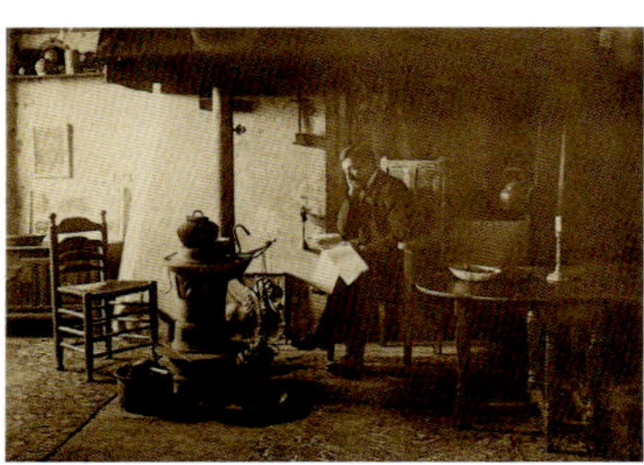

CAT. 33 Unidentified photographer

Piet Mondrian in the living area of his studio at 10 Rembrandtplein, Amsterdam, c. 1905 (?)
(see p. 94)

Salt print, 12 x 16.9 cm

The Hague, RKD, Piet Mondrian Archive (0740), inv. 56

Mondrian kept this studio from February 1905 to June 1906. There are no further clues as to the dating. In cat. 34, Mondrian's hair seems longer and his beard fuller. Growing his hair and beard longer is associated with the period from 1906 to mid-1910: cf. cats 35–42. We therefore date this photo earlier than cat. 34.

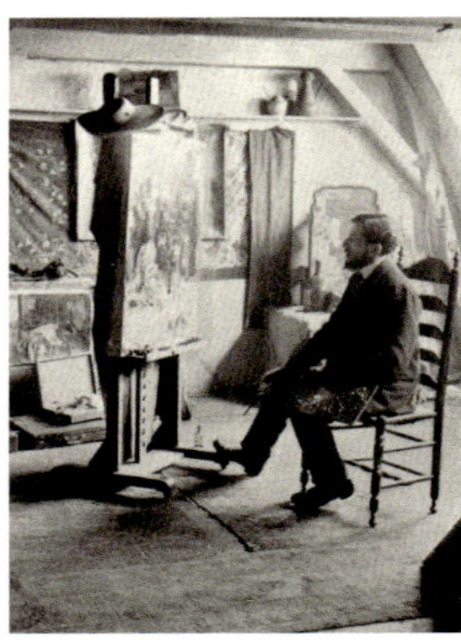

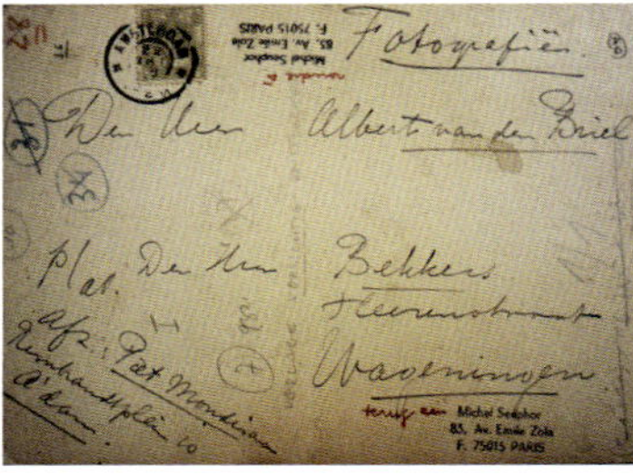

CAT. 34 Unidentified photographer

Piet Mondrian in his studio at 10 Rembrandtplein, Amsterdam, c. March 1906 (see pp. 94–5)

Verso, in Piet Mondrian's handwriting: '*Fotografiën.* / Den heer *Albert van den Briel* / p/a Den heer *Bekkers.* / Heerenstraat / *Wageningen.*', 'Afz.: *Piet Mondriaan* / Rembrandtplein 10 / *A'dam.*'; postmark: 'AMSTERDAM / 22 MRT 0[5/6?] / 1-2[v]'; stamp (2x), with inscription 'terug aan'/'rendre à': 'Michel SEUPHOR / 83, Av. Emile Zola / F. 75015 PARIS'

A vintage print has not been traced. The reproduction of the original photo shown here was taken by Frans Postma during a visit to Michel Seuphor in the early 1990s.

It is not clear from the postmark on the back whether the year is 1905 or 1906; the month 'March' ('MRT') is, however, legible. Although Janssen has suggested that the photograph was taken when Mondrian won the Willink van Collen Prize in April 1906 (Janssen 2016, pp. 256 and 349), the still life seen in the photograph does not appear finished. We therefore date the picture to around March 1906, which means it would have been taken before the artist won the prize.

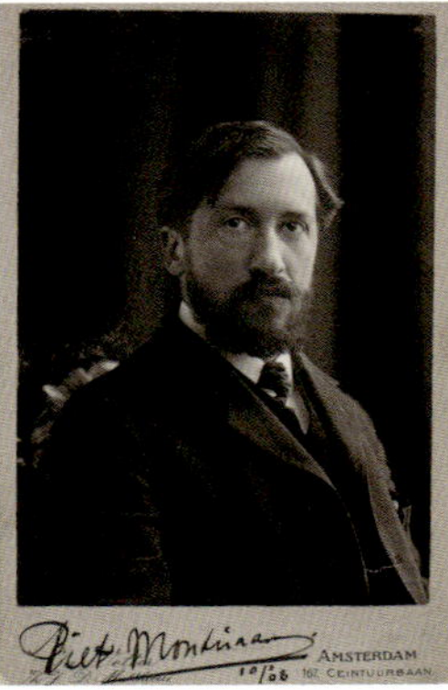

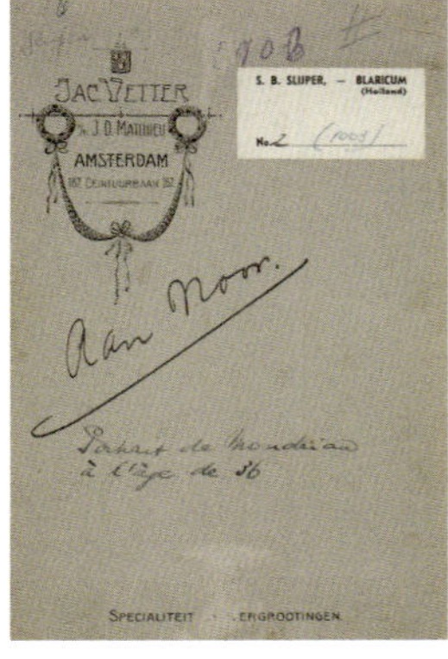

CAT. 35 Fotografisch atelier Jac. Vetter

Portrait of Piet Mondrian, autumn 1907 (see p. 96)

Gelatin developing-out paper, 16.5 x 10.5 cm (mount)

Recto, in Piet Mondrian's handwriting: '*Piet Mondriaan / 10/'08*'; verso: *'Aan Noor' ('To Noor')*

The Hague, RKD, Collectie Preciosafoto's Piet Mondriaan

We date this photograph to the autumn of 1907, based on the assumption that it was taken for use in Lurasco's book, which was published in December 1907 (see p. 22).

Publication: F. M. Lurasco, *Onze Moderne Meesters* (Amsterdam 1907), n.p.

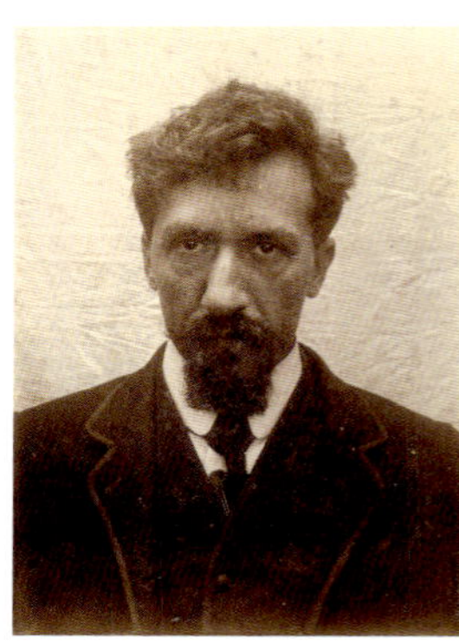

CAT. 36 Unidentified photographer

Portrait of Piet Mondrian, c. 1908
(see p. 96)

Recto, in Eva de Benefditty's handwriting: 'P. Mondriaan 1910'

Private collection

This photograph belongs to a private collection and was not available for further examination. Technical data is therefore lacking.

Although Eva de Benedітty dated it to 1910 (see inscription), the photograph was probably taken around 1908. Personal contact between Mondrian and De Benedітty ceased in June 1909, although Mondrian wrote her a few more letters in 1910 (see Entrop 2003, p. 42). We date the picture to around 1908 based on the style of Mondrian's hair and beard. This differs from cats 37–40, where he has a centre parting, which he adopted in the course of 1908.

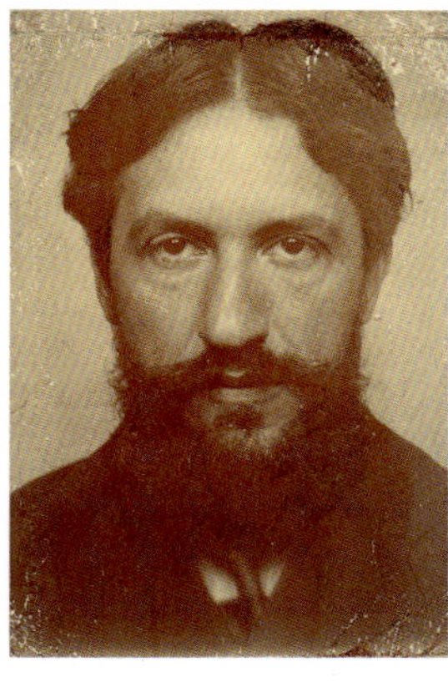

CAT. 37 Unidentified photographer

Portrait of Piet Mondrian with beard and centre parting, c. 1908
(see p. 97)

Gelatin printing-out paper, 15.5 x 10.2 cm

Verso, in Piet Mondrian's handwriting (?): '*Piet Mondriaan*'

The Hague, RKD, Cis and Leo Heijdenrijk Archive (0787)

See Coppes 2012, pp. 90–91 regarding the relationship between the two connected pictures (cats 37–8) and the drawn *Self-Portrait* of 1908–9 (A637).

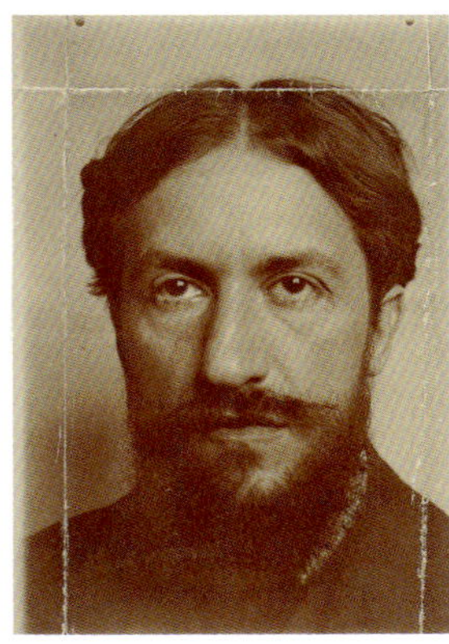

CAT. 38 Unidentified photographer

Portrait of Piet Mondrian with beard and centre parting, c. 1908
(see p. 97)

Gelatin printing-out paper, 17.6 x 12.5 cm

Verso, in Piet Mondrian's handwriting (?): '*Piet Mondrian*'

The Hague, RKD, Piet Mondrian Archive (0740), inv. 58

The spelling of the surname with a single 'a' – a change that Mondrian only decided to make in 1912 – indicates that the inscription must have been added after that date. See also cat. 37.

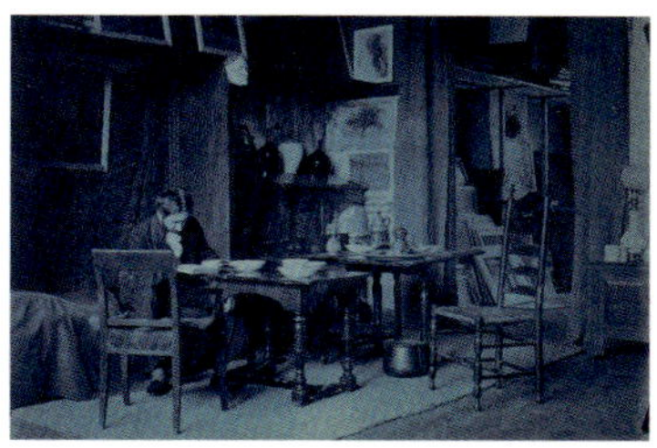

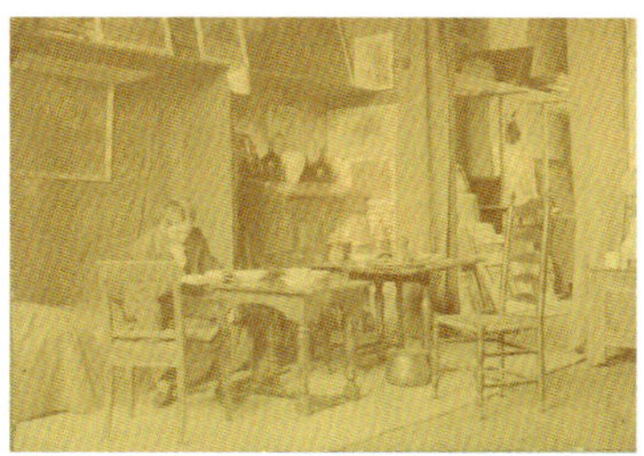

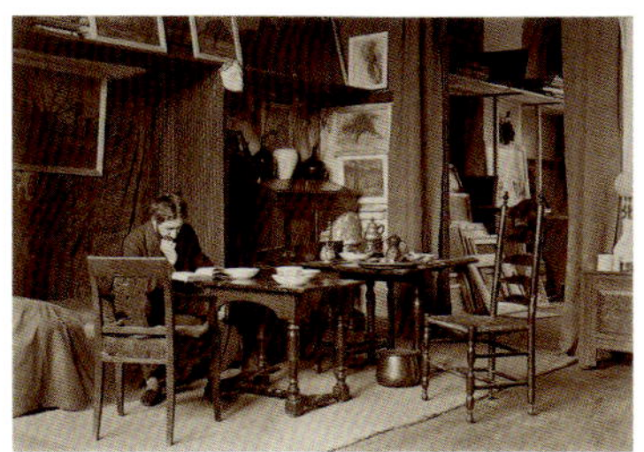

CAT. 39.1; CAT. 39.2; CAT. 39.3
Reinier Drektraan

Piet Mondrian in the living area of his studio at 421 Sarphatipark, Amsterdam, autumn 1908
(see pp. 98–9)

(1) Cyanotype, 14.4 x 19.7 cm; (2) salt print, 14.4 x 19.7 cm; (3) unidentified

(1) Verso, stamp: 'R. DREKTRAAN, Kuiperstraat 60'

(1) The Hague, RKD, Piet Mondrian Archive (0740), inv. 57; (2) Otterlo, Kröller-Müller Museum; (3) private collection

Janssen has dated this photograph to the autumn of 1908, arguing that Mondrian had it taken to publicize his first big exhibition at the Stedelijk Museum, Amsterdam (Janssen 2013, p. 109).

Three contemporary copies of the picture are known, printed using different techniques. The one in the Kröller-Müller Museum has the same kind of mount as the cyanotype in the RKD collection. Reinier Drektraan's stamp on the back is only found on the RKD print; the stamp on the back of the Kröller-Müller Museum copy has been scratched out. The third print, which belongs to a private collection, was not available for further examination. Technical data is therefore lacking.

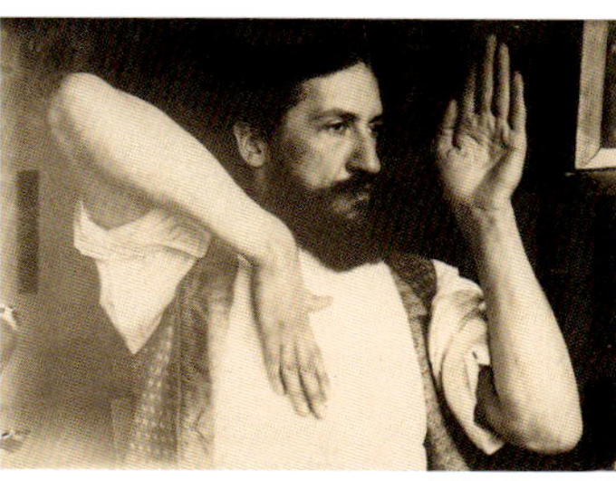

CAT. 40 Alfred Waldenburg

Phrenological portrait of Piet Mondrian, c. April 1909
(see p. 100)

Gelatin printing-out paper, 13 x 18 cm

Recto, in Alfred Waldenburg's handwriting: 'fecit Dr med Alfred Waldenburg Berlin 1909'; verso, in Harry Holtzman's handwriting (?): 'Dalcroze? / Eurhythmics'

The Hague, RKD, Piet Mondrian Archive (0740), inv. 59

Based on Mondrian's letters to Aletta de Iongh, this photograph will have been taken shortly before 16 May 1909 (Coppes 2020, p. 26, n. 29).

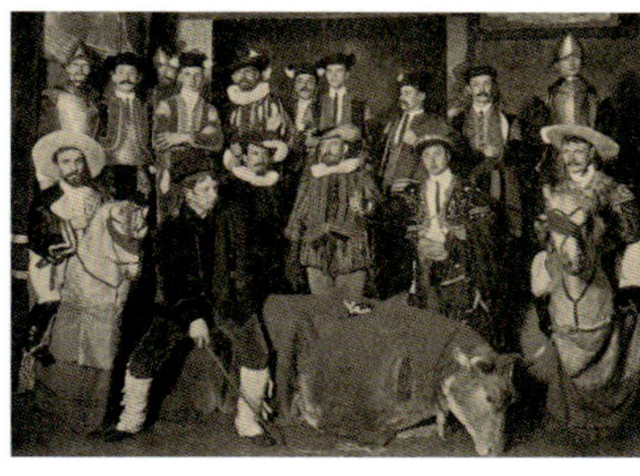

CAT. 41 Unidentified photographer

***Tableau vivant* at the Spanish-themed party of the Sint Lucas artists' association, 13 November 1909** (see p. 47)

The picture was reproduced in the magazine *De Kunst*, captioned: 'Participants in the bullfight. From left to right, front row: Filarski, Monnickendam, Piet Mondrian, Benner, Hoogerwaard, Bergman; second row: L. C. Mondriaan, M. Citroen, Bakker, Poortenaar, Breitenstein, Van de Wall Perné, Colnot, Smorenburg, Oscar Haberer, M. Butter.' The 'bullfight' staged by Mondrian was one of the highlights of the fancy-dress evening.

A vintage print has not been traced; the photograph is only known thanks to its publication in *De Kunst*, which provides the date. Mondrian's brother Louis ('L. C.') was an 'art-loving member' of the society and was thus also able to take part in the play (Coppes 2018, p. 124).

Publication: N. H. Wolf, '"Spanje" in "Sint-Lucas". 't Jaarlijksch feest', *De Kunst*, vol. 2, no. 95 (20 November 1909), n.p.

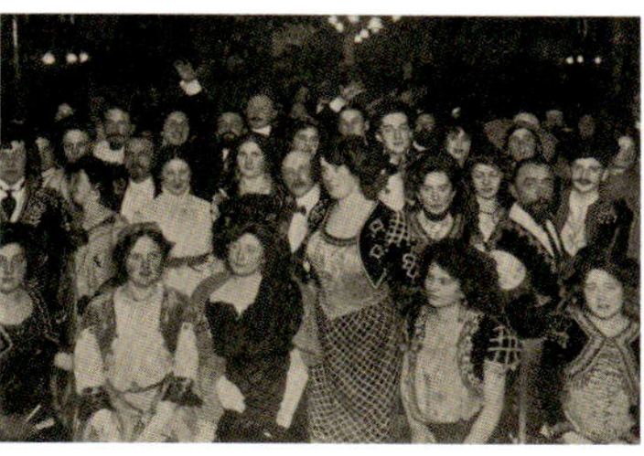

CAT. 42 Unidentified photographer

Spanish-themed party of the Sint Lucas artists' association, 13 November 1909

The picture was reproduced in the magazine *De Kunst*, captioned: 'View of the room after supper. The ladies include Mrs Maris, Mrs Knap, Mrs Clignett, Miss Ansingh, Miss Letsch, and the gentlemen Simon Maris, Piet Mondrian, J. P. Nord Thomson, G. C. Vrint, G. van Pelt, L. Saalborn, C. M. Garms and P. Clignett.' Mondrian can be seen at the back, on the left, with a Van Dyck beard and ruff.

A vintage print has not been traced; the photograph is only known thanks to its publication in *De Kunst*.

See also cat. 41.

Publication: N. H. Wolf, '"Spanje" in "Sint-Lucas". 't Jaarlijksch feest', *De Kunst*, vol. 2, no. 95 (20 November 1909), n.p.

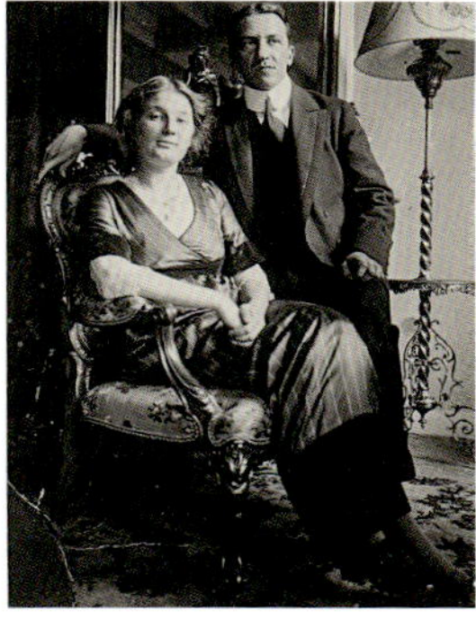

CAT. 43 Unidentified photographer

Portrait of Greta Heijbroek and Piet Mondrian, c. September 1911
(see p. 101)

Gelatin developing-out paper, 12 x 9.1 cm

The Hague, RKD, Piet Mondrian Archive (0740), inv. 134

According to a note by Harry Holtzman on the back, this print came into his possession in July 1958 through a cousin of Greta Heijbroek.

For the dating, see Welsh/Joosten 1998-I, p. 132, 1998-II, p. 100.

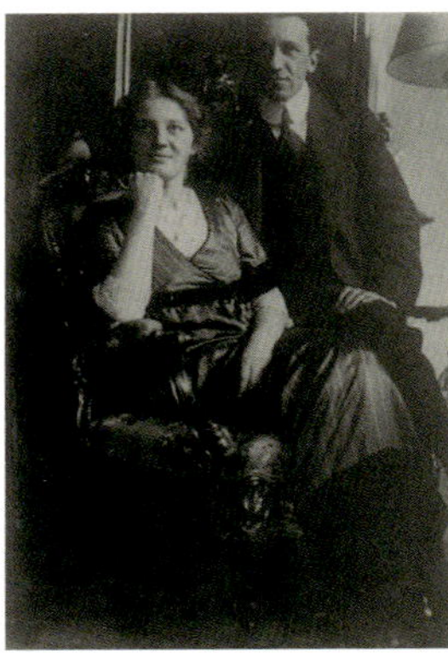

CAT. 44 Unidentified photographer

Portrait of Greta Heijbroek and Piet Mondrian, c. September 1911

Private collection

A vintage print has not been traced; the photograph reproduced here is a later print (The Hague, RKD, Joop Joosten Archive (0838), inv. 808).

For the dating, see cat. 43.

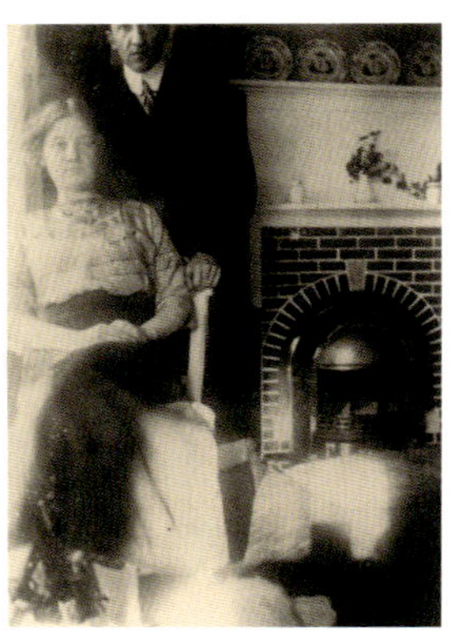

CAT. 45 Unidentified photographer

Portrait of Greta Heijbroek and Piet Mondrian, c. September 1911

Verso, in unidentified handwriting: 'Helaas met een half hoofd!' ('Alas, with half a head!') (cf. Hanssen 2017, fig. 5, n.p.)

Private collection

The picture was not available for further research. Technical data is therefore lacking. The reproduction was made available by L. Hanssen. See Hanssen 2017.

For the dating, see cat. 43.

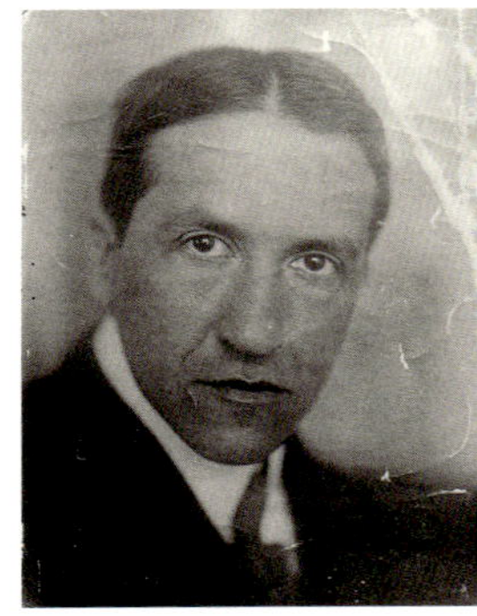

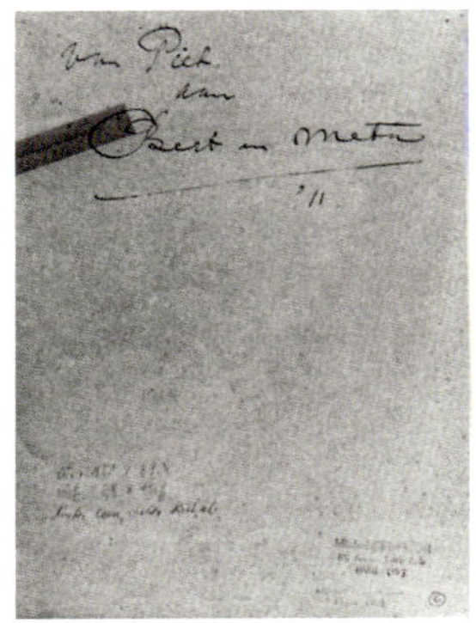

CAT. 46 Unidentified photographer

Portrait of Piet Mondrian, 1911 (see p. 102)

Verso, in Piet Mondrian's handwriting: 'Van Piet / aan / *Bert en Meta* / '11' ('From Piet / to / Bert and Meta / [19]11'); stamp (2x): 'Michel SEUPHOR / 83 Avenue Emile Zola / PARIS (15e)'

A vintage print has not been traced; the photograph reproduced here is a later print (The Hague, RKD, Joop Joosten Archive (0838), inv. 808).

The dating is based on Mondrian's dedication to Bert and Meta van den Briel. It cannot be ruled out, however, that the picture was taken as early as the autumn of 1910, after Mondrian changed his appearance.

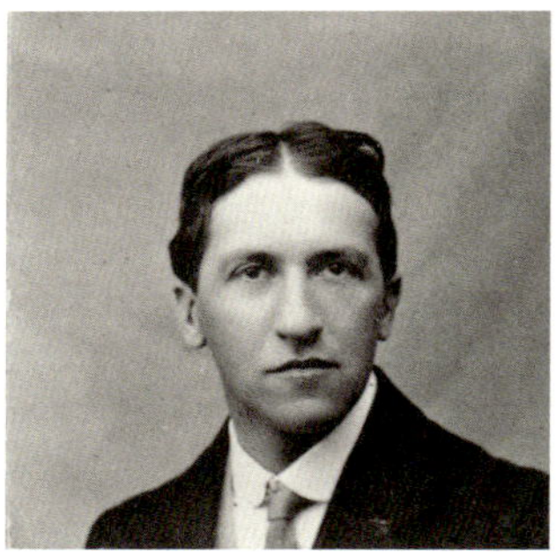

CAT. 47 Unidentified photographer

Portrait of Piet Mondrian, 1912 (?)
(see p. 102)

Paris, Archives des Musées Nationaux, Musée du Louvre (Série LL)

The picture is known from Mondrian's copyist card for the Louvre, which was issued to him on 1 June 1912. It is likely to have been taken shortly before that date.

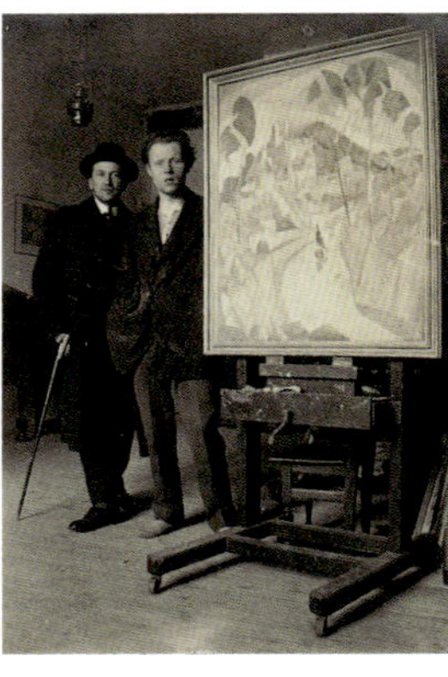

CAT. 48 Conrad Kickert

Piet Mondrian and Lodewijk Schelfhout in the latter's studio, 1912
(see p. 103)

Gelatin developing-out paper, 11.8 x 8.4 cm

The Hague, RKD, Lodewijk Schelfhout Archive (0278), inv. 271

Schelfhout completed his painting *View of Villeneuve-lès-Avignon* – seen here on the easel – in 1912, and so we date the photograph to that year.

In May 1912, Schelfhout moved from his studio on Avenue du Maine to one on Rue du Départ. It is not clear at which of these locations the photograph was taken.

See also Almering-Strik 2018, pp. 53–5, 162.

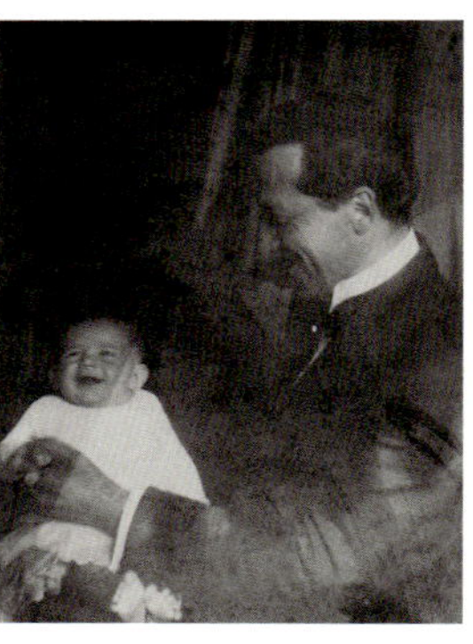

CAT. 49 Unidentified photographer

Piet Mondrian with Hugues Raymond Colin on his knee, September–October 1914 (see p. 102)

Private collection

The picture was not available for further research. Technical data is therefore lacking. The reproduction was made available by L. Hanssen. Dated to September or October 1914 based on Hanssen 2015 (photograph 17, between pp. 192 and 193, cf. the publication's online notes).

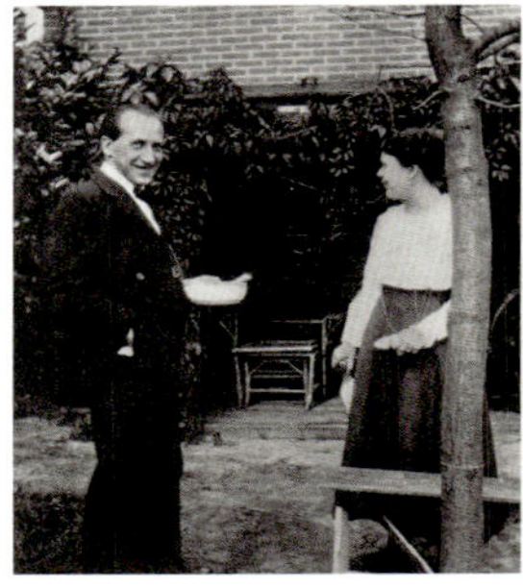

CAT. 50 Unidentified photographer

Piet Mondrian with an unidentified woman, between August 1914 and the end of June 1919

A vintage print has not been traced; the photograph is only known thanks to its publication in Wijsenbeek 1968.

Given Mondrian's hairstyle and estimated age, the picture must date from the period August 1914 to the end of June 1919, which he spent in the Netherlands. The brick wall in the background also looks Dutch.

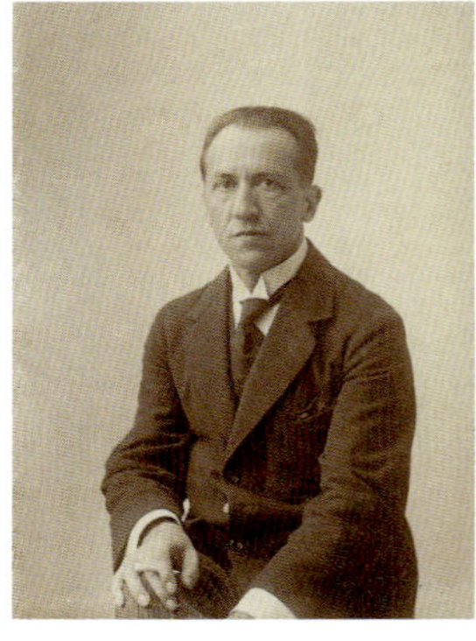

CAT. 51 Unidentified photographer (Peter Alma?)

Portrait of Piet Mondrian, c. 1918 (?)
(see p. 103)

Gelatin printing-out paper, 9.7 x 7.2 cm

Verso: 'C. M.'

The Hague, RKD, Collectie Preciosafoto's Piet Mondriaan

We know from an undated letter from Mondrian to Theo van Doesburg (c. March 1922) that the artist Peter Alma took a portrait photo of Mondrian. This could be it.

Since the picture is also known from Mondrian's residence permit in Paris, it must have been taken prior to June 1919, and hence in the Netherlands. Given the uncertainty about both the photographer and the timing, we have dated the photograph to around 1918.

The initials in the inscription are probably those of Carel Mondriaan, from whose estate this print might have come.

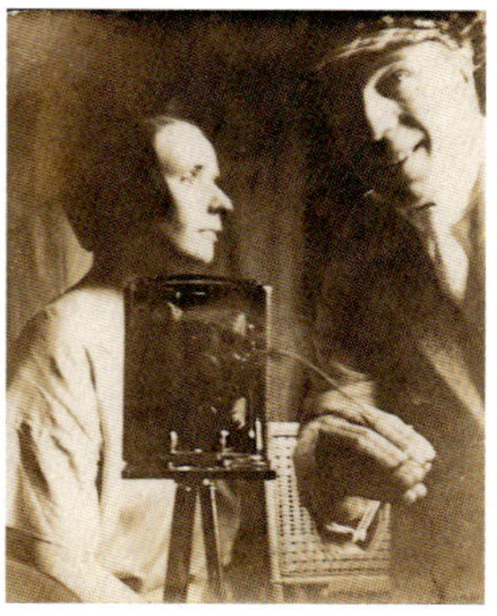

CAT. 52 Theo van Doesburg

Self-portrait of Theo and Nelly van Doesburg in Piet Mondrian's studio, between 28 March and 9 April 1921 (see p. 109)

Gelatin developing-out paper, 9.6 x 7.5 cm

Verso, in Nelly van Doesburg's handwriting: 'Does+Nelly / in het atelier / van Mondriaan / 1921' ('[Van] Does[burg] and Nelly in Mondrian's studio, 1921')

The Hague, RKD, Theo and Nelly van Doesburg Archive (0408), inv. 1515

On a second print, verso, in Nelly van Doesburg's handwriting: 'bij / Mondriaan / Does + / Nelly' ('at Mondrian's, [Van] Does[Burg] and Nelly') (The Hague, RKD, Theo and Nelly van Doesburg Archive (0408), inv. 1515).

The picture must date from Theo and Nelly van Doesburg's visit to Mondrian between 28 March and 9 April 1921 (Ottevanger 2008, p. 322; Welsh/Joosten 1998-II, pp. 116, 121).

It was evidently taken using a mirror.

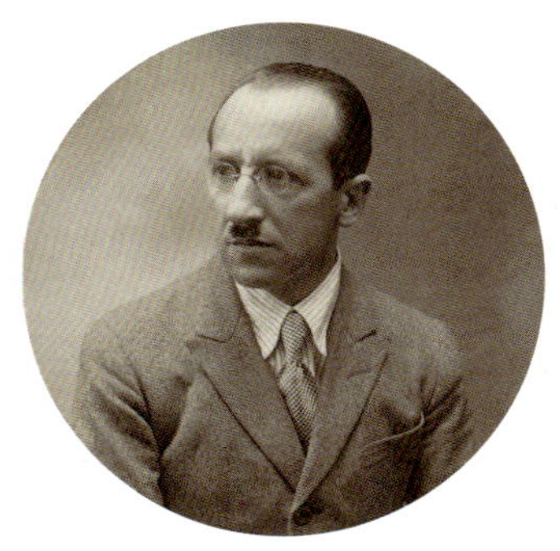

CAT. 53 Unidentified photographer

Portrait of Piet Mondrian, c. 1922 (see p. 110)

Gelatin developing-out paper, 7.9 x 8 cm

The Hague, RKD, Theo and Nelly van Doesburg Archive (0408), inv. 1678

Dating based on the strong resemblance to Mondrian's appearance in cat. 54, a photograph taken in 1922. Mondrian does not seem to have worn a pince-nez before 1922. The eyewear makes its first appearance in cats 53–4.

Publication: 'P. Mondriaan', *De Stijl*, vol. 7, no. 79/84 (1927), pp. 35–7; photograph on p. 35.

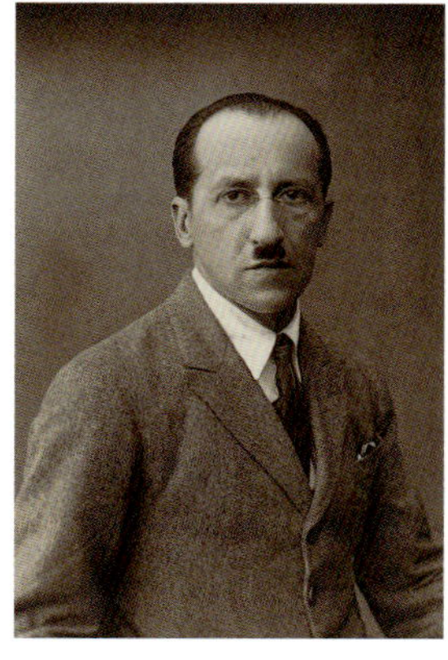

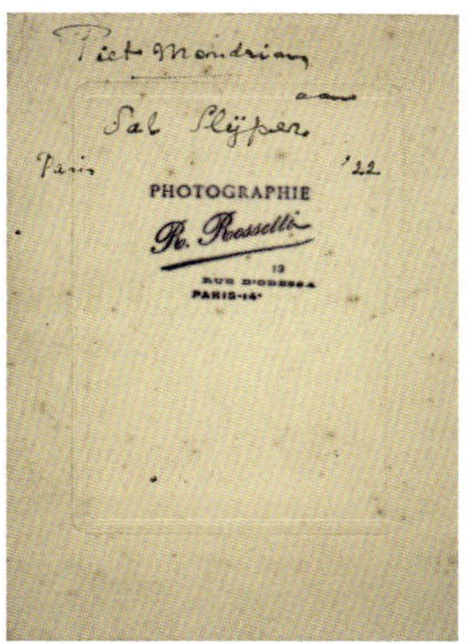

CAT. 54 Photographie R. Rossetti

Portrait of Piet Mondrian, summer (June?) 1922 (see p. 111)

Gelatin printing-out paper, 10.8 x 7.5 cm

Stamp recto: 'R. Rossetti'; verso, in Piet Mondrian's handwriting: '*Piet Mondrian* / aan [to] / Sal Slijper / Paris '22'; stamp: 'PHOTOGRAPHIE / R. Rossetti / 13 / RUE D'ODESSA / PARIS-14e'

The Hague, RKD, Sal Slijper Archive (0150), inv. 536

Second print: identical stamps; verso, in Piet Mondrian's handwriting: '*Piet Mondrian* 16 juin 22'. (The Hague, RKD, inv. RKD-PF-143)

A *terminus ante quem* is provided by the date on the second print of the portrait (16 June 1922). We have therefore dated it to summer (June?) 1922.

Publication: Piet Mondrian, 'Schilderkunst', *De Stijl*, vol. 5, no. 12 (December 1922), p. 179 (cut-out).

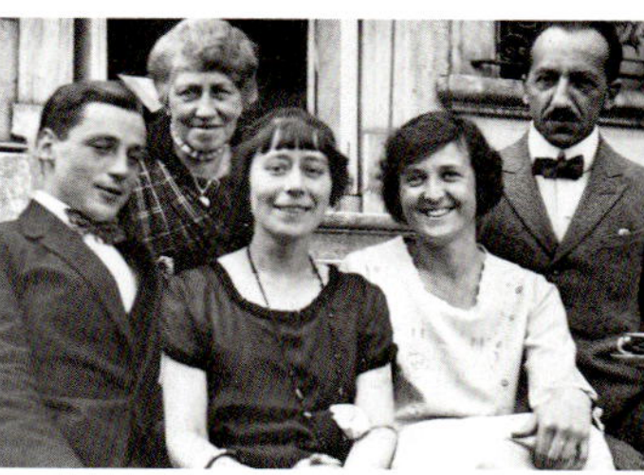

CAT. 55 Unidentified photographer

Company in the Colin-Penning family's garden, summer 1922 (see p. 113)

Verso, in unidentified handwriting: 'Piet Mondrian (à droite) à Clamart chez M et Mme Colin du Terrail en 1922'

A vintage print has not been traced; the photograph reproduced here is a later print (The Hague, RKD, Herbert Henkels Archive (0620), inv. 442).

Dating based on the note on the back and the light clothing worn in this and subsequent photographs. It corresponds with Mondrian's appearance in the photograph, including the toothbrush moustache.

See Henkels 1987, p. 208; Hanssen 2015, pp. 85, 185; Colin 2021, p. 49.

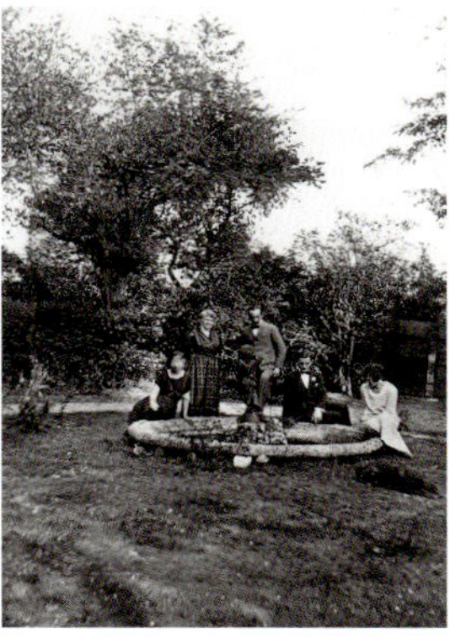

CAT. 56 Unidentified photographer

Company in the Colin-Penning family's garden, summer 1922 (see p. 112)

A vintage print has not been traced; the photograph reproduced here is a later print (The Hague, RKD, Herbert Henkels Archive (0620), inv. 442).

For the dating, see cat. 55.

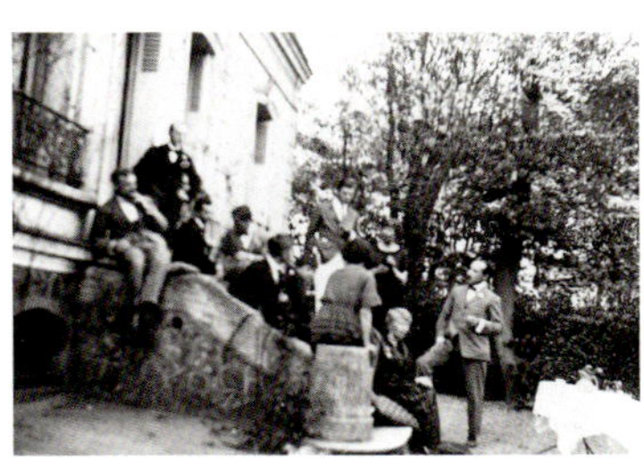

CAT. 57 Unidentified photographer

Company in the Colin-Penning family's garden, summer 1922

A vintage print has not been traced; the photograph reproduced here is a later print (The Hague, RKD, Herbert Henkels Archive (0620), inv. 442).

For the dating, see cat. 55.

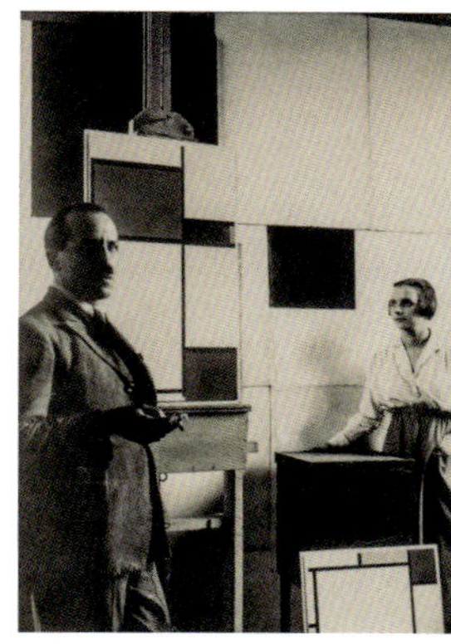

CAT. 58 Theo van Doesburg

Piet Mondrian and Nelly van Doesburg in Mondrian's studio, early May 1923 (see p. 114)

A vintage print has not been traced; the photograph reproduced here is a later print (The Hague, RKD, Joop Joosten Archive (0838), inv. 809).

Theo van Doesburg had been staying with Mondrian 'for the past week' on 7 May 1923 (Ottevanger 2008, p. 426). The painting leaning against the cabinet, *Tableau 2* (B146, 1922), was exhibited at the Grosse Berliner Kunstausstellung in Berlin from 19 May 1923, where a German collector bought it. Allowing a week for transport, the photograph could have been taken around 12 May at the latest; we therefore date it to the beginning of May 1923.

Publication: Piet Mondrian, 'Den huif naar den wind', *De Stijl*, vol. 6, no. 6/7 (August 1924), pp. 86–8 (cut-out).

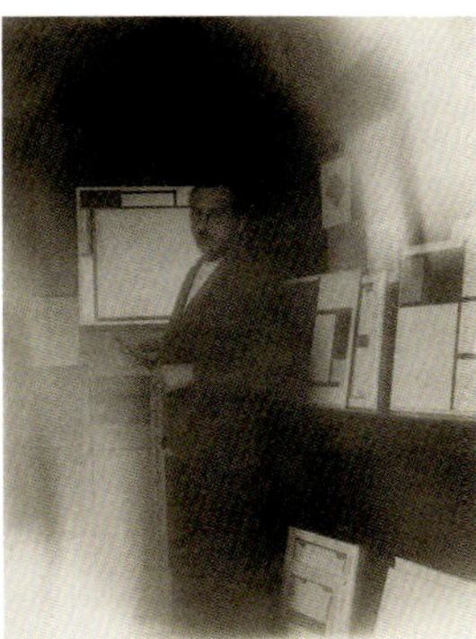

CAT. 59 César Domela

Piet Mondrian in his studio, December 1923 (see p. 115)

Gelatin developing-out paper, 10.4 x 7.7 cm

Verso, in César Domela's handwriting: 'Mondriaan 1924'

The Hague, RKD, César Domela Archive (0076), inv. 299

Domela later dated the photograph to 1924, but it must have been taken in 1923. Mondrian's letters to Til Brugman and Sal Slijper show that the painting *Tableau* (B150), visible on the right, might have been in the Netherlands since late December 1923 or January 1924. Partly for this reason, the photograph had already been dated to December 1923 (De Jongh-Vermeulen 2019, p. 72).

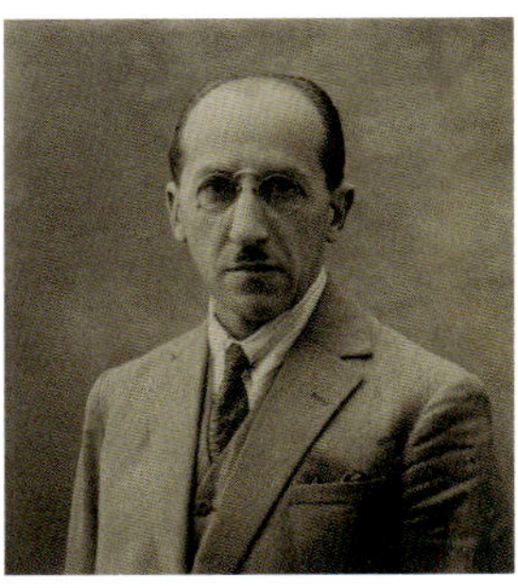

CAT. 60 Unidentified photographer

Portrait of Piet Mondrian, c. 1924 (?) (see p. 115)

Gelatin developing-out paper, 6.5 x 5.2 cm

The Hague, RKD, Sal Slijper Archive (0150), inv. 536

The dating of this photograph is not certain. Mondrian looks older here than in Rossetti's picture from the spring (June?) of 1922 (cat. 54). The photograph probably dates from before around November 1924, when he had two new pairs of glasses made, 'one for nearby and one for far away, with imitation tortoiseshell frames. Nicer than a lorgnon [pince-nez]' (letter from Piet Mondrian to Til Brugman, 13 November 1924 (The Hague, RKD, Til Brugman Archive (0607)). Despite this, Mondrian can still be seen in several photographs wearing a pince-nez. He bade a final farewell to the toothbrush moustache in or shortly before 1928.

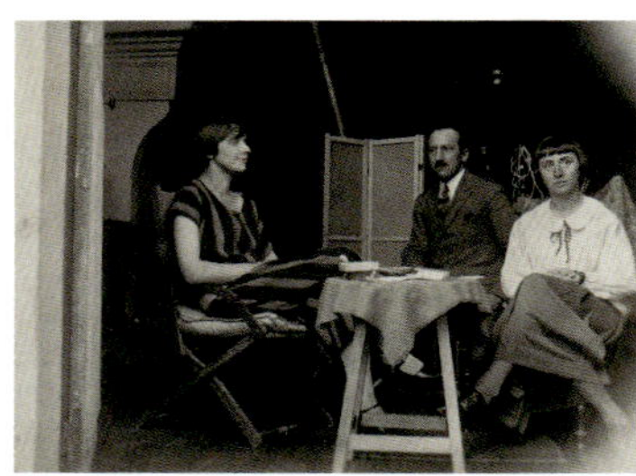

CAT. 61 Theo van Doesburg

Nelly van Doesburg, Piet Mondrian and the German artist Hannah Höch in the Van Doesburgs' studio, 27 April 1924 (see p. 116)

Gelatin developing-out paper, 8 x 10.7 cm

Verso, in Hannah Höch's handwriting: 'bei Does Mondrian im Atelier Paris 1924 Nelly Doesburg Mondrian H. Höch' ('at [Van] Does[burg's], Mondrian in the studio, Paris, 1924, Nelly Doesburg, Mondrian, H. Höch')

Berlin, Berlinische Galerie, Nachlass Hannah Höch, inv. BG HHC-F 285/79

Hannah Höch's travel diary records that she was with the Van Doesburgs in Clamart on Sunday 27 and Monday 28 April 1924. Mondrian joined them on the Sunday.

See Ottevanger 2008, p. 460, n. 16; Roters 1995, pp. 156–58

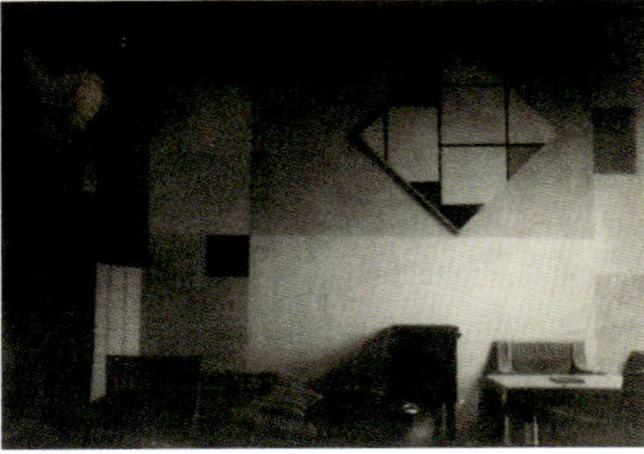

CAT. 62 Georges Vantongerloo

Piet Mondrian's studio, July–August 1924 (see p. 117)

A vintage print has not been traced; the photograph reproduced here is a later print (The Hague, RKD, Joop Joosten Archive (0838), inv. 814).

Georges Vantongerloo visited Paris in July and August 1924. Judging by the first version of *Lozenge Composition* (B151, 1924) on the wall, the photograph must have been taken during that visit. Mondrian substantially adjusted the canvas after the summer of 1924, making the lines wider, for example. For that reason, we date the photograph to July–August 1924.

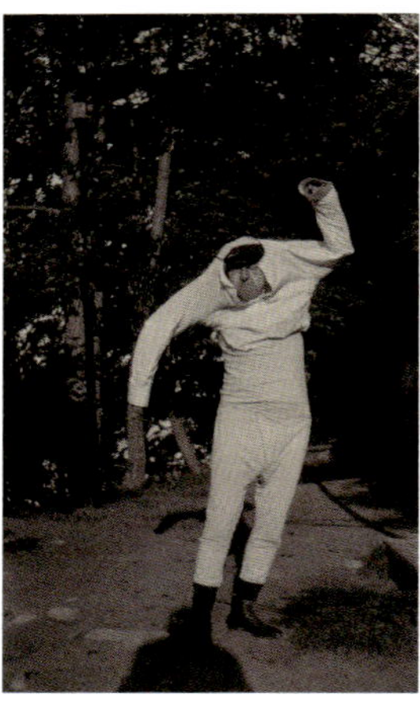

CAT. 63 Agatha Zethraeus

Piet Mondrian in Agatha Zethraeus's garden, Clamart, c. 1925 (see p. 118)

Collodion printing-out paper, 10.8 x 6.2 cm

Verso, in Agatha Zethraeus's handwriting: 'Ten gevolge van plaatsruimte / was ik steeds gedwongen een zeer / gewichtig artikel buitenhuis aan te trekken. – Mijn op de foto zicht- / bare "Schurbartbinde" [sic] geeft een idee / welk een zorg ik aan mijn / uiterlijk besteed. / P. Mondriaan' ('In view of the space, I was always obliged to put on a weighty article outdoors. The moustache guard visible in the picture gives an idea of the care I pay to my appearance. P. Mondrian')

The Hague, RKD, Collectie Preciosafoto's Piet Mondriaan

The painter Agatha Zethraeus, from whose estate this photograph originates, was a friend of Mondrian's. Around 1925, she spent some time in Clamart, near Paris. The photograph is likely to have been taken around that time, hence its dating to about 1925.

The moustache guard (*Schnurrbartbinde*) mentioned in the inscription on the back was worn by gentlemen to keep their whiskers in shape overnight. Any moustache Mondrian might have been sporting at this time is thus hidden from view.

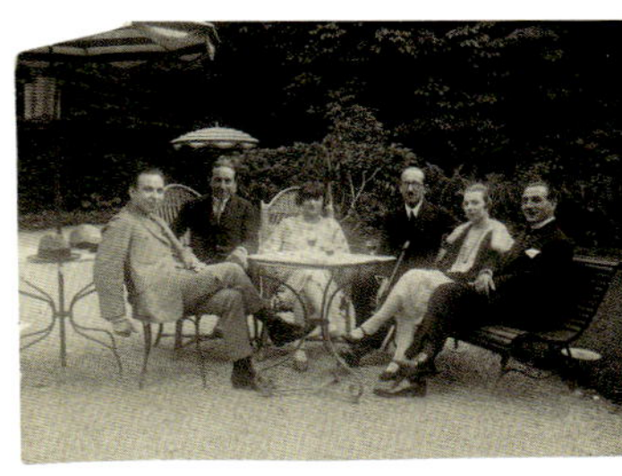

CAT. 64 Liesbeth Sanders-Herzberg

Mondrian and friends in a garden in Saint-Germain-en-Laye, 15 July 1925 (see p. 119)

Gelatin developing-out paper, 7.2 x 9.7 cm

Verso, in unidentified handwriting: 'In de tuin [in the garden] Av. des Loges. St. Germain en Laye / 15 ~~Aug~~ Julie 1925 / v.l.n.r.: [left to right] / P.F.S.; J. & Frie; Piet M.; Tine & Georges van Tongerlo'

The Hague, RKD, Collectie Preciosafoto's Piet Mondriaan

The 15 July 1925 date is based on the inscription.

See also cats 65–6, which were taken during the same visit by Mr and Mrs Sanders and Mr and Mrs Tas.

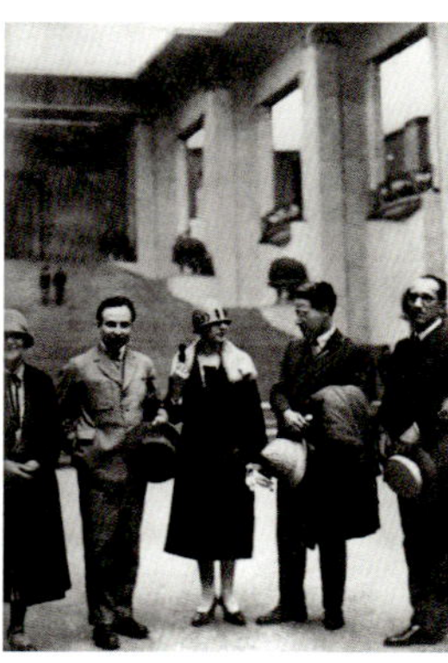

CAT. 65 Liesbeth Sanders-Herzberg (?)

Mondrian and friends at the Grand Palais during a visit to the Exposition des Arts Décoratifs, Paris, c. July 1925

Left to right: Lucia Moholy-Nagy (?), Paul Sanders, Tine Vantongerloo, László Moholy-Nagy, Piet Mondrian and Georges Vantongerloo.

A vintage print has not been traced; the photograph reproduced here is a later print (The Hague, RKD, Joop Joosten Archive (0838), inv. 809).

The photograph was taken on the occasion of the same visit by the Sanders and the Tases.

See also cats 64 and 66.

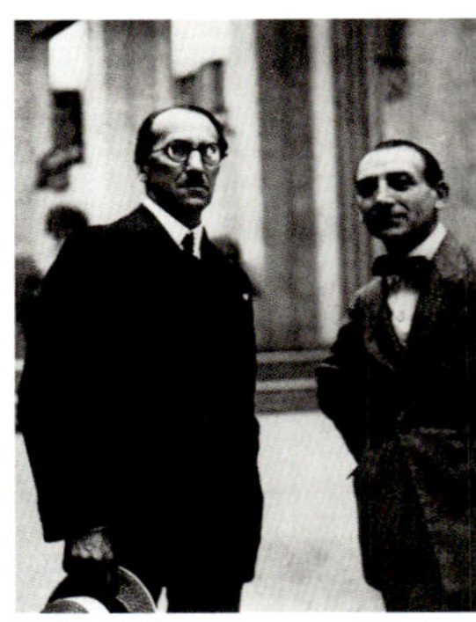

CAT. 66 Liesbeth Sanders-Herzberg (?)

Piet Mondrian and Georges Vantongerloo at the Grand Palais during a visit to the Exposition des Arts Décoratifs, Paris, c. July 1925

A vintage print has not been traced; the photograph reproduced here is a later print (The Hague, RKD, Joop Joosten Archive (0838), inv. 809).

The photograph was taken on the occasion of the same visit by the Sanders and the Tases.

See also cats 64–5.

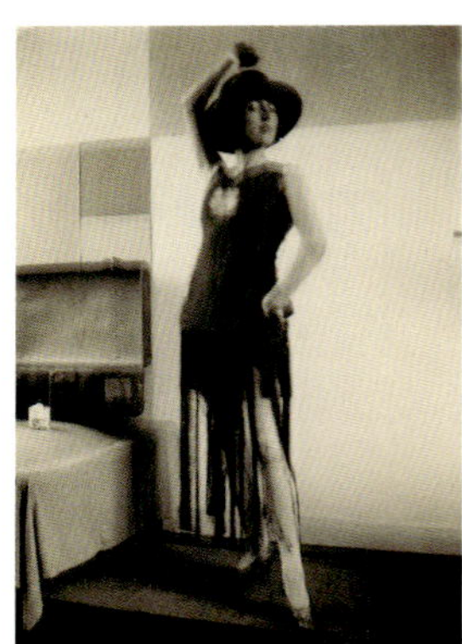

CAT. 67 Unidentified photographer (César Domela?)

The dancer Kamares (Willy van Aggelen) in Piet Mondrian's studio, late December 1925 (see p. 120)

Gelatin developing-out paper, 6.6 x 4.4 cm

University of Amsterdam, Theatre Collection, Wilhelmina van Aggelen Archive, inv. 15

A similar photograph was taken in Theo van Doesburg's studio between 21 and 28 December 1925. We assume that the pictures in Mondrian's studio (cats 67–72) were taken around the same time, probably by César Domela (De Jongh-Vermeulen 2019, pp. 98–9).

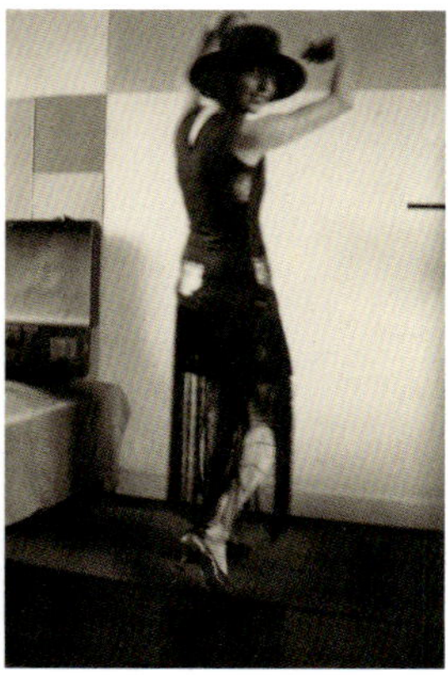

CAT. 68 Unidentified photographer (César Domela?)

The dancer Kamares (Willy van Aggelen) in Piet Mondrian's studio, late December 1925 (see p. 120)

Gelatin developing-out paper, 6.6 x 4.4 cm

See also cat. 67.

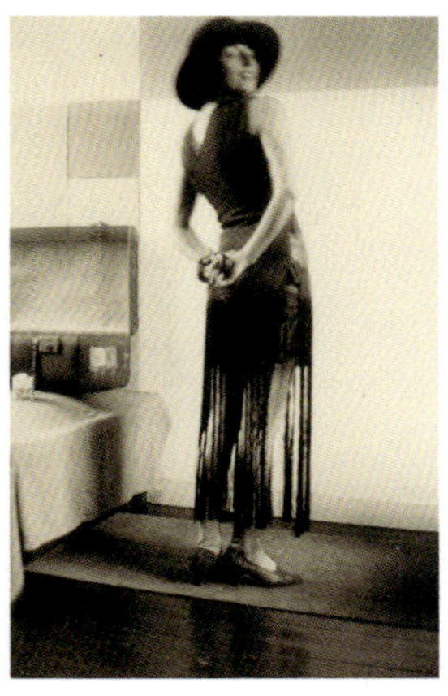

CAT. 69 Unidentified photographer (César Domela?)

The dancer Kamares (Willy van Aggelen) in Piet Mondrian's studio, late December 1925 (see p. 120)

Gelatin developing-out paper, 6.6 x 4.4 cm

See also cat. 67.

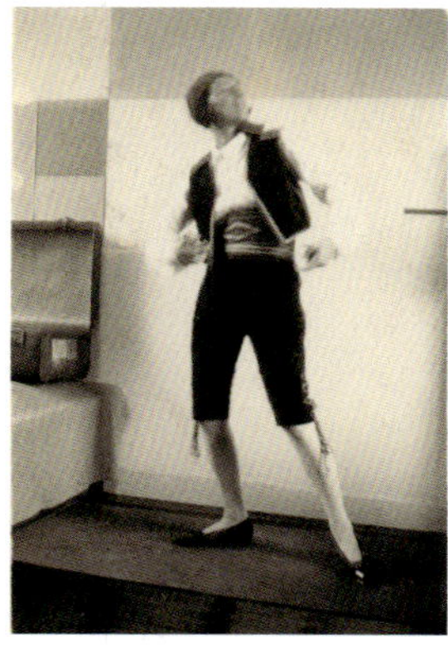

CAT. 70 Unidentified photographer (César Domela?)

The dancer Kamares (Willy van Aggelen) in Piet Mondrian's studio, late December 1925 (see p. 120)

Gelatin developing-out paper, 6.6 x 4.4 cm

See also cat. 67.

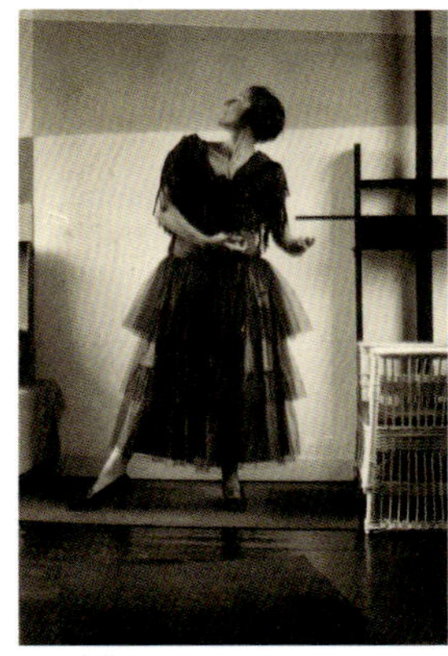

CAT. 71 Unidentified photographer (César Domela?)

The dancer Kamares (Willy van Aggelen) in Piet Mondrian's studio, late December 1925 (see p. 120)

Gelatin developing-out paper, 6.6 x 4.4 cm

See also cat. 67.

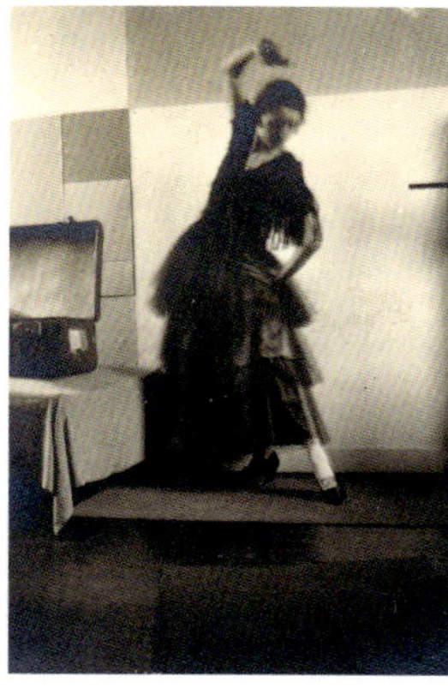

CAT. 72 Unidentified photographer (César Domela?)

The dancer Kamares (Willy van Aggelen) in Piet Mondrian's studio, late December 1925 (see p. 120)

Gelatin developing-out paper, 6.6 x 4.4 cm

See also cat. 67.

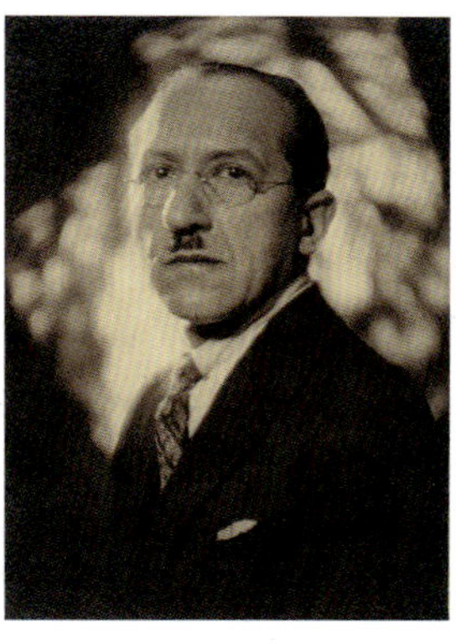

CAT. 73 Max Winisky

Portrait of Piet Mondrian, c. 1926 (see p. 121)

Gelatin developing-out paper, 17.8 x 12.5 cm

Recto, in unidentified handwriting (Max Winisky?): '12 rue Bréa', signed 'MAX'

The Hague, RKD, Piet Mondrian Archive (0740), inv. 62

Since Mondrian is wearing the same glasses as in other photographs taken in 1926, we date the picture to around that year (see also cats 82–3).

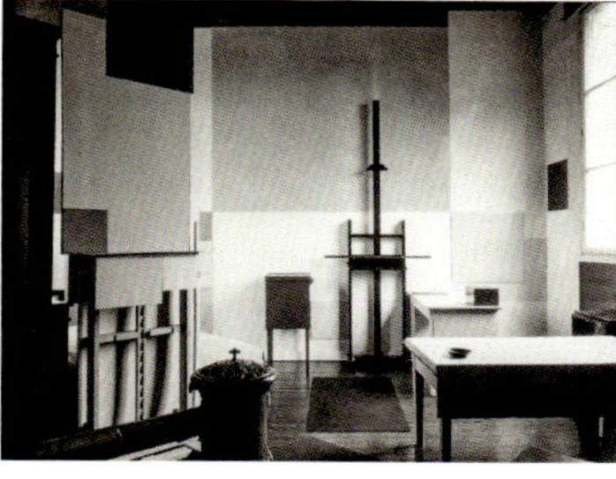

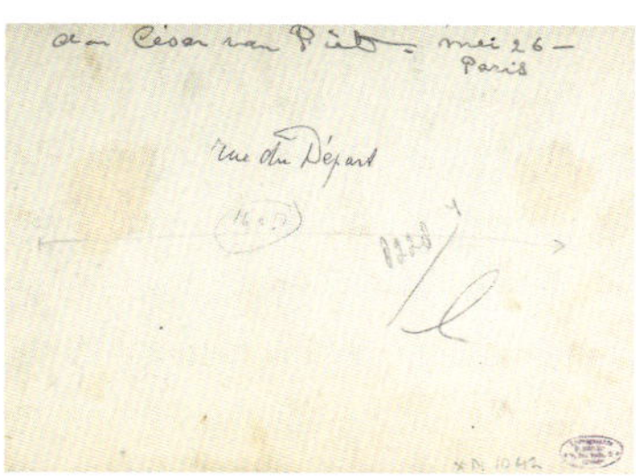

CAT. 74 Pierre Delbo

Piet Mondrian's studio, c. late November 1925–March 1926 (see p. 123)

Gelatin developing-out paper, 16.5 x 21.8 cm

Verso, in Piet Mondrian's handwriting: 'Aan [to] César van Piet. mei [May] 26. / Paris'; stamp: 'Photographie / P. DELBO / 9, Rue Vavin, / Paris-VIe'

The Hague, RKD, César Domela Archive (0076), inv. 299

The photograph belongs to a series with cats 75–6.

Mondrian wrote to the architect J. J. P. Oud on 10 November 1925 that he planned to paint his wicker armchairs (Paris, Fondation Custodia, inv. 1972-A.). The chairs in cats 75–76 are already white. A studio photograph taken in early April 1926 shows that the layout of the back wall had changed by then (see cat. 77). Delbo's photos must therefore date from between the end of November 1925 and the end of March 1926. See also pp. 34–5.

Publications: Hannes Meyer, 'Die neue Welt', *Das Werk*, vol. 13, no. 7 (July 1926), pp. 205–24; Piet Mondrian, 'Neo-Plasticisme. De Woning – De Straat – De Stad', *Internationale Revue i10*, vol. 1, no. 10 (October 1927), pp. 12–18; Jean Gorin, 'La Fonction plastique dans l'architecture future', *Cercle et Carré*, no. 3 (June 1930), n.p.

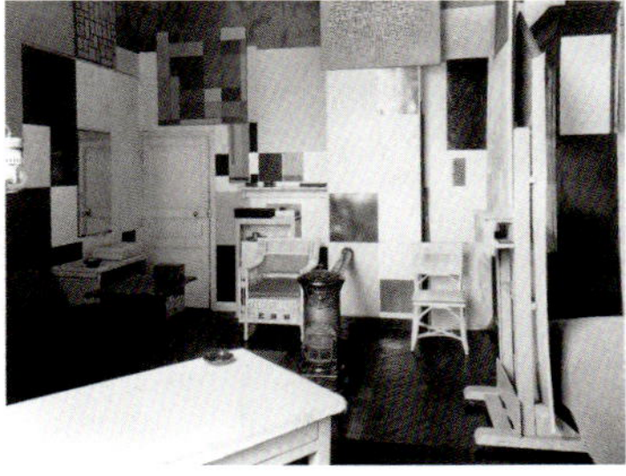

CAT. 75 Pierre Delbo

Piet Mondrian's studio, c. late November 1925–March 1926 (see p. 124)

Gelatin developing-out paper, 16.5 x 21.8 cm

Zurich, EHT/gta Archiv, Nachlass Alfred Roth, inv. 131_T_1_3_F_3.5

This photograph belongs to a series with cats 74 and 76. For more information, see cat. 74.

Publication: *Der Querschnitt*, vol. 8, no. 2 (February 1928), photo section after p. 124.

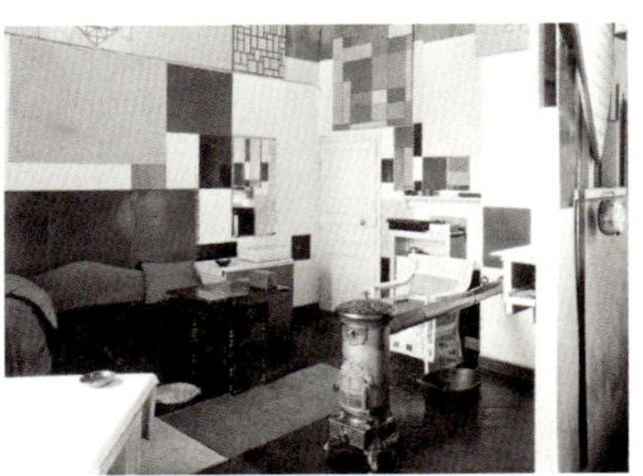

CAT. 76 Pierre Delbo

Piet Mondrian's studio, c. late November 1925–March 1926
(see p. 125)

A vintage print has not been traced; the photograph reproduced here is a later print (The Hague, RKD, Joop Joosten Archive (0838), inv. 814).

This photograph belongs to a series with cats 74 and 75. For further information, see cat. 74.

Publication: Anonymous [W. F. A. Röell], 'Bij Piet Mondriaan. Het kristalheldere atelier. Apologie van den Charleston', *De Telegraaf* (12 September 1926) (montage with cat. 78; see p. 34, ill. 36).

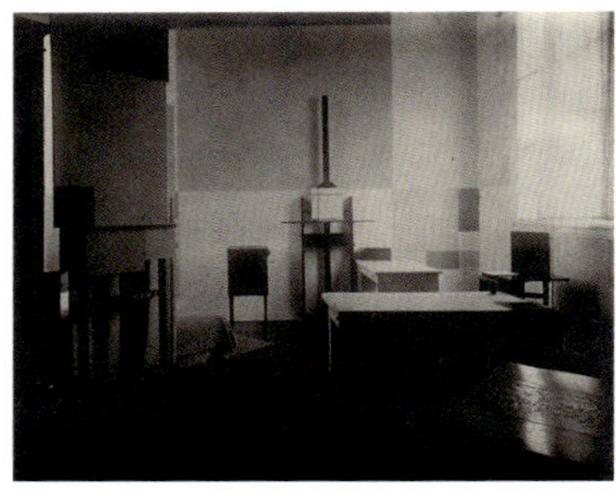

CAT. 77 Unidentified photographer

Piet Mondrian's studio, 7 April 1926
(see p. 126)

Gelatin developing-out paper, 12.1 x 14.9 cm

Verso, in Katherine Dreier's handwriting: 'Mondrian's Studio – / He would not pose *in* it'. The other inscription is a printing instruction (see also cat. 78)

Yale, Beinecke Rare Book & Manuscript Library, Katherine S. Dreier Papers/Société Anonyme Archive, YCAL MSS 101. Box 109, folder 2641

Katherine Dreier visited Mondrian on 7 April 1926 (Welsh/Joosten 1998-I, p. 132; Wieczorek 2020, p. 158).

Based on the inscription on the back of cat. 78, this picture has previously been attributed to Man Ray, who frequently took commissioned photographs and was a friend of Katherine Dreier (Hanssen 2015, pp. 319–20). However, the photograph's technical shortcomings, caused by the strong lighting from the right, argue against this. Perhaps Dreier took the picture herself.

Publication: Katherine Dreier, 'Mondrian – Holland', *International Ex[h]ibition of Modern Art Arranged by the Société Anonyme for the Brooklyn Museum* (New York (Brooklyn Museum) 1926), pp. 48–9 (montage with cat. 78, both of them back to front).

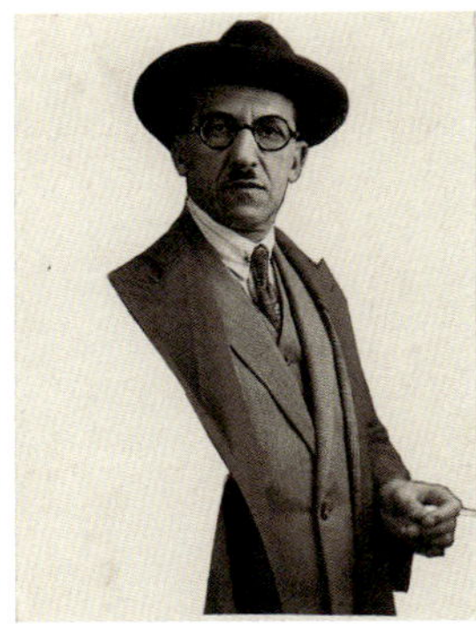

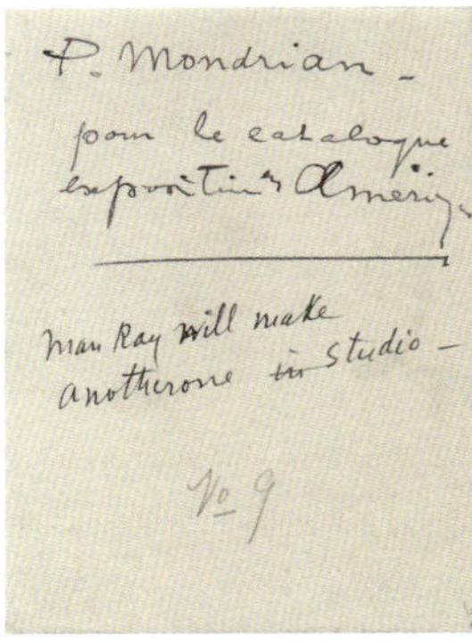

P. Mondrian –
pour le catalogue
exposition Amérique

Man Ray will make
another one in studio –

No 9

CAT. 78 Unidentified photographer

Portrait of Piet Mondrian, c. September 1926 (see p. 127)

Gelatin developing-out paper, 14 x 10.3 cm (mount)

Verso, in Piet Mondrian's handwriting: 'P. Mondrian. / Pour le catalogue / *exposition en Amérique*'; in Katherine Dreier's handwriting: 'Man Ray will make / another one in Studio'

Yale, Beinecke Rare Book & Manuscript Library, Katherine S. Dreier Papers/Société Anonyme Archive, YCAL MSS 101. Box 109, folder 2641

This cut-out is the only surviving version of the photograph. Katherine Dreier might have asked Mondrian for a portrait photo after he refused to pose in his studio (see inscription on cat. 77). No further evidence has been found for the claim that it was Man Ray who took this photo (Hanssen 2015, pp. 319–20).

The picture was published in the Dutch newspaper *De Telegraaf* on 12 September 1926. On the assumption that the picture was taken shortly before this, we date it to around September 1926.

Publications: Anonymous [W. F. A. Röell], 'Bij Piet Mondriaan. Het kristalheldere atelier. Apologie van den Charleston', *De Telegraaf* (12 September 1926) (montage with cat. 76); Katherine Dreier, 'Mondrian – Holland', *International Ex[h]ibition of Modern Art Arranged by the Société Anonyme for the Brooklyn Museum* (New York (Brooklyn Museum) 1926), pp. 48–9 (montage with cat. 77, both of them back to front).

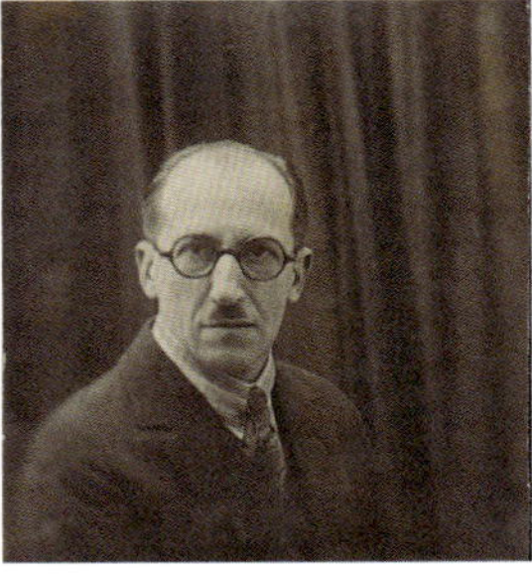

CAT. 79 Unidentified photographer (Charles Karsten?)

Portrait of Piet Mondrian, c. summer/autumn 1926 (see p. 127)

Gelatin developing-out paper, 4.1 x 3.7 cm

Verso, in unidentified handwriting: 'Piet Mondriaan'

Rotterdam, Het Nieuwe Instituut, Charles Karsten Archive, inv. KARS_e5.127-1

Although the picture comes from the estate of the architect Charles Karsten, who took several photographs of Mondrian, it is not certain that he was the author of this image.

It has previously been dated to around 1930 (Hoek 1996, p. 114), but Mondrian had not worn a moustache since around 1928. The photograph is likely to have been taken around the same time as cat. 78: the painter is wearing the same tie and glasses in both pictures. We therefore date it to around summer/autumn 1926.

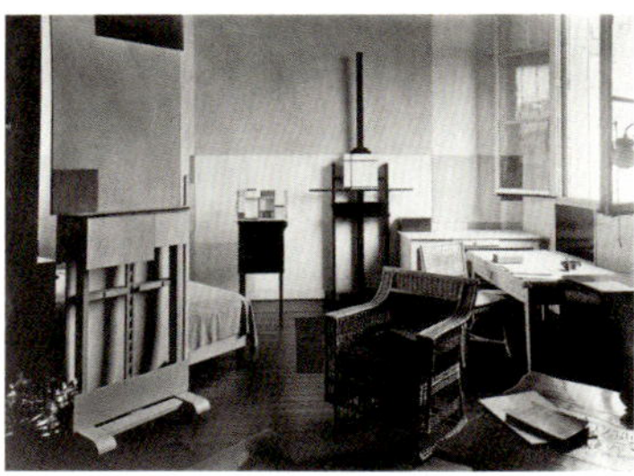

CAT. 80 André Kertész

Piet Mondrian's studio, 19 (?) August 1926 (see p. 129)

A vintage print has not been traced; the photograph reproduced here is a later print (The Hague, RKD, Joop Joosten Archive (0838), inv. 814).

While the dating of the photograph has been contested in the past, it is highly likely to have been taken in the summer of 1926. The earliest mention of a visit to Mondrian by Kertész, in the latter's diary, dates from 19 August 1926 (see p. 128). The open window suggests a summer's day, and so we have assumed that the photograph was taken on that date. This is consistent with the publications on the table in the foreground: Seuphor's poetry collection came out in July 1926 (Henkels 1976, pp. 49, 141; Hanssen 2015, p. 274, n. 2–3); according to Seuphor, the photograph was actually taken on the date of publication, but he wrongly stated that the book was published in October/November (Postma 1995, p. 14). The issue of *Das Werk* appeared in July 1926.

See also cats 81–2.

Publication: Henry van Loon, 'Piet Mondriaan, de mensch, de kunstenaar', *Maandblad voor Beeldende Kunsten*, vol. 4, no. 7 (July 1927), pp. 195–99.

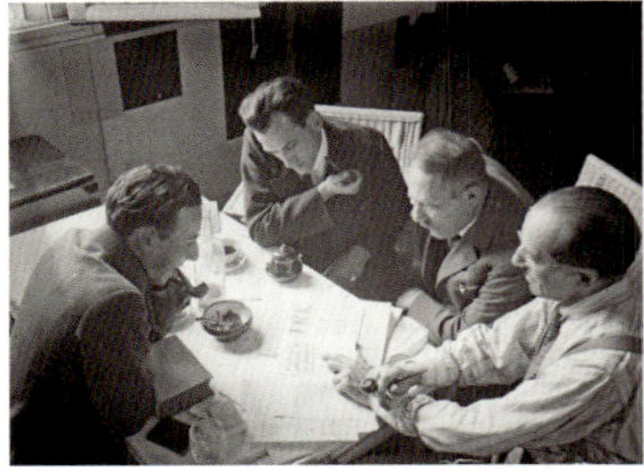

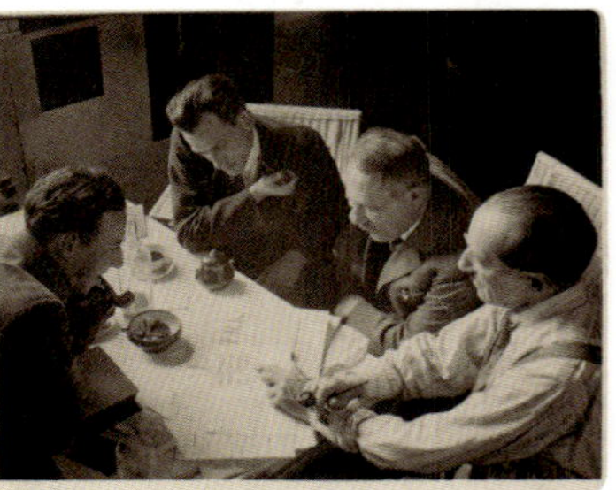

CAT. 81.1; CAT. 81.2 André Kertész

Michel Seuphor, Gyula Zilzer, unidentified man and Piet Mondrian in Mondrian's studio, 19 (?) August 1926 (see p. 130)

(1) Gelatin dry-plate negative, 9 x 12 cm; (2) gelatin developing-out paper, 8.3 x 10.2 cm

(2) Recto: signed 'A. Kertész Paris'

(1) Paris, Médiathèque du Patrimoine et de la Photographie, inv. 72L000687; (2) New Orleans Museum of Art, inv. 73173

This photograph is likely to have been taken on the same day as cat. 80, given Michel Seuphor's poetry book and the offprint of *Das Werk* on the table, and also the wide-open window. It too has therefore been dated to (probably) 19 August 1926.

The earlier identification of the unidentified man as Louis Saalborn (De Mondenard 2010, p. 119) has been rejected based on other portraits of Saalborn from that time. Gyula Zilzer has also been mistakenly identified in the past as the poet Juozas Tysliava (ibid.).

A large print of this picture featured along with cats 92–3 and 96 in the first exhibition of Kertész's work at the Paris gallery Au Sacre du Printemps in March 1927.

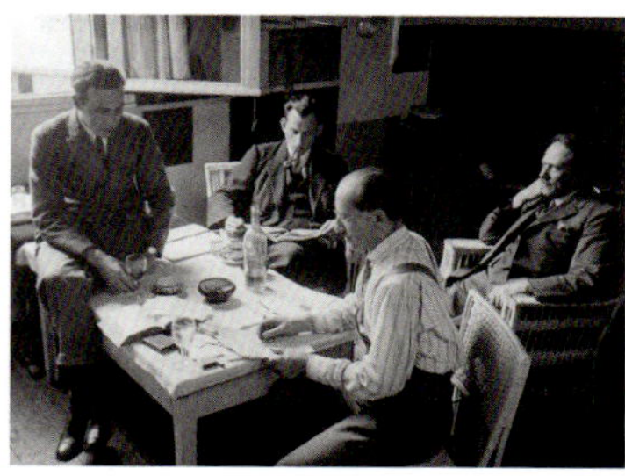

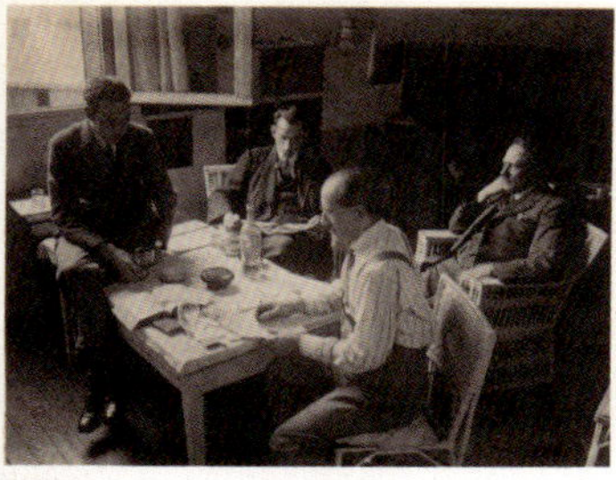

CAT. 82.1; CAT. 82.2 André Kertész

Michel Seuphor, Gyula Zilzer, Piet Mondrian and unidentified man in Mondrian's studio, 19 (?) August 1926 (see p. 131)

(1) Gelatin dry-plate negative, 9 x 12 cm; (2) gelatin developing-out paper, 8.6 x 10.7 cm

(2) Verso, in Michel Seuphor's handwriting: 'Zilzer / Seuphor / Mondrian / x / Aout 1926 / Kertesz' and 'avant 40'

(1) Paris, Médiathèque du Patrimoine et de la Photographie, inv. 72L000688; (2) private collection (?)

For the identification, see also cat. 81.

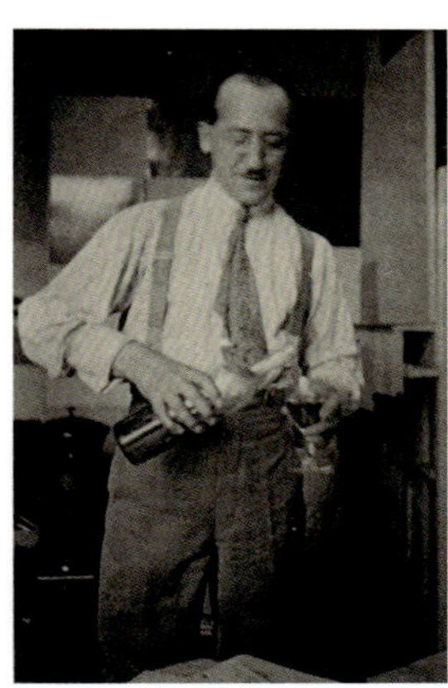

CAT. 83 André Kertész

Piet Mondrian, pouring wine, 19 (?) August 1926 (see p. 132)

Gelatin developing-out paper, 12 x 7.5 cm

Verso, in Michel Seuphor's handwriting: 'Mondrian / août 26 / foto Kertész' and 'avant 40'

Private collection

Given what Mondrian is wearing, this photograph must have been taken on the same date as cats 81–2; see those entries for more information.

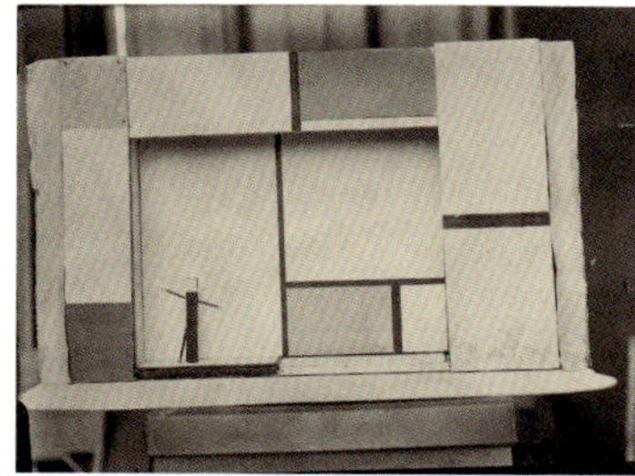

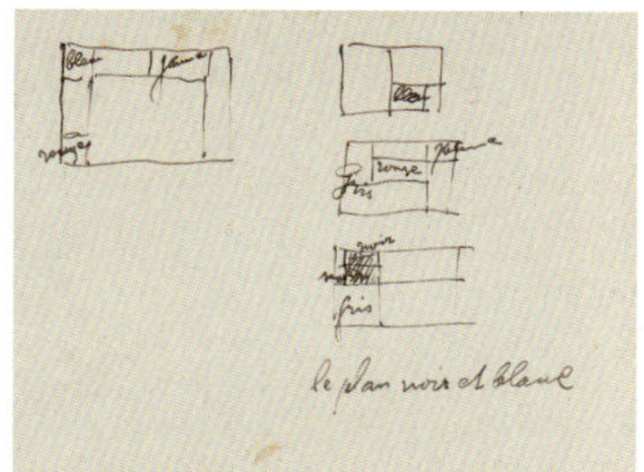

CAT. 84 André Kertész

Model of Mondrian's stage design for Seuphor's play *L'Ephémère est éternel*, first act, between 19 August and 20 December 1926 (see p. 133)

Gelatin developing-out paper, 8.9 x 11.9 cm

Private collection (?)

Verso: four sketches of the stage set and the three acts; colour notes; below, in Piet Mondrian's handwriting: 'le plan noir et blanc'. See also the supporting illustration.

A *post quem* is provided by Kertész's earliest documented visit to Mondrian on 19 August 1926 (Coppes/Jansen 2020, p. 84 and p. 91, n. 15). The *ante quem* is offered by a letter from Mondrian to J. J. P. Oud, in which he states that he gave several prints to the French architect Robert Mallet-Stevens (letter Piet Mondrian to J. J. P. Oud, 20 December 1926, Paris, Fondation Custodia, inv. 1972-A.428).

The model is also visible in cats 80 and 121.

See also cats 85–6.

Publications: *Documents internationaux de l'esprit nouveau*, no. 1 (1927), p. 34; *Maandblad voor Beeldende Kunsten*, 4 (1927) no. 7, p. 196; *7 Arts* 6 (1928), no. 19, p. 3.

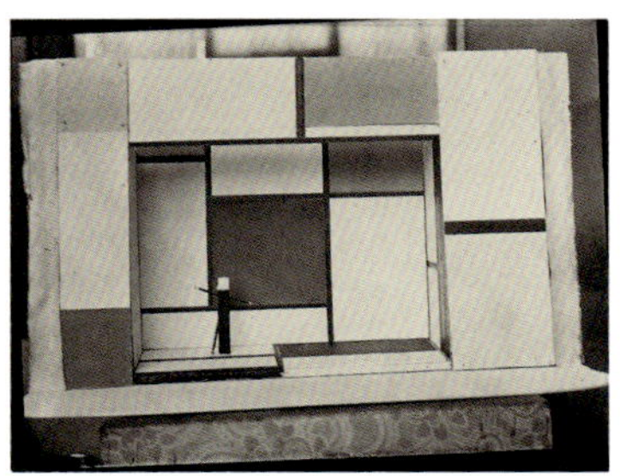

CAT. 85 André Kertész

Model of Mondrian's stage design for Seuphor's play *L'Ephémère est éternel*, second act, between 19 August and 20 December 1926 (see p. 133)

Gelatin developing-out paper, 8.9 x 11.9 cm

Private collection (?)

See also cats 84 and 86.

Publications: *Documents internationaux de l'esprit nouveau*, no. 1 (1927), p. 34; *Maandblad voor Beeldende Kunsten*, 4 (1927) no. 7, p. 196; *7 Arts* 6 (1928), no. 19, p. 3.

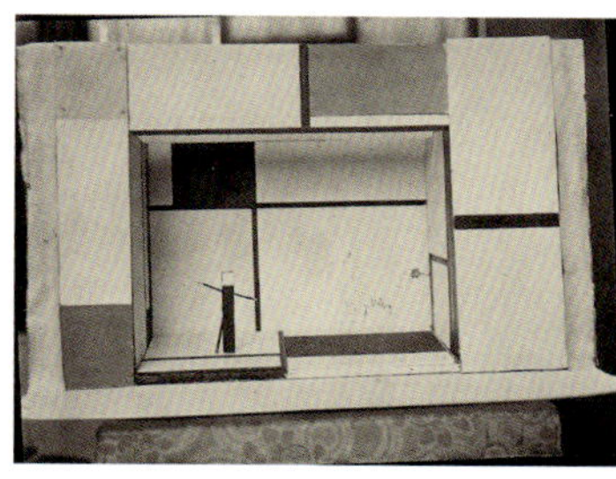

CAT. 86 André Kertész

Model of Mondrian's stage design for Seuphor's play *L'Ephémère est éternel*, third act, between 19 August and 20 December 1926 (see p. 133)

Gelatin developing-out paper, 8.9 x 11.9 cm

Private collection (?)

See also cats 84–5.

Publications: *Documents internationaux de l'esprit nouveau*, no. 1 (1927), p. 34; *Maandblad voor Beeldende Kunsten*, 4 (1927) no. 7, p. 196; *7 Arts* 6 (1928), no. 19, p. 3.

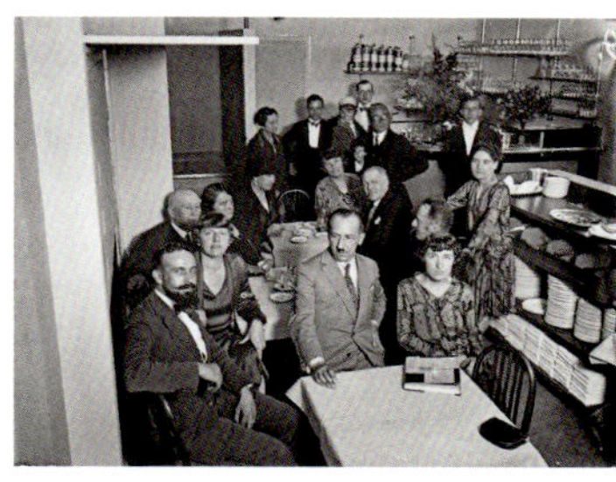

CAT. 87 André Kertész

Company at the opening of the restaurant Bij Leo Faust, 2 September 1926 (see p. 134)

Gelatin dry-plate negative, 9 x 12 cm

Paris, Médiathèque du Patrimoine et de la Photographie, inv. 72L000686

The restaurant opened on 2 September 1926.

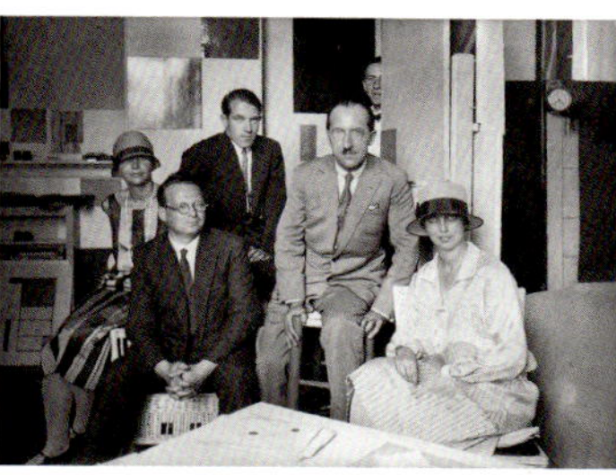

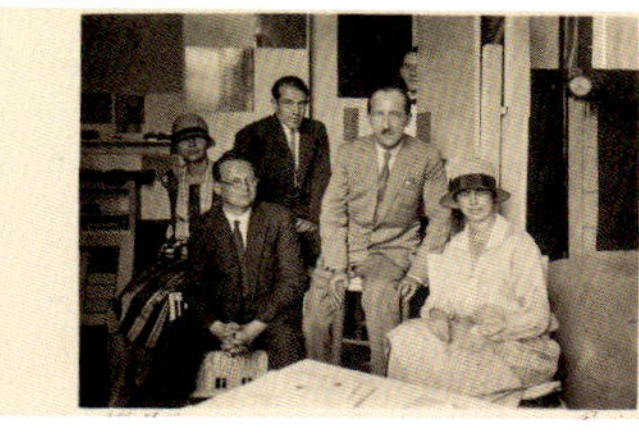

CAT. 88.1; CAT. 88.2 André Kertész

Company in Piet Mondrian's studio, 2 September 1926 (?) (see p. 135)

(1) Gelatin dry-plate negative, 9 x 12 cm; (2) gelatin developing-out paper, 8.6 x 13.7 cm

(1) Paris, Médiathèque du Patrimoine et de la Photographie, inv. 72L000604; (2) Kunstmuseum Stuttgart, Archiv Baumeister, inv. ab-f-009-064-o

(2) Recto: gesigneerd 'A Kertész Paris'

The back of a later print (c. 1955) from Michel Seuphor's estate is inscribed in his handwriting: 'Photo: Kertesz Août 1926'. Mondrian's clothes match those he is wearing in cat. 87, which was taken on 2 September 1926. Although the painter is dressed in the same suit in cat. 89, it is not certain whether the pictures were taken on the same day.

A colour lithograph after Mondrian's painting *Tableau I* (B126, 1921) can be seen on the floor rear left. It came from *Der Sieg der Farbe: die entscheidende Zeit unserer Malerei in 40 farbigen Lichtdrucken* by Adolf Behne, which was published in 1923.

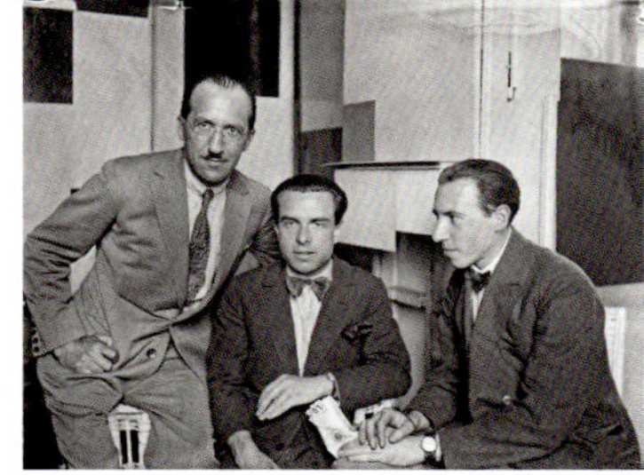

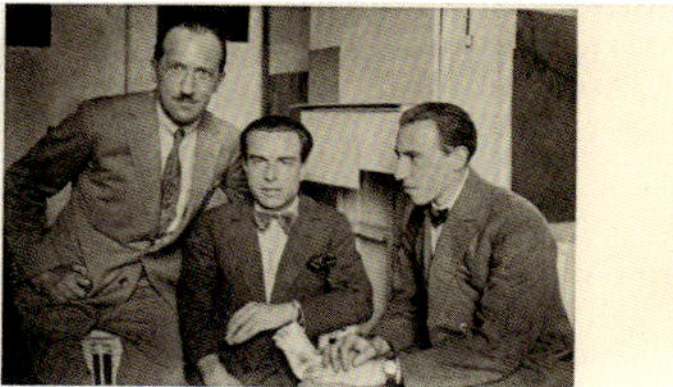

CAT. 89.1; CAT. 89.2 André Kertész

Piet Mondrian, Enrico Prampolini and Michel Seuphor in Mondrian's studio, 2 September 1926 (?)

(see p. 136)

(1) Gelatin dry-plate negative, 9 x 12 cm; (2) gelatin developing-out paper, 8 x 11 cm

(2) Recto: signed 'A. Kertész Paris'

(1) Paris, Médiathèque du Patrimoine et de la Photographie, inv. 72L000603; (2) Houston, The Museum of Fine Arts, The Manfred Heiting Collection, inv. 2002.260

For the dating, see cat. 88.

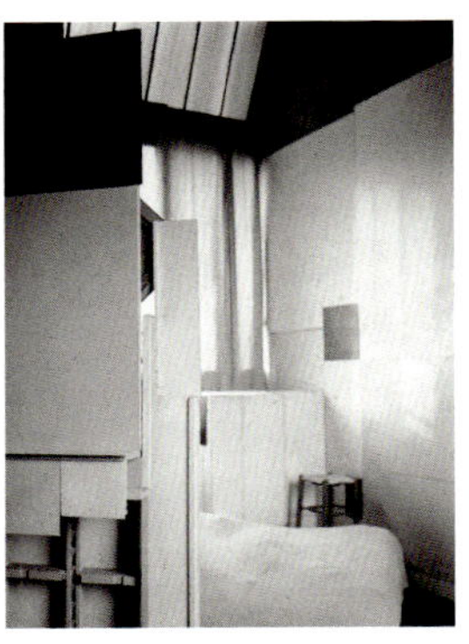

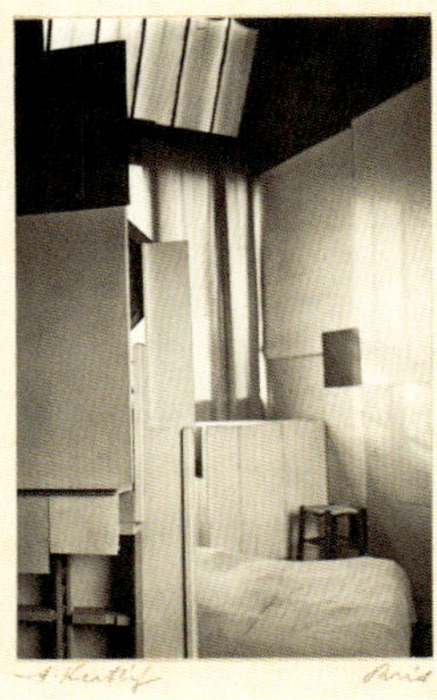

CAT. 90.1; CAT. 90.2 André Kertész

Piet Mondrian's studio, between September 1926 and mid-February 1927 (see p. 137)

(1) Gelatin dry-plate negative, 12 x 9 cm; (2) gelatin developing-out paper, 10.8 x 6.7 cm

(2) Recto: signed 'A. Kertész Paris'

(1) Paris, Médiathèque du Patrimoine et de la Photographie, inv. 72L000533; (2) New York, The Metropolitan Museum of Art, Gilman Collection, inv. 2005.100.180

The dating of this and the following photographs is uncertain, but they must have been taken after the previous series from 19 (?) August 1926, given the large number of people present in the latter, compared to the stillness of these photographs. Some of the pictures in the series were exhibited at the gallery Au Sacre du Printemps in March 1927, and so they must have been taken by mid-February at the latest. In the absence of further evidence, we date cats 90–99 to between September 1926 and mid-February 1927.

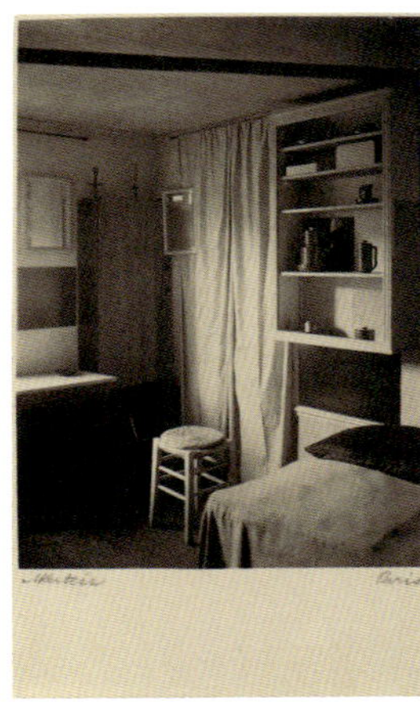

CAT. 91 André Kertész

Piet Mondrian's living quarters, between September 1926 and mid-February 1927 (see p. 138)

Gelatin developing-out paper, 13.7 x 8.2 cm

Recto: signed 'A. Kertész Paris'

New York, The Metropolitan Museum of Art, Gift of Harry Holtzman, inv. 1986.1225.2

For the dating, see cat. 90.

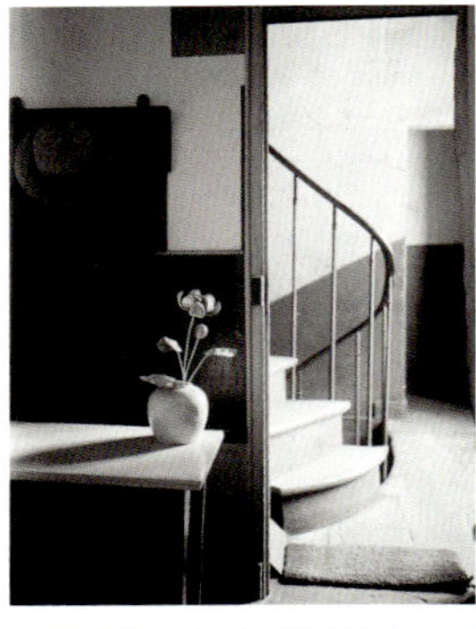

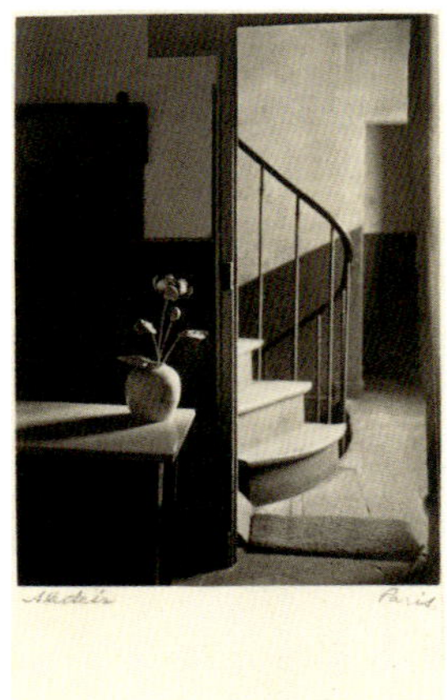

CAT. 92 André Kertész

***Chez Mondrian, Paris*, between September 1926 and mid-February 1927** (see p. 139)

(1) Gelatin dry-plate negative; (2) gelatin developing-out paper

(1) 12 x 9 cm; (2) 13.3 x 8.1 cm

(2) Recto: signed 'A. Kertész Paris'

(1) Paris, Médiathèque du Patrimoine et de la Photographie, inv. 72L000126; (2) New York, The Metropolitan Museum of Art, Gift of Harry Holtzman, inv. 1986.1225.1

For the dating, see cat. 90.

A large print of this picture featured, along with cats 81, 93 and 96, in the first exhibition of Kertész's work at the Paris gallery Au Sacre du Printemps in March 1927. In May 1928 Kertész exhibited the photograph again at the Salon de l'Escalier in Paris.

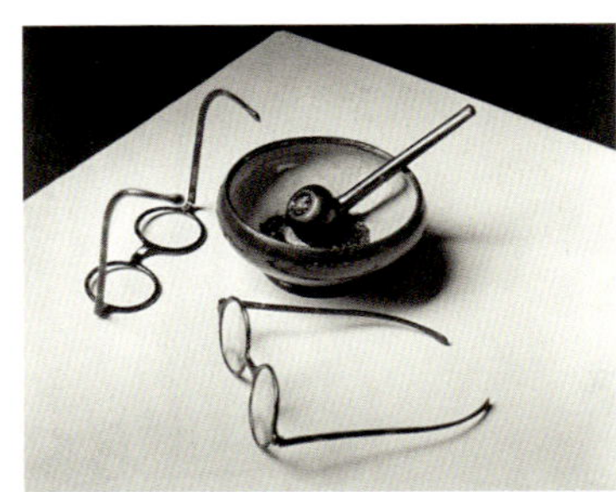

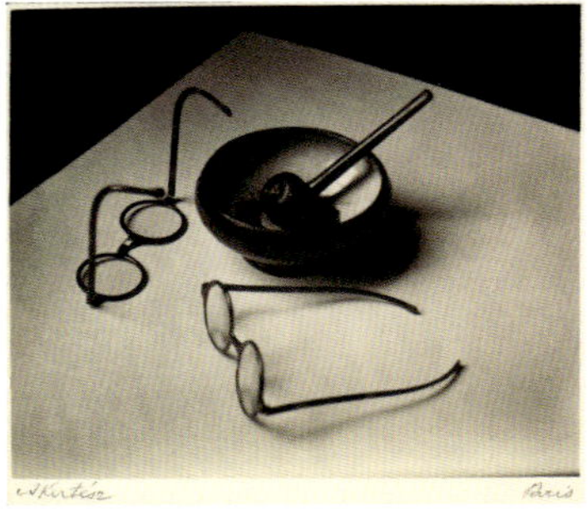

CAT. 93.1; CAT. 93.2 André Kertész

***Les Lunettes et la pipe de Mondrian/ Nature morte*, between September 1926 and mid-February 1927** (see p. 140)

(1) Gelatin dry-plate negative, 9 x 12 cm; (2) gelatin developing-out paper, 8.5 x 13.6 cm

(2) Recto: signed 'A. Kertész Paris'; verso, in André Kertész's handwriting: 'Kertesz I X / dans le Studio Mondrian'

(1) Paris, Médiathèque du Patrimoine et de la Photographie, inv. 72L000123; (2) New York, The Museum of Modern Art, Thomas Walther Collection, inv. 1721.2001

For the dating, see cat. 90.

A large print of this picture featured, along with cats 81, 92 and 96, in the first exhibition of Kertész's work at the Paris gallery Au Sacre du Printemps in March 1927.

A print of the photograph was included in January 1929 in the travelling exhibition 'Fotografie der Gegenwart', which was held in cities including Essen, Berlin, Frankfurt, Dresden, Leipzig and London.

From 18 May 1929, another print was part of the equally prominent travelling exhibition 'Film und Foto', organized by the Deutsche Werkbund and shown in Stuttgart, Zurich, Vienna, Zagreb and Tokyo, amongst others.

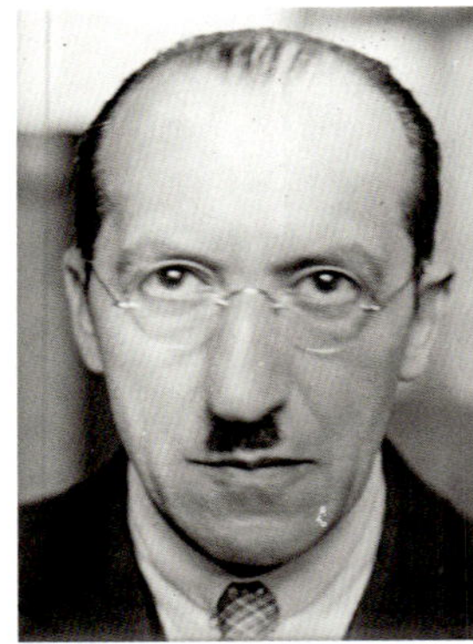

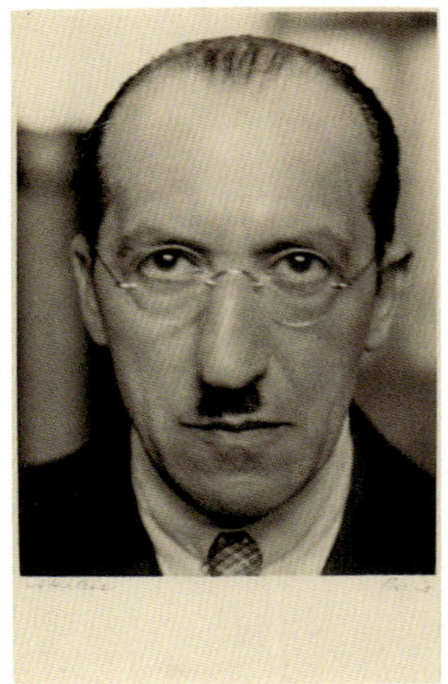

CAT. 94.1; CAT. 94.2 André Kertész

Portrait of Piet Mondrian, between September 1926 and mid-February 1927 (see p. 141)

(1) Gelatin dry-plate negative, 12 x 9 cm; (2) gelatin developing-out paper, 13.2 x 8.2 cm

(2) Recto: signed 'A. Kertész Paris'; verso: 'P. Mondrian 1926'

(1) Paris, Médiathèque du Patrimoine et de la Photographie, inv. 72L000824; (2) New York, The Museum of Modern Art, Thomas Walther Collection, inv. 1720.2001

For the dating, see cat. 90.

The portraits in cats 94–6 and 99 were taken during the same session.

Technical examination reveals that Kertész edited the negative: the creases around Mondrian's mouth and his hairline were retouched. According to Reinhold, adjustment was 'unnecessary to the composition and more likely was added to produce a more flattering likeness' (Reinhold 2014, pp. 6–7, figs 15–17).

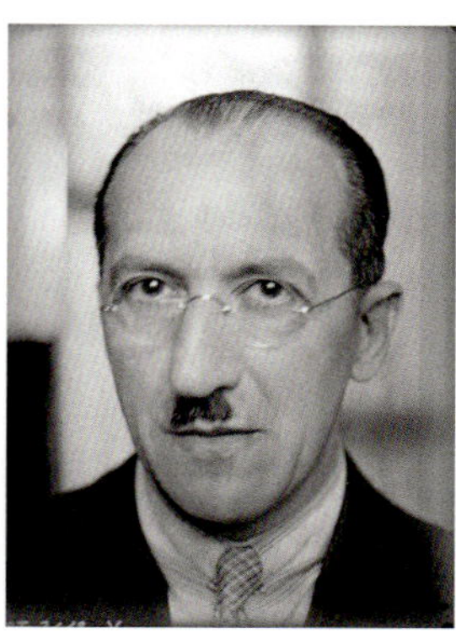

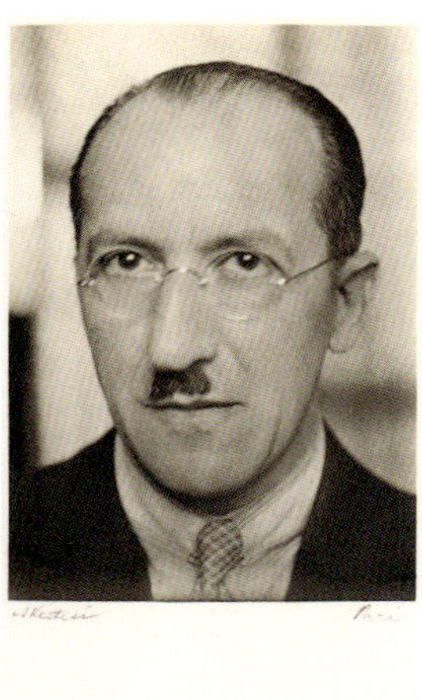

CAT. 95.1; CAT. 95.2 André Kertész

Portrait of Piet Mondrian, between September 1926 and mid-February 1927 (see p. 141)

(1) Gelatin dry-plate negative, 12 x 9 cm; (2) gelatin developing-out paper, 13.2 x 8.2 cm

(2) Recto: signed 'A. Kertész Paris'

(1) Paris, Médiathèque du Patrimoine et de la Photographie, inv. 72L003612; (2) Los Angeles, The J. Paul Getty Museum, inv. 93.XM.21.1

For the dating, see cat. 90.

For the portrait series, see cat. 94.

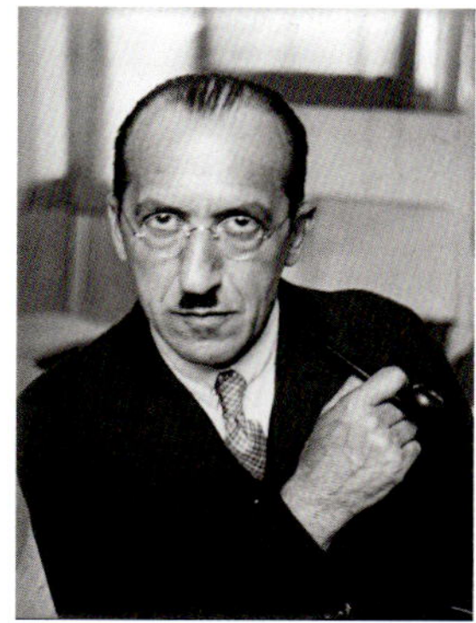

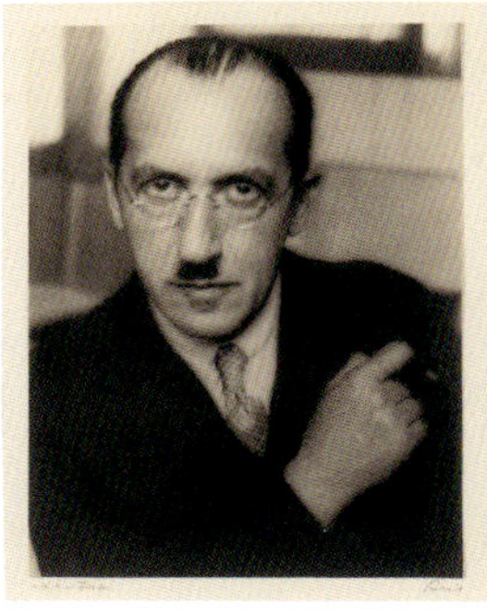

CAT. 96.1; CAT. 96.2 André Kertész

Portrait of Piet Mondrian, between September 1926 and mid-February 1927 (see p. 142)

(1) Gelatin dry-plate negative, 12 x 9 cm; (2) gelatin developing-out paper, 22.7 x 18.4 cm

(2) Recto: signed 'A. Kertész Paris'

(1) Paris, Médiathèque du Patrimoine et de la Photographie, inv. 72L000459; (2) The Fred Jones Jr Museum of Art at the University of Oklahoma, Gift of Dr and Mrs Richard L. Sandor, 2000

For the dating, see cat. 90.

For the portrait series, see cat. 94.

A large print of this picture featured along with cats 81 and 92—3 in the first exhibition of Kertész's work at the Paris gallery Au Sacre du Printemps in March 1927.

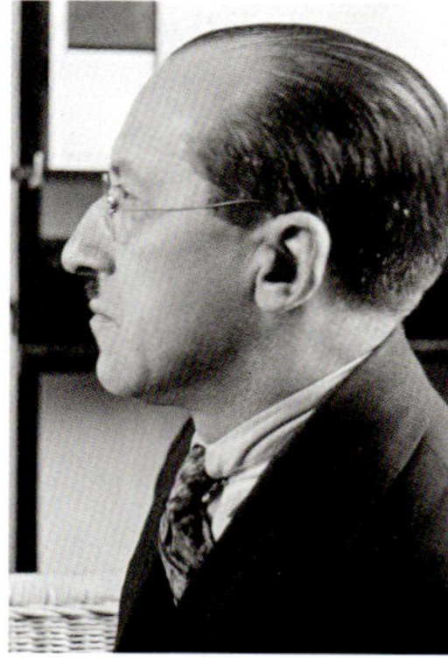

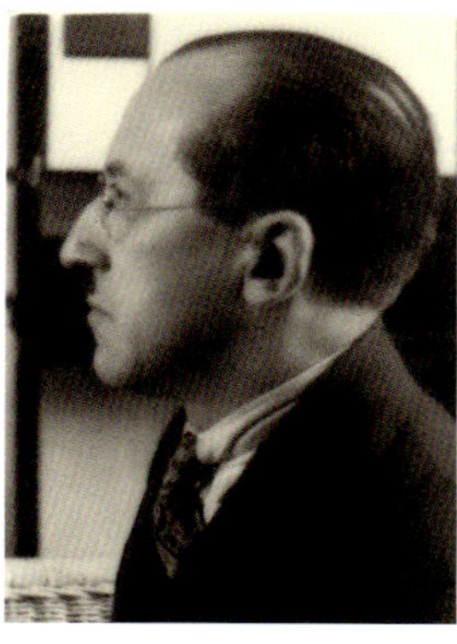

CAT. 97.1; CAT. 97.2 André Kertész

Portrait of Piet Mondrian, between September 1926 and mid-February 1927 (see p. 143)

1) Gelatin dry-plate negative, 12 x 9 cm; (2) gelatin developing-out paper, 13.2 x 8.2 cm

(2) Recto: signed 'A. Kertész Paris'; verso, in Kertész's handwriting: 'Mondrian'

(1) Paris, Médiathèque du Patrimoine et de la Photographie, inv. 72L000663; (2) Estate of André Kertész

For the dating, see cat. 90.

For the portrait series, see cat. 94.

Composition (B186, 1927) can be seen on the easel behind Mondrian. The lowest horizontal line is missing, indicating that the painting was not finished at the time the photograph was taken.

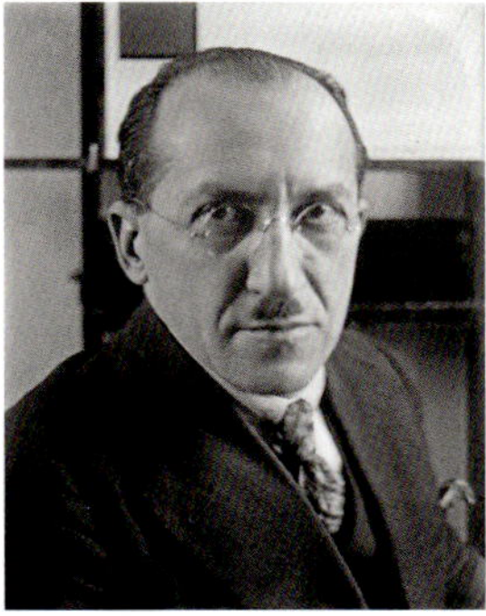

CAT. 98 André Kertész

Portrait of Piet Mondrian, between September 1926 and mid-February 1927 (see p. 144)

Gelatin dry-plate negative, 12 x 9 cm

Paris, Médiathèque du Patrimoine et de la Photographie, inv. 72L000822

For the dating, see cat. 90.

For the portrait series, see cat. 94.

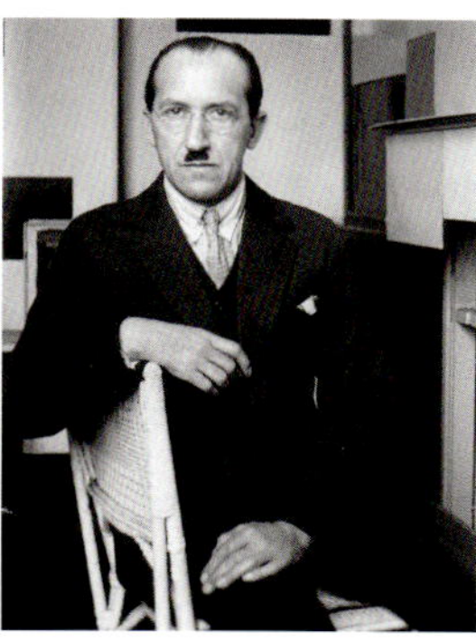

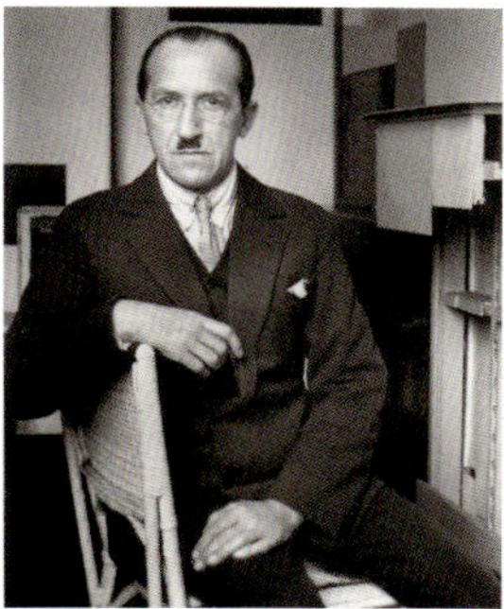

CAT. 99.1; CAT. 99.2 André Kertész

***Mondrian*, between September 1926 and mid-February 1927** (see p. 145)

(1) Gelatin dry-plate negative, 12 x 9 cm; (2) gelatin developing-out paper, 24.7 x 19.7 cm

(2) Verso, in Kertész's handwriting: 'André Kertész / 1926'. According to the J. Paul Getty Museum, the inscription was added later.

(1) Paris, Médiathèque du Patrimoine et de la Photographie, inv. 72L000383; (2) Los Angeles, The J. Paul Getty Museum, inv. 84.XM.193.25

For the dating, see cat. 90.

For the portrait series, see cat. 94.

A large print in the J. Paul Getty Museum collection shares the dimensions of the photograph that Kertész exhibited at the gallery Au Sacre du Printemps in 1927 (cat. 96), and is thus likely to have been part of that exhibition.

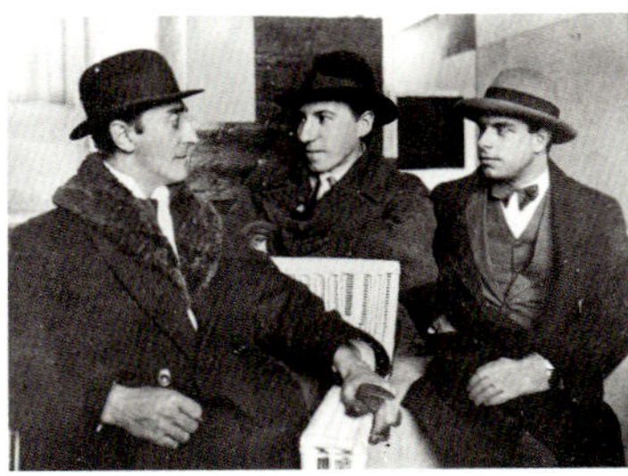

CAT. 100 André Kertész

Paul Dermée, Michel Seuphor and Enrico Prampolini in Piet Mondrian's studio, winter 1926–27 (see p. 146)

A vintage print has not been traced; the photograph reproduced here is a later print (The Hague, RKD, Joop Joosten Archive (0838), inv. 814).

The magazine *Documents internationaux de l'esprit nouveau* only survived for one issue (January 1927), and so we date the photograph of its editors to the winter of 1926–27.

The photograph can be linked to several other pictures of Dermée, Seuphor and Prampolini that Kertész took in the winter of 1926–27. It is the only one, however, to have been shot in Mondrian's studio.

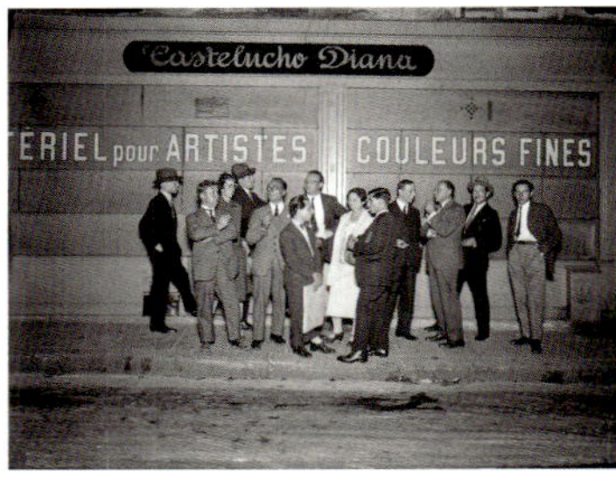

CAT. 101 André Kertész

Company after the opening of the 'Photo-Kertész' exhibition in the gallery Au Sacre du Printemps, 12 March 1927 (see pp. 146–47)

Gelatin dry-plate negative, 9 x 12 cm

Paris, Médiathèque du Patrimoine et de la Photographie, inv. 72L000457

This photograph has long been titled 'Après l'inauguration à la galerie "Au Sacre du Printemps"'. The gallery in question opened on 12 March 1927. The location of the picture is 16 Rue de la Grande Chaumière, a fifteen-minute walk from the gallery, which was located at 5 Rue du Cherche-Midi.

Hanssen dates the photograph to 20 August 1927, arguing that it was taken on the publication of Michel Seuphor's book of poetry *Diaphragme intérieur et un drapeau*. The latter appeared in July 1926, however (Hanssen 2015, p. 274, n. 2–3; see also Henkels 1976, p. 141).

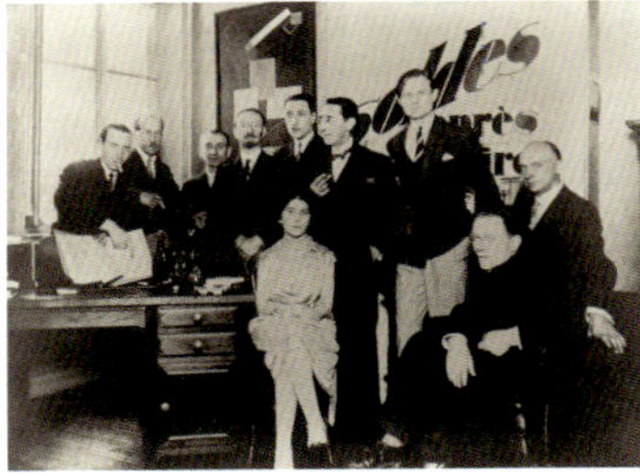

CAT. 102 Stanislaw Londynski

Company at Paul Dermée's house, Paris, c. July 1927 (see p. 148)

A vintage print has not been traced; the photograph reproduced here is a later print (The Hague, RKD, Joop Joosten Archive (0838), inv. 809).

The photograph is thought to date from around July 1927 (Welsh/Joosten 1998-II, p. 137).

Cat. 103 was also taken on that occasion.

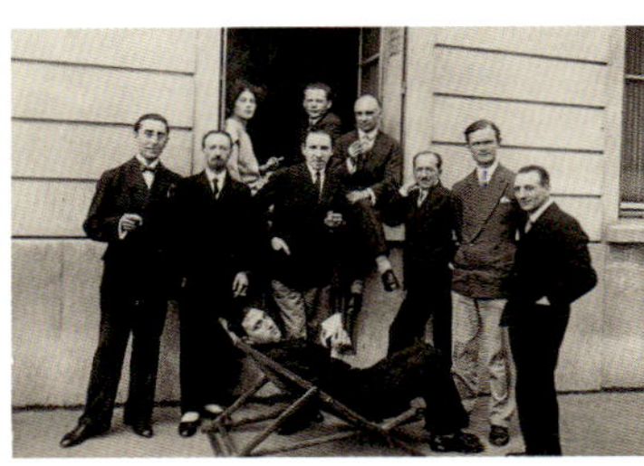

CAT. 103 Stanislaw Londynski

Company in front of Paul Dermée's house, Paris, c. July 1927 (see p. 149)

Gelatin developing-out paper, 11.8 x 16.3 cm

Private collection

For the dating, see cat. 102.

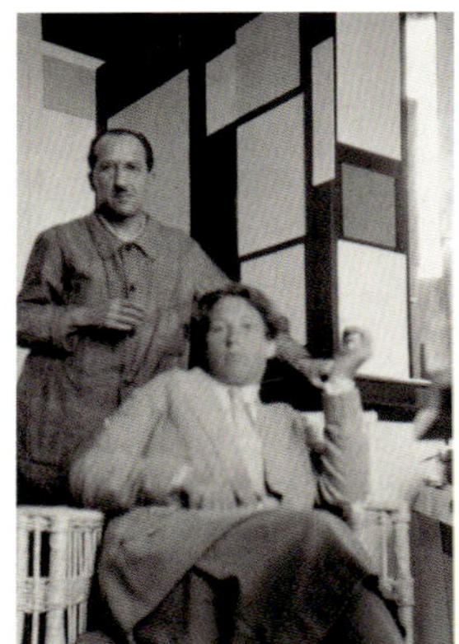

CAT. 104 Hannah Höch

Piet Mondrian and Til Brugman in Mondrian's studio, September 1927 (see p. 150)

Gelatin developing-out paper, 8 x 5.4 cm

Verso, in Hannah Höch's handwriting: 'Til u. Mondrian. / Sept. 27. / Atelier Mondrian / Foto: Höch'

Berlin, Berlinische Galerie, Nachlass Hannah Höch, inv. BG-HHC F 132/79,b

The Dutch poet Til Brugman and the German artist Hannah Höch visited Mondrian in September 1927 en route to Grenoble (Rehorst 1989, pp. 41–52; Welsh/Joosten 1998-II, p. 137).

A separate cut-out print of the photo with Mondrian's portrait was likewise made, which – along with a second print of this shot – also belongs to the Hannah Höch archive.

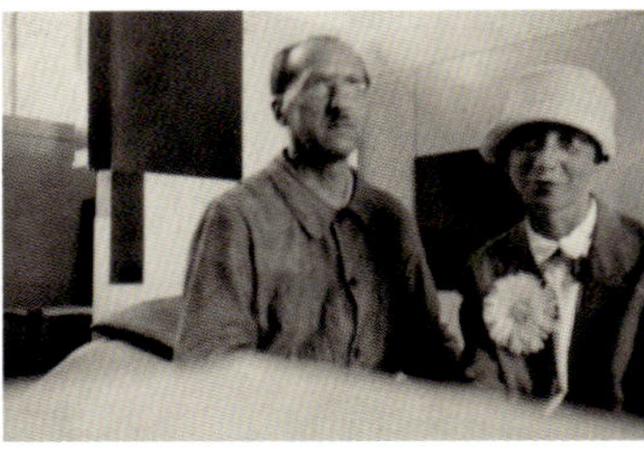

CAT. 105 Til Brugman (?)

Piet Mondrian and Hannah Höch in Mondrian's studio, September 1927 (see p. 150)

Gelatin developing-out paper, 3.8 x 5.9 cm

Verso, in Hannah Höch's handwriting: 'Hannah Höch u. Mondrian. Paris / ~~1~~9.27. / Atelier Mondrian'

Berlin, Berlinische Galerie, Nachlass Hannah Höch, inv. BG-HHC F 114/79,b

For the dating, see cat. 104.

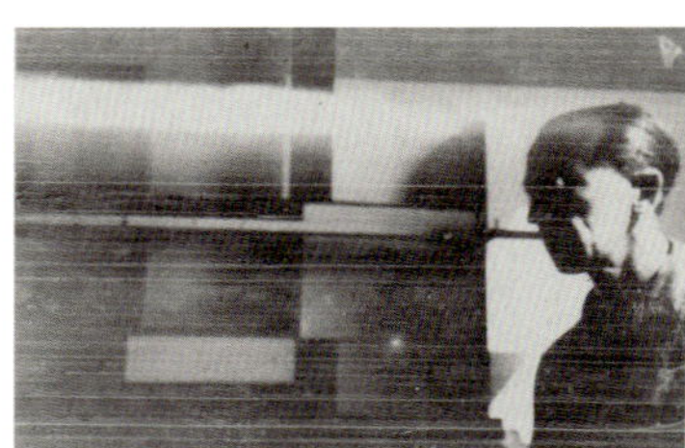

CAT. 106 Hannah Höch

Portrait of Piet Mondrian, September 1927

Gelatin developing-out paper, dimensions unknown (according to the Berlinische Galerie)

Verso, in Hannah Höch's handwriting: 'Mondrian, Paris, / in seinen / Atelier / Foto: / Höch'

Berlin, Berlinische Galerie, Nachlass Hannah Höch, inv. BG-HHC F 133/79,b

For the dating, see cat. 104.

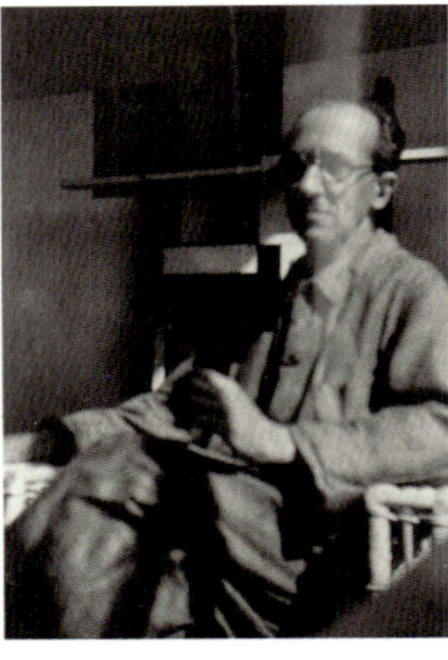

CAT. 107 Hannah Höch

Portrait of Piet Mondrian, September 1927 (see p. 151)

Gelatin developing-out paper, dimensions unknown (according to the Berlinische Galerie)

Verso, in Hannah Höch's handwriting: 'Mondrian 1926 / in Paris. / Foto: Höch'

Berlin, Berlinische Galerie, Nachlass Hannah Höch, inv. BG-HHC F 133/79,d

Although the date '1926' is inscribed on the back, this picture must have been taken during Höch and Brugman's visit to Mondrian in September 1927. See cat. 104.

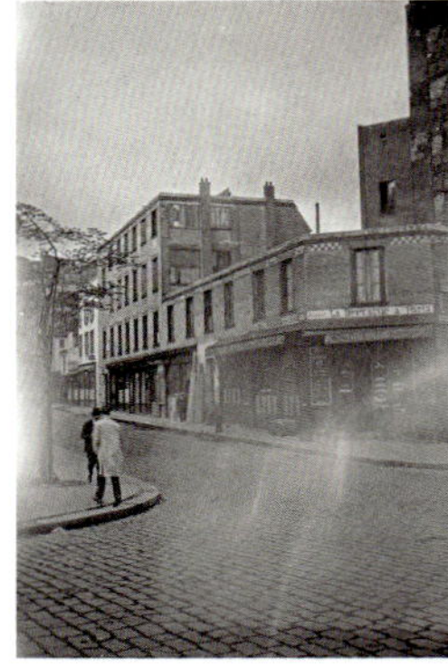

CAT. 108 Alfred Roth

Studio complex at 26 Rue du Départ, spring 1928 (see p. 152)

Gelatin developing-out paper, 15.7 x 10.6 cm

Zurich, ETH, gta Archiv, Nachlass Alfred Roth, inv. 131_T_1_3_F_3.3

Alfred Roth met Mondrian in April 1928 (Roth 1973, pp. 128–30; Welsh/Joosten 1998-II, p. 139). He was employed in Le Corbusier's studio until the end of June 1928. The following month he moved to Sweden (Lemoine 1994, p. 11; Roth 1973, p. 145). The photograph must thus have been taken in the spring of 1928, as supported by the limited amount of foliage on the tree on the left.

A frontal shot can be found in cat. 143.

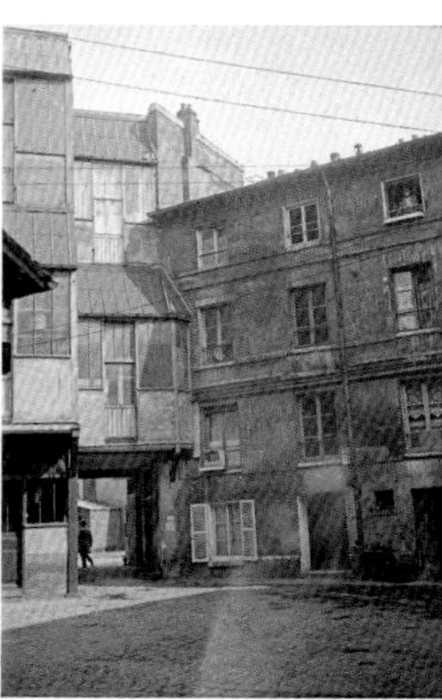

CAT. 109 Alfred Roth

Courtyard of the studio complex at 26 Rue du Départ, spring 1928 (see p. 152)

Gelatin developing-out paper, 12.5 x 8.3 cm

Zurich, ETH, gta Archiv, Nachlass Alfred Roth, inv. 131_T_1_3_F_3.10

For the dating, see cat. 108.

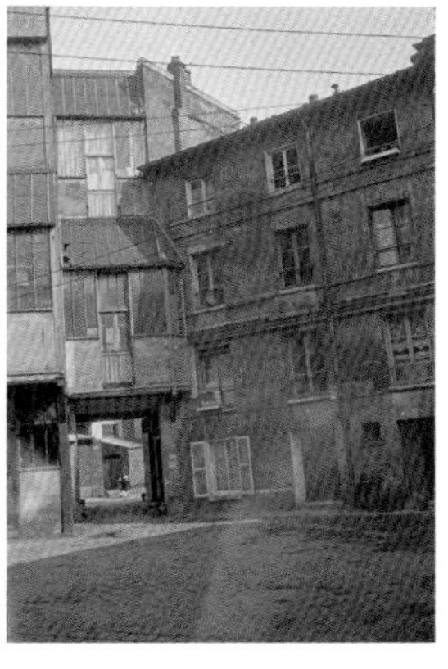

CAT. 110 Alfred Roth

Courtyard of the studio complex at 26 Rue du Départ, spring 1928 (see p. 153)

Gelatin developing-out paper, 12.5 x 8.3 cm

Zurich, ETH, gta Archiv, Nachlass Alfred Roth, inv. 131_T_1_3_F_3.1

For the dating, see cat. 108, and for the location of Mondrian's studio, cat. 109.

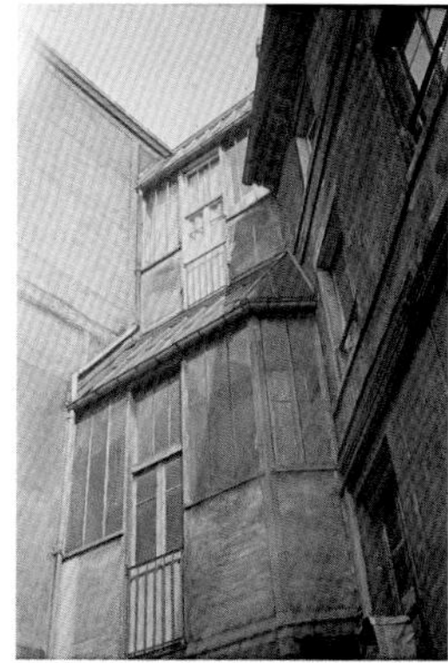

CAT. 111 Alfred Roth

Window of Piet Mondrian's studio (top floor), viewed from the courtyard at 26 Rue du Départ, spring 1928 (see p. 153)

Gelatin developing-out paper, 12.5 x 7.9 cm

Zurich, ETH, gta Archiv, Nachlass Alfred Roth, inv. 131_T_1_3_F_3.4

For the dating, see cat. 108.

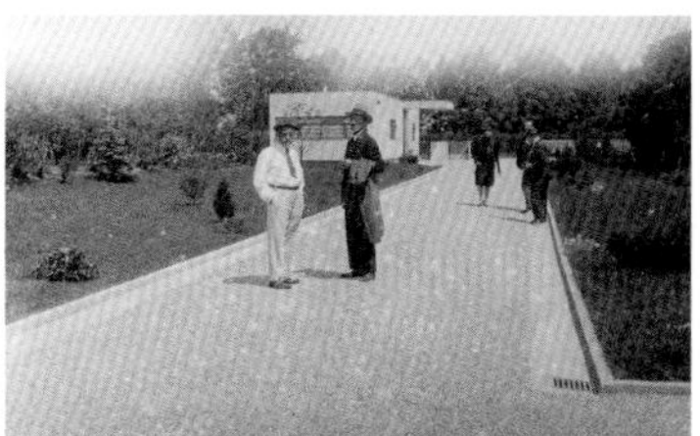

CAT. 112 Alfred Roth

Michael Stein and Piet Mondrian at the entrance of Villa Stein-de Monzie, Garches, 1 July 1928 (see pp. 154–55)

Gelatin developing-out paper, 7.1 x 11.7 cm

Zurich, ETH, gta Archiv, Nachlass Alfred Roth, inv. 131_T_1_3_F_2.2

The visit occurred on 1 July 1928.

Cf. Roth 1973, p. 137.

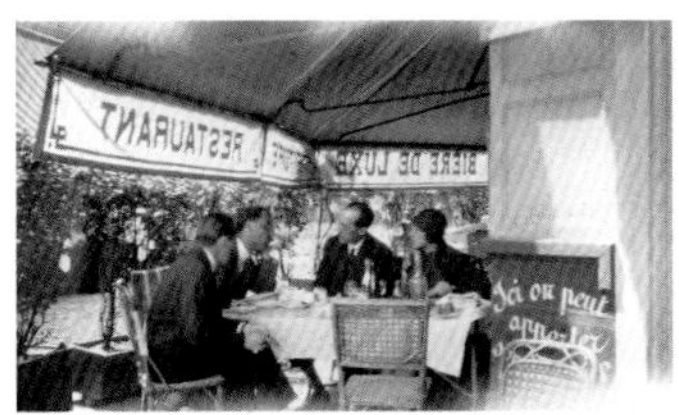

CAT. 113 Ernest Weissmann (?)

Alfred Roth, Mart Stam, Piet Mondrian and an unidentified woman (Stam's wife Lena Lebeau?) on a terrace, 1 July 1928 (see p. 155)

Gelatin developing-out paper, 7.3 x 10.1 cm

Zurich, ETH, gta Archiv, Nachlass Alfred Roth, inv. 131_T_1_3_F_2.5

The picture was taken before or after the visit to Villa Stein-de Monzie on 1 July 1928 (see cat. 112), probably by Ernest Weissmann, who was also present but does not appear in the photo.

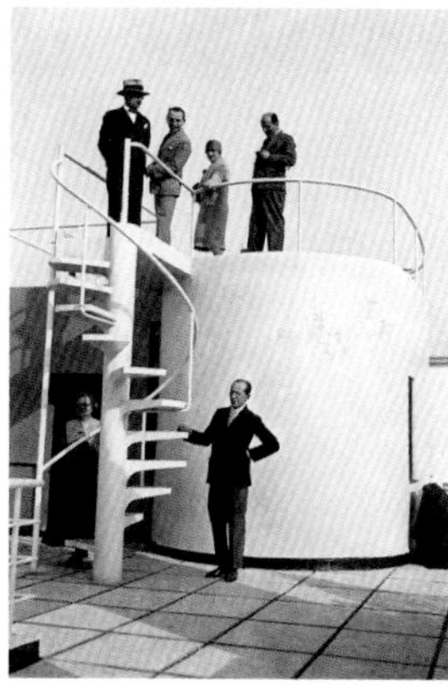

CAT. 114 Unidentified photographer

Company on the roof terrace of Villa Stein-de Monzie, Garches, early September 1928 (see p. 157)

Gelatin developing-out paper, 15 x 10 cm

Paris, Fondation Le Corbusier, Villa Stein-de Monzie, inv. L1-10, 75

The photograph was taken during a two-week visit by Lissitzky and his wife to Paris in early September 1928 (Welsh/Joosten 1998-II, p. 140).

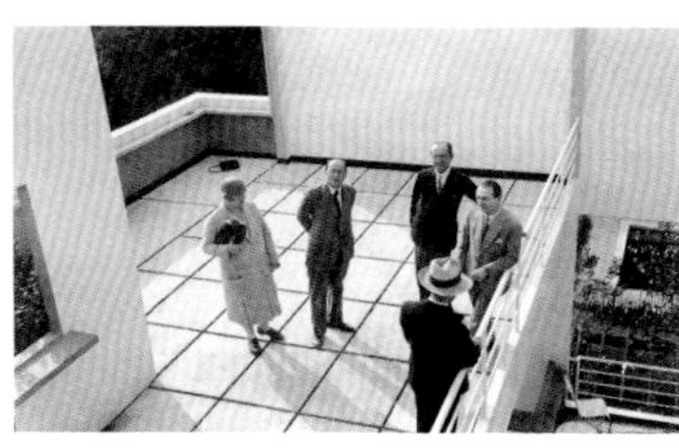

CAT. 115 Unidentified photographer

Company on the roof terrace of Villa Stein-de Monzie, Garches, early September 1928 (see p. 156)

Gelatin developing-out paper, 10 x 15 cm

Paris, Fondation Le Corbusier, inv. L1-10

For the dating, see cat. 114.

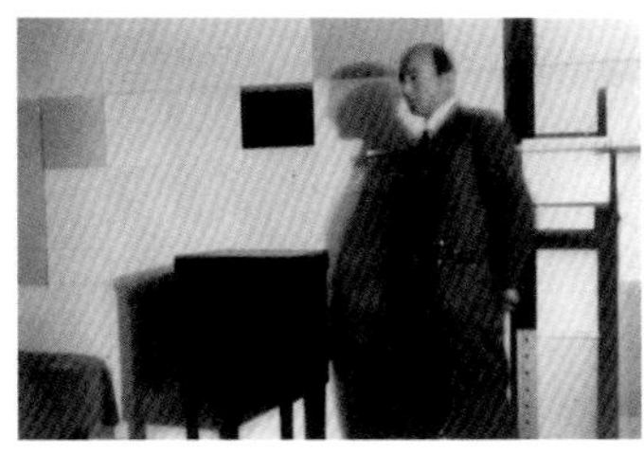

CAT. 116 Sophie Lissitzky-Küppers (?)

El Lissitzky in Piet Mondrian's studio, early September 1928

A vintage print has not been traced; the photograph reproduced here is a later print (The Hague, RKD, Joop Joosten Archive (0838), inv. 815.

The photograph might have been taken on the same day as the trip to Garches (see cat. 114).

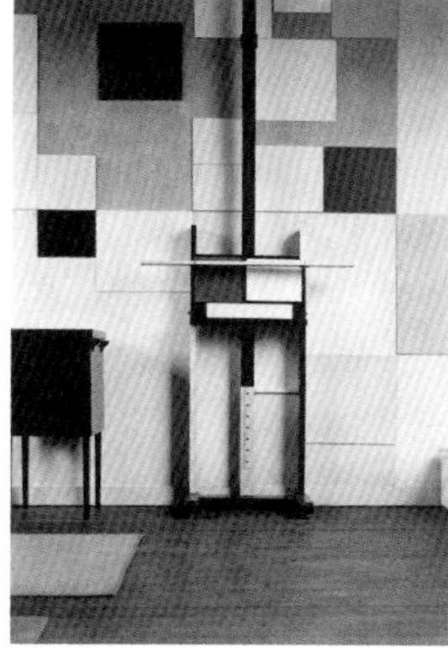

CAT. 117 Sigfried Giedion

Piet Mondrian's studio, September 1928 (see p. 158)

Gelatin developing-out paper, 14.3 x 9.4 cm

Verso, in unidentified handwriting: 'Piet Mondrians / atelier in Paris.'

Zurich, ETH, gta Archiv, Familienarchiv Sigfried Giedion und Carola Giedion-Welcker, inv. 43B-K-1930-12-19

Sigfried Giedion and Carola Giedion-Welcker visited Mondrian in September 1928 (Welsh/Joosten 1998-II, p. 140). The photograph must have been taken on that occasion.

Publication: Carola Giedion-Welcker, 'Die Kunst des zwanzigsten Jahrhunderts. Experimentierzelle – Zeitseismograf', *Das Kunstblatt*, vol. 14, no. 3 (March 1930), p. 66.

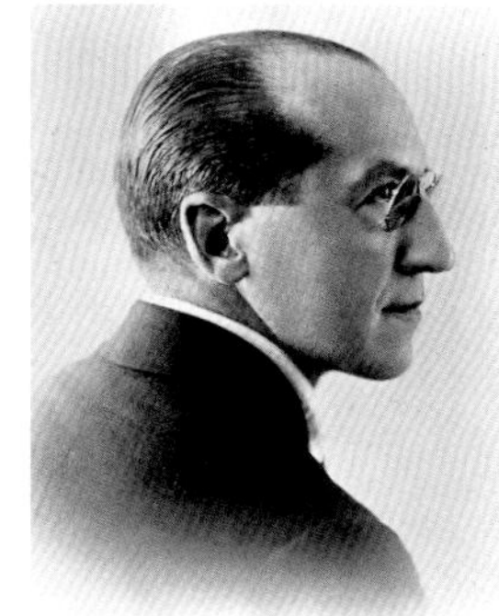

CAT. 118 Unidentified photographer

Portrait of Piet Mondrian, c. 1929 (see p. 159)

A vintage print has not been traced; the photograph reproduced here is a later print (The Hague, RKD, Joop Joosten Archive (0838), inv. 809).

We date this photograph to about 1929 based on its reproduction in August 1929 in the *Chicago Tribune*. It accompanied an article there by the American journalist and artist John Xceron, who presumably met Mondrian earlier that year (Coppes 2012, pp. 49–51). Mondrian's appearance is very similar to the portrait photograph that Michel Seuphor took in 1929 (cat. 119). He is wearing the same pince-nez, for instance, in both pictures.

The photograph has been attributed in the past to André Kertész and also to an otherwise unidentified photographer by the name of 'Muguet'. For stylistic reasons,

Kertész is not likely to have been the author. As far as we know, moreover, Mondrian and Kertész had no further contact after 1927.

Publication: John Xceron: 'Who's Who Abroad: Piet Mondrian', *Chicago Tribune, European Edition* (12 August 1929).

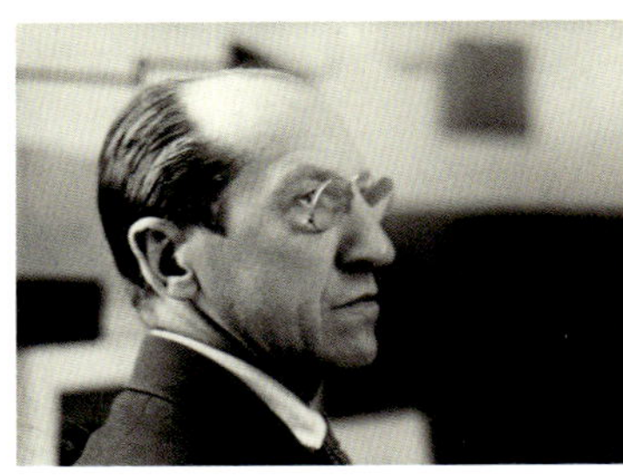

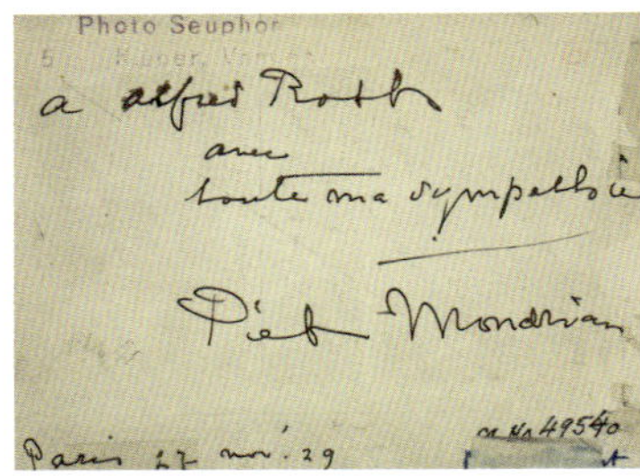

CAT. 119 Michel Seuphor

Portrait of Piet Mondrian, mid-1929 (?) (see p. 159)

Gelatin developing-out paper, 7.8 x 10.4 cm

Verso, in Piet Mondrian's handwriting: 'a Alfred Roth / avec / toute ma sympathie / Piet Mondrian / Paris 27 nov. '29'; stamp: 'Photo Seuphor / 5 rue *Kléber*, Vanves'

The Hague, RKD, Collectie Preciosafoto's Piet Mondriaan

The dedication on the back means the picture must have been taken no later than November 1929.

Publications: Piet Mondrian, 'L'Art réaliste et l'art superréaliste (la morphoplastique et la néoplastique)', *Cercle et Carré*, no. 2 (15 April 1930), p. [3]; Sven Backlund, 'Piet Mondrian', *Hyresgästen*, vol. 9, no. 20 (15 October 1931), pp. 1, 3.

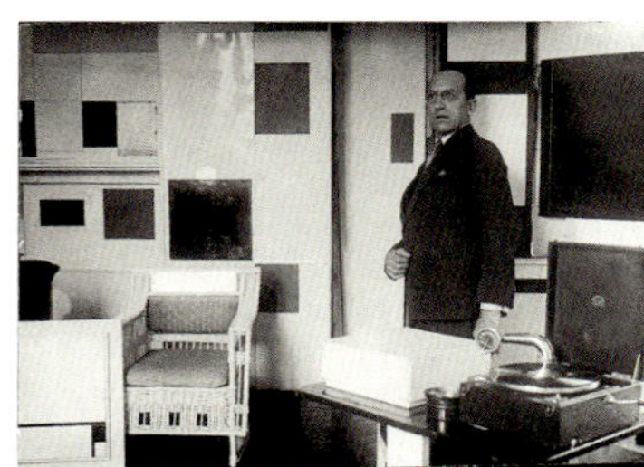

CAT. 120 Rosie Ney (?)

Piet Mondrian in his studio, mid-1929 (?) (see p. 160)

Gelatin developing-out paper, 12.3 x 17 cm

The Hague, RKD, Piet Mondrian Archive (0740), inv. 64

The attribution to the Hungarian photographer Rosie Ney is based on a letter from Mondrian to Michel Seuphor on 14 March 1930: 'Et je voudrais que mad. Ney faisait une photo de mon atelier: elle a bien réussi l'autre fois.' ('I would like Madame Ney to take a photo of my studio: she did it very well the other time.') (Photocopy of letter in The Hague, RKD, Mondrian Correspondence Project Archive (0613), inv. 075). See cats 130–33 for other photographs that might be attributable to Ney.

The picture must have been taken before the end of October 1929, as the painting *Composition I, with Red and Black* (B214), which is partly visible in the lower left, was exhibited in Amsterdam from 2 November to 2 December and subsequently sold. In this absence of further information, we provisionally date the photograph to 7mid-1929.

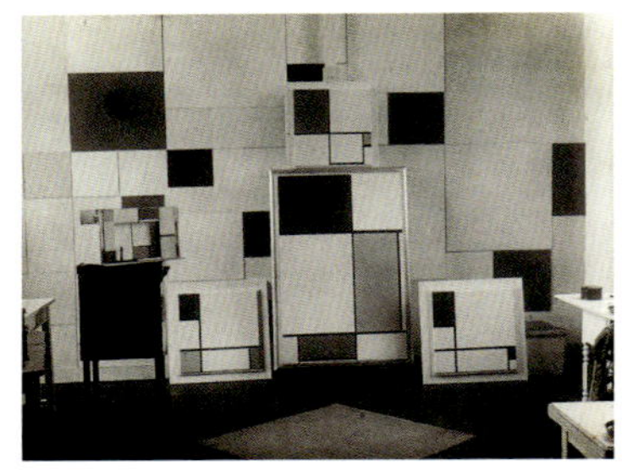

CAT. 121 Charles Karsten

Piet Mondrian's studio, c. summer 1929 (see p. 161)

Gelatin developing-out paper, 16.5 x 21 cm

Collection Matthijs Erdman, Amsterdam

In the week of 21 October, Mondrian sent the paintings that can be seen in this photograph to Amsterdam, where they were displayed for several weeks beginning on 2 November at the A.S.B. (Architecture, Painting, Sculpture) exhibition at the Stedelijk Museum. The architect Charles Karsten, one of the organizers of the exhibition, had selected works by Mondrian some months earlier. He took two photographs on that occasion, one of which (cat. 122) was reproduced in the catalogue. Bearing in mind the time needed to compile and print the catalogue, the pictures must date from no later than September 1929.

In November 1929, Mondrian sent a print of this photograph to Paul Citroen for use in his book *Palet*. See below.

Publications: Piet Mondriaan, 'L'Art réaliste et l'art superréaliste', in Paul Citroen, *Palet. Een boek gewijd aan de hedendaagsche Nederlandsche schilderkunst* (Amsterdam 1931), pp. 76–82; Sven Backlund, 'Piet Mondrian', *Hyresgästen*, vol. 9, no. 20 (15 October 1931), pp. 1–3; Piet Mondrian, 'De werkelijke waarde der tegenstellingen', *Kroniek van hedendaagsche kunst en kultuur*, vol. 5, no. 3 (December 1939), pp. 34–6.

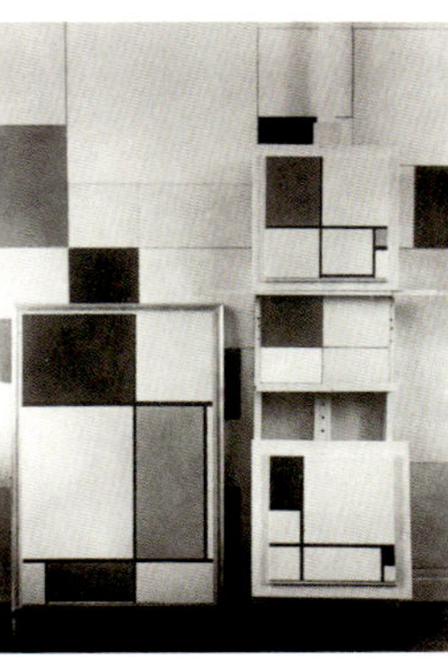

CAT. 122 Charles Karsten

Piet Mondrian's studio, c. summer 1929 (see p. 162)

A vintage print has not been traced; the photograph reproduced here is a later print (The Hague, RKD, Joop Joosten Archive (0838), inv. 815).

For the dating, see cat. 121.

Publications: *Catalogus 1929: 2de tentoonstelling A.S.B.* (exhib. cat. Stedelijk Museum 1929), n.p.; 'Réponse de Piet Mondrian', *Cahiers d'Art*, vol. 6, no. 1 (January 1931), pp. 41–3.

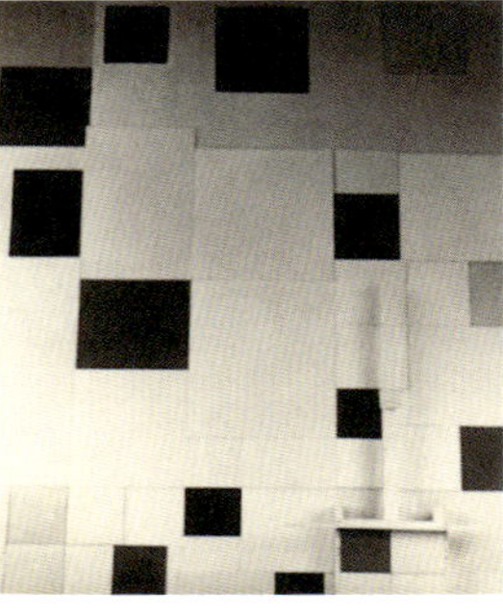

CAT. 123 Unidentified photographer

Piet Mondrian's studio, c. summer 1929 (see p. 163)

Gelatin developing-out paper, 13.8 x 11.8 cm

The Hague, RKD, Piet Mondrian Archive (0740), inv. 63

Dating based on the similar state of the wall decoration to that in cats 121–22.

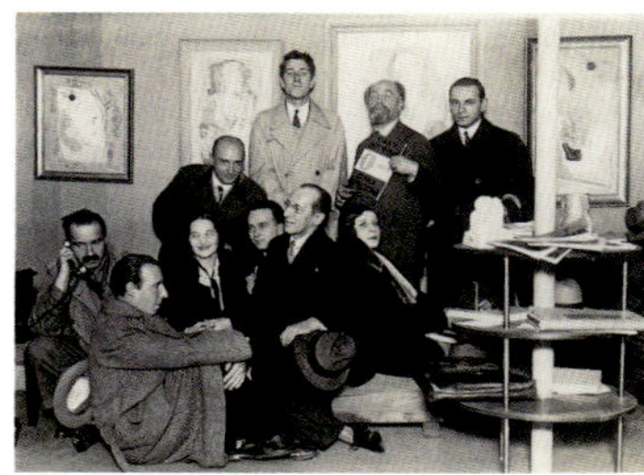

CAT. 124 Stanislaw Londynski

Company at the opening of Gustave Buchet's exhibition at Galerie Zak, Paris, 22 November 1929 (see pp. 164–65)

Gelatin developing-out paper, 16.8 x 22.8 cm

Private collection

The Swiss artist Gustave Buchet's exhibition at Galerie Zak opened on 22 November 1929.

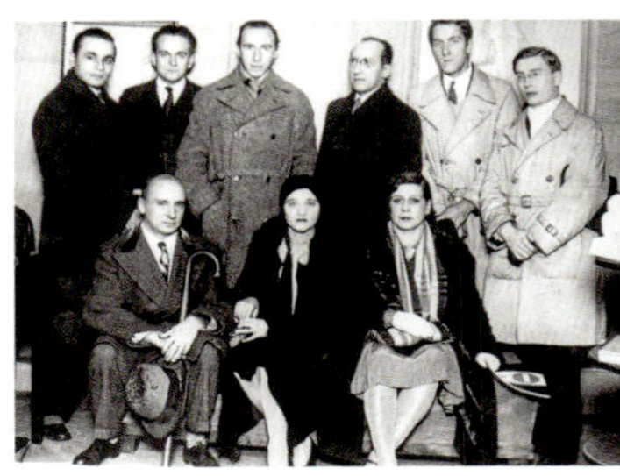

CAT. 125 Stanislaw Londynski

Company at the opening of Gustave Buchet's exhibition at Galerie Zak, Paris, 22 November 1929 (see p. 166)

A vintage print has not been traced; the photograph reproduced here is a later print (The Hague, RKD, Joop Joosten Archive (0838), inv. 809).

For the dating, see cat. 124.

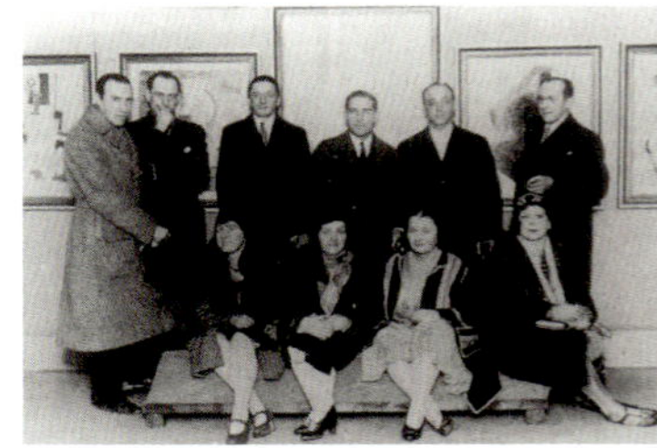

CAT. 126 Stanislaw Londynski

Company at the opening of Gustave Buchet's exhibition at Galerie Zak, Paris, 22 November 1929

A vintage print has not been traced; the image reproduced here is a photocopy of the photograph (The Hague, RKD, Joop Joosten Archive (0838), inv. 809).

Left to right, sitting: three unidentified women, Florence Henri; standing: Michel Seuphor, two unidentified men, Gustave Buchet, unidentified man, Piet Mondrian.

For the dating, see cat. 124.

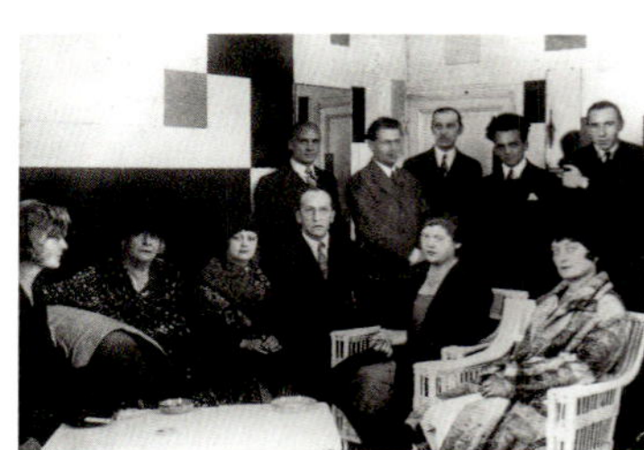

CAT. 127 Henri Glarner

Company in Piet Mondrian's studio, c. autumn 1929 (see p. 167)

A vintage print has not been traced; the photograph reproduced here is a later print (The Hague, RKD, Joop Joosten Archive (0838), inv. 815).

See Welsh/Joosten 1998-II, p. 142, for the identification.

Michel Seuphor introduced several of the people in the photograph to Mondrian in August–September 1929 (ibid.). We assume that this group photo was taken some time after that.

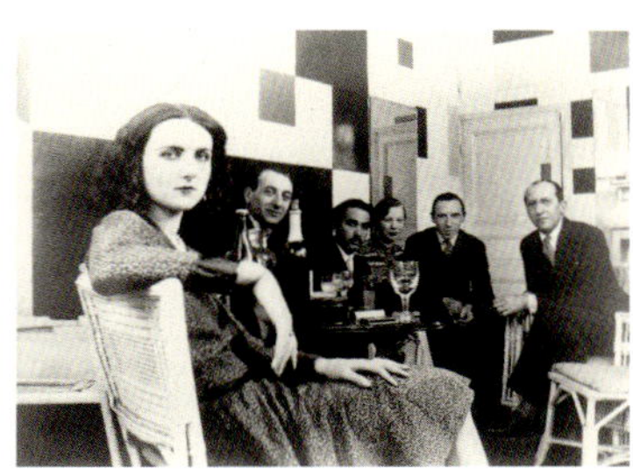

CAT. 128 Florence Henri (?)

Company in Piet Mondrian's studio, c. autumn 1929
(see p. 168)

A vintage print has not been traced; the photograph reproduced here is a later print (The Hague, RKD, Joop Joosten Archive (0838), inv. 809).

Florence Henri, who was also present, is missing from the photograph, making it likely that she took it; see also cat. 129.

Although it is a different company than on cat. 127, Seuphor seems to be the connecting factor here as well. Moreover, the decoration of the studio is very similar in both photos. We therefore use the same date for both photos.

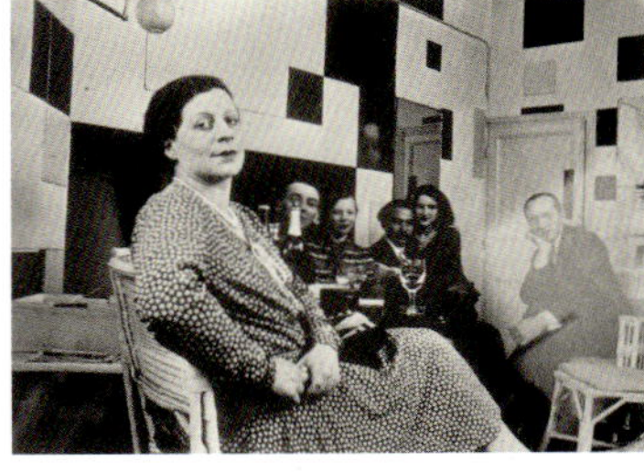

CAT. 129 Michel Seuphor (?)

Company in Piet Mondrian's studio, c. autumn 1929 (see p. 169)

A vintage print has not been traced; the photograph reproduced here is a later print (The Hague, RKD, Joop Joosten Archive (0838), inv. 809).

For the dating, see cat. 128.

Michel Seuphor, who was also present, is missing from the photograph, making it likely that he took it; see also cat. 128.

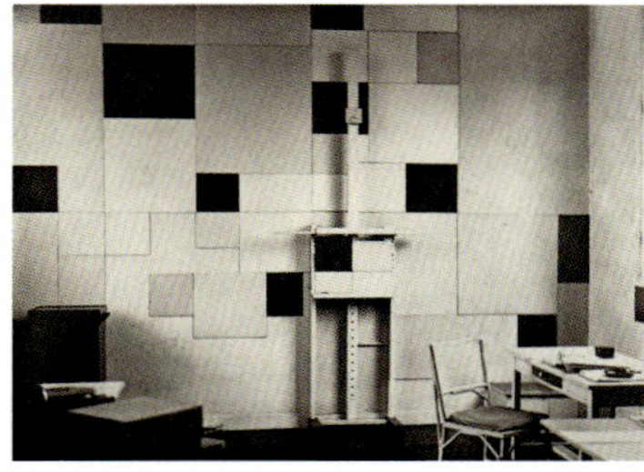

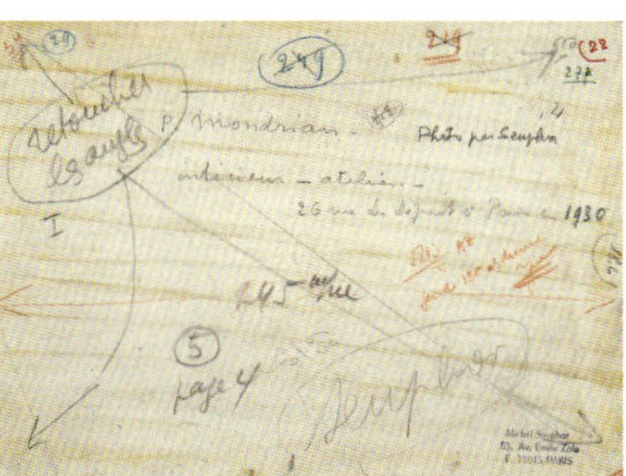

CAT. 130 Michel Seuphor or Rosie Ney

Piet Mondrian's studio, c. March–April 1930 (see p. 171)

Gelatin developing-out paper, 17.9 x 23.8 cm

Verso, in Piet Mondrian's handwriting: 'P. Mondrian. / interieur – atelier. – / 26 rue du Départ à Paris en 1930', where the year has been corrected from '1925'; in Seuphor's handwriting: 'Photo par Seuphor'; stamp: 'Michel Seuphor / 83, Av. Emile Zola / F. 75015 PARIS'

Berlin, Galerie Berinson

The photograph will have been taken some time before it was published in June 1930. Cats 131–33 must date from the same period, as they show the wall decoration in the same state; cat. 131 was taken during the same session as this one. We have linked these four photographs to a letter from Mondrian to Seuphor dated 14 March 1930: 'Et je voudrais que mad. Ney faisait une photo de mon atelier: elle a bien réussi l'autre fois.' ('I would like Madame Ney to take a photo of my studio: she did it very well the other time.') (Photocopy of letter in The Hague, RKD, Mondrian Correspondence Project Archive (0613), inv. 075). This means, however, that it is not certain whether it was Michel Seuphor himself or Rosie Ney who took the pictures. While the photograph is labelled 'Photo par Seuphor' on the back, it is evident from cat. 135 that this does not necessarily indicate authorship.

Publication: Jean Gorin, 'La Fonction plastique dans l'architecture future', *Cercle et Carré*, no. 3 (June 1930), [pp. 2 and 9].

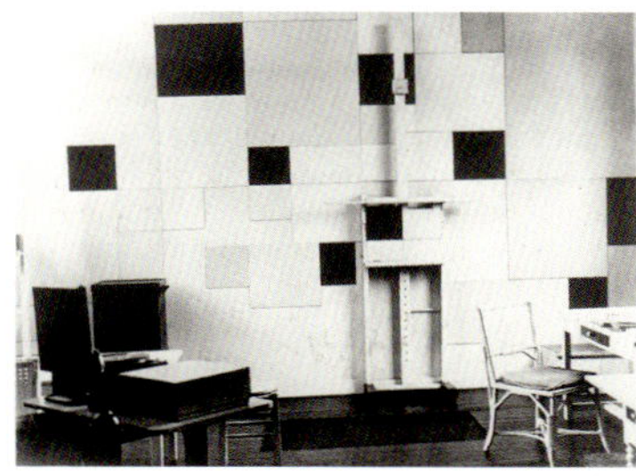

CAT. 131 Michel Seuphor or Rosie Ney

Piet Mondrian's studio, c. March–April 1930 (see p. 172)

Gelatin developing-out paper, 7.8 x 10.1 cm

Private collection

The picture was taken during the same session as cat. 130.

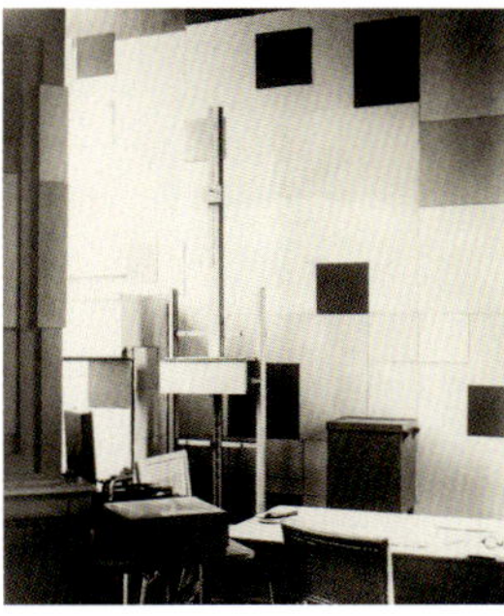

CAT. 132 Michel Seuphor or Rosie Ney

Piet Mondrian's studio, c. March–April 1930 (see p. 170)

Gelatin developing-out paper, 25.3 x 20.4 cm

The Hague, RKD, Robert P. Welsh Archive (0632), inv. 449

It cannot be determined for certain whether this is a vintage print or a later one. Other prints of the photograph are not known.

The picture was taken from precisely the same spot as cat. 133. The striking difference between the two in the grey values of the rear wall surfaces is attributable to the use of a filter (presumably for the colour yellow). Seuphor wrote in this respect: 'If you did not use the filter, it was totally wrong. Blue turned out light, yellow dark, and the red also dark' (Postma 1995, p. 14). See Wieczorek 2020, pp. 162–63 for the use of colour filters.

See also cat. 130.

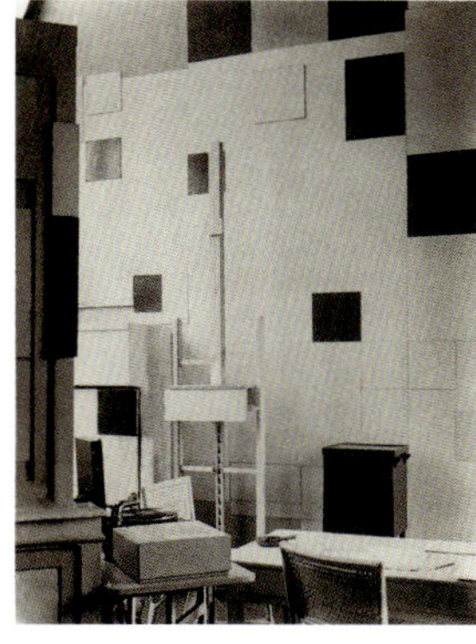

CAT. 133 Michel Seuphor or Rosie Ney

Piet Mondrian's studio, c. March–April 1930 (see p. 173)

Gelatin developing-out paper, 21.4 x 16.4 cm

The Hague, RKD, Robert Welsh Archive (0632), inv. 449

It cannot be determined for certain whether this is a vintage print or a later one. Other prints of the photograph are not known.

See also cats 130 and 132.

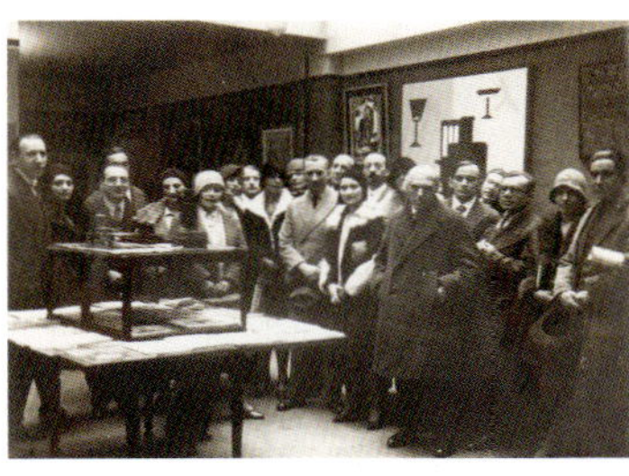

CAT. 134 Ina Bandy

Company at the opening of the Cercle et Carré exhibition at Galerie 23, Paris, 18 April 1930

Gelatin developing-out paper, 17.1 x 23.4 cm

Verso, in Michel Seuphor's handwriting: 'Photo prise par Seuphor'; stamp: 'INA BANDY / 29, QUAI D'ANJOU, 29 / ODÉ. 38-29 PARIS-IVe'

Private collection (?)

Left to right: Michel Seuphor, Vera Idelson, Georges Vantongerloo, Pierre Daura, Marcelle Cahn, Franciska Clausen, Florence Henri, Nechama Szmuszkowicz, Sophie Taeuber-Arp, Ingeborg Bjarnason, Hans Arp, Piet Mondrian, Nadia Grabowska, Luigi Russolo, Wanda Wolska, Joaquín Torres-García, Friedrich Vordemberge-Gildewart, Stefan Moszczynski, Jean Gorin, Manolita Piña Torres-García, Germán Cueto.

Despite Seuphor's claim that he took the picture (see inscription), we believe that Ina Bandy was the photographer. This is supported by the fact that Seuphor himself is in the picture.

See Welsh/Joosten 1998-II, p. 145, for the identification.

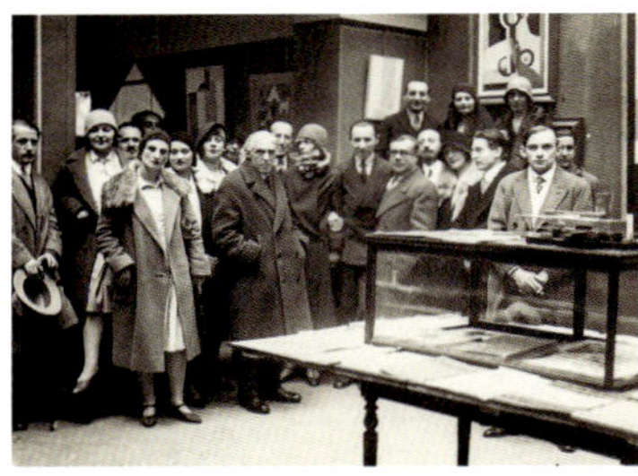

CAT. 135 Ina Bandy

Company at the opening of the Cercle et Carré exhibition at Galerie 23, Paris, 18 April 1930 (see p. 174)

Gelatin developing-out paper, 18 x 23.8 cm

Recto, Michel Seuphor's handwriting: 'Seuphor 1930'

Collection Matthijs Erdman, Amsterdam

See also cat. 134.

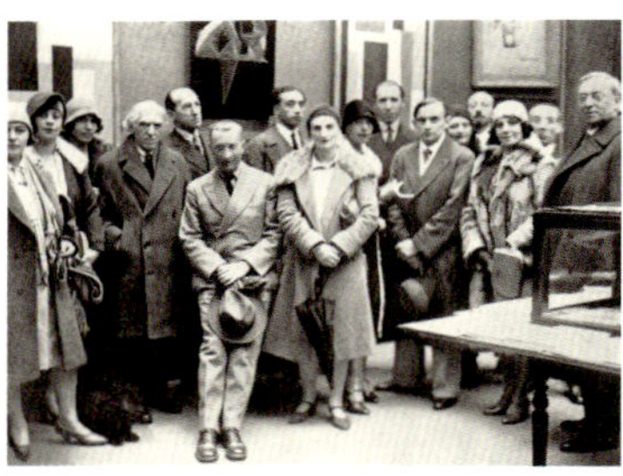

CAT. 136 Ina Bandy

Company at the opening of the Cercle et Carré exhibition at Galerie 23, Paris, 18 April 1930 (see p. 175)

Gelatin developing-out paper, 17.1 x 23.1 cm

Private collection (?)

Identification is based on the inscription on another print (Drouot auctioneers, Paris, 10 November 2017, lot 73).

See also cat. 134.

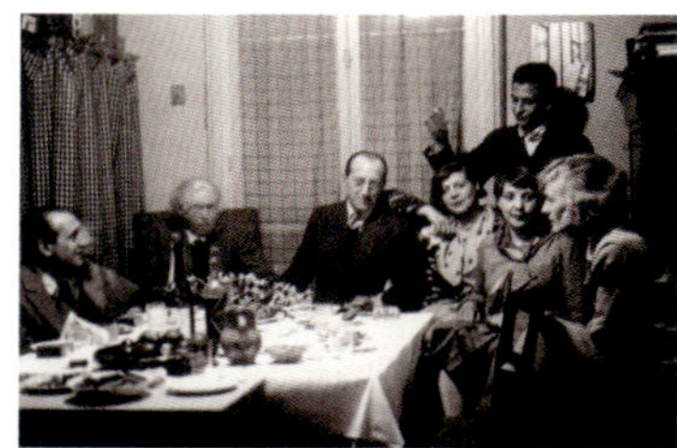

CAT. 137 Michel Seuphor

Company in Michel Seuphor's home, Vanves, April 1930 (see p. 176)

Gelatin developing-out paper, 18 x 23.8 cm

Recto, in Michel Seuphor's handwriting: 'Seuphor 1929'

Collection Matthijs Erdman, Amsterdam

For the identification, see Welsh/Joosten 1998-II, p. 145; Leal 2010, p. 310.

Since Cercle et Carré disbanded in the summer of 1930, this photograph must date from the period when it was still active; in accordance with Welsh/Joosten 1998 and Leal 2010, we thus date this and the following photograph to April 1930.

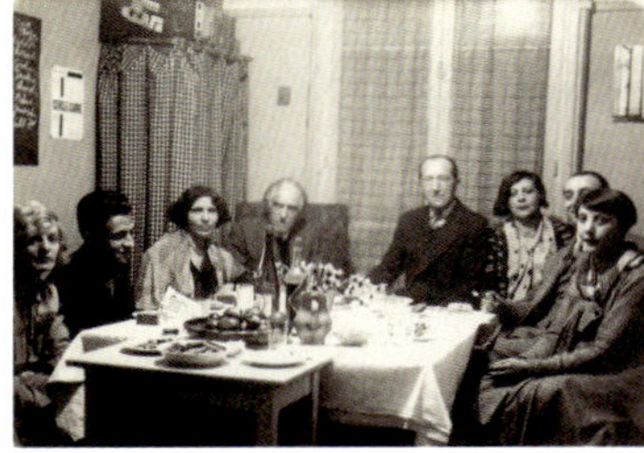

CAT. 138 Michel Seuphor

Company in Michel Seuphor's home, Vanves, April 1930 (see p. 177)

Recto, in Michel Seuphor's handwriting: 'Seuphor 1929'

Gelatin developing-out paper, 18 x 23.8 cm

Collection Matthijs Erdman, Amsterdam

For dating and identification, see cat. 137.

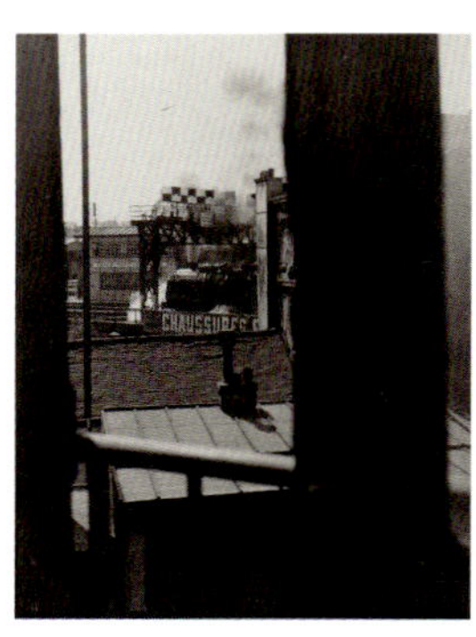

CAT. 139 László Moholy-Nagy

Gare Montparnasse viewed from Piet Mondrian's studio, summer 1927 or summer 1930 (see p. 178)

Gelatin developing-out paper, 30 x 24.1 cm

The Hague, Kunstmuseum Den Haag, inv. 0487331

There is some uncertainty regarding the dating of this and the other photograph that Moholy-Nagy took of the view from Mondrian's studio (cat. 140). Possible dates are either 1927 (see Leal 2010, p. 19, 301) or the summer of 1930 (see Janssen 2008, p. 230).

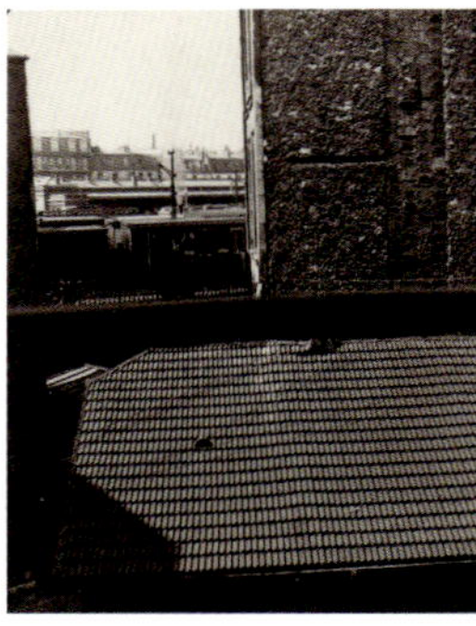

CAT. 140 László Moholy-Nagy

Gare Montparnasse viewed from Piet Mondrian's kitchen window, summer 1927 or summer 1930 (see p. 179)

Gelatin developing-out paper, 30 x 24.1 cm

The Hague, Kunstmuseum Den Haag, inv. 0487333

For the dating, see cat. 139.

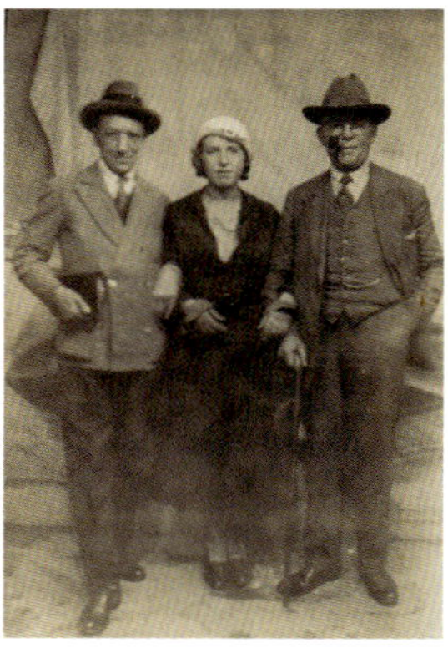

CAT. 141 Unidentified photographer

Piet Mondrian, an unidentified woman and Berend Groeneveld, c. 1930 (see p. 180)

Gelatin developing-out paper, 12.9 x 8.9 cm

Verso, in Berend Groeneveld's handwriting: 'I am in the middle of two Hollandais / Et c'est pour ça / Que je me sens très gaie / I am sorry that You / are not here / We have with You / Together much / plaisir. / Servus = / Goodby / Berend Gvelt. / Singer / S.'

The Hague, RKD, Simon Maris and Family Archive (0257), inv. 93

The dating of this picture is taken from the scant literature on Maris, Mondrian and Groeneveld (Gorter 1998, p. 37).

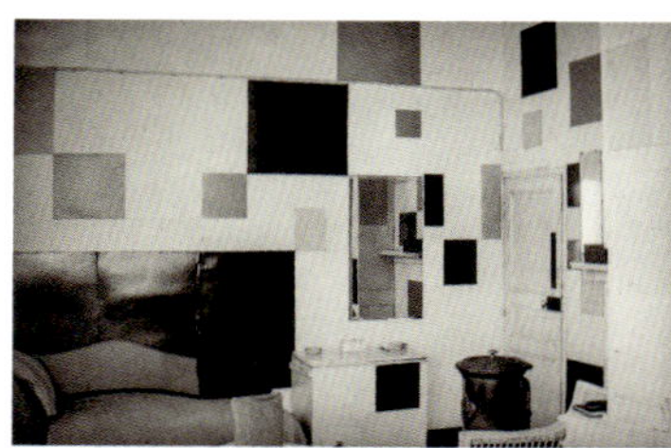

CAT. 142 Jan van den Briel

Piet Mondrian's studio, 1931 (see p. 181)

Gelatin developing-out paper, 16.7 x 23.8 cm

Recto, lower left on support in unidentified handwriting: 'atelier 1931'

The Hague, RKD, Collectie Preciosafoto's Piet Mondriaan

It cannot be determined for sure whether this is a vintage print or a later one. Other prints of the photograph are not known.

Attribution and dating are drawn from Henkels 1988, p. 18.

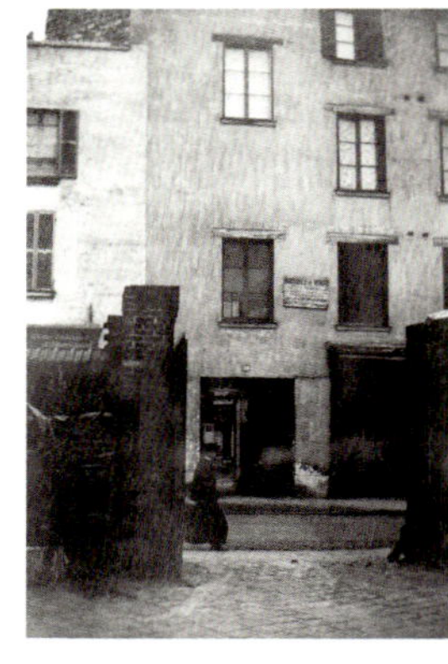

CAT. 143 Jan van den Briel

Studio building on Rue du Départ, 1931 (see p. 180)

Gelatin developing-out paper, 10.7 x 7.4 cm

The Hague, RKD, Collectie Preciosafoto's Piet Mondriaan

It cannot be determined for sure whether this is a vintage print or a later one. Other prints of the photograph are not known.

Attribution to Jan van den Briel is based on a note by Robert Welsh, who received the photograph from Mondrian's friend Albert van den Briel (The Hague, RKD, Robert Welsh Archive (0632), inv. 449); we assume that the picture was taken during the same visit to Mondrian in 1931 as cat. 142.

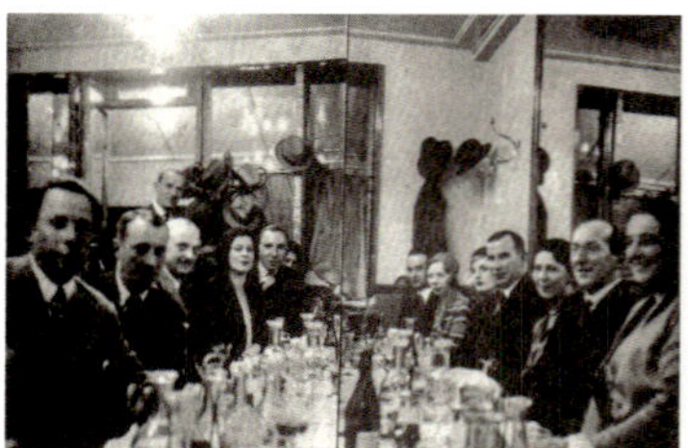

CAT. 144 Unidentified photographer

Company at Café Voltaire, Paris, May 1931 (see p. 182)

Gelatin developing-out paper, 18 x 24 cm

Paris, Bibliothèque Kandinsky, Fonds Robert et Sonia Delaunay, inv. DEL 84

For the identification see Welsh/Joosten 1998-II, p. 149; Leal 2010, p. 311.

The technical details come from Leal

2010, p. 353. This is thought to be a later print and not an original. The image consists of two prints.

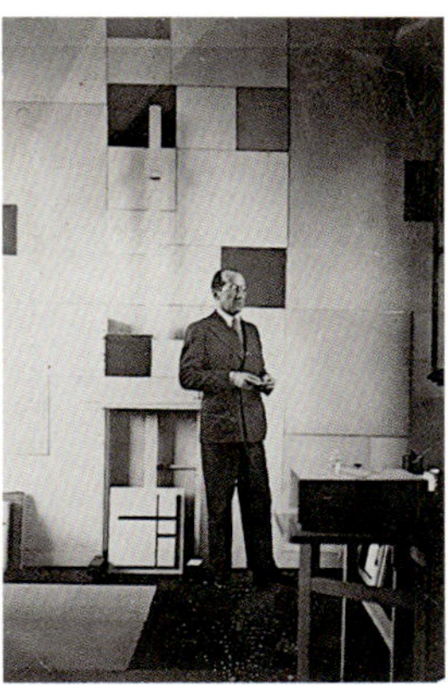

CAT. 145 Charles Karsten

Piet Mondrian in his studio, August 1931 (see p. 183)

Gelatin developing-out paper, 5.5 x 3.7 cm

Verso, on mount, in Charles Karsten's handwriting: 'Atelier Piet Mondriaan / Aug '41'

Het Nieuwe Instituut, Rotterdam, Charles Karsten Archive, inv. KARS_e3.238-3

The August 1931 date is based on the inscription.

See Welsh/Joosten 1998-II, p. 150.

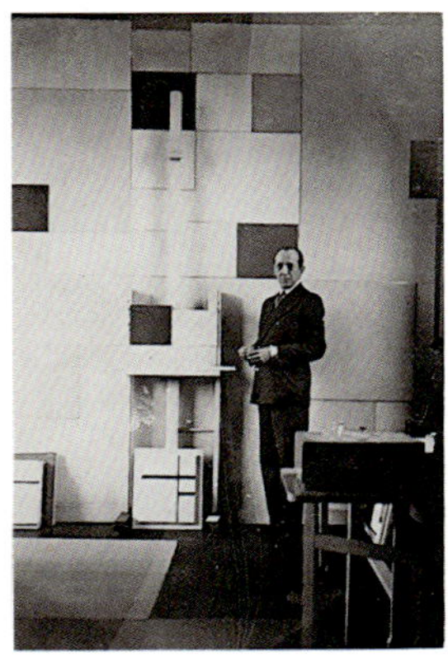

CAT. 146 Charles Karsten

Piet Mondrian in his studio, August 1931 (see p. 183)

Gelatin developing-out paper, 5.5 x 3.7 cm

Rotterdam, Het Nieuwe Instituut, Charles Karsten Archive, inv. KARS_e3.238-3

See also cat. 145.

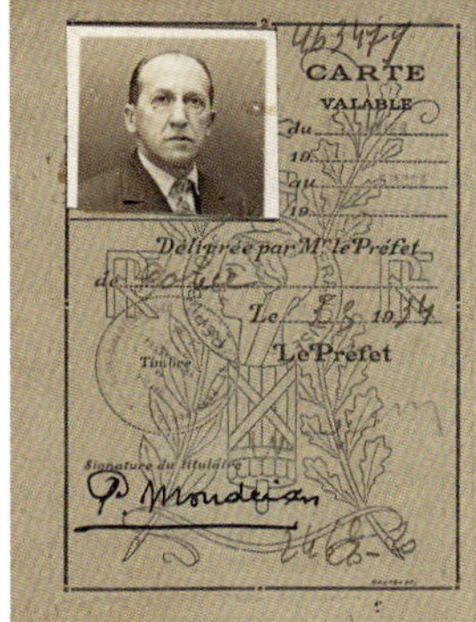

CARTE
VALABLE
Délivrée par M. le Préfet
Le Préfet
P. Mondrian

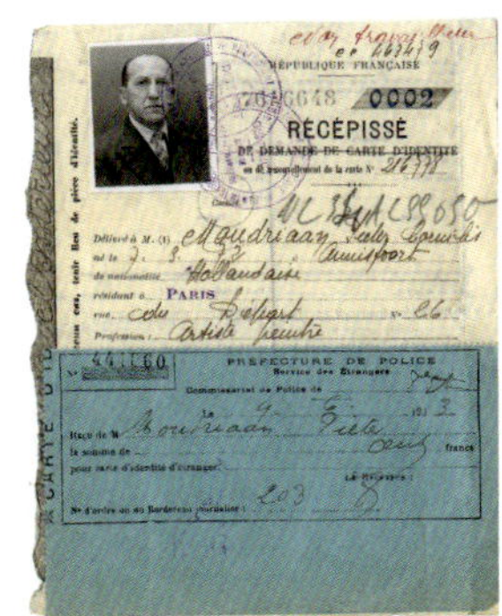

RÉPUBLIQUE FRANÇAISE
RÉCÉPISSÉ
DE DEMANDE DE CARTE D'IDENTITÉ
PARIS
PRÉFECTURE DE POLICE

CAT. 147.1; CAT. 147.2 Unidentified photographer

Portrait of Piet Mondrian, c. June 1933 (see p. 183)

Gelatin developing-out paper, dimensions unknown

(1) Paris, Archives et Musée de la Préfecture de Police de Paris, Service de la Mémoire et des Affaires Culturelles, inv. IC5-463479; (2) Yale, Beinecke Rare Book & Manuscript Library, Piet Mondrian Papers, GEN MSS 1102, Series II, Box 4, Folder 94

Dating to about June 1933 is based on the date of the blue receipt: 9 June 1933.

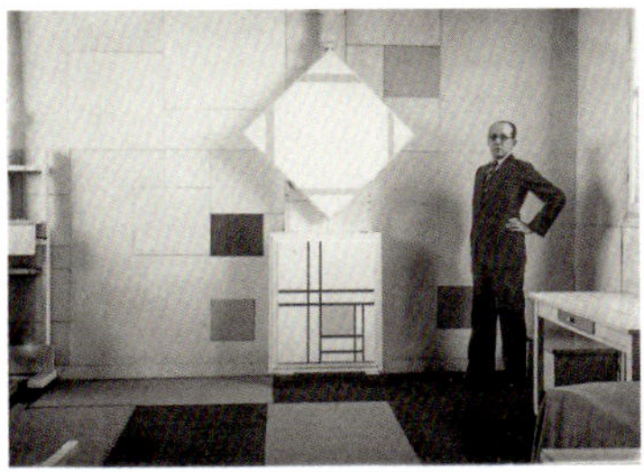

CAT. 148 Charles Karsten

Mondrian in his studio, September/ October 1933 (see p. 184)

Gelatin developing-out paper, 8.9 x 13.9 cm

Verso, partially illegible, in unidentified handwriting: 'Marcelle de [xxxxxxx] A'dam'

Rotterdam, Het Nieuwe Instituut, Charles Karsten Archive, inv. KARS_e3.238-2

The architect Charles Karsten published the photograph in the autumn of 1933 in the magazine *De 8 en Opbouw*, with which he was associated. It is assumed that he took this picture and cat. 149 some time earlier, during an undocumented visit to Mondrian (Welsh/Joosten 1998-II, p. 155). Another possibility is that they were taken when Karsten came to collect the diamond-shaped painting in early October (Wijnia 2018, p. 120).

Publication: 'Cavalcade', *De 8 en Opbouw*, vol. 4, no. 22 (28 October 1933), p. 197.

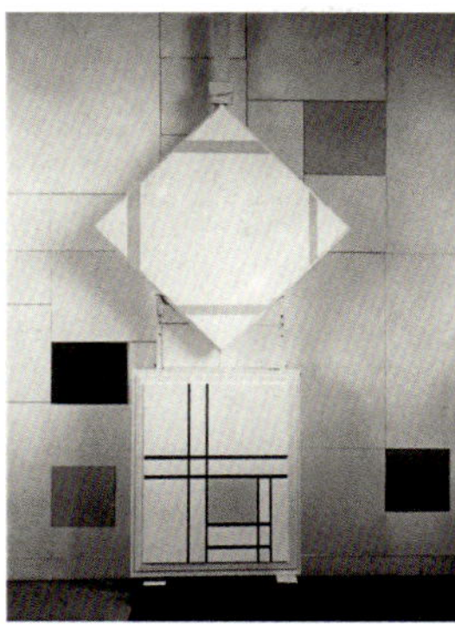

CAT. 149 Charles Karsten

Piet Mondrian's studio, with *Lozenge Composition with Four Yellow Lines* (B241) and *Composition with Double Lines and Yellow* (B242) on the easel, September/October 1933 (see p. 185)

Gelatin developing-out paper, 10 x 8.1 cm

Rotterdam, Het Nieuwe Instituut, Charles Karsten Archive, inv. KARS_e3.238-1

See also cat. 148.

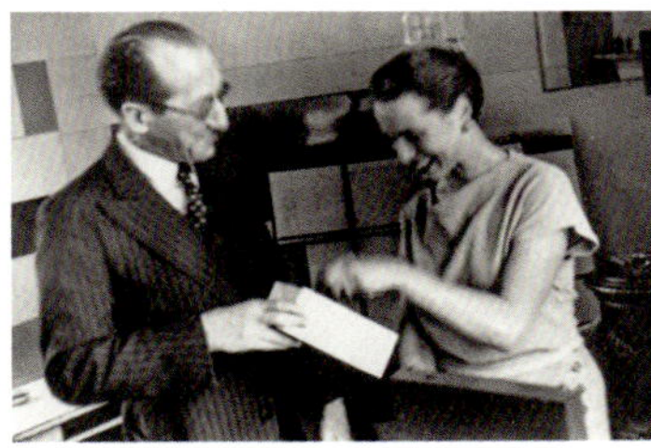

CAT. 150 Eugene Lux

Piet Mondrian and Gwendolyn Lux in Mondrian's studio, c. March–May 1934 (see p. 187)

Gelatin developing-out paper, 7.9 x 12 cm

The Hague, RKD, Piet Mondrian Archive (0740), inv. 65

Letters from Mondrian to the Luxes show that they were in direct contact around March–May 1934 (The Hague, RKD, Eugene and Gwen Lux Archive). All the pictures in this series (cats 150–71) must have been taken in that period. See also Welsh/Joosten 1998-II, pp. 155–56.

Mondrian wrote to Eugene and Gwen Lux on 27 July 1934: 'Les photos de Mr. Gallatin sont bien mais ne pas si vivantes que les votres et trop académiques' ('Mr Gallatin's photos [cats 172–73] are good but not as lively as yours and too academic'; The Hague, RKD, Eugene and Gwen Lux Archive (0954), inv. 3).

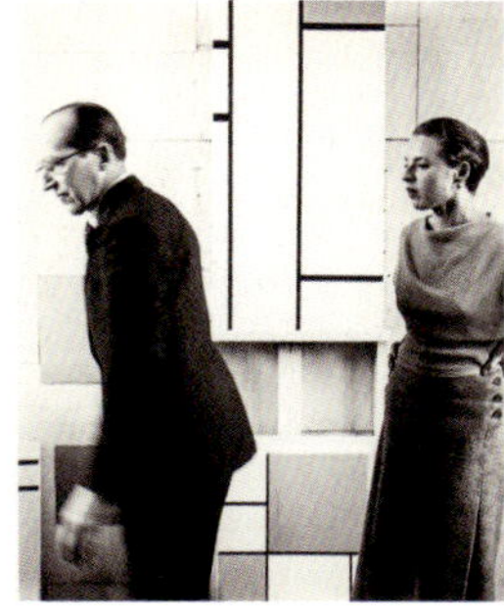

CAT. 151 Eugene Lux

Piet Mondrian and Gwendolyn Lux in Mondrian's studio, c. March–May 1934 (see p. 189)

A vintage print has not been traced; the photograph reproduced here is a later print (The Hague, RKD, Joop Joosten Archive (0838), inv. 810).

For the dating, see cat. 150.

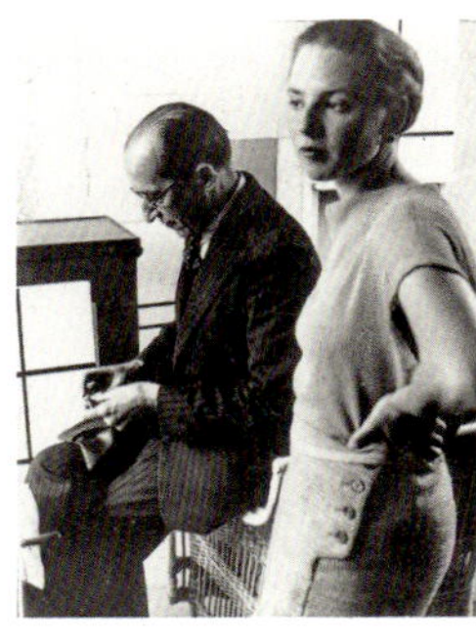

CAT. 152 Eugene Lux

Piet Mondrian and Gwendolyn Lux in Mondrian's studio, c. March–May 1934 (see p. 188)

Gelatin developing-out paper, 11.7 x 8.8 cm

Verso, in Gwen Lux's handwriting: '*To my dear / friend Mondrian / Gwen Lux*'

The Hague, RKD, Piet Mondrian Archive (0740), inv. 65

For the dating, see cat. 150.

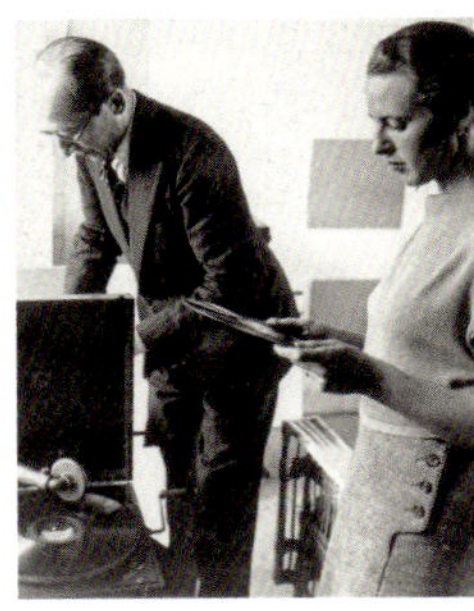

CAT. 153 Eugene Lux

Piet Mondrian and Gwendolyn Lux in Mondrian's studio, c. March–May 1934 (see p. 188)

Gelatin developing-out paper, 10.7 x 8.9 cm

Verso, in unidentified handwriting: 'Gwen Lux'

The Hague, RKD, Piet Mondrian Archive (0740), inv. 65

For the dating, see cat. 150.

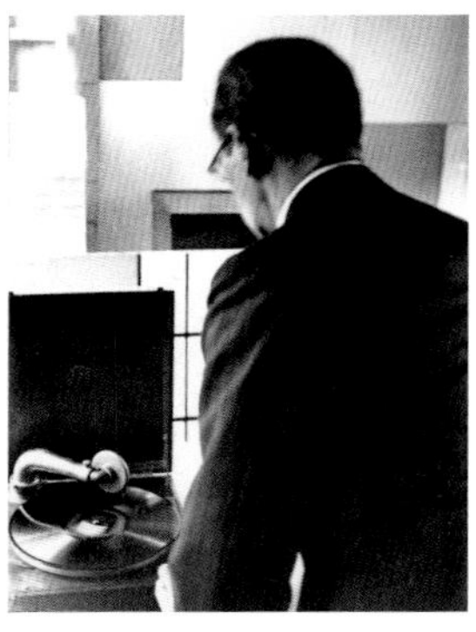

CAT. 154 Eugene Lux

Piet Mondrian with gramophone, c. March–May 1934 (see p. 190)

Gelatin developing-out paper, 11.4 x 8.7 cm

The Hague, RKD, Piet Mondrian Archive (0740), inv. 65

For the dating, see cat. 150.

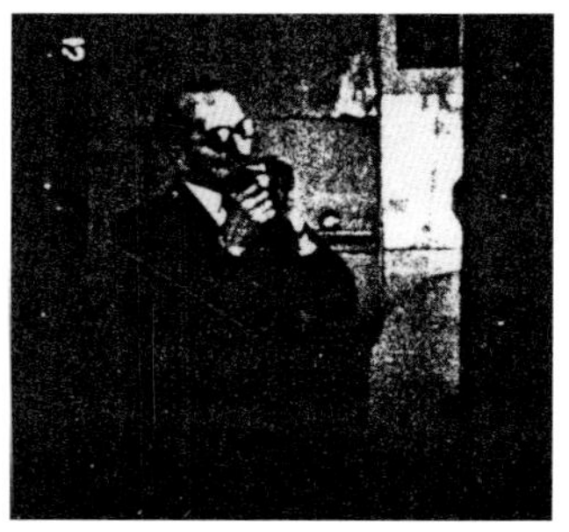

CAT. 155 Eugene Lux

Portrait of Piet Mondrian, c. March–May 1934

This image comes from a negative strip that also includes cats 156-57.

Neither the negative itself nor vintage prints of cats 155–56 have been traced; the sole source is a photocopy of a contact print of the negative strip (The Hague, RKD, Joop Joosten Archive (0838), inv. 810).

For the dating, see cat. 150.

For the lowermost photograph, see cat. 157.

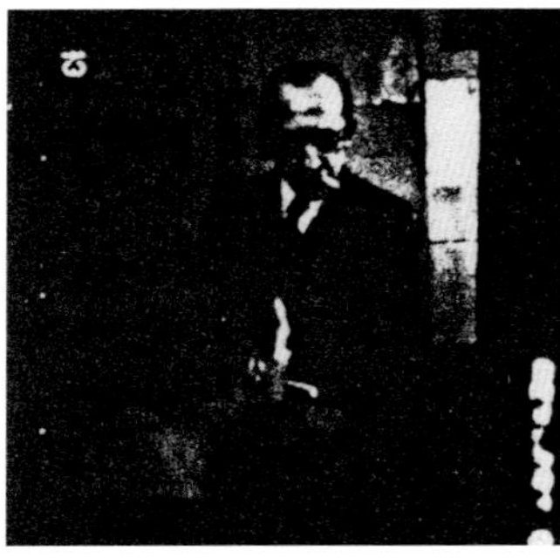

CAT. 156 Eugene Lux

Portrait of Piet Mondrian, c. March–May 1934

For the dating, see cat. 150.

See cats 155 and 157.

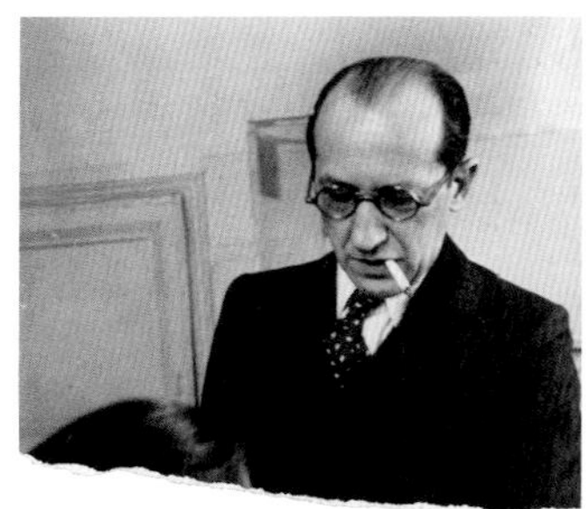

CAT. 157 Eugene Lux

Piet Mondrian and Gwendolyn Lux in Mondrian's studio, c. March–May 1934
(see p. 190)

Gelatin developing-out paper, 7.1 x 8.8 cm

Verso, in unidentified handwriting: 'Paris? Gwen Lux'

The Hague, RKD, Piet Mondrian Archive (0740), inv. 65

The full negative is part of the strip that also contains cats 155–56.

For the dating, see cat. 150.

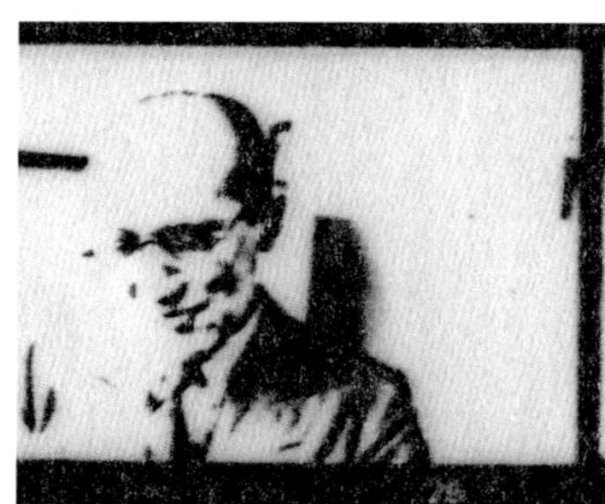

CAT. 158 Eugene Lux

Portrait of Piet Mondrian, c. March–May 1934

This image comes from a negative strip that also includes cats 159–61. No vintage prints of cats 158–59 have been traced; the sole source is a photocopy of a contact print of the negative strip (The Hague, RKD, Joop Joosten Archive (0838), inv. 810). The order of cats 158–61 is based on the negative strip.

For the dating, see cat. 150.

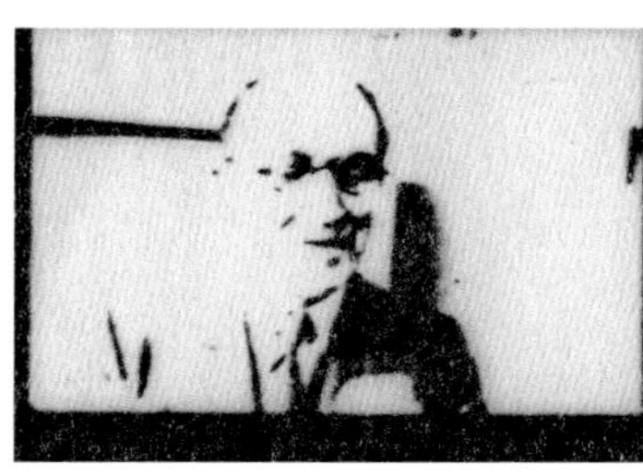

CAT. 159 Eugene Lux

Portrait of Piet Mondrian, c. March–May 1934

See also cat. 158.

For the dating, see cat. 150.

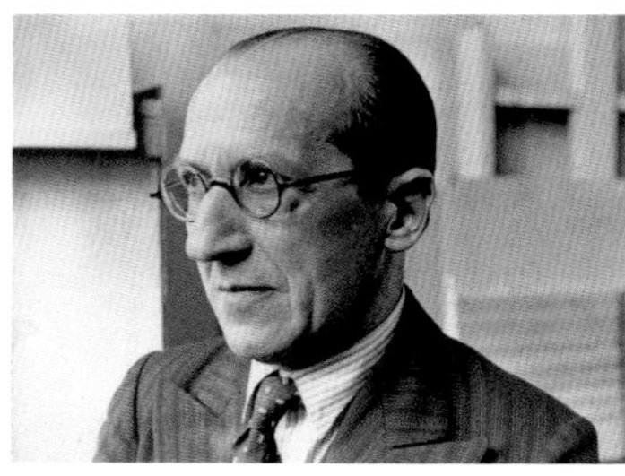

CAT. 160 Eugene Lux

Portrait of Piet Mondrian, c. March–May 1934 (see p. 191)

Gelatin developing-out paper, 17.9 x 24.3 cm

The Hague, RKD, Piet Mondrian Archive (0740), inv. 66

For the dating, see cat. 150.

Two prints of this picture are part of Mondrian's estate.

See also cat. 158.

Publication: Edouard Mesens, 'E. L. T. Mesens Presents Living Art in England', *London Bulletin*, nos 8–9 (January–February 1939), p. 29.

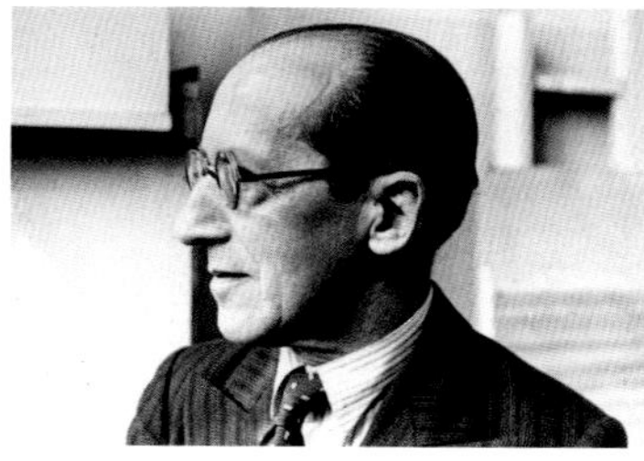

CAT. 161 Eugene Lux

Portrait of Piet Mondrian, c. March–May 1934 (see p. 191)

Gelatin developing-out paper, 8.8 x 11.2 cm

Verso, in unidentified handwriting: *'early / 1930ies / Paris'*

The Hague, RKD, Piet Mondrian Archive (0740), inv. 66

For the dating, see cat. 150.

See also cat. 158.

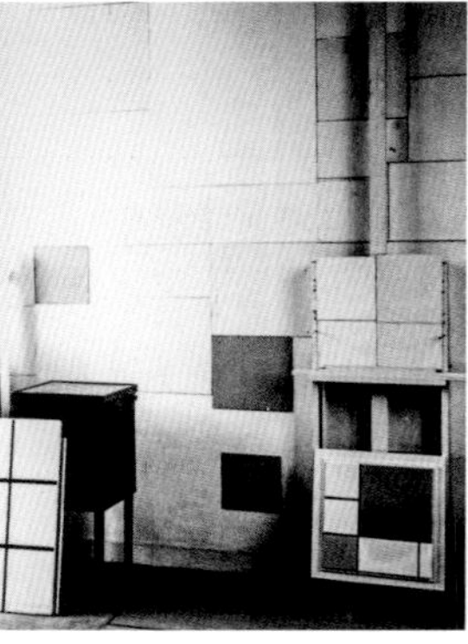

CAT. 162 Eugene Lux

Piet Mondrian's studio, c. March–May 1934 (see p. 192)

A vintage print has not been traced; the photograph reproduced here is a later print (The Hague, RKD, Joop Joosten Archive (0838), inv. 818).

For the dating, see cat. 150.

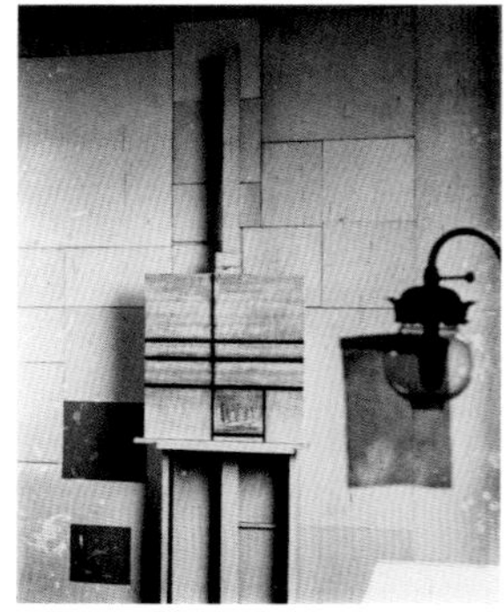

CAT. 163 Eugene Lux

Piet Mondrian's studio, c. March–May 1934 (see p. 193)

A vintage print has not been traced; the photograph reproduced here is a later print (The Hague, RKD, Joop Joosten Archive (0838), inv. 818).

For the dating, see cat. 150.

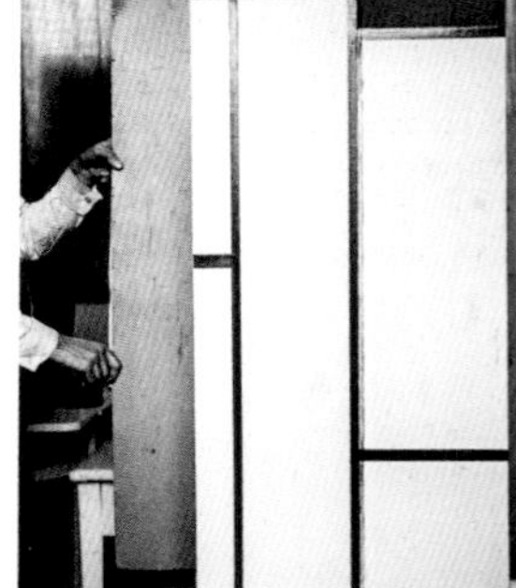

CAT. 164 Eugene Lux

***Composition A (No. I), with Red* (B260) unfinished in Mondrian's studio, c. March–May 1934**
(see p. 194)

A vintage print has not been traced; the photograph reproduced here is a later print (The Hague, RKD, Joop Joosten Archive (0838), inv. 818).

For the dating, see cat. 150.

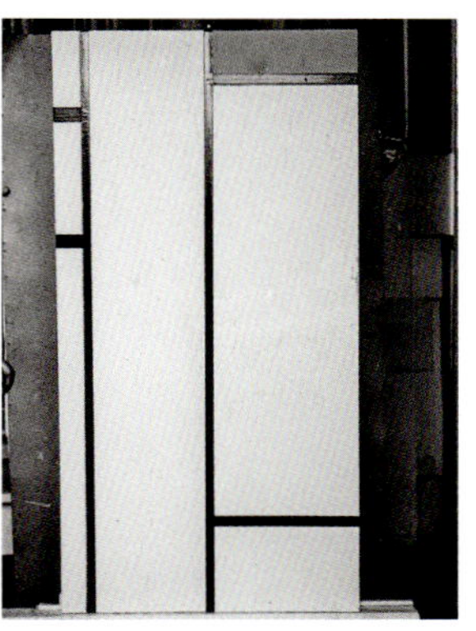

CAT. 165 Eugene Lux

***Composition (No. III) blanc-jaune* (B257) unfinished in Mondrian's studio, c. March–May 1934**
(see p. 195)

A vintage print has not been traced; the photograph reproduced here is a later print (The Hague, RKD, Joop Joosten Archive (0838), inv. 818).

For the dating, see cat. 150.

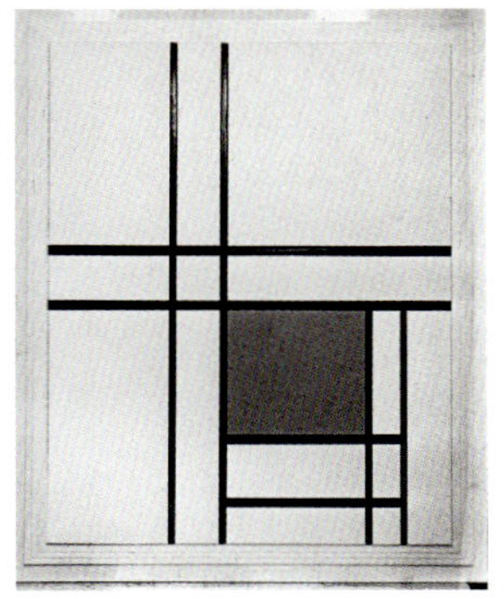

CAT. 166 Eugene Lux

***Composition with Double Lines and Yellow* (B242) in Mondrian's studio, c. March–May 1934** (see p. 195)

A vintage print has not been traced; the photograph reproduced here is a later print (The Hague, RKD, Joop Joosten Archive (0838), inv. 818).

For the dating, see cat. 150.

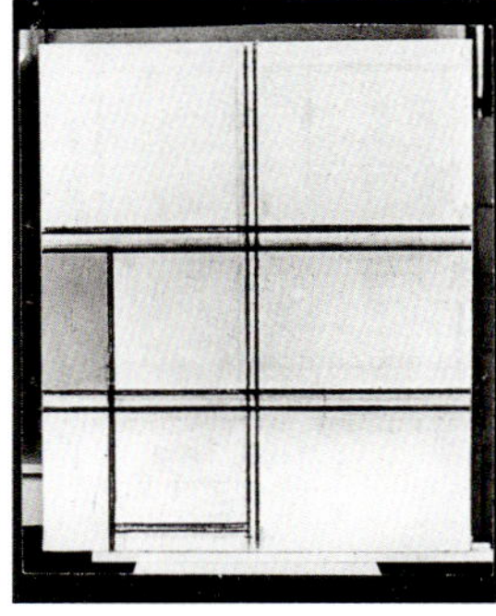

CAT. 167 Eugene Lux

***Composition* (B252) unfinished in Mondrian's studio, c. March–May 1934** (see p. 196)

A vintage print has not been traced; the photograph reproduced here is a later print (The Hague, RKD, Joop Joosten Archive (0838), inv. 818).

For the dating, see cat. 150.

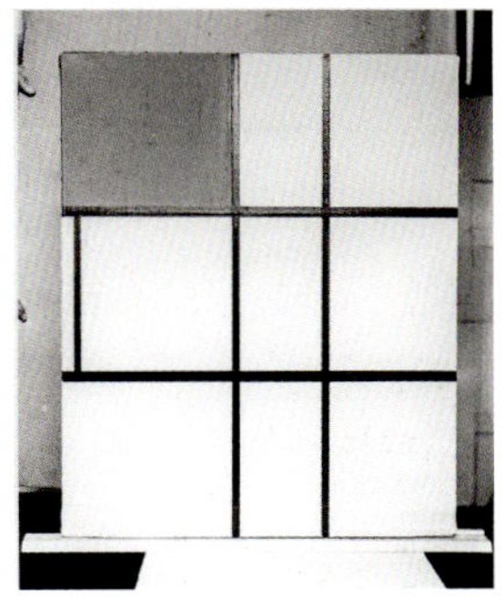

CAT. 168 Eugene Lux

***Composition B/(No. II), with Red* (B254) unfinished in Mondrian's studio, c. March–May 1934**

(see p. 196)

A vintage print has not been traced; the photograph reproduced here is a later print (The Hague, RKD, Joop Joosten Archive (0838), inv. 818).

For the dating, see cat. 150.

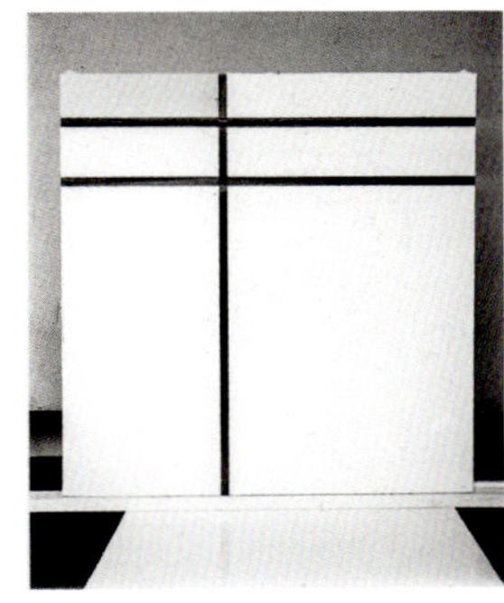

CAT. 169 Eugene Lux

***Composition A, with Double Line and Yellow* (B253) unfinished in Mondrian's studio, c. March–May 1934** (see p. 197)

A vintage print has not been traced; the photograph reproduced here is a later print (The Hague, RKD, Joop Joosten Archive (0838), inv. 818).

For the dating, see cat. 150.

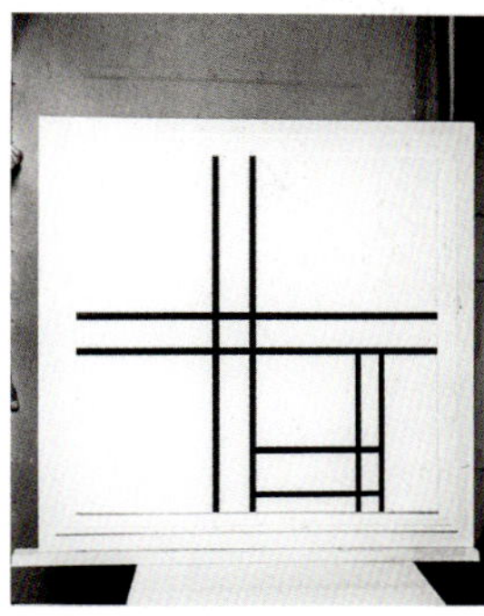

CAT. 170 Eugene Lux

***Composition in Black and White, with Double Lines* (B243) in Mondrian's studio, c. March–May 1934**
(see p. 197)

A vintage print has not been traced; the photograph reproduced here is a later print (The Hague, RKD, Joop Joosten Archive (0838), inv. 818).

For the dating, see cat. 150.

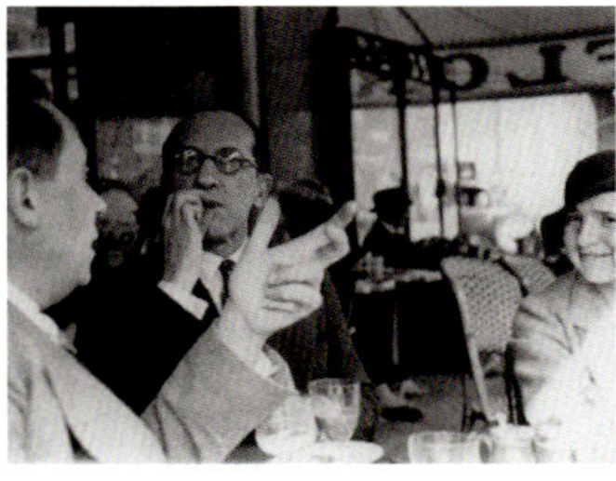

CAT. 171 Eugene Lux

Robert Delaunay, Piet Mondrian and an unidentified woman on the terrace of Café de Flore, Paris, c. March–May 1934 (see p. 198)

A vintage print has not been traced; the photograph reproduced here is taken from Portevin 2010, p. 20.

For the dating, see cat. 150.

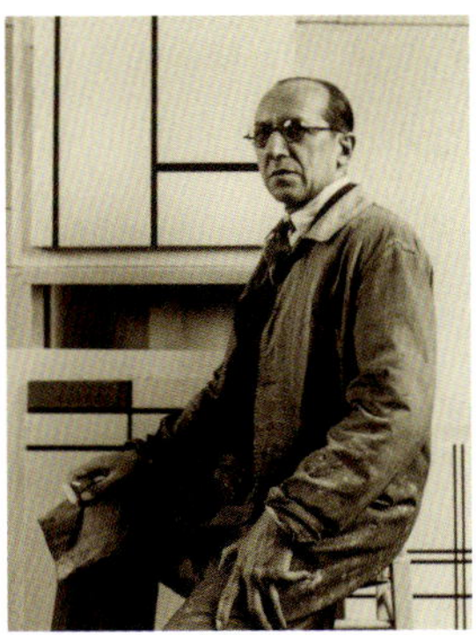

CAT. 172 Albert Eugene Gallatin

Portrait of Piet Mondrian, June 1934
(see p. 199)

Gelatin developing-out paper, 18 x 13 cm

Recto, signed: 'Gallatin / June 1934'

Paris, Bibliothèque Kandinsky, Centre Pompidou, Fonds photographique A. E. Gallatin, inv. FGP GALL 3287 (20)

The dating is based on the inscription.

This and the following photograph by Albert Gallatin (cat. 173) must have been taken before 26 June 1934: Mondrian thanked him for sending it in a letter of that date (New York, New York Historical Society collection). See p. 62, note 75, for the French text of the letter to Gallatin. In a letter of 27 July 1934 to the Luxes, Mondrian said he found Gallatin's photographs 'too academic' (The Hague, RKD, Eugene Lux and Gwen Lux Archive (0954), inv. 3).

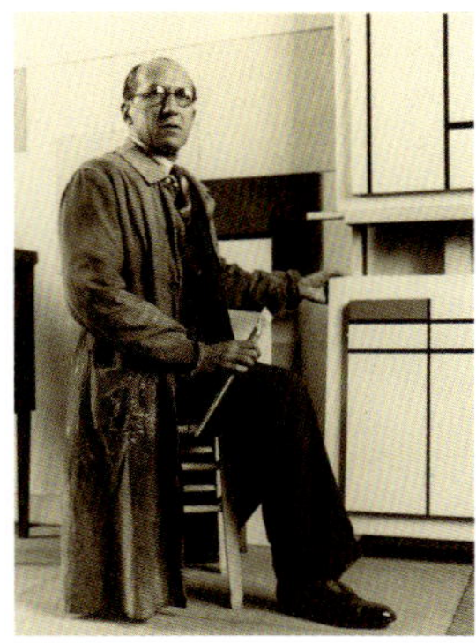

CAT. 173 Albert Eugene Gallatin

Portrait of Piet Mondrian, June 1934
(see p. 200)

Gelatin developing-out paper, 17.8 x 12.9 cm

Philadelphia Museum of Art, A. E. Gallatin Collection, inv. 1952-61-132

See also cat. 172.

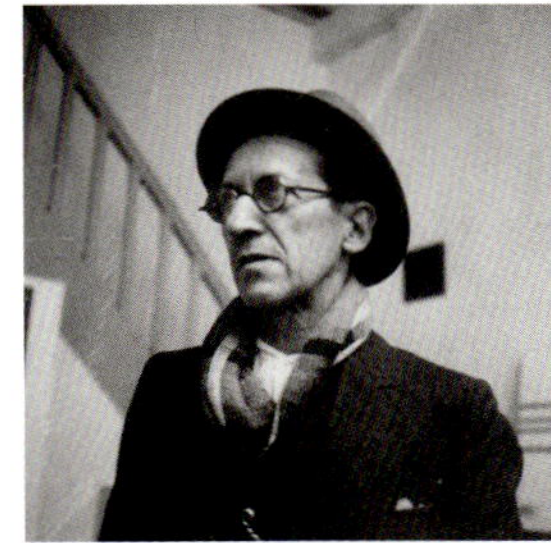

CAT. 174 Kurt Schwitters

Portrait of Piet Mondrian, between 20 and 24 March 1936
(see p. 201)

Gelatin developing-out paper, 6 x 6 cm

Verso, in Kurt Schwitters' handwriting: 'bitte gelegentlich an Mondrian' ('Please [give] to Mondrian if you get chance')

Sprengel Museum Hannover, Kurt Schwitters Archive, inv. KSA 2003.20

According to his French visa, Mondrian moved into this studio on 278 Boulevard Raspail on 20 March 1936 (Welsh/Joosten 1998-II, p. 163). Schwitters wrote to the art collectors Oskar and Annie Müller-Widmann on 24 March, informing them that he had visited Mondrian and enclosing this photograph. The picture must thus have been taken between 20 and 24 March 1936. The scarf Mondrian is wearing in the photo supports a date in early spring 1936.

On 7 July 1936, Schwitters wrote to the Müller-Widmanns: 'Die Fotos an Tschi[chold] [...] und Mondrian bitte ich gelegentlich weiter zu geben. Besten Dank.' ('Please pass on the photos to Tschi[chold] [...] and Mondrian if you get chance. Thanks.'). This tallies with the message on the verso.

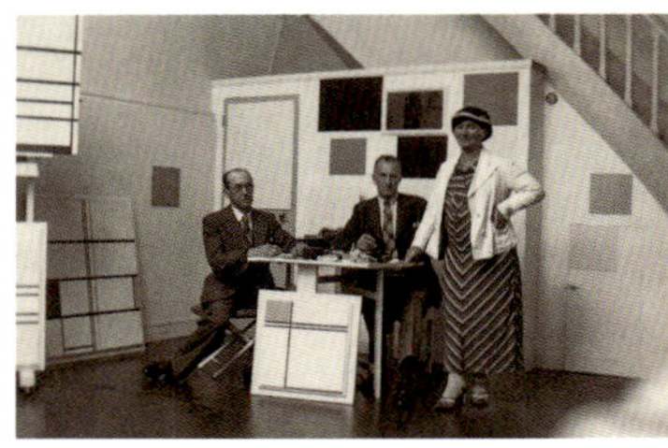

CAT. 175 Unidentified photographer

Piet Mondrian, Carel Mondriaan and his fiancée Maria van den Berg in Mondrian's studio, August 1936 (see p. 202)

Gelatin developing-out paper, 5.4 x 7.8 cm

Verso, in Carel Mondriaan's handwriting: 'Atelier van m'n broer in Parijs / Bezoek augs. 1936.' ('My brother's studio in Paris / Visit August 1936.')

The Hague, RKD, Carel Mondriaan Archive (0929), inv. 23

This and the following picture (cat. 176) may have been taken using a self-timer.

The dating is based on the inscription. A receipt was also found among Carel Mondriaan's papers from the Paris hotel *Raspail*, dated '27 Août 1936'.

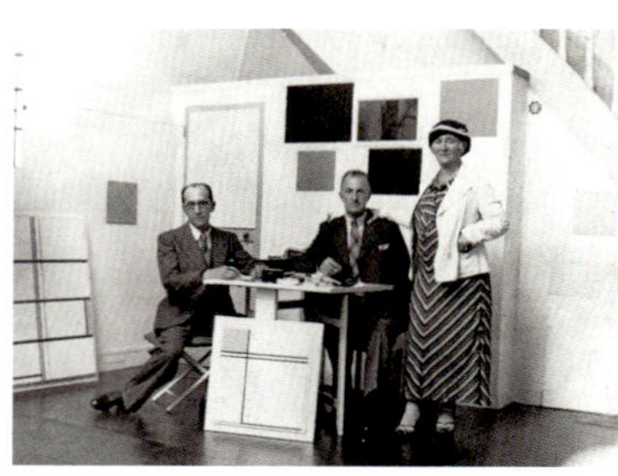

CAT. 176 Unidentified photographer

Piet Mondrian, Carel Mondriaan and his fiancée Maria van den Berg in Mondrian's studio, August 1936

Gelatin developing-out paper, 15 x 20 cm

Verso, in Harry Holtzman's handwriting: '[Piet Mondrian with / Carel and Mary Mondriaan, / in his studio on Rue du Depart, / Paris]'

Yale, Beinecke Rare Book & Manuscript Library, Piet Mondrian Papers. The authors have seen. At the time of publication, the photograph was not available at the Library. The authors examined it personally in 2015.

See also cat. 175.

Holtzman was mistaken in his note on the back: the photograph was taken in the studio at 278 Boulevard Raspail.

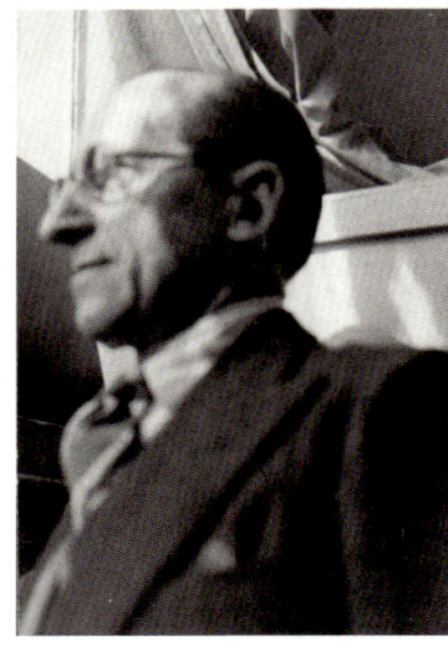

CAT. 177 Unidentified photographer

Portrait of Piet Mondrian, c. 1937 (see p. 203)

Gelatin developing-out paper, 8.6 x 6 cm

The Hague, RKD, Piet Mondrian Archive (0740), inv. 67

This photograph came from Piet Mondrian's estate.

The low perspective in this and the next picture (cat. 178) tallies with Cas Oorthuys's photographs (cats 182–85) and might indicate the use of a camera such as (in Oorthuys's case) a Rolleiflex, which had a matt glass viewfinder on the top. Further details are not known.

Based on the similarities with Oorthuys's pictures and the one taken by Kurt Schwitters in March 1936 (cat. 174), in which Mondrian is wearing the same glasses, we date the photograph to around 1937.

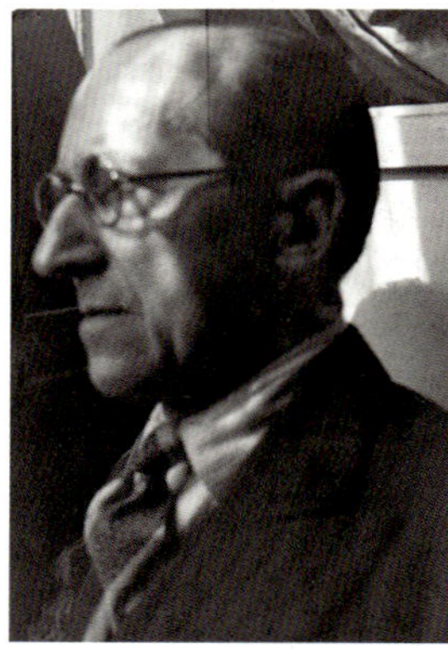

CAT. 178 Unidentified photographer

Portrait of Piet Mondrian, c. 1937 (see p. 203)

Gelatin developing-out paper, 8.6 x 6 cm

The Hague, RKD, Piet Mondrian Archive (0740), inv. 67

See also cat. 177.

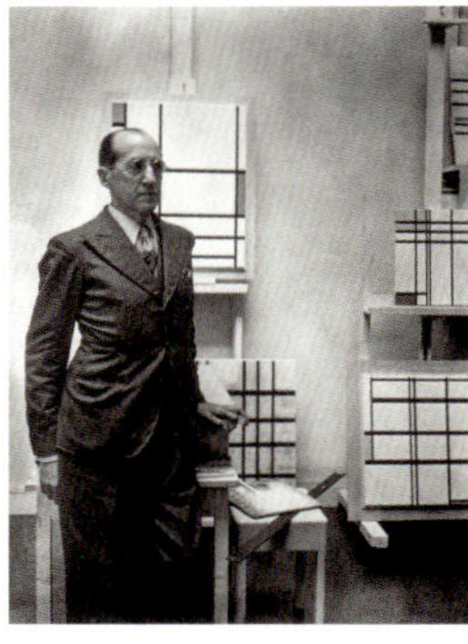

CAT. 179 Rogi André (Rosza Klein)

Piet Mondrian in his studio, c. June–July 1937 (see p. 204)

Gelatin developing-out paper, 40 x 30.1 cm

Paris, Centre Pompidou, Centre de Création Industrielle, inv. AM1982-307

The exhibition at the Jeu de Paume, on the occasion of which the photographs was taken, opened on 30 July. This photograph was probably taken in the weeks leading up to the opening and has therefore been dated to around June–July 1937.

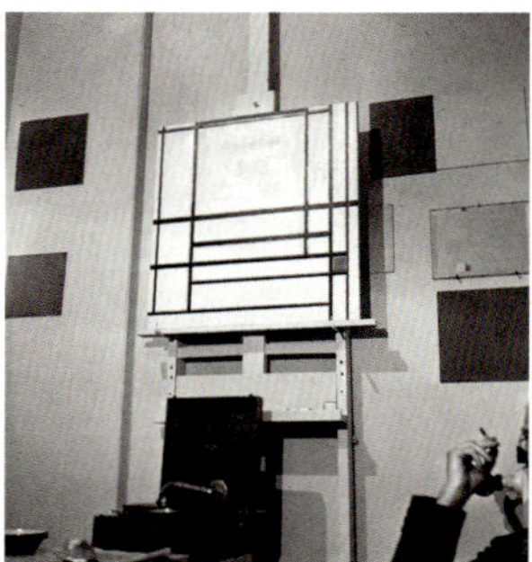

CAT. 180 Cas Oorthuys

Piet Mondrian's studio with *Composition of Lines with Red (Unfinished)* (B278) on the easel, August (?) 1937 (see p. 206)

Gelatin developing-out paper (contact print), 6.1 x 5.7 cm

Rotterdam, Nederlands Fotomuseum, inv. CAS-3005-7

Peter Alma and the photographer Cas Oorthuys visited Mondrian in the summer (probably August) of 1937 (Welsh/Joosten 1998-II, p. 168).

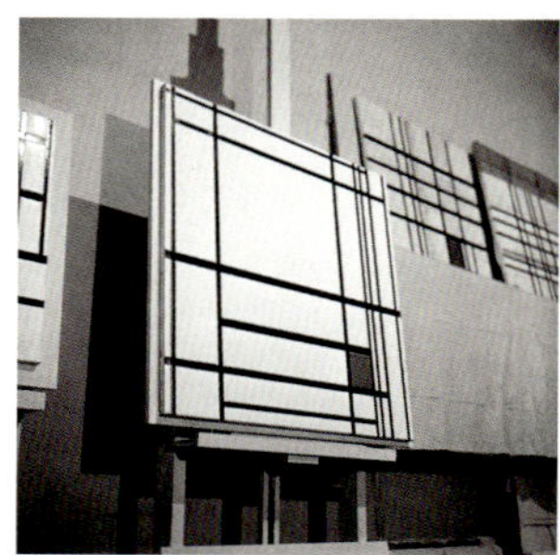

CAT. 181 Cas Oorthuys

Piet Mondrian's studio with *Composition de lignes et couleur: III* (B277) on the easel, August (?) 1937 (see p. 207)

Gelatin developing-out paper (contact print), 6.1 x 5.7 cm

Rotterdam, Nederlands Fotomuseum, inv. CAS-3005-6

For the dating, see cat. 180.

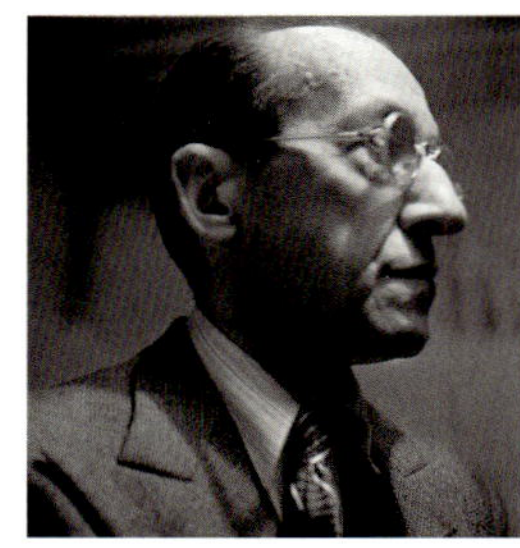

CAT. 182 Cas Oorthuys

Portrait of Piet Mondrian, August (?) 1937 (see p. 208)

Gelatin developing-out paper (contact print), 6.1 x 5.7 cm

Rotterdam, Nederlands Fotomuseum, inv. CAS-3005-2

For the dating, see cat. 180.

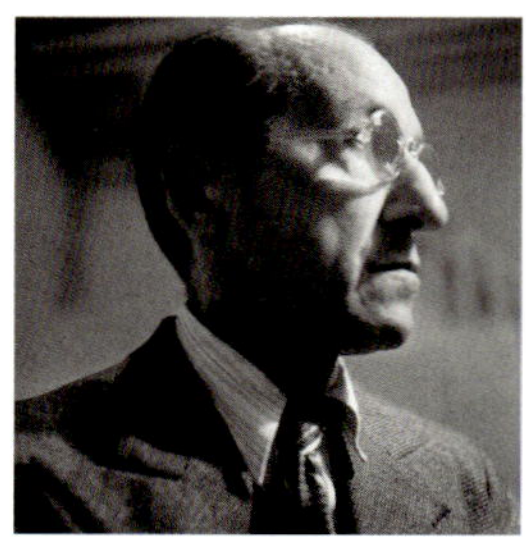

CAT. 183 Cas Oorthuys

Portrait of Piet Mondrian, August (?) 1937 (see p. 208)

Gelatin developing-out paper (contact print), 6.1 x 5.7 cm

Rotterdam, Nederlands Fotomuseum, inv. CAS-3005-5

For the dating, see cat. 180.

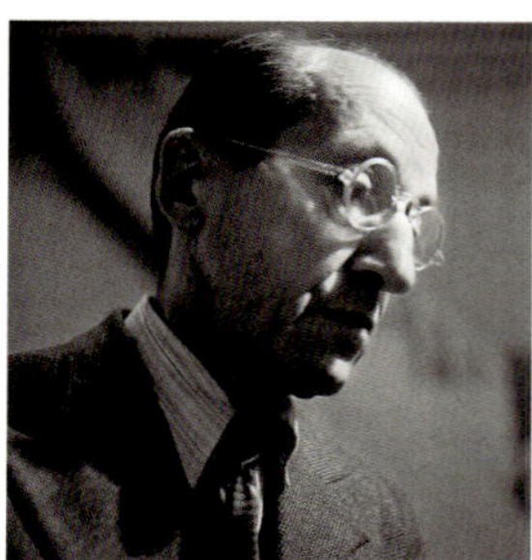

CAT. 184 Cas Oorthuys

Portrait of Piet Mondrian, August (?) 1937 (see p. 208)

Gelatin developing-out paper (contact print), 6.1 x 5.7 cm

Rotterdam, Nederlands Fotomuseum, inv. CAS-3005-3

For the dating, see cat. 180.

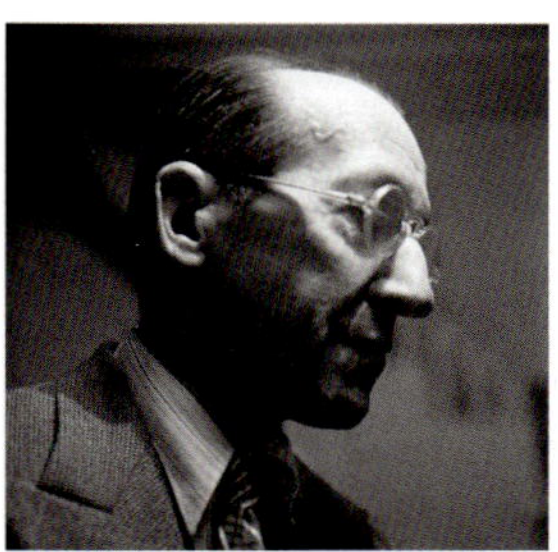

CAT. 185 Cas Oorthuys

Portrait of Piet Mondrian, August (?) 1937 (see p. 208)

Gelatin developing-out paper (contact print), 6.1 x 5.7 cm

Rotterdam, Nederlands Fotomuseum, inv. CAS-3005-4

For the dating, see cat. 180.

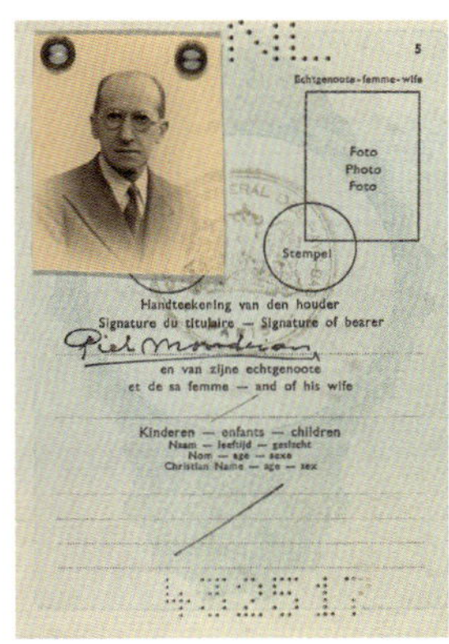

CAT. 186 Unidentified photographer

Piet Mondrian's passport photo, 12 September 1938 (see p. 209)

Gelatin developing-out paper, 6.1 x 5.1 cm

Verso, stamp: '12 SEPT 193[8]'

The Hague, RKD, Anna Bergman Archive (0662), inv. 30

Dating based on the stamp on the back.

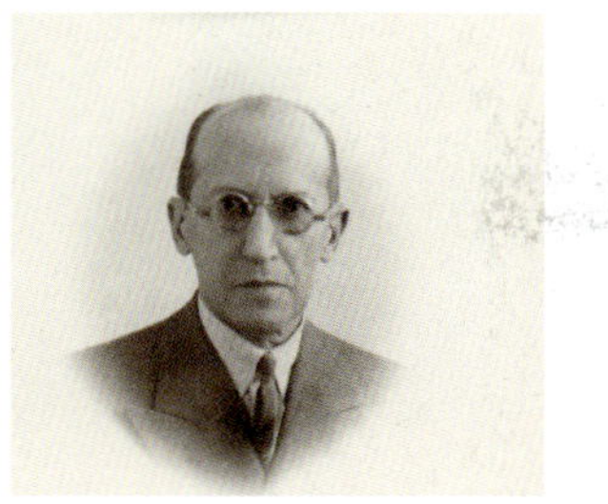

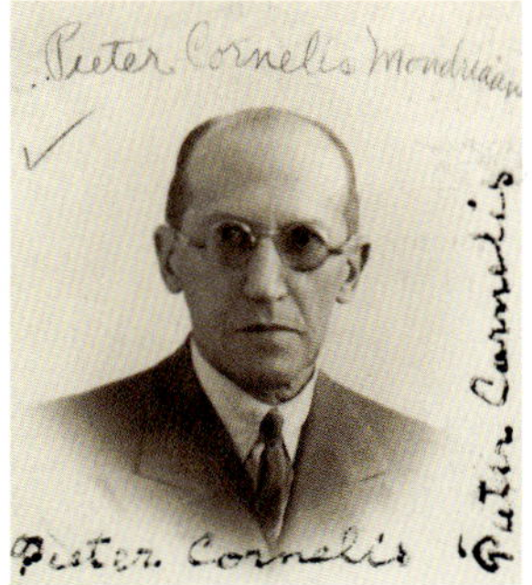

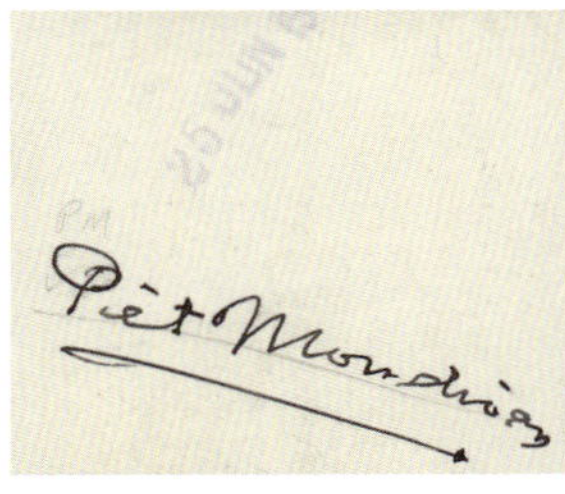

CAT. 187.1; CAT. 187.2 Portraits by Jerome photography studio, London

Portrait of Piet Mondrian, 25 June 1940

Gelatin developing-out paper, 6.6 x 7 cm

(1) Verso, in Piet Mondrian's handwriting: '*Piet Mondrian*'; stamp: '25 JUN 19[40]'; envelope, stamp: '*Portraits by* / Jerome'; (2) recto, in Piet Mondrian's handwriting: 'Pieter Cornelis Mondriaan / Pieter Cornelis (2x)', verso, stamp: '25 JUN 19[40]'

(1) and (2) The Hague, RKD, Piet Mondrian Archive (0740), inv. 68

Six prints of this passport photo have been preserved in the Piet Mondrian archive, two of which the artist signed once or several times. They were intended for the official documents required for his upcoming emigration to the United States (see cat. 188). One was used for his Immigrant Identification Card.

The dating is provided by the stamp on the back.

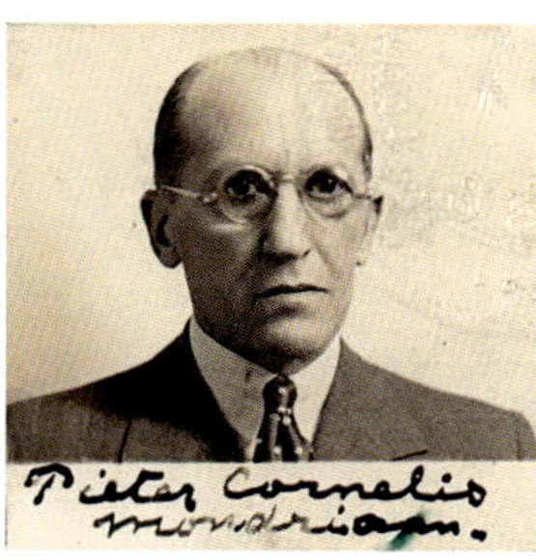

CAT. 188 Unidentified photographer

Portrait of Piet Mondrian, between 24 August and 22 September 1941 (see p. 215)

Gelatin developing-out paper, 4.4 x 4.5 cm

Recto, in Piet Mondrian's handwriting: 'Pieter Cornelis / Mondriaan.'

Yale, Beinecke Rare Book & Manuscript Library, Piet Mondrian Papers, GEN MSS 1102, Series II, Box 4, Folder 106

Mondrian had this passport photo taken on his application for US citizenship.

An earlier photograph could not be used in this instance, as Mondrian noted in a letter to Harry Holtzman: 'I got my naturarization [sic] papers back from the Department because the photos must be not older than 30 days' (letter dated 25 April 1941; The Hague, RKD, Piet Mondrian Archive (0740), inv. 117).

Mondrian's application for US citizenship is dated 22 September 1941. Since the photograph could not be older than thirty days, we have dated it to between 24 August and 22 September of that year.

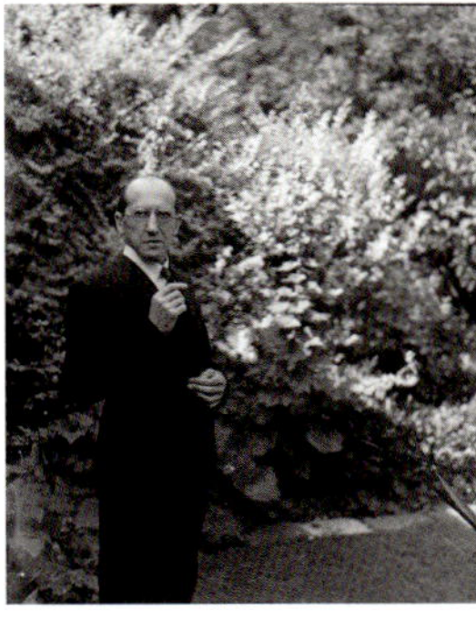

CAT. 189 Harry Holtzman

Piet Mondrian in the garden of Harry and Eileen Holtzman's summer home in Great Barrington, autumn 1940 (?) (see p. 217)

Gelatin developing-out paper, 10.8 x 8.2 cm

Verso, in Harry Holtzman's handwriting: '1941. / Photo by Harry Holtzman / 1941 / at / Holtzman's / house in / Great Barrington, / Mass.'

The Hague, RKD, Piet Mondrian Archive (0740), inv. 69

It is clear from the notes on the back of the vintage print found among Mondrian's papers that the photograph was taken in the garden of Harry and Eileen Holtzman's summer home in Great Barrington, Massachusetts.

The precise date is not known. Mondrian's only documented visit there occurred 'a few weeks after his arrival in the United States' (Pitts Rembert 1970, pp. 44–5). If the photograph was taken during that stay, the date is more likely to have been autumn 1940 rather than 1941 as stated on the back.

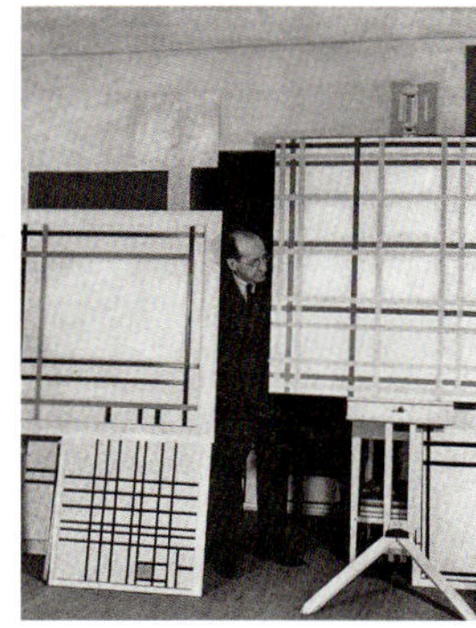

CAT. 190 Emery Muscetra

Piet Mondrian in his studio with recent works, c. October 1941 (see p. 218)

A vintage print has not been traced; the photograph is known solely from Janis's publication.

The otherwise unknown Emery Muscetra took three pictures of Mondrian in his studio on Sidney Janis's request (cats 190–92). They were intended to illustrate an article on Parisian émigrés in New York that Janis was working on for *Decision* magazine.

Since the article was published in November 1941, we date the photographs to around October of that year (Welsh/ Joosten 1998-II, p. 176).

Publication: Sidney Janis, 'School of Paris Comes to U.S.', in *Decision: A Review of Free Culture*, vol. 1, nos 5/6 (November/ December 1941), pp. 85–95.

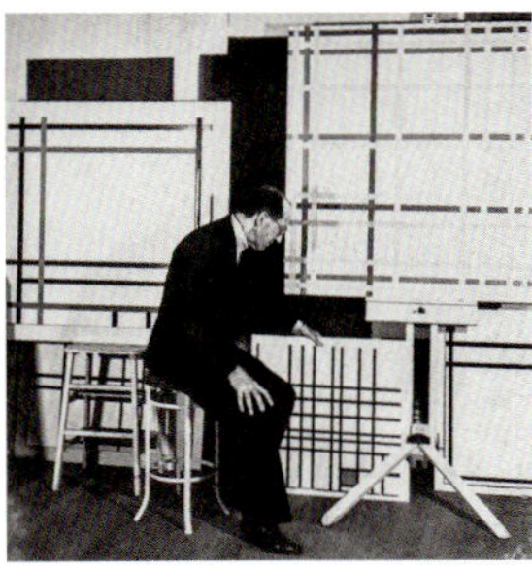

CAT. 191 Emery Muscetra

Piet Mondrian in his studio with recent works, c. October 1941 (see p. 219)

A vintage print has not been traced; the photograph reproduced here is a later print (The Hague, RKD, Joop Joosten (0838), inv. 811).

See also cat. 190.

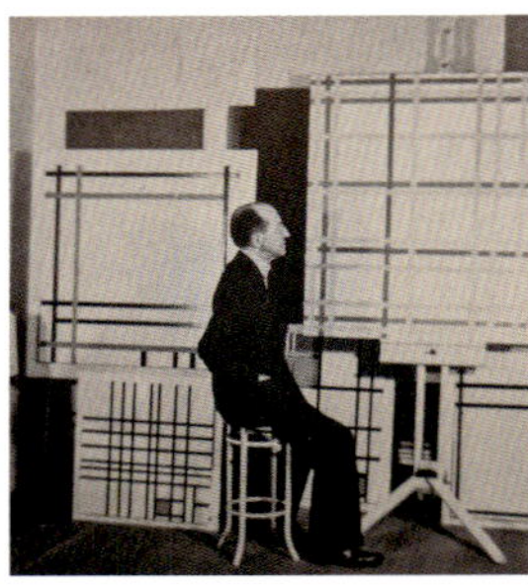

CAT. 192 Emery Muscetra

Piet Mondrian in his studio with recent works, c. October 1941

A vintage print has not been traced; the photograph reproduced here is a later print (The Hague, RKD, Joop Joosten (0838), inv. 811).

For more information, see cat. 190.

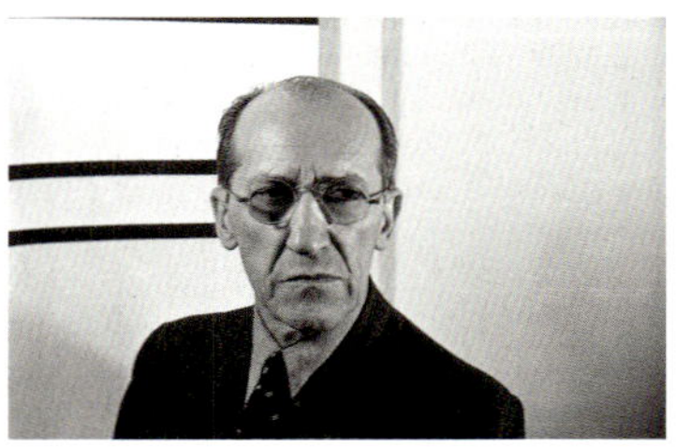

CAT. 193 Harry Holtzman

Portrait of Piet Mondrian in Holtzman's studio, between 4 October 1940 and May 1942 (see p. 220)

Contact print from a 35 mm negative, 2.4 x 3.6 cm

Private collection

The series of photographs making up cats 193–223 were taken during a single session. There are too few indicators, however, for a secure dating. The *post quem* is 3 October 1940, the date on which Mondrian arrived in New York. One of the photographs in the series, meanwhile, was published no later than 1 June 1942 in Peggy Guggenheim's collection catalogue, *Art of This Century* (see cat. 195). We therefore date the series between 4 October 1940 and May 1942.

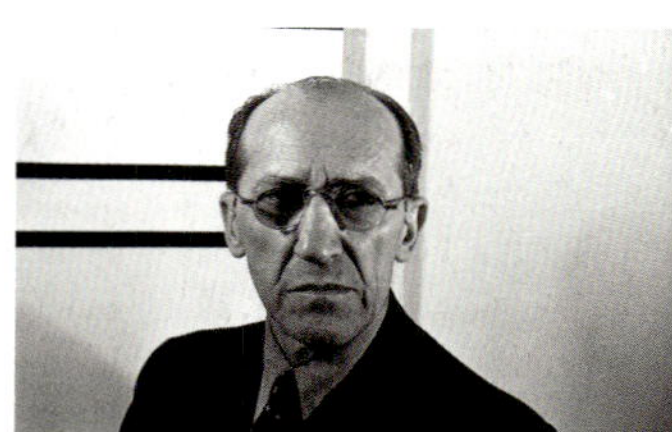

CAT. 194 Harry Holtzman

Portrait of Piet Mondrian in Holtzman's studio, between 4 October 1940 and May 1942 (see p. 220)

Contact print from a 35 mm negative, 2.4 x 3.6 cm

Private collection

For the dating, see cat. 193.

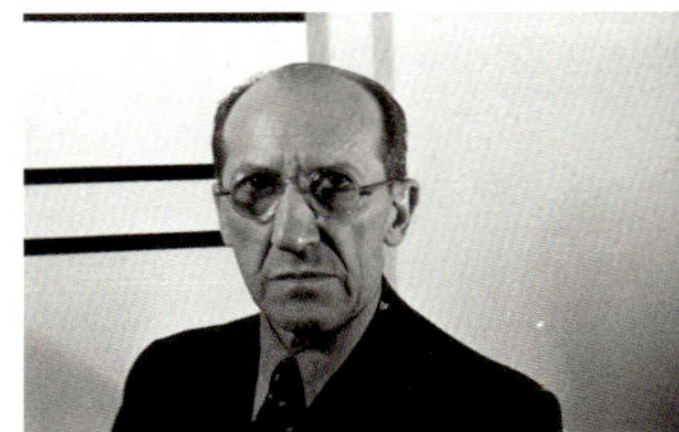

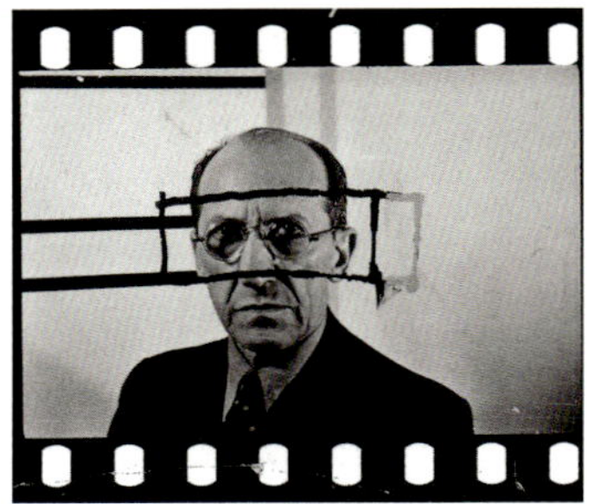

CAT. 195.1; CAT. 195.2 Harry Holtzman

Portrait of Piet Mondrian in Holtzman's studio, between 4 October 1940 and May 1942 (see p. 31)

(1) Gelatin developing-out paper, 8 x 11 cm; (2) Contact print from a 35 mm negative, 2.4 x 3.6 cm

(1) and (2) Private collection

For the dating, see cat. 193.

The cut-out of Mondrian's eyes marked on the negative was published no later than 1 June 1942 in Peggy Guggenheim's collection catalogue *Art of This Century*.

Mondrian wrote to the Holtzmans that he was satisfied with the result: 'The book is well done, I think and "the eyes" are in also. But mine are not so good as Harry has made the original photo. In general, the others are still worse' (letter to Harry and Eileen Holtzman, 1 June 1942, The Hague, RKD, Piet Mondrian Archive (0740), inv. 121).

Publication: Peggy Guggenheim, 'Piet Mondrian', in Peggy Guggenheim (ed.), *Art of This Century: Objects – Drawings – Photographs – Paintings – Sculpture – Collages, 1910 to 1942* (New York (Art of This Century Gallery) 1942), pp. 54–5, photograph p. 54 (cut-out).

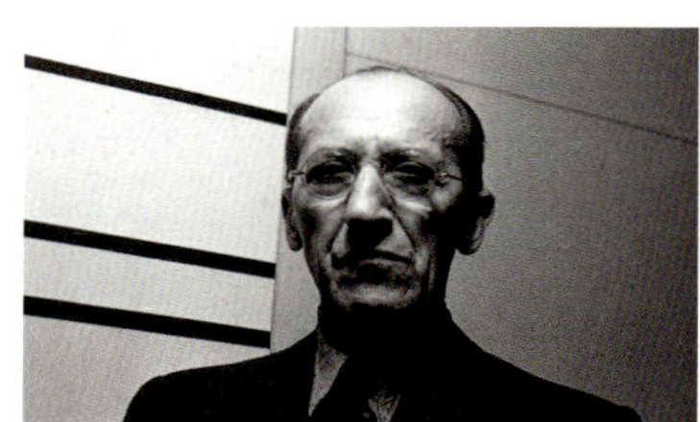

CAT. 196 Harry Holtzman

Portrait of Piet Mondrian in Holtzman's studio, between 4 October 1940 and May 1942 (see p. 220)

Contact print from a 35 mm negative, 2.4 x 3.6 cm

Private collection

For the dating, see cat. 193.

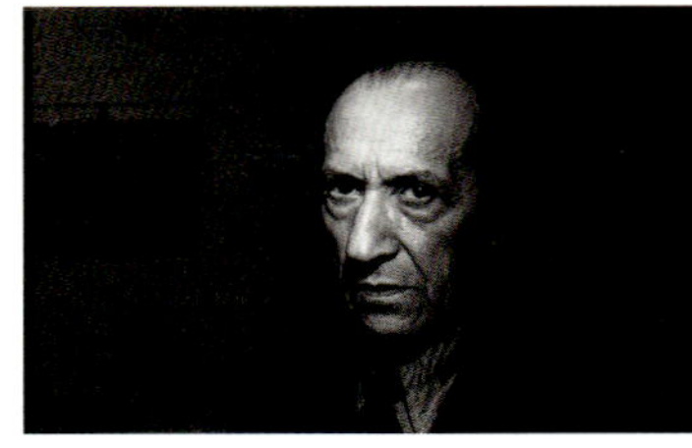

CAT. 197 Harry Holtzman

Portrait of Piet Mondrian in Holtzman's studio, between 4 October 1940 and May 1942
(see p. 220)

Contact print from a 35 mm negative, 2.4 x 3.6 cm

Private collection

For the dating, see cat. 193.

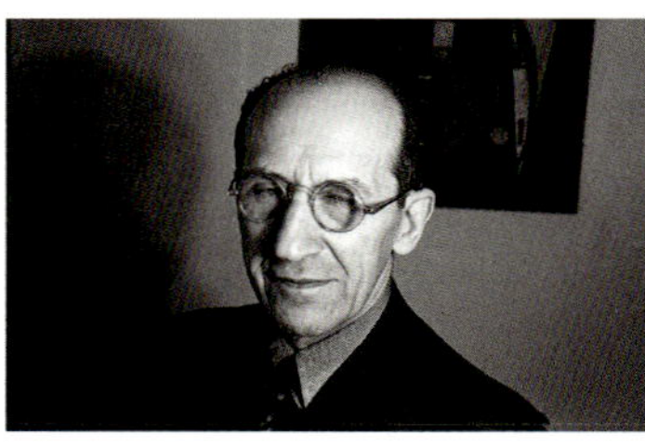

CAT. 198 Harry Holtzman

Portrait of Piet Mondrian in Holtzman's studio, between 4 October 1940 and May 1942
(see p. 221)

Contact print from a 35 mm negative, 2.4 x 3.6 cm

Private collection

For the dating, see cat. 193.

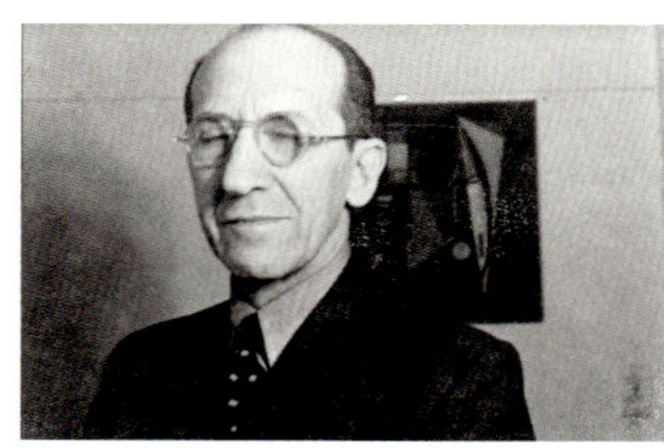

CAT. 199 Harry Holtzman

Portrait of Piet Mondrian in Holtzman's studio, between 4 October 1940 and May 1942
(see p. 221)

Contact print from a 35 mm negative, 2.4 x 3.6 cm

Private collection

For the dating, see cat. 193.

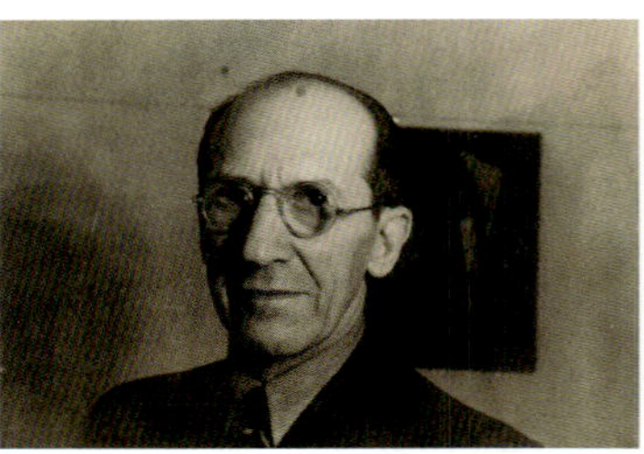

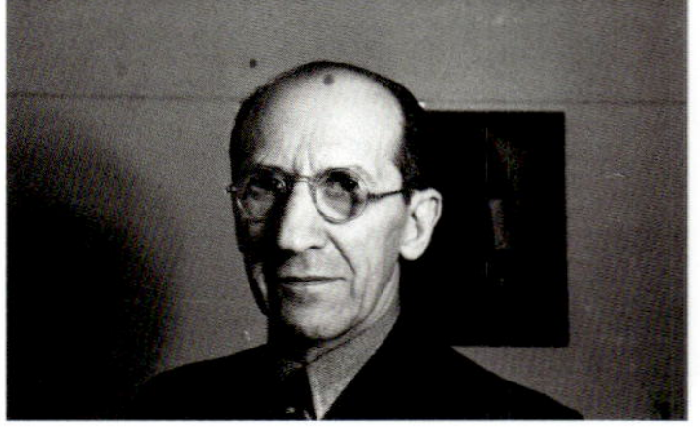

CAT. 200.1; CAT. 200.2 Harry Holtzman

Portrait of Piet Mondrian in Holtzman's studio, between 4 October 1940 and May 1942
(see p. 221)

(1) Gelatin developing-out paper, 8 x 11 cm; (2) contact print from a 35 mm negative, 2.4 x 3.6 cm

(1) and (2) Private collection

For the dating, see cat. 193.

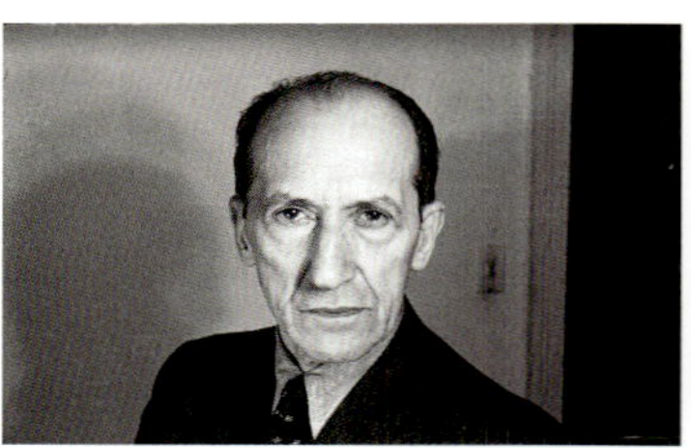

CAT. 201 Harry Holtzman

Portrait of Piet Mondrian in Holtzman's studio, between 4 October 1940 and May 1942

Contact print from a 35 mm negative, 2.4 x 3.6 cm

Private collection

For the dating, see cat. 193.

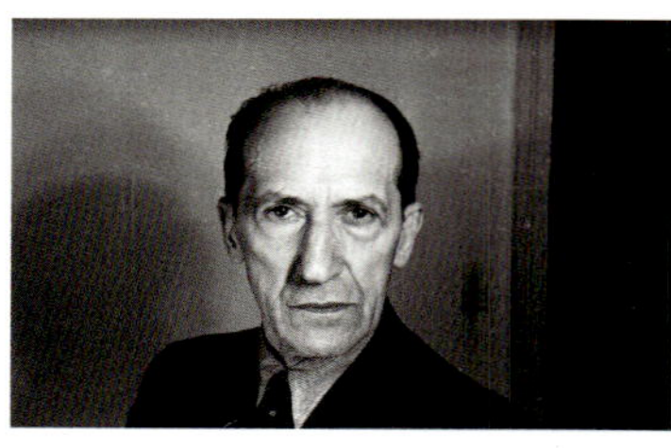

CAT. 202 Harry Holtzman

Portrait of Piet Mondrian in Holtzman's studio, between 4 October 1940 and May 1942
(see p. 221)

Contact print from a 35 mm negative, 2.4 x 3.6 cm

Private collection

For the dating, see cat. 193.

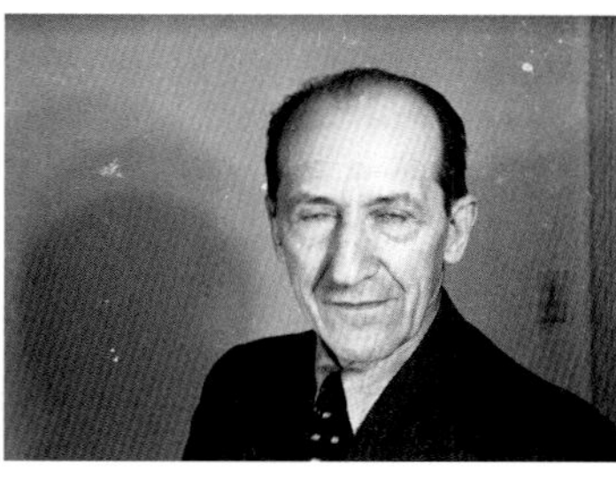

CAT. 203 Harry Holtzman

Portrait of Piet Mondrian in Holtzman's studio, between 4 October 1940 and May 1942

Contact print from a 35 mm negative, 2.4 x 3.6 cm

Private collection

For the dating, see cat. 193.

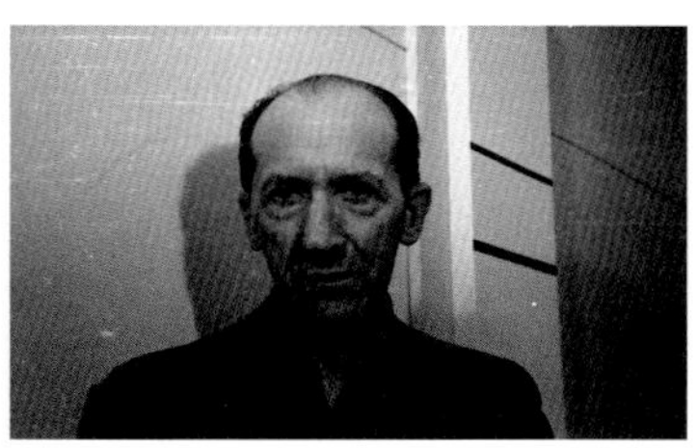

CAT. 204 Harry Holtzman

Portrait of Piet Mondrian in Holtzman's studio, between 4 October 1940 and May 1942

Contact print from a 35 mm negative, 2.4 x 3.6 cm

Private collection

For the dating, see cat. 193.

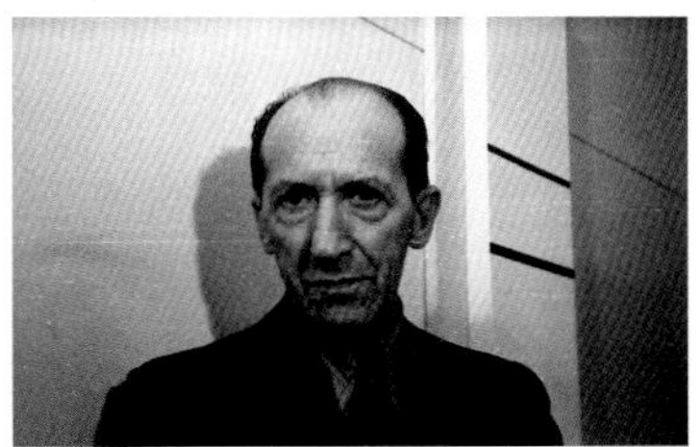

CAT. 205 Harry Holtzman

Portrait of Piet Mondrian in Holtzman's studio, between 4 October 1940 and May 1942

Contact print from a 35 mm negative, 2.4 x 3.6 cm

Private collection

For the dating, see cat. 193.

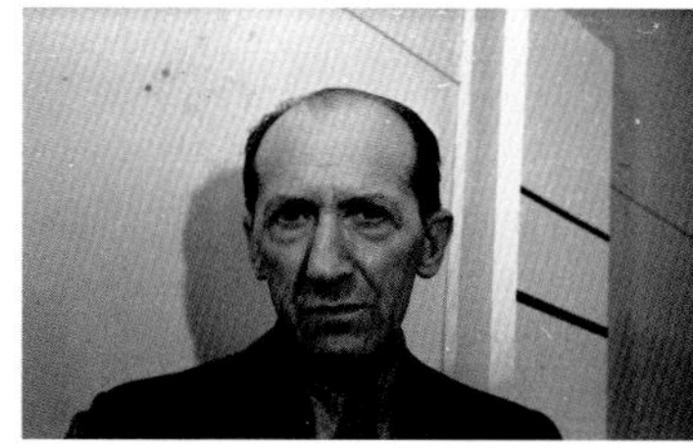

CAT. 206 Harry Holtzman

Portrait of Piet Mondrian in Holtzman's studio, between 4 October 1940 and May 1942

Contact print from a 35 mm negative, 2.4 x 3.6 cm

Private collection

For the dating, see cat. 193.

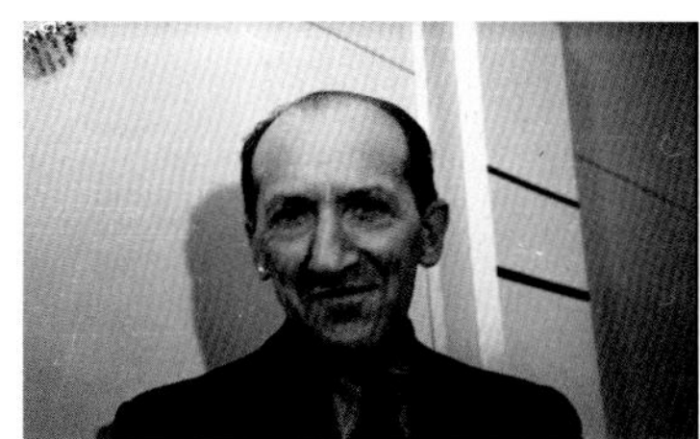

CAT. 207 Harry Holtzman

Portrait of Piet Mondrian in Holtzman's studio, between 4 October 1940 and May 1942

Contact print from a 35 mm negative, 2.4 x 3.6 cm

Private collection

For the dating, see cat. 193.

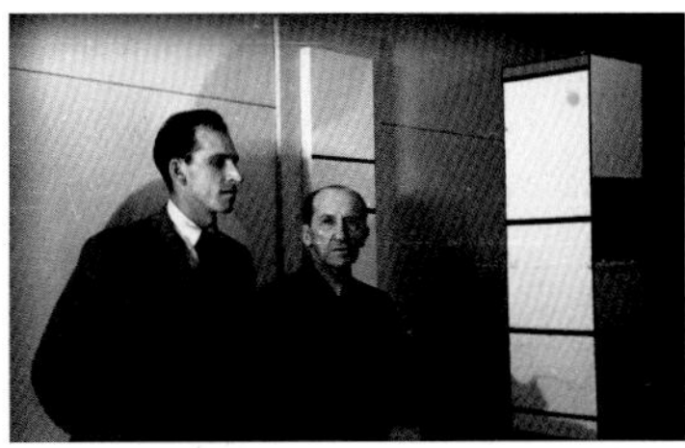

CAT. 208 Harry Holtzman

Harry Holtzman and Piet Mondrian in Holtzman's studio, between 4 October 1940 and May 1942

Contact print from a 35 mm negative, 2.4 x 3.6 cm

Private collection

For the dating, see cat. 193.

The series of double portraits of Holtzman and Mondrian (cats 208–15) was reportedly taken by Holtzman using a self-timer (e-mail Madalena Holtzman to the authors, 18 February 2022).

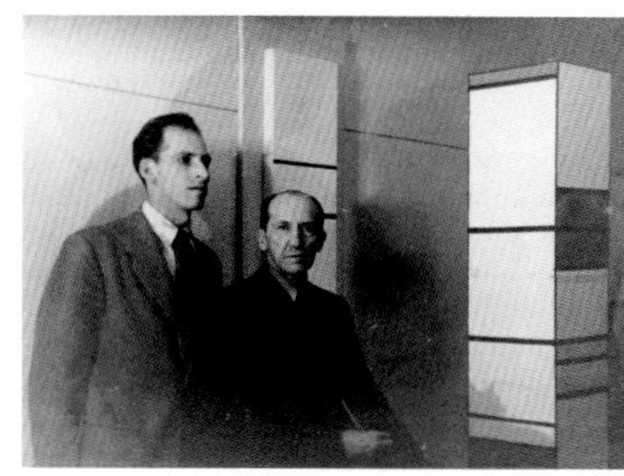

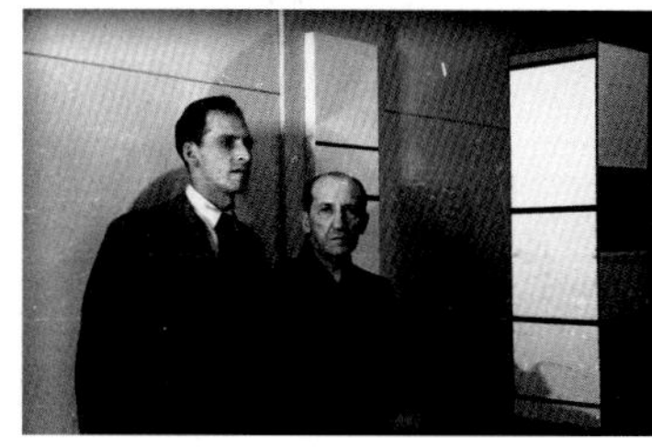

CAT. 209.1 ; CAT. 209.2 Harry Holtzman

Harry Holtzman and Piet Mondrian in Holtzman's studio, between 4 October 1940 and May 1942

(1) Gelatin developing-out paper, 22 x 25 cm; (2) Contact print from a 35 mm negative, 2.4 x 3.6 cm

(1) and (2) Private collection

For the dating, see cat. 193. See also cat. 208.

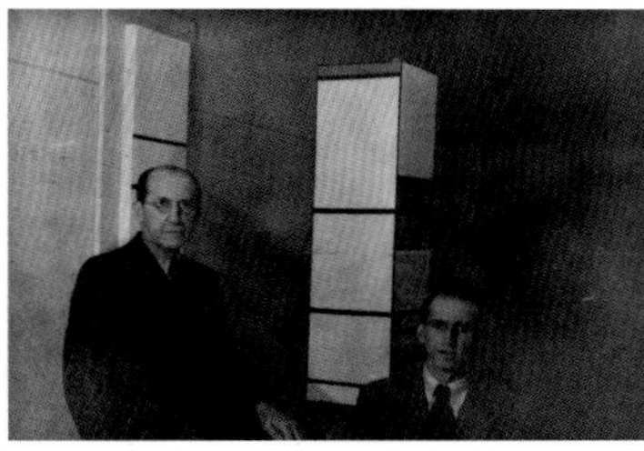

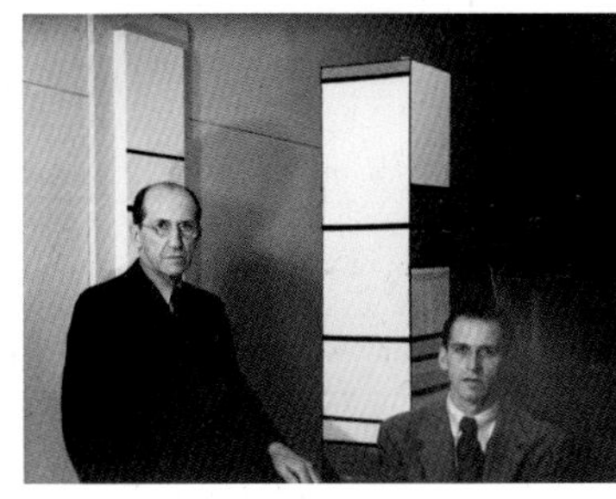

CAT. 210.1; CAT. 210.2 Harry Holtzman

Piet Mondrian and Harry Holtzman in Holtzman's studio, between 4 October 1940 and May 1942

(1) Gelatin developing-out paper, 8 x 11 cm; (2) Contact print from a 35 mm negative, 2.4 x 3.6 cm

(1) and (2) Private collection

For the dating, see cat. 193. See also cat. 208.

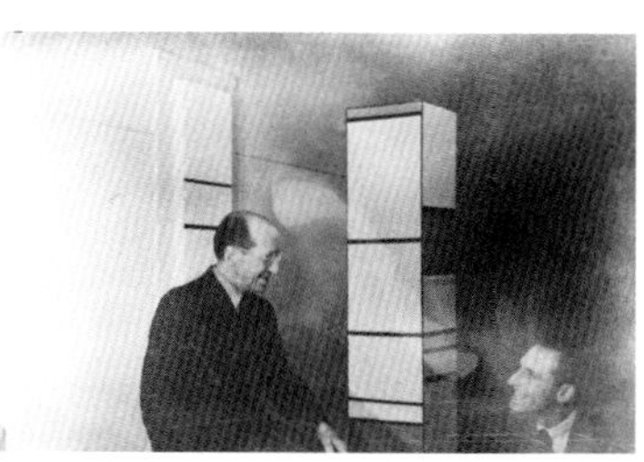

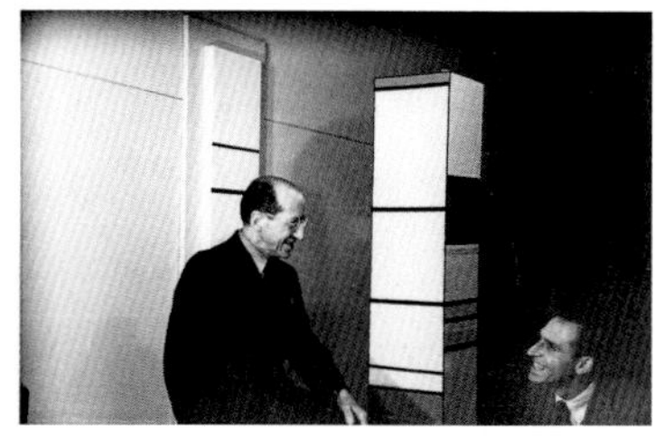

CAT. 211.1; CAT. 211.2 Harry Holtzman

Piet Mondrian and Harry Holtzman in Holtzman's studio, between 4 October 1940 and May 1942
(see p. 223)

(1) Gelatin developing-out paper, 22 x 25 cm; (2) Contact print from a 35 mm negative, 2.4 x 3.6 cm

(1) and (2) Private collection

For the dating, see cat. 193. See also cat. 208.

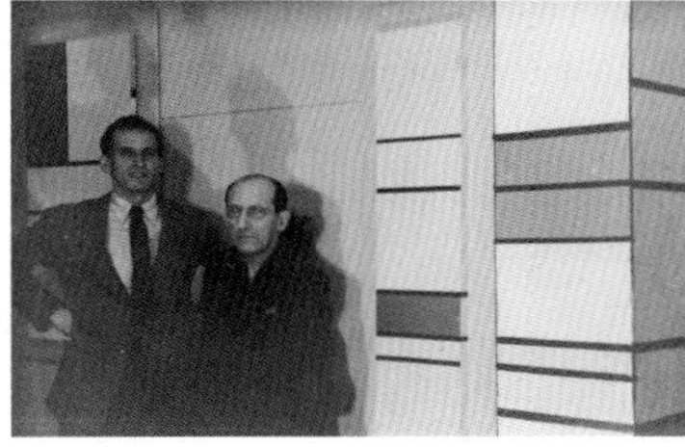

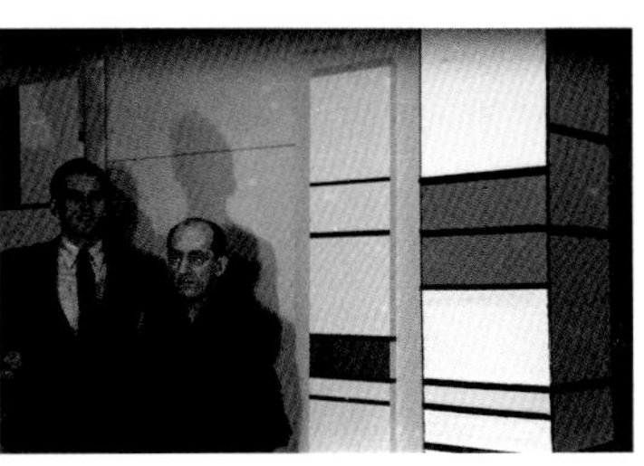

CAT. 212.1; CAT. 212.2 Harry Holtzman

Harry Holtzman and Piet Mondrian in Holtzman's studio, between 4 October 1940 and May 1942

(1) Gelatin developing-out paper, 22 x 25 cm; (2) Contact print from a 35 mm negative, 2.4 x 3.6 cm

(1) and (2) Private collection

For the dating, see cat. 193. See also cat. 208.

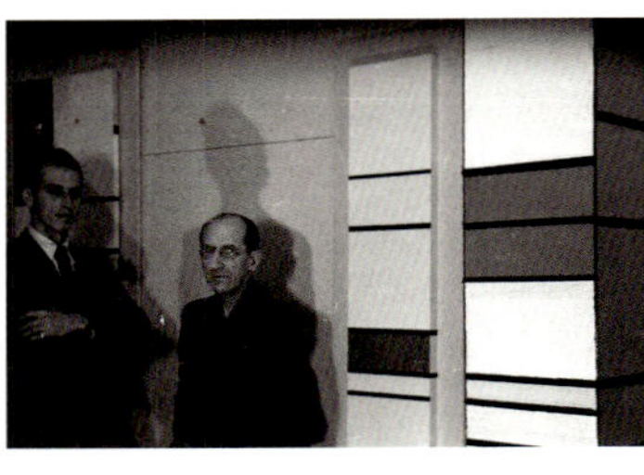
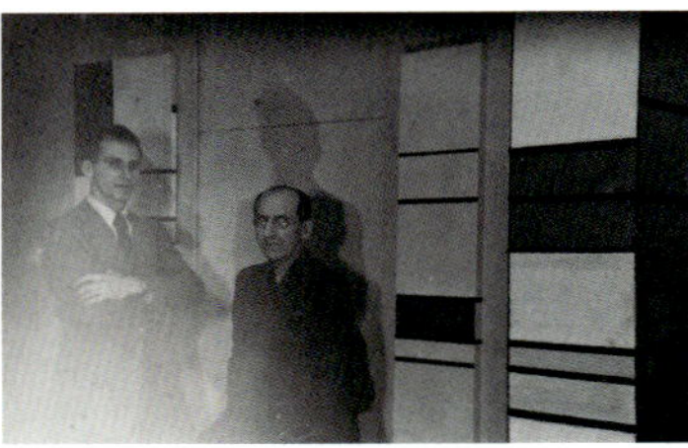

CAT. 213.1; CAT. 231.2 Harry Holtzman

Harry Holtzman and Piet Mondrian in Holtzman's studio, between 4 October 1940 and May 1942

(1) Gelatin developing-out paper, 22 x 25 cm; (2) Contact print from a 35 mm negative, 2.4 x 3.6 cm

(1) and (2) Private collection

For the dating, see cat. 193. See also cat. 208.

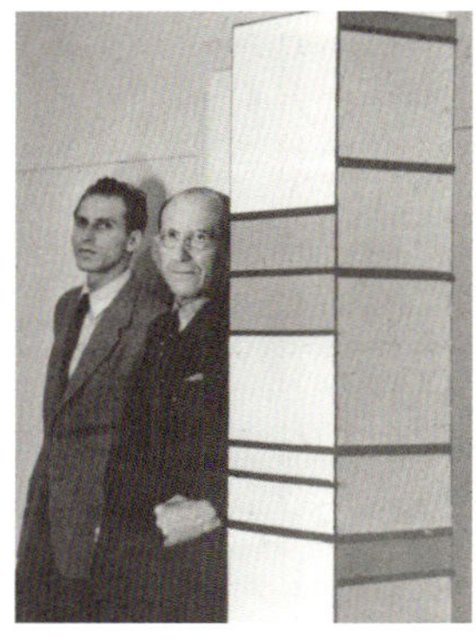
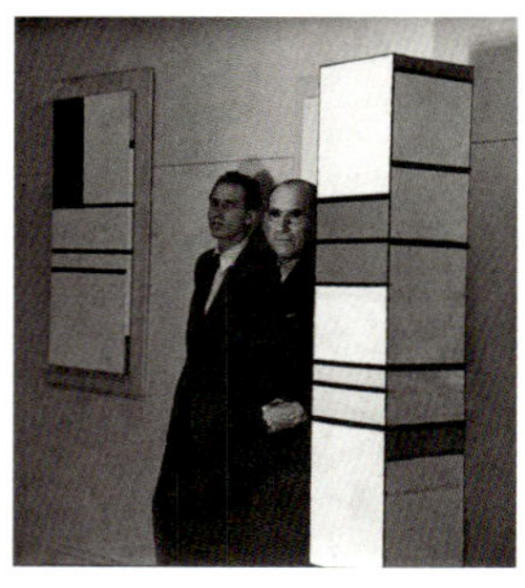

CAT. 214.1; CAT. 214.2 Harry Holtzman

Harry Holtzman and Piet Mondrian in Holtzman's studio, between 4 October 1940 and May 1942
(see p. 222)

(1) Gelatin developing-out paper, 25 x 19 cm (cut out); (2) Contact print from a 35 mm negative, 3.6 x 2.4 cm

(1) and (2) Private collection

For the dating, see cat. 193. See also cat. 208.

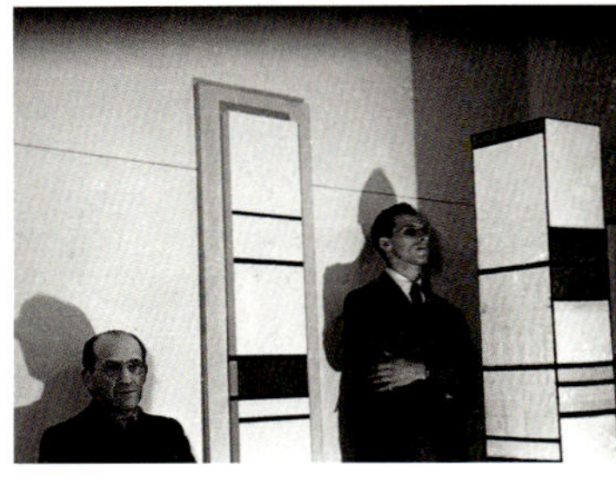

CAT. 215 Harry Holtzman

Piet Mondrian and Harry Holtzman in Holtzman's studio, between 4 October 1940 and May 1942
(see p. 223)

Contact print from a 35 mm negative, 2.4 x 3.6 cm

Private collection

For the dating, see cat. 193. See also cat. 208.

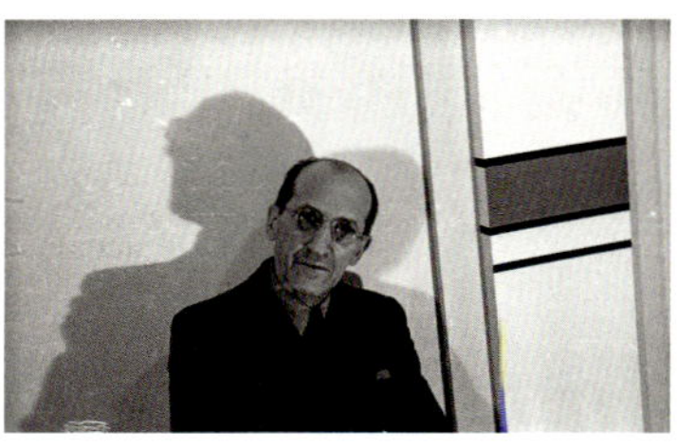

CAT. 216 Harry Holtzman

Portrait of Piet Mondrian in Holtzman's studio, between 4 October 1940 and May 1942
(see p. 225)

Contact print from a 35 mm negative, 2.4 x 3.6 cm

Private collection

For the dating, see cat. 193.

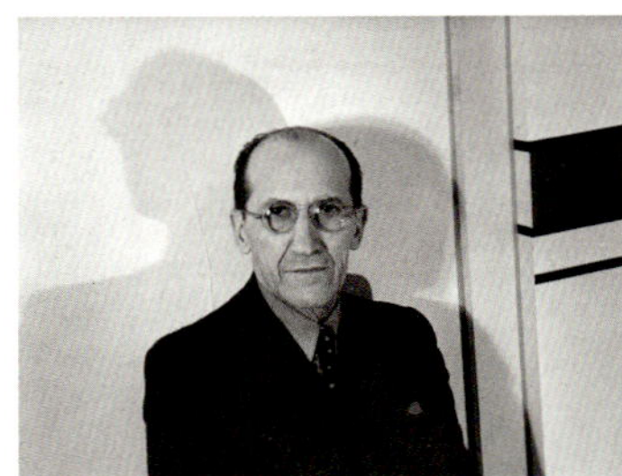
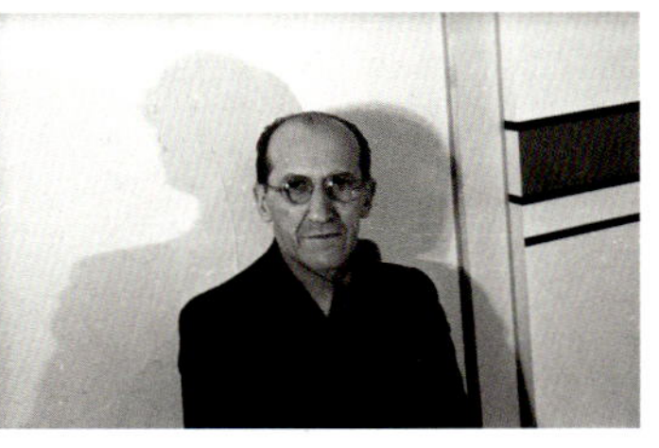

CAT. 217.1; CAT. 217.2 Harry Holtzman

Portrait of Piet Mondrian in Holtzman's studio, between 4 October 1940 and May 1942
(see p. 225)

(1) Gelatin developing-out paper, 22 x 25 cm; (2) Contact print from a 35 mm negative, 2.4 x 3.6 cm

(1) and (2) Private collection

For the dating, see cat. 193.

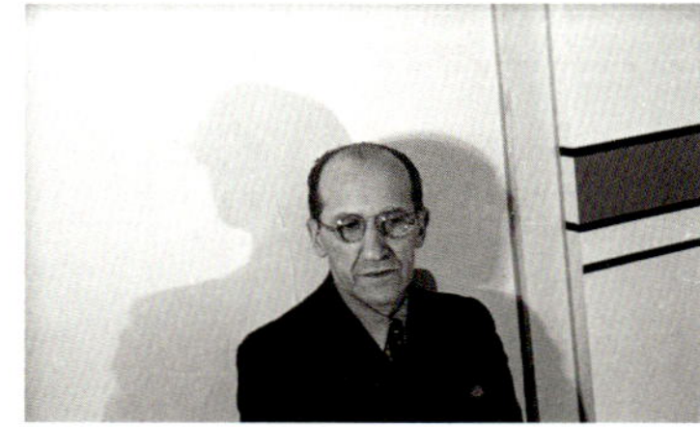

CAT. 218 Harry Holtzman

Portrait of Piet Mondrian in Holtzman's studio, between 4 October 1940 and May 1942 (see p. 224)

Contact print from a 35 mm negative, 2.4 x 3.6 cm

Private collection

For the dating, see cat. 193.

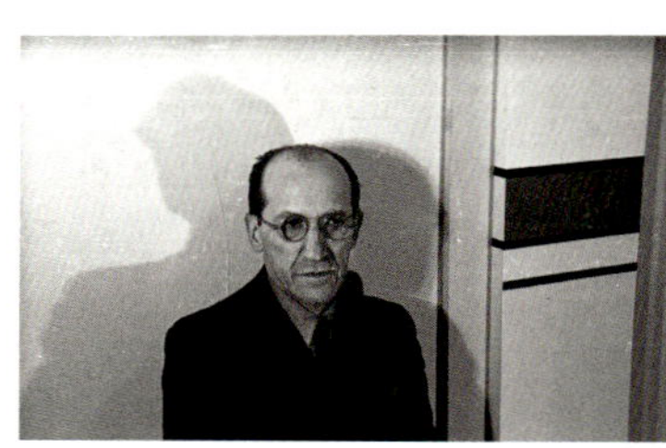

CAT. 219 Harry Holtzman

Portrait of Piet Mondrian in Holtzman's studio, between 4 October 1940 and May 1942 (see p. 225)

Contact print from a 35 mm negative, 2.4 x 3.6 cm

Private collection

For the dating, see cat. 193.

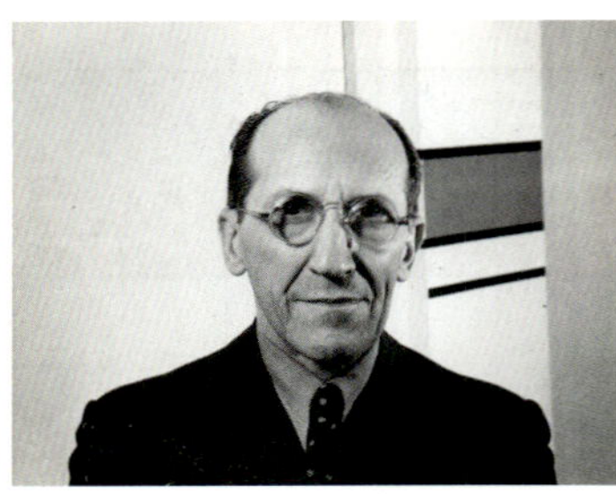
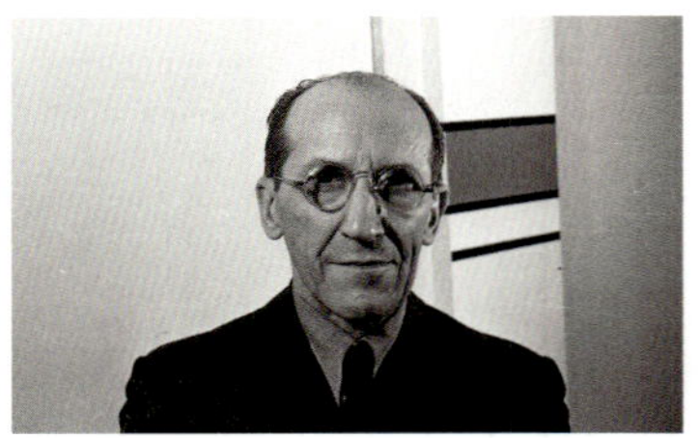

CAT. 220.1; CAT. 220.2 Harry Holtzman

Portrait of Piet Mondrian in Holtzman's studio, between 4 October 1940 and May 1942
(see p. 225)

(1) Gelatin developing-out paper, 22 x 25 cm; (2) Contact print from a 35 mm negative, 2.4 x 3.6 cm

(1) and (2) Private collection

For the dating, see cat. 193.

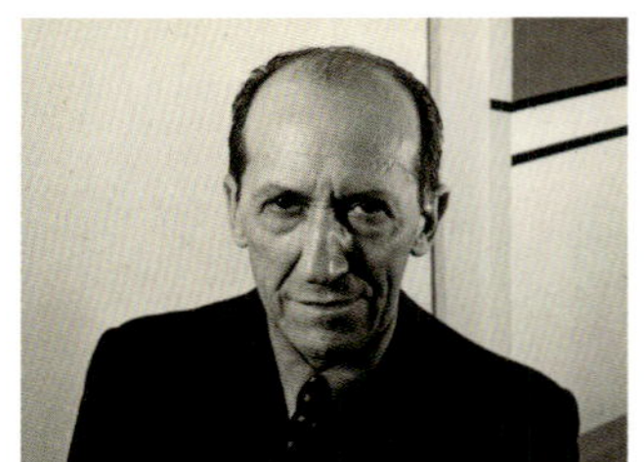
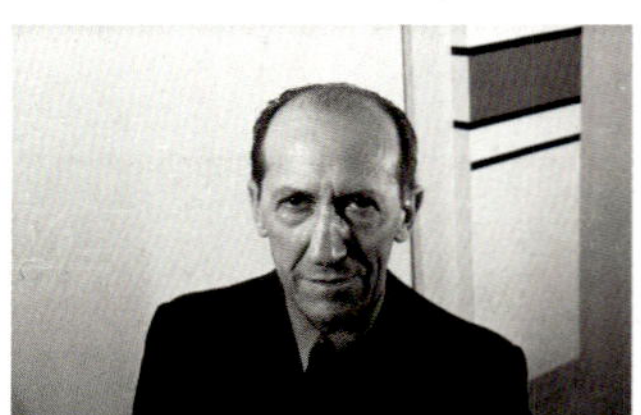

CAT. 221.1; CAT. 221.2 Harry Holtzman

Portrait of Piet Mondrian in Holtzman's studio, between 4 October 1940 and May 1942
(see p. 224)

(1) Gelatin developing-out paper, 19 x 25 cm; (2) Contact print from a 35 mm negative, 2.4 x 3.6 cm

(1) and (2) Private collection

For the dating, see cat. 193.

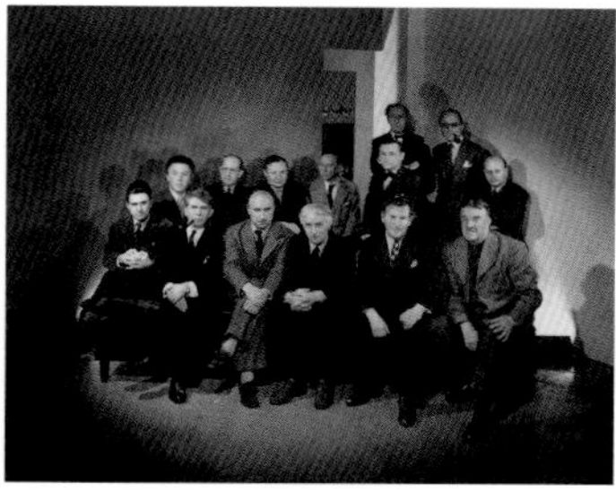

CAT. 222 George Platt Lynes

Group portrait of participants in the 'Artists in Exile' exhibition, c. February 1942 (see p. 226)

Technique and dimensions unknown

Washington, DC, Smithsonian Institution, Archives of American Art, George Platt Lynes photographs, 1926–1950, REEL 153

The session took place in George Platt Lynes's photography studio prior to the 'Artists in Exile' exhibition, which ran from 3 to 28 March at the Pierre Matisse Gallery, New York. The details are drawn from an article in *Art News* (Frost 1942): 'The photograph of the Artists in Exile in the show's catalogue unites the most diverse factors in the European artistic scene (and represents, incidentally, a diplomatic triumph for Pierre Matisse who posed the subjects at George Platt Lynes' studio one agitated morning).' For this reason, we date the photo to around February 1942.

For the identification, see p. 227.

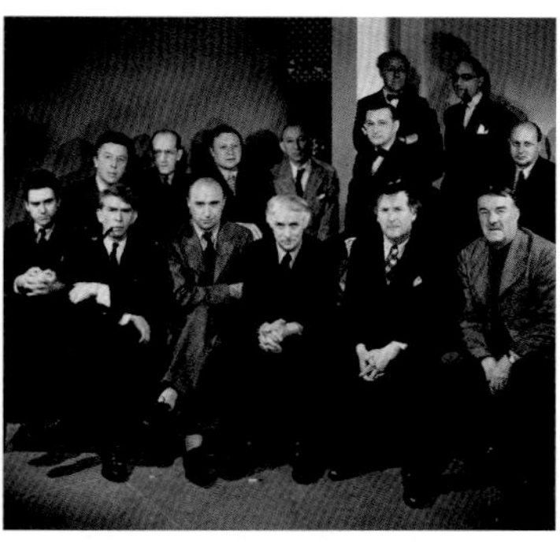

CAT. 223 George Platt Lynes

Group portrait of participants in the 'Artists in Exile' exhibition, c. February 1942

Technique and dimensions unknown

Washington, DC, Smithsonian Institution, Archives of American Art, George Platt Lynes photographs, 1926–1950, REEL 153

For the identification, see p. 227. For the dating, see cat. 222.

Publications: *Artists in Exile* (exhib. cat. New York 1942); 'Artists in Exile Hold Stimulating Show', *Art Digest*, 16, no. 12 (15 March 1942), pp. 9–10.

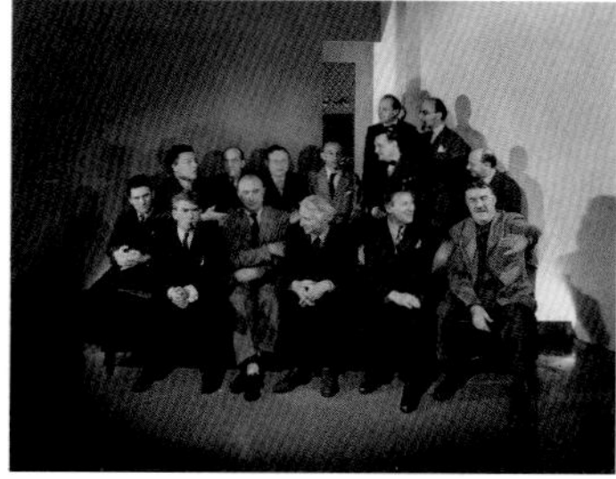

CAT. 224 George Platt Lynes

Group portrait of participants in the 'Artists in Exile' exhibition, c. February 1942 (see p. 227)

Technique and dimensions unknown

Washington, DC, Smithsonian Institution, Archives of American Art, George Platt Lynes photographs, 1926–1950, REEL 153

For the identification, see p. 227. For the dating, see cat. 222.

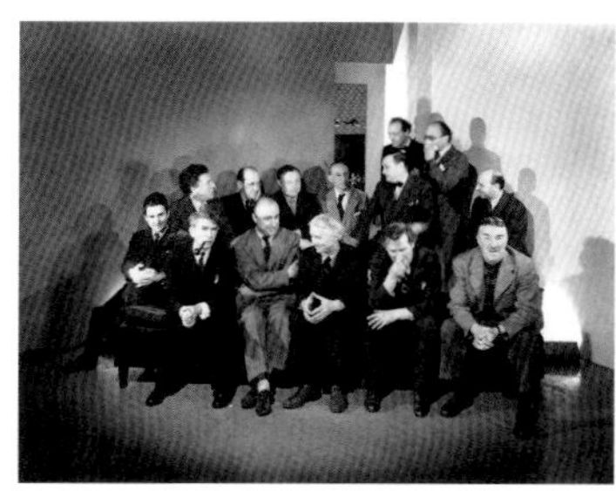

CAT. 225 George Platt Lynes

Group portrait of participants in the 'Artists in Exile' exhibition, c. February 1942

Gelatin developing-out paper, 20.5 x 25.5 cm

Paris, Centre Pompidou, Bibliothèque Kandinsky, inv. FGP BRE 1851

For the identification, see p. 227. For the dating, see cat. 222.

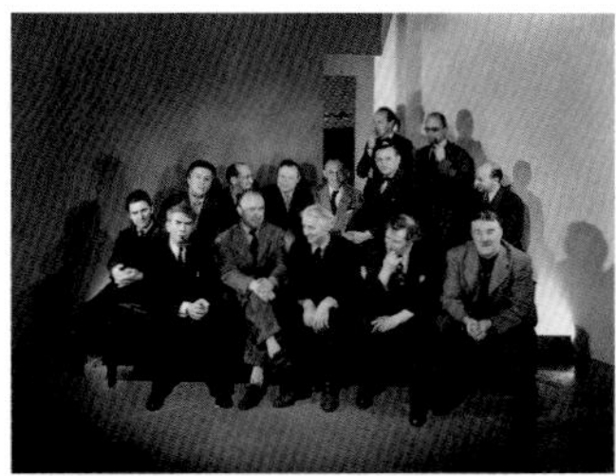

CAT. 226 George Platt Lynes

Group portrait of participants in the 'Artists in Exile' exhibition, c. February 1942

Technique and dimensions unknown

Washington, DC, Smithsonian Institution, Archives of American Art, George Platt Lynes photographs, 1926–1950, REEL 153

For the identification, see p. 227. For the dating, see cat. 222.

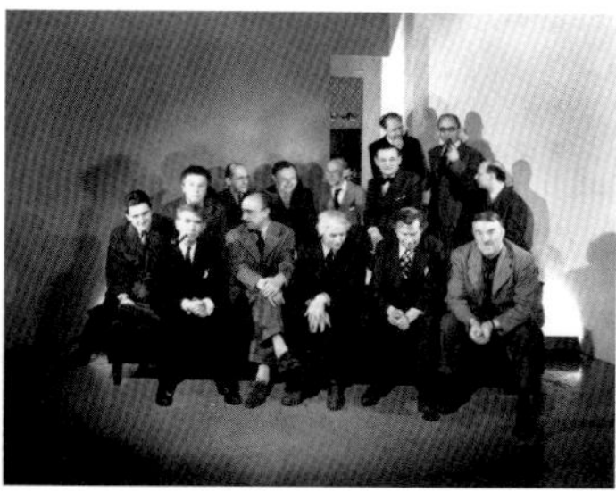

CAT. 227 George Platt Lynes

Group portrait of participants in the 'Artists in Exile' exhibition, c. February 1942

Technique and dimensions unknown

Washington, DC, Smithsonian Institution, Archives of American Art, George Platt Lynes photographs, 1926–1950, REEL 153

For the identification, see p. 227. For the dating, see cat. 222.

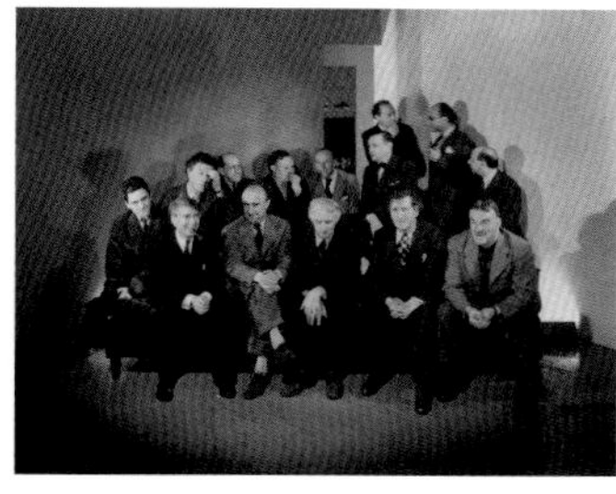

CAT. 228 George Platt Lynes

Group portrait of participants in the 'Artists in Exile' exhibition, c. February 1942 (see p. 228)

Technique and dimensions unknown

Washington, DC, Smithsonian Institution, Archives of American Art, George Platt Lynes photographs, 1926–1950, REEL 153

For the identification, see p. 227. For the dating, see cat. 222.

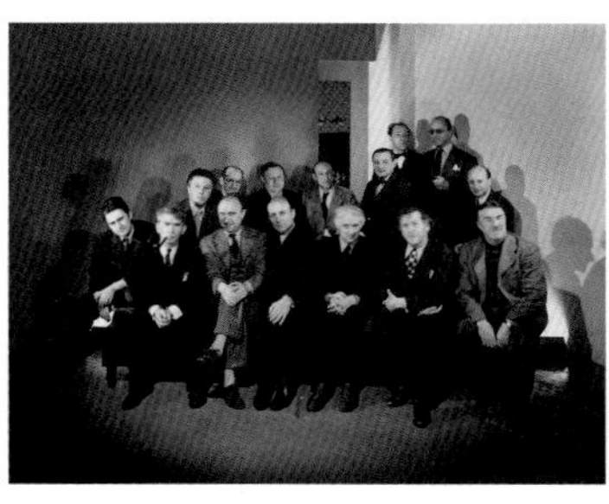

CAT. 229 George Platt Lynes

Group portrait of participants in the 'Artists in Exile' exhibition, c. February 1942 (see p. 229)

Technique and dimensions unknown

Washington, DC, Smithsonian Institution, Archives of American Art, George Platt Lynes photographs, 1926–1950, REEL 153

For the identification, see p. 229. For the dating, see cat. 222.

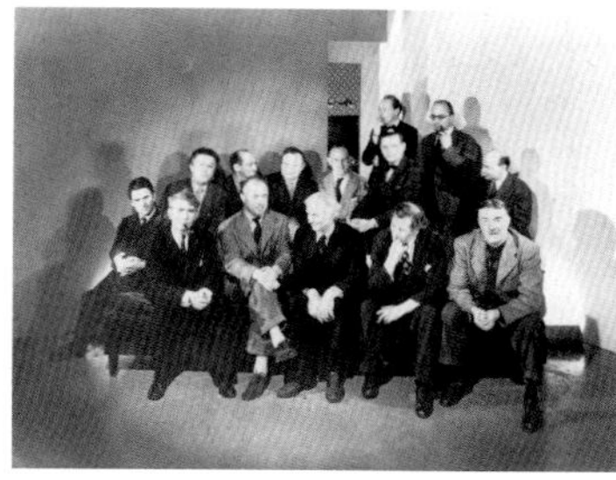

CAT. 230 George Platt Lynes

Group portrait of participants in the 'Artists in Exile' exhibition, c. February 1942

Technique and dimensions unknown

Washington, DC, Smithsonian Institution, Archives of American Art, George Platt Lynes photographs, 1926–1950, REEL 153

For the identification, see p. 227. For the dating, see cat. 222.

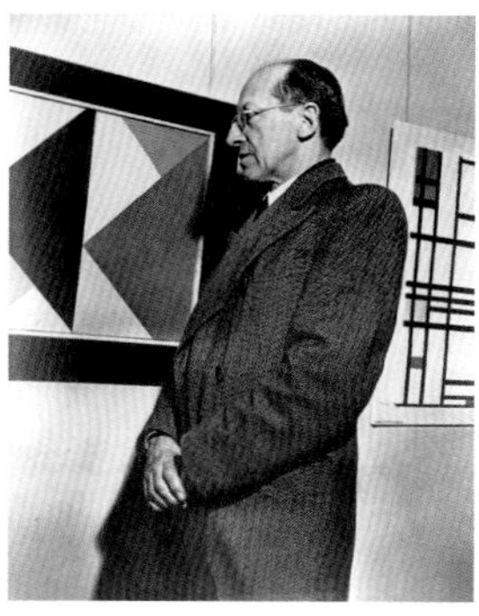

CAT. 231 Lisette Model

Piet Mondrian at the opening of the 'Masters of Abstract Art' exhibition, 1 April 1942 (see p. 231)

A vintage print has not been traced; the photograph reproduced here is a later print (The Hague, RKD, Collectie Kunstenaarsportretten Piet Mondriaan).

The exhibition was a fundraiser for the American Red Cross and was held at Helena Rubinstein's New Art Center from 1 April to 15 May 1942.

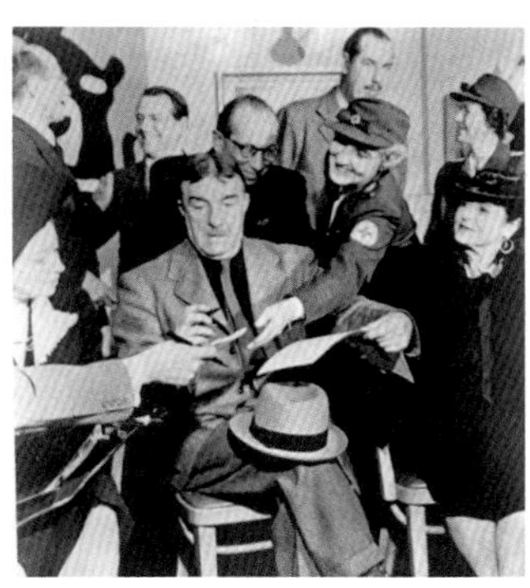

CAT. 232 Lisette Model

Fernand Léger signing autographs at the opening of the 'Masters of Abstract Art' exhibition, 1 April 1942 (see p. 230)

Gelatin developing-out paper, 22 x 19.6 cm

Verso: Hans Richter collection stamp

Private collection (?)

For the exhibition, see cat. 231.

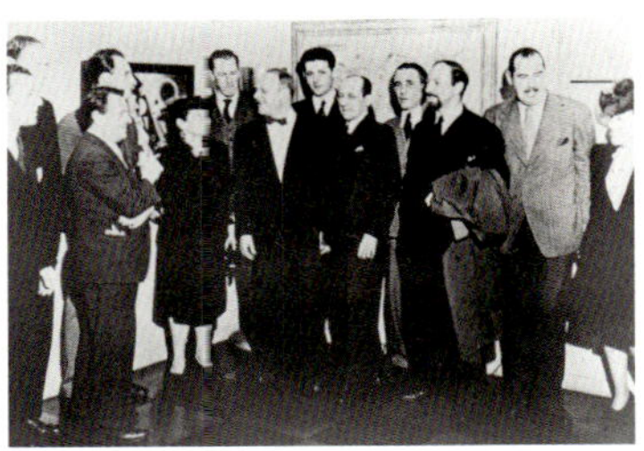

CAT. 233 Lisette Model

Group photograph at the opening of the 'Masters of Abstract Art' exhibition, 1 April 1942

Left to right: Stephan Lion, George Morris, Fritz Glarner, Harry Holtzman, Helena Rubinstein, unidentified man, Carl Holty, Burgoyne Diller, Piet Mondrian, Hans Richter, John Ferren, Charles Shaw, Gertrude Greene.

A vintage print has not been traced; the photograph reproduced here is a later print (The Hague, RKD, Collectie Kunstenaarsportretten Piet Mondriaan).

The identification is drawn in part from Welsh/Joosten 1998-II, p. 177.

For the exhibition, see cat. 231.

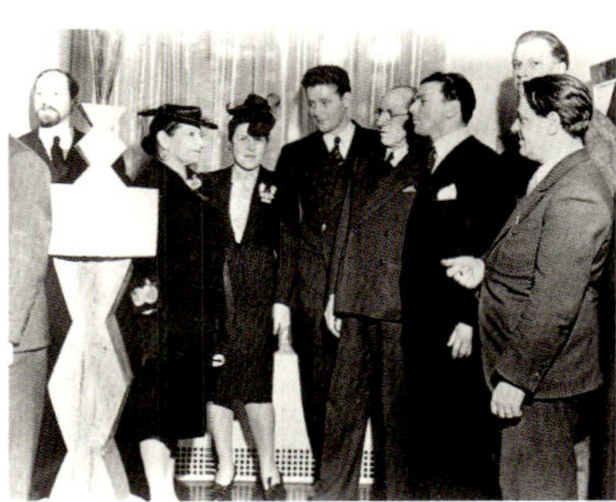

CAT. 234 Lisette Model

Group photograph at the opening of the 'Masters of Abstract Art' exhibition, 1 April 1942 (see p. 232)

A vintage print has not been traced; the photograph reproduced here is a later print (The Hague, RKD, Artist Portraits Piet Mondrian Collection).

For the exhibition, see cat. 231.

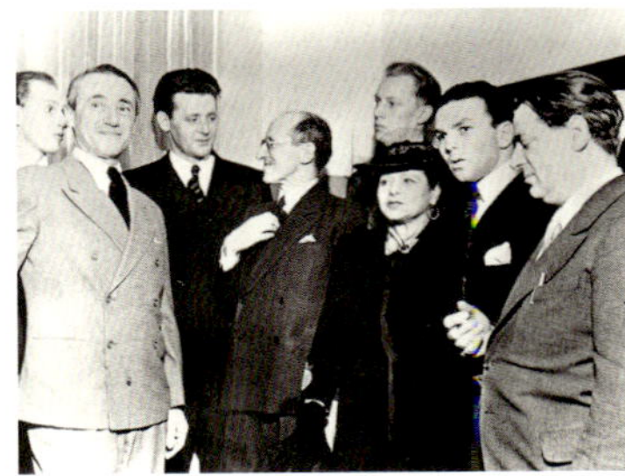

CAT. 235 Lisette Model

Group photograph at the opening of the 'Masters of Abstract Art' exhibition, 1 April 1942 (see p. 232)

A vintage print has not been traced; the photograph reproduced here is a later print (The Hague, RKD, Collectie Kunstenaarsportretten Piet Mondriaan).

For the exhibition, see cat. 231.

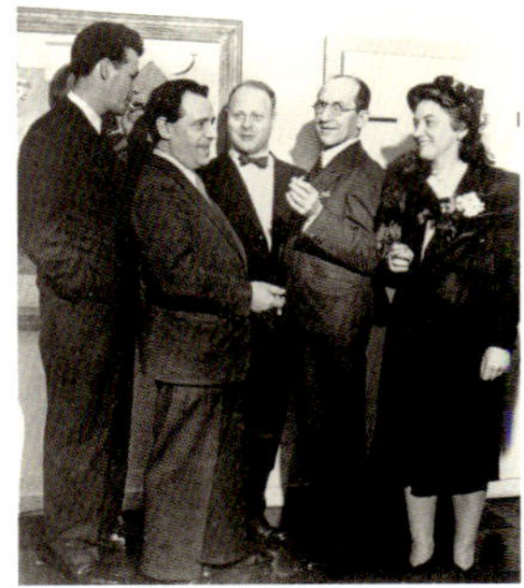

CAT. 236 Lisette Model

Group photograph at the opening of the 'Masters of Abstract Art' exhibition, 1 April 1942 (see p. 233)

A vintage print has not been traced; the image reproduced here is a photocopy of the photograph (The Hague, RKD, Collectie Kunstenaarsportretten Piet Mondriaan).

For the exhibition, see cat. 231.

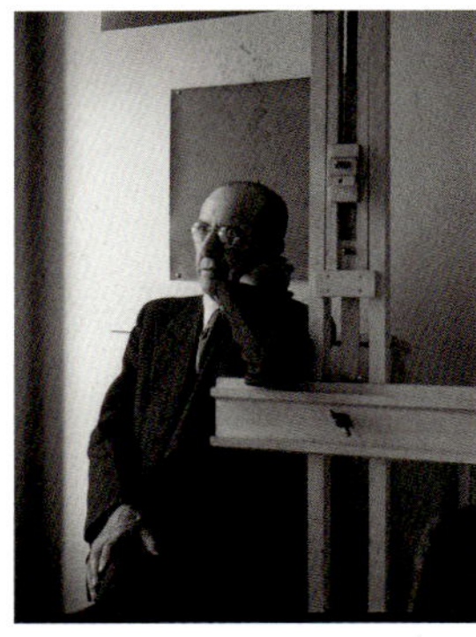

CAT. 237 Arnold Newman

Portrait of Piet Mondrian in his studio, between 29 April and 7 May 1942 (see p. 235)

Gelatin developing-out paper, 12.1 x 9.3 cm

The Hague, RKD, Herbert Henkels Archive (0620), inv. 445

Mondrian wrote to Harry Holtzman on Monday, 27 April 1942: 'I get just a letter from a Mr Newman who is making a serie of portraits of artists in New-York and would like to include me.' (The Hague, RKD, Piet Mondrian Archive (0740) inv. 120.) He wrote to Newman that same day to inform him that he would be available 'next Wednesday or Thursday' (copy, The Hague, RKD, Mondrian Correspondence Project Archive (0613), inv. 60). It is not clear whether Mondrian meant 'this coming Wednesday' or 'Wednesday next week'. Consequently, the series of photographs classified as cats 237–44 date either from 29 or 30 April, or 6 or 7 May 1942.

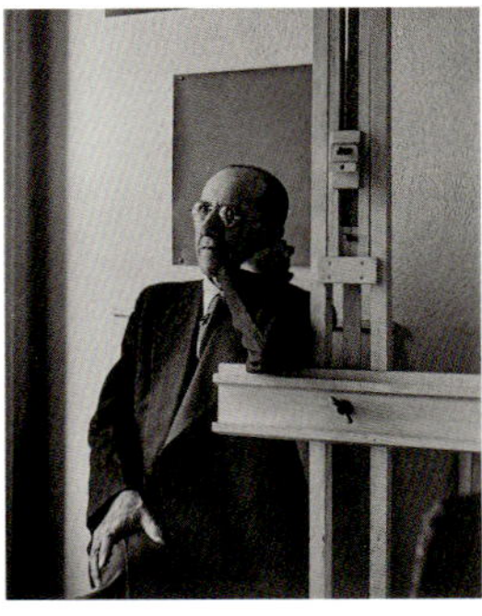

CAT. 238 Arnold Newman

Portrait of Piet Mondrian in his studio, between 29 April and 7 May 1942

Gelatin developing-out paper, 12.5 cm x 10 cm

Verso, stamp: '© ARNOLD NEWMAN [...]'

Amsterdam, Rijksmuseum, inv. RP-F-2008-9

For the dating, see cat. 237.

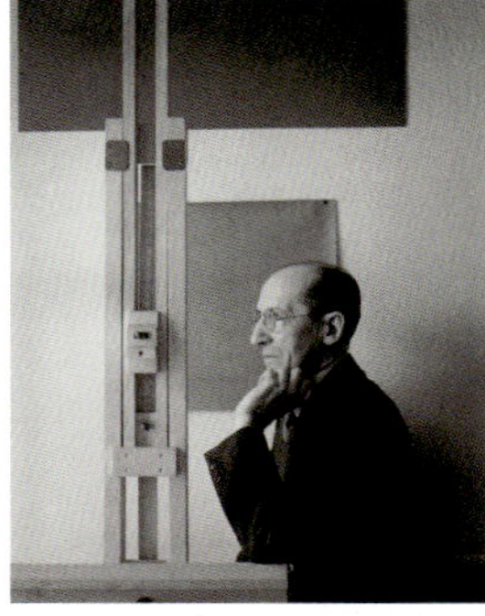

CAT. 239 Arnold Newman

Portrait of Piet Mondrian in his studio, between 29 April and 7 May 1942 (see p. 237)

Gelatin developing-out paper, 12.1 x 9.3 cm

Recto: 'not printed'

The Hague, RKD, Herbert Henkels Archive (0620), inv. 445

For the dating, see cat. 237.

Publication: H. Felix Kraus, 'Mondriaan: A Great Modern Dutch Painter', *Knickerbocker Weekly*, 2, no. 20 (21 September 1943), pp. 24–5.

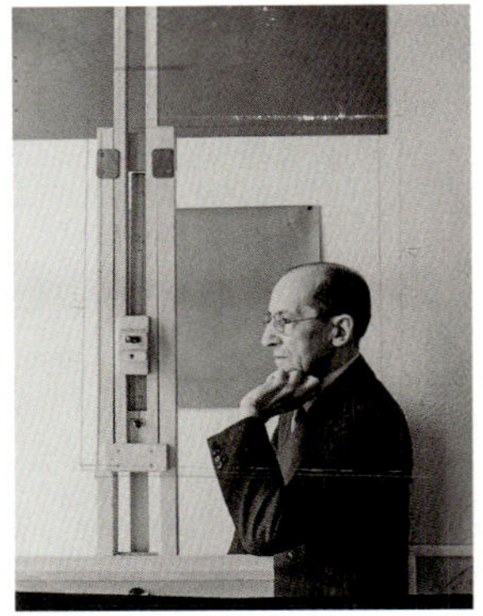

CAT. 240 Arnold Newman

Portrait of Piet Mondrian in his studio, between 29 April and 7 May 1942 (see p. 236)

Gelatin developing-out paper, 12.5 cm x 10 cm

Verso, stamp: '© ARNOLD NEWMAN [...]'

Amsterdam, Rijksmuseum, inv. RP-F-2008-9

For the dating, see cat. 237.

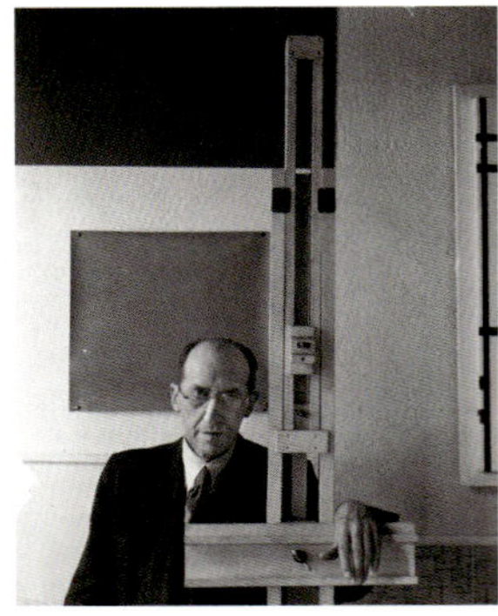

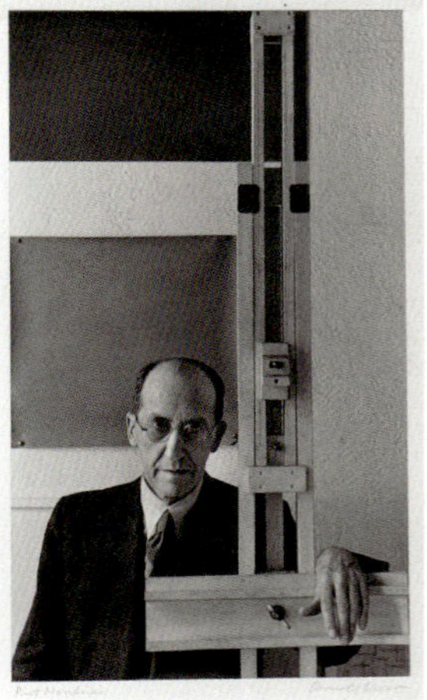

CAT. 241.1; CAT. 241.2 Arnold Newman

Portrait of Piet Mondrian in his studio, between 29 April and 7 May 1942 (see p. 238)

Gelatin developing-out paper, (1) 25 x 20 cm; (2) 24.6 x 14.3 cm, 43.2 x 35.5 cm (mount)

(2) Recto: 'Piet Mondrian', signed 'Arnold Newman'

(1) The Hague, RKD, Herbert Henkels

Archive (0620), inv. 445; (2) Art Institute of Chicago, inv. 1956.1125

For the dating, see cat. 237.

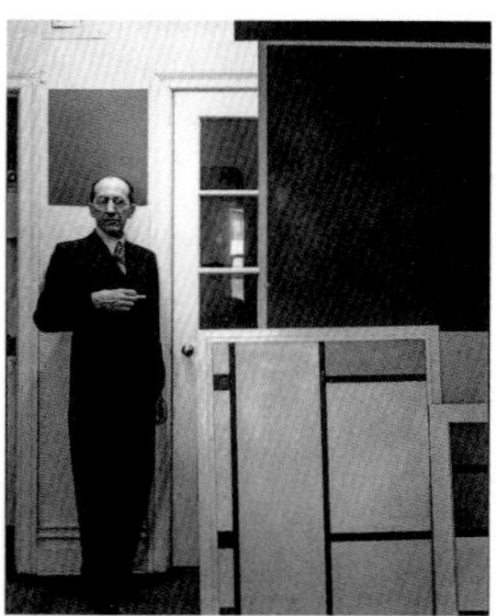

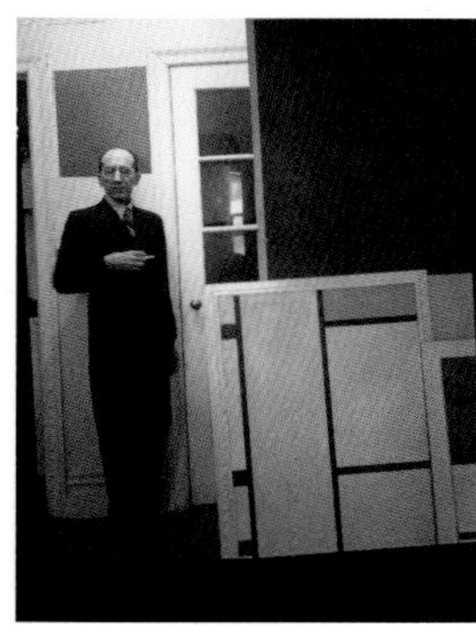

CAT. 242.1; CAT. 242.2 Arnold Newman

Portrait of Piet Mondrian in his studio, between 29 April and 7 May 1942

Gelatin developing-out paper, (1) 12.2 x 9.3 cm; (2) 24.4 x 16.6 cm, 43 x 35.4 cm (mount)

(2) Recto: 'Mondrian 1942', signed '© Arnold Newman'

(1) The Hague, RKD, Herbert Henkels Archive (0620), inv. 445; (2) Philadelphia Museum of Art, inv. 1945-72-48

For the dating, see cat. 237.

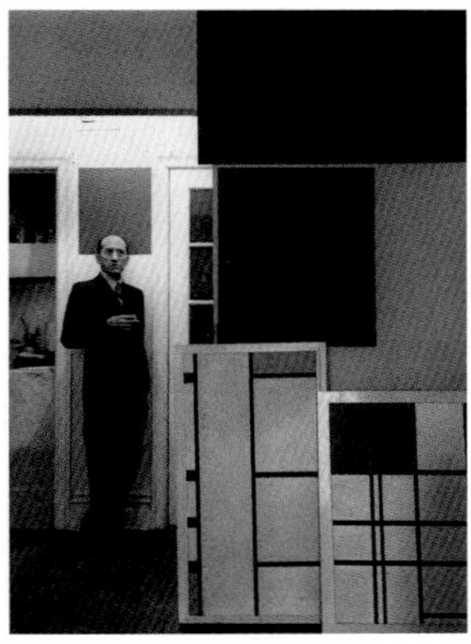

CAT. 243 Arnold Newman

Portrait of Piet Mondrian in his studio, between 29 April and 7 May 1942 (see p. 239)

Gelatin developing-out paper, 33 x 24 cm, 35.2 x 26.5 cm (mount)

Recto: 'Mondrian 1942', signed '© Arnold Newman'

Houston, The Museum of Fine Arts, The Allan Chasanoff Photographic Collection, inv. 91943

For the dating, see cat. 237.

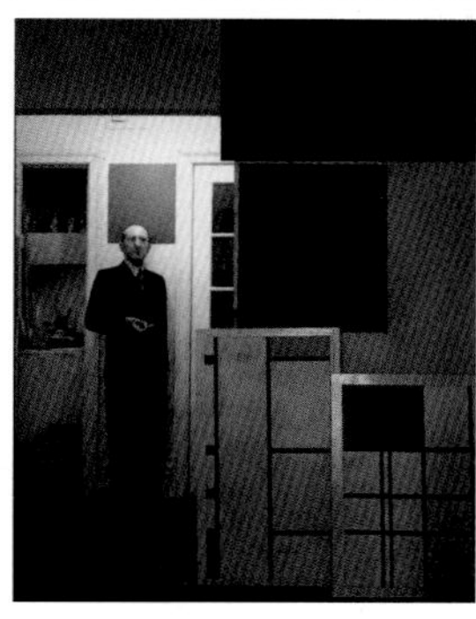

CAT. 244 Arnold Newman

Portrait of Piet Mondrian in his studio, between 29 April and 7 May 1942

Gelatin developing-out paper, 12.1 x 9.3 cm

The Hague, RKD, Herbert Henkels Archive (0620), inv. 445

For the dating, see cat. 237.

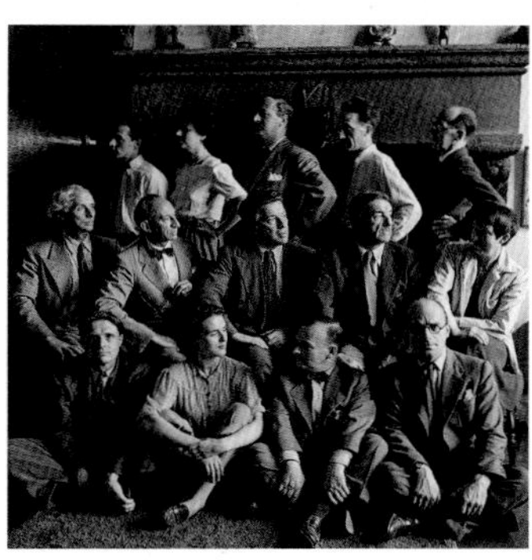

CAT. 245 Hermann Landshoff

***Die Surrealisten*, c. July 1942**
(see p. 241)

Gelatin developing-out paper, 11.5 x 10.8 cm

Munich, Münchner Stadtmuseum, Sammlung Fotografie/Archiv Landshoff, inv. FM-2012/200-190

The photograph has been dated in the past to around July 1942, based on Marcel Duchamp's arrival in New York on 25 June 1942 (Welsh/Joosten 1998-II, p. 178). Another possibility is that it was taken in autumn 1942 as part of the preparations for the 'Art of This Century' exhibition, which opened on 20 October at Peggy Guggenheim's gallery (Kranzfelder 2013, p. 67). In view of the summer clothes that some of the artists are wearing, we will stick to the first dating.

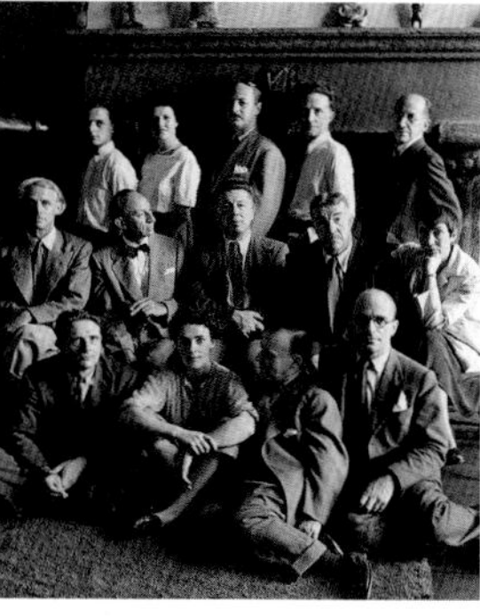

CAT. 246 Hermann Landshoff

***Die Surrealisten*, c. July 1942**
(see p. 242)

Gelatin developing-out paper, 13.5 x 10.6 cm

Munich, Münchner Stadtmuseum, Sammlung Fotografie/Archiv Landshoff, inv. FM-2012/200-182

For identification and dating, see cat. 245.

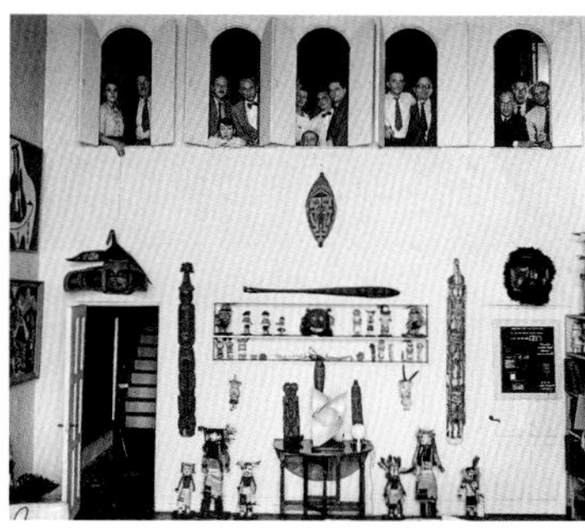

CAT. 247 Hermann Landshoff

Group photograph at Peggy Guggenheim's house, c. July 1942
(see p. 243)

Gelatin developing-out paper, 10 x 10.9 cm

Munich, Münchner Stadtmuseum, Sammlung Fotografie/Archiv Landshoff, inv. FM-2012/200-191

For the dating, see cat. 245.

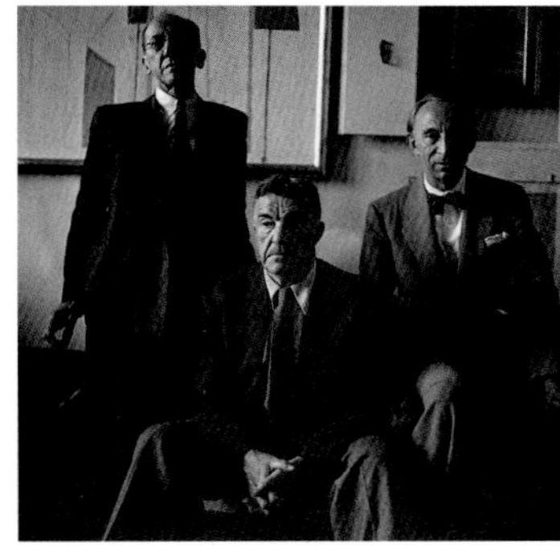

CAT. 248 Hermann Landshoff

Piet Mondrian, Fernand Léger and Amédée Ozenfant at Peggy Guggenheim's house, c. July 1942
(see p. 244)

Gelatin developing-out paper, 10.4 x 10.3 cm

Munich, Münchner Stadtmuseum, Sammlung Fotografie/Archiv Landshoff, inv. FM-2012/200-194

For the dating, see cat. 245.

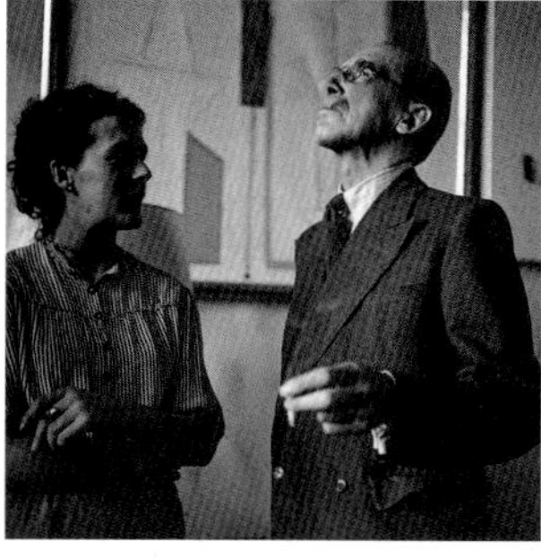

CAT. 249 Hermann Landshoff

Leonora Carrington and Piet Mondrian at Peggy Guggenheim's house, c. July 1942 (see p. 245)

Gelatin developing-out paper, 10.8 x 10.5 cm

Munich, Münchner Stadtmuseum, Sammlung Fotografie/Archiv Landshoff, inv. FM-2012/200-198

For the dating, see cat. 245.

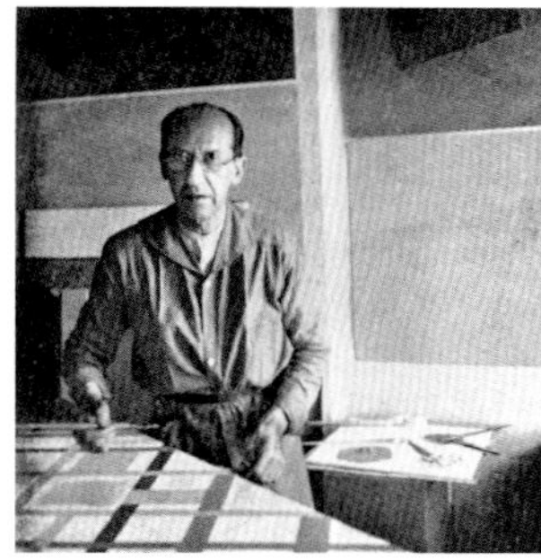

CAT. 250 Kate Steinitz

Piet Mondrian working on *Victory Boogie Woogie* (B324), between June and the end of August 1942
(see p. 247)

Washington, DC, Smithsonian Institution, Steinitz-Schwitters Papers

No vintage print of this photograph has been traced; the reproduction shown here is a later print (The Hague, RKD, Joop Joosten Archive (0838), inv. 811). Given the similarities in the subject of the picture and Mondrian's clothes compared to five other photographs attributed to Kate Steinitz, we assume that she also took this one. In total, therefore, six photographs of Kate Steinitz's visit to Mondrian are known (cats 250–55), four of which are on a page in an album belonging to the Schwitters-Steinitz Collection of the National Gallery of Art in Washington (cats 251–53 and 255).

Mondrian thanked Kate Steinitz in a letter dated 19 December 1942 for 'the pictures' she had sent him (letter from Mondrian to Steinitz, Washington, DC, Smithsonian Institution, Kate Steinitz Papers).

This photograph allows the series to be dated, as it shows Mondrian working on the painting *Victory Boogie Woogie*. He embarked on it in June 1942 and initially set up the work as a composition of intersecting coloured lines, as can be seen in the photo. In October 1942, he broke the lines up into blocks. Since Steinitz moved to the West Coast in August 1942, the photographs can be dated between June and the end of August 1942.

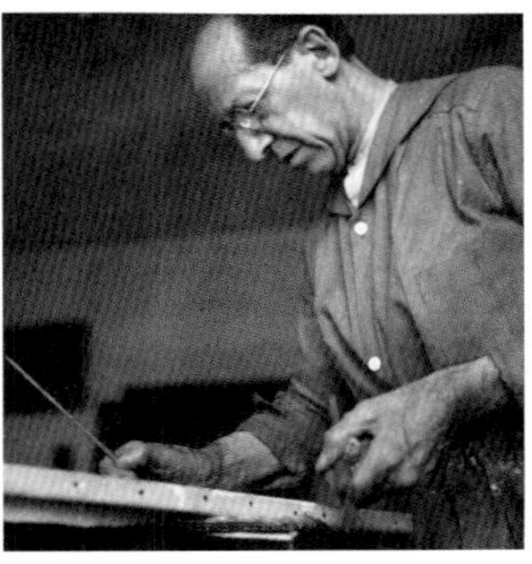

CAT. 251 Kate Steinitz

Piet Mondrian working on *Victory Boogie Woogie* (B324), between June and the end of August 1942 (see p. 246)

Gelatin developing-out paper, 12 x 8.5 cm

Recto, in Kate Steinitz's handwriting: 'Mondrian / New York'

Washington DC, National Gallery of Art (Library), Schwitters-Steinitz Collection

See also cat. 250.

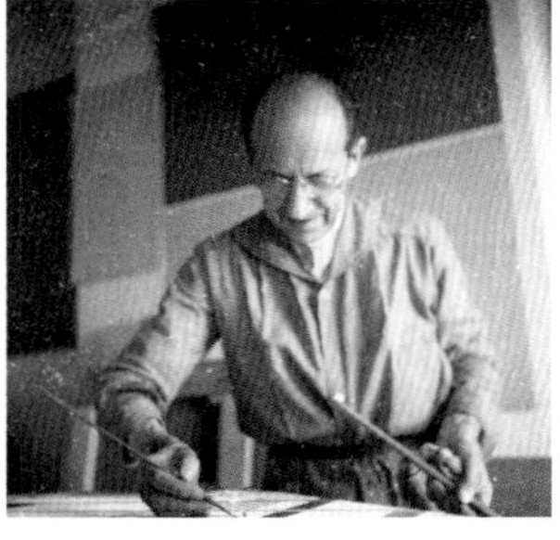

CAT. 252 Kate Steinitz

Piet Mondrian working on *Victory Boogie Woogie* (B324), between June and the end of August 1942 (see p. 247)

Gelatin developing-out paper, 11.5 x 11.5 cm

Washington, DC, National Gallery of Art (Library), Schwitters-Steinitz Collection

See also cat. 250.

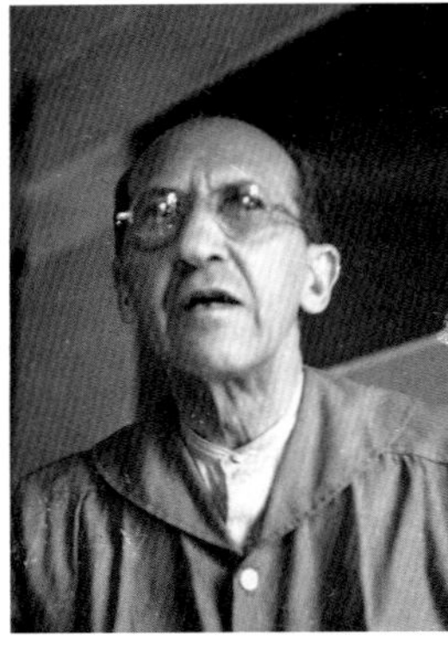

CAT. 253 Kate Steinitz

Portrait of Piet Mondrian, between June and the end of August 1942 (see p. 248)

Gelatin developing-out paper, 11.8 x 8.4 cm

Washington, DC, National Gallery of Art (Library), Schwitters-Steinitz Collection

See also cat. 250.

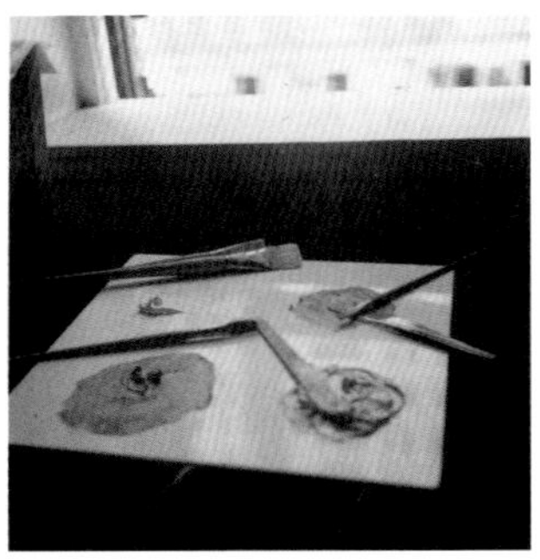

CAT. 254 Kate Steinitz

Piet Mondrian's palette, between June and the end of August 1942 (see p. 249)

Gelatin developing-out paper, 5.9 x 5.7 cm

The Hague, RKD, Piet Mondrian Archive (0740), inv. 72

On 19 December 1942, Mondrian wrote to Steinitz: 'I thank you for the pictures. When enlarged the "palette" will be not so bad I think.' (Letter from Mondrian to Steinitz, Washington, DC, Smithsonian Institution, Kate Steinitz Papers.) He had previously written to her about the palette too: 'I have no palette but a white stone' (undated letter from Mondrian to Steinitz, ibid.).

The way the tools and the blobs of paint are arranged on the palette is identical to cat. 255.

See also cat. 250.

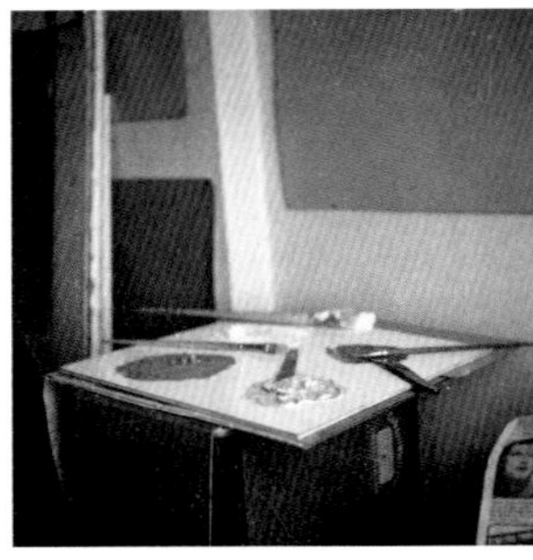

CAT. 255 Kate Steinitz

Mondrian's palette, between June and the end of August 1942 (see p. 249)

Gelatin developing-out paper, 11.7 x 11.2 cm

Washington, DC, National Gallery of Art (Library), Schwitters-Steinitz Collection

See also cats 250 and 254.

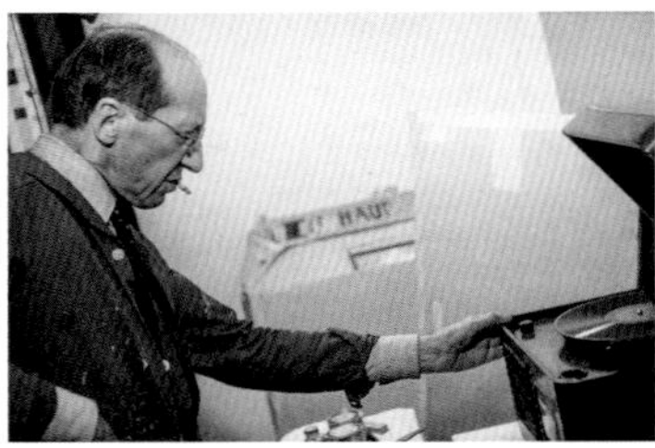

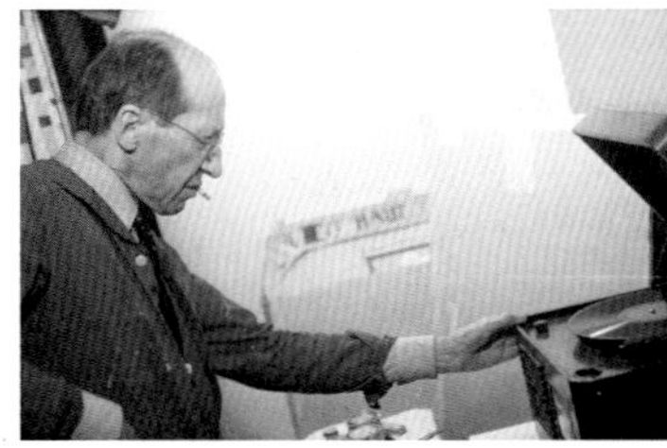

CAT. 256.1; CAT. 256.2 Fritz Glarner

Piet Mondrian in his studio with his gramophone, between c. late 1942 and mid-March 1943 (see p. 251)

(1) Gelatin developing-out paper, 12.6 x 20.8 cm; (2) contact print from 35 mm negative, 2.4 x 3.6 cm

(1) Verso, in Harry Holtzman's handwriting (?): 'Glarner'

(1) The Hague, RKD, Piet Mondrian Archive (0740), inv. 70; (2) Zurich, Kunsthaus, Glarner Archiv, no inv., sheet 6, strip 2, negative 3

Fritz Glarner's extensive series of photos of Mondrian and his studio (cats 256–95) cannot be securely dated. It has previously been assigned a date shortly before 22 March 1943, partly because the painting *Trafalgar Square* (B[294]322), which can be seen in cats 291–95, was displayed from that day at the Valentine Gallery.
The painting as shown in the picture is not finished, however (Cooper/Spronk 2001, pp. 70, 233–34). We have therefore opted for a somewhat broader dating.

See also cat. 276.

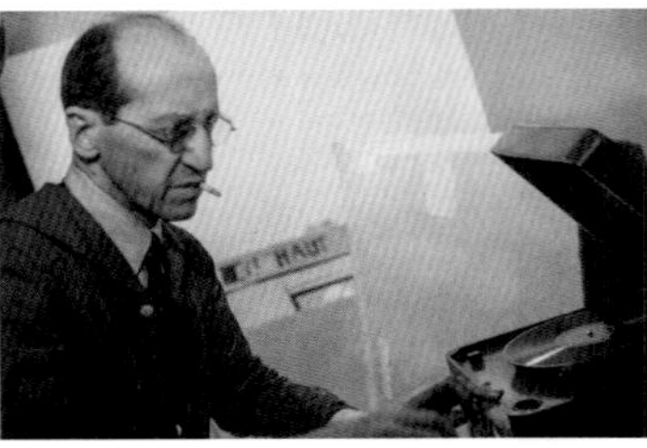

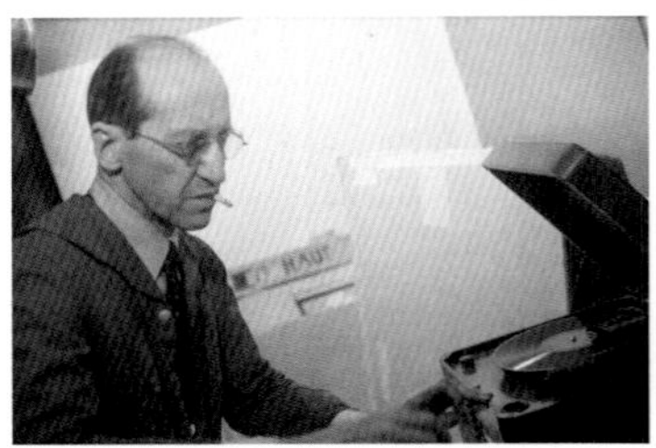

CAT. 257.1; CAT. 257.2 Fritz Glarner

Piet Mondrian in his studio with his gramophone, between c. late 1942 and mid-March 1943

(1) Gelatin developing-out paper, 12.7 x 20.8 cm; (2) contact print from 35 mm negative, 2.4 x 3.6 cm

(1) Verso, in Harry Holtzman's handwriting (?): 'Glarner'

(1) The Hague, RKD, Piet Mondrian Archive (0740), inv. 70; (2) Zurich, Kunsthaus, Glarner Archiv, no inv., sheet 6, strip 2, negative 4

For the dating, see cat. 256.

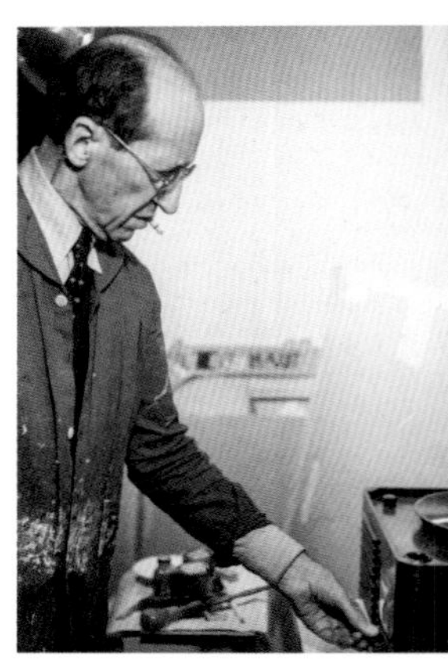

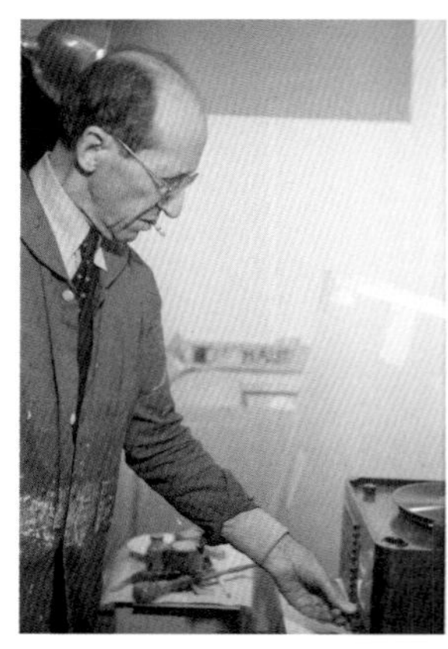

CAT. 258.1; CAT. 258.2 Fritz Glarner

Piet Mondrian in his studio with his gramophone, between c. late 1942 and mid-March 1943

(1) Gelatin developing-out paper, 20.8 x 12.6 cm; (2) contact print from 35 mm negative, 3.6 x 2.4 cm

(1) Verso, in Harry Holtzman's handwriting (?): 'Glarner'

(1) The Hague, RKD, Piet Mondrian Archive (0740), inv. 70; (2) Zurich, Kunsthaus, Glarner Archiv, no inv., sheet 6, strip 2, negative 5

For the dating, see cat. 256.

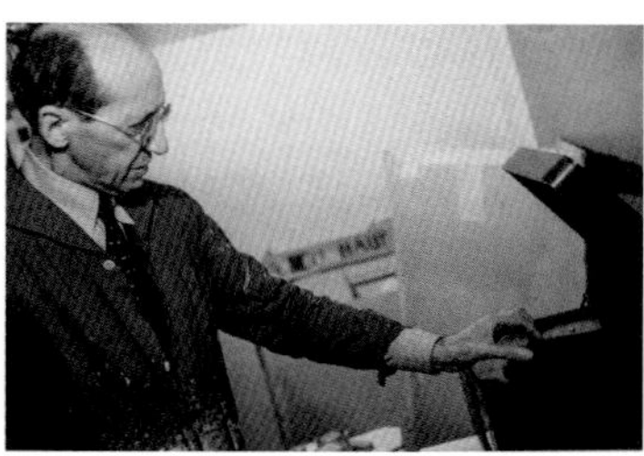

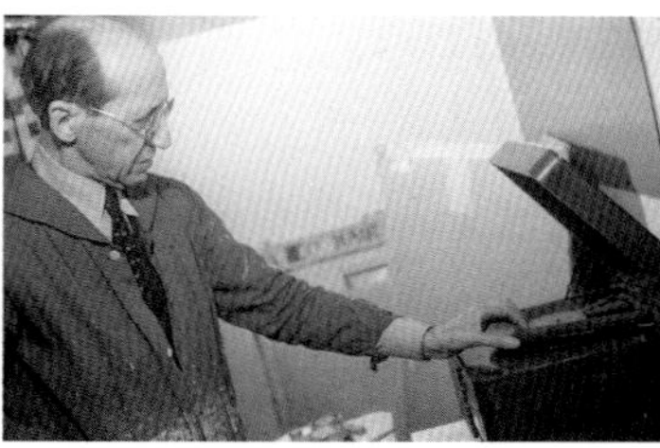

CAT. 259.1; CAT. 259.2 Fritz Glarner

Piet Mondrian in his studio with his gramophone, between c. late 1942 and mid-March 1943

(1) Gelatin developing-out paper, 12.7 x 20.8 cm; (2) contact print from 35 mm negative, 2.4 x 3.6 cm

(1) Verso, in Harry Holtzman's handwriting (?): 'Glarner'

(1) The Hague, RKD, Piet Mondrian Archive (0740), inv. 70; (2) Zurich, Kunsthaus, Glarner Archiv, no inv., sheet 6, strip 2, negative 6

For the dating, see cat. 256.

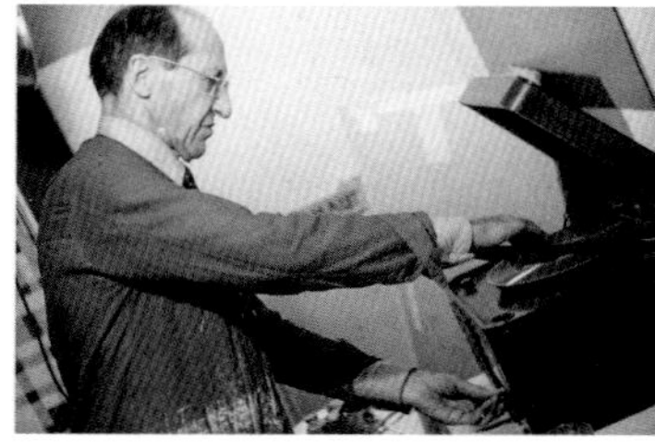

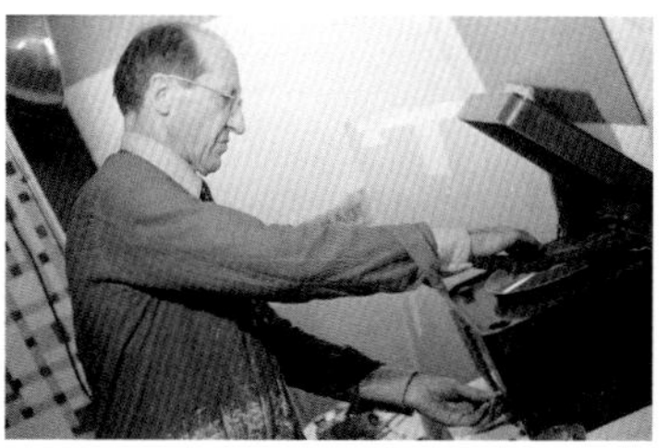

CAT. 260.1; CAT. 260.2 Fritz Glarner

Piet Mondrian in his studio with his gramophone, between c. late 1942 and mid-March 1943

(1) Gelatin developing-out paper, 12.8 x 20.8 cm; (2) contact print from 35 mm negative, 2.4 x 3.6 cm

(1) Verso, in Harry Holtzman's handwriting (?): 'Glarner'

(1) The Hague, RKD, Piet Mondrian Archive (0740), inv. 70; (2) Zurich, Kunsthaus, Glarner Archiv, no inv., sheet 6, strip 2, negative 7

For the dating, see cat. 256.

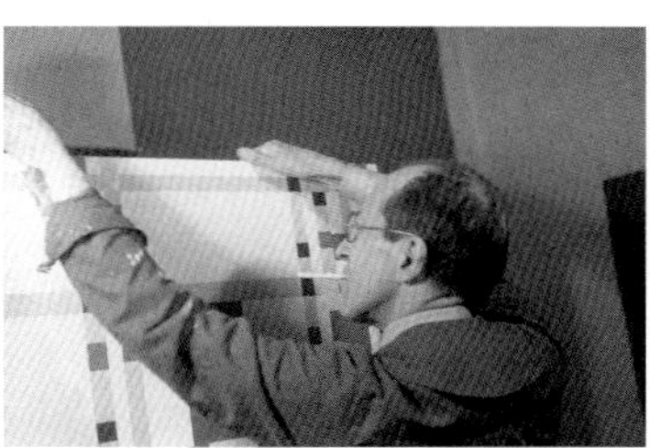

CAT. 261 Fritz Glarner

Piet Mondrian in his studio, with *Broadway Boogie Woogie* (B323), between c. late 1942 and mid-March 1943 (see p. 252)

Contact print from a 35 mm negative, 2.4 x 3.6 cm

Zurich, Kunsthaus, Glarner Archiv, no inv., sheet 6, strip 3, negative 8

For the dating, see cat. 256.

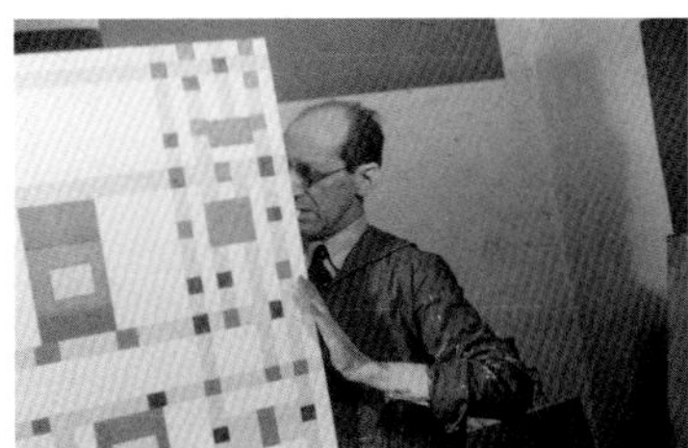

CAT. 262 Fritz Glarner

Piet Mondrian in his studio, with *Broadway Boogie Woogie* (B323), between c. late 1942 and mid-March 1943

Contact print from a 35 mm negative, 2.4 x 3.6 cm

Zurich, Kunsthaus, Glarner Archiv, no inv., sheet 6, strip 3, negative 9

For the dating, see cat. 256.

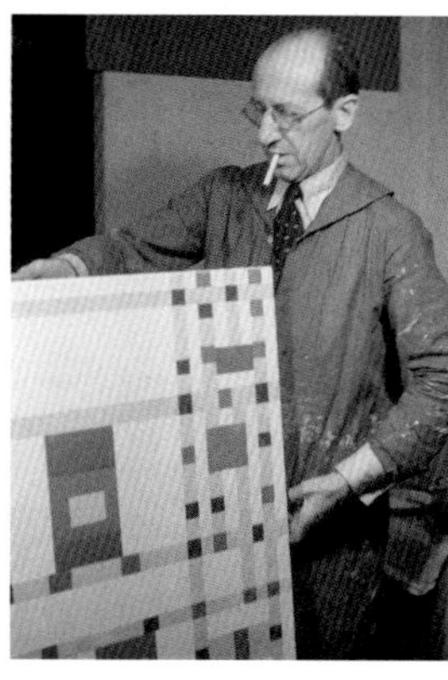

CAT. 263 Fritz Glarner

Piet Mondrian in his studio, with *Broadway Boogie Woogie* (B323), between c. late 1942 and mid-March 1943 (see p. 252)

Contact print from a 35 mm negative, 3.6 x 2.4 cm

Zurich, Kunsthaus, Glarner Archiv, no inv., sheet 6, strip 3, negative 10

For the dating, see cat. 256.

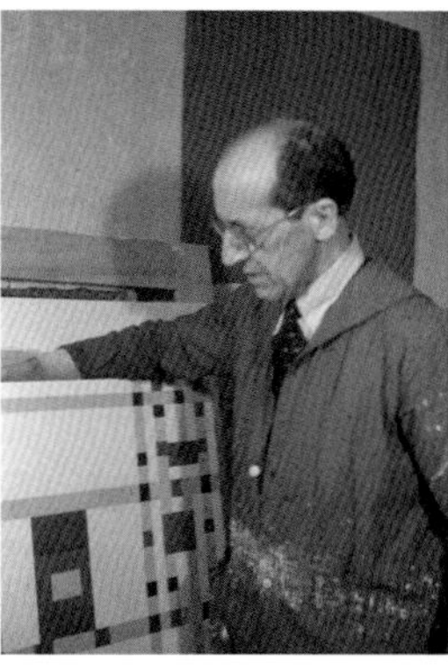

CAT. 264 Fritz Glarner

Piet Mondrian in his studio, with *Broadway Boogie Woogie* (B323), between c. late 1942 and mid-March 1943

Contact print from a 35 mm negative, 3.6 x 2.4 cm

Zurich, Kunsthaus, Glarner Archiv, no inv., sheet 6, strip 3, negative 11

For the dating, see cat. 256.

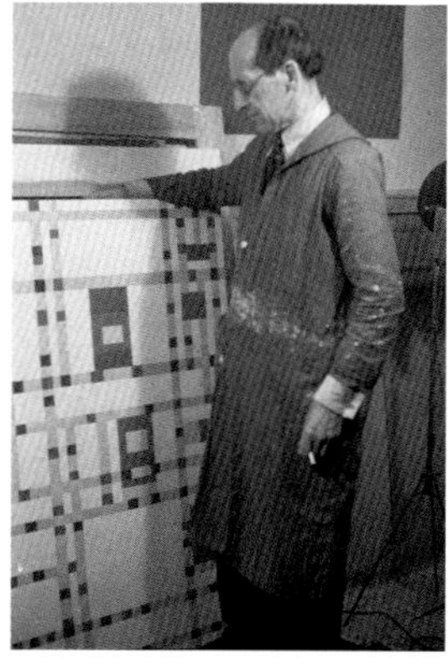

CAT. 265 Fritz Glarner

Piet Mondrian in his studio, with *Broadway Boogie Woogie* (B323), between c. late 1942 and mid-March 1943 (see p. 253)

Contact print from a 35 mm negative, 3.6 x 2.4 cm

Zurich, Kunsthaus, Glarner Archiv, no inv., sheet 6, strip 3, negative 12

For the dating, see cat. 256.

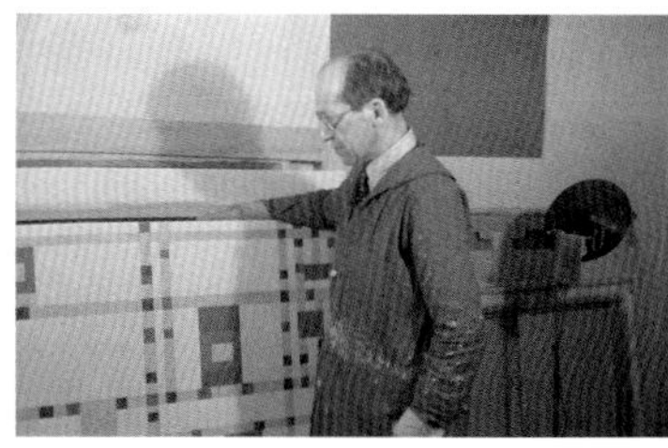

CAT. 266 Fritz Glarner

Piet Mondrian in his studio, with *Broadway Boogie Woogie* (B323), between c. late 1942 and mid-March 1943

Contact print from a 35 mm negative, 2.4 x 3.6 cm

Zurich, Kunsthaus, Glarner Archiv, no inv., sheet 6, strip 4, negative 13

For the dating, see cat. 256.

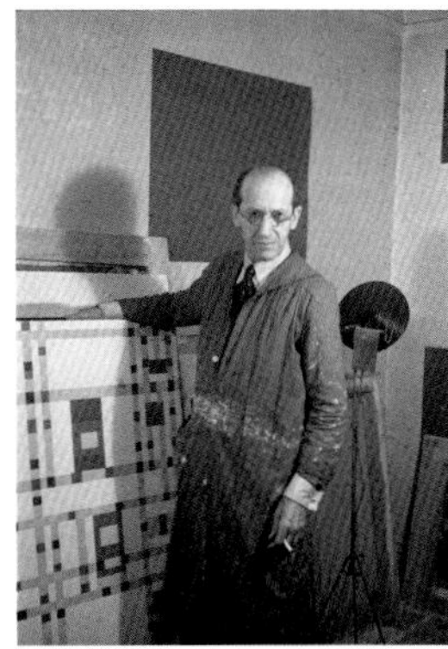

CAT. 267 Fritz Glarner

Piet Mondrian in his studio, with *Broadway Boogie Woogie* (B323), between c. late 1942 and mid-March 1943 (see p. 253)

Contact print from a 35 mm negative, 3.6 x 2.4 cm

Zurich, Kunsthaus, Glarner Archiv, no inv., sheet 6, strip 4, negative 14

For the dating, see cat. 256.

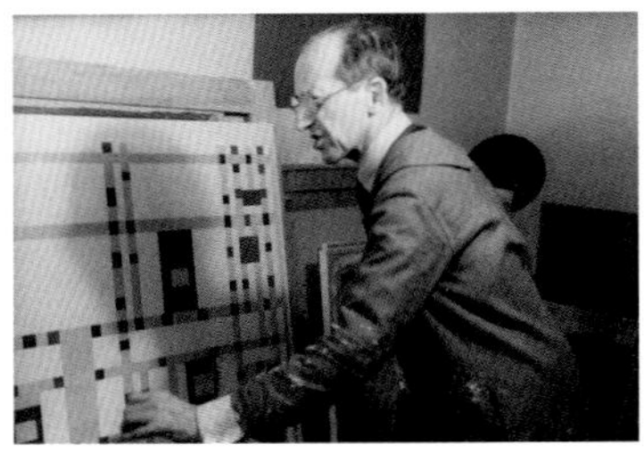

CAT. 268 Fritz Glarner

Piet Mondrian in his studio, with *Broadway Boogie Woogie* (B323), between c. late 1942 and mid-March 1943

Gelatin developing-out paper, 16.2 x 22.8 cm

Private collection

For the dating, see cat. 256.

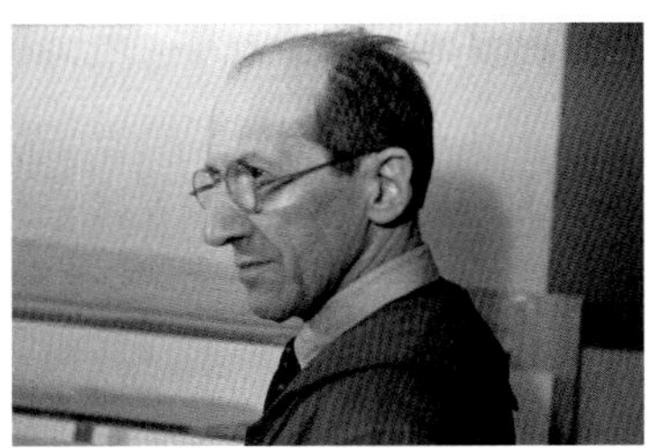

CAT. 269 Fritz Glarner

Piet Mondrian in his studio, between c. late 1942 and mid-March 1943

Contact print from a 35 mm negative, 2.4 x 3.6 cm

Zurich, Kunsthaus, Glarner Archiv, no inv., sheet 6, strip 4, negative 15

For the dating, see cat. 256.

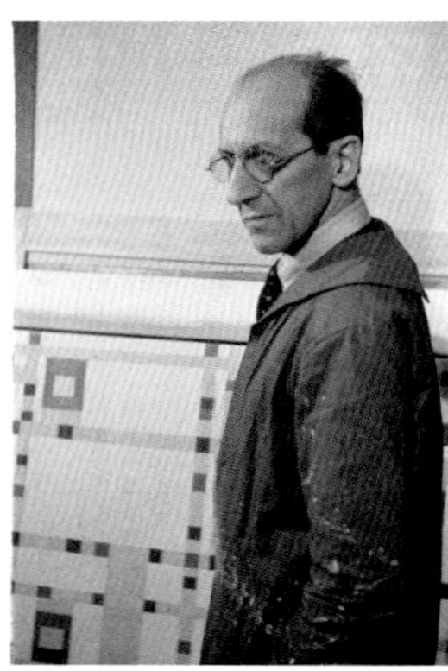

CAT. 270 Fritz Glarner

Piet Mondrian in his studio, between c. late 1942 and mid-March 1943 (see p. 255)

Contact print from a 35 mm negative, 3.6 x 2.4 cm

Zurich, Kunsthaus, Glarner Archiv, no inv., sheet 6, strip 4, negative 16

For the dating, see cat. 256.

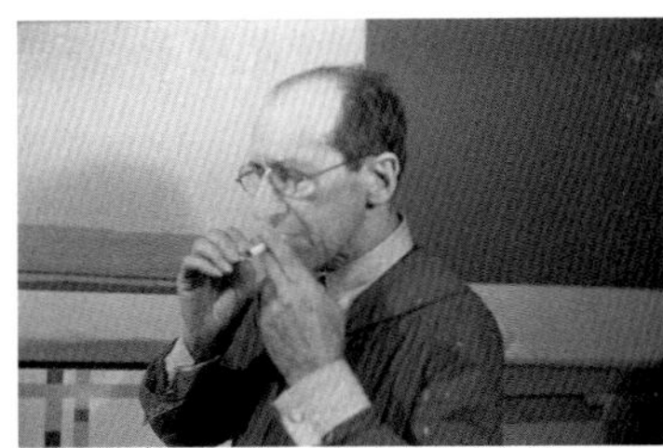

CAT. 271 Fritz Glarner

Piet Mondrian in his studio, between c. late 1942 and mid-March 1943

Contact print from a 35 mm negative, 2.4 x 3.6 cm

Zurich, Kunsthaus, Glarner Archiv, no inv., sheet 6, strip 4, negative 17

For the dating, see cat. 256.

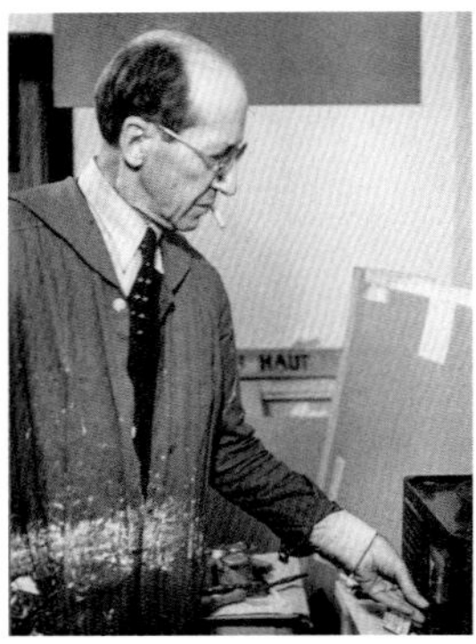

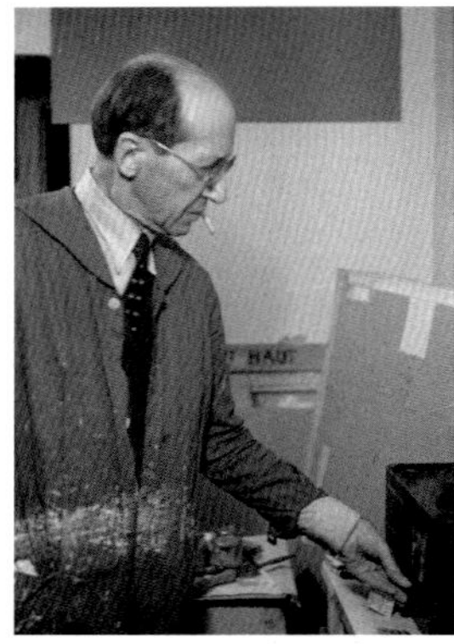

CAT. 272.1; CAT. 272.2 Fritz Glarner

Piet Mondrian in his studio with his gramophone, between c. late 1942 and mid-March 1943 (see p. 254)

(1) Gelatin developing-out paper, 17.3 x 11.8 cm; (2) contact print from a 35 mm negative, 3.6 x 2.4 cm

(1) Verso, in Harry Holtzman's handwriting (?): 'Glarner'

(1) The Hague, RKD, Piet Mondrian Archive (0740), inv. 70; (2) Zurich, Kunsthaus, Glarner Archiv, no inv., sheet 6, strip 5, negative 18

For the dating, see cat. 256.

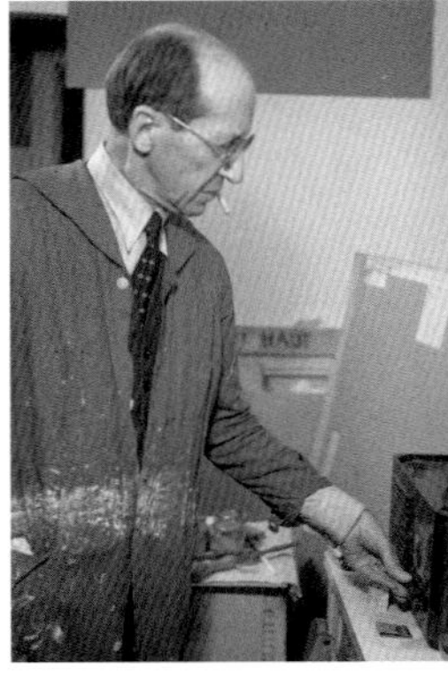

CAT. 273 Fritz Glarner

Piet Mondrian in his studio with his gramophone, between c. late 1942 and mid-March 1943

Contact print from a 35 mm negative, 3.6 x 2.4 cm

Zurich, Kunsthaus, Glarner Archiv, no inv., sheet 6, strip 5, negative 19

For the dating, see cat. 256.

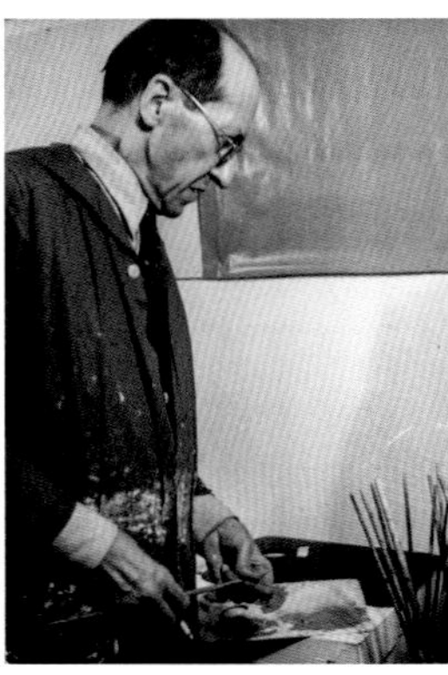

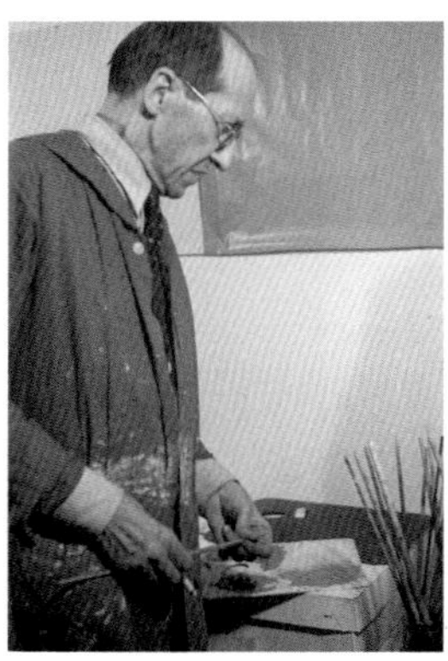

CAT. 274.1; CAT. 274.2 Fritz Glarner

Piet Mondrian working in his studio, between c. late 1942 and mid-March 1943

(1) Gelatin developing-out paper, 17.3 x 11.8 cm; (2) contact print from a 35 mm negative, 3.6 x 2.4 cm

(1) The Hague, RKD, Piet Mondrian Archive (0740), inv. 70; (2) Zurich, Kunsthaus, Glarner Archiv, no inv., sheet 6, strip 5, negative 20

For the dating, see cat. 256.

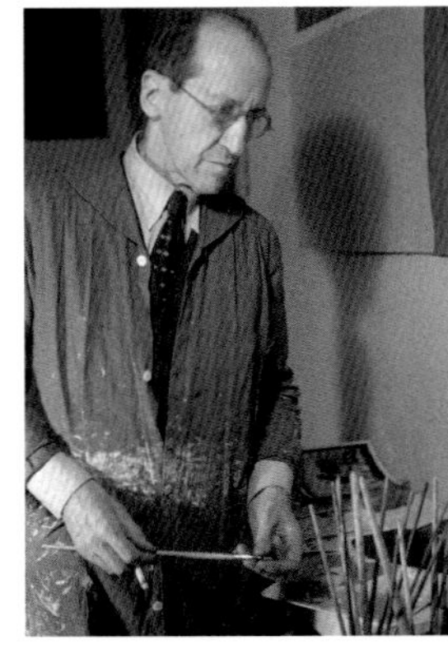

CAT. 275 Fritz Glarner

Piet Mondrian working in his studio, between c. late 1942 and mid-March 1943 (see p. 256)

Contact print from a 35 mm negative, 3.6 x 2.4 cm

Zurich, Kunsthaus, Glarner Archiv, no inv., sheet 6, strip 5, negative 21

For the dating, see cat. 256.

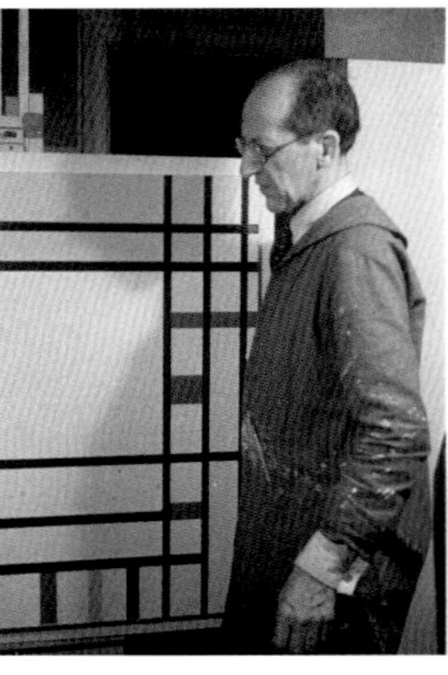

CAT. 276 Fritz Glarner

Piet Mondrian in his studio, with *Place de la Concorde* (B321), between c. late 1942 and mid-March 1943 (see p. 257)

Contact print from a 35 mm negative, 3.6 x 2.4 cm

Zurich, Kunsthaus, Glarner Archiv, no inv., sheet 6, strip 6, negative 23

For the dating, see cat. 256.

Like *Trafalgar Square* (B[294]322; see cat. 256), *Place de la Concorde* (B[283]321, behind Mondrian) also featured from the end of March 1943 in the exhibition at the Valentine Gallery. The photograph shows that the frame had not yet been widened, as Mondrian would do later (Cooper/Spronk 2001, p. 222).

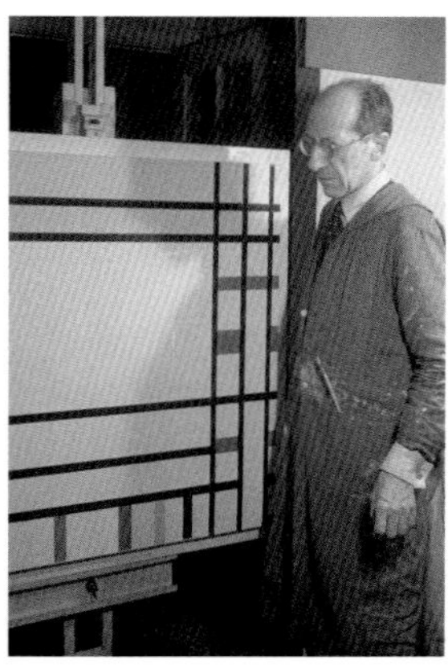

CAT. 277 Fritz Glarner

Piet Mondrian in his studio, with *Place de la Concorde* (B321), between c. late 1942 and mid-March 1943

Contact print from a 35 mm negative, 3.6 x 2.4 cm

Zurich, Kunsthaus, Glarner Archiv, no inv., sheet 6, strip 6, negative 24

For the dating, see cat. 256.

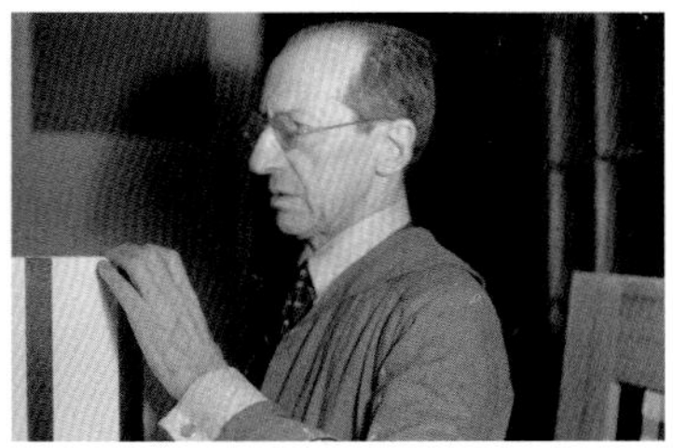

CAT. 278 Fritz Glarner

Piet Mondrian in his studio, between c. late 1942 and mid-March 1943 (see p. 258)

Contact print from a 35 mm negative, 2.4 x 3.6 cm

Zurich, Kunsthaus, Glarner Archiv, no inv., sheet 8, strip 1, negative 37

For the dating, see cat. 256.

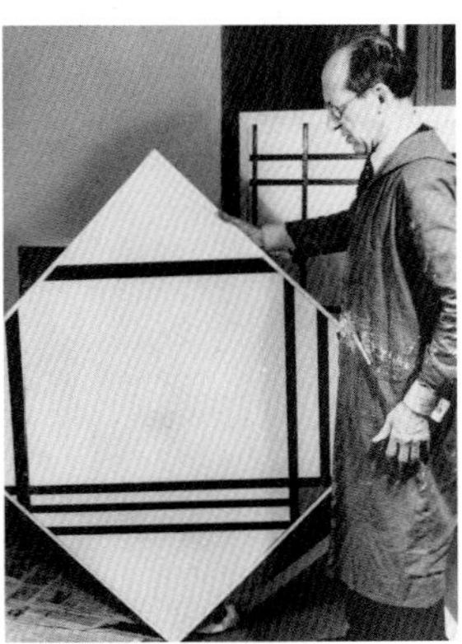

CAT. 279 Fritz Glarner

Piet Mondrian in his studio, with *Picture No. III* (B282), between c. late 1942 and mid-March 1943

Contact print from a 35 mm negative, 3.6 x 2.4 cm

Zurich, Kunsthaus, Glarner Archiv, no inv., sheet 6, strip 6, negative 25

For the dating, see cat. 256.

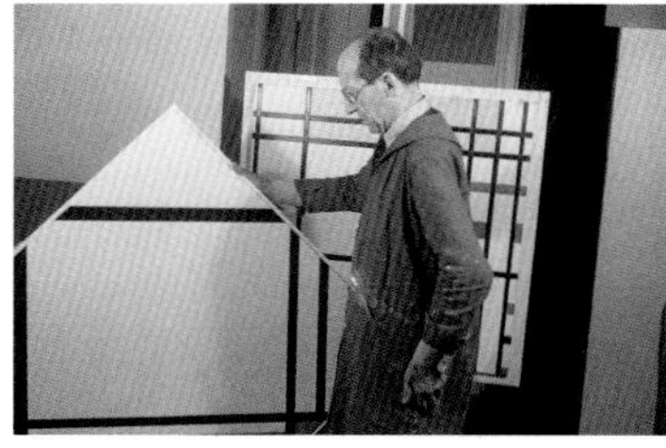

CAT. 280 Fritz Glarner

Piet Mondrian in his studio, with *Picture No. III* (B282), between c. late 1942 and mid-March 1943 (see p. 259)

Contact print from a 35 mm negative, 2.4 x 3.6 cm

Zurich, Kunsthaus, Glarner Archiv, no inv., sheet 6, strip 6, negative 26

For the dating, see cat. 256.

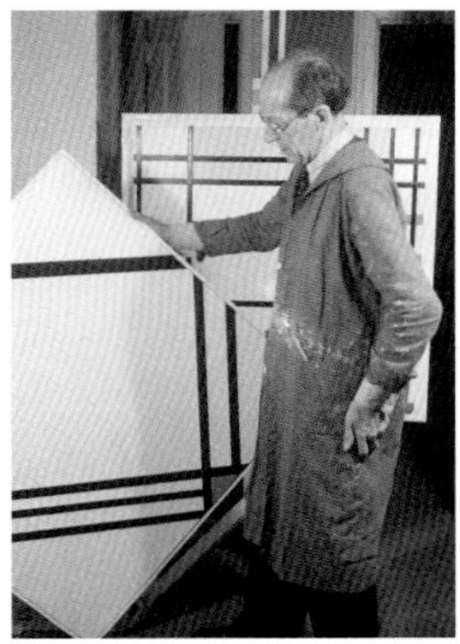

CAT. 281 Fritz Glarner

Piet Mondrian in his studio, with *Picture No. III* (B282), between c. late 1942 and mid-March 1943

Contact print from a 35 mm negative, 3.6 x 2.4 cm

Zurich, Kunsthaus, Glarner Archiv, no inv., sheet 6, strip 6, negative 27

For the dating, see cat. 256.

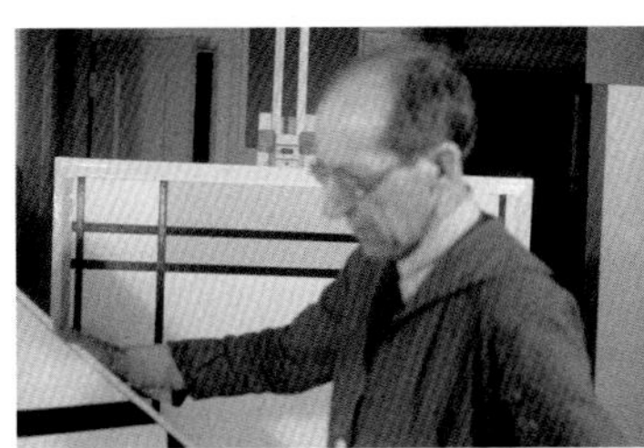

CAT. 282 Fritz Glarner

Piet Mondrian in his studio, with *Picture No. III* (B282), between c. late 1942 and mid-March 1943 (see p. 258)

Contact print from a 35 mm negative, 2.4 x 3.6 cm

Zurich, Kunsthaus, Glarner Archiv, no inv., sheet 6, strip 7, negative 28

For the dating, see cat. 256.

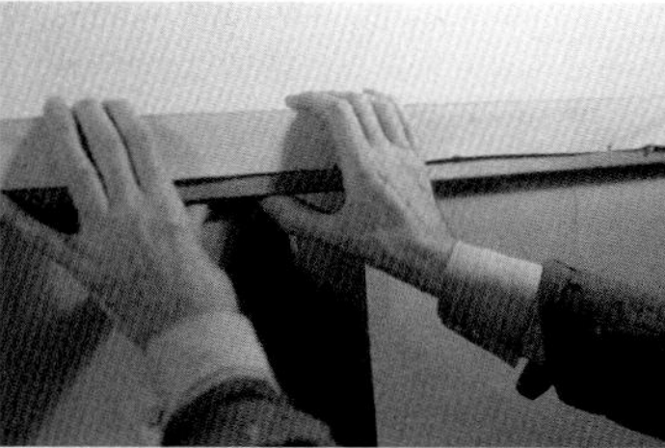

CAT. 283 Fritz Glarner

The hands of Piet Mondrian, between c. late 1942 and mid-March 1943 (see p. 260)

Contact print from a 35 mm negative, 2.4 x 3.6 cm

Zurich, Kunsthaus, Glarner Archiv, no inv., sheet 6, strip 7, negative 29

For the dating, see cat. 256.

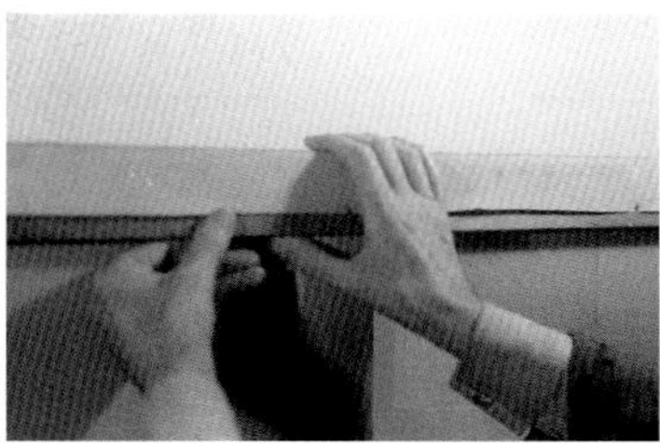

CAT. 284 Fritz Glarner

The hands of Piet Mondrian, between c. late 1942 and mid-March 1943 (see p. 260)

Contact print from a 35 mm negative, 2.4 x 3.6 cm

Zurich, Kunsthaus, Glarner Archiv, no inv., sheet 6, strip 7, negative 30

For the dating, see cat. 256.

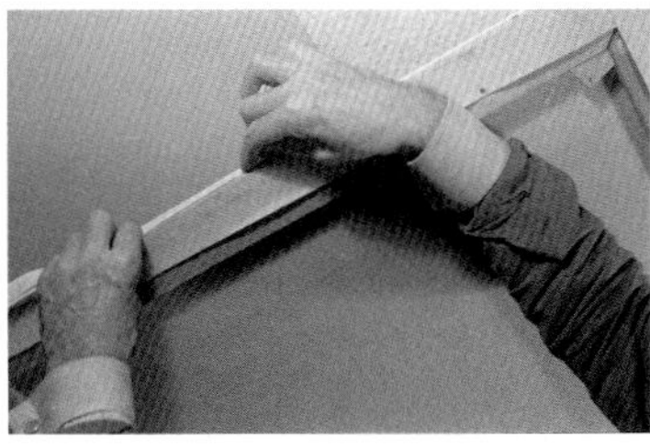

CAT. 285 Fritz Glarner

The hands of Piet Mondrian, between c. late 1942 and mid-March 1943 (see p. 261)

Contact print from a 35 mm negative, 2.4 x 3.6 cm

Zurich, Kunsthaus, Glarner Archiv, no inv., sheet 6, strip 7, negative 31

For the dating, see cat. 256.

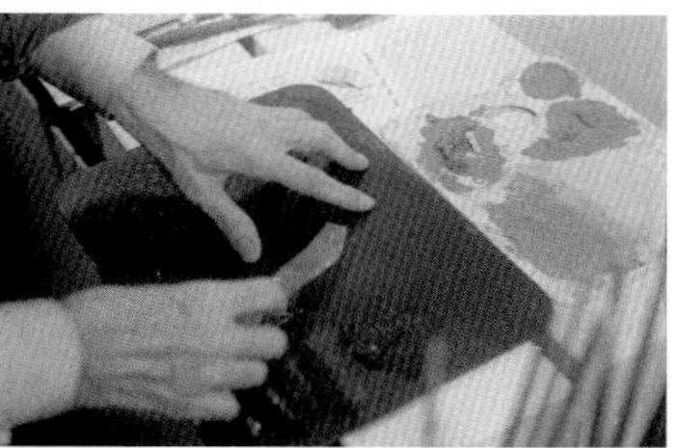

CAT. 286 Fritz Glarner

The hands of Piet Mondrian, between c. late 1942 and mid-March 1943 (see p. 261)

Contact print from a 35 mm negative, 2.4 x 3.6 cm

Zurich, Kunsthaus, Glarner Archiv, no inv., sheet 6, strip 7, negative 32

For the dating, see cat. 256.

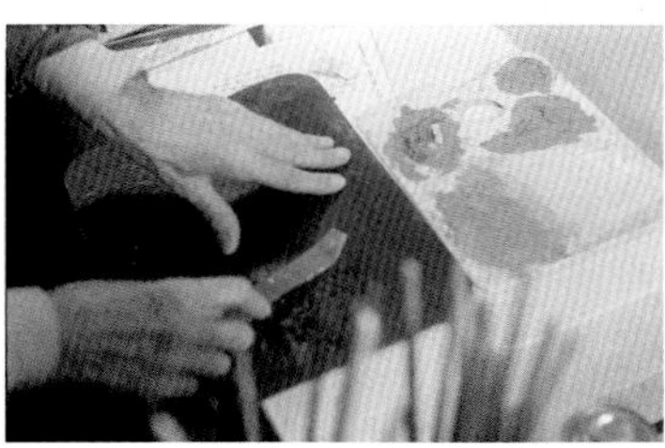

CAT. 287 Fritz Glarner

The hands of Piet Mondrian, between c. late 1942 and mid-March 1943 (see p. 260)

Contact print from a 35 mm negative, 2.4 x 3.6 cm

Zurich, Kunsthaus, Glarner Archiv, no inv., sheet 8, strip 1, negative 33

For the dating, see cat. 256.

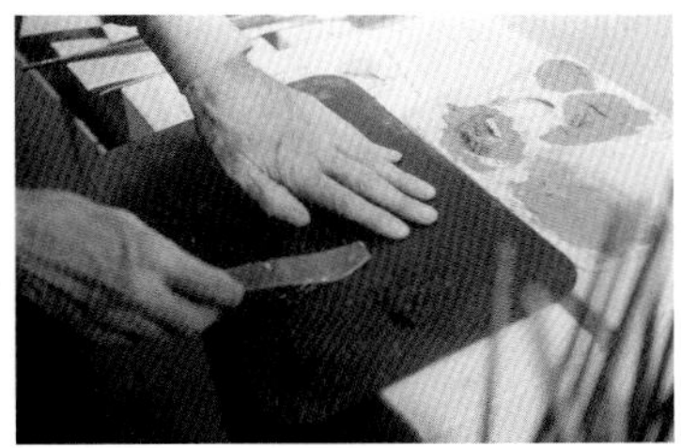

CAT. 288 Fritz Glarner

The hands of Piet Mondrian, between c. late 1942 and mid-March 1943 (see p. 260)

Contact print from a 35 mm negative, 2.4 x 3.6 cm

Zurich, Kunsthaus, Glarner Archiv, no inv., sheet 8, strip 1, negative 34

For the dating, see cat. 256.

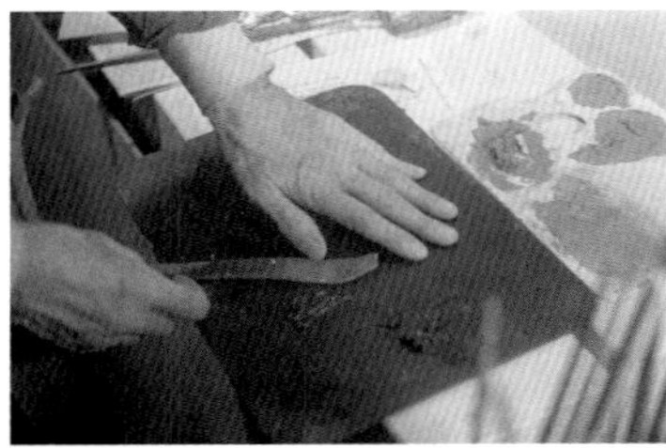

CAT. 289 Fritz Glarner

The hands of Piet Mondrian, between c. late 1942 and mid-March 1943 (see p. 261)

Contact print from a 35 mm negative, 2.4 x 3.6 cm

Zurich, Kunsthaus, Glarner Archiv, no inv., sheet 8, strip 1, negative 35

For the dating, see cat. 256.

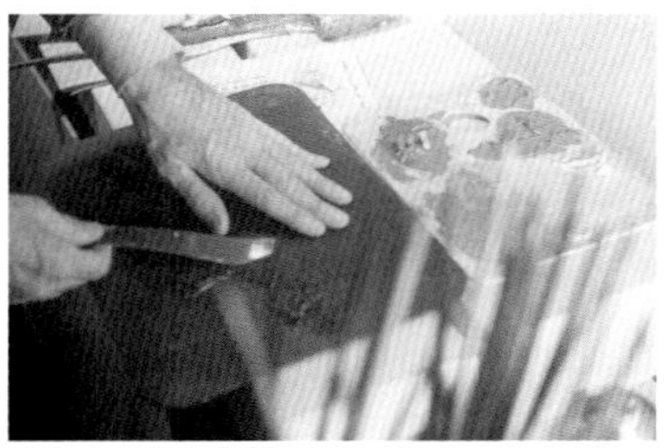

CAT. 290 Fritz Glarner

The hands of Piet Mondrian, between c. late 1942 and mid-March 1943 (see p. 261)

Contact print from a 35 mm negative, 2.4 x 3.6 cm

Zurich, Kunsthaus, Glarner Archiv, no inv., sheet 8, strip 1, negative 36

For the dating, see cat. 256.

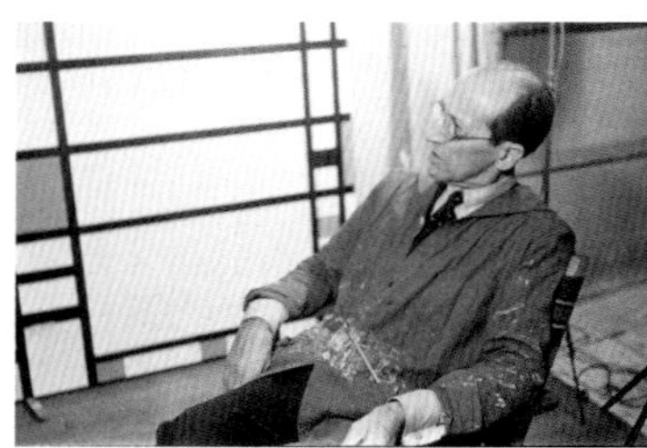

CAT. 291 Fritz Glarner

Piet Mondrian in his studio, between c. late 1942 and mid-March 1943

Contact print from a 35 mm negative, 2.4 x 3.6 cm

Zurich, Kunsthaus, Glarner Archiv, no inv., sheet 10, strip 5, negative 2

For the dating, see cat. 256.

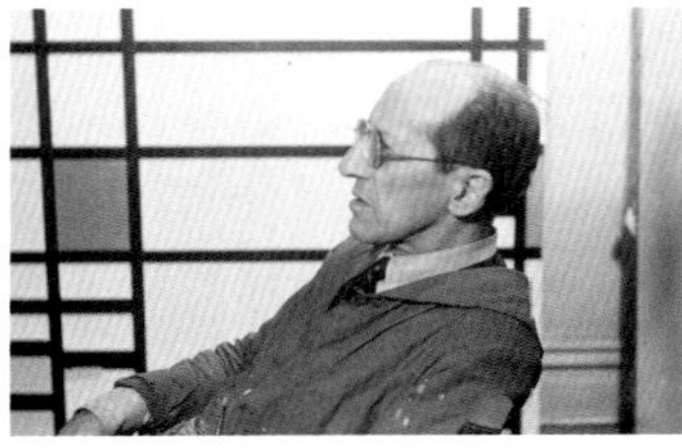

CAT. 292 Fritz Glarner

Piet Mondrian in his studio, between c. late 1942 and mid-March 1943
(see p. 262)

Contact print from a 35 mm negative, 2.4 x 3.6 cm

Zurich, Kunsthaus, Glarner Archiv, no inv., sheet 10, strip 5, negative 3

For the dating, see cat. 256.

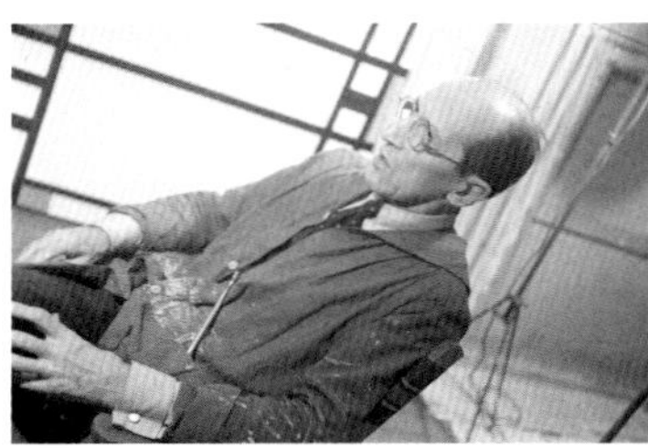

CAT. 293 Fritz Glarner

Piet Mondrian in his studio, between c. late 1942 and mid-March 1943

Contact print from a 35 mm negative, 2.4 x 3.6 cm

Zurich, Kunsthaus, Glarner Archiv, no inv., sheet 10, strip 5, negative 4

For the dating, see cat. 256.

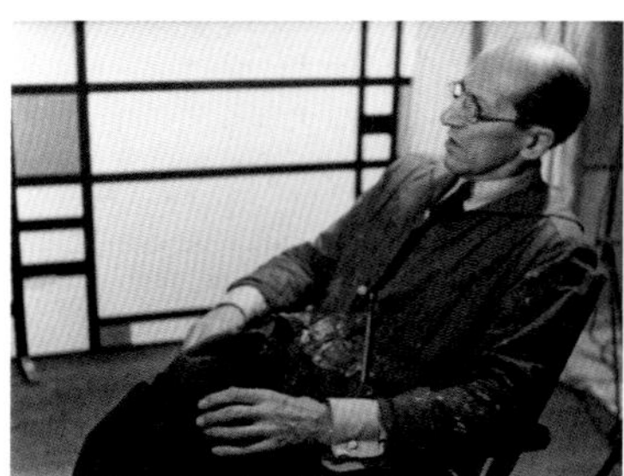

CAT. 294 Fritz Glarner

Piet Mondrian in his studio, between c. late 1942 and mid-March 1943
(see p. 263)

Gelatin developing-out paper, 8.4 x 10.6 cm

Private collection

For the dating, see cat. 256.

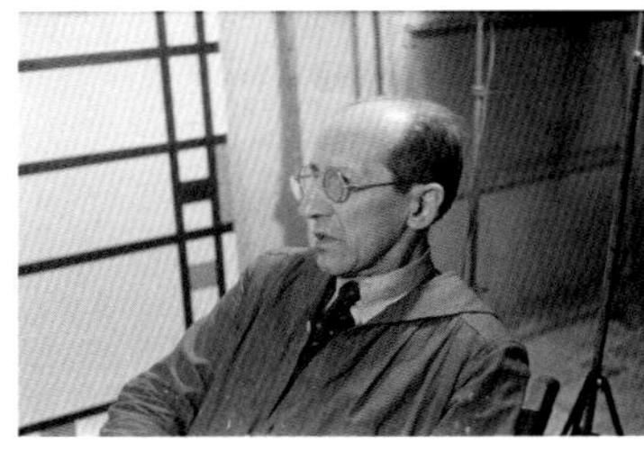

CAT. 295 Fritz Glarner

Piet Mondrian in his studio, between c. late 1942 and mid-March 1943

Contact print from a 35 mm negative, 2.4 x 3.6 cm

Zurich, Kunsthaus, Glarner Archiv, no inv., sheet 10, strip 5, negative 6

For the dating, see cat. 256.

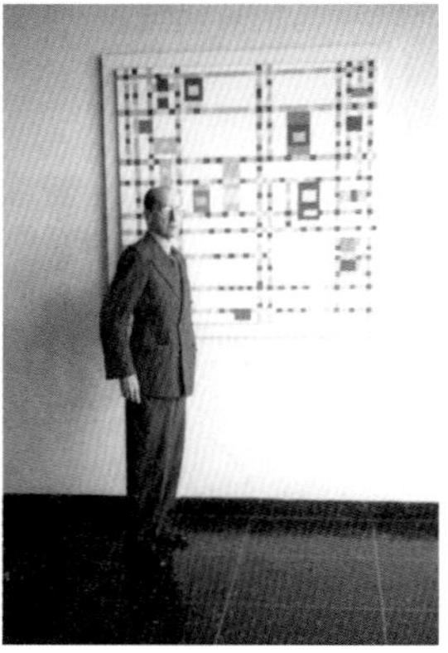

CAT. 296 Elizabeth 'Bobsy' Goodspeed Chapman

Piet Mondriaan in the Museum of Modern Art, with *Broadway Boogie Woogie* (B323), October 1943
(see p. 264)

Gelatin developing-out paper, 13 x 8,5 cm

Recto (to the right of photograph), in Elizabeth Goodspeed's handwriting: '1943 / Oct- / New / York'; see also cat. 299.

Collection Robert Storr

In October 1943 Mondrian and Elizabeth 'Bobsy' Fuller Goodspeed (later Chapman) visited the Museum of Modern Art in New York, which had acquired the *Broadway Boogie Woogie* painting earlier in 1943 thanks to an anonymous donation. The cats 303–4 photographs must have been prior to or after that visit. The cats 296–304 photographs are part of a photo album, in which 296–99 and 303–4 are mounted on a page, and 300–2 on another page.

The date is taken from the caption above.

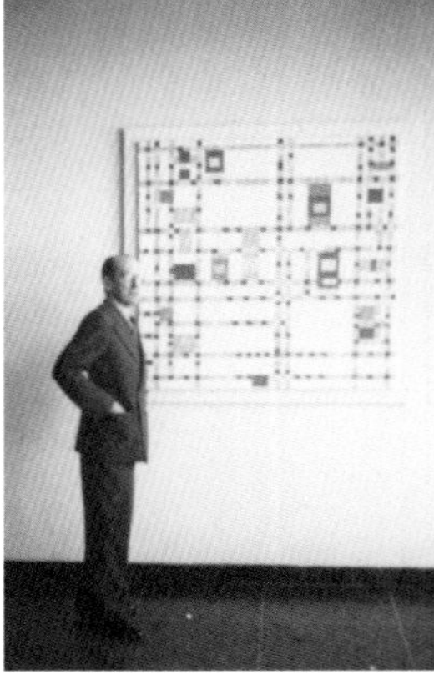

CAT. 297 Elizabeth 'Bobsy' Goodspeed Chapman

Piet Mondriaan in the Museum of Modern Art, with *Broadway Boogie Woogie* (B323), October 1943
(see p. 264)

Gelatin developing-out paper, 13 x 8,5 cm

Collection Robert Storr

See also cats 296 and 299.

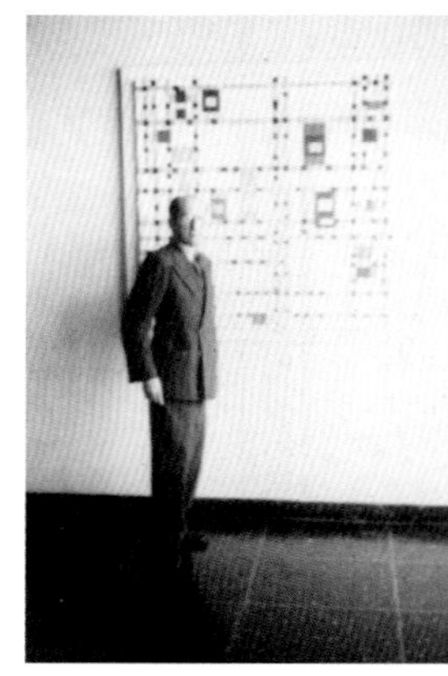

CAT. 298 Elizabeth 'Bobsy' Goodspeed Chapman

Piet Mondrian in the Museum of Modern Art, with *Broadway Boogie Woogie* (B323), October 1943
(see p. 264)

Gelatin developing-out paper, 13 x 8,5 cm

Collection Robert Storr

See also cats 296 and 299.

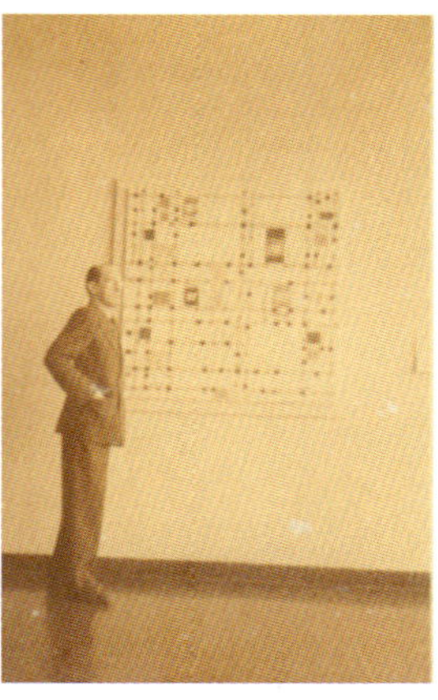

CAT. 299 Elizabeth 'Bobsy' Goodspeed Chapman

Piet Mondriaan in the Museum of Modern Art, with *Broadway Boogie Woogie* (B323), October 1943 (see p. 264)

Gelatin developing-out paper, 12 x 6,9 cm
Recto (to the right of photograph, but pertaining to cats 296–99), in Elizabeth Goodspeed's handwriting: 'Piet / Mondrian / and his / "Boogie / Woogie" / 1942 / – / 1943 / at the / Museum / of / Modern / Art'

Collection Robert Storr

See also cat. 296.

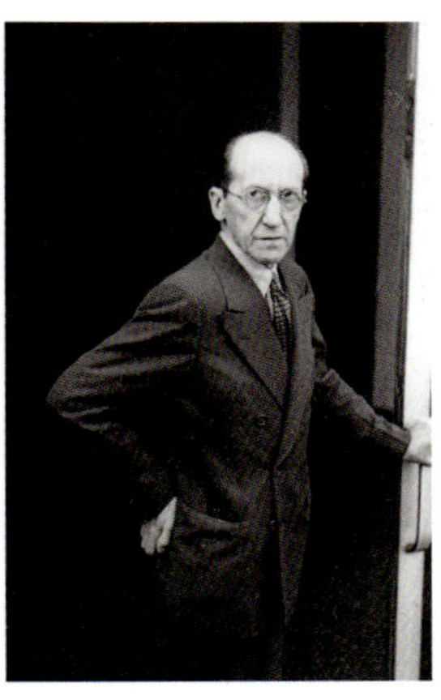

CAT. 300 Elizabeth 'Bobsy' Goodspeed Chapman

Piet Mondrian at the entrance to the Museum of Modern Art's sculpture garden, October 1943 (see p. 265)

Gelatin developing-out paper, 13 x 8,5 cm

Recto (above photograph), in Elizabeth Goodspeed's handwriting: 'Museum of Modern Art'; (beneath photograph): 'Piet Mondrian'

Collection Robert Storr

See also cat. 296.

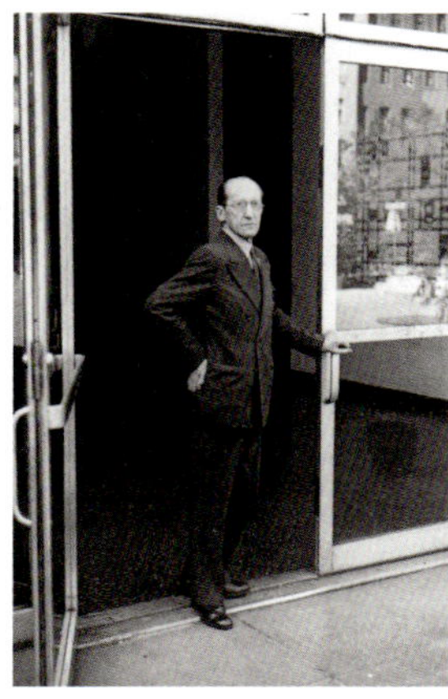

CAT. 301 Elizabeth 'Bobsy' Goodspeed Chapman

Piet Mondrian at the entrance to the Museum of Modern Art's sculpture garden, October 1943 (see p. 265)

Gelatin developing-out paper, 13 x 8,5 cm

Collection Robert Storr

See also cat. 296. For the caption, see cat. 300.

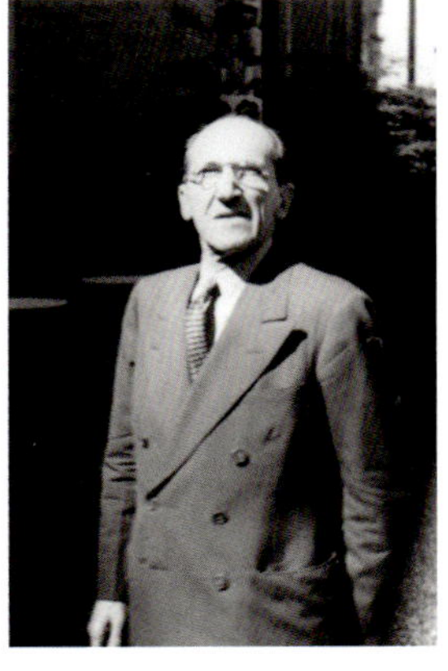

CAT. 302 Elizabeth 'Bobsy' Goodspeed Chapman

Piet Mondrian in the Museum of Modern Art's sculpture garden, October 1943 (see p. 265)

Gelatin developing-out paper, 13 x 8,5 cm

Collection Robert Storr

See also cat. 296.

For the caption, see cat. 300.

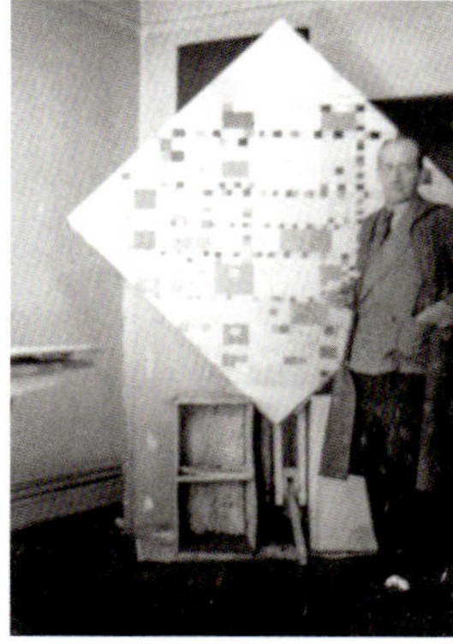

CAT. 303 Elizabeth 'Bobsy' Goodspeed Chapman

Piet Mondrian in his studio, next to *Victory Boogie Woogie* (B324), October 1943 (see p. 264)

Gelatin developing-out paper, 10,9 x 7,6 cm

Recto (beneath the photograph) in Elizabeth Goodspeed's handwriting: 'In his studio'

Collection Robert Storr

See also cat. 296.

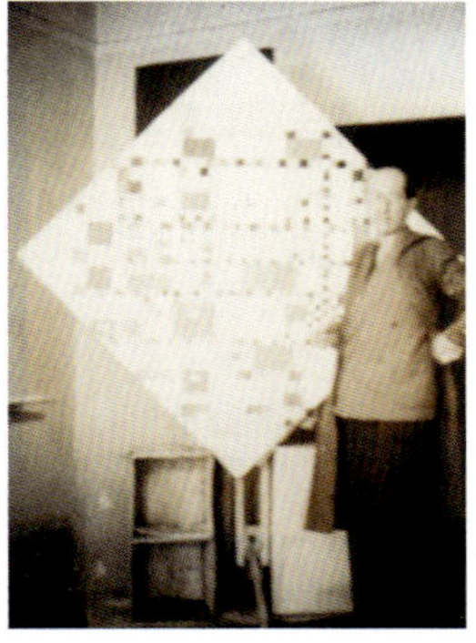

CAT. 304 Elizabeth 'Bobsy' Goodspeed Chapman

Piet Mondriaan in his studio, with *Victory Boogie Woogie* (B324), October 1943 (see p. 264)

Gelatin developing-out paper, 10,7 x 7,4 cm
Recto (beneath the photograph) in Elizabeth Goodspeed's handwriting: 'Boogie Woogie 1943'

Collection Robert Storr

See also cat. 296.

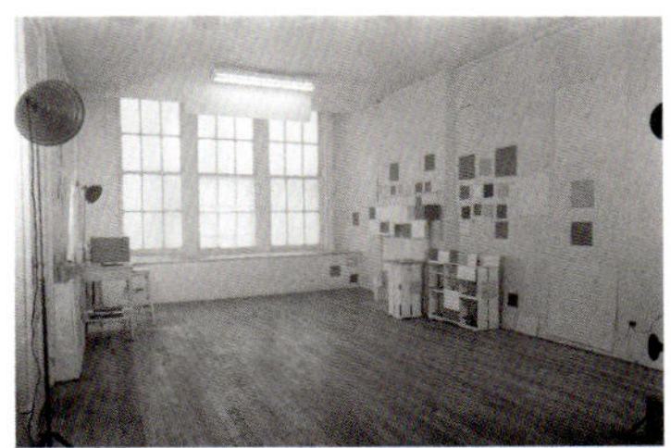

CAT. 305 Fritz Glarner

Mondrian's studio after his death, between 2 February and 21 March 1944 (see pp. 268–69)

Contact print from a 35 mm negative, 2.4 x 3.6 cm

Zurich, Kunsthaus, Glarner Archiv, no inv., sheet 2, strip 7, negative [illegible]; sheet 10, strip 1, negatives 29–32

The precise date of the session or sessions when Glarner shot his series of pictures is not known; see p. 266.

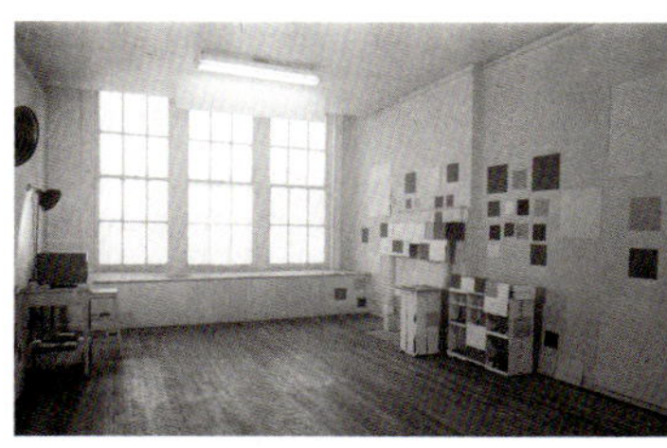

CAT. 306 Fritz Glarner

Mondrian's studio after his death, between 2 February and 21 March 1944

Contact print from a 35 mm negative, 2.4 x 3.6 cm

Zurich, Kunsthaus, Glarner Archiv, no inv., sheet 10, strips 1–3, negatives 33–40

For the dating, see cat. 305.

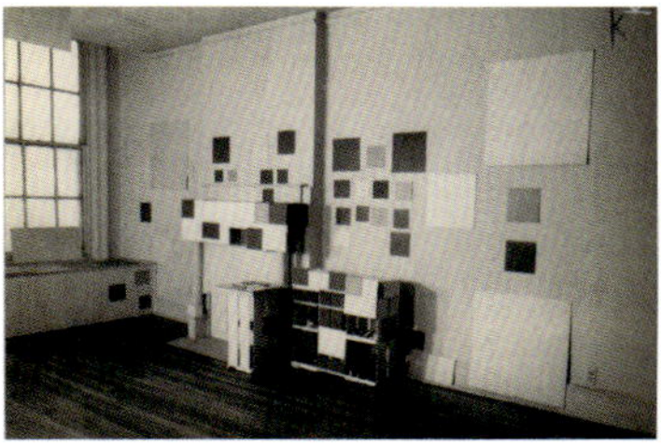

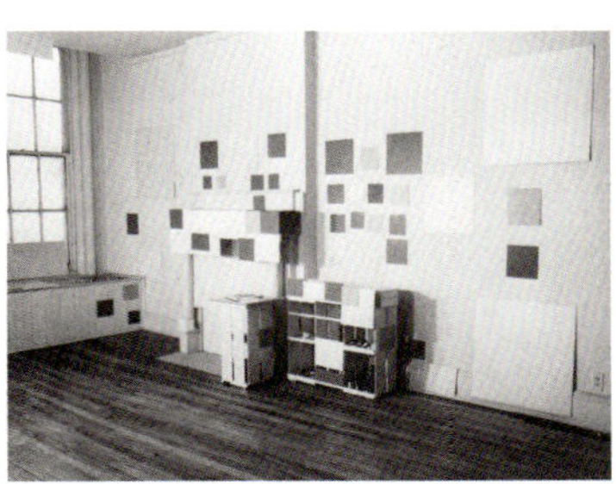

CAT. 307.1; CAT. 307.2 Fritz Glarner

Mondrian's studio after his death, between 2 February and 21 March 1944

(1) Gelatin developing-out paper, 7.6 x 10.7 cm; (2) contact print of a 35 mm negative, 2.4 x 3.6 cm

(1) Private collection; (2) Zurich, Kunsthaus, Glarner Archiv, no inv., sheet 4, strips 6–7, negatives 3–5

For the dating, see cat. 305.

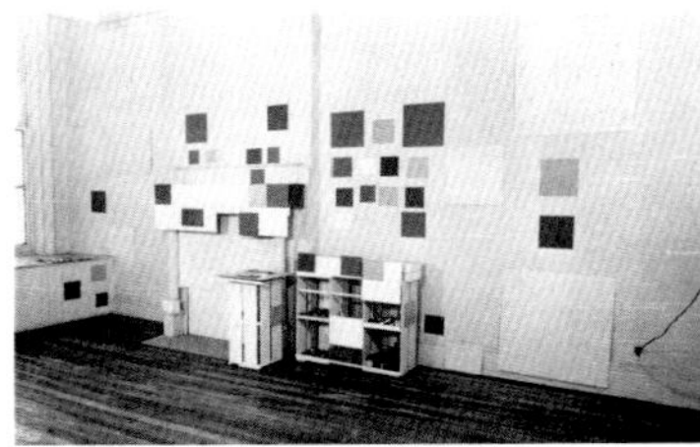

CAT. 308 Fritz Glarner

Mondrian's studio after his death, between 2 February and 21 March 1944
(see p. 270)

Contact print from a 35 mm negative, 2.4 x 3.6 cm

Zurich, Kunsthaus, Glarner Archiv, no inv., sheet 4, strips 6–7, negatives 4–5

For the dating, see cat. 305.

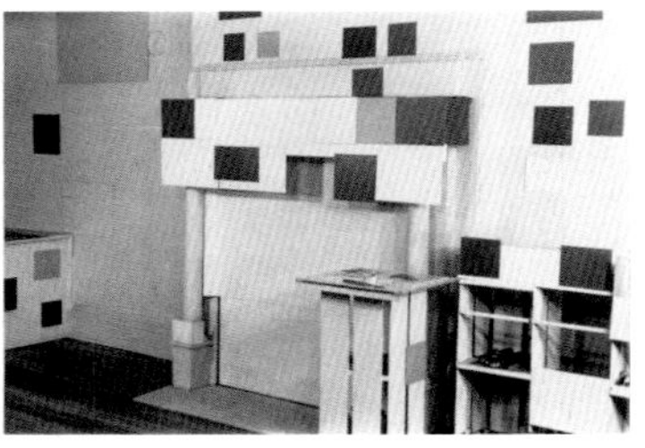

CAT. 309 Fritz Glarner

Mondrian's studio after his death, with his palette table in the middle, and a shelf-unit with painting materials on the right, between 2 February and 21 March 1944
(see p. 271)

Contact print from a 35 mm negative, 2.4 x 3.6 cm

Zurich, Kunsthaus, Glarner Archiv, no inv., sheet 1, strip 5, negatives 30–31

For the dating, see cat. 305.

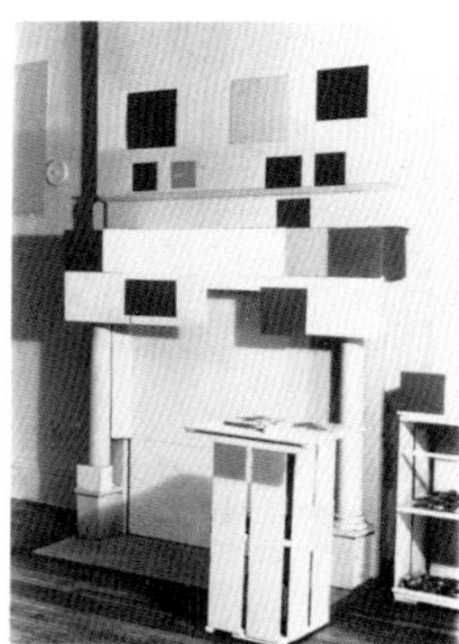

CAT. 310 Fritz Glarner

Mondrian's studio after his death, with his palette table in the foreground, between 2 February and 21 March 1944

Contact print from a 35 mm negative, 3.6 x 2.4 cm

Zurich, Kunsthaus, Glarner Archiv, no inv., sheet 10, strip 7, negatives 25–8

For the dating, see cat. 305.

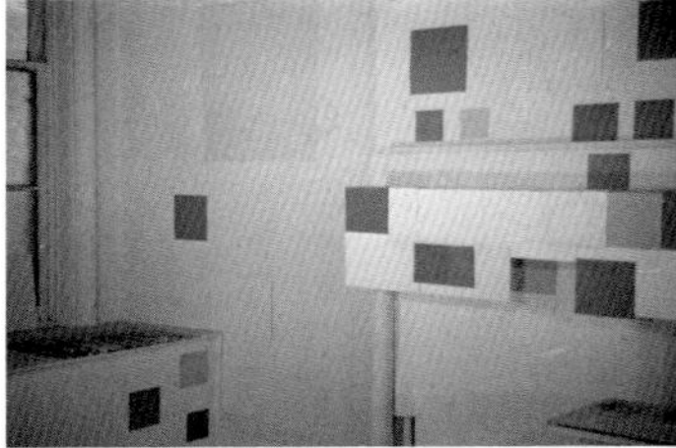

CAT. 311 Fritz Glarner

Mondrian's studio after his death; on the left, in front of the window, several dozen paintbrushes, between 2 February and 21 March 1944

Contact print from a 35 mm negative, 2.4 x 3.6 cm

Zurich, Kunsthaus, Glarner Archiv, no inv., sheet 11, strip 4, negative 3

For the dating, see cat. 305.

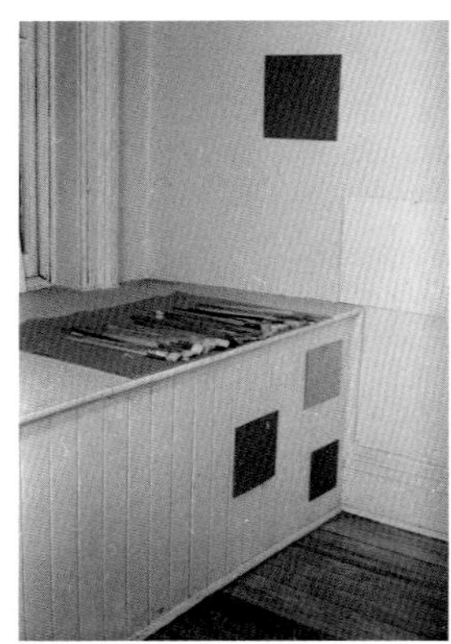

CAT. 312 Fritz Glarner

Paintbrushes in Mondrian's studio after his death, between 2 February and 21 March 1944 (see p. 272)

Contact print from a 35 mm negative, 3.6 x 2.4 cm

Zurich, Kunsthaus, Glarner Archiv, no inv., sheet 10, strip 6, negative 23

For the dating, see cat. 305.

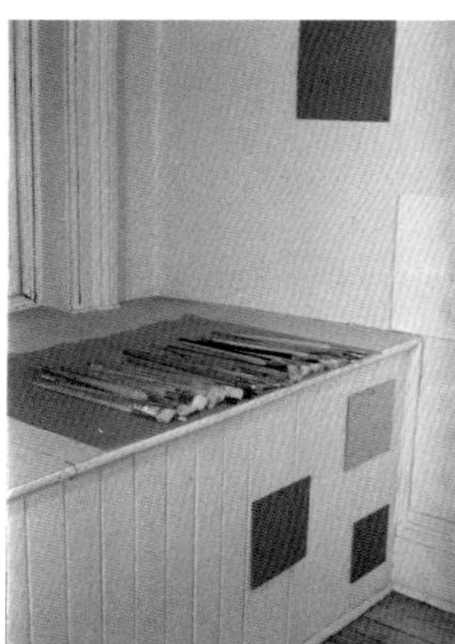

CAT. 313 Fritz Glarner

Paintbrushes in Mondrian's studio after his death, between 2 February and 21 March 1944

Contact print from a 35 mm negative, 3.6 x 2.4 cm

Zurich, Kunsthaus, Glarner Archiv, no inv., sheet 10, strip 7, negative [24]

For the dating, see cat. 305.

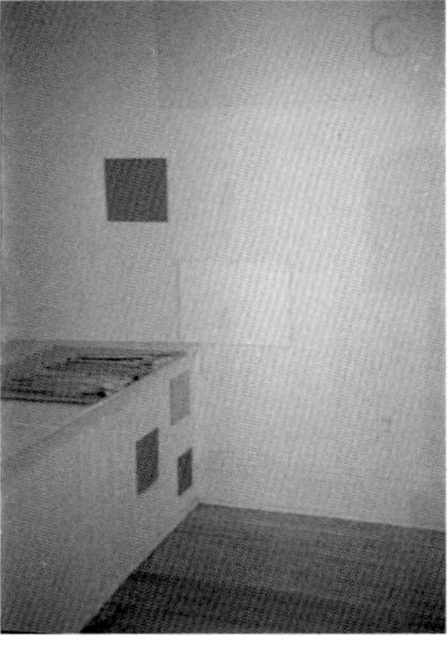

CAT. 314 Fritz Glarner

Paintbrushes in Mondrian's studio after his death, between 2 February and 21 March 1944

Contact print from a 35 mm negative, 3.6 x 2.4 cm

Zurich, Kunsthaus, Glarner Archiv, no inv., sheet 11, strip 3, negative 1

For the dating, see cat. 305.

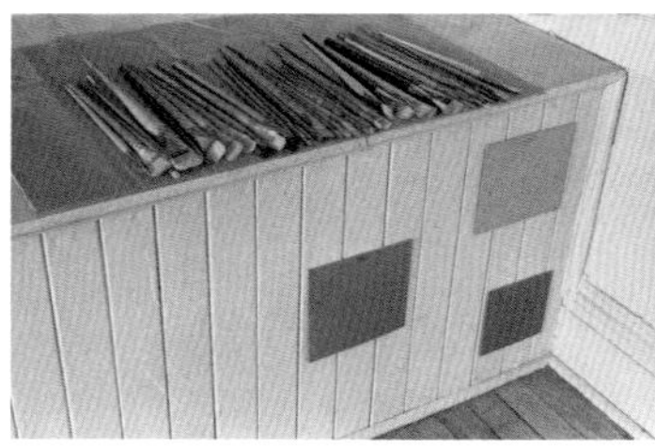

CAT. 315 Fritz Glarner

Paintbrushes in Mondrian's studio after his death, between 2 February and 21 March 1944 (see p. 273)

Contact print from a 35 mm negative, 2.4 x 3.6 cm

Zurich, Kunsthaus, Glarner Archiv, no inv., sheet 1, strip 6, negative 37

For the dating, see cat. 305.

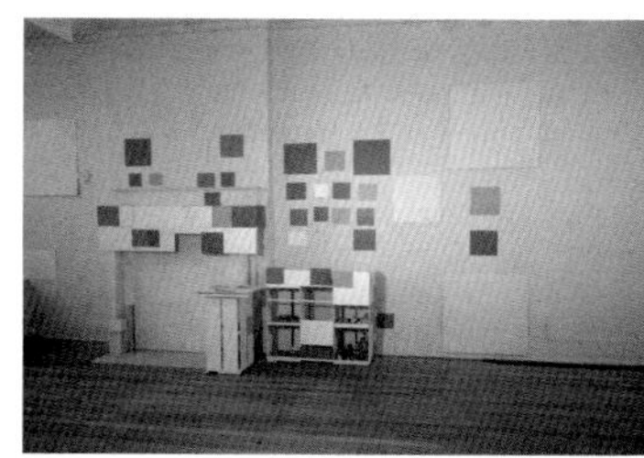

CAT. 316 Fritz Glarner

Mondrian's studio after his death; view of the east wall, with his palette table in front of the fireplace, alongside a shelf-unit with painting materials, between 2 February and 21 March 1944
(see pp. 274—75)

Contact print from a 35 mm negative, 2.4 x 3.6 cm

Zurich, Kunsthaus, Glarner Archiv, no inv., sheet 4, strip 2, negatives 24–8

For the dating, see cat. 305.

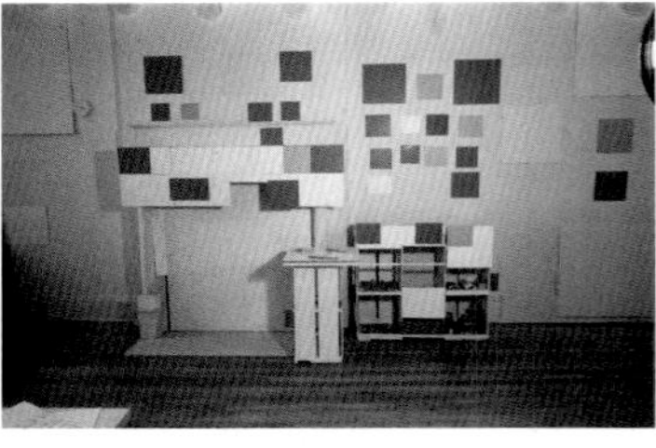

CAT. 317 Fritz Glarner

Mondrian's studio after his death; view of the east wall, with his palette table in front of the fireplace, alongside a shelf-unit with painting materials, between 2 February and 21 March 1944

Contact print from a 35 mm negative, 2.4 x 3.6 cm

Zurich, Kunsthaus, Glarner Archiv, no inv., sheet 4, strip 3, negatives 29–33

For the dating, see cat. 305.

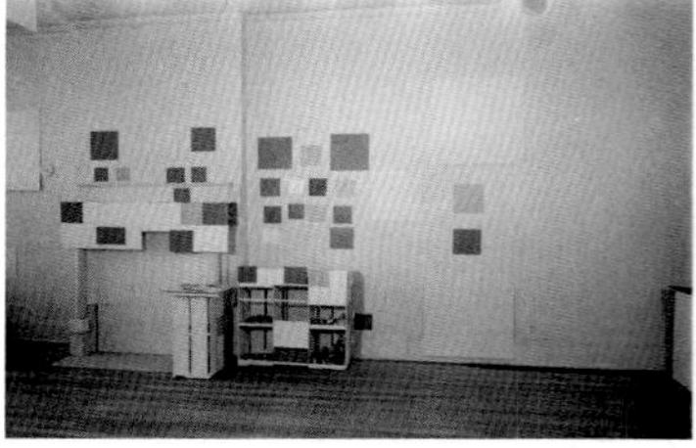

CAT. 318 Fritz Glarner

Mondrian's studio after his death; view of the east wall, with his palette table in front of the fireplace, alongside a shelf-unit with painting materials, between 2 February and 21 March 1944

Contact print from a 35 mm negative, 2.4 x 3.6 cm

Zurich, Kunsthaus, Glarner Archiv, no inv., sheet 1, strip 2, negative 22

For the dating, see cat. 305.

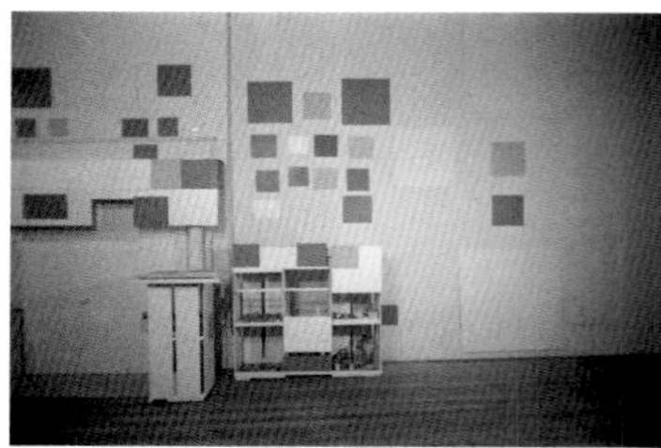

CAT. 319 Fritz Glarner

Mondrian's studio after his death; view of the east wall, with his palette table in front of the fireplace, alongside a shelf-unit with painting

materials, between 2 February and 21 March 1944
Contact print from a 35 mm negative, 2.4 x 3.6 cm
Zurich, Kunsthaus, Glarner Archiv, no inv., sheet 11, strip 7, negatives 17–19
For the dating, see cat. 305.

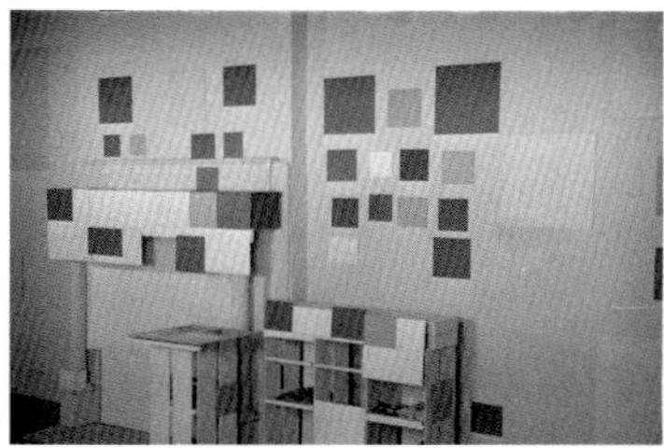

CAT. 320 Fritz Glarner
Mondrian's studio after his death; decoration of the east wall, with his palette table in front of the fireplace and, to the right, a shelf-unit with painting materials, between 2 February and 21 March 1944
Contact print from a 35 mm negative, 2.4 x 3.6 cm
Zurich, Kunsthaus, Glarner Archiv, no inv., sheet 11, strip 5, negative 7
For the dating, see cat. 305.

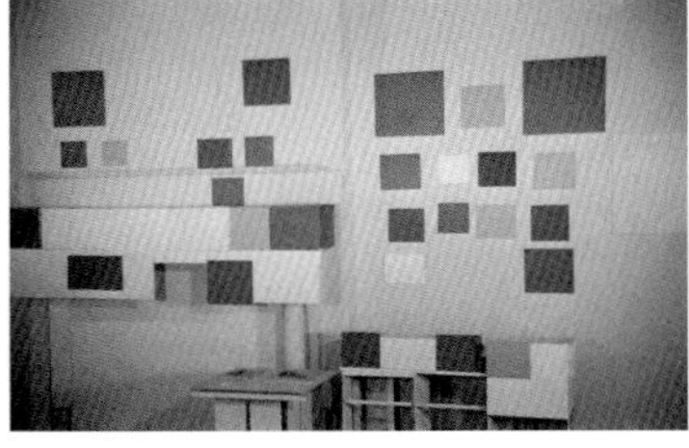

CAT. 321 Fritz Glarner
Mondrian's studio after his death; decoration of the east wall, with his palette table in front of the fireplace and, to the right, a shelf-unit with painting materials, between 2 February and 21 March 1944
Contact print from a 35 mm negative, 2.4 x 3.6 cm
Zurich, Kunsthaus, Glarner Archiv, no inv., sheet 11, strip 3, negative 43
For the dating, see cat. 305.

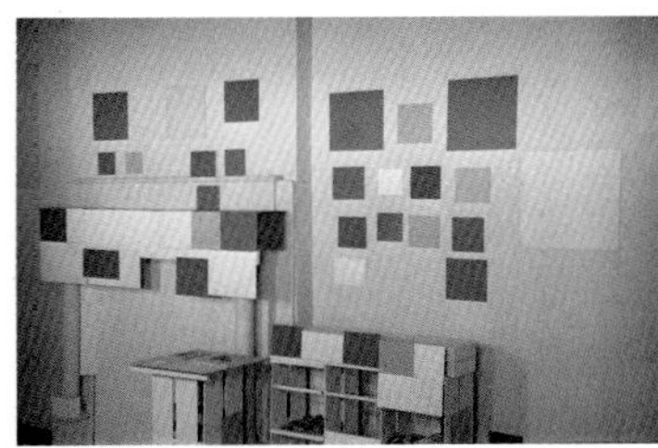

CAT. 322 Fritz Glarner
Mondrian's studio after his death; decoration of the east wall, with his palette table in front of the fireplace and a shelf-unit with painting materials to the right, between 2 February and 21 March 1944
Contact print from a 35 mm negative, 2.4 x 3.6 cm
Zurich, Kunsthaus, Glarner Archiv, no inv., sheet 11, strip 4, negative 5
For the dating, see cat. 305.

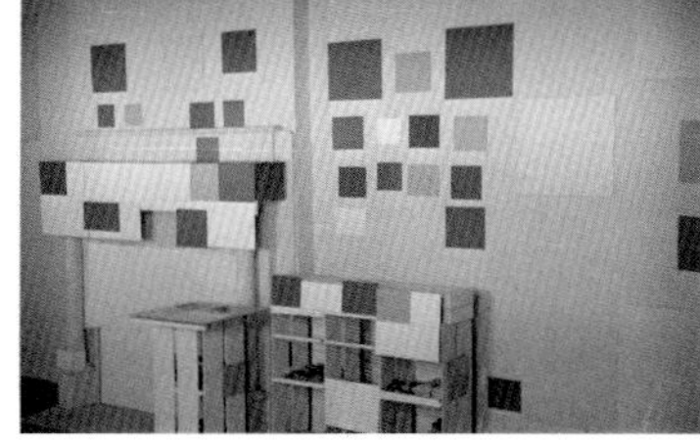

CAT. 323 Fritz Glarner
Mondrian's studio after his death; decoration of the east wall, with his palette table in front of the fireplace and, to the right, a shelf-unit with painting materials, between 2 February and 21 March 1944
Contact print from a 35 mm negative, 2.4 x 3.6 cm
Zurich, Kunsthaus, Glarner Archiv, no inv., sheet 11, strip 4, negative 6
For the dating, see cat. 305.

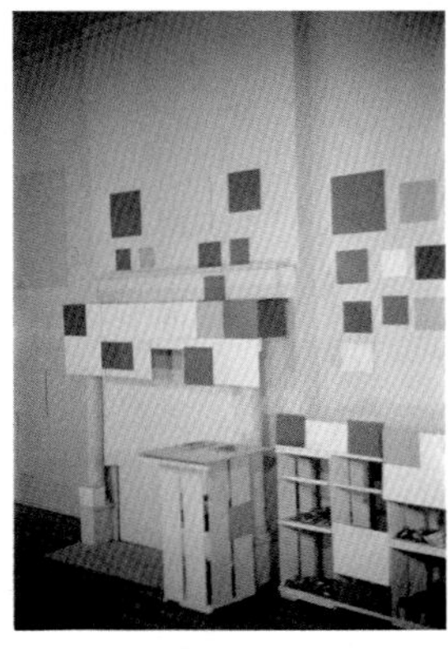

CAT. 324 Fritz Glarner
Mondrian's studio after his death; decoration of the east wall, with his palette table in front of the fireplace and, to the right, a shelf-unit with painting materials, between 2 February and 21 March 1944
(see p. 273)
Contact print from a 35 mm negative, 3.6 x 2.4 cm
Zurich, Kunsthaus, Glarner Archiv, no inv., sheet 11, strip 4, negative 2
For the dating, see cat. 305.

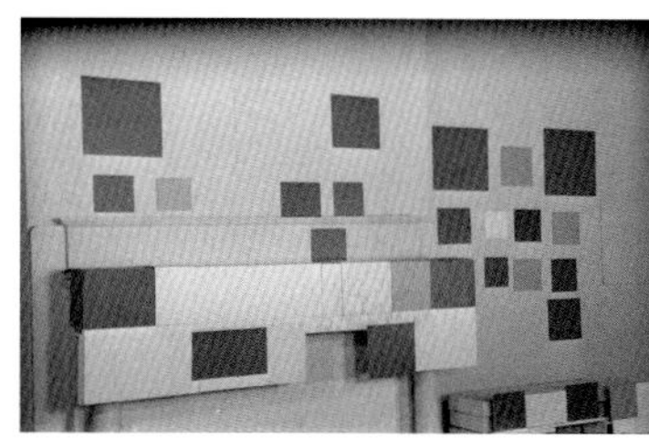

CAT. 325 Fritz Glarner
Mondrian's studio after his death; decoration of the east wall, between 2 February and 21 March 1944
Contact print from a 35 mm negative, 2.4 x 3.6 cm
Zurich, Kunsthaus, Glarner Archiv, no inv., sheet 11, strip 5, negative 11
For the dating, see cat. 305.

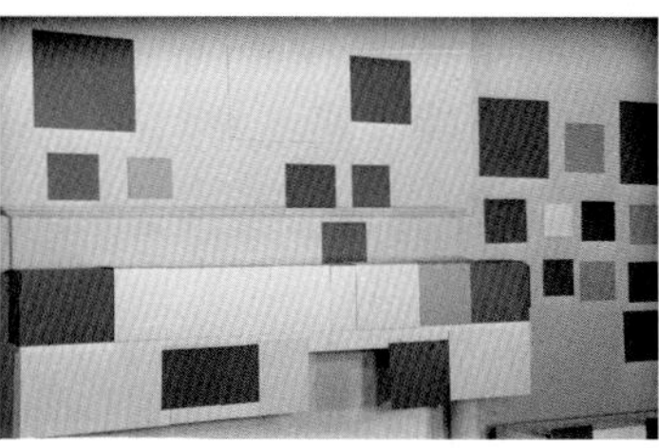

CAT. 326 Fritz Glarner
Mondrian's studio after his death; decoration of the east wall, between 2 February and 21 March 1944
Contact print from a 35 mm negative, 2.4 x 3.6 cm
Zurich, Kunsthaus, Glarner Archiv, no inv., sheet 11, strip 5, negative 10
For the dating, see cat. 305.

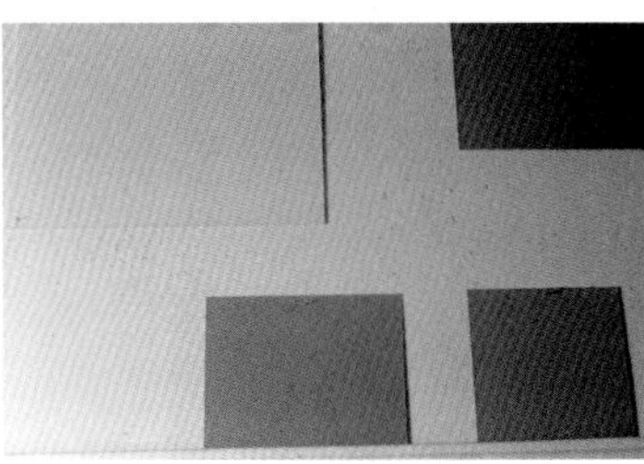

CAT. 327 Fritz Glarner
Mondrian's studio after his death; decoration of the east wall (detail), between 2 February and 21 March 1944
Contact print from a 35 mm negative, 2.4 x 3.6 cm
Zurich, Kunsthaus, Glarner Archiv, no inv., sheet 11, strip 2, negatives 40–42
For the dating, see cat. 305.

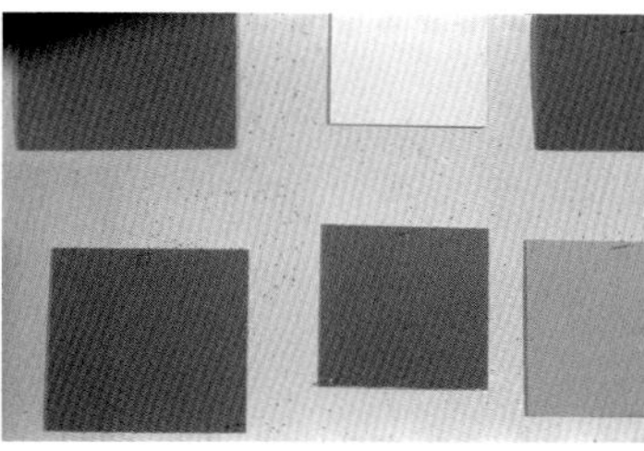

CAT. 328 Fritz Glarner
Mondrian's studio after his death; decoration of the east wall (detail), between 2 February and 21 March 1944
Contact print from a 35 mm negative, 2.4 x 3.6 cm
Zurich, Kunsthaus, Glarner Archiv, no inv., sheet 1, strip 6, negatives 34–5
For the dating, see cat. 305.

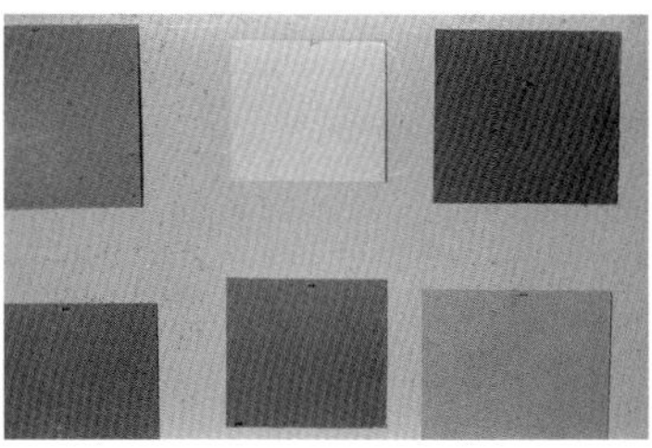

CAT. 329 Fritz Glarner
Mondrian's studio after his death; decoration of the east wall (detail), between 2 February and 21 March 1944
Contact print from a 35 mm negative, 2.4 x 3.6 cm
Zurich, Kunsthaus, Glarner Archiv, no inv., sheet 11, strips 1–2, negatives 34–9
For the dating, see cat. 305.

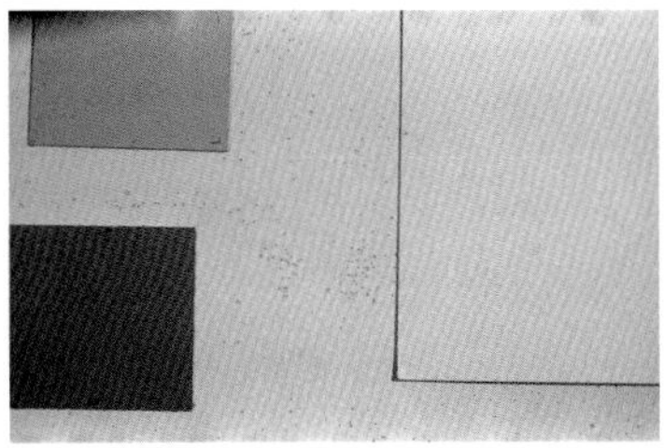

CAT. 330 Fritz Glarner
Mondrian's studio after his death; decoration of the east wall (detail), between 2 February and 21 March 1944
Contact print from a 35 mm negative, 2.4 x 3.6 cm
Zurich, Kunsthaus, Glarner Archiv, no inv., sheet 1, strip 5, negatives 32–3
For the dating, see cat. 305.

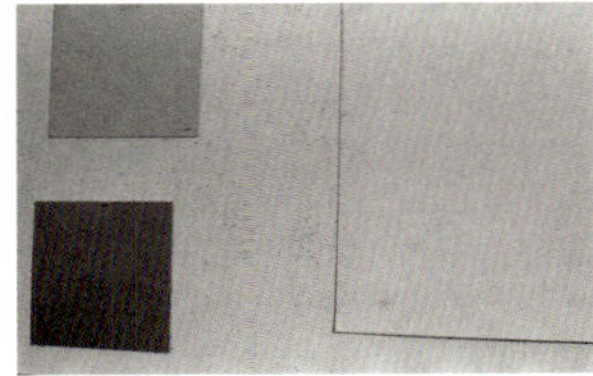

CAT. 331 Fritz Glarner

Mondrian's studio after his death; decoration of the east wall (detail), between 2 February and 21 March 1944

Contact print from a 35 mm negative, 2.4 x 3.6 cm

Zurich, Kunsthaus, Glarner Archiv, no inv., sheet 1, strip 6, negative 36

For the dating, see cat. 305.

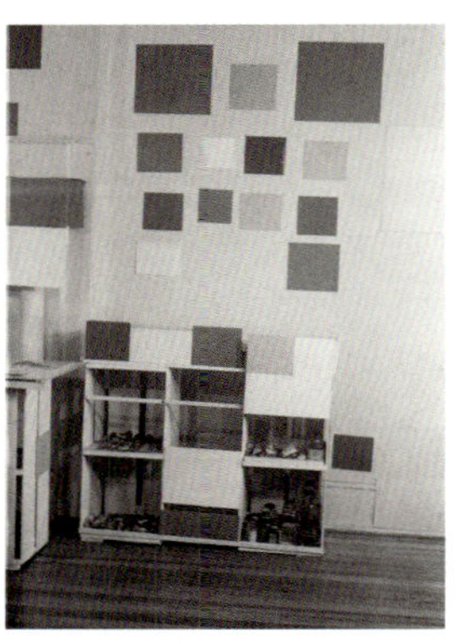

CAT. 332 Fritz Glarner

Mondrian's studio after his death; decoration of the east wall and a shelf-unit with painting materials, between 2 February and 21 March 1944

Contact print from a 35 mm negative, 3.6 x 2.4 cm

Zurich, Kunsthaus, Glarner Archiv, no inv., sheet 1, strip 5, negative 29

For the dating, see cat. 305.

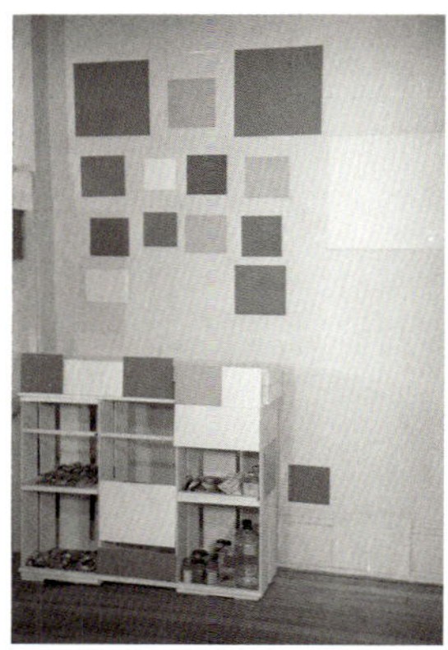

CAT. 333 Fritz Glarner

Mondrian's studio after his death; decoration of the east wall and a shelf-unit with painting materials, between 2 February and 21 March 1944

Contact print from a 35 mm negative, 3.6 x 2.4 cm

Zurich, Kunsthaus, Glarner Archiv, no inv., sheet 11, strip 4, negative 4

For the dating, see cat. 305.

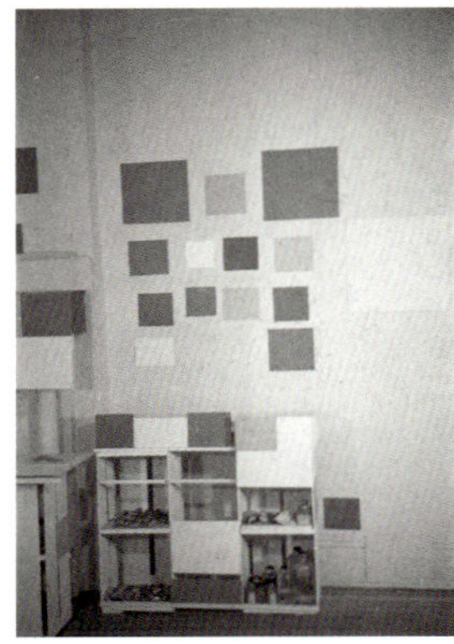

CAT. 334 Fritz Glarner

Mondrian's studio after his death; decoration of the east wall and a shelf-unit with painting materials, between 2 February and 21 March 1944

Contact print from a 35 mm negative, 3.6 x 2.4 cm

Zurich, Kunsthaus, Glarner Archiv, no inv., sheet 11, strip 3, negative 44

For the dating, see cat. 305.

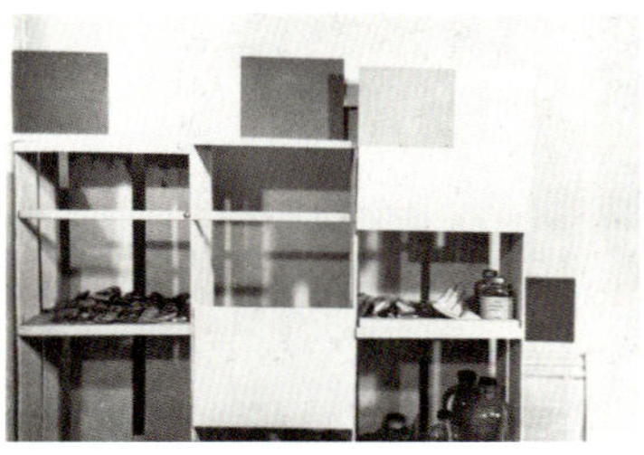

CAT. 335 Fritz Glarner

Shelf-unit with Mondrian's painting materials in his studio after his death, between 2 February and 21 March 1944

No vintage print of this photograph has been traced; the reproduction shown here is a later print (The Hague, RKD, Collectie Kunstenaarsportretten)

For the dating, see cat. 305.

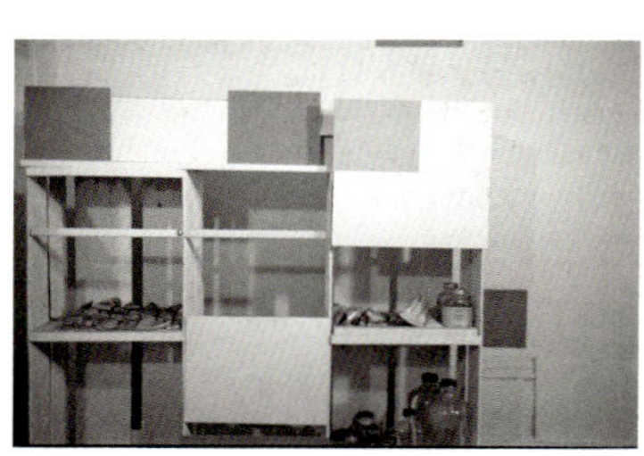

CAT. 336 Fritz Glarner

Shelf-unit with Mondrian's painting materials in his studio after his death, between 2 February and 21 March 1944 (see p. 276)

Contact print from a 35 mm negative, 2.4 x 3.6 cm

Zurich, Kunsthaus, Glarner Archiv, no inv., sheet 11, strip 3, negative 42

For the dating, see cat. 305.

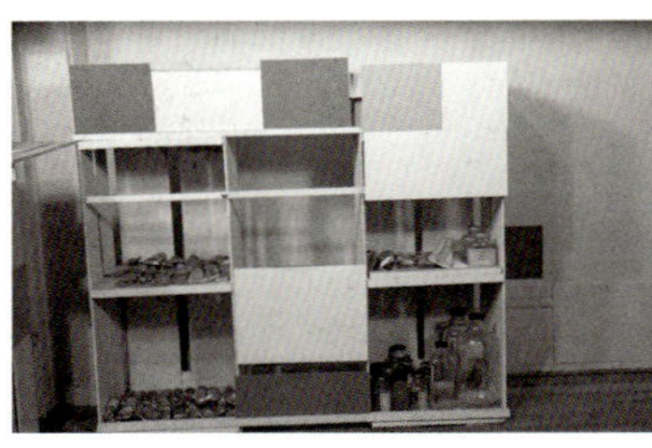

CAT. 337 Fritz Glarner

Shelf-unit with Mondrian's painting materials in his studio after his death, between 2 February and 21 March 1944

Contact print from a 35 mm negative, 2.4 x 3.6 cm

Zurich, Kunsthaus, Glarner Archiv, no inv., sheet 11, strip 6, negative 14

For the dating, see cat. 305.

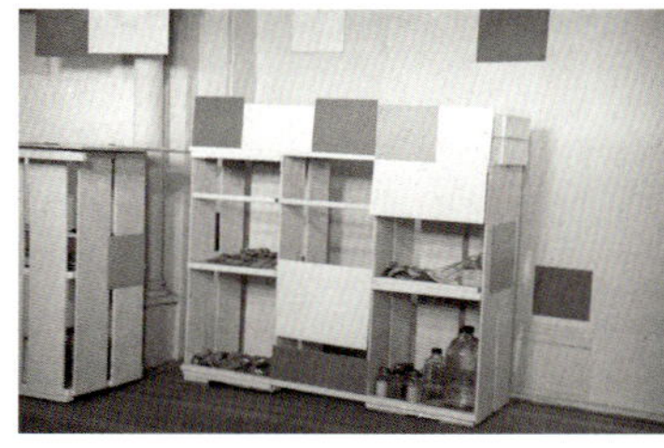

CAT. 338 Fritz Glarner

Palette table and shelf-unit with Mondrian's painting materials in his studio after his death, between 2 February and 21 March 1944

Contact print from a 35 mm negative, 2.4 x 3.6 cm

Zurich, Kunsthaus, Glarner Archiv, no inv., sheet 11, strip 5, negative 8

For the dating, see cat. 305.

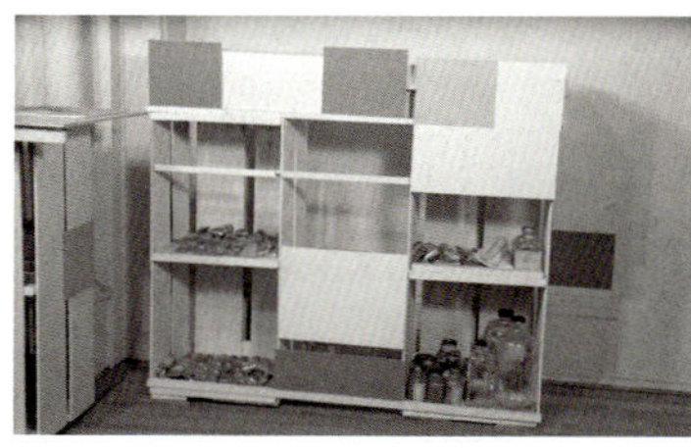

CAT. 339 Fritz Glarner

Palette table and shelf-unit with Mondrian's painting materials in his studio after his death, between 2 February and 21 March 1944

Contact print from a 35 mm negative, 2.4 x 3.6 cm

Zurich, Kunsthaus, Glarner Archiv, no inv., sheet 11, strip 6, negative 15

For the dating, see cat. 305.

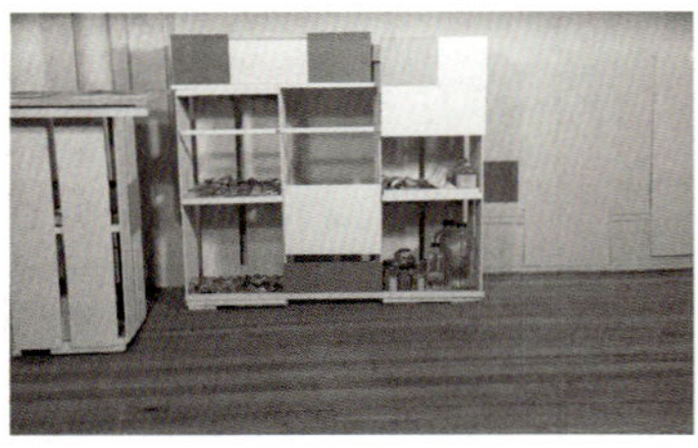

CAT. 340 Fritz Glarner

Palette table and shelf-unit with Mondrian's painting materials in his studio after his death, between 2 February and 21 March 1944

Contact print from a 35 mm negative, 2.4 x 3.6 cm

Zurich, Kunsthaus, Glarner Archiv, no inv., sheet 11, strip 6, negative 16

For the dating, see cat. 305.

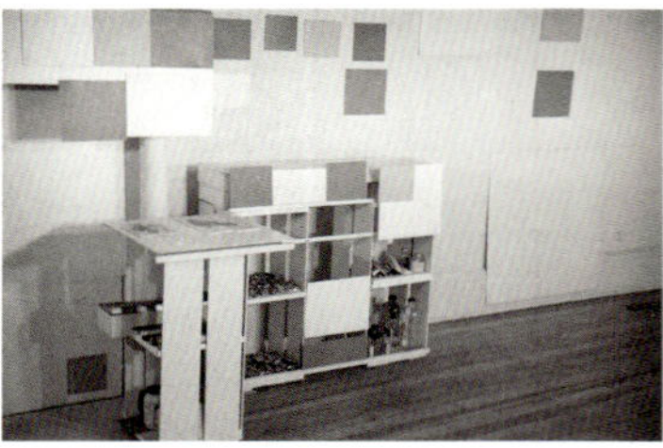

CAT. 341 Fritz Glarner

Palette table and shelf-unit with Mondrian's painting materials in his studio after his death, between 2 February and 21 March 1944

Contact print from a 35 mm negative, 2.4 x 3.6 cm

Zurich, Kunsthaus, Glarner Archiv, no inv., sheet 11, strip 5, negative 9

For the dating, see cat. 305.

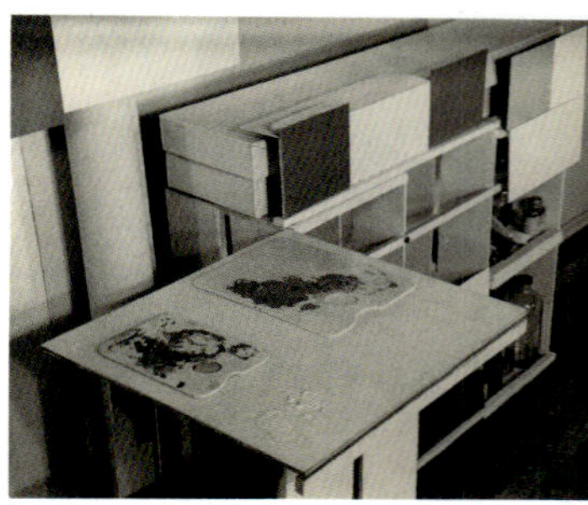

CAT. 342 Fritz Glarner

Palette table with palettes and a shelf-unit with painting materials in Mondrian's studio after his death, between 2 February and 21 March 1944

Gelatin developing-out paper, 7 x 8.3 cm
Private collection

For the dating, see cat. 305.

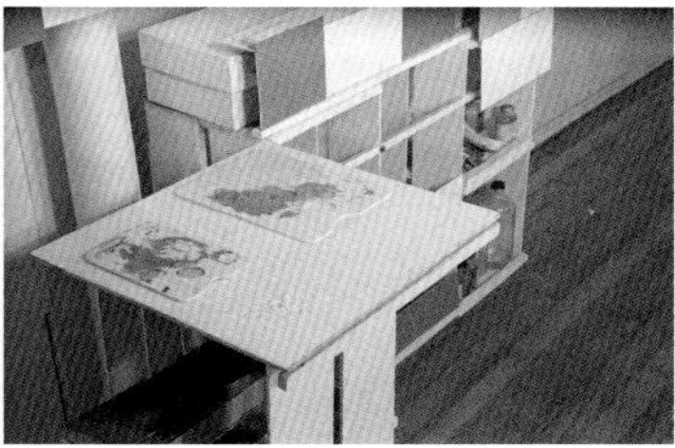

CAT. 343 Fritz Glarner

Palette table with palettes and a shelf-unit with painting materials in Mondrian's studio after his death, between 2 February and 21 March 1944 (see p. 277)

Contact print from a 35 mm negative, 2.4 x 3.6 cm

Zurich, Kunsthaus, Glarner Archiv, no inv., sheet 11, strip 6, negative 13

For the dating, see cat. 305.

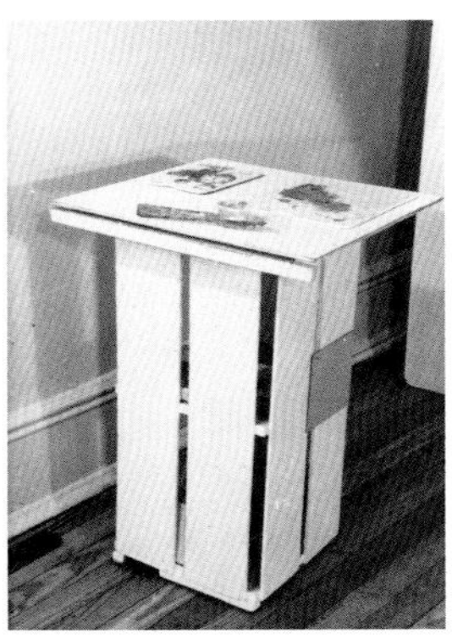

CAT. 344 Fritz Glarner

Palette table with palettes and a palette knife in Mondrian's studio after his death, between 2 February and 21 March 1944 (see p. 276)

Contact print from a 35 mm negative, 3.6 x 2.4 cm

Zurich, Kunsthaus, Glarner Archiv, no inv., sheet 9, strip 1, negatives 41–2

For the dating, see cat. 305.

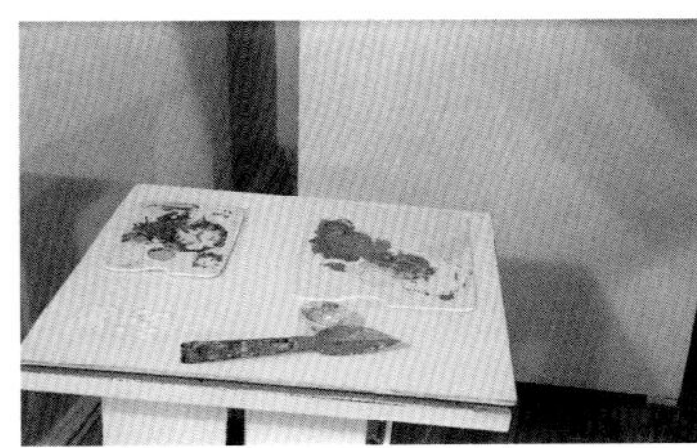

CAT. 345 Fritz Glarner

Palette table with palettes and a palette knife in Mondrian's studio after his death, between 2 February and 21 March 1944

Contact print from a 35 mm negative, 2.4 x 3.6 cm

Zurich, Kunsthaus, Glarner Archiv, no inv., sheet 9, strip 1, negative 43

For the dating, see cat. 305.

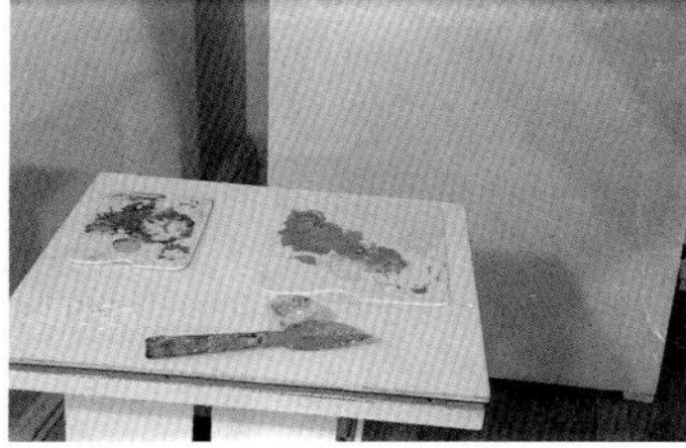

CAT. 346 Fritz Glarner

Palette table with palettes and a palette knife in Mondrian's studio after his death, between 2 February and 21 March 1944

Contact print from a 35 mm negative, 2.4 x 3.6 cm

Zurich, Kunsthaus, Glarner Archiv, no inv., sheet 9, strip 1, negative 4[4]

For the dating, see cat. 305.

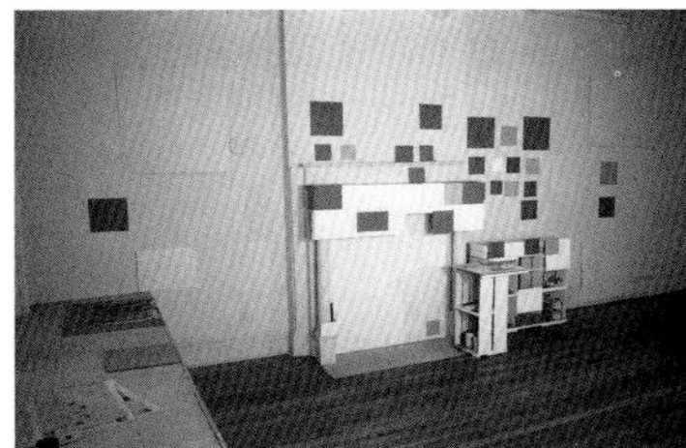

CAT. 347 Fritz Glarner

Mondrian's studio after his death, east wall, between 2 February and 21 March 1944 (see p. 278)

Contact print from a 35 mm negative, 2.4 x 3.6 cm

Zurich, Kunsthaus, Glarner Archiv, no inv., sheet 4, strips 5–6, negatives 42–4, 1–2

For the dating, see cat. 305.

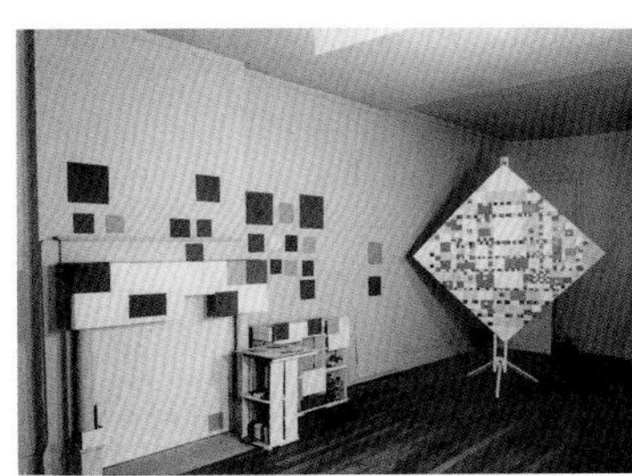

CAT. 348 Fritz Glarner

Mondrian's studio after his death, east wall, with *Victory Boogie Woogie* (B324) on the easel, between 2 February and 21 March 1944 (see p. 279)

Gelatin developing-out paper, 7.8 x 9.9 cm

Private collection

For the dating, see cat. 305.

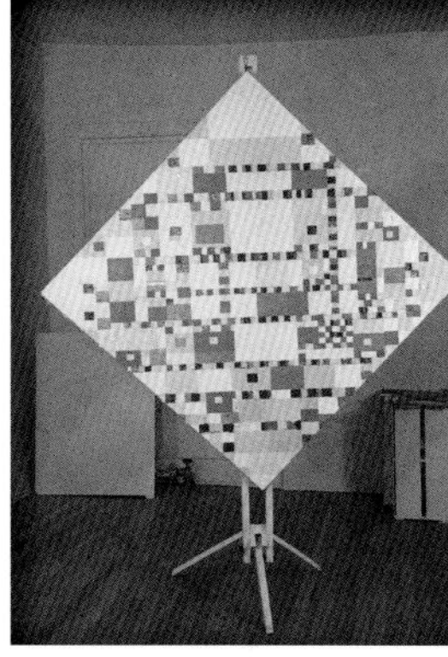

CAT. 349 Fritz Glarner

***Victory Boogie Woogie* (B324) on the easel in Mondrian's studio after his death, between 2 February and 21 March 1944**

Contact print from a 35 mm negative, 3.6 x 2.4 cm

Zurich, Kunsthaus, Glarner Archiv, no inv., sheet 10, strip 6, negative 21

For the dating, see cat. 305.

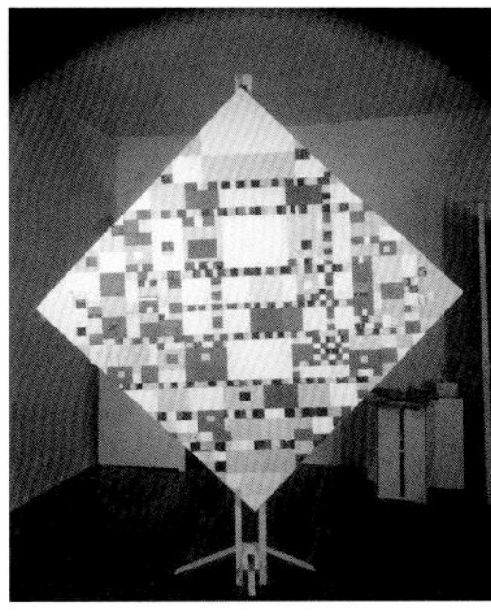

CAT. 350 Fritz Glarner (?)

***Victory Boogie Woogie* (B324) on the easel in Mondrian's studio after his death, between 2 February and 21 March 1944**

No vintage print of this photograph has been traced; the reproduction shown here is from Van Bommel 2011, p. 132 (courtesy Amsterdam University Press).

Although this photograph was previously attributed to Fritz Glarner, the quality of the shot is noticeably better than the other photographs attributed to Glarner. Moreover, the negative was not found in the Glarner Archiv in the Kunsthaus in Zurich. The attribution to Glarner is therefore with reservations.

For the dating, see cat. 305.

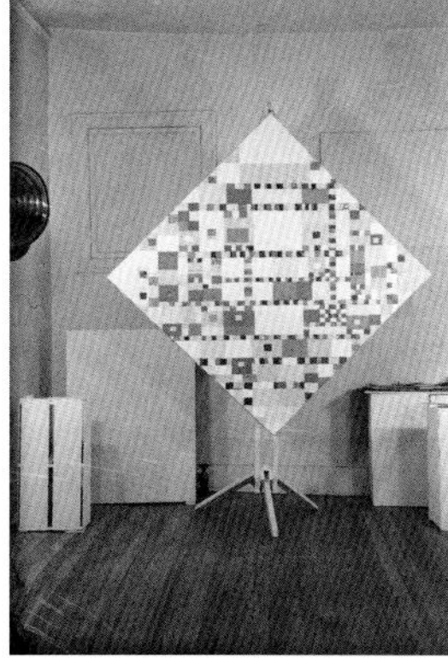

CAT. 351 Fritz Glarner

***Victory Boogie Woogie* (B324) on the easel in Mondrian's studio after his death, between 2 February and 21 March 1944**

Contact print from a 35 mm negative, 3.6 x 2.4 cm

Zurich, Kunsthaus, Glarner Archiv, no inv., sheet 9, strip 1, negative 40

For the dating, see cat. 305.

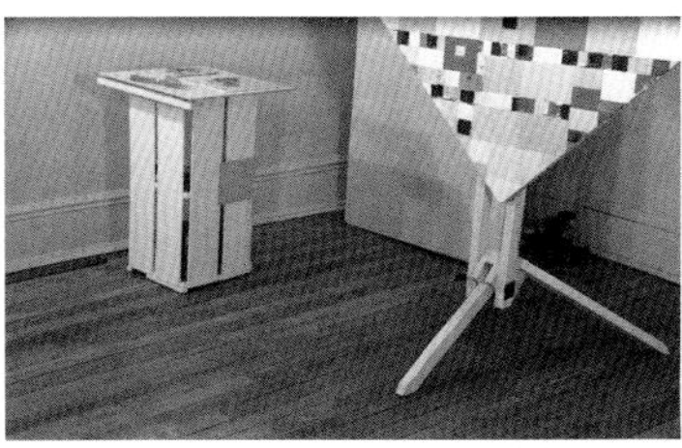

CAT. 352 Fritz Glarner

Palette table with palettes and palette knife next to *Victory Boogie Woogie* (B324) in Mondrian's studio after his death, between 2 February and 21 March 1944 (see p. 280)

Contact print from a 35 mm negative, 2.4 x 3.6 cm

Zurich, Kunsthaus, Glarner Archiv, no inv., sheet 9, strip 2, negatives 1–3

For the dating, see cat. 305.

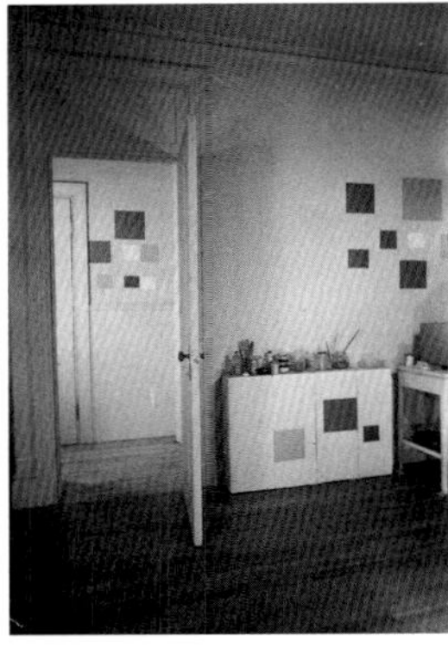

CAT. 353 Fritz Glarner

Part of the west wall of Mondrian's studio after his death, with a view through to the landing, between 2 February and 21 March 1944

Contact print from a 35 mm negative, 3.6 x 2.4 cm

Zurich, Kunsthaus, Glarner Archiv, no inv., sheet 1, strip 4, negatives [38]–41

For the dating, see cat. 305.

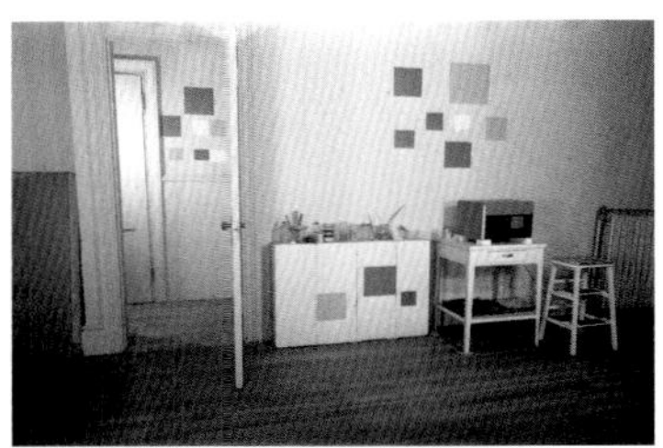

CAT. 354 Fritz Glarner

Part of the west wall and furniture in Mondrian's studio after his death, with a view through to the landing, between 2 February and 21 March 1944 (see p. 281)

Contact print from a 35 mm negative, 2.4 x 3.6 cm

Zurich, Kunsthaus, Glarner Archiv, no inv., sheet 12, strips 3–4, negatives 24–9

For the dating, see cat. 305.

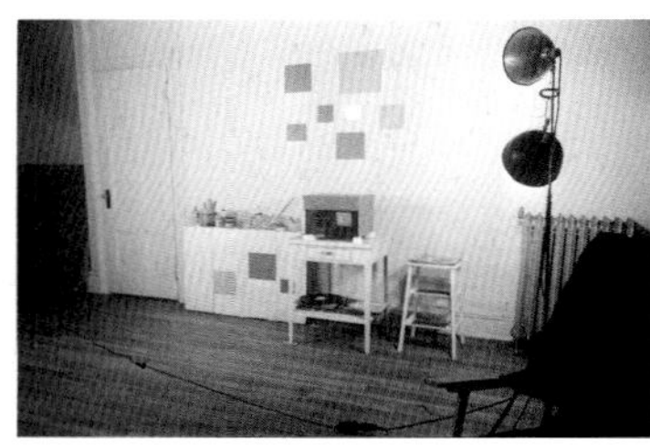

CAT. 355 Fritz Glarner

West wall of Mondrian's studio after his death, with furniture and gramophone, between 2 February and 21 March 1944

Contact print from a 35 mm negative, 2.4 x 3.6 cm

Zurich, Kunsthaus, Glarner Archiv, no inv., sheet 12, strip 3, negatives 35–7; strip 2, negative 38

For the dating, see cat. 305.

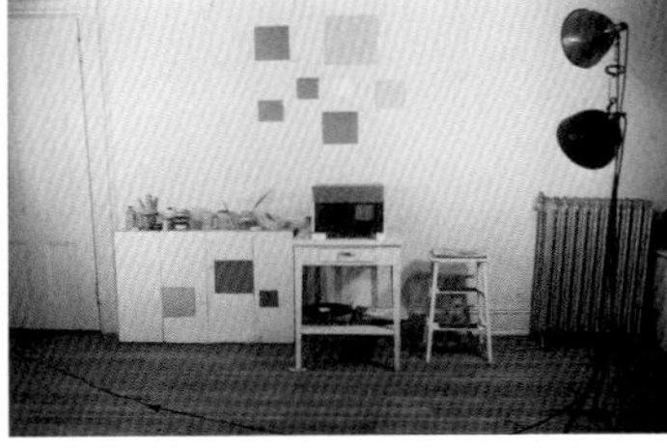

CAT. 356 Fritz Glarner

West wall of Mondrian's studio after his death, with furniture and gramophone, between 2 February and 21 March 1944

Contact print from a 35 mm negative, 2.4 x 3.6 cm

Zurich, Kunsthaus, Glarner Archiv, no inv., sheet 12, strips 4–5, negatives 30–34

For the dating, see cat. 305.

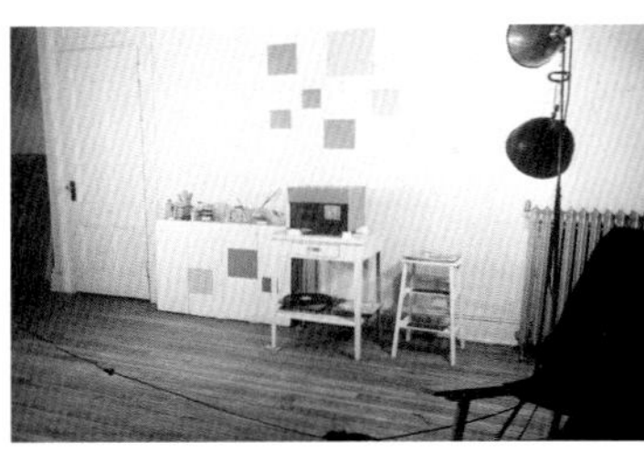

CAT. 357 Fritz Glarner

West wall of Mondrian's studio after his death, with furniture and gramophone, between 2 February and 21 March 1944

Contact print from a 35 mm negative, 2.4 x 3.6 cm

Zurich, Kunsthaus, Glarner Archiv, no inv., sheet 12, strip 2, negatives 39–40

For the dating, see cat. 305.

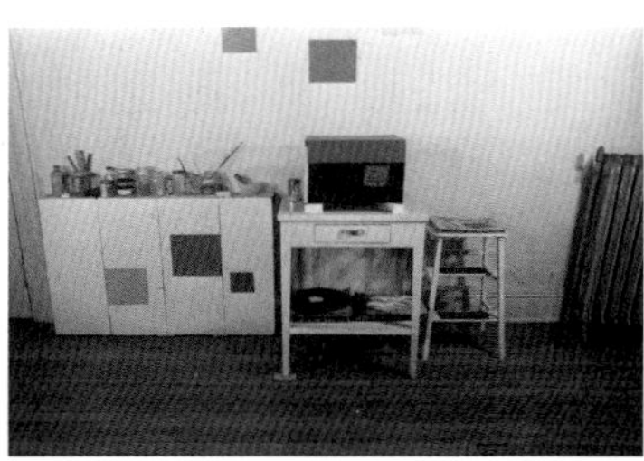

CAT. 358 Fritz Glarner

West wall of Mondrian's studio after his death, with furniture and gramophone, between 2 February and 21 March 1944

Contact print from a 35 mm negative, 2.4 x 3.6 cm

Zurich, Kunsthaus, Glarner Archiv, no inv., sheet 12, strip 6, negative 43

For the dating, see cat. 305.

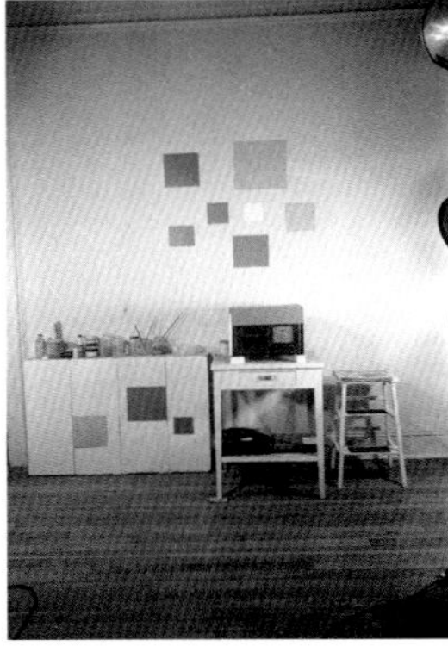

CAT. 359 Fritz Glarner

West wall of Mondrian's studio after his death, with furniture and gramophone, between 2 February and 21 March 1944 (see p. 280)

Contact print from a 35 mm negative, 3.6 x 2.4 cm

Zurich, Kunsthaus, Glarner Archiv, no inv., sheet 12, strip 1, negative 15

For the dating, see cat. 305.

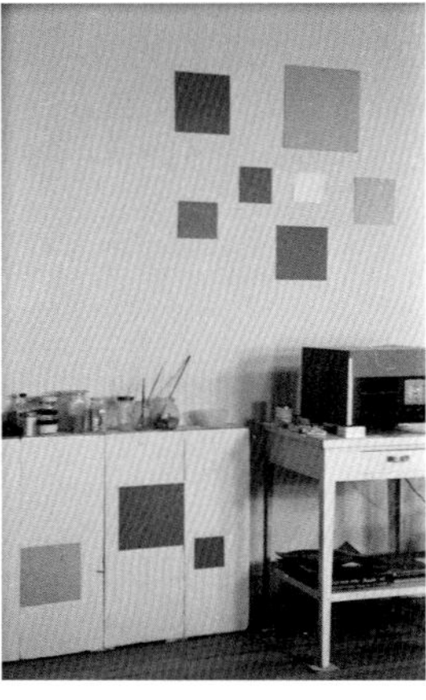

CAT. 360 Fritz Glarner

West wall of Mondrian's studio after his death, with furniture and gramophone, between 2 February and 21 March 1944

Contact print from a 35 mm negative, 3.6 x 2.4 cm

Zurich, Kunsthaus, Glarner Archiv, no inv., sheet 9, strips 4–5, negative 15

For the dating, see cat. 305.

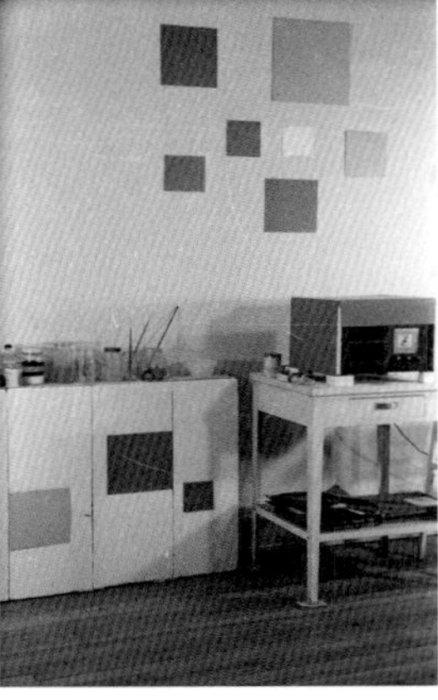

CAT. 361 Fritz Glarner

West wall of Mondrian's studio after his death, with furniture and gramophone, between 2 February and 21 March 1944

Contact print from a 35 mm negative, 3.6 x 2.4 cm

Zurich, Kunsthaus, Glarner Archiv, no inv., sheet 9, strip 5, negative 19

For the dating, see cat. 305.

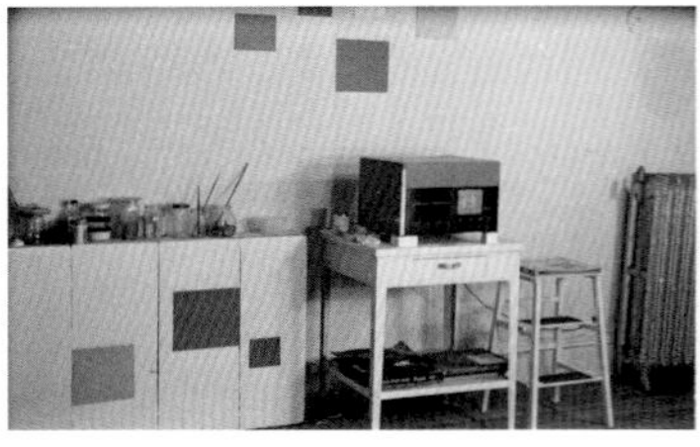

CAT. 362 Fritz Glarner

Decoration of the west wall and furniture in Mondrian's studio after his death, between 2 February and 21 March 1944

Contact print from a 35 mm negative, 2.4 x 3.6 cm

Zurich, Kunsthaus, Glarner Archiv, no inv., sheet 9, strip 4, negative 12

For the dating, see cat. 305.

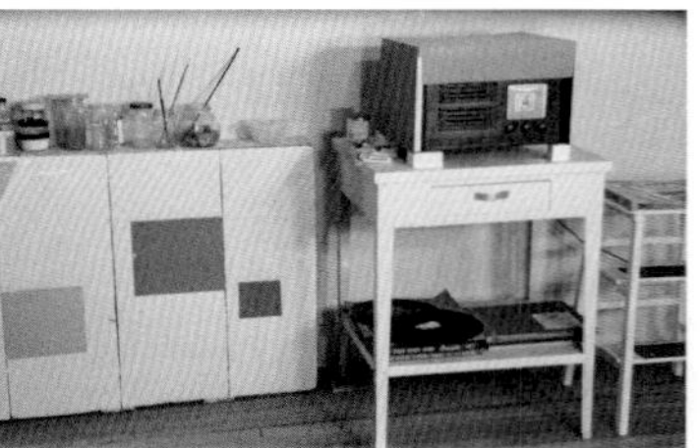

CAT. 363 Fritz Glarner

Furniture in Mondrian's studio after his death, between 2 February and 21 March 1944

Contact print from a 35 mm negative, 2.4 x 3.6 cm

Zurich, Kunsthaus, Glarner Archiv, no inv., sheet 9, strip 2, negative 4

For the dating, see cat. 305.

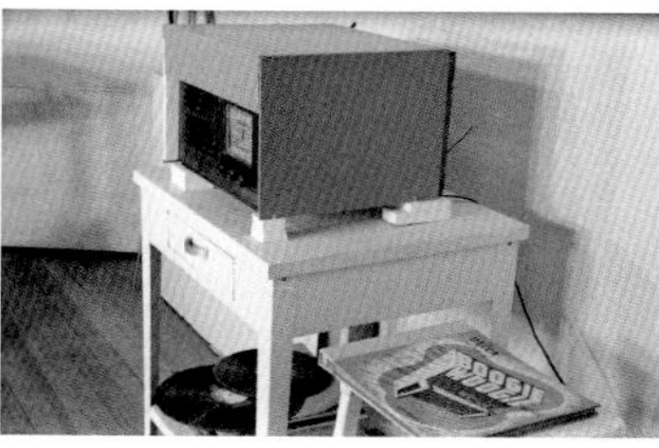

CAT. 364 Fritz Glarner

Mondrian's gramophone after his death, between 2 February and 21 March 1944 (see p. 281)

Contact print from a 35 mm negative, 2.4 x 3.6 cm

Zurich, Kunsthaus, Glarner Archiv, no inv., sheet 9, strip 3, negative 6

For the dating, see cat. 305.

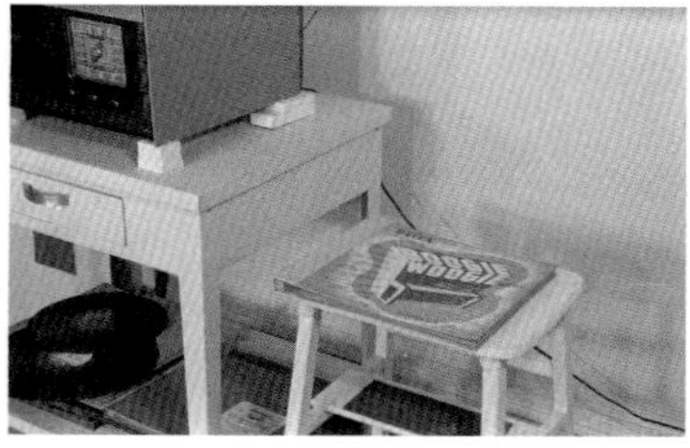

CAT. 365 Fritz Glarner

Mondrian's gramophone after his death, between 2 February and 21 March 1944

Contact print from a 35 mm negative, 2.4 x 3.6 cm

Zurich, Kunsthaus, Glarner Archiv, no inv., sheet 9, strips 3–4, negative 9

For the dating, see cat. 305.

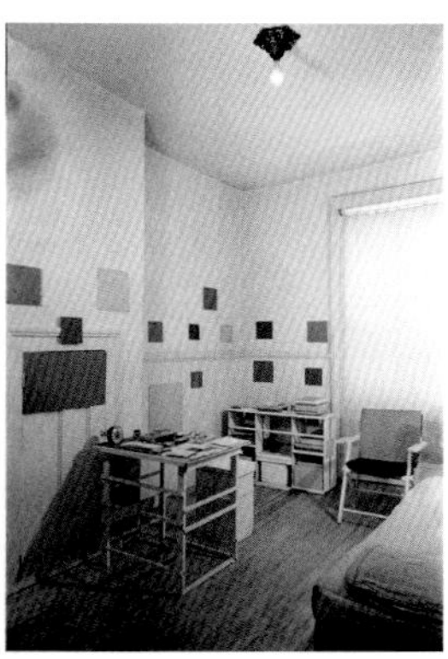

CAT. 366 Fritz Glarner

Mondrian's living quarters after his death, between 2 February and 21 March 1944 (see p. 282)

Contact print from a 35 mm negative, 3.6 x 2.4 cm

Zurich, Kunsthaus, Glarner Archiv, no inv., sheet 1, strips 1–2, negative 20

For the dating, see cat. 305.

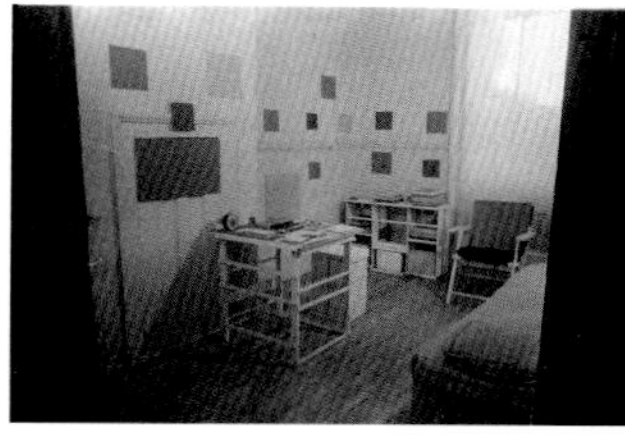

CAT. 367 Fritz Glarner

Mondrian's living quarters after his death, between 2 February and 21 March 1944

Contact print from a 35 mm negative, 2.4 x 3.6 cm

Zurich, Kunsthaus, Glarner Archiv, no inv., sheet 1, strip 1, negatives 16–18

For the dating, see cat. 305.

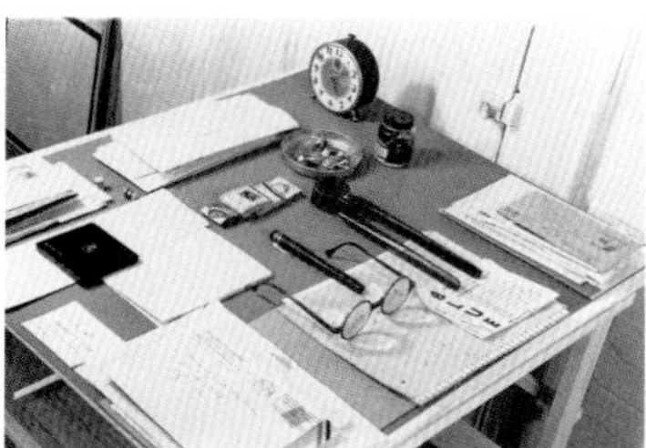

CAT. 368 Fritz Glarner

Writing table in Mondrian's living quarters after his death, between 2 February and 21 March 1944

Contact print from a 35 mm negative, 2.4 x 3.6 cm

Zurich, Kunsthaus, Glarner Archiv, no inv., sheet 3, strip 5, negative 13

For the dating, see cat. 305.

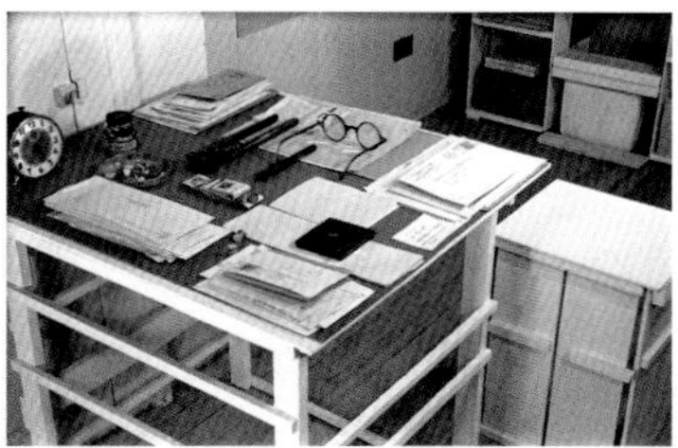

CAT. 369 Fritz Glarner

Writing table in Mondrian's living quarters after his death, between 2 February and 21 March 1944
(see p. 283)

Contact print from a 35 mm negative, 2.4 x 3.6 cm

Zurich, Kunsthaus, Glarner Archiv, no inv., sheet 3, strip 3, negatives 4–7

For the dating, see cat. 305.

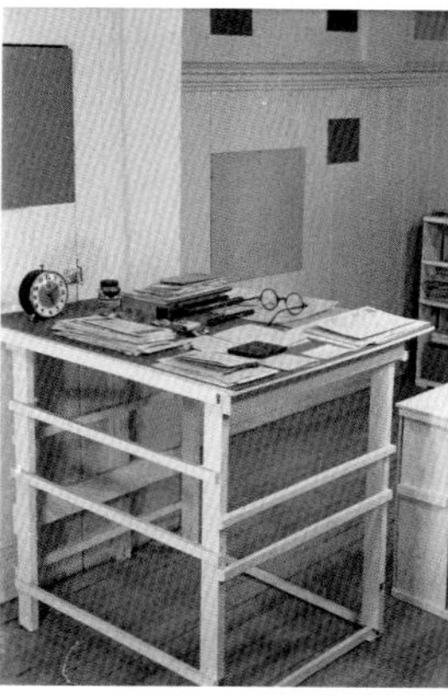

CAT. 370 Fritz Glarner

Writing table in Mondrian's living quarters after his death, between 2 February and 21 March 1944

Contact print from a 35 mm negative, 3.6 x 2.4 cm

Zurich, Kunsthaus, Glarner Archiv, no inv., sheet 3, strips 2–3, negative 44

For the dating, see cat. 305.

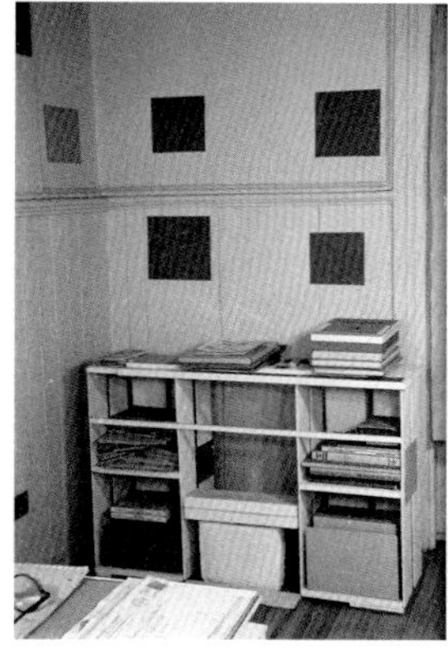

CAT. 371 Fritz Glarner

Bookcase in Mondrian's living quarters after his death, between 2 February and 21 March 1944
(see p. 284)

Contact print from a 35 mm negative, 3.6 x 2.4 cm

Zurich, Kunsthaus, Glarner Archiv, no inv., sheet 3, strips 1–2, negative 41

For the dating, see cat. 305.

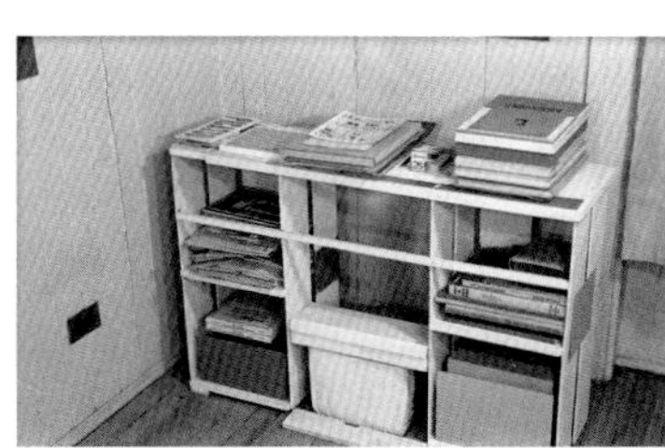

CAT. 372 Fritz Glarner

Bookcase in Mondrian's living quarters after his death, between 2 February and 21 March 1944

Contact print from a 35 mm negative, 2.4 x 3.6 cm

Zurich, Kunsthaus, Glarner Archiv, no inv., sheet 3, strip 4, negatives 8–12

For the dating, see cat. 305.

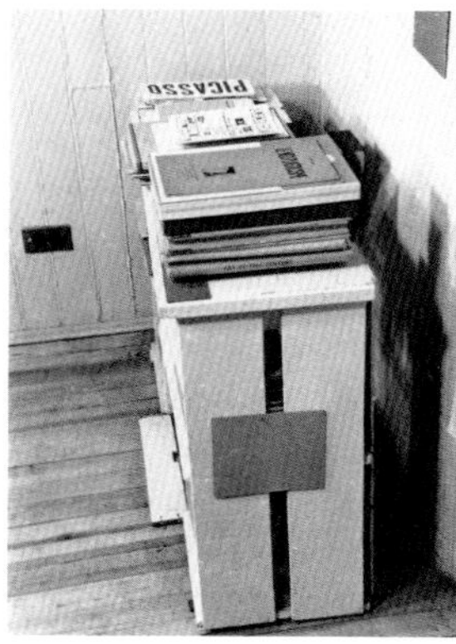

CAT. 373 Fritz Glarner

Bookcase in Mondrian's living quarters after his death, between 2 February and 21 March 1944
(see p. 285)

Contact print from a 35 mm negative, 3.6 x 2.4 cm

Zurich, Kunsthaus, Glarner Archiv, no inv., sheet 3, strips 5–6, negatives 17–21

For the dating, see cat. 305.

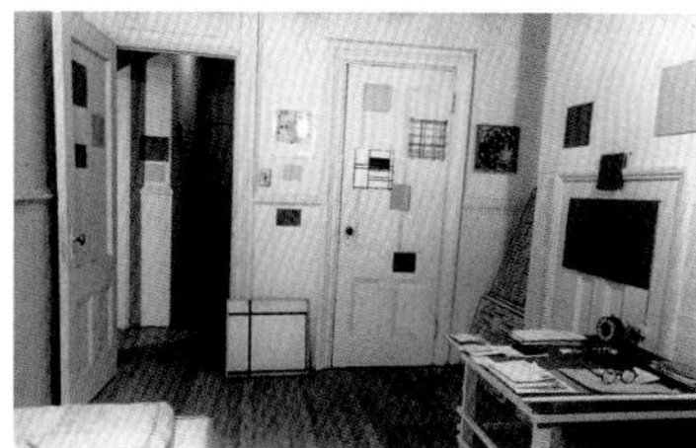

CAT. 374 Fritz Glarner

Mondrian's living quarters after his death, between 2 February and 21 March 1944 (see pp. 286–87)

Gelatin developing-out paper, 7 x 10.2 cm

Private collection

For the dating, see cat. 305.

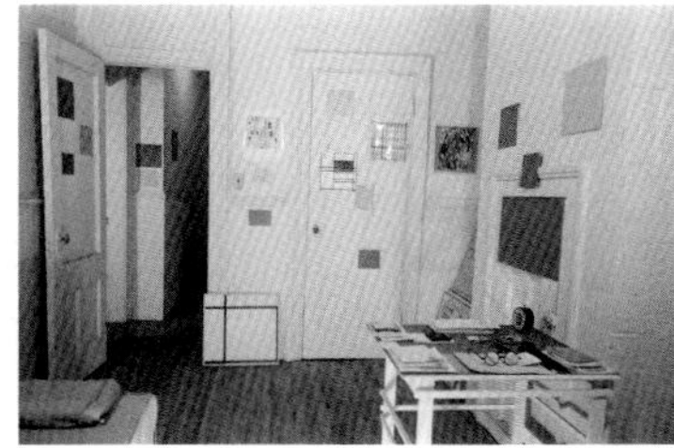

CAT. 375 Fritz Glarner

Mondrian's living quarters after his death, between 2 February and 21 March 1944

Contact print from a 35 mm negative, 2.4 x 3.6 cm

Zurich, Kunsthaus, Glarner Archiv, no inv., sheet 12, strips 6–7, negatives 1–4

For the dating, see cat. 305.

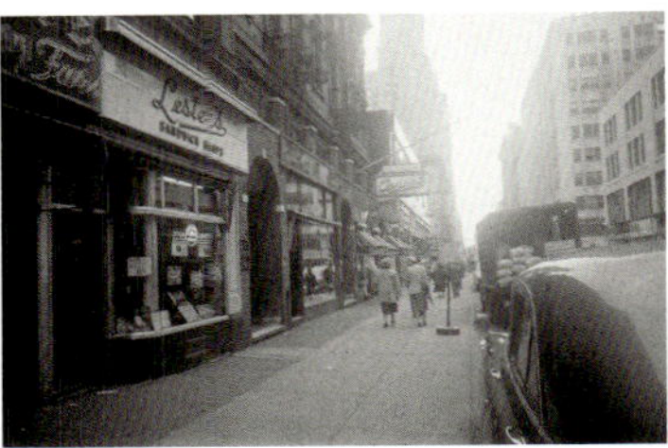

CAT. 376 Fritz Glarner

View of East 59th Street; on the left, the archway leading to Mondrian's studio and apartment at no. 15, between 2 February and 21 March 1944 (see p. 288)

Contact print from a 35 mm negative, 2.4 x 3.6 cm

Zurich, Kunsthaus, Glarner Archiv, no inv., sheet 1, strip 3, negative 12

For the dating, see cat. 305.

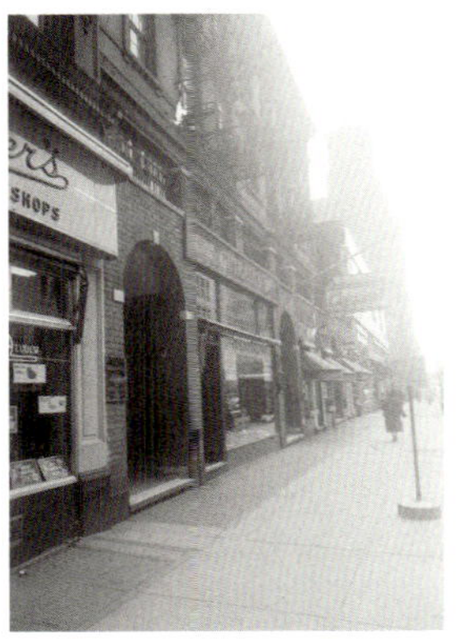

CAT. 377 Fritz Glarner

View of East 59th Street; on the left, the archway leading to Mondrian's studio and apartment at no. 15, between 2 February and 21 March 1944

Contact print from a 35 mm negative, 3.6 x 2.4 cm

Zurich, Kunsthaus, Glarner Archiv, no inv., sheet 1, strip 7, negative 25

For the dating, see cat. 305.

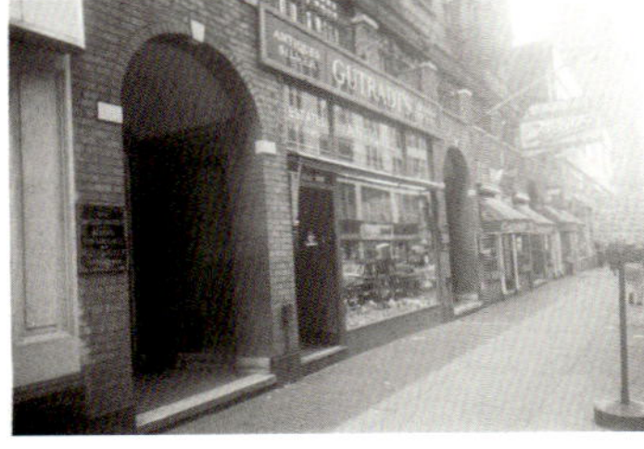

CAT. 378 Fritz Glarner

View of East 59th Street; on the left, the archway leading to Mondrian's studio and apartment at no. 15, between 2 February and 21 March 1944

Contact print from a 35 mm negative, 2.4 x 3.6 cm

Zurich, Kunsthaus, Glarner Archiv, no inv., sheet 1, strip 3, negative 11

For the dating, see cat. 305.

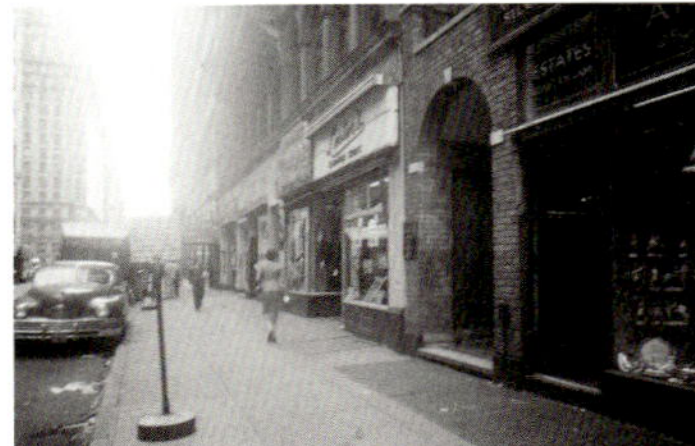

CAT. 379 Fritz Glarner

View of East 59th Street; on the right, the archway leading to Mondrian's studio and apartment at no. 15, between 2 February and 21 March 1944

Contact print from a 35 mm negative, 2.4 x 3.6 cm

Zurich, Kunsthaus, Glarner Archiv, no inv., sheet 1, strip 3, negative 13

For the dating, see cat. 305.

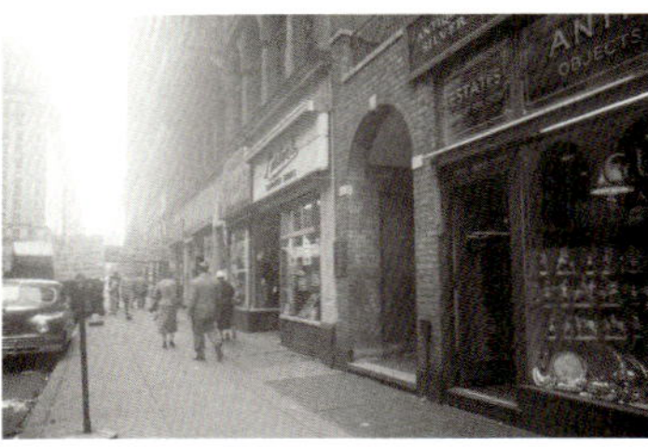

CAT. 380 Fritz Glarner

View of East 59th Street; on the right, the archway leading to Mondrian's studio and apartment at no. 15, between 2 February and 21 March 1944

Contact print from a 35 mm negative, 2.4 x 3.6 cm

Zurich, Kunsthaus, Glarner Archiv, no inv., sheet 1, strip 3, negative 14

For the dating, see cat. 305.

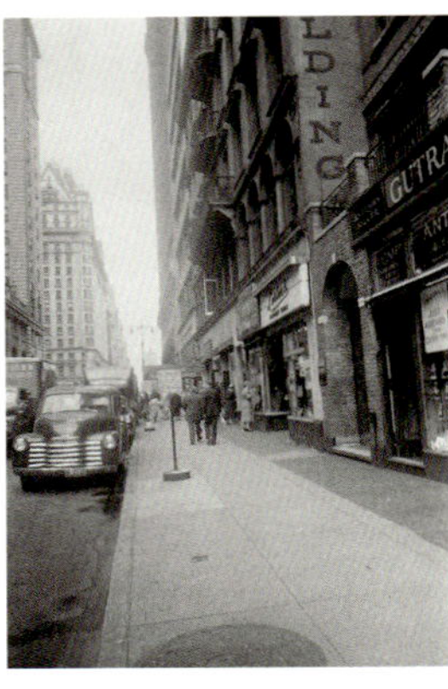

CAT. 381 Fritz Glarner

View of East 59th Street; on the right, the archway leading to Mondrian's studio and apartment at no. 15, between 2 February and 21 March 1944 (see p. 289)

Contact print from a 35 mm negative, 3.6 x 2.4 cm

Zurich, Kunsthaus, Glarner Archiv, no inv., sheet 1, strip 7, negative 24

For the dating, see cat. 305.

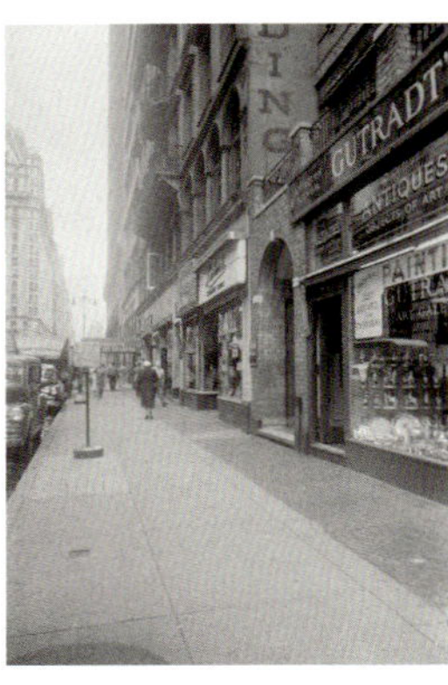

CAT. 382 Fritz Glarner

View of East 59th Street; on the right, the archway leading to Mondrian's studio and apartment at no. 15, between 2 February and 21 March 1944

Contact print from a 35 mm negative, 3.6 x 2.4 cm

Zurich, Kunsthaus, Glarner Archiv, no inv., sheet 1, strip 7, negative 27

For the dating, see cat. 305.

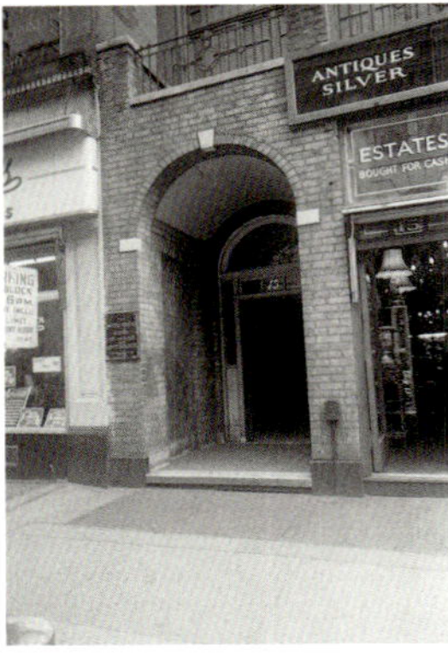

CAT. 383 Fritz Glarner

The entrance to Mondrian's final address, 15 East 59th Street, between 2 February and 21 March 1944 (see p. 289)

Contact print from a 35 mm negative, 3.6 x 2.4 cm

Zurich, Kunsthaus, Glarner Archiv, no inv., sheet 1, strip 7, negative 26

For the dating, see cat. 305.

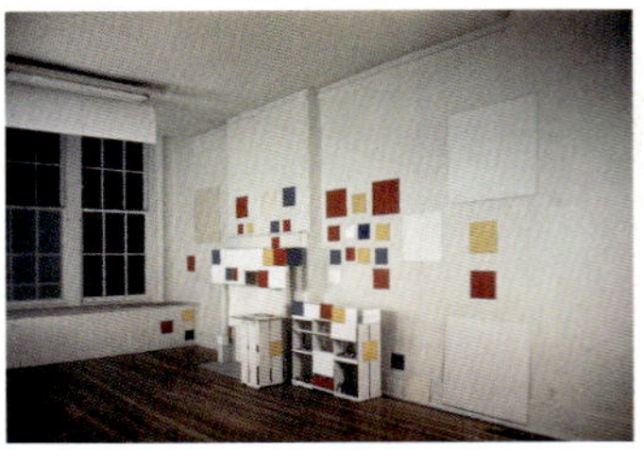

CAT. 384 Harry Holtzman

Mondrian's studio after his death, between 2 February and 21 March 1944 (see pp. 290–91)

Colour slide from original Kodachrome transparency, 2.3 x 3.4 cm

The Hague, RKD, Nico Crama Archive

The precise date of the session or sessions when Holtzman shot his series of pictures is not known; see Posthumous Photographs, p. 266.

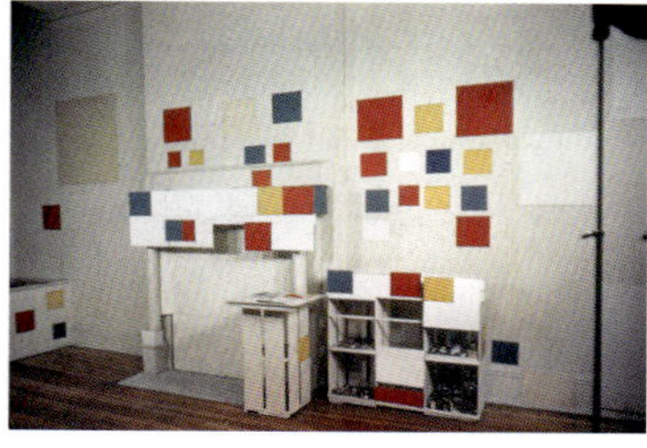

CAT. 385 Harry Holtzman

Mondrian's studio after his death, with his palette table and a shelf-unit with painting materials, between 2 February and 21 March 1944
(see p. 292)

Colour slide from original Kodachrome transparency, 2.3 x 3.4 cm

The Hague, RKD, Nico Crama Archive

For the dating, see cat. 384.

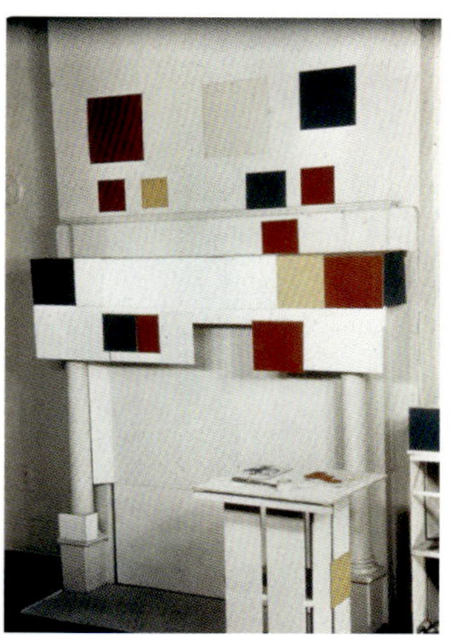

CAT. 386 Harry Holtzman

Mondrian's studio after his death, with his palette table in the foreground, between 2 February and 21 March 1944
(see p. 293)

Colour slide from original Kodachrome transparency, 3.4 x 2.3 cm

The Hague, RKD, Nico Crama Archive

For the dating, see cat. 384.

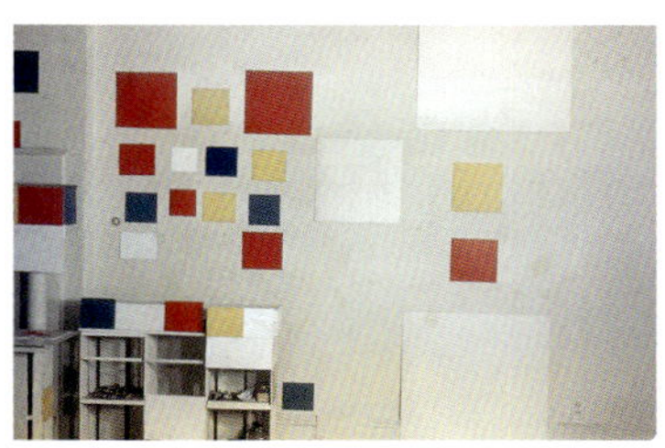

CAT. 387 Harry Holtzman

Wall decoration and furniture in Mondrian's studio after his death, between 2 February and 21 March 1944
(see p. 293)

Colour slide from original Kodachrome transparency, 2.3 x 3.4 cm

The Hague, RKD, Nico Crama Archive

For the dating, see cat. 384.

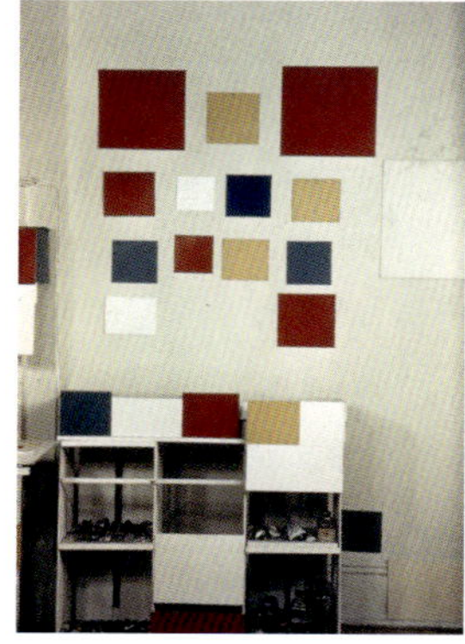

CAT. 388 Harry Holtzman

Wall decoration and shelf-unit with painting materials in Mondrian's studio after his death, between 2 February and 21 March 1944
(see p. 294)

Colour slide from original Kodachrome transparency, 3.4 x 2.3 cm

The Hague, RKD, Nico Crama Archive

For the dating, see cat. 384.

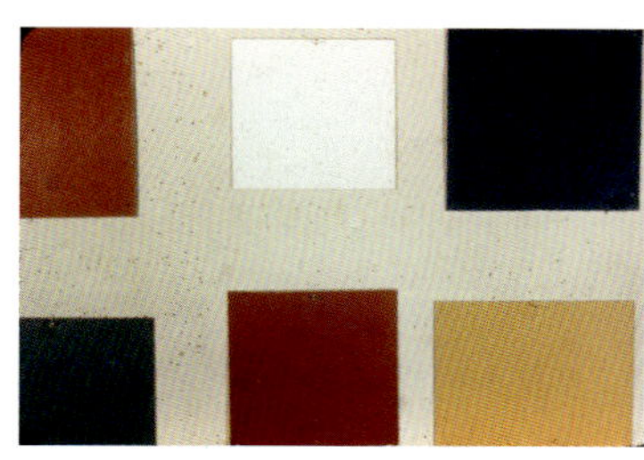

CAT. 389 Harry Holtzman

Mondrian's studio after his death; decoration of the east wall (detail), between 2 February and 21 March 1944

Colour slide from original Kodachrome transparency, 2.3 x 3.4 cm

The Hague, RKD, Nico Crama Archive

For the dating, see cat. 384.

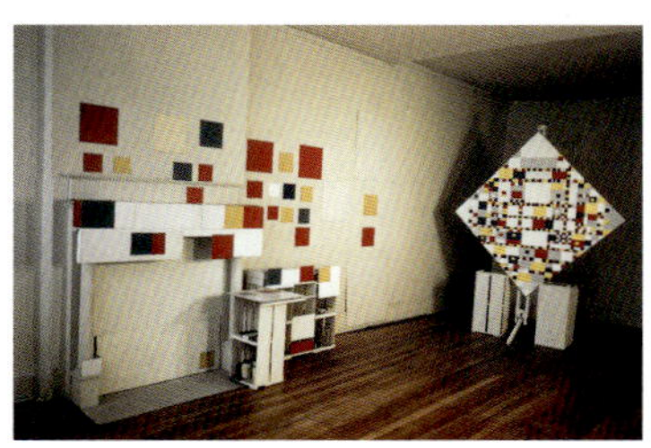

CAT. 390 Harry Holtzman

Mondrian's studio after his death, with *Victory Boogie Woogie* (B324) on the easel, between 2 February and 21 March 1944 (see p. 298)

Colour slide from original Kodachrome transparency, 2.3 x 3.4 cm

The Hague, RKD, Nico Crama Archive

For the dating, see cat. 384.

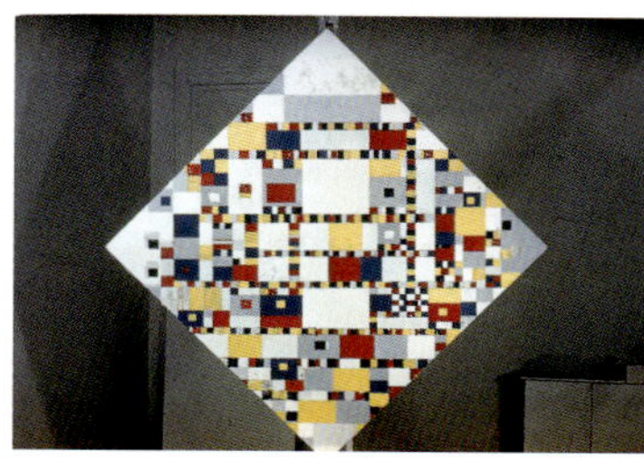

CAT. 391 Harry Holtzman

***Victory Boogie Woogie* (B324) in Mondrian's studio after his death, between 2 February and 21 March 1944** (see p. 295)

Colour slide from original Kodachrome transparency, 2.3 x 3.4 cm

The Hague, RKD, Nico Crama Archive

For the dating, see cat. 384.

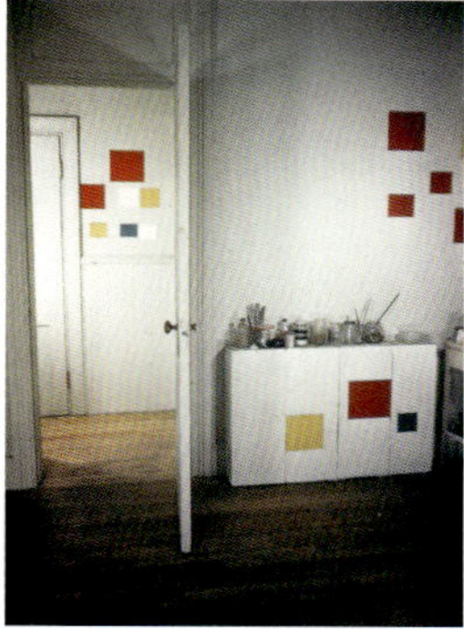

CAT. 392 Harry Holtzman

Decoration of walls and furniture in Mondrian's studio after his death, between 2 February and 21 March 1944 (see p. 296)

Colour slide from original Kodachrome transparency, 3.4 x 2.3 cm

The Hague, RKD, Nico Crama Archive

For the dating, see cat. 384.

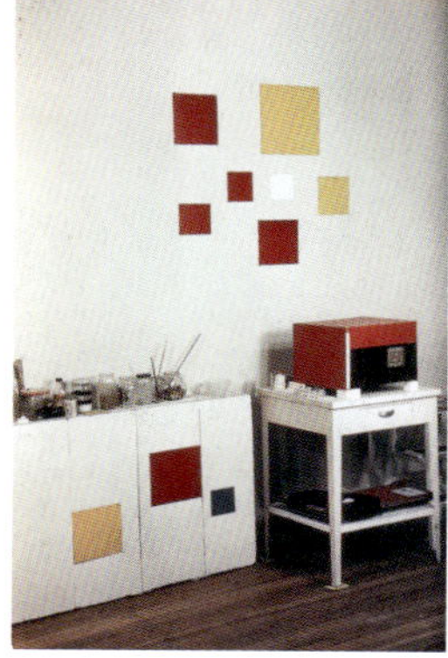

CAT. 393 Harry Holtzman

Wall decoration and furniture in Mondrian's studio after his death, between 2 February and 21 March 1944 (see p. 297)

Colour slide from original Kodachrome transparency, 3.4 x 2.3 cm

The Hague, RKD, Nico Crama Archive

For the dating, see cat. 384.

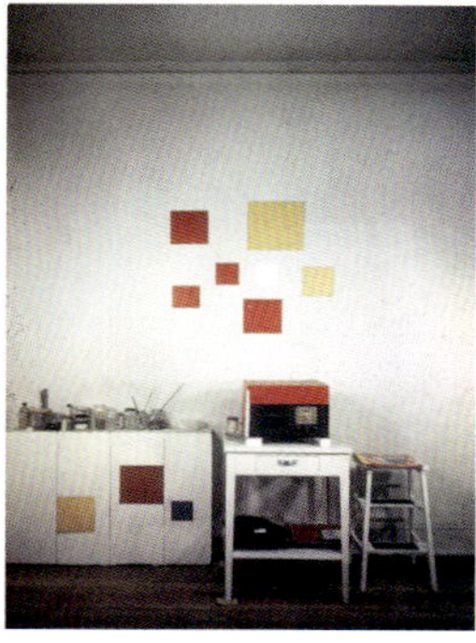

CAT. 394 Harry Holtzman

Wall decoration and furniture in Mondrian's studio after his death, between 2 February and 21 March 1944 (see p. 297)

Colour slide after original Kodachrome transparency, 3.4 x 2.3 cm

The Hague, RKD, Nico Crama Archive

For the dating, see cat. 384.

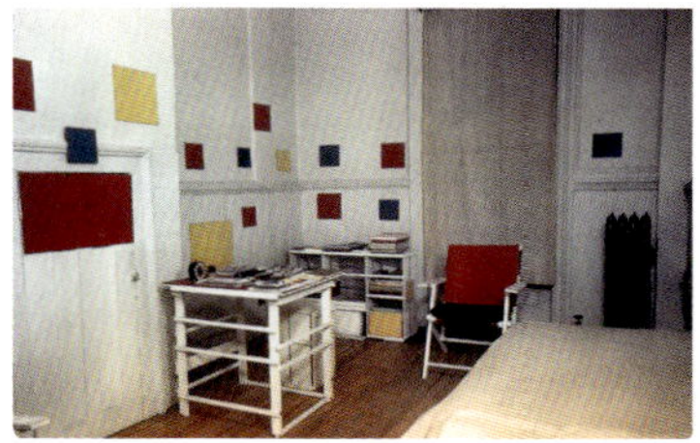

CAT. 395 Harry Holtzman

Mondrian's living quarters after his death, between 2 February and 21 March 1944 (see p. 299)

Colour slide from original Kodachrome transparency, 2.3 x 3.4 cm

The Hague, RKD, Nico Crama Archive

For the dating, see cat. 384.

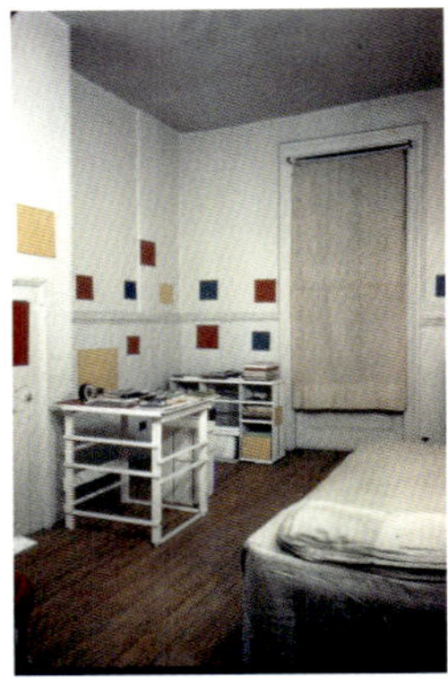

CAT. 396 Harry Holtzman

Mondrian's living quarters after his death, between 2 February and 21 March 1944

Colour slide after original Kodachrome transparency, 3.4 x 2.3 cm

The Hague, RKD, Nico Crama Archive

For the dating, see cat. 384.

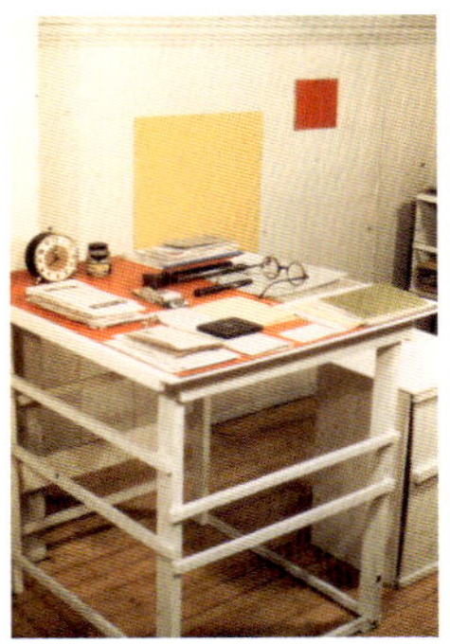

CAT. 397 Harry Holtzman

Writing table in Mondrian's living quarters after his death, between 2 February and 21 March 1944

Colour slide after original Kodachrome transparency, 2.8 x 2.2 cm

Private collection

For the dating, see cat. 384.

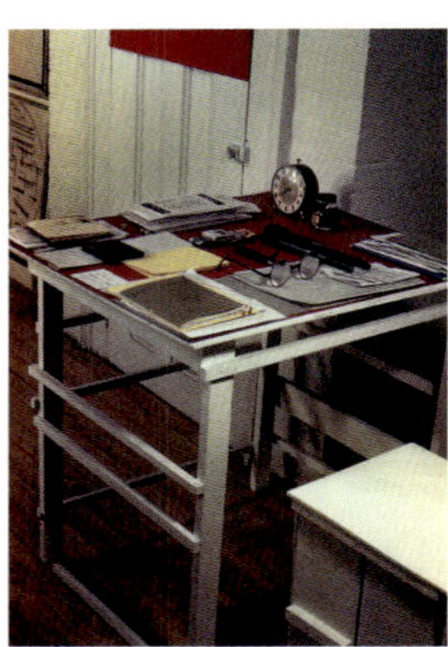

CAT. 398 Harry Holtzman

Writing table in Mondrian's living quarters after his death, between 2 February and 21 March 1944 (see p. 300)

Colour slide from original Kodachrome transparency, 3.4 x 2.3 cm

The Hague, RKD, Nico Crama Archive

For the dating, see cat. 384.

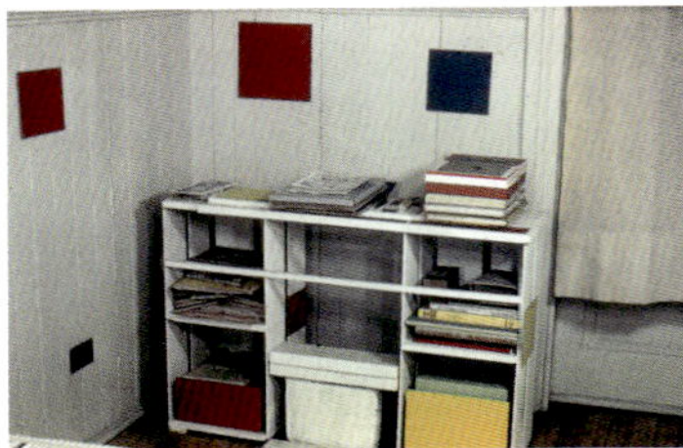

CAT. 399 Harry Holtzman

Bookcase in Mondrian's living quarters after his death, between 2 February and 21 March 1944 (see p. 301)

Colour slide from original Kodachrome transparency, 2.3 x 3.4 cm

The Hague, RKD, Nico Crama Archive

For the dating, see cat. 384.

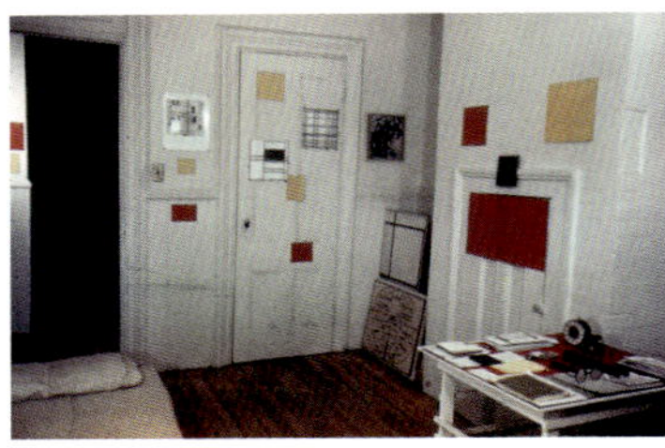

CAT. 400 Harry Holtzman

Mondrian's living quarters after his death, between 2 February and 21 March 1944 (see p. 302)

Colour slide from original Kodachrome transparency, 2.3 x 3.4 cm

The Hague, RKD, Nico Crama A-chive

For the dating, see cat. 384.

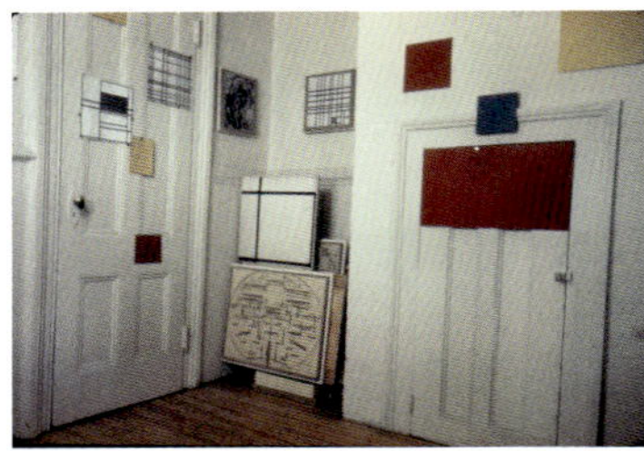

CAT. 401 Harry Holtzman

Corner of Mondrian's living quarters after his death, with wall decoration and several (reproductions) of his works, between 2 February and 21 March 1944

Colour slide from original Kodachrome transparency, 2.3 x 3.4 cm

The Hague, RKD, Nico Crama Archive

For the dating, see cat. 384.

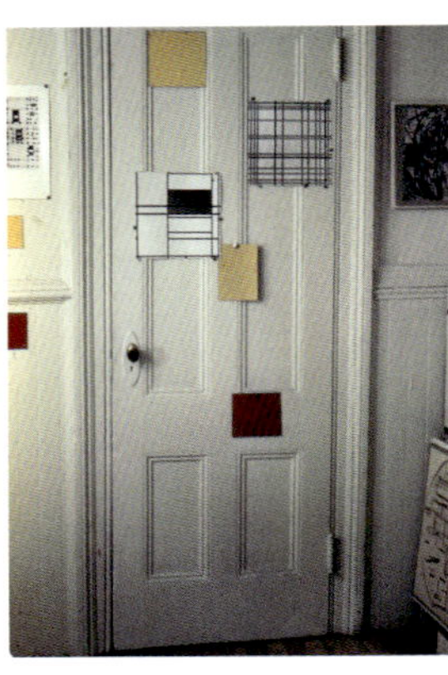

CAT. 402 Harry Holtzman

The door of Mondrian's living quarters after his death, between 2 February and 21 March 1944 (see p. 303)

Colour slide from original Kodachrome transparency, 3.4 x 2.3 cm

The Hague, RKD, Nico Crama Archive

For the dating, see cat. 384.

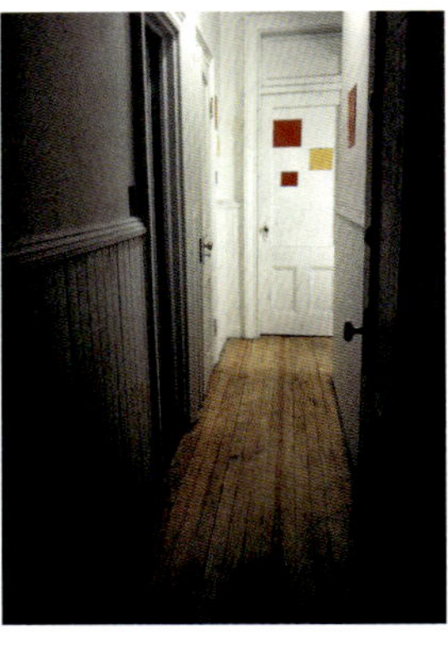

CAT. 403 Harry Holtzman

The corridor of Mondrian's apartment after his death, between 2 February and 21 March 1944 (see p. 303)

Colour slide from original Kodachrome transparency, 3.4 x 2.3 cm

The Hague, RKD, Nico Crama Archive

For the dating, see cat. 384.

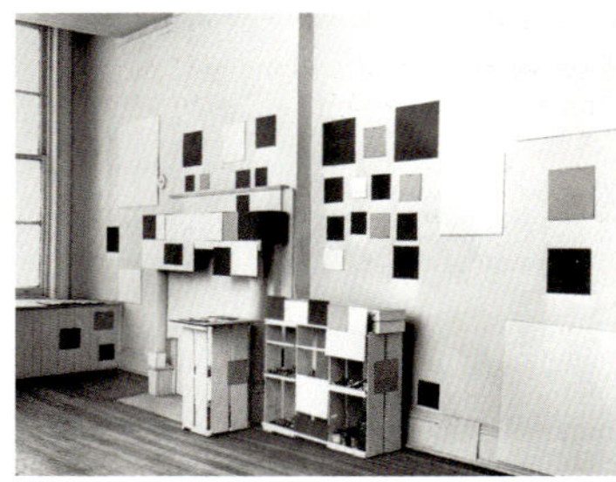

CAT. 404 Fernand Fonssagrives

Mondrian's studio after his death, between 22 March and c. 3 May 1944 (see p. 304)

A vintage print has not been traced. The photograph reproduced here is a later print (Winterswijk, Museum Villa Mondriaan).

Mondrian's studio was opened to interested parties for about six weeks beginning on 22 March. The fashion shoot (cats 408–11) that Fernand Fonssagrives did for *Town & Country* magazine must have taken place in that period. On the same occasion, he took three pictures of the studio without a model present and one of the late painter's living quarters (cats 404–7).

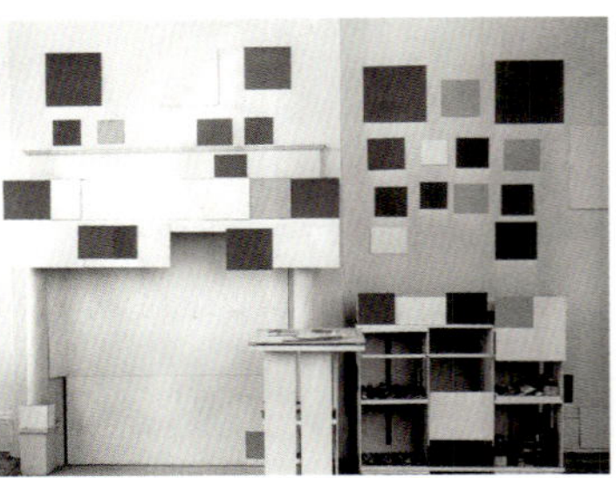

CAT. 405 Fernand Fonssagrives

Mondrian's studio after his death, between 22 March and c. 3 May 1944 (see p. 305)

A vintage print has not been traced. The photograph reproduced here is a later print (Winterswijk, Museum Villa Mondriaan).

See cat. 404.

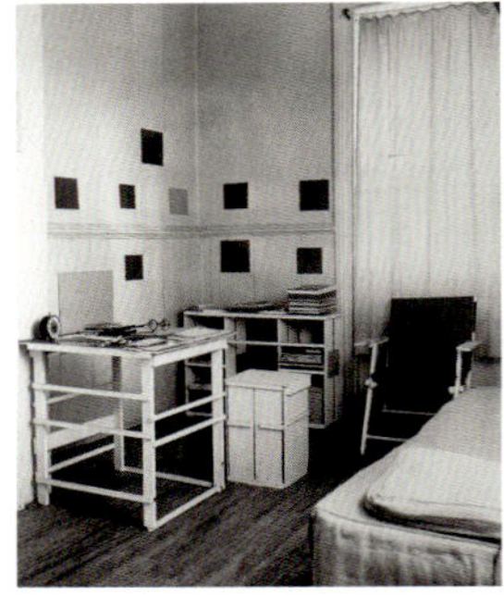

CAT. 406 Fernand Fonssagrives

Mondrian's living quarters after his death, between 22 March and c. 3 May 1944 (see p. 306)

A vintage print has not been traced. The photograph reproduced here is a later print (Winterswijk, Museum Villa Mondriaan).

See cat. 404.

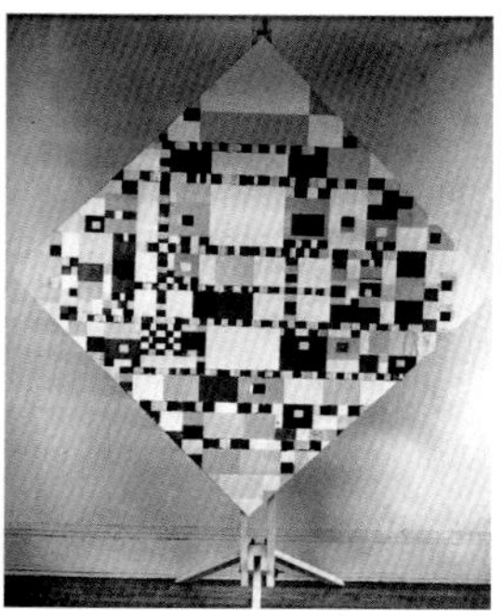

CAT. 407 Fernand Fonssagrives

Victory Boogie Woogie **(B324) in Mondrian's studio after his death, between 22 March and c. 3 May 1944** (see p. 307)

A vintage print has not been traced. The photograph reproduced here is a later print (Winterswijk, Museum Villa Mondriaan).

See cat. 404.

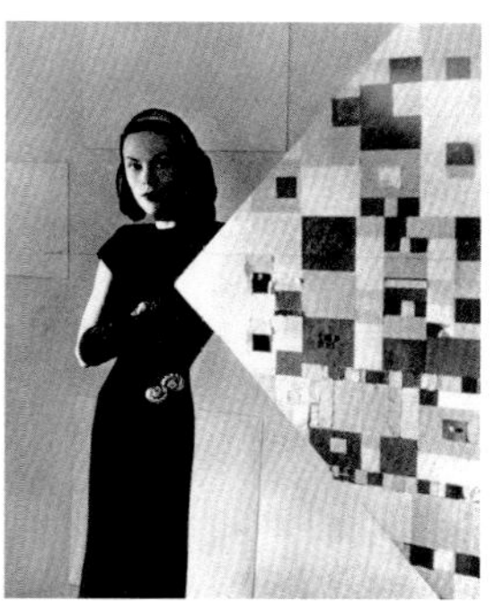

CAT. 408 Fernand Fonssagrives

Model next to *Victory Boogie Woogie* (B324) in Mondrian's studio after his death, between 22 March and c. 3 May 1944 (see p. 308)

A vintage print has not been traced; the photograph is known only from the fashion feature in *Town & Country* magazine. The photograph reproduced here is a later print (Winterswijk, Museum Villa Mondriaan).

See cat. 404.

Publication: 'Black Is Right', in *Town & Country* (June 1944).

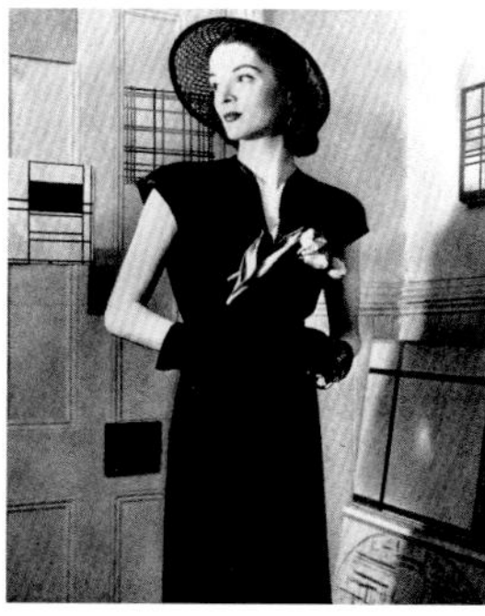

CAT. 409 Fernand Fonssagrives

Model in Mondrian's living quarters after his death, between 22 March and c. 3 May 1944 (see p. 308)

A vintage print has not been traced; the photograph is known only from the fashion feature in *Town & Country* magazine. The photograph reproduced here is a later print (Winterswijk, Museum Villa Mondriaan).

See cat. 404.

Publication: 'Black Is Right', in *Town & Country* (June 1944).

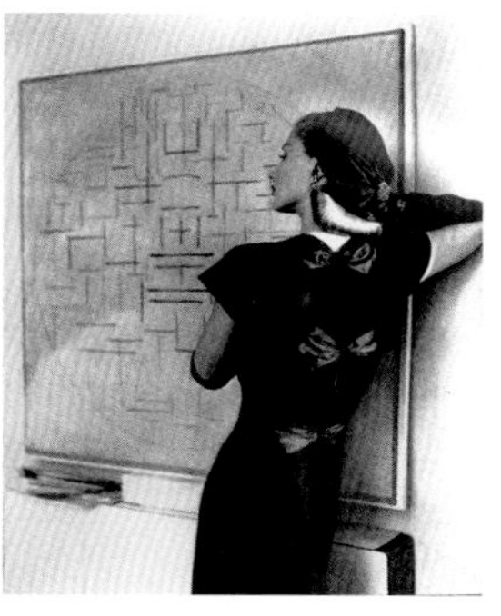

CAT. 410 Fernand Fonssagrives

Model in front of *Composition in Circle* (B75) in Mondrian's studio after his death, between 22 March and c. 3 May 1944 (see p. 309)

A vintage print has not been traced; the photograph is known only from the fashion feature in *Town & Country* magazine. The photograph reproduced here is a later print (Winterswijk, Museum Villa Mondriaan).

See cat. 404.

Publication: 'Black Is Right', in *Town & Country* (June 1944).

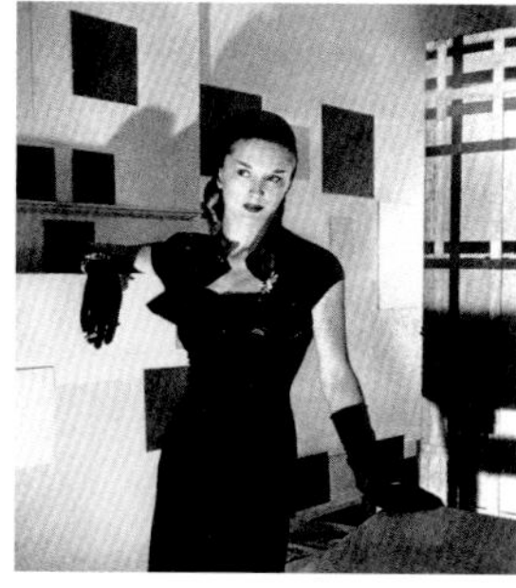

CAT. 411 Fernand Fonssagrives

Model next to *New York City 1* (B300) in Mondrian's studio after his death, between 22 March and c. 3 May 1944 (see p. 309)

A vintage print has not been traced; the photograph is known only from the fashion feature in *Town & Country* magazine. The photograph reproduced here is a later print (Winterswijk, Museum Villa Mondriaan).

See cat. 404.

Publication: 'Black Is Right', in *Town & Country* (June 1944).

>> Detail of cat. 121

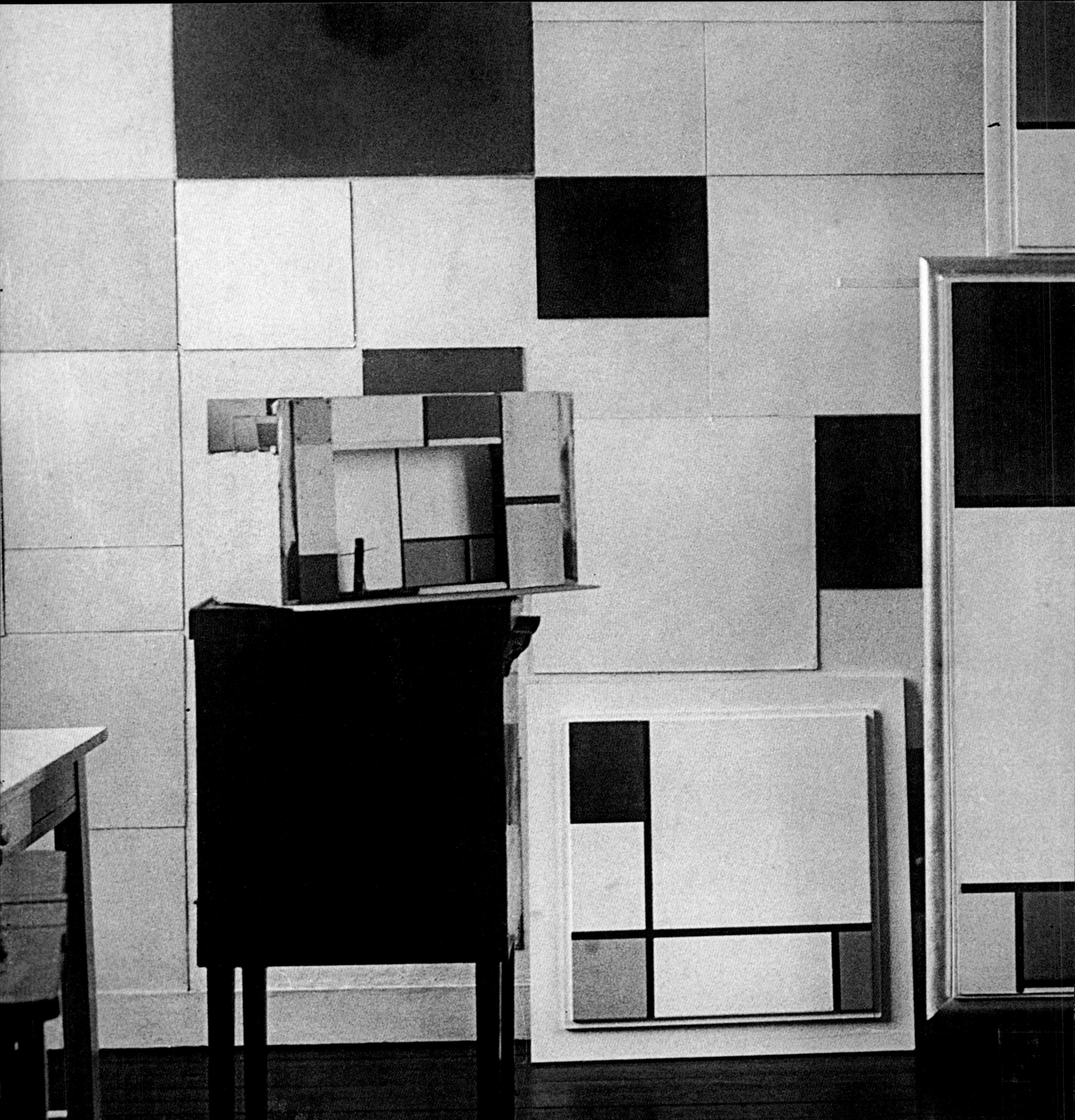

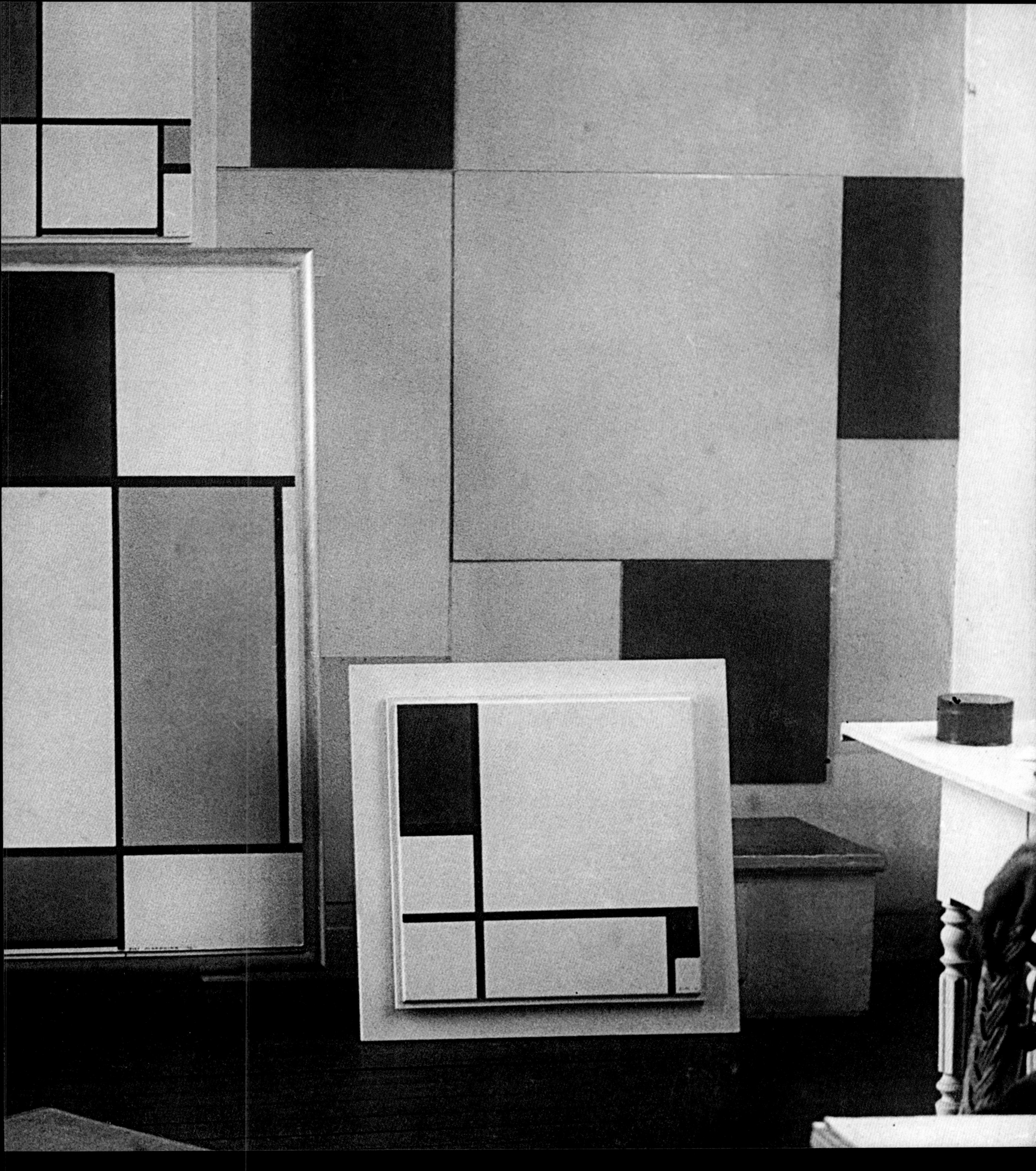

Bibliography

Almering-Strik 2018
L. M. Almering-Strik, *Lodewijk Schelfhout. Nederlands eerste kubist*, Zwolle 2018

Anonymous 1926
[Anonymous], 'Liste des exposants', *Le Photographe. La Revue technique des professionnels*, 163 (5 February 1926)

Anonymous 1933
[Anonymous], 'Simon Maris 60 jaar', *Algemeen Handelsblad*, 21 May 1933

Anonymous 1944
[Anonymous], 'Studio', *The New Yorker*, 15 April 1944, pp. 20–22

Baldassari 1997
Anne Baldassari, *Le Miroir noir. Picasso, sources photographiques 1900–1928*, Paris 1997

Bax 1994
Marty Bax, 'Mondriaan en zijn vrienden', in Robert Welsh et al., exh. cat. *Mondriaan aan de Amstel 1892–1912*, Amsterdam (Gemeentearchief) 1994, pp. 22–42.

Blotkamp 2006
Carel Blotkamp, 'Het atelier als zelfportret', in: Mariëtte Haveman et al. (eds), *Ateliergeheimen. Over de werkplaats van de Nederlandse kunstenaar vanaf 1200 tot heden*, Lochem/Amsterdam 2006, pp. 340–59

Blotkamp 2010
Carel Blotkamp, 'L'Atelier de Mondrian, ou La Retraite d'un flâneur', in: Leal 2010, pp. 99–107

Bool 1994
Flip Bool, 'Foto'en typografie in *i10*', in: Toke van Helmond (ed.), *i10. Sporen van de avant-garde*, Heerlen 1994, pp. 67–77

Boom 1996
Mattie Boom, 'A New Art: Photography in the Nineteenth Century', in: Mattie Boom & Hans Rooseboom (eds), *A New Art: Photography in the 19th Century. The Photo Collection of the Rijksmuseum, Amsterdam*, Amsterdam 1996, pp. 16–30

Boom/Rooseboom 2012
Mattie Boom & Hans Rooseboom, 'Acquisitions Photography 2008–11', *The Rijksmuseum Bulletin*, vol. 60 no. 2 (2012), pp. 167–91

Borhan 1994
Pierre Borhan, *André Kertész: His Life and Works*, Boston 1994

Bowness 1989
Alan Bowness, *Conditions of Success: How the Modern Artist Rises to Fame*, London 1989

Bramly 2012
Serge Bramly, 'Préface', in: exh. cat. *Mondrian*, Paris (Paviotfoto) 2012, n.p.

Citroen 1931
Paul Citroen, *Palet. Een boek gewijd aan de hedendaagsche Nederlandsche schilderkunst*, Amsterdam 1931

Colin 2021
Anne Colin du Terrail, *Raymond Colin, artiste peintre (1886–1929). Biographie*, E-book (pdf) 2021

Cooper/Spronk 2001
Harry Cooper & Ron Spronk, exh. cat. *Mondrian: The Transatlantic Paintings*, Cambridge, MA (Harvard University Art Museums)/Dallas, TX (Dallas Art Museum) 2001, New Haven/Cambridge 2001

Coppes 2010
Wietse Coppes, 'Photographies, reproductions et portraits. L'Image que Mondrian veut donner de lui-même', in: Leal 2010, pp. 145–57

Coppes 2012
'Het "wetenschappelijk-technische laboratorium" van Piet Mondriaan. Het atelier op 26, rue du Départ ten tijde van het bezoek van Alexander Calder', in: exh. cat. *Alexander Calder. De grote ontdekking*, The Hague (Gemeentemuseum) 2012, pp. 38–51

Coppes 2018
Wietse Coppes, 'Mondriaan als toreador', in: Yvonne Bleyerveld et al. (eds), *Schatten van het RKD. Nederlands Instituut voor Kunstgeschiedenis*, Den Haag 2018, pp. 124–25

Coppes 2020
Wietse Coppes, 'De uitzonderlijke levenswandel van "schedelmeter" Alfred Waldenburg', *Rode haring*, 1 (June 2020), pp. 18–33

Coppes/Jansen 2020
Wietse Coppes & Leo Jansen, 'The Colour of Black-and-White. An Unknown Sketch of a Well-Known Set Design', in: Sjoerd van Faassen et al. (eds), *Dutch Connections: Essays on International Relationships in Architectural History in Honour of Herman van Bergeijk*, Delft 2020, pp. 79–92

Daniel 1998
Malcolm Daniel (ed.), *Edgar Degas: Photographer*, New York 1998

Darwent 2012
Charles Darwent, *Mondrian in London: How British Art Nearly Became Modern*, London 2012

De Jongh-Vermeulen 2019
Ankie de Jongh-Vermeulen, 'Cesar Domela's verzwegen verblijf in Berlijn', in: *Eigenbouwer. Tijdschrift voor de goede smaak*, no. 7 (June 2017), pp. 59–79

De Mondenard 2010
Anne de Mondenard, 'L'Odyssée d'une icône. Trois photographies d'André Kertész', in: Leal 2010, pp. 111–12

Draaijer 2022
Nick Draaijer, *De geheime portretten van Mondriaan. Een familiegeschiedenis*, Amsterdam/Antwerpen 2022

Dreier 1926
Katherine S. Dreier, exh. cat. *International Exhibition of Modern Art Arranged by the Société Anonyme*, New York (Brooklyn Museum) 1926

Droste/Opel 2019
Magdalena Droste & Nicole Opel (eds), *Bauhaus 1919–1933*, Berlin/Cologne 2019

Easton 2011
Elizabeth W. Easton (ed.), *Snapshot: Painters and Photography 1888–1915*, New Haven/London 2011

Entrop 2003:
Marco Entrop, 'Verliefde ogen zien Mondriaan. Uit het dagboek van Eva de Beneditty', in: *De parelduiker*, vol. 8 no. 1 (2003), pp. 28–45.

Ernst 1984
Jimmy Ernst, *A Not-So-Still Life*, New York 1984

Ewing et al. 2012
William A. Ewing et al., *Masterclass: Arnold Newman*, London 2012

Flukinger 2013
Roy Flukinger, *Arnold Newman: At Work*, Austin 2013

Forgács 1994
Éva Forgács, 'Als zeepbellen. Het conflict tussen Kállai en Moholy-Nagy in de discussie over de verhouding tussen schilderkunst en fotografie in *i10*, 1927', in: Toke van Helmond (ed.), *i10. Sporen van de avant-garde*, Heerlen 1994, pp. 83–8

Forman 1971
Nessa Forman, 'An Explosion of Colors in Paint and Frames', *The Sunday Bulletin*, Philadelphia (January 1971)

Frost 1942
Rosamund Frost, 'First Fruits of Exile: What Recent Emigré Artists Have Done in America', *Art News*, 15 March 1942, pp. 23, 32.

Gasser 2007
Martin Gasser, 'Herdeg, Hugo P.', entry in *Historisches Lexikon der Schweiz* (HLS), version 11 December 2007 (https://hls-dhs-dss.ch/de/articles/027250/2007-12-11/, accessed 15 March 2022)

Giedion-Welcker 1930
C. Giedion-Welcker, 'Die Kunst des zwanzigsten Jahrhunderts. Experimentierzelle — Zeitseismograf', *Das Kunstblatt*, vol. 14 no. 3 (March 1930), pp. 65–70

Gorin 1930
J. A. Gorin, 'La Fonction de l'art plastique dans l'architecture future', *Cercle et Carré*, no. 3 (30 June 1930), p. [3]

Gorter 1998
Paul Gorter, 'Mies Maris' vergeten Mondriana (vervolg)', *Jong Holland*, no. 3 (1998), pp. 35–47

Gorter 2017
Paul Gorter, *Kunstenaarsvereniging Sint Lucas. De onbekende jaren 1885–1908*, Amsterdam 2017

Gorter 2020
Paul Gorter, *Piet Mondriaan and Simon Gorter: The Photographs Discovered at the Home of Mies Maris in 1997*, E-book 2020

Guggenheim 1942
Peggy Guggenheim, 'Piet Mondrian', in: idem, exh. cat. *Art of This Century: Objects — Drawings — Photographs — Paintings — Sculpture — Collages, 1910 to 1942*, New York (Art of This Century Gallery) 1942, pp. 54–5

Hanssen 2015
Léon Hanssen, *De schepping van een aards paradijs. Piet Mondriaan 1919–1938*, Amsterdam/Antwerpen 2015

Hanssen 2017
Léon Hanssen, *Alleen een wonder kan je dragen. Over het sublieme bij Mondriaan*, Rimburg/Amsterdam 2017.

Harrison/Denne 2002
Helen A. Harrison & Constance Ayers Denne, *Hamptons Bohemia: Two Centuries of Artists and Writers on the Beach*, San Francisco 2002

Haus 1990
Andreas Haus, 'Laszlo Moholy-Nagy', in: Jeannine Fiedler (ed.), *Photography at the Bauhaus*, Cambridge (MA) 1990, pp. 15–18

Hekking 1982
S. Hekking, *Cas Oorthuys fotograaf 1908–1975*, Amsterdam 1982

Henkels 1976
Herbert Henkels (ed.), *Seuphor*, Antwerpen 1976

Henkels 1987
Herbert Henkels, exh. cat. *Mondrian from Figuration to Abstraction*, Tokyo (The Seibu Museum of Art) et al. 1987

Henkels 1988
Herbert Henkels (ed.), *'t is alles een groote eenheid, Bert. Piet Mondriaan, Albert van den Briel en hun vriendschap aan de hand van brieven, documenten en fragmenten*, Haarlem 1988

Henkels 1993
Herbert Henkels, exh. cat. *Mondrian in New York*, Tokyo (Tokoro Gallery) 1993

Hoek 1982
Els Hoek, 'Piet Mondriaan', in: Carel Blotkamp (ed.), *De beginjaren van De Stijl, 1917–1922*, Utrecht 1982, pp. 47–82

Hoek 1996
Els Hoek, 'Piet Mondriaan', in: Carel Blotkamp (ed.), *De vervolgjaren van De Stijl, 1922–1932*, Amsterdam/Antwerp 1996, pp. 114–52

Holtzman/James 1986
Harry Holtzman & Martin S. James (ed.), *The New Art — The New Life: The Collected Writings of Piet Mondrian*, Boston 1996

Janis 1941
Sidney Janis, 'School of Paris Comes to U.S.', *Decision: A Review of Free Culture*, vol. 1 no. 5/6 (November/December 1941), pp. 85–95

Janssen 2008
Hans Janssen, *Mondriaan in het Gemeentemuseum Den Haag*, The Hague 2008

Janssen 2013
Hans Janssen, exh. cat. *Mondriaan in Amsterdam, 1892–1912*, Amsterdam (Amsterdam Museum) 2013

Janssen 2016
Hans Janssen, *Piet Mondriaan. Een nieuwe kunst voor een ongekend leven*, Amsterdam 2016

Jooren 2016
Marieke Jooren, 'Alma, lotgeval van De Stijl?', in: idem (ed.), exh. cat. *Peter Alma. Van De Stijl naar communisme*, Arnhem 2016, pp. 8–24

Kállai 1927
Ernst Kállai, 'Malerei und Fotografie', *i10*, no. 4 (April 1927), pp. 148–57

Kertész/Adam 1985
André Kertész & Peter Adam, *Kertész on Kertész: A Self-Portrait*, London 1985

Kettering 2006
Alison McNeil Kettering, *Rembrandts groepsportretten*, Zwolle 2006

Kisters 2017
Sandra Kisters, *The Lure of the Biographical: On the (Self-)Representation of Modern Artists*, Amsterdam 2017

Klee 1925
Exh. cat. *Paul Klee. 39 aquarelles de Paul Klee illustrant le mot du peintre seront exposées pour la première fois en France*, Paris (Galerie Vavin-Raspail) 1925

Knight 1989
Terry W. Knight, 'Transformations of De Stijl Art: The Paintings of Georges Vantongerloo and Fritz Glarner', *Environment and Planning B: Planning and Design*, vol. 16 no. 1 (1989), pp. 51–98

Kranzfelder 2013
Ivo Kranzfelder, 'Europäer in New York. Zu einigen Künstlerportraits von Hermann Landshoff', in: Pohlmann/Landshoff 2013, pp. 67–72

Lansing/Colman 2013
Amy Kurtz Lansing & Benjamin Colman, exh. cat. *Harry Holtzman and American Abstraction*, Old Lyme (Florence Griswold Museum) 2013

Leal 2010
Brigitte Leal (ed.), exh. cat. *Mondrian*, Paris (Centre Pompidou, Musée National d'Art Moderne) 2010

Le Coultre 2015
Martijn F. Le Coultre, *De hut van Mondriaan. Laren-Blaricum 1914–1919*, Laren/Naarden 2015

Leijerzapf 1984
Ingeborg Leijerzapf (ed.), *Geschiedenis van de Nederlandse fotografie in monografieën en thema-artikelen*, 8 vol., Alphen aan de Rijn 1984

Lurasco 1907
F. J. Lurasco (ed.), *Onze moderne meesters*, Amsterdam 1907

Mali et al. 1994
Anco Mali et al., *Pieter Cornelis Mondriaan senior 1839–1921. Een gedreven vader*, Amersfoort/Winterswijk 1994

Mathews 1974
Oliver Mathews, *The Album of Carte-de-Visite and Cabinet Portrait Photographs 1854–1914*, London 1974

McCauley Lee/Canaan 2004
Eric McCauley Lee & Rima Canaan, *The Fred Jones Jr Museum of Art at the University of Oklahoma: Selected Works*, Oklahoma 2004

Meyer 1926
Hannes Meyer, 'Die neue Welt', *Das Werk*, vol. 13 no. 7 (July 1926), pp. 205–24

Moholy-Nagy 1922
László Moholy-Nagy, 'Produktion — Reproduktion', *De Stijl*, vol. 5 no. 7 (July 1922), pp. 98–100

Moholy-Nagy 1925
László Moholy-Nagy, *Malerei Fotografie Film*, Berlin 1925

Mondriaan 1918
Piet Mondriaan, 'De Nieuwe Beelding in de schilderkunst', *De Stijl*, vol. 1 no. 11 (September 1918), pp. 125–32

Mondriaan 1927
Piet Mondriaan, 'Neo-Plasticisme. De Woning — De Straat — De Stad', *Internationale Revue i10*, vol. 1 no. 10 (October 1927), pp. 12–18

Mondrian 1924
P. Mondrian, 'De huif naar den wind', in *De Stijl*, vol. 6 no. 6/7 (1924), pp. 86–8

Mondrian 1926
Piet Mondrian, 'Die Malerei und ihre praktische "Realisierung"', *ABC: Beiträge zum Bauen*, series 2 no. 2 (May 1926), p. 5

Mondrian et al. 1927
Piet Mondrian et al., 'Diskussion über Ernst Kállai's Artikel "Malerei und Fotografie"', *i10*, vol. 1 no. 6 (June 1927), pp. 227–36

Newman 1996
[Arnold Newman], 'Newman on Mondrian', *Art News Magazine* (February 1996), p. 28

Newman/Geldzahler 1980
A. Newman & H. Geldzahler (Foreword), *Artists: Portraits from Four Decades*, New York 1980

Opbouw 1933
De 8 en Opbouw, vol. 4 no. 22 (28 October 1933), p. 197

Origines 1937
Exh. cat. *Origines et développement de l'art international indépendant*, Paris (Musée du Jeu de Paume) 30 July–31 October 1937

Ottevanger 2008
Alied Ottevanger (ed.), *'De Stijl overal absolute leiding'. De briefwisseling tussen Theo van Doesburg en Antony Kok*, Bussum 2008

Phillips et al. 1985
Sandra S. Phillips et al., *André Kertész: Of Paris and New York*, Chicago 1985

Pitts Rembert 1970
Virginia Pitts Rembert, *Mondrian, America, and American Painting*, Ph.D. Columbia University, New York 1970

Pohlmann/Landshoff 2013
Ulrich Pohlmann & Andreas Landshoff, exh. cat. *Hermann Landshoff. Portrait Mode Architektur. Retrospektive 1930–1970*, München (Münchner Stadtmuseum) 2013

Portevin 2010
Jeanne-Marie Portevin, 'Repères biographiques', in: *Télérama hors-série. Piet Mondrian au Centre Pompidou*, 2010, p. 20

Postma 1995
Frans Postma, *26, Rue du Départ: Mondrian's Studio in Paris, 1921–1936*, Berlin 1995

Querido 1909
Israel Querido, 'Van Menschen en Dingen. Een schilders-studie. Spoor, Mondriaan en Sluijters', *De Controleur*, vol. 20 no. 1004 (23 October 1909), n.p.

Rehorst 1989
Chris Rehorst, 'Hannah Höch und die Niederlande', in: Elisabeth Moortgat & Cornelia Thater-Schulz (eds), exh. cat. *Hannah Höch 1889–1978. Ihr Werk, ihr Leben, ihre Freunde*, Berlin (Berlinische Galerie) 1989, pp. 41–52

Reinhold 2014
Nancy Reinhold, 'Exhibition in a Pocket: The *Cartes Postales* of André Kertész', in: Mitra Abbaspour et al. (eds), *Object: Photo. Modern Photographs: The Thomas Walther Collection 1909–1949. An Online Project of The Museum of Modern Art*, New York (The Museum of Modern Art) 2014, https://www.moma.org/interactives/objectphoto/assets/essays/Reinhold.pdf

Röell 1920
Anoniem [W. F. A. Röell], 'Een bezoek bij Piet Mondriaan', *Het Vaderland*, 9 July 1920

Röell 1926
Anoniem [W. F. A. Röell], 'Bij Piet Mondriaan. Het kristalheldere atelier. Apologie van den Charleston', *De Telegraaf*, 12 September 1926

Rooseboom 2019
Hans Rooseboom, *Lichtjaren. Een geschiedenis van de fotografie*, Amsterdam 2019

Roters 1995
Eberhard Roters et al. (eds), *Hannah Höch: eine Lebenscollage 1921–1945*, Stuttgart 1995

Roth 1973
Alfred Roth, *Begegnung mit Pionieren. Le Corbusier, Piet Mondrian, Adolf Loos, Josef Hoffmann, Auguste Perret, Henry van de Velde*, Basel/Stuttgart etc. 1973

Sarl 1998
Timm Sarl, 'A New World of Pictures: The Use and Spread of the Daguerrotype Process', in: Michel Frizot (ed.), *A New History of Photography*, Cologne 1998, pp. 33–50

Seuphor 1971
Michel Seuphor, *Cercle et Carré*, Paris 1971

Seuphor 1988
Michel Seuphor, *Une vie à angle droit*, Paris 1988

Société 1926-1
Société des artistes indépendants. Catalogue de la 37e exposition au Palais de Bois, Porte Maillot, Paris 1926 (gallica.bnf.fr/ark:/12148/bpt6k9656486d.texteImage)

Société 1926-2
Société des artistes français. Explication des ouvrages de peinture, sculpture, architecture, gravure et lithographie des artistes vivants, Paris 1926

Troy 2013
Nancy J. Troy, *The Afterlife of Piet Mondrian*, Chicago 2013

Van Deene 1977
Jan F. van Deene, 'Rechtvaardiging', in: *Centraal Museum Utrecht Mededelingen*, no. 16–17, Utrecht 1977, pp. 1–87

Van den Dorpel et al. 1989
M. van den Dorpel et al., *Het Nederlandse fotoportret 1860–1915. Een handleiding bij het dateren en bewaren van portretfoto's*, The Hague 1989

Van Loon 1922
Henri van Loon, 'Bij Piet Mondriaan', *Nieuwe Rotterdamsche Courant*, 23 March 1922

Van Loon 1946
Maud van Loon, 'Mondriaan, zoals hij leefde te Parijs', *De Groene*, 7 December 1946, n.p.

Welsh/Joosten 1998-I, -II, -III
Robert P. Welsh & Joop M. Joosten, *Piet Mondrian: Catalogue Raisonné*. Vol. 1: *Catalogue Raisonné of the Naturalistic Works (until early 1911)*; Vol. 2: *Catalogue Raisonné of the Work of 1911–1944*; Vol. 3: *Appendix*, New York 1998

Wieczorek 2014
Marek Wieczorek, 'Mondrian's Studio Utopia, 26 Rue du Départ', in: exh. cat. *Mondrian and His Studios: Colour in Space*, Liverpool (Tate Modern) 2014, pp. 46–67

Wieczorek 2020
Marek Wieczorek, 'Color and Line: Recovering Mondrian's Lost Paintings and Broader Arc', in: exh. cat. *Mondrian & De Stijl*, Madrid (Museo Reina Sofia) 2020, pp. 140–45

Wijnia 2018
Lieke Wijnia, 'Bringing Mondrian's "Lozenge Composition with Yellow Lines" to the Netherlands', *The Burlington Magazine*, vol. 160 no. 1379 (February 2018), pp. 118–25

Wijsenbeek 1968
L. J. F. Wijsenbeek, *Piet Mondrian*, Recklinghausen 1968

Xceron 1929
John (Jean) Xceron, 'Who's Who Abroad: Piet Mondrian', *Chicago Daily Tribune* (European Edition), 12 August 1929

Index

Acknowledgments

Compiling and publishing this book in three languages has been a complex operation, which we could not have brought to a successful conclusion without the help of many people. We would like to begin by thanking the following for the vital content, information and practical support they have provided: Flip Bool, Harry Cooper, Niels Coppes, Vicky Foster, Clarissa Frascadore, Akiko Hakuno, Louise Henriksen, the late Hans Janssen, Avi Keitelman, Laurens Kleine Deters, Alexandra Kostromina, Bas Mühren, Marieke de Natris, Charlotte Rixten, Jana Roovers, Wim van Sinderen, Jet Sloterdijk, Nancy J. Troy, Marek Wieczorek and Aurora Wilson Dyer Gough.

We are similarly grateful to Sabine Craft-Giepmans and Chris Stolwijk at the RKD — Netherlands Institute for Art History and to Karina van Dalen-Oskam, Lex Heerma van Voss, Dirk van Miert and Mariken Teeuwen at the Huygens Institute, Royal Netherlands Academy of Arts and Sciences (KNAW) for the generosity with which they created the necessary possibilities within these respective institutions.

For their excellent translations and meticulous editing, we thank Ted Alkins, Bruno Bernaerts, Dorine Duyster, Ann Kay, Anne-Laure Vignaux and Martine Wezenbeek.

Our gratitude is also due to Franca Candrian, Anne Colin du Terrail, Matthijs Erdman, Paul Gorter, Léon Hanssen, Madalena Holtzman, Alain Paviot and Robert Storr for kindly sharing visual material, without which this book would have been significantly less comprehensive. The same goes for the many public institutions who provided us with scans of photographs from their collections. They are listed in the photographc credits (p. 366).

We are also indebted to the International Music and Art Foundation for the crucial financial support it provided, and especially to Walter Feilchenfeldt for mediating in that process.

And our special gratitude is deserved by the team at Tijdsbeeld publishers: Ronny Gobyn, Jan Martens, Ann Mestdag and Griet Van Haute. We are full of admiration for the lucid and attractive design Griet has created for this complex book. And last, but by no means least, we thank the project coordinator Ann Mestdag. The warmest words could not do justice to her tireless efforts at every stage of this project. It is no exaggeration to say that *Mondrian and Photography* could not have been published without her.

Wietse Coppes
Leo Jansen

Photographic credits

The publishers have made every effort to comply with copyright regulations. Anyone believing that they are entitled to affirm rights is requested to contact the RKD — Netherlands Institute for Art History, The Hague.

Amsterdam, Matthijs Erdmann: cats 121, 135, 137–38

Amsterdam, Rijksmuseum: cats 238, 240

Amsterdam, Universiteit van Amsterdam, Theatercollectie, Archief Wilhelmina van Aggelen, Museum purchase funded by the Caroline Wiess Law Accessions Endowment Fund, The Manfred Heiting Collection: cats 67–72

Berljn, Berlinische Galerie: cats 61, 104–07

Berlin, Galerie Berinson: cat. 130

Brooklyn (NY), Higher Pictures Generation: cat. 97.2

Charenton-le-Pont, Médiathèque du Patrimoine et de la Photographie / © RMN-Grand palais, Photo © Ministère de la Culture - Médiathèque du patrimoine et de la photographie, Dist. RMN-Grand Palais / André Kertész: fig. 25; cats 81.1, 82.1, 87, 88.1, 89.1, 90.1, 92.1, 93.1, 94.1, 95.1, 96.1, 97.1, 98, 99.1, 101

Courtesy Amsterdam University Press, Amsterdam: cat. 350

Courtesy Anne Collin du Terrail: cats 55–57

Courtesy Paul Gorter: cats 6, 16, 32

Courtesy Léon Hanssen: cats 45, 49

Courtesy Lempertz Auction House, Cologne: cats 84–86

Courtesy Galerie Françoise Paviot, Paris: cats 83, 103, 124, 131, 135, 268, 294, 307.1, 342, 348, 374

Courtesy Robert Storr / Photo Alexander Harding Photography, Cheshire (CT): cats 296–304

Hannover, Sprengel Museum, Kurt Schwitters Archiv / Photo Herling/Herling/ Werner: cat. 174

Houston, The Museum of Fine Arts, The Allen Chasanoff Photographic Collection: cat 243

Houston, The Museum of Fine Arts, The Manfred Hefting Collection: cat 89.2

Los Angeles, The J. Paul Getty Museum: fig. 26; cats 95.2, 99.2

Munich, Münchner Stadtmuseum, Sammlung Fotografie/Archiv Landshoff / Photo bpk: cats 245–49

New Haven (CT), Yale University, Beinecke Rare Book and Manuscript Library: fig. 3; cats 77–8, 147.2, 176, 188

New Orleans Museum of Art, Museum purchase, Women's Volunteer Committee Fund, 73.173: cat. 81.2

New York, The Metropolitan Museum of Art, Gilman Collection / Scala, Florence: cats 90.2, 91

New York, The Museum of Modern Art, Digital image © 2023 The Museum of Modern Art, New York/Scala, Florence: cats 90.2, 93.2, 94.2

Norman (OK), The Fred Jones Jr. Museum of Art at the University of Oklahoma, Gift of Dr. And Mrs. Richard L. Sandor: cat. 96.2

Paris, Archives et Musée de la Préfecture de Police de Paris, Service de la mémoire et des affaires culturelles: cat. 147.1

Paris, Bibliothèque historique de la Ville de Paris: fig. 37

Paris, Bibliothèque Kandinsky, Centre Pompidou, Fonds Photographique A.E. Gallatin / RMN: cats 172, 225

Paris, Centre Pompidou, Centre de Création industrielle / Photo © Centre Pompidou, MNAM-CCI, Dist. RMN-Grand Palais / Georges Meguerditchian: cat. 179

Paris, Centre Pompidou, MNAM-CCI Bibliothèque Kandinsky, Dist. RMN-Grand Palais / Fonds général photo: cat. 225

Parijs, Fondation Le Corbusier / © FLC/ADAGP: cats 114–15

Rotterdam, Het Nieuwe Instituut, Archief Charles Karsten: cats 79, 145–46, 148–49

Rotterdam, Nederlands Fotomuseum / © Cas Oorthuys: cats 180–85

Philadelphia Museum of Art: cat. 242.2

Philadelphia Museum of Art, A.E. Gallatin Collection: cat. 173

Otterlo, Kröller-Müller Museum: cat. 39.2

Stuttgart, Kunstmuseum Stuttgart, Archiv Baumeister: cat. 88.2

The Hague, Kunstmuseum: figs 17, 20; cats 139–40

The Hague, Nationaal Archief, Collectie Spaarnestad: cat. 31

The Hague, RKD — Nederlands Instituut voor Kunstgeschiedenis, Photo Vicky Foster: figs 6–7, 15, 53–4, 65, 68–74; cats 1–5, 7–14, 17–30, 33–5, 37–8, 39.1, 40, 43–4, 46, 48, 50–60, 62–6, 73–4, 76, 80, 100, 102, 116, 118–20, 122–23, 125–29, 131–33, 141–43, 150–70, 175, 177–78, 186–87, 189, 230, 231, 233–36, 237, 239, 241.1, 242.1, 244, 254, 256.1, 257.1, 258.1, 259.1, 260.1, 272.1, 274.1, 335, 384–96, 398–403

Washington, National Gallery of Art Library: cats 250–53, 255

Winterswijk, Courtesy Villa Mondriaan: figs 8–9; cats 222, 224, 226–29, 404–11

Zurich, EHT / gta Archiv, Nachlass Alfred Roth: cats 75, 108–13, 117

Zurich, Kunsthaus Zürich, Glarner Archiv: cats 256.2, 257.2, 258.2, 259.2, 260.2, 261–67, 269–71, 272.2, 273, 274.2, 275–95, 305–06, 307.2, 308–34, 336–47, 349, 351–73, 375–83

Colophon

Authors
Wietse Coppes
Leo Jansen
in collaboration with Clarissa Frascadore, Laurens Kleine Deters

Book design and typesetting
Griet Van Haute

Cover design
Rutger Fuchs

Translation
Ted Alkins

Copy-editing
Ann Kay

Photography RKD — Netherlands Institute for Art History, The Hague
Vicky Foster

Picture research
Wietse Coppes, Akiko Hakuno, Ann Mestdag
in collaboration with Aurora Wilson Dyer Gough

Colour separation, printing and binding
Graphius, Ghent

Printed on Magno Volume 150 g
Typeset in Satoshi

First published as *Mondriaan en fotografie. De kunstenaar in beeld* by Tijdsbeeld, Ghent and RKD — Netherlands Institute for Art History, The Hague

Coordination Tijdsbeeld
Ronny Gobyn
Ann Mestdag

Coordination RKD — Netherlands Institute for Art History, The Hague
Chris Stolwijk
Sabine Craft-Giepmans

MIX
Paper
FSC® C014767

This publication was published with the support of:

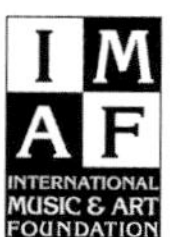

International Music & Art Foundation

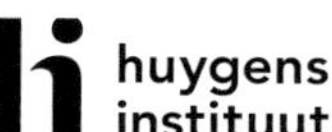

Huygens Instituut voor Nederlandse Geschiedenis en Cultuur (KNAW)

English edition first published by
Hatje Cantz Verlag GmbH
Mommsenstraße 27
10629 Berlin
www.hatjecantz.com
A Ganske Publishing Group Company

ISBN 978-3-7757-5400-2

Cover: Company at the opening of Gustave Buchet's exhibition at Galerie Zak, Paris, 22 November 1929 (detail). Photograph: Stanislaw Londynski (cat. 124)